PAGE 50 **ON THE ROAD**

ON GUIDE
stings

TOP EXPERIENCES MAP

Port Douglas & the Daintree p353
Cape York Peninsula & the Savannah Way p387
Cairns, Islands & Highlands p304
Townsville to Innisfail p262
Whitsunday Coast p225
Journeys into the Outback p407
Capricorn Coast p198
Fraser Island & the Fraser Coast p169
Noosa & the Sunshine Coast p142
Around Brisbane p97
Brisbane p52
Gold Coast p115

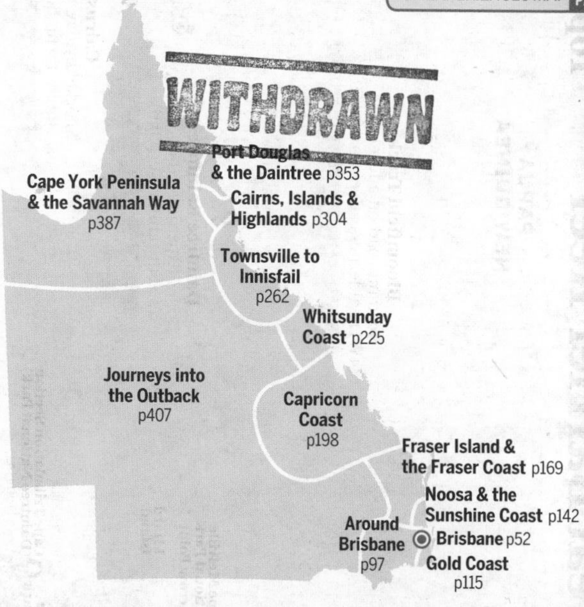

PAGE 455 **SURVIVAL GUIDE**

VITAL PRACTICAL INFORMATION TO HELP YOU HAVE A SMOOTH TRIP

Deadly & Dangerous...... 456
Directory A–Z.................. 459
Transport........................ 467
Index.........
Map Legen

THIS EDITION WRITTEN AND RESEARCHED BY

Regis St Louis

Sarah Gilbert, Catherine Le Nevez, Olivia Pozzan

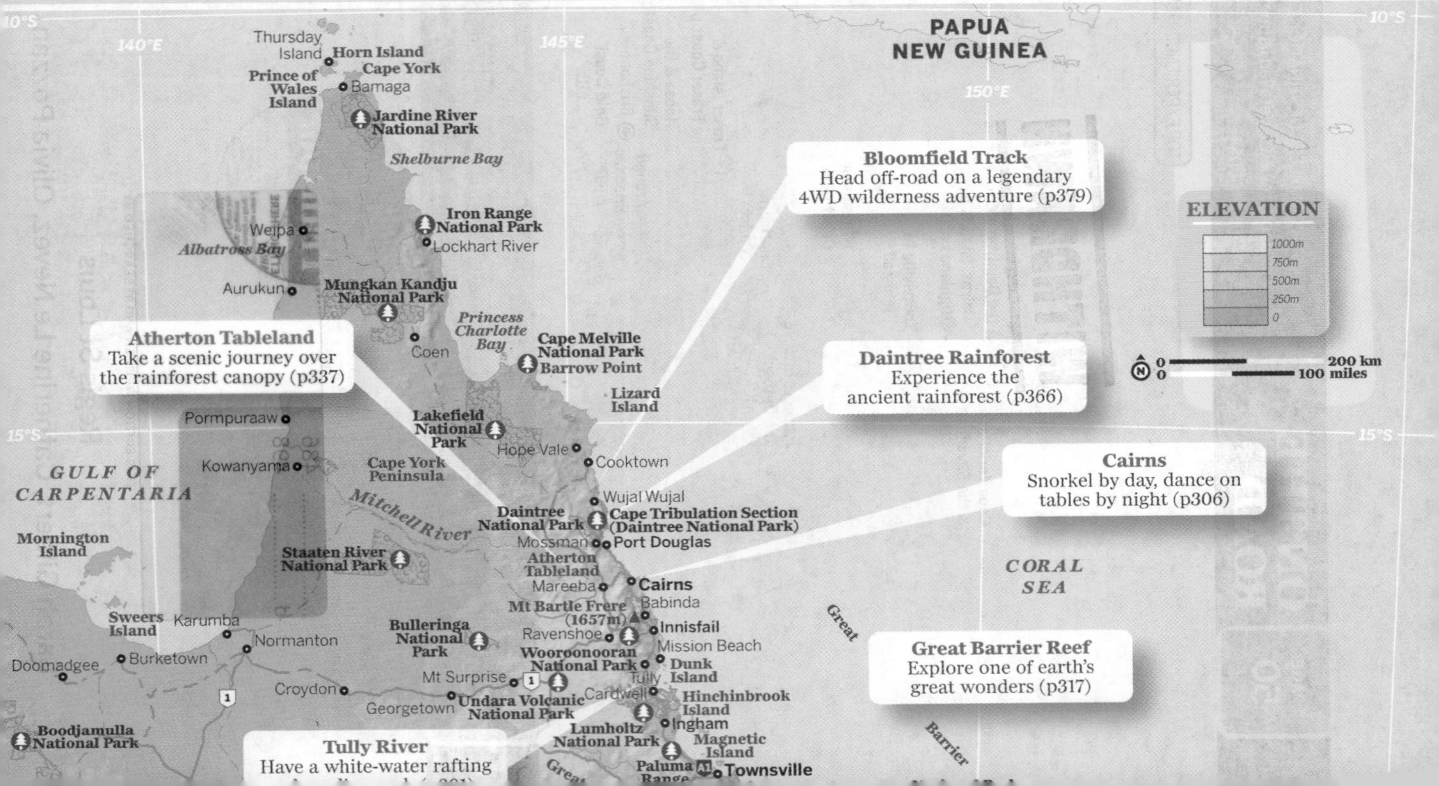

Bloomfield Track
Head off-road on a legendary 4WD wilderness adventure (p379)

Atherton Tableland
Take a scenic journey over the rainforest canopy (p337)

Daintree Rainforest
Experience the ancient rainforest (p366)

Cairns
Snorkel by day, dance on tables by night (p306)

Great Barrier Reef
Explore one of earth's great wonders (p317)

Tully River
Have a white-water rafting

ELEVATION
1000m
750m
500m
250m
0

0 200 km
0 100 miles

10°S
15°S
140°E
145°E
150°E
PAPUA NEW GUINEA
Thursday Island
Horn Island
Cape York
Prince of Wales Island
Bamaga
Jardine River National Park
Shelburne Bay
Weipa
Albatross Bay
Iron Range National Park
Lockhart River
Aurukun
Mungkan Kandju National Park
Coen
Princess Charlotte Bay
Cape Melville National Park
Barrow Point
Lizard Island
Pormpuraaw
Lakefield National Park
Hope Vale
Cooktown
GULF OF CARPENTARIA
Kowanyama
Cape York Peninsula
Mitchell River
Wujal Wujal
Daintree National Park
Cape Tribulation Section (Daintree National Park)
Mossman
Port Douglas
Mornington Island
Staaten River National Park
Atherton Tableland
Mareeba
Cairns
CORAL SEA
Mt Bartle Frere (1657m)
Babinda
Innisfail
Great
Sweers Island
Karumba
Normanton
Bulleringa National Park
Ravenshoe
Mission Beach
Burketown
Doomadgee
Wooroonooran National Park
Dunk Island
Tully
Mt Surprise
Croydon
Georgetown
Undara Volcanic National Park
Cardwell
Hinchinbrook Island
Ingham
Boodjamulla National Park
Lumholtz National Park
Magnetic Island
Paluma Range
Townsville
Barrier

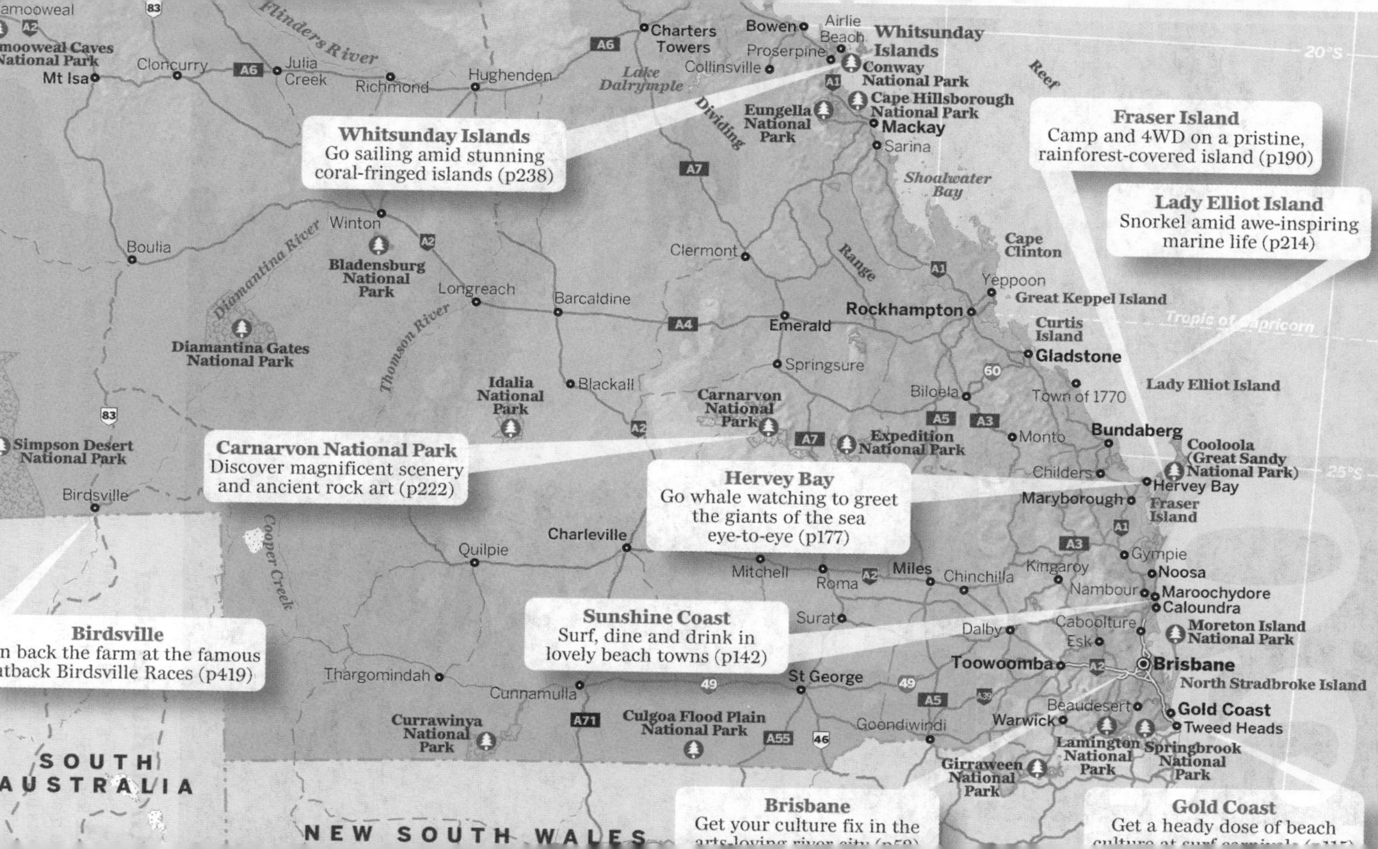

Whitsunday Islands
Go sailing amid stunning coral-fringed islands (p238)
Fraser Island
Camp and 4WD on a pristine, rainforest-covered island (p190)
Lady Elliot Island
Snorkel amid awe-inspiring marine life (p214)
Carnarvon National Park
Discover magnificent scenery and ancient rock art (p222)
Hervey Bay
Go whale watching to greet the giants of the sea eye-to-eye (p177)
Sunshine Coast
Surf, dine and drink in lovely beach towns (p142)
Birdsville
Win back the farm at the famous outback Birdsville Races (p419)
Brisbane
Get your culture fix in the
Gold Coast
Get a heady dose of beach
Camooweal
Camooweal Caves National Park
Mt Isa
Cloncurry
Julia Creek
Richmond
Hughenden
Flinders River
Charters Towers
Lake Dalrymple
Bowen
Airlie Beach
Proserpine
Collinsville
Whitsunday Islands
Conway National Park
Cape Hillsborough National Park
Eungella National Park
Mackay
Sarina
Dividing
Range
Reef
Shoalwater Bay
Cape Clinton
Winton
Bladensburg National Park
Boulia
Diamantina River
Diamantina Gates National Park
Longreach
Thomson River
Barcaldine
Clermont
Emerald
Springsure
Rockhampton
Yeppoon
Great Keppel Island
Curtis Island
Gladstone
Tropic of Capricorn
Lady Elliot Island
Town of 1770
Biloela
Blackall
Idalia National Park
Carnarvon National Park
Expedition National Park
Monto
Bundaberg
Cooloola (Great Sandy National Park)
Childers
Hervey Bay
Maryborough
Fraser Island
Simpson Desert National Park
Birdsville
Cooper Creek
Charleville
Quilpie
Mitchell
Roma
Miles
Chinchilla
Kingaroy
Gympie
Noosa
Nambour
Maroochydore
Caloundra
Surat
Dalby
Caboolture
Esk
Moreton Island National Park
Toowoomba
Brisbane
North Stradbroke Island
Thargomindah
Cunnamulla
St George
Goondiwindi
Beaudesert
Warwick
Gold Coast
Tweed Heads
Currawinya National Park
Culgoa Flood Plain National Park
Girraween National Park
Lamington National Park
Springbrook National Park
SOUTH AUSTRALIA
NEW SOUTH WALES
20°S
25°S

20 TOP EXPERIENCES

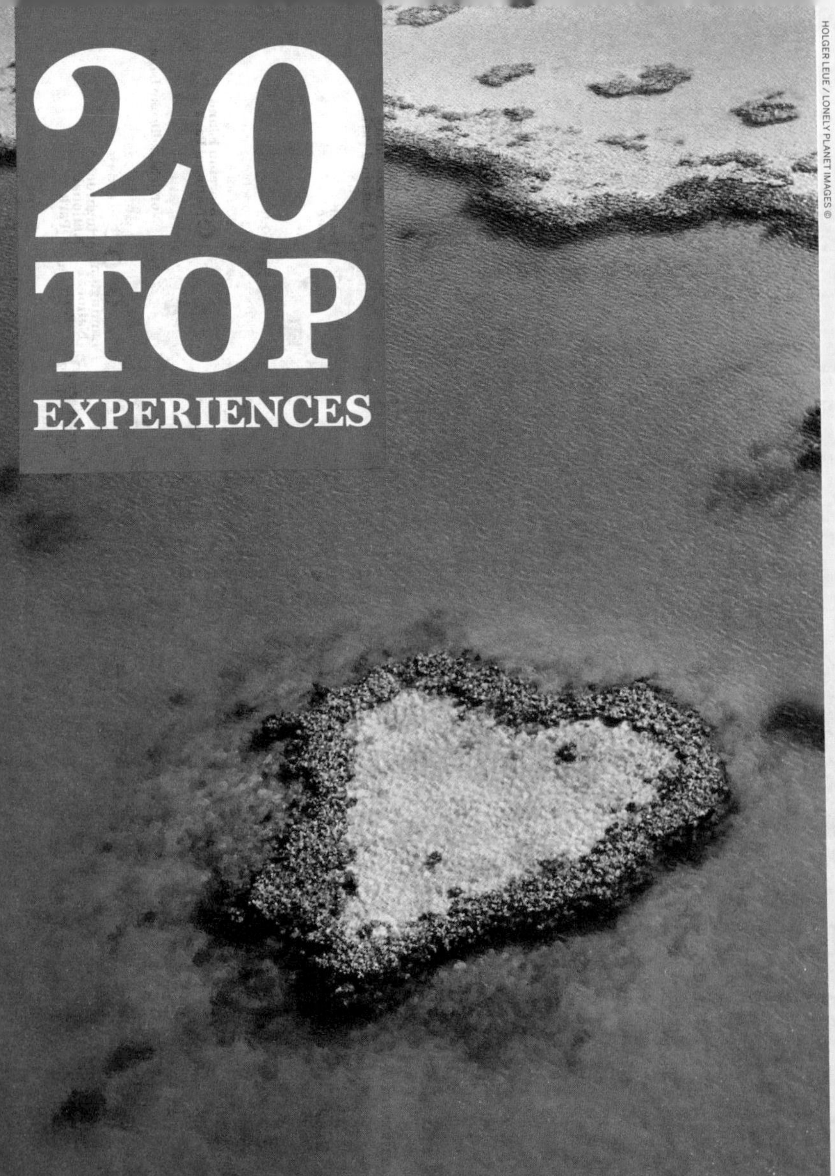

HOLGER LEUE / LONELY PLANET IMAGES ©

Great Barrier Reef

1 Stretching more than 2000km up the Queensland coastline, the awe-inspiring Great Barrier Reef (p317) is one of the world's great wonders. Among the best ways to experience it: donning a mask and fins and delving into the vivid undersea kingdom for a close-up view of dazzling corals, sea turtles, sharks, rays and tropical fish of every colour and size. You can also explore the reef by sailboat, take a scenic flight, gaze at marine life through a glass-bottomed semisubmersible and linger in a resort (or camp) on a remote coral-fringed island. Hardy Reef (p256)

PAUL DYMOND / LONELY PLANET IMAGES ©

The Daintree Rainforest

2 Fan palms, ferns and mangroves are just some of the 3000 or so plant species in the ancient, World Heritage–listed Daintree Rainforest (p366), which is alive with a chorus of birds, insects and frogs. Guided day walks, wildlife-spotting night tours, mountain treks, interpretive boardwalks, canopy walks, self-guided walking trails, 4WD trips, horse riding, kayaking, croc-spotting cruises and tropical-fruit orchard tours and tastings are among the many ways to experience one of the most extraordinary ecosystems on the planet.

Brisbane

3 Brisbane (p52) is an arts-loving city with a packed calendar of food and music festivals, top dance and theatre performances, cutting-edge exhibitions (such as at the Queensland Art Gallery, pictured) and big-name concerts. There's great sports events and plenty of ways to enjoy the subtropical climate year-round. The river city boasts vibrant open-air markets, colourful boutiques and a fantastic cafe scene, while award-winning restaurants and burgeoning nightlife means you'll never run out of options when the sun goes down.

Island Hopping in the Whitsundays

RICHARD I'ANSON / LONELY PLANET IMAGES ©

4 Sailing across the shimmering blue waters of the Coral Sea, ounging beside the pool in a luxury sland resort, playing castaway on a secluded beach...there are so many ways to enjoy the beautiful Whitsunday Islands (p238). One of the best is from the deck of a sailing boat, basking in the warm sunshine and balmy sea air while deciding upon which perfect sandy bay to anchor in. Whether snorkelling the coral reef, swimming at gorgeous Whitehaven Beach, or savouring the brilliant sunsets, there's only one word to describe the Whitsundays: divine!

RICHARD I'ANSON / LONELY PLANET IMAGES ©

Surfers Paradise

5 Surfers (p122) is the bling capital of Queensland, a commercial spend-happy zone filled with tacky tourist shops, enormous shopping malls, towering high-rises and throbbing nightclubs. Slip into a sequinned bikini, slide on the faux-gold jewellery, slap on a pair of high heels and you'll fit right in. Surfers' kitschy attractions and nonstop action promise no respite, but if you make the time to peer beneath the Gold Coast's brash facade, you'll find the heavenly blue skies, golden beaches and perfect surf that gave the town its name.

Sunshine Coast

6 The endless summers and surfer-chic culture of the Sunshine Coast (p142) bewitch all who step onto its sandy shores. There's a wholesomeness to the Sunny Coast that's as natural and unaffected as its idyllic surf beaches and balmy sea breezes. Early mornings see a steady flow of surfers, joggers, cyclists and walkers making the most of the beach scene and cappuccino culture. Noosa (pictured), the coast's boutique resort town, where barefoot surfers mingle effortlessly with the designer-clad beach elite, is the elegant yet unpretentious star of this sandy crown.

RICHARD I'ANSON / LONELY PLANET IMAGES ©

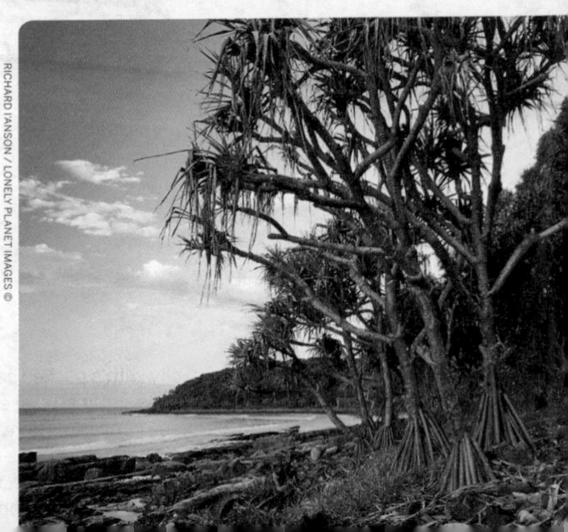

Fraser Island

7 Fraser Island (p190) is an ecological wonderland created by drifting sand, where wild dogs roam free and lush rainforest grows on sand. It's a primal island utopia, home to a profusion of wildlife, including the purest strain of dingo (pictured) in Australia. The best way to explore the island is in a 4WD – cruising up the seemingly endless beaches and bouncing along sandy inland tracks. Tropical rainforest, pristine freshwater pools and beach camping under the stars will bring you back to nature.

Whale Watching in Hervey Bay

8 During most of the year Hervey Bay (p178) is a sleepy seaside village with a remarkably long sandy beach and a flat, shallow sea. That all changes in mid-July, when migrating humpback whales (pictured) cruise into the bay to frolic and cavort and thousands of tourists cruise out onto the water to watch them play. It's one of the best whale-watching regions in the world, and seeing these aqua-acrobats waving, blowing, breaching and having fun is breathtaking.

xploring the Cape York Peninsula

It's the wild and rugged frontier of Australia, a landscape of climatic extremes, croc-infested rivers and stark but beautiful scenery. The overland journey through the untamed wilderness Cape York (p390) and along the legendary Old Telegraph Track is an epic northern safari bound turn you as wild and feral as the land. It's an exhilarating experience to fly the flag at the Tip of stralia, a fitting end to the challenge of rough corrugated dirt roads, difficult creek crossings and les and miles of raw Australian beauty.

urf Carnivals on the Gold Coast

10 They're the bronzed gods of the surf, the beefcakes of the sea, the uberfit icons of Australia's beach-crazed culture. Since their beginnings in 1907, Australia's surf lifesavers have volved into superfit, superbuff athletes, pitting their skills against each other in seasonal surf arnivals (p124) – gruelling events involving ocean swimming, beach running and surfboat racing. 's hard work but makes for an extraordinary – and sensorily pleasing – spectator sport for the est of us limp squids.

BOB CHARLTON / LONELY PLANET IMAGES ©

Lady Elliot Island

11 This ecofriendly resort island (p214) is one of the loveliest and most peaceful places to experience the Great Barrier Reef. Snorkel straight off Lady Elliot's white sands: the living reef that surrounds the tiny coral cay is teeming with tropical fish, turtles and the island's resident manta rays. At hatching time (January to April) you can see baby turtles (pictured) scamper across the sand, and humpback whales pass by from June to October. Getting to the island is equally memorable, with a scenic flight over the turquoise reef-filled waters.

Carnarvon National Park & Gorge

12 Carnarvon Gorge (p222) is a wonderland for bushwalkers, birdwatchers and nature lovers. Offering a huge range of walks, the gorge is filled with diverse ecosystems tucked away in hidden canyons, while cliff tops offer soaring views over the countryside. Pretty-faced wallabies scamper about the gorge floor, while at night, spotlights reveal gliders soaring from tree to tree. Aboriginals have been visiting this sacred place for at least 20,000 years, and have left remarkable stencil art that can be admired in several of the area's caves.

ANDREW PEACOCK / LONELY PLANET IMAGES ©

WALTER BIBIKOW / JON ARNOLD IMAGES LTD / ALAMY

Town of 1770

13 Built on the site of Captain Cook's landing, this idyllic village (p215) and the wildlife-rich peninsula surrounding it remain largely unspoilt. Outdoor adventure comes in many forms, from sea kayaking to surfing great breaks off nearby Agnes Water. Four national parks in the area offer superb bushwalking, and 1770 also makes a fine base for boat trips out to dive or snorkel the southern Barrier Reef. At the end of the day, the sleepy township has one bar with VIP views of the prettiest sunsets on the east coast.

afting the Tully River

4 Two things make rafting the Tully River (p291) the wildest white-water ride in the country. First, Tully is the wettest region in Australia, as evidenced by the 7.9m-high gumboot at the rance to the town. Yes, Tully has recorded that much rain in a single year! Second, rafting trips timed to coincide with the release of the river's hydroelectric floodgates. So on the off chance not raining, you're still guaranteed thrills (and possibly some spills) on Grade 4 rapids all r long.

LAWRIE WILLIAMS / LONELY PLANET IMAGES ©

MARTIN COHEN / LONELY PLANET IMAGES ©

Wildlife Watching in North Queensland

15 The further north you head in Queensland, the more deadly, dangerous or just damn big the creatures become. Human-height cassowaries (p294) strut through the rainforest, whopping crocs (p301) inhabit the waterways, while the country's largest snakes slither across the land. Even the insects are huge, like hand-sized Ulysses butterflies. And north Queensland is home to over 50 different kinds of tree frog (pictured), including the world's largest of its species, the giant tree frog.

RICHARD I'ANSON / LONELY PLANET IMAGES ©

Kuranda

16 You can drive or catch a bus from Cairns to the rainforest village of Kuranda (p338) in around half an hour. But that would be missing the point. Kuranda is as much about the journey as it is the destination. Hop into a gondola on the 7.5km-long Skyrail Rainforest Cableway, browse Kuranda's markets for arts, crafts and gourmet goodies, then wind your way back down to Cairns through picturesque mountains and 15 tunnels on the Kuranda Scenic Railway (pictured).

Hinchinbrook Island: Walkers' Holy Grail

17 Queensland has plenty of resort islands where you can sprawl on a sunlounge. But if you're up for something more active, consider hiking the Thorsborne Trail (p289) on Hinchinbrook, Australia's only island national park. Running from the north of the island to its southern tip, the Thorsborne is not for the faint-hearted – prepare to cross creeks, draw water and protect your food from ravenous rats. End-to-end, allow three nights at bush camp sites along the ungraded 32km-long track. Hiker numbers are limited, so book ahead.

WILL SALTER / LONELY PLANET IMAGES ©

SIMON FOALE / LONELY PLANET IMAGES ©

Reef- & Party-Loving Cairns

18 Early morning in Cairns (p304), you're boarding a boat out to the reef, mid-morning you're snorkelling or diving amid the coral. Late afternoon, you're heading back to shore after an action-packed day. But it's not over: you and your new friends order a sundowner and decide on one of Cairns' multitude of restaurants for an alfresco dinner. Then you're ready to hit this hedonistic city's bars, pubs and clubs, and end up dancing until dawn. Suddenly it's early morning, and time to do it all over again...

The Birdsville Races

19 What started in 1882 as a run for stock horses has today morphed into a massive event (p419), attracting up to 7000 spectators who pile into the one-pub town for four days of dusty track racing and boozing. The race weekend is in early September, though in recent years heavy rains have flooded out the event. But even when equine flu stopped the horses turning up in 2007, crowds still thronged to Birdsville to pitch tents in the dust, drink beer and see old mates.

ANDREW WATSON / LONELY PLANET IMAGES ©

FRASER HALL / ROBERT HARDING WORLD IMAGERY / ALAMY

Bloomfield Track 4WD Adventure

20 Buckle up for one of Australia's great 4WD journeys. The track (p379), which runs from Cape Tribulation to Cooktown, is a bumpy 80km of creek crossings, precipitous mountain climbs and sheer drops, with plenty of diversions along the way, including waterfalls, Aboriginal-guided cultural tours, national-park walking trails and the welcome sight of the legendary Lion's Den pub near the northern end. If you want to max out the adventure, a handful of camping grounds, cabins and lodges are scattered along the route.

welcome to Queensland

From the surf-loving beaches of the Gold Coast to the wildlife-rich rainforests of the Daintree, Queensland spreads a dazzling array of natural and cultural wonders. The hardest part is deciding where to begin…

Enchanting Landscapes

Queensland's most famous attraction is the astounding aquatic wonderland of the Great Barrier Reef, which stretches for more than 2000km along the coast. The Sunshine State is also home to hundreds of islands, harbouring a remarkable variety of landscapes: giant sand dunes, colourful fringing reefs, and surreal forests growing right in the sand. You'll find idyllic island getaways, remote ocean-fronting camp sites and family-friendly resorts. Back on the mainland, bewitching national parks dot the landscape, with lush rainforests, soaring mountains, sparkling lakes and a staggering array of wildlife that rates from cute and cuddly (koalas) to downright fearsome (crocs). Gateway to the state is the easy-going river city of Brisbane, whose urban charms (great dining, nightlife and the arts) meld seamlessly with the natural environment (riverside cliffs, parklands and botanic gardens). In the south, the glitz and high energy of the Gold Coast vies with the laid-back beach towns of the Sunshine Coast.

Big Adventures

The great outdoors holds endless possibilities in Queensland. You can don a mask and fins and explore some of the most stunning underwater landscapes on Earth. There's adrenaline-charged white-water rafting in the north, and smooth and scenic kayaking all along the coast. Bushwalking and hiking are first-rate, whether you opt for a challenging multiday trek on one of the state's scenic Great Walks, or hit a shorter trail through rainforests and gorges, up mountains or along bush-lined lakes and rivers. You can go sailing through the turquoise waters of the Whitsundays, stopping at powdery white-sand beaches along the way; or take on a 4WD adventure, plying the 'beach highway' of Fraser Island, exploring the great open skies of the outback or jostling along the rutted Bloomfield Track en route to the Tip of Australia.

Eat, Drink & Be Merry

With a great cafe scene, sprawling food markets and riverside restaurants serving temptations from every corner of the globe, Brisbane is redefining itself as a foodie destination. The city's alter ego arrives after sundown, when nightclubs, lounges and bars light up the capital. Elsewhere in the state you'll find culinary rewards great and small, from seafood feasts along the coast to sizzling steaks in the outback. Superb dining rooms are sprinkled all over Queensland, from Noosa (which also has a worthwhile food festival) to Port Douglas (with memorable waterside restaurants). Although little known abroad, the Granite Belt has been producing some superb award-winning wines in recent years, with dozens of vineyards open for tasting (plus orchards, berry farms and cheesemakers).

need to know

Currency

» Australian dollar ($)

Language

» English

When to Go?

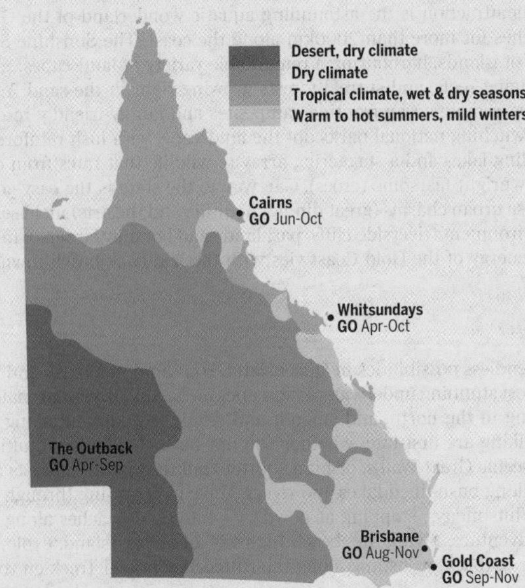

High Season (Jun–Sep)

» Busiest time. Bigger crowds and higher accommodation prices.

» Best time to see migrating whales.

» Good underwater visibility and warm temperatures (but sometimes windy) on Great Barrier Reef.

Shoulder Season (Apr–May & Oct–Nov)

» Warm pleasant temperatures, with long beach days.

» Fewer crowds, and prices drop slightly.

Low Season (Dec–Mar)

» Hot, humid climate and abundant rainfall in the north.

» Stinger season (officially November to May) makes swimming unsafe from Agnes Water north.

» Outback travel is unsafe; some roads close.

Your Daily Budget

Budget less than

$75

» Dorm beds: $20–$30; camping: from $5.50

» Free activities (concerts, museums)

» Youth cards save on sights and transport

Midrange

$150–$250

» Double room in midrange hotel: $100–$180

» Dinner in decent restaurants: $50–$80 for two

» Car hire from $30 per day

Top end over

$250

» Lodging in a resort: from $200

» Dining in top restaurants: $80 per person

» Activities: sailing the Whitsundays (from $300 per night), diving course ($650), outback 4WD trip ($200 per day)

Money

» ATMs widely available. Credits cards accepted at most lodgings, restaurants and shops.

Visas

» All visitors except for New Zealanders need a visa (available online through www.immi.gov.au).

Mobile Phones

» Local SIM cards can be used in Australian and European phones. Of the main providers, Telstra has the most extensive network.

Driving

» Drive on the left; steering wheel is on the right side of the car.

Websites

» **Lonely Planet** (www.lonelyplanet.com/australia/queensland) Destination information, hotel bookings, travel forum, photos.

» **Courier Mail** (www.couriermail.com.au) Brisbane's daily, with current affairs.

» **Queensland Holidays** (www.queenslandholidays.com.au) Extensive Queensland coverage: accommodation, attractions and tours.

» **Queensland Parks and Wildlife Service** (www.derm.qld.gov.au) National parks and conservation areas.

Exchange Rates

Canada	C$1	$1
Europe	€1	$1.37
Japan	¥100	$1.22
New Zealand	NZ$1	$0.78
UK	UK£1	$1.60
USA	US$1	$1

For current exchange rates see www.xe.com.

Important Numbers

To call any regular number, dial the area code, followed by the 8-digit number.

Emergency ☎000

Queensland area code ☎07

Country Code (Australia) ☎61

Reverse-charge call ☎1800-REVERSE (738 3773)

International access code ☎0011

Arriving in Queensland

» **Brisbane** (p95)

Airtrain – every 15 to 30 minutes from 6am to 8pm; $15

Coachtrans shuttle bus (to CBD hotels) – every 30 minutes; $15

Taxis – around $40

» **Gold Coast** (Coolangatta Airport, p117)

Gold Coast Tourist Shuttle – meets arriving flights; $18

» **Cairns** (p329)

Sun Palm shuttle – meets arriving flights; $10 to Cairns, $35 to Port Douglas

Taxis – $20 to $30 to Cairns

Top Tips for Safe Travel

» Don't swim off northern beaches during stinger season (November to May).

» Avoid driving between dusk and dawn, when wildlife might cross your path.

» Take care in the water; the surf can be strong with dangerous ocean currents (and swim between the flags).

» Don't forget your motion-sickness tablets (if you need them) before boating on the Great Barrier Reef.

» Remember to bring sunscreen, a hat and sunglasses to deflect fierce UV radiation – and don't forget to slather on repeatedly (especially the backs of the legs) when snorkelling or diving; better yet, use a full-length wetsuit (sunscreen isn't great for the reef).

» Make sure you have travel insurance for any adrenaline-charged activities, such as bungee jumping, white-water rafting or rock climbing.

» Bring a lightweight rain jacket for tropical downpours.

if you like...

Beaches

With over 7000km of coastline, Queensland has a dazzling array of beaches, from hedonistic, people-packed sands in the south to remote tropical beauties in the north. You'll find sun-kissed shores of every type: picture-perfect white powdery sands fronting azure seas, magnificent surf spots and wild, idyllic seafront inviting endless walks.

Surfers Paradise The brash and buzzing heart of the Gold Coast is a mecca for young sun-worshippers (p122).

Rainbow Beach This picturesque and wild beach has coloured-sand cliffs that give the town its name (p172).

Whitehaven Beach The jewel of the Whitsundays and one of Australia's loveliest beaches, with powdery, white sand and crystal-clear waters (p258).

Four Mile Beach It's nearly impossible not to reach for your camera when stepping onto this long, photogenic beach backed by palms in Port Douglas (p355).

Etty Bay Framed by rocky headlands and lush rainforest, this beautiful and little-known beach is a great spot to spy cassowaries (p299).

Islands

Home to hundreds of islands, Queensland boasts some spectacular getaways of the powdery-sand-and-palm-fringed variety. Magical bushwalks, magnificent wildlife, deserted beaches and cinematic aquatic beauty (colourful coral reefs, whale and dolphin watching) are just a few draws.

North Stradbroke Island A quick trip from Brisbane with whale watching, long beach walks along deserted sands and swimming in forest-ringed lakes (p101).

Fraser Island The world's largest sand island, and setting for 4WD adventures, has giant dunes, freshwater lakes and abundant wildlife (p190).

Whitsundays Book in at one of the islands' top resorts, or board a sailboat and explore as many of these pristine islands as you can (p238).

Lady Musgrave Island Ringed by the Great Barrier Reef and reachable by light aircraft, this remote island is a great place to play castaway (p214).

Dunk Island Home to a national park and a high-end resort, Dunk has excellent walking trails, snorkelling in coral gardens and good birdwatching (p298).

Aquatic Adventures

Idyllic coral cays, surf-pounded tropical islands and the magnificent Great Barrier Reef provide never-ending opportunities for aquatic adventure. Surfing, diving, snorkelling, kayaking, reef walks and wildlife watching – few places on earth can compete with Queensland's enormous bounty.

Diving Book a passage out to the Great Barrier Reef and go diving amid some of the most striking underwater scenery on the planet (p29).

Surfing Grab a board (or take a few lessons) and hit the amazing breaks along the southern coast – don't miss Mooloolaba and Noosa (p155 and p144).

Watch sea turtles in the wild Get an awe-inspiring view of loggerhead hatchlings as they lumber down to the sea at Mon Repos, one of the most important nesting sites in Australia. (p188).

Sea kayaking Take an adventurous two-day sea-kayaking trip from Cow Bay out to Snapper Island (p370).

» View fascinating ancient Aboriginal rock art at the Art Gallery, Carnarvon Gorge (p223)

CHRIS BELL / LONELY PLANET IMAGES ©

Indigenous Culture

Queensland provides some fine ways to experience the age-old culture of the first Australians. You can take a Dreaming tour through spiritually rich native sites, gaze upon ancient rock art or hit the Brisbane galleries where a new generation of Aboriginal artists are making their mark.

Kuku Yalanji Dreamtime Walks Take a guided walk through lush Mossman Gorge, learning about bush tucker and Dreaming legends from knowledgable Indigenous guides (p364).

Suzanne O'Connell Gallery See works from some of the nation's most talented Aboriginal artists at this gallery in Brisbane's New Farm district (p64).

Mungalla Station Take an Aboriginal-led tour through the rainforest, then book in for a traditional meal offered by the local Nywaigi culture north of Townsville (p285).

Carnarvon Gorge Get a close-up view of stunning rock art inside the twisted gorges of this ancient wonderland (p223).

Festivals & Events

No matter the season, Queenslanders find cause for revelry, whether celebrating the return of the whales during their annual migration, watching dusty horseraces in the outback or digging their heels in the sand during a full-moon bash. For more causes for carousing, see p19.

Brisbane Festival Brisbane's biggest celebration (held in September) features fireworks over the river and three weeks of concerts, theatre, dance and other events (p72).

Hervey Bay Whale Festival This seductive town celebrates the reappearance of the whales with live concerts, a street parade and kids fest (p181).

Full-moon parties For a memorable all-night experience, Base Backpackers draws hundreds of revellers to the sand during its wild monthly party on Magnetic Island (p277).

Birdsville Races The tiny outback town brings plenty of good cheer (and no shortage of booze) to this fun, four-day horse-racing event (p419).

Food & Drink

Temptation comes in many forms when it comes to food and drink in Queensland. The vast coastline yields a seafood bounty. You'll also find award-winning (but little known) wines, food festivals and a plethora of great restaurants. For more on the culinary scene see p450.

Oskars Perched over the beach, this Gold Coast charmer is the place to sample some of Queensland's finest seafood (p132).

Noosa Food & Wine Festival This lovely Sunshine Coast town serves up a gluttonous eat-drink-and-be-merry fest in May (p147).

XXXX Brewery tour Learn the history of Queensland's favourite beverage during a brewery tour – with plenty of sampling at the end (p70).

Mojo's Reason enough to venture to the northern tropics, this fantastic French-Australian restaurant serves up inventive and delectable fusion fare (p365).

Granite Belt wineries Queensland does indeed have vineyards, and this cool mountainous region is a great place to sample some superb wines (p107).

If you like... dinosaurs, head to the Lark Quarry Dinosaur Trackways in the outback for a look at thousands of dino footprints made 95 million years ago (p415)

Family Fun

Queensland has a wealth of options to keep both kids and adults entertained when travelling around the state. Top picks include high-action theme parks, whale-watching cruises, aquariums and a world-class zoo. For more tips on travelling with children see p42.

Theme parks There's nonstop adventure in the Gold Coast's theme parks, with refreshing water parks, aquatic shows and plenty of heart-racing roller coasters (p120).

Underwater World The largest oceanarium in the southern hemisphere is a great place to see sharks, stingrays, dazzling fish and more (p155).

Australia Zoo Allow a full day for the massive Australia Zoo, Queensland's temple to all creatures great and small (p153).

Whale watching In season (July through October) you're almost sure to see whales on a scenic cruise from Hervey Bay or Redcliffe (p181 and p99).

Daydream Island Resort Unlike many Whitsunday Islands' resorts, this one welcomes children with open arms, offering heaps of activities for the kids (p252).

Scenic Journeys

Getting from point A to point B can entail big adventures in Queensland. You can plan an itinerary by train, 4WD, boat or even sky gondola, taking in awe-inspiring scenery along the way.

4WD to Cape York One of Australia's great wilderness adventures is the off-road journey to the tip of Australia. Experienced drivers can go it alone. You can also join a tour (p390).

Sailing the Whitsundays This stunning archipelago is one of Australia's most magical places to sail. You can hire a bareboat or join a multi-day tour (p239).

Train to Cairns The *Sunlander* keeps the golden era of train travel alive on its scenic 30-hour journey between Brisbane and Cairns (p476).

Seaplane to Lizard Island The journey to this spectacular island – home to both campgrounds and a 5-star resort – is memorable, with a seaplane landing on Watsons Bay (p476).

Skyrail to Kuranda This 7.5km-long gondola ride sails over the rainforest canopy on its journey between Cairns and Kuranda (p342).

A Touch of Luxury

If you'd like to live it up and have some cash to spend, Queensland would be quite interested in making your acquaintance. A growing number of first-rate resorts vie for top honours when it comes to guest pampering.

Daintree Eco Lodge & Spa This splendid rainforest retreat has it all – boutique villas, a high-end spa and guided walks led by members of the Kuku Yalanji community (p368).

Pumpkin Island You'll have this privately owned island largely to yourself if you overnight in one of the cosy eco-friendly cabins (p210).

Mouses House In Gold Coast's Springbrook National Park, these charming cedar cottages set in the misty forest seem like something out of a fairy tale (p139).

Paradise Bay This eco-resort has just 10 beautifully sited bungalows and manages to deliver a heavy dollop of luxury while still doing good by the environment (p251).

month by month

Top Events

1 **Brisbane Festival**, September

2 **Cairns Festival**, August

3 **Woodford Folk Festival**, December

4 **Noosa Food & Wine Festival**, May

5 **Cooktown Discovery Festival**, June

January

Heat and humidity are hallmarks everywhere in the state. While the north experiences monsoonal rains – the Daintree region virtually shuts down and much of the outback remains inaccessible – holidaying families pack the southern beaches.

Big Day Out

This huge open-air music concert tours Australia, stopping over for one day at the Gold Coast, usually in late January. It attracts big-name international acts and dozens of attention-grabbing local bands and DJs. Buy tickets well in advance (www.bigdayout.com).

Australia Day

As elsewhere on the continent, Queenslanders celebrate the arrival of the First Fleet (in 1788) over the barbie on 26 January. Big towns often host events; Brisbane stages live concerts in the South Bank Parklands, followed by fireworks.

February

High temperatures and frown-inducing humidity continue. It's still the cyclone season (from December to April) anywhere north of the tropic line. Brisbanites flock to the Gold or Sunshine Coast beaches on weekends.

Tropfest

The world's largest short-film festival comes to Brisbane for one day in late January. The free event kicks off with a live performance, with screenings afterwards. It all happens in the South Bank Parklands (www.tropfest.com).

May

The end of the wet season brings folks outdoors in the tropical north, while in the south they get their last full days at the beach before colder temperatures arrive.

Noosa Food & Wine Festival

One of the Australia's best regional culinary fests happens over three days in mid-May in food-loving Noosa, with cooking demonstrations, wine tasting, cheese exhibits and plenty of feasting on gourmet fare. There are live concerts at night.

Wintermoon Festival

In a pretty bush setting north of Mackay, this family-friendly music fest features three stages, with musicians playing folk and world music. Most people camp, which adds to the appeal as impromptu performances happen around the grounds. It's held yearly over the Labour Day weekend (www.wintermoonfestival.com).

June

The tourist season kicks into high gear as visitors from southern states head to the warm tropical north, with beaches now stinger-free. Prices are higher and lodgings fill quickly. Southeast Queensland has cooler, mild temperatures.

Cooktown Discovery Festival

This weekend event commemorates Captain Cook's

landing in 1770, with a lively re-enactment by costumed local performers, both of Aboriginal and European ancestry. Highlights include fireworks, garden parties and Indigenous heritage activities – 'campfire yarns', performances, and food stalls, including bush tucker (www.cooktowndiscovery festival.com.au).

Laura Aboriginal Dance Festival

Held every odd-numbered year (2013, 2015 etc), this colourful festival celebrates Aboriginal culture in Cape York through dance, song, ceremony and performance. It takes place in Laura, 330km north of Cairns (www.lauradance festival.com).

July

July sees even bigger numbers of out-of-state visitors to Queensland, fleeing colder southern climes for the north.

Mareeba Rodeo

Around since 1949, this two-day event is one of Australia's biggest rodeos. It has all the crowd favourites – bull riding, steer wrestling, cattle shows – plus sideshows, rides and stalls. Mareeba is located an hour's drive west of Cairns (www. mareebarodeo.com.au)

August

Peak season continues in Queensland, particularly in the north, where temperatures remain mild and rainfall is minimal. In the south, cooler weather continues, making for brisk days on the coast.

Ekka

The Royal Queensland Show brings the country fair to Brisbane at this festive fun-for-all 10-day event. Fireworks, concerts, fashion parades, theme-park rides, crafts and food – plus prize-winning livestock – all pull in the big crowds (www.ekka.com.au).

Cairns Festival

Running for three weeks from late August to early September, this massive arts-and-culture fest brings a stellar program of music, theatre, dance, comedy, film, Indigenous art and public exhibitions. Outdoor events held in public plazas, parks and gardens make good use of Cairns' tropical setting (www.festivalcairns. com.au).

Hervey Bay Whale Festival

One of the world's best whale-watching towns pays homage to its favourite cetacean in this popular early-August fest. Top events: an illuminated evening street parade, a kids festival and free concerts on the seafront (www.herveybaywhale festival.com.au).

Mt Isa Rodeo

Kick up your heels and join the down-home fun at this country rodeo in the heart of the outback. You'll be treated to bareback bronco riding, steer wrestling, roping, bull riding, barrel racing, a parade and live bands playing country music (www.isaro deo.com.au).

September

Peak tourist season begins to tail off in September, as the weather generally remains mild across the country. September brings out some well-known festivals, including the superb Brisbane Festival.

Brisbane Festival

One of Australia's largest and most diverse arts festivals runs for 22 days in September and features an impressive array of concerts, plays, dance performances and fringe events around the city. It kicks off with 'Riverfire', an elaborate fireworks show over the river (www.brisbanefestival. com.au).

Valley Fiesta

Fortitude Valley, Brisbane's buzzing nightlife district, hosts this weekend-long arts extravaganza with free outdoor concerts, craft and indie designer markets, fashion parades, art exhibitions and other events that showcase the city's more creative side (www.valley fiesta.com).

Wallaby Creek Festival

In late September, this three-day festival features blues, roots and world sounds. There's a kids festival, adult workshops (didgeridoo making, fire twirling), performance artists, acrobats and more. It's held in a lush tropical setting near Rossville, 40km south of Cooktown (www.wallabycreekfestival.org.au).

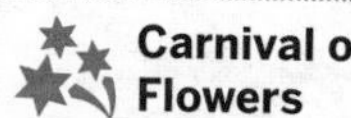

Carnival of Flowers

This 10-day fest in Toowoomba celebrates the return of spring to southeast Queensland. The highlight is the floral parade, with its magnificent flower-covered floats. There's also a food-and-wine component, concerts, free open-air cinema and elaborate blooming displays all over 'the garden city' (www.tcof.com.au).

Birdsville Races

This long-running event (first held in 1882) brings horse-racing lovers from across the country to the dusty outback town of Birdsville. It's held over one weekend in early September with a live local band kicking things off (www.birdsvilleraces.com.au).

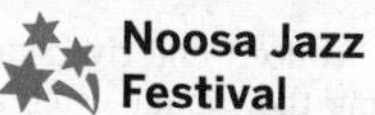

Noosa Jazz Festival

Lovely Noosa becomes a music mecca during this long-running jazz festival held in early September. Over 90 different performances are staged in town, showcasing the talents of national and international artists alike, both in indoor and outdoor venues. Some events are free.

October

October spells the tail end of the dry season in the north, with temperatures on the rise. Warmer weather blankets the south though beach days remain few and nights remain cool.

Coolangatta Gold

The Ironman of surf lifesaving, the Coolangatta Gold is a gruelling test of endurance that includes a 23km surf-ski paddle, a 3.5km swim and various beach runs – adding up to some 465.6km in all. The event is open to the public, so anyone can enter (www.coolangattagold.com.au).

November

Stinger season arrives in November and runs through to May in northern Queensland (north of Agnes Water). With the beginning of the wet season, Cooktown and the outback have limited services until May. School holidays (mid-November through to December) bring mayhem to the Gold Coast.

Noosa Multi Sport Festival

More than 50,000 flock to the small Sunshine Coast town of Noosa for this three-day event celebrating fitness and healthy living. Fun runs, bike races and a challenging triathlon are the big attractions, plus live music, cooking demonstrations, a fashion show and kids activities (www.usmevents.com.au).

December

The summer arrives, bringing soaring temperatures and humidity. The wet season is well underway in northern Queensland (anywhere north of Townsville), making travel there exceedingly unpleasant. Summer holidays bring abundant visitors to the southern beaches.

Woodford Folk Festival

One of the Sunshine Coast's biggest gatherings, the Woodford Folk Festival stages a diverse collection of performers playing folk sounds from across the globe. There's also dance, food, performance art, workshops, discussions and more. The festival runs 27 December to 1 January (www.woodfordfolkfestival.com).

Whether you've got six days or 60, these itineraries provide a starting point for the trip of a lifetime. Want more inspiration? Head online to www.lonelyplanet.com/thorntree to chat with other travellers.

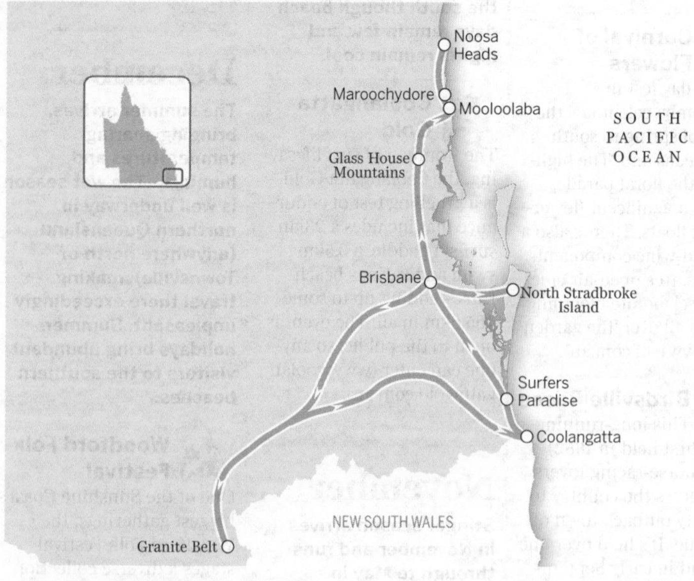

10 Days

The Sensational South

Begin in **Brisbane** for a dose of culture, taking in art exhibits, a concert and riverside dining, followed by nightlife in **Fortitude Valley**. After exploring the capital, catch a boat to **North Stradbroke Island** for whale watching, sea kayaking and idyllic beach walks. Back on the mainland, head west to the cool (bring a jacket), scenic **Granite Belt** for wine tasting and bushwalks in national park. Head east to the **Gold Coast**, stopping in laid-back **Coolangatta** before continuing north to the party centre of **Surfers Paradise**. Let loose your inhibitions (and your stomach) at the **Gold Coast Theme Parks**.

After the Gold Coast people parade, continue north to the **Glass House Mountains** for striking panoramas (and rock-climbing for the intrepid). Nearby is the fantastic **Australia Zoo**, which is well worth visiting. Next hit **Mooloolaba**, home to sun, surf and a super-friendly beach vibe; its northern beach neighbour, **Maroochydore**, is also enchanting. Another half-hour north and you reach **Noosa**, a classy resort town with sublime beaches, well-preserved national park (home to sometimes-spotted koalas) and first-class cuisine.

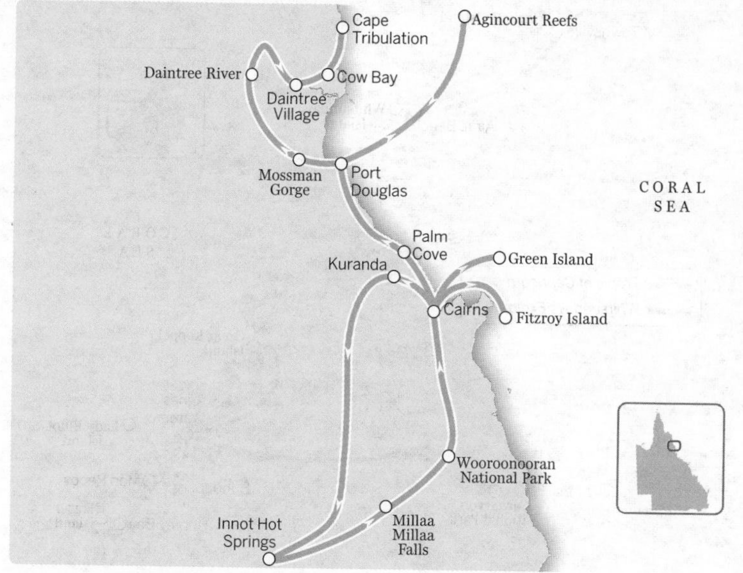

Two Weeks

Rainforest & Reef

Australia's reef-diving capital and gateway to the ancient tropical rainforests to the north, **Cairns** is an obligatory stop on almost any itinerary through Queensland. Spend a few days in the buzzing town, visiting its lush botanic gardens, enjoying good meals and getting a taste of the town's brash nightlife. Take day trips to **Green** and **Fitzroy Islands**, with reef-trimmed shores, verdant vegetation and lovely beaches. Book a snorkelling or dive trip to the **Great Barrier Reef** (ideally the outer reef) or plan a few days on a live-aboard expedition to **Cod Hole**, one of Australia's best dive spots. You can also plan adventure activities like white-water rafting and skydiving.

After a few days in Cairns, head inland via gondola cableway or scenic railway to **Kuranda** for rainforest walks and browsing the popular markets. Spend a few days exploring the region (though you'll need your own wheels), soaking in **Innot Hot Springs**, visiting picturesque **Millaa Millaa falls** and hiking in spectacular **Wooroonooran National Park**.

Head back to the coast and treat yourself to a night in a peaceful resort in lovely **Palm Cove**, just north of Cairns. Continue an hour further north to **Port Douglas**, a peaceful holiday town with a beautiful beach. It's also a base for boat trips to the outer reef with first-rate catamarans heading to **Agincourt Reefs**.

After a few nights eating, drinking and relaxing in Port Douglas, hit the road. The first stop is **Mossman Gorge**, where lush lowland rainforest surrounds the photogenic Mossman River. Sign up for a memorable **Kuku-Yalanji Dreamtime walk**, run by the Indigenous Kuku-Yalanji.

Go north to the **Daintree River**. Take a crocodile-spotting cruise and stop for lunch in the **Daintree Village**. Afterwards, continue back to the river, where you'll cross by vehicle ferry to the northern side. From here drive north (carefully, as this is cassowary country) toward Cape Tribulation. Stop at the **Daintree Discovery Centre** to learn about this magnificent area. The lovely beach at nearby **Cow Bay** is also worth a detour. Continue north, taking a bit of refreshment at the **Daintree Ice Cream Company**. The last stop is **Cape Tribulation**, a magnificent meeting of rainforest and reef. Spend a few nights taking in the splendour at one of the fine lodges tucked in the rainforest.

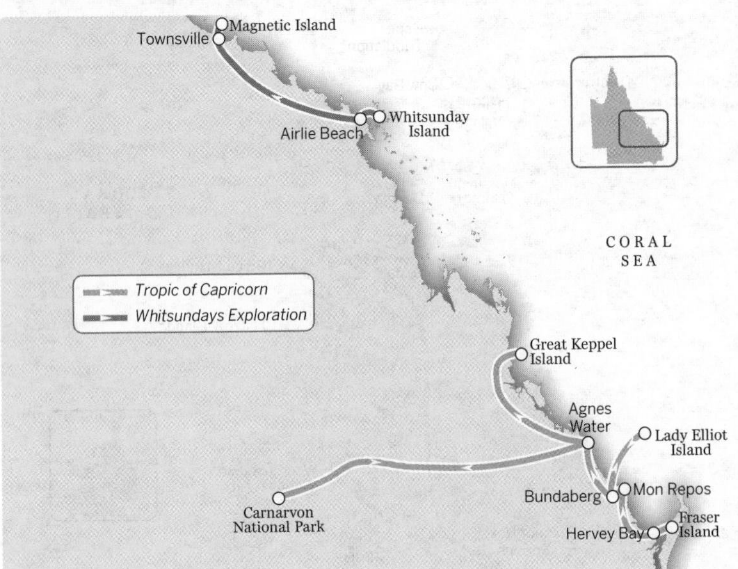

Two Weeks

Tropic of Capricorn

Start the adventure in **Hervey Bay**, a pleasant seaside town with good swimming beaches and superb whale-watching cruises from here in season (July to October). Next, prepare for big adventure (either hiring a 4WD or joining a tour) on **Fraser Island**, home to massive dunes, beach 'highways', memorable bushwalks and crystal-clear lakes. After Fraser, head north to **Mon Repos**, where you can see massive loggerhead turtles nesting or new hatchlings dashing into the sea (November to March). The old-fashioned country town of **Bundaberg** is next; don't miss a tour of the famous **Bundaberg Rum Distillery**. From Bundaberg, catch a flight to **Lady Elliott Island** with magnificent snorkelling and diving amid marine-rich coral gardens. Back on the mainland, go north to **Agnes Water**, a charming town with good surf and white-sand beaches. Refreshed, take the long drive west to **Carnarvon National Park**, with its dramatic gorges and mesmerising Aboriginal rock paintings. The last stop is **Great Keppel Island**, a stunningly beautiful and pristine island with fine beaches and forest-covered hills.

One to Two Weeks

Whitsundays Exploration

Fly to **Airlie Beach**, and indulge in a bit of the town's youthful nightlife, while researching boats heading out to the **Whitsunday Islands**. A multiday trip is a great option as you can explore remote islands that you and your fellow crew will have to yourself. Make sure your boat's itinerary includes a stop on **Whitsunday Island** for a memorable swim off stunning **Whitehaven Beach**, one of the prettiest beaches in Australia. After cruising the islands, book a night or two at an island resort. For something more adventurous, you could also sign on for an overnight kayaking trip out to one of the islands.

After Airlie Beach, pack yourself up and continue north around three hours to **Townsville**. Explore the waterfront promenade, visit the superb Reef HQ Aquarium, scale Castle Hill and soak up the fine dining scene. If you're an experienced diver, book a spot on a boat out to dive the famous **Yongala wreck dive**. End your journey on **Magnetic Island**, an unpretentious island with easygoing beach villages, abundant wildlife and scenic bushwalking tracks.

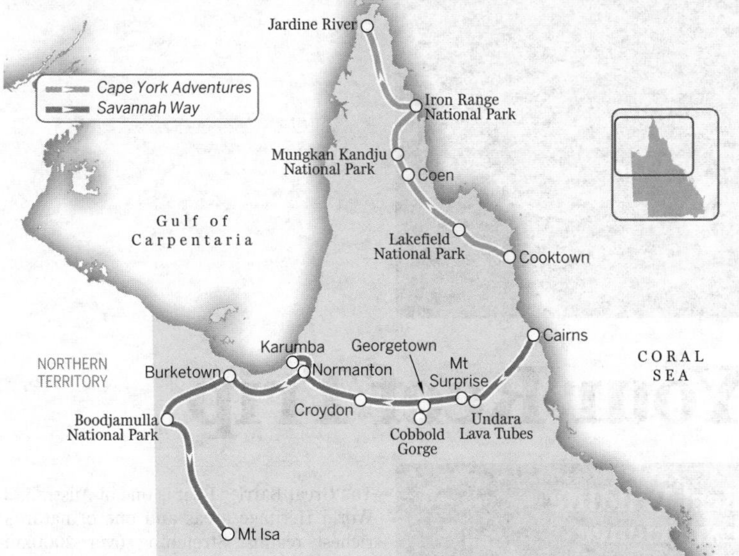

One to Two Weeks

Savannah Way

This route crosses a remote part of northern Queensland to the Gulf of Carpentaria and makes a great add-on to the Rainforest & Reef tour if time allows. Apart from a couple of detours, it's a sealed road, accessible to all vehicles.

From **Cairns**, the first stop is the fascinating **Undara Lava Tubes**, where you can walk through ancient volcanic formations. Continue west through the old mining towns of **Mt Surprise**, **Georgetown** and **Croydon**, but don't miss the detour to dramatic **Cobbold Gorge**, with swimming holes, wildlife and rugged cliffs. Back on the highway, **Normanton** is a good barra fishing town on the Normanton River, but continue another 70km to remote **Karumba** on the Gulf of Carpentaria for unparalleled angling and super sunsets. If you have a 2WD, you can head south on the sealed Matilda Hwy to Cloncurry and then west to Mt Isa. Otherwise, hit the dirt on the Savannah Way west to **Burketown** for the morning glory, then make your way southwest to **Boodjamulla National Park**, where you can canoe in the stunning gorge, camp and explore fossil sites. Continue south on 4WD tracks to the Barkly Hwy and southeast to civilisation at **Mt Isa**, the outback's biggest town.

One to Two Weeks

Cape York Adventures

To cover the magnificent, pristine ground from Cooktown to Cape York you'll need a 4WD to get you off the beaten track.

Begin your northern adventure in the fascinating frontier settlement of **Cooktown**. Then head northwest on McIver Rd into Queensland's second-largest national park: isolated **Lakefield National Park**, with rich wildlife and great outdoor activities, including superb barramundi fishing and croc-spotting.

From the north end of the park, head west to the Peninsula Development Rd and drive north 100km to **Coen**, the Cape's 'capital' and gateway to the Rokeby section of **Mungkan Kandju National Park**. Continue another 100km or so and turn east onto Archer Rd to **Iron Range National Park**, Australia's largest conservation area of lowland tropical forest, with spectacular bird life and flora.

To reach the top of the Cape you need to drive the extent of Telegraph Rd (about 200km), which skirts Jardine River National Park. Here you can swim in the gorgeous (croc-free) natural pools at Twin Falls. Once you cross the **Jardine River**, set up camp on the beach at Seisia or Punsand Bay and savour the final leg of the rugged trip to the tip of Australia.

Your Reef Trip

Best Wildlife Experience

Watching protected sea turtles hatch and make their first daring dash to the water on Lady Elliot Island or Heron Island, then, while snorkelling or diving, watching their older relatives glide gracefully through the ocean.

Best Snorkelling Experience

Taking a fast catamaran from Airlie Beach out to Knuckle Reef or a seaplane to Hardy Reef and immersing yourself in some of the word's best snorkelling spots.

Best View from Above

Soaring above the Reef on a scenic flight from Cairns and watching its huge and vivid mass carpet the sea beneath you.

Most Tranquil Experience

Exploring the southern end of the Great Barrier Reef, especially Fitzroy Reef Lagoon.

Best Sailing Experience

Sailing from Airlie Beach through the Whitsunday Islands and exploring exquisite fringing reefs on the islands' perimeters.

The Great Barrier Reef is one of Australia's World Heritage areas and one of nature's richest realms. Stretching over 2000km from just south of the tropic of Capricorn (near Gladstone) to just south of Papua New Guinea, it is the most extensive reef system in the world, and made entirely by living organisms.

There is a multitude of ways to see the magnificent spectacle of the Reef. Diving and snorkelling are far and away the best methods of getting up close and personal with the menagerie of marine life and dazzling corals. Immersing yourself in the sea furnishes you with the most exhilarating appreciation of just how wonderful and rich this community is. The unremarkable surface of the water belies the colourful congestion less than a metre or so beneath.

You can also surround yourself with fabulous tropical fish without getting wet on a semi-submersible or glass-bottomed boat, which provides windows to the underwater world below. Alternatively, you can go below the ocean's surface inside an underwater observatory, or stay up top and take a reef walk.

Another spectacular way to see the Reef while staying dry is on a scenic flight. Soaring high provides a macroperspective of the Reef's beauty and size and allows you to see the veins and networks of coral connecting and ribboning out from one another.

When to Go

High season on the Great Barrier Reef is from June to December. The best overall visibility is from August to January.

From December to March **northern Queensland** (north of Townsville) has a distinct wet season, bringing oppressive heat and abundant rainfall (from July to September it's drier and cooler). Cyclones can occur from November to March but are not common and shouldn't prevent you from going (an effective cyclone warning system is in place in the Pacific).

Anytime is generally good to visit the **Whitsundays**. Winter (June to August) can be pleasantly warm, but you will occasionally need a jumper during the day and a light jacket at night. South of the Whitsundays, summer (December to March) can be hot and humid, but the wet season doesn't extend as far south as the Whitsundays.

Southern and **central Queensland** experience mild winters (June to August) – pleasant enough for diving or snorkelling in a wetsuit.

Picking Your Spot

It's said you could dive here every day of your life and still not see all of the Great Barrier Reef. Individual chapters in this book provide in-depth information, but the following are some of the most popular and remarkable spots from which to access the Reef. Bear in mind that individual areas change over time, depending on the weather or any recent damage.

Mainland Gateways

There are several mainland gateways to the Reef, all offering slightly different experiences or activities. Deciding which to choose can be difficult – so here's a brief overview, ordered from south to north.

Agnes Water & Town of 1770 (p215) are small towns and good choices if you want to escape the crowds. From here tours head to Fitzroy Reef Lagoon, one of the most pristine sections of the Reef, where visitor numbers are still limited. The lagoon is excellent for snorkelling but also quite spectacular viewed from the boat.

Gladstone (p211) is a slightly bigger town but still a relatively small gateway. It's an excellent choice for avid divers and snorkellers, being the closest access point to the southern or Capricorn reef islands and innumerable cays, including Lady Elliot Island.

Airlie Beach (p243) is a small town with a full rack of sailing outfits. The big attraction here is spending two or more days aboard a boat and seeing some of the Whitsunday Islands' fringing coral reefs. The surrounding scenery is sublime, but you'll only see the edges of the Reef. There are, however, a number of fast-catamaran operators that zoom across 60km to reach reefs that provide outstanding snorkelling, swimming and diving.

Airlie is also friendly to all wallets, so whether you're a five- or no-star traveller, there'll be a tour to match your budget.

Townsville (p264) is a renowned gateway among divers. Whether you're learning or experienced, a four- or five-night onboard diving safari around the numerous islands and pockets of the Reef is a great choice. In particular, Kelso Reef and the wreck of the SS *Yongala* are teeming with marine life. There are also a couple of day-trip options on glass-bottomed boats, but for more choice you're better off heading to Cairns. **Reef HQ** (p265), which is basically a version of the Reef in an aquarium, is also here.

Mission Beach (p291) is closer to the Reef than any other gateway destination. This small, quiet town offers a few boat and diving tours to sections of the outer reef. Although the choice isn't huge, neither are the crowds, so you won't be sharing the experience with a fleet of other vessels.

Cairns (p306) is undeniably the main launching pad for Reef tours: there is a bewildering number of operators here. You can do anything from relatively inexpensive day trips on large boats to intimate five-day luxury charters. The variety of tours covers a wide section of the Reef, with some operators going as far north as Lizard Island. Inexpensive tours are likely to travel to inner reefs, ie those close to the mainland, which tend to be more damaged than outer reefs. Scenic flights also operate out of Cairns. Bear in mind, though, that this is the most popular destination, so unless your budget stretches to a private charter you'll be sharing the experience with many others.

Port Douglas (p355) is a swanky resort town and a gateway to the Low Isles and Agincourt Reef, an outer ribbon reef featuring crystal-clear water and particularly stunning corals. Although Port Douglas is

USEFUL WEBSITES

» **Dive Queensland** (www.dive-queensland.com.au) Queensland's dive tourism association, with info on dive locations, dive operators, live-aboards and diving schools.

» **Tourism Queensland** (www.queenslandholidays.com.au) Official state tourism portal with listings for accommodation and attractions.

» **Great Barrier Reef Marine Park Authority** (www.gbrmpa.gov.au) Reef-related info on climate change, conservation, tourism and fisheries.

» **Queensland Parks & Wildlife Services** (www.derm.qld.gov.au) Info, including permits and how to get there, for all national parks.

» **Australian Bureau of Meteorology** (www.bom.gov.au) The latest info (and annual statistics) on rainfall, temperatures and weather conditions.

smaller than Cairns, it's very popular and has a wealth of tour operators. Diving, snorkelling and cruising trips tend to be classier, pricier and less crowded than in Cairns. You can also take a scenic flight from here.

Cooktown (p380) is another one for divers. The town's lure is its close proximity to Lizard Island (see p385). Although you can access the island from Cairns, you'll spend far less time travelling by boat if you go from here. Cooktown's relatively remote location means there are only a handful of tour operators and small numbers of tourists, so your experience is not likely to be rushed or brief. The only drawback is that the town and its tour operators shut down between November and May for the wet season.

Islands

Speckled throughout the Reef is a profusion of islands and cays that offer some of the most stunning access to the Reef. Here is a list of some of the best islands, travelling from south to north.

For more information on individual islands, see the Whitsunday Coast (p225), Capricorn Coast (p198), Townsville to Innisfail (p262), Cairns, Islands & Highlands (p304) and Port Douglas & The Daintree Rainforest (p353) chapters.

The coral cay of **Lady Elliot Island** (p214) is the most southerly of the Reef islands. It's awe-inspiring for bird-watchers, with some 57 species living on the island. Sea turtles also nest here and it's possibly the best location on the Reef to see manta rays. It's also a famed diving spot. There's a simple, pricey camping resort here, but you can also visit Lady Elliot on a day trip from Bundaberg.

Heron Island (p214) is a tiny coral cay sitting amid a huge spread of reef. It's a diving mecca, but the snorkelling is also good and it's possible to do a reef walk from here.

Heron is a nesting ground for green and loggerhead turtles and home to some 30 species of birds. It's an exclusive, utterly tranquil place, and the sole resort on the island charges accordingly.

Hamilton Island (p254), the daddy of the Whitsundays, is a sprawling resort laden with infrastructure. While this doesn't create the most intimate atmosphere, there is a wealth of tours going to the outer reef. It's also a good place to see patches of the Reef that can't be explored from the mainland. Families are extremely well catered for.

Hook Island (p252) is an outer Whitsunday Island surrounded by fringing reefs. There is excellent swimming and snorkelling here, and the island's sizeable bulk provides plenty of good bushwalking. There's affordable accommodation on Hook and it's easily accessed from Airlie Beach, making it a top choice for those on a modest budget.

Orpheus Island (p287) is a national park and one of the Reef's most exclusive, tranquil and romantic hideaways. This island is particularly good for snorkelling – you can step right off the beach and be surrounded by the Reef's colourful marine life. Clusters of fringing reefs also provide plenty of diving opportunities.

Green Island (p335) is another of the Reef's true coral cays. The fringing reefs here are considered to be among the most beautiful surrounding any island, and the diving and snorkelling are quite spectacular. Covered in dense rainforest, the entire island is national park. Bird life is abundant, with around 60 species to be found. The resort on Green Island is well set up for reef activities; several tour operators offer diving and snorkelling cruises and there's also an underwater observatory. The island is accessible as a day trip from Cairns.

Lizard Island (p385) is remote, rugged and the perfect place to escape civilisation. It has a ring of talcum-white beaches, remarkably blue water and few visitors. It's also world-renowned as a superb scuba-diving location, with what is arguably Australia's best-known dive site at Cod Hole (p386), where you can swim with docile potato cod weighing as much as 60kg. Pixie Bommie is another highly regarded dive site on the island.

Snorkellers will also get an eyeful of marine life here all around the island, with giant clams, manta rays, barracudas and dense schools of fish abundant in the waters just offshore.

If you're staying overnight you need to have deep pockets or no requirements whatsoever – it's either five-star or luxury bush camping.

Diving & Snorkelling the Reef

Much of the diving and snorkelling on the Reef is boat-based, although there are some excellent reefs accessible by walking straight off the beach of some islands scattered along the Great Barrier. Free use of snorkelling gear is usually part of any cruise to the Reef and you can typically fit in around three hours of underwater wandering. Overnight or 'live-aboard' trips obviously provide a more in-depth experience and greater coverage of the reefs. If you want to do more than snorkel but don't have a diving certificate, many operators offer the option of an introductory dive, which is a guided dive where an experienced diver conducts an underwater tour. A solid lesson in safety and procedure is given beforehand and you don't require a five-day Professional Association of Diving Instructors (PADI) course or a 'buddy'.

Boat Excursions

Unless you're staying on a coral-fringed island in the middle of the Great Barrier Reef, you'll need to join a boat excursion – either on a daytrip or on a multi-day live-aboard – to experience the Reef's real beauty. Daytrips leave from many places along the coast, as well as from island resorts (see p27 for prime gateways) and typically include the use of snorkelling gear, snacks and a buffet lunch, with scuba diving an optional extra. Many boats also offer an introductory scuba dive on the Reef, escorted by a divemaster, which can be a great way to get a taste of diving. On some boats a naturalist or marine biologist presents a talk on the Reef's ecology.

Boat trips vary dramatically in passenger numbers, type of vessel and quality – which is reflected in the price – so it's worth getting all the details before committing to a particular trip. When selecting a tour, consider the vessel (motorised catamaran or sailing ship), the number of passengers (from six to 400), what extras are offered and the destination. The outer reefs are usually more pristine. Inner reefs often show signs of damage from humans, coral bleaching and coral-eating crown-of-thorns starfish. Some companies that are only licensed to visit the

TOP SNORKELLING SITES

Some nondivers may wonder if it's really worth going to the Great Barrier Reef 'just to snorkel'. The answer is a resounding yes. There are some fantastic sites for snorkellers – in fact, much of the rich, colourful coral lies just underneath the surface (as coral needs bright sunlight to flourish) and is easily accessible. Here's a round-up of the top snorkelling sites:

- Fitzroy Reef Lagoon
- Heron Island
- Keppel Island
- Lady Elliot Island
- Lady Musgrave Island
- Hook Island
- Hayman Island
- Lizard Island
- Border Island (Whitsundays)
- Hardy Reef (Whitsundays)
- Knuckle Reef (Whitsundays)
- Michaelmans Reef (Cairns)
- Hastings Reef (Cairns)
- Norman Reef (Cairns)
- Saxon Reef (Cairns)
- Opal Reef (Port Douglas)
- Agincourt Reef (Port Douglas)
- Mackay Reef (Port Douglas)

MOTION SICKNESS

If you're prone to motion sickness, be sure to bring medication or acupressure wristbands with you, as boat rides out to the Reef can be a little rough. Some swear by herbal ginger remedies, while others say they don't work. Take your tablets 30 minutes before boarding – once you're on the water, it's generally too late.

inner reef have cheaper tours; in most cases you get what you pay for. Some operators offer the option of a trip in a glass-bottomed boat or semi-submersible.

Many boats have underwater cameras for hire – although you'll save money by hiring these on land (better yet, purchase an underwater housing case for your digital camera if you plan to take a lot of pictures). Some boats also have professional photographers on board who will dive with you and take high-quality shots of you in action.

Live-Aboards

If you're eager to do as much diving as possible, a live-aboard is an excellent option. This allows reef-goers the chance to dive around three dives per day, plus the occasional night dive, and visit more remote parts of the Great Barrier Reef. Trip lengths vary from one to 12 nights. The three-day/three-night voyages, which allow up to 11 dives (nine day and two night dives), are among the most common. Some go on exploratory trips, others run a set route and may use fixed moorings or pontoons, while others are more impromptu.

It is worth checking the various options as some boats offer specialist itineraries following marine life and events such as minke whales or coral spawning, or offer trips to more remote spots like the far northern reefs, Pompey Complex, Coral Sea Reefs or Swain Reefs.

It's recommended to go with operators who are Dive Queensland members: this ensures they follow a minimum set of guidelines. See www.dive-queensland.com.au for the latest membership list. Ideally, they are also accredited by the Ecotoursim Association of Australia (www.ecotourism.org.au).

Popular departure points for live-aboard dive vessels, along with the locales they visit:

» **Bundaberg** – the Bunker Island group, including Lady Musgrave and Lady Elliot Islands, possibly Fitzroy, Llewellyn and rarely visited Boult Reefs or Hoskyn and Fairfax Islands.

» **1770** – Bunker Island group.

» **Gladstone** – Swains and Bunker Island group.

» **Mackay** – Lihou Reef and the Coral Sea.

» **Airlie Beach** – the Whitsundays, Knuckle Reef and Hardy Reef.

» **Townsville** – *Yongala* wreck, plus canyons of Wheeler Reef and Keeper Reef.

» **Cairns** – Cod Hole, Ribbon Reefs, the Coral Sea and possibly far northern reefs.

» **Port Douglas** – Osprey Reef, Cod Hole, Ribbon Reefs, Coral Sea and possibly the far northern reefs.

Dive Courses

In Queensland there are numerous places where you can learn to dive, take a refresher course or improve your skills. Dive courses in Queensland are generally of a high standard, and all schools teach either PADI or Scuba Schools International (SSI) qualifications. Which certification you choose isn't as important as choosing a good instructor, so be sure to seek local recommendations and meet with the instructor before committing to a program.

One of the most popular places to learn is Cairns, where you can choose between courses for the budget-minded (four-day courses from around $450) that combine pool training and reef dives, to longer, more intensive courses that include reef diving on a live-aboard (five-day courses including three-day/two-night live-aboard are around $825).

Other places where you can learn to dive, and then head out on the Reef include the following:

» Bundaberg

» Mission Beach

» Townsville

» Airlie Beach

» Hamilton Island

» Magnetic Island

» Port Douglas

For more details on Dive Courses, see p310.

Safety Guidelines for Diving

Before embarking on a scuba-diving, skin-diving or snorkelling trip, carefully consider the following points to ensure a safe and enjoyable experience:

» If scuba diving, make sure you have a current diving certification card from a recognised scuba-diving instructional agency.

» Ensure you're healthy and feel comfortable diving.

» Obtain reliable information from a reputable local dive operation about the physical and environmental conditions at the dive site, such as water temperature, visibility and tidal movements, and find out how local divers deal with these considerations.

» Be aware that underwater conditions vary significantly from one region, or even site, to another. Seasonal changes can significantly alter any site and dive conditions. These differences influence the way divers dress for a dive and what diving techniques they use.

» Be aware of local laws, regulations and etiquette with regards to marine life and the environment.

» Dive only at sites within your realm of experience. If available, engage the services of a competent, professionally trained dive instructor or divemaster.

Diving for Nondivers

Several operators from Cairns use systems that allow nondivers to 'dive' using surface-supplied air systems. With helmet diving, hoses provide fresh surface air to divers via astronaut-like helmets so you can breathe normally and your face and hair stay dry (you can even wear glasses). There's also no need to know how to swim as you'll be walking on a submerged platform, 4m to 5m below the surface. Walks typically last 15 to 20 minutes, and are conducted under the guidance of a qualified dive instructor. Prices start at around $140. Anyone older than 12 and over 140cm tall can participate, although as with scuba diving, certain medical conditions will prohibit participation (asthma, heart disease, pregnancy, epilepsy). For operators, see p311.

Picking the Right Resort

The Great Barrier Reef is home to over a dozen island resorts, offering varying levels of comfort and style. Although most options sit squarely in the luxury category, there are some affordable stays for those who are seeking a beautiful setting, but don't mind

KEY DIVING DETAILS

Diving & Flying

Remember that your last dive should be completed 24 hours before your flight – even in a balloon or for a parachute jump – in order to minimise the risk of residual nitrogen in the blood that can cause decompression injury. On the other hand, it's fine to dive soon after arriving by air.

Insurance

Find out whether or not your insurance policy classifies diving as a dangerous sport and excludes it. For a nominal annual fee, the **Divers Alert Network** (DAN; www.diversalertnetwork.org) provides insurance for medical or evacuation services required in the event of a diving accident. DAN's hotline for diving emergencies is ✆800 088 200.

Visibility

Coastal areas: 1m to 3m
Several kilometres offshore: 8m to 15m
Outer edge of the Reef: 20m to 35m
Coral Sea: 50m and beyond

Water Temperature

In the north, the water temperature is warm all year round, from around 24°C to 30°C. Going south it gradually gets cooler, dropping to 20°C to 28°C in winter.

middle-of-the-road accommodation, like that offered on Lady Elliot Island.

Where to stay depends not only on your budget, but also what sort of activities you have in mind. Some resorts are small and secluded (and don't allow children), which can be ideal for a tropical getaway doing little more than swinging in a hammock, basking on powdery sand beaches and sipping tropical cocktails. If this sounds ideal, try Orpheus or Hayman Islands. Other resorts have a busier vibe and offer a wide range of activities, from sailing and kayaking to helicopter joy rides, plus restaurants and even some nightlife. If this is more to your liking, try Hamilton Island.

You'll find the widest selection of resorts in the Whitsundays (p238).

Camping on the Great Barrier Reef

Pitching a tent on an island is a unique and affordable way to experience the Great Barrier Reef. If you don't mind roughing it a bit, you can enjoy an idyllic tropical setting at a fraction of the price of the five-star island resort that may be located down the road from the campground. Campsite facilities range from virtually nothing to showers, flush toilets, interpretive signage and picnic tables. Most islands are remote, so ensure you are adequately prepared for medical and general emergencies.

Wherever you stay, you'll need to be self-sufficient, bringing your own food and drinking water (5L per day per person is recommended). Weather can often prevent planned pickups, so have enough supplies to last an extra three or four days in case you get stranded.

As a general reminder, all the islands have fragile ecosystems, so camp only in designated areas, keep to marked trails and take out all that you brought in. Fires are banned so you'll need a gas stove or similar.

You'll need to reserve campsites well in advance. National park camping permits can be reserved online through **QPWS** (☎13 74 68; www.derm.qld.gov.au). Here are our top camping picks.

Whitsunday Islands (p242) Nearly a dozen beautifully sited camping areas, scattered on the islands of Hook, Whitsunday and Henning.

MAKING A POSITIVE CONTRIBUTION TO THE REEF

The Great Barrier Reef is incredibly fragile and it's worth taking some time to educate yourself on responsible practices while you're there. Here are a few of the more important sustainable practices, but this is by no means an exhaustive list.

» Whether on an island or in a boat, take all litter with you – even biodegradable material like apple cores – and dispose of it back on the mainland.

» Remember that it is an offence to damage or remove coral in the marine park.

» Don't touch or harass marine animals and be aware that if you touch or walk on coral you'll damage it. It can also create some nasty cuts. Never rest or stand on coral.

» If you have a boat, be aware of the rules in relation to anchoring around the reef, including 'no anchoring areas'. Be very careful not to damage coral when you let down the anchor.

» If you're diving, check that you are weighted correctly before entering the water and keep your buoyancy control well away from the reef. Ensure that equipment such as secondary regulators and gauges aren't dragging over the reef.

» If you're snorkelling (and especially if you are a beginner) practice your technique away from coral until you've mastered control in the water.

» Hire a wetsuit rather than slathering on sunscreen, which can damage the reef.

» Watch where your fins are – try not to stir up sediment or disturb coral.

» Do not enter the water near a dugong, including when swimming or diving.

» Note that there are limits on the amount and types of shells that you can collect.

TOP REEF DIVE SPOTS

The Great Barrier Reef is home to some of the world's best diving sites. Here are a few of our favourite spots to get you started:

» **SS Yongala** – a sunken shipwreck that has been home to a vivid marine community for more than 90 years.

» **Cod Hole** – go nose-to-nose with a potato cod.

» **Heron Island** – join a crowd of colourful fish straight off the beach.

» **Lady Elliot Island** – with 19 highly regarded dive sites.

» **Pixie Bommie** – delve into the after-five world of the Reef by taking a night dive.

Capricornia Cays Camping available on three separate coral cays including Masthead Island, North West Island and Lady Musgrave Island (p214) – a fantastic, uninhabited island that's limited to a maximum 40 campers.

Dunk Island (p298) Equal parts resort and national park with good swimming, kayaking and hiking.

Fitzroy Island (p336) Resort and national park with short walking trails through bush and coral just off the beaches.

Frankland Islands (p337) Coral-fringed island with white-sand beaches off Cairns.

Lizard Island (p385) Stunning beaches, magnificent coral and abundant wildlife, but generally you must arrive by plane.

Orpheus Island (p287) Secluded island (accessible by air) with pretty tropical forest and superb fringing reef.

Queensland Outdoors

Best Wildlife Spotting

Whales and dolphins off Hervey Bay
Koalas on Magnetic Island
Cassowaries in the Daintree
Platypuses in Eungella National Park
Dingoes on Fraser Island

Top Five Aquatic Activities

Surfing at Noosa
Kayaking at North Stradbroke Island
Sailing around the Whitsundays
Diving on the Great Barrier Reef
Fishing on Lake Tinaroo

Best Activities for Daredevils

Bungee jumping at Surfers Paradise
Skydiving over Caloundra
Parasailing over the Gold Coast
White-water rafting on the Tully River
Cruising the highway of Fraser Island in a 4WD

Best National Parks for Bushwalking

Wooroonooran
Carnarvon
Lamington
Springbrook
Girraween

Home to ancient rainforests, magnificent tropical islands, rugged mountains and the stunning Great Barrier Reef, Queensland harbours some of Australia's best sites for outdoor adventure. Scuba diving and snorkelling are extremely popular activities and a great way to view the rich aquatic life off the coast, while surfing here is world-class. There's also great whale watching, sailing, fishing and loads of other waterside activities. Islands come in hundreds of varieties, from sparkling, reef-fringed beauties to massive sand-dune-laden national parks whose interior is accessible only by 4WD. You can camp on deserted beaches, surf amazing breaks or paddle a kayak through dense mangroves. Heading inland, you'll find superb bushwalking in rainforests, trekking and rock-climbing around craggy peaks and white-water rafting on rushing rivers. Those looking for something a little different can go skydiving, parasailing or even hunt for precious stones in Queensland's gem fields.

Bushwalking & Trekking

Bushwalking is a popular activity in Queensland year-round, and there are some superb settings for taking in the scenery, from short 1km walks to multi-

WALK	DIFFICULTY	DISTANCE	DURATION	SCENERY
Carnarvon	hard	86km	6-7 days	dramatic sandstone gorges, Aboriginal rock paintings, panoramic ridgelines
Fraser Island	hard	90km	up to 8 days	rainforests, coloured sands, picturesque lakes, towering sand dunes
Gold Coast Hinterland	moderate	55km	3 days	palm-filled valleys, mist-covered mountains, cliff-top views, waterfalls, crystal-clear rivers
Mackay Highlands	moderate	50km	4-6 days	rainforest, gorges, steep escarpments, rolling farmlands
Sunshine Coast Hinterland	moderate	58km	4 days	scenic Blackall Range, waterfalls, eucalypt forest, subtropical rainforest & fine views
Wet Tropics	moderate	100km	6 days	waterfalls, gorges, views & World Heritage rainforest at Girringun National Park
Whitsunday	hard	30km	3 days	lowland tropical rainforest, rocky creeks, lush palm valleys, views, rugged Conway Range (inside Conway National Park)

day treks with camping along the way. National parks and state forests are some of the best places for walking. See p444 for contact details and more information.

There are some celebrated tracks for experienced walkers in Queensland. Bear in mind that these can be difficult and the conditions for some require substantial bushwalking smarts. In northern Queensland the 32km ungraded Thorsborne Trail (p289) on Hinchinbrook Island is a spectacular bushwalking retreat. Walker numbers are limited for this trail at any one time. The Thorsborne traverses a gamut of environments, including remote beaches, rainforests and creeks, amid spectacular mountain scenery. Other multi-day treks are part of the Great Walks of Queensland.

Less experience is needed for the myriad trails on Magnetic Island (p275), where koalas and bird life are prolific.

When to Go

Walking in the southern half of the state is feasible and pleasant all year round due to the accommodating climate. Regardless of the time of year, however, you should always take plenty of drinking water with you.

From the Capricorn Coast north, the best time to go walking is from April to September as things can get pretty hot and sticky during the summer, particularly in the wet season between the months of November and February. Longer walking tracks are often closed at this time of year, and even shorter tracks require advance planning to take into account the harsher conditions.

Summer is also the most prolific period for bushfires, which represent a constant threat throughout Queensland. **Queensland Parks & Wildlife Service** (QPWS; www.derm.qld.gov.au) can advise you on current alerts; also check out p456 for more information.

Great Walks of Queensland

An initiative of the state government, the Great Walks of Queensland is the result of a $16.5 million campaign to create a world-class set of walking tracks. These highlight some of the state's most striking scenery from lush tropical forests to pristine beaches, with sparkling lagoons and wildlife-rich bushland all part of the journey.

The walks are designed to allow bushwalkers to experience rainforests and bushlands without disturbing the ecosystems. There's no admission charge to do the walks, though you will have to book well in advance for a campsite permit (which costs $5.15 per person per night). For complete details, including walk descriptions, mapping details and campsite bookings, contact QPWS.

Bushwalking Books & Resources

An excellent way to explore the region is by contacting a local bushwalking club, such as the **Brisbane Bushwalkers Club** (www.bbw.org.au), which welcomes new members to join group outings. The following guidebooks are a good starting point for your own bushwalking adventure:

» *Take a Walk in South-East Queensland* (2009) by John & Lyn Daly covers more than 170 walks, including overnight treks as well as easy, moderate and hard day hikes in 22 national parks in Brisbane, Gold Coast, Sunshine Coast and Fraser Coast regions.

» *Tropical Walking Tracks* (2007) by Kim Dungey and Jane Whytlaw includes dozens of walks outside Cairns, Kuranda and Cooktown, in the Daintree area and in the Atherton Tableland.

» Lonely Planet's *Walking in Australia* (2006) describes 60 walks of different lengths and difficulty in various parts of the country, including walks through three of Queensland's World Heritage–listed sites.

» *50 Walks in North Queensland* (2000) by Tyrone Thomas highlights the Wet Tropics Rainforests, with graded walks covering regions from Cape Tribulation in the north to Mackay in the south, plus seven islands in the Great Barrier Reef.

Diving & Snorkelling

The Queensland coast boasts enough spectacular dive sites to make you giddy. The Great Barrier Reef offers some of the world's best diving and snorkelling, and there are dozens of operators vying to teach you to scuba dive or provide you with the ultimate dive safari. There are also some 1600 shipwrecks along the Queensland coast, revealing vivid and densely populated marine metropolises for you to explore. For details on diving in the Great Barrier Reef see p26.

You can snorkel just about everywhere along Queensland's coast; it requires minimum effort and anyone can do it. Many diving locations, such as those in the table opposite, are also popular snorkelling sites.

Diving is generally good year-round although during the wet season, usually December to March, floods can wash a lot of mud out into the ocean and visibility for divers and snorkellers is sometimes obscured.

Stinger Warning

All water activities, including diving and snorkelling, are affected by stingers (box jellyfish), which are found year-round off the Queensland coast and in river mouths, from Agnes Water north. They are dangerous and should not be taken lightly. Look for the stinger-resistant enclosures at beaches during the peak stinger season, which runs from November to May. Never enter the water at beaches that have been closed due to the presence of stingers, and consider using a full-body lycra suit if you must go in the water during stinger season. For more information see p456.

Diving Courses

Every major town along the coast has one or more diving schools, but standards vary, so it's worthwhile doing some research before signing up. Diving professionals are notoriously fickle and good instructors move around from company to company – ask around to see which one is currently well regarded.

When choosing a diving course, look carefully at how much of your open-water experience will be out on the Reef. Many of the budget courses only offer shore

SITE	DIVE OPERATORS	FEATURES	PAGE
North Stradbroke Island	Manta Lodge (www.mantalodge.com.au)	manta rays, leopard & grey nurse sharks, humpback whales, turtles, dolphins, hard & soft corals	p101
Moreton Island	Dive In Sports at Tangalooma (www.tangalooma.com)	Tangalooma Wrecks, good snorkelling site	p104
South Port	Diving the Gold Coast (www.divingthegoldcoast.com.au)	abundant marine life, including rays, sharks, turtles & 200 fish species	p117
Mooloolaba	Scuba World (www.scubaworld.com.au)	dive with sharks & rays at Underwater World; or wreck dive a sunken warship off the coast	p155
Hervey Bay	Dive Hervey Bay (diveherveybay.com.au)	shallow caves, schools of large fish, wreck dives, turtles, sea snakes, stone fish, rays, trevally	p177
Rainbow Beach	Wolf Rock Dive Centre (www.wolfrockdive.com.au)	one of Australia's top diving destinations, with grey nurse sharks, turtles, manta rays, giant gropers amid volcanic pinnacles	p172
Bundaberg	Bundaberg Aqua Scuba (www.aquascuba.com.au)	wreck dives, gropers, turtles, rays, live-aboard dive boat	p188

dives, which are often less interesting than open-water dives. At the other end of the scale, on the most expensive courses you can live aboard a boat or yacht for several days, with all your meals included in the price. Normally you have to show that you can tread water for 10 minutes and swim 200m before you can start a course. Most schools will also require that you undertake a medical, which usually costs extra (around $55 to $80).

Prices

A four- or five-day **Professional Association of Diving Instructors** (PADI; www.padi.com) course leading to a recognised open-water certificate costs anything from $275 to $800. The Bundaberg area is among the cheapest places to learn.

For certified divers, trips and equipment hire are available just about everywhere. You'll need evidence of your qualifications, and some places may also ask to see your logbook. Renting gear and going on a two-tank day dive generally costs between $75 and $190.

See the table above for popular diving and snorkelling locations outside the Great Barrier Reef.

Surfing & Kite-Surfing

From a surfer's point of view, Queensland's Great Barrier Reef is one of nature's most tragic mistakes – it's effectively a 2000km-long breakwater! Mercifully, there are some great surf beaches along the coast in southern Queensland. The Gold Coast has great breaks as does virtually the entire shoreline of the Sunshine Coast. Look out for a copy of Mark Warren's definitive *Atlas of Australian Surfing*, available in a portable format or as a large coffee-table book.

You can hire boards from almost any surf shop along the coast, and op shops in surf resorts are usually full of used boards. Unless you're taking lessons, it's probably best to start off with boogie boarding and work your way up, as surfing isn't as easy as it looks. Always ask locals and lifesavers about the severity of breaks – broken boards and limbs are not uncommon, particularly among inexperienced surfers with high ambitions.

Caloundra and Noosa are increasingly popular venues for kite-surfing. You can also take kite-surfing lessons just outside Brisbane, in Redcliffe (p99).

Good Surf Breaks

» **Coolangatta** (p133) is a popular surfing haunt for Gold Coast locals, particularly Kirra Beach.

» **Burleigh Heads** (p131) has serious waves, which require some experience.

» **Caloundra** (p152) to **Mooloolaba** (p155) is a good strip with fine breaks.

» **Noosa** (p144) is popular among longboarders, with good wave action at Sunshine Beach and the point breaks around the national park, especially during the cyclone swells of summer (December to February).

» **North Stradbroke Island** (p101) is harder to get to, but has good surf beaches that tend to be less crowded than the Gold Coast and Sunshine Coast beaches.

» **Agnes Water & the Town of 1770** (p215) is where you can actually surf off the Great Barrier Reef, which at this point of its stretch does create some excellent breaks. This spot is strictly for old hands, though; the walls can get pretty hairy, you have to swim well out from shore and you may be sharing your personal space with the odd reef shark.

Surfing Lessons

If you're new to the sport, the best way to find your feet is with a few lessons, and there are dozens of surf schools in south-east Queensland. Two of the best spots to learn, mostly because the waves are kind to beginners, are Surfers Paradise (p122) and Noosa (p144). Two-hour lessons typically cost between $50 and $65 and five-day courses for the really keen generally cost between $180 and $250.

Rafting, Kayaking & Canoeing

White-Water Rafting

The mighty Tully, North Johnstone and Russell Rivers between Townsville and Cairns are renowned white-water-rafting locations, benefiting from the very high rainfall in the area. The Tully is the most popular of the three and has Grade 3 to 4 rapids. This means the rapids are moderate, but require continuous manipulation of the raft to stay upright. Most of the guides who operate tours here have internationally recognised qualifications and safety is fairly high on their list of priorities. This said, you don't need any experience to take part, just a desire for a rush. You also need to be older than 13 on the Tully (or age 10 on the Russell).

You can do full-day rafting day trips for about $130 on the Russell River, or $185 on the Tully, including transfers. See Cairns (p291) and Tully (p291) for more details.

Kayaking & Canoeing

Kayaking and canoeing are also popular activities in Queensland. There are numerous operations along the coast that offer paddling expeditions along idyllic waterways and lakes, or out through the calm Barrier Reef waters – sometimes from the mainland to offshore islands. There are also plenty of companies that operate guided tours of the waters off the Gold and Sunshine Coasts.

A few recommended places to go paddling in Queensland are listed in the table opposite.

Sailing

Queensland's waters are pure utopia for seafarers of all abilities, offering some of the most spectacular sailing locations in the world. The hands-down winner of the state's many picture-postcard spots is the Whitsunday Islands. These 74 idyllic gems are surrounded by a translucent blue sea that, at times, has a seamless and uninterrupted horizon. There are countless charters and boat operators based at Airlie Beach, the gateway to the islands.

Tours

You'll find plenty of day tours that hop between two or three islands, but the three-day/two-night all-inclusive cruises are much better value and provide a greater appreciation of just how beautiful the area is. You can also choose between tours that sleep their passengers onboard or ones that dock at an island resort for the night.

The greatest benefit of joining a tour is that you do not require any sailing expertise – some outfits will get you to participate under guidance, but you can be a complete landlubber and still enjoy a true sailing experience. The range of tours is huge and, as with most activities,

SITE	TYPE	OPERATOR	FEATURES	PAGE
North Stradbroke Island	kayaking	Straddie Adventures (www.straddieadventures.com.au)	mangroves & lovely coastline, dolphins, sea turtles, rays	p101
Great Sandy National Park	kayaking & canoeing	Elanda Point (www.elanda.com.au)	high-backed dunes, wildflowers, mangroves, rainforests	p163
Whitsunday Islands	sea kayaking	Salty Dog (www.saltydog.com.au)	one-day & multiday trips exploring Molle Islands, amid coral reefs, dolphins, turtles, sea eagles	p241
Noosa	kayaking	Noosa Ocean Kayak (www.noosakayaktours.com)	sea kayak tours amid dolphins, turtles on Laguna Bay; river kayaking on Noosa River	p146
Magnetic Island	kayaking	Magnetic Island Sea Kayaks (www.seakayak.com.au)	exploring the picturesque bays of the island	p276
Mission Beach	kayaking	Coral Sea Kayaking (www.coralseakayak.com.au)	day paddles to & around Dunk Island, multiday trips to stunning Hinchinbrook Island	p293

the smaller the number of passengers the greater the price. As a general guide, day tours cost around $160 for adults and $60 for children. Three-day, two-night sailing packages typically start from around $500 per person.

For complete details see p239.

Chartering a Boat

It's fairly easy to charter your own boat at Airlie Beach, but be warned: that glassy sea has the potential to turn nasty and, regardless of what operators say, braving the ocean solo should only be attempted by sailors with some experience.

If you're lacking the skills but still want a far more intimate experience than a tour, consider chartering your own boat and hiring a skipper to do all the hard work for you. The cost of a 'bareboat' (unskippered) charter will set you back somewhere between $550 and $1100 per day, depending on the size of the boat.

There's also a sizeable local sailing scene around Manly (p100), just south of Brisbane, or you can explore some of the islands off the Far North Queensland coast on board a chartered boat or cruise from Port Douglas (p357).

Bungee Jumping & Skydiving

There are plenty of opportunities for adrenaline junkies to get a hit in Queensland. Surfers Paradise is something of a bungee mecca, offering brave participants a host of creative spins on the original bungee concept. Another hot spot is Cairns. A jump will generally cost you between $100 and $140.

Tandem skydiving provides one of the most spectacular ways to get an eyeful of Queensland's colourful palette. Prices depend on the height of your jump. Most novices start with a jump of 9000ft, which provides up to 28 seconds of freefall and costs around $250. You can also do 11,000ft or even 14,000ft, which affords 60 seconds of freefall, reaching speeds up to 200km/h; this one costs around $350. Caloundra is one of the most popular spots in Queensland to skydive, and the set-up there allows you to land right on the beach.

Popular locations for skydiving include the following:

» Caloundra (p152)

» Surfers Paradise (p122)

» Brisbane (p66)
» Airlie Beach (p244)
» Mission Beach (p292)
» Cairns (p312)

Paragliding, Hang-Gliding & Parasailing

You'll see paragliding at many locations along the Queensland coast, but one of the best spots for it is above the Carlo Sandblow at Rainbow Beach (p178), where championship competitions are held every January. Tandem paragliding flights there generally last around 20 to 30 minutes and cost around $150.

There are only a handful of outfits offering hang-gliding tandem flights. One unique option is run by **South East Queensland Hang-gliding** (www.hangglidequeensland.com.au) at Canungra in the Gold Coast hinterland (see p136). Hang-gliders are pulled by ultralight aircraft to 1000m, then released for a 20-minute glide back to earth, with striking views of Mt Tamborine. Flights cost $275. Paragliding is also offered in the same locale by **Paragliding Queensland** (www.pgqld.com.au; tandem flights $260).

Parasailing is another exhilarating way to view the coast from above. Outfits operate out of the Gold Coast and many other beach resorts along the coast.

Fishing

Fishing in all its forms is incredibly popular in Queensland, especially in coastal areas. More than a few Queensland families spend entire summers living out of the back of their 4WDs while trying their luck in the surf breaks. There are also plenty of dams and freshwater bodies that provide good fishing haunts.

The barramundi (or 'barra') is Australia's premier native sport fish, partly because of its tremendous fighting qualities and partly because it's delicious! Note that the minimum size for barramundi is 58cm to 60cm in Queensland depending on where you're fishing – there are also bag limits, and the barra season is closed in most places from 1 November to 31 January. Barramundi fishing is excellent in the coastal and estuarine waters of Far North Queensland, where both fishing resorts and commercial operators offer sports-fishing trips.

The heavy-tackle season runs from September to December.

Where to Fish & Local Resources

The Great Barrier Reef has traditionally been a popular fishing ground, but zoning laws introduced in July 2004 have tightened the area of reef that can be fished, in response to concerns about environmental damage and overfishing.

There are also limitations on the number of fish you can catch and their size,

GEM HUNTING

Fossicking (hunting for precious stones) is a novel pastime in certain areas of Queensland, where tall tales and legendary finds – like the $90 million blue sapphire unearthed in 1930 – lure dilettante diggers with the thought of striking it rich. Most of Queensland's gem fields are in relatively remote areas, and a visit here can be a big adventure and possibly even profitable. And if you don't strike it lucky with rubies, opals or sapphires you're bound to meet some fascinating characters along the way.

Queensland's main fossicking areas are the gem fields around Sapphire and Rubyvale (about 300km inland from Rockhampton; p220), the Yowah Opal Fields (deep in the southern outback, 150km west of Cunnamulla); and the topaz fields around Mt Surprise and Georgetown (about 300km southwest of Cairns; p402).

Before you start digging, you'll need a miner's right or 'fossicking licence'; most caravan parks in the fossicking areas can sort you out with a licence or you can visit any office of the **Department of Mines & Energy** (☎3237 1434; www.dme.qld.gov.au; 1-month licence adult/family $6.50/9.25). Note that fossicking is strictly a no-go in national parks.

and restrictions on the type of gear you can use. You also need to be aware of which fish are protected entirely from fishing. The easiest way to find out what you can catch, where and how is to contact the nearest QPWS office.

For information on weather and tide conditions and what's biting, tune in to local radio stations. Weekly reports for popular fishing spots along the Queensland coast can be found online at www.fishingmonthly.com.au.

Top Fishing Spots

- » North Stradbroke Island (p101)
- » Fraser Island (p171)
- » Rainbow Beach (p172)
- » Lake Tinaroo (p351)
- » Lakefield National Park (p393)

Charters & Tours

Reef-, River- & Land-Based Fishing Charters

- » North Stradbroke Island (p101)
- » Caloundra (p152)
- » Rainbow Beach (p172)
- » Port Douglas (p359)
- » Hamilton Island (p254)
- » Dingo Beach (p258)
- » Maroochydore (p155)

Fishing Tours

- » Main Beach (p117)
- » North Stradbroke Island (p101)

Travel with Children

Best Regions for Kids

Brisbane

A gateway to kiddie adventure with boat rides, an artificial lagoon, hands-on museums and a koala sanctuary.

Gold Coast

Kids will love the thrilling rides and watery action of five massive theme parks just north of Surfers Paradise.

Noosa & the Sunshine Coast

Animal lovers shouldn't miss Australia Zoo, followed by a visit to Mooloolaba's dazzling Underwater World.

Fraser Island & the Fraser Coast

Kids will love going eye-to-eye with giants of the deep on a whale-watching cruise from Hervey Bay.

Cairns, Islands & Highlands

Rainforest walks, a swimming lagoon, playgrounds and boat trips to the reef or islands. Memorable trips to Kuranda.

Port Douglas & the Daintree

Crocodile-spotting cruises along the Daintree River, Great Barrier Reef trips and fascinating exploring in the Daintree Discovery Centre.

Like Australia as a whole, Queensland generally welcomes families with young travellers. The state has superb attractions for all ages: bucket-and-spade fun at beaches all along the coast, Gold Coast theme parks, zoos and wildlife sanctuaries where you can have close encounters (including koala cuddling) with Australia's finest, leisurely boat rides, eye-popping aquariums and hands-on science museums, bushwalks (easy-going and challenging alike), camping adventures, and plenty of other activities likely to wow the young ones.

Queensland for Kids

Child- and family-friendly activities are listed throughout this guide in the On the Road chapters, and Brisbane has a section devoted specifically to kids (p67).

Dining with Children

Children are usually more than welcome at midrange restaurants, cafes and bistros, surf and RSL clubs as well as pubs, where they can have a casual counter meal. High chairs are fairly common. Many fine-dining restaurants don't welcome small children.

Most places that welcome children don't have separate kids' menus, and those that do usually offer food straight from the deep fryer, such as crumbed chicken and chips. You may be better advised to find something on the main menu and have the kitchen adapt the dish to suit your child's needs.

The best news for travelling families is that there are plenty of free or coin-operated barbecues in parks. Beware of weekends and public holidays when fierce battles can erupt over who is next in line for the barbecue.

Change Facilities & Cots

All cities and most major towns have centrally located public rooms where mothers (and sometimes fathers) can go to nurse their baby or change its nappy (diaper); check with the local visitors centre or city council for details. While many Australians have a relaxed attitude about breastfeeding or nappy changing in public, others frown on it.

Many motels and the better-equipped caravan parks have playgrounds and swimming pools, and can supply cots (cribs) and baby baths – motels may also have in-house children's videos and childminding services. Top-end hotels and many (but not all) midrange hotels are well versed in the needs of guests who have children. B&Bs, on the other hand, often market themselves as sanctuaries from all things child-related.

Babysitting

If you want to leave Junior behind for a few hours, some of Queensland's numerous licensed child-care agencies have places set aside for casual care. To find them, check under Baby Sitters and Child Care Centres in the *Yellow Pages* telephone book, or phone the local council for a list. Licensed centres are subject to government regulation and usually adhere to high standards; to be on the safe side, it's best to avoid unlicensed ones.

One recommended agency on the south coast is **Gold Coast Baby Sitters** (☎5563 3382; www.goldcoastbabysitters.com.au), which provides certified babysitters and nannies who specialise in hotel babysitting all along the Gold Coast. All have a government-issued suitability certificate and a first-aid certificate. They can sit for between three hours and overnight, but you'll need to give 24 hours' notice. Rates start at $17 per hour, plus $20 booking fee.

Discounts for Children

Child concessions (and family rates) often apply for such things as accommodation, tours, admission fees, and air, bus and train transport, with some discounts as high as 50% off the adult rate. However, the definition of 'child' can vary from under 12 to under 16 years. Many popular sights (such as the Australia Zoo) also have discount rates for families, which will save a few dollars compared to buying individual tickets.

Accommodation concessions generally apply to children under 12 years sharing the same room as adults. On the major airlines, infants travel free provided they don't occupy a seat – child fares usually apply between the ages of two and 11 years. Most sights also give free admission to children under two years.

Necessities

Medical services and facilities in Queensland are of a high standard, and items such as baby food, formula and disposable nappies are widely available in urban centres. Major hire-car companies will supply and fit booster seats for you, for which you'll be charged around $20 for up to three days' use, with an additional daily fee for longer periods.

Lonely Planet's *Travel with Children* contains plenty of useful information.

Children's Highlights

Outdoor Adventure

» Sea kayaking in the gentle waters of the Gold Coast Broadwater or along the idyllic Noosa River

» Horse riding along bush trails in the Gold Coast hinterland or along the beach near Noosa

» Snorkelling the Great Barrier Reef on a boat trip from Port Douglas

» Taking a 4WD camping adventure on Fraser Island

» Ogling life-sized dinosaur models and ancient fossils on the Dinosaur Trail in the outback

Theme Parks

» Dreamworld – take in thrilling rides and see an IMAX show

» Whitewater World – cool off in this aquatic theme park

» Warner Bros Movie World – enjoy movie-themed rides and mingle with VIP cartoon characters

» Sea World – watch performing seals and see sharks, dugongs and polar bears up close

Rainy-Day Activities

» Exploring the museums in Brisbane, including the hands-on Sciencentre and the Maritime Museum, where you can clamber through the narrow corridors of a Navy frigate

» Watching sharks, seals and other marine life at Underwater World on the Sunshine Coast

» Visiting Townsville's Reef HQ aquarium for a look at the wonders of the Great Barrier Reef

» Seeing birds, wallabies, crocs and other critters at the indoor Cairns Wildlife Dome

Eating

» Eating fish and chips on laid-back Burleigh Heads beach

» Gorging on freshly made ice cream at Daintree Ice Cream Company

» Visiting fruit and berry farms and a chocolate-making master in the Granite Belt

» Snacking on goodies at one of Brisbane's sprawling weekend markets

Planning

Weather, crowds and stingers are all important considerations when planning a Queensland family getaway. The south coast (Gold and Sunshine Coasts) can be great fun any time of year, though it gets a little chilly during the winter (June to August), making for unpredictable beach days (water temperature can get to around 19°C, with air temperatures on sunny days in the low 20s).

Winter, on the other hand, is the best (but busiest) time to visit tropical Queensland, with clear nights, stinger-free beaches and an absence of the oppressive heat, humidity and monsoonal downpours that characterise the summer months (December to March).

Travelling during school holidays can be maddening – particularly in the Gold and Sunshine Coasts. If possible avoid peak times when Australian vacationers are likely to be swarming into the state.

regions at a glance

Planning a trip to Queensland can be a daunting task, given the state's massive size and the wide array of attractions scattered across its 1.9 million sq km. The more populous south has surf-loving beaches, good dining and nightlife, and outdoor adventures in lush hinterland rainforests. Further north, you'll find spectacular islands, including Fraser Island, the Whitsundays and the less-visited coral-fringed islands of the Capricorn Coast. Speaking of coral, you can arrange trips to the Great Barrier Reef from the Capricorn Coast northwards. Key gateways such as Cairns and Port Douglas are also close to picturesque islands and World Heritage rainforests. For rugged adventures (road trips, nights camping under stars), there's the outback, as well as the wild Cape York Peninsula.

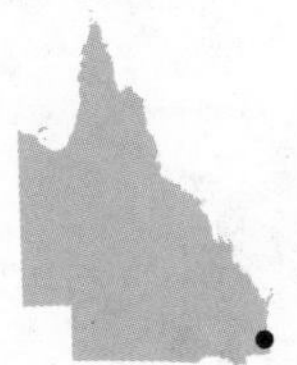

Brisbane

Arts & Culture ✓✓✓
Food & Wine ✓✓✓
Nightlife ✓✓✓

Arts & Culture

Catch world-class dance, theatre and concerts in Brisbane, and see an array of artwork (from old-world masterpieces to cutting-edge Aboriginal works) at museums and galleries around town. In the summer, Brisbane hosts free outdoor shows and film screenings.

Food & Wine

First-rate chefs, delectable ingredients from the fertile countryside and lovely riverside settings combine for exquisite dining in Queensland's capital. No matter what you're craving – seafood, sushi, Vietnamese, modern Australian or simply a rich cup of coffee – you'll find it in Brisbane.

Nightlife

Nights out in Brisbane can mean many things: from lounging at a riverside bar to partying in Fortitude Valley. There's live jazz, indie-rock shows and stylish lounges where DJs spin eclectic sounds to a laid-back crowd.

p52

Around Brisbane

Islands ✓✓
Outdoor Activities ✓✓
Food & Wine ✓✓✓

Islands

In Moreton Bay, North Stradbroke Island offers excellent surfing, sea-kayaking and beach walks, while Moreton Island has a full-service resort offering lots of activities. You can also visit the former prison island of St Helena.

Outdoor Activities

Top ways to spend a sun-drenched day include whale watching in Moreton Bay, running or cycling along the Redcliffe Peninsula and scenic bushwalking in Girraween National Park. North Stradbroke and Moreton Islands offer even more outdoor adventures.

Food & Wine

In the lovely rolling countryside of the Granite Belt, dozens of vineyards have free tastings. You'll also find fruit growers, cheesemakers and gourmet chocolate. In Manly and Redcliffe, seafood rules, and it's a great place to sample Moreton Bay bugs.

p97

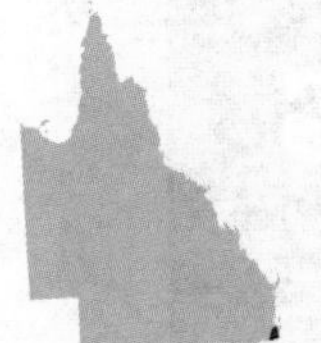

Gold Coast

Surfing ✓✓✓
Theme Parks ✓✓✓
Nightlife ✓✓

Surfing

With a sublime climate and excellent surf beaches fronting the glittering strip of high-rises, the Gold Coast is a surfing nirvana. Top picks include Burleigh Heads, Kirra, Rainbow Bay and Snapper Rocks.

Theme Parks

Spinning loops, dizzying rides and wet-water thrills are guaranteed to test the staunchest stomach at the Gold Coast's ostentatious theme parks. Adrenalin junkies shouldn't miss Dreamworld's Big 6 Thrill Rides, Wet'n'Wild's Kamikaze and WhiteWater World's Hydrocoaster.

Nightlife

Après-surf, the giddy Gold Coast kicks into overdrive with loud alfresco eateries, street music and a celebratory crowd – young and old alike – looking to party. After sundown, a Surfers Paradise nightclub is a prime spot to catch the action.

p115

Noosa & the Sunshine Coast

Surfing ✓✓✓
Beaches ✓✓✓
Scenery ✓✓✓

Surfing

A relaxed surfer ethos rules the sunny Sunshine Coast. At Noosa, the national park forms a stunning backdrop to the peeling right-hand point waves off its many breaks, while Mooloolaba and Maroochydore are other top surf spots.

Beaches

Noosa's north-facing main beach is idyllic, with calm blue waters and a sugar-fringed shore. Mooloolaba has a popular swimming beach, especially for kiddies. To escape the crowds, head to the pristine sands between Coolum and Peregian.

Scenery

The splendid beaches of the Sunshine Coast merge into native bushland, subtropical rainforest and the forested ridges of the hinterland. See it up close on hikes in the rainforest, or up the craggy peaks of the Glass House Mountains.

p142

Fraser Island & the Fraser Coast

Wildlife ✓✓✓
Whale Watching ✓✓✓
Island Safaris ✓✓✓

Wildlife

Known for its long, sandy beaches and spectacular national parks, the Fraser Coast is home to egg-laying sea turtles (at Mon Repos), wild dingoes (Fraser Island) and migrating whales and dolphins (Fraser Island and Hervey Bay).

Whale Watching

With their playful antics – breaching, blowing, fin-waving and tail-slapping – migrating humpback whales seem like giant puppies of the sea. You can see them up close on a boat tour from Hervey Bay.

Island Safaris

Fashioned by the wind and sea, Fraser Island has rainforest, massive dunes and lovely lakes but no roads, meaning a 4WD adventure is the only way to see it.

p169

Capricorn Coast

Scenery ✓✓✓
Rock Art ✓✓✓
Islands ✓✓

Scenery

Great Keppel Island has powdery white-sand beaches and dense bushland. Carnarvon National Park is a wildlife-rich wonderland of verdant scenery, while Byfield has deserted beaches and sublime canoeing. Blackdown Tableland National Park is worth a trip for the hidden waterholes and soaring views.

Rock Art

Carnarvon Gorge is one of Australia's great outdoor art galleries. Aboriginal stencils adorn the walls of several caves, providing a fascinating monument to the civilisation whose presence here goes back 20,000 years.

Islands

Tiny, coral-ringed Lady Musgrave Island has superb snorkelling, as does densely vegetated Heron Island, while Pumpkin Island is the place to play Robinson Crusoe. Great Keppel Island has fantastic bushwalking.

p198

Whitsunday Coast

Islands ✓✓✓
Sailing ✓✓✓
Snorkelling ✓✓✓

Islands

With 74 tropical beauties to choose from, the Whitsunday Islands group is a utopia for beach castaways and cocktail-swilling resort types. Whether bushwalking, kayaking or lounging, all island trips must eventually lead to Whitehaven Beach.

Sailing

Surrounding the archipelago of the Whitsunday Islands, translucent blue seas seem incomplete without a snow-white yacht sailing into the picture. The wind, the sea, the beckoning sandy bays… the Whitsundays are sailing- and island-hopping heaven.

Snorkelling

Snorkelling the fringing reef around the islands is as good as, if not better than, snorkelling the Great Barrier Reef. In this psychedelic underwater world, tropical fish flit through a vibrantly coloured landscape of coral, polyps, anemones and otherworldly marine life.

p225

Townsville to Innisfail

Beaches ✓✓✓
Architecture ✓✓
National Parks ✓✓

Beaches
Along the coast you'll find vast, sandy expanses such as Mission Beach and intimate coves like Etty Bay. Offshore you'll find standout beaches on high-end Orpheus Island and lovable Dunk Island.

Architecture
Historic architecture in the region includes the grand gold-rush-era streetscapes of Charters Towers, beautiful 19th-century buildings in Townsville, and Australia's highest concentration of art deco architecture in Innisfail.

National Parks
Hiking, camping, swimming and picnicking opportunities abound in the region's cache of national parks. Top picks include bushwalking paradise Hinchinbrook Island and the rainforest-covered peaks of Paluma Range National Park.

p262

Cairns, Islands & Highlands

Underwater Worlds ✓✓✓
Food & Wine ✓✓
Nightlife ✓✓

Snorkelling & Diving
Every day, Cairns' flotilla of boats ferries passengers to the dazzling underwater world of the Great Barrier Reef. To escape the crowds, join a live-aboard vessel to explore more remote sections of the reef.

Food & Wine
Many of the Atherton Tableland's farms, factories, orchards and plantations, including tropical-fruit-wine producers, can be visited on tours – or simply taste their produce at restaurants throughout this lush region.

Nightlife
Sipping tropical cocktails overlooking the water, listening to jazz in loungey surrounds, partying hard at bars and pubs or seriously shaking it on the dance floor – Cairns is the nightlife hub of the Far North.

p304

Port Douglas & the Daintree

Indigenous Culture ✓✓✓
Fishing ✓✓
Wildlife Watching ✓✓✓

Indigenous Culture
A number of Aboriginal-led tours can take you on a spiritual journey through this ancient rainforest region, offering an insight into the area's rich Indigenous culture. Mossman Gorge's Kuku Yalanji Dreamtime Walks are fabulous.

Fishing
Reef fishing, river fishing, beach casting, helifishing, or just throwing in a line off the jetty – if you want to catch your own dinner, you'll be spoilt for choice in this region.

Wildlife Watching
Thousands of wildlife species inhabit the rainforest's incredible ecosystem, including roaming cassowaries, and saltwater crocodiles (gulp) cruising the waterways.

p353

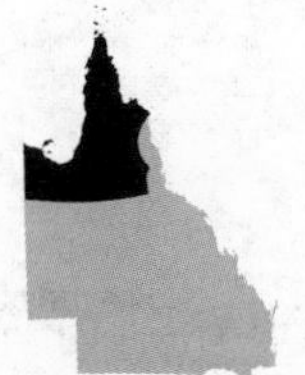

Cape York Peninsula & the Savannah Way

Scenery ✓✓✓
Fishing ✓✓✓
History ✓✓

Scenery

Queensland's last frontier is a patchwork of rainforest, palm-fringed beaches and tropical savannah overlaid by wild, snaking rivers. Monsoonal rains turn it all into a vast isolated wetland for months on end. This is Australia in the raw.

Fishing

Fishing here is legendary, with barramundi the main catch, but there's plenty of sports fish ready to snag themselves on the nearest hook. It's mandatory to crack the tab on a coldie (local speak for 'have a beer') to get the fish biting...

History

The echoes of WWII, early pioneers and explorers, pearl divers and shipwrecks permeate the Cape. Lonely tombstones and unmarked graves attest to the extreme hardships faced by those who tried to tame this wild land.

p387

Journeys into the Outback

Scenery ✓✓
Dinosaurs ✓✓✓
Outback Pubs ✓✓✓

Scenery

Queensland's outback is home to some ruggedly beautiful scenery, with big skies and fiery sunsets, where you can find peace in the great open spaces and star-filled nights. You can take it all in on a 4WD trip, camping at remote spots along the way.

Dinosaurs

Hughenden, Richmond and – best of all – Winton offer boundless delights to the amateur palaeontologist, with museums that do these small towns proud.

Outback Pubs

Made world famous by *Crocodile Dundee*, the outback pub – with its timber walls, wide verandah, tin roof and gruff patrons – is the stuff of legend. For several of the best, head to Barcaldine.

p407

Look out for these icons:

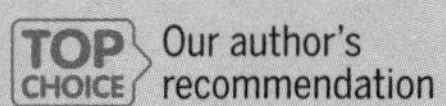

Our author's recommendation

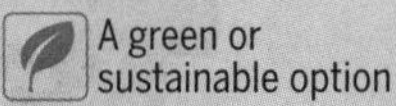
A green or sustainable option

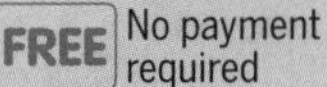

No payment required

BRISBANE 52

AROUND BRISBANE 97

REDCLIFFE 99

MANLY & ST HELENA ISLAND 100

NORTH STRADBROKE ISLAND 101

MORETON ISLAND 104

GRANITE BELT 106

Stanthorpe & Ballandean .106

TOOWOOMBA 111

AROUND TOOWOOMBA ... 114

Highfields & Crows Nest .. 114

Jondaryan Woolshed Complex 114

GOLD COAST 115

Southport & Main Beach 117

South Stradbroke Island .. 121

Surfers Paradise 122

Broadbeach 129

Burleigh Heads & Currumbin 130

Coolangatta 133

GOLD COAST HINTERLAND 136

Tamborine Mountain 137

Springbrook National Park 138

Lamington National Park 140

NOOSA & THE SUNSHINE COAST .. 142

Noosa 144

Bribie Island 151

Glass House Mountains .. 151

Caloundra 152

Mooloolaba & Maroochydore 155

Coolum 160

Peregian & Sunshine Beach 161

Cooloola Coast 162

Eumundi 163

SUNSHINE COAST HINTERLAND 165

Montville 166

Mapleton 168

FRASER ISLAND & THE FRASER COAST 169

FRASER COAST 171

Gympie 171

Rainbow Beach 172

Maryborough 175

Hervey Bay 177

Childers 184

Bundaberg 186

FRASER ISLAND 190

CAPRICORN COAST. 198

Rockhampton 200

Yeppoon 205

Great Keppel Island 208

Gladstone 211

Southern Reef Islands 213

Agnes Water & Town of 1770 215

CAPRICORN HINTERLAND 218

Emerald 219

Gemfields 220

Carnarvon National Park 222

WHITSUNDAY COAST 225

Mackay 227

Eungella 234

Stoney Creek 235

Eungella National Park ... 235

Brampton Island 236

Newry Island Group 238

THE WHITSUNDAYS 238

Midge Point 243

Proserpine 243

Airlie Beach 243

Conway National Park 251

Long Island 251

Hook Island 252

Daydream Island 252

South Molle Island 253

Hamilton Island 254

Hayman Island 256

Lindeman Island 257

Whitsunday Island 258

Bowen 259

TOWNSVILLE TO INNISFAIL 262

Townsville 264

MAGNETIC ISLAND 275

SOUTH OF TOWNSVILLE 280

WEST OF TOWNSVILLE .. 280

Ravenswood 281

Charters Towers 281

NORTH OF TOWNSVILLE 284

See the Index for a full list of destinations covered in this book.

On the Road

Paluma Range National Park 284
Ingham & Around 285
Lucinda 287
Orpheus Island 287
Cardwell & Around 288
Hinchinbrook Island 289
Goold & Garden Islands . 290
Tully 290
Mission Beach 291
Dunk Island 298
Bedarra Island 299
Mission Beach to Innisfail 299
Innisfail & Around 300

CAIRNS, ISLANDS & HIGHLANDS 304

CAIRNS 306
SOUTH OF CAIRNS 329
Babinda 330
Bramston Beach 330
Wooroonooran National Park 331
CAIRNS' NORTHERN BEACHES 331
Machans Beach 331
Holloways Beach 332
Yorkeys Knob 332
Trinity Beach & Around . . . 332
Clifton Beach 333
Palm Cove 333
Ellis Beach 335
ISLANDS OFF CAIRNS . . . 335
Green Island 335
Fitzroy Island 336
Frankland Islands 337
ATHERTON TABLELAND 337
Kuranda 338
Mareeba 342
Atherton & Around 344
Ravenshoe 347
Millaa Millaa 347
Malanda & Around 348
Yungaburra 349
Lake Tinaroo 351

PORT DOUGLAS & THE DAINTREE 353

PORT DOUGLAS 355
NORTH OF PORT DOUGLAS 363
Mossman 364
Julatten 365
Mossman to the Daintree . 365
THE DAINTREE 366
Daintree Village 367
Daintree River to Cape Tribulation 370
Cape Tribulation 373
NORTH TO COOKTOWN . . 377
Inland Route 377
Coastal Route 379
Cooktown 380
Lizard Island Group 385

CAPE YORK PENINSULA & THE SAVANNAH WAY 387

CAPE YORK PENINSULA . 390
Lakeland to Musgrave 392
Musgrave to Archer River 393
Archer River to Lockhart River 394
Archer River to Weipa . . . 394
Archer River to Bramwell Junction 395
Bramwell Junction to Jardine River 395
Northern Peninsula Area . 397
Torres Strait Islands 397
THE SAVANNAH WAY 400
Mt Garnet to Undara 401
Mt Surprise 402
Georgetown 402
Normanton 404
Normanton to Burketown 404
Burketown to the Border 406

JOURNEYS INTO THE OUTBACK 407

Charters Towers to Cloncurry 409
Cloncurry 409
Mt Isa 410
Mt Isa to Charleville 413
Winton 413
Longreach 415
Barcaldine 417
Charleville 418
THE CHANNEL COUNTRY 418
Mt Isa to Birdsville 419
Birdsville 419
Birdsville Track 420
Simpson Desert National Park 420
Birdsville to Charleville . . 420

Brisbane

Includes »

Sights 53
Activities 65
Courses 67
Quirky Brisbane 67
Tours 70
Festivals & Events 72
Sleeping 72
Eating 78
Drinking..............84
Entertainment 87
Shopping............. 90

Best Places to Eat

» E'cco (p79)
» Ortiga (p82)
» Lark (p83)
» Mondo Organics (p84)
» Watt (p82)

Best Places to Stay

» Treasury (p72)
» Portal (p72)
» Emporium (p75)
» Limes (p75)
» Il Mondo (p77)

Why Go?

One of Australia's most underrated destinations, Brisbane is an easy-going city with a vibrant arts scene, burgeoning nightlife and first-rate dining, with lush gardens, iconic sights and historic buildings woven into the landscape.

Brisbanites are an active bunch and make good use of the temperate climate and riverside setting. You can go jogging, cycling and kayaking, wander through outdoor markets or relax on palm-fringed artificial beaches just a short jaunt from the high-rises looming over the Brisbane River.

Brisbane's chefs cater to a global palate, and eating and drinking is all about the open-air experience. Many restaurants, bars and cafes have back gardens, riverside views, or sidewalk seating on tree-lined streets.

As an epicentre of the arts, Brisbane is no longer just 'a big country town' of decades past. Instead you'll find world-class museums, theatres, live-music venues, massive sporting events and heaps of unique fare – open-air cinema, outdoor concerts, colourful festivals and more.

When to Go

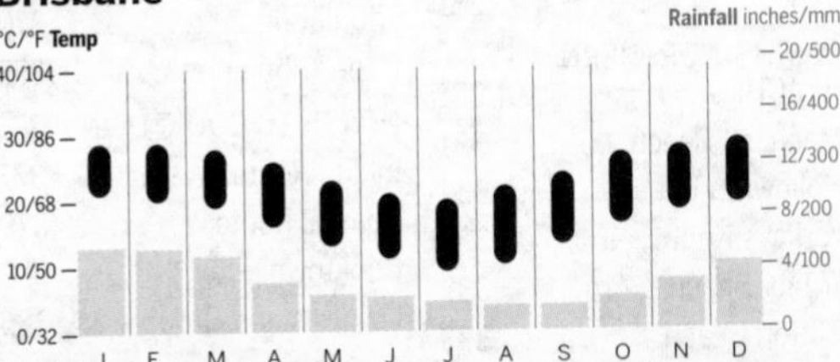

January With high heat and humidity Brisbane swelters during the summer; locals head for the coast.

May Cooler, milder temperatures arrive (you'll need a jacket at night), continuing till August.

September Springtime brings pleasant temperatures and a massive arts-and-music event.

History

The first settlement in the Brisbane area was established at Redcliffe on Moreton Bay in 1824 as a penal colony for Sydney's more recalcitrant convicts. After struggling with inadequate water supplies and hostile Aborigines, the colony was relocated to the banks of the Brisbane River, the site of the city centre today, but suffered at the hands of numerous crooked warders and was abandoned in 1839. The Moreton Bay area was thrown open to free settlers in 1842, marking the beginning of Brisbane's rise to prominence, and the start of trouble for the region's Aborigines.

By the time of Queensland's separation from New South Wales in 1859, Brisbane had a population of around 6000. Huge wealth flowed into the city from the new pastoral and gold-mining enterprises in the Darling Downs, and grandiose buildings were erected to reflect this new-found affluence. The frontier-town image was hard to shake off, however, and it wasn't until the 1982 Commonwealth Games and Expo '88 that Brisbane's reputation as a cultural centre became recognised. Brisbane has now cemented its place as Australia's third-largest city, with a population of around two million.

Sights

Most of Brisbane's major sights are in the CBD or inner-city suburbs. A walk through the city centre will reveal Brisbane's colonial history and architecture, while a ferry ride or bridge walk across the river lands you in South Bank, home to both stellar art museums and peaceful parkland (complete with attractive artificial swimming lagoons). Chinatown and Brunswick St, both in Fortitude Valley, provide healthy doses of dining, nightlife, shopping and gallery-hopping.

CITY CENTRE

City Botanic Gardens PARK

(Map p56; Alice St; ⌚24hr, free guided tours 11am & 1pm Mon-Sat) These expansive gardens are a mass of green lawns, towering Moreton Bay figs, bunya pines, macadamia trees and other tropical flora, descending gently from the Queensland University of Technology (QUT) campus. A network of paths throughout enables strollers, joggers, picnickers, cyclists and in-line skaters to make their way to quiet spots for respite, or to nowhere in particular. The pretty **Mangrove Boardwalk**, a wooden walkway skirting the riverbank on the eastern rim, is lit until midnight. The glow provides good opportunities to spot tame possums in the trees.

Riverfront LANDMARK

The former docks area northeast of the CBD is one of the most attractive and lively areas in the city. The striking, domed **Customs House** (Map p56; www.customshouse.com.au; 399 Queen St; admission free; ⌚10am-4pm) from 1886–89 is so aesthetically pleasing it's hard to imagine it was used as a functional building. As the name suggests, for almost a century this was where all ships heading into Brisbane's port were required to pay duties.

Further south are the **Riverside Centre** and **Eagle Street Pier** complexes (Map p56). Despite the rather dated-looking highrises soaring above, this is an attractive riverside site and home to some noteworthy restaurants as well as casual cafes and bars where you can take in the view. A good time to come here is on Sunday morning, when the area becomes a busy craft market. There are ferry terminals at both complexes.

City Hall & King George Square LANDMARK

Brisbane City Hall (Map p56; 266 George St; admission free; ⌚lift & viewing tower 10am-3pm) is a gracious sandstone edifice overlooking **King George Square**. Built in 1930, its splendour is not only skin deep; when you enter be sure to draw your eyes from the marble staircase upwards to the kaleidoscopic roof and gothic art deco light fittings. There's an observation platform up in the bell tower, which affords brilliant views across the city. At research time, City Hall was undergoing extensive restoration and remained closed to visitors.

Museum of Brisbane MUSEUM

(Map p56; 157 Ann St; admission free; ⌚10am-5pm) Around the corner from City Hall, this museums illuminates the city from a variety of viewpoints, with interactive exhibits that explore both social history and the current cultural landscape. Expect a spread of craftwork, video art, sculpture, photography and installations by local and international artists.

Roma Street Parkland PARK

(Map p56; www.romastreetparkland.com; 1 Parkland Blvd; admission free; ⌚24hr, free guided tours 10am & 2pm) This park is a veritable feast of flora inhabiting 16 hectares of the northern edge of the city. Apparently it's the biggest urban subtropical garden in the world. Broken into 16 precincts, the park offers visitors the opportunity to explore lily gardens, an Indian-inspired tea and coffee plantation,

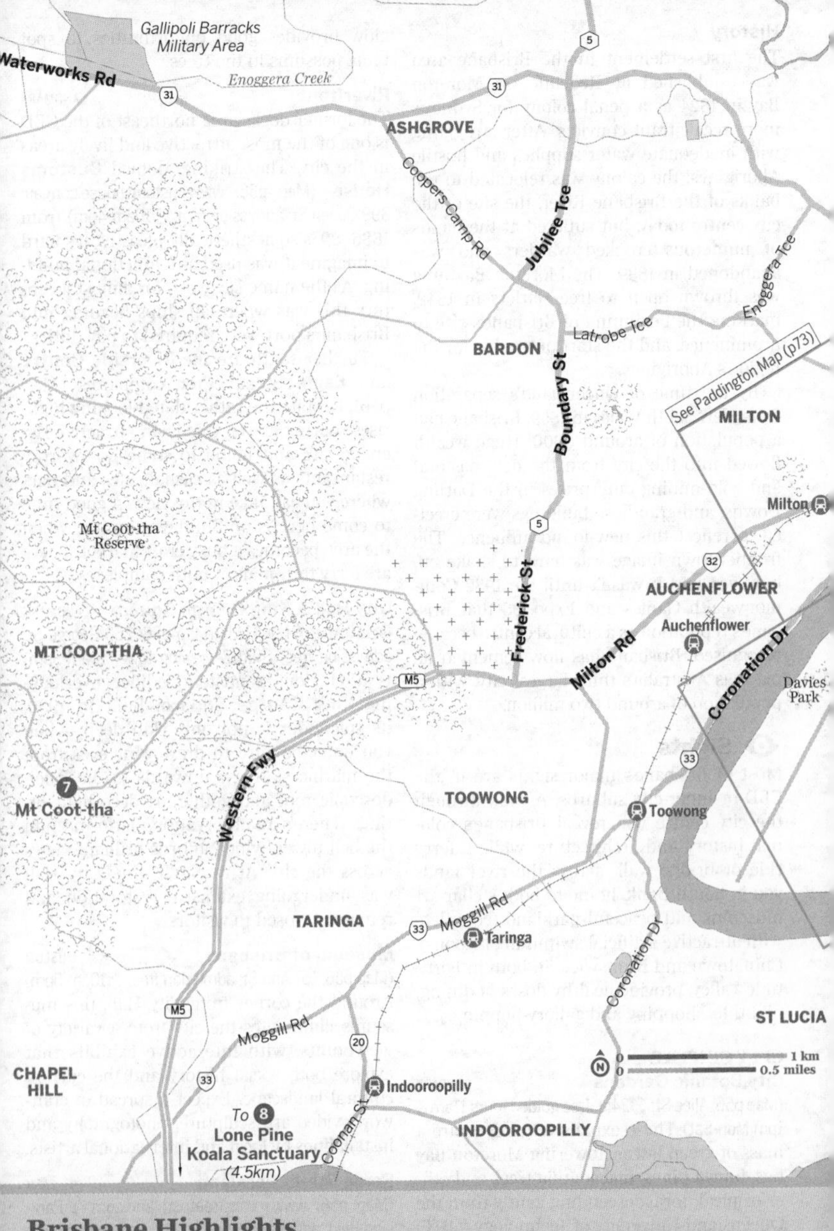

Brisbane Highlights

1. Strolling the mangrove boardwalk through the tropical foliage at the **City Botanic Gardens** (p53)
2. Wandering the enormous floors of the world-class **Gallery of Modern Art** (p59)
3. Booking a table at one of Brisbane's best restaurants in **New Farm** (p81)
4. Taking in the heady bar and club scene in **Fortitude Valley** (p85)
5. Running, walking or cycling along the **riverside path** (p59)

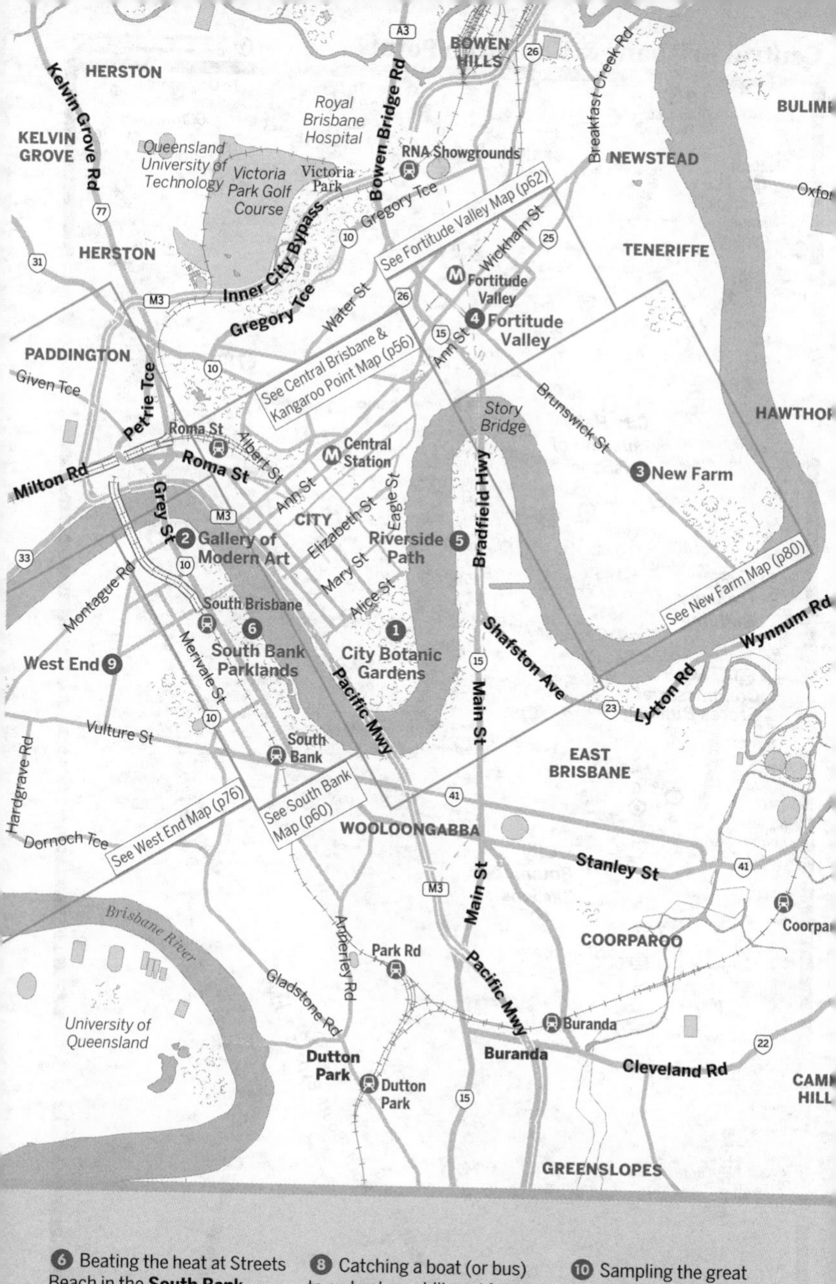

6 Beating the heat at Streets Beach in the **South Bank Parklands** (p59)

7 Going bush in the city: exploring wilderness at **Mt Coot-tha** (p61)

8 Catching a boat (or bus) to go koala-cuddling at **Lone Pine Koala Sanctuary** (p63)

9 Lunching lazily in the **West End** (p84) with a side of jazz and bohemia

10 Sampling the great produce of Queensland, and taking in the buzzing atmosphere at an outdoor **market** (p92)

Central Brisbane & Kangaroo Point

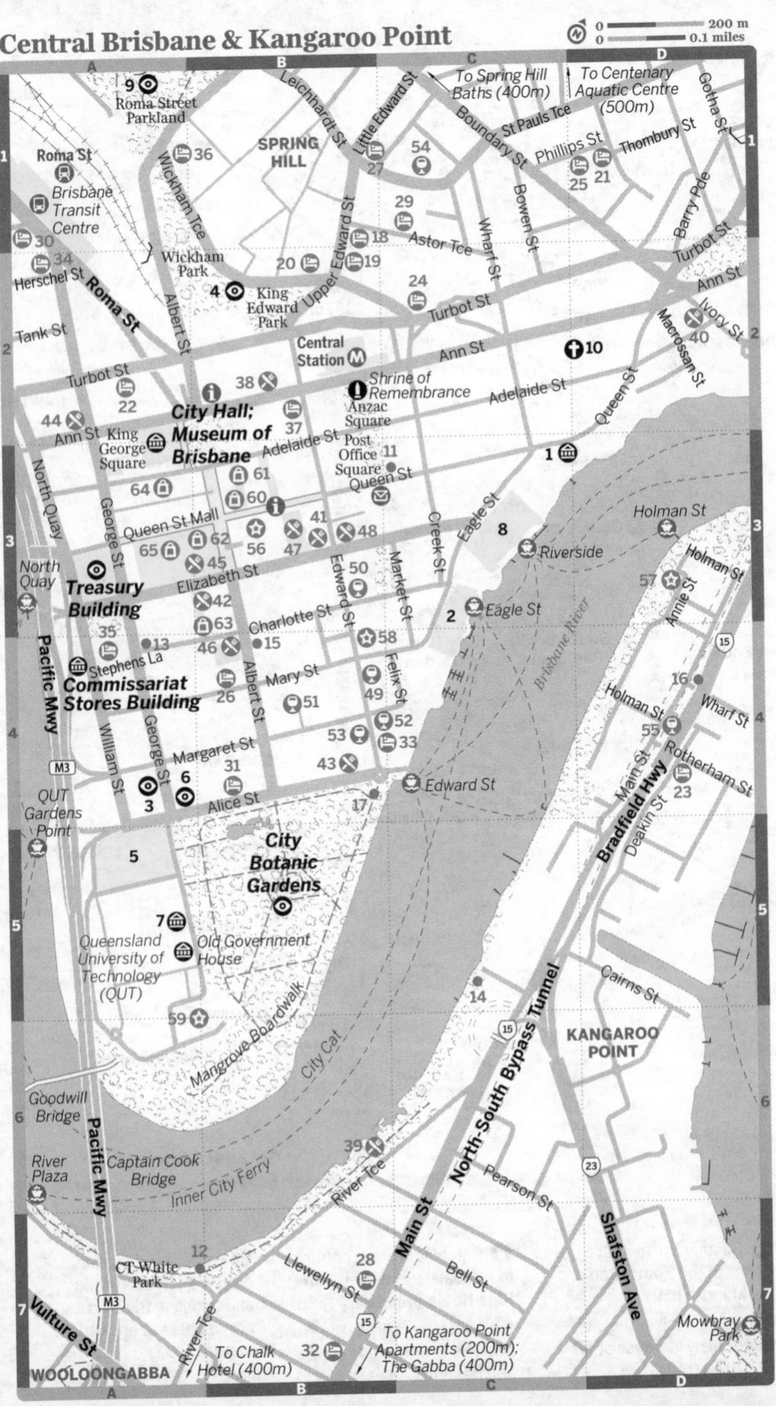

Central Brisbane & Kangaroo Point

Top Sights

City Botanic Gardens B5
City Hall A3
Commissariat Stores Building A4
Museum of Brisbane A3
Treasury Building A3

Sights

1 Customs House C3
2 Eagle Street Pier C4
Kookaburra River Queens .... (see 2)
Land Administration Building .... (see 35)
3 Mansions A4
4 Old Windmill & Observatory B2
5 Parliament House A5
6 Queensland Club A4
7 QUT Art Museum A5
8 Riverside Centre C3
9 Roma Street Parkland A1
10 St John's Cathedral D2

Activities, Courses & Tours

11 City Sights Tour Departure Point C3
12 Cliffs Rock-Climbing Area A7
13 Pancake Manor A4
14 Riverlife Adventure Centre C5
15 Skatebiz B4
16 Story Bridge Adventure Climb D4
17 Valet Cycle Hire B4

Sleeping

18 Acacia Inner-City Inn B1
19 Annie's Inn B2
20 Astor Metropole B2
21 Dahrl Court D1
22 Explorers Inn A2
23 Il Mondo D4
24 Inchcolm Hotel C2
25 Kookaburra Inn D1
26 M on Mary B4
27 Metropolitan Motor Inn B1
28 Paramount Motel B7
29 Portal C1
30 Q Resorts Abbey Apartments A1
31 Quay West Suites Brisbane B4
32 Queensland Motel B7
Soho Motel .... (see 36)
33 Stamford Plaza Brisbane C4
34 Tinbilly A2
35 Treasury A4
36 Urban Brisbane A1
37 X-Base Brisbane Central B2
X-Base Brisbane Embassy .... (see 41)

Eating

38 Bleeding Heart Gallery B2
Cha Cha Char .... (see 2)
39 Cliffs Cafe B6
40 E'cco D2
41 Embassy Hotel B3
42 Govinda's B3
43 Il B4
44 Java Coast Café A2
45 Myer Centre Food Court B3
46 Spoon Espresso Deli B4
Verve Cafe & Bar .... (see 58)
47 Wintergarden Centre Food Court B3
48 Woolworths B3

Drinking

49 Belgian Beer Cafe B4
50 Exchange Hotel B3
51 Laneway B4
52 Moo Moo B4
53 Port Office Hotel B4
54 Sportsman's Hotel C1
55 Story Bridge Hotel D4

Entertainment

56 Brisbane City Myer Centre B3
57 Brisbane Jazz Club D3
58 Metro Arts Centre B4
59 QUT Gardens Theatre A6
Ticketek .... (see 45)

Shopping

60 Australia the Gift B3
Australian Geographic .... (see 45)
61 Brisbane Arcade B3
Eagle St Pier Markets .... (see 2)
62 Egg Records B3
63 Elizabeth Arcade B3
64 Record Exchange A3
65 RM Williams A3

a rockery, native gardens and much more. There are also activities for mums and bubs, and plenty of public barbecues so you can do the very Australian picnic thing.

Southeast of the Parkland, on Wickham Tce, is the 1828 **Old Windmill & Observatory** (Map p56), one of the oldest buildings in Brisbane. Due to a design flaw, the sails were too heavy for the wind to turn, and a

WHEN IT RAINS, IT POURS: BRISBANE FLOOD 2011

Wild weather in the Sunshine State in December 2010 and January 2011 caused major flooding throughout Queensland with many towns inundated and isolated throughout the state. Brisbane did not escape the onslaught, recording its biggest flood since 1974. The usually placid Brisbane River became a swirling torrent of brown water sweeping boats, pontoons and other debris downstream towards the sea. Flood water streamed into the CBD's riverfront areas while in low-lying suburbs only rooftops remained above the waterline. More than 30,000 homes were affected by the floods. Popular attractions such as South Bank Parklands and the Riverside Centre were also affected, while the Riverwalk, the section of floating walkway of the riverside path, was destroyed. Along the river front, the city's ferry terminals suffered substantial damage, with many docks swept away, disrupting Brisbane's busy ferry services. After the clean-up, restoration and reconstruction of damaged areas proceeded rapidly. In many parts of the city little evidence remains of the 2011 floods.

convict-powered treadmill was briefly employed before the mill was abandoned. The building was converted to a signal post and later a meteorological observatory.

Treasury Casino to Queensland University of Technology LANDMARK

At the western end of the Queen St Mall, overlooking the river, is Brisbane's magnificent Italian Renaissance–style **Treasury Building** (Map p56). It has a lavish facade, with commanding balconies and columns. The treasury now contains an entirely different kind of money spinner: Conrad's 24-hour casino.

In the block southeast of the casino, Conrad also occupies the equally gorgeous former **Land Administration Building** (Map p56). Here, however, it's been converted to one of the city's classiest hotels, the Treasury (see p72).

Closer to the water is another of Brisbane's historic gems: the **Commissariat Stores Building** (Map p56; 115 William St; adult/child $5/2.50; ⏲10am-4pm Tue-Fri). Built by convicts in 1829, it was used as a government store until 1962. Today it houses a museum that follows the development of the Moreton Bay settlement, which eventually became Brisbane. The ground floor delves into the history of the Moreton Bay penal colony, which incarcerated repeat offenders from all over the country during the 1820s.

Continuing south along George St, on the right immediately after the junction with Margaret St, is the **Mansions** (Map p56), a beautiful and unusual three-storey terrace built in 1890. Look out for the cats on top of the parapet at each end of the building. Opposite is the imposing Greek-revival facade of the **Queensland Club** (Map p56).

One block south of the Mansions, **Parliament House** (Map p56; www.parliament.qld.gov.au; cnr Alice & George Sts; admission free) occupies a suitably regal position overlooking the City Botanic Gardens. Set against a tropical backdrop, its grand, sand-coloured facade is quite magnificent and arguably Brisbane's most stunning historical piece of architecture. The structure dates from 1868 and was built in French Renaissance style with a roof clad in Mt Isa copper. Free guided tours are available on demand between 9am and 4pm Monday to Friday, which is the only way you'll get to peek inside.

Virtually next door, within the Queensland University of Technology (QUT) campus, is the **QUT Art Museum** (Map p56; 2 George St; admission free; ⏲10am-5pm Tue-Fri, noon-4pm Sat & Sun). Modest in size, this gallery showcases contemporary art in all its mediums and 'isms'. There's a definite lean towards Australian works, but temporary exhibits by international artists are also displayed.

SOUTH BANK

TOP CHOICE **Cultural Centre** MUSEUMS & CONCERT HALL

On South Bank, just over Victoria Bridge from the CBD, the Cultural Centre is the epicentre of Brisbane's cultural confluence. It's a huge compound that includes a concert and theatre venue, an enormous conference and convention centre and a modern concrete edifice containing three museums and the Queensland State Library. Right next to this is yet another art mecca, the Gallery of Modern Art.

A good place to start is the **Queensland Museum** (Map p60; www.southbank.qm.qld.

gov.au; cnr Grey & Melbourne Sts; admission free; ⌚9.30am-5pm), which occupies imaginations with all manner of curiosities. Queensland's history is given a once-over with an interesting collection of exhibits, including a skeleton of the state's own dinosaur, *Muttaburrasaurus,* and the *Avian Cirrus,* the tiny plane in which Queensland's Bert Hinkler made the first England-to-Australia solo flight in 1928. Upstairs there's an enlightening, if not distressing, display on Queensland's endangered species, as well as a reconstruction of the host of mammoth marsupials that roamed these shores more than 100,000 years ago. There are also good temporary exhibits on the likes of bug, beetle and butterfly parades, or dinosaur skeletons from around the globe.

The museum also houses the excellent **Sciencentre** (Map p60; admission adult/child/family $12/9/40), with over 100 hands-on, interactive exhibits that delve into life science and technology in fun, thought-provoking ways.

Inside an austere chunk of concrete, the **Queensland Art Gallery** (Map p60; www.qag.qld.gov.au; Melbourne St, South Brisbane; admission free; ⌚10am-5pm Mon-Fri, 9am-5pm Sat & Sun) houses a fine permanent collection, mostly of domestic and European artists. The gallery showcases Australian art from the 1840s through to the 1970s, and the 1st floor is devoted to celebrated Australian artists; you can view works by masters including Sir Sydney Nolan, Arthur Boyd, William Dobell and George Lambert.

The **Gallery of Modern Art** (Map p60; Stanley Place; admission free; ⌚10am-5pm Mon-Fri, 9am-5pm Sat & Sun) is housed in an enormous building flooded with natural light, which contrasts wood, concrete and brushed steel in its contemporary design. Exhibition halls showcase Australian art from the 1970s to modern times in a variety of changing exhibitions and media: painting, sculpture and photography sit alongside video, installation and film. You can enjoy the sublime river and city views from various onsite cafes.

South Bank Parklands PARK

(Map p60; admission free; ⌚dawn-dusk) This beautiful swathe of green park skirts the western side of the Brisbane River. It suffered flood damage during the 2011 flood, but restoration of facilities proceeded quickly. A good thing, as this popular spot is home to cultural attractions, fine eateries, small rainforests, hidden lawns and gorgeous flora. Scattered throughout are barbecues and climbing gyms where youngsters swarm like bees to honey. A scenic esplanade offers spectacular views of the city and the whole area is laden with atmosphere and character.

The stand-out attraction is the **Streets Beach** (Map p60), an artificial swimming hole that resembles a tropical lagoon, with an attractive landscaping of trees, bridges and rockeries. The beach even has its own lifeguards, but the lack of rips, undertows and sharks tends to keep the drama to a minimum. It gets packed on weekends.

Nearby, **Stanley Street Plaza** (Map p60) is a renovated section of historic Stanley St lined with cafes, shops and restaurants; buskers draw crowds in the summer.

On Friday evening and all day Saturday and Sunday there's a large and popular **craft and clothing market** in the plaza.

The **Suncorp Piazza** (Map p60) is an outdoor theatre that screens international sporting events regularly and movies during school holidays, both for free. It's also a venue for concerts and performances.

The Parklands are located within easy walking distance of the CBD. You can also get there by CityCat or City Ferry, or by bus or train from the transit centre or Central Station.

Maritime Museum MUSEUM

(Map p60; Sidon St, South Brisbane; adult/child $8/3.50, dry dock $4/2; ⌚9.30am-4.30pm) This museum, at the western end of the South Bank promenade, has a wide range of displays on maritime adventures (and misadventures) along the state's coast. A daunting

RIVERSIDE PATH

One of the best ways to see the city is to stroll, cycle or jog along the riverside path. You can plot a day out following one side of the river and head back on the other side. Don't miss a stroll through the South Bank Parklands, and up to Kangaroo Point, passing below the rock-climbing cliffs (a good pitstop is the Cliffs Cafe). Nearly every bridge has a separate pedestrian lane separate from traffic, including the Story Bridge, which has a magnificent views of downtown. Frequent ferry docks means you can always hop on a boat when you're ready to call it a day.

South Bank

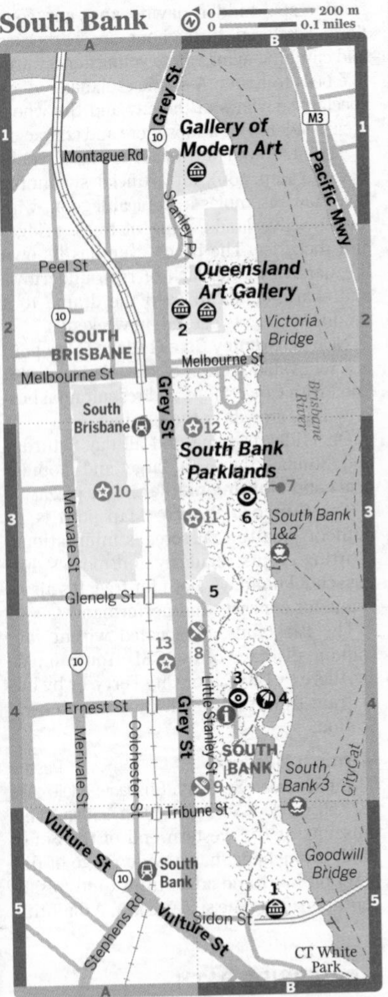

South Bank

Top Sights

Gallery of Modern Art B1
Queensland Art Gallery B2
South Bank Parklands B3

Sights

1 Maritime Museum B5
2 Queensland Museum A2
Sciencentre .... (see 2)
3 Stanley Street Plaza B4
4 Streets Beach B4
5 Suncorp Piazza B3
6 Wheel of Brisbane B3

Activities, Courses & Tours

7 River City Cruises B3

Eating

8 Ahmet's B4
9 Piaf B4

Entertainment

10 Brisbane Convention & Exhibition Centre A3
11 Queensland Conservatorium B3
12 Queensland Performing Arts Centre B3
13 South Bank Cinema A4

Shopping

South Bank Lifestyle Markets ..... (see 3)

highlight is the sizable map showing the location of more than 1500 shipwrecks (mostly victims of the Reef) in Queensland's waters since 1791. It's worth shelling out a little extra to tour the dry dock – the highlight of the museum is undoubtedly clambering around the fascinating rooms of the HMAS *Diamantina,* a restored 1944 navy frigate.

Wheel of Brisbane FERRIS WHEEL

(Map p60; www.thewheelofbrisbane.com.au; Russell St, South Brisbane; adult/child $15/10; ⌚11am-9pm) For a memorable view over Brisbane, take a ride on the riverside Wheel, located a few steps from the Queensland Performing Arts Centre (QPAC). The enclosed gondolas rise to a height of 60m, where you'll have a striking 360-degree panorama of the city; rides last 12 to 15 minutes and include audio commentary of Brisbane sights.

FORTITUDE VALLEY & NEW FARM

For over a decade the alternative neighbourhoods of Fortitude Valley and nearby New Farm have been the hub of all things contemporary and cool, thanks to a confluence of artists, restaurateurs and various fringe types flooding the area.

During the day the action is concentrated on **Brunswick Street Mall** (Map p62), a pedestrianised arcade full of pavement cafes, bars and shops. The northeast section of Fortitude Valley and New Farm is more pleasant though – James and Brunswick Sts are good places to begin your exploration.

Alongside the funky restaurants and bars, Brisbane's very own **Chinatown** occupies only one street (Duncan St) but exhibits the same flamboyance and flavour of its counterparts in Sydney and Melbourne. The Ann St end is guarded by an exquisite Tang dynasty archway and oriental lions. Chinese landscaping throughout includes pagodas and a waterfall.

Just west of the Valley, **St John's Cathedral** (Map p56; 373 Ann St; admission free; ⌚9.30am-4.30pm, tours 10am & 2pm Mon-Sat, 2pm Sun) is a beautiful piece of 19th-century Gothic Revival architecture. Inside the church is a magnificent fusion of carved timber and stained glass. The building is a true labour of love – construction began in 1906 and ended in March 2009, making it one of the last cathedrals of its architectural style to be built.

New Farm, just east of the Valley along Brunswick St, is packed with bars and restaurants that cater to an eclectic but generally well-moneyed crowd. At the eastern end of Brunswick St, **New Farm Park** (Map p80) is a large, open parkland with playgrounds, picnic areas and gas barbecues, jacaranda trees and rose gardens.

GREATER BRISBANE

Newstead House — HISTORIC SITE

(☎3216 1846; www.newsteadhouse.com.au; cnr Breakfast Creek Rd & Newstead Ave, Newstead; adult/child/family $6/4/15; ⌚10am-4pm Mon-Thu, 2-5pm Sun) On a breezy hill overlooking the river, Brisbane's best-known heritage site dates from 1846 and is beautifully fitted out with Victorian furnishings, antiques, clothing and period displays. It's surrounded by manicured gardens and has superb water vistas. It's located north of the centre, in Newstead Park. On Sundays, Devonshire tea is served on the verandah.

Mt Coot-tha Reserve — NATURE RESERVE

About 7km west of the city centre, Mt Coot-tha Reserve is a 220-hectare bush reserve that's teeming with wildlife (mostly of the possum and bush-turkey variety). Aside from the chunk of wilderness, the big attractions here are a massive planetarium and the spectacular lookout. The latter affords panoramic daytime views of Brisbane and a few bits beyond, and at night, a sea of twinkling lights blanketing the terrain for miles. The lookout is accessed via Samuel Griffith Dr and has wheelchair access.

There are picnic spots with tables and barbecues scattered throughout the park. One of the nicest is **Simpson Falls**, set in a gentle valley and surrounded by scrub. In less of a bush enclave but with a thick carpet of lawn is **Hoop Pine**. Bigger than both is **JC Slaughter Falls**, where you can create an alfresco banquet amid oodles of trees and grass. The turn-off to JC Slaughter Falls is just north of Sir Samuel Griffith Dr.

At the end of the road you can access the circuitous, 1.5km **Aboriginal Art Trail**, which takes you past eight art sites with work by local Aboriginal artists, including tree carvings, rock paintings and a ceremonial

BRISBANE IN...

Two Days

Start with breakfast in Brisbane's bohemian **West End**, and then saunter across to **South Bank Parklands**. Take in an exhibit at the **Cultural Centre**, then head to a riverside eatery. Take a stroll (or a swim) at **Streets Beach** and explore the parklands. Afterwards, jump on a ferry to the **Brisbane Powerhouse** in New Farm for a bite or perhaps a show.

On day two head downtown for a gander at the mix of old and new architecture, visiting **City Hall**, **King George Square** and the **Treasury Building**, before strolling through the lush **Botanic Gardens**. Finish the day with a brew at the **Belgian Beer Cafe** and a banquet in Fortitude Valley's **Chinatown**.

Four Days

On day three check out cafe culture in **New Farm**, then delve into the shopping or gallery scene in nearby Fortitude Valley. Spend the afternoon exploring **Mt Coot-tha Reserve** and the **Brisbane Botanic Gardens**. Then head back to **Fortitude Valley** for fine dining, and work it all off in one of the Valley's late-night bars.

On day four take a cruise upriver to **Lone Pine Koala Sanctuary**. Recount the day's events over a beer at the **Breakfast Creek Hotel** and then gravitate to Paddington for cocktails and a bite at the **Lark**.

Fortitude Valley

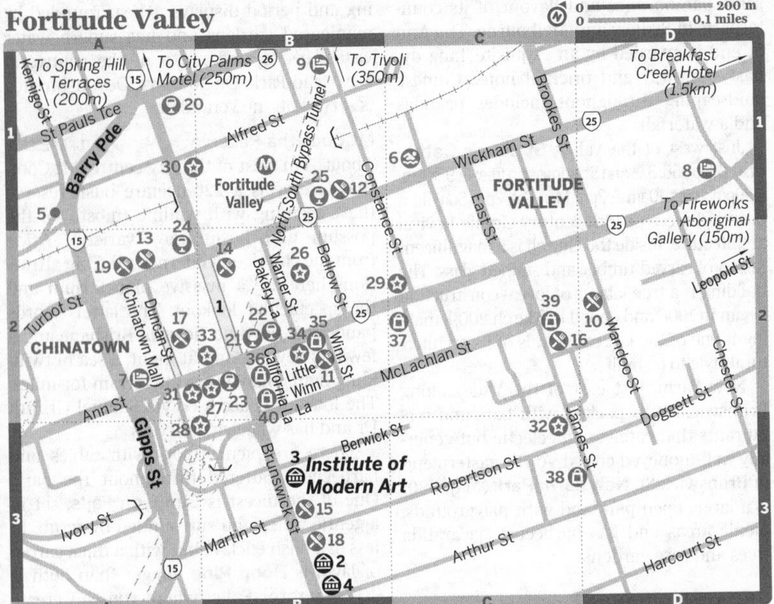

dance pit. Also here is the **JC Slaughter Falls Track** (3.4km return), which leads through the reserve to the lookout. It's quite steep in several sections; decent walking shoes are recommended.

The very beautiful **Brisbane Botanic Gardens** (admission free; ⌚8am-5pm, free guided walks 11am & 1pm Mon-Sat) cover 50 hectares and include over 20,000 species of plants. The plethora of mini ecologies, which include cactus, Japanese and herb gardens, rainforests and arid zones, make you feel like you're traversing the globe's landscape in all its vegetated splendour. There is also a compact tropical dome in which exotic palms soar above you like science-fiction props. Don't miss the weeping fig in the exotic rainforest section and keep an eye out for geckos scuttling across your path as you wander through. There's an excellent restaurant on site, **Botanical** (mains $15-24), serving breakfast, lunch and snacks, overlooking a lily-pad-filled lagoon.

Also within the gardens, the **Sir Thomas Brisbane Planetarium** (⌚10am-4pm Tue-Fri, 11am-7.30pm Sat, 11am-4pm Sun) is Australia's largest planetarium. There's a great observatory here and the shows inside the **Cosmic Skydome** (adult $7-14, child $7-9) will make you feel like you've stepped on board the *Enterprise*. Outside of show times, you can explore the small museum with photographs of star systems, a replica of Neil Armstrong's *Apollo 11* suit, and a screening room that shows short space-related clips.

To get here via public transport, take bus 471 from bus stop 40 on Adelaide St, opposite King George Sq ($3.90, 25 minutes, hourly Monday to Friday, five services Saturday and Sunday). The bus drops you off in the lookout car park and stops outside the Brisbane Botanic Gardens en route.

D'Aguilar Range National Park

NATURE RESERVE

Brisbanites suffering from suburban malaise satiate their wilderness cravings at this 35,000-hectare park in the D'Aguilar Range, 10km north of the city centre. Comprising both South D'Aguilar and Mt Mee, it's a great area for bushwalking, cycling, horse riding, camping and scenic drives. At the park entrance the **Walkabout Creek Visitor Centre** (☎camping permits 13 7468; www.derm.qld.gov.au; 60 Mt Nebo Rd) has information about **camping** (per person $5.15) and maps of the park. If you plan to camp, keep in mind that it is bush camping, without any facilities: campers need to obtain permits prior to arrival by telephone or online. Note, these are remote, walk-in camp sites, and

Fortitude Valley

Top Sights
- Institute of Modern Art B3

Sights
- 1 Brunswick Street Mall B2
- 2 Jan Murphy Gallery B3
- 3 Judith Wright Centre for Contemporary Arts B3
- 4 Philip Bacon Gallery B3

Activities, Courses & Tours
- C!rca .... (see 3)
- James St Cooking School .... (see 39)
- 5 Rocksports A1
- 6 Valley Pool C1

Sleeping
- 7 Bunk Backpackers A2
- 8 Emporium D1
- 9 Limes B1

Eating
- 10 Campos D2
- 11 Flamingo B2
- 12 Garuva B1
- James St Market .... (see 39)
- 13 Kuan-Yin Tea House A2
- 14 McWhirter's Marketplace B2
- 15 Ortiga B3
- 16 Spoon Deli C2
- 17 Thai Wi-Rat A2
- 18 Tibetan Kitchen B3
- 19 Vietnamese Restaurant A2
- Wagamama .... (see 8)

Drinking
- 20 Alloneword A1
- 21 Bowery B2
- Cru Bar .... (see 39)
- 22 La Ruche B2
- 23 Press Club B2
- 24 Sky Room A2
- 25 Wickham Hotel B1

Entertainment
- Beat MegaClub .... (see 34)
- Birdie Num Num Bar & Nightclub. (see 7)
- 26 Church B2
- 27 Cloudland B2
- Electric Playground .... (see 26)
- 28 Family B3
- 29 Fringe Bar C2
- 30 Globe A1
- 31 Monastery A2
- 32 Palace Centro C3
- 33 X&Y Bar B2
- 34 Zoo B2

Shopping
- 35 Blonde Venus B2
- Brunswick Street Markets .... (see 1)
- 36 Butter Beats B2
- 37 Dogstar C2
- Emporium .... (see 8)
- 38 Francis Leon C3
- 39 James St Market C2
- 40 Maiocchi B2

you need to hike between 1km and 10km to reach them.

The bird life is a big lure here and it's a beautiful spot for a barbecue. There are **walking trails** ranging from a few hundred metres to 13km, including the 6km Morelia Track at Manorina day-use area and the 5km Greene's Falls Track at Mt Glorious.

Beside the visitor centre is **Walkabout Creek** (adult/child/family $6/3/15), a wildlife centre where you can see a resident platypus up close, as well as turtles, green tree frogs, lizards, pythons and gliders. There's also a small but wonderful walk-through aviary. It's an outstanding alternative to a zoo.

To get here catch bus 385 ($5.30, 30 minutes), which departs from Roma St Station hourly from 10.22am to 3.22pm (services start at 8.47am on weekends). The bus stops outside the visitor centre, and the last departure back to the city is at 4.48pm (3.53pm on weekends). There are two park walks (1.5km and 5km) available from the visitor centre; other walks are a fair distance away, so you'll need your own transport.

Lone Pine Koala Sanctuary NATURE RESERVE
(☎3378 1366; Jesmond Rd, Fig Tree Pocket; adult/child/family $30/21/80; ⊙8.30am-5pm) About 12km southwest of Brisbane's CBD, this wildlife sanctuary is an easy half-day trip. It's the world's largest koala sanctuary and with more than 130 of the cute and cuddly bears you won't be lacking photo opportunities. A cuddle costs an extra, but irresistible, $16 (including photos), and you can hand feed the tame kangaroos for around $1 per bag of pellets. Keeping the koalas and roos company are wombats, possums, dingoes,

ART GALLERIES OF BRISBANE

Brisbane has a small but growing array of private galleries and exhibition spaces, where you can get an eyeful of both the mainstream and the cutting-edge. The best and biggest is the **Institute of Modern Art** (Map p62; ☎3252 5750; www.ima.org.au; ⏰11am-5pm Tue-Sat, to 8pm Thu), a noncommercial gallery with an industrial exhibition space and regular showings by local artists. It's housed inside the **Judith Wright Centre for Contemporary Arts** (Map p62; ☎3872 9000; www.judithwrightcentre.com.au; 420 Brunswick St, Fortitude Valley), which is another excellent venue for live performance of all genres.

Other places to explore the city's art scene include **Suzanne O'Connell Gallery** (Map p62; www.suzanneoconnell.com; 93 James St; ⏰11am-4pm Wed-Sat), a well-respected gallery tucked away in New Farm. It specialises in Indigenous art, with stunning works from artists all across Australia. There are regular openings, and it's a good source for information.

Milani (www.milanigallery.com.au; 54 Logan Rd, Woolloongabba; ⏰11am-6pm Tue-Sat) is a superb gallery with cutting-edge Aboriginal and contemporary artwork. The well respected **Philip Bacon** (Map p62; www.philipbacongalleries.com.au; 2 Arthur St, Fortitude Valley; ⏰10am-5pm Tue-Sat) gallery has 19th-century and modern Australian paintings and sculpture.

Fireworks (Map p62; www.fireworksgallery.com.au; 52 Doggett St, Newstead; ⏰10am-6pm Tue-Fri, 10am-4pm Sat) specialises in both Aboriginal art and more mainstream contemporary pieces. It's just a short stroll from James St. **Jan Murphy** (Map p62; www.janmurphygallery.com.au; 486 Brunswick St, Fortitude Valley; ⏰10am-5pm Tue-Sat) is another leading exhibition space in the heart of the Valley's gallery district.

Tasmanian Devils, raptors, a platypus and sheep and sheepdogs. Frequent presentations (birds of prey, sheep sheering, koala talks) give added insight. The sanctuary is set in gorgeous parklands beside the river.

To get here catch bus 430 ($4.70, 43 minutes, hourly), which leaves from the Queen St bus station, or bus 445 ($4.70, 37 minutes, hourly), from stop 40 on Adelaide St near King George Sq.

Alternatively, **Mirimar II** (☎1300 729 742; www.miramar.com; incl park entry per adult/child/family $60/35/180) cruises to the sanctuary along the Brisbane River from North Quay, next to Victoria Bridge. There's recorded commentary along the way. It departs daily at 10am, returning from Lone Pine at 1.45pm. One-way passage is half-price.

Alma Park Zoo — ZOO

(☎3204 6566; www.almaparkzoo.com.au; Alma Rd, Dakabin; adult/child/family $20/21/85; ⏰9am-4pm) You can bond with a multicultural mix of furred and feathered brethren at this zoo, 28km north of the city centre. Inhabiting 16 hectares of subtropical gardens is a large collection of native birds and mammals, including koalas, kangaroos, emus and dingoes. Among the impressive representation of beautiful exotics are Malaysian sun bears, tamarin and squirrel monkeys and leopards. You can touch many of the animals, and feeding times are all between 10.30am and 3pm.

To get here via public transport catch the Zoo Train (on the Caboolture line), which leaves from Roma St Station daily at 9am ($6.70, 45 minutes) and connects with the free zoo bus at Dakabin station.

Daisy Hill Koala Centre — NATURE RESERVE

(☎3299 1032; www.derm.qld.gov.au; Daisy Hill Rd, Daisy Hill Forest Reserve; admission free; ⏰10am-4pm) Located about 25km southeast of the city, this centre has informative displays and a number of fat and happy-looking koalas, but it's no zoo. The surrounding area is an important koala habitat and part of a 435-hectare conservation park. The centre is designed to acquaint visitors with koalas on a much more comprehensive level than just a cuddle and photo encounter.

Once you've delved into their world you can head out into the reserve and spot them in the wild. There are also lovely picnic and bushwalking spots, plus plenty of opportunities to see bird life and other furry natives.

Activities

Brisbane's climate and geography are perfect for outdoor activities and the city's relatively flat incline and numerous parks and gardens enable you to walk, cycle, skate, swim and scale walls to your heart's content.

Riverlife Adventure Centre ADVENTURE CENTRE
(Map p56; ☎3891 5766; www.riverlife.com.au; Naval Stores, Kangaroo Point) A good one-stop shop for a wide range of activities, located near the Kangaroo Point cliffs. It offers rock climbing ($45 per session), abseiling (rapelling, $39) and kayaking instruction ($39), and hires out bicycles (per 90 minutes/four hours $15/30), kayaks (per 90 minutes $25) and in-line skates (per 90 minutes/four hours $20/40). It also has kayaking excursions followed by a BBQ on weekend nights, and Sunday brunch-and-activity deals.

Rock Climbing & Abseiling

Rock climbing is a very popular pastime in Brisbane, and you can do the Spiderman dance in spectacular fashion at the **cliffs rock-climbing area** (Map p56), on the southern banks of the Brisbane River at Kangaroo Point. These pink volcanic cliffs are allegedly 200 million years old and, regardless of your level of expertise, joining the other scrambling figures is good (and exhilarating!) fun. The cliffs are floodlit until midnight or later. Several operators offer climbing and abseiling instruction here, and there are great climbing sights further afield (notably in the Glasshouse Mountains).

Near the cliffs, the **Riverlife Adventure Centre** (Map p56; www.riverlife.com.au; Naval Stores, River Tce, Kangaroo Point) provides lessons.

Other operators:

Adventures Around Brisbane ABSEILING, ROCK CLIMBING
(☎1800 689 453; www.adventuresaroundbrisbane.com.au; climbing $35) Holds rock-climbing introductory courses and meets at the base of the cliffs. It also has an introduction to abseiling course, and lead climbs to Glass House Mountains and Mt Tinbeerwah.

Adventure Seekers ABSEILING, ROCK CLIMBING
(☎1300 855 859; www.adventureseekers.com.au; half-day climb or abseil $110) Runs half-day abseiling and rock climbing (separately) at Kangaroo Point. Also offers two-hour abseiling sessions at dusk ($59).

BRISBANE BY BIKE

Brisbane is one of Australia's most bike-friendly cities, with over 900km of bikeways and bike paths, including scenic routes that follow the Brisbane River. Pick up free maps at the **Transport Information Centre** (cnr Ann & Albert Sts, CBD). A good starter takes you from the City Botanic Gardens, across the Goodwill Bridge and out to the University of Queensland. It's about 7km one way and you can stop for a beer at the Regatta pub in Toowong.

Bicycles are allowed on Citytrains, except on weekdays during peak hours. You can also take bikes on CityCats and ferries for free, but cycling in malls is a no-no.

Brisbane's new bike-sharing program **City Cycle** (www.citycycle.com.au) kicked off in 2010, with a network of 2000 bikes at 150 bike stations across Brisbane. To check out a bike, go online and purchase a one-day subscription ($11), which you can then use at any station. Bikes are free for the first half-hour (and you can ride all day for free, as long as bikes are returned within half-hour intervals). After the first half-hour, prices rise exponentially ($2.20 for 31 to 60 minutes, $6 for 60 to 90 minutes, $11 for 91 to 120 minutes, etc). Long-term visitors can sign up for three-month ($28) or one-year ($61) subscriptions. The only catch: you must wear a helmet or risk a hefty fine. Visit the website for a list of places to purchase one.

If you'd rather not hassle with City Cycle, here are several reputable hire outfits, with helmet and bike lock included.

Bicycle Revolution (Map p76; www.bicyclerevolution.org.au; 294 Montague Rd, West End; per day/week $35/150) Non-profit, worker-owned shop that sells and hires out eye-catching, handsomely restored vintage bikes.

Valet Cycle Hire (Map p56; ☎0408 003 198; cnr Edward & Alice Sts; per hr/2hr/day $18/24/42) Located at entrance to Botanic Gardens. Tandems, children's bikes and baby seats available. It also delivers bikes to hotels (half-day/full day $45/55).

TOP FIVE WILDERNESS DAY TRIPS NEAR BRISBANE

If Brisbane is becoming a bit hectic for you and you want to reacquaint yourself with nature, consider these easy day trips out of the city:

North Stradbroke Island (p101) An idyllic and little-developed island with great surfing, coastal walks, whale watching, diving and bushwalking.

Gold Cost hinterland (p136) A vast sea of dense forest with wonderful walking makes a great antidote to urban grit.

Glass House Mountains (p151) Volcanic crags sprout from humid green surrounds in these lovely mountains with hikes to their craggy peaks. Australia Zoo is also here.

D'Aguilar Range National Park (p62) Commune with nature barely outside the city limits; walking tracks take you into the heart of this well-managed park.

Girraween National Park (p110) Walks amid towering boulders, enchanting forests and colourful wildflowers in springtime.

You can also climb indoors at **Urban Climb** (Map p76; ☎3844 2544; www.urbanclimb.com.au; 2/220 Montague Rd, West End), or **Rocksports** (Map p62; ☎3216 0462; 224 Barry Pde, Fortitude Valley). Casual climbs cost around $18.

Swimming

Aside from the artificial lagoon at the South Bank Parklands, Brisbane has plenty of more conventional pools. Choices include:

Centenary Aquatic Centre SWIMMING
(off Map p56; 400 Gregory Tce, Spring Hill; adult/child $5/4; ⏲5.30am-7pm Mon-Fri, 7am-4pm Sat & Sun) This is the best pool in town, with an Olympic-sized lap pool, a kids pool and a diving pool with a high tower.

Splash Leisure SWIMMING
(www.splash.com.au; 375 Hamilton Rd, Chermside; pool adult/child $7.50/5, water park adult/child $11/9; ⏲pool 5.30am-7pm Mon-Fri, 7am-5pm Sat & Sun, water park 10am-3pm Sat & Sun) Water park with slides and tube rides. Great for families. Indoor swimming pool also open daily.

Spring Hill Baths SWIMMING
(off Map p56; 14 Torrington St, Spring Hill; adult/child $4.50/3.20; ⏲6.30am-7pm Mon-Thu, to 6pm Fri, 8am-5pm Sat, 8am-1pm Sun) Heated year-round, these old-fashioned baths are among the oldest in the southern hemisphere.

Valley Pool SWIMMING
(Map p62; 432 Wickham St, Fortitude Valley; adult/child $4.50/3.20; ⏲5.30am-7pm Mon-Fri, 7.30am-6pm Sat & Sun) With a 50m outdoor pool.

In-Line Skating

Skaters reclaim the streets on Wednesday nights with **Planet Inline** (☎3217 3571; www.planetinline.com) skate tours ($15) starting at 7.15pm from the top of the Goodwill Bridge. It also runs a Saturday morning breakfast club tour ($15), and Sunday afternoon tours that differ each week and last about three hours ($15).

You can hire skates and equipment from **Skatebiz** (Map p56; ☎3220 0157; www.skatebiz.com.au; 101 Albert St, Brisbane; per 2/24hr $13/25) or **Riverlife Adventure Centre** (Map p56; ☎3891 5766; www.riverlife.com.au; Naval Stores, River Tce, Kangaroo Point).

Skydiving & Ballooning

Brisbane Skydiving Centre SKYDIVING
(☎1300 788 555; www.jumpthebeachbrisbane.com.au; from $310) Picks up from the CBD and offers tandem skydives over Brisbane, landing on the beach in Redcliffe.

Ripcord Skydivers SKYDIVING
(☎3399 3552; www.ripcord-skydivers.com.au; from $295) Also picks up from the CBD and offers tandem skydives over Brisbane, landing on the beach in Redcliffe.

Fly Me to the Moon BALLOONING
(☎3423 0400; www.brisbanehotairballooning.com.au) Offers one-hour ballooning trips over Brisbane costing $298 per person on weekdays and $348 on weekends. Free pick-up and breakfast included.

Golf

Victoria Park Golf Course GOLF
(☎3252 9891; Herston Rd, Herston) The most central public course, immediately north of Spring Hill; 18 holes cost $23 during the week and $27.50 on weekends. Club hire is another $28 for a full set or $16 for a half set.

St Lucia Golf Links GOLF
(☎3403 2556; cnr Carawa St & Indooroopilly Rd, St Lucia) About 8km south of the city centre.

Indooroopilly Golf Club GOLF
(☎3721 2173; Meiers Rd, Indooroopilly) Also about 8km south of the city centre.

Courses

James St Cooking School COOKING
(Map p62; ☎3252-8850; www.jamesstcookingschool.com.au; James St Markets, Fortitude Valley; 3hr class $125-135) Among James St popular offerings – both hands-on and demonstration classes – are three-hour courses on cooking modern Australian, French, Thai, seafood or 'beer and BBQing'. The school also offers cooking classes for kids (accompanied by a parent).

Mondo Organics COOKING
(Map p76; ☎3844 1132; www.mondo-organics.com.au; 166 Hardgrave Rd, West End; 2hr class $105-125) Award-winning chefs teach a wide range of skills at these hands-on two-hour classes. You can master the basics of cooking Japanese, Italian, Persian, vegetarian and other dishes. One-hour wine appreciation classes ($35 to $55) explore an equally broad field, from Spanish reds to summer cocktails.

Quirky Brisbane

National Festival of Beers BEER FESTIVAL
(www.nfb.com.au; Story Bridge Hotel; per person $25) Brisbane has many a cultural festival event on its annual calendar, but perhaps none quite as close to Australians' hearts as this event held over three days in mid-September. Beer lovers gather to pay homage to the golden honey and are indulged with brews from around 45 Australian breweries – both macro and micro. There's also a fairly impressive entertainment line-up to enhance the mood, and the University of Beer, where you can receive invaluable tuition from the top brewers.

Australia Day Cockroach Races RACING EVENT
(www.cockroachraces.com.au) Many Australians mistakenly believe the Melbourne Cup is the 'race that stops a nation', but any self-respecting Brisbanite can tell you this tag really belongs to these annual races held at the Story Bridge Hotel every 26 January. The

BRISBANE FOR CHILDREN

One of the best attractions for children is the **Cultural Centre** (p58). Here the Queensland Museum runs some fantastic, hands-on programs for little tackers during school holidays. The incorporated Sciencentre is made for inquisitive young minds and will keep them inventing, creating and discovering for hours. The Queensland Art Gallery has a Children's Art Centre in which it runs regular programs throughout the year.

C!RCA (Map p62; ☎3852 3110; www.circa.org.au; 420 Brunswick St, per day $80) offers action-packed 'circus classes' (tumbling, balancing, jumping, trapeze work) for budding young performers at the Judith Wright Centre in Fortitude Valley.

Bookings are essential for this one: budding thespians can unfurl some creative vigour of another genre at dance and theatre workshops at the **Brisbane Powerhouse** (p90).

The **South Bank Parklands** (p59) has the safe and child-friendly Streets Beach and a scattering of jungle-gym playgrounds with rubber surfaces. There are more imaginative playgrounds in the **Roma Street Parkland** (p53).

The river is a big plus. Many children will enjoy a river-boat trip, especially if it's to **Lone Pine Koala Sanctuary** (p63), where they can cuddle up to one of the lovable creatures. Similarly, a trip to **Alma Park Zoo** (p64) or the **Daisy Hill Koala Centre** (p64) will keep them engaged with local and foreign wildlife.

The **Brisbane City Council** (www.brisbane.qld.gov.au) runs Chill Out, a program of activities for 10- to 17-year-olds during the school holidays, and **Visible Ink** (www.visible-ink.org), an ongoing program with activities and events designed for 12- to 16-year-olds.

The free monthly booklet *Brisbane's Child* (www.brisbaneschild.com.au) has information about Brisbane for parents. Click onto the Bub Hub website (www.bubhub.com.au) for comprehensive information for new parents, including everything from clinic contacts and locations, prenatal care and activities for newborns to toddlers.

Daycare or babysitting options include **Dial an Angel** (☎1300 721 111; www.dialanangel.com) and **Care4Kidz** (www.careforkidz.com.au/brisbane/babysitting.htm).

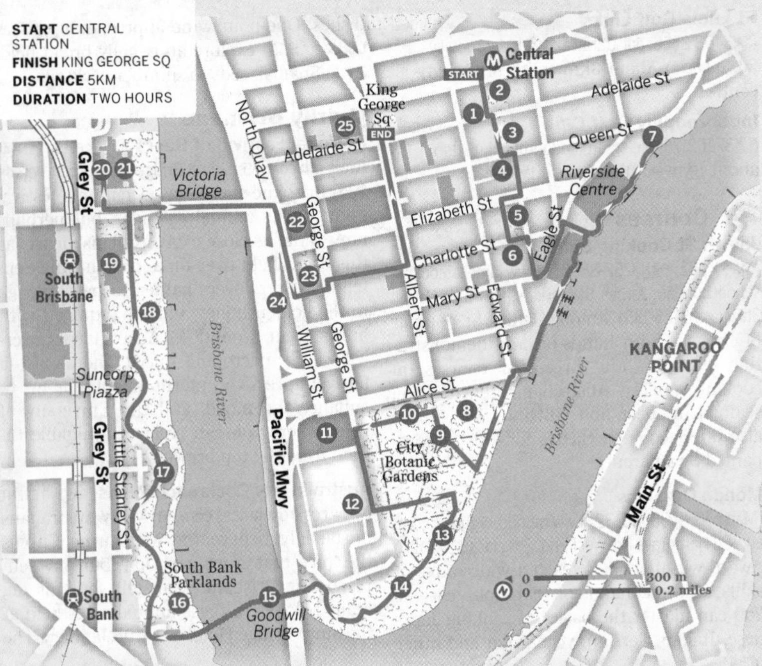

Walking Tour
A Stroll from the CBD to South Bank

With its downtown parks, riverside cycle paths, historic buildings and gentle landscape, Brisbane is a great place to explore on foot. The city council produces the fold-out *Brisbane City Walk* with itinerary and description of 30 historic and cultural highlights. Alternatively, the following walk covers about 5km and takes a couple of hours.

Starting at Central Station, head due south, cross the road and descend the steps into 1 **Anzac Square**, where locals, city workers and ibises mill about the grassy patches and shady trees. At the northwestern end of the park, the 2 **Shrine of Remembrance** is a Greek Revivalist cenotaph where an eternal flame burns in remembrance of Australian soldiers who died in WWI.

Take the pedestrian bridge over the road at the southeastern corner of the square, which leads into 3 **Post Office Square**. Heading in the same direction, cross Queen St to Brisbane's historic 4 **GPO**, which is still in use. Walk down the small alley that skirts the eastern side of the post office through to Elizabeth St. Cross the road and explore the beautiful 5 **St Stephen's Cathedral** and the adjoining St Stephen's Chapel. Built in 1850, the chapel is Brisbane's oldest church and was designed by English architect Augustus Pugin, who designed London's Houses of Parliament. The cathedral was built in 1874.

Walk through the grassy courtyard behind the cathedral until you reach Charlotte St. Take a left and the first right onto Market St. The small cafe on the corner, the 6 **Market Street Cafe**, is a fine place to grab a coffee or a snack. Continue to Eagle St, then take a left, walk to the first light and turn right. Cross the busy road, and walk through the high-rises of Eagle St Pier until you reach the waterfront. From here jog north to have a look at the elegant 7 **Customs House**, a historic 19th-century building that occasionally hosts art exhibitions. Head south again and take in the city views to your right and the river views to your left.

When you get to Edward St Pier take a stroll through the 8 **City Botanic Gardens**, a lush area of fig trees, bunya pines and wide lawns. As you enter, you'll have fantastic views of the river and docked boats to your left. After about 50m, take the path to the 9 **rotunda**, where you'll find a stand with free brochures detailing sights within the park. Head towards the park's Albert St entrance, but take a left for a stroll around the 10 **Ornamental Ponds**. Keep your eyes peeled for ducks, ibises and the odd curlew. After passing the lakes take a peak at Queensland's regal, copper-topped 11 **Parliament House**. You can also pop inside and see when the next free tour is going. Afterwards, continue along the paved road skirting the park and onto the campus of Queensland University of Technology (QUT), where you'll find the beautifully restored 12 **Old Government House**. Built in 1860, this is one of Queensland's most important heritage structures and was the first public building designed and built in the budding colony. The rooms on the main level are largely empty. Head upstairs to visit the William Robinson Gallery showcasing the superb landscapes of one of Queensland's finest living painters. Wind your way back through the gardens, where you'll pass the elegant 13 **Jemmy Morrill and Brolgas sculpture**. Morrill was the sole survivor of a shipwreck on the Great Barrier Reef in 1846. Aboriginal people found him and he lived with them for 17 years before returning to a European settlement in Queensland. He went on to play a pivotal role in improving relations between Aboriginal peoples and early settlers.

Keep to the river to take a stroll along the pretty 14 **Mangrove Boardwalk**, a wooden walkway with fine river views. When the boardwalk ends, get back on the main path and continue toward the pedestrian-only 15 **Goodwill Bridge**. Cross the bridge, admiring the view from the middle (watch for speeding cyclists). On the other side, you'll be on the edge of the pleasant and pretty 16 **South Bank Parklands**. Stroll amid flowering vines and shade trees and have a look at 17 **Streets Beach**, a handsomely landscaped artificial swimming lagoon. If you're feeling peckish, you can stop in for a snack at one of many restaurants and cafes in the park (there are even more options on Little Stanley St). Otherwise, continue on towards Victoria Bridge. If time allows, you can take a spin on the 18 **Wheel of Brisbane**, providing excellent views over the city from its 60m-high climb. You might also duck into the 19 **Queensland Performing Arts Centre (QPAC)** to see if any upcoming shows pique your interest; the enormous museum complex of the Cultural Centre that connects to QPAC (via walkways over Melbourne St) is worth a day's exploring in its own right. Here you'll find the massive 20 **Queensland Museum**, packed with state treasures including dinosaur bones unearthed in the north, displays on Queensland's unique flora and fauna, and *Avian Cirrus*, Bert Hinkler's tiny plane that made the first England-to-Australia solo flight. Parents with kids in tow will want to head downstairs to the hands-on Sciencentre. Nearby, the 21 **Queensland Art Gallery** showcases exquisite landscapes and portraits by Australian and European artists dating back to the mid-19th century.

Once you've gotten a taste of South Bank, cross the Victoria Bridge, which will take you to the 22 **Treasury Building**, a magnificent Italian Renaissance design that today houses a 24-hour casino. Turn right onto William St and you'll pass another spectacular Italian Renaissance building, the 23 **Land Administration Building**. Across William St is another slice of Brisbane history, the 24 **Commissariat Stores Building**, which was built by convicts in 1829 and used as a government store until the 1960s.

Just south of the Land Administration Building, a small unnamed alley cuts through to George St. Turn left on George St and then immediately right onto Charlotte St. Continue along Charlotte St and then turn left onto Albert St to head into the heart of Brisbane's lively CBD. You'll pass outdoor cafes, bookshops and multistorey shopping centres, including the Myer Centre. Queen St Mall is packed with more stores, eateries and multilevel shopping emporiums. Cross this street and head two blocks further northwest into King George Sq. On your left is the final stop of the day, 25 **City Hall**, a striking sandstone building from the 1930s that was undergoing restoration when we passed through. If it's open, take the lift up to the top of the bell tower and soak up the views over the CBD. Otherwise, head to one of the cafes overlooking the square for a much-deserved pick-me-up following the day's exploring.

heart-stopping line-up includes no fewer than 14 races plus additional competitions such as Miss Cocky and the Cocky Day Costume Competition.

Great Brisbane Duck Race RACING EVENT
No, the locals have not figured out a way to train waddling water birds to become elite athletes. This is a *rubber* duckie race, an annual event on the Brisbane Festival calendar. You get to 'adopt a duck' for $5 and spur it down the river (strictly a vocal affair), willing it to defeat its competitors and become the first to cross the line. The competition is fierce – an estimated 20,000 ducks fight for the winner's crown each year. If you happen to be the lucky caretaker of the victor, you'll be rewarded for your efforts with a new car! If your duck performed at a substandard level, you get to go home knowing you helped raise invaluable funds for the Princess Alexandra Hospital Foundation, which benefits from all the proceeds.

Brisbane Go Club CLUB
(http://brisbane.go.org.au) This club meets every Wednesday night at the Romanesque revival-style **Pancake Manor** (Map p56; ☎3221 6433; 18 Charlotte St) for several hours of tuition and competition of the Chinese board game…plus pancakes. You can go along to watch the masters in action ($1) or even participate and give some of them a run for their money.

Tours

There are all sorts of organised tours of Brisbane and the surrounding areas on offer – ask at any of the visitor centres for brochures and details. Most of the tour-bus companies have offices in the Brisbane Transit Centre.

City Tours

City Sights Tour BUS
(day tickets per adult/child $25/20) A hop-on-hop-off shuttle bus taking in 19 of Brisbane's major landmarks. Tours depart every 45 minutes between 9am and 3.45pm from Post Office Sq on Queen St (Map p56). The same ticket covers you for unlimited use of CityCat ferry services.

Ghost Tours WALKING, BUS
(☎3344 7265; www.ghost-tours.com.au; walking/coach tour $25/75) Hosts 90-minute guided walking tours or 2½-hour bus tours of Brisbane's haunted heritage: murder scenes, cemeteries, eerie arcades and the infamous Boggo Rd Gaol. Offers several tours a week; bookings are essential.

Tours and Detours Bus CITY HIGHLIGHTS
(☎1300 363 436; www.toursanddetours.com.au; adult/child $90/55) Runs a Brisbane highlights tour, which takes in many of the city's historical buildings, sights and gardens, as well as a river cruise. The tour lasts three hours and includes hotel pick-up.

Brisbane Lights Tours NIGHT
(☎3822 6028; www.brisbanelightstours.com; adult/child from $45/25) Zips you around the city and beyond to Mt Coot-tha to admire Brisbane in all its glittering nighttime glory. The tour covers a lot of ground including buzzing Paddington, South Bank, Fortitude Valley, various lookouts and even a river cruise past the illuminated cliffs of Kangaroo Point.

Story Bridge Adventure Climb SCENIC
(Map p56; ☎1300 254 627; www.storybridgeadventureclimb.com.au; adult/child from $89/76) Gives bridge climbers 2½ hours of exhilarating (or terrifying) views over Brisbane and beyond, to the Glass House Mountains in the north and Gold Coast hinterland to the south, from the upper reaches of the city's premier bridge.

Brewery Tours

Castlemaine-Perkins XXXX Brewery BREWERY
(Map p73; ☎3361 7597; www.xxxxalehouse.com.au; cnr Black & Paten Sts; adult/child $22/15; ⏰hourly 11am-4pm Mon-Fri & 6pm Wed, 12.30pm, 1pm & 1.30pm Sat) Adult entry includes four ales to quench your thirst at the end of the tour, so leave the car at home. The brewery also offers weekend beer and barbecue tours, which includes lunch ($35). Call or go online for details. It's a 20-minute walk west from the transit centre, or you can take the Citytrain to Milton station. Wear enclosed shoes.

Carlton & United Brewhouse BREWERY
(☎3826 5858; cnr Mulles Rd & Pacific Hwy, Yatala; entry with/without transfer bus $35/20; ⏰10am, noon & 2pm Mon-Fri). Apparently this is one of the most technologically advanced breweries in the world, pumping out three million bottles of the good stuff a day. Just to see this much liquid gold in one spot is awesome enough – Homer Simpson eat your heart out – but this tour also includes free beer at the end.

River Cruises

Coasting up and down the Brisbane River is a great way to see the pretty peaks and troughs of the city.

Kookaburra River Queens CRUISES
(Map p56; ☎3221 1300; www.kookaburrariverqueens.com; lunch/dinner cruises per person from $49/75) Chug up and down the river in restored wooden paddle steamers. Meals are a three-course seafood and carvery buffet, and there's live entertainment (bands, DJs, dancing) on evening cruises. It usually departs from the Eagle St Pier. At the time of research the cruise was temporarily operating from Bretts Wharf due to flood damage to the pier. Check the departure point when booking.

River City Cruises CRUISES
(Map p60; ☎0428 278 473; www.rivercitycruises.com.au; South Bank Parklands Jetty A; adult/child/family $25/15/60) If you just want the sights without the fancy fuss then River City Cruises has 1½-hour cruises with commentary, departing South Bank at 10.30am and 12.30pm (plus 2.30pm during the summer).

Steam Train

Steam locomotives TRAINS
(☎3432 5100; www.theworkshops.qm.qld.gov.au; adult/child $19/10) One Sunday a month, beautifully restored steam trains head out of Roma St Station for one-hour chugs around town. Go online for the latest schedule.

Hinterland Tours

Moreton Bay Escapes NATURE
(☎1300 559 355; www.moretonbayescapes.com.au; per person $109) This company offers several walking day trips out of Brisbane and into surrounding rainforest. The Rainforest Discovery Bushwalk includes the awesome Natural Arch, the waterfalls of Springbrook National Park and the intriguing pin-prick glow worms; Lamington Day Hike includes the ancient forests of Lamington National Park, a World Heritage–listed rainforest. There is also the option for a two-day tour spending a night in the rainforest. Also check out p105.

Araucaria Ecotours NATURE
(☎5544 1283; www.learnaboutwildlife.com) Eighteen kilometres east of Rathdowney in the Gold Coast hinterland, Araucaria offers three-day naturalist-led wilderness tours in the Mt Barney National Park area. The tour picks up in Brisbane every Wednesday morning and calls in at the Daisy Hill Koala Centre on the way down to the rainforests of the Border Ranges. The cost is $418 per person for camping accommodation, or $528 in a two-bed cabin. This company also operates day tours including Bushwalking in Brisbane ($110) and Coochiemudlo Island ($110), which both include lunch.

For information on more hinterland tours see p165 and p137.

BRISBANE FESTIVAL

Brisbane's streets become a hurly-burly of colour, flair, flavour and fireworks during the city's biggest arts event of the year – the Brisbane Festival (formerly known as Riverfest). Running over three weeks in September, the festival is one of Australia's biggest. In 2010 there were over 330 performances and 60-odd events, featuring over 2000 artists – who hailed from all over Australia, plus the UK, the USA, Ireland, Cuba, Ireland, Belgium and Indonesia, among other countries. Art exhibitions, dance, theatre, opera, symphonies, circus performers and vaudeville all add to the eclectic scene, with street events and free concerts around town.

The festival is opened each year with a bang – literally. Staged over the Brisbane River, with vantage points from South Bank, the city and West End, Riverfire is a massive fireworks show with dazzling visual choreography and a synchronised soundtrack.

Other events combine Indigenous culture with contemporary performance to pay homage to the river and celebrate cultural collaboration. Leading restaurants come together to engage in outstanding culinary events, while music plays the role of a constant backdrop throughout the festival – with artists performing everything from jazz to hip-hop to electronic soundscapes. The city's live-music venues also fill their play list on a nightly basis.

For more information click onto www.brisbanefestival.com.au.

Festivals & Events

Information on festivals and events in Brisbane can be found at visitors centres or at www.ourbrisbane.com/whatson.

Chinese New Year NEW YEAR
Always a popular event in the Valley in January/February.

Tropfest SHORT FILMS
(www.tropfest.com) Nationwide short-film festival telecast live at South Bank in mid-February.

Queensland Winter Racing Carnival HORSE RACING
(www.queenslandracing.com.au) From late April to late June there are major horse-race meetings each weekend at both Doomben and Eagle Farm Racecourses, including the Brisbane Cup in mid-May.

Paniyiri Festival GREEK CULTURE
(paniyiri@thegreekclub.com.au) Greek cultural festival with dancing, food and music. Held in late May at Musgrave Park in West End.

Brisbane Pride Festival GAY, LESBIAN
(www.pridebrisbane.org.au) Brisbane's fabulously flamboyant gay and lesbian celebration, held in June.

Queensland Music Festival MUSIC
(www.queenslandmusicfestival.com.au) Outstanding celebration of the world of music, held over 17 days in July in odd-numbered years.

'Ekka' Royal National Agricultural (RNA) Show AGRICULTURE
(www.ekka.com.au) The country comes to town in early August with competitions, wood chopping and rides.

Brisbane International Film Festival FILM
(www.biff.com.au) Ten days of quality films in August.

Brisbane Festival ARTS
(www.brisbanefestival.com.au) Brisbane's major festival of the arts, with buskers, performances, music and concerts held in September. See the boxed text on p72 for more information.

Valley Fiesta FOOD, MUSIC
(www.valleyfiesta.com.au) Food and music festival held in Chinatown and Brunswick St Mall in mid-September.

Sleeping

Brisbane has an excellent selection of accommodation options that will suit any budget. Most are outside the CBD, but more often than not they're within walking distance or have good public-transport connections.

The inner suburbs have their own distinct flavours. Spring Hill, just north of the CBD, is quiet and within easy striking distance of downtown and Fortitude Valley. Petrie Tce and Paddington, just west of the city centre, combine trendy restaurants and rowdy bars. Staying in the alternative neighbourhoods of Fortitude Valley and nearby New Farm places you next door to Chinatown and in the city's most concentrated nightlife scene. West End, south of the river, has a decidedly chilled-out, slightly bohemian atmosphere and some great cafes and restaurants.

In a pinch, North Kangaroo Point has inexpensive motels lining the busy highway feeding into the Story Bridge.

Prices vary widely for midrange lodging. You can often score the best deals on www.wotif.com. Many places give cheaper rates on weekends.

CITY CENTRE

TOP CHOICE **Treasury** LUXURY HOTEL $$$
(Map p56; ☎3306 8888; www.treasurybrisbane.com.au; 130 William St; r $200-349; ❄@) Brisbane's classiest hotel is in the beautifully preserved former Land Administration Building. Every room is unique and awash with heritage features, with high ceilings, framed artwork on the walls and polished wood furniture and elegant furnishings. Even the standard rooms are quite spacious. The best rooms have river views.

Portal BOUTIQUE HOTEL $$
(Map p56; ☎3009 3400; www.portalhotel.com.au; 52 Astor Tce; d from $160; ❄wi-fi) Behind the ultra-modern black-and-white facade, this newish boutique hotel has contemporary rooms with a nice overall design and thoughtful touches (original artwork in each room, iPod docking stations, free wi-fi, hair straighteners for the gals). There's also a women-only floor. The downside: some rooms are quite small. The bar-restaurant on the ground floor is an atmospheric spot for a drink.

Urban Brisbane BOUTIQUE HOTEL $$
(Map p56; ☎3831 6177; www.hotelurban.com.au; 345 Wickham Tce; d from $170; ❄wi-fi pool) Fresh from a $10-million makeover in 2008, the Urban Brisbane has stylish rooms kitted out in masculine tones with balconies and high-end fittings (super-comfortable beds, oversized LCD TVs, fuzzy bathrobes). There's

Paddington

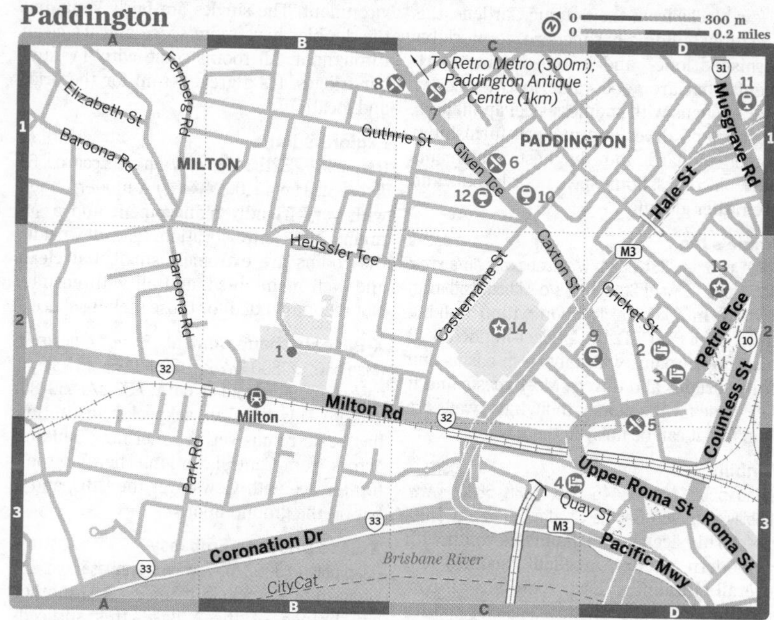

Paddington

Activities, Courses & Tours

1 Castlemaine-Perkins XXXX Brewery ... B2

Sleeping

2 Aussie Way Hostel ... D2
3 Banana Benders Backpackers ... D2
Brisbane City Backpackers ... (see 4)
4 Brisbane City YHA ... C3

Eating

5 Barracks ... D2
6 Fundies ... C1
7 Lark ... C1
8 Sol Breads ... B1

Drinking

9 Caxton Hotel ... D2
10 Iceworks ... C1
11 Normanby Hotel ... D1
12 Paddo Tavern ... C1

Entertainment

Barracks ... (see 5)
13 Brisbane Arts Theatre ... D2
Sit Down Comedy Club ... (see 12)
14 Suncorp Stadium ... C2

a heated outdoor pool and a bar with live music on Friday nights.

Quay West Suites Brisbane APARTMENTS **$$$**
(Map p56; ☎3853 6000; www.mirvachotels.com; 132 Alice St; 1-/2-bedroom ste $275/385;) This sophisticated hotel has opulent self-contained units with modern kitchens, fully equipped laundries, numerous TVs and stereos, and spectacular views. The refined interiors aim for luxury, and the extras include a lovely pool and gymnasium. Staff are gracious.

Stamford Plaza Brisbane HOTEL **$$$**
(Map p56; ☎3221 1999; www.stamford.com.au; cnr Edward & Margaret Sts; r from $225;) At the southern end of the city, the Stamford has a historic facade in front of a modern tower. The indulgent rooms have antique touches, large beds and plenty of atmosphere. On site is a gym, an art gallery, a hair-and-beauty salon, a bar and several restaurants.

M on Mary APARTMENTS **$$**
(Map p56; ☎3503 8000; www.monmary.com.au; 70 Mary St; apt from $170;) Handily located

a few blocks from the Botanic Gardens, this 43-storey building has modern, comfortably furnished one- and two-bedroom apartments that are good value for the money. Full kitchens with stainless-steel appliances, washer and dryer and modern furnishings come standard and the best apartments have balconies. Some have poor layouts and are rather gloomy.

Annie's Inn B&B $

(Map p56; ☎3831 8684; www.babs.com.au/annies; 405 Upper Edward St; d $88, s/d without bathroom $68/78) In a central location within walking distance of the CBD, this budget-minded B&B has simple rooms with tiny wash basins and frilly curtains and duvets. Most guests find it fair value for the money, though the walls are thin and it can be noisy in the morning.

Tinbilly HOSTEL $

(Map p56; ☎1800 446 646, 3238 5888; www.tinbilly.com; 466 George St; dm $22-30, d $100; ❄@) This sleek hostel flaunts its youth with a modern interior, excellent facilities and overall cleanliness. Each room has air-con, a bathroom and individual lockers, and it's wheelchair-accessible. There's also a travel agency and a popular bar, which is one big party place – with live bands, DJs and open-mic nights.

Inchcolm Hotel HOTEL $$$

(Map p56; ☎3226 8888; www.theinchcolm.com.au; 73 Wickham Tce; r $160-250; ❄≋) This elegant heritage hotel retains elements from its early-20th-century past (including an old-fashioned cage elevator), but the rooms have been renovated extensively. Those in the newer wing tend to have more space and more light courtesy of huge windows, while the rooms in the older wing have more character. There's also a rooftop pool and a respected in-house restaurant.

Q Resorts Abbey Apartments APARTMENTS $$

(Map p56; ☎3236 0600; www.qresorts.com.au; 160 Roma St; 1-bed apt from $180; ❄@≋) The Abbey is a good place to stay if you can score a refurbished apartment, which have a clean, contemporary feel, with spacious bedrooms, washing machines and dryers and comfy lounge suites. The older quarters are too battered to recommend.

Acacia Inner-City Inn B&B $

(Map p56; ☎3832 1663; www.acaciainn.com; 413 Upper Edward St; d $100, s/d without bathroom $75/85) This well-maintained B&B has small, motel-style rooms in a functional environment. The singles are fairly snug, but the doubles have more space and it's clean throughout. All rooms come with TVs and bar fridges. It's a great set-up for the price and location.

Explorers Inn HOTEL $$

(Map p56; ☎3211 3488; www.explorers.com.au; 63 Turbot St; d from $100; ❄@wi-fi) A modern hotel with very friendly management and a supreme city-centre location. The downside: the rooms are extremely small, but clean and well maintained, and all with ensuite. Not recommended for those seeking space.

X-Base Brisbane Central HOSTEL $

(Map p56; ☎1800 242 273, 3211 2433; www.stayatbase.com; 398 Edward St; dm $27-32, s/d $50/80; ❄@wi-fi) This colossal backpacker institution has basic rooms set in a heritage building across from Central Station. There's a rooftop terrace with views over the CBD, and a bar on the ground floor.

X-Base Brisbane Embassy HOSTEL $

(Map p56; ☎3002 5777; www.stayatbase.com; 214 Elizabeth St; dm $31-35, d $85-99; ❄) Another city branch of the X-Base, this spruced-up place is quieter than other hostels, and new carpets and a fresh paint job make it feel somewhat like a hotel. There's a large screening room for films, and a sun deck with BBQ and city views.

Astor Metropole HOTEL $$

(Map p56; ☎3144 4000; www.astorhotel.com.au; 193 Wickham Tce; r $90-170; P❄@) Good range of rooms – check into a Tower room for great views and 4½-star facilities.

Metropolitan Motor Inn HOTEL $$

(Map p56; ☎3831 6000; www.metropolitanmotorinn.com; 106 Leichhardt St, Spring Hill; r $110-170; P❄@) Business hotel with trim, comfortable rooms, set with striped duvets and opening onto sizeable balconies. Check internet for specials.

Soho Motel MOTEL $$

(Map p56; ☎3831 7722; www.sohobrisbane.com.au; 333 Wickham Tce; r $107-140; P❄@) Smart, boxy, compact rooms; nice little balconies.

PETRIE TERRACE

Aussie Way Backpackers HOSTEL $

(Map p73; ☎3369 0711; 34 Cricket St; dm/s/d with shared bathroom $28/55/68; ❄@) This small hostel is set in a picturesque, two-storey timber Queenslander, built in 1872. The rooms are spacious and handsomely furnished – some with four-poster beds and throw pillows.

It feels more like a guesthouse than a hostel, with a laid-back crowd and a great outdoor area. No children.

Brisbane City Backpackers HOSTEL $
(Map p73; ☎1800 062 572; www.citybackpackers.com; 380 Upper Roma St; dm $21-30, s or d from $79; ❄@☎≋) This place is popular, and makes good use of outdoor spaces – the rooftop has sun lounges and river views, and there's a pool with barbecue. Rooms and dorms are generally well kept, ranging from four- to 30-bed, plus private and ensuite rooms. The on-site bar has something going on most nights including live music on weekends. Free internet access.

Brisbane City YHA HOSTEL $
(Map p73; ☎3236 1004; www.yha.com.au; 392 Upper Roma St; dm $32-40, tw & d $83-100; ❄@☎≋) This top-notch, clean and well-run hostel was refurbished in 2009, and now has a rooftop pool and sundeck with river views. Rooms range from three- to 10-bed dorms, and there's a cafe-bar on site where you can meet other travellers. The loud-speaker wake-up call at 9.30am is a drag.

Banana Benders Backpackers HOSTEL $
(Map p73; ☎1800 241 157, 3367 1157; www.bananabenders.com; 118 Petrie Tce; dm/d $30/72; ❄@☎) This friendly, down-to-earth backpackers has basic rooms and a great deck with top city views. Owners can help you find work. A bit out of the way, it's a 10-minute uphill slog from the Brisbane Transit Centre.

SPRING HILL

Spring Hill Terraces GUESTHOUSE $$
(Map p62; ☎3854 1048; www.springhillterraces.com; 260 Water St; budget/std r $85/110, studio/terrace unit $130/160; ❄@☎≋) Travellers give high marks for the good old-fashioned service and fairly priced accommodation at this friendly place. It offers motel-style rooms and units, all set amid greenery within 10-minutes' walk of the Valley. The terrace units (miniature townhouses) are best with balconies and leafy courtyards.

Dahrl Court APARTMENTS $$
(Map p56; ☎3830 3400; www.dahrlcourt.com.au; 45 Phillips St; apt from $155; ❄☎) Tucked into a quiet, leafy pocket of Spring Hill, this boutique complex offers good value for its roomy accommodation. The sizable apartments are fully self-contained with kitchens and heritage aesthetics throughout (two with balconies).

Kookaburra Inn GUESTHOUSE $
(Map p56; ☎3832 1303; www.kookaburra-inn.com.au; 41 Phillips St; s/d with shared bathroom $55/72; ❄☎@) This small and friendly two-level guesthouse has simple rooms with a wash basin and fridge and shared clean bathrooms. There's a lounge, guest kitchen and an outdoor patio. Overall, it's a good budget option for those looking to escape the dormitory experience.

FORTITUDE VALLEY

Emporium LUXURY HOTEL $$$
(☎3253 6999; www.emporiumhotel.com.au; 1000 Ann St; d from $270; ❄@≋) A short walk to both Brunswick and James Sts, the first-rate Emporium has uber-modern rooms set with high-end fittings and loads of creature comforts – luxurious king-sized beds, Bose audio systems, marble kitchenettes – and there's a heated outdoor lap pool, cocktail lounge and good eating and shopping options in the same complex.

Limes BOUTIQUE HOTEL $$$
(Map p62; ☎3852 9000; www.limeshotel.com.au; 142 Constance St; d from $229; ❄@☎≋) A stylish newcomer to the Valley, the architecturally intriguing Limes Hotel has handsomely outfitted rooms that make good use of tight space – each has plush furniture, kitchenettes and thoughtful extras (iPod docks, free wi-fi, l'Occitane bath products, a free gym pass). The narrow rooms also have a balcony or private courtyard (with hammock). The rooftop bar is smashing.

Bunk Backpackers HOSTEL $
(Map p62; ☎3257 3644; www.bunkbrisbane.com.au; cnr Ann & Gipps St; dm $15-33, s/d $65/75; ❄@☎≋) This highly rated hostel has generous dorms with bathrooms, good mattresses, gleaming kitchens and funky decor. Being steps from Brisbane's best nightlife, Bunk attracts a festive, socially minded crowd; and weekends are noisy. Dorms sleep from four to 20, and there's also a fabulous bar (Birdee Num Num), swimming pool and spa. It's also wheelchair friendly.

City Palms Motel MOTEL $
(off Map p62; ☎3252 1338; www.citypalmsmotel.com; 55 Brunswick St; d from $90; ❄) Fringed by palm trees on busy Brunswick St, this little motel has cool, dark rooms with kitchenettes. Some rooms are in better shape than others. It's a decent location if you want to

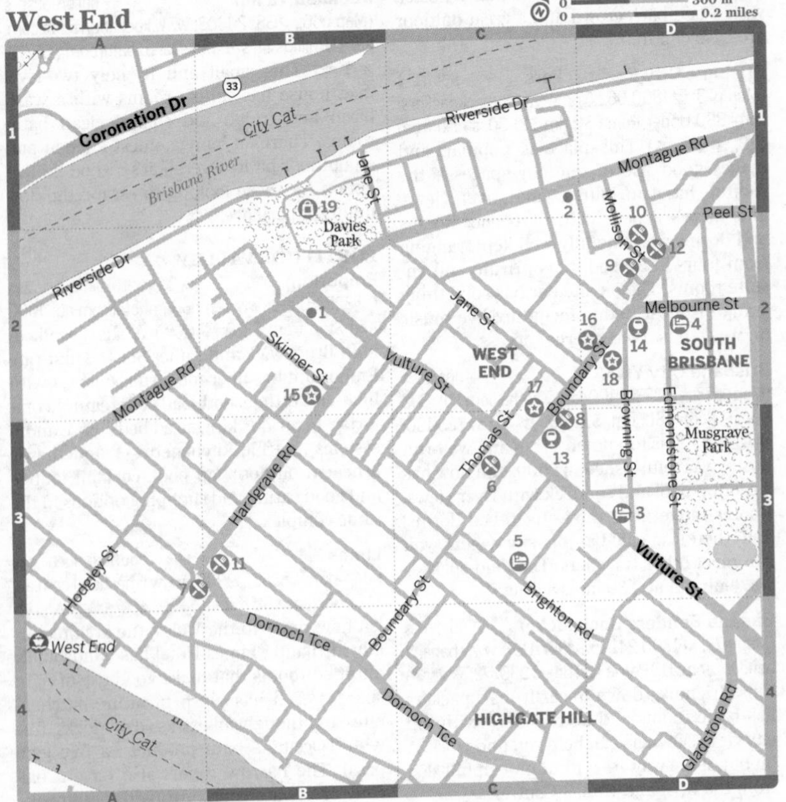

West End

Activities, Courses & Tours

1 Bicycle Revolution B2
Mondo Organics Cooking Courses .... (see 11)
2 Urban Climb C1

Sleeping

3 Brisbane Backpackers Resort D3
4 Edmondstone Motel D2
5 Somewhere to Stay C3

Eating

6 Black Star C3
7 Caravanserai A3
8 Forest C3
9 Gunshop Cafe D2
10 Kafe Meze D2
11 Mondo Organics B3
12 Three Monkeys D2

Drinking

Archive Beer Boutique & Bistro (see 18)
13 Lock'n'Load C3
14 Lychee Lounge D2

Entertainment

15 Cafe Checocho B2
16 Hi-Fi D2
17 Music Kafe C2
18 Uber D2

Shopping

19 West End Markets B1

be close to the Valley, but can be noisy – so request a room at the back.

NEW FARM

Bowen Terrace GUESTHOUSE $

(Map p80; ☎3254 0458; www.bowentceaccommodation.com; 365 Bowen Tce; dm/s/d $35/60/85, deluxe r $99-145; P@≋) A beautifully restored Queenslander, this guesthouse is tucked away in a quiet area of New Farm. The friendly owners have installed TVs and bar fridges in every room and there's a lovely back deck overlooking the pool. Excellent value for money.

Allender Apartments APARTMENTS $$

(Map p80; ☎3358 5832; www.allenderapartments.com.au; 3 Moreton St; studio/1-bedroom apt $130/160; ❄) Allender's studios and one-bedroom apartments are a mixed bag. In the plain yellow-brick building are simply furnished but clean rooms in need of an update. More attractive are the heritage apartments in the adjoining Fingal House, a 1918 Queenslander with polished wood floors, oak furniture and access to a private verandah or courtyard.

SOUTH BANK & WEST END

Edmondstone Motel MOTEL $$

(Map p76; ☎3255 0777; www.edmondstonemotel.com.au; 24 Edmondstone St, South Bank; s/d $109/119; ❄@≋) A 10-minute walk from both the South Bank parklands and West End, the Edmondstone Motel is excellent value for its comfortable, completely renovated rooms. The quarters are small with yellow-brick walls, but make good use of space. All have new mattresses, kitchenettes, LCD TVs and most have small balconies. There's a small pool and BBQ as well.

Somewhere to Stay HOSTEL $

(Map p76; ☎1800 812 398, 3846 2858; www.somewheretostay.com.au; 47 Brighton Rd, West End; dm $19-27, s $44-49, d $54-74; @≋) Big and breezy, there's more than 50 rooms in this enormous white Queenslander home with a very laid-back vibe.

Brisbane Backpackers Resort HOSTEL $

(Map p76; ☎3844 9956; www.brisbanebackpackers.com.au; 110 Vulture St, West End; dm $25-32, d/tr $99/120; ❄@≋) The best feature of this popular hostel is the pool and spa, with a tiled outdoor area and a bar right next door. The rooms themselves are basic but generally well maintained. The hostel provides a courtesy bus, tours, meals and plenty of amusement. It's a short stroll to the bars and cafes of West End.

KANGAROO POINT

Il Mondo HOTEL $$

(Map p56; ☎3392 0111; www.ilmondo.com.au; 25 Rotherham St; r/apt $160/250; ❄@≋) In a fine location near the Story Bridge, this boutique hotel has handsome three- and four-star rooms with a contemporary, minimalist design, high-end fixtures and plenty of space. The cheaper options are standard hotel rooms while the more expensive are self-contained apartments. From here, it's a quick ferry ride to the Eagle St Pier or Edward St in the CBD; you can also stroll over the Story Bridge. Il Mondo often has excellent deals online.

Paramount Motel HOTEL $

(Map p56; ☎3393 1444; www.paramountmotel.com.au; 649 Main St; d/tw/f $98/120/160; ❄≋) This clean and comfy complex has bright, cheerfully furnished rooms with fully equipped kitchens. There's a barbecue by the pool and the staff are friendly and helpful.

Queensland Motel HOTEL $

(Map p56; ☎3391 1061; www.queenslandmotel.id.au; 777 Main St; d/tr $98/109; ❄≋) The nicely maintained Queensland Motel offers large, brightly coloured rooms with good beds. Try to get a room on the top floor where you'll be greeted by rustling palm trees while enjoying coffee on the balcony.

Kangaroo Point Apartments APARTMENTS $

(off Map p56; ☎1800 676 855, 3391 6855; www.kangaroopoint.com; 819 Main St; apt $125-165; ❄≋) These contemporary serviced apartments have very obvious pluses and minuses. On the plus side: prices are excellent for the smart modern flats with balconies; and there are two pools. Unfortunately, it's set on a busy highway and isn't very peaceful.

OUTER BRISBANE

Fern Cottage B&B $$

(☎3511 6685; www.ferncottage.net; 89 Fernberg Rd, Paddington; s/d $115/140; ❄@) Fern Cottage is a beautifully renovated Queenslander with a splash of Mediterranean ambience. The rooms are utterly cushy and there's a lush garden retreat out the back with a shady balcony. Rooms have a cottage appeal and the burgundy room is the pick of the bunch: it's upstairs, spacious and has a great balcony. Nothing is too much trouble for the friendly

LOCAL KNOWLEDGE

PHILIP JOHNSON: HEAD CHEF AT E'CCO

Kitchens are great, there's always a melting pot of ideas – you work with different chefs, and things evolve over the years.

Claim to Fame

Winning *Gourmet Traveller's* Restaurant of the Year award in 1997. Some people say that's what helped put Brisbane's restaurant scene on the map. I hate to look at it like that but I think the rest of the country took notice: 'there must be some decent places to eat up there in Brisbane'. A well-known food critic said you couldn't eat north of Paddington – as in Paddington, Sydney. That changed a bit that year.

Cooking Style

Modern Australian, it has Italian influences, and there's always a bit of Asian in it owing to our proximity, plus a bit of Mediterranean.

Dining Scene in Brisbane

It's amazing. Brisbane is a city that has grown up in the last 15 years. I think for years we were considered playing second fiddle to Sydney and Melbourne, now I think we have great restaurants with top quality and service.

Other Favourite Restaurants

Something casual I love is Alto at the Powerhouse. Ortiga has just opened and it is fantastic.

hosts, who also have self-catering apartments available close by.

Newmarket Gardens Caravan Park CAMPGROUND $
(☎3356 1458; www.newmarketgardens.com.au; 199 Ashgrove Ave, Ashgrove; powered/unpowered sites $33/31, cabins $95-116; ❄@) This clean site doesn't have many trees, but it is just 4km north of the city centre, and is connected to town by several bus routes and the Citytrain (Newmarket station).

Eating

Brisbane's CBD has a number of fine eating options, but there is also an extensive array of culinary offerings outside the city centre.

In the Valley you'll find inexpensive cafes and a smorgasbord of Asian flavours on offer, thanks to Chinatown. Nearby, stylish New Farm is becoming *the* place to eat out in Brisbane with a large selection of multicultural eateries, including some very fine restaurants. West End is a distinctly cosmopolitan corner, with trendy cafes and eclectic cuisine. In every pocket of town, eateries take advantage of Brisbane's perfect winter climate with open-air courtyards or tables out on the street.

For self-caterers,there's a Coles Express on Queen St, just west of the mall, and a Woolworths (Map p56) on Edward St in the city. In Fortitude Valley there's a great produce market inside **McWhirters Marketplace** (Map p62; cnr Brunswick & Wickham Sts). The Asian supermarkets in Chinatown mall also have an excellent range of fresh vegies, Asian groceries and exotic fruit.

Not a potato, asparagus, pear or Lisbon lemon sits out of place at the upmarket **James St Market** (Map p62; James St, Fortitude Valley). It's pricey, but the quality is excellent and there's a good seafood shop here.

CITY CENTRE

There are food courts in the major shopping malls offering multicultural quick eats. The best are between Queen and Elizabeth Sts on the ground floor of the Wintergarden Centre (Map p56) and on Level E (the ground floor) of the Myer Centre (Map p56). Both places have hugely popular sushi bars and kiosks selling noodles, curries and kebabs, as well as more familiar Aussie standards such as fish and chips, roast meats and gourmet sandwiches. You can eat well for less than $12 in any of these places and the malls are open seven days.

E'cco MODERN AUSTRALIAN $$$
(Map p56; ☎3831 8344; 100 Boundary St; mains $43; ⏰lunch Tue-Fri, dinner Tue-Sat) One of the finest restaurants in the state, award-winning E'cco is a must for any culinary aficionado. Masterpieces on the menu include Milly Hill lamb rump with baby beetroot, roast pumpkin, blue cheese and pine nuts. The interior is suitably swish and you'll need to book well in advance.

Embassy Hotel PUB FARE $
(Map p56; 188 Edward St; mains $10-18; ⏰lunch & dinner) With red tones, cubed seating and polished wood, this groovy hotel dishes out some excellent pub nosh and is popular with city folk and travellers alike. Flash-fried calamari comes with a lime and chilli dipping sauce, or savour tried-and-true fav-ourites like fish and chips or juicy steak burgers.

Cha Cha Char STEAK $$$
(Map p56; ☎3211 9944; Eagle St Pier; mains $30-50; ⏰lunch Mon-Fri, dinner daily) Wallowing in awards, this long-running favourite serves Brisbane's best steaks, along with first-rate seafood and roast game meats. The elegant semicircular dining room has floor-to-ceiling windows with waterfront views. It's classy without being pretentious.

II MODERN AUSTRALIAN $$$
(Map p56; ☎3210 0600; cnr Edward & Alice Sts; mains $40-45; ⏰lunch Mon-Fri, dinner Mon-Sat) This elegant award-winning restaurant near the City Botanic Gardens serves delectable fare – largely locally sourced – with imaginative flourishes. Start off with fresh oysters with yuzu dipping sauce, followed by market-fresh fish or grilled Darling Downs sirloin with field mushrooms and red wine jus. The service is first-rate, and there's a superb wine list.

Govinda's VEGETARIAN $
(Map p56; Upstairs, 99 Elizabeth St; all-you-can-eat buffet $12; ⏰11am-3pm & 5-7.30pm Mon-Thu, 11am-8.30pm Fri, 11am-2.30pm Sat; ✎) This Hare Krishna eatery is a peaceful spot to dine inexpensively on vegetarian curry, veggie puffs, dahl-lentil soup, salad, pappadams with chutneys and fruit pudding.

Bleeding Heart Gallery CAFE $
(Map p56; www.bleedingheart.com.au; 166 Ann St; mains $6-8; ⏰8am-5pm Mon-Fri; ᯤ) Set back from Ann St in a charming, two-storey Queenslander, this spacious cafe and gallery has a bohemian vibe and hosts art openings, occasional concerts and other events. The verandah makes a fine setting for coffee, salads and sandwiches, and all profits go toward charitable and community projects.

Java Coast Cafe CAFE $
(Map p56; 340 George St; mains $9-14; ⏰7.30am-3.30pm Mon-Fri) Head to the peaceful back garden with its fountain, subtropical plants and Buddha statues for an escape from the bustling CBD. Good coffee, teas, plus sandwiches and light meals with Asian accents.

Verve Cafe & Bar ITALIAN $$
(Map p56; ☎3221 5691; 109 Edward St; mains $17-22; ⏰lunch Mon-Fri, dinner Mon-Sat) This groovy subterranean venue is a bar-cafe-restaurant fusion with muted tunes and tones, and excellent service with a real buzz during the day. The menu includes imaginative salads, pastas, pizzas and risottos. Try the sand crab and snapper risotto with lemon and fresh thyme. The crowd is arty and relaxed.

Spoon Espresso Deli DELI $
(Map p56; ☎3012 7322; cnr Albert & Charlotte Sts; breakfast $4-7, lunch $8; ⏰7am-5pm Mon & Tue, to 6pm Wed-Fri, 8am-3pm Sat, 8am-2pm Sun) This wee nook has all sorts of daytime yummies including Moroccan couscous salad and gourmet variations on the humble sandwich, such as the delightful BLAT – a BLT with avocado. There's vegetarian lasagne, fishcakes and freshly squeezed juices

PORTSIDE WHARF

A few ferry stops downriver from New Farm Park lies **Portside Wharf** (www.portsidewharf.com.au; 39 Hercules St, Hamilton), Brisbane's cruise ship terminal and home to a handful of upmarket restaurants that are beautifully sited overlooking the river. Standouts include **Sono** (☎3268 6655; mains $30-58; ⏰lunch Wed-Sun, dinner Tue-Sun), one of Brisbane's best Japanese restaurants; **Wilsons Boathouse** (☎3868 4480; mains $33-50; ⏰lunch & dinner), serving award-winning seafood; and **Byblós** (☎3268 2223; mains $29-35; ⏰lunch & dinner Tue-Sun), a trendy spot specialising in Lebanese and Mediterranean fare. Portside also houses the five-screen **Dendy Cinemas** (www.dendy.com.au) and a few shops and cafes. To reach the complex, take the CityCat ferry to Brett's Wharf, and follow the riverside path 500m further east.

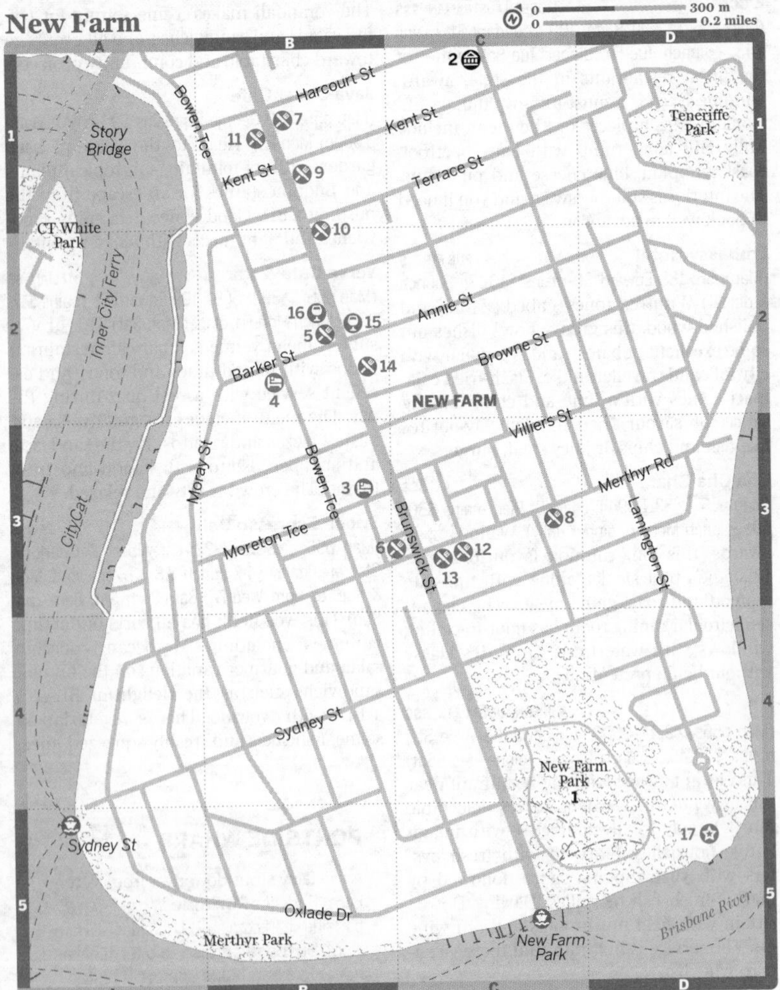

too. Seating spills out of full-length windows and onto the pavement outside.

CHINATOWN & FORTITUDE VALLEY

Although better known for its nightlife, the Valley has some excellent eateries, particularly in the Chinatown area (mostly Duncan and Wickham Sts), where the scent of curries and exotic spices lure would-be passers-by. Skip Brunswick St mall, which is lined with run-of-the-mill take-away and pub fare.

Vietnamese Restaurant VIETNAMESE $
(Map p62; 194 Wickham St; mains $8-15; lunch & dinner) Aptly if unimaginatively named, this is indeed *the* place in town to eat Vietnamese, with exquisitely prepared dishes served to an always crowded house. The real delights are to be found on the 'Authentic Menu'. The shredded beef in spinach rolls is tops, as is any dish containing the word 'sizzling'. BYO and licensed.

Kuan-Yin Tea House VEGETARIAN $
(Map p62; 198 Wickham St; mains $8-10; 11.30am-5pm Mon & Sat, 11.30am-7pm Wed-Fri, to 3pm Sun;) This is a warmly lit place with wood panelling and a bamboo-lined ceiling, where a cross-section of Brisbanites (Asian families, hipster couples, travel writers) comes for

New Farm

Sights

1 New Farm Park....................C4
2 Suzanne O'Connell Gallery....................C1

Sleeping

3 Allender Apartments....................B3
4 Bowen Terrace....................B2

Eating

5 Anise....................B2
6 Arriva....................C3
7 BurgerUrge....................B1
8 Cafe Bouquiniste....................C3
9 Café Cirque....................B1
Chang Thai Restaurant....................(see 10)
10 Himalayan Cafe....................B2
11 Pintxo....................B1
12 Smoke....................C3
13 Vue....................C3
Watt....................(see 17)
14 Wok On Inn....................B2

Drinking

15 Alibi Room....................B2
Alto Bar....................(see 17)
16 Gertie's....................B2

Entertainment

17 Brisbane Powerhouse....................D5

Shopping

Jan Power's Farmers Market.....(see 17)

flavourful vegetarian noodle soups, dumplings and mock-meat rice dishes. Great tea and (non-alcoholic) drink selection.

Garuva FUSION $$
(Map p62; ☎3216 0124; 324 Wickham St; mains $24; ⏰dinner) Garuva's rainforested foyer leads to tables with cushioned seating concealed by silk curtains. There's a rather 'Arabian Nights' feel to the place, with dim lighting, loungey beats and subdued banter (more raucous on weekends). The menu leans toward Asian fusion – sweet-potato and bean curry, warm Thai beef salad, coconut prawns – and all dishes are large entrée size, meant for sharing. Hunt out the cool, hidden cocktail bar lurking in the recesses. Reserve ahead on weekends.

Cafe Cirque CAFE $$
(Map p80; 618 Brunswick St; breakfast mains $14-17; ⏰8am-4pm) One of the best breakfast spots (served all day) in town, it serves rich coffees, delectable omelettes, eggs Benedict, pancakes and French toast, plus daily specials, along with open-faced sandwiches and gourmet salads for lunch. It's a buzzing, two-level space with wood floors, whirring coffee machines, a few front tables and long lines on weekends.

Campos CAFE $$
(Map p62; 11 Wandoo St; mains $17-22; ⏰7am-4pm) Brisbanites are a famously divided bunch, but when it comes to coffee, most agree that Campos serves among the best, if not *the* best in town. Drink rich brews at the small indoor-outdoor alley cafe (behind James St Market), with tasty breakfast and lunch fare.

Flamingo CAFE $
(Map p62; 5B Winn St; mains $9-15; ⏰7.30am-4pm) Tucked down a tiny lane off Ann St, the Flamingo is a buzzing little cafe with black and pink walls, a boho vibe and cheerfully profane wait staff. Eclectic neighbourhood regulars linger over fresh juices, strong coffees and omelettes or filling panini at outdoor tables scattered on the tiny lane.

Spoon Deli CAFE $$
(Map p62; 22 James St; breakfast $10-15, mains $14-21; ⏰5.30am-7pm Mon-Fri, to 6pm Sat & Sun) Inside James St market, this upmarket deli serves deliciously rich pasta, salads, soup and colossal paninis and focaccias. The fresh juices are a liquid meal unto themselves. Diners munch their goodies amid the deli produce at oversized square tables or low benches skirting the windows, which flood the place with sunlight. You'll feel hungry as soon as you walk in.

Tibetan Kitchen TIBETAN $
(Map p62; ☎3358 5906; 454 Brunswick St; mains $14-18; ⏰dinner; ✓) Tasty Tibetan fare amid prayer flags and colourful environs.

Thai Wi-Rat THAI $
(Map p62; ☎3257 0884; Beirne Bldg, Chinatown Mall; dishes $10-14; ⏰10am-9pm) This hole-in-the-wall joint cooks up good Thai and Laotian takeaway, including *Pla Dook Yang* (grilled whole catfish).

Wagamama ASIAN FUSION $$
(Map p62; Emporium Centre, 1000 Ann St; mains $14-20; ⏰lunch & dinner) Classy noodle restaurant with communal tables. It's perpetually busy for its quality, well-priced food.

NEW FARM

New Farm is one of the best areas to eat in the city and has seen an explosion of new eateries in recent years. It has a certain self-inflated feel to it, but genuine, creative, good-value options can still be found, and it has a much nicer atmosphere than parts of the Valley.

Ortiga SPANISH **$$$**

(Map p62; ☎3852 1155; 446 Brunswick St; sharing plates $18-36; ⊙dinner Tue-Sun) One of Brisbane's best new restaurants, Ortiga opened in 2010 to much fanfare. You can dine in the stylish upstairs tapas bar with rustic wood tables and exposed brick walls or head to the elegant subterranean dining room where chefs work their magic in an open kitchen. Top picks include *cochinillo* (slow-cooked suckling pig), *pulpo a gallega* (Galician-braised octopus) and whole slow-cooked lamb shoulder. There's also the real-deal *jamon iberico de bellota puro* – cured from black pigs who've feasted exclusively on acorns. Superb (40-page) wine list.

Anise FRENCH **$$$**

(Map p80; ☎3358 1558; 697 Brunswick St; mains $36-42; ⊙5pm-1am Sun-Wed, noon-1pm Thu-Sat) This uber-stylish 21-seat restaurant and wine bar features an award-winning menu of seasonally inspired Gallic fare. Patrons plant themselves around the narrow bar and feast on amuse-bouches (hors d'œuvres) like oysters and Alsace foie-gras, followed by grass-fed Black Angus beef, fresh fish of the day or slow-braised spring lamb.

Watt MODERN AUSTRALIAN **$$$**

(Map p80; ☎3358 5464; Brisbane Powerhouse; mains $24-34; ⊙lunch Tue-Sun, dinner Tue-Sat, breakfast Sat & Sun) On the lower level of the Powerhouse Arts precinct, this stylish riverside spot serves award-winning modern Australian fare. Start with the Queensland spanner crab or crispy duck salad before moving on to lamb striploin, seafood pasta or the daily catch perfectly grilled.

Cafe Bouquiniste CAFE **$**

(Map p80; 121 Merthyr Rd; mains $8-10; ⊙8am-5.30pm) Set in the front room of a charming Queenslander, this tiny cafe and bookseller has oodles of charm, if not much space – just a few tables and sofas set amid bookshelves, gift items and crinkled newspapers. The coffee is fantastic, service is friendly, and the prices are right for the breakfast fare, toasted sandwiches, savoury tarts and cakes. Bouquiniste has a loyal following of creative types, young and old, who largely hail from New Farm.

Pintxo SPANISH **$$**

(Map p80; 561 Brunswick St; tapas $4-6; ⊙lunch Fri-Sun, dinner Tue-Sun) Grab a seat around the long, narrow bar and choose your freshly prepared tapas as it glides past at this casual, welcoming Spanish spot on Brunswick St. Hot plates are made to order, with standouts like pancetta-wrapped shrimp, grilled scallops or pork-and-veal meatballs. Spanish wines, sangria and cocktails match nicely.

Smoke BBQ **$$**

(Map p80; ☎3358 1922; 85 Merthyr Rd; mains $20-35; ⊙lunch & dinner Tue-Sun) The smell of hickory hangs in the air of this small, buzzing, always-packed restaurant serving American-style BBQ. Tender short ribs, pulled pork and charcoal chicken (with vodka barbecue sauce) are highlights, along with requisite sides like coleslaw, mac and cheese and cornbread. It's all nicely done, though if you're from Memphis you might balk at the prices.

Himalayan Cafe NEPALESE **$**

(Map p80; ☎3358 4015; 640 Brunswick St; mains $15-23; ⊙dinner Tue-Sat; ☑) Set in a sea of prayer flags and colourful cushions, this friendly, unfussy restaurant serves authentic Tibetan and Nepalese fare such as *momo cha* (steamed dumplings), sherpa chicken (curry and sour cream), and tender *fhaiya darkau* (lamb with veggies, coconut milk and spices). It gets rave reviews and kids are welcome.

Chang Thai Restaurant THAI **$**

(Map p80; ☎3254 4342; cnr Brunswick & Terrace Sts; mains $11-15; ⊙dinner) You can dine alfresco at tables out front or in the dining room. Importantly the Thai food is an excellent standard and the Pad Thai is particularly good, with large chunky vegetables. All the classic Thai dishes are covered and it does some mouth-watering seafood specialities.

Vue MODERN AUSTRALIAN **$$**

(Map p80; ☎3358 6511; 1/83 Merthyr Rd; mains $12-16; ⊙7am-10pm Tue-Sat, to 6pm Sun & Mon) The outside dining curls around into the mall at this trendy New Farm eatery, where large open windows give it an airy feel. Its best feature is the reasonably priced food, which is even more reasonable from 4pm to 6pm Wednesday to Friday and 4pm to 9.30pm Tuesday and Saturday, when all pizza and pasta dishes are $12. Try the marinated-lamb pizza with caramelised onion, olives, capsicum, rocket and spiced yoghurt. Bands on Friday night turn it into Merthyr Rd's premium entertainment venue.

THE BARRACKS

The site that once served as a gaol (1860 to 1883), then a police depot (until the 1940s) sat derelict for years before reopening as a mixed-use development in 2008, following a $120 million overhaul. Housing three heritage-listed buildings from its former days, the **Barracks** (Map p73; www.thebarracks.info; Petrie Tce) was hailed an immediate success (and garnered national awards) in the realm of urban renewal, and Brisbanites have embraced it as their own – curious history and all.

The Barracks houses cafes and restaurants (both casual and high-end), a six-screen cinema, a supermarket, a bookshop, a wine shop and other specialty stores. The restaurants and adjoining bars draw crowds on weekend nights, and the one-stop complex has obvious appeal during rainy days. It's located around the corner from Roma St Station, and just a short stroll from the nightlife along Caxton St.

Arriva ITALIAN $$
(Map p80; 3254 1599; 84 Methyr Rd; mains $17-22; dinner Tue-Sun) Cheap it ain't, genuine it is. Diners are always packed into this Italian place even on weeknights for the authentic articles that come from the efficient kitchen. This is pizza like Papa used to make and pasta that even Mama would approve of.

Wok on Inn ASIAN FUSION $
(Map p80; 728 Brunswick St; mains $11-14; lunch Sun-Fri, dinner daily) With a lovely shaded front courtyard this industrious and popular noodle bar is the New Farm spot for some fast noodles. Choose your noodle, your cooking style (including Mongolian) and your meat/veg combo. There's also a regular $7.50 lunch special.

BurgerUrge BURGERS $
(Map p80; 542 Brunswick St; mains $9-13; lunch Fri-Sun, dinner Tue-Sun;) Among the city's best burgers, with a wealth of options to choose from: lamb; chicken, avocado and bacon; classic beef; and veggie options (grilled tofu, portabella, aubergine and goats cheese). Good milkshakes too.

PETRIE TERRACE & PADDINGTON

Lark MODERN AUSTRALIAN $$
(Map p73; 3369 1299; 267 Given Tce; small plates $8-26; 4pm-midnight Tue-Thu, noon-midnight Fri-Sun) Situated in a converted colonial-style cottage, the Lark is an award-winning restaurant that's praised for both its inventive fusion fare and its artfully prepared cocktails. Share plates from the 'grazing' (tapas) menu, such as Wagyu sliders or spinach and fetta risotto balls, followed by yoghurt-baked barramundi or tempura prawns with wakame salad. There's also outdoor seating.

Fundies MODERN AUSTRALIAN $
(Map p73; 219 Given Tce; mains around $10; 7.30am-4pm Mon-Sat, 8am-3pm Sun;) Combining an organic food store and cafe, this is the place to get your organic brekky or lunch and then stock up on healthy groceries. Try the big breakfast with tofu scramble or the curry lentil burger for lunch.

Sol Breads CAFE $
(Map p73; 20 Latrobe Tce; mains $8.50; 7am-4pm Mon-Sat, to 3pm Sun;) This sunny bakery and cafe serves up organic and vegetarian fare – fresh baked croissants, muffins and pastries, plus muesli and fruit for breakfast, and a lunch menu of daily salads and soups, savoury tarts, calzone and pizza slices. There's also a small balcony out the back.

SOUTH BANK & KANGAROO POINT

Open-air cafes and restaurants are scattered along parklands. On the edge of the greenery, Grey St is also packed with eating and snacking options.

Ahmet's TURKISH $$
(Map p60; 3846 6699; 164 Grey St; mains $20-28; lunch & dinner) On restaurant-lined Grey St, Ahmet's serves delectable Turkish fare amid a riot of colours. The pide (oven-baked Turkish pizza) here is sublime – try the *kusbasi* pide (spicy lamb) or the sizzling *karisik izgara* (mixed grill), and baklava for dessert. There's belly dancing on Friday and Saturday nights, plus live 'gypsy-jazz' on Thursday nights.

Piaf FRENCH $$
(Map p60; 3846 5026; 186 Grey St; mains $22; 7am-late) A laid-back bistro with a loyal following, Piaf serves a small selection (just five mains and a few salads and lighter fare) of good-value contemporary fare. Recent hits: duck breast with braised

red cabbage, broccolini and blueberry sauce; pumpkin gnocchi with spinach and cherry tomatoes; and Niçoise salad with confit tuna. Eat inside the Zen-like dining room or sit at the umbrella-shaded outside tables.

Cliffs Cafe MODERN AUSTRALIAN $
(Map p56; 3 River Tce; mains $12-17; ⏲7am-5pm) A steep climb up from Kangaroo Point park, this cliff-top cafe has superb views over the river. Cyclists, joggers, young families – all are welcome at this casual open-air spot, where thick burgers, battered barramundi and chips, salads, desserts and good coffee are among the standouts.

WEST END

Restaurants, cafes and bars line Boundary St, between Jane and Vulture Sts.

Mondo Organics MODERN AUSTRALIAN $$
(off Map p76; ☎3844 1132; 166 Hardgrave Rd; mains $26-38; ⏲lunch Fri-Sun, dinner Wed-Sat, breakfast Sat & Sun) Using the highest-quality organic and sustainable produce, Mondo Organics earns high marks for its delicious seasonal menu. Recent hits include pumpkin, leek and ricotta tortellini; lamb rack with wild mushroom risotto; ocean trout with shaved fennel and saffron-infused mashed potatoes.

Gunshop Cafe MODERN AUSTRALIAN $$
(Map p76; ☎3844 2241; 53 Mollison St; mains $24-33; ⏲7am-2pm Mon, 7am-late Tue-Sat, 7am-12.30pm Sun) A beautiful repurposing of a former gunshop, this trendy eatery has exposed brick walls, sculptural-like ceiling lamps and an inviting garden in back. Menu changes daily and features ingredients sourced from local markets. Recent hits: eggs Benedict with vodka-cured ocean trout, grass-fed rib filet with roast mushrooms, and grilled emperor with braised leek and bacon.

Caravanserai TURKISH $$
(off Map p76; ☎3217 2617; 1-3 Dornoch Tce; mains $25-33; ⏲lunch Thu-Sun, dinner Tue-Sun) Richly woven tablecloths, red walls and candlelit tables create a warm and inviting atmosphere at this standout Turkish restaurant. Meze platters are great for sharing (with humus, babagounosh, artichokes, dolma and more). Dine on the back verandah for pleasant river views.

Kafe Meze GREEK $$
(Map p76; ☎3844 1720; 56 Mollison St; mains $27-29; ⏲lunch & dinner) This indoor-outdoor Greek restaurant delivers fresh flavours and tastes of the Mediterranean. Tapas-style is a good way to sample a range of dishes, like grilled haloumi, marinated octopus, calamari and tzatziki with pita bread.

Forest VEGAN $
(Map p76; 124 Boundary St; mains $5-9; ⏲10am-9pm; ✎) A youthful vegan-loving crowd heads to this casual cafe-bar. Menu highlights include curries, veggie burgers, 'no-bull' (meatless) pies, samosas, and daily specials (such as veg chilli and baked dishes), plus desserts; it also has organic beer and wine.

Three Monkeys CAFE $
(Map p76; 58 Mollison St; mains $12-15; ⏲9.30am-10pm) This laid-back bohemian teahouse is steeped in pseudo-Moroccan decor and ambience. Low lighting, rustic wood furnishings and tiny nooks make a fine setting for delicious cake and coffee – or heartier pizzas, focaccia and panini. There's also a courtyard in back.

Black Star CAFE $
(Map p76; 44 Thomas St; ⏲7am-3pm Mon, to 5pm Tue-Fri, to late Sat, 8am-3pm Sun) A neighbourhood favourite, West End's most popular roastery has excellent coffee, outdoor tables, all-day breakfast and live music on Saturday nights.

Drinking

The prime drinking destination in Brisbane is Fortitude Valley, with its lounges, bars hosting live music, and nightclubs. New Farm also has a burgeoning nightlife scene, while the CBD attracts a festive after-work crowd. New Farm has some fine bars, attracting a mostly neighbourhood crowd.

CITY CENTRE

Belgian Beer Cafe BAR
(Map p56; cnr Mary & Edward Sts; ⏲noon-late) Tin ceilings, wood-panelled walls and globe lights lend an old-fashioned charm to the front room of this buzzing space, while out back, the inviting split-level beer garden provides a laid-back setting for sampling fine brews (including 30-plus Belgian beers) and high-end bistro fare (charcuterie plates, croque monsieurs, steamed mussels with white wine and garlic).

Laneway BAR
(Map p56; Spencer Ln off Margaret St; ⏲6pm-midnight Mon-Sat) Concealed down a narrow

lane and hidden above the high-end restaurant Euro, Laneway is a secret hideaway where well-dressed barstaff whip up artful cocktails (try the spiced fig and VSOP cognac Barnum's Lane) for a well-dressed but unpretentious crowd. A nice bonus: silent films play on the building facing the open-sided bar.

Moo Moo RESTAURANT-WINE BAR
(Map p56; cnr Margaret & Edwards Sts; ⏲6pm-midnight Mon-Sat) Located inside the heritage Port Office building, this stylish high-end grill restaurant has an inviting open-air lounge on the lane out back, with a trickling fountain and fairy lights. A laid-back crowd comes here for the 90-plus wines by the glass.

Port Office Hotel BAR
(Map p56; cnr Edward & Margaret Sts) The industrial edge of this renovated city pub is spruced up with swathes of dark wood and jungle prints. Pull up a stool or find a bench early and settle in for the evening, when a mixed crowd usually descends.

Exchange Hotel BAR
(Map p56; 131 Edward St) This spacious city pub remains popular with a big cross-section of drinking socialisers.

FORTITUDE VALLEY

Press Club COCKTAIL BAR
(Map p62; www.thepressclub.net.au; 339 Brunswick St; ⏲5pm-late Thu-Sat) A mainstay of Valley nightlife, the Press Club is an elegant spot filled with amber hues, leather sofas and ottomans, glowing chandeliers and fabric-covered lanterns, giving it a touch of Near Eastern glamour. Live music happens on Thursdays – check out jazz, funk or rockabilly – while DJs spin on Friday and Saturday nights. No cover charge.

La Ruche COCKTAIL BAR
(Map p62; 680 Ann St) French for 'the hive', La Ruche is indeed a buzzing place, where a well-dressed crowd banters over nicely mixed cocktails and tasty bistro-style tapas plates. The main room channels *Alice in Wonderland* with wildly sculpted chandeliers and elegantly mismatched furniture, while there's a spacious (smokers') courtyard out the back and a small, cosy retreat upstairs.

Alloneword BAR
(Map p62; www.alloneword.com.au; 188 Brunswick St) On a seedy stretch of Brunswick, this underground spot is the antidote to sleek cocktail bars taking over the Valley. The front room is pure whimsy: vintage wallpaper, velvety banquettes and a mirrored ceiling over the bar, while the back patio hosts artful graffiti murals and DJs inspiring (and inspired by?) the young, dance-loving crowd.

Sky Room COCKTAIL BAR
(Map p62; level 2, 234 Wickham St; ⏲5pm-late Wed-Sun) Overlooking one of the Valley's liveliest corners, the Sky Room is a rambling lounge of pot plants, lime green couches and chairs, a long wooden bar and a balcony complete with flickering tiki torches. The cocktail menu leans toward tropical drinks, while DJs play a mix of old-school, danceable rock to a generally laid-back crowd. Bottled beer is served in a brown paper bag.

Bowery COCKTAIL BAR
(Map p62; 676 Ann St) Exposed brick walls, gilded mirrors and antique chandeliers lend a classy, old-fashioned vibe to this long narrow bar on bustling Ann St. The cocktails are top-notch (and priced accordingly), and there's a tiny patio out the back. Live jazz bands play during the week (Tuesday to Thursday), while DJs spin on weekends.

Cru Bar COCKTAIL BAR
(Map p62; 2 James St) Located on the corner of James St market, this buzzing upmarket space has a superb wine list (with a wine shop next door) and an airy, open design that makes a fine setting for drinks or a bite (with excellent nouveau Australian dishes) before heading deeper into the Valley.

WEST END

Lychee Lounge COCKTAIL BAR
(Map p76; 94 Boundary St) Sink into the lush furniture and stare up at the macabre dolls'-head chandeliers at this exotic oriental lounge-bar. Mellow beats, mood lighting and an open frontage to Boundary St create an ideal setting for imbibing the delightfully inventive cocktails.

Lock 'N' Load BAR-RESTAURANT
(Map p76; www.locknloadbistro.com.au; 142 Boundary St; ⏲10am-late) This classic all-wood two-storey gastro-pub gathers a friendly mixed crowd most nights. Changing local artwork lines the walls, while bands play on the small front stage most nights. There's a leafy garden out the back

and seating on the upstairs balcony for prime viewing over West End's liveliest street. You can order tasty bistro fare in the restaurant.

Archive Beer Boutique & Bistro BAR-RESTAURANT
(Map p76; 100 Boundary St) Nestled beneath the nightclub Uber, Archive pays homage to all-Aussie beers (over 80 varieties), with a superb selection of award-winning pilseners and Bavarian-style ales. Books and framed prints adorn the lounge area, while the newspaper-covered walls by the pool tables may make you feel like you're inside a birdcage. There's also tasty bistro fare.

NEW FARM & BREAKFAST CREEK

Alto Bar BAR-RESTAURANT
(Map p80; www.brisbanepowerhouse.org; Brisbane Powerhouse, New Farm) Inside the arts-loving Brisbane Powerhouse, this open, upstairs bar has an enormous balcony overlooking the river that makes a mighty fine vantage point, no matter the weather. There's a full menu of creative Australian cooking, and always something happening at the Powerhouse.

Alibi Room CAFE-BAR
(Map p80; 720 Brunswick St, New Farm; ⊙7am-late; 📶) A fine alternative to the Valley's chi-chi lounges, this quirky eat-drink spot gathers an eclectic crowd most days, particularly on $2-taco Tuesday nights. You'll also find creative cocktails, a good beer and wine menu, free wi-fi, tasty snacks (plus breakfast all day) and cool window seating opening onto Brunswick St, making it a great spot for people watching.

Gertie's COCKTAIL BAR
(Map p80; 699 Brunswick St, New Farm; ⊙4pm-midnight Tue-Sun) A sophisticated New Farm affair, Gertie's has comfy seating, warm subdued lighting, top-notch cocktails and live acoustic music on weekends. It's a great place to meet for a drink when starting out the night.

Breakfast Creek Hotel BAR-RESTAURANT
(off Map p62; 2 Kingsford Smith Dr; ⊙lunch & dinner) In a great rambling building dating from 1889, this historic pub is a Brisbane institution. Built in French Renaissance style, the pub encompasses various bars (including a beer garden and an art deco 'private bar' where you can still drink draft beer tapped from a wooden keg). The stylish, modern Substation No 41 bar serves boutique beers and cocktails.

PETRIE TERRACE, PADDINGTON & AROUND

Normanby Hotel BAR
(off Map p73; 1 Musgrave Rd, Red Hill) Opposite the train station of the same name, this rambling hotel is pure Queensland. Without doubt its best feature is the colossal, modern beer garden, which packs a celebratory crowd on weekends. The huge bar upstairs is a mishmash of brick and art deco with sawdust floor and a mishmash of modern touches. Live bands draw big crowds on Sunday.

Iceworks BAR
(Map p73; cnr Given Tce & Dowse St, Paddington) Former home of the Ithaca Iceworks, this splashy watering hole has a long, white-tiled bar with 20 beers on draft and an open-sided interior that packs crowds on weekends – particularly during Broncos games at nearby Suncorp Stadium.

Paddo Tavern BAR
(Map p73; 186 Given Tce, Paddington) The clientele is local but the decor in this huge pub is kitschy Wild West. An odd marriage, sure, but the punters lap it up along with icy beers, footy telecasts, pool tables and rockin' Sunday sessions. There's a wide outside area and open plan inside.

Caxton Hotel BAR
(Map p73; 38 Caxton St, Petrie Tce) This unpretentious but stylish pub is hugely popular on Friday and Saturday nights, when the buzz of the heaving crowd wafts out the wide-open bay windows onto the street. Expect mainstream music in the background and sports on the telly.

KANGAROO POINT & SOUTH BANK

Story Bridge Hotel BAR
(Map p56; 200 Main St, Kangaroo Point) This beautiful old pub beneath the bridge at Kangaroo Point is the perfect place for a pint after a long day exploring. There are several different spaces, including a traditional bistro, an alfresco drinking, snacking spot and the popular Outback Bar – a casual beer garden that hosts live jazz on Sundays (from 3pm).

Chalk Hotel BAR
(off Map p56; www.chalkhotel.com.au; 735 Stanley St, Woolloongabba) On weekends, fun-loving crowds descend on this huge South Brisbane hotspot, which is three blocks west

GAY & LESBIAN BRISBANE

While Brisbane can't compete with the prolific gay and lesbian scenes in Sydney and Melbourne, what you'll find here is quality rather than quantity.

Most action, centred in Fortitude Valley, is covered by the fortnightly **Q News** (www.qnews.com.au). **Queensland Pride** (www.queenslandpride.gaynewsnetwork.com.au), another gay publication, takes in the whole of the state. **Queer Radio** (www.4zzzfm.org.au), a radio show on Wednesday from 9pm to 11pm on FM102.1, is another source of information on the city. For lesbian news and views, **Dykes on Mykes** precedes it (7pm to 9pm).

Major events on the year's calendar include the **Queer Film Festival** (www.bqff.com.au) held in April, which showcases gay, lesbian, bisexual and transgender films and videos, and the **Brisbane Pride Festival** (www.pridebrisbane.org.au), which happens in June. Pride attracts up to 25,000 people every year, and peaks during the parade held midfestival.

Brisbane's most popular gay and lesbian venue is the **Wickham Hotel** (Map p62; cnr Wickham & Alden Sts, Fortitude Valley), a classic old Victorian pub with good dance music, drag shows and dancers. The Wickham celebrates the Sydney Mardi Gras and the Pride Festival in style and grandeur.

Other good options:

Beat MegaClub CLUB
(Map p62; ☎3852 2661; 677 Ann St, Fortitude Valley) Gay friendly.

Family CLUB
(Map p62; ☎3852 5000; 8 McLachlan St, Fortitude Valley) On Sundays, this popular club hosts 'Fluffy', which is Brisbane's biggest gay dance party.

Sportsman's Hotel PUB
(Map p56; 130 Leichhardt St, Spring Hill) Another fantastically popular gay venue, with a different theme or show for each night of the week.

of the Gabba. Its three levels provide atmospheres for all types, including an open beer garden. If you're a Brisbane Lions fan, you're on home turf.

☆ Entertainment

Brisbane pulls almost all of the international bands heading to Oz and the city's clubs have become nationally renowned. There's also plenty of theatre. Pick up copies of the free entertainment papers *Time Off* (www.timeoff.com.au), *Rave* (www.ravemag.com.au) and *Scene* (www.scenemagazine.com.au) from any cafe in the Valley.

The *Courier Mail* also has daily arts and entertainment listings, and a comprehensive 'What's On In Town' section each Thursday. The city council also publishes a bimonthly *Live* guide, listing arts and culture events, many free.

Ticketek (☎13 28 49; http://premier.ticketek.com.au) is an agency that handles phone bookings for many major events, sports and performances. You can pick up tickets from the Ticketek booth at the back of the Myer Centre (Map p56).

To ensure you can get into Brisbane's nightspots, carry proof of age and (especially if you're male) avoid wearing tank-tops, shorts or thongs (flip-flops). It's also best not to rock up in a big group of guys.

Nightclubs

Brisbane is proud of its nightclub scene – most clubs are open Thursday to Sunday nights, are adamant about ID and charge between $7 and $25 cover. The alternative scene is centred on the Valley, and attracts a mixed straight and gay crowd.

Cloudland NIGHTCLUB
(Map p62; 641 Ann St, Fortitude Valley; ⏲11.30am-late Wed-Sun) Like stepping into a cloud forest (or at least the Ann St version of it), this sprawling, multilevel nightclub has a huge open plant-filled lobby with retractable roof, a wall of water and wrought-iron birdcage-like nooks sprinkled about; you'll also find a rooftop garden, a cellar bar and plenty of other spots for whiling away the night. Cloudland aims for a slightly more sophisticated 25-and-up crowd.

DON'T MISS

MOONLIGHT CINEMA

One of the best ways to spend a warm summer night in Brisbane is with a picnic basket amid the festive crowd at the **Moonlight Cinemas** (www.moonlight.com.au; adult/child $15/11). Between December and February, New Farm Park near the Powerhouse plays host to outdoor film screenings – new releases, indies and cult classics – from Wednesday to Sunday nights, right around sundown (7pm). Tickets go on sale in the first week of November. You can bring food, but no alcohol is allowed in the cinema.

Monastery NIGHTCLUB
(Map p62; ☎3257 7081; 621 Ann St, Fortitude Valley) After a sensible refurbishment giving easier access to the bar and more grooving space, Monastery really does look like a monastery inside (apart from the heaving, sweaty hordes churning up the dance floor) with its iconic, plush design and gothic lighting. Lucid soundscapes, especially electro-house from classy resident and international DJs, keep the fans coming back.

Family NIGHTCLUB
(Map p62; ☎3852 5000; 8 McLachlan St, Fortitude Valley) One of Brisbane's best nightclubs, the music scene here is phenomenal. Family exhilarates dance junkies every weekend on four levels with two dance floors, four bars, four funky themed booths and a top-notch sound system. Elite DJs from home and away frequently grace the decks, including the Stafford Brothers with their predominantly 'hands in the air' house mixes, and Baby Gee, who hangs out on the fringes of the club circuit and has won many accolades for his intelligent mix of genres.

Fringe Bar NIGHTCLUB
(Map p62; ☎3252 9833; cnr Ann & Constance Sts, Fortitude Valley) A wildly groovy place, the '70s decor slapped up with style lends itself to swaying punters at this Brisbane institution. Thursday night is gaining popularity among the younger set determined to thumb their nose at a conventional weeknight out: from 8pm to 10pm you can catch some of the city's upcoming live bands, then DJs play funky house and electro into the wee hours. If you prefer a dose of retro or top of the pops, try weekend nights.

Uber NIGHTCLUB
(Map p76; ☎3846 6680; 100 Boundary St, West End) Brisbane's latest club, Uber is cool indeed, with a stylish decor and patrons to match. It's a bit decadent like an old-style boutique hotel, with its brushed steel and polished dark wood. The music varies but weekends are dedicated to pure main-room house. The best thing about the plush cocktail-lounge bar is the balcony perched in prime viewing position over the comings and goings in the heart of the West End.

Birdie Num Num Bar & Nightclub BAR, NIGHTCLUB
(Map p62; www.birdeenumnum.com.au; 608 Ann St, Fortitude Valley) Part of the Bunk Backpackers complex, it's filled with backpackers and students for nightly rowdiness. It packs big crowds (Brisbanites included) on weekends.

Beat MegaClub NIGHTCLUB
(Map p62; ☎3852 2661; 677 Ann St, Fortitude Valley) Five dance floors, six bars and hardcore techno equals the perfect place for dance junkies who like their beats hard. It's popular with the gay and lesbian crowd with regular drag performances, but Beat is welcoming to all and we've received good traveller feedback about this place.

Two places next door to each other on Warner St, popular with the younger set, and in the heart of the Valley are the **Church** (Map p62; ☎1300 784 860; 25 Warner St), which is set in an old cathedral and pulls some impressive DJs spinning house and electro; and **Electric Playground** (Map p62; ☎1300 784 860; 27 Warner St), which has been newly renovated and has a great light-and-sound set up. Look for the mirror ball and red carpet out the front. It takes the music (and itself) a bit more seriously than its neighbour.

Live Music

Brisbane's love affair with live music began long before three lanky lads sang harmonic ditties and called themselves the Bee Gees. In recent years successful acts, including Katie Noonan, Kate Miller-Heidke and Pete Murray, have illustrated Brisbane's musical diversity and evolution. You can get in early to see history in the making at any number of venues. Cover charges start at around $5.

Hi-Fi ROCK
(Map p76; www.thehifi.com.au; 125 Boundary St, West End) In 2009 Melbourne's popular rock

venue opened an outpost in Brisbane's hipster-loving West End. The modern, minimalist space has unobstructed sight lines and a decent line-up of local and international talent (hosting the likes of the Bronx, Guttermouth, Concrete Blond and the Charlatans).

Zoo ECLECTIC
(Map p62; www.thezoo.com.au; 711 Ann St, Fortitude Valley; ⏲Wed-Sat) Since 1992 Zoo has been delivering a quality alternative venue for Brisbane's music connoisseurs. The long queues here start early for a good reason: whether you're into hard rock, hip hop, acoustic, reggae or electronic soundscapes, Zoo has a gig for you. It's one of your best chances to hear some raw local talent.

Brisbane Jazz Club JAZZ
(Map p56; ☎3391 2006; www.brisbanejazzclub.com.au; 1 Annie St, Kangaroo Point) Beautifully sited overlooking the river, this tiny club has been a beacon for jazz purists since 1972. The space is small and intimate, and anyone who's anyone in the jazz scene plays here when they're in town. Sets happen Thursday to Sunday nights; there's usually a cover charge of $15 to $20.

X&Y Bar ECLECTIC
(Map p62; ☎3257 1259; www.xandybar.com.au; 648 Ann St, Fortitude Valley) This welcoming and unpretentious bar aims to attract an eclectic crowd owing to its nondiscriminatory door policy. It features a mix of live music (mostly indie rock) and DJs, and there's always something going on.

Tivoli ECLECTIC
(☎3852 1711; www.thetivoli.net.au; 52 Costin St, Fortitude Valley) International artists such as Nick Cave and Noel Gallagher have graced the stage at this elegant old art deco venue built in the early 20th century. Hosting a range of touring acts, you're likely to see quality comedy here too. All tickets are sold through Ticketek.

Cafe Checocho LIVE MUSIC
(Map p76; 69 Hardgrave Rd, West End; ⏲3-10pm Mon, 10am-10pm Tue-Sat; 📶) Serving up chess, coffee and chocolate *(che-co-cho)*, this charming, lived-in cafe also has live music most nights (jazz, blues, world).

Music Kafe LIVE MUSIC
(Map p76; www.themusickafe.com; 185 Boundary St, West End) Live music most days with blues, rock, jazz and folk, plus open-mic nights (currently Wednesdays).

Brisbane Convention and Exhibition Centre ARENA
(Map p60; www.bcec.com.au; cnr Merivale & Glenelg Sts, South Bank) When the big guns are in town they rock the 8000-seat auditorium.

Globe LIVE MUSIC
(Map p62; www.globetheatre.com.au; 220 Brunswick St, Fortitude Valley) An old cinema converted into a live-music venue; gigs on weekends.

Cinemas

There are open-air movies screened over summer in the South Bank Parklands (p89) and in New Farm Park (p88).

Palace Centro CINEMA
(Map p62; www.palacecinemas.com.au; 39 James St, Fortitude Valley) Screens art-house films and has a Greek film festival at the end of November.

Palace Barracks CINEMA
(Map p73; www.palacecinemas.com.au; Petrie Tce) Shows a mix of Hollywood and alternative fare near Roma St Station.

South Bank Cinema CINEMA
(Map p60; www.cineplex.com.au; cnr Grey & Ernest Sts, South Bank) The cheapest cinema for mainstream flicks; tickets cost about a third less than at other places.

Dendy Cinema CINEMA
(www.dendycinema; 39 Hercules St, Hamilton) Shows mainstream fare at Portside Wharf.

Brisbane City Myer Centre CINEMA
(Map p56; Level 3, Myer Centre) On Queen St Mall, also shows mainstream blockbusters.

Performing Arts

Brisbane is well stocked with theatre venues, most of them located at South Bank. For bookings at the Queensland Performing Arts

BRISBANE OPEN-AIR

For six weeks in March and April each year, the South Bank Parklands hosts **Brisbane Open Air** (www.brisbaneopenair.com.au), which brings a line-up of film screenings and live bands to the Rainforest Green. Live acoustic or DJ sets kick off around 5.45pm, with films starting at dusk, around 6.45pm. Buy tickets online to avoid sell-outs and arrive early to snag a seat. Food and alcohol are sold at stands on the green.

Centre and all South Bank theatres, contact **Qtix** (☎13 62 46; www.qtix.com.au).

Queensland Performing Arts Centre THEATRE, LIVE MUSIC

(QPAC; Map p60; ☎3840 7444; www.qpac.com.au; Cultural Centre, Stanley St, South Bank) This centre consists of three venues and features concerts, plays, dance and performances of all genres. Catch anything from flamenco to *West Side Story* revivals.

Queensland Conservatorium LIVE MUSIC

(Map p60; ☎3735 6111; www.griffth.edu.au/concerts; 16 Russell St, South Bank; ⌚Mar-Oct) South of the Queensland Performing Arts Centre, the Conservatorium hosts opera, as well as national and international artists playing classical, jazz, rock and world music. Many concerts are free.

Brisbane Powerhouse THEATRE, LIVE MUSIC

(Map p80; ☎3358 8600; www.brisbanepowerhouse.org; 119 Lamington St, New Farm) The former 1940 power station continues to bring electricity to the city – albeit in the form of nationally acclaimed theatre, music and dance productions. There are loads of happenings at the Powerhouse – many free – and the venue, with its several bar-restaurants, enjoys a beautiful setting overlooking the Brisbane River.

Metro Arts Centre THEATRE

(Map p56; ☎3002 7100; www.metroarts.com.au; level 2, 109 Edward St) This progressive venue hosts community theatre, local dramatic pieces, dance and art shows. It's a good spot to head for a taste of Brisbane's creative performance talent.

QUT Gardens Theatre THEATRE

(Map p56; ☎3138 4455; www.gardenstheatre.qut.com; QUT, 2 George St) This university theatre plays host to touring national and international productions as well as performances from the university's dramatic, musical and dance companies.

Brisbane Arts Theatre THEATRE

(Map p73; ☎3369 2344; www.artstheatre.com.au; 210 Petrie Tce, Petrie Tce) Amateur theatre performances along the lines of Shakespeare and Dickens are held here.

Sit Down Comedy Club COMEDY

(Map p73; ☎3369 4466; www.standup.com.au; Paddo Tavern, Given Tce, Paddington) There are a few comedy venues, the most prominent being this well-established one at the Paddo Tavern.

Sport

Like most other Australians, Brisbanites are sports-mad. You can see interstate cricket matches and international test cricket at the **Gabba** (Brisbane Cricket Ground; off Map p56; www.thegabba.org.au; 411 Vulture St) in Woolloongabba, south of Kangaroo Point. If you're new to the game, try and get along to a 20/20 match, which is cricket in its most explosive form. The cricket season runs from October to March.

During the other half of the year, rugby league is the big spectator sport. The Brisbane Broncos play home games at **Suncorp Stadium** (Map p73; www.suncorpstadium.com.au; 40 Castlemaine St, Milton).

Once dominated by Victorian teams, the Australian Football League (AFL) has been challenged by the Brisbane Lions, who have tasted success in recent years. You can watch them live at a home game at the Gabba between March and September. Also calling Suncorp home is the Queensland Roar football (soccer) team, attracting massive crowds in recent years. The domestic football season lasts from August to February.

Shopping

Brisbane is home to splendid riverside markets, eye-catching boutiques and galleries, and one-of-a-kind shops selling everything from indie fashions to indigenous artwork, with vintage apparel, new and used books, rare vinyl and much more.

Paddington Antique Centre ANTIQUES

(off Map p73; 167 Latrobe Tce, Paddington) Inside a former cinema, the city's biggest antique emporium houses over 50 dealers selling all manner of treasure/trash from the past. Clothes, jewellery, dolls, books, artwork, lamps, musical instruments, toys, clothing, glassware, ceramics, carpets, military stuff and much more lie waiting to be unearthed.

Blonde Venus CLOTHING

(Map p62; 707 Ann St, Fortitude Valley) One of the top boutiques in Brisbane, Blonde Venus has been around for 20-plus years, stocking a well-curated selection of both indie and couture labels. Look for Australian designs by Third Millennium, Josh Goot and Akira; with international pieces by Fred Perry, Patricia Field and Betsey Johnson among others.

Francis Leon CLOTHING

(Map p62; 65 James St, Fortitude Valley) One of Brisbane's most promising emerging labels, Francis Leon has unique and art-

SHOPPING THE STREETS

City Centre The CBD has a wide mix of high- and low-brow, including emporiums selling boomerangs, didgeridoos and other Australiana. Numerous boutiques crowd the upmarket Elizabeth Arcade (Map p56), between Elizabeth and Charlotte Sts, and the plusher, split-level Brisbane Arcade (Map p56), between the Queen St Mall and Adelaide St.

Fortitude Valley The intersection of Ann and Brunswick Sts in Fortitude Valley houses trendy shops selling local and international designers. Nearby James St, just south of the James St Market, also has some fine upmarket shops.

Paddington Boutiques, vintage stores and antique shops extend along Latrobe Tce, just west of Given Tce.

fully designed pieces – skirts, dresses, tops as well as jewellery. And all samples are made in-house.

Dogstar CLOTHING
(Map p62; www.dogstar.com.au; 713 Ann St, Fortitude Valley) The Japanese-born designer of the beautiful pieces in this shop has infused more than a touch of her land of birth into their designs. Beautiful fabrics and fine details feature prominently in skirts, jackets, wraps and tunics.

Maiocchi CLOTHING
(Map p62; 370 Brunswick St, Fortitude Valley) This is a great little store for individual pieces without the price tag of its glamorous neighbours.

Retro Metro CLOTHING
(off Map p73; 27 Latobe Tce, Paddington) Along Paddington's boutique-lined main street, Retro Metro stocks a wide selection of vintage wear, including cowboy boots, suits, cocktail dresses, handbags and jewellery. High-end collectible pieces as well as records, vases and other knick-knacks are across the street (34 Latrobe Tce).

RM Williams CLOTHING
(Map p56; Level 1, Myer Centre, Queen St Mall) One of the best-known makers of Aussie gear, this store stocks high-quality boots, hats, oilskins, moleskins, belts, jumpers and flannelette shirts.

Australia the Gift SOUVENIRS
(Map p56; 150 Queen St Mall) This is the biggest vendor of this kind of souvenir in the city. It carries extensive stocks of mass-produced Australiana.

Australian Geographic SOUVENIRS
(Map p56; Level 2, Myer Centre, 91 Queen St) Stocks everything from books and calendars on Australian flora and fauna to glow-in-the-dark dinosaurs.

Emporium BOUTIQUES, FOOD
(Map p62; 1000 Ann St, Fortitude Valley) This retail centre has more than 35 boutique shops and eateries. Check out Coaldrake's, a well-stocked family-owned bookshop with an espresso bar, or grab a Turkish pizza at Mecca Bah.

Record Exchange MUSIC
(Map p56; Level 1, 65 Adelaide St, CBD) Record Exchange is home to an astounding collection of vinyl, plus CDs, DVDs, posters and other memorabilia.

Other music shops:

Egg Records MUSIC
(Map p56; Level 1, 121 Queen St Mall, CBD) Well-organized collection of LPs, CDs and memorabilia.

Butter Beats MUSIC
(Map p62; 368 Brunswick St, Fortitude Valley) Handy location in the Valley.

Information

Bookshops

Archives Fine Books (40 Charlotte St) You could get lost in here for hours: fantastic range of secondhand books, boasting one million titles.

Avid Reader (www.avidreader.com.au; 193 Boundary St, West End) Diverse selection, excellent cafe and frequent readings and other events.

Borders Bookstore (162 Albert St) Sizable branch of this reliable chain.

Folio Books (www.foliobooks.com.au; 80 Albert St) Small bookshop with eclectic offerings.

World Wide Maps & Guides (Shop 30, Anzac Sq Arcade, 267 Edward St; ⏲closed Sun) Good assortment of travel guides and maps.

Emergency

Ambulance (☎000, 1300 369 003)
Fire (☎000, 3247 5539)
Lifeline (☎13 11 14)

MARKET-LOVERS' GUIDE TO BRISBANE

James Street Market FOOD

(Map p62; James St, New Farm; ⏲8.30am-6pm) Paradise for gourmands, this small but beautifully stocked market has gourmet cheeses, a bakery/patisserie, fruits, vegetables, and lots of gourmet goodies. The fresh seafood counter serves excellent sushi and sashimi.

Jan Power's Farmers Market FOOD

(Map p80; Brisbane Powerhouse, 119 Lamington St, New Farm; ⏲7am-noon every 2nd & 4th Sat of the month) Don't miss this excellent and deservedly popular farmers market if it's on when you're in town: over 120 stalls selling fresh produce, local wines, jams, juices, snacks (waffles, sausages, desserts, coffees) and much more. The CityCat takes you straight there.

Valley Laneway Markets CLOTHING, FOOD

(www.valleylanewaymarkets.com.au; Fortitude Valley; ⏲10am-4pm Sun) Launched in late 2010, this youthful market celebrates the Valley's alternative cultural scene, with live music, food stalls and new and vintage clothing and other goods for sale. Find it on three hidden laneways: Little Winn Lane, California Lane and Bakery Lane.

West End Markets FOOD

(Map p76; Davies Park, cnr Montague Rd & Jane St; ⏲6am-2pm Sat) This sprawling flea market has loads of fresh produce, herbs, flowers, organic foodstuffs, clothing and bric-a-brac. It's an apt representation of the diverse West End and a good place for noshing, with stalls selling a wide range of cuisines; there's also live music in the park.

South Bank Lifestyle Markets FOOD

(Map p60; Stanley St Plaza, South Bank; ⏲5pm-10pm Fri, 10am-5pm Sat, 9am-5pm Sun) These popular markets have a great range of clothing, craft, art, handmade goods and interesting souvenirs. Over 80 stalls are set up in rows of colourful tents.

Brunswick Street Markets CLOTHING, ACCESSORIES

(Map p62; Brunswick & Ann Sts, Fortitude Valley; ⏲8am-4pm Sat & Sun) These colourful markets fill the mall in Fortitude Valley with a diverse collection of crafts, clothes, books, records and miscellaneous works by budding designers.

Eagle Street Pier Markets SOUVENIRS, ACCESSORIES

(Map p56; Eagle St Pier, CBD; ⏲7am-4pm Sun) Set along the pedestrian lanes hugging the river, the Sunday Eagle St Pier markets have dozens of stalls, selling glassware, handicrafts, art, juices, snacks and live music.

Police (☎000) City (☎3224 4444; 67 Adelaide St); Fortitude Valley (☎3131 1200; Brunswick St Mall); headquarters (☎3364 6464; 200 Roma St)

RACQ (☎13 19 05, breakdown 13 11 11) City (GPO Bldg, 261 Queen St); St Pauls Tce (300 St Pauls Tce) Roadside service.

Internet Access

Wireless internet access is widely available at many hotels and cafes, though it's increasingly rare to find *free* wi-fi.

Brisbane Square Library (266 George St) Free internet terminals and wi-fi access.

Global Gossip City (290 Edward St; ⏲9am-11pm Mon-Sat, 10am-10pm Sat & Sun); Fortitude Valley (312 Brunswick St; ⏲9am-11pm) $4 per hour with membership; gets cheaper the more you use it. Plenty of terminals and cheap-call phone booths.

Internet City (Level 4, 132 Albert St; per hr $4; ⏲24hr) Cheap broadband access.

IYSC (128 Adelaide St; 60c per 10min, $3 per hr; ⏲8.30am-8.30pm Mon-Fri, 9.30am-8.30pm Sat & Sun)

State Library of Queensland South Bank; ⏲10am-8pm Mon-Thu, to 5pm Fri-Sun) Quick 20-minute terminals or free wi-fi.

Medical Services

Brisbane Sexual Health Clinic (☎3837 5611; Biala City Community Health Centre, 270 Roma St)

Pharmacy on the Mall (☎3221 4585; 141 Queen St; ⏲7am-9pm Mon-Thu, to 9.30pm Fri, 8am-9pm Sat, 8.30am-6pm Sun)

Queensland Statewide Sexual Assault Helpline (☎1800 010 120)

Royal Brisbane & Women's Hospital (☎3636 8111; cnr Butterfield St & Bowen Bridge Rd, Herston; ⏲24hr casualty ward)

Travel Clinic (☎1300 369 359, 3211 3611; 1st fl, 245 Albert St; ⏲7.30am-7pm Mon-Thu, to 6pm Fri, 8.30am-5pm Sat, 9.30am-5pm Sun)

Travellers' Medical & Vaccination Centre (TMVC; ☎3815 6900; 75 Astor Tce, Spring Hill; ⏲8am-5pm Mon, Tue, Thu & Fri, 8.30am-8pm Wed, 8am-1.30pm Sat)

Money

There are foreign-exchange bureaus at Brisbane Airport's domestic and international terminals, as well as ATMs that take most international credit cards. For after-hours foreign exchange, the tellers in the Treasury Casino are there 24 hours a day. ATMs are prolific throughout Brisbane.

American Express (☎1300 139 060; Shop 3, 156 Adelaide St)

Travelex (☎3210 6325; Shop 149F, Myer Centre, Queen St Mall)

Post

Australia Post (☎13 13 18; 261 Queen St; ⏲7am-6pm Mon-Fri) This branch, the General Post Office (GPO), has poste restante.

Tourist Information

Brisbane Visitor Information Centre (☎3006 6290; Queen St Mall; ⏲9am-5.30pm Mon-Thu, to 7pm Fri, to 4.30pm Sat, 9.30am-4pm Sun) Located between Edward and Albert Sts. Great one-stop info counter for all things Brisbane.

Naturally QLD (☎1300 130 372; 160 Ann St; ⏲8.30am-5pm Mon-Fri) The Queensland Parks & Wildlife Service (QPWS) runs this excellent information centre. You can get maps, brochures and books on national parks and state forests, as well as camping information and Fraser Island permits.

South Bank Visitors Centre (www.visitsouthbank.com.au; Stanley St Plaza, South Bank Parklands; ⏲9am-5pm)

Travel Agencies

Flight Centre (☎3221 8900; www.flightcentre.com.au; 170 Adelaide St)

STA Travel (☎134 782; www.statravel.com.au); City (☎3229 2499; Shop G11, Queen Adelaide Bldg, 59 Adelaide St); Myer Centre (☎3229 6066; Shop 40, Myer Centre, Ground Level, Queen St Mall)

YHA Membership & Travel office (☎3236 1680; 450 George St; ⏲9am-6pm Mon-Fri, 10am-4pm Sat) Tours, YHA membership and YHA hostel bookings.

Travellers with Disabilities

The city centre is commendably wheelchair friendly and Brisbane City Council (BCC) produces the *Brisbane Mobility Map*. It's usually available from the **BCC Customer Services Centre** (☎3403 8888, TTY 3403 8422; www.brisbane.qld.gov.au; 266 George St; ⏲9am-5pm Mon-Fri).

The **Disability Information Awareness Line** (DIAL; ☎1800 177 120, 3224 8444, TTY 3896 3471; www.disability.qld.gov.au) provides information on disability services and support throughout Queensland. Its phone lines are open from 9am to 5pm Monday to Friday. DIAL also publishes the quarterly *Connect* magazine.

Information about disabled access on public transport can be obtained from **Trans-Info** (☎13 12 30; www.transinfo.qld.gov.au).

Getting There & Away

The Brisbane Transit Centre (Map p56), 500m northwest of the city centre, is the main terminus and booking point for all long- distance buses and trains, as well as Citytrain services. Central Station is also an important hub for trains.

Air

Brisbane's main airport is about 16km northeast of the city centre at Eagle Farm, and has separate international and domestic terminals almost 3km apart, linked by the **Airtrain** (☎3215 5000; www.airtrain.com.au; tickets $4), which runs every 15 to 30 minutes. It's a busy international arrival and departure point with frequent flights to Asia, Europe, Pacific islands, North America, New Zealand and Papua New Guinea. See p467 for details of international airlines that fly into Brisbane.

Several airlines link Brisbane to the rest of the country. **Qantas** (☎13 13 13; www.qantas.com.au; 247 Adelaide St) has an extensive network, connecting Brisbane with Sydney (1½ hours), Melbourne (2½ hours), Adelaide (2½ hours), Canberra (two hours), Hobart (four hours), Perth (five hours) and Darwin (four hours).

Virgin Blue (☎13 67 89; www.virginblue.com.au) also flies between Brisbane and Australian capital cities.

Jetstar (☎13 15 38; www.jetstar.com.au) connects Brisbane with the same cities as Virgin Blue (except Perth) as well as Cairns.

The new kid on the block, **Tiger Airways** (☎9335 3033; www.tigerairways.com.au), is a Singapore-based budget carrier that will hopefully shake up the airline market in Australia and bring about better budget fares for travellers. It currently flies from Melbourne to the Gold Coast and Sunshine Coast but may well have started a Brisbane service by the time you read this.

Qantas, Virgin Blue and Jetstar all fly to towns and cities within Queensland, especially the more popular coastal destinations and the Whitsunday Islands. For flight details to and from Brisbane see individual destination Getting There & Away sections throughout this book.

Macair (☎1300 622 247; www.macair.com.au) flies to many destinations in the Queensland outback, including Mt Isa (four hours).

See p467 for more details on flying to and from Brisbane and around Queensland.

Bus

Bus companies have booking desks on the 3rd level of the Brisbane Transit Centre. **Greyhound Australia** (☎13 14 99; www.greyhound.com.au) is the main company on the Sydney–Brisbane run; you can go via the New England Hwy (17 hours) or the Pacific Hwy (16 hours) for $125. **Premier Motor Service** (☎13 34 10; www.premierms.com.au) operates the same routes, often with slightly cheaper deals.

You can also travel between Brisbane and Melbourne ($230, 24 to 28 hours) or Adelaide ($300, 40 hours), although competitive airfares may enable you to fly for the same price or less.

Heading south to Byron Bay, there are four daily buses from Brisbane airport ($50, three hours) and the Brisbane Transit Centre on **Byron Easy Bus** (www.byroneasybus.com.au).

North to Cairns, Premier Motor Service runs one direct service daily and Greyhound runs four. The approximate fares and journey times to places along the coast are as follows:

DESTINATION	DURATION	ONE-WAY FARE
Cairns	29hr	$255
Hervey Bay	5½hr	$65
Noosa Heads	2½hr	$30
Mackay	16½hr	$165
Rockhampton	11½hr	$115
Townsville	23hr	$215

There are also daily services to the Northern Territory: it's a 48-hour trip to Darwin ($540) via Longreach ($140, 17 hours) and Mt Isa ($190, 27 hours).

AIRPORT TO THE GOLD COAST & BEYOND **Coachtrans** (☎3358 9700; www.coachtrans.com.au) operates the Airporter direct services from Brisbane Airport to the Gold Coast (adult/child $32/20). Services meet every major flight and will drop you anywhere on the Gold Coast.

AIRPORT TO THE SUNSHINE COAST **Sun-Air Bus Service** (☎5477 0888; www.sunair.com.au) is one of several operators with direct services from Brisbane Airport to the Sunshine Coast (see p151).

Car & Motorcycle

There are five major routes, numbered from M1 to M5, into and out of the Brisbane metropolitan area. The major north–south route, the M1, connects the Pacific Hwy to the south with the Bruce Hwy to the north, but things get a bit confusing as you enter the city.

Coming from the Gold Coast, the Pacific Hwy splits into two at Eight Mile Plains. From here, the South East Freeway (M3) runs right into the centre, skirting along the riverfront on the western side of the CBD before emerging on the far side as Gympie Arterial Rd.

If you're just passing through, take the Gateway Motorway (M1) at Eight Mile Plains, which bypasses the city centre to the east and crosses the Brisbane River at the Gateway Bridge ($3 toll). From either direction, the Eagle Farm exit on the northern side of the bridge provides a quick route to the Valley and CBD. Just north is the turn-off to Brisbane Airport. The Gateway Motorway and Gympie Arterial Rd meet in Bald Hills, just south of the Pine River, and merge to form the Bruce Hwy.

Heading inland, the Ipswich Motorway (M2) branches off the M1 south of the centre and crosses the M3 before snaking off southwest to Ipswich and the Darling Downs. For a quick route from the city, pick up Milton Rd at the northwestern tip of the CBD and follow it out to the M5, which runs south to meet the Ipswich Motorway at Wacol (Milton Rd is also the way to get to Mt Coot-tha).

HIRE All of the major companies – **Hertz** (☎13 30 39), **Avis** (☎13 63 33), **Budget** (☎13 27 27), **Europcar** (☎13 13 90) and **Thrifty** (☎1300 367 227) – have offices at the Brisbane Airport terminals and throughout the city.

There are also several smaller companies in Brisbane that advertise slightly cheaper deals:

Abel Rent A Car (☎1300 13 14 29, 3832 3666; www.abel.com.au; Roma St) Attached to the Brisbane Transit Centre

Ace Rental Cars (☎1800 620 408, 3868 3833; www.acerentals.com.au; 330 Nudgee Rd, Hendra)

East Coast Car Rentals (☎1800 028 881, 3839 9111; www.eastcoastcarrentals.com.au; 76 Wickham St, Fortitude Valley)

Train

Brisbane's main station for long-distance trains is the Brisbane Transit Centre. For reservations and information visit the **Queensland Rail Travel Centre** (☎131 617; www.qr.com.au) Central Station (☎3235 1323; Ground fl, Central Station, 305 Edward St; ⏲8am-5pm Mon-Fri); Roma St (☎3235 1331; Brisbane Transit Centre, Roma St; ⏲6am-5pm Mon-Fri). You can also make reservations online or over the phone.

For details of intrastate train services to and from Brisbane, see p475.

Getting Around

To/From the Airport

The easiest way to get to and from the airport is the **Airtrain** (☎3215 5000; www.airtrain.com.au; adult/child $15/7.50; ⏲6am-7.30pm), which runs every 15 to 30 minutes from the airport to Fortitude Valley, Central Station, Roma St Station and other key destinations. There are also half-hourly services to the airport from Gold Coast Citytrain stops.

If you prefer door-to-door service, **Coachtrans** (☎3358 9700; www.coachtrans.com.au) runs regular shuttle buses between the airport and any hotel in the CBD. It costs $15 per adult and $8 per child. A taxi into the centre from the airport will cost around $40.

Bicycle

See p65 for information on cycling in and around Brisbane.

Car & Motorcycle

There is ticketed two-hour parking on many streets in the CBD and in the inner suburbs, but the major thoroughfares become clearways (ie parking is prohibited) during the morning and afternoon rush hours. If you do park in the street, pay close attention to the times on the parking signs, as Brisbane's parking inspectors take no prisoners. Parking is free in the CBD during the evening.

Parking is cheaper around South Bank than the city centre.

Queensland's motoring association is the RACQ, which provides insurance, maps and a breakdown service.

Public Transport

Brisbane boasts a world-class public transport network, and information on bus, train and ferry routes and connections can be obtained from the **Transit Information Centre** (www.translink.com.au; cnr Ann & Albert Sts).

Bus and ferry information is also available at the Brisbane Visitor Information Centre, the bus station information centre under the Queen St Mall, and the Queensland Rail Travel Centre.

GO CARD

If you plan to use public transport for more than a few trips, you'll save money by purchasing a Go Card ($5). Purchase the card, add credit and then use it on city buses, trains and ferries, and you'll save over 30% off individual fares. The handy cards are sold (and can be recharged) at transit stations and news agents.

Note that you'll save even more if you travel off-peak when using the Go Card (an adult ticket travelling in Zone 1 will cost $3.90/2.65/2.33 using a paper ticket/Go Card/Go Card travelling off-peak).

Fares on buses, trains and ferries operate on a zone system. There are 23 zones in total, but the city centre and most of the inner-city suburbs fall within Zone 1, which means most fares will be $3.90/2 per adult/child or $2.65/1.33 with the Go Card. If travelling in Zone 2, tickets are $4.60/2.30 per adult/child or $3.11/1.56 with the Go Card.

BOAT The 2011 Brisbane flood damaged a number of pontoons and ferry terminals along the Brisbane River. Limited CityCat and City Ferry services resumed operating soon after, but many ferry terminals remained off-line at the time of research. It is anticipated most, if not all, services will be operating by mid-to-late 2011. Check with **TransLink** (☎13 12 30; www.translink.com.au) for updates to services and timetables.

Resumption of normal services would see the blue CityCat catamarans run every 20 to 30 minutes between 5.45am and 11pm from the University of Queensland in the west to Bretts Wharf in the east, and back. Stops along the way include North Quay (for Queen St Mall), South Bank, Riverside (for the CBD) and New Farm Park. CityCats are wheelchair accessible at all stops except for West End, QUT Gardens Point, Riverside, Bulimba and Brett's Wharf.

The Inner City Ferries zigzag back and forth across the river between North Quay, near the Victoria Bridge, and Mowbray Park. Services start at about 6am Monday to Sunday, and run until about 11pm. There are also several cross-river ferries; most useful is the Eagle St Pier to Thornton St (Kangaroo Point) service. Check the TransLink website for updated information on ferry services.

Like all public transport, fares are based on zones. Most stops you'll need will be city-based and therefore in Zone 1.

BUS The Loop, a free bus that circles the city area and stops at QUT, the Queen St Mall, City Hall, Central Station and Riverside, runs every 10 minutes on weekdays between 7am and 6pm.

The main stop for local buses is in the basement of the Myer Centre. You can also pick up most of the useful buses from the colour-coded stops along Adelaide St, between George and Edward Sts.

Useful buses from the city centre include buses 195, 196, 197 and 199 to Fortitude Valley and New Farm, which leave from Adelaide St between King George Sq and Edward St.

TRAIN The fast Citytrain network has seven lines, which run as far as Nambour, Cooroy and Gympie in the north (for the Sunshine Coast), and Nerang and Robina in the south (for the Gold Coast). Other routes include Rosewood (for Ipswich) and Cleveland (for the North Stradbroke Island ferry). The lines to Pinkenba, Shorncliffe and Ferny Grove are mainly for suburban commuters.

The Airtrain service integrates with the Citytrain network in the CBD and along the Gold Coast line. All trains go through the Roma St Station inside the Brisbane Transit Centre and Central Station in the city, and Brunswick St Station in Fortitude Valley.

Trains run from around 4.30am, with the last train on each line leaving Central Station between 11.30pm and midnight. On Sunday the last trains run at around 10pm.

Taxi

There are usually plenty of taxis around the city centre, and there are taxi ranks at the Brisbane Transit Centre and at the top end of Edward St, by the junction with Adelaide St.

You can book a taxi by telephone ($1 booking fee). Try **Black & White** (☎13 10 08) or **Yellow Cab Co** (☎13 19 24). Most cabs have Eftpos capabilities.

Around Brisbane

Includes »

Redcliffe............. 99
Manly & St Helena Island 100
North Stradbroke Island 101
Moreton Island 104
Granite Belt 106
Stanthorpe & Ballandean.......... 106
Toowoomba 111
Around Toowoomba.. 114
Highfields & Crows Nest 114
Jondaryan Woolshed Complex............ 114

Best Places to Eat

» Morgans (p99)
» Fish Cafe (p100)
» Look (p104)
» Shiraz (p109)

Best Places to Stay

» Pandanus Palms Resort (p103)
» Stradbroke Island Beach Hotel (p103)
» Tangalooma Wild Dolphin Resort (p105)
» Happy Valley (p108)

Why Go?

Just outside the city, Brisbane has some enchantingly diverse areas that make for a fine day or overnight trip. Thirty minutes east of the CBD, you reach the edge of Moreton Bay, where you can explore laid-back coastal towns, linger over a seafood feast or book a cruise exploring the marine-rich waters of the bay. The lovely islands just offshore provide a wide range for activities – sea-kayaking, snorkelling, surfing, bushwalking, camping or just lounging on pretty beaches.

West of the city and perched high on the Great Dividing Range you'll find Toowoomba, a large and charming country town with wide tree-lined streets, stately homes and magnificent gardens.

In the Granite Belt south of there, vineyards and orchards thrive in the cold, crisp air. This is the heart of Queensland's wine country, with boutique wineries, fruit farms and cosy cottages. Nearby, balancing boulders and spring wildflowers attract bushwalkers.

When to Go

Toowoomba

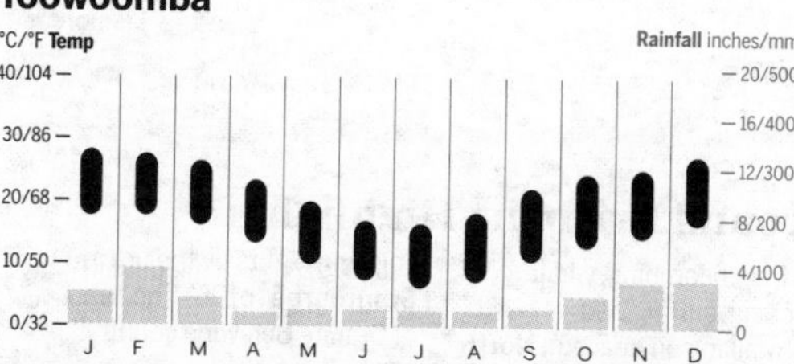

January As Queensland bakes, cooler climates in Toowoomba make for a fine escape.

July Cooler weather and peak season for whale watching, with sure sightings in Moreton Bay.

September Spring blossoms in the Granite Belt with a floral festival and blooming wildflowers.

Around Brisbane Highlights

1 Beachcombing, whale watching, surfing and bushwalking on peaceful **North Stradbroke Island** (p101)

2 Hand-feeding dolphins, sand-boarding and lazing about under swaying palms on **Moreton Island** (p104)

3 Sampling bold reds and farm-fresh produce and enjoying nights by the fire in **Stanthorpe** (p106), the heart of Granite Belt wine country.

4 Bushwalking amid the pristine beauty of **Girraween National Park** (p110)

5 Celebrating the return of spring during the colourful Carnival of Flowers in **Toowoomba** (p111)

6 Feasting on fresh seafood, then strolling along the pretty esplanade at **Manly** (p100)

7 Discovering the local lore in a fascinating history museum, followed by whale watching at **Redcliffe** (p99)

8 Taking a spooky ghost tour on the former island prison of **St Helena** (p100)

REDCLIFFE

POP 56,000

As the state's first European settlement, the Redcliffe Peninsula, located on the bay 35km north of the state capital, talks up its historical credentials. They're pretty organised up here with informative tourist centres and a surprisingly good museum. Redcliffe, a picturesque jut of land doused in an ambling, happy coastal ambience, makes a great break from the urban lashings of Brisbane and that's what it's mainly used for. Particularly good for families, the area has calm beaches ideal for the kids.

Sights & Activities

A pedestrian and cycle path hugs the peninsula's shore from Scarborough in the north to Redcliffe Point in the centre. **Bike hire** (per hour $8; 8.30am-4.30pm) is available on weekends on the path near Sutton's Beach. It's the most scenic way to see the area, and there are frequent stairs to the shops and cafes on the esplanade atop the slight slope. On the way you can stretch your legs on the sizeable **Redcliffe Jetty**, which has had several makeovers since its beginnings in 1885. A few hundred metres south of the jetty sits **Settlement Cove Lagoon**, a small lagoon with various pools, playground and barbecues. Understandably it's a fantastic spot for families.

At the base of the peninsula, on Clontarf Beach, the Redcliffe Visitor Information Centre feeds the voracious local pelicans every day at 10am.

The small but interesting **Redcliffe Historical Museum** (75 Anzac Ave; admission free; 10am-4pm Tue-Sun) details the peninsula's history through information boards, artefacts and a great series of personal accounts from locals.

For a scenic trip onto the bay, sign up for a one-day Moreton Island cruise with **Dolphin Wild** (3880 4444; www.dolphinwild.com.au; adult/child $115/65) which includes boating around the bay, stopping at Moreton Island for snorkelling the wrecks, lunch and beach time, then returning at 3.30pm. From July to October, **Brisbane Whale Watching** (3880 0477; www.brisbanewhalewatching.com.au; adult/child incl lunch $135/95) takes passengers on a high-speed catamaran to see the humpbacks on their annual migration. Trips depart Redcliffe Jetty.

If you're feeling adventurous, sign up for an adrenalin-pumping ride with **Brisbane Kite School** (3284 1186; www.brisbanekiteschool.com.au; cnr Hornibrook Esplanade & Elizabeth Ave), which has a kite-surf school on the peninsula; a two-hour lesson is $180 to $200.

Sleeping & Eating

Waltzing Matilda MOTEL $

(3283 7177; www.waltzingmatildamotel.com.au; 109 Margate Parade, Margate Beach; r $90-125) This battered place has seen better days, but at the price it's good value. The rooms worth chasing here are the upstairs sea-facing ones, with small balconies and water views making the worn carpets and ageing decor behind you fade into insignificance.

Pale Pacific Holiday Units APARTMENTS $

(3284 7743; www.palepacificholidayunits.com.au; 159 Margate Pde, Margate Beach; apt $90-120;) These four old-fashioned units are very well kitted-out, including TVs and full kitchens, and make a good option for families or couples. The two-bedroom units have sea-facing balconies, and because the whole place is on a corner it catches the afternoon sea breeze.

Morgans SEAFOOD $$$

(3203 5744; Bird of Passage Pde, Scarborough; mains $32-50; lunch & dinner) An emporium of the freshest seafood, here you'll find Morgans Seafood Restaurant, a sushi bar, fish market and seafood takeaway. If you want the full splurge, the award-winning restaurant with verandah overlooking the marina is ideal, otherwise line up at the takeaway and eat among the vigorous seagulls at outdoor tables.

Information

The main **Redcliffe Visitor Information Centre** (Pelican Park, Hornibrook Esplanade, Clontarf) is at the base of the peninsula. There's also another smaller, central **branch** (cnr Redcliffe Pde & Irene St) in Redcliffe.

Getting There & Around

Translink buses 680, 690 and 310 service the Redcliffe area, including Scarborough, from Brisbane ($6.70, one hour). You can also do a train-bus combo from either Sandgate or Petrie stations.

Vehicle ferries to Moreton Island leave from Scarborough at the northern tip of the headland.

MANLY & ST HELENA ISLAND

POP 4200

Just a few kilometres south of the Brisbane River mouth, Manly's large marina makes a good base for trips into Moreton Bay, including yacht rides. The town is delightful, with an assortment of eating and drinking establishments; seafood rules most of the kitchens.

The esplanade (north and south of the marina), with various pools and parks, makes for good walking or cycling in either direction with water and island views, and scenic cliffs around East Coast Marina.

Manly is also the gateway to little St Helena Island, only 6km from the mouth of the Brisbane River. A high-security prison until 1932, St Helena still has the remains of several **prison buildings**, plus parts of Brisbane's first **tramway**, built in 1884. The old trams were pulled by horses, but these days a tractor pulls the coaches as part of the island tour.

Sights & Activities

Various sailing companies offer day trips out on Moreton Bay. **Solo** (☎0432 122 333; www.solosail.com.au; adult/child $125/89) operates all-day tours in its racing yacht *Solo*, which has won the Sydney-to-Hobart yacht race. Tours depart at 7.15am and return at 5.30pm, and include snorkelling, swimming and lazing about on Moreton Island, plus lunch.

Manly Eco Cruises (☎3396 9400; www.manlyecocruises.com) takes folk out on the MV *Getaway*, for two-hour champagne breakfast cruises (adult/child $35/17). It also runs St Helena tours (day/evening from $39/99).

The **Royal Queensland Yacht Squadron** (☎3396 8666; www.rqys.com.au; 578 Royal Esplanade), south of the centre, has yacht races every Wednesday afternoon, and many of the captains are happy to take visitors on board for the ride. Sign on in the Yachties Bar before 12.30pm. You may also be able to pick up a yacht ride along the coast from here: the club has a noticeboard where people advertise for crew. And if you're interested in learning to sail, this is a great choice (private lesson $120). Another port of call is the **Wynnum-Manly Yacht Club** (☎3393 5708).

A number of operators offer trips to St Helena, including **AB Sea Cruises** (☎3893 1240; www.sthelenaisland.com.au; ⏲9.15am Mon-Fri, 10am Sat & Sun), with day trips to St Helena from Manly Harbour. The tour includes a tramway ride and a 'dramatised tour' of the prison (adult/child $70/40), complete with floggings if you so desire. Its ghost tour ($90/50) departs on Friday and Saturday evening. **Cat-O'-Nine-Tails** (☎1300 438 787; www.catoninetails.com.au; William Gunn Jetty, Manly) offers similar tours.

Sleeping & Eating

Manly Harbour Backpackers HOSTEL **$**

(☎1800 800 157; www.manlyharbourbackpackers.com.au; 45 Cambridge Pde; dm $25-30, d/tr $75/90) Upstairs on Manly's main strip, this is a laid-back hostel in a great old property right on the main drag, with attractive common areas, and lots of activities on offer. Recently spruced up dorms have six to eight beds; some are en suite. Also here is the excellent **Manly Deck** (mains around $20; ⏲lunch Fri-Sun, dinner Tue-Sun), a bar-restaurant that does $8 meals for backpackers most nights.

Manly Hotel HOTEL **$$**

(☎3249 5999; www.manlyhotel.com; 54 Cambridge Pde, Manly; mains $20-33; ⏲lunch & dinner) This is a much classier joint than it appears from outside, with floor-to-ceiling windows and high-end pub grub (oven-baked lamb shank, barramundi). There are also excellent front and rear beer gardens, and live music on weekends. It also has a large range of well-maintained rooms (single $70 to $120, double $85 to $135).

Fish Cafe SEAFOOD **$$$**

(☎3893 0195; cnr Cambridge Pde & Esplanade; mains $32-44; ⏲lunch & dinner daily, breakfast Sat & Sun) For the best fish and chips ($12) in town, get a takeaway (local whiting is recommended), trot across the road and pull up a seat overlooking the marina. If you prefer to eat at the elegant restaurant next-door, tuck into memorable seafood dishes such as rich bouillabaisse, wild river barramundi or succulent Moreton Bay bugs.

Information

The **tourist information office** (43 Cambridge Pde; ⏲9am-5pm Mon-Fri, 10am-3pm Sat & Sun) is very helpful.

Getting There & Around

The best way to get to Manly is by train, which departs from Brisbane's Roma St or Central Stations ($3.60, 40 minutes, approximately half-hourly). It's a 10-minute walk from the station to the waterfront, down Cambridge Pde. Bicycle hire is available from Manly Pool (1 Fairlead Cres, per hr/day $15/35), on the waterfront.

NORTH STRADBROKE ISLAND

POP 3000

'Straddie' is one of Moreton Bay's gems. A lovely sand island that is frequently turned into a playground by Brisbanites escaping the urban grind for the weekend, it's large enough to absorb this influx of visitors and has some genuinely pristine wilderness areas. If you want to get some sun on your back the beaches here are excellent and there are some great walking tracks to sublime inland lakes. The wild southeastern coast is the spot where 4WD drivers churn up the sands. Given its popularity with mainlanders there are also some fabulous accommodation and dining options.

North and South Stradbroke Islands used to be joined, but a savage storm severed the sand spit between the two in 1896. Sand mining used to be a major industry, although these days only the southwest of the island is mined. For information on South Stradbroke, see p121.

Sights & Activities

Straddie's most obvious lure is a string of beautiful **beaches**. At Point Lookout there's a series of points and bays along the headland, and endless stretches of white sand. Cylinder Beach and Amity Point generally provide calm swimming opportunities, while Main Beach churns some good swells and breaks for **surfing**. There are also unpatrolled and exposed breaks all along Eighteen Mile Beach. Manta Lodge YHA hires out surfboards.

Straddie Adventures (☎3409 8414; www.straddieadventures.com.au; 112 East Coast Rd, Point Lookout) offers sea-kayaking trips including snorkelling stops ($60) around Straddie, and sand-boarding ($30). It also hires gear (snorkel, kayaks, bikes, surfboards).

Manta Lodge & Scuba Centre (☎3409 8888; www.mantalodge.com.au; 1 East Coast Rd), based at the YHA, offers snorkelling for $85 inclusive of a three-hour boat trip and all the gear. Open-water dive courses cost $520, while a trip with two dives for certified divers goes for $185. The centre will also hire out snorkel gear ($25) if you already know what you're doing. Some of the diving sites are spectacular, with sightings of grey nurse and leopard sharks, turtles, tropical fish and other marine life common.

The island is also famous for its **fishing**, and the annual Straddie Classic, held in August, is one of Australia's richest and best-known fishing competitions.

Straddie Super Sports (☎3409 9252; Bingle Rd, Dunwich) hires out fishing gear from $25 per day. See p102 for fishing tours.

With a 4WD you can drive all the way down the eastern beach to Jumpinpin, the channel that separates North and South Stradbroke, a legendary fishing spot. Access is via George Nothling Dr or Tazi Rd. 4WD permits cost $44 and are available from the Dunwich visitor information centre. You can also call **Redlands Tourism** (☎3821 2730) to purchase one.

There is a good walk around the **North Gorge** (30 minutes) on the headland at Point Lookout, and porpoises, dolphins, manta rays and sometimes whales can be spotted from up here. In fact Point Lookout is one of the best land-based **whale-watching** sites in Queensland.

Dunwich, on the western coast, is where the ferries dock and is home to the **North Stradbroke Historical Museum** (Welsby Rd; adult/child $3.50/1; ⌚10am-2pm Tue-Sat), near the post office. The museum is definitely worth an hour or two's browsing, with stories of shipwrecks, harrowing voyages, life in the 'benevolent asylum' and an introduction to the rich Aboriginal history of the island. An oddball collection of island artefacts includes the skull of a sperm whale, washed up along Main Beach in 2004.

The eastern beach, known as **Eighteen Mile Beach**, is open to 4WD vehicles and campers, and there are lots of walking tracks and old 4WD roads on the northern half of the island. Just off the road from Dunwich to the beach, **Blue Lake** is the glittering centrepiece of the Blue Lake National Park. It's reached by a 2.7km walking trail through the forest, starting from a car park, well signed off the side of the road. There's a wooden viewing platform affording great views and the lake is surrounded by a forest of paperbarks, eucalypts and banksias. Keep an eye out for swamp wallabies. The freshwater lake is a beautiful spot for a swim, if you don't mind the spooky unseen depths.

Point Lookout

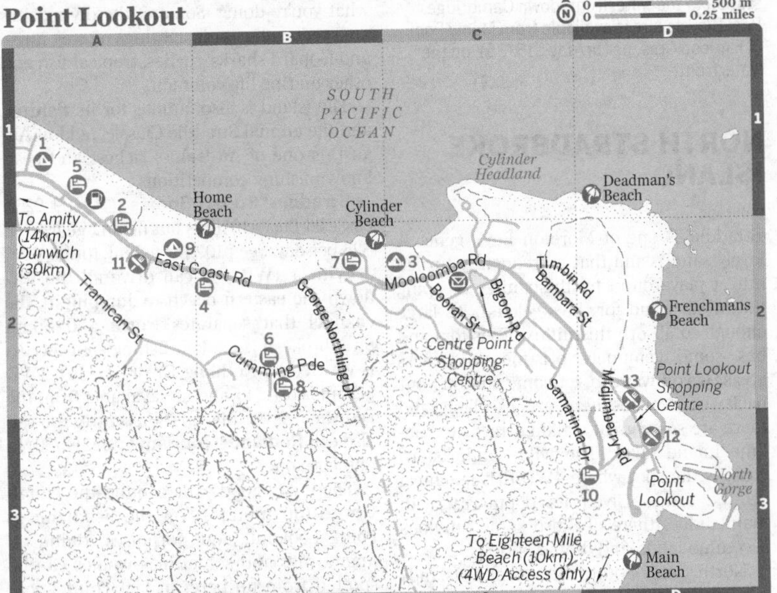

Point Lookout

Activities, Courses & Tours

Scuba Centre .... (see 5)
Straddie Adventures .... (see 2)

Sleeping

1 Adder Rock Camping Area A1
2 Anchorage on Straddie A1
3 Cylinder Beach Camping Area C2
4 Domain Stradbroke Resort B2
5 Manta Lodge YHA A1
6 Pandanus Palms Resort B2
7 Stradbroke Island Beach Hotel B2
8 Straddie Views B&B B2
9 Thankful Rest Camping Area A2
10 Whale Watch Ocean Beach Resort D3

Eating

Amis .... (see 6)
11 Bowls Club A2
Harlequin .... (see 4)
12 Fishes D3
13 Look D2

There's also good swimming at **Brown Lake**, about 3km along Tazi Rd from Dunwich. Favoured by families and only a short 2WD from the road, the water here is very brackish, hence the name. There are picnic benches, barbecues, a playground and a sandy beach that's good for paddling.

For both lakes, take the road opposite to the ferry terminal. If you're coming from Point Lookout turn right to the ferry and left to get to the lakes.

If you want to hike the 20km across the island from Dunwich to Point Lookout, a number of dirt-track loops break the monotony of the bitumen road. A pleasant diversion is a visit to the **Myora Springs**, which are surrounded by lush vegetation and walking tracks, near the coast about 4km north of Dunwich.

Tours

A number of tour companies offer good 4WD tours of the island. Generally these take in a strip of the eastern beach and visit several freshwater lakes. All tour operators will collect you from either the ferry at Dunwich or your accommodation.

North Stradbroke Island 4WD Tours 4WD
(☎3409 8051; straddie4wd@bigpond.com) Operates 4WD tours as well fishing tours. Half-day tours cost $35/20 per adult/child; fishing tours run $45/30.

Point Lookout Fishing Charters FISHING (☎3409 8353, 0407 376 091) Organises six-hour fishing trips that cost $160 per person.

Straddie Kingfisher Tours FISHING, WHALE WATCHING (☎3409 9502; www.straddiekingfishertours.com.au; adult/child $79/59) Operates six-hour 4WD and fishing tours; also has whale-watching tours in season.

Sleeping

Almost all of the island's accommodation is in Point Lookout, strung along 3km of coastline. Note that during low season you can get just one night's accommodation at many places, but it's far more expensive than booking multiple nights.

Pandanus Palms Resort APARTMENTS $$$ (☎3409 8106; www.pandanus.stradbrokeresorts.com.au; 21 Cumming Pde; apt $245-315;) Perched high above the beach, with a thick tumble of vegetation beneath, the large two-bed townhouses here are a good size and boast modern furnishings. It is well worth paying the extra for ocean-fronting accommodation, as these have private yards with barbecues and marvellous views. Excellent restaurant onsite.

Straddie Views B&B $$ (☎3409 8875; www.northstradbrokeisland.com/straddiebb; 26 Cumming Pde; r from $150) Several suites are available in this friendly B&B run by a couple of Straddie locals. Rooms are an excellent size – probably double that of most B&B rooms. Inside you get cane furniture, a breakfast menu and little touches like wine glasses on the bed filled with chocolates awaiting your arrival. Breakfast in the morning is served on the upstairs deck with fantastic water views.

Stradbroke Island Beach Hotel HOTEL $$$ (☎3409 8188; www.stradbrokeislandbeachhotel.com.au; East Coast Rd; d $230-310;) Straddie's only hotel has an intriguing modern design (taking its inspiration from the often-sited manta rays), with 12 cool, inviting rooms in muted colour schemes, each with high-end fixtures and a balcony (it's worth the $40 extra for sea views). The open bar downstairs with outdoor beer garden and 'sail' roof is a delight, and makes you feel like you're almost on the beach itself. There is a restaurant and spa here as well.

Domain Stradbroke Resort APARTMENTS $$ (☎3415 0000; www.stradbrokedomain.com; 43 East Coast Rd; villa from $167;) Large ultra-modern villas are set in a leafy compound and backed by forest here. Each villa (or 'shack' as the one-bedrooms are called) features blond woods, original artwork and outdoor deck with barbecue. Unfortunately, there isn't much space between villas, and the layouts for two-bedrooms are a little zany, with a completely separate building for the master bedroom.

Manta Lodge YHA HOSTEL $ (☎3409 8888; www.mantalodge.com.au; 1 East Coast Rd; dm/d $30/78; @) This large hostel near the beach is clean and well kept, and has excellent facilities, including a dive school on the doorstep. There are four-, six- and eight-bed dorms and the owners are happy to close off small dorms to couples or friends who don't want to share, and just charge a bit extra.

Straddie Holiday Parks CAMPGROUND $ (☎1300 551 253; unpowered/powered sites $35/40, cabins $109-165) There are seven camping grounds on the island operated by this outfit, but the most attractive are those grouped around Point Lookout. The **Adder Rock Camping Area** and the **Thankful Rest Camping Area** both overlook lovely Home Beach, while the **Cylinder Beach Camping Area** sits right on one of the island's most popular beaches. There are also several cheaper sites (from $15 per night) accessible by 4WD only. Sites should be booked well in advance.

Anchorage on Straddie APARTMENTS $$ (☎3409 8266; www.anchorage.stradbrokeresorts.com.au; East Coast Rd; two nights $235-400;) The friendly managers of these large self-contained apartments with balconies keep the place shipshape and there's a boardwalk from the hotel grounds straight to the beach. For sea views, ask for a room on the third level.

Whale Watch Ocean Beach Resort APARTMENTS $$$ (☎1800 450 004, 3409 8555; www.whalewatchresort.com.au; Samarinda Dr; apt per night $369; @) Sublime and secluded three-bedroom apartments with stylish furniture and large decks.

Eating

There are only a handful of dining choices; with most places in Point Lookout.

TOP CHOICE **Amis** MODERN AUSTRALIAN **$$$**
(☎3409 8600; 21 Cummings Pde; mains $28-36; ⊙dinner Wed-Sun) For a memorable meal on Straddie, Amis is hard to top, combining north African and Asian accents with fresh local produce. The menu is small but features standouts like Queensland kangaroo loin fillet, chargrilled prawns on bamboo, fish of the day and crispy duck confit. Inside you'll find a thatched roof, large windows, and efficient, smooth and friendly service.

Look MODERN AUSTRALIAN **$$**
(☎3415 3390; 29 Mooloomba Rd; lunch mains $12-18, dinner mains $25-30; ⊙breakfast & lunch daily; dinner Thu-Sat) This seems to be the hub of Point Lookout during the day, with funky tunes in the background and great outdoor seating with breezy water views. Look's menu has daily specials, spicy seafood dishes, antipasto sharing platters and creative salads. It's an elegant but relaxed affair.

Fishes SEAFOOD **$$**
(East Coast Rd; mains $15-20; ⊙9am-7pm Sat-Mon, 9am-4pm Tue-Thu; wi-fi) True to its name, Fishes serves scrumptious fish and chips, with outdoor seating across the road from the entrance to the stunning North Gorge Walk. There's free wi-fi, binocular hire ($10 for four hours) and bike hire ($22 for four hours).

Island Fruit Barn CAFE **$**
(Bilinga Rd, Dunwich; mains $10-14; ⊙7am-4pm) On the main road in Dunwich, the Island Fruit Barn is a casual and welcoming little spot that serves excellent breakfasts, smoothies, salads and sandwiches using high-quality ingredients. The tiny gourmet grocery is a good place to stock up on goodies.

Harlequin FUSION **$$**
(East Coast Rd; mains $16-24; ⊙breakfast & lunch) Harlequin is a classy little eatery with a pleasant outdoor deck abutting the Domain resort. The menu features an eclectic mix of light bistro fare as well as fresh salads, seafood and curry dishes.

Bowls Club PUB FARE **$**
(East Coast Rd; mains $10-26; ⊙lunch & dinner) For tasty, casual meals that won't break the budget head to the friendly Bowls Club, with pub fare and different baked meals nightly.

Information

There are three small settlements on the island: Dunwich, Amity Point and Point Lookout, which are all grouped around the northern end of the island. Point Lookout, on the main surf beach, is the nicest place to stay. Apart from the beach, the southern part of the island is closed to visitors because of mining.

Getting There & Away

The gateway to North Stradbroke Island is the seaside suburb of Cleveland. Regular **trains** (www.transllink.com.au) run from Central or Roma St to Cleveland station ($6.70, one hour) and buses to the ferry terminals (10 minutes) meet the trains at Cleveland station.

Several ferry companies head across to Straddie. **Stradbroke Ferries** (☎3488 5300; www.stradbrokeferries.com.au) goes to Dunwich almost every hour from about 6am to 6pm ($19 return, 25 minutes). It also has a slightly less frequent vehicle ferry (per vehicle including passengers return $135, 40 minutes) from 5.30am to 5.30pm.

The **Gold Cat Stradbroke Flyer** (☎3286 1964; www.flyer.com.au) also runs an almost-hourly catamaran service from Cleveland to One Mile Jetty ($19 return, 25 minutes), 1km north of central Dunwich.

Getting Around

Local buses (☎3409 7151) meet the ferries at Dunwich and One Mile Jetty and run across to Point Lookout ($9.50 return). The last bus to Dunwich leaves Point Lookout at about 6.45pm, later on Friday. There's also the **Stradbroke Cab Service** (☎0408 193 685), which charges $60 for the trip from Dunwich to Point Lookout. **Fishes** (East Coast Rd, Point Lookout) hires out bikes ($15/30/99 per hour/day/five days). The **Islander Holiday Resort** (☎3409 8388; islander@stradbrokeresorts.com.au; East Coast Rd, Point Lookout) hires out a car for $70 a day; scooters are also available.

MORETON ISLAND

POP 300

If you're not going much further north in Queensland than Brisbane but want a slice of tropical paradise, slip over to this blissful island. Dazzling white-sand beaches are backed by Australian bush tumbling down to the sands, while the water itself is coloured patchy jade and indigo and, once you're in it, crystal clear. Apart from a few rocky headlands, it's all sand, with Mt Tempest, the highest coastal sand hill in the world, towering to 280m. The island hosts prolific bird life, and at its northern tip is a lighthouse, built in 1857. Off the western coast are the rusty hulking Tangalooma Wrecks, which provide good snorkelling and diving.

The best part about the island is its lack of development, with 90% of it a national park. The island sees far fewer visitors than Stradbroke, with mostly families, Asian tourists and grey nomads dropping anchor.

Sights & Activities

The main draw of the island is **Tangalooma**, halfway down the western side of the island, a popular tourist resort sited at an old whaling station. The only other settlements, all on the western coast, are **Bulwer**, near the northwestern tip, **Cowan Cowan**, between Bulwer and Tangalooma, and **Kooringal**, near the southern tip.

The following activities are all based at the resort.

The main attraction is the **wild-dolphin feeding** that takes place each evening around sundown. Usually about eight or nine dolphins swim in from the ocean and take fish from the hands of volunteer feeders. You have to be a guest of the resort to participate, but onlookers are welcome.

Also here is the **Marine Research & Education Centre**, which has a display on the diverse marine and bird life of Moreton Bay. You can pick up a map of the island showing walking trails. There's a desert trail (two hours) and a bush walk (1½ hours), both leaving from the resort, as well as a longer walk to Water Point (four hours) on the east coast. It's also worth making the strenuous trek to the summit of Mt Tempest, 3km inland from Eagers Creek.

You can hire snorkelling gear from **Dive In Sports** (per day $10) and immerse yourself amid the colourful coral and marine life of the Tangalooma Wrecks. If you prefer to view things from on top of the water, it also has kayaks for $10 per hour. If you're into more adventurous playthings, check out **Club Toys**, which hires out catamarans ($15 per hour), surf skis and motorboats ($20 per hour).

For an aerial view of the bay, book a sightseeing flight with **Tangalooma Helicopter Service** (flight per person $70-285).

Tours

Most day and two-day tours depart from Brisbane or the Gold Coast.

Tangatours DIVING, SNORKELLING
(Tangalooma Wild Dolphin Resort) Offers 1½-hour snorkelling trips around the Tangalooma Wrecks ($35) and introductory diving trips for qualified divers. You can also do an open-water PADI dive course here.

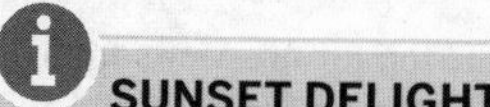

SUNSET DELIGHT

For flaming sunset views over the water, head up to the top of Kangaroo Lodge, which is within the Tangalooma Resort complex. Tangalooma on Moreton Island is one of the few places around Brisbane that faces west over the bay, giving wonderful water sunsets, with the Tangalooma Wrecks looking quite surreal in the foreground.

Micat SNORKELLING, WALKING
(☎3909 3397; www.micat.com.au; 1-day tours adult/child from $155/95, 2-day camping tours from $299) Offers tours of the island with heaps of activities thrown in, including snorkelling, sand-boarding and bushwalking. The two-day tour means you camp overnight.

Sunrover Expeditions NATURE, CAMPING
(☎1800 353 717, 3203 4241; www.sunrover.com.au; adult/child $120/100) A friendly and reliable 4WD-tour operator with good day tours, which include lunch. Also operates two-day (adult/child $195/150) and three-day camping tours (adult/child $250/225). Both of these options include meals.

Moreton Bay Escapes NATURE, CAMPING
(☎1300 559 355; www.moretonbayescapes.com.au; 1-day tours adult/child from $165/125, 2-day camping tours $249/149)

Sleeping & Eating

There are a few holiday flats and houses for rent at Kooringal, Cowan Cowan and Bulwer. To see what's on offer, including current pricing arrangements, go to www.moretonisland.com/accommodation.html.

Tangalooma Wild Dolphin Resort
HOTEL, APARTMENTS $$$
(☎1300 652 250, 3637 2000; www.tangalooma.com; 1-night packages from $310; ❄@≋) Fringed with grass leading onto the beach, and thatched umbrellas and swaying palm trees providing shade, this aging resort is the only formal setup on the island. There's a plethora of options available, starting with pretty bland hotel-style rooms in Kookaburra Lodge. If you go for one of these, get a

room near the top for fine views from your balcony. A step up are the units and suites, where you'll get beachside access and rooms kitted out in cool, contemporary decor with good facilities. Both include kitchens in an open-plan living style. Look for online deals through www.wotif.com.

The resort has several eating options, including the **Coffeeshop** (snacks $6; ⏲lunch) for sandwiches, wraps and pies; the **Beach House Rotunda** (mains $25-35; ⏲dinner) for something more substantial, or **Tursiops Restaurant** (all-you-can-eat $35; ⏲dinner) for buffet-style dining.

There are 10 national park **camping grounds** (sites per person/family $6/21), all with water, toilets and cold showers; of these, five are on the beach. For information and camping permits, book online (www.derm.qld.gov.au), contact the DERM office in Brisbane (☎1300 130 372; level 3, 400 George St, CBD) or call ☎13 74 68. Camping permits must be arranged before you get to the island.

The shops at Kooringal and Bulwer are expensive, so bring what you can from the mainland.

Information

Moreton Island has no paved roads, but 4WD vehicles can travel along the beaches and a few cross-island tracks – seek local advice about tides and creek crossings before venturing out. You can get Queensland Parks & Wildlife Service (QPWS) maps from the vehicle-ferry offices or the information desk at the Marine Research & Education Centre at Tangalooma. Vehicle permits for the island cost $40 and are available through the ferry operators, online (www.derm.qld.gov.au) or at a DERM office (in Brisbane: level 3, 400 George St). Note that ferry bookings are *mandatory* if you want to take a vehicle across.

Getting There & Around

A number of ferries operate from the mainland. The **Tangalooma Flyer** (☎3268 6333; www.tangalooma.com; return day trip adult/child from $45/25) is a fast catamaran operated by the Tangalooma Resort. It makes the 1¼-hour trip to the resort on Moreton Island daily from a dock at Eagle Farm, at Holt St off Kingsford Smith Dr. A bus (adult/child one-way $19/9) to the Flyer picks up passengers from Brisbane CBD hotels and the Roma St Transit Centre starting around 8am. A return service is also available. Depending on the group size, a taxi may be cheaper. Bookings are essential (☎3637 2000).

The **Moreton Venture** (☎3909 3333; www.moretonventure.com.au; vehicle & passengers return $190-265; ⏲8.30am daily) is a vehicle ferry that runs from Howard-Smith Dr, Lyton, at the Port of Brisbane, to Tangalooma. It returns from the island at 3.30pm daily. There are additional departures on Friday and Sunday.

The new vehicle ferry **Amity Trader** (☎0487 227 437; www.amitytrader.com; vehicle & passengers return $100) sails between Amity and Kooringal on Moreton Island's southern tip. Call for times and to reserve a spot.

There is one 4WD taxi driver operating **Moreton Island Tourist Services** (☎3408 2661; www.moretonisland.net.au). One-way trips range from $40 to $180.

GRANITE BELT

Located just west of the Great Dividing Range, the Granite Belt is home to rolling hillsides sprinkled with vineyards and orchards that thrive in the cold, crisp air. This is the heart of Queensland's wine country and the lush countryside is dotted with apple, pear, plum and peach trees, cosy cottages and boutique wineries. Further south, on the NSW border, balancing boulders and spring wildflowers attract bushwalkers to the dramatic Girraween National Park.

Stanthorpe & Ballandean

POP 4800

Queensland's coolest town (literally), at an altitude of 915m, is one of its least-known tourist hotspots. With a distinct four-season climate, Stanthorpe is a popular winter retreat where normally sweltering Queenslanders can cosy in front of a fire or warm up with a fine red wine from one of the more than 50 boutique wineries in the region. In 1860 an Italian priest planted the first grapevine in the Granite Belt but it wasn't until the influx of Italian immigrants in the 1940s (bringing with them a

WHEN TO GO

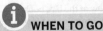

If you plan to visit a fair number of vineyards, consider planning your visit to the Granite Belt on the weekend. Although prices are slightly higher for lodging then, you'll have access to all the vineyards and restaurants, many of which close on weekdays.

TOP VINEYARDS & GRANITE BELT DELICACIES

With dozens of wineries offering free tastings, you could easily spend a week or more sampling the great fruits of the region – and still just scratch the surface. For those who have only a day or two in the area, here's a roundup of our favourite spots. All are on the free map available at the tourist office.

Ravens Croft (www.ravenscroftwines.com.au; 274 Spring Creek Rd, Stanthorpe; ⏲10.30am-4.30pm Fri-Sun Sep-Jan, Wed-Sun Feb-Aug) Friendly, highly respected winemaker with superb reds (Petit Verdot, Cabernet Sauvignon, port) and whites (including a top-notch Verdelho). With its own resident koala ('Blinky') in the bush out back.

Ballandean (www.ballandeanestate.com; Sundown Rd, Ballandean; ⏲9am-5pm) One of Queensland's oldest and biggest wineries, with many award-winning vintages and a good restaurant. Also offers free winery tours (11am, 1pm and 3pm).

Boireann (www.boireannwinery.com.au, the Summit; ⏲10am-4.30pm Fri-Mon) Handmade premium reds rank among the finest in the region (and awarded five stars by Australian wine authority James Halliday).

Pyramids Road (www.pyramidsroad.com.au; Pyramids Rd, Wyberba; ⏲10am-4.30pm) On the road to Girraween National Park, Pyramids makes a fine detour; the reds are excellent, with a notable Mourvèdre and a widely praised 'Bernie's Blend' (Cabernet, Shiraz and Mourvèdre).

Robert Channon (www.robertchannonwines.com.au; 32 Bradley Ln, Stanthorpe; ⏲11am-4pm) Lots of trophy-winning wines, and a fine lunch restaurant with views over a pretty lake.

Felsberg Winery (www.felsberg.com.au; 116 Townsend Rd, Glen Aplin; ⏲9.30am-4.30pm) The setting is striking: a hilltop Bavarian-style chalet with lovely views over the countryside. Good wines (try the unusual sparkling red cuvée rouge), and a restaurant serving seasonal fare (lunch daily, dinner Fridays and Saturdays).

Golden Grove (www.goldengrovee.com.au; 337 Sundown Rd, Ballandean; ⏲9am-5pm) Well-established family-run estate with many unique varieties, including an excellent Nero d'Avola, a vine native to Sicily.

Tobin (www.tobinwines.com.au; cnr Ricca & Sundown Rds, Ballandean; ⏲9am-5pm) Laid-back boutique vineyard with a mighty fine tempranillo.

Granite Belt Dairy Farmhouse (cnr Amiens Rd & Duncan Ln, Thulimbah; ⏲10am-4pm) What's wine without cheese? The Granite Belt's best cheesemaker spreads a tasty array of the good stuff – all available for sampling. It also makes fantastic milkshakes and cheesecake and sells fresh-baked bread, chutneys and other picnic fare.

Heavenly Chocolate (2117 Pyramids Rd, Wyberba; ⏲10am-4pm Fri-Mon) Chocolate makes a fine accompaniment to a full-bodied red, and Heavenly prepares decadent handmade chocolates and fudge – plus 21 different creamy hot chocolates for those cold winter days.

Bramble Patch (www.bramblepatch.com.au; 381 Townsend Rd, Glen Aplin; ⏲10am-4pm) Berry grower worth visiting for the ice cream with homemade berry compote, waffles with berries and of course fresh fruits (November to April), jams and relishes.

lifetime of viticultural nous) that the wine industry truly began. Today Stanthorpe and the tiny village of Ballandean, less than 20km south of town, boast a flourishing 'wine tourism' industry – a term describing small, boutique wineries that offer cellar door sales, and often on-site dining and vineyard performances and events, and boutique accommodation.

But it's not all wine and song: the Granite Belt's changing seasons also make it a prime fruit-growing area and there's plenty of fruit-picking available for backpackers who don't mind chilly mornings.

Sights & Activities

Wine-tasting is a must-do in Queensland's premier wine region, as is a drive through the spectacular Granite Belt landscape. If you plan on swilling one too many, opt for a tour.

For nonalcoholic pursuits, the **Stanthorpe Heritage Museum** (12 High St; adult/child $5/2.50; 10am-4pm Wed-Fri, 1-4pm Sat, 9am-1pm Sun), on the northern outskirts of town, gives a comprehensive insight into Stanthorpe's tin-mining and grazing past. Well-preserved old buildings from the 1800s include a slab-timber jail, a shepherd's hut and a school house. There's a moving display on Stanthorpe (and Australia) losses in the wars, and homemade 'make-do' pieces – toys, kitchen items, pillow cases, curtains – showing local ingenuity during scarce times.

The **Granite Belt Maze** (364 Old Warwick Rd; adult/child $15/12; 9.30am-4.30pm Thu-Tue), 8.5km north of town, is as kitschy as a hedged maze can be but the kids will love it.

The **Stanthorpe Regional Art Gallery** (4681 1874; Lock St; 10am-4pm Mon-Fri, to 1pm Sat & Sun), northwest of the post office, has a small collection of works by local artists.

While you're in town, take a stroll through the parkland around Quart Pot Creek, near the visitors centre. The park is full of cool-climate trees and in autumn the leaves are ablaze with colour.

Tours

Several companies run day tours of the wineries, with lunch included, out of Stanthorpe ($70 to $85) and Brisbane ($145):

Filippo's Tours WINE
(4683 3130; www.filippostours.com.au) Also has overnight packages (per person $285).

Granite Belt Winery Tours WINE
(0428 282 871; www.granitebeltwinerytours.com.au) Personalised tours from Brisbane or Stanthorpe.

Granite Highlands Maxi Tours WINE
(4681 3969; www.maxitours.com.au) Offers a range of options including overnight packages (per person $260)

Festivals & Events

The main event in the Granite Belt spans an entire season. Winter (June to August) is the **Brass Monkey Season**, with a parade of music events and food fiestas in town and at various wineries.

The **Apple & Grape Festival** (www.appleandgrape.org) is a three-day harvest festival held every even-numbered year in March where you can celebrate the 37,000 tonnes of apples produced here each year.

Many of the wineries hold regular performances and events; check with the visitors centre for details. One of the largest wineries, **Ballandean Estate Wines** (4684 1226; www.ballandeanestate.com; Sundown Rd, Ballandean) hosts **Priscilla in the Vineyard** (March), **Opera in the Vineyard** (May) and **Jazz in the Vineyard** (October), all with copious amounts of food and wine.

The **Sicilian Vintage Lunch** held in February at **Golden Grove Estate** (4684 1291; www.goldengrovee.com.au; Sundown Rd, Ballandean) celebrates the start of the vintage Italian-style with grape stomping, Italian music and a three-course Sicilian lunch.

Sleeping

Oddly, the Granite Belt high season is during the cooler months (May through September), when Queenslanders head to mountain cabins for a dose of frigid temperatures and cosying up by the fire. Prices are higher then, and are higher on weekends year-round.

TOP CHOICE **Happy Valley** CABINS **$$**
(4681 1370; www.happyvalleyretreat.com; Glenlyon Dr; cabin midweek $170, weekend $190-230) Some 4km west of Stanthorpe (signposted off the Texas road), this fine complex offers secluded, beautifully sited timber cabins, all with their own bathrooms, wood fires and verandahs. It stands on a bush property studded with granite outcrops, and has a good restaurant. Children are welcome at this friendly, laid-back place.

Diamondvale B&B Cottages B&B **$$**
(4681 3367; www.diamondvalecottages.com.au; 26 Diamondvale Rd; d from $180;) In a bucolic setting of bushland outside of Stanthorpe, Diamondvale is a friendly place with four lovely cottages, each with charming old-fashioned details, a wood-burning fireplace, kitchen and verandah. You can follow the creek 2km and stroll into town.

Azjure BOUTIQUE INN **$$$**
(4684 1232; www.azjure.com.au; 165 Sundown Rd, Ballandean; d $250-330;) This award-winning retreat has three beautifully designed ultra-modern freestanding cabins, affording fine views of the serene landscape. Each has a large open-layout, floodlit windows, veran-

LOCAL KNOWLEDGE

MARK RAVENSCROFT, WINEMAKER & FOUNDER OF RAVENS CROFT WINES

What attracted you to the Granite Belt?

I came to this region 12 years ago. I had tasted the wines, seen the potential and land was cheap and the opportunity was there to start my own place.

What's unique about this growing region?

The area is one of the highest grape growing regions in Australia. It has really cool nights, which is great for natural acidity. Granite belt wines can hold their own against any other Australian wines.

Any favourite wines from Queensland?

My favourite wine would have to be my 2002 Reserve Cabernet Sauvignon as it was my first trophy winner and gold medal at a national show. Other Granite Belt wines to look out for are wines from Pyramids Road winery – especially its Mourvèdre – and Boireann Wines.

What does the future hold for Granite Belt wineries?

As we have really only been recognised in the last 10 years I see a great future for GB wines.

What do you like to do in the area during your time off?

Time off – yeah right! I do a bit of bushwalking in Girraween National Park, but not enough!

Any tips for travellers coming here?

Try to go to as many of the smaller wineries as possible as they are mostly very individual wines. Use a car as the tour companies usually only visit the bigger ones.

dah with barbecue and high-end fittings (including a spa tub with views).

Murray Gardens MOTEL, CABINS **$$**
(☎4681 4121; www.murraygardens.com.au; 10 Pancor Rd; motel $80-120, cottages $120-240; ❄📶) This good-value option is set on 20 acres of natural bushland on the outskirts of town. You can choose between a motel room or a fully self-contained cottage with a fireplace or gas heating. Except for the bird life, it's very quiet.

Briar Rose Cottages INN **$$**
(☎4683 6334; www.briarrosecottages.com.au; 66 Wallangarra Rd; d Sun-Thu $95, Fri & Sat $110) These cute cottages are small in size but big on romance. Both the two-bedroom front cottage and the one-bedroom back cottage have log fires, feather doonas and stacks of charm.

Country Style CABINS, CAMPGROUND **$**
(☎4683 4358; www.countrystyleaccommodation.com.au; 27156 New England Hwy; cabin/camping/caravan $90/20/25; @) It's nothing fancy, but the price is right for this nicely landscaped option amid 12 acres of bushland north of Ballandean. Cabins are basic motel-style, with small kitchens and wood-burning fires. And there are some nicely set unpowered campsites overlooking the Severn River. It's located on the highway to Ballandean, 10km south of Stanthorpe.

Vineyard Cottages & Café CABINS **$$**
(☎4684 1270; www.vineyardcottages.com.au; 28126 New England Hwy; cottage $195-245, 2-bedroom cottage $320-375) On the northern outskirts of Ballandean, you'll find seven attractive, heritage-style brick cottages with spas and private verandahs overlooking several acres of English-style gardens. There is also a good restaurant (open for dinner Wednesday to Sunday) that has a fine reputation for its fresh, seasonal menu.

Eating

Shiraz MODERN AUSTRALIAN **$$**
(☎4684 1000; 28200 New England Hwy, Ballandean; mains $33-35; ⏲lunch & dinner Wed-Sun) Most foodie-loving locals rank Shiraz as the area's best restaurant, with a small warmly lit dining room and a tiny menu with exquisitely turned out fare – Black Angus rib fillet, rack of lamb, mouth-watering scallops and tender grilled barramundi. Small but

WORTH A TRIP

GIRRAWEEN NATIONAL PARK

A short drive east of Ballandean, Girraween National Park is home to towering granite boulders, pristine forests and brilliant blooms of springtime wildflowers – all of which make a marvellous setting for a walk. Wildlife is abundant and there are 17km of trails to take you to the top of some of the surreal granite outcrops. The shortest path is a 3km walk and scramble up the 1080m Pyramids, while the granddaddy of Girraween walks is the 10.4km trek to the top of Mt Norman (1267m).

Ballandean and Stanthorpe are an easy drive, but there are some excellent places to stay in the area.

Girraween Environmental Lodge (☎4684 5138; www.girraweenlodge.com.au; Pyramids Rd, Ballandean; cabin $260) is an ecofriendly bushland retreat set on 400 acres adjacent to the national park. The self-contained timber cabins, made largely of recycled timber, are ultracomfy and have wood heaters and private decks with barbecues. There's also an outdoor spa and plunge pool. There's no restaurant at the lodge but you can buy a range of gourmet frozen meals, barbecue packs and breakfast baskets.

Wisteria Cottage (☎4684 5121; www.wisteriacottage.com.au; 2117 Pyramids Rd; cottages incl breakfast $180) has three beautiful wooden chalet-style cottages in a large paddock with grazing cattle. The cabins have wide verandahs, cosy fireplaces and sleep up to six people. There's also a fine chocolate shop onsite.

Girraween Country Inn (☎4683 7109; www.girraweencountryinn.com.au; Eukey Rd; d incl breakfast from $115) is a two-storey, chalet-style guesthouse set on 40 acres of bushland on the northern edge of the park. It oozes old-world charm with a warm and welcoming restaurant downstairs, and eight guestrooms upstairs. To get here, turn off the New England Hwy at Ballandean and follow Eukey Rd for 9km.

There are also two good camping grounds in the park, which teem with wildlife and have drinking water, barbecues and hot showers.

The **visitors centre** has information on the park and walking tracks. Camping permits can be obtained at the self-registration stands in the park. Although winter nights here can be cold, it's hot work climbing the boulders, so take plenty of water.

To reach the park, head 8km south of Ballandean, turn left on Pyramids Rd, and continue another 7km to the park entrance.

well-chosen wine list. It's on the highway just north of Ballandean, opposite the dinosaur statue.

Patty's on McGregor MODERN AUSTRALIAN **$$**
(☎4681 3463; 2 McGregor Tce; mains $28-36; ⏲dinner Thu-Sat) A long-running Stanthorpe favourite, Patty's serves a changing selection of beautifully prepared dishes with Eastern accents – lamb curry, Tassie salmon with grilled vegetables, grilled prawns, and always one vegetarian dish of the day. Black-and-white tile floors, candlelit tables and artwork on the walls, sets the scene inside the cosy dining room.

Queensland College of Wine Tourism MODERN AUSTRALIAN **$$**
(☎4685 5050; cnr New England Hwy & Caves Rd; mains $15-34; ⏲10am-3pm Tue-Sun) The chic Cellar Door Bistro features the delectable handiwork of student chefs at the college. The multicourse tasting menu ($38) is great value and features flavourful dishes using locally sourced ingredients when possible. Each course comes with one of the college's award-winning Bianca Ridge wines, which are produced in-house. It's an elegant and welcoming setting, with a flickering fire and floor-to-ceiling windows overlooking the vineyard.

Barrel Room MODERN AUSTRALIAN **$$**
(☎4684 1326; Ballandean Estate Wines, Sundown Rd, Ballandean; mains $18-29; ⏲10am-4pm Wed-Mon, 6-8pm Fri & Sat) This cosy restaurant, framed by 140-year-old floor-to-ceiling wine barrels, makes a fine setting for a decadent meal and a bottle or two of winery's excellent vintages. Confit duck with gorgonzola polenta, tiger prawn risotto and pan-fried Rannoch farm quail are a few recent hits from the changing seasonal menu.

Anna's Restaurant ITALIAN **$$**
(☎4681 1265; cnr Wallangarra Rd & O'Mara Tce; mains $19-33; ⏲dinner Tue-Sat) A family-run,

Italian BYO restaurant set in a pretty Queenslander, Anna's is famous locally for its weekend buffets ($30 to $35), where you can gorge on antipasto platters, hearty pasta and a vast array of veal, poultry and seafood dishes. Midweek, the fireplace and candle-lit tables make for more intimate dining.

L'Aquila PIZZA, CAFE **$$**
(☎4681 0356; 130 High St; pizzas $11-20; ⏲9am-5pm Sun-Thu, to 9pm Fri & Sat) On Stanthorpe's main street, easy-going L'Aquila is a good choice for smooth coffees, filling breakfasts, sandwiches, wraps, salads, burgers and light fare for lunch, or decent pizzas for dinner on weekends (with takeaway Tuesday to Sunday).

Information

Maryland St is the main thoroughfare in town. Most of the wineries are located south of Stanthorpe around Ballandean. You can get a winery-trail map from the **Stanthorpe visitors centre** (www.granitebeltwinecountry.com.au; Leslie Pde; ⏲9am-5pm) just south of the creek. For alternative wine-tasting, pick up a map of the **Strange Bird Wine Trail**, listing 20 or so wineries growing unusual varieties (Tempranillo, Sylvaner, Viognier, Gewurtzraminer, Malbec etc). There's also a **Nude Food** guide, which lists produce and gourmet sellers and restaurant-wineries.

Getting There & Around

Greyhound Australia (☎1300 473 946; www.greyhound.com.au) and **Crisps Coaches** (☎4661 8333; www.crisps.com.au) stop at the Shell garage on the corner of Folkestone and Maryland Sts. There are buses to Warwick (45 minutes), Toowoomba (2¼ hours), Brisbane (3½ hours) and Tenterfield in NSW (1½ hours), where you can pick up the Kirklands bus to Byron Bay. Brisbane to Stanthorpe costs $60 (3½ hours).

TOOWOOMBA

POP 129,000

Perched on the edge of the Great Dividing Range, 700m above sea level, Toowoomba is a large and charming country town, with wide tree-lined streets, stately homes and friendly down-to-earth locals. The air is distinctly crisper on the range, and in spring the town's numerous gardens blaze with colour. Not only is the 'Garden City' Queensland's largest and oldest inland city, it is also the birthplace of that archetypal Aussie cake, the lamington.

Sights & Activities

Toowoomba's fabulous public parks and gardens have rightly earned it the moniker 'the Garden City'. The **Ju Raku En Japanese Garden** (West St; ⏲7am-dusk) is a tranquil and beautiful spot several kilometres south of the centre at the University of Southern Queensland. Designed by a Japanese professor in Kyoto, the 5-hectare garden has a peaceful lake, picturesque bridges and Zen-like strolling paths.

The pretty **botanic gardens** (cnr Lindsay & Campbell Sts) occupy the northeast corner of Queens Park. In autumn, the changing leaves blaze with colour. Test your senses at the **Laurel Bank Park** (cnr Herries & West Sts), which has a scented garden for the visually impaired.

Toowoomba's other great parks are the **Escarpment Parks** that are strung along the eastern edge of the plateau. **Picnic Point**, located on the eastern outskirts of town, is the most accessible and has outstanding views over the Lockyer Valley. There's a cafe and **restaurant** (⏲breakfast & lunch daily, dinner Fri & Sat) here as well as ample picnic grounds. All Escarpment Parks have walking trails; collect a free map at the visitors centre.

Immediately north of Queens Park, the newly expanded **Cobb & Co Museum** (27 Lindsay St; adult/child $13/7; ⏲10am-4pm) houses an impressive carriage collection with interactive displays depicting town life and outback travel in the horse-drawn age. The museum also has a blacksmith forge, photographic displays of early Toowoomba and other Queensland towns and an Aboriginal collection – shields, axe heads, boomerangs – plus animated films relating Dreaming stories.

A walk through Toowoomba's city precinct with its stately late-19th-century sandstone buildings (including the **old post office** and **courthouse**) is a pleasant way to while away an hour or so. The visitors centre publishes a series of *A Walk Through History* brochures. The ghoulishly inclined might also want to pick up a copy of *Tombstone Trails,* a self-guided tour through Toowoomba's cemetery and the gravesites of its early pioneers.

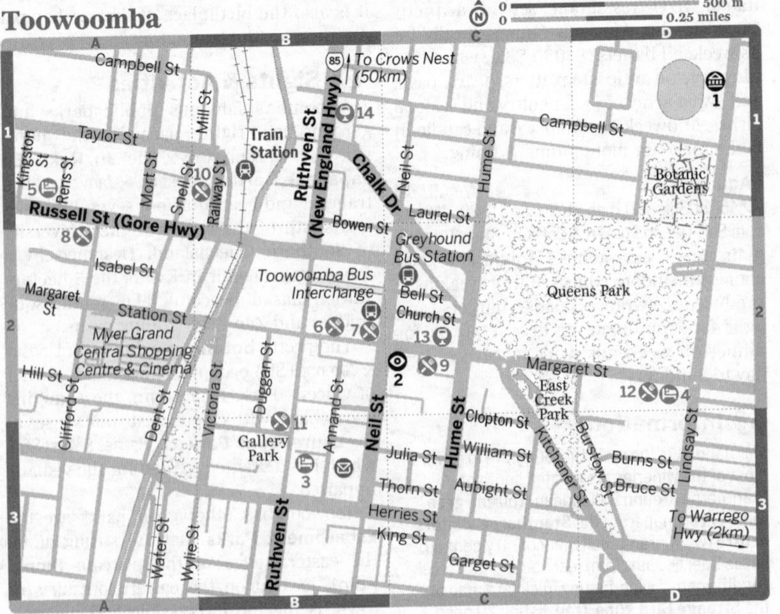

Toowoomba

Sights

1 Cobb & Co Museum D1
2 Court House C2
Old Post Office .... (see 9)

Sleeping

3 Burke & Wills Hotel B3
4 Park Motor Inn D2
5 Vacy Hall A1

Eating

6 Bon Amici B2
7 Cube Hotel B2
8 Gip's A2
9 GPO Café & Bar C2
10 Metro Café B1
11 Oxygen Café B3
12 Park House Café D2

Drinking

13 Fibber Magee C2
14 Spotted Cow B1

Festivals & Events

Toowoomba's **Carnival of Flowers** (www.carnivalofflowers.com.au) is a colourful celebration of spring held during the last week in September. It includes floral displays, a grand parade, exhibition gardens and a food and wine festival.

Sleeping

The Warrego Hwy (which turns into James St) is sprinkled with serviceable motels, which you'll pass driving in from Brisbane.

TOP CHOICE **Vacy Hall** GUESTHOUSE $$
(☎4639 2055; www.vacyhall.com.au; 135 Russell St; d $98-225; wi-fi) Just uphill from the town centre, this magnificent 1880s mansion offers 12 heritage-style rooms with loads of romantic old-world charm. A wide verandah wraps around the house, all rooms have private bathrooms and some even have their own fireplaces. Free wi-fi.

Burke & Wills Hotel HOTEL $$
(☎4632 2433; www.burkeandwillshotel.com.au; 554 Ruthven St; d $140-220; air-con, wi-fi) Nicely located in the centre of town, this is a six-storey hotel with comfortably furnished standard rooms as well as a few luxury spa suites. The hotel has two bars, two restaurants, 24-hour reception and gaming facilities.

Park Motor Inn MOTEL $$
(☎4632 1011; www.parktoowoomba.com.au; 88 Margaret St; s/d $96/108; air-con) This comfortably furnished motel has a handy location opposite leafy Queens Park. The rooms have all

the usual features and the bathrooms have full-length mirrors. It's close to a couple of popular cafes.

Toowoomba Motor Village Tourist Park CAMPGROUND & CABINS $
(☎4635 8186; www.toowoombamotorvillage.com.au; 821 Ruthven St; campsites $20-31, cabins & units $55-100) This excellent modern park is 2.5km south of the centre, but is very well equipped and has terrific views.

Eating

The best assortment of restaurants is along Margaret St, between Ruthven and Hume.

Park House Café MODERN AUSTRALIAN $$
(☎4638 2211; 92 Margaret St; mains $19-34; ⊙breakfast & lunch daily, dinner Wed-Sat) Facing Queens Park, this chic cottage cafe has a lovely verandah and seating on the front patio for pleasant alfresco dining. Gourmet sandwiches, hearty salads (like seared lamb with fetta and roasted pumpkin), pastas, and grilled meats, seafood and daily specials are the big draw. Generous pours of wines by the glass.

GPO Café & Bar MODERN AUSTRALIAN $$
(☎4659 9240; 140 Margaret St; mains $30-40; ⊙breakfast & lunch Mon-Sat, dinner Wed-Sat) Set in a heritage building with a relaxing verandah and an intimate dining room, GPO serves flavourful dishes like herb-crusted Atlantic salmon, beautifully grilled steaks, and seafood dishes with Asian touches.

Cube Hotel MODERN AUSTRALIAN $$
(cnr Margaret & Neil Sts; mains $22-34; ⊙lunch & dinner) On the main floor of this multilevel eating and drinking space, the Stone Grill serves delectably fresh lamb, scallops, eye filet or marinated crocodile plus vegetables that you grill up tableside atop the 400°C stone grill. On weekend nights the Cube hosts a dance club; there are several other bars and a wide upstairs verandah.

Gip's MODERN AUSTRALIAN $$$
(☎4638 3588; 120 Russell St; mains $30-38; ⊙lunch daily, breakfast Mon-Fri, dinner Mon-Sat) Set in the billiard room of this historic Clifford House, Gip's is an elegant restaurant serving locally sourced delicacies – Moreton Bay bugs, Junee farm lamb rump, braised Bangalow pork belly. You can dine amid jacaranda trees in the garden courtyard on warm days.

FREAK OF NATURE: TOOWOOMBA'S INLAND TSUNAMI

On 10 January 2011 a wall of water raged through Toowoomba's town centre in an unprecedented weather event that has been likened to an inland tsunami. The wild weather that inundated Queensland in December 2010 and January 2011 caused floods throughout the state and in the capital, Brisbane, and heralded a flash flood of epic proportions that took Toowoomba completely by surprise. Cars were tossed around like corks, people clung to trees and signposts, and houses were washed off their stumps. The torrential wall of water swept through the Lockyer Valley devastating the small towns of Grantham and Murphys Creek. Despite its ferocity the inland tsunami left little lasting damage in Toowoomba, but it is a day the Garden City will never forget.

Bon Amici CAFE, LIVE MUSIC $
(191 Margaret St; light meals $6-12; ⊙8am-late) For a stiff drink or a good coffee (with delectable cakes) settle down at this red-walled, cruisy cafe. There's often live music in the evenings.

Oxygen Café CAFE $
(cnr Ruthven & Little Sts; mains $9-16; ⊙7.30am-2.30pm Tue-Sun; 🖉) This colourful breezy cafe serves organic fare: filling breakfasts (scrambled eggs and ocean trout roe), juices and smoothies, burgers (vegetarian, grilled yellow fin tuna) and sandwiches. Good tea selection.

Metro Café CAFE $
(☎4632 0090; 15 Railway St; mains $10-18; ⊙breakfast & lunch) Opposite the train station, this trendy cafe serves gourmet sandwiches and salads, vegetarian fare (like lentil burgers), all-day breakfasts and good coffee. Outdoor seating in front.

Drinking

Spotted Cow BAR
(cnr Ruthven & Campbell Sts) A lively spot for a drink or a bite, the Spotted Cow is a Toowoomba favourite for its extensive drinks menu (including 70 different beers) and tasty bistro fare (try the 1kg pot of mussels).

Fibber Magee BAR

(153 Margaret St) If you fancy a beer without the fuss, this agreeable, Irish-themed pub is popular and central, and there's a garden out the back.

Information

Downtown Toowoomba centres around Ruthven St (part of the north–south New England Hwy) and Margaret St.

Toowoomba visitors centre (86 James St) Located southeast of the centre, at the junction with Kitchener St. Very helpful.

Getting There & Away

Toowoomba is 126km west of Brisbane on the Warrego Hwy.

Bus

Greyhound Australia (1300 473 946; www.greyhound.com.au; 28-30 Neil St; one-way $20-31) and **Toowoomba Transit Coaches** (4699 4700; www.ttcoaches.com.au; Neil St; one-way from $25) provide daily services between Brisbane and Toowoomba.

AROUND TOOWOOMBA

Highfields & Crows Nest

North of Toowoomba the New England Hwy travels the ridges of the Great Dividing Range, passing through a series of small villages on the road to Crows Nest. One of these villages, Highfields (12km from Toowoomba), is little more than a satellite cluster of houses and a small shopping centre but it's worth stopping at the charming **Chocolate Cottage and Café** (4630 8729; 10475 New England Hwy; 8.30am-5pm Wed-Mon) for a light lunch, wicked handmade chocolates and great views over the escarpment.

Another 38km north, the pretty little township of Crows Nest hosts the **World Worm Races** (www.crowsnestfestival.com.au) every October. The **Crows Nest Falls National Park** is far more impressive, with a gushing waterfall in an area of eucalypt forest punctuated by craggy granite outcrops. There are some scenic walking tracks (ranging from 2km to 4.5km) and refreshing swimming holes, and you can camp. The park is about 6km east of town. For accommodation there's the **Crows Nest Caravan Park** (4698 1269; www.crowsnestcaravanpark.com.au; New England Hwy; campsites $22, cabins $60-105) and **Crows Nest Motel** (4698 1399; www.crowsnestmotel.com.au; 7547 New England Hwy; d/apt $98/124).

Jondaryan Woolshed Complex

Fresh from a $2 million refurbishment, the huge **Jondaryan Woolshed Complex** (4692 2229; www.jondaryanwoolshed.com; 264 Evanslea Rd; adult/child $13/8; 10am-4pm) showcases the rich pastoral traditions of Queensland. Built in 1859, it's the state's oldest operating woolshed and offers a fascinating glimpse back in time. It's located 45km northwest of Toowoomba on the Warrego Hwy.

The woolshed played a pivotal role in the history of the Australian Labor Party as it was here in 1890 that the first of the legendary shearers' strikes began. Today the woolshed is the centrepiece of a large tourist complex with an interesting collection of rustic old buildings, antique farm and industrial machinery (including a mighty, steam-driven 'roadburner', which applied the first tarmac to many of Australia's roads) and weekend blacksmithing and shearing demonstrations.

The best time to arrive is at 10.30am or 1.30pm, when the shed hosts demonstrations – shearing in the woolshed, wagon rides, blacksmithing, sheepdogs working, wool spinning and the like.

There are several rustic accommodation choices, all organised through the Woolshed reception. The **shearers quarters** (dm $17, linen extra $15) are basic rooms around an open-sided communal cooking and dining shelter with sawdust-covered floors. They score top marks for atmosphere, and there are a few comforts such as hot showers and toilets. There are also self-contained **cabins** ($95-150) with a kitchenette and en suite or you can **camp** (up to 4 people $11-14) or stay in a **safari tent** ($29-36). You need to bring your own swag or bedroll if you camp.

Jondaryan hosts a number of annual events, including a nine-day **Australian Heritage Festival** in late August and early September, a **New Year's Eve bush-dance**, an **Australia Day** celebration, a **Working Draught Horse Expo** in June and a **Big Sunday** country brunch every third Sunday of the month.

Gold Coast

Includes »

Southport & Main Beach 117
South Stradbroke Island 121
Surfers Paradise 122
Broadbeach 129
Burleigh Heads & Currumbin 130
Coolangatta 133
Gold Coast Hinterland....... .. 136
Tamborine Mountain........... 137
Springbrook National Park 138
Lamington National Park 140

Why Go?

Boasting 35 beaches and 300 sunny days a year, the Gold Coast promises its four million annual visitors a taste of the quintessential Aussie lifestyle of sun, surf and fun. Behind a long ribbon of beach stretching from South Stradbroke Island to the New South Wales border is a shimmering strip of high-rises, theme parks and nonstop action. The undisputed capital is Surfers Paradise where the fun sucks you into a relentless spin and spits you back out exhausted. But the brash commercialism and relentless pace won't appeal to everyone. The hype diminishes outside the epicentre, with Broadbeach's beach-chic and Burleigh Heads' seaside charm mellowing into Coolangatta's laid-back surfer ethos.

The beaches are spectacular, with excellent surfing at Burleigh Heads, Currumbin, Kirra and Duranbah. South Stradbroke Island also has some great waves, and a long uncrowded beach. And in the lush, subtropical hinterland, Lamington and Springbrook National Parks have rainforest walks, waterfalls and cosy mountain retreats.

Best Places to Eat

» Moo Moo (p129)
» Oskars (p132)
» Elephant Rock Café (p133)

Best Places to Stay

» Komune (p134)
» Vibe Hotel (p125)
» Palazzo Versace (p120)
» Mouses House (p139)
» Wave (p129)

When to Go

Surfers Paradise

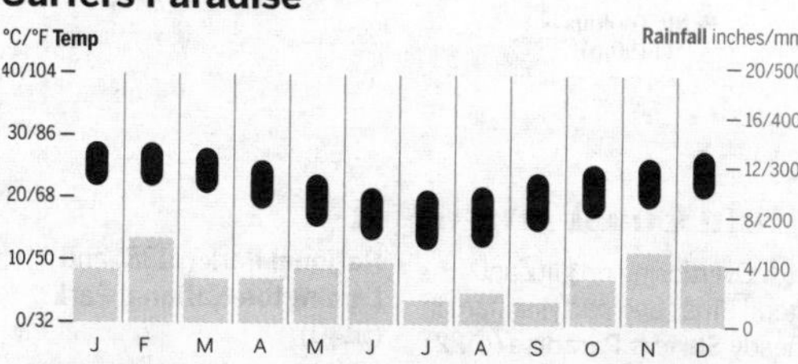

January Music buffs will favour the Big Day Out in January.

October Watch and drool as fit bods compete in the Coolangatta Gold Surf Life Saving event.

Mid-November School-leavers head to Surfers Paradise for a month-long party.

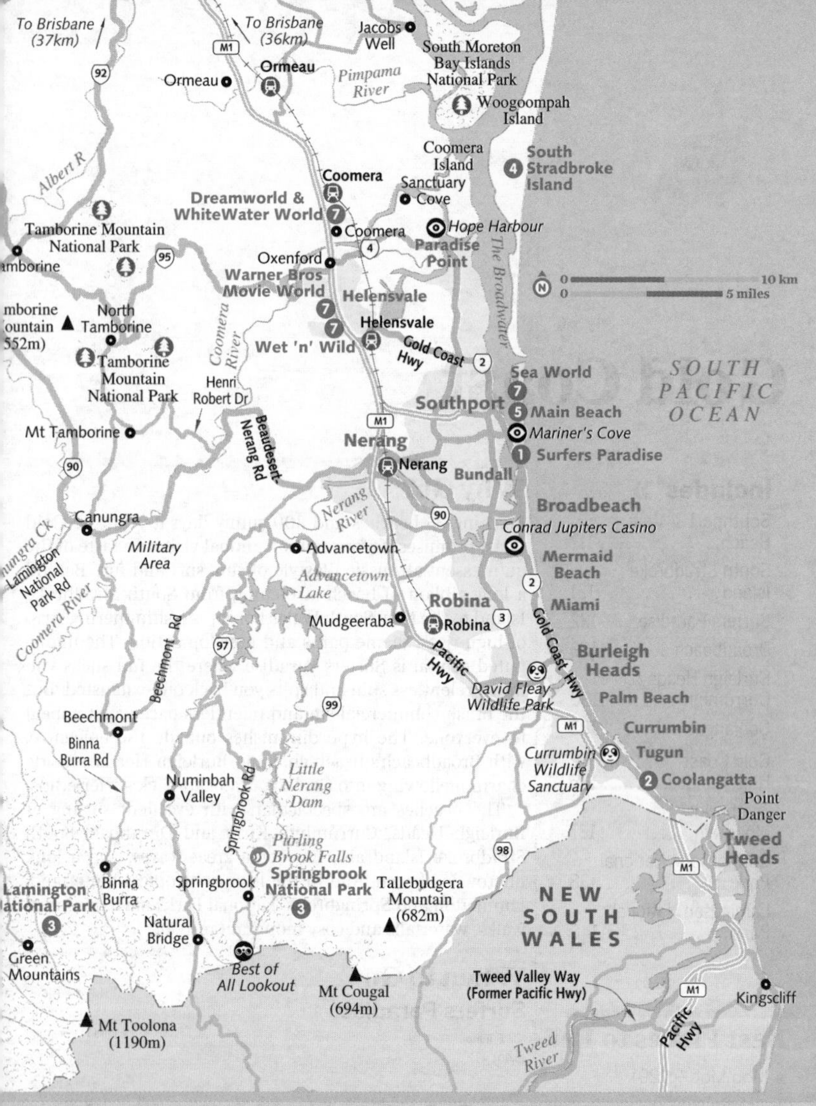

Gold Coast Highlights

1. Overdosing on glitz and good times and partying hard in heady **Surfers Paradise** (p122)
2. Surfing the breaks and soaking up the famous Gold Coast sunshine at **Coolangatta** (p133)
3. Bushwalking through deep gorges and towering rainforests in **Springbrook National Park** (p138) and **Lamington National Park** (p140)
4. Getting away from the crowds on **South Stradbroke Island's** (p121) looong stretch of golden beach
5. Luxuriating in the opulent **Palazzo Versace** (p120) at Main Beach
6. Blissing out with a mind-body-soul makeover in a hinterland **spa retreat** (p139)
7. Flying on roller coasters, losing yourself in Hollywood and getting wet and wild at the Gold Coast **theme parks** (p123)

Dangers & Annoyances

Car theft is a major problem all the way along the Gold Coast; park in well-lit areas and don't leave valuables in your vehicle.

The Gold Coast turns into party central for thousands of school leavers between mid-November and mid-December during 'schoolies week'. Although it's generally a lot of fun for those celebrating, it can be hell for everyone else.

Getting There & Away

AIR

The Gold Coast international airport at Coolangatta is 25km south of Surfers Paradise. **Qantas** (13 13 13; www.qantas.com), **Jetstar** (13 15 38; www.jetstar.com.au) and **Virgin Blue** (13 67 89; www.virginblue.com) fly from Sydney and Melbourne. **Tiger Airways** (03 9335 3033; www.tigerairways.com) has flights from Melbourne.

BUS

Long-distance buses stop at the bus transit centres in Southport, Surfers Paradise and Coolangatta. **Greyhound Australia** (1300 473 946; www.greyhound.com.au) has frequent services to/from Brisbane ($20, 1½ hours), Byron Bay ($30, 2½ hours) and Sydney ($150, 15 hours). **Premier Motor Service** (13 34 10; www.premierms.com.au) serves the same routes.

Coachtrans (1300 664 700, 3358 9700; www.coachtrans.com.au) operates a direct service from Brisbane airport (one way $43.50) to anywhere on the Gold Coast and also has services from Brisbane City to Surfers ($32, 1½ hours) or to the theme parks. Transfers from the Gold Coast to Byron Bay are $60 one way and take 2½ hours.

Con-x-Ion (5556 9888; www.con-x-ion.com) operates a similar service from Brisbane airport (one way $44) to the Gold Coast or to theme parks.

TRAIN

Citytrain services link Brisbane to Helensvale ($12.40, one hour), Nerang ($12.90, one hour) and Robina stations ($15, 1 hour 20 minutes) roughly every half-hour. **Surfside Buslines** (13 12 30; www.translink.com.au) runs regular shuttles from the train stations down to Surfers ($4 to $5) and beyond, and to the theme parks.

Getting Around

TO/FROM THE AIRPORT

Coachtrans (3358 9700; www.coachtrans.com.au) operates a shuttle between Tweed Heads and Brisbane, with stops along the way, including Dreamworld, Movie World and Wet'n'Wild. **Gold Coast Tourist Shuttle** (1300 655 655, 5574 5111; www.gcshuttle.com.au; adult/child/family $18/9/45) meets every flight into Coolangatta Airport and operates door-to-door transfers to most Gold Coast accommodation. It also offers a Freedom Pass, which includes return transfers to your accommodation plus unlimited theme-park transfers and unlimited Surfside Buslines travel from $67/34/168 per adult/child/family for three days.

BUS

Surfside Buslines (13 12 30; www.translink.com.au) runs a frequent service up and down the Gold Coast Hwy from Tweed Heads, stopping at Dreamworld, Sanctuary Cove and Paradise Point.

TAXI

Ring 13 10 08 for taxi services on the Gold Coast.

Southport & Main Beach

POP 24,100

Sheltered from the ocean by a long sandbar (known as the Spit) and the Broadwater estuary, Southport is a relatively quiet residential enclave 4km north of Surfers Paradise. There's not much to do here and it's a long way from the beach but it can be a good base if you want to escape the nonstop frenzy of Surfers.

Main Beach, just south of Southport, marks the gateway to the Spit and the high-rise tourist developments. The Spit runs 3km north, dividing the Broadwater from the South Pacific Ocean. The ocean side of the Spit is relatively untouched, backed by a long strip of natural bushland, and has excellent beaches and surf. At the southern end of the Spit is the Sea World theme park, while the upmarket shopping complex of Marina Mirage is near Mariner's Cove and the marina, the departure point for cruises and other water-based activities.

Activities

Mariner's Cove is the place to book all water activities. The easiest way to sift through the plethora of operators is to book at the **Mariner's Cove Tourism Information & Booking Centre** (5571 1711; Mariner's Cove; 8.30am-4.30pm). Some recommended activities include the following:

Cruising & Fishing

Tall Ship SAILING

(5532 2444; www.tallship.com.au; Mariner's Cove Marina; full-day cruises adult/child from $129/79) Cruises to South Stradbroke Island on yachts dressed up to look like tall ships. Half-day cruises also available. Combine parasailing with a tall ship experience for $50. Also has whale-watching cruises.

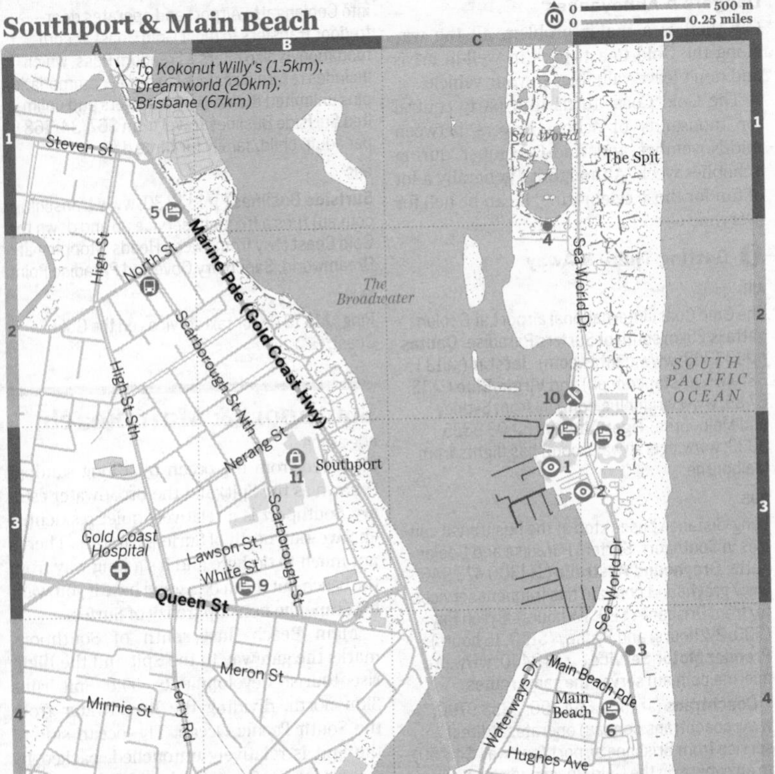

Mirage Boat Hire BOATING
(☎5591 2553; www.mirageboathire.com.au; Mariner's Cove Marina) Skipper your own half-cabin cruiser (from $100 for two hours), speedboat (from $150 per hour) or barbecue pontoon (half-day $275).

Gone Fishing FISHING
(☎5510 9611; www.gonefishing.net.au; 4/5hr tours $95/120, full-day tours $185)

Helicopter Flights

Gold Coast Helitours HELICOPTER FLIGHTS
(☎5591 8457; www.goldcoasthelitours.com.au; Mariner's Cove Marina) Flights range from five minutes (adult/child $54/39), 30 minutes ($249/189) and 45 minutes ($375/270). This is the only company to offer tandem skydiving out of a helicopter at 10,000ft.

Sea World Helicopters HELICOPTER FLIGHTS
(☎5588 2224; Sea World Dr, Main Beach) Offers five-minute (adult/child $59/49) to 30-minute ($285/225) flights.

Dreamworld Helicopters HELICOPTER FLIGHTS
(☎5529 4744; www.dreamworld.com.au; Pacific Hwy, Coomera)

Surfing & Kayaking

Balunjali KAYAKING
(☎5533 8527; www.balunjali.com.au; half-day tour adult/child $89/77) Includes an interpretative Aboriginal cultural experience, kayaking to South Stradbroke Island, snorkelling and a traditional billy tea.

Australian Kayaking Adventures KAYAKING
(☎0412 940 135; www.australiankayakingadventures.com.au; half-day tours to South Stradbroke Island $85) Includes breakfast on the beach.

Southport & Main Beach

Sights

1 Marina Mirage C3
2 Mariner's Cove D3

Activities, Courses & Tours

3 1st Wave Surfing D4
Broadwater Canal Cruises .... (see 2)
GC Hovercraft Tours & Watersports .... (see 2)
Gold Coast Helitours .... (see 2)
Jet Ski Safaris .... (see 2)
Mirage Boat Hire .... (see 2)
Paradise Jet Boating .... (see 2)
Queensland Scuba Diving Company .... (see 2)
4 Sea World C2
Sea World Helicopters .... (see 4)
Sea World Whale Watch .... (see 4)
Seabreeze Sports .... (see 2)
Spirit of Gold Coast .... (see 2)
Tall Ship .... (see 2)

Sleeping

5 Harbour Side Resort A1
6 Main Beach Tourist Park D4
7 Palazzo Versace C3
8 Sheraton Mirage Resort & Spa D3
Surfers Paradise YHA at Main Beach .... (see 2)
9 Trekkers B3

Eating

Fisho's .... (see 2)
Max Brenner Chocolate Bar .... (see 1)
10 Peter's Fish Market C2
Saks .... (see 1)
Sunset Bar & Grill .... (see 1)

Drinking

Fisherman's Wharf Tavern .... (see 2)

Shopping

11 Australia Fair Shopping Centre B3

Information

Mariner's Cove Tourism Information & Booking Centre .... (see 2)
Post Office .... (see 11)

1st Wave Surfing SURFING
(☎0412 729 747; www.firstwavesurfing.com.au; Main Beach Pavilion; 2hr lessons $50) Next to Main Beach Surf Life Saving Club (SLSC). Also rents out boards.

Water Sports

Jet Ski Safaris JET SKIING
(☎5526 3111; www.jetskisafaris.com.au) Tours from 40 minutes ($70) to 1½ hours ($100) and 2½ hours ($160) around the region's islands and mangroves. Overnight camping safaris to South Stradbroke Island are $325. Prices given are per person.

GC Hovercraft Tours & Watersports HOVERCRAFTING
(☎1300 559 931; www.goldcoasthovercraft.com; 30min ride adult/child/family $55/40/150, 45min ride $60/45/170)

Paradise Jet Boating JETBOATING
(☎1300 538 2621, 5526 3190; Mariner's Cove Marina; 45min rides $63) Serious speed, spins and beach-blasting on a jetboat.

Seabreeze Sports WATER SPORTS
(☎5527 1099; www.seabreezesports.com.au; jet ski, jetboat & parasailing packages $115, Broadwater cruise adult/child $45/25)

Shane's Watersports World WATER SPORTS
(☎5591 5225; www.shaneswatersports.com.au) Jet-ski hire from $75 per half-hour. Range of adventure watersports packages.

Queensland Scuba Diving Company DIVING
(☎5526 7722; www.qldscubadive.com.au; Mariner's Cove Marina; dives from $99)

Surfer's Paradise Divers DIVING
(☎5591 7117; Mariners Cove; intro dive $120) English and Japanese instructors.

Whale Watching

Whale watching is available June to November.

Spirit of Gold Coast WHALE WATCHING
(☎5572 7755; www.goldcoastwhalewatching.com; adult/child $89/59)

Australian Whale Watching WHALE WATCHING
(☎1300 422 784; www.australianwhalewatching.com.au; 3hr cruises adult/child $95/60)

Sea World Whale Watch WHALE WATCHING
(☎5588 2224; adult/child $99/77, including entry to Sea World $110/88)

GOLD COAST IN...

Two Days

On day one take your pick of being dunked, rolled or spun a thousand different ways at one of the **Gold Coast theme parks**. After freshening up, and dinner at one of the al fresco restaurants in Circle on Cavill, it's time to hit the party-scene big time. Fortunately, nearly all of Surfers' **nightclubs** are within stumbling distance of each other on Orchid Ave.

If you're still up for action the next day, Mariner's Cove at **Main Beach** has a plethora of water sports but if you want to chill instead, sit back on the **Aquaduck** for a kitschy (but fun) land and water-based tour of Surfers. Or simply take in the sky-high view from the **QDeck**. Have lunch at **Elephant Rock Café** overlooking Currumbin Beach, then spend the afternoon getting friendly with Australia's native critters at **Currumbin Wildlife Sanctuary**. Tonight, try your luck at **Jupiters Casino** or take in a show at the **theatre**.

Four Days

On day three spend the morning surfing the coast's legendary waves at **Burleigh** or **Coolangatta**. Lunch at **Oskars** overlooking the beach before packing an overnight bag and taking a leisurely drive into the hinterland. For a romantic stay in a fairytale cottage head to **Mouses House** in Springbrook National Park. Serious hikers may prefer the walks in **Lamington National Park**.

On day four take the meandering drive to **Tamborine Mountain** to browse the arts and crafts cottage set. A Devonshire tea is mandatory but stock up on home-made chocolates, fudges and jams before returning to the beach for a late afternoon swim.

Tours

Broadwater Canal Cruises RIVER CRUISES
(☎0410 403 020; adult/child $35/18) Cruises to Tiki Village Wharf in Surfers Paradise. Depart from Mariner's Cove at 10.30am and 2pm. The two-hour tour includes a buffet-style Devonshire tea.

Wyndham Cruises RIVER CRUISES
(☎5539 9299; www.wyndhamcruises.com.au; adult/child/family $45/25/115) Two-hour cruise up to and around the Broadwater with morning or afternoon tea included.

Sleeping

Palazzo Versace RESORT $$$
(☎1800 098 000, 5509 8000; www.palazzoversace.com; Sea World Dr, Main Beach; d $480-585, ste/condos from $685/1300; ❄@≋) The Palazzo is quite simply pure extravagance, from the sumptuous rooms to the equally indulgent restaurants and bars. Everything from the pool furniture to the buttons on the staff uniforms has Donatella Versace's glamorous mark on it.

Sheraton Mirage Resort & Spa RESORT $$$
(☎1800 073 535, 5591 1488; www.starwoodhotels.com/sheraton; Sea World Dr, Main Beach; d from $215, ste $500-650; ❄@≋) If you must have direct beach access this is the only five-star resort on the coast that will do. The rooms are classy and spacious. Spa aficionados will get their fix at the Golden Door Spa & Health Club at Mirage Resort.

Harbour Side Resort MOTEL $$
(☎5591 6666; www.harboursideresort.com.au; 132 Marine Pde, Southport; studio $90, 1-/2-bedroom apt $120/160; ❄@≋) Disregard the overwhelming brick facade and busy road; within this sprawling property you'll find pastel-hued units with oodles of room. The kitchens are well equipped and the complex also has a laundry and tennis courts.

Surfers Paradise YHA at Main Beach HOSTEL $
(☎5571 1776; www.yha.com.au/hostels; 70 Sea World Dr, Main Beach; dm/d & tw $25/$69.50; @) In a great position overlooking the marina, here you only have to drop over the balcony to access the plethora of water sports, cruises and tours on offer. There's a free shuttle bus, barbecue nights every Friday, and the hostel is within staggering distance of the Fisherman's Wharf Tavern.

Trekkers HOSTEL $
(☎1800 100 004, 5591 5616; www.trekkersbackpackers.com.au; 22 White St, Southport; dm/d & tw

$27/70; @⊠) You could bottle the friendly vibes of this beautiful Queenslander and make a mint. The building is looking a bit tired but the communal areas are homey and the garden is a mini-oasis.

Main Beach Tourist Park CARAVAN PARK $$
(☎5667 2720; www.gctp.com.au/main; Main Beach Pde, Main Beach; unpowered/powered sites from $33/36, cabins from $140; ❄⊠) Just across the road from the beach, this caravan park is a favourite with families. It's a tight fit between sites but the facilities are good. Rates are for two people.

Eating

Marina Mirage has a good choice of cosy cafes and swish restaurants. The cheapest place to eat is the food court in the Australia Fair Shopping Centre. Opposite the shopping centre, Southport Central on Scarborough St has a cluster of cool cafes.

Saks ITALIAN $$$
(☎5591 2755; Marina Mirage, 74 Sea World Dr, Main Beach; mains $30-50; ⊙lunch & dinner) Head straight for the deck where tall glass windows offer uninterrupted views of the marina. The brief but sophisticated menu boasts seafood, steak and good Italian fare.

Max Brenner Chocolate Bar CAFE $
(☎5591 1588; Marina Mirage, Main Beach; snacks $5-15; ⊙10am-10pm Mon-Fri, 9am-midnight Sat & Sun) Slaves of the 'dark master' will revel in this decadent cafe given over to all things chocolate. Naughty cakes and desserts are best accompanied with 'choctails' – mocktails drowned in chocolate.

Sunset Bar & Grill MODERN AUSTRALIAN $$
(☎5528 2622; Marina Mirage, Main Beach; dishes $8-25; ⊙7am-6pm) If your wallet has taken a beating at the exclusive boutiques in the mall, you'll be glad to find this little place right on the water. Steaks, burgers and seafood dishes are all reasonably priced.

Fisho's SEAFOOD $
(☎5571 0566; Mariner's Cove, Main Beach; dishes under $13; ⊙lunch & dinner Mon-Fri, breakfast Sat & Sun) Attached to the Fisherman's Wharf Tavern, Fisho's serves up reliable staples such as burgers, and fish and chips for $15. It transforms into a partying hot spot with live music on weekends.

Peter's Fish Market SEAFOOD $
(☎5591 7747; Sea World Dr, Main Beach; meals $10-16; ⊙9am-7.30pm) A no-nonsense fish market selling fresh and cooked seafood in all shapes and sizes at reasonable prices.

Drinking

Fisherman's Wharf Tavern PUB
(Mariner's Cove, Main Beach) The famous Sunday Sessions at this styled-up tavern have live music on the deck overlooking the Broadwater.

Kokonut Willy's BAR
(360 Marine Pde, Southport) Plastic coconut palms and castaway decor equals cocktail bar (of course!). In the Grand Hotel at the northern end of Southport, this cute bar has views over the water. The attached restaurant has a decent menu (mains $20 to $25) while the bar next door has live music most nights.

Information

Gold Coast Hospital (☎5571 8211; 108 Nerang St, Southport)

Post office (☎13 13 18; Marina Mirage; Shop 301, Australia Fair Shopping Centre, Southport; ⊙9am-5pm Mon-Wed & Fri, to 6pm Thu, to 2pm Sat, 10.30am-2pm Sun)

Getting There & Away

Coaches stop at the Southport Transit Centre on Scarborough St, between North and Railway Sts. Catch local Surfside buses from outside the Australia Fair Shopping Centre on Scarborough St.

South Stradbroke Island

This narrow, 20km-long sand island is a largely undeveloped tranquil contrast to the developed mainland sprawl of the Gold Coast tourist strip. At the northern end, the narrow channel separating it from North Stradbroke Island (p101) is popular for fishing, while at the southern end, the tip of the long sandbar known as the Spit is only 200m away. There are two resorts, a camping ground and plenty of bush, sand and sea to satisfy anglers, surfers, bushwalkers and kayakers. Cars aren't permitted on the island so you'll have to walk or cycle to get around.

Couran Cove Island Resort (☎1800 268 726, 5509 3000; www.couran.com; d from $260; ❄⊠) is an exclusive luxury resort with all guests' rooms perched on the water's edge. There are four restaurants, a day spa, a private marina and guided nature walks. Rates don't include ferry transfers (adult/child $50/25 return) from Hope Harbour at the northern end of the Gold Coast. Ferries leave at 11am, 2.30pm and 6pm and return at 9.30am, 1pm, 5pm and 7pm.

For something less extravagant, you can head to the **Couran Point Island Beach Resort** (☎5501 3555; www.couranpoint.com.au; d from $150;), which has colourful and comfortable hotel rooms, and slightly larger units with kitchenettes. All rates include use of nonmotorised facilities but do not include ferry transfers (adult/child $25/10 return). Day-trippers can access the resort facilities (adult/child/family $55/25/150, including bistro lunch). The ferry leaves Marina Mirage daily at 10am and returns at 4pm.

Surfers Paradise

POP 18,510

Sprouting out of the commercial heart of the Gold Coast is the signature high-rise settlement of Surfers Paradise. Here the pace is giddy and frenetic, a brash pleasure dome of nightclubs, shopping and relentless entertainment. Imagine Miami or Ibiza shifted down under, and you'll have some idea of what to expect. But with so much bling and glitz in your face, be prepared to part with your cash. About the only time you won't is if one of the famous 'meter maids' – pretty young things in gold-lamé bikinis – feeds your expired parking meter.

If sun-worship is your thing, head to the beach early as the density of towering high-rises shades the sand from midafternoon. Not that it matters; the beach is no longer the main attraction. If you're not here for the nearby theme parks, you're here to party! Surfers is the acknowledged party hub of the Gold Coast, happily catering to all demographics, from 40-somethings getting squiffy on martinis to Gen Ys dropping pills on the dance floor and schoolies cutting loose on the beach. The backpacker places particularly go all out to ensure that the town goes off every night of the week, but after a while the excessive party scene becomes repetitive.

If you're after a relaxing beach holiday, head further south.

Sights

Surfers' sights are usually spread across beach towels but for an eagle-eye scope, zip up to the **QDeck** (☎5582 2713; Q1 Building, Hamilton Ave; adult/child/family $19/11/49; ⌚9am-9pm Sun-Thu, to midnight Fri & Sat). From a height of 230m you have a spectacular 360-degree panorama of the Gold Coast and its hinterland. On a clear day you can see north to Brisbane and south to Byron Bay. Wander around the glass-enclosed deck and you'll learn other interesting titbits, like the Q1 is the world's 21st tallest building, the arc lights illuminating the spine can be seen 200km away, and it takes 43 seconds to reach the observation deck on the 77th floor. There's a cafe and bar so there's no need to hurry back to earth.

The kiddies will like **Infinity** (☎5538 2988; www.infinitygc.com.au; Chevron Renaissance, cnr Surfers Paradise Blvd & Elkhorn Ave; adult/child/family $24.90/16.90/69.90; ⌚10am-10pm), a walk-through maze cleverly disguised by an elaborate sound-and-light show.

The **Gold Coast Art Gallery** (☎5581 6567; www.gcac.com.au; Gold Coast Arts Centre, 135 Bundall Rd; ⌚10am-5pm Mon-Fri, 11am-5pm Sat & Sun), about 1.5km inland, displays excellent temporary exhibitions.

Activities

You won't be bored in Surfers. Apart from swimming at the beach it's action all the way.

Surfing & Kayaking

Cheyne Horan School of Surf SURFING
(☎1800 227 873, 0403 080 484; www.cheynehoran.com.au; The Esplanade; 2hr lessons $45) World Champion surfer Cheyne Horan offers excellent tuition.

Go Ride a Wave SURFING
(☎1300 132 441, 5526 7077; www.gorideawave.com.au; Cavill Ave Mall; surfing or kayaking 2hr lessons from $55; ⌚9am-5pm) Also rents out surfboards, kayaks, beach chairs and umbrellas.

Brad Holmes Surf Coaching SURFING
(☎5539 4068, 0418 757 539; www.bradholmessurfcoaching.com; 90min lessons $75) Also caters to disabled surfers.

Splash Safaris Sea Kayaking KAYAKING
(☎0407 741 748; half-day tours $85) Tour includes kayaking, snorkelling, fish-feeding, bushwalking and morning or afternoon tea.

Airborne Activities

Champagne breakfast follows a flight over the Gold Coast hinterland.

Balloon Down Under BALLOON FLIGHTS
(☎5593 8400; www.balloondownunder.com.au; 1hr flights adult/child $310/200)

GOLD COAST THEME PARKS

Test your lung capacity (or better yet, the kids') on the thrilling rides and swirling action at the five American-style theme parks just north of Surfers. Discount tickets are sold in most of the tourist offices on the Gold Coast; the 3 Park Super Pass (adult/child $177/115) covers entry to Sea World, Movie World and Wet'n'Wild. Be aware that most parks do not allow visitors to bring their own food and drink onto the premises.

Dreamworld (Map p116; ☎5588 1111; www.dreamworld.com.au; Pacific Hwy, Coomera; adult/child $72/47; ⏲10am-5pm) Skip breakfast if you plan on tackling the Big 6 Thrill Rides, which include the Claw (a giant pendulum that swings you nine storeys high at 75km/h) and the Giant Drop (a terminal-velocity machine where you free-fall from 38 storeys). It's not all rides, though – there's an interactive tiger show and an IMAX theatre. A two-day world pass (adult/child $99/69) lets you jump between Dreamworld and WhiteWater World as often as you like.

WhiteWater World (Map p116; ☎5588 1111; www.whitewaterworld.com.au; Pacific Hwy, Coomera; adult/child $45/30; ⏲10am-4pm) Next door to Dreamworld, this aquatic theme park is the place to take the kids on a hot summer day. There's the Hydrocoaster (a rollercoaster on water), and the Green Room, where you'll spin in a tube through a tunnel, then drop 15m down a green water funnel. Get caught in the Rip or splash around in the surging swells in the Cave of Waves.

Sea World (Map p118; ☎5588 2222, show times 5588 2205; www.seaworld.com.au; Sea World Dr, Main Beach; adult/child $75/50; ⏲10am-5pm) See Australia's only polar bears in this aquatic park, along with dugongs, sharks and performing seals and dolphins. There are dizzying rides, of course, but for a unique hands-on experience book an Animal Adventure with a marine-mammal trainer.

Warner Bros Movie World (Map p116; ☎5573 8485; www.movieworld.com.au; Pacific Hwy, Oxenford; adult/child $75/50; ⏲10am-5pm) 'Hollywood on the Gold Coast' boasts more movie-themed rides than movie-set action but the kids will love meeting their favourite movie legends and Loony Tunes characters.

Wet'n'Wild (Map p116; ☎5573 2255; www.wetnwild.com.au; Pacific Hwy, Oxenford; adult/child $55/35; ⏲10am-5pm Feb-Apr & Sep-Dec, to 4pm May-Aug, to 9pm 27 Dec-25 Jan) If the beach is too sedate, this colossal water-sports park offers plenty of creative ways to get wet. You can launch from a 15m-high platform in a tube and blast down a 40m tunnel, or swirl through the Black Hole, or zoom down Mammoth Falls in a big rubber ring. If all that sounds too energetic, catch a movie in a tube at the Dive'n'Movies.

Balloon Aloft BALLOON FLIGHTS
(☎5578 2244; www.balloonaloft.net; 1hr flights adult/child $310/195)

Adrenaline Action

Movie Stunt Experience STUNTS
(☎0415 999 626; www.moviestuntexperience.com; half-day $149, full-day $299, free pick-up & drop-off) Be an action hero for the day, abseiling commando-style through windows, flying on wires, jumping from buildings and being set on fire.

Jetboat Extreme JETBOATING
(☎5538 8890; www.jetboatextreme.com.au; 1hr rides adult/child $50/35) Slides and spins across the water in a turbo-charged, twin-jet-powered, custom-built jetboat.

Whale Watching

Whales in Paradise WHALE WATCHING
(☎3880 4455; www.whalesinparadise.com; adult/child $95/60; ⏲Jun-Nov) Leaves central Surfers for 3½ hours of whale-watching action.

Horse Riding

Gumnuts Horseriding HORSE RIDING
(☎5543 0191; www.gumnutsfarm.com.au; Biddaddaba Creek Rd; adult/child $110/75) Damper, billy tea, lunch and transfers to accommodation throughout the Gold Coast.

Numinbah Valley Adventure Trails HORSE RIDING
(☎5533 4137; www.numinbahtrails.com; adult/child $75/65) Three-hour horse-riding treks through beautiful rainforest and river

Surfers Paradise

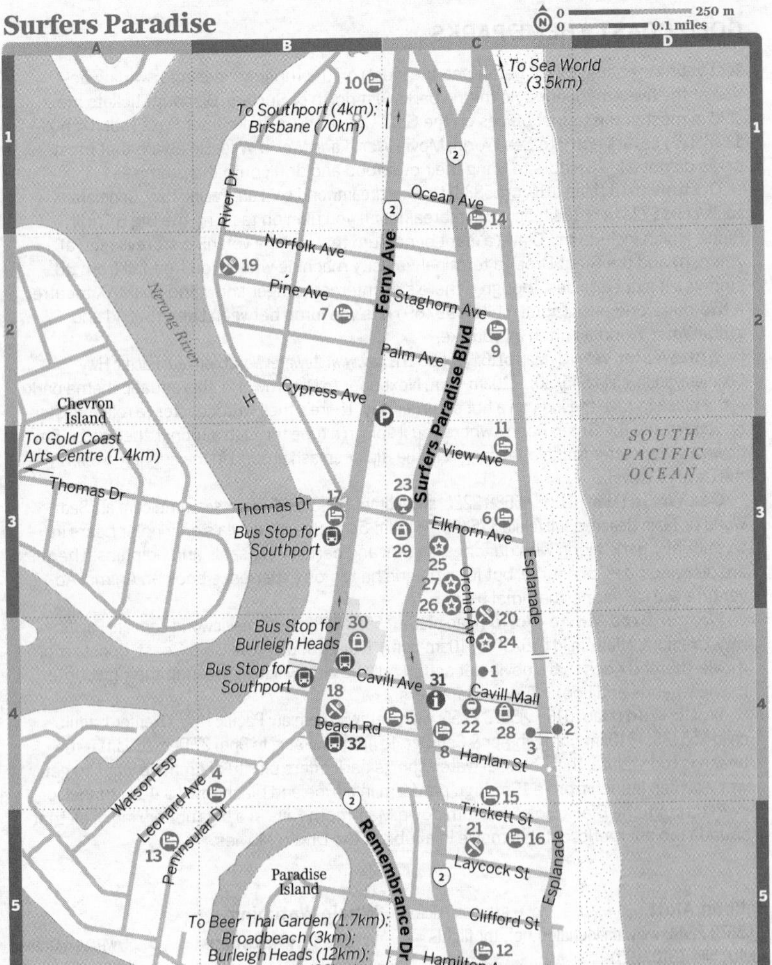

scenery in the Numinbah Valley, 30km south of Nerang.

Tours

A kitschy way to explore Surfers is on the **AquaDuck** (☎5539 0222; www.aquaduck.com.au; 7a Orchid Ave; adult/child $35/26), a semi-aquatic bus (or a boat on wheels) that moves effortlessly from the road to the river and back again.

You can also access the Gold Coast hinterland with a number of tour operators from Surfers Paradise. See p137 for more information.

Festivals & Events

Big Day Out MUSIC
(www.bigdayout.com) Huge international music festival in late January.

Quicksilver Pro-Surfing Competition SURFING
See some of the world's best surfers out on the waves in mid-March.

Surf Life-Saving Championships SURF LIFE-SAVING
Also in mid-March, expect to see some stupidly fit people running about wearing very little.

Surfers Paradise

Sights
QDeck .... (see 12)

Activities, Courses & Tours
1 AquaDuck C4
2 Cheyne Horan School of Surf C4
3 Go Ride a Wave C4
Infinity .... (see 29)

Sleeping
4 Backpackers in Paradise B4
5 Breakfree Cosmopolitan Resort C4
6 Chateau Beachside C3
7 Cheers Backpackers B2
8 Courtyard Marriott C4
9 International Beach Resort C2
10 Marriott Resort B1
11 Olympus C3
12 Q1 Resort C5
13 Sleeping Inn Surfers A5
14 Surf 'n' Sun Backpackers C1
15 Surfers International Apartments C4
16 Trickett Gardens Holiday Inn C5
17 Vibe Hotel B3

Eating
18 Asian Bites B4
Baritalia .... (see 29)
19 Bumbles Café B2
20 Central Lounge Bar & Restaurant C4
Fishnets Café .... (see 30)
Kamikaze Teppanyaki .... (see 30)
Surfers Sandbar .... (see 6)
21 Tandoori Place C5

Drinking
22 Beer Garden C4
23 Clock Hotel C3

Entertainment
24 Cocktails & Dreams C4
25 MP's C3
26 Sin City C3
27 Vanity C3

Shopping
28 Centro Surfers Paradise C4
29 Chevron Renaissance Shopping Centre C3
30 Circle on Cavill B4

Information
Gold Coast Accommodation Service .... (see 5)
31 Gold Coast Information & Booking Centre C4
Travellers Central .... (see 32)

Transport
32 Transit Centre B4

Gold Coast International Marathon MARATHON
This marathon is held in July.

Coolangatta Gold IRONMAN
October. See the boxed text, p125.

Schoolies SCHOOL-LEAVERS PARTY
Month-long party by school-leavers from mid-November to mid-December. Generally involves lots of alcohol and unruly behaviour.

Sleeping

Surfers is riddled with self-contained units. In peak season, rates skyrocket and there's usually a two- or three-night minimum stay. Low season rates are quoted in the following reviews.

The **Gold Coast Accommodation Service** (☎5592 0067; www.goldcoastaccommodationservice.com; Shop 1, 1 Beach Rd) can arrange and book accommodation and tours.

TOP CHOICE **Vibe Hotel** BOUTIQUE HOTEL $$
(☎5539 0444; www.vibehotels.com.au; 42 Ferny Ave; d from $140; ❄@≋) You won't miss this chocolate and lime-green high-rise on the Nerang River, a vibrant gem among the bland plethora of hotels and apartments. The rooms are subtle-chic and the poolside is the spot for sundowners. The aqua-view rooms have superb vistas over the river.

Q1 Resort APARTMENTS $$$
(☎1300 792 008, 5630 4500; www.q1.com.au; Hamilton Ave; 1-/2-/3-bedroom apt from $252/340/500; ❄@≋) Spend a night in the world's second-tallest residential tower. This stylish 80-storey resort is a modern mix of metal, glass and fabulous wrap-around views. All units have glass-enclosed balconies. There's a lagoon-style pool, a fitness centre and a day spa.

Surfers International Apartments APARTMENTS $$

(☎1800 891 299, 5579 1299; www.surfers-international.com.au; 7-9 Trickett St; 1-/2-bedroom apt 3-night minimum stay from $450/630; @≋) This high-rise, just off the beach, has large, comfortable apartments with full ocean views. The complex comes with a small gym and a rooftop pool. This is a good option, close to everything.

Chateau Beachside APARTMENTS $$

(☎5538 1022; www.chateaubeachside.com.au; cnr Elkhorn Ave & The Esplanade; d/studio/1-bedroom apt $145/160/175, minimum 2-night stay; ❄@≋) Right in the heart of Surfers, this seaside complex is an excellent choice. All the newly renovated studios and apartments have ocean views and the 18m pool is a bonus.

Marriott Resort RESORT $$$

(☎5592 9800; www.marriott.com.au; 158 Ferny Ave; d/ste from $295/640; ❄@⌔≋) Just north of the centre, this resort is ridiculously sumptuous, from the sandstone-floored foyer with punka-style fans to the lagoon-style pool, complete with artificial white-sand beaches and a waterfall.

Trickett Gardens Holiday Inn APARTMENTS $$

(☎5539 0988; www.trickettgardens.com.au; 24-30 Trickett St; s/d $150/185; ❄≋) This friendly low-rise block is great for families, with a central location and well-equipped, self-contained units. It's so tranquil it's hard to believe you're close to Surfers' frantic action.

Courtyard Marriott HOTEL $$$

(☎1800 074 317, 5579 3499; www.marriott.com; cnr Surfers Paradise Blvd & Hanlan St; d/ste from $195/245; ❄@⌔≋) Right in the centre of Surfers, this plush top-end hotel is attached to the Centro Shopping Complex and offers all the luxury you would expect in this price range, including sea views, and spa baths in the top-price suites.

Olympus APARTMENTS $$

(☎5538 7288; www.olympusapartments.com.au; 62 The Esplanade; d $130-180; @⌔≋) Just 200m north of Elkhorn Ave and opposite the beach, this high-rise block has well-kept, spacious apartments with one or two bedrooms.

International Beach Resort APARTMENTS $$

(☎1800 657 471, 5539 0099; www.internationalresort.com.au; 84 The Esplanade; apt $125-204; ❄@⌔≋) A seafront high-rise, this place is just across from the beach, and has good studios and one- and two-bedroom units.

Breakfree Cosmopolitan Resort APARTMENTS $$

(☎5570 2311; www.breakfree.com.au; cnr Surfers Paradise Blvd & Beach Rd; 1-bedroom/2-bedroom apt from $238/378, minimum 2-night stay; ❄≋) Set back from the beach a tad but still very central, this complex contains 55 privately owned, self-contained apartments, each uniquely furnished by the owners. There's also a barbecue area, a spa and a sauna. It can be noisy at night.

Sleeping Inn Surfers HOSTEL $

(☎1800 817 832, 5592 4455; www.sleepinginn.com.au; 26 Peninsular Dr; dm $22-26, d with/without bathroom $78/68; @≋) The newly renovated rooms are comfortable and all dorms have their own ensuite and well-equipped kitchen. Request the four-bed dorm if you don't want to share the bathroom with a large number of people. There's free limo pick-up from the transit centre.

Surfers Paradise Backpackers Resort HOSTEL $

(☎1800 282 800, 5592 4677; www.surfersparadisebackpackers.com.au; 2837 Gold Coast Hwy, Surfers Paradise; dm/d $23/74; @⌔≋) This purpose-built hostel with sauna, tennis court, pool room and bar has newly renovated rooms and self-contained apartments. It's family-friendly, offers good security, free laundry facilities and has a free courtesy bus to and from the transit centre. It's about 1.5km from the town centre.

Backpackers in Paradise HOSTEL $

(☎5538 4344; www.backpackersinparadise.com; 40 Peninsular Dr; dm/d from $20/65; @≋) The mini-cinema is a major drawcard in this party hostel. The rooms and bathrooms were all undergoing much-needed renovations at the time of research, which should lift its standards and make this a comfortable hostel. The on-site convenience store is a bonus.

Surf 'n' Sun Backpackers HOSTEL $

(☎1800 678 194, 5592 2363; www.surfnsun-goldcoast.com; 3323 Surfers Paradise Blvd; dm/d $25/65; @⌔≋) Looking dowdy, worn and tired, this is still a very friendly family-run business and is close to Surfers' beach and bars. All dorms are six-share with a TV and bathroom, and the pool is the hub of the lazy-day action.

Cheers Backpackers HOSTEL $

(☎1800 639 539, 5531 6539; www.cheersbackpackers.com.au; 8 Pine Ave; dm $22-32, d $60-90; @≋) Amid the friendly blur of theme nights, karaoke, pool comps, pub crawls, happy hours and barbecues, you might miss the grotty bathrooms. But if partying is the main attraction then you probably won't mind.

Eating

Self-caterers will find supermarkets in **Centro Surfers Paradise** (Cavill Ave Mall), **Chevron Renaissance Shopping Centre** (cnr Elkhorn Ave & Gold Coast Hwy) and **Circle on Cavill** (cnr Cavill & Ferny Ave).

Baritalia ITALIAN $$
(☎5592 4700; Shop 15, Chevron Renaissance Building, cnr Elkhorn Ave & Surfers Paradise Blvd; mains $10-25; ⊙breakfast, lunch & dinner) The perfect spot for people-watching, this al fresco Italian-style bar and restaurant has rustic wooden benches and an atmosphere to match. The coffee is *perfetto,* and the good-value Friday night special includes a plate of pasta or risotto with a glass of wine.

Kamikaze Teppanyaki JAPANESE $$
(☎5592 0888; Circle on Cavill, Surfers Paradise Blvd; dishes $8-27; ⊙lunch & dinner) This very popular al fresco Japanese restaurant dishes up teppan vegetables, steamed rice, kamikaze salad, miso soup, and ginger and sesame sauce with every main meal.

Bumbles Café CAFE $$
(☎5538 6668; 21 River Dr; dishes $11-25; ⊙7am-4pm) One of the few tranquil spots in Surfers, this cute cafe is located in a quiet nook opposite the Nerang River. The menu isn't extensive but has some interesting global temptations.

Surfers Sandbar MODERN AUSTRALIAN $$
(cnr Elkhorn Ave & The Esplanade; dishes $8-20; ⊙breakfast, lunch & dinner) The ocean views gives this cafe, bar and restaurant the edge over most Surfers' eateries. The menu gravitates towards burgers, beer-battered fish and chips, and light seafood meals but forgo the rather impersonal indoor restaurant and dine al fresco. Or just order a coldie and enjoy the sea breeze.

Fishnets Café SEAFOOD $
(Circle on Cavill, 3/38 Surfers Paradise Blvd; dishes $7-13; ⊙lunch & dinner) Forget the paper plates and plastic cutlery – the fish and chips, octopus salad, and fresh fish fillets at this outdoor eatery in the heart of the Circle are excellent value.

Central Lounge Bar & Restaurant FUSION $$
(☎5592 3228; 27 Orchid Ave; mains lunch $11-20, dinner $20-32; ⊙lunch Fri-Sun, dinner Tue-Sun) This central restaurant and lounge bar is a cool place to indulge in a long lunch. Tables and chairs spill into the centre of the mall so passers-by can watch you having a good time. Salads, steaks and beer-battered fish and chips are on offer. The resident DJ creates a fusion of cool tunes to smooth you into the weekend club scene.

Beer Thai Garden THAI $$
(☎5538 0110; cnr Chelsea Ave & Gold Coast Hwy; mains $15-25; ⊙dinner) Reputed to dish up the best Pad Thai on the coast, this lovely restaurant brims with atmosphere. Two glitzy elephants flank the entrance, and soft lighting makes the most of the outdoor Thai garden bar. Good value and easy on the pocket. It's south down the Gold Coast Hwy.

Tandoori Place INDIAN $$
(☎5538 0808; Aegean Resort, Laycock St; mains $15-25; ⊙lunch & dinner; ✎) An Indian restaurant that boasts a swag of awards and is highly recommended by locals has to be a winner. On the extensive menu you'll find seafood, poultry, lamb, beef and hot, hot, *hot* vindaloo roo. Vegetarians are also spoiled for choice.

Asian Bites ASIAN FUSION $
(9 Beach Rd; dishes $4-15; ⊙lunch & dinner) For a quick, cheap meal without fanfare, this hole-in-the-wall cafe promises a taste of Asia in every bite. Pick from over 43 Chinese, Malaysian and Singaporean dishes.

Drinking

Beer Garden BAR
(Cavill Ave) A very popular watering hole, the upstairs Beer Garden isn't a garden but a huge barn-like affair overlooking Cavill Ave. It's the place to start a night of clubbing.

Clock Hotel PUB
(cnr Elkhorn Ave & Surfers Paradise Blvd) From the bar inside you won't see the parade of Aussie icons (kangaroo, emu, swagman and koala) emerging from the clocktower on the hour, every hour, but you'll certainly hear the bells tolling... Time for another cocktail...or wine...or beer...

Northcliffe SLSC SURF CLUB
(Garfield Tce) A little south of Cavill Mall, this surf club sits directly on the beach. It's large and modern with zero intimacy but the expansive ocean views go well with a coldie on a hot day.

Entertainment

Orchid Ave is Surfers' main bar and nightclub strip. Cover charges are usually between $10 and $20 and Wednesday and Saturday are generally the big party nights.

You can take the hassle out of your big night out with **Wicked Club Crawl** (5580 8422; www.wickedclubcrawl.com.au; tickets $30-50) or **Plan B Party Tours** (0400 685 501; www.planbtours.com; tickets $30). Every Wednesday, Friday and Saturday the teams organise a club crawl to five or six nightclubs (including free entry for the rest of the week), a free drink and pizza at each venue, party games and loads of fun.

Backpackers Big Night Out (www.goldcoastbackpackers.net; tickets $30) hosts a similar club crawl on Wednesdays and Saturdays, exclusively for backpackers. A party bus picks you up from your hostel and that's when the party begins. Tickets are available only through Gold Coast Association hostels and get you free entry into four nightclubs, a free drink and pizza at each venue, and other goodies.

Nightclubs

Vanity NIGHTCLUB

(26 Orchid Ave) Formerly the Bedroom, Vanity is one of the hottest clubs in town, priding itself on beautiful people and upmarket glam.

Sin City NIGHTCLUB

(22 Orchid Ave) A newcomer on the party scene, this Vegas-style nightclub is the place to be seen.

Cocktails & Dreams NIGHTCLUB

(15 Orchid Ave) One of the oldest clubs in town, it still draws a regular crowd of party animals.

MP's NIGHTCLUB

(Forum Arcade, 26 Orchid Ave) This popular gay club has cheap drinks and drag shows. On Friday and Saturday it fills with a happy, mixed crowd soaking up a generic nightclub atmosphere.

Theatre

Gold Coast Arts Centre THEATRE

(5588 4000; www.gcac.com.au; 135 Bundall Rd) This excellent centre, beside the Nerang River, has two cinemas, a restaurant, a bar and a 1200-seat theatre, which regularly hosts impressive theatrical productions.

Information

The Gold Coast Hwy splits either side of Surfers, with Surfers Paradise Blvd taking southbound traffic and Remembrance Dr, which then becomes Ferny Ave, taking northbound traffic.

Internet access costs $4 to $5 per hour.

American Express (Amex; 1300 139 060; Pacific Fair Shopping Centre, Hooker Blvd, Broadbeach) Two kilometres south of Surfers.

Email Centre (5538 7500; Orchid Ave; 9am-10pm)

Gold Coast Information and Booking Centre (5538 4419; Cavill Ave Mall; 8.30am-5pm Mon-Fri, to 5pm Sat, 9am-4pm Sun) Information booth; also sells theme-park tickets.

Our High Speed Internet (5504 7992; 3063 Surfers Paradise Blvd; 9am-11pm)

Paradise Medical Clinic (5592 3999; Centro Surfers Paradise, Cavill Ave Mall; 8.30am-5pm Mon-Fri, 9am-12.30pm Sat)

Post office (13 13 18; Shop 165, Centro Surfers Paradise, Cavill Ave Mall; 9am-5.30pm Mon-Fri, to 12.30pm Sat)

Surfers Paradise Day & Night Medical Centre (5592 2299; 3221 Surfers Paradise Blvd; 7am-11pm)

Travellers Central (5538 3274; www.travellerscentral.com.au; Surfers Paradise Transit Centre, cnr Beach Rd & Remembrance Dr; 9am-7pm) Help with accommodation and tours for travellers of all budget ranges.

Getting There & Away

The transit centre is on the corner of Beach Rd and Remembrance Dr. All the major bus companies have desks here. For more information on buses and trains, see p121.

Getting Around

Car hire costs around $30 to $50 per day. You can also hire scooters and mopeds. Some of the many operators:

Avis (13 63 33, 5539 9388; cnr Ferny & Cypress Aves)

Budget (1300 362 848, 5538 1344; cnr Ferny & Palm Aves)

Discover Gold Coast Scooter & Car Rentals (5538 0003; Shop 188, Centro Shopping Centre, Surfers Paradise) Scooters from $30 per hour, cars from $39 per day.

Getabout Rentals (5504 6517; Shop 9, The Mark, Orchid Ave) Also rents out scooters and bikes and organises motorcycle tours of the Broadwater area (from $60 for 30 minutes to $280 per half-day).

Mopeds City (5592 5878; 103 Ferny Ave) Hires out brand-new mopeds (per hour/day $30/70).

Red Back Rentals (☎5592 1655; Transit Centre, cnr Beach & Cambridge Rds)

Red Rocket Rent-A-Car (☎1800 673 682, 5538 9074; Centre Arcade, 16 Orchid Ave) Also rents out scooters (per day $30) and bicycles (per day $12).

Broadbeach

POP 3800

Only a few kilometres south of Surfers, bling gives way to upmarket glam. Boutique shops and fashionable cafes line the Broadbeach streets while open stretches of green parkland separate the fine sandy beach from the esplanade. This is where Gold Coast locals wine and dine, and for a taste of the stylish beach-and-sun lifestyle it's exquisite.

Shopaholics will find two of the coast's major shopping centres (Oasis and Pacific Fair) within easy reach of the beach. Broadbeach is also a good alternative to Surfers if you want a peaceful night's sleep.

Sights & Activities

Conrad Jupiters Casino CASINO
(☎5592 8100; www.conrad.com.au; Gold Coast Hwy; admission free; ⏲24hr) Hundreds of thousands of optimistic gamblers filter through this mammoth temple to Mammon every year and leave with their pockets slightly lighter and their addiction briefly sated. This was the first legal casino in Queensland, and it features more than 100 gaming tables, including blackjack, roulette, two-up and craps, and hundreds of bleeping poker machines. Also here is **Jupiters Theatre** with live music and glamorous dinner shows. You have to be over 18 years of age to enter, and the usual dress codes apply – no thongs (flip-flops), vests or ripped clothes. A monorail runs here from the Oasis Shopping Centre.

Sleeping

Wave APARTMENTS $$$
(☎5555 9200; www.thewavesresort.com.au; 89-91 Surf Parade; r $225-550, minimum 3-night stay; ❄@📶≋) You can't miss this spectacular high-rise with its wave-inspired design towering over Broadbeach's glam central. These luxury apartments make full use of the coast's spectacular views, especially from the sky pool on the 34th floor.

Hi-Ho Beach Apartments APARTMENTS $$
(☎5538 2777; www.hihobeach.com.au; 2 Queensland Ave; 1-/2-bedroom apt $150/180; ≋) A great choice for location, close to the beach and Broadbeach's cafe scene. Standard apartments are looking weary but the renovated superior and executive apartments are very comfortable.

Conrad Jupiters RESORT $$$
(☎1800 074 344, 5592 8130; www.conrad.com.au; Gold Coast Hwy; r $220-1240, penthouse ste $3100; ❄@📶≋) If you hit the jackpot at the casino downstairs, splash out on the luxury penthouse suite at this landmark Gold Coast icon. The hotel's facilities include seven restaurants, five bars and a professional gym and health centre.

A'Montego Mermaid Beach Motel MOTEL $$
(☎5575 1577; www.mermaidbeachmotel.com.au; 2395 Gold Coast Hwy; r from $100; ❄≋📶) This small, personable motel has spotless units that are a mark above the surrounding litter of cheapie options.

Eating

Broadbeach's culinary scene is a class above Surfers'.

1two3 MEDITERRANEAN $$
(☎5538 4123; Phoenician Building, 90 Surf Parade; dishes $10-30; ⏲breakfast, lunch & dinner) This new concept Mediterranean dining and lounge bar offers three portion sizes with every dish – taster, entrée and main. Great concept, great atmosphere, and live music every night.

Moo Moo STEAKHOUSE $$$
(☎5539 9952; Broadbeach on the Park, 2685 Gold Coast Hwy; mains $30-60; ⏲lunch & dinner) A mecca for serious carnivores, Moo Moo's signature dish is a 1kg Wagyu rump steak rubbed with spices, char-grilled until smoky, then roasted and carved at the table. Beef connoisseurs will drool over the Master Kobe rib fillet, a luxury beef produced from a long period of grain feeding of Wagyu beef. Vegetarians will be happy with the seafood and pasta dishes on the menu.

Manolas Brothers Deli DELI $
(19 Albert Ave; dishes $8-25; ⏲breakfast & lunch, deli open 7am-6pm) Cosmopolitan delicacies fill every nook and cranny on the ceiling-high shelves in this sumptuous gourmet deli-cafe. Park yourself at the massively long central table to salivate over the juicy olives, antipasti, imported cheeses and decadent homemade cakes and biscuits. Health freaks will love the salads and juices.

OUTBACK ON THE COAST

You don't need to travel long distances into the dusty heart of Australia to experience the outback. The venue at the **Australian Outback Spectacular** (☎133 386; Pacific Hwy, Oxenford; adult/child incl dinner $99.95/69.95; ⏱shows start 6.45pm Tue-Sat) has been built to resemble a traditional outback shearing shed and the backdrops and props (you even get a stockman's hat to wear) reflect the Australian landscape. The Man from Snowy River comes to life when stockmen and -women (in Akubras and Driza-bones) show off their superb horsemanship, crack bullwhips and muster stampeding cattle. Dinner is typical outback tucker – damper and barbecue steak. It's a 'bonza' night out and you even get to keep the hat!

Koi FUSION $$
(☎5570 3060; Wave Building, cnr Surf Parade & Albert Ave; mains $24-40; ⏱breakfast, lunch & dinner) For serious people-watching, morning lattes or sunset cocktails, this cruisy cafe and lounge bar is the happening place. Gourmet pizzas and tapas rub shoulders with an interesting contemporary menu where seafood features prominently. Live music on Sunday afternoons draws the après-beach crowd.

Champagne Brasserie FRENCH $$
(☎5538 3877; 2 Queensland Ave; mains $20-40; ⏱lunch Tue-Fri, dinner Tue-Sat) This lively, unassuming restaurant could have been plucked from a French village, and dishes up traditional French fare with a modern twist. The house specialty – roasted duck breast infused with honey toffee, cinnamon, vanilla, cardomom and star anise – is highly recommended.

Three Beans Espresso CAFE $
(Phoenician Building, 90 Surf Pde; dishes $5-10; ⏱24hr) Serious coffee!

☆ Entertainment

Dracula's Theatre Restaurant THEATRE
(☎5575 1000; www.draculas.com.au; 1 Hooker Blvd; dinner & show $83) For the ghoulishly inclined, this restaurant offers a fang-tastically good time. Be entertained by both the vampirish cabaret act and fetishly dressed wait-staff while sinking your fangs into fiendish-sounding dishes including the restaurant's signature diabolical and delicious Death by Chocolate. What better way to die?

Burleigh Heads & Currumbin

POP 7600 & 2600

A little further south and the true essence of the Gold Coast – far removed from the frenzied party atmosphere of Surfers – permeates the chilled-out surfie town of Burleigh Heads. With its cheery cafes and beachfront restaurants overlooking a gorgeous stretch of white sand, and its small but beautiful national park on the rocky headland, Burleigh Heads charms everyone.

In the right weather conditions, the headland here produces a spectacular right-hand point break, famous for its fast, deep barrel rides, but it definitely isn't for beginners. The shore is lined with vicious black rocks and the rip is ferocious.

Currumbin, 6km south of Burleigh Heads, is a sleepy little town, and a great spot for a relaxing family holiday, especially as the kids can swim in the calm waters of Currumbin Creek. Currumbin Alley is known as a good spot for stand-up paddleboarding and for learner-surfers.

◉ Sights

Currumbin Wildlife Sanctuary WILDLIFE PARK
(☎5534 1266; www.cws.org.au; Gold Coast Hwy, Currumbin; adult/child $49/31; ⏱8am-5pm) Here you can see Australian native animals in natural bush and rainforest habitats. Tree kangaroos, koalas, emus, wombats and other cute-and-furries are joined daily by flocks of brilliantly coloured rainbow lorikeets, which take great delight in eating out of your hand. There are informative and interactive shows throughout the day (did you know the scrub python can swallow prey four times the size of its head?), and there is also an Aboriginal dance show. One of the best ways to see the sanctuary is on a Wildnight Tour (adult/child $89/59), when the native nocturnal animals go about their business.

David Fleay Wildlife Park WILDLIFE PARK
(☎5576 2411; West Burleigh Rd; adult/child/senior/family $17.10/7.95/10.30/43.45; ⏱9am-5pm) Run by the Queensland Environmental Protection Agency this park has 4km of walking tracks through mangroves and rainforest and plenty of educational and

Burleigh Heads

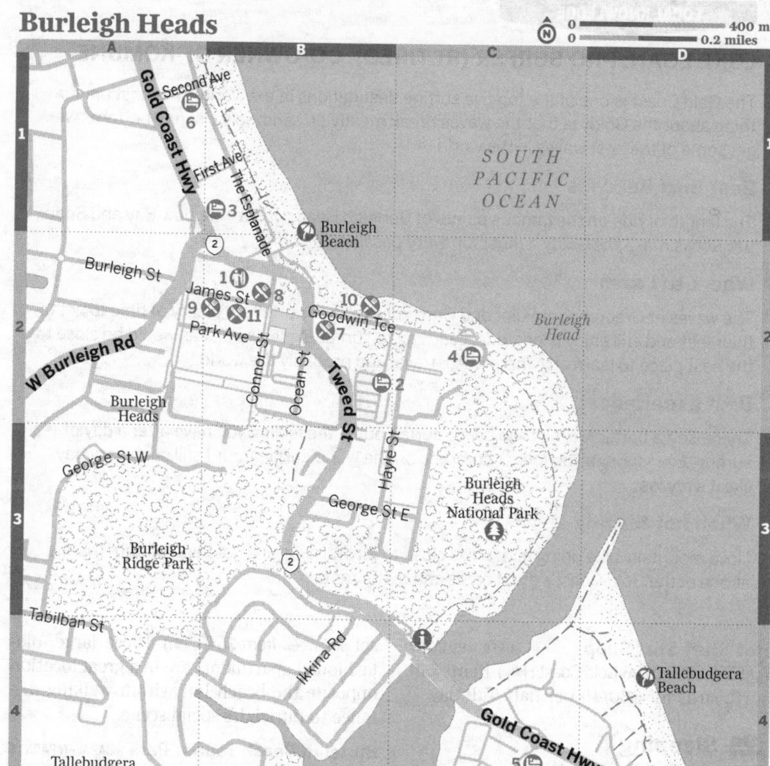

informative shows throughout the day. It's an excellent opportunity to experience Australian fauna. The park is named after its founder, Australian naturalist David Fleay, the first person to breed the platypus in captivity (at Healesville Sanctuary in Victoria). The park runs a research and breeding program for rare and endangered species, although no platypus have successfully been bred here.

Activities

The right-hand point break at Burleigh Heads is the best wave here, but it's usually crowded with pro surfers. There are plenty of other waves to practise on along the beach.

Surfing Services Australia SURFING LESSONS (☎5535 5557; www.surfingservices.com.au; adult/child $35/25) Surfing lessons at Currumbin Alley every weekend at 8am and 10am.

Burleigh Heads

Activities, Courses & Tours

1 Hot Stuff Surf Shop B2

Sleeping

2 Burleigh Beach Tourist Park B2
3 Burleigh Palms Holiday Apartments B1
4 Hillhaven Holiday Apartments C2
5 Tallebudgera Creek Tourist Park C4
6 Wyuna A1

Eating

7 Bluff Café B2
8 Fishmongers B2
9 Govinda's B2
Mermaids on the Beach .... (see 10)
10 Oskars B2
11 Zullaz B2

Drinking

Pointbreak .... (see 10)

LOCAL KNOWLEDGE

LUKE EGAN: PRO SURFER (RETIRED), CO-OWNER OF KOMUNE

The Gold Coast is one of the top five surfing destinations in the world. The most unique thing about the Goldy is that the waves break mostly on sand, so for sandy bottoms we get some of the best waves in the world.

Best Surf Beaches

The length of ride on the famous points of Burleigh Heads, Kirra, Rainbow Bay and Snapper Rocks make the Goldy a must for every passionate surfer.

Where to Learn

The waves at Greenmount Point and Currumbin allow first-timers plenty of time to get to their feet and still enjoy a long ride. Learning to surf at these two places would be close to the best place to learn anywhere in Australia, and probably the world.

Best Experience

There isn't a better feeling than being 'surfed out' – the feeling you have after a day of surfing. Even though I no longer compete on the world surfing tour I still surf every day like it's my last.

When not Surfing

I love mountain-bike riding in the hills close to Mt Warning, and catching up with friends at one of the Gold Coast's great cafes and restaurants.

Hot Stuff Surf Shop SURFBOARD RENTAL
(☎5535 6899; 1706 Gold Coast Hwy) Rents out surfboards for $30/40 per half-/full day.

Sleeping

Hillhaven Holiday Apartments APARTMENTS $$
(☎5535 1055; www.hillhaven.com.au; 2 Goodwin Tce, Burleigh Heads; d $170, minimum 3-night stay; @) The pick of these upmarket apartments is the gold deluxe room at $300 per night. Situated on the headland adjacent to the national park these apartments have a grand view of Burleigh Heads. There's no through traffic so it's ultraquiet yet only 150m to the beach and cafe scene.

Burleigh Palms Holiday Apartments APARTMENTS $$
(☎5576 3955; www.burleighpalms.com; 1849 Gold Coast Hwy, Burleigh Heads; 1-bedroom apt per night/week from $130/550, 2-bedroom apt from $160/660;) Even though they're on the highway, these large and comfortable self-contained units are close to the beach, and are solid value. The owner is a mine of information and is happy to organise tours and recommend places to visit.

Wyuna APARTMENTS $$
(☎5535 3302; www.wyunaapartments@bigpond.com; 82 The Esplanade, Burleigh Heads; 2-bedroom apt per week from $640;) These large, old-fashioned apartments are in a great location opposite the beach but within walking distance to Burleigh's social scene.

Burleigh Beach Tourist Park CARAVAN PARK $
(☎5667 2750; www.goldcoasttouristparks.com.au; Goodwin Tce, Burleigh Heads; unpowered/powered sites $29/36, cabins from $115; @) This council-run park is snug, but it's in a great spot. Get in quick to bag a shady site. The good news is that you can stumble to the beach and the barbies are free. Rates are for two people.

Tallebudgera Creek Tourist Park CARAVAN PARK $
(☎5667 2700; www.goldcoasttouristparks.com.au; 1544 Gold Coast Hwy, Burleigh Heads; unpowered/powered sites $29/36, cabins from $115; @) This sprawling park is colossal but it's well laid out with its own road system and sits right on the banks of Tallebudgera Creek. Rates are for two people.

Eating

Oskars SEAFOOD $$$
(☎5576 3722; 43 Goodwin Tce, Burleigh Heads; dishes $20-50; lunch & dinner) One of the Gold Coast's finest, this elegant restaurant (right on the beach) constantly lands a coveted place on best-dining lists from

all quarters, and for good reason. Against elevated, sweeping views of the coastline you'll dine on a changing selection of seafood dishes.

Elephant Rock Café MODERN AUSTRALIAN $$
(5598 2133; 776 Pacific Pde, Currumbin; mains $16-34; breakfast & lunch daily, dinner Tue-Sat;) A cool cafe specialising in Mod Oz and 'gourmet vegetarian' cuisine (gluten sufferers will want to head here), this trendy cafe morphs from beach-chic by day to ultrachic at night. You can watch the moon rise over the ocean from the top deck or just enjoy the sound of waves lapping the beach.

Mermaids on the Beach MEDITERRANEAN $$
(5520 1177; 31 Goodwin Tce, Burleigh Heads; mains $23-36; breakfast, lunch & dinner) Another gem directly on the beach, the beautiful white sands of Burleigh Heads spread out from your feet down to the water's edge. Have the fruit platter for breakfast and for dinner sample interesting Mediterrasian dishes like prawn and lemon tortellini. Outside meal hours this is a snappy beach bar.

Zullaz FUSION $$
(5535 3511; 50 James St; mains $11-28; lunch Fri, dinner Tue-Sat) The menu is as exotic as the decor in this funky bar-cum-restaurant. The Polynesian, Moroccan and Indian dishes sound tantalising but be brave and order the Jamaican goat curry. Cocktails are just as exotic.

Bluff Cafe CAFE $$
(1/66 Goodwin Tce; dishes $10-30; breakfast, lunch & dinner) Start the day with a morning coffee at this popular and breezy cafe just opposite the beach. Après-surfing head back here for a mouth-watering gourmet pizza.

Govinda's INDIAN $
(20 James St; dishes $7-13; 11.30am-8pm) You can't go wrong with a large combo of three dishes for just $13 at this tiny Indian restaurant. Zero atmosphere but your taste-buds won't complain.

Fishmongers SEAFOOD $
(9 James St, Burleigh Heads; dishes $8-17; lunch & dinner) This fishmonger/fish-and-chip shop/restaurant is the business. Select your seafood bites from the display and then eat them hot down by the beach. Or sit down at a table in the unpretentious restaurant and tuck into the seafood fishermans basket for $13.50.

Drinking

Pointbreak BAR
(43 Goodwin Tce) Nothing beats a sundowner on the deck at this chic waterfront bar and restaurant. Live music Sunday arvos, surf flicks Wednesday nights, and DJ Fridays make this the coolest point break in Burleigh.

Information

QPWS Information Centre (5535 3032; 1711 Gold Coast Hwy; 9.30am-3pm Mon & Wed, 9am-3pm Tue, Thu & Fri, 9am-noon Sat & Sun) At the northern end of Tallebudgera Creek.

Coolangatta

POP 4870

Coolangatta is a laid-back seaside resort on Queensland's southern border, proud of its good surf beaches and tight community. With a sleek makeover transforming the esplanade, this once sleepy town is now the pick of the Gold Coast. If you want to bypass the glam and party scene, catch the best waves on the coast, or just kick back on the beach, you've found the spot. North of the point, Kirra has a beautiful long stretch of beach with challenging surf. Heading south, there are good views down the coast from Point Danger, the headland at the end of the state line.

Activities

The most difficult break here is Point Danger, but Kirra Point often goes off and there are gentler breaks at Greenmount Beach and Rainbow Bay. Learn to surf with **Walkin' on Water** (5534 1886, 0418 780 311; www.walkinonwater.com; 2hr group lesson per person $40). Former professional surfer and Australian surfing team coach Dave Davidson of **Gold Coast Surf Coaching** (0417 191 629) promises to get you up and surfing in your first lesson.

Cooly Surf (5536 61470; cnr Marine Pde & Dutton St; 9am-5pm) hires out high-performance surfboards as well as malibu surfboards (half-/full day $30/45) and stand-up paddleboards ($40/55).

Cooly Dive (5599 4104; www.coolydive.com.au; cnr McLean & Musgrave Sts; 8am-6pm) offers guided dives ($180), snorkelling ($85) as well as PADI dive courses. **Coolangatta Whale Watch** (5599 4104; www.coolangattawhalewatch.com.au; cnr McLean & Musgrave Sts; 3hr cruise adult/child $85/60;

Coolangatta

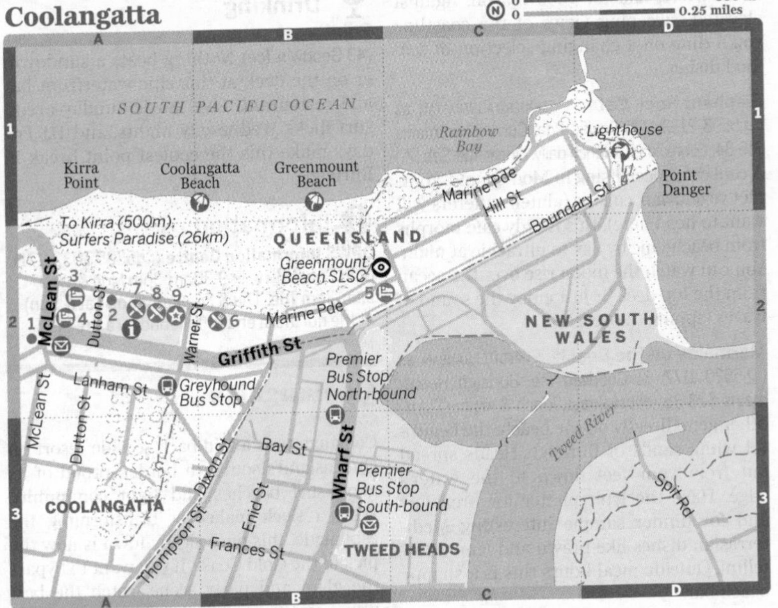

Coolangatta

Activities, Courses & Tours

Coolangatta Whale Watch............(see 1)
1 Cooly Dive............A2
2 Cooly Surf............A2

Sleeping

3 Beach House Seaside Resort............A2
4 Coolangatta Sands Hostel............A2
5 Komune............B2

Eating

6 Bellakai............B2
7 Earth 'n' Sea Pizza & Pasta............A2
Grill'd............(see 2)
8 O-Sushi............A2

Entertainment

9 Coolangatta Hotel............A2

8am-6pm) runs from June to the end of October.

You can get high with **Gold Coast Skydive** (5599 1920; Coolangatta Airport; tandem jumps from $325).

Tours

Catch-A-Crab RIVER CRUISES
(5599 9972; www.catchacrab.com.au; adult/child $55/36) Has great half-day tours along the Terranora Inlet of the Tweed River. The cruise involves mud-crab catching (try to say that in a hurry), fishing, pelican feeding and, if the tides permit, yabbie hunting.

Rainforest Cruises RIVER CRUISES
(5536 8800; www.goldcoastcruising.com) Has a number of cruise options ranging from crab catching to surf 'n' turf lunches on rainforest cruises along the Tweed River. Cruises start from $35 for two hours.

Sleeping

TOP CHOICE **Komune** BOUTIQUE HOTEL $$
(5536 6764; www.komuneresorts.com; 146 Marine Pde, Coolangatta; dm from $45, 2-bedroom apt $220, penthouse $695, penthouse & Sky-House party room $1500, breakfast included;) The beach-funk decor, tropical poolside and a 'no shirt, no shoes, no problem' mantra, makes this the ultimate surf retreat. The new concept in accommodation – from budget dorms (including a girls-only dorm), self-contained apartments, and a hip penthouse begging for a party – attracts a broad range of travellers, and fosters eclectic friendships. With superb ocean views, great staff and a cosy movie *sala* (outdoor-style room), you won't want to leave.

COOLANGATTA GOLD

The Gold Coast beaches are the natural habitats of Speedo-clad surf life-savers and bronzed bikini babes. At any time, a stroll along the beach promises a visual flesh-feast but in October the eye-candy barometer zooms into the stratosphere when the superfit and superbuff strut their stuff at the famous Coolangatta Gold. It's the Ironman of surf life-saving, one of the most gruelling physical events on the planet, and an incredible eye-candy extravaganza for the rest of us mere mortals.

First run in 1984 to promote a best-forgotten movie of the same name, the race got off to a shaky start before its firm placement on the annual Surf Life Saving Australia racing calendar in 2005. From Surfers Paradise, the 46.6km race involves a gruelling surf-ski paddle to Greenmount, beach runs, an ocean swim, a board paddle and a final 10km beach run back to Surfers. The women's event, raced over a distance of 25.5km, is just as punishing. After a torturous three hours or so, winners of the Coolangatta Gold earn the right to be gods of the sand and legends of the surf.

Coolangatta Sands Hostel HOSTEL $
(☎5536 7472; www.coolangattasandshostel.com.au; cnr Griffith & McLean Sts; dm from $30, d $72) Above the Coolangatta Sands Hotel and directly opposite the beach, this clean, airy and pleasant hostel is a good choice. The Queenslander balcony has comfortable daybeds to catch the sea breeze. As well as a free shuttle to and from the airport, there are plenty of incentives – free surf lessons and free trips to Nimbin, Mt Warning and Byron Bay.

Beach House Seaside Resort APARTMENTS $$
(☎5590 2111; www.classicholidayclub.com.au; 52 Marine Pde, Coolangatta; s/d from $150/180;) Although it belongs to a holiday club, this apartment complex often has rooms available to nonmembers. Recently refurbished, the units are bright and airy, fully self-contained and sleep up to six people. Also within the complex is a gym, spa and sauna.

Meridian Tower APARTMENTS $$
(☎1300 785 599, 5536 9400; www.meridiantower.com.au; 6 Coyne St, Kirra; 1-/2-bedroom apt per week from $795/910;) This tall tower block (the first in Kirra), opposite the beautiful Kirra beach, has spacious and airy fully self-contained apartments with large north-facing balconies. There's a spa, a sauna and tennis courts. Outside peak season, shorter stays are available.

Coolangatta YHA HOSTEL $
(☎5536 7644; www.coolangattayha.com; 230 Coolangatta Rd, Bilinga; dm $25-32, s $38-42, d $60-67, all incl breakfast;) A looong 4km haul from the bustle, this well-equipped YHA is favoured by surf junkies (of all vintages) who overdose on the excellent breaks across the road. You can also hire boards ($25 per day) and bikes. Courtesy transfers from Coolangatta are available.

Kirra Vista Holiday Units APARTMENTS $$
(☎5536 7375; www.kirravista.com.au; 12-14 Musgrave St, Kirra; d $150;) Forget the drab exterior, the renovated units in this small complex are a welcome surprise. All rooms have ocean views but be sure to book the renovated units.

Kirra Beach Tourist Park CARAVAN PARK $
(☎5667 2740; www.goldcoasttouristparks.com.au; Charlotte St, Kirra; unpowered/powered sites $29/34, cabins from $115;) This large council-run park has plenty of trees and a well-stocked open-air camp kitchen. The modern self-contained cabins are good value. There's also a TV room, barbecues and volleyball and basketball courts. Rates are for two people.

Eating

Marine Pde is lined with al fresco cafes and restaurants.

Bread'n'butter TAPAS $$
(☎5599 4666; 76 Musgrave St, Kirra; tapas $14-19; ⌚dinner daily, lunch Sat & Sun) Head upstairs to the balcony where mood lighting and chill tunes make this Spanish tapas bar perfect for a drink or a light meal. The pizzas are tasty and the tapas are huge. On Friday and Saturday nights, a DJ turns upstairs into a lively bar scene.

Mist MODERN AUSTRALIAN $$$
(☎5536 8885; cnr Douglas & Musgrave Sts, Kirra; tapas $10-23, mains $36-42; ⌚breakfast, lunch & dinner) The Mod Oz cuisine is creative, innovative and sassy, the curtained alcoves, arty chandeliers and eclectic decor is stylish

beach-chic. Cocktails are spot-on but tapas servings can be a bit light.

Bellakai MODERN AUSTRALIAN $$
(☎5531 5177; Marine Pde; meals $12-30; ⏰breakfast, lunch & dinner) This casual and relaxed cafe has great ocean views to complement a menu based on fresh local produce. At night soft candlelight adds a touch of romance to the restaurant's crisp white decor. Meals can be inconsistent but the coffee is excellent.

O-Sushi JAPANESE $
(66-80 Marine Pde, Coolangatta; sushi rolls from $2.80, mains $8-21; ⏰lunch & dinner) Boasting Japanese chefs and authentic Japanese cuisine, this perky sushi bar is about as stylish as a sushi bar can get. Try the *kushi-yaki* (traditional Japanese grill).

Earth'n'Sea Pizza & Pasta PIZZA $$
(☎5536 3477; Marine Pde, Coolangatta; mains $17-33; ⏰lunch & dinner) A hot summer night, a balmy sea breeze, a cold beer and a sizzling pizza – what better way to top off a day at the beach? Voted Best Pizza Restaurant on the Gold Coast, it has 22 gourmet pizzas on offer – you can't go wrong.

Grill'd BURGERS $
(Showcase on the Beach, Marine Pde; burgers $9-13; ⏰11am-10pm) Burgers of every description, including low-fat and vegan burgers.

☆ Entertainment

Coolangatta Hotel NIGHTCLUB
(cnr Marine Pde & Warner St) One of the hottest spots on the Gold Coast, the 'Cooly' has legendary Sunday sessions, and the Balcony nightclub attracts some of the biggest acts in the music industry.

Information

Coolangatta visitors centre (☎5569 3380; Shop 22, Showcase on the Beach, Griffith St; ⏰8.30am-5pm Mon-Fri, 9am-3pm Sat, 9am-noon Sun)

Post office (☎13 13 18) Coolangatta (cnr Griffith & McLean Sts); Tweed Heads (Tweed Mall)

Showcase Medical Centre (☎5536 6771; Shop 41-2, Showcase on the Beach Centre; ⏰7.30am-4pm Mon-Fri)

Getting There & Away

Greyhound (☎1300 473 946; www.greyhound.com.au) bus stop is in Warner St, while **Premier** (☎13 34 10; www.premierms.com.au) coaches stop in Wharf St.

GOLD COAST HINTERLAND

Inland from the surf, sand and half-naked bods on the Gold Coast beaches, the densely forested and unspoiled mountains of the McPherson Range feel like a million miles away. The range forms a natural barrier between the eastern coastline and the rolling green hills of the Darling Downs, and is a subtropical paradise of rainforests, waterfalls, panoramic lookouts and amazing wildlife. Closest to the coast, Springbrook is arguably the wettest place in southeast Queensland and the villages that speckle this area are influenced by the cooler air and vast sea of dense forest. Lamington National Park attracts bird-watchers, nature-lovers and serious hikers while Tamborine Mountain lures the craft cottage set. In winter, cosy cabins and fireplaces attract romantic weekenders.

Centrally located between Tamborine Mountain and Lamington National Park (at the junction of the approach roads to Green Mountains and Binna Burra) is the small town of Canungra where you'll find the **Canungra tourist information office** (☎5543 5156; cnr Kidston St & Lawson Lane; ⏰9am-4pm). Stop here to pick up walking track maps and information on the region.

Sights & Activities

If you're heading up to Green Mountains, **O'Reilly's Canungra Valley Vineyards** (☎5543 4011; Lamington National Park Rd), owned by the O'Reilly family (of O'Reilly's Rainforest Guesthouse fame), is housed in an old homestead and is open daily for tastings and sales.

Gumnuts Horseriding (☎5543 0191; www.gumnutsfarm.com.au; Biddaddaba Creek Rd) operates half-day (adult/child $65/45) and full-day (adult/child $110/75) horse rides, which include damper, billy tea (lunch on the full-day ride) and transfers to accommodation throughout the Gold Coast. Night tours include a barbecue and foot-stomping bush dances.

If you've got the gumption, **Paragliding Queensland** (☎5543 4000; www.pgqld.com.au) and **SE Queensland Hang Gliding** (☎5543 5631; www.hangglidequeensland.com.au; 66 Kidston St) both offer tandem flights for $220.

WORTH A TRIP

MT BARNEY NATIONAL PARK

In the rugged dry eucalypt woodlands of the Western Rim, Mt Barney National Park is a World Heritage site and one of Queensland's largest areas of pristine wilderness. A very different landscape to the lush Eastern Rim, the park and its seven peaks (the tallest reaching 1359m) attracts serious bushwalkers. Note that some of the tracks are poorly marked and you will need sound navigational skills to hike in this rough terrain.

Yellow Pinch Reserve picnic area is at the base of Mt Barney, Queensland's second-highest mountain. There's a reasonably easy 5km walk from the car park to a swimming hole on Barney Creek. A good base is **Mt Barney Lodge** (5544 3233; www.mtbarneylodge.com.au; Upper Logan Rd; unpowered sites $12, cabins $120, homestead for 4 people $300) with two picturesque homesteads and two rustic cabins.

Bushwalkers will find a basic **camping ground** (per person $5.15) in the national park. Purchase permits in advance (13 74 68; www.derm.qld.gov.au).

To reach the national park from Tamborine Mountain, drive 20km southwest on the Mt Lindesay Hwy through the small cattle centre of Beaudesert and continue 30km south to Rathdowney. Here you'll find the **Rathdowney Information Centre & Historical Museum** (5544 1222; Mt Lindesay Hwy; 9am-2pm Mon-Fri, 9am-4pm Sat & Sun). Drive about 1km south of Rathdowney and turn right onto the Boonah-Rathdowney Rd. After about 8km Upper Logan Rd veers off to the left and takes you into Mt Barney National Park.

3584; 9am-3.30pm Sat & Sun; Green Mountains 5544 0634; 9-11am & 1-3.30pm Mon-Fri).

Sleeping & Eating

There's a national-park camping ground close to O'Reilly's, and bush camping is permitted in several areas within the park, but only a limited number of permits (per person $5.15) are issued. Camping permits can be obtained by self-registering on site, from the ranger at Green Mountains, or by booking online. During weekends and school holidays all permits must be booked in advance. Note that there is no national park camping available in the Binna Burra section.

Binna Burra Mountain Lodge

GUESTHOUSE $$

(1300 246 622, 5533 3622; www.binnaburralodge.com.au; Binna Burra Rd, Beechmont; unpowered/powered sites $24/30, safari tents from $55, d incl breakfast with/without bathroom $250/190) Stay in the lodge, rustic log cabins or in a tent surrounded by forest in this atmospheric mountain retreat. The central restaurant (mains $20 to $35; open breakfast and dinner) has good views over the national park. While here, try the lodge's 'senses trail' for the blind, indulge in the Rejoove Day Spa, or learn to abseil. Other activities include guided walks, flying-fox flights and free nightly nature documentaries. Transport to and from the lodge can be arranged upon request.

O'Reilly's Rainforest Retreat

GUESTHOUSE $$$

(1800 688 722, 5502 4911; www.oreillys.com.au; Lamington National Park Rd; guesthouse s/d from $163/278, villas 1-/2-bedroom from $400/435, minimum 2-night stay; @) Established in 1926, this famous guesthouse at Green Mountains is still run by the O'Reilly family. The original guesthouse (looking dated and faded) still manages to retain its old-world rustic charm – and sensational views – but there's also a choice of luxury villas. The Discovery Centre runs daily activities including guided rainforest walks, glow-worm walks, 4WD tours, flying-fox and giant swing rides (all at added cost), and free nightly nature documentaries. There's a day spa, a bar and a plush restaurant (mains $25 to $40; open breakfast, lunch and dinner).

Getting There & Away

Mountain Coach Company (5524 4249; return day trip adult/child $69/39) has a daily service from the Gold Coast to O'Reilly's via Tamborine Mountain (one hour). To stay overnight at O'Reilly's, the transfer fee is $45 each way.

Noosa & the Sunshine Coast

Includes »

Noosa.............144
Bribie Island........151
Glass House Mountains..........151
Caloundra..........152
Mooloolaba & Maroochydore......155
Coolum...........160
Peregian & Sunshine Beach.............161
Cooloola Coast......162
Eumundi..........163
Sunshine Coast Hinterland.........165
Maleny............165
Montville...........166
Mapleton...........168

Best Places to Eat

» Spirit House Restaurant (p164)

» Humid (p149)

» Berardo's (p149)

» Wasabi (p149)

» Bella Venezia (p158)

Best Places to Stay

» Secrets on the Lake (p167)

» Islander Noosa Resort (p147)

» Hidden Valley B&B (p164)

Why Go?

If your idea of the perfect summer holiday involves lazy days in the sun, sand between your toes, and fish and chips on the beach then pack a smile, ditch the bling and immerse yourself in the laid-back beach-chic culture of the refreshingly natural and unaffected Sunshine Coast.

From the tip of Bribie Island, the 'Sunny Coast' stretches north for one hundred golden kilometres to the Cooloola Coast, just beyond the exclusive, leafy resort town of Noosa. The coast is perfect for surfing and swimming, and Mooloolaba, with its popular beach, outdoor eateries and cafes, is a firm favourite with holidaying Australian families.

Forming a stunning backdrop to this spectacular coastline are the ethereal Glass House Mountains and, a little further north, the Sunshine Coast hinterland, home to the forested folds and ridges, gorges and waterfalls, lush green pastures and quaint villages of the Blackall Range.

When to Go

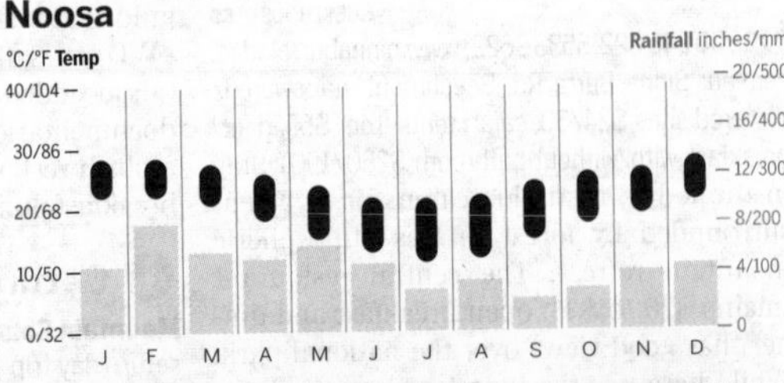

May Satisfy indulgent gustatory cravings at the Noosa Food & Wine Festival.

August–September Noosa's streets fill with music during the four-day Noosa Jazz Festival.

DecemberCelebrate the year's end eclectically, and alternately, at the Woodford Folk Festival.

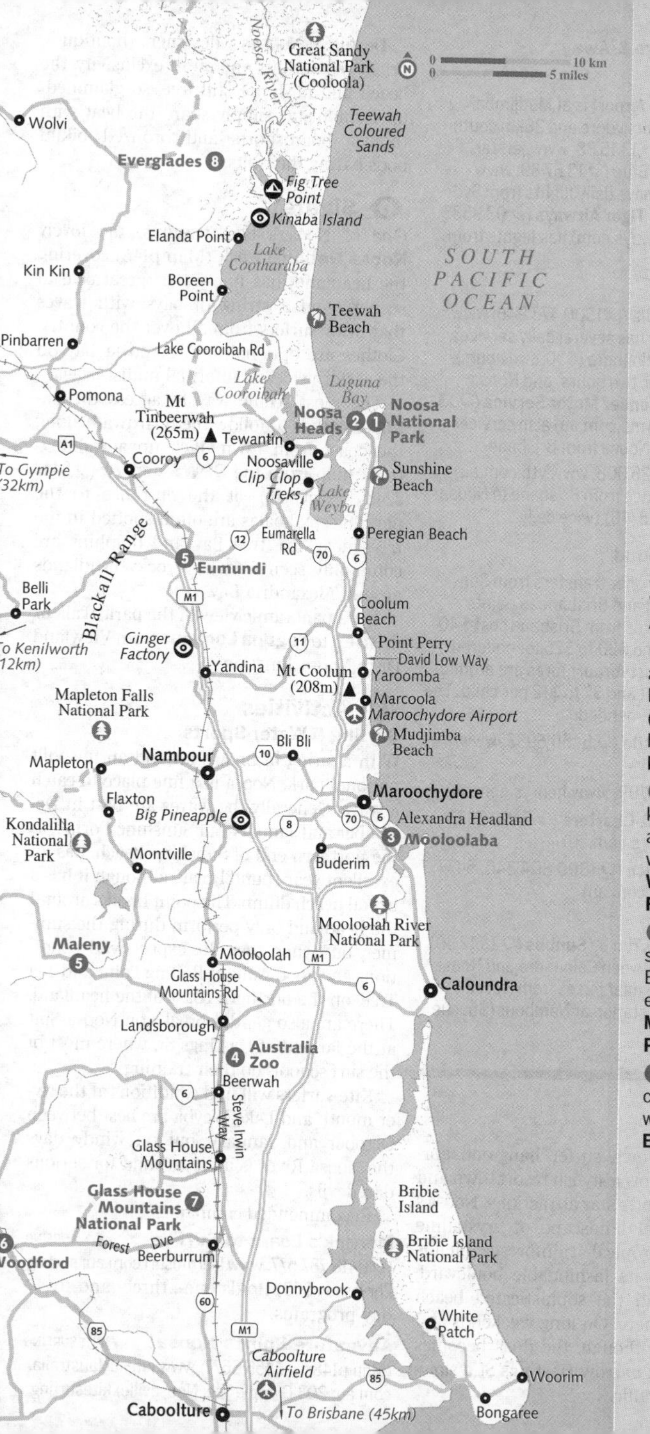

Noosa & the Sunshine Coast Highlights

1. Bushwalking through **Noosa National Park** (p144) spotting koalas in the trees and dolphins in the bay
2. Wining and dining at Noosa's swish **restaurants and cafes** (p149)
3. Surfing, sunning and lapping up the beach-cafe scene in **Mooloolaba** (p155)
4. Finding your inner crocodile (and other wild critters) at the wonderful wildlife sanctuary of **Australia Zoo** (p153)
5. Savouring the alternative vibe at the **Eumundi markets** (p163) and the funky hinterland town of **Maleny** (p165)
6. Donning flares, kaftans, and wild new-age hippie-chic at the wonderfully eclectic **Woodford Folk Festival** (p165)
7. Hiking to the summit of Mount Beerwah in the ethereal **Glass House Mountains National Park** (p151)
8. Kayaking or canoeing the quiet waters of the Noosa **Everglades** (p147)

Getting There & Away

AIR

The Sunshine Coast Airport is at Mudjimba, 10km north of Maroochydore and 26km south of Noosa. **Jetstar** (☎13 15 38; www.jetstar.com.au) and **Virgin Blue** (☎13 67 89; www.virginblue.com.au) have daily flights from Sydney and Melbourne. **Tiger Airways** (☎03 9335 3033; www.tigerairways.com) has flights from Melbourne.

BUS

Greyhound Australia (☎1300 473 946; www.greyhound.com.au) has several daily services from Brisbane to Caloundra ($30, two hours), Maroochydore ($30, two hours) and Noosa ($32, 2½ hours). **Premier Motor Service** (☎13 34 10; www.premierms.com.au) also services Maroochydore and Noosa from Brisbane.

Veolia (☎1300 826 608; www.vtb.com.au) has an express service from Brisbane to Noosa (one way/return $25/46) twice daily.

Getting Around

Several companies offer transfers from Sunshine Coast Airport and Brisbane to points along the coast. Fares from Brisbane cost $40 to $50 for adults and $20 to $25 for children. From Sunshine Coast Airport fares are around $15 to $25 per adult and $7 to $12 per child. The following are recommended:

Col's Airport Shuttle (☎5450 5933; www.airshuttle.com.au)

Henry's (☎5474 0199; www.henrys.com.au)

Noosa Transfers & Charters (☎5450 5933; www.noosatransfers.com.au)

Sun-Air Bus Service (☎1800 804 340, 5477 0888; www.sunair.com.au)

The blue minibuses run by **Sunbus** (☎13 12 30) buzz frequently between Caloundra and Noosa. Sunbus also has regular buses from Noosa across to the train station at Nambour ($5, one hour) via Eumundi.

Noosa

POP 9110

Once a little-known surfer hang-out, gorgeous Noosa is now a stylish resort town and one of Queensland's star attractions. Noosa's stunning natural landscape of crystalline beaches and tropical rainforests blends seamlessly with its fashionable boulevard, Hastings St, and the sophisticated beach elite who flock here. On long weekends and school holidays, though, the flock becomes a migration and narrow Hastings St a slow-moving file of traffic.

Despite Noosa's designer boutiques, pricey restaurants and air of exclusivity, the beach and bush are still free, so glammed-up fashionistas simply share the beat with thongs, boardshorts and bronzed bikini bods baring their bits.

Sights

One of Noosa's best features, the lovely **Noosa National Park** (Map p145) covering the headland, has fine walks, great coastal scenery and a string of bays with waves that draw surfers from all over the country. Clothes are optional at Alexandria Bay on the eastern side, an informal nudist beach.

The most scenic way to access the national park is to follow the boardwalk along the coast from town. Pick up a walking-track map from the **QPWS centre** (☎5447 3243; 9am-3pm), at the entrance to the park. Sleepy koalas are often spotted in the trees near Tea Tree Bay and dolphins are commonly seen from the rocky headlands around Alexandria Bay.

For a panoramic view of the park, walk or drive up to **Laguna Lookout** from Viewland Dr in Noosa Junction.

Activities

Surfing & Water Sports

With a string of breaks around an unspoilt national park, Noosa is a fine place to catch a wave. Generally the waves are best in December and January but Sunshine Corner, at the northern end of Sunshine Beach, has an excellent year-round break, although it has a brutal beach dump. The point breaks around the headland only perform during the summer, but when they do, expect wild conditions and good walls at Boiling Point and Tea Tree, on the northern coast of the headland. There are also gentler breaks on Noosa Spit at the far end of Hastings St, where most of the surf schools do their training.

Kite-surfers will find conditions at the river mouth and Lake Weyba are best between October and January, but on windy days the Noosa River is a playground for serious daredevils.

Recommended companies:

Merrick's Learn to Surf SURFING
(☎0418 787 577; www.learntosurf.com.au; surfing 2hr lesson $60) Holds one-, three- and five-day programs.

Adventure Sports Noosa KITESURFING
(Map p148; ☎5455 6677; www.kitesurfaustralia.com.au; 203 Gympie Tce, Noosaville; kitesurfing

Noosa Heads

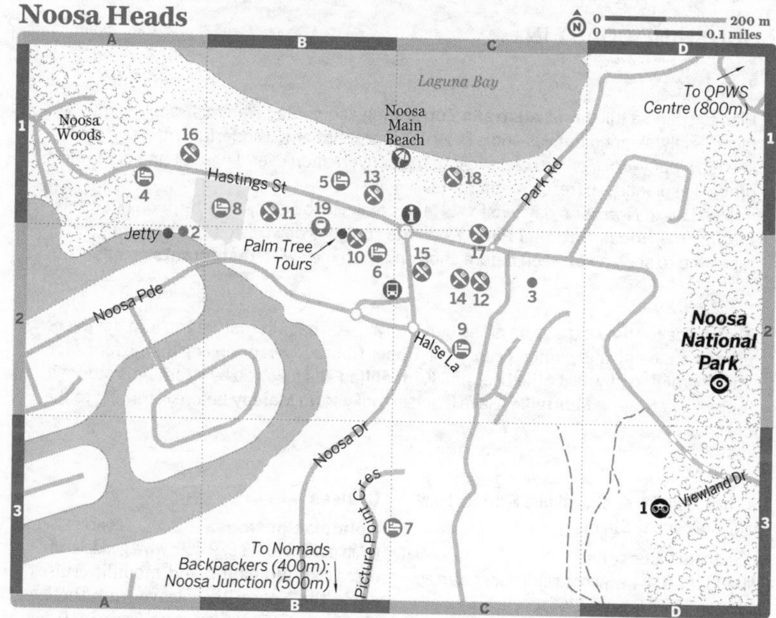

Noosa Heads

Top Sights

Noosa National Park D2

Sights

1 Laguna Lookout D3

Activities, Courses & Tours

Gondolas of Noosa .... (see 2)
2 Noosa Ferry A2
3 Noosa Longboards C2

Sleeping

4 #2 Hastings St A1
5 Accom Noosa B1
6 Emerald B2
7 Picture Point Terraces C3
8 Sheraton Noosa Resort B1
9 YHA Halse Lodge C2

Eating

10 Aromas B2
11 Bay Village Shopping Centre Food Court B1
12 Berardo's C2
13 Berardo's on the Beach B1
Bistro C .... (see 13)
14 Café Le Monde C2
15 Gaston C2
16 Lindoni's A1
17 Massimo's C2
18 Noosa Heads SLSC C1

Drinking

Cato's .... (see 8)
19 Zachary's B1

2½hr lesson $150, stand-up paddleboarding 2hr $50) Also hires out kayaks (half day $35) and bikes (two hours $19).

Go Ride A Wave SURFING
(☎1300 132 441; www.gorideawave.com.au; 2hr surf lesson $60, surfboard hire 2hr $25, stand-up paddleboard hire 1hr $25)

Noosa Adventures & Kite-Surfing KITESURFING
(☎0458 909 012; www.noosakitesurfing.com.au; 2hr/8hr kitesurfing lesson $160/440)

Noosa Longboards SURFING
(Map p145; ☎5447 2828; www.noosalongboards.com; 255 Hastings St, Noosa; 2hr surfing lesson

SUNSHINE COAST IN....

Two Days

Plan to spend a full day at **Australia Zoo** getting acquainted with Australia's slimy-faced, scaly-skinned natives and a bevy of other weird and wonderful critters. Then see how many 'crikeys' you can slip into the conversation over dinner at one of **Mooloolaba's** esplanade al fresco restaurants.

Head up to **Noosa** on day two to surf the breaks followed by an afternoon bushwalk through the **Noosa National Park**. When the sun goes down stroll along Hastings St, take time to see and be seen before choosing from the swish **restaurants** on offer.

Four Days

The choice for the next two days lies between a rustic back-to-nature trip into the **Everglades**, canoeing and camping along the Upper Noosa River; or driving up the range for an easy rainforest walk to the beautiful **Kondalilla Falls** followed by a romantic stay in a boutique cottage in **Montville**. Have lunch in funky town **Maleny** before returning to the coast.

$60, half-/full-day surfboard hire $35/50, body-board hire per day $10)

Noosa Surf Lessons SURFING
(☎0400 182 614; www.noosasurflessons.com.au; 2hr lesson $75, 3 lessons $165)

Canoeing & Kayaking

The Noosa River is excellent for canoeing; it's possible to follow it up through Lakes Cooroibah and Cootharaba, and through the Cooloola Section of Great Sandy National Park.

Noosa Ocean Kayak Tours KAYAKING
(☎0418 787 577; www.learntosurf.com.au; 2hr tours $66, kayak hire per day $55) Tours around Noosa National Park and along the Noosa River.

Kayak Noosa KAYAKING
(Map p148; ☎0448 567 321; www.kayaknoosa.com; 194 Gympie Tce, Noosaville; 2hr sunset kayak $60, half-/full-day guided kayak tour $95/155) Tours around Noosa National Park. Also hires out kayaks (single/double two hours $25/40).

Adventure Activities

Noosa Ocean Rider SPEEDBOAT
(Map p148; ☎0438 386 255; cnr Gympie Tce & Weyba Rd, Noosaville; 1hr $70) Thrills and spills on a very fast and powerful speedboat.

Noosa Bike Hire & Tours MOUNTAIN BIKING
(☎5474 3322; www.bikeon.com.au; tours $95) Half-day mountain-bike tours along the Noosa Trail Network and along the Noosa Enduro 100km course.

Cruises

Gondolas of Noosa GONDOLA CRUISES
(Map p145; ☎0412 929 369; www.gondolasofnoosa.com) Romantic and moonlit cruises along the Noosa River leave from the Sheraton Jetty. Prices start from $150 for an hour; add extra for nibbly platters and champagne.

Noosa Ferry RIVER CRUISES
(☎5449 8442) Bring your own alcohol while cruising the waters of Noosa Sound on the popular Sunset Cruise (per person $19.50; Tuesday to Saturday) Also has 90-minute round-trip cruises to Tewantin from the Sheraton Jetty.

Horse Riding & Camel Safaris

Clip Clop Treks HORSE RIDING
(☎0429 051 544; www.clipcloptreks.com.au; Eumarella Rd, Lake Weyba; 2hr rides $90) Offers horse rides around (and in) Lake Weyba and the surrounding bush. For more information on horse rides (and camel rides) on the beach and in the bush, see p162.

☞ Tours

Fraser Island

A number of operators offer trips to Fraser Island via the Cooloola Coast.

Fraser Island Adventure Tours 4WD
(☎5444 6957; www.fraserislandadventuretours.com.au; day tour $170) Has won several industry awards for its day tour to Eli Creek and Lake McKenzie and packs as much punch as a two-day tour.

Trailblazer Tours 4WD
(☎1800 639 518, 5499 9595; www.trailblazertours.com.au; 3-day safaris per person $330) Operates small group tours and can pick up and drop off at either Noosa or Rainbow Beach. Also offers two-day safaris for $260. Popular with backpackers.

Discovery Group 4WD
(☎5449 0393; www.thediscoverygroup.com.au; day tour adult/child $159/115) Visit the island in a big black 4WD truck. Guided rainforest walk at Central Station, visits Lakes Birrabeen and McKenzie.

For more information about tours to Fraser Island, see the boxed text (p195).

If you're cashed up and want to do it the spectacular way, **Air Fraser Island** (☎1800 247 992; www.airfraserisland.com.au) and **Sunshine Aviation** (☎5450 5665; www.sunshineaviation.com.au) offer fly-drive packages including flights to Fraser Island and 4WD hire for self-guided day trips. Tours cost $250 to $300 per person.

Everglades

The passage of the Noosa River that cuts into the Great Sandy National Park is poetically known as the 'river of mirrors' or the Everglades. It's a great place to launch a kayak and camp along the many **national park campgrounds** (www.derm.qld.gov.au; per person/family $5.15/20.60) along the riverbank. Otherwise take a tour:

Discovery Group BOAT CRUISE
(☎5449 0393; www.thediscoverygroup.com.au; day tour adult/child $155/105) Includes a 4WD trip along the coloured sands and a boat cruise in the Everglades. On Wednesday and Saturday, visit the Eumundi markets and cruise the Everglades in the afternoon (per person $125).

Kanu Kapers KAYAKING
(☎5485 3328; www.kanukapersaustralia.com; 11 Toolara St, Boreen Point; per person from $145, overnight trip $145) Guided or self-guided kayaking trips into the Everglades. Kayak hire per day from $65.

Scenic Tours

The Eumundi markets are popular on Wednesdays and Saturdays. A couple of companies throw in an extra dash of pizzazz:

Boomerang Tours SCENIC
(☎1800 763 077; per person $59) Following the 'hippie trail', visits Eumundi markets, Kondalilla Falls, Montville and Mary Cairncross Reserve. Includes sausage sizzle lunch.

On the Prowl Surf n Adventures SCENIC
(☎0450 279 623; www.ontheprowl.com.au; per person $59) Follow a stint at the Eumundi markets with two hours of surfing, kayaking or wake-boarding. After lunch, swim in hinterland waterfalls, before stopping for a beer on the way home.

Festivals & Events

Noosa Food & Wine Festival GASTRONOMIC
(☎5447 5666; www.noosafoodandwine.com.au) A three-day tribute to all things of gastronomic and culinary delight. In May.

Noosa Long Weekend CULTURAL
(☎5474 9941; www.noosalongweekend.com) Ten-day festival of arts, culture, food and fashion in June/July.

Noosa Jazz Festival MUSIC
(☎5449 9189; www.noosajazz.com.au) Four-day annual jazz festival, attracting artists from around the globe and held in late August and early September.

Noosa Triathlon TRIATHLON
(☎5449 0711; www.usmevents.com.au) Week-long sports festival in early November culminating in the very popular triathlon.

Sleeping

Accom Noosa (Map p145; ☎1800 072 078; www.accomnoosa.com.au; Shop 5, Fairshore Apartments, Hastings St, Noosa Heads) has an extensive list of private holiday rentals that are good for stays of three nights or more.

With the exception of backpackers' hostels, accommodation prices can rise by 50% in busy times and 100% in the December to January peak season. During these times most places require a minimum two- or three-night stay. Low season rates are quoted.

Islander Noosa Resort RESORT **$$**
(Map p148; ☎5440 9200; www.islandernoosa.com.au; 187 Gympie Tce, Noosaville; 2-/3-bedroom villa $178/205; ❄@🛜🏊) Set on 4 acres of lush tropical gardens, with a central tropical pool and wooden boardwalks meandering through the trees to your comfortable bungalow, this resort is excellent value. It's bright and cheerful and packs a cocktail-swilling, island-resort ambience.

Picture Point Terraces APARTMENTS **$$$**
(Map p145; ☎5449 2433; www.picturepointterraces.com.au; 47 Picture Point Cres, Noosa Heads;

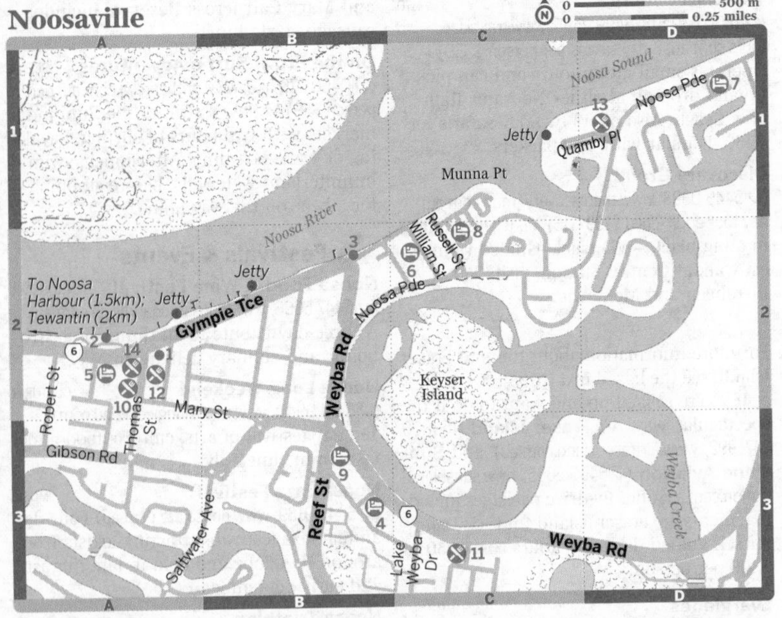

Noosaville

Activities, Courses & Tours

1 Adventure Sports Noosa ... A2
2 Kayak Noosa ... A2
3 Noosa Ocean Rider ... B2

Sleeping

4 Anchor Motel Noosa ... B3
5 Islander Noosa Resort ... A2
6 Noosa Backbackers Resort ... C2
7 Noosa Parade Holiday Inn ... D1
8 Noosa River Caravan Park ... C2
9 Noosa River Retreat ... B3

Eating

10 Burger Bar ... A2
11 Humid ... C3
12 Red on Thomas ... A2
13 Ricky's River Bar & Restaurant ... D1
14 Thomas Corner ... A2
Wasabi ... (see 13)

2-/3-bedroom apt from $410/480;) On high ground behind Noosa these ultra-chic apartments with all the mod cons have fantastic views over the rainforest to Laguna Bay. The private spa bath on the balcony is the ideal spot for a sunset cocktail. There's a seven-night minimum stay in high season.

#2 Hastings St APARTMENTS **$$$**
(Map p145; 5448 0777; www.2hastingsst.com.au; 2 Hastings St, Noosa Heads; units from $225;) These two-bedroom, two-bathroom units at the Noosa Woods end of Hastings St are great value as a four-share. Units overlook the river or the woods, and you're within a short walk of everything. Minimum two-night stay.

Sheraton Noosa Resort RESORT **$$$**
(Map p145; 5449 4888; www.starwoodhotels.com/sheraton; 14-16 Hastings St, Noosa Heads; r $255;) As expected, this five-star hotel has tastefully decorated rooms with suede fabrics, fabulous beds, balconies, kitchenettes and spas. The hotel houses the popular bar Cato's as well as a day spa.

YHA Halse Lodge HOSTEL **$**
(Map p145; 1800 242 567, 5447 3377; www.halselodge.com.au; 2 Halse Lane, Noosa Heads; members/nonmembers dm $29/32, d $78/86; meals $10-15;) Elevated from Hastings St by a steeeep driveway, this splendid colonial-era timber Queenslander is a legend on the backpacker route. There are three- and six-

bed dorms as well as doubles and a lovely wide veranda. The bar is a mix-and-meet bonanza and serves great meals.

Emerald APARTMENTS **$$$**
(Map p145; ☎1800 803 899, 5449 6100; www.emeraldnoosa.com.au; 42 Hastings St, Noosa Heads; 1-bedroom apt from $255; ❄@📶🏊) The stylish Emerald has indulgent rooms bathed in ethereal white and sunlight. Expect clean, crisp edges and exquisite furnishings. All one-, two- and three-bedroom apartments are fully self-contained but ask for a balcony with a view.

Anchor Motel Noosa MOTEL **$$**
(Map p148; ☎5449 8055; www.anchormotelnoosa.com.au; cnr Anchor St & Weyba Rd, Noosaville; r from $115; ❄🏊📶) There's no escaping the nautical theme in this colourful motel. Blue-striped bedspreads, porthole windows and marine motifs may inspire you to wear stripes and cut-offs while grilling prawns on the barbie.

Noosa Parade Holiday Inn APARTMENTS **$$**
(Map p148; ☎5447 4177; www.noosaparadeholidayinn.com; 51 Noosa Pde, Noosa Heads; r $125; ❄🏊📶) Not far from Hastings St, these large, bright apartments are good value. The pleasant and cool interiors are clad in bold colours and face away from the street and passing traffic.

Noosa River Retreat APARTMENTS **$$**
(Map p148; ☎5474 2811; www.noosariverretreat.net; cnr Weyba Rd & Reef St, Noosaville; studio $110; ❄@📶🏊) Your buck goes a long way at this orderly complex, which houses spick, span and spacious units. On site are a central barbecue and a laundry, and the corner units are almost entirely protected by small native gardens.

Nomads Backpackers HOSTEL **$**
(☎5447 3355; www.nomadshostels.com; 44 Noosa Dr, Noosa Junction; dm from $26; @📶🏊) One of the Nomads chain, this hostel has the usual trademarks – popular bar, central location and party atmosphere. You can't get less than an eight-bed dorm but you'll be partying so hard it won't matter. There's a tour desk on site.

Noosa Backpackers Resort HOSTEL **$**
(Map p148; ☎1800 626 673, 5449 8151; www.noosabackpackers.com; 9-13 William St, Noosaville; dm/d $25/58; @🏊) The concrete courtyard that greets you on arrival here isn't particularly welcoming but this is a quiet and pleasant hostel in the backstreets of Noosaville. It's looking decidedly tired, and the six-bed dorms and doubles all have shared bathrooms.

Noosa River Caravan Park CARAVAN PARK **$**
(Map p148; ☎5449 7050; Russell St, Noosaville; unpowered/powered sites $31/39; 📶) On the banks of the Noosa River, this park has the closest camping facilities to Noosa but although it's in a pretty spot the caravan park's rules and regulations might make you think twice before pitching your tent.

Eating

You can eat well for around $10 at the **Bay Village Shopping Centre food court** (Map p145; Hastings St, Noosa Heads). Self-caterers can stock up at the Noosa Fair Shopping Centre in Noosa Junction.

Berardo's MODERN AUSTRALIAN **$$$**
(Map p145; ☎5447 5666; Hastings St; mains $30-42; ⊙dinner) Beautiful Berardo's is culinary Utopia, from the sun-dappled setting swimming in elegance to the heavenly food. Soft music from the grand piano and delicate dishes made from fresh local produce will have you swooning in gustatory ecstasy.

Humid MODERN AUSTRALIAN **$$**
(Map p148; ☎5449 9755; 195 Weyba Rd, Noosaville; mains $25-30; ⊙lunch & dinner Wed-Sun) It might feel as though you're eating inside a designer warehouse in this high-ceilinged, two-storey restaurant but the food begs to differ. The Italian influences are subtle and classy and Humid is consistently rated as one of the best restaurants in Noosa.

Gaston MODERN AUSTRALIAN **$$**
(Map p145; 5/50 Hastings St; mains $17-25; ⊙breakfast, lunch & dinner) This casual al fresco bar and bistro is highly recommended by the locals. It's also a great place to watch the passing parade of beautiful people.

Berardo's on the Beach MODERN AUSTRALIAN **$$**
(Map p145; ☎5448 0888; on the beach, Hastings St; mains $20-36; ⊙breakfast, lunch & dinner) Reminiscent of the French Riviera, this stylish bistro is only metres from the waves. Classy without being pretentious, this is Noosa in a seashell. The Mod Oz menu uses local produce with a focus on seafood.

Wasabi JAPANESE **$$**
(Map p148; ☎5449 2443; 2 Quamby Place, Noosaville; mains $20-33; ⊙dinner Tue-Sun, lunch Fri & Sat) The must-try is this award-winning Japanese restaurant's signature dish, Hiramasa Ponzu: kingfish sashimi slices on a long glass plank, drizzled with toasted sesame

seeds, fried ginger chips, sliced green onions and citrusy soy ponzu dressing.

Red on Thomas FUSION **$$**
(Map p148; 4 Thomas St, Noosaville; mains $15-25; ⌚lunch & dinner Tue-Sun) A popular venue for Noosaville locals, this casual street eatery is always busy. Consistently good food with an emphasis on seafood and pizza, and a large selection of cocktails are guaranteed to make anyone happy.

Thomas Corner MODERN AUSTRALIAN **$$**
(Map p148; cnr Thomas St & Gympie Tce, Noosaville; mains $15-31; ⌚lunch & dinner) A newcomer to Noosaville's 'Eat Street', this casual al fresco restaurant oozes trendy-chic with its rough concrete floor and concrete and wooden furnishings. The relaxed menu showcases simple dishes without fuss but with style.

Bistro C MODERN AUSTRALIAN **$$**
(Map p145; ☎5447 2855; on the beach, Hastings St; mains $25-35; ⌚breakfast, lunch & dinner) The menu at this yuppie beachfront brasserie is an eclectic blend of everything that seems like a good idea at the time. The legendary egg-fried calamari is still popular.

Ricky's River Bar & Restaurant
MODERN AUSTRALIAN **$$$**
(Map p148; ☎5447 2455; Noosa Wharf, 2 Quamby Pl; mains $30-40; ⌚lunch & dinner) In a perfect location on the Noosa River, this elegant restaurant has a simple, well-executed menu favouring local produce like Noosa spanner-crab spaghettini. The tapas menu is tantalising.

Café Le Monde MODERN AUSTRALIAN **$$**
(Map p145; Hastings St; mains $15-28; ⌚breakfast, lunch & dinner) There's not a fussy palate or dietary need that isn't catered for on Café Le Monde's enormous menu. The large, open-air patio buzzes with diners digging into burgers, seared tuna steaks, curries, pastas, salads and plenty more. Come for daily happy-hour drinks between 4pm and 6pm.

Lindoni's ITALIAN **$$$**
(Map p145; ☎5447 5111; Hastings St; mains $20-50; ⌚dinner) Behind the gothic candelabra guarding the entrance, this romantic Italian restaurant has a Mediterranean courtyard for intimate candlelit dining. The cuisine favours the lighter southern Italian style – think Positano and the Amalfi coast – with lashings of *amore*.

Aromas CAFE **$**
(Map p145; 32 Hastings St; mains $10-28; ⌚breakfast, lunch & dinner) This European-style cafe is unashamedly ostentatious with chandeliers, faux-marble tables and cane chairs deliberately facing the street so patrons can ogle the passing foot traffic. There's the usual array of *panini*, cakes and light meals but most folk come for the coffee and the atmosphere.

Noosa Heads SLSC PUB FARE **$$**
(Map p145; Hastings St; mains $10-28; ⌚breakfast Sat & Sun, lunch & dinner daily) Perfect beach views from the deck.

Massimo's GELATI **$**
(Map p145; Hastings St; gelati $2-4; ⌚9am-10pm) Definitely one of the best *gelaterias* in Queensland.

Burger Bar BURGERS **$**
(Map p148; 4 Thomas St, Noosaville; burgers $10-15; ⌚11am-9pm) Informal and quirky venue, dishing up hormone-free, vegetarian, and weird and wonderful Burgerian delights.

Drinking & Entertainment

Zachary's BAR
(Map p145; 30 Hastings St, Noosa Heads) This shabby-chic, second-storey 'gourmet pizza bar' is a favourite meeting place and night-starter.

KB's BAR
(44 Noosa Dr, Noosa Junction) Noosa's backpackers and other free spirits start their nightly revelry at this popular hostel bar. Live rock fills every crevice several nights a week; when it doesn't, the place hums to the harmony of beer jugs and beery banter.

Cato's COCKTAIL BAR
(Map p145; Sheraton, 16 Hastings St) As well as a decadent cocktail list, Cato's boasts over 30 wines by the glass. The place can get noisy, especially on Friday nights when live music draws the crowds.

The J THEATRE
(☎5455 4455; www.thej.com.au; 60 Noosa Dr, Noosa Junction) The J, aka The Junction, showcases a broad range of artistic, cultural and musical performances from world and rock to classical. Check the website for event details.

Information

Noosa has an amazing number of roundabouts and it's easy to get lost. Broadly speaking, Noosa encompasses three zones: Noosa Heads (around Laguna Bay and Hastings St), Noosaville (along the Noosa River) and Noosa Junction (the administrative centre).

Noosa visitors centre (Map p145; ☎5430 5020; www.visitnoosa.com.au; Hastings St; ⏰9am-5pm)

Palm Tree Tours (Map p145; ☎5474 9166; www.palmtreetours.com.au; Bay Village Shopping Centre, Hastings St; ⏰9am-5pm) Very helpful tour desk. Can book tours, accommodation and bus tickets.

Post office (91 Noosa Dr)

Urban Mailbox (Ocean Breeze, Noosa Dr, Noosa Heads; per 15min $3; ⏰8am-8pm) Super-expensive internet access.

ℹ Getting There & Away

Long-distance buses stop at the bus stop near the corner of Noosa Dr and Noosa Pde (Map p145). **Greyhound Australia** (☎1300 473 946; www.greyhound.com.au) has several daily connections from Brisbane ($32, 2½ hours) while **Premier Motor Service** (☎13 34 10; www.premierms.com.au) has one ($23, 2½ hours). **Veolia** (☎1300 826 608; www.vtb.com.au) has an express service from Brisbane to Noosa (one way/return $25/46) twice daily.

At the time of research a new transit centre was under construction in Noosa Dr, Noosa Junction. Once completed, long-distance buses will arrive here.

Sunbus (☎13 12 30) has frequent services to Maroochydore ($5, one hour) and the Nambour train station ($5, one hour).

ℹ Getting Around

Bicycle

Noosa Bike Hire and Tours (☎5474 3322; www.bikeon.com.au; per 4hr/day $29/39) hires out bicycles from several locations in Noosa including Nomads Backpackers. Alternatively, bikes are delivered to and picked up from your door for free.

Boat

Noosa Ferry (☎5449 8442) operates ferries between Noosa Heads and Tewantin (one way adult/child/family $13/4.50/30, all-day pass $19.50/5.50/45; 30 minutes). Tickets include onboard commentary, so the ferry provides a tour as well as being a people-mover.

Bus

During the peak holiday seasons – 26 December to 10 January and over Easter – there are free shuttle buses every 10 to 15 minutes between Weyba Rd, just outside Noosa Junction, travelling all the way to Tewantin, and stopping just about everywhere in between. Sunbus has local services that link Noosa Heads, Noosaville, Noosa Junction and Tewantin.

Car

Car rental starts from around $60 per day.

Avis (☎5447 4933; Shop 1, Ocean Breeze Resort, cnr Hastings St & Noosa Dr, Noosa Heads)

Budget (☎5474 2820; 52 Mary St, Noosaville)

Hertz (☎5447 2253; 12 Eenie Creek Rd, Noosaville)

Thrifty (Accom Noosa, Shop 5, Fairshore Apartments, Hastings St, Noosa Heads)

Bribie Island

POP 15,920

This slender island at the northern end of Moreton Bay is popular with young families, retirees and those with a cool million or three to spend on a waterfront property. It's far more developed than Stradbroke or Moreton Islands but the **Bribie Island National Park** on the northwestern coast has some beautifully remote **national park camping areas** (www.derm.qld.gov.au; per person/family $5.15/20.60). Note that access is by 4WD only.

There's no 4WD hire on the island and 4WD permits (per week/year $37.65/117.60) can be purchased online (www.derm.qld.gov.au). You can also purchase permits at **Bribie Passage Kiosk and Boat Hire** (☎5497 5789; 23 Kalmakuta Dr, Sandstone Point; ⏰6am-4pm Mon-Fri, 5.30am-5.30pm Sat & Sun). **Bribie Island visitors centre** (☎3408 9026; www.bribie.com.au; Benabrow Ave, Bellara; ⏰9am-4pm Mon-Fri, 9am-3pm Sat, 9.30am-1pm Sun) has more information.

The **Inn Bongaree** (☎3410 1718; www.innbongaree.com.au; 25 Second Ave, Bongaree; s/d $50/65) is a great budget option or you can stay at **Sylvan Beach Resort** (☎3408 8300; www.sylvanbeachresort.com.au; d from $170; ❄@🏊), which has comfortable self-contained units across the road from the beach.

There are plenty of restaurants. For proper Aussie tucker, try the **Bribie Island RSL** (99 Toorbul St, Bongaree; mains $10-20; ⏰lunch & dinner).

Frequent Citytrain services run from Brisbane to Caboolture where a Trainlink bus connects to Bribie Island.

Glass House Mountains

The ethereal volcanic crags of the Glass House Mountains rise abruptly from the subtropical plains 20km northwest of Caboolture. In Dreamtime legend the highest of the 16 pointy peaks and domes, Mt

UNEXPECTED TREASURE: ABBEY MUSEUM

The impressive art and archaeology collection in the **Abbey Museum** (☎5495 1652; www.abbeymuseum.asn.au/home.htm; 1 The Abbey Pl; adult/child $8.80/5; ⊙10am-4pm Mon-Sat) spans the globe and would be at home in any of the world's famous museums. Once the private collection of Englishman John Ward, the pieces – including neolithic tools, medieval manuscripts and even an ancient Greek foot-guard (one of only four in the world) – will have you scratching your head in amazement.

Near the museum, the **Abbey Church** has more original stained glass from Winchester Cathedral than what is actually left in the cathedral. In July, you can make merry at Australia's largest medieval festival, held on the grounds.

The Abbey Museum is on the road to Bribie Island, 6km from the Bruce Hwy (M1) turn-off where you'll find the **Caboolture Warplane Museum** (☎5499 1144; Hangar 104, Caboolture Airfield, McNaught Rd; adult/child/family $8/5/18; ⊙9am-3pm), which has a collection of restored WWII warplanes, all in flying order.

Beerwah, is the mother of this family of mountain spirits. It's worth diverting off the Bruce Hwy (M1) onto the slower Steve Irwin Way (formerly the Glass House Mountains Rd) to snake your way through dense pine forests and green pastureland for a close-up view of these spectacular volcanic plugs.

The **Glass House Mountains National Park** is broken into several sections (all within cooee of Beerwah) with picnic grounds and lookouts but no camping grounds. The peaks are reached by a series of sealed and unsealed roads known as Forest Dr, which heads inland from Steve Irwin Way.

Sights & Activities

A number of signposted walking tracks reach several of the peaks but be prepared for some steep and rocky trails. **Mt Beerwah** (556m) is the most trafficked but has a section of open rock face that may increase the anxiety factor. The walk up **Ngungun** (253m) is more moderate but the views are just as sensational, while **Tibrogargan** (364m) is probably the best climb with a challenging scramble and several amazing lookouts from the flat summit. Rock climbers can usually be seen scaling Tibrogargan, Ngungun and Beerwah (for climbing information, visit www.qurank.com). **Mt Coonowrin** (aka 'crook-neck'), the most dramatic of the volcanic plugs, is closed to the public.

Sleeping & Eating

With only basic accommodation available, the Glass House Mountains are best visited as a day trip.

Glasshouse Mountains Holiday Village CARAVAN PARK $
(☎5496 9338; www.glasshousemountainsholidayvillage.com.au; 778 Steve Irwin Way, Glasshouse Mountains; unpowered/powered sites $25/35, cabins from $110; ❄≋) This park has comfortable, self-contained cabins, pretty sites and spectacular mountain views. Facilities include barbecues, a tennis court and a small cafe.

Glasshouse Mountains Tavern PUB FARE $$
(10 Reed St, Glasshouse Mountains; mains $15-25; ⊙lunch & dinner) This welcoming pub cooks up good pub nosh. The open fire keeps things cosy during winter and a peppering of outdoor seating is great for a midday middy on sunny days.

Caloundra

POP 20,140

Straddling a headland at the southern end of the Sunshine Coast, Caloundra is slowly shedding its staid retirement-village image without losing its sleepy seaside charm. Excellent fishing in Pumicestone Passage (the snake of water separating Bribie Island from the mainland) and a number of pleasant surf beaches make it a popular holiday resort for both families and water-sports action fans.

Sights & Activities

Caloundra's beaches curve around the headland so you'll always find a sheltered beach no matter how windy it gets. **Bulcock Beach**, just down from the main street and pinched by the northern tip of Bribie Island, captures a good wind tunnel, making it popular with kitesurfers. There's a lovely promenade on the foreshore that extends around to **Kings Beach** where there's a kiddie-friendly interactive water feature, and a free saltwater swimming pool on the rocks. The coastal track continues around the headland towards Currimundi. Depending on the conditions, **Moffat Beach** and **Dickey Beach** have the best surf breaks.

Q Surf School SURFING
(☎0404 869 622; www.qsurfschool.com; 1hr lesson $45, 3 lessons $120) Also offers stand-up paddleboarding (one-hour lesson $55).

Blue Water Kayak Tours KAYAKING
(☎5494 7789; www.bluewaterkayaktours.com; half-/full-day tours $75/150, minimum 4 people) Kayak across the channel to explore the northern tip of Bribie Island National Park.

Caloundra Cruise BOAT CRUISE
(☎5492 8280; www.caloundracruise.com; Maloja Ave Jetty; adult/child/family $20/10/45, 2½hr eco-explorer cruise adult/child $44/20) Cruise into Pumicestone Passage.

Sunshine Coast Skydivers SKYDIVING
(☎5437 0211; www.sunshinecoastskydivers.com.au; dives from $220) If you're mad enough to step out of a plane, you can be filmed in the process.

Queensland Air Museum MUSEUM
(☎5492 5930; www.qam.com.au; Caloundra Airport; adult/child/family $10/6/24; ⏲10am-4pm) Plenty of planes to keep budding aviators happy for hours.

DON'T MISS

CREATURE FEATURE: AUSTRALIA ZOO

Just north of Beerwah is one of Queensland's, if not Australia's, most famous tourist attractions.

Australia Zoo (☎5494 1134; www.australiazoo.com.au; Steve Irwin Way, Beerwah; adult/child/family $49/29/146; ⏲9am-4.30pm) is a fitting homage to its founder, and zany celebrity wildlife enthusiast, Steve Irwin. As well as all things slimy and scaly the zoo has an amazing wildlife menagerie complete with a Cambodian-style Tiger Temple, the Asian-themed Elephantasia, as well as the famous crocoseum. There are macaws, birds of prey, giant tortoises, snakes, otters, camels, and more crocs and critters than you can poke a stick at. Plan to spend a full day at this amazing wildlife park.

Various companies offer tours from Brisbane and the Sunshine Coast (see p165). The zoo operates a free courtesy bus from towns along the coast, as well as from the Beerwah train station (bookings essential).

Sleeping

There are plenty of high-rise apartments to choose from in Caloundra. There's often a minimum three- to five-night stay in high season. High season rates are quoted.

Rolling Surf Resort APARTMENTS $$$
(☎5491 9777; www.rollingsurfresort.com; Levuka Ave, Kings Beach; 1-/2-bedroom apt $240/400; ❄@📶🏊) This ultrachic resort directly on the beach has *très* modern furnishings, fantastic views and a heated pool. Be king of Kings Beach in the three-bedroom penthouse suite. In high season there's a minimum five-night stay.

City Centre Motel MOTEL $$
(☎5491 3301; 20 Orsovar Tce; d $100-119; ❄) The closest motel to the city centre holds no surprises but it's a small complex and the rooms, although basic, are comfortable.

Caloundra Backpackers HOSTEL $
(☎5499 7655; www.caloundrabackpackers.com.au; 84 Omrah Ave; dm/d $28/65; @📶) A newcomer to Caloundra, the dorms here are adequate, there's a comfy lounge and two decent kitchens. Plus you get free bike, surfboard and stand-up paddleboard hire. Budding masterchefs can pit their culinary skills against each other at the Friday night cooking comp.

Dicky Beach Family Holiday Park CARAVAN PARK $
(☎5491 3342; www.dicky.com.au; 4 Beerburrum St; unpowered/powered sites $32/35, cabins from $90; ❄🏊📶) You can't get any closer to one of Caloundra's most popular beaches. The brick cabins are as ordered and tidy as the grounds and there's a small swimming pool for the kids. Rates are for two people.

Belaire Place APARTMENTS $$
(☎5491 8688; www.belaireplace.com; 34 Minchinton St; apt from $175; ❄🏊📶) Overlooking Bulcock Beach, these spacious, one-bedroom apartments might have a poky design but you can watch the action on the beach from the large balcony. It's walking distance to the beach, cafes and restaurants.

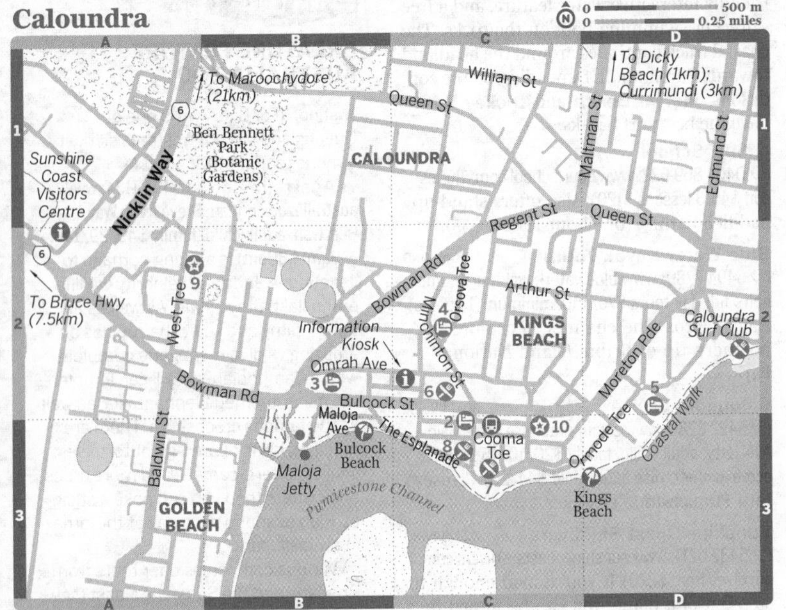

Caloundra

Activities, Courses & Tours

1 Caloundra Cruise B3

Sleeping

2 Belaire Place C3
3 Caloundra Backpackers B2
4 City Centre Motel C2
5 Rolling Surf Resort D2

Eating

6 Chilli Jam Café C2
7 La Dolce Vita C3
Saltwater@Kings .... (see 5)
8 Tides C3

Entertainment

9 Caloundra RSL A2
10 CBX C3

Eating

The newly spruced-up Bulcock Beach esplanade has a number of al fresco cafes and restaurants, all with perfect sea views.

Saltwater@Kings CAFE $$
(☎5437 2260; 8 Levuka Ave, Kings Beach; mains $16-35; ⏲breakfast, lunch & dinner) The playful menu at this casual beachside cafe promises nude oysters, spiced chook salad and a range of 'voluptuous dishes'. Perfect for lunch straight off the beach.

La Dolce Vita ITALIAN $$
(☎5438 2377; Shop 1, Rumba Resort, The Esplanade, Bulcock Beach; mains $20-35; ⏲breakfast, lunch & dinner) This modern Italian restaurant has a stylish black-and-white theme but it's best to sit outdoors behind the large glass windowed booth for al fresco dining with gorgeous sea views. Try the *gambari alio olio peperoncini* (prawns with garlic, oil and chilli peppers).

Tides SEAFOOD $$$
(☎5438 2304; 26 The Esplanade, Bulcock Beach; mains $35-50; ⏲lunch & dinner) For fine dining, exquisite seafood and stunning views of the Pumicestone Passage treat yourself to Tides. The non-fishy dishes are just as tempting as Neptune's bounty.

Chilli Jam Café CAFE $
(51 Bulcock St; mains $8-14; ⏲breakfast & lunch) A friendly couple from Yorkshire run this popular cafe where you can devour a range of gourmet sandwiches, wraps, salads and burgers.

Entertainment

CBX PUB
(12 Bulcock St) Queensland's only beer exchange hovers somewhere between an RSL

and a surf club. The bar works like a stock exchange, with beer prices rising and falling depending on demand. Live bands and DJs on weekends make this the local party scene.

Caloundra RSL CLUB
(19 West Tce) Some RSLs are small and unassuming affairs – not this one. With enough flamboyance to outdo Liberace, Caloundra's award-winning RSL has a number of restaurants and bars including the groovy 1970s-style Lava Lounge Bar. The glitzy atmosphere can be a little overwhelming.

Information

Hotspot Internet Café (☎5499 6644; Shop 8, 51 Bulcock St; per hr $6; ⏰9am-5pm Mon-Fri, to 3pm Sat)

Sunshine Coast visitors centre (☎5478 2233; 7 Caloundra Rd; ⏰9am-5pm) On the roundabout at the entrance to town. There's also a kiosk in the main street.

Getting There & Away

Greyhound (☎1300 473 946; www.greyhound.com.au) buses from Brisbane ($32, two hours) stop at the **bus terminal** (☎5491 2555; Cooma Tce). **Sunbus** (☎13 12 30) has frequent services to Noosa ($5.80, 1½ hours) via Maroochydore ($3.20, 50 minutes).

Mooloolaba & Maroochydore

POP 10,250 & 16,360

Mooloolaba has seduced many a 'sea-changer' with its sublime climate, golden beach and cruisy lifestyle. The locals here are proud of their surfing roots and relaxed beach culture. Just take a morning walk on the foreshore and you'll find walkers and joggers, suntans and surfboards, and a dozen genuine smiles before breakfast.

Mooloolaba and Maroochydore, along with Alexandra Headland and Cotton Tree, form the Maroochy region. While Maroochydore takes care of the business end, Mooloolaba steals the show. Eateries, boutiques and pockets of low-rise resorts and apartments have spread along the Esplanade, transforming this once-humble fishing village into one of Queensland's most popular holiday destinations. In summer Maroochy bursts with families indulging in good fishing and surf beaches, but it quickly reverts back to the tranquil epitome of coastal Oz for the remainder of the year.

Sights & Activities

Beaches SURFING
Serious beach-goers are spoilt for choice, especially on the beautiful Mooloolaba beach. If the surf's up, kiddies will find relatively calm water at the **Spit** at the southern end of the beach.

There are good surf breaks along the strip – one of Queensland's best for longboarders is the **Bluff**, the prominent point at Alexandra Headland. The beach breaks from Alex to Maroochydore are consistent even in a southerly, while **Pincushion** near the Maroochy River mouth can provide an excellent break in the winter offshore winds.

Ex-HMAS Brisbane DIVING
As well as surfing, diving onto the wreck of a sunken warship, the ex-HMAS *Brisbane* is incredibly popular. Sunk in July 2005, the wreck lies in 28m of water, and its funnels are only 4m below the surface.

Underwater World OCEANARIUM
(Map p159; The Wharf, Mooloolaba; www.underwaterworld.com.au; adult/child/family $32/22/90; ⏰9am-5pm) In the largest tropical oceanarium in the southern hemisphere, you can swim with seals, dive with sharks or simply marvel at the ocean life outside the 80m-long transparent underwater tunnel. There's a touch tank, seal shows and educational spiels to entertain both kids and adults.

Scuba World DIVING
(Map p159; ☎5444 8595; www.scubaworld.com.au; The Wharf, Mooloolaba; dives from $99; ⏰9am-5pm Mon-Sat, 10.30am-4pm Sun) Arranges shark dives (certified/uncertified divers $195/225) at Underwater World, coral dives off the coast and a wreck dive off the ex-HMAS *Brisbane*. PADI courses available.

Robbie Sherwell's XL Surfing Academy SURFING
(☎5478 1337; www.robbiesherwell.com.au; 1hr lesson private/group $95/45) Gets your toes wet.

Suncoast Kiteboarding KITEBOARDING
(☎0412 985 858; www.suncoastkiteboarding.com.au; 2hr lesson $180) At Cotton Tree, Noosa and Caloundra.

Sunshine Coast Kitesurfing Academy KITESURFING
(☎5479 2131; www.sunshinecoastkitesurfing.com.au; 1½hr lesson $150) At the mouth of the Maroochy River.

Sunreef DIVING
(☎5444 5656; www.sunreef.com.au; 110 Brisbane Rd, Mooloolaba; PADI Open Water Diver course

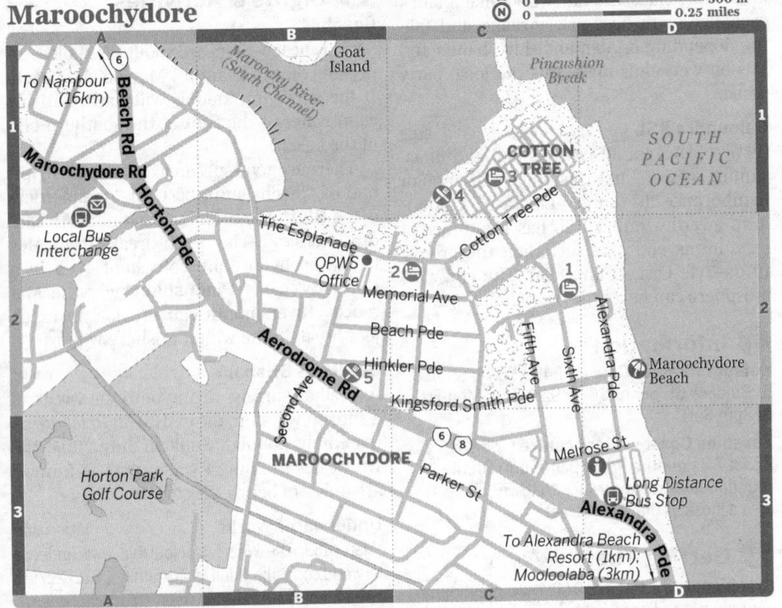

Maroochydore

Sleeping

1 Coral Sea Apartments........................C2
2 Cotton Tree Beach House Backpackers........................C2
3 Cotton Tree Caravan Park........................C1

Eating

4 Boat Shed........................C1
5 India Today........................B2

$595) Offers two dives ($145) on the wreck of the sunken warship, the ex-HMAS *Brisbane*. Also runs night dives on the wreck.

Hire Hut WATER SPORTS
(Map p159; ☎5444 0366; www.oceanjetski.com.au; The Wharf, Parkyn Pde, Mooloolaba) Hires out kayaks (two hours $25), stand-up paddleboards (two hours $35), jet skis (one hour $100) and boats (per hour/half-day $42/75)

Sunshine Coast Bike & Board Hire SPORTING HIRE
(☎0439 706 206; www.adventurehire.com.au) Hires bikes (per day $30), kayaks (per day $40) and surfboards (per day $25).

Swan's Boat Hire BOAT HIRE
(☎5443 7225; 59 Bradman Ave, Maroochydore; half-/full day $146/226; ⊙6am-6pm) On the Maroochy River. Also hires out kayaks (one hour/half-day $20/60).

Tours

Boat Cruises

Steve Irwin's Whale One WHALE WATCHING
(Map p159; ☎1300 27 45 39; www.whaleone.com.au; adult/child/family $135/75/330) Sunrise whale-watching cruises are available in September and October.

Canal Cruise BOAT CRUISES
(Map p159; ☎5444 7477; www.mooloolabacanalcruise.com.au; The Wharf, Mooloolaba; adult/child/family $18/6/45; ⊙11am, 1pm & 2.30pm) Cruises past the glitterati canal houses on the Mooloolah River. Bring your own alcohol and nibblies on the sundowner cruise (one hour $16/5/40).

Cruiz Away River Tours BOAT CRUISES
(Map p159; ☎5444 7477; www.cruisemooloolaba.com.au; The Wharf, Mooloolaba; ecotours adult/child $39/27, sunset cruise $30) Birdwatching and nature cruises on the Mooloolah River National Park.

Kayaking

Aussie Sea Kayak Company KAYAKING
(Map p159; ☎0407 049 747; www.ausseakayak.com.au; The Wharf, Mooloolaba; 4hr tour $65, 2hr

sunset paddle $45) Kayaking around Mooloolaba, Noosa Everglades, and multiday trips to North Stradbroke, Fraser and Moreton Islands.

Fraser Island

Fraser Island Adventure Tours 4WD
(☎5444 6957; www.fraserislandadventuretours.com.au; day tour $170) Has won several industry awards for its day tour to Eli Creek and Lake McKenzie and packs as much punch as a two-day tour. Pick-up points along the coast from Caloundra to Noosa.

Sleeping

During school holidays, rates can double, and most places require a minimum two- or three-night stay. Low season prices are quoted.

Landmark Resort RESORT $$
(Map p159; ☎1800 888 835, 5444 5555; www.landmarkresort.com.au; cnr Esplanade & Burnett St, Mooloolaba; studio/1-bedroom apt from $175/195; ❄@📶🏊) Nothing compares to the ocean views from these breezy apartments. The resort sits above Mooloolaba's trendy eateries and is only 20m from the beach. There's a heated lagoon-style pool, and a rooftop spa and barbecue.

Seamark on First APARTMENTS $$$
(Map p159; ☎5457 8600; www.seamarkresort.com.au; 29 First Ave, Mooloolaba; 1-bedroom apt from $180; ❄🏊📶) One street back from Mooloolaba's fashionable Esplanade this stylish and modern resort is bright, airy and spacious. Most apartments have ocean views – sit on the balcony and watch the moonrise over the water. There's a two-night minimum stay.

Kyamba Court Motel MOTEL $$
(Map p159; ☎5444 0202; www.kyambacourtmotel.com.au; 94 Brisbane Rd, Mooloolaba; d Mon-Fri $95, Sat $130; ❄🏊📶) Although this motel is on a busy road, it also fronts the canal where you can lounge around in comfort while throwing a few shrimps on the barbie. The rooms are large, comfortable and clean. It's a short walk into town and to the beach. Great value.

Coral Sea Apartments APARTMENTS $$
(Map p156; ☎5479 2999; www.coralsea-apartments.com; 35-7 Sixth Ave, Maroochydore; 1-/2-bedroom from $160/190; ❄@🏊) These yawning two- and three-bedroom apartments occupy a lovely spot close to Maroochy Surf Club and the beach. Inside you'll find tasteful decor and the balconies are plenty big and breezy.

Alexandra Beach Resort RESORT $$
(☎5475 0600; www.breakfreealexandrabeach.com.au; cnr Alexandra Pde & Pacific Tce, Alexandra Headland; studio/1-bedroom apt $170/199; ❄@📶🏊) Directly opposite the beach, these large and comfy apartments open onto either a courtyard or a balcony, but can be quite noisy. The 150m tropical-lagoon pool comes with a pool bar! There's a two-night minimum stay.

Mooloolaba Beach Backpackers HOSTEL $
(Map p159; ☎5444 3399; www.mooloolababackpackers.com; 75 Brisbane Rd, Mooloolaba; dm/d $28/70; @📶🏊) Some dorms have en suites, some don't, and although the rooms look a bit tired, the amount of freebies (bikes, kayaks, surfboards, stand-up paddleboards and breakfast) more than compensates. Besides, it's only 500m from the beachside day- and night-life.

Cotton Tree Beach House Backpackers HOSTEL $
(Map p156; ☎5443 1755; www.cottontreebackpackers.com; 15 The Esplanade, Cotton Tree; dm/d $26/55) The vibe is as warm as the brightly painted common-room walls and the atmosphere as laid-back as the fat Lab lolling on the sofa. Opposite a park and a river, this renovated century-old Queenslander is clean and homey and oozes charm. Note the free surfboards, kayaks and bikes.

Cotton Tree Caravan Park CARAVAN PARK $
(Map p156; ☎1800 461 253, 5443 1253; www.maroochypark.qld.gov.au; Cotton Tree Pde, Cotton Tree; unpowered/powered sites from $25/28, cabins $125-160) This baby sits right on the beach at the mouth of the Maroochy River. In summer it resembles a teeming suburb but it's a grassy spot with great facilities. Rates are for two people.

Mooloolaba Beach Caravan Park CARAVAN PARK $
(Map p159; ☎1800 441 201, 5444 1201; www.maroochypark.qld.gov.au; Parkyn Pde, Mooloolaba; powered sites from $35) This little beauty fronts lovely Mooloolaba Beach. It also runs a tiny van site at the northern end of the Esplanade that has the best location and views of any accommodation in town. Prices are for two people.

Eating

Bella Venezia ITALIAN $$$
(Map p159; ☎5444 5844; 95 Esplanade, Mooloolaba; mains $25-38; ⏰lunch & dinner) This understated yet casually chic restaurant with a funky wine bar spreads across an arcade cul-de-sac. The menu is extensive, and exclusively Italian, with exquisite dishes such as Moreton Bay Bug ravioli.

Boat Shed SEAFOOD $$
(Map p156; ☎5443 3808; Esplanade, Cotton Tree; mains $25-35; ⏰lunch daily, dinner Mon-Sat) A shabby-chic gem located on the banks of the Maroochy River, it's great for sunset drinks beneath the sprawling cotton tree. Seafood is the star of the menu and a must-try is the coconut-battered prawns with roasted banana and caramelised rum syrup. After dinner, roll back to the outdoor lounges for dessert and some seriously romantic star-gazing.

India Today INDIAN $$
(Map p156; ☎5452 7054; 91 Aerodrome Rd, Maroochydore; mains $15-22; ⏰lunch Thu-Sat, dinner daily) You can't miss the masses of fairy lights decorating this restaurant on Maroochydore's main drag. Be prepared for the brightly and chaotically coloured visual feast of Indian cloths, textiles, paintings and wall hangings waiting inside. The butter chicken with the chef's special sauce is delicious.

Nude CAFE $
(Map p159; Shop 3, Esplanade, Mooloolaba; dishes $6-18; ⏰breakfast & lunch) Occupying the prime position on the esplanade, this casual al fresco cafe is the ideal spot for people-watching, and for ocean views with your latte. Salads, wraps, gourmet sandwiches and naughty cakes will satisfy your post-swimming munchies.

Via Italia ITALIAN $$
(Map p159; ☎5477 7343; Shop 13, Peninsular Apartments, Esplanade, Mooloolaba; mains $17-25; ⏰breakfast, lunch & dinner) This stylish but casual outdoor restaurant opposite the beach is in the thick of the action. Come for a sundowner at the central bar. The gourmet pizzas will tempt you to linger on.

Karma Waters MODERN AUSTRALIAN $$
(Map p159; Mantra, Esplanade, Mooloolaba; mains $21-32; ⏰breakfast, lunch & dinner) Another outdoor eatery along the lively esplanade, Karma Waters dishes up Mod Oz cuisine with a Portuguese influence. The influence isn't always apparent but the meals are tasty. Try the seared Atlantic salmon with lemon caper butter sauce.

Raw Energy CAFE $
(Map p159; Mantra, Esplanade, Mooloolaba; dishes $6-18; ⏰breakfast & lunch) In this popular beachside cafe pretty young things serve up tofu, tempeh and gluten-free with 'zinger' juices. Muffin addicts will think they've found The One. Forget fast, but since this is the best coffee on the strip it's definitely worth the wait.

Thai Seasons THAI $
(Map p159; ☎5444 4611; 10 River Esplanade, Mooloolaba; mains $10-12; ⏰dinner) Affectionately known as 'dirty Thai', don't be put off by the plastic outdoor setting and grubby exterior. You have to grab your own cutlery, but this unpretentious restaurant dishes out the best Thai food in town. If it's crowded, order takeaway and head for the picnic tables overlooking Mooloolaba's main beach.

Drinking & Entertainment

Soave BAR
(Map p159; 17-19 Brisbane Rd, Mooloolaba) The place to meet for after-work drinks or to fuel up for a Friday night on the town. The gourmet pizza menu is matched with an impressive cocktail list.

Mooloolaba SLSC SURF CLUB
(Map p159; Esplanade, Mooloolaba; ⏰10am-10pm Sun-Thu, to midnight Fri & Sat) A traditional Aussie icon, the surf club somehow seamlessly morphs from a midweek good-value family outing to a weekend singles pick-up joint where local bands play 1980s dance music every Friday night. The floor-to-ceiling windows on the deck provide stunning views.

Fridays NIGHTCLUB
(Map p159; The Wharf, Parkyn Pde, Mooloolaba; ⏰Tue-Sat) It's loud, tacky and incredibly popular with backpackers and locals.

Information

The Mooloolaba Esplanade seamlessly morphs into Alexandra Pde along the beachfront at Alexandra Headland ('Alex' to the locals), then flows into Aerodrome Rd and the main CBD of Maroochydore. Cotton Tree is at the mouth of the Maroochy River.

Email Central Internet Lounge (19 The Esplanade, Cotton Tree; per hr $5; ⏰9am-8pm)

Post office Mooloolaba (☎13 13 18; cnr Brisbane Rd & Walan St); Maroochydore (Sunshine Plaza, Horton Pde)

Mooloolaba

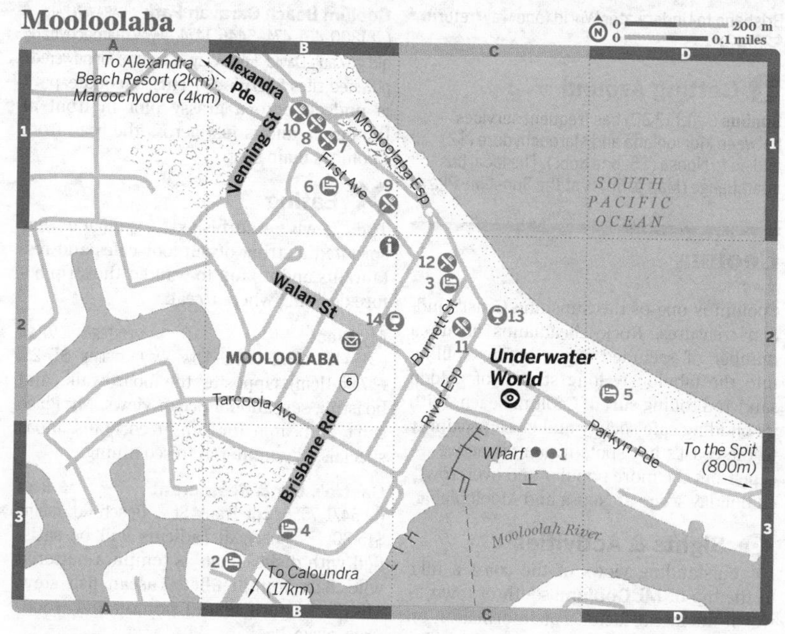

Mooloolaba

Top Sights

Underwater World C2

Activities, Courses & Tours

1 Aussie Sea Kayak Company C3
Canal Cruise .... (see 1)
Cruiz Away River Tours .... (see 1)
Hire Hut .... (see 1)
Scuba World .... (see 1)
Steve Irwin's Whale One .... (see 1)

Sleeping

2 Kyamba Court Motel B3
3 Landmark Resort C2
4 Mooloolaba Beach Backpackers B3
5 Mooloolaba Beach Caravan Park D2
6 Seamark on First B1

Eating

7 Bella Venezia B1
8 Karma Waters B1
9 Nude B1
10 Raw Energy B1
11 Thai Seasons C2
12 Via Italia C2

Drinking

13 Mooloolaba SLSC C2
14 Soave B2

Entertainment

Fridays .... (see 1)

QPWS office (Map p156; ☎5443 8940; 29 The Esplanade, Cotton Tree; ⊙8.30am-4.30pm Mon-Fri)

Sunshine Coast Visitor Information Centre (☎1800 644 969; www.maroochytourism.com; ⊙9am-5pm); Maroochydore (Map p156; cnr Sixth Ave & Melrose Sts); Mooloolaba (Map p159; cnr Brisbane Rd & First Ave); Sunshine Coast Airport (Friendship Dr, Marcoola)

Getting There & Away

Long-distance buses stop in front of the **Sunshine Coast Visitor Information Centre** (cnr Sixth Ave & Melrose St, Maroochydore). **Greyhound Australia** (☎1300 473 946; www.greyhound.com.au) and **Premier Motor Services** (☎13 34 10; www.premierms.com.au) run to and from Brisbane. Veolia (☎1300 826 608; www.vtb.com.au) has a direct service from

Brisbane to Underwater World (one way/return $23/42).

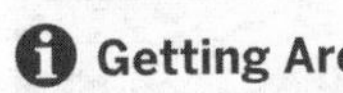

Getting Around

Sunbus (☎13 12 30) has frequent services between Mooloolaba and Maroochydore ($2) and on to Noosa ($5, one hour). The local bus interchange (Map p156) is at the Sunshine Plaza.

Coolum

POP 7180

Coolum is one of the Sunshine Coast's hidden treasures. Rocky headlands create a number of secluded coves before spilling into the fabulously long stretch of golden sand and rolling surf of Coolum beach. With its budding cafe society and close proximity to the coast's hot spots it's an attractive escape from the more popular and overcrowded holiday scene at Noosa and Mooloolaba.

Sights & Activities

For outstanding views of the coast a hike to the top of **Mt Coolum**, south of town, is worth the sweat factor. For information on how to get there, try the **visitors centre** (David Low Way; 9am-5pm Mon-Fri, 10am-4pm Sat).

Coolum Surf School (☎5446 5279; www.coolumsurfschool.com.au; 2hr lesson $50, 3-/5-day package $135/180) gets you standing on a board; the school also hires out stand-up paddleboards (24 hours $50).

Skydive Ramblers (☎5446 1855; www.skydiveforfun.com; jumps from 10,000/14,000ft $350/399) will throw you out of a plane at a ridiculous height. Savour the coastal view before a spectacular beach landing.

Sleeping

Villa Coolum MOTEL $

(☎5446 1286; www.villacoolum.com; 102 Coolum Tce, Coolum Beach; r $79-99;) Hidden behind a leafy veranda, these modest bungalows have spacious motel-style rooms fronting a long balcony. The refurbished rooms are good value.

Beach Retreat APARTMENTS $$

(☎5471 7700; www.beachretreatcoolum.com; 1750 David Low Way; d from $250 for minimum 2-night stay;) With ocean views and within walking distance to the esplanade eateries, these spacious apartments are in a great location. The central pool area is handy for rough beach weather. Standby one-night rates are available.

Coolum Beach Caravan Park CARAVAN PARK $

(☎1800 461 474, 5446 1474; www.maroochypark.qld.gov.au; David Low Way, Coolum; unpowered/powered sites $32/35;) This adequate park is nudged onto a grassy plot in front of the beach, and is just across the road from Coolum's main strip.

Eating

The newly refurbished esplanade has sprouted a string of outdoor cafes and restaurants and it's fun to wander the strip before deciding where to eat.

My Place MEDITERRANEAN $$

(☎5446 4433; David Low Way; mains $17-25; 7am-11pm) Opposite the boardwalk, and boasting sensational ocean views, My Place can't be beaten for sunset cocktails, tapas specials, or summer al fresco dining.

Castro's Bar & Restaurant ITALIAN $$

(☎5471 7555; cnr Frank St & Beach Rd; mains $15-30; dinner) All radicals will be satisfied with dishes such as tempura-battered wild Barramundi fillet, Tuscan fish stew, Middle Eastern seared salmon and wood-fired pizza.

Raw Energy CAFE $

(David Low Way; mains $6-14; breakfast & lunch) Après-surf, tuck into a raw energy lunch

THE HEAD IN THE SEA

Along the Maroochy coast you'll see a small rocky island a little way offshore of Mudjimba, near Coolum. Mudjimba Island is also known to locals as 'Old Woman Island' but according to Aboriginal legend this rocky outcrop is in fact the head of a mighty warrior, Coolum. It seems Coolum and Ninderry were two warriors in love with the same woman, Maroochy. Ninderry kidnapped her, Coolum rescued her, and in retaliation Ninderry knocked off his head.

This, of course, angered the gods who promptly turned Ninderry into a rock and Coolum into a mountain. From where it was catapulted 1km into the sea, Coolum's head became Mudjimba Island. Maroochy, grief-stricken, fled into the mountains and wept a river of tears – the Maroochy River. And where the old woman of 'Old Woman Island' came from is anybody's guess.

where the menu is full of salads, tofu and all things healthy.

Peregian & Sunshine Beach

POP 2800 & 2360

Fifteen kilometres of uncrowded, unobstructed beach stretches north from Coolum to Sunshine Beach and the rocky northeast headland of Noosa National Park. Peregian clusters around a small village square with only a few cafes and restaurants, its lack of nightlife a drawcard for holidaying families. This is the place for long solitary beach walks, good surf breaks, fresh air and sunshine – and it's not uncommon to see whales breaking offshore.

A little further north the laid-back latte ethos of Sunshine Beach attracts Noosa locals escaping the summer hordes. Beach walks morph into bush walks over the headland; a postprandial stroll through the **Noosa National Park** takes an hour to reach Alexandria Bay and two hours to Noosa's Laguna Bay. Road access to the park is from McAnally Dr or Parkedge Rd.

Sights & Activities

The **Peregian Originals** (www.eastcoastoriginals.org.au) is a changing line-up of both popular and obscure local, national and international bands. Attracting earth mothers, surfers and lovers of good music, these free Sunday afternoon sessions (first and third Sundays of the month) in the park in front of the Peregian SLSC have become a summer classic. Check the website for performance dates and details.

Learn to surf with **Wavesense** (☎0414 369 076; www.wavesense.com.au), twice voted Surfing Australia Surf School of the Year. For an extra thrill try **Kitesurfing** (☎1300 548 369, 0400 404 040; 1hr lesson $65).

Sleeping

It's hard to book anything less than a two-night stay in Sunshine Beach's holiday apartments.

Andari APARTMENTS $$$
(☎5474 9996; www.andari.com.au; 19-21 Belmore Tce, Sunshine Beach; 2-bedroom apt $200;) This quiet retreat of townhouses is set in shady, subtropical gardens. The apartments are light and airy, overlook the beach, and are a short stroll to cafes and restaurants.

Sunshine Beach

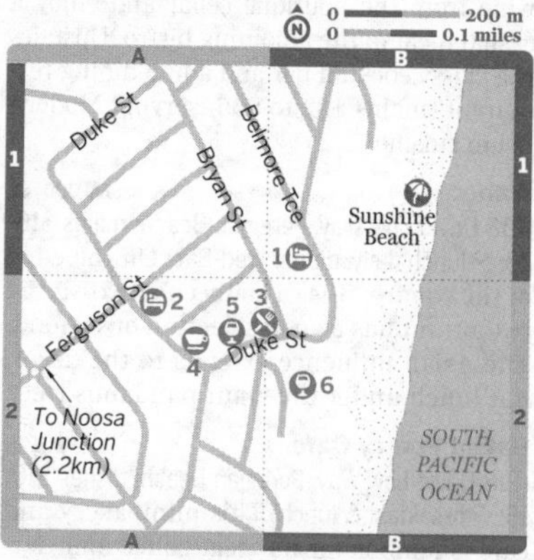

Sunshine Beach

Sleeping
1 Andari B1
2 Dolphins Beach House A2

Eating
3 Embassy XO A2

Drinking
4 Costa Noosa A2
5 Marble Bar Bistro A2
6 Sunshine Beach SLSC B2

Pacific Blue Apartments APARTMENTS $$
(☎5448 3611; www.pacificblueapartments.com.au; 236 David Low Way, Peregian Beach; r from $130;) Close to the pub *and* the beach, Pacific Blue has cheerful two-bedroom units, all self-contained and with a healthy amount of space.

Dolphins Beach House HOSTEL $
(☎5447 2100; www.dolphinsbeachhouse.com; 14 Duke St, Sunshine Beach; dm $24-26, d $65-75;) This cosy backpacker hostel is nestled in a patch of tropical gardens, and reflects the Asian and Mexican influences of its well-travelled owner. The rooms are basic and clean, there's plenty of kitchen space, it's close to cafes and the beach, and only a short bus ride to Noosa. Don't come looking for party central (there's no bar), but instead chill out before rejoining the frenzy of the backpacker trail.

Eating

Embassy XO MEDITERRANEAN $$
(☎5455 4460; cnr Duke & Bryan Sts, Sunshine Beach; mains $15-25; lunch & dinner) An innovative concept for the Sunshine Coast is

this chic bistro wine bar. Select a bottle of wine from the boutique cellar and enjoy a casual meal in the adjoining bistro. Upstairs is a classy cocktail bar and a fine-dining restaurant (mains $32 to $36) serving Modern Asian cuisine.

Wahoo SEAFOOD **$$**

(218 David Low Way, Peregian Beach; mains $16-23; ⊙lunch daily, dinner Wed-Sat) On the edge of the square, this casually cool two-storey restaurant has a good selection of seafood. The Asian influence extends to the decor. Eat lunch under the giant pandanus tree.

Baked Poetry Cafe CAFE **$**

(218 David Low Way, Peregian Beach; dishes $10-16; ⊙breakfast & lunch) This minibakery and cafe is famous for its great coffee and German sourdough bread. The *eier im glass* is a Frankfurt breakfast special where your soft-boiled eggs arrive in a glass alongside a plate of bacon, grilled tomato and cheese.

Drinking

Marble Bar Bistro BAR

(40 Duke St; tapas $12-19; ⊙noon-late) Kick back in a cushioned lounge or perch yourself at one of the marble benches at this cruisy cocktail and tapas bar sans door or walls. Pizzas are popular.

Costa Noosa CAFE

(26 Duke St, Sunshine Beach) The best coffee on the entire Sunshine Coast. Say no more.

Sunshine Beach SLSC SURF CLUB

(Duke St) The Sunday afternoon sessions are legendary, with live music, dancing and outstanding ocean views.

Cooloola Coast

Stretching for 50km between Noosa and Rainbow Beach, the Cooloola Coast is a long, remote strip of sandy beach backed by the Cooloola Section of the **Great Sandy National Park**. Although it's undeveloped, the 4WD and tin-boat sets flock here in droves so it's not always as peaceful as you might imagine. If you head off on foot or by canoe along the many inlets and waterways, however, you'll soon escape the crowds.

From the end of Moorindil St in Tewantin, the **Noosa North Shore Ferry** (☎5447 1321; pedestrians/cars one way $1/6; ⊙5.30am-12.20am Fri & Sat, to 10.20pm Sun-Thu) shuttles folk across the river to Noosa North Shore. The trip takes a matter of minutes; if you're sporting a caravan on the back of your car it's an extra $6 to $8. Most people head here for activities along the Noosa River and on Lake Cooroibah. If you have a 4WD you can drive along the beach to Rainbow Beach (and on up to Inskip Point to the Fraser Island ferry), but you'll need a permit (www.derm.qld.gov.au; per day/week/month $10/25/40). You can also buy a permit from the **Noosa visitors centre** (☎5430 5020; www.visitnoosa.com.au; Hastings St; ⊙9am-5pm) but it'll cost extra. Finally, check the tide times before setting out.

On the way up the beach you'll pass the **Teewah coloured sand cliffs**, estimated to be about 40,000 years old.

LAKE COOROIBAH

A couple of kilometres north of Tewantin, the Noosa River widens into Lake Cooroibah. If you take the Noosa North Shore Ferry, you can drive up to the lake in a conventional vehicle and camp along sections of the beach.

Camel Company Australia (☎0408 710 530; www.camelcompany.com.au; Beach Rd, North Shore, Tewantin; 1hr rides adult/child $60/45, 2hr rides $80/60) has beach camel rides. **Noosa Horseriding** (☎0438 710 530; www.noosahorseriding.com.au; 1/2hr rides $65/95, half-day rides $195) has rides in the beach and the bush.

Noosa Equathon (☎5474 2665; www.equathon.com; 1½hr beach ride $85, 1hr beach & bush ride $110) also offers multiday rides.

Noosa North Shore Retreat (☎5447 1225; www.noosanorthshoreretreat.com.au; Beach Rd; unpowered/powered sites from $15/24, r from $145, cabins from $65; ❄@≋) is a sprawling park with a variety of sleeping options and is in a great location on Lake Coorooibah. There's a minimum two-night stay on weekends.

Recycled materials have been used to build the basic dorms at **Gagaju Backpackers** (☎1300 302 271, 5474 3522; www.travoholic.com/gagaju; 118 Johns Dr, Tewantin; unpowered sites/dm $10/15; @), a no-frills riverside wilderness camp. If you want a rugged experience (complete with composting toilets) this will suit. Bring mozzie repellent!

LAKE COOTHARABA & BOREEN POINT

Cootharaba is the biggest lake in the Cooloola Section of Great Sandy National Park, measuring about 5km across and 10km in length. On the western shores of the lake and at the southern edge of the national park, Boreen Point is a relaxed little community with several places to stay and to eat. The lake is the gateway to the Noosa Everglades, offering bushwalking, canoeing and bush camping.

Kanu Kapers (☎5485 3328; www.kanukapersaustralia.com; 11 Toolara St, Boreen Point; kayak hire per day $65) offers guided or self-guided kayaking trips (per person $145, overnight trip $145) into the Everglades.

Cooloola Adventures (☎5485 3164; www.cooloolaadventures.com.au; 20 Boreen Point Pde, Boreen Point; canoe hire per day per person $99, 3-day camping safari $139) hires out canoes and kayaks for self-guided trips. The company also operates a water taxi to Kinaba (one way/return $15/30).

The two self-contained units at **Lake Cootharaba Gallery Units** (☎5485 3153; 64 Laguna St, Boreen Point; r per night from $99) are homey and practical. The gallery is a tad eccentric, linen costs extra, and there's a minimum two-night stay.

On the river, the quiet and simple **Boreen Point Camping Ground** (☎5485 3244; Dun's Beach, Teewah St, Boreen Point; unpowered/powered sites $15/22) is dominated by large gums and native bush. Take a right turn off Laguna St onto Vista St and bear right at the lake. Rates are for two people.

Apollonian Hotel (☎5485 3100; Laguna St, Boreen Point; mains $10-24; ⏲lunch & dinner) is a gorgeous old pub with sturdy timber walls, shady verandas and a beautifully preserved interior. The pub grub is tasty and popular. Come for the famous Sunday spit-roast lunch.

From Boreen Point, an unsealed road leads another 5km to **Elanda Point**.

GREAT SANDY NATIONAL PARK – COOLOOLA SECTION

The Cooloola Section of Great Sandy National Park covers more than 54,000 hectares from Lake Cootharaba north to Rainbow Beach. It's a varied wilderness area with long sandy beaches, mangrove-lined waterways, forest, heath and lakes, all featuring plentiful birdlife – including rarities such as the red goshawk and the grass owl – and lots of wildflowers in spring.

The Cooloola Way, which runs from Tewantin up to Rainbow Beach, is open to 4WD vehicles unless there's been heavy rain – check with the rangers before setting out. Most people prefer to bomb up the beach, though you're restricted to a few hours either side of low tide. You'll need a permit (www.derm.qld.gov.au; per day/week/month $10/25/40). Make sure you check the tides as many a 4WD has met a wet end at high tide.

Although there are many 4WD tracks to lookout points and picnic grounds, the best way to see Cooloola is by boat or canoe along the numerous tributaries of the Noosa River. Boats can be hired from Tewantin and Noosa (along Gympie Tce), and Boreen Point.

There are some fantastic walking trails starting from Elanda Point on the shore of Lake Cootharaba, including the 46km Cooloola Wilderness Trail to Rainbow Beach and a 7km trail to an unstaffed QPWS information centre at Kinaba.

Before you go, pop into the **QPWS Great Sandy Information Centre** (☎5449 7792; 240 Moorindil St, Tewantin; ⏲8am-4pm), which can provide information on park access, tide times and fire bans within the park. The centre issues car and camping permits for both Fraser Island and Great Sandy National Park but these are best booked online (www.derm.qld.gov.au).

The park has a number of camping grounds, many of them along the river. The most popular (and best-equipped) camping grounds are Fig Tree Point (at the northern end of Lake Cootharaba), Harry's Hut (about 4km upstream) and Freshwater (about 6km south of Double Island Point) on the coast. You can also camp (per person/family $5.15/20.60) at designated zones on the beach if you're driving up to Rainbow Beach. Apart from Harry's Hut, Freshwater and Teewah Beach, all sites are accessible by hiking or river only.

Eumundi

POP 490

Sweet little Eumundi is a quaint highland village with a quirky New Age vibe greatly amplified during its famous market days. The historic streetscape blends well with modern cafes, unique boutiques, silversmiths, crafts-people and body-artists doing their thing. Once you've breathed Eumundi air don't be surprised if you feel a sudden urge to take up beading or body-painting.

Sights & Activities

The **Eumundi markets** (⏲6.30am-2pm Sat, 8am-1pm Wed) attract thousands of visitors to their 300-plus stalls and have everything from hand-crafted furniture and jewellery to homemade clothes and alternative-healing booths.

The town's other claim to fame is Eumundi Lager, originally brewed in the Imperial Hotel. Nowadays it's made down at Yatala on the Gold Coast but you can still sample it on tap at the **Imperial Hotel** (Memorial Dr).

Beautiful glass sculptures and other works of art are on display at **Tina Cooper Glass** (5442 8110; www.tinacooper.com; 106 Memorial Dr; 9am-4pm Sat-Wed, 10am-3pm Thu, 11am-3pm Sun). On Saturdays you can see glass-blowing artists at work.

Murra Wolka Creations (5442 8691; www.murrawolka.com; 39 Memorial Dr; 9am-4.30pm Mon-Fri) is Aboriginal-owned and operated. Here you can buy boomerangs and didgeridoos hand-painted by indigenous artists. They can also arrange dance performances by the Gubbi Gubbi dancers.

Kiddies will love a visit to the **Ginger Factory** (5446 7100; www.gingerfactory.com.au; 50 Pioneer Rd, Yandina; admission free; 9am-5pm). There are train rides, factory and plantation tours and, of course, a huge range of ginger products and souvenirs on sale. To get there, take the Bruce Hwy (M1) south from Eumundi.

About 10km northwest of Eumundi, the little village of **Pomona** sits in the shadow of looming Mt Cooroora (440m). Every year hardy athletes run to the summit to claim the title of 'King of the Mountain'.

In the village itself, the wonderful **Majestic Theatre** (5485 2330; www.majestictheatre.com.au; 3 Factory St, Pomona; Tue-Fri) is one of the only places in the world where you can see a silent movie accompanied by the original Wurlitzer organ soundtrack. For 21 years (until 2007) the theatre played only one film – Rudolph Valentino's *The Son of the Sheikh,* every Thursday night. Talkies are now screened but the focus remains firmly on the silent screen. For a step back in history, catch a **screening** (tickets $15, meal deal $27; 7.30pm) of the iconic *The Son of the Sheikh* on the first Thursday of each month.

Sleeping

Hidden Valley B&B B&B $$

(5442 8685; www.eumundibed.com; 39 Caplick Way; r $175-195;) This not-so-hidden retreat is on 1.5 hectares of land only 400m from Eumundi on the Noosa road. Inside this attractive Queenslander you can choose a themed room to match your mood – Aladdin's Cave, the Emperors Suite or the Hinterland Retreat. All have private balconies but there are simpler rooms (from $140) in the converted railcar in the garden. You'll love the attention to detail.

Harmony Hill Station B&B $$

(5442 8685; www.eumundibed.com; 81 Seib Rd; carriage $150;) Perched on a hilltop in a 5-hectare property, this restored and fully self-contained 1912 purple railway carriage is the perfect place to relax or to romance. Share the grounds with grazing kangaroos, watch the sunset from Lover's Leap, share a bottle of wine beneath a stunning night sky...or even get married (the owners are celebrants!). Breakfast and dinner hampers are available on request.

Eating

TOP CHOICE **Spirit House Restaurant** ASIAN $$$

(5446 8994; 20 Ninderry Rd, Yandina; mains $28-36; lunch daily, dinner Wed-Sat) This legendary restaurant is at Yandina, 11km south of Eumundi. The subtropical surrounds create a delightful Southeast Asian setting while the kitchen concocts divine Thai- infused innovations. Order the shared dining plates ($10) to sample all the exquisite offerings. If you feel inspired sign up for a cooking class.

Azzurro ITALIAN $$

(69 Memorial Dr; mains $13-28; breakfast Wed, Sat & Sun, lunch Tue-Sun, dinner Wed-Sat) Recommended by the locals, this breezy Italian restaurant has simple *panini* and salads as well as delicious-sounding dishes like roasted ducks breast with wilted radicchio and wild mushroom risotto.

Sala Thai THAI $

(Memorial Dr; dishes $10-16; lunch & dinner Tue-Sun) An excellent Thai restaurant that dishes up consistently good quality meals and comes highly recommended by the locals can't be missed. Enough said.

Berkelouw Café CAFE $

(5442 8422; 87 Memorial Dr; dishes $5-15; breakfast & lunch) One of the few cafes to open every day, this is the place for coffee, cakes and muffins. Take your coffee for a browse through the wonderful Berkelouw Books next door.

Drinking

Joe's Waterhole PUB

(www.musicliveatjoes.com; Memorial Dr) Built in 1891 this old pub has weathered over a century to attract big-name national and international musicians. Check the website for details.

WOODSTOCK DOWN UNDER

The famous **Woodford Folk Festival** features a huge diversity of over 2000 national and international performers playing folk, traditional Irish, indigenous and world music, as well as buskers, belly dancers, craft markets, visual-arts performances, environmental talks and a visiting squad of Tibetan monks. The festival is held on a property near the town of Woodford from 27 December to 1 January each year. Camping grounds are set up on the property with toilets, showers and a range of foodie marquees but be prepared for a mud bath if it rains. The festival is licensed, so leave your booze at home.

Tickets cost around $97 per day ($116 with camping) and can be bought online, at the gate or the **festival office** (☎5496 1066). Check online at www.woodfordfolkfestival.com for a program of performances.

Woodford is 35km northwest of Caboolture. Shuttle buses run regularly from the Caboolture train station to and from the festival grounds.

Information

Discover Eumundi Heritage and Visitors Centre (☎5442 8762; Memorial Dr; ⊙10am-4pm Mon-Fri, 9am-3pm Sat, 10am-2pm Sun) Also houses the museum (admission free).

Getting There & Away

Sunbus (☎13 12 30) runs hourly from Noosa Heads ($3.20, 40 minutes) and Nambour ($4.10, 30 minutes). A number of tour operators visit the Eumundi markets on Wednesdays and Saturdays.

SUNSHINE COAST HINTERLAND

Reaching heights of 400m and more, the Blackall Range forms a stunning backdrop to the Sunshine Coast's popular beaches, a short 50km away. A relaxed half- or full-day circuit drive from the coast follows a winding road along the razorback line of the escarpment, passing through quaint mountain villages and offering spectacular views of the coastal lowlands. The villages (some suffering an overdose of kitschy craft shops and Devonshire tearooms) are worth a visit but the real attraction is the landscape, with its lush green pastures and softly folded valleys and ridges, and the waterfalls, swimming holes, rainforests and walks in the national parks. Cosy cabins and B&Bs are popular weekend retreats, especially during winter.

Tours

Plenty of tour companies operate through the hinterland and will pick up from anywhere along the Sunshine Coast.

Boomerang Tours SCENIC
(☎1800 763 077; per person $59) Following the 'hippie trail', visits Kondalilla Falls, Montville, Mary Cairncross Reserve, as well as the Eumundi markets. Includes sausage sizzle lunch.

Storeyline Tours SCENIC
(☎5474 1500; www.storeylinetours.com.au; adult/child $90/55) Runs small-group tours to Montville and nearby rainforests, and trips to the Glass House Mountains.

Off Beat Rainforest Tours SCENIC
(☎5473 5135; www.offbeattours.com.au; adult/child $155/100) 4WD ecotours to Conondale National Park, including morning tea, a gourmet lunch and transfers.

Maleny

POP 1300

Perched high in the heart of the rolling green hills of the Blackall Range, Maleny is an intriguing melange of artists, musicians and creative souls, the ageing hippie scene, rural 'tree-changers' and cooperative ventures. Its quirky bohemian edge underscores a thriving commercial township that has well and truly moved on from its timber and dairy past without yielding to the tacky heritage developments and ye olde tourist-trap shoppes that have engulfed nearby mountain villages. There's a strong sense of community with amazing support for local 'co-ops' and environmental concerns, and equally stubborn resistance to amorphous corporations.

Sights & Activities

Mary Cairncross Scenic Reserve (Mountain View Rd) is a pristine rainforest shelter spread over 52 hectares southeast of town. Walking tracks snake through the rainforest and there's a healthy population of birdlife and unbearably cute pademelons.

Maleny Bookshop (39 Maple St; ⊙10am-4pm) is the sort of secondhand bookshop where gems are found hidden among the eclectic assortment of used, out-of-print and antiquarian books.

Sleeping

Maleny Lodge Guest House B&B $$
(5494 2370; www.malenylodge.com; 58 Maple St; s incl breakfast $155-180, d incl breakfast $180-205;) This rambling B&B boasts myriad gorgeous rooms with cushy, four-poster beds and lashings of stained wood and antiques. There's an open fire for cold winter days and an open pool house for warm summer ones.

Relax at the Cabin BOUTIQUE CABIN $$$
(5499 9377; www.kingludwigs.com.au; cabin $350) Only 3km from Maleny this secluded cabin is set in pine forest on 8 hectares of land. The spa, fireplace and large, comfy bed dominate the living room, and a wall of glass doors opens onto a wide timber deck. Your favourite wines, a range of beers and a welcoming cheese platter greet your arrival, and little luxuries like fluffy bathrobes and heated towel-racks are a classy touch.

Morning Star Motel MOTEL $$
(5494 2944; www.morningstarmotel.com; 2 Panorama Pl; r $88-110) The rooms at this comfortable and clean motel have outstanding coastal views, and the deluxe suites also have spas. Wheelchair accessible.

Ocean View Tourist Park CARAVAN PARK $
(1300 769 443, 5494 1171; www.oceanviewtouristpark.com; Maleny-Landsborough Rd; unpowered/powered sites $27/30, cabins $100;) Conveniently close to Australia Zoo, the coast and the hinterland, this tourist park also has magnificent views of the Glass House Mountains and Sunshine Coast beaches. Rates are for two people.

Eating

There are several good cafes along Maple St as well as a co-op selling organic fruit and vegetables.

TOP CHOICE **Up Front Club** CAFE $
(31 Maple St; dishes $10-20; breakfast, lunch & dinner) This cosy cafe injects funk by the bucketful into Maleny's main strip, with organic breads and tofu and tempeh salads. Live music takes to the stage Friday to Sunday nights and you'll catch anything from reggae to a bout of folk. Musicians are welcome to join in the blackboard sessions for 15 minutes of fame, and possibly a cash prize, on Monday evenings.

Terrace INTERNATIONAL $$$
(5494 3700; cnr Mountain View & Maleny-Landsborough Rds; mains $25-50; lunch & dinner) One of Queensland's best, this award-winner serves delectable seafood and has spectacular views of the Glass House Mountains. If you're ravenous try the Moreton Bay bugs, king prawns, salmon and barramundi served on a sizzling granite tile with root vegetables and polenta salad.

Bombay Mahal INDIAN $$
(5494 3670; 76 Maple St; mains $20-32; dinner Thu-Tue) This intimate Indian restaurant in an old chapel on the main street is filled with the aroma of exotic spices and delicious curries.

King Ludwigs Restaurant GERMAN $$
(5499 9377; www.kingludwigs.com.au; 401 Mountain View Rd; mains $29-35; lunch Wed-Sun, dinner Fri & Sat) Klaus and Barbara have a passion for good food, German beer and welcoming Bavarian hospitality. A schnapps (or two) in the rustic Bavarian bar will prime your taste buds for the mouth-watering dishes on the menu, including the legendary Bavarian potato cream soup with Frankfurt sausage. The views of the Glass House Mountains are sensational.

Monica's Café CAFE $
(11/43 Maple St; mains $10-20; breakfast & lunch) Snazzy Monica's blackboard menu promises innovative dishes and has gluten-free options. Sit outside to soak up the town's cruisy vibe or take a seat at the long wooden table indoors. There's also a cosy nook upstairs.

Colin James Fine Foods DELI $
(37 Maple St; dishes $8-17; 9am-5pm Mon-Fri, to 4pm Sat & Sun) This deli, cafe and fromagerie serves light meals, sandwiches and melts. The fromagerie has over 200 cheeses begging to be sampled, and the gelati are wicked.

Information

Visitors centre (5499 9033; 23 Maple St; 10am-3pm) At the Maleny Community Centre.

Montville

POP 860

It's hard to imagine that the chintzy mountain village of Montville with its fudge emporiums, Devonshire tearooms and cottage crafts began life under the dramatic name of Razorback – until you arrive at the town's spectacular ridge-top location 1640ft above

WORTH A TRIP

KENILWORTH

In the Mary River Valley west of the Blackall Range, Kenilworth is a small country town with the merest whiff of an alternative vibe. There's not much to do in town, as all the action takes place outdoors – canoeing the Mary River, bushwalking and camping in the Conondale Range, or horse riding in the Mary Valley.

The **Kenilworth visitors centre** (☎5446 0122; Elizabeth St; ⏲10am-3pm) has walking-trail maps and information on various activities. In town, sample locally made cheese and yogurt at **Kenilworth Country Foods** (☎5446 0144; 45 Charles St; ⏲9am-4pm Mon-Fri, 10.30am-3pm Sat & Sun) and be sure to take a wedge of wickedly good cheese on your camping trip. A lovely camp site can be found on the banks of the Obi Obi Creek, 10km east of town on the Obi Obi Rd. Look for the large grassy area just past the bridge at crossing 2 and (bonus) you don't need a permit. But if you plan to camp in the Kenilworth State Forest or Conondale National Park you will need a permit (☎13 74 68; www.derm.qld.gov.au; per person $5.15).

Horse riders will want to stay at **Kenilworth Homestead** (☎5446 0555; www.kenilworthhomestead.com.au; 2760 Eumundi-Kenilworth Rd; dm $55, 2-bedroom cottage $150), where you can also set up camp (per person $9) by the Mary River.

McGinn's of Kenilworth (☎5446 0025; 11 Elizabeth St; mains $8-23; ⏲breakfast & lunch) is a shady spot for lunch or coffee and cake.

Kenilworth is 18km west of Mapleton on the Obi Obi Rd.

sea level. While Montville's cottage-industry makeover won't appeal to everyone, its subtropical setting is pleasantly attractive and the rainforests, waterfalls and hiking trails in the Kondalilla National Park will appeal to bushwalkers and birdwatchers.

A five-minute drive south of town, **Baroon Pocket Dam** is a lovely spot for a picnic and the (now flooded) site of the ancient Bunya nut festivals, when Aboriginal tribes would gather to feast on the sacred Bunya nut and hold corroborees, rituals and marriages. Baroon Pocket Dam is also the start of the 32km Sunshine Coast Hinterland Great Walk. It's a 10km walk from the dam through lush rainforest (or a 3km drive northwest of Montville) to **Kondalilla National Park** and the popular **Kondalilla Falls**. Stretch out on the lawns here for a picnic or take a cool rainforest walk to a swimming hole at the head of the falls. Check for leeches when you get out!

The **information centre** (☎5478 5544; 198 Main St; ⏲10am-4pm) in town can help you find cottage accommodation.

Sleeping

Romance comes at a hefty price on the range.

TOP CHOICE **Secrets on the Lake** BOUTIQUE COTTAGE $$$
(☎5478 5888; www.secretsonthelake.com.au; 207 Narrows Rd; midweek/weekend from $200/250; ❄) These magical, hand-crafted wooden treehouses hidden among the foliage have all the ingredients for romance – sunken spas, log fires and stunning views of Lake Baroon. There's a complimentary champagne breakfast hamper, and freshly baked muffins are delivered to your cabin each morning.

Narrows Escape BOUTIQUE COTTAGE $$$
(☎5478 5000; www.narrowsescape.com.au; Narrows Rd; midweek/weekend $285/320; ❄) Also near the lake, these rainforest cottages come with life's little luxuries – breakfast hampers with organic produce, aromatherapy massages, spa baths and log fires. Swinging in the hammock on the deck or gazing at the canopy through the ceiling skylights, you're always immersed in nature.

Treehouses of Montville BOUTIQUE COTTAGE $$$
(☎1800 444 350; www.treehouses.com.au; Kondalilla Falls Rd; from $235) Near the entrance to Kondalilla National Park, these beautiful self-contained treehouses are hidden in a secluded patch of rainforest. Each cabin has a fireplace, spa and private wooden deck. There's also a restaurant for romantic candlelit dining.

Clouds of Montville MOTEL $$
(☎5442 9174; www.cloudsofmontville.com.au; 166 Balmoral Rd; r midweek/weekend $155/185; ❄) Set on 2 hectares, Clouds has a range of accommodation options from motel-style

rooms with a kitchenette to fully self-contained cottages complete with a wood fire and spa. Cottage stays include breakfast and complimentary transport to nearby restaurants.

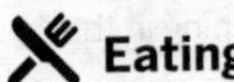

Eating

Poets Café CAFE $$

(☎5478 5479; 167 Main St; mains $16-32; ⊙breakfast & lunch daily, dinner Fri) Perhaps Coleridge or one of the poets painted on the ceiling dreamt of a French pavilion with white trim. Today's poets sip frothy lattes while browsing the gourmet menu in this charming cafe.

Edge Restaurant CAFE $$

(127-133 Main St; mains $14-25; ⊙breakfast & lunch) Perched on the edge of the escarpment, this restaurant in the Mayfield complex has stupendous views of the fabulous green hinterland and blue ocean in the distance.

Mapleton

The tiny village of Mapleton is perched at the northern end of the Blackall Range. It has a couple of craft and pottery galleries and flanks the **Mapleton Falls National Park**. In the park, Pencil Creek cascades 120m over an escarpment to form Mapleton Falls. The lookout has views over the Obi Obi Valley. In spring, look for peregrine falcons roosting on the edges of the falls. A number of walking trails, including the Sunshine Coast Hinterland Great Walk, start here.

Taman Sari (☎5478 6868; www.tamansari.com.au; Obi Obi Rd; d per night $345, minimum 2-night stay) has two private pavilions in a luxurious Asian-inspired rainforest sanctuary overlooking the Obi Obi Valley. Behind the impressive wooden doors the attention to detail is extraordinary, from the heated towel racks to the huge spa room with its pebbled floor.

Just north of Mapleton, **Lilyponds Holiday Park** (☎1800 003 764, 5445 7238; www.lilyponds.com.au; 26 Warruga St; unpowered/powered sites from $33/33, cabins $95-125) overlooks the Mapleton Lily Ponds and has self-contained cabins or you can camp in the avocado orchard. Camping rates are for two people.

Lunch on the wide veranda of the **Mapleton Tavern** (cnr Maleny-Montville & Obi Obi Rds; mains $16-25; ⊙lunch daily, dinner Mon-Sat), an iconic pink Queenslander, comes with sweeping views of the hinterland and the ocean in the distance.

Fraser Island & the Fraser Coast

Includes »

Fraser Coast 171
Gympie 171
Rainbow Beach 172
Maryborough 175
Hervey Bay 177
Childers.............184
Burrum Coast National Park.......186
Bundaberg 186
Around Bundaberg 190
Fraser Island........190

Best Places to Eat

» Waterview Bistro (p174)
» Cafè Tapas (p183)
» Black Dog Café (p183)

Best Places to Stay

» Kingfisher Bay Resort (p193)
» Debbie's Place (p173)
» Beachfront Tourist Parks (p181)

Why Go?

Nature buffs will beeline it to World Heritage–listed Fraser Island, the world's largest sand island. Four-wheel driving along the east coast or through inland forests reveals an island paradise sculpted by wind and surf; a mystical land of giant dunes, ancient rainforests and luminous lakes.

Across the calm waters of the Great Sandy Strait, Hervey Bay is the launch pad to Fraser. There's a whiff of burgeoning beach-cafe culture, but at heart it's a mellow coastal community riding on the back of the annual humpback whale migrations. Further south, Rainbow Beach is a refreshingly unaffected seaside village and an alternative departure point for Fraser Island. Fishing, swimming, boating and camping are hugely popular along the stretch of coastline.

Inland, agricultural fields surround old-fashioned country towns steeped in history. Bundaberg, the largest city in the region, overlooks a sea of waving sugar cane and is famous for its fiery, golden rum.

When to Go

Bundaberg

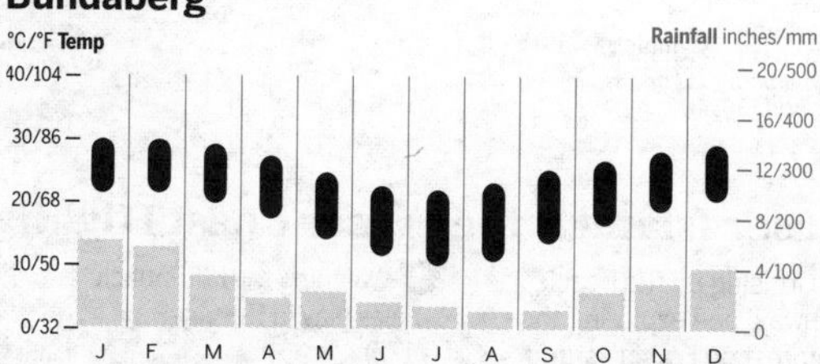

March–November Sunny skies and mild winters make this a great time to visit Fraser Island.

July–November Watch humpback whales frolic in the sea. The best time for sightings is August to October.

November–March Spy on turtles laying eggs in the sand at Mon Repos.

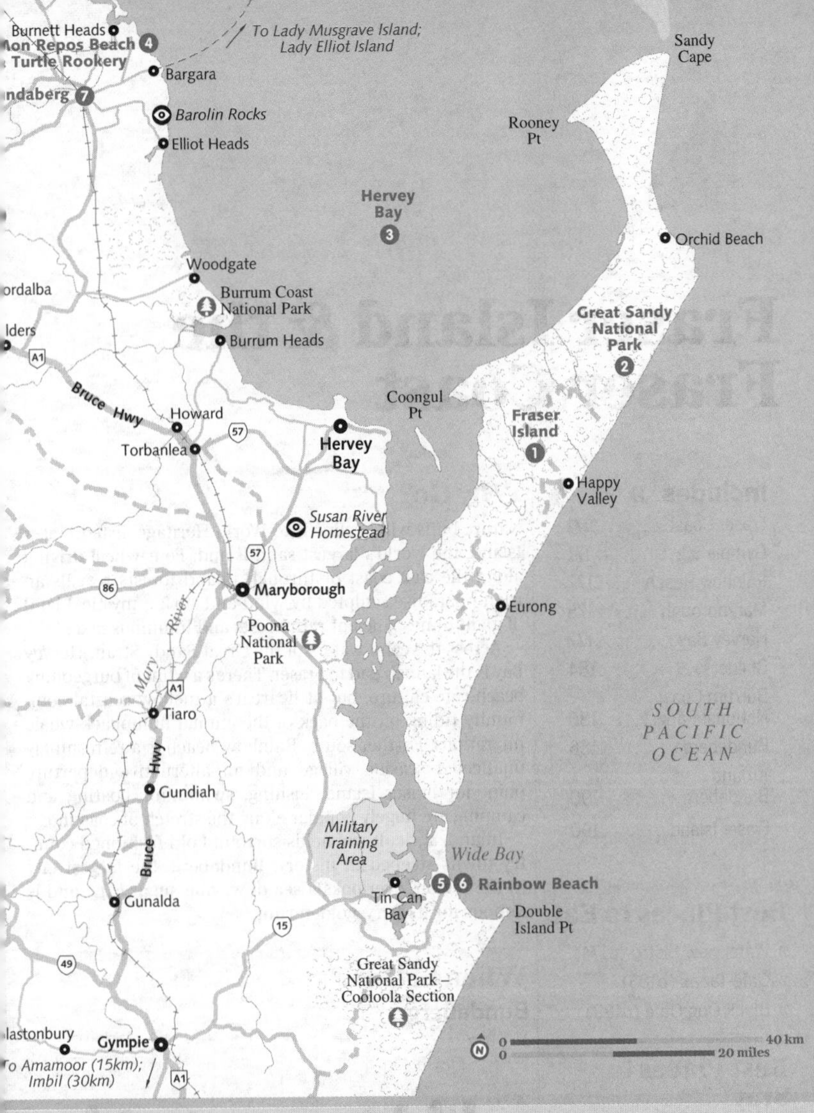

Fraser Island & the Fraser Coast Highlights

1 Cruising up the beach 'highway', and exploring the rainforest on **Fraser Island** (p190), the world's largest sand island

2 Beach camping under the stars in the **Great Sandy National Park** (p172)

3 Watching the humpback whales play in **Hervey Bay** (p177)

4 Spotting loggerhead-turtle hatchlings erupt from the sand at **Mon Repos Beach & Turtle Rookery** (p188)

5 Soaking up the laid-back beach scene and views of the spectacular coloured sand cliffs at **Rainbow Beach** (p172)

6 Diving with grey-nurse sharks, manta rays and turtles off Rainbow Beach at **Wolf Rock** (p173)

7 Drinking liquid-gold sugar cane at the rum distillery in **Bundaberg** (p186) and remaining upright

Getting There & Away

AIR

Qantas (13 13 13; www.qantas.com.au) flies to Bundaberg and Hervey Bay from Brisbane.

Virgin Blue (13 67 89; www.virginblue.com.au) has direct flights to Hervey Bay from Sydney.

BUS

Greyhound Australia (13 20 30; www.greyhound.com.au) and **Premier Motor Service** (13 34 10; www.premierms.com.au) both have regular coach services along the Bruce Hwy (A1) with stops at all the major towns. They also detour off the highway to Hervey Bay and Rainbow Beach.

TRAIN

Queensland Rail (13 22 32, 1300 13 17 22; www.traveltrain.com.au) has frequent services between Brisbane and Rockhampton passing through the region. Choose between the high-speed *Tilt Train* or the more sedate *Sunlander*. For details see the Getting There & Away sections of the relevant towns and cities.

FRASER COAST

Mixing coast and country, the Fraser Coast runs the gamut from coastal beauty, beachfront national parks and tiny seaside villages to sugar-cane fields, farmlands and old-fashioned country towns. Along this stretch of coastline, mellow Hervey Bay draws the biggest crowds with its easy access to Fraser Island and thrilling whale-watching action. Nestled in a picturesque bay south of Hervey Bay, pretty little Rainbow Beach, with its stunning coloured sand cliffs, is even closer to Fraser and has a good surf beach.

Far removed from the cruisy beach scene, Maryborough and Gympie are inland country towns steeped in history and heritage. A little further north, Bundaberg rises out of a sea of sugar-cane fields, fruit orchards and vegetable patches. Seasonal picking and harvesting attract long-staying backpackers, or maybe the pull is Bundaberg's wickedly famous rum!

Gympie

POP 10,930

Gympie's gold once saved Queensland from near-bankruptcy, but that was in the 1860s and not much has happened since. A few period buildings line the main street but most travellers on the Bruce Hwy bypass the town centre.

Sights & Activities

Woodworks Forestry & Timber Museum MUSEUM

(5483 7691; cnr Fraser Rd & Bruce Hwy; adult/student $10/5; 10am-4pm Wed-Sun) On the highway south of town, this unusual museum displays memorabilia and equipment from the region's old logging days. The highlight of the museum (and perhaps the lowlight of the industry) is a cross-section of a magnificent kauri pine that lived through the Middle Ages, Columbus' discovery of America and the industrial revolution, only to be felled in the early 20th century.

Gympie Gold Mining & Historical Museum MUSEUM

(5482 3995; 215 Brisbane Rd; adult/child/family $10/5/25; 9am-4pm) History buffs will be interested in this large collection of mining equipment and functioning steam-driven engines.

Valley Rattler TRAIN RIDE

(5482 2750; www.thevalleyrattler.com; half-day tours per adult/child $20/10, day tours $47/23.50) This restored 1923 steam train leaves from the old Gympie train station on Tozer St every Wednesday and Sunday morning at 10am and chugs through the pretty Mary Valley to the tiny township of Imbil 40km away. The return trip takes 5½ hours, with lunch, caffeine and souvenir stops. On Saturday, half-day tours (departing 9.30am, 11.30am and 1.45pm) only go as far as Amamoor, 20km away.

Festivals & Events

Muster COUNTRY MUSIC

(www.muster.com.au) This annual country-music hoedown is held over six days in late August each year, in the Amamoor Creek State Forest Park.

Sleeping & Eating

Gympie Muster Inn MOTEL $$

(5482 8666; 21 Wickham St; d $135;) If you don't want to camp at the Muster, or if you're passing through town, this large, central motel won't be memorable but it'll be comfortable enough.

Capelli on Duke MODERN AUSTRALIAN $$

(5482 9515; 13 Alfred St; mains $24-32; lunch Fri & Sun, dinner Wed-Sat) The deck under the shady jacaranda is perfect for long lunches or you can dine in the snazzy red-and-white themed interior. Enjoy a range of delicious tapas with a selection from the international wine list.

Kingston House Restaurant MODERN AUSTRALIAN $$

(☎5483 6733; 11 Channon St; mains $18-29; ⏰lunch & dinner Wed-Sun) Nestled inside a beautifully renovated, sprawling Queenslander, this restaurant is pure class. The menu features delicious dishes using local produce and has a boutique wine list.

Emilia CAFE $

(☎5482 8885; 201 Mary St; mains $8-20; ⏰8am-5pm Mon-Fri) What Italian deli-cafe isn't adorned with heavy brocade, ornate gold-framed mirrors, a tempting range of imported deli items – and excellent espresso?

Information

Gympie Cooloola Tourism (☎1800 444 222, 5482 5444; www.cooloola.org.au) Matilda (Matilda Service Centre, Bruce Hwy; ⏰9am-5pm); Lake Alford (Bruce Hwy, Gympie; ⏰9am-4.30pm) Both branches are on the Bruce Hwy south of town. They also stock the free *Heritage Walking Tour Map*, which details Gympie's relics of the gold-mining days.

If you fancy you've got the Midas touch, the Lake Alford centre can fix you up with a gold-fossicking licence ($6.50 per month), gold-panning equipment ($5.50 per day) or even a gold detector ($50 per day).

Getting There & Around

Cooloola Connections (☎5481 1667; www.coolconnect.com.au) Operates transfers from Brisbane Airport and the Sunshine Coast Airport to Gympie (one way $75).

Greyhound Australia (☎1300 473 946; www.greyhound.com.au) Has numerous daily services from Brisbane ($40, 3½ hours), Noosa ($22, two hours) and Hervey Bay ($33, 1¾ hours).

Polley's Coaches (☎5480 4500; Pinewood Ave) Has buses from Gympie to Rainbow Beach ($15, 1¾ hours), departing from the RSL on Mary St at 1.15pm on weekdays.

Premier Motor Service (☎13 34 10; www.premierms.com.au) Operates the same routes (once daily). Long-distance coaches stop at the bus shelter in Jaycee Way, behind Mary St.

Traveltrain (☎1300 131 722; www.traveltrain.com.au) Operates the *Tilt Train* (adult/child $42/20, 2½ hours, Sunday to Friday) and the *Sunlander* (adult/child $42/20, 3¼ hours, three weekly), which travel from Brisbane to Gympie on their way to Rockhampton and Cairns.

Rainbow Beach

POP 1000

Gorgeous Rainbow Beach is a tiny town at the base of the Inskip Peninsula with spectacular multicoloured sand cliffs overlooking its rolling surf and white sandy beach. Still relatively untouched, the town's friendly locals, relaxed vibe and convenient access to Fraser Island (only 10 minutes by barge) and the Cooloola Section of the Great Sandy National Park has made this a rising star of Queensland's coastal beauty spots.

Sights & Activities

Coloured Sand Cliffs BEACH

The town is named for these majestic cliffs, which can be found by walking 2km south of the surf club along the beach. The cliffs arc their red-hued way around Wide Bay, offering a sweeping panorama from the lighthouse at Double Island Point to Fraser Island in the north. A 600m track along the cliffs at the southern end of Cooloola Dr leads to the **Carlo Sandblow**, a spectacular 120m-high dune.

Great Sandy National Park NATURE RESERVE

The Cooloola Section (p163) has a number of national park **campsites** (www.derm.qld.gov.au; per person/family $5.15/20.60), including beach camping. Book permits online. You'll also need a **4WD permit** (www.derm.qld.gov.au; per day/week/month $10/25/40). Bushwalkers will find tracks throughout the national park (maps from the QPWS office), including the 46.2km **Cooloola Wilderness Trail**, which starts at Mullens car park (off Rainbow Beach Rd) and ends near Lake Cooloola.

Double Island Point & Tin Can Bay FISHING

There's a good surf break at Double Island Point but fishing is the most popular activity here. The vast shoreline provides abundant beach fishing and really serious anglers can access Tin Can Bay inlet from either the Carlo Point or Bullock Point boat ramps. Both are just north of town.

Rainbow Paragliding PARAGLIDING

(☎5486 3048, 0418 754 157; www.paraglidingrainbow.com; glides $150) This outfit offers tandem glides above the Carlo Sandblow, where the state championships are held every December. If you get hooked you can do a one-day introduction ($240) or an eight-day full licensed course ($1600).

Skydive Rainbow Beach SKYDIVING
(☎0418 218 358; www.skydiverainbowbeach.com; 8000ft/10,000ft/14,000ft dives $260/295/334) Get your knees in the breeze and land on the main beach.

Wolf Rock Dive Centre DIVING
(☎5486 8004; www.wolfrockdive.com.au; double dive charter from $160) Experienced divers will love the adrenalin dives at Wolf Rock, a congregation of four volcanic pinnacles off Double Island Point. It is widely regarded as one of Queensland's best scuba-diving sites and teems with gropers, turtles, manta rays and harmless grey-nurse sharks. The endangered grey-nurse shark is found here all year round.

Rainbow Dreaming INDIGENOUS CULTURE
(☎0427 069 041; ⏲by appointment) Soak up some Indigenous culture at Fraser's on Rainbow YHA hostel with cultural talks and Dreamtime legends while you spend half a day fashioning or painting a didgeridoo or boomerang.

Rainbow Beach Dolphin View Sea Kayaking KAYAKING, SURFING
(☎0408 738 192; 4hr tours per person $85) Go on a kayaking safari or rent a kayak (half day $65). If you'd rather surf with the dolphins, it also runs the **Rainbow Beach Surf School** (two-hour session $55). Board hire is $15 per hour or $40 per day.

Carlo Canoes CANOEING
(☎5486 3610; per half-/full day $30/45) Hire a canoe at Carlo's if you want to do your own exploring.

Tours

Surf & Sand Safaris SCENIC
(☎5486 3131; www.surfandsandsafaris.com.au; adult/child $70/35) Runs 4WD tours through the national park and along the beach to the coloured sands and lighthouse at Double Island Point.

Dolphin Ferry Cruise BOAT CRUISE
(☎0428 838 836; www.dolphinferrycruise.net.au; 3hr cruise adult/child $30/15; ⏲7.20am & 9.30am) These houseboats cruise across the inlet from Carlo Point to Tin Can Bay. The highlight of the trip is hand-feeding Mystique, a wild Indo-Pacific Humpback dolphin who makes regular breakfast visits to the Tin Can Bay marina.

Sleeping

TOP CHOICE **Debbie's Place** B&B $
(☎5486 3506; www.rainbowbeachaccommodation.com.au; 30 Kurana St; d/ste/3-bedroom apt from $79/89/99; ❄) This beautiful timber Queenslander, dripping with pot plants, has charming fully self-contained rooms with private entrances and verandahs. The effervescent Debbie is a mine of information and makes this a cosy home away from home. The new apartments next door are large and comfortable.

Rainbow Ocean Palms Resort APARTMENTS $$$
(☎5486 3211; www.rainbowoceanpalms.com; 105 Cooloola Dr; 1-/2-bedroom apt from $200/300; ❄≋) Making the most of the panoramic ocean views, these luxury apartments have a modern, contemporary design and feature loads of glass, light and space. It overlooks the national park, you can see the ocean from your spa, and there's a great restaurant next door.

Plantation Resort APARTMENTS $$$
(☎5486 9000; www.plantationresortatrainbow.com.au; 1 Rainbow Beach Rd; apts from $260; ❄@≋) These swish apartments have perfect ocean views and the outdoor cane settings and white plantation-themed rooms will have you reaching for the nearest gin and tonic. It's classy beach-chic and smack bang in the middle of town.

Rainbow Shores Resort RESORT $$$
(☎5486 3999; www.rainbowshores.com.au; 12 Rainbow Shores Dr; r per week from $875, villas & beach houses per week from $1200; ❄≋) For luxury in the bush, this is the place. Accommodation options include standard holiday units, funky, individual three-bedroom beach houses and stylish split-level villas. On site is a nine-hole golf course, tennis courts, barbecues, a restaurant and plenty of bush. There's a minimum five-night stay in high season.

Rainbow Sands Holiday Units MOTEL $$
(☎5486 3400; 42-46 Rainbow Beach Rd; d/1-bedroom apt $95/125; ❄📶≋) This low-rise, palm-fronted complex has standard motel rooms with poolside glass doors and bar fridges, and self-contained units with full laundries for comfortable longer stays. The owners are utterly genuine and helpful.

Pippies Beach House HOSTEL $
(☎1800 425 356, 5486 8503; www.pippiesbeachhouse.com.au; 22 Spectrum St; dm/d $24/65;

(❄≋) With only 12 rooms, this small, superchilled hostel is the place to relax between surfing, diving and bushwalking. It's clean and the bathrooms are large. Take a Fraser Island trip with Pippies and you get two nights free accommodation at the hostel. Other bonuses include free breakfasts and water toys, and plenty of space in the garden for tents and vans ($12 per person).

Dingo's Backpacker's Resort HOSTEL $
(☎1800 111 126, 5486 8222; www.dingosatrainbow.com; 20 Spectrum Ave; dm/d $22/65; ❄@≋) The vivacious English manager keeps the bar hopping in this party hostel. There's live music every Wednesday and Saturday night, a Balinese-style gazebo for recovery, free tours to Carlo Sandblow, free pancake breakfasts and cheap meals every night.

Fraser's on Rainbow YHA HOSTEL $
(☎1800 100 170, 5486 8885; www.frasersonrainbow.com; 18 Spectrum St; dm/d from $25/65; @≋) In a converted motel this hostel has roomy dorms and a pleasant, relaxed atmosphere. Locals join guests for a tipple at the sprawling outdoor bar, and you can also buy cheap meals every night.

Rainbow Beach Holiday Village CARAVAN PARK $
(☎1300 366 596, 5486 3222; www.beach-village.com; 13 Rainbow Beach Rd; unpowered/powered sites from $27/34, cabins from $90; ❄≋) This excellent park spreads over 2 hectares, overlooking the beach and ocean. There's enough foliage for a small jungle, the cabins are fully self-contained and it's extremely popular. Rates are for two people.

Great Sandy National Park CAMPGROUND $
(www.derm.qld.gov.au; campsites per person/family $5.15/20.60) The Cooloola Section has a number of national park campsites including a wonderful stretch of beach camping along Teewah Beach. Book permits online. You'll also need a 4WD permit (www.derm.qld.gov.au; per day/week/month $10/25/40).

Rainbow Beach Hire-a-Camp CAMPGROUND $
(☎5486 8633; www.rainbow-beach.org) Camping on the beach is one of the best ways to experience this part of the coast but if you don't have camping gear, don't despair. As well as hiring out equipment, this company can set up your tent and campsite, organise camping permits, and break camp for you when you're done.

Eating

Self-caterers will find a supermarket on Rainbow Beach Rd.

TOP CHOICE **Waterview Bistro** MODERN AUSTRALIAN $$
(☎5486 8344; Cooloola Dr; mains $26-35; ⏲breakfast & lunch Sun, lunch & dinner Wed-Sat) Sunset drinks are a must at this swish restaurant with sensational views of Fraser Island from its hilltop perch. The small menu changes regularly and offers carnivores and vegetarians alike something delicious to complement the view.

Rainbow Beach Hotel PUB FARE $$
(1 Rainbow Beach Rd; mains $20-35; ⏲lunch & dinner) The spruced-up pub carries on the plantation theme with ceiling fans, palm trees, timber floors and cane furnishings. The restaurant is bright, airy and serves up traditional pub grub. Have a sunset drink on the upstairs balcony.

Shak CAFE $$
(12 Rainbow Beach Rd; mains $10-30; ⏲breakfast, lunch & dinner) This popular cafe perfectly encapsulates Rainbow's laid-back surfer chic, serving delicious smoothies, vegie burgers and fish in various guises.

Information

QPWS office (☎5486 3160; Rainbow Beach Rd; ⏲8am-4pm)

Rainbow Beach visitors centre (☎5486 3227; 8 Rainbow Beach Rd; ⏲7am-5pm) Privately run, very helpful and can organise tours.

Shell Tourist Centre (☎5486 8888; Rainbow Beach Rd; ⏲8am-5pm) At the Shell service station; tour bookings and barge tickets for Fraser Island.

Tribal Travel (☎1800 559 987; www.tribaltravel.com.au; Rainbow Beach Rd; ⏲7am-7pm summer, 9am-7pm winter) Next to the Rainbow Beach Hotel. Book buses, accommodation, tours and activities.

Getting There & Around

Greyhound Australia (☎1300 473 946; www.greyhound.com.au) has several daily services from Brisbane ($65, five hours), Noosa ($33, 2½ hours) and Hervey Bay ($30, 1½ hours). **Premier Motor Service** (☎13 34 10; www.premierms.com.au) has less-expensive services. **Cooloola Connections** (☎5481 1667; www.coolconnect.com.au) runs a shuttle bus to Rainbow Beach from Brisbane Airport ($110, three hours) and Sunshine Coast Airport ($65, two hours). **Polley's Coaches** (☎5480 4500) has buses from Gympie ($15, 1¾ hours).

Most 4WD-hire companies will also arrange permits, barge costs ($90 return per vehicle) and hire out camping gear. Some recommended companies:

All Trax 4WD Hire (☎5486 8767; Rainbow Beach Rd) At the Shell service station.

Rainbow Beach Adventure Centre 4WD Hire (☎5486 3288; www.adventurecentre.com.au; Rainbow Beach Rd; ⊙7am-5pm)

Safari 4WD (☎1800 689 819, 5486 8188; 3 Karoonda Ct)

Maryborough

POP 21,500

Born in 1847, Maryborough is one of Queensland's oldest towns, and its port was the first shaky step ashore for thousands of 19th-century free settlers looking for a better life in the new country. Heritage and history are Maryborough's fortes, the pace of yesteryear reflected in its beautifully restored colonial-era buildings and gracious Queenslander homes.

This big old country town is also the birthplace of PL Travers, creator of everyone's favourite umbrella-wielding nanny, Mary Poppins.

Sights

Portside HISTORIC SITE

In the historic port area beside the Mary River, Portside has 13 heritage-listed buildings, parklands and museums. Today's tidy colonial-era buildings and landscaped gardens paint a different picture from Maryborough's once-thriving port and seedy streets filled with sailors, ruffians, brothels and opium dens. The **Portside Centre** (☎4190 5730; cnr Wharf & Richmond Sts; ⊙10am-4pm Mon-Fri, 10am-1pm Sat & Sun), located in the former **Customs House**, has interactive displays on Maryborough's history. Part of the centre but a few doors down, the **Bond Store Museum** also highlights key periods in Maryborough's history. Downstairs is the original packed-earth floor and even some liquor barrels from 1864. Lining the streets around Portside are many fine old buildings including Queensland's oldest **post office** (cnr Bazaar & Wharf Sts), built in 1866, and the revival-style **Woodstock House** on Richmond St.

Mary Poppins statue MONUMENT

On the street in front of the neoclassical **former Union Bank** (birthplace of *Mary Poppins* author, PL Travers) is a life-size statue of the acerbic character Travers created, rather than the saccharine-sweet Disney version.

Maryborough Military & Colonial Museum MUSEUM

(106 Wharf St; adult/child $5/2; ⊙9am-3pm) Check out the only surviving three-wheeler Girling car. Originally built in London in 1911, this fully restored model zips along at a blistering 29km/h. The museum also houses a replica Cobb & Co coach and one of the largest military libraries in Australia.

Queens Park PARK

With a profusion of glorious trees, including a banyan fig that's more than 140 years old, this is a pleasant spot for a picnic. Chug through the park on the **Mary Ann** (adult/child $3/2), a life-sized replica of Queensland's first steam engine, built in Maryborough in 1873. It operates on the last Sunday of each month and every Thursday. Kiddies will love the **Melsa** (per person $1)

GETTING BACK TO NATURE

Want to know how to best appreciate the unspoilt natural landscape of Fraser Island and the Fraser Coast?

» Go native on Fraser Island – hike the **Fraser Island Great Walk** (p175), join a **guided walk** (p195) or make like a castaway on an **island campsite** (p194) – you'll be amazed at the beauty of the star-studded night sky.

» Spot the dog – there's something utterly magical about spotting an endemic species in its natural habitat. **Dingoes** (p192) are the cool cats of the dog world but keep your distance, their bite *is* worse than their bark.

» Be a nocturnal voyeur – spy on egg-laying loggerhead **turtles** (p188) and their itty-bitty offsprings' mad dash to the sea.

» Play with big fish – watch the majestic **humpback whales** (p178) frolic in the ocean waters, then head back to Hervey Bay and party yourself into a beached-whale possie.

miniature steam engines that chug through the park on the last Sunday of the month.

Artscape ART GALLERY
(10am-4pm Mon-Fri, to 1pm Sat & Sun) Next to the Military Museum, this gallery has exhibitions by local and national artists and sculptors.

Heritage Centre NOTABLE BUILDING
(4123 1842; cnr Wharf & Richmond Sts; 9am-4pm Mon-Fri) If tracing your genealogical tree is a priority, the Heritage Centre stores colonial immigration records from ships' logs; and if dear old great-great-granddaddy arrived in Australia courtesy of Her Majesty's prison system, you'll find convict records as well.

Mary River Parklands PARK
On the riverfront in front of Portside look for a cluster of ships' bollards painted to resemble colonial figures.

Customs House Hotel NOTABLE BUILDING
(Wharf St) One of the oldest portside hotels is currently a nightclub, but it was once an opium den and is rumoured to have a resident ghost (or maybe the nightly beats have driven it away).

Brennan & Geraghty MUSEUM
(64 Lennox St; adult/child/family $5.50/2.50/13.50; 10am-3pm) This National Trust–classified store traded for 100 years before closing its doors. The museum is filled with tins, bottles and packets, including early Vegemite jars and curry powder from the 1890s, all crammed onto the ceiling-high shelves. Look for the 1885 tea packet from China, the oldest item in the store.

Tours

Tea with Mary CITY
(1800 214 789, 4190 5730; per person $12.50) You get more than a morning cuppa on this tour. A costumed guide spills the beans on the town's past on a tour of the historic precinct. Admission charges and morning tea are included in the cost.

Maryborough Riverboat Cruises RIVER CRUISES
(4123 1523; www.maryboroughrivercruise.com; 1hr tour $20, 2hr lunch cruise $35; 10am, noon & 2pm Tue-Sun) Informed commentaries are provided while you cruise past heritage homes and historic buildings along the Mary River.

Ghostly Tours & Tales GHOST TALES
(1800 214 789, 4190 5742; tour incl progressive dinner $75). On the last Saturday of each month you can get spooked on a torch-lit tour of the city's grisly murder sites, opium dens, haunted houses and cemetery.

Guided walks CITY
(9am Mon-Sat) Free walks depart from the City Hall every morning and take in the town's sights.

Sleeping

Eco Queenslander RENTAL HOUSE $$
(0438 195 443; www.ecoqueenslander.com; 15 Treasure St; house $120-140) Bypass the impersonal motels and get your own cosy home. In a lovely converted Queenslander with a comfy lounge, full kitchen, laundry and a cast-iron bathtub, you won't want to leave. Eco-features include solar power, rainwater tanks, energy efficient lighting and bikes for you to use.

McNevin's Parkway Motel MOTEL $$
(1800 072 000, 4122 2888; www.mcnevins.com.au; 188 John St; r from $110;) This well-run complex is popular with business folk but the fresh, light motel rooms are comfortable, regardless of your reason for staying. A step up in style and price are the smart executive suites, which have separate bedrooms and spas.

Blue Shades Motor Inn MOTEL $$
(4122 2777; 35 Ferry St; r from $100;) A close second to the Parkway, this large motel complex has a range of accommodation, from generic and simple motel rooms to family and modern executive rooms.

Arkana Motel MOTEL $
(4121 2261; www.arkanamotel.com.au; 46 Ferry St; r from $90;) Located just out of the town centre, this good-value motel has no surprises and is a reasonably comfortable option.

Wallace Motel & Caravan Park CARAVAN PARK $
(4121 3970; www.wallacecaravanpark.com.au; 22 Ferry St; unpowered/powered sites $20/25, cabins $75-85;) This pleasant park spreads across a gentle slope underneath a bevy of towering trees. Modern cabins, self-contained motel units and camp kitchens cater to all tastes. Rates are for two people.

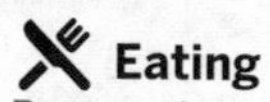

Eating

Basement TAPAS $
(☎4121 0002; 389 Kent St; tapas $9; ⊙4.30pm-midnight Thu-Sat) Descend the stairs to this ultra-chic tapas bar with its mood lighting, leather lounges and high-set steel benches and you'll think you've stepped into the big city. This is the in-place for after-work drinks and 'Mediterrasian'-inspired tapas.

Toast CAFE $
(199 Bazaar St; dishes $5-10; ⊙6am-4pm Mon-Sat, 7-10pm Fri & Sat) Stainless-steel fittings, polished cement floors and coffee served in paper cups stamp the metro-chic seal on this cafe. Sushi, gourmet focaccias and yummy sweet treats are on offer but the main attraction is the best coffee you'll find in town.

Port Residence MODERN AUSTRALIAN $$
(☎4123 5001; Customs House, Wharf St; mains $15-30; ⊙breakfast, lunch & dinner Thu-Sun) An elegant restaurant and tea room in the old Customs House residence. Light meals and traditional Aussie favourites like scones and tea are served on the shady verandah, which has lovely views over the Mary River Parklands.

Muddy Waters Café SEAFOOD $$
(☎4121 5011; 71 Wharf St; mains $15-32; ⊙breakfast & lunch Tue-Sat, dinner Thu-Sat) The shady riverfront deck and the summery menu, with tempting seafood dishes such as Heineken-battered barramundi and salt-and-pepper squid, will keep you happy at this classy cafe.

White Lion Pub PUB FARE $$
(37 Walker St; mains $12-30; ⊙lunch & dinner Tue-Sat) Don't mistake this warm, friendly local for just another generic pub. The cosy restaurant and beer garden has an extensive menu with both steaks and seafood popular with the locals.

☆ Entertainment

Brolga Theatre THEATRE
(☎4122 6060; 5 Walker St) For a touch of culture, this strikingly contemporary theatre hosts musical and theatrical events.

Information

The **Maryborough/Fraser Island visitors centre** (☎1800 214 789, 4190 5742; City Hall, Kent St; ⊙9am-5pm Mon-Fri, to 1pm Sat & Sun) in the 100-year-old City Hall is extremely helpful and has free copies of comprehensive self-guided walking tours.

Kent St is the main strip but you'll find Portside has most of the museums and the Mary River Parklands are along Wharf St.

Getting There & Away

Both the *Sunlander* ($60, five hours, three weekly) and the *Tilt Train* ($60, 3½ hours, Sunday to Friday) connect Brisbane with the Maryborough West station, 7km west of the centre. There's a shuttle bus into town from the main bus terminal beside the Maryborough train station on Lennox St.

Greyhound Australia (☎1300 473 946; www.greyhound.com.au) and **Premier Motor Service** (☎13 34 10; www.premierms.com.au) have buses to Gympie ($30, one hour), Bundaberg ($40, three hours) and Brisbane ($64, 4½ hours).

Wide Bay Transit (☎4121 3719) has hourly services between Maryborough and the Urangan Marina in Hervey Bay ($8, one hour) every weekday, with fewer services on the weekend. Buses depart Maryborough from outside the City Hall in Kent St.

Hervey Bay

POP 41,225

Like its English Casanova namesake, Hervey Bay is a seductive charmer that's difficult to resist. A warm subtropical climate, long sandy beaches, calm blue ocean and a relaxed and unpretentious local community lure all sorts – backpackers, families and sea-changing retirees – to its shores. Throw in the chance to see the majestic humpback whales frolicking in the water, and the town's convenient access to the World Heritage–listed Fraser Island, and it's easy to understand how this once-sleepy fishing village seduces without even trying.

Don't bother packing a surfboard though: Fraser Island shelters Hervey Bay from the ocean surf, and the sea here is shallow and completely flat – perfect for kiddies and postcard summer holiday pics.

Sights

The beach and related activities are the big lure in Hervey Bay, but there a couple of attractions.

Reef World AQUARIUM
(☎4128 9828; Pulgul St, Urangan; adult/child $18/9, shark dives $40; ⊙9.30am-4pm) A small aquarium stocked with some of the Great Barrier Reef's most colourful characters, including a giant 18-year-old groper. You can also take a dip with lemon, whaler and other nonpredatory sharks.

Hervey Bay

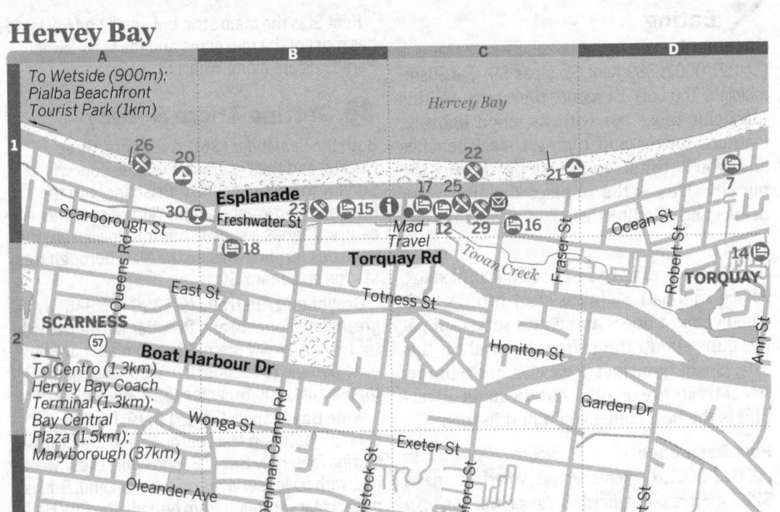

Vic Hislop's Greath White Shark and Whale Expo SHARK EXHIBIT
(553 The Esplanade, Urangan; adult/child $15/7; ⌚8.30am-5.30pm) For an informative, but slightly kitschy, peek at what hides beneath the sea visit the acclaimed Sharkman's collection of all things Jaws-like. If the newspaper clippings of gruesome shark attacks don't make you shudder maybe the 5.6m frozen Great White in the freezer will!

Wetside PARK
(www.widebaywater.qld.gov.au/quicklinks/wetsidewatereducationpark; The Esplanade, Scarness) On a hot day the kids will want to flock to this wet spot on the foreshore. There's plenty of shade, fountains, tipping buckets and a boardwalk with water infotainment (you'll learn such gems as your brain and a beef steak have almost the same amount of water). The waverider (per person $5) is the only place to surf in Hervey Bay. Wetside is open most afternoons and longer on weekends, with an after-sunset lightshow on Fridays and Saturdays. Opening hours vary from month to month so check the website for current details.

Botanic Gardens GARDEN
(Elizabeth St, Urangan; ⌚6.30am-8.30pm) Dense foliage, walking tracks, a few lagoons and over 80 visiting bird species makes the gardens a pleasant picnic spot. There's also a small but beautiful **orchid house** (admission $2; ⌚10am-3.45pm Mon-Fri) and an Aboriginal bush-tucker garden.

Akarra Lagoons NATURE RESERVE
Wallabies, kangaroos and goannas roam around this reserve, 5km north along the Burrum Heads Rd, and more than 170 species of birds visit the grounds.

Scrub Hill Community Farm FARM
(☎4124 6908; Scrub Hill Rd; ⌚by appointment) Operated by the Korrawinga Aboriginal Community, the farm is an initiative designed to provide Hervey Bay's Indigenous community with training and employment in tourism and related industries. There are bush tucker and medicine tours, farm tours and cultural performances. It's a good idea but the sporadic and inconsistent nature of the operation means tours are often unavailable.

Activities

Whale Watching

Hervey Bay is touted as the 'whale-watching capital of the world'. After fleeing the Antarctic winter to mate and calve in the warmer waters off northeastern Australia,

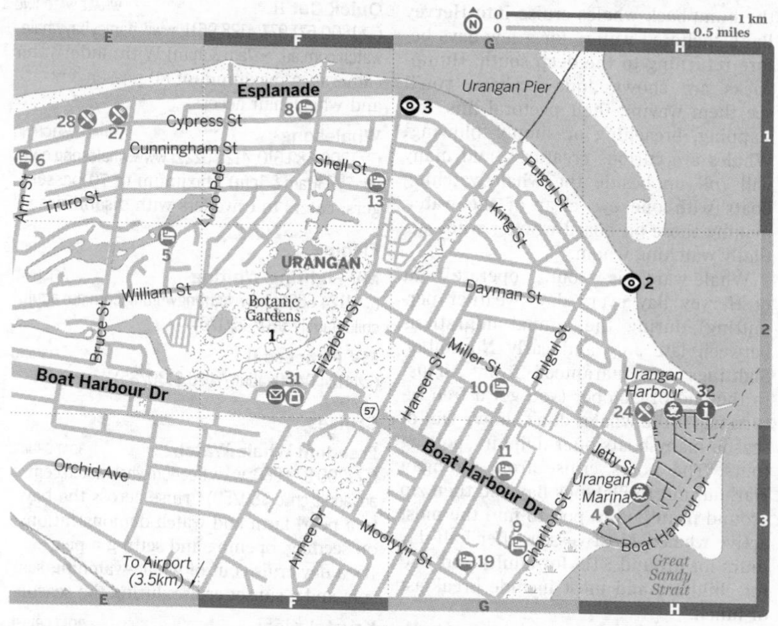

Hervey Bay

Sights

1 Botanic Gardens F2
2 Reef World H2
3 Vic Hislop's Great White Shark & Whale Expo G1

Activities, Courses & Tours

Aquavue .... (see 22)
Blue Dolphin Marine Tours .... (see 32)
Enzo's on the Beach .... (see 26)
Freedom Whale Watch .... (see 32)
4 Krystal Klear H3
MV Tasman Venture .... (see 32)
Quick Cat II .... (see 32)
Spirit of Hervey Bay .... (see 32)
That's Awesome .... (see 32)
Whalesong .... (see 32)

Sleeping

5 Alexander Lakeside B&B E2
6 Arlia Sands Apartments E1
7 Australis Shelly Bay Resort D1
8 Bay B&B F1
9 Boat Harbour Resort G3
10 Chamomile B&B G2
11 Colonial Village YHA G3
12 Fraser Roving C1
13 Grange Resort F1
14 Happy Wanderer Village D2
15 La Mer Beachfront Apartments B1
16 Next Backpackers C1
17 Nomads C1
18 Palace Backpackers B2
19 Quarterdecks Harbour Retreat G3
20 Scarness Beachfront Tourist Park A1
21 Torquay Beachfront Tourist Park C1

Eating

22 Aquavue C1
23 Black Dog Cafe B1
24 Cafe Baleana H2
25 Cafe Tapas C1
Club Crepery .... (see 29)
26 Enzo's on the Beach A1
27 Pier Restaurant E1
28 Raging Bull Stonegrill E1
29 Simply Wok C1

Drinking

30 Hoolihan's A1

Shopping

31 Urangan Central Shopping Centre F2

Information

32 Whale Watch Tourist Centre H2

the humpback whales cruise into Hervey Bay's sheltered waters for a few days before returning to the deep south. Humpbacks are showy aqua-acrobats; you'll see them waving their pectoral fins, tail slapping, breaching or simply 'blowing'. Whales are curious creatures, and many will roll up beside the whale-watching boats with one eye clear of the water, making those on board wonder who's actually watching whom.

Whale-watching tours operate out of Hervey Bay every day (weather permitting) during the annual migrations between late July and early November. Sightings are guaranteed from August to the end of October (you get a free return trip if the whales don't show). Out of season many boats offer dolphin-spotting tours. The boats cruise from Urangan Harbour out to Platypus Bay and then zip around from pod to pod to find the most active whales. Most vessels offer half-day tours for around $115 for adults and $60 for children, and most include breakfast or lunch.

Tour bookings can be made through your accommodation or the information centres.

Some recommended operators:

Spirit of Hervey Bay WHALE WATCHING
(☎1800 642 544; www.spiritofherveybay.com; ⌚8.30am & 1.30pm) The largest vessel with the greatest number of passengers. Has an underwater hydrophone and underwater viewing window.

That's Awesome WHALE WATCHING
(☎1800 653 775; www.awesomeadventure.com.au; ⌚7am, 10.30am, 2.30pm) This rigid inflatable boat speeds out to the whales faster than any other vessel. The low deck level means you're nearly eyeball-to-eyeball with the big fish.

MV Tasman Venture WHALE WATCHING
(☎1800 620 322; www.tasmanventure.com.au; ⌚8.30am & 1.30pm) Maximum of 80 passengers; underwater microphones and viewing windows.

Blue Dolphin Marine Tours WHALE WATCHING
(☎4124 9600; www.bluedolphintours.com.au; ⌚7.30am) Maximum 20 passengers on a 10m catamaran.

Freedom Whale Watch WHALE WATCHING
(☎1300 879 960; www.freedomwhalewatch.com.au; adult/child $120/80; ⌚9.30am) Maximum of 40 passengers.

Quick Cat II WHALE WATCHING
(☎1800 671 977, 4128 9611; www.herveybaywhalewatch.com.au; ⌚7am & 1pm) With underwater cameras, a maximum of 80 passengers and wheelchair access.

Whalesong WHALE WATCHING
(☎1800 689 610, 4125 6222; www.whalesong.com.au; ⌚7.30am & 1pm) Maximum of 70 passengers; caters to travellers with disabilities.

Fishing

MV Fighting Whiting FISHING
(☎4124 6599; www.fightingwhiting.com.au; adult/child/family $70/35/170)

MV Princess II FISHING
(☎4124 0400; adult/child $130/85)

Cruises

Freedom Whale Watch BOAT CRUISE
(☎1300 879 960; www.freedomwhalewatch.com.au; adult/child $80/50) Cruise across the bay to a pearl farm and watch demonstrations on seeding, opening and setting a pearl. It's a day cruise out of whale-watching season, and a sunset cruise during the season.

Krystal Klear BOAT CRUISE
(☎4128 9800; 5hr tour adult/child $90/50) Leaving from the Urangan Marina, this day trip on a 40ft glass-bottomed boat includes snorkelling, coral viewing and an island tropical barbecue.

Watersports

Aquavue WATERSPORTS
(☎4125 5528; www.aquavue.com.au; The Esplanade, Torquay) Hires out SeaKarts (per hour $50), kayaks (per hour $20) and jet skis (per 15 minutes $50). A guided Fraser Island jet ski tour costs $320.

Enzo's on the Beach WATERSPORTS
(☎4124 6375; 351a The Esplanade, Scarness) Offers kitesurfing lessons ($130 per 1½ hours) and paddleboarding (lesson or hire per hour $30 or two hours $40). Also hires out kayaks and surf skis.

Scenic Flights

Air Fraser Island SCENIC FLIGHT
(☎1800 247 992, 4125 3600; www.airfraserisland.com.au) Whale-watching flights and scenic flights over Fraser Island from $70.

MI Helicopters SCENIC FLIGHT
(☎1800 600 345; www.mihelicopters.com.au) Scenic flights from 10 minutes ($95) to one hour. Flights of 35 minutes ($255) and longer take you over Fraser Island.

Fraser Coast Microlites SCENIC FLIGHT
(☎1300 732 801) Ditch the metal shell and take a flight from $75 (20 minutes).

Other Activities

Hervey Bay Skydivers SKYDIVING
(☎1300 558 616, 4183 0119; www.herveybayskydivers.com.au) Tandem skydives for $250 from 10,000ft and $270 from 14,000ft. Add an extra $30 for skydives over the beach.

Susan River Homestead HORSE RIDING
(☎4121 6846; www.susanriver.com; Hervey Bay-Maryborough Rd) Located halfway between Maryborough and Hervey Bay. Horse-riding packages (adult/child $220/165) include accommodation, all meals and use of the on-site swimming pool and tennis courts. Two-hour rides cost $85.

Tours

Fraser Island is the big drawcard here and practically every tour operator, hotel, hostel and information centre can organise your trip. See boxed text (p195) for more information.

Lady Elliot Island ISLAND TRIP
(☎1800 072 200, 5536 3644; www.ladyelliot.com.au; per person $299) A popular day trip. Includes at least five hours on the Great Barrier Reef, a glass-bottomed boat or snorkel tour, lunch and use of the resort's facilities.

Tory's Tours SIGHTSEEING
(☎4128 6500; www.torystours.com.au; adult/child $99/85) On Mondays and Fridays visits the Bundaberg Rum Distillery. Every Wednesday, feed the dolphins on a trip to Tin Can Bay.

Festivals & Events

Hervey Bay Whale Festival CULTURAL
(www.herveybaywhalefestival.com.au) Celebrate the return of the whales at this festival, held over a week at the start of August.

Sleeping

Quarterdecks Harbour Retreat APARTMENTS $$
(☎4197 0888; www.quarterdecksretreat.com.au; 80 Moolyyir St, Urangan; 1-/2-/3-bedroom villas $150/195/225; ❄📶≋) These excellent villas are stylishly furnished with a private courtyard, all the mod cons you could wish for and little luxuries like fluffy bathrobes. Backing onto a nature reserve, it's quiet apart from the wonderful bird life, and only a cooee from the beach. The accommodation and tour packages are great value. Pets welcome.

Beachfront Tourist Parks CARAVAN PARK $
(www.beachfronttouristparks.com.au; unpowered/powered sites $23/31); Pialba (☎4128 1399); Scarness (☎4125 1578); Torquay (☎4128 1274) Fronting onto Hervey Bay's exquisitely long sandy beach, all three of these shady parks have the best ocean views, and the Torquay site is smack bang in the heart of the action.

Australis Shelly Bay Resort APARTMENTS $$
(☎4125 4533; www.shellybayresort.com.au; 466 The Esplanade, Torquay; 1-/2-bedroom units $125/170; ❄@≋) The bold, cheerful self-contained units at this complex are clean and spacious. All rooms have water views and with the beach just across the road this is one of the best options in town. There's also an Indian restaurant on site.

Bay B&B B&B $$
(☎4125 6919; www.baybedandbreakfast.com.au; 180 Cypress St, Urangan; s $75, d $135-150; ❄@≋) This great-value B&B is run by a friendly, well-travelled Frenchman. Guest rooms are in a comfy annexe out the back, and breakfast is served on an outdoor patio in a tropical garden, surrounded by birds and masses of greenery. Families can take over the separate fully self-contained unit. Breakfast crepès are delicious, and dinners are available on request.

Colonial Village YHA HOSTEL $
(☎1800 818 280; www.cvyha.com; 820 Boat Harbour Dr, Urangan; unpowered/powered sites $18/24, dm/d/cabins from $20/54/85; ❄@≋) This excellent YHA is set on 8 hectares of tranquil bushland, close to the marina and only 50m from the beach. It's a lovely spot, thick with ambience, possums and parrots. Facilities include a spa, tennis and basketball courts, and a funky bar. Breakfast is free and dinners cost $8 to $10.

Grange Resort RESORT $$$
(☎4125 2002; www.thegrange-herveybay.com.au; cnr Elizabeth & Shell Sts, Urangan; 1-/2-bedroom villas $195/225; ❄📶≋) Reminiscent of a stylish desert resort with fancy split-level condos and filled with life's little luxuries, this place is close to the beach and to town. Glossy kitchens and bathrooms, stainless-steel appliances, plump couches, spacious boudoirs and commodious decks are the norm. Also has some great specials.

SEXY HUMPBACKS

Males 'strutting their stuff' are nothing new in the animal kingdom: think of a hummingbird's song, a peacock's dance or the local surf club on a Friday night. But unlike land-based animals, giant marine mammals are limited to how (and what) they can strut. In the case of the humpback whale, singing seems to be the best option.

Dr Mike Noad from the University of Queensland, a leading international expert on the humpback, sums up a male whale's song as 'an acoustic version of a peacock's tail. It's complex and very beautiful but meaningless except as a way to show off.' Songs last 10 to 20 minutes and are often repeated continuously for hours on end.

Since only males sing (and only during the breeding migrations), it's a likely bet these bulls are crooning for a mate. After a season of song and sex the male's job is done, leaving the cows responsible for raising their calves.

Not so different from the surf club after all.

Quick whale facts:

» Three whales form a pod, a dozen form a pulse.

» Calves drink up to 600 litres of milk per day.

» Young reach sexual maturity at seven to 10 years of age.

» Pregnant females have a gestation period of 10 months.

Alexander Lakeside B&B B&B **$$**
(☎4128 9448; www.herveybaybedandbreakfast.com.au; 29 Lido Pde, Urangan; r $135-165; ❄📶) In a quiet street, this warm and friendly B&B offers lakeside indulgence where turtles come a-visiting in the morning. There's a heated lakeside spa, two spacious rooms with en suites and two luxury self-contained suites. Guests also have access to a kitchen and laundry.

Chamomile B&B B&B **$$**
(☎4125 1602; www.chamomile.com.au; 65a Miller St; s $105, d $130-155) In a stately Queenslander with long timber verandahs, this quaint B&B with its country-floral decor will have you reminiscing of favourite aunts baking home-made cookies. There are plenty of cosy retreats and a tropical garden filled with birdsong.

La Mer Beachfront Apartments APARTMENTS **$$**
(☎1800 100 181, 4128 3494; www.lamer.com.au; 396 The Esplanade, Torquay; 1-/2-bedroom apt from $150/200; ❄📶🏊) With colours this bold you'll think you're in the Mediterranean. The rainbow scheme continues indoors but it's actually quite pleasant. The apartments are large, comfortable and have fully equipped kitchens. Choose between poolside or beachfront units.

Arlia Sands Apartments APARTMENTS **$$**
(☎4125 4360; www.arliasands.com.au; 13 Ann St, Torquay; 1-/2-bedroom apts $135/145; ❄🏊) This refurbished series of units contains plush furniture and spacious modern bathrooms. It's off the main drag yet close to the beach and shops and is *trés* quiet.

Boat Harbour Resort APARTMENTS **$$**
(☎4125 5079; www.boatharbourresort.net; 651-652 Charlton St, Urangan; apt $115-135; ❄📶🏊) Close to the Urangan marina, these timber studios and cabins are set on attractive grounds. The studios have sizeable decks out the front and the roomy villas are great for families.

Palace Backpackers HOSTEL **$**
(☎1800 063 168, 4124 5331; www.palaceadventures.com; 184 Torquay Rd, Scarness; dm/d $25/55; ❄@🏊) These self-contained units (with doubles, three-, four- and six-bed-dorms) are set in tropical gardens and are only a short walk to the beach. Each unit has its own bathroom, kitchen and lounge. Good deals for Fraser Island tours.

Happy Wanderer Village CARAVAN PARK **$**
(☎4125 1103; www.happywanderer.com.au; 105 Truro St, Torquay; unpowered/powered sites from $30/35, cabins/villas from $64/121; ❄📶🏊) The manicured lawns and profuse gum-tree cover at this large park make for great tent sites. The cabins and villas are clean and roomy and the spotless facilities include a spa, free barbecues and a laundry. Rates are for two people. Wheelchair accessible.

Next Backpackers HOSTEL **$**
(☎4125 6600; www.nextbackpackers.com.au; 10 Bideford St, Torquay; dm $20-32, d $69; ❄@📶)

Having won a swag of awards, you'd expect this modern hostel to be a cut above the usual suspects. With polished wooden floors, ultraclean roomy rooms and a well-equipped stainless-steel kitchen, it certainly is. There's a 'girls only' dorm and a bar open until midnight.

Nomads HOSTEL $
(☎4125 3601; www.nomadshostels.com; 408 The Esplanade, Torquay; dm/d from $18/60; ❄@📶🏊) This sprawling complex directly opposite the beach has all bases covered. Low-level housing clusters around the colonial-style bar, central pool and shady barbecue area. The tour desk can organise packages (with a free night if you book the half-day whale-watching tour) and self-drive Fraser Island tours to their permanent campsite on Fraser Island.

Fraser Roving HOSTEL $
(☎1800 989 811, 4125 6386; www.fraserroving.com; 412 The Esplanade, Torquay; dm $23-25, d with/without bathroom $60/65; @🏊) Although the rooms are stark and spartan, Fraser's party vibe continues undiminished. The hostel is a maze of corridors, but you're definitely in the heart of the action. Tuck into the all-you-can-eat Mexican for $11.90 every night of the week.

Eating

Self-caterers can stock up at the supermarkets inside the Centro, Urangan Central and Bay Central Plaza shopping centres.

TOP CHOICE **Black Dog Café** FUSION $$
(☎4124 3177; 381 The Esplanade, Torquay; mains $14-33; ⏲lunch & dinner) The ambience is funk, the menu is Zen. The East-meets-West dishes feature sushi, Japanese soup, fresh burgers, curries, club sambos and seafood salads and will tame any black dog.

Cafè Tapas TAPAS $$
(417 The Esplanade, Torquay; tapas $7; ⏲lunch & dinner) This slick venue has funky artwork, dim lighting, red couches and low tables flickering with coloured lights. Come for Asian-inspired tapas and linger longer for drinks and music.

Enzo's on the Beach CAFE $
(351a The Esplanade, Scarness; mains $8-20; ⏲6.30am-5pm) A shabby-chic outdoor cafe with a superb beachfront location where you can dine on focaccias, wraps, healthy salads and light meals or just sip a coffee and wallow in the perfect ocean views. Active sorts can hire kayaks, surf skis and paddleboards or learn kitesurfing.

Aquavue CAFE $
(415a The Esplanade, Torquay; mains $8-13; ⏲breakfast & lunch) Another outdoor cafe on the beachfront offering unbeatable sea views and the usual assortment of sandwiches and light meals. There are plenty of water toys for hire.

Café Balaena CAFE $$
(Shop 7, Terminal Bldg, Buccaneer Ave, Urangan; mains $10-25; ⏲breakfast & lunch daily, dinner Thu-Mon) This waterfront cafe at the marina provides expansive views, atmosphere with a decidedly laid-back twist and wallet-friendly prices. The menu ranges across the board with a good dose of seafood.

Raging Bull Stonegrill STEAKHOUSE $$
(☎4194 6674; 486 The Esplanade, Torquay; mains $20-40; ⏲dinner) This interactive dining experience whereby a slab of meat, chicken or fish cooks on a hot rock on your plate will make carnivores feel righteously healthy. Don't forget to eat your greens.

Pier Restaurant SEAFOOD $$
(☎4128 9699; 573 The Esplanade, Urangan; mains $20-40; ⏲dinner Mon-Sat) Although sitting opposite the water, the Pier makes little use of its ocean views but this à la carte restaurant does have an interesting seafood menu (crocodile and Hervey Bay scallops) and is deservedly popular.

Simply Wok ASIAN $$
(417 The Esplanade, Torquay; mains $14-25; ⏲breakfast, lunch & dinner) Noodles, stir-fries, seafood and curries will satisfy any cravings for Asian cuisine, and there's an all-you-can-eat hot buffet for $15.90.

Club Crepery SEAFOOD $
(417 The Esplanade, Torquay; mains $10-16; ⏲9am-4pm) This tiny hole-in-the-wall cafe has wicked seafood crepes. Try the club berry stack for breakfast.

Drinking

Hoolihan's PUB
(382 The Esplanade, Scarness). Like all good Irish pubs, Hoolihan's is wildly popular, especially with the backpacker crowd. Maybe it's got something to do with its hard-drinking ethos and carbo-laden meals.

Information

Hervey Bay covers a string of beachside suburbs – Point Vernon, Pialba, Scarness, Torquay and Urangan – but behind the flawless beachfront and pockets of sedate suburbia, the outskirts of town dissolve into an industrial jungle. Unfortunately, when you enter town on the Maryborough–Hervey Bay Rd, the only way to reach the beach is through this frenzied traffic snarl.

Hervey Bay Visitor Information Centre (☎1800 811 728, 4125 9855; www.herveybaytourism.com.au; cnr Urraween & Maryborough Rds; ⊙9am-5pm) Helpful and professional tourist office on the outskirts of town.

Hervey Bay visitors centre (☎1800 649 926, 4124 4050; 401 The Esplanade, Torquay; internet per hr $4; ⊙8.30am-8.30pm Mon-Fri, 9am-6.30pm Sat & Sun) Privately run booking office with internet access. Very friendly. Call anytime.

Mad Travel (☎4125 3601; 408 The Esplanade, Torquay; internet per hr $4; ⊙7am-11pm) Located at Nomads. Offers internet access and is a booking agent for tours and activities.

Post office (☎4125 1101; 414 The Esplanade, Torquay) Branches also at Pialba and Urangan.

Whale Watch Tourist Centre (☎1800 358 595, 4128 9800; Urangan Marina, Urangan; ⊙7.30am-6pm) At the marina; it's privately run and has good information on whale-watching tours.

Getting There & Away

Air

Hervey Bay airport is off Booral Rd, Urangan, on the way to River Heads.

Qantas (☎13 13 13; www.qantas.com.au) has several daily flights to/from Brisbane. **Virgin Blue** (☎13 67 89; www.virginblue.com.au) flies daily from Sydney.

Boat

Boats to Fraser Island leave from River Heads, about 10km south of town, and Urangan Marina (see p196). Most tours leave from Urangan Harbour.

Bus

Long-distance buses depart **Hervey Bay Coach Terminal** (☎4124 4000; Central Ave, Pialba). **Greyhound Australia** (☎1300 473 946; www.greyhound.com.au) and **Premier Motor Service** (☎13 34 10; www.premierms.com.au) have several services to/from Brisbane ($75, 5½ hours), Maroochydore ($50, 3½ hours), Bundaberg ($24, 1½ hours) and Rockhampton ($95, six hours).

Tory's Tours (☎4128 6500; www.torystours.com.au) has twice-daily services to Brisbane airport ($65).

Wide Bay Transit (☎4121 3719) has hourly services from Urangan Marina (stopping along The Esplanade) to Maryborough ($8, one hour) every weekday, with fewer services on weekends.

Trainlink buses connect Maryborough West train station with the Coach Terminal ($8, 45 minutes).

Getting Around

Car & Motorcycle

Seega Rent a Car (☎4125 6008; 463 The Esplanade) has small cars from $40 to $55 a day. Plenty of rental companies makes Hervey Bay the best place to hire a 4WD for Fraser Island:

Aussie Trax (☎1800 062 275; 56 Boat Harbour Dr, Pialba)

Fraser Magic 4WD Hire (☎4125 6612; www.fraser-magic-4wdhire.com.au; 5 Kruger Crt, Urangan)

Hervey Bay Rent A Car (☎4194 6626) Also rents out scooters ($30 per day).

Safari 4WD Hire (☎1800 689 819, 4124 4244; www.safari4wdhire.com.au; 102 Boat Harbour Dr, Pialba)

Childers

POP 1350

Surrounded by lush green fields and rich red soil, Childers is a charming little town, its main street lined with tall, shady trees and lattice-trimmed historical buildings. Backpackers flock here for fruit-picking and farm work, although, sadly, Childers is remembered most for the 15 backpackers who perished in a fire in the Palace Backpackers Hostel in June 2000.

Sights & Activities

Childers Palace Memorial & Art Gallery ART GALLERY

(72 Churchill St; ⊙9am-4pm Mon-Fri, to 3pm Sat & Sun) There is now a moving memorial in the restored building, including poignant images of the backpackers who perished.

Old Pharmacy MUSEUM

(90 Churchill St; ⊙9am-3.30pm Mon-Fri) A pharmacy operated here from 1894 to 1982. The original chemist was also the town dentist, vet, optician and local photographer. The dispensary has been restored to its original layout and showcases torturous dental gear, medicines dating back to the 1800s, dispensing flasks, and a detailed prescription book.

Isis Historical Complex HISTORIC PARK
(Taylor St; adult/child $2/free; ⏲9am-noon Mon-Fri) A mock historical town, with cottages, a general store and a post office. You'll also find the delightful **Figtree Treasures** out front with a range of interesting antiques.

The lovely 100-year-old **Federal Hotel** (cnr Churchill and North Sts) has batwing doors while a bronze statue of two fighting pig dogs sits outside the **Grand Hotel** (110 Churchill St).

On the last Sunday in July, Childers' main street is swamped with street performers, musicians, dancers, and food and craft stalls during its annual **Festival of Cultures**, which draws over 50,000 people.

Sleeping & Eating

Sugarbowl Caravan Park CARAVAN PARK $
(☎4126 1521; 4660 Bruce Hwy; unpowered/powered sites $20/22, cabins $66; @☒) A little out of town, this caravan park has spectacular views over the surrounding countryside. There's plenty of space and a good scattering of foliage between sites. Many farm-working backpackers stay here.

Childers Tourist Park & Camp CARAVAN PARK/CAMPGROUND $
(☎4126 1371; 111 Stockyard Rd; unpowered/powered sites $24/25, on-site vans $66) This very clean and friendly place is a better option for farm-working backpackers, but you'll need a car. Rates are for two people.

Mango Hill B&B B&B $$
(☎4126 1311; www.mangohillcottages.com; 8 Mango Hill Dr; s/d $90/120; ☒) For warm, country hospitality, stay at these cute cane-cutter cottages situated 4km south of town. They are decorated with handmade wooden furniture, country decor and comfy beds that ooze charm and romance. A bottle of preservative-free, organic wine from the on-site boutique winery, **Hill of Promise Estate** (⏲cellar door 10am-4pm, or by appointment), goes well with the picture-pretty views from the cottage verandah.

Kapé Centro CAFE $
(65 Churchill St; mains $9-15; ⏲breakfast & lunch) Stop for lunch in the old post office building, where light meals, salads and pizzas are served up on the verandah.

Mammino's ICE CREAM $
(115 Lucketts Rd; ⏲9am-5pm) On your way out of town take a detour to this farm for wickedly delicious homemade macadamia-nut ice cream. Lucketts Rd is off the Bruce Hwy just south of Childers.

Information

Childers Visitors Information Centre (☎4130 4660; ⏲9am-4pm Mon-Fri, to 3pm Sat & Sun) Beneath the Childers Palace Memorial & Art Gallery.

Getting There & Away

Childers is 50km southwest of Bundaberg. **Greyhound Australia** (☎1300 473 946) and

WORTH A TRIP

TIN CAN BAY

For a pleasant backroads coastal drive, head out of Rainbow Beach along Rainbow Beach Rd, turn north onto Tin Can Bay Rd and after 10km you'll reach the idyllic and quiet fishing village of Tin Can Bay. Sitting at the southern tip of the Great Sandy Strait, it's the perfect place to escape the beaten track.

Mystique, the resident dolphin, makes regular breakfast visits to the Tin Can Bay marina boat ramp and monitored feeding takes place from 8am to 10am.

Sleepy Lagoon Hotel/Motel (☎5486 4124; 12-16 Bream Rd; d $50-85) has both budget and motel accommodation, or you could live it up at **Dolphin Waters** (☎5486 2600; www.dolphinwaters.com.au; 40-1 The Esplanade; d from $125; ❄☒📶), which has spotless, self-contained units. Fishing enthusiasts can fish from dawn to dusk and beyond on the fully self-contained houseboats from **Tin Can Bay Houseboats** (☎5486 2669; www.tincanbayhouseboats.com.au; Norman Point; minimum 2 nights $890).

The seafood platter at **Snappers on the Marina** (☎5486 4400; 1 Oyster Pde; mains $12-30; ⏲lunch & dinner Thu, Fri & Mon) is a Neptunian feast and the marina restaurant has lovely water views.

Leaving town on Tin Can Bay Rd, turn north towards Maryborough for a pleasant 65km country drive through pine forests and lush greenery.

Premier Motor Service (☎13 34 10) both stop at the Shell service station north of town and have daily services to/from Brisbane ($75, 6½ hours), Hervey Bay ($18, one hour) and Bundaberg ($18, 1½ hours).

Burrum Coast National Park

The attractive Burrum Coast National Park covers two sections of coastline on either side of the little village of **Woodgate**, 37km east of Childers. Woodgate's charming old stilt-houses line the Esplanade, which fronts an incredibly beautiful 16km stretch of white sandy beach. Nothing happens here and it's perfect for family summer holidays. The Woodgate section of the national park begins at the southern end of the Esplanade, and has nice beaches, good fishing and a **camping ground** (per person $5.50) at Burrum Point, reached by a 4WD-only track. There are more isolated bush-camping areas in the Kinkuna section of the park, a few kilometres north of Woodgate, and you'll need a 4WD to reach them. Book camping permits online at www.derm.qld.gov.au.

Woodgate Beach Tourist Park (☎4126 8802; www.woodgatebeachtouristpark.com; 88 The Esplanade; unpowered/powered sites $27/29, cabins $85-95, beachfront villas $110; ❄@) is a tidy, tranquil park close to the national park and opposite the beach. Rates are for two people.

Woodgate Beach Hotel-Motel (☎4126 8988; 195 The Esplanade; d $90), at the northern end of the Esplanade, has a block of reasonable motel units just across from the beach, and dishes up decent pub grub.

Bundaberg

POP 46,960

Boasting a sublime climate, coral-fringed beaches and waving fields of sugar cane, 'Bundy' should feature on the Queensland tourist hit parade. But this old-fashioned country town feels stuck in a centuries-old time warp and nothing much seems to happen here. The pleasant main strip is a wide, palm-lined street, and the surrounding countryside forms a picturesque chequerboard of rich, red volcanic soil, small crops and sugar cane stretching pancake-flat to the coastal beaches 15km away. Born out of these cane fields is the famous Bundaberg Rum, a potent and mind-blowing liquor bizarrely endorsed by a polar bear but as iconically Australian as Tim Tams and Vegemite.

Hordes of backpackers flock to Bundy for fruit-picking and farm work; others quickly pass through on their way to family summer holidays at the nearby seaside villages.

Sights

Bundaberg Rum Distillery DISTILLERY
(☎4131 2999; www.bundabergrum.com.au; Ave St; self-guided tour adult/child $15/7.50; ⏲9am-3.30pm Mon-Fri, to 2.30pm Sat & Sun) Bundaberg's biggest claim to fame is the iconic Bundaberg Rum – you'll see the Bundy Rum polar bear on billboards all over town. Aficionados of the good stuff can see the vats where liquid gold is made. Guided **tours of the factory & museum** (adult/child $25/12.50) depart every hour from 10am to 3pm each day. Tours follow the rum's production from start to finish; each of the 290 vats on site contains 69,000L of maturing rum. If the heady fumes don't get you, the free sample at the end of the tour will.

Hinkler Hall of Aviation MUSEUM
(☎4130 4400; www.hinklerhallofaviation.com; Botanic Gardens, Mt Perry Rd; adult/child/family $15/10/40; ⏲9am-4pm) Situated within the grounds of the Botanic Gardens, this modern museum has multimedia exhibits, a flight simulator, and informative displays that chronicle the life of Bundaberg's famous son and pioneer solo aviator, Bert Hinkler. Hinkler made the first solo flight between England and Australia in 1928. There's even a fragment from Hinkler's glider which was aboard the fated *Challenger* Space Shuttle when it exploded soon after take-off in 1986.

Hummock LANDMARK
From the lookout on top of this extinct volcano (the only hill (96m) in this flat landscape), you see Bundaberg's patchwork fields of sugar cane and small crops spread against an ocean backdrop. During the cane-harvest season from July to November, the horizon blazes with spectacular and incredibly quick-lived and furious cane fires.

Bundaberg Barrel BREWERY
(☎4154 5480; www.bundaberg.com; 147 Bargara Rd; adult/child $12.50/5.50; ⏲9am-4.30pm Mon-Sat, 10am-3pm Sun) Not quite as famous as the rum (probably because it's nonalcoholic) is Bundaberg Ginger Beer. To see how the ginger is mushed, crushed, brewed and fer-

Bundaberg

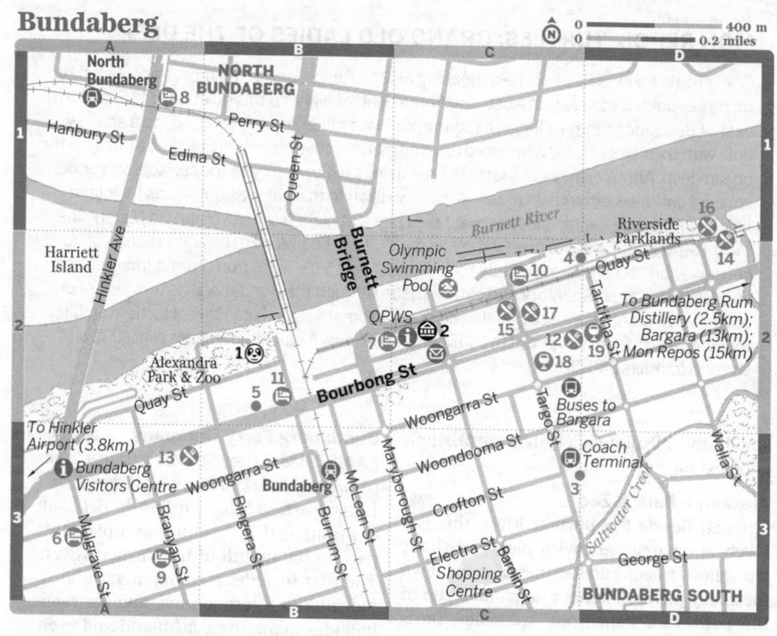

Bundaberg

Sights

1 Alexandra Park & Zoo B2
2 Bundaberg Regional Art Gallery C2

Activities, Courses & Tours

Australian Divers .... (see 3)
3 Bundaberg Aqua Scuba C3
4 Bundaberg Ferry Company C2
5 Dive Musgrave B2

Sleeping

6 Bundaberg Spanish Motor Inn A3
7 Cellblock Backpackers B2
8 Feeding Grounds Backpackers A1
9 Inglebrae A3
10 Quality Hotel C2
11 Villa Mirasol B2

Eating

12 Indulge C2
13 Les Chefs A3
14 Restaurant D1
15 Spicy Tonight C2
16 Spinnaker Restaurant & Bar D1
17 Teaspoon C2

Drinking

18 Central Hotel C2
19 Club Hotel D2

mented, visit the Barrel. At least the free samples won't give you a head rush.

Botanic Gardens GARDEN
(Mt Perry Rd; ⏲5.30am-6.45pm Sep-Apr, 6am-6.30pm May-Aug) Two kilometres north of the town centre is a green oasis of tropical shrubs, towering trees and flowering gardens surrounding a few small lakes. Within the grounds are a number of museums including the **Hinkler House Museum** (adult/child $5/2; ⏲10am-4pm) inside Bert Hinkler's Southampton house; the **Bundaberg & District Historical Museum** (adult/child $4/2; ⏲10am-4pm), which has plenty of colonial-era antiques; and the **Fairymead House Sugar Museum** (adult/child $4/2; ⏲10am-4pm), which documents the development of the sugar-cane industry.

Bundaberg Regional Art Gallery ART GALLERY
(☎4130 4750; www.brag-brc.org.au; 1 Barolin St; ⏲10am-5pm Mon-Fri, 11am-3pm Sat & Sun) This

MON REPOS' TURTLES: GRAND OLD LADIES OF THE DEEP

Going turtle takes on a whole new meaning at Mon Repos, one of the most important natural turtle rookeries in eastern Australia. At the dead of night on this quiet beach 15km northeast of Bundaberg, female loggerheads lumber laboriously up the sand, scoop a shallow hole with their flippers, lay a hundred or so eggs, then cover them up before returning to the ocean deep. About eight weeks later the hatchlings dig their way to the surface, and under cover of darkness emerge en masse to scurry down to the water as quickly as their little flippers allow. Egg-laying and hatching takes place at night from November to March. The **Mon Repos visitors centre** (4159 1652; 7.30am-6pm Mon-Fri) has information on turtle conservation and organises nightly tours (adult/child $10/5.25) from 7pm during the season. Bookings are mandatory and can be made through the Bundaberg visitors centre or online at www.bookbundabergregion.com.au. Alternatively, you can take a turtle-watching tour with **Foot Prints Adventures** (4152 3659; www.footprintsadventures.com.au; adult/child incl transfers $48/30).

small (and purple) gallery has surprisingly good exhibitions.

Alexandra Park & Zoo PARK

(Quay St) Beside the Burnett River, this is a lovely sprawling park with plenty of shady trees, flower beds and swathes of green lawn for a lazy picnic. There's also a small zoo at the park with kangaroos, wallabies, birds and deer.

Activities

About 16km east of Bundaberg, the small beach hamlet of Bargara has good diving and snorkelling at Barolin Rocks and in the Woongarra Marine Park.

Dive Musgrave DIVING

(1800 552 614; www.divemusgrave.com.au; 239 Bourbong St; per person $698) Offers three-day trips for experienced divers to Lady Musgrave and the Bunker group of islands.

Bundaberg Aqua Scuba DIVING

(4153 5761; www.aquascuba.com.au; Shop 1, 66 Targo St) Offers four-day, PADI open-water diving courses for $265, but this only includes shore dives. Advanced open-water dive courses cost from $295.

Australian Divers DIVING

(4152 4064; 66 Targo St) A PADI course here costs $400.

Tours

Lady Elliot Island ISLAND TRIP

(1800 072 200, 5536 3644; www.ladyelliot.com.au; adult/child $299/162) The flying day trip to Lady Elliot Island includes at least five hours on the Great Barrier Reef, a glass-bottomed boat or snorkel tour, lunch and use of the resort's facilities.

Bundaberg Ferry Company RIVER CRUISE

(4152 9188; 3 Quay St; 2½hr tours per adult/child/family $25/13/70; 9.30am Wed & Fri, 1.30pm Tue & Fri-Sun) The *Bundy Belle*, an old-fashioned ferry, chugs at a pleasant pace to the mouth of the Burnett River. The tour includes a commentary and morning or afternoon tea, and the scenery includes mangroves, farmland and even the Bundaberg Rum Distillery.

Sleeping

There are plenty of midrange motels on the Bundaberg–Childers Rd into town. Bundaberg's hostels cater to working backpackers; most hostels arrange harvest work and stays of one week or longer are the norm. Check the hostels carefully before deciding as standards vary considerably.

Inglebrae B&B $$

(4154 4003; www.inglebrae.com; 17 Branyan St; r incl breakfast $110-140;) For old-world English charm in a glorious Queenslander, this delightful B&B is just the ticket. Polished timber and stained glass seep from the entrance into the rooms, which come with high beds and small antiques. Breakfasts are big and hot, and are served on the lovely verandah.

Quality Hotel HOTEL $$

(4155 8777; www.burnettmotel.com.au; 7 Quay St; r $185-200;) This modern pit stop is popular with conferences and travelling business folk, but the good facilities and decor set it apart from just about every other option in town. The rooms are quite stylish and there's a gym, a sauna, and a licensed restaurant and cocktail bar overlooking the Burnett River.

Cellblock Backpackers HOSTEL $
(☎1800 837 773, 4154 3210; cnr Quay & Maryborough Sts; dm per night/week from $27/160, d $66; ❄@≋) Doing time has never been so good! This arresting hostel in Bundy's heritage-listed former lock-up is a swish resort with plasma-screen TVs, a trendy pool bar and clean, modern facilities. The seven restored jail cells (grab the padded cell!) lack windows (of course) but are great for couples. The hostel arranges harvest work and the bathrooms are remarkably clean considering most backpackers drag farm soil home from a day in the fields.

Feeding Grounds Backpacker HOSTEL $
(☎4152 3659; www.footprintsadventures.com.au; 4 Hinkler Ave; dm $30) The smallest hostel in Bundaberg is a friendly, family-run affair in a converted and extended house. It's a bit cramped but a new purpose-built hostel was under construction in the backyard at the time of research. The environmentally conscious owner of the hostel runs Footprints Adventures turtle tours. Combined accommodation and tour packages are available.

Villa Mirasol MOTEL $$
(☎4154 4311; www.villa.net.au; 225 Bourbong St; r from $149; ❄@≋) The Mexican theme is evident in this ochre-coloured, centrally located motel. Aztec motifs decorate the rooms and the executive suites come with a spa. Wheelchair accessible.

Bundaberg Spanish Motor Inn MOTEL $$
(☎4152 5444; www.bundabergspanishmotorinn.com; 134 Woongarra St; s/d$85/95; ❄≋) In a quiet side street off the main drag, this Spanish hacienda-style motel is great value. All units are self-contained and all rooms overlook the central pool.

Eating

Les Chefs INTERNATIONAL $$
(☎4153 1770; 238 Bourbong St; mains $27; ⌚lunch Tue-Fri, dinner Mon-Sat) One for the carnivores, this upmarket, intimate restaurant goes global, treating diners to duck, veal, seafood, chicken and beef dishes à la Nepal, Mexico, France, India and more. It's immensely popular so make a reservation.

Spinnaker Restaurant & Bar MODERN AUSTRALIAN $$
(☎4152 8033; 1a Quay St; dishes $10-40; ⌚lunch Tue-Fri, dinner Tue-Sat) With a picturesque perch above the Burnett River, this is a great choice for a long lunch or an intimate dinner. Or just have a sundowner at the bar and nibble on a selection of tapas.

Spicy Tonight FUSION $
(☎4154 3320; 1 Targo St; dishes $12-20; ⌚lunch & dinner Mon-Sat) Bundaberg's spicy little secret combines Thai and Indian cuisine with hot curries, vindaloo, tandoori and a host of vegetarian dishes.

Restaurant MODERN AUSTRALIAN $$
(☎4154 4589; cnr Quay & Toonburra Sts; mains $25-35; ⌚dinner Tue-Sat) Once a rowing shed, this riverside bar and restaurant serves up simple Mod Oz cuisine. The interior can be a bit dim but the outdoor tables on the timber deck make a lovely spot for a quiet drink. Live music plays on weekends.

Indulge CAFE $
(80 Bourbong St; dishes $9-16; ⌚breakfast & lunch) Scrumptious pastries, fancy brekkies, decent coffee and consistently good food draw in the crowds. Can be busy and crowded.

Teaspoon CAFE $
(10 Targo St; mains $5-10; ⌚8am-5pm Mon-Sat) This funky little cafe has the best coffee in town.

Drinking & Entertainment

You won't go thirsty in Bundaberg. There's a host of pubs with glorious exteriors and the locals will probably provide all the animation you need.

Central Hotel PUB
(18 Targo St) Strut your stuff on the dance floor at Bundy's hottest nightclub. Pretty young things and backpackers crowd in here every weekend.

Club Hotel PUB
(cnr Tantitha & Bourbong Sts) The lounge bar has laid-back lounges and chill-out music; an inner-city vibe in country Bundy.

Information

Bundaberg Email Centre (☎4153 5007; 197 Bourbong St; internet per hr $4; ⌚10am-10pm)

Bundaberg visitors centre (☎1300 722 099, 4153 8888; www.bundabergregion.info; 271 Bourbong St; ⌚9am-5pm)

Cosy Corner Internet Cafe (☎4153 5999; Barolin St; internet per hr $4; ⌚8am-7pm Mon-Fri, 9am-5pm Sat, 11am-5pm Sun)

Post office (☎4151 6708; cnr Bourbong & Barolin Sts)

QPWS (☎4131 1600; 46 Quay St)

Getting There & Around

Air

Bundaberg's **Hinkler Airport** (Takalvan St) is about 4km southwest of the centre. There are several flights each day between Bundaberg and Brisbane with **Qantaslink** (☎13 13 13; www.qantas.com.au).

Bus

The coach terminal is in Targo Street. Both **Greyhound Australia** (☎1300 473 946; www.greyhound.com.au) and **Premier Motor Service** (☎13 34 10; www.premierms.com.au) have daily services connecting Bundaberg with Brisbane ($95, seven hours), Hervey Bay ($24, 1½ hours), Rockhampton ($75, four hours) and Gladstone ($50, 2½ hours).

Local bus services are handled by **Duffy's Coaches** (☎4151 4226). It has numerous services every weekday to Bargara ($5, 35 minutes), leaving from the back of Target on Woongarra St and stopping around town.

Train

Both the *Sunlander* ($68, seven hours, three weekly) and the *Tilt Train* ($68, five hours, Sunday to Friday) travel from Brisbane to Bundaberg on their respective routes to Cairns and Rockhampton.

Around Bundaberg

In many people's eyes, the beach hamlets around Bundaberg are more attractive than the town itself. Some 25km north of the centre is **Moore Park**, with wide, flat beaches. To the south is the very popular **Elliot Heads** with a nice beach, rocky foreshore and good fishing. Locals and visitors also flock to **Mon Repos** to see baby turtles hatching from November to March.

BARGARA

POP 5530

Some 16km east of Bundaberg lies the cruisy beach village of Bargara, a picturesque little spot with a good surf beach, a lovely esplanade and a few snazzy cafes. Recent years have seen a few high-rises sprout up along the foreshore but the effect is relatively low-key. Families find Bargara attractive for its clean beaches and safe swimming, particularly at the 'basin', a sheltered artificial rock pool.

In a great location opposite the esplanade, **Kacy's Bargara Beach Motel** (☎1800 246 141, 4130 1111; www.bargaramotel.com.au; cnr See & Bauer Sts; d from $119, 2-bedroom apt from $199; ❄📶🏊) offers a range of accommodation from pleasant motel rooms to self-contained apartments. Downstairs is the tropically themed **Kacy's Restaurant and Bar** (mains $12-32; ⊙breakfast & dinner daily, lunch Fri-Sun), where you can sip cocktails on the capacious timber deck.

Otherwise, the large sprawling grounds of the **Bargara Beach Caravan Park** (☎4159 2228; www.bargarabeach.com.au; Nielson Park, Bargara; unpowered/powered sites $22/28, cabins $85) covers 6.5 hectares, so you're bound to find room to pitch a tent.

FRASER ISLAND

The region's Aborigines call it K'Gari (paradise). Sculpted from wind, sand and surf, the striking blue freshwater lakes, crystalline creeks, giant dunes and lush rainforests of this gigantic sandbar form an enigmatic island paradise unlike any other in the world. Created over hundreds of thousands of years from sand drifting off the east coast of mainland Australia, Fraser Island is the largest sand island in the world (measuring 120km by 15km) and the only place where rainforest grows on sand.

Inland, the vegetation varies from dense tropical rainforest and wild heath to wetlands and wallum scrub, with 'sandblows' (giant dunes over 200m high), mineral streams and freshwater lakes opening onto long sandy beaches fringed with pounding surf. The island is home to a profusion of birdlife and wildlife including the purest strain of dingo in Australia, while offshore waters teem with dugongs, dolphins, sharks and migrating humpback whales.

This island Utopia, however, is marred by an ever-increasing volume of 4WD traffic tearing down the beach and along sandy inland tracks. With over 350,000 people visiting the island each year, Fraser can sometimes feel like a giant sandpit with its own peak hour and congested beach highway.

Fraser Island

Sleeping

1 Dilli Village Fraser Island C6
2 Eurong Beach Resort C5
3 Fraser Island Beachhouses C5
4 Fraser Island Wilderness Retreat C4
5 Frasers@Cathedral Beach C4
6 Kingfisher Bay Resort B5
7 Sailfish on Fraser C4

Fraser Island

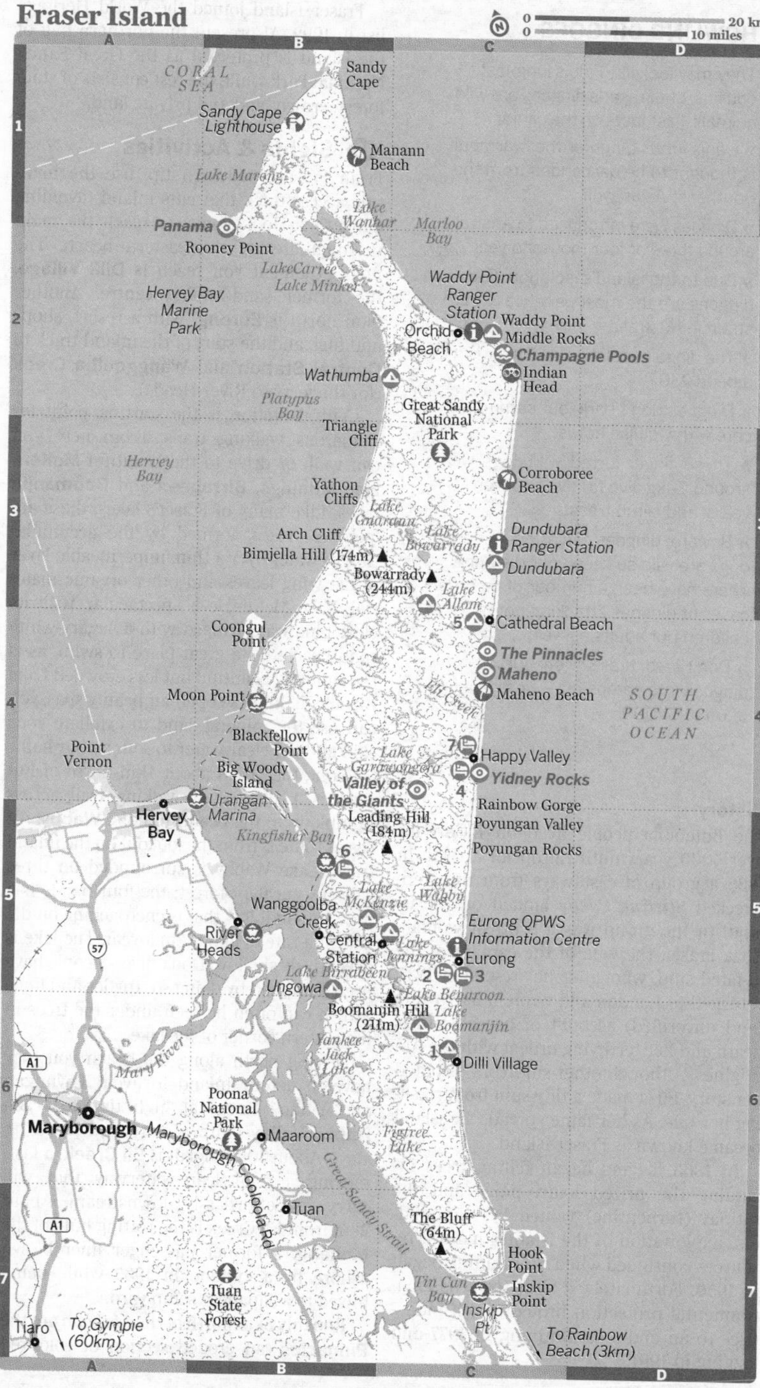

0 20 km
0 10 miles
CORAL SEA
Sandy Cape
Sandy Cape Lighthouse
Manann Beach
Lake Marong
Lake Wanhar
Marloo Bay
Panama
Rooney Point
LakeCarree
Lake Minker
Hervey Bay Marine Park
Waddy Point Ranger Station
Waddy Point
Orchid Beach
Middle Rocks
Champagne Pools
Indian Head
Wathumba
Platypus Bay
Great Sandy National Park
Triangle Cliff
Hervey Bay
Corroboree Beach
Yathon Cliffs
Lake Gnarann
Lake Bowarrady
Arch Cliff
Dundubara Ranger Station
Bimjella Hill (174m)
Dundubara
Bowarrady (244m)
Lake Allom
Cathedral Beach
Coongul Point
The Pinnacles
Maheno
Eli Creek
Moon Point
Maheno Beach
SOUTH PACIFIC OCEAN
Blackfellow Point
Point Vernon
Happy Valley
Lake Garawongera
Big Woody Island
Valley of the Giants
Yidney Rocks
Hervey Bay
Urangan Marina
Rainbow Gorge
Leading Hill (184m)
Poyungan Valley
Kingfisher Bay
Poyungan Rocks
Lake Wabby
Lake McKenzie
Wanggoolba Creek
Eurong QPWS Information Centre
River Heads
Central Station
Lake Jennings
Eurong
57
Lake Birrabeen
Ungowa
Lake Benaroon
Boomanjin Hill (211m)
Lake Boomanjin
Yankee Jack Lake
Mary River
Dilli Village
A1
Poona National Park
Maryborough
Maryborough Cooloola Rd
Maaroom
Figtree Lake
Great Sandy Strait
Tuan
A1
The Bluff (64m)
Hook Point
Tin Can Bay
Inskip Point
Inskip Pt
Tuan State Forest
Tiaro
To Gympie (60km)
To Rainbow Beach (3km)

HOWLING DINGOES

They may look like Fido's long-lost cousins, but Fraser's dingoes are wild animals. Fast facts on the canid:

» *Canis lupus dingo* or the 'warragul' is thought to be descended from the Southeast Asian wolf.

» Dingoes were introduced to Australia around three or four thousand years ago.

» Due to the island's isolation, Fraser's dingoes are the most genetically pure strain in Australia.

» The dingo population on Fraser is around 230.

» Dingoes don't bark, but communicate with wolflike howls.

» These ginger-furred 'wild dogs' weigh around 20kg, live for five to seven years, and climb trees.

» Beware: dingoes can attack! These dogs are wild so keep your distance. There have been a number of recorded cases of dingoes attacking not only children but adults as well.

» Don't feed, tease or encourage dingoes into campsites – or face a fine of up to $4000.

History

The Butchulla people lived on K'Gari for over 5000 years until European arrival. In 1836 a group of castaways from the shipwrecked *Stirling Castle* landed on the island. In the group was a Scottish woman, Eliza Fraser, the wife of the captain of the ill-fated ship, who, after her rescue in 1837, returned to London and wrote a harrowing (and unverified) account of her husband's death and her terrifying ordeal with the Aborigines. Although other survivors disputed her story, Eliza made a tidy sum from retelling her tale. As her fame spread, the island became known as Fraser Island.

In 1863 loggers began felling trees including the prized kauri pines and the satinay (turpentine) valued by shipbuilders. Exploitation of the island's natural resources continued when sandmining began in 1950. Fortunately, a shift towards environmental protection brought both industries to an end – sandmining in 1977 and logging in 1991.

Fraser Island joined the World Heritage list in 1992. At present the northern half of the island is protected as the Great Sandy National Park while the rest consists of state forest, crown land and private land.

Sights & Activities

From Fraser's southern tip, use the high-tide access track that cuts inland (avoiding dangerous Hook Point) to reach the main thoroughfare on the eastern beach. The first settlement you reach is **Dilli Village**, the former sand-mining centre. Another 9km north is **Eurong**, with a resort, shops and fuel, and the start of the inland track to **Central Station** and **Wanggoolba Creek** (for the ferry to River Heads).

Central Station is the starting point for numerous walking trails. From here you can walk or drive to the beautiful **McKenzie**, **Jennings**, **Birrabeen** and **Boomanjin** lakes. Like many of Fraser's lakes, these are 'perched' lakes, formed by the accumulation of water over a thin, impermeable layer of decaying leaves and other organic material. Lake McKenzie is spectacular, with its clear blue water ringed with a sugary-white sand beach. It's a great place to swim, as is the similarly beautiful but less crowded Lake Birrabeen. In these open-air beauty spas, you can use the mineral sand to exfoliate your skin and the clear water to soften your hair.

Along the beach about 4km north of Eurong is a signposted walking trail across sandblows to the beautiful **Lake Wabby**. An easier route is from the lookout on the inland track. Lake Wabby is surrounded on three sides by eucalypt forest; the fourth side is a massive sandblow that is encroaching on the lake at a rate of about 3m a year. The lake is deceptively shallow. Don't dive – people have been paralysed by doing so. Turtles and huge catfish can often be seen under the trees in the eastern corner of the lake.

Driving north along the beach you may have to detour inland to avoid Poyungan and Yidney Rocks at high tide to reach **Happy Valley** (with a store and places to stay). About 10km north is **Eli Creek**, a fast-moving, crystal-clear waterway that will carry you effortlessly downstream. About 2km from Eli Creek is the rotting hulk of the **Maheno**, a former passenger liner blown ashore by a cyclone in 1935 while being towed to a Japanese scrap yard.

Roughly 5km north of the *Maheno* are the **Pinnacles** (an eroded section of coloured

WORTH A TRIP

CANIA GORGE NATIONAL PARK

About 225km west of Bundaberg, the small Cania Gorge National Park preserves a range of habitats from dry eucalyptus forest and rugged sandstone escarpments to deep gullies filled with mosses and ferns. The scenery is spectacular, wildlife is plentiful and there are numerous walking trails to impressive rock formations.

You can't camp at the park itself, but **Cania Gorge Tourist Retreat** (☎4167 8110; www.caniagorgeretreat.com.au; Cania Rd, Monto; unpowered/powered sites $20/26, cabins $90; @☎) is nestled in a sandstone gorge close to the park entrance and walking trails.

If you don't want to camp, the nearest town is **Monto**, 26km southeast, where the **Colonial Motor Inn & Restaurant** (☎4166 1377; 6 Thomson St; r $85) has decent motel rooms.

sand cliffs), and a further 10km is **Dundubara**, with a ranger station and a very good camping ground. Another 20km along the beach is the rock outcrop of **Indian Head**, the best vantage point on the island. Sharks, manta rays, dolphins and whales (during the migration season) can often be seen from the top of the headland.

From Indian Head the trail branches inland passing **Champagne Pools**, the only safe spot on the island for saltwater swimming. The trail leads back to **Waddy Point** and **Orchid Beach**, the last settlement on the island.

Many tracks north of this are closed for environmental protection. The 30km of beach up to the northern tip of **Sandy Cape** and its lighthouse is off limits to hire vehicles. The beach from Sandy Cape to Wathumba is closed to all vehicles, as is the road from Orchid Beach to Platypus Bay.

On the island you can take a scenic flight with **MI Helicopters** (☎1800 600 345, 4125 1599; www.mihelicopters.com.au; 25min flight $240) or with **Air Fraser** (☎1800 600 345, 4125 3600; 10min flights from $70).

Sleeping & Eating

Sailfish on Fraser APARTMENTS $$$
(☎4127 9494; www.sailfishonfraser.com.au; Happy Valley; d from $230-250, extra person $10;) Any notions of rugged wilderness and roughing it will be forgotten quick smart at this plush, indulgent retreat. These two-bedroom apartments (which sleep up to six people) are cavernous and classy, with wall-to-wall glass doors, spas, mod cons, mod furnishings and an alluring pool.

Kingfisher Bay Resort RESORT $$
(☎1800 072 555, 4194 9300; www.kingfisherbay.com; Kingfisher Bay; d $160, 2-bedroom villa $198; @) This elegant eco-resort has hotel rooms with private balconies, and sophisticated two- and three-bedroom timber villas that are elevated to limit their environmental impact. The villas and spacious holiday houses are utterly gorgeous and some even have spas on their private decks. There's a three-night minimum stay in high season. The resort has restaurants, bars and shops and operates two different daily ranger-guided eco-accredited tours of the island (adult/child $169/99).

Fraser Island Beachhouses RENTAL HOUSE $$
(☎1800 626 230, 4127 9205; www.fraserislandbeachhouses.com.au; Eurong Second Valley; studio per 2 nights $300, 2-bedroom house per 2 nights from $700;) Another luxury option, this complex contains sunny, self-contained units kitted out with polished wood, cable TVs and ocean views. Rates start with studios and climb to $900 for two-bedroom beachfront houses.

Eurong Beach Resort RESORT $$
(☎1800 111 808, 4120 1600; www.eurong.com.au; Eurong; r $140, 2-bedroom apt $199; mains $17.50-50; ⏰breakfast, lunch & dinner; @) Bright, cheerful Eurong is the main resort on the east coast and the most accessible for all budgets. At the cheaper end of the market are simple motel rooms and units, while comfortable, fully self-contained apartments are good value for families. There is a cavernous restaurant, a bar, two pools and tennis courts. Guided 4WD tours (accommodation included) leave daily. The resort also has a bottle shop, a petrol station and a general store.

Fraser Island Wilderness Retreat HOSTEL $
(☎4127 9144; Happy Valley; dm $30, mains $20-25; ⏰lunch & dinner; @) This wilderness-retreat-turned-backpackers has dorms (sleeping up to six) in nine timber lodges. The cabins cascade down a gentle slope amid plenty of tropical foliage, and there's a bistro and bar.

SAND SAFARIS: EXPLORING FRASER ISLAND

The only way to explore Fraser Island is with a 4WD vehicle. For most travellers there are three transport options: tag-a-long tours, organised tours or 4WD hire.

Please be aware of your environmental footprint. When choosing how to visit this precious natural landscape bear in mind that the greater the number of individual vehicles driving on the island, the greater the environmental damage.

Tag-a-Long Tours

The original self-drive tours where 4WD convoys headed off for a three-day, two-night camping safari were incredibly popular with backpackers. However, due to a spate of fatal vehicular accidents on Fraser Island in the past few years, new laws were introduced changing the original self-drive tours into tag-a-long tours where a maximum of five vehicles follow a lead vehicle with an experienced guide and driver.

Advantages include flexibility; you can make new friends fast. The disadvantages are that new laws have increased the cost of these tours. And if your group doesn't get along it's a long three days. Inexperienced drivers get bogged in sand all the time but this can be part of the fun.

Rates hover around $300 to $320 and exclude food, fuel and alcohol. Check if permits are included in the price. Some operators also throw in a couple of nights' free accommodation. Recommended operators:

Colonial Village YHA (☎1800 818 280, 4125 1844; www.cvyha.com; Hervey Bay)

Dingo's Backpacker's Resort (☎1800 111 126, 5486 8200; www.dingosatrainbow.com; Rainbow Beach)

Fraser Roving (☎1800 989 811, 4125 6386; www.fraserroving.com.au; Hervey Bay)

Next Backpackers (☎4125 6600; www.nextbackpackers.com.au; Hervey Bay)

Nomads (☎1800 354 535, 4125 3601; www.nomadshostels.com; Hervey Bay)

Palace Adventures (☎1800 063 168, 4124 5331; www.palaceadventures.com; Hervey Bay)

Pippies Beach House (☎1800 425 356, 5486 8503; www.pippiesbeachhouse.com.au; Rainbow Beach)

Organised Tours

Tours leave from Hervey Bay, Rainbow Beach and Noosa and cover the highlights: rainforests, Eli Creek, Lakes McKenzie and Wabby, the coloured Pinnacles and the *Maheno* shipwreck.

Camping

Supplies on the island are limited and costly. Campers, particularly, should stock up well. Be prepared for mosquitoes and march flies.

Camping permits are required at QPWS camping grounds and any public area (ie along the beach). The most developed **QPWS camping grounds** (per person/family $5.15/20.60), with coin-operated hot showers, toilets and barbecues, are at Waddy Point, Dundubara and Central Station. Campers with vehicles can also use the smaller camping grounds with fewer facilities at Lake Boomanjin, Ungowa and Wathumba on the western coast. Walkers' camps (for hikers only) are set away from the main campgrounds along the Fraser Island Great Walk trail (p175). The trail map lists the campsites and their facilities. Camping is permitted on designated stretches of the eastern beach, but there are no facilities. Fires are prohibited, except in communal fire rings at Waddy Point and Dundubara, and to utilise these you'll need to bring your own firewood in the form of untreated, milled timber. All rates following are for two people.

Dilli Village Fraser Island CAMPGROUND $
(☎4127 9130; Dilli Village; unpowered sites $20, bunkrooms $40, cabins $100) Managed by the University of the Sunshine Coast, Dilli Village offers good sites on a softly sloping camping ground. The facilities are as neat as a pin and the cabins are ageing but accommodating.

Advantages include minimum fuss and expert commentary, and you can return to Rainbow Beach or Noosa. The downside is that during peak season you could share the experience with 40 others.

Among the many ecocertified operators:

Footprints on Fraser (☎1300 765 636; www.footprintsonfraser.com.au; 4-/5-day walk $1375/1825) Highly recommended guided walking tours of the island's natural wonders.

Cool Dingo Tours (☎1800 072 555, 4194 9222; www.cooldingotour.com; 2-/3-day tour $328/405) Overnight at lodges with option to stay extra nights on the island. Party in the Dingo Bar!

Kingfisher Bay Tours (☎1800 072 555, 4120 3333; www.kingfisherbay.com; day tours adult/child $169/99) Fraser Island–based ranger-guided ecotours.

Fraser Explorer Tours (☎1800 249 122, 4194 9222; www.fraserexplorertours.com.au; 1-/2-day tour $175/312) Highly recommended.

Fraser Experience (☎1800 689 819, 4124 4244; www.fraserexperience.com; 2-day tours $295) Small groups and more freedom about the itinerary.

4WD Hire

You can hire a 4WD from Hervey Bay, Rainbow Beach and even on Fraser Island. All companies require a hefty bond, usually in the form of a credit-card imprint, which you *will* lose if you drive in salt water – don't even think about running the waves!

A driving-instruction video will usually be shown. Fraser has had some nasty accidents, often due to speeding, and new laws restrict the speed limit to 80km/h on the beach and 30km/h inland. Note that there is a maximum limit of eight passengers to a hire 4WD vehicle and seatbelts are mandatory (or face fines of up to $300).

Advantages include complete freedom to roam the island and escape the crowds. The disadvantage is that you may find you have to tackle beach and track conditions that even experienced drivers find challenging.

Rates for multiday rentals start at around $150 a day and most companies also rent camping gear. See Car & Motorcycle (p184) and Getting There & Around (p174) for rental companies in Hervey Bay and Rainbow Beach. On the island, **Kingfisher Bay 4WD Hire** (☎4120 3366) hires out 4WDs from $175/280 per half-/full day.

Frasers@Cathedral Beach CAMPGROUND **$$** (☎4127 9177; Cathedral Beach; unpowered sites $29-39, powered sites $39-49, cabins $145-180; @) This spacious, privately run park with its abundant, flat, grassy sites is a fave with families. The excellent facilities include large communal barbecue areas and spotless amenities. The quaint, comfortable cabins come with private picnic tables.

ℹ Information

A 4WD is necessary to drive on Fraser Island. General supplies and expensive fuel are available from stores at Cathedral Beach, Eurong, Kingfisher Bay Resort, Happy Valley and Orchid Beach. Most stores stock some camping and fishing gear, and those at Kingfisher Bay, Eurong, Happy Valley and Orchid Beach sell alcohol. There are public telephones at these locations and at most camping grounds.

Treat all tap, lake and stream water before drinking (either by boiling for five to 10 minutes or with water-treatment tablets). There is no pharmacy or resident doctor on the island.

The main ranger station, **Eurong QPWS Information Centre** (☎4127 9128), is at Eurong. Others can be found at **Dundubara** (☎4127 9138) and **Waddy Point** (☎4127 9190). Office hours vary.

The **Fraser Island Taxi Service** (☎4127 9188) operates all over the island. A one-way fare from Kingfisher Bay Resort to Eurong costs $80. Bookings essential.

If your vehicle breaks down, call **Fraser Island Breakdown** (☎4127 9173) or the **tow-truck service** (☎4127 9449, 0428 353 164), both based in Eurong.

FRASER ISLAND GREAT WALK

Opened in 2004, the Fraser Island Great Walk is a stunning way to see this enigmatic island in all its diverse colours. The trail undulates through the island's interior for 90km from Dilli Village to Happy Valley. Broken up into sections of 6km to 16km, plus some side trails off the main sections, it follows the pathways of Fraser Island's original inhabitants, the Butchulla people, and passes underneath rainforest canopies, through shifting dunes and alongside some of the island's vivid lakes.

From Dilli Village, a 6.3km track cuts inland, affording brilliant views of the island from Wongi Sandblow en route to Lake Boomanjin. Over the next 7.2km leg you begin to leave the dry scribbly-gum woodlands and forests (regenerating from logging and mining) behind as you enter the rainforest to Lake Benaroon.

The third section travels for 7.5km, following the western shore of Lake Benaroon before zig-zagging along Lake Birrabeen's southern shore. The trail continues on an old logging road, dwarfed by towering satinay forests and brush box, to Central Station.

From here you have two options to Lake McKenzie. If you turn west you'll walk via Basin Lake (6.6km), which is a popular haunt for turtles. If you turn east the trail takes a lengthy route through Pile Valley (11.3km).

The fifth section sweeps for 11.9km in a slight arc from Lake McKenzie back towards the island's eastern coast and Lake Wabby. This leg reveals some of the island's most stunning rainforest, as well as the east-coast dunes that buffer Lake Wabby from the coast. The next section to the Valley of the Giants is 16.2km long and passes beneath some of Fraser's oldest and largest trees.

The seventh leg (13.1km) tags along an old tramline to Lake Garawongera, uncovering evidence of the earliest logging camps on the island. Another 6.6km, mostly downhill through open forests and dunes, takes you to the end of the trail at Happy Valley.

The Great Walk trail is mostly stable sand and not particularly difficult, but the island has the potential to throw a few whammies your way. Weather conditions, notably heavy rain, can affect the track, although this can be a blessing as it firms up the patches of soft sand on the trail. Before you go, pick up the *Fraser Island Great Walk* brochure from a QPWS office (or download it from www.derm.qld.gov.au) and seek updates on the track's conditions.

Permits

You will need permits for vehicles (per month/year $40.00/198.00) and camping (per person/family $6.00/21.00), and these must be purchased before you arrive. It's best to purchase the permits online at www.derm.qld.gov.au or contact **QPWS** (☎13 74 68). Permits aren't required for private camping grounds or resorts. Permit-issuing offices include the following:

Bundaberg QPWS Office (☎4131 1600; 46 Quay St)

Great Sandy Information Centre (☎5449 7792; 240 Moorinidil St, Tewantin; ⊙8am-4pm) Near Noosa.

Marina Kiosk (☎4128 9800; Buccaneer Ave, Urangan Boat Harbour, Urangan; ⊙6am-6pm)

Maryborough QPWS (☎4121 1800; 20 Tennyson St; ⊙8.30am-5pm Mon-Fri)

Rainbow Beach QPWS (☎5486 3160; Rainbow Beach Rd)

River Heads Information Kiosk (☎4125 8485; ⊙6.15-11.15am & 2-3.30pm) Ferry departure point at River Heads, south of Hervey Bay.

Getting There & Away

Air

Air Fraser Island (☎1800 247 992, 4125 3600; www.airfraserisland.com.au) charges from $125 for a return flight (20 minutes each way) to the island's eastern beach, departing Hervey Bay airport.

Boat

Several large vehicle ferries connect Fraser Island to the mainland. Most visitors use the two services that leave from River Heads (about 10km south of Hervey Bay) or from Inskip Point near Rainbow Beach.

Fraser Island Barges (☎1800 227 437, 4194 9300; www.fraserislandferry.com.au; vehicle & 4 passengers return $150, additional passengers $11) makes the 30-minute crossing from River Heads to Wanggoolba Creek on the western coast of Fraser Island. It departs daily from River Heads at 8.30am, 10.15am and 4pm, and returns from the island at 9am, 3pm and 5pm. The same company also operates a service from the Urangan Marina in Hervey Bay to Moon Point on Fraser Island but car-hire companies won't allow you to drive their cars here so it's limited to car owners and hikers. Rates are the same as for the service from River Heads to Wanggoolba Creek. Pedestrian fare is $36 return.

Kingfisher Vehicular Ferry (☎1800 072 555, 4194 9300; www.fraserislandferry.com; pedestrian adult/child return $50/25, vehicle & 4 passengers return $150, additional passengers $11) operates a vehicle and passenger ferry which makes the 50-minute crossing from River Heads to Kingfisher Bay Resort daily, departing at 6.45am, 9am, 12.30pm, 3.30pm, 6.45pm and 9.30pm and returning at 7.50am, 10.30am, 2pm, 5pm, 8.30pm and 11pm.

Coming from Rainbow Beach, the operators **Rainbow Venture & Fraser Explorer** (☎4194 9300; pedestrian/vehicle return $10/80) and **Manta Ray** (☎5486 8888; vehicle return $90) both make the 15-minute crossing from Inskip Point to Hook Point on Fraser Island continuously from about 7am to 5.30pm daily.

Capricorn Coast

Includes »

Rockhampton 200
Yeppoon 205
Great Keppel Island 208
Gladstone 211
Southern Reef Islands 213
Agnes Water & Town of 1770 215
Eurimbula & Deepwater National Parks 218
Capricorn Hinterland 218
Emerald 219
Gemfields 220
Carnarvon National Park 222

Best Places to Eat

» Shio Kaze (p206)

» Ferns Hideaway (p208)

» Tree Bar (p217)

» Saigon Saigon By the River (p202)

Best Places to Stay

» Svendsen's Beach (p209)

» Waterpark Farm (p208)

» Surfside Motel (p206)

» Criterion Hotel (p201)

» Agnes Water Beach Caravan Park (p216)

Why Go?

The stunning powdery white beaches and aqua-blue waters of the tropical islands and coral cays of the Capricorn Coast superbly fit the picture-postcard image. The peaceful islands of the southern Great Barrier Reef – Heron and Lady Elliot in particular – offer some of the best snorkelling and diving in Queensland, while remote beaches and windswept national parks can be found along the entire Capricorn coastline.

Inland from the coast is cattle and coal country, with steakhouses aplenty and vast coal deposits that fuel the region's booming economy. In amongst it all are gemfields filled with precious zircons, amethysts, rubies and sapphires.

Rising above the inland plains, the weathered plateaus of the Great Dividing Range form spectacular sandstone escarpments, especially around the Carnarvon and Blackdown Tableland National Parks, where ancient Aboriginal rock art, deep gorges and waterfalls abound.

When to Go

Rockhampton

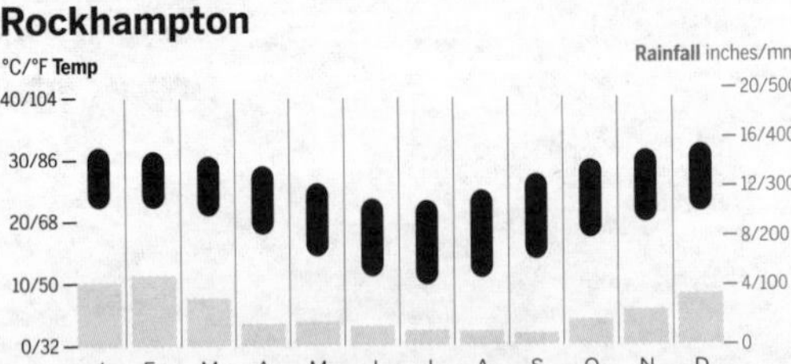

March–May Carnarvon Gorge is full after the wet season and wildlife abounds.

September–November The waters are warming and the weather is still relatively mild.

December–February Temperatures soar and stingers are the scourge of beach swimmers.

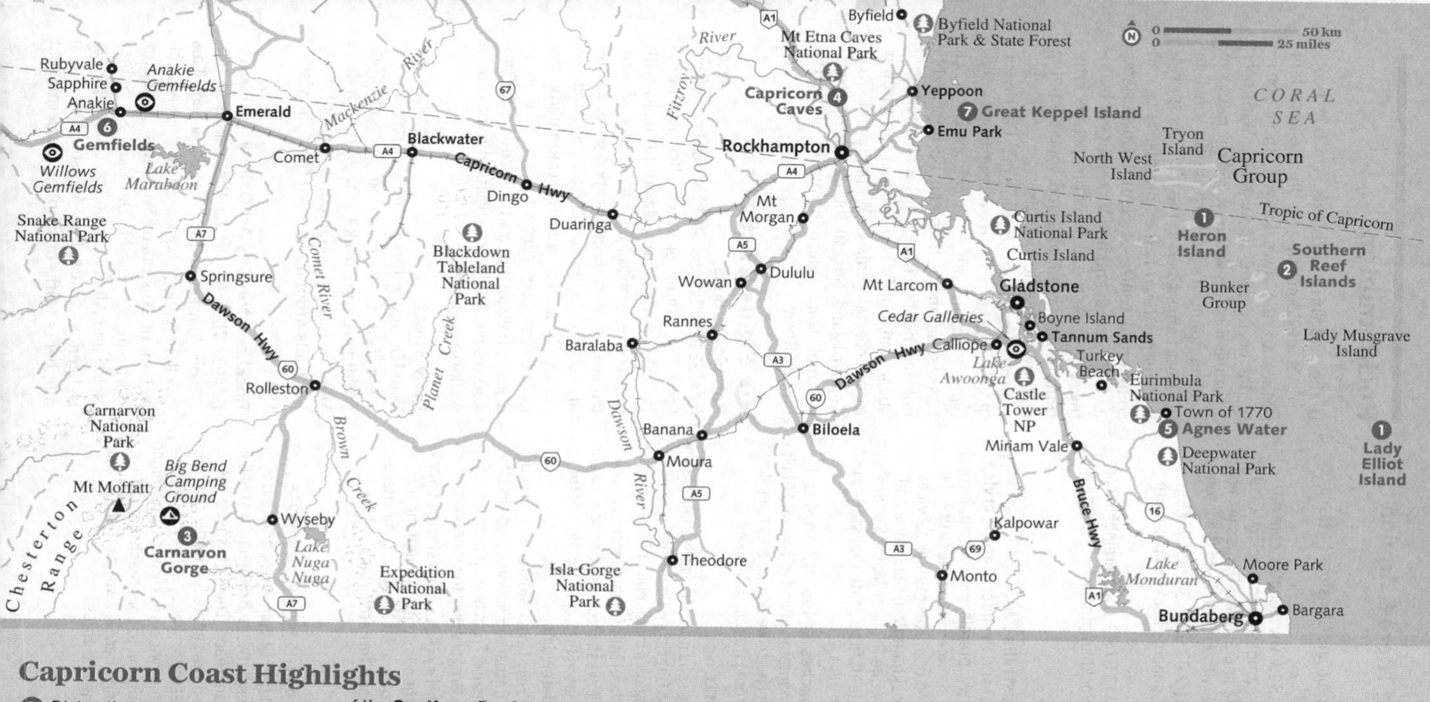

Capricorn Coast Highlights

1. Diving the spectacular underwater coral gardens of **Heron Island** (p214) and **Lady Elliot Island** (p214)
2. Playing castaway on the [illegible] cays of the **Southern Reef Islands** (p213)
3. Discovering ancient Aboriginal rock art and hiking through the twisting sandstone canyon of **Carnarvon Gorge** (p222)
4. Spelunking through tight tunnels and cathedral caverns in the **Capricorn Caves** [illegible]
5. Surfing and chilling at Queensland's most northerly surf beach, **Agnes Water** (p215)
6. Fossicking for sapphires [illegible] Rubyvale in the **Gemfields** (p220)
7. Beachcombing and sun worshipping on laid-back **Great Keppel Island** (p208)

Getting There & Around

AIR

Both Rockhampton and Gladstone have major domestic airports.

Qantas (☎13 13 13; www.qantas.com.au) Connects Rockhampton with Mackay, Gladstone, Brisbane and Sydney; Qantaslink connects Brisbane with Emerald and Gladstone.

Tiger Airways (☎03 9335 3033; www.tigerairways.com) Connects Rockhampton with Melbourne.

Virgin Blue (☎13 67 89; www.virginblue.com.au) Connects Rockhampton with Brisbane and Sydney.

BUS

Greyhound Australia (☎13 20 30; www.greyhound.com.au) and **Premier Motor Service** (☎13 34 10; www.premierms.com.au) have regular coach services along the Bruce Hwy (A1). Greyhound operates regular services to and from Rockhampton, Gladstone and Agnes Water, while Premier Motor Service runs a Brisbane–Cairns route that stops at Rockhampton.

Paradise Coaches (☎4933 1127) makes the run from Rockhampton inland to Emerald (daily) and Longreach (twice weekly). It also operates a daily service from Emerald to Mackay.

CAR & MOTORCYCLE

The Bruce Hwy runs north to south about 50km inland from the Capricorn Coast, and passes through the region's major hub of Rockhampton.

The major inland route is the Capricorn Hwy (A4), which follows the tropic of Capricorn west from Rockhampton through Emerald and the Gemfields to Barcaldine.

The Dawson Hwy from Gladstone takes you west towards Carnarvon National Park and the town of Springsure. From here, it's a short 66km stretch on the Gregory Hwy to Emerald.

The Burnett Hwy (A3), which starts at Rockhampton and heads south through the old gold-mining town of Mt Morgan, is an interesting and popular alternative route to take to Brisbane.

TRAIN

Queensland Rail (☎1800 872 467, 3235 1122; www.queenslandrail.com.au) operates frequent services between Brisbane, Townsville, Cairns and Longreach. The high-speed *Tilt Train* and the more sedate *Sunlander* operate on the coastal route. The *Spirit of the Outback* leaves Brisbane twice weekly and turns inland from Rockhampton to Longreach. For details, see the Getting There & Away sections of the relevant towns and cities.

Rockhampton

POP 74,500

If the wide-brimmed hats, cowboy boots and V8 utes don't tip you off, the large bull statues around town let you know you're in the 'beef capital' of Australia. With over 2.5 million cattle within a 250km radius of Rockhampton, it's no surprise the smell of bulldust hangs thick in the air. This sprawling country town is the administrative and commercial centre of central Queensland, its wide streets and fine Victorian-era buildings reflecting the region's prosperous 19th-century heyday of gold and copper mining and the beef cattle industry.

Straddling the tropic of Capricorn, 'Rocky' marks the start of the tropics but, lying 40km inland and lacking coastal sea breezes, summers here can be unbearably hot and humid. Rocky has a smattering of attractions but is best seen as the gateway to the coastal gems of Yeppoon and Great Keppel Island. Stay in the old part of town to enjoy some charming walks along the Fitzroy River.

Sights & Activities

Botanic Gardens GARDEN

(☎4922 1654; Spencer St; admission free; ⏱6am-6pm) Just south of town, Rockhampton's Botanic Gardens are a beautiful oasis with impressive banyan figs, tropical and subtropical rainforest, landscaped gardens and lily-covered lagoons. The formal Japanese garden is a Zen zone of tranquillity, the **cafe** (⏱8am-5pm) serves tea and cake under a giant banyan fig, and the **zoo** (⏱8.30am-4.30pm) has koalas, wombats, dingoes and a walk-through aviary.

Quay Street HISTORIC STREET

Wander down this historic street in the town centre, with its grand sandstone buildings dating back to the gold-rush days. You can pick up leaflets that map out walking trails around the town from the visitor centres.

Rockhampton City Art Gallery ART GALLERY

(☎4927 7129; 62 Victoria Pde; admission free; ⏱10am-4pm Tue-Fri, 11am-4pm Sat & Sun) This excellent gallery boasts an impressive collection of Australian paintings, including works by Sir Russell Drysdale, Sir Sidney Nolan and Albert Namatjira. Contemporary Indigenous artist Judy Watson also has a number of works on display. The permanent collection is supplemented by innovative temporary exhibitions, for which there are varying admission charges.

Dreamtime Cultural Centre MUSEUM
(☎4936 1655; www.dreamtimecentre.com.au; Bruce Hwy; adult/child $13.50/6.50; ⏰10am-3.30pm Mon-Fri, tours 10.30am & 1pm) Located about 7km north of town, this rewarding Indigenous Australian and Torres Strait Islander heritage display centre provides a fascinating insight into local Indigenous history. The centre is set on 12 hectares of natural bushland and ancient tribal sites, and exhibits sandstone displays of the archaeology and mythology of the Aboriginal people. The recommended 90-minute tour includes boomerang throwing.

Archer Park Rail Museum MUSEUM
(☎4922 2774; Denison St; adult/child/family $6.60/4.50/15; ⏰9am-4pm Sun-Fri) This museum is housed in the former train station, which was built in 1899. The station's story and that of the unique Purrey steam tram are told through photographs and displays.

Central Queensland Military & Artefacts Association MUSEUM
(☎4921 0648; 40 Archer St; adult/concession $5/4; ⏰9am-4pm) Next door to the rail museum, it displays Australia's involvement in various military campaigns and wars. During WWII Rockhampton was home to 76,000 US servicemen, and there's plenty of American memorabilia on display. Look out for some interesting 'trench art' pieces: cups, letter openers, ashtrays and some weird imaginative statuettes fashioned from discarded ammo casings, bullet shells and the like.

Heritage Village HISTORIC PARK
(☎4936 1026; Bruce Hwy; adult/child/family $7.70/4.50/22.70; ⏰9am-4pm) Located 10km north of the city centre is a museum of replica historical buildings set in lovely landscaped gardens; it even has townspeople at work in period garb. There's also a visitor centre here.

Kershaw Gardens GARDEN
(☎4936 8254; via Charles St; admission free; ⏰6am-6pm) Just north of the Fitzroy River this is an excellent botanical garden devoted to Australian native plants. Its attractions include artificial rapids, a rainforest area, a fragrant garden and heritage architecture.

Rock Pool Water Park AMUSEMENT PARK
(☎4928 2261; www.rockpoolwaterpark.com.au; 330-360 Berserker St; adult/child $4.50/3.50; ⏰6am-6pm) If you're stuck in Rocky on a warm day, this park offers a multitude of pools, slides and other outdoor activities.

Mt Archer NATURE RESERVE
As a backdrop to the city, Mt Archer rises 604m out of the landscape northeast of Rockhampton, offering stunning views of the city and hinterland from the summit, especially at night. It's a national park with walking trails weaving through eucalypts and rainforest abundant in wildlife. Rockhampton City Council publishes a brochure about the park, which is available from visitor centres.

Tours

Little Johnny's Tours & Rentals NATURE
(☎0414 793 637; www.littlejohnnystours.com) Runs trips to many nearby attractions, such as Byfield and the Capricorn Caves, and also does minibus runs between Rockhampton Airport and Yeppoon.

Capricorn Coast Trail Rides HORSERIDING
(☎0413 483 850, 4939 2611; www.cctrailrides.com.au) Runs horseback tours through local bushland.

Festivals & Events

Beef Australia AGRICULTURE
(www.beefaustralia.org) Held every three years (the next one will be in May 2012), this is a huge exposition of everything beefy.

Jazz on Quay MUSIC
(www.jazzonquay.com.au) Held in September.

Sleeping

The northern and southern approach roads to Rocky are lined with numerous motels but choose somewhere in the old centre, south of the river, if you want to stroll the elegant palm-lined streets overlooking the Fitzroy River. Most hotels and many motels have their own eateries attached.

Criterion Hotel HOTEL $
(☎4922 1225; www.thecriterion.com.au; 150 Quay St; r $55-80, motel r $125-150; ❄) The Criterion is Rockhampton's grandest old pub with an elegant foyer and function room, a friendly bar and great bistro (Bush Inn Bar & Grill). Its top two storeys have dozens of period rooms, some of which have been lovingly restored but, although the rooms have showers,

the toilets are down the hall. If you're not into period rooms, the hotel also has a number of 4.5-star motel rooms.

Rockhampton YHA HOSTEL $
(4927 5288; www.yha.com.au; 60 MacFarlane St; dm $22, d $50-67;) The Rocky YHA is well looked after, with a spacious lounge and dining area and a well-equipped kitchen. It has six- and nine-bed dorms as well as doubles and cabins with bathrooms, and there's a large patch of lawn to toss a ball around. The hostel arranges tours, offers courtesy pick-ups from the bus station, and is an agent for Premier and Greyhound buses.

Denison Hotel BOUTIQUE HOTEL $$
(4923 7378; www.denisonhotel.com.au; 233 Denison St; r $165-200;) This freshly renovated 1885 Victorian home is an easy walk from Quay St. Its stately rooms have four-poster beds and plasma TVs, and the hotel's Rolls Royce can pick you up from the airport or station.

Goldston House B&B $$
(4921 4186; www.goldstonhouse.com.au; cnr George & Derby Sts; r incl breakfast $165-200;) Set in a gracious old Queenslander just a dozen blocks from Quay St, Goldston House's suites are well equipped, roomy and stylish. Rates include free airport transfers.

Coffee House MOTEL, APARTMENTS $$
(4927 5722; www.coffeehouse.com.au; 51 William St; r $160-189;) Popular with the business traveller, the Coffee House features beautifully appointed motel rooms, self-contained apartments and spa suites in central Rocky. There's a popular and stylish cafe-restaurant/wine bar on-site.

Southside Holiday Village CARAVAN PARK, CABINS $
(1800 075 911, 4927 3013; www.sshv.com.au; Lower Dawson Rd; 2-person unpowered/powered/en-suite sites $25/32/42, cabins $62-102;) This is one of the city's best caravan parks. It has neat, self-contained cabins and villas with elevated decking, large grassed campsites, a courtesy coach and a good camp kitchen. It's about 3km south of the town centre.

Rockhampton Plaza Hotel HOTEL $$
(4927 5855; www.rockhamptonplaza.com.au; 161-167 George St; r $115-155;) The Plaza has well-appointed, pretty typical four-star hotel rooms that overlook a park. There's a bar and restaurant, and it's located just a short stroll southwest of the centre and close to the train station.

Central Park Motel MOTEL $$
(4927 2333; www.centralparkmotel.com.au; 224 Murray St; r $135-170;) In a quiet street opposite a park but close to the town centre, this motel has large rooms and suites catering for singles to families. A good choice for a good night's sleep.

Motel 98 MOTEL $$
(4927 5322; www.98.com.au; 98 Victoria Pde; r $155-195;) The smart Motel 98 has well-appointed, spacious rooms positioned around the pool. The motel's restaurant, Cassidy's, has a terrace overlooking the river and a sound reputation as one of the best eateries in town.

Oxford Hotel HOSTEL $
(4922 1837; cnr East & Denham Sts; dm $25;) Downtown Backpackers is located above this boisterous pub, offering basic, budget accommodation right in the centre of town. VIP members receive discounts, you can get pizzas at the bar and there's live music every weekend.

Eating & Drinking

Saigon Saigon By the River ASIAN $$
(4927 0888; www.saigonbytheriver.com; Quay St, near cnr Denham St; mains $15-20; lunch & dinner Wed-Mon) This two-storey bamboo hut overlooks the Fitzroy River and offers pan-Asian food with local ingredients like kangaroo and crocodile served in a sizzling steamboat (pre-ordering is required for these exotic dishes). If you're not up for Australian native or reptile, try the crispy chicken or the king prawns.

Criteron Hotel PUB, STEAKHOUSE $$
(4922 1225; www.thecriterion.com.au; 150 Quay St; dishes $10-40; lunch & dinner) The Criterion's front bar is a friendly place to grab a beer, while its Bush Inn Bar & Grill has a modern Western theme with stone floors, wooden booths and tables, and huge steaks to match – like the $38 Kilo Challenge. There are plenty of nonsteak options, including slabs of barra, chicken dishes and pizzas. There's regular live music later in the week.

Pacino's ITALIAN $$
(4922 5833; cnr Fitzroy & George Sts; mains $19-39; dinner Tue-Sun) This stylish Italian restaurant oozes Mediterranean warmth with its stone floors, wooden tables and potted fig trees. A class act for an intimate dinner of delicious Italian cooking featuring favourites

like osso bucco and pasta cooked a dozen different ways.

Cassidy's SEAFOOD, STEAKHOUSE $$
(☎4927 5322; www.98.com.au; 98 Victoria Pde; mains $18-46 ⊙breakfast daily, lunch Mon-Fri, dinner Mon-Sat) One of Rocky's finest and part of Motel 98, this licensed dining room features modern Australian kangaroo, steak, lamb and seafood dishes. Sit inside or on the terrace overlooking the Fitzroy River.

Thai Tanee THAI $$
(☎4922 1255; cnr William & Bolsover Sts; mains $15-28; ⊙dinner) This unpretentious restaurant is recommended by the locals for consistently good Thai food; it has a yum cha special for Sunday brunch.

O'Dowd's Irish Pub PUB
(☎4927 0344; 100 William St) Live bands (with nary a skerrick of an Irish tune) play on Friday and Saturday nights in the dark wooden saloon bar. Upstairs there's backpacker accommodation (doubles from $65).

Ginger Mule BAR
(☎4927 7255; 8 William St; ⊙4pm-late Wed-Sat) An urban-chic wine and tapas bar, this place draws the Friday night cocktail crowd.

Heritage Hotel PUB
(☎4927 6996; cnr William & Quay Sts) This grand old pub with iron-lattice balconies has a stylish cocktail lounge with river views and outdoor tables. After-work drinks can linger on to dinner in the tavern, where the extensive menu includes pizzas, burgers and lamb shank pie as well as the ubiquitous steak.

☆ Entertainment

Great Western Hotel PUB
(☎4922 3888; www.greatwesternhotel.com.au; 39 Stanley St) Looking like a spaghetti-western film set, this century-old pub is home to Rocky's cowboys and cowgals. Out back there's a rodeo arena where every Wednesday (which is also two-for-one meal night in the bistro) and Friday night you can watch cowboys being tossed in the air by bucking bulls and broncos. Touring bands occasionally rock here, and you can get tickets online.

Stadium CLUB
(☎4927 9988; 234 Quay St; admission after 10pm $12; ⊙till late Fri & Sat) Next door to the Heritage Hotel, this is the place most partygoers head to after the pubs. It's a large, flashy club with a sporty theme – you dance on a mini basketball court.

Pilbeam Theatre THEATRE
(☎4927 4111; Victoria Pde) This plush 967-seat theatre is located in the Rockhampton Performing Arts Complex and hosts national and international acts. Its Italian restaurant is recommended by the locals.

Birch Carrol & Coyle Cinemas CINEMA
(☎4926 6977; cnr Bruce Hwy & Stockland St) This multiscreen cinema is in the Stockland Shopping Centre in north Rocky and shows mostly mainstream blockbusters.

WORTH A TRIP

CAPRICORN CAVES & BENT-WING BATS

In the Berserker Range, 24km north of Rockhampton near the Caves township, the amazing **Capricorn Caves** (☎4934 2883; www.capricorncaves.com.au; Caves Rd; adult/child $26/13; ⊙9am-4pm) are not to be missed. These ancient caves honeycomb a limestone ridge, and on a guided tour through the caverns and labyrinths you'll see cave coral, stalactites, dangling fig-tree roots and little insectivorous bats. The highlight of the one-hour cathedral tour is the beautiful natural rock cathedral where a haunting rendition of 'Amazing Grace' is played to demonstrate the cavern's incredible acoustics. Every December traditional Christmas carol singalongs are held in the cathedral. Also in December, around the summer solstice (1 December to 14 January), sunlight beams directly through a 14m vertical shaft into Belfry Cave creating an electrifying light show. If you stand directly below the beam, reflected sunlight colours the whole cavern with whatever colour you're wearing.

Daring spelunkers can book a two-hour adventure tour ($60) which takes you through tight spots with names such as 'Fat Man's Misery'. You must be at least 16 years old for this tour.

The Capricorn Caves complex has barbecue areas, a pool, a kiosk and **accommodation** (unpowered/powered sites $27/32, cabins from $160).

Information

Capricorn Visitor Centre (☎4921 2311; Gladstone Rd; ⏰9am-5pm) Helpful centre on the highway beside the tropic of Capricorn marker, 3km south of the town centre.

CQ Net(☎4922 5988; 29 William St; per hr $5; ⏰9am-3.30pm & 5pm-late Mon, Tue, Thu & Fri) Internet access.

Department of Environment & Resource Management (DERM; ☎13 74 68; www.derm.qld.gov.au; 61 Yeppoon Rd, North Rockhampton) About 7km northwest of central Rockhampton. Formerly called the Queensland Parks & Wildlife Service.

Post Office (☎13 13 18; 150 East St; ⏰9am-5pm Mon-Fri)

Rockhampton Library (☎4936 8265; 232 Bolsover St; ⏰9.15am-5.30pm Mon, Tue & Fri, 1-8pm Wed, 9.15am-8pm Thu, 9.15am-4.30pm Sat) Free internet access, but you need to book.

Rockhampton Visitor Centre (☎4922 5339; 208 Quay St; ⏰8.30am-4.30pm Mon-Fri, 9am-4pm Sat & Sun) Capricorn Visitor Centre's sister branch is located in the beautiful former customs house in central Rocky.

Getting There & Away

Air

Qantas, Tiger Airways and Virgin Blue connect Rockhampton with various cities. See p200 for more details.

Bus

Greyhound Australia (☎13 20 30; www.greyhound.com.au) has regular services from Rocky to Mackay ($60, four hours), Brisbane ($114, 11 hours) and Cairns ($178, 18 hours). All services stop at the **Mobil Service Station** (91 George St). **Premier Motor Service** (☎13 34 10; www.premierms.com.au) operates a Brisbane–Cairns service, stopping at Rocky.

Paradise Coaches (☎4933 1127) makes a daily run from Rocky to Emerald ($48, four hours). Services leave from the Mobil Service Station.

Young's Bus Service (☎4922 3813) to Yeppoon ($12.10, 45 minutes) includes a loop through Rosslyn Bay and Emu Park. Young's also has buses to Mt Morgan ($12.10, 50 minutes, Monday to Friday). Buses depart from the Kern Arcade in Bolsover St.

Train

Queensland Rail (☎1800 872 467, 3235 1122; www.queenslandrail.com.au) runs the *Tilt Train*, which connects Rockhampton with Brisbane (from $119, 7½ hours, Sunday to Friday) and Cairns (from $266, 16 hours, twice weekly). The slower *Sunlander* connects Rockhampton with Brisbane three times per week, and has a sleeper service between Rockhampton and Cairns (from $252, 20 hours). The *Spirit of the Outback* also connects Rockhampton with Brisbane (from $119), Emerald ($65, five hours, twice weekly) and Longreach ($130, 14 hours, twice weekly).

The train station is 450m southwest of the city centre.

RINGERS & COWBOYS: FARMSTAYS

Kick up some red dust on a fair dinkum Aussie outback cattle station and find out the difference between a jackeroo, ringer, stockman and cowboy. On a farmstay you're immersed in the daily activities of a working cattle station, riding horses and motorbikes, mustering cattle, fencing, and cooking damper and billy tea over a campfire. Before you know it, you'll find yourself looking for a ute, swag and blue dog to go with your RM Williams boots and high-crowned Akubra.

Myella Farmstay (☎4998 1290; www.myella.com; Baralaba Rd; 3/7days incl meals & activities $360/750, day trips $110; ❄@≋), 125km southwest of Rockhampton, gives you a taste of the outback on a 10.5-sq-km farm. The package includes bush explorations by horseback, motorcycle and 4WD, meals, accommodation in a renovated homestead with polished timber floors and a wide verandah, farm clothes and free transfers from Rockhampton. You get lots of kangaroo exposure at the on-site kangaroo rehab centre that cares for orphaned joeys.

At **Kroombit Lochenbar Station** (☎4992 2186; www.kroombit.com.au; dm $27, d with/without bathroom $84/68, 2-day & 2-night package incl dm, meals & activities per person $280; ❄@≋), 35km east of Biloela, Kroombit Park covers 2 hectares of eucalypt bushland on the 40-sq-km Lochenbar Cattle Station. There are several farmstay packages to choose from and you can pitch a tent or stay in a bush-timber or upmarket cabin. While soaking up the Aussie experience, you can learn to crack a whip, throw a boomerang or loop a lasso, and earn your spurs on a mechanical bucking bull. Rates include pick-up from Biloela.

Getting Around

Rockhampton Airport is 5km south of the city centre. **Sunbus** (☎4936 2133) runs a reasonably comprehensive city bus network operating all day Monday to Friday and Saturday morning. All services terminate in Bolsover St, between William and Denham Sts. You can pick up a timetable at the visitor centre.

There's also a taxi service in town, **Rocky Cabs** (☎13 10 08).

Around Rockhampton

Capricorn Caves is well worth the trip, and is easily reachable from both Rockhampton and Yeppoon.

Mt Morgan (population 244) has two claims to fame: it was once the richest gold mine in the world, and it was home to the first Australian soldier to die on foreign soil. A lucky stockman struck gold here in 1880, and open-cut operations continued until 1981. In its time the mine produced 225 tonnes of gold and 360,000 tonnes of copper. The Boer War is long over and the big mountain of gold is now a big crater. Although the town is heritage-listed, the 19th-century buildings are a rather sorry-looking lot, and about the only reason to stop by is to see the former mine. The mine can only be visited with **TMC Tours** (☎4938 1823; www.tmctours.com.au; adult/child/family $27/12/66; ⏲by appointment), whose tours leave from the old train station (bookings essential) and take in the town's sights, the open-cut mine and a large man-made cavern with dinosaur footprints on the roof.

If you're interested in the town's history, the **Mt Morgan Historical Museum** (☎4938 2122; 87 Morgan St; adult/child $5/1; ⏲10am-4pm), an unmistakable yellow building with a large yellow dinosaur on the roof, has an extensive collection of photographs, old mining equipment and artefacts.

The **visitor centre** (☎4938 2312; Railway Pde; ⏲9am-4pm) is located in the lovely old train station.

Yeppoon

POP 13,290

Pretty little Yeppoon is a small seaside town with a long beach, calm waters and an attractive hinterland of volcanic outcrops, pineapple patches and grazing lands. The handful of quiet streets, sleepy motels and beachside cafes attract Rockhamptonites beating the heat and tourists heading for Great Keppel Island only 13km offshore.

Sights & Activities

Mill Gallery GALLERY

(☎4939 1311; www.millgallery.com.au; 31 Normanby St; ⏲9am-4pm Tue-Sun) This gallery is run by a collective of local artists who exhibit their own work and that of other artists in a gallery at Yeppoon's old post office.

Cooberrie Park NATURE RESERVE

(☎4939 7590; www.cooberriepark.com.au; Woodbury Rd; adult/child/family $25/15/65; ⏲10am-3pm) About 15km north of Yeppoon this is a small wildlife sanctuary on 2 hectares of bushland. You can see kangaroos, wallabies and peacocks wandering freely through the grounds. You can also feed the critters (with the park's prepackaged food) and, for an extra cost, hold a furry koala or some slithering reptiles.

Snorkelling Cruises SNORKELLING

Rosslyn Bay is also the departure point for the ferry to Great Keppel Island and for yacht charters and tours. **Funtastic Cruises** (☎0438 909 502; www.funtasticcruises.com; full-day cruise adult/child $90/75) operates full-day snorkelling trips to Middle Island on board its 17m catamaran, with a two-hour stopover on Great Keppel Island, morning and afternoon tea, and all snorkelling equipment. It can also organise camping drop offs to islands en route. **Sail Capricornia** (☎0402 102 373; www.keppelbaymarina.com.au; full-day cruise incl lunch adult/child $115/75) offers snorkelling cruises on board a 12m yacht as well as sunset and overnight cruises.

Capricorn Coast Trail Rides HORSE RIDING

(☎0413 483 850, 4939 2611; www.cctrailrides.com.au) You can see the local sights on horseback with Capricorn Coast Trail Rides, offering one- and two-hour rides ($40/70) on weekends as well as occasional longer rides. They set out from the Oaks Caltex Service Station, about halfway along the Yeppoon to Rockhampton road.

Golf GOLF

Golfers should check out Rydges Capricorn Resort.

Sleeping

There are beaches, caravan parks, backpackers, motels and holiday units along the 19km of coastline running south from Yeppoon to Emu Park. A fairly complete listing can be found at www.yeppooninfo.com.au.

Surfside Motel MOTEL $

(☎4939 1272; 30 Anzac Pde; r $90-95; ❄@🛜≋) Across the road from the beach and close to town, this 1950s strip of lime-green motel units epitomises summer holidays at the beach. And it's terrific value – the rooms are spacious and unusually well equipped, complete with toaster, hair dryer and free wi-fi.

Driftwood Motel & Holiday Units MOTEL $$

(☎4939 2446; www.driftwoodunits.com.au; 5-7 Todd Ave; r $99-130; ❄≋) Huge self-contained units at motel prices with beach frontage make Driftwood a great bargain. There are good family units with separate bedrooms and there's a children's playground, but be aware that there's a four-night minimum stay in high season.

While Away B&B B&B $$

(☎4939 5719; www.whileawaybandb.com.au; 44 Todd Ave; s/d incl breakfast $115/140; ❄) With four good-sized rooms and an immaculately clean house with wheelchair access, this B&B is a perfect, quiet getaway. There are complimentary nibbles, tea, coffee, port and sherry as well as generous breakfasts. There are no facilities for kids.

Beachfront 55 APARTMENTS $$

(☎4939 1403; www.beachfront55.com.au; 55 Todd Ave; units $139, villas from $285; ❄) North of town, these comfortable fully self-contained units each come with a private barbecue and courtyard. There's also a large villa that comfortably sleeps six; with a private pool and garden view, it has ocean glimpses, but is very close to the manager's quarters.

Rydges Capricorn Resort RESORT $$$

(☎1800 075 902, 4925 2525; www.capricornresort.com; Farnborough Rd; d $179-350; ❄≋) This is a large and lavish golf resort about 8km north of Yeppoon. Its accommodation ranges from standard hotel rooms to plush self-contained apartments. There's a huge pool, a gym and several bars and restaurants – locals rave about the sushi. Package deals are available, and booking online gets you the best deal. The resort's two immaculate golf courses are open to the public at $80 for 18 holes, which includes a motorised buggy. Club hire costs another $15.

Beachside Caravan Park CARAVAN PARK $

(☎4939 3738; Farnborough Rd; 2-person unpowered sites $21, powered sites $26-29) This basic but neat little camping park, north of the town centre, boasts a beachfront location. It has good amenities and grassed sites with some shade but no cabins or on-site vans.

Rosslyn Bay Inn APARTMENTS $$

(☎4933 6333; www.rosslynbayinn.com.au; Vin E Jones Dr; r $145-155; ❄≋) Located at the marina, this place has comfortable studio rooms and one- and two-bedroom units, as well as a bar and restaurant, Beaches (open lunch and dinner).

Eating & Drinking

Shio Kaze JAPANESE $$

(☎4939 5575; 18 Anzac Pde; per head about $25; ⏲lunch & dinner Wed-Sun) Delicious, fresh, great-value sushi served overlooking the beach. BYO alcohol.

Thai Take-Away THAI $$

(☎4939 3920; 24 Anzac Pde; mains $12-20; ⏲dinner) A deservedly popular Thai BYO restaurant where you can sit outside on the footpath, catch a sea breeze, and satisfy those chilli and coconut cravings. There's a large selection of seafood dishes and snappy service.

Megalomania MODERN AUSTRALIAN $$

(☎4939 2333; Arthur St; mains $22-36; ⏲11am-late) Another ultracool urban hang-out with a stone floor, slatted wooden blinds and an urban-islander vibe, this is a great place for a drink or dinner. The menu changes weekly.

Keppel Bay Sailing Club PUB FARE $

(☎4939 9537; Anzac Pde; mains $11-37; ⏲lunch & dinner) Choose between the beachfront clubhouse and deck with good steaks and seafood, such as mouth-watering crumbed coral trout, or cross the road for a cheap buffet meal and the din of countless pokies at Spinnakers.

Shore Thing BREAKFAST, SANDWICHES $

(☎4939 1993; 6 Normanby St; mains under $14; ⏲breakfast & lunch) A breezy little cafe on the main street dishing up sandwiches, focaccias, wraps and big breakfasts.

Strand Hotel PUB

(☎4939 1301; cnr Anzac Pde & Normanby St) The battered Strand has live music every weekend and serves $10 counter meals at lunch and dinner, but it's especially known for its Sunday evening parrilla, an Argentine-style barbecue with music to match.

Entertainment

Footlights Theatre Restaurant THEATRE (☎4939 2399; www.footlights.com.au; 123 Rockhampton Rd; dinner & show $90) Footlights hosts a three-course meal and a two-hour, comedy-variety show every Friday and Saturday night.

Little Theatre THEATRE (www.yeppoonlittletheatre.org.au; 64 William St) This theatre puts on occasional amateur productions; tickets are available at Yellow Door.

Information

Capricorn Coast Visitor Centre (☎1800 675 785, 4939 4888; www.capricorncoast.com.au; Scenic Hwy; ⏲9am-5pm) Located beside the Ross Creek roundabout at the entrance to the town, the vistor centre has plenty of information on the Capricorn Coast and Great Keppel Island, and can help you book accommodation and tours.

Yellow Door (☎4939 4805; 11 Normanby St) Sells new and used books and CDs, and runs a book exchange. It also has internet access for $5 per hour.

Yeppoon Library (☎4939 3433; 78 John St) Free internet access.

Getting There & Away

Yeppoon is 43km northeast of Rockhampton. **Young's Bus Service** (☎4922 3813; www.youngsbusservice.com.au) runs frequent buses from Rockhampton ($12 one way) to Yeppoon and down to the Keppel Bay marina (www.keppelbaymarina.com.au).

If you're heading for Great Keppel Island or the Great Barrier Reef, some ferry operators will transport you between your accommodation and Keppel Bay marina. Otherwise, if you're driving, there's a free car park at the marina. For secure undercover parking, the **Great Keppel Island Security Car Park** (☎4933 6670; 422 Scenic Hwy; per day from $12) is located on the Scenic Hwy south of Yeppoon, close to the turn-off to Keppel Bay marina.

Around Yeppoon

The drive south from Yeppoon and Rosslyn Bay passes three fine headlands with good views: **Double Head**, **Bluff Point** and **Pinnacle Point**. After Pinnacle Point the road crosses **Causeway Lake**, a saltwater inlet where you can hire fishing boats, bait and tackle for a spot of estuary fishing.

Emu Park (population 2967), 19km south of Yeppoon, is the second-largest township on the coast, but there's not much here, apart from more good views and the **Singing Ship** memorial to Captain Cook – a curious monument of drilled tubes and pipes that emit mournful whistling and moaning sounds in the breeze. **Emus Beach Resort** (☎4939 6111; www.emusbeachresort.com; 92 Pattinson St; dm $24-27, d/tr/q $75/95/100;) is a superlative backpackers, with a pool, kitchen, barbecue and a travel booking service; it also offers tours to the local crocodile farm. Otherwise, **Bell Park Caravan Park** (☎4939 6202; bellpark@primus.com.au; Pattinson St; unpowered/powered sites $18/22, cabins $84) has spacious sites, clean amenities and comfortable cabins just a stone's throw from the beach.

Emu Park Pizza & Pasta (☎4938 7333; Hill St; pizzas $10-22; ⏲dinner) is an unprepossessing restaurant but the pizzas attract locals from Yeppoon.

Fifteen kilometres along the Emu Park–Rockhampton road, the **Koorana Crocodile Farm** (☎4934 4749; www.koorana.com.au; Coowonga Rd; adult/child $22/11; ⏲tours 10.30am & 1pm) can be explored via the informative guided tours. Get there early to sample croc kebabs, croc ribs or a croc pie at the restaurant.

Byfield

Tiny Byfield consists of a general store, a school and a cluster of houses. The main attractions in this largely undeveloped region are the **Byfield National Park** and **State Forest**. It's a pleasant 40km drive north from Yeppoon through the pine plantations of the Byfield State Forest with turn-offs along the way to various picnic areas. North of Byfield, the Shoalwater Bay military training area borders the forest and park, and is strictly off limits.

The Byfield National Park and State Forest form the **Byfield coastal area**, a wild and scenic region of rocky headlands, long sandy beaches, massive dunes, heath land, forest, mangrove-lined estuaries, rainforested creeks and granite mountains. The main waterway, Waterpark Creek, supplies Rockhampton's town water, and is a magnificent place to go canoeing. There are five **campgrounds** (☎13 74 68; www.qld.gov.au/camping;

per person/family $4.50/18) to choose from: Upper Stoney Creek, Red Rock, Waterpark Creek, Nine Mile Beach and Five Rocks, all of which must be prebooked. Both Nine Mile Beach and Five Rocks are on the beach and you'll need a 4WD to access them. When conditions are right, there's decent surf at Nine Mile.

Nob Creek Pottery (☎4935 1161; 216 Arnolds Rd; admission free; ⊙9am-5pm), just south of Byfield, is a unique working pottery and gallery nestled in leafy rainforest where you can watch the potters at work. The giant kiln here resembles an enormous sleeping dragon; the gallery showcases hand-blown glass, woodwork and jewellery, and the handmade ceramics are outstanding.

Waterpark Eco-Tours & Farm (☎4935 1171; www.waterparkecotours.com; 201 Waterpark Creek Rd; 2-3hr tours $25, cabin $110; ❄) has excellent river trips in an electric-powered boat so you can experience the rainforest in complete silence. The tour also includes a horse-drawn carriage ride around a working tea-tree plantation, demonstration of tea-tree oil distillation, a safari bus trip to the farm's historic sites, and morning tea. If you find it hard to leave the genuine hospitality on offer, there's a fully self-contained timber cabin on the 97-hectare farm where you can swing in a hammock, swim in the creek or just relax in the outdoor spa.

Byfield Creek Lodge (☎4935 1117; www.byfieldcreeklodge.com.au; 32 Richters Rd; d incl breakfast from $150; ❄) is an African-themed B&B set on 3 hectares of rainforest overlooking Byfield Creek. In the two-bedroom cabin, you can soak in the outdoor spa after a day of bushwalking, canoeing or four-wheel driving through the national park.

Signposted just north of Byfield, **Ferns Hideaway** (☎4935 1235; www.fernshideaway.com.au; 67 Cahills Rd; 2-person unpowered sites $24, d $150; ❄≋) is a secluded oasis in immaculate gardens that offers canoeing and walks. The homestead has a quality à la carte **restaurant** (mains $18-32; ⊙lunch & afternoon tea Wed-Sun, dinner Sat, breakfast Sun) featuring live music on weekends, while nestled among the trees are self-contained cabins with wood fires. There are also double rooms with shared facilities; or you can camp, with hot showers included in the tariff. Restaurant patrons and those staying on-site have free access to all facilities, including canoes.

Byfield General Store & Café (☎4935 1190; 223 Byfield Rd; ⊙8am-6pm Wed-Mon, to 2pm Tue) has basic grocery supplies and a simple courtyard cafe serving pies, sandwiches and highly recommended burgers. You can get fuel here and also some very good information about the national park.

Great Keppel Island

Great Keppel Island is a stunningly beautiful island with rocky headlands, forested hills and a fringe of powdery white sand lapped by clear azure waters. Numerous 'castaway' beaches ring the 14-sq-km island, while natural bushland covers 90% of the interior. A string of huts and accommodation options sit behind the trees lining the main beach but the developments are low-key and relatively unobtrusive. Only 13km offshore, and with good snorkelling, swimming and bush walking, Great Keppel is an easily accessible, tranquil island retreat.

The sprawling Great Keppel Island Resort was once the centre of activity here, but it closed suddenly in 2008, leaving an increasingly dilapidated shell, and making for a much quieter island. The resort isn't set to reopen any time soon.

Sights

The beaches of Great Keppel rate among Queensland's best. Take a short stroll from **Fisherman's Beach**, the main beach, and you'll find your own deserted stretch of white sand. There is fairly good coral and excellent fish life, especially between Great Keppel and Humpy Island to the south. A 30-minute walk south around the headland brings you to **Monkey Beach**, where there's good snorkelling. A walking trail from the southern end of the airfield takes you to **Long Beach**, perhaps the island's best beach.

There are several bushwalking tracks from Fisherman's Beach; the longest and perhaps most difficult leads to the 2.5m 'lighthouse' near **Bald Rock Point** on the far side of the island (three hours return).

You can see an **underwater observatory** off Middle Island, close to Great Keppel. A confiscated Taiwanese fishing junk was sunk next to the observatory to provide a haven for fish.

Activities

The **Watersports Hut** on the main beach hires out snorkelling equipment, kayaks and

Great Keppel Island

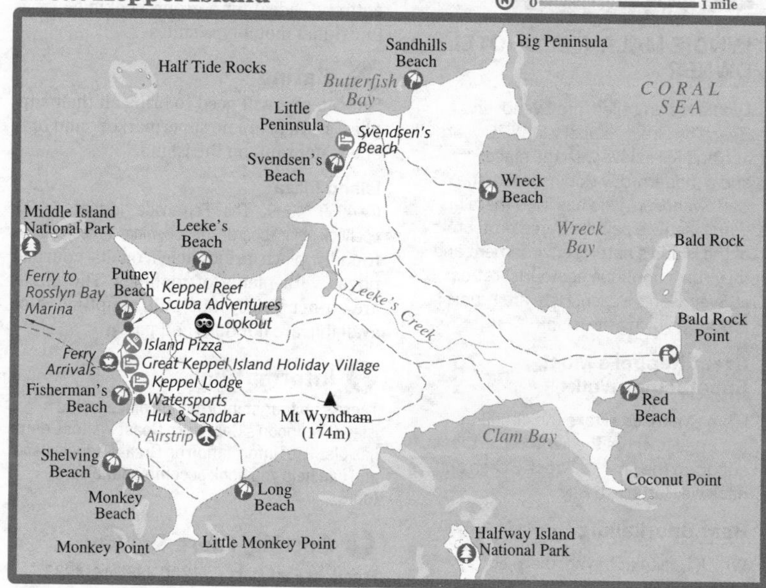

catamarans, and runs banana rides. You can buy drinks and ice creams at the **Sandbar** here and watch the sun set over the water.

Keppel Reef Scuba Adventures (☎4939 5022, 0408 004 536; www.keppeldive.com; Putney Beach) offers introductory dives (per person $200), snorkelling trips (per person $50), and also hires out snorkelling gear (per day $15).

Tours

Freedom Fast Cats (☎1800 336 244, 4933 6244; wwwfreedomfastcats.com) operates a coral cruise to the best location of the day (depending on tides and weather), which includes viewing through a glass-bottomed boat and fish feeding. The cruise (adult/child $63/42) leaves from Keppel Bay marina. Freedom also runs full-day cruises (adult/child $130/85) including coral viewing, fish feeding, snorkelling, boom netting and a barbecue lunch, as well as wave-jumping, thrill-seeking trips on the fast boat *Wild Duck* (35-minute ride adult/child $25/20).

Sleeping

Without Great Keppel Island Resort, accommodation options are somewhat limited. Holiday homes can be rented through the **Capricorn Coast Visitor Centre** (☎1800 675 785, 4939 4888; www.capricorncoast.com.au; Scenic Hwy; ⏲9am-5pm) in Yeppoon. Six- and eight-bedroom homes can be rented in their entirety or the rooms can be rented as individual motel-style suites.

Svendsen's Beach CABINS $
(☎4938 3717; www.svendsensbeach.com; Svendsen's Beach; cabins 3 nights, minimum 3-night stay $285) This secluded boutique castaway retreat has two luxury tent-bungalows on separate elevated timber decks overlooking lovely Svendsen's Beach. The environmentally friendly operation has solar heating, wind generators, rainwater tanks and an eco-fridge, and the communal beach-kitchen has a barbecue and stove-top. The artistic owner has fashioned decorative wooden sculptures and furnishings including a quaint candlelit bush-bucket shower. It's the perfect place for snorkelling, bushwalking and romantic getaways. Transfers from the ferry drop-off at Fisherman's Beach are included in the tariff.

Great Keppel Island Holiday Village HOSTEL, CABINS $
(☎4939 8655; www.gkiholidayvillage.com.au; dm $35, r & tents $85, cabins with bathroom $140, 2-bedroom houses from $220) Offers various

LOCAL KNOWLEDGE

LYNDIE MALAN: ECOHOTEL OWNER

Lyndie Malan sailed into Svendsen's Beach on Great Keppel Island 20 years ago and fell in love with the place... and a modern-day Robinson Crusoe, Carl Svendsen, who has lived there his entire life. The pair are fierce protectors of the island's natural environment and they run a boutique ecotourist retreat at Svendsen's Beach. Here are Lyndie's tips for enjoying the island:

Great Keppel's Most Spectacular Walk

From Svendsen's, take the circuit up the ridge towards the lighthouse, then cut down the spur to Wreck Beach and back via Butterfish Bay.

Best Snorkelling Spots

Wreck Beach at the northern end, or Butterfish Bay.

Your Favourite Secret Swimming Spot

Secret Beach – yes, it's really called that! Ask for directions...

Great Keppel's Most Adorable Animal

Flatback turtle hatchlings – they're very cute!

Its Most Dangerous Beast

Mosquitos – they are the world's most dangerous.

types of good budget accommodation, including four-bed dorms and cabins that sleep three people. There's a two-night minimum. It's a very friendly, relaxed place with shared bathroom facilities and a decent communal kitchen and barbecue area. Snorkelling gear is free and the village runs motorised canoe trips around Middle Island ($30 per person).

Keppel Lodge GUESTHOUSE **$$**
(☎4939 4251; www.keppellodge.com.au; Fisherman's Beach; s $90-100, d $110-130, each additional person $50) A pleasant open-plan house with four large bedrooms (with bathrooms) branching from a large communal lounge and kitchen. The house is available in its entirety – ideal for a group booking – or as individual motel-type suites.

Eating

Self-caterers will need to bring all their supplies, as there are no supermarkets, and only one restaurant, on the island.

Island Pizza PIZZA **$**
(☎4939 4699; The Esplanade; dishes $6-30; ⏲check blackboard for opening times) This friendly place prides itself on its gourmet pizzas with plenty of toppings. The pizzas are rather pricey but still tempting. Also available are hot dogs and pasta.

Information

There's no tourist information office on the island. Yeppoon's Capricorn Coast Visitor Centre has plenty of information on Great Keppel Island and can help you book accommodation and tours.

Getting There & Away

Freedom Fast Cats (☎1800 336 244, 4933 6244; www.freedomfastcats.com; return fare per adult/concession/child/family $49/41/29/127) departs the Keppel Bay marina in Rosslyn Bay (7km south of Yeppoon) for Great Keppel Island each morning, returning that same afternoon (call ahead for precise times). If you have booked accommodation, check that someone will meet you on the beach to help with your luggage.

Other Keppel Bay Islands

Great Keppel is the largest of 18 stunning continental islands dotted around Keppel Bay, all within 20km of the coast. Unlike coral cay islands, which are formed by the build up of tiny fragments of coral, algae and other reef plants and animals, continental islands were originally rocky outcrops of the mainland ranges.

These beautiful islands feature clean, white beaches and impossibly clear water ranging from pale turquoise through to deep indigo blue. Several have fringing coral reefs excellent for snorkelling or diving. You can visit **Middle Island**, with its underwater observatory, or **Halfway** and **Humpy Islands** if you're staying on Great Keppel. Some of the islands are national parks where you can maroon yourself for a few days of self-sufficient camping.

To camp on a national-park island, you need to take your own supplies, including water. Camper numbers on each island are restricted. For information and permits, call **DERM** (☎13 74 68; www.qld.gov.au/camping).

The second-largest of the group and one of the most northerly is **North Keppel Island**. It covers 6 sq km and is a national park. The most popular camping spot is Considine Beach on the northwestern coast, which has toilets and a shower. There are a few small palms and other scattered trees but shade is limited. Take insect repellent.

Other islands with camping grounds include Humpy, Miall and Middle.

Pumpkin Island (☎4939 4413; www.pumpkinisland.com.au; camping per person $20, cabins $300-480) is a tiny, privately owned island just south of North Keppel. It has five simple, cosy cabins with water and solar power, and each has a gas stove, fridge and barbecue. All you need to bring is food and linen. There's also a small campsite with its own private beach, hot water and barbecue. Transfers to the island are $90 return and there's a minimum two-night stay.

Gladstone

POP 28,810

On first impression, the industrial town of Gladstone, with its busy port, coal- and bauxite-loading terminals, oil tanks, power station and alumina refineries, is rather uninspiring. Sometimes first impressions are right. There's little to keep you in town; head straight for the marina, the main departure point for boats to the southern coral cay islands of Heron, Masthead and Wilson on the Great Barrier Reef. What little action there is can be found at the end of Gondoon St, with its restaurants and bars.

Sights & Activities

If you have some time to spare before or after island hopping, drive up to the **Auckland Point Lookout** for views over Gladstone harbour, the port facilities and shipping terminals. A brass tablet at the lookout maps the harbour and its many islands.

Toondoon Botanic Gardens (☎4971 4444; Glenlyon Rd; admission free; ⌚9am-6pm Oct-Mar, 8.30am-5.30pm Apr-Sep), about 7km south of town, comprise 83 hectares of rainforest, lakes and Australian native plants. There's a visitor centre, an orchid house and free one-hour guided tours between February and November (tours can be booked at the gardens or visitor centre). The gardens have wheelchair access.

If you are in the area, market days (ask the visitor centre for dates) at the **Calliope River Historical Village** (☎4975 7428; Dawson Hwy, Calliope; admission $2; ⌚8am-4pm), 26km south of Gladstone, are hugely popular. Held six times a year, the 200-plus stalls of arts, crafts, clothes, jewellery and local produce attract over 3000 people. While here you can wander around the village's restored heritage buildings, including an old pub (licensed on market days), church, schoolhouse and a slab hut.

Agnes Water and Town of 1770, south of Gladstone, are the place to be for a seaside break, but Gladstone's local beaches will do if you just need a quick trip out of town. Tannum Sands (20km southeast of Gladstone) is the local beachside hang-out, and its long stretch of beachside parkland is dotted with barbecues and playgrounds. Across the Boyne River, Boyne Island is even quieter but both areas are popular with fishing and boating enthusiasts. If you're overnighting in Gladstone this can be an attractive alternative, although dining options are limited.

Created by the construction of the Awoonga Dam in 1984, **Lake Awoonga** is a popular recreational area 30km south of Gladstone. Backed by the rugged **Mt Castle Tower National Park**, the lake, which is stocked with barramundi, has a scenic setting with landscaped picnic areas, a cafe, barbecues, walking trails and birdlife. You can hire canoes, boats and fishing gear from the **Lake Awoonga Caravan Park** (☎4975 0155; www.lakeawoongacaravanpark.com.au; Lake Awoonga Rd, Benaraby; 2-person unpowered/powered sites $20/29, d cabins from $75).

Tours

Gladstone's big-ticket industries, including the alumina refineries, aluminium smelter, power station and port authority, open their doors for free industry tours. The one- or 1½-hour tours start at different times on different days of the week depending on the industry. Book at the visitor centre.

Fishing, diving and sightseeing cruises to the Swains and Bunker Island groups are the speciality of the 20m **MV Mikat** (☎4972 3415; www.mikat.com.au). Cruises are a minimum of three days with all meals catered, and there's a licensed bar on board. Trips leave from the marina. **Capricorn**

ART DETOUR

Cedar Galleries (☎4975 0444; www.cedargalleries.com.au; Bruce Hwy; ⏲9am-4pm Thu-Sun) is a tranquil artists' bush retreat where you can watch painters and sculptors at work in hand-built, slab-hut studios. To unleash your creative genius, you can take art and craft classes with visiting artists (call ahead to book) or just browse the gardens and the gallery. There's also a cafe, beautiful hand-crafted wedding chapel, kids' jumping castle, herd of friendly alpacas and winery cellar door but no accommodation, although aspiring artists are welcome to pitch a tent or sleep on the floor. If you're here on the last Sunday of the month, you can watch local musicians do their thing at the monthly Sunday session (admission $12, includes barbecue dinner).

This unique artists' colony (114km south of Gladstone) is signposted off the Bruce Hwy, 7km southeast of Calliope.

Star Cruises (☎4978 0499) and **Rob Benn Charters** (☎4972 8885) also offer charter trips with fishing, diving, snorkelling and reef-viewing experiences.

As well as operating services to Curtis Island, **Curtis Ferry Services** (☎4972 6990; www.curtisferryservices.com.au) has a morning **coffee cruise** (adult/child $18/10; ⏲10.40am Apr-Oct) leaving the marina every Wednesday, taking in the highlights of the Gladstone harbour.

Sleeping

Gladstone Backpackers HOSTEL $
(☎4972 5744; www.gladstonebackpackers.com; 12 Rollo St; dm/d $25/65; @) This fairly central hostel has recently undergone renovations with more to come. It's a friendly, family-run place in an old Queenslander, with a large kitchen, clean bathrooms and an airy outside deck. There's free use of bicycles and free pick-ups from the marina, bus, train and airport. You're sure to feel part of the family by the time you leave.

Barney Beach Caravan Park CARAVAN PARK $
(☎4972 1366; www.barneybeach.com.au; 10 Friend St; 2-person powered sites $37, cabins $150-205; @) About 2km east of the city centre and close to the foreshore, this is the most central of the caravan parks. It's large and tidy, with a good camp kitchen and excellent self-contained accommodation. There are complimentary transfers to the marina for guests visiting Heron Island. Buslink Queensland runs buses here.

Auckland Hill B&B B&B $$$
(☎4972 4907; www.ahbb.com.au; 15 Yarroon St; s/d $230/260;) This sprawling, comfortable Queenslander has six spacious rooms with king-sized beds. Each is differently decorated; there is a spa suite and one with wheelchair access. Breakfasts are hearty and the mood is relaxed.

Harbour City Motel MOTEL $$
(☎4976 7100; 20-24 William St; s/d $115/125) If you must stay in Gladstone, this is a decent motel in the centre of town. The large rooms have modern bathrooms and the motel has a licensed steakhouse.

Tannum Beach Caravan Village CARAVAN PARK $
(☎4973 7201; www.tannumvillage.com.au; The Esplanade; unpowered/powered sites $29/35; cabins from $95;) A shady riverside site 500m from the beach.

Boyne Island Motel & Villas MOTEL $$
(☎4973 7444; www.boynemotel.com.au; 3 Orana Ave; d $95, 1-/2-bedroom villas $125/175;) Roomy self-contained cabins in tropical gardens close to the beach.

Eating & Drinking

Tables On Flinders SEAFOOD $$
(☎4972 8322; 2 Oaka La; mains $20-39; ⏲lunch Tue-Fri, dinner Tue-Sat) This delightful, cosy restaurant specialises in seafood and does it well. Tasty mudcrabs are served steamed with hot butter, garlic cream or Singapore-style chilli. The quality, value and ambience draw visiting suits and romantic couples.

Library Square Brasserie MODERN AUSTRALIAN $$
(☎4972 8611; 56 Goondoon St; mains $22-30; ⏲lunch Mon-Fri, dinner Mon-Sun) The varied menu at this local favourite can be enjoyed at outside tables with live music on show in the square on Thursday and Friday nights.

Scotties Bar & Restaurant MODERN AUSTRALIAN $$
(☎4972 9999; 46 Goondoon St; mains $12-35; ⏲dinner Mon-Sat, lunch Fri only) Thai, Mediterranean, steak, seafood and pasta: this popular restaurant, with a decidedly blue theme, has an eclectic and always changing

menu that includes a couple of vegetarian options. The walls bear interesting local artwork and you can sit on the outside deck in the main street.

Gladstone Yacht Club PUB FARE $
(☎4972 8611; 1 Goondoon St; mains $12-24; ⊙lunch & dinner) The Yacht Club is a popular place to wine and dine on a budget, and with good reason. The steak, chicken, pasta and seafood are tasty and generous; there are daily buffet specials and you can eat on the deck overlooking the water.

Information

DERM (☎4971 6500; 3rd fl, 136 Goondoon St; ⊙8.30am-4.30pm Mon-Fri) Provides information on all the southern Great Barrier Reef islands as well as the area's mainland parks.

Gladstone City Library (☎4976 6400; 39 Goondoon St; ⊙9.30am-5.45pm Mon-Fri, to 7.45pm Thu, 9am-4.30pm Sat) Free internet access, but you must book in advance.

Post Office (☎13 13 18; Valley Shopping Centre, Goondoon St)

Visitor Centre (☎4972 9000; Bryan Jordan Dr; ⊙8.30am-5pm Mon-Fri, 9am-5pm Sat & Sun) Located at the marina, the departure point for boats to Heron Island.

Getting There & Away

Air

Qantaslink (☎13 13 13; www.qantas.com.au) has several daily flights between Brisbane and Gladstone (70 minutes) and two daily flights between Rockhampton and Gladstone (25 minutes). The airport is 7km from the town centre.

Boat

Curtis Ferry Services (☎4972 6990; www.curtisferryservices.com.au) has services to Curtis Island five days per week. The ferry leaves from the Gladstone marina and stops at Farmers Point on Facing Island en route. Transport to North West and Masthead Islands can be arranged on request.

You can also access the islands with various charter operators.

If you've booked a stay on Heron Island, the resort operates a launch (adult/child $110/55, two hours), which leaves the Gladstone marina at 11am daily.

Bus

Greyhound Australia (☎13 20 30; www.greyhound.com.au) has several coach services from Brisbane ($105, 10½ hours), Bundaberg ($45, 1½ hours) and Rockhampton ($34, 2½ hours). The terminal for long-distance buses is at the Mobil Service Station, on the Dawson Hwy about 200m southwest of the centre.

Train

Queensland Rail (☎1800 872 467, 3235 1122; www.queenslandrail.com.au) has daily north- and southbound services passing through Gladstone. The *Tilt Train* stops in Gladstone from Brisbane ($108, 6½ hours) and Rockhampton ($34, one hour). The more sedate *Sunlander* and *Spirit of the Outback* trains take far longer.

Getting Around

Gladstone Airport is 7km southwest of town. **Buslink Queensland** (☎4972 1670) has four daily services from the airport into town. Catch bus 2 or 3 and expect to pay from $1 to $3 depending on the route.

In general, public transport to places around Gladstone is very limited. Buslink Queensland runs local bus services on weekdays only, including a service along Goondoon St to Barney Point (and the rather unattractive Barney Beach), which stops out the front of the caravan park there. To book a taxi, phone **Blue & White Taxis** (☎13 10 08).

Southern Reef Islands

If you've ever had 'castaway' dreams of tiny coral atolls fringed with sugary white sand and turquoise-blue seas, you've found your island paradise in the southern Great Barrier Reef islands. From beautiful Lady Elliot Island, 80km northeast of Bundaberg, secluded and uninhabited coral reefs and atolls dot the ocean for about 140km up to Tryon Island, east of Rockhampton.

Several cays in this part of the reef are excellent for snorkelling, diving and just getting back to nature – though reaching them is generally more expensive than reaching islands nearer the coast. Some of the islands are important breeding grounds for turtles and seabirds, and visitors should be aware of the precautions taken to ensure the wildlife's protection, outlined in the relevant DERM information sheets.

Camping is allowed on Lady Musgrave, Masthead and North West national-park islands, and campers must be totally self-sufficient. Numbers are limited, so it's advisable to apply well ahead for a camping permit ($5.15/20.60 per person/family). Contact the **DERM** (☎13 74 68; www.qld.gov.au/camping) to book.

Access is from Town of 1770 and Gladstone.

DETOUR: CURTIS ISLAND

Curtis Island, just across the water from Gladstone, can't be confused with a resort island. Apart from swimming, fishing and curling up with a good book, its only real drawcard is the annual appearance of rare flatback turtles on its eastern shores between November and January. Camping permits can be booked via **DERM** (☎13 74 68; www.qld.gov.au/camping) and rental accommodation can be arranged by calling **Capricorn Lodge** (☎4972 0222; lodges from $100). **Curtis Ferry Services** (☎4972 6990; www.curtisferryservices.com.au; return adult/child/family $30/22/84) connects the island with Gladstone on Monday, Wednesday, Friday, Saturday and Sunday.

LADY ELLIOT ISLAND

On the southern frontier of the Great Barrier Reef, Lady Elliot is a 40-hectare vegetated coral cay popular with divers, snorkellers and nesting sea turtles. The island is a breeding and nesting ground for many species of tropical seabirds but its stunning underwater landscape is the main attraction. Divers can walk straight off the beach to explore an ocean bed of shipwrecks, coral gardens, bommies (coral pinnacles or outcroppings) and blowholes, and abundant marine life including barracuda, giant manta rays and harmless leopard sharks.

Lady Elliot Island is not a national park, and camping is not allowed. Your only option is the low-key **Lady Elliot Island Resort** (☎1800 072 200; www.ladyelliot.com.au; per person $160-326). Accommodation at this no-frills resort is in basic tent cabins, simple motel-style units or more expensive two-bedroom, self-contained suites. Rates include breakfast and dinner, snorkelling gear and some tours. A three-night minimum stay applies over Christmas and New Year.

The only way to reach the island is in a light aircraft. Seair (book through the resort) flies guests to the resort from Bundaberg and Hervey Bay ($254/136 per adult/child return). You can also visit the island on a day trip from Bundaberg and Hervey Bay for $300/170 (the price includes a range of tours and activities as well as lunch and snorkelling gear).

LADY MUSGRAVE ISLAND

Wannabe castaways look no further – this is the perfect desert island! This tiny 15-hectare cay 100km northeast of Bundaberg sits on the western rim of a stunning, turquoise-blue reef lagoon renowned for its safe swimming, snorkelling and diving. A white-sand beach fringes a dense canopy of pisonia forest brimming with roosting birdlife, including terns, shearwaters and white-capped noddies. Birds nest from October to April, while green turtles nest from November to February.

The uninhabited island is part of the Capricornia Cays National Park and there is a DERM campground on the island's west side. The campground has bush toilets but little else and campers must be totally self-sufficient, even bringing their own water. Numbers are limited to 40 at any one time, so apply well ahead for a permit with **DERM** (☎13 74 68; www.qld.gov.au/camping). Online bookings can be made – search under Capricornia Cays National Park. Don't forget to bring a gas stove as fires are not permitted on the island.

Day trips to Lady Musgrave depart from the Town of 1770 marina.

HERON & WILSON ISLANDS

With the underwater reef world accessible directly from the beach, Heron Island is famed for superb scuba diving and snorkelling, although you'll need a fair amount of cash to visit. A true coral cay, it is densely vegetated with pisonia trees and surrounded by 24 sq km of reef. There's a resort and research station on the northeastern third of the island; the remainder is national park.

Heron Island Resort (☎4972 9055, 1800 737 678; www.heronisland.com; s/d incl breakfast from $399/479) covers the northeastern third of the island. Its comfortable accommodation is suited to families and couples; the Point Suites have the best views. Meal packages are extra, and guests will pay $200/100 per adult/child for launch transfer, or $440/270 for helicopter transfer. Both are from Gladstone.

Wilson Island (www.wilsonisland.com; s/d from $671/918), also part of a national park, is an exclusive wilderness retreat with six permanent tents and solar-heated showers. There are excellent beaches and superb snorkelling. The only access is from Heron Island and you'll need to buy a combined Wilson–Heron package and spend at least two nights on Wilson Island. Transfers between Wilson and Heron Islands are included in the tariff.

OTHER ISLANDS

There are three other islands in this group worth mentioning, all major nesting sites for loggerhead turtles and various seabirds, notably shearwaters and black noddies. The turtles nest between November and February, the birds between October and April. All three islands allow self-sufficient camping with limited facilities.

Southwest of Heron Island, 45-hectare, uninhabited **Masthead Island** is the second largest of the nine vegetated cays in the Capricorn Group. Camping is permitted from Easter to October; there is a limit of 50 campers and bookings are essential.

At 106 hectares, **North West Island** is the second-biggest cay on the reef. Formerly a guano mine and turtle-soup factory, it is now a national park popular with campers. There's a limit of 150 campers and camping is closed from 26 January to Easter. There are no scheduled services to North West; contact **Curtis Ferry Service** (☎4972 6990; www.curtisferryservices.com.au) at the Gladstone marina to arrange transport, or **DERM** (☎13 74 68; www.qld.gov.au/camping) for details on suitable launches and barges to access the island.

Tryon Island is a tiny, beautiful, 11-hectare national park cay north of North West Island. There is a camping ground, but the island is currently closed to visitors to allow for revegetation. Check with DERM for the latest details.

Agnes Water & Town of 1770

POP 1620

Surrounded by national parks, sandy beaches and the blue Pacific, the twin coastal towns of Agnes Water and Town of 1770 are among Queensland's most appealing seaside destinations. The tiny settlement of Agnes Water has a lovely white-sand beach, the east coast's most northerly surf beach, while the even tinier Town of 1770 (little more than a marina!) marks Captain Cook's first landing in Queensland.

This area provides good access to the southern end of the reef, including the Fitzroy Reef Lagoon. The 'Discovery Coast' is a popular nook for surfing, boating and fishing away from the crowds. To get here, turn east off the Bruce Hwy at Miriam Vale, 70km south of Gladstone. It's another 57km to Agnes Water and a further 6km to the Town of 1770.

Sights

Miriam Vale Historical Society Museum (☎4974 9511; Springs Rd, Agnes Water; adult/child $3/free; ⌚1-4pm Mon & Wed-Sat, 10am-4pm Sun) displays a small collection of artefacts, rocks and minerals, as well as extracts from Cook's journal and the original telescope from the first lighthouse built on the Queensland coast.

Activities & Tours

The action around here happens on and in the water. Agnes Water is Queensland's northernmost surf beach. A Surf Life Saving Club patrols the main beach and there are often good breaks along the coast.

Round Hill Creek at the Town of 1770 is a calm anchorage for boats. Charter boats are available for fishing, surfing, snorkelling and diving trips to the southern Great Barrier Reef, with Lady Musgrave Island about 1½ hours offshore. There's good fishing and mudcrabbing upstream.

Reef 2 Beach Surf School SURFING
(☎4974 9072, 0402 328 515; www.reef2beachsurf.com; 1/10 Round Hill Rd, Agnes Water) Learn to surf on the gentle breaks of the main beach with the highly acclaimed Reef 2 Beach Surf School. A three-hour group surfing lesson is $17, and surfboard hire is $20 for four hours.

Lazy Lizard Surf School SURFING, KAYAKING
(☎0488 177 000; www.lazylizardsurfschool.com.au) Offers lessons for smaller groups (up to 12 people, $33 for half day). The same outfit runs **1770 Liquid Adventures** (☎0428 956 630; www.1770liquidadventures.com.au), which offers a spectacular twilight kayaking tour. For $40, you get a lesson in sea kayaking, riding the waves just off 1770, before retiring to the beach for drinks and snacks as the sun sets – keep an eye out for dolphins. You can also rent kayaks for $40 per half day.

Dive 1770 DIVING
(☎4974 9359; www.dive1770.com) Offers dive courses (PADI open-water $250) and Great Barrier Reef dives (from $30).

1770 Underwater Sea Adventures DIVING
(☎1300 553 889; www.1770underseaadventures.com.au) Offers a range of dive courses, and

STINGERS

The potentially deadly Chironex box jellyfish and irukandji, also known as sea wasps or marine stingers, inhabit Queensland's coastal waters north of Agnes Water (occasionally further south) from around October to April, and swimming is not advisable during these times. Fortunately, swimming and snorkelling are usually safe around the reef islands throughout the year; however, the rare and tiny (1cm to 2cm across) irukandji has been sighted on the outer reef and islands. For more information on stingers and treatment, see p456.

Great Barrier Reef and wreck dives ($160 including snorkel gear and meals, plus $25 per dive and $30 for gear rental).

1770 Marina Café BOAT HIRE
(☎4974 9227; half-/full day $65/95) Hires out aluminium dinghies.

Hooked on 1770 CRUISE
(☎4974 9794) Hooked on 1770 has full- and half-day fishing and scenic charters starting at $55 per person.

ThunderCat 1770 WATER SPORTS
(☎0427 177 000; adult/child $85/65) Adrenaline junkies will love wave jumping, surfing and slalom running in a surf racing boat. The action is toned down slightly on the Action Adventurer and even more so on the Wilderness Explorer tours, where you visit secluded beaches, learn some local history and explore 1770's pristine waterways and national park coastline. Tours and activities can be tailored and combined to include diversions like tube riding and even wearable 'sumo suits' that have swimmers spinning like crazy as they are towed behind boats.

Scooteroo CHOPPER RIDE
(☎4974 7697; www.scooterrootours.com; 21 Bicentennial Dr; 3hr chopper ride $55; pick-up's at around 2.45pm) Back on land, straddle a chopper and cover the back roads around Agnes Water in the coolest way possible. On the 60km tour you ride the mean beast along country back-roads for scenic views of the coast and hinterland, with plenty of kangaroos and wallabies to see. All you need is a car licence as the machines are fully automatic and you don't have to worry about changing gears. Wear long pants and closed-in shoes.

Wyndham Aviation SCENIC FLIGHT
(1¼hr flight per person $85) A flight over the headland in a Skyhawk three-seater Cessna light aircraft with Wyndham Aviation is a popular activity. From your aerial viewpoint you can often spot dolphins and turtles swimming in the water and you get to land on a secluded beach. Book flights through your accommodation.

1770 Larc Tours CRUISE
(☎4974 9422; www.1770larctours.com.au) From the Town of 1770 marina, this outfit runs fun full-day tours in its amphibious vehicles. The tours take in Middle Island, Bustard Head and Eurimbula National Park, and operate Monday, Wednesday and Saturday. It costs $148/88 per adult/child, including lunch. It also runs daily one-hour sunset cruises ($35/16) and sandboarding safaris (Thursday and Sunday, $85 per person). Larc Tours also runs the **MV James Cook** (www.1770jamescook.com.au), a 14m vessel that sleeps up to 10 people for tours of up to seven days.

Lady Musgrave Cruises CRUISE, SNORKELLING
(☎4974 9077; www.1770reefcruises.com; Captain Cook Dr; adult/child $175/85) Excellent day trips to Lady Musgrave Island aboard the *Spirit of 1770*. It takes 1¼ hours to get there and five hours is spent at the island and its stunning blue lagoon. Coral viewing in a semi-submersible, lunch, morning and afternoon tea, snorkelling and fishing gear are provided on the cruises, which depart the Town of 1770 marina every morning at 8am. For an extra cost you can go diving. Island camping transfers are also available for $320 per person.

Sleeping

Agnes Water Beach Caravan Park CARAVAN PARK, CABINS $
(☎4974 9132; www.agneswaterfirstpoint.com.au; Jeffrey Court, Agnes Water; unpowered sites $30, powered sites $35-59, en suite cabins $120-250) This park has tented cabins on stilts that must offer some of the best-value beachfront rooms around. Each cabin comes with its own deck, equipped with gas barbecue. The camp's toilet and shower facilities are clean and new.

Sandcastles 1770 Motel & Resort RESORT $$
(☎4974 9428; www.sandcastles1770.com.au; 1 Grahame Colyer Dr, Agnes Water; motel r from $90,

villas & beach-home apt from $160-650; ❄@≋) Set on 4 hectares of landscaped gardens and subtropical vegetation, Sandcastles has a range of accommodation options from motel-style rooms to luxury beach apartments and villas. The funky one- to four-bedroom Balinese-themed villas are large and airy and open onto a central courtyard, and some have private pools. There's also a popular on-site restaurant, Kahunas, as well as a small cafe open for breakfast and lunch.

Cool Bananas HOSTEL $
(☎4974 7660; www.coolbananas.net.au; 2 Springs Rd, Agnes Water; dm $26; @) This Balinese-themed backpackers has roomy six- and eight-bed dorms, open and airy communal areas, and is only a five-minute walk to the beach and shops. Otherwise, you can laze the day away in a hammock in the tropical gardens.

Backpackers 1770 HOSTEL $
(☎4974 9132; www.the1770backpackers.com; 7 Agnes St, Agnes Water; dm/d $25/55; @) This small backpackers is large on hospitality and friendly staff. A few dorms have en suites, there's no extra charge for linen or cutlery and the toilet paper is two-ply! The hostel is 700m from the beach, close to shops and has plans for expansion.

1770 Southern Cross Tourist Retreat HOSTEL $
(☎4974 7225; www.1770southerncross.com; 2694 Round Hill Rd, Agnes Water; dm/d incl breakfast $25/75, 2-night minimum stay; @≋) More of an ecoresort than a backpackers, this excellent retreat is set on 6.5 hectares of bushland 2.5km out of town. The three- and four-bed dorms are in clean, airy timber cabins (all with en suites). There's an open-air meditation *sala* (where you'll sometimes see visiting Buddhist monks), an ultracool communal chill-out zone, kangaroos on the grounds, and a free shuttle bus to town. Bike hire is free or you can hire a scooter, and you can swim or fish in the lake. Highly recommended.

Mango Tree Motel MOTEL $$
(☎4974 9132; www.mangotreemotel.com; 7 Agnes St, Agnes Water; r from $135; ❄) Only 100m from the beach, this good-value motel offers large self-contained rooms (sleeping up to six) with the option of continental breakfast.

1770 Camping Grounds CARAVAN PARK $
(☎4974 9286; www.1770campinggrounds.com; Captain Cook Dr, Town of 1770; 2-person unpowered/powered sites $33/38) A large but peaceful park with sites right by the beach and plenty of shady trees.

Sovereign Lodge BOUTIQUE HOTEL $$
(☎4974 9257; www.1770sovereignlodge.com; 1 Elliot St, Town of 1770; d $165-280; ❄≋) This lovely boutique accommodation has a range of immaculate self-contained rooms, some with excellent views from its hill-top perch. There's also a Balinese 'body temple' here where, among other offerings, you can be massaged, wrapped in clay, rubbed with hot rocks and scrubbed with salt.

Agnes Water Beach Club APARTMENTS $$
(☎4974 7355; www.agneswaterbeachclub.com.au; 3 Agnes St, Agnes Water; 1-/2-bedroom apt from $145/190; ❄@≋) In a good location close to cafes, restaurants and the beach, these new luxury apartments have modern kitchens, large private balconies and courtyards, and a spa and barbecue area beside the pool.

Beach Shacks APARTMENTS $$
(☎4974 9463; www.1770beachshacks.com; 578 Captain Cook Dr, Town of 1770; d from $178) These delightful self-contained tropical 'shacks' are made of timber, cane and bamboo. They offer grand ocean views and magnificent private accommodation just a minute's walk from the water.

Eating

Tree Bar MODERN AUSTRALIAN $$
(☎4974 7446; 576 Captain Cook Dr, Town of 1770; mains $14-38; ⊙breakfast, lunch & dinner) This little salt-encrusted waterfront diner has plenty of charm and an atmospheric bar. Seafood is its prime offering.

Deck MODERN AUSTRALIAN $$
(☎4974 9157; 584 Captain Cook Drive, Town of 1770; mains $20-30; ⊙dinner Tue-Sun) Locally caught seafood, served inside or alfresco among the palms, is accompanied by delicious sides or nestled in perfectly cooked pasta. Great service and candlelit tables make this a romantic option.

Yok Attack THAI $$
(☎4974 7454; Shop 22, Endeavour Plaza, cnr Captain Cook Dr & Round Hill Rd, Agnes Water; mains $17-25; ⊙lunch & dinner Thu-Tue) This simple Thai restaurant is very popular with the locals and is highly recommended.

Getaway Garden Cafe MODERN AUSTRALIAN $
(☎4974 9232; 303 Bicentennial Drive, Agnes Water; mains $8-27; ⏰breakfast, lunch & dinner Sun-Thu, breakfast & lunch Fri) The airy outdoor cafe serves delectable cakes for afternoon tea and is a short walk from several deserted beaches. It also hosts regular lamb-on-a-spit nights; call ahead to book.

Kahunas Pizza Bar & Grill MODERN AUSTRALIAN $$
(☎4974 9428; 1 Grahame Colyer Dr, Agnes Water; mains $15-38; ⏰dinner) At Sandcastles 1770 Motel & Resort, Kahunas is a popular choice, especially for beer and pizza on a hot night. There's plenty of meat on the char-grill and an excellent seafood plate.

Latino Caffe SANDWICHES $
(☎4974 7000; Endeavour Plaza, Agnes Water; mains $8-13; ⏰breakfast & lunch) Serves wraps, salads, open grills and sandwiches.

Agnes Water Tavern PUB FARE $$
(☎4974 9469; 1 Tavern Rd, Agnes Water; mains $22-28; ⏰lunch & dinner) The large bistro in the tavern offers massive steaks and classic seafood baskets without much atmosphere, but the shaded outdoor dining area is quite nice and the bar is a good place to meet the locals.

Information

Agnes Water Library (☎4902 1501; Rural Transaction Centre, 3 Captain Cook Rd; ⏰9am-4.30pm Mon-Fri) Next door to the visitor centre, the library has free internet access – half an hour, booked in advance. Both the library and the visitor centre are due to move some time in 2011 – check at the next door service station for their new address.

Agnes Water Visitor Centre (☎4902 1533; Rural Transaction Centre, 3 Captain Cook Rd; ⏰8.30am-5pm Mon-Fri, 9am-5pm Sat & Sun) Opposite Endeavour Plaza.

Hub Café Centre (☎4974 7460; Endeavour Plaza, cnr Round Hill Rd & Captain Cook Dr, Agnes Water) Serves some of the best coffee in town, with half an hour's worth of internet thrown in for free (otherwise, $5 an hour).

Getting There & Away

Bus

Only one of several daily **Greyhound Australia** (☎13 20 30; www.greyhound.com.au) buses detours off the Bruce Hwy to Agnes Water; the direct bus from Bundaberg ($24, 1½ hours) arrives opposite Cool Bananas at 6.10pm. Others, including **Premier Motor Service** (☎13 34 10; www.premierms.com.au), drop passengers at Fingerboard Rd.

Eurimbula & Deepwater National Parks

South of Agnes Water is Deepwater National Park, an unspoiled coastal landscape with long sandy beaches, freshwater creeks, good fishing spots and two camping grounds. It's also a major breeding ground for loggerhead turtles, which dig nests and lay eggs on the beaches between November and February. You can watch the turtles laying and see hatchlings emerging at night between January and April, but you need to observe various precautions outlined in the DERM park brochure (obtainable at the office in Town of 1770).

The northern park entrance is 8km south of Agnes Water and is only accessible by 4WD. It's another 5km to the basic camping ground at Middle Rock (no facilities) and a further 2km to the Wreck Rock camping ground and picnic areas, with rain and bore water and composting toilets. Wreck Point can also be accessed from the south by 2WD vehicles via Baffle Creek.

The 78-sq-km Eurimbula National Park, on the northern side of Round Hill Creek, has a landscape of dunes, mangroves and eucalypt forest. There are two basic camping grounds, one at Middle Creek with toilets only and the other at Bustard Beach with toilets and limited rainwater. The main access road to the park is about 10km southwest of Agnes Water.

Middle Rock in Deepwater and Middle Creek in Eurimbula have self-registration stands but you must obtain permits for the other camping grounds from the **DERM** (☎13 74 68; www.qld.gov.au/camping).

CAPRICORN HINTERLAND

Aboriginal rock art, spectacular sandstone cliffs, deep gorges and precious gemstones are just some of the surprises to be found in the dry Central Highlands west of Rockhampton.

The area was first settled by miners chasing gold and copper around Emerald and sapphires around Anakie, but coal, cattle and grain are its lifeblood today. The national parks of Carnarvon, south of Emerald, and the Blackdown Tableland, southeast of the coal-mining centre of Blackwater, are rugged sandstone escarpments with breathtaking vistas and ancient Aboriginal rock art.

The Capricorn Hwy (A4) runs inland from Rockhampton, virtually along the tropic to Emerald, where rock-hounds will want to try their luck fossicking for sapphires and rubies in the world's richest sapphire fields.

Blackdown Tableland National Park

The Blackdown Tableland is an amazing sandstone plateau that rises out of the flat plains to a height of 600m. It features stunning panoramas, great bushwalks, waterfalls, Aboriginal rock art and eucalypt forests. There's also a good camping ground here.

The park is 150km west of Rockhampton. The turn-off to the park is signposted off the Capricorn Hwy, 11km west of Dingo and 35km east of Blackwater. From here, it's 23km to the top, the last 8km of which are steep, winding and often slippery. Caravans are not recommended.

At the top you come to the breathtaking **Horseshoe Lookout**, with picnic tables, barbecues and toilets. There's a walking trail starting here to **Two Mile Falls** (2km).

Munall Campground (☎13 74 68; www.qld.gov.au/camping; per person/family $4.50/18) is about 8km on from Horseshoe Lookout. It has pit toilets and fireplaces but you'll need to bring drinking water, firewood and/or a fuel stove. Several walking trails start from the campground. You must have a permit to camp and the campsite must be prebooked.

Not far from the turnoff to the park is Blackwater, where the **Blackwater International Coal Centre** (☎4982 7755; www.bicc.com.au; tours per adult/child/family $18/10/50 ⏲9am-5pm) showcases the booming Australian coal industry via an interpretive centre and tours of the working coal mine.

Emerald

POP 11,000

Sitting on the edge of the Gemfields, Emerald is not, as you would expect, a fossicking ground for the precious green gemstones. Instead its name comes from Emerald Creek, in turn named after a local prospector, Jack Emerald. Once little more than a railway siding, the town has grown into a major centre for the surrounding mining and agricultural industries. As well as cattle, the rich soil supports sunflowers, citrus trees, grapes and cotton.

A series of destructive fires between 1936 and 1968 destroyed many of Emerald's century-old buildings and rebuilding has given the town a relatively modern, but not terribly aesthetic, appearance. One exception is the restored 1900 Emerald Railway Station in the centre of town.

Sights & Activities

The town's sights are quite limited but you cannot miss the world's largest replica of **van Gogh's Sunflowers** (Moreton Park, Dundas St), which is positioned on a 25-metre easel next to the visitor centre. The painting celebrates the Central Highlands' reputation as a major sunflower producer.

Also near the visitor centre, **Emerald Pioneer Cottage & Museum** (☎4982 1050; 3 Clermont St; ⏲2-4pm Mon-Fri Apr-Oct) has a collection of historic buildings including the town's first church and jail.

Outside the Town Hall in Egerton St is a section of **fossilised tree** estimated to be 250 million years old.

The living vegetation isn't quite that ancient at the **Emerald Botanic Gardens** (☎4982 8333; Capricorn Hwy), on the banks of the Nogoa River. Six kilometres of walking tracks weave through 12 themed gardens, a bush chapel and 10 Federation Pillars (depicting Australian identity since Federation). As the only botanic gardens in the central western district of Queensland, this is one of the few green, shady and pleasant spots for a picnic lunch.

Waterholes and billabongs are always a welcome sight in the dry lands of central Queensland. About 18km southwest of Emerald you can water-ski, fish for barra, and try your hand at crayfishing (the lake is stocked with the famous red-claw crayfish) in Queensland's second-largest artificial lake, **Lake Maraboon**. As well as a boat ramp and attractive picnic areas, there's also a holiday village here.

Sleeping & Eating

There are plenty of motels to choose from in Emerald.

Route 66 MOTEL **$$**

(☎4987 7755; www.route66motorinn.com.au; 2 Opal St; r from $145; ❄@☒) Just metres from the riverside botanic gardens, this new motel has comfortable suites, movies on demand, a licensed restaurant – the works. It's an easy walk to the main street and the train station.

Lake Maraboon Holiday Village CARAVAN PARK, CABINS $

(☎4982 3677; www.discoveryholidayparks.com.au; Fairbairn Dam Access Rd; unpowered & powered sites $30, cabins $100-200; ❄✉) Overlooking Lake Maraboon, this large park has a kiosk and a fully licensed restaurant (open Wednesday to Sunday). You can also hire a boat for a spot of fishing.

Emerald Cabin & Caravan Village CARAVAN PARK, CABINS $

(☎4982 1300; fax 4987 5320; 64 Opal St; 2-person unpowered/powered sites $25/30, cabins $90; ❄) Closer to town, this is a large park only a pitching wedge from the golf course and a short stroll to the public pool. It has rows of neat cabins, immaculate amenities and a shaded camping area with a camp kitchen and barbecue.

Pritchard Road Country Resort RESORT $

(☎4982 1707; motel707@bigpond.com; 17 Ruby St; r incl breakfast with/without ensuite $85/60; ❄✉) A decent budget option, this friendly place just out of the town centre caters mostly to miners. There's a $20 roast served nightly.

Crepe & Coffee Club MODERN AUSTRALIAN $

(☎4987 7017; Briel St; dishes $12-16; ⏲breakfast & lunch) This welcoming cafe is set in the courtyard of a plant and flower shop, and is a pleasant place to enjoy crepes, salads, sandwiches and burgers. The coffees are huge – and pricey.

Information

Central Highlands Visitor Centre (☎4982 4142; Clermont St; ⏲9am-5pm Mon-Sat, 10am-2pm Sun) Located in Morton Park, has information on the Gemfields and Carnarvon National Park.

Library (☎4982 8347; 44 Borilla St; ⏲noon-5.30pm Mon, 10am-5.30pm Tue, Thu & Fri, 10am-8pm Wed, 9am-noon Sat) For free internet access, prebook a computer at the library.

Getting There & Away

Emerald lies on the Capricorn Hwy 260km west of Rockhampton. Without a car it's difficult to travel to and around Emerald, the Gemfields and the Central Highlands. **Paradise Coaches** (☎4933 1127) has a daily run to/from Rockhampton ($48, four hours) and Mackay. Paradise also has a twice-weekly run to Longreach.

The *Spirit of the Outback* train stops in Emerald on its Rocky-to-Longreach run every Tuesday and Saturday, and again on the return trip on Monday and Thursday. The Rockhampton-to-Emerald leg costs $94 and takes five hours. The Emerald-to-Longreach leg costs $97.90 and takes nine hours.

Qantaslink (☎13 13 13; www.qantas.com.au) flies between Brisbane and Emerald several times a day.

Gemfields

The richest sapphire fields in the world cover 900 sq km of the hot, dry, scrubby plains a short drive west of Emerald. In the small, ramshackle Gemfield townships of Anakie, Sapphire, Rubyvale and Willows, you'll hear tall tales and true of incredible finds of rubies, zircons and sapphires worth squillions. The famous 'Black Star of Queensland', an 1165-carat blue sapphire worth a cool $90 million was found here by a 14-year-old boy in 1930. Legend has it the boy's father, thinking the gemstone was a worthless black crystal, used it as a doorstop for many years until its real worth was discovered. If you can stand the flies, heat and dust, you can try your hand at fossicking for the next big one – or at least unearth a likely doorstop.

To go fossicking you need a **licence** (adult/family $5.80/8.20) from the Emerald Courthouse or one of the Gemfields' general stores or post offices. You can obtain camping permits from the same places, which allow you to pitch a tent anywhere in the fields. Basic fossicking equipment includes sieves, a pick and shovel, water and a container. You can bring this with you or hire it when you arrive.

Fossicking is hard work and an easier alternative is to buy a bucket of 'wash' (mine dirt in water) from one of the fossicking parks to hand-sieve and wash. Otherwise you can just go 'specking', searching for stones sparkling on the surface, a good idea after heavy rains.

The most popular times to visit are the drier, cooler months from April to September.

Sights & Activities

Unsurprisingly, the only activity in the Gemfields is, well, looking for gems.

Miners Heritage Walk-in Mine MINE

(☎4985 4444; Heritage Rd; adult/child $12.50/5; ⏲9am-5pm) About 2km north of Rubyvale, the excellent walk-in mine has informative 30-minute underground tours throughout the day during which you descend into a maze of tunnels 18m beneath the surface. Then you can try your luck with a bucket of wash.

Fascination FOSSICKING
(☎4985 4675; 72 Keilambete Rd, Rubyvale; per couple $75) Conducts day-long, self-drive fossicking tours which include licences, equipment and guiding. You supply your own transport, food and drink.

Pat's Gems FOSSICKING
(☎4985 4544; www.patsgems.com.au; 1056 Rubyvale Rd, Sapphire; ⏲8.30am-5pm) Located 1km north of Sapphire, Pat's Gems has buckets of dirt for $8 each or six buckets for $40. It also has fossicking gear available for hire. There's a pleasant cafe here and accommodation as well.

Festivals & Events

In the second week in August, Anakie hosts the annual **Gemfest Festival of Gems** (www.gemfest.com.au), featuring exhibitions and sales of gems, jewellery, mining and fossicking equipment, art and craft markets, and entertainment.

Sleeping & Eating

Pat's Gems CABINS $
(☎4985 4544; www.patsgems.com.au; 1056 Rubyvale Rd; cabins $75; ❄) Bunk down in one of four newly furnished cabins after rummaging through the wash on-site. The cabins are small but cosy and have polished wood floors, and you can use the camp barbecue and kitchen area. The **Scrub Blush Café** (⏲ 8.30am-5pm) at Pat's Gems dishes up sandwiches, burgers, cake and coffee, and you can eat alfresco under the shade.

Rubyvale Gem Gallery APARTMENTS $$
(☎4985 4388; www.rubyvalegemgallery.com; 7 Keilambete Rd, Rubyvale; apt from $125; ❄) The couple who run this gallery cut and set their gems on the premises. You can watch jewellers at work and can arrange group tours to their underground mine. The accommodation, in the centre of Rubyvale, is comfortable.

Gemseekers Caravan Park CARAVAN PARK, CABINS $
(☎4985 4175; www.gemseekers.com.au; 10 Vane Tempest Rd, Rubyvale; 2-person unpowered/powered sites $22/24, d cabins from $100; ❄@) There are some excellent campsites amid the attractive lawns and gardens here, as well as barbecues and a camp kitchen. There are also self-contained cabins with facilities for travellers with disabilities.

Ramboda Homestead B&B $$
(☎4985 4154; ramboda@bigpond.com; Capricorn Hwy, Anakie; s/d incl breakfast $70/100) Just east of Anakie, this is an attractive old timber homestead on a working cattle property. The B&B has country-style bedrooms with shared bathrooms, and dinners can be organised by prior arrangement.

Rubyvale Holiday Units MOTEL, APARTMENTS $
(☎4985 4518; www.rubyvaleholiday.com.au; 35 Heritage Rd, Rubyvale; d motel $90, 1-/2-bedroom apt $115/150; ❄≋) Spacious motel and self-contained units, about 1km north of Rubyvale. The friendly owners are experienced miners and gem cutters. They have a small gem shop and provide a gem-cutting service.

New Royal Hotel HOTEL, CABINS $$
(☎4985 4754; 2 Keilambete Rd, Rubyvale; d $110, extra person $15; ❄) The attractive New Royal has four cosy, self-contained log cabins (with open fires) in keeping with the theme of the pub. Good counter lunches and dinners are served daily, with the usual fare of steak, chicken and pasta.

Sapphire Caravan Park CARAVAN PARK, CABINS $
(☎4985 4281; www.sapphirecaravanpark.com.au; 57 Sunrise Rd, Sapphire; 2-person unpowered/powered sites $20/25, cabins $60-130) In an attractive bush setting near Sapphire, these cabins are built from 'billy boulders', the smooth, round stones common to the area. They're simple and rustic but comfortable. There are good communal amenities, barbecues and a large camp kitchen with fridge and freezer.

Information

The Gemfields townships are little more than a cluster of streets, houses, general stores and service stations.

In Anakie, 42km west of Emerald on the Capricorn Hwy, the **Big Sapphire Gemfields Visitor Centre** (☎4985 4525; www.bigsapphire.com.au; 1 Anakie Rd; ⏲8am-6pm) has information, maps and fossicking licences, and hires out fossicking equipment.

In Sapphire, 10km north of Anakie, the **Sapphire Trading Post** (☎4985 4179; 2 Centenary Dr) also has fossicking and camping licences, camping and mining supplies, as well as food, fuel and gas.

A further 8km north is Rubyvale, the main town of the Gemfields. Willows is 38km southwest of Anakie.

Getting There & Away

Without a car it's difficult to get to or around the Gemfields as there are no regular bus services. But **Paradise Coaches** (☎4933 1127) will do drop-offs at Anakie on its twice-weekly run between Rockhampton and Longreach ($14, 35 minutes). You can also arrive by train on the twice-weekly *Spirit of the Outback* service ($12.10, one hour 20 minutes).

Springsure

POP 1150

Springsure, located 66km south of Emerald, has a striking backdrop of sunflower fields and granite mountains. An outcrop of Mt Zamia, part of the escarpment overlooking the town, was named the Virgin Rock by early settlers who claimed to have seen an image of the Virgin Mary in the rock face. Although erosion and weathering have taken their toll on the rocky vision, with a bit of imagination (helped along with a few rums) you might have a spiritual experience.

About 10km southwest of Springsure is the **Old Rainworth Fort** (☎4984 1674; off Wealwandangie Rd; adult/child $7/3; ⏲9am-2pm Fri-Wed Mar-Nov), built by settlers following the Wills Massacre of 1861 when 19 settlers were killed in a conflict with Aborigines on Cullin-La-Ringo Station northwest of Springsure.

You'll most likely spend the night at Emerald or at Carnarvon National Park, but if you find yourself in Springsure at bedtime, you could do worse than the **Queen's Arms Hotel** (☎4984 1533; www.queensarmshotel.com.au; 14 Charles St; s/d $66/88; ❄). This old pub on the highway that skirts the town has modern, comfortable rooms and shared facilities. Otherwise, you can choose from a couple of budget motels and the **Springsure Roadhouse & Caravan Park** (☎4984 1418; fax 4984 1418; 86 William St; 2-person unpowered/powered sites $15/25).

Heading 70km southeast of Springsure you'll reach the tiny township of Rolleston, your last source of fuel and supplies before turning off for Carnarvon National Park. If you stay on the Dawson Hwy, you reach Biloela after another 212km.

Carnarvon National Park

The rugged Carnarvon National Park, in the middle of the Great Dividing Range, features dramatic sandstone-gorge scenery and magnificent Aboriginal rock paintings and carvings. The 298,000-hectare national park, located 250km south of Emerald, is where you'll find the impressive Carnarvon Gorge and the less accessible sections of Mt Moffatt, Ka Ka Mundi and Salvator Rosa.

Dangers & Annoyances

The best time to visit the national park is during the dry, cooler months from April to October but be prepared for hot days and cold nights (temperatures can fall below freezing). Unsealed roads can become impassable in heavy rains.

Be aware there is no fuel at Carnarvon. Fuel up at either Rolleston (the northern access point) or Injune (the southern access point).

There is no mobile phone coverage in this area but emergency calls can be made by dialling ☎112.

Sights & Activities

Carnarvon Gorge NATIONAL PARK

Carved by water running through soft sandstone, Carnarvon Gorge is an amazing oasis of deep pools, river oaks, flooded gums, and delicate ferns and mosses, snaking through 30km of semiarid terrain. The towering 200m-high cliffs change colour throughout the day and seasons.

Situated about 3km into the Carnarvon Gorge section of the park, there's a **visitor centre** (☎4984 4505; ⏲8-10am & 3-5pm) and a scenic picnic and camping ground. The main walking track starts beside the visitor centre and follows Carnarvon Creek through the gorge. Detours lead to various points of interest, such as the **Moss Garden** (3.6km), **Ward's Canyon** (4.8km), the **Art Gallery** (5.6km) and **Cathedral Cave** (9.3km).

Allow *at least* a whole day for a visit. Basic groceries and ice are available at Takarakka Bush Resort.

Mt Moffatt NATIONAL PARK

The more westerly, rugged Mt Moffatt section of the park has some beautiful scenery and diverse vegetation and fauna, and **Kenniff Cave**, which is an important Aboriginal archaeological site with stencil paintings on the rock walls. It's believed Aborigines lived here as long as 19,000 years ago.

EXPLORING CARNARVON GORGE'S TRAILS & ROCK ART

Over millions of years, Carnarvon Creek and its tributaries have carved 30km of twisting gorges and waterfalls through the soft sedimentary rock of stunning Carnarvon Gorge. Massive, crumbling, yellow-white sandstone cliffs up to 200m high conceal a 'lost world' of giant cycads, cool moss gardens, king ferns and rare palms. Some 21km of well-maintained walking trails allow access to the gorge's majestic scenery, wildlife and poignant Aboriginal art, offering several days' worth of rewarding exploration.

The 2km **nature trail** is an easy stroll starting at the visitor centre, best done in the early morning when platypuses can be glimpsed where the trail crosses Carnarvon Creek. For a more energetic start to the day, head up to **Boolimba Bluff** (6.5km return) for a magnificent view of the cliffs. For longer walks, start early and be aware of the hot midafternoon temperatures and the possibility of violent afternoon storms in summer. The many side trails to narrow tributary gorges, waterfalls and art sites should not be missed. If you have the gear, camp at **Big Bend** camping ground so you can spend more time exploring.

The permanent creek in the gorge supports abundant wildlife, including platypuses, gliders, eastern grey kangaroos and smaller macropods, as well as a multitude of brightly coloured birds. If one plant epitomises Carnarvon's 'lost world' feel, it is the prehistoric-looking zamia cycad, *Macrozamia moorei,* which can grow for over 400 years. After developing a method to neutralise its toxins, the local Aborigines made this cone a staple of their diet.

Vivid reminders of the rich Indigenous culture of the gorge can be found in the remarkable rock engravings, freehand drawings and mouth-sprayed stencils of the gorge's caves. The **Art Gallery** features more than 2000 stencils, paintings and engravings along 62m of rock wall. It is one of the finest examples of stencil art in Australia, showing boomerangs, axes, arms and hands. The **Cathedral Cave**, near Big Bend camping ground, is an enormous rock shelter with numerous stencils and an intriguing figure painting. Smaller **Baloon Cave**, which also features stencilling, can be reached from a car park east of the visitor centre.

Tours

Sunrover Expeditions CAVES

(☎1800 353 717; www.sunrover.com.au; per person incl meals $940) Runs a five-day camping safari into Carnarvon Gorge between March and October. Or you can choose to stay at the Takarakka Bush Resort ($1200) or the Wilderness Lodge ($1600).

Carnarvon Gorge Tours CAVES

(☎4984 4529; www.ausnatureguides.com; from $20) Run by knowledgeable local Simon Ling. As well as giving afternoon talks on the geology, biology and anthropological history of the gorge (around twilight at Takarakka's firepit), he takes evening spotlighting tours where you'll see gliders swooshing from tree to tree along with many other nocturnal creatures that call the gorge home.

Sleeping & Eating

Carnarvon Gorge Visitor Area & Big Bend Camping Ground CAMPGROUND $

(☎13 74 68; www.qld.gov.au/camping; sites per adult/family $4.50/18) The area around the visitor centre is open to camping only during the Easter, June–July and September–October school holidays; bookings are essential. The isolated Big Bend camping ground is a 10km walk up the gorge, about 500m upstream from Cathedral Cave. It is open all year and campers require permits and bookings. There are toilets here but no showers and fires are not permitted so you will need a fuel stove.

Mt Moffatt Camping Ground CAMPGROUND $

(☎13 74 68; www.qld.gov.au/camping; sites per adult/family $4.50/18) In the Mt Moffatt section of the national park, camping with a permit is allowed at four sites, but you need to be completely self-sufficient and a 4WD and extra fuel are advisable. Bookings are essential and can be made online.

Takarakka Bush Resort CARAVAN PARK, CABINS $

(☎4984 4535; www.takarakka.com.au; Wyseby Rd; unpowered sites $28-34, powered sites $34-41, cabins $95-220) About 5km from the picnic ground, Takarakka is a picturesque bush oasis with a big open camping area and a ring of simply furnished, elevated canvas cabins (BYO linen) with private verandahs. There's a large camp kitchen and dining area (BYO cutlery and plates), barbecues and hot showers. The reception sells drinks, groceries, ice and gas. The resort also runs guided tours (check with reception for details).

Carnarvon Gorge Wilderness Lodge LODGE **$$**

(☎1800 644 150, 4984 4503; www.carnarvon-gorge.com; Wyseby Rd; per person from $150; ⊙closed Dec-Feb; ☒) This upmarket safari-style accommodation, located near the park entrance, offers attractive cabins nestled in the bush. You have the option of a full-board package (per person from $155 to $300), and there is an on-site restaurant and bar. Guided tours and walks are also available.

ℹ Getting There & Away

There is no bus service to Carnarvon, so unless you're on a tour you'll need your own transport.

Rolleston, 136km southeast of Emerald on the Dawson Hwy, is the northern access point. From Rolleston to Carnarvon Gorge the road is bitumen for 70km then unsealed for 25km. The unsealed section of road is suitable for conventional vehicles and caravans in dry weather but can become impassable after heavy rain.

Injune, 90km north of Roma, is the southern access point. From Injune and Wyseby, the road is bitumen all the way.

To get into the Mt Moffatt section of the park, there are two roads from Injune: one through Womblebank Station (mostly unsealed), the other via Westgrove Station (all unsealed). There are no through roads from Mt Moffatt to Carnarvon Gorge or the park's other remote sections.

Whitsunday Coast

Includes »

Mackay 227
Eungella 234
Brampton Island 236
Cape Hillsborough National Park 238
The Whitsundays ... 238
Airlie Beach 243
Daydream Island ... 252
South Molle Island .. 253
Hamilton Island 254
Hayman Island 256
Lindeman Island 257
Whitsunday Island .. 258
Bowen 259

Best Places to Eat

» Bommie Restaurant (p255)

» Alain's Restaurant (p248)

» Fish D'vine (p248)

Best Places to Stay

» Qualia (p254)

» Paradise Bay (p251)

» Hayman Island Resort (p256)

» Platypus Bushcamp (p236)

» Water's Edge Resort (p246)

Why Go?

In the calm waters of the Coral Sea, the beautiful Whitsunday Islands are one of Australia's greatest natural tourist attractions. Opal-jade waters and white sandy beaches fringe the forested domes of these 'drowned' mountains where you can camp in secluded bays as a modern-day castaway, laze in a tropical island resort, snorkel, dive, or set sail and island-hop through this stunning archipelago. Beneath the shimmering seas are swarms of tropical fish and the world's largest coral garden in the Great Barrier Reef Marine Park. The gateway to the islands, Airlie Beach, is a vibrant backpacker hub with a continual parade of changing faces and a throbbing nightlife. Further north lie the unspoilt coastal gems of Hydeaway Bay and Cape Gloucester.

South of Airlie, and overlooking a sea of sugar cane, Mackay is a typical Queensland coastal town with palm-lined streets. There's not much to do here but it's a handy base for trips to Finch Hatton Gorge and Eungella National Park – lush hinterland oases where platypuses play in the wild.

When to Go

Mackay

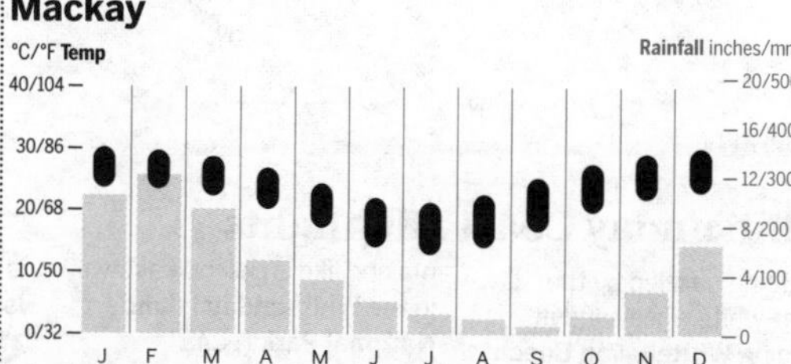

June–October The perfect time to enjoy sunny skies, calm days, mild weather and stinger-free seas.

August Boats skim across the water, and parties spill into the street during Airlie Beach Race Week.

September–October Optimal conditions for kayaking around the islands.

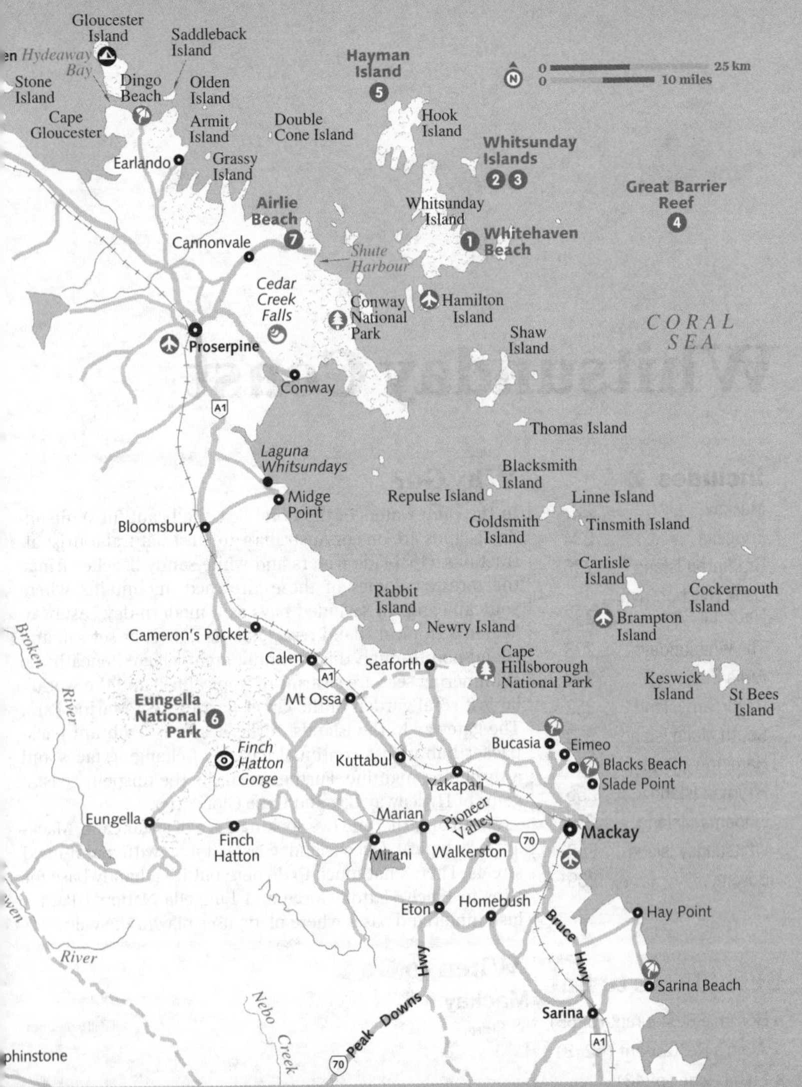

Whitsunday Coast Highlights

1 Being dazzled by the bright-white silica sand at stunning **Whitehaven Beach** (p258)

2 Sailing through the magnificent aquamarine waters of the **Whitsunday Islands** (p239)

3 Camping under the stars, hiking nature trails, and making like an island castaway in the **Whitsunday Islands National Park** (p242)

4 Diving and snorkelling the island's fringing reefs or the outer **Great Barrier Reef** (p239)

5 Sipping cocktails by the pool at the luxurious tropical island resort of **Hayman Island** (p256)

6 Waiting patiently for a glimpse of a shy platypus and walking in the misty rainforest at **Eungella National Park** (p235)

7 Getting wet, swilling beer and partying hard in fun-lovin' **Airlie Beach** (p243)

Getting There & Around

AIR

Mackay airport (www.mackayairport.com.au) is a major domestic hub, and **Qantas** (☎13 13 13; www.qantas.com), **Jetstar** (☎13 15 38; www.jetstar.com.au) and **Virgin Blue** (☎13 67 89; www.virginblue.com.au) have regular flights to/from the major centres, while **Tiger Airways** (☎03-9335 3033; www.tigerairways.com.au) flies to Mackay from Melbourne.

If you're heading for the Whitsundays, Qantas, Jetstar and Virgin Blue have frequent flights to Hamilton Island, where there are boat/air transfers to all the other islands. You can also fly into Proserpine (aka Whitsunday Coast) on the mainland. From there you can take a charter flight to the islands, or a bus to Airlie Beach or nearby Shute Harbour.

There's also the Whitsunday airport, a small airfield near Airlie Beach, with regular services to the islands.

BOAT

Airlie Beach and Shute Harbour are the main launching pads for boat trips to the Whitsundays; see p243 for details.

BUS

Greyhound Australia (☎1300 473 946; www.greyhound.com.au) and **Premier Motor Service** (☎13 34 10; www.premierms.com.au) operate regular coach services along the Bruce Hwy (A1) with stops at all the major towns. They also detour off the highway from Proserpine to Airlie Beach.

TRAIN

Queensland Rail (☎13 22 32, 1300 131 7 22; www.queenslandrail.com.au) has frequent services between Brisbane and Townsville/Cairns passing through the region. Choose between the high-speed *Tilt Train* or the more sedate *Sunlander*. For details see the Getting There & Away sections of the relevant towns and cities.

Mackay

☎07 / POP 66,880

An attractive town with palm-lined streets and art deco buildings, Mackay doesn't quite make the tourist hit-list. Instead, this big country coastal town caters more to the surrounding agricultural and mining industries. Although the redeveloped marina tries to entice with alfresco restaurants and outdoor cafes along its picturesque promenade, Mackay is more a convenient base for excursions out of town. It's only a 1½-hour drive to the Whitsundays, a short flight to pretty Brampton Island, and a scenic drive among the sugar-cane fields to Pioneer Valley and Eungella National Park.

Sights & Activities

Mackay's impressive **art deco architecture** owes much to a devastating cyclone in 1918, which flattened many of the town's buildings. Enthusiasts should pick up a copy of *Art Deco Mackay* from the Town Hall Visitor Information Centre (p231). History buffs should also grab the brochure *A Heritage Walk in Mackay,* which guides you around 20 of the town's historic sites.

There are good views over the harbour from **Mt Basset Lookout** and at **Rotary Lookout** in North Mackay.

Artspace Mackay ART GALLERY
(Map p228; www.artspacemackay.com.au; Gordon St; admission free; ⏲10am-5pm Tue-Sun) Mackay's small regional art gallery showcases works from local and visiting artists. Browse the extensive collection of art books and art before grazing at **Foodspace** (⏲9am-3pm Tue-Sun), the in-house licensed cafe.

Mackay Regional Botanic Gardens GARDEN
(Lagoon St; admission free) Covering 33 hectares, 3km south of the city centre, this is an impressive 'work in progress'. There are several themed gardens, including a **tropical shade garden** (⏲8.45am-4.45pm).

Bluewater Lagoon SWIMMING
(Map p228; admission free; ⏲9am-5.45pm) With marine stingers plying the ocean waters during the summer, Mackay has followed in the footsteps of Airlie Beach and Cairns by creating a designated safe swimming area. The pleasant man-made lagoon near Caneland Shopping Centre has fountains, waterslides, grassed picnic areas and a cafe.

Mackay Marina MARINA
(Mackay Harbour) The lively marina is a thriving precinct where locals rub shoulders with inquisitive tourists. It's a pleasant place to wine and dine with a waterfront view, or to simply picnic in the park and stroll along the breakwater.

Stoney Creek Farm Stay HORSE RIDING
(☎4954 1177; www.stoneycreekfarmstay.com; Peak Downs Hwy) This popular horse-riding centre offers three-hour trail rides for $85. Rides pass through picturesque, undulating bush. The three-day all-inclusive trail ride ($290) is particularly recommended. Stoney Creek is 28km southwest of Mackay, and it's accessible by bus; call ahead for directions.

Central Mackay

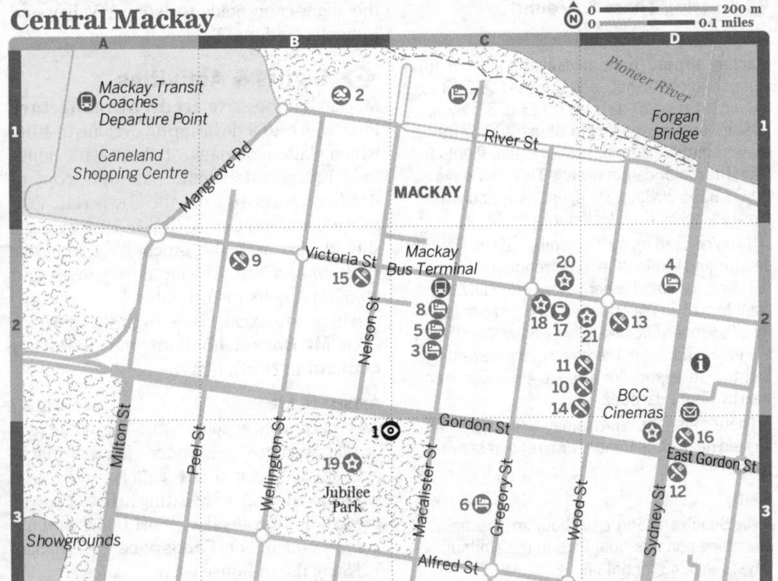

Central Mackay

Sights

1 Artspace Mackay B3

Activities, Courses & Tours

2 Bluewater Lagoon B1

Sleeping

3 Coral Sands Motel C2
4 Gecko's Rest D2
5 International Lodge Motel C2
6 Mackay Grande Suites C3
7 Mid City Motor Inn C1
8 Quest C2

Eating

9 Austral Hotel B2
10 Burp Eat Drink D2
11 Cafe La De Da D2
12 Fish D'vine D3
Foodspace .... (see 1)
Hot Wok .... (see 3)
13 Kevin's Place D2
14 Montezuma's C2
15 Nelsons Seafood Café B2
16 Oscar's on Sydney D3

Drinking

17 Gordi's Café & Bar C2

Entertainment

18 Code C2
19 Mackay Entertainment & Convention Centre B3
20 Mainstreet C2
21 Platinum Lounge D2

Beaches & Swimming

Mackay has plenty of beaches, although not all of them are ideal for swimming. The best ones are about 16km north of Mackay at Blacks Beach, Eimeo and Bucasia (p233).

Town Beach is the closest to the city centre; to get there, follow Gordon St all the way east from the centre. There is a sandy strip, but the water is very shallow and subsides a long way out at low tide, leaving a long stretch of mudflats. **Illawong Beach**, 2km further south, is a more attractive proposition. A better option is **Harbour Beach**, 6km north of the centre and just south of the Mackay Marina. The beach here is patrolled and there's a foreshore reserve with picnic tables and barbecues.

Tours

Farleigh Sugar Mill INDUSTRIAL TOUR
(☎4959 8360; adult/child/family $22/12/59; 2hr tours 9am, 11am, 1pm Jun-Nov) In the cane-crushing season you can see how the sweet crystals are made. Learn all about the history, production and technology, but dress prepared for a working mill, which means long sleeves, long pants and enclosed shoes. The mill is 10km northwest of Mackay.

Jungle Johno Eco Tours SCENIC TOUR
(☎4944 1230; tours $75) The elusive platypus is the Holy Grail of this expedition. You'll be taken deep into the national park to spot these shy, amphibious creatures in their natural habitat. You'll also get to swim under crystal-clear waterfalls and see other wildlife such as kingfishers, turtles and water dragons. The seven-hour day trips, operating from Gecko's Rest (p230), include Finch Hatton Gorge and are a good way to see the best bits of Eungella and surrounds in one day.

Reeforest Adventure Tours SCENIC TOUR
(☎1800 500 353, 4959 8360; www.reeforest.com) The day-long Platypus & Rainforest Eco Safari ($145 per person) explores Finch Hatton Gorge and visits the platypuses of Broken River. It includes lunch at a secluded bush retreat near the gorge and an interpretive walk. The tour also departs from Airlie Beach ($145). Another option is a day tour to Cape Hillsborough ($145), which features Aboriginal middens, stone fish-traps and a bush-tucker trail.

Tiger Moth SCENIC FLIGHT
(☎4998 5677; www.mackaytiger.com.au) For a scenic view of the coast and cane-fields, take to the skies in a yellow 1943 De Havilland Tiger Moth.

Festivals & Events

Each year around May the **Wintermoon Folk Festival** (☎4958 8390; www.wintermoonfestival.com; day tickets adult/child $60/free) is held at Camerons Pocket, 70km north of Mackay. This is a great opportunity to hear local and interstate musicians fiddle, strum and sing their stuff. Most people make a weekend of it and camp near the festival grounds (additional cost). Discounted prepaid tickets can be bought from the **Mackay Entertainment & Convention Centre** (MECC; ☎4961 9777; www.mackayecc.com.au; Alfred St), or you can buy tickets at the festival.

Sleeping

Getting a bed in Mackay isn't easy. The city's accommodation can often be booked solid with mineworkers enjoying some time off. There are oodles of budget and midrange motels strung along busy Nebo Rd south of the centre. The budget options (around $75 a double) post their prices out the front.

Clarion Hotel Mackay Marina HOTEL $$$
(☎4955 9400; www.mackaymarinahotel.com; Mulherin Dr, Mackay Harbour; d $245-445; ❄@📶🏊) The Clarion is the darling of the marina precinct and it's not hard to see why. All rooms have spacious showers and balconies and all the mod cons you'd expect of a hotel of international standing. Couples should try the Pamper Package ($455), which includes accommodation in a spa suite, sparkling wine and chocolates, a 30-minute massage, a hot breakfast and noon checkout. You may not want to leave your room.

Coral Sands Motel MOTEL $$
(☎4951 1244; www.coralsandsmotel.com.au; 44 Macalister St; s/d $110/120; ❄📶🏊) One of the better midrange options in Mackay, the Coral Sands boasts ultrafriendly management and large rooms in a central location. The pool looks like it has seen better days, but with the river, shops, pubs and cafes so close to your doorstep, you won't care.

Ocean Resort Village RESORT $$
(☎1800 075 144, 4951 3200; www.oceanresortvillage.com.au; 5 Bridge Rd, Illawong Beach; apt $95-105, 2-bedroom apt $140; ❄🏊) This is a good-value beachside resort comprising 34 self-contained apartments (studio, and one- and two-bedroom) set amid lush, tropical gardens. It features two pools, barbecue areas and half-court tennis.

Quest APARTMENTS $$$
(☎4829 3500; www.questmackay.com.au; 38 Macalister St; studios $168, 1-/2-bedroom apts from $198/280; ❄@🏊) The ideal choice for comfort; choose from modern, spacious apartments with full kitchen facilities or huge studios with a kitchenette. There's classy decor and grand views over the city.

Mackay Grande Suites HOTEL $$$
(☎4969 1000; www.mackaygrandesuites.com.au; 9 Gregory St; r $205, 1-bedroom from $245; ❄@🏊) Mackay's long-awaited addition to the top end of the scale in the city centre doesn't

disappoint with its stylish decor and modern amenities. Splash out and try the spa suite ($310 to $390) with its huge plasma TV and balcony with panoramic vistas.

International Lodge Motel MOTEL $$
(☎4951 1022; internationallodge@bigpond.com; 40 Macalister St; r from $105;) Behind the unimpressive facade are clean, bright and cheerful motel rooms. This is a good-value option that's close to the city's restaurants and bars.

Mid City Motor Inn MOTEL $$
(☎4951 1666; stay@midcitymotel.com.au; 2 Macalister St; r $114-180;) Looking tired but comfortable, this motel is in a superb location beside the river promenade, and it's only a short stroll into the town centre.

Ocean International RESORT $$
(☎1800 635 104, 4957 2044; www.oceaninternational.com.au; 1 Bridge Rd, Illawong Beach; d $170-270;) On the beach, close to the airport and only 3km south of the centre, this four-star, four-storey complex overlooks Sandringham Bay and the Coral Sea. There's an excellent restaurant and cocktail bar, a spa and sauna, a business centre and a tropical poolside setting.

Illawong Beach Resort RESORT $$
(☎4957 8427; www.illawong-beach.com.au; 73 Illawong Dr, Illawong Beach; 2-bedroom villas from $140;) Choose from a garden or beachside unit in quiet, clean, spacious surroundings. The resort is looking tired but the villas are fully self-contained and roomy.

Gecko's Rest HOSTEL $
(☎4944 1230; www.geckosrest.com.au; 34 Sydney St; dm/s/d $24/55/90;) Bustling and busy, Gecko's almost bursts at the seams with adventurous travellers stopping over on their way up north or down the coast. The place is looking slightly grubby but the four-bed dorms each have a small fridge, and there's a large kitchen and a huge rooftop balcony area. Jungle Johno Eco Tours (p229) run from here.

Eating

Burp Eat Drink MODERN AUSTRALIAN $$$
(☎4951 3546; www.burp.net.au; 86 Wood St; mains $32-40; lunch & dinner Tue-Fri, dinner Sat) A swish Melbourne-style restaurant in the tropics, Burp has a small but tantalising menu. The contemporary dishes include an interesting assortment of sharing plates such as Japanese eggplant stuffed with prawns and oyster sauce.

Kevin's Place ASIAN $$
(☎4953 5835; cnr Victoria & Wood Sts; mains $18-25; lunch & dinner Mon-Fri, dinner Sat) Sizzling, spicy Singaporean dishes and efficient, revved-up staff combine with the building's colonial ambience and the tropical climate to create a Raffles-esque experience.

Angelo's on the Marina ITALIAN $$
(☎4955 5600; www.angelosonthemarina.com.au; Mulherin Dr, Mackay Marina; mains $20-30; lunch & dinner daily, breakfast Sat & Sun) A large, lively restaurant in a delightful marina setting, with an extensive range of pasta and a mouth-watering Mediterranean menu.

Fish D'vine SEAFOOD $$
(☎4953 4442; www.fishdvine.com.au; Sydney St; mains $12-25; lunch & dinner) This original concept fish cafe and rum bar serves up fresh fish in various guises as well as all things nibbly from Neptune's realm. If you don't want to sample one of the 100 rums on offer, there are plenty of other potent beverages.

Montezuma's MEXICAN $
(☎4944 1214; www.montezumas.com.au/mackay.htm; 94 Wood St; mains $10-19; lunch & dinner) Although it's a chain, this Mexican-influenced restaurant just around the corner from the cinema, is an ideal choice for a pre- or after-movie feed. Dim lighting adds to the cosy atmosphere and the snug booths offer some intimacy, if that's what you're after.

Austral Hotel PUB FARE $$
(☎4951 3288; www.theaustralhotel.com.au; 189 Victoria St; mains $17-31, steaks $23-41; lunch & dinner) You won't get a better cut of meat in Mackay than at the Austral. Huge plates of prime Aussie beef fill your plate in a genuine pub surrounding with cold draught beer to wash it down. Of course, there's the usual assortment of seafood and chicken dishes if cooked cow doesn't do it for you.

Cafe La De Da CAFE $
(☎4944 0203; 70 Wood St; meals $14-26; breakfast & lunch, dinner Fri & Sat) Always busy, always good. True to its name, La De Da whiles away its time nonchalantly serving generous mains such as seafood, big steaks, curries, salads and the obligatory wraps and sandwiches. The breakfasts won't leave you hungry.

Oscar's on Sydney FUSION $
(☎4944 0173; cnr Sydney & Gordon Sts; mains $10-21; ⏰breakfast & lunch) The delicious *poffertjes* (authentic Dutch pancakes with traditional toppings) are still going strong at this very popular corner cafe but don't be afraid to give the other dishes a go.

Hot Wok ASIAN FUSION $
(☎4951 1663; 44 Macalister St; mains $10-16; ⏰lunch Tue-Fri, dinner daily) For Chinese and Thai cuisine, this is the place to go. Good food, good value but no atmosphere – get a takeaway.

Nelson's Seafood Café SEAFOOD $
(☎4953 5453; cnr Victoria & Nelson Sts; mains $9-15; ⏰10.30am-7.30pm Mon-Thu & Sun, 9.30am-8pm Fri & Sat) To call Nelson's a fish-and-chip shop would be a gross injustice. This is seafood with a twist. The crumbed scallops are nearly as big as tennis balls!

Drinking

Sails Sports Bar BAR
(Mulherin Dr, Mackay Harbour) This outdoors bar with sports memorabilia on the walls can get rowdy at night, but it's a great place on Sunday arvo with live music and a marina outlook.

Gordi's Café & Bar PUB
(85 Victoria St) Order a $5 schooner and pull up a stool at this big open-air bar overlooking Victoria St's comings and goings.

Satchmo's at the Reef BAR
(Mulherin Dr, Mackay Harbour) A classy wine-and-tapas bar full of boaties and featuring live music on Sunday afternoon.

Entertainment

Code NIGHTCLUB
(99 Victoria St; www.thecodenightclub.com.au; ⏰10pm-3am) Don your glad rags to slink into this classy nightclub.

Platinum Lounge NIGHTCLUB
(83 Victoria St; ⏰7pm-3am Wed-Sat, 5pm-2am Sun) On the 1st floor above the corner of Victoria and Wood Sts, the Platinum Lounge is still the most popular nightclub in town.

Mainstreet NIGHTCLUB
(148 Victoria St; www.mainstreetnightclub.com.au; ⏰Thu-Sat) Live music and DJs.

Mackay Entertainment & Convention Centre LIVE MUSIC, THEATRE
(☎4961 9777; www.mackayecc.com.au; Alfred St; ⏰box office 9am-5pm Mon-Fri, 10am-1pm Sat) The city's main venue for live performances; phone the box office to find out what's on.

Information

Mackay City Library (☎4961 9387; Gordon St; ⏰9am-5pm Mon & Fri, 10am-6pm Tue, 10am-8pm Thu, 9am-3pm Sat) Internet access is free for the first 20 minutes. Bookings essential.

Mackay Queensland Parks & Wildlife Service (QPWS;☎4944 7800; www.derm.qld.gov.au; 30 Tennyson St) It's best to book camp sites online.

Mackay Visitor Information Centre (☎4944 5888; www.mackayregion.com; 320 Nebo Rd; ⏰8.30am-5pm Tue-Fri, 9am-5pm Mon, 9am-4pm Sat & Sun) About 3km south of the centre. Internet access.

Post Office (☎13 13 18; Sydney St) Near the corner of Gordon St.

Town Hall Visitor Information Centre (☎4951 4803; townhall@mackayregion.com; 63 Sydney St; ⏰9am-5pm Mon-Fri, to noon Sat & Sun) Also has internet access.

Getting There & Away

The train station, airport, and visitors centre are all about 3km south of the city centre.

Air

Jetstar (☎13 15 38; www.jetstar.com.au) and **Virgin Blue** (☎13 67 89; www.virginblue.com.au) have flights from Brisbane, while **Tiger Airways** (☎03-9335 3033; www.tigerairways.com.au) has flights from Melbourne. **Qantas** (☎13 13 13; www.qantas.com.au) has direct flights most days between Mackay and Brisbane, Rockhampton and Townsville.

Bus

Long-distance buses stop at the **Mackay Bus Terminal** (☎4944 2144; cnr Victoria & Macalister Sts; ⏰7am-6pm Mon-Fri, to 4pm Sat), where tickets can also be booked. **Greyhound Australia** (☎1300 473 946; www.greyhound.com.au) and **Premier Motor Service** (☎13 34 10; www.premierms.com.au) travel up and down the coast between Brisbane ($200, 17 hours) and Cairns ($170, 13 hours), stopping in Mackay.

Train

Queensland Rail (☎13 22 32, 1300 13 17 22; www.queenslandrail.com.au) has several services stopping at Mackay on its way between Brisbane and Townsville/Cairns. The speedy *Tilt Train* departs at 6.50am on Tuesday and Saturday heading to Cairns ($190, 12 hours) via Townsville ($110, 5½ hours), and 8.50pm on Sunday and Wednesday heading to Brisbane

($240, 13 hours). Fares shown are adult business class.

The *Sunlander* departs at 2.25am heading to Cairns on Monday and Wednesday and 5.35am on Friday. Brisbane-bound, it departs Mackay at 11.30pm on Tuesday, Thursday and Saturday. Adult fares between Mackay and Brisbane (17 hours) are $160/220 in seat/sleeper berth.

Getting Around

Avis (☎4951 1266; www.avis.com.au), **Budget** (☎4951 1400; www.budget.com.au), **Europcar** (☎4952 6269; www.europcar.com.au), **Hertz** (☎4951 3334; www.hertz.com.au) and **Redspot** (☎4998 5799; www.redspotcars.com.au) all have counters at the airport.

Mackay Transit Coaches (☎4957 3330) has several services around the city, and also connecting the city with the harbour and the northern beaches; pick up a timetable from one of the visitor centres. Routes begin from Caneland Shopping Centre and there are many signposted bus stops, but you can hail a bus anywhere along the route as long as there is room for it to pull over. There's a free service on Sunday, running to all the major tourist sights. Signal for the driver to pull over anywhere along the route on Gordon St and Nebo Rd.

For a taxi, call **Mackay Taxis** (☎13 13 08). Count on about $20 for a taxi from either the train station or the airport to the city centre.

Around Mackay

Nestled at the foothills of the Connors Range, about 40km south of Mackay, **Sarina** (pop 3290) is worth a half-day visit to see the mini sugar mill. Otherwise it's chiefly a service centre for the surrounding sugar-cane farms and home to CSR's Plane Creek sugar mill and ethanol distillery. Ethyl alcohol from Sarina may end up in fuel, Philippine gin or Japanese sake. The helpful **Sarina Tourist Art & Craft Centre** (☎4956 2251; Railway Sq, Bruce Hwy; ⏲9am-5pm) showcases local handicrafts and assists with information.

Take a tour of a mini sugar mill at **Sarina Sugar Shed** (☎4943 2801; www.sarinasugarshed.com.au; Railway Sq; adult/child $18/9; ⏲tours 9.30am, 10.30am, noon & 2pm Mon-Sat), the only miniature sugar-processing mill and distillery of its kind in Australia. After the tour enjoy a complimentary tipple at the distillery.

There's a small **museum** (☎4956 2436; adult/child $4/1; ⏲9.30am-2pm Tue, Wed & Fri) housing some interesting exhibits from times gone by. It's next to the Sarina Tourist Art & Craft Centre.

Architectural enthusiasts will appreciate the old **National Bank building** on Central St. It was originally established in the mill grounds, but was moved in 1910 to its present location. The gorgeous old **train station** is worth a look, too.

If you do find yourself staying the night, the **Tramway Motel** (☎4956 2244; 110 Broad St; s/d $100/105; ❄📶🏊), off the Bruce Hwy just north of town, has clean, bright units and family rooms ($150).

Only a few kilometres southeast of Sarina, **Armstrong Beach Caravan Park** (☎4956 2425; 66 Melba St; sites $25-30) is the closest coastal van park to Sarina. Prices are for two people.

The **Diner** (☎4956 1990; 11 Central St; mains $4-6; ⏲4am-6pm Mon-Fri, to 10am Sat) is an iconic rustic roadside shack and is the oldest eatery in town. Meals are still cooked on a wood stove and if the wind blows in the right direction and you cop a whiff, you'll want to grab something here. Although it looks a bit ramshackle, the diner has been quelling the appetites of famished mill workers for decades. To find it, take the turn-off to Clermont in the centre of town and look for the tin shack on your left, just before the railway crossing.

There are a number of low-key beachside settlements a short drive east of Sarina, where the clean, uncrowded beaches and mangrove-lined inlets provide excellent opportunities for exploring, fishing, and spotting wildlife such as sea eagles and nesting marine turtles. Nature takes a back seat at Hay Point, which is dominated by the largest coal-exporting facility in the southern hemisphere.

Set on the shores of Sarina Inlet, **Sarina Beach** is a laid-back coastal village that boasts a long beach, a general store and service station, and a boat ramp at the inlet.

Fernandos Hideaway (☎4956 6299; www.sarinabeachbb.com; 26 Captain Blackwood Dr; B&B s $100, d $130-140; ❄🏊) is a Spanish hacienda perched on a rugged headland offering magnificent coastal views and absolute beachfront. The living room is cluttered with an eclectic collection of souvenirs from the well-travelled (and eccentric) owner and includes a suit of armour and a stuffed lion. Choose between the panoramic double with a spa in the bathroom, and a double or family room that share a bathroom.

WORTH A TRIP

SUGAR COUNTRY

It's 36km from Sarina to Mackay via the Bruce Hwy (A1), but a longer alternative route takes you deep into the cane fields and past several points of interest. Take the turn-off to Homebush, 2km north of Sarina on the Bruce Hwy. The road is narrow and is regularly crossed by cane-train tracks, so drive carefully, particularly during harvest (July to November).

After about 24km you'll see the signpost to one of the area's main attractions: located about 800m off the main road is **Polstone Sugar Cane Farm** (4959 7298; Masotti's Rd; adult/child/family $15/7/40; tours 1.30pm Mon, Wed & Fri Jun-Oct), where you can take a two-hour tour in a covered wagon to see how sugar cane is grown and harvested and how sugar is produced.

Further on, the **General Gordon Hotel** (4959 7324; Homebush Rd, Homebush), an impressive old country pub in a sea of sugar cane, has been serving thirsty locals and travellers for ages. It's a popular stop for lunch, too. Shortly after the pub take the turn-off to the left, cutting north to the Peak Downs Hwy and Walkerston. When you reach the highway you'll have to backtrack a few kilometres to reach historic **Greenmount Homestead** (4959 2250; adult/child/concession $6/2/4; 9.30am-12.30pm Sun-Fri), a classic Queenslander built by the Cook family in 1915 on the property where Mackay's founder, John Mackay, first settled in 1862. It was reopened in 2001 after extensive restorations. To head back to Mackay, return to Walkerston and keep going until you reach the Bruce Hwy.

Located at the northern end of the Esplanade, most rooms at the **Sarina Beach Motel** (4956 6266; sarbeach@mackay.net.au; The Esplanade; d $100-135;) are looking dated, but they are spacious, and look out over a wide expanse of lawn that stretches down to the beach.

Mackay's Northern Beaches

The coastline north of Mackay is made up of a series of headlands and bays. The small residential communities strung along here are virtually outer suburbs of Mackay. There are some reasonably good beaches for swimming and fishing, and the prevailing winds keep the kitesurfers happy.

Blacks Beach unfolds for 6km, so stretch those legs and claim a piece of Coral Sea coast for a day. Of the several accommodation options, **Blue Pacific Resort** (1800 808 386, 4954 9090; www.bluepacificresort.com.au; 26 Bourke St, Blacks Beach; studios $155, 1-/2-bedroom units $175/225;) has bright and cheerful units directly on the beach. The spa studios are popular, the two-bedroom units are great value, and all rooms have self-catering facilities.

Close by is **Seawinds Caravan Park** (4954 9334; sites $21-31, cabins $82-101;) This attractively located park was undergoing major renovations at the time of research and looks set to be the pick of the van parks, with tent sites overlooking a gloriously long stretch of beach. Rates given are for two people.

At the northern end of Blacks Beach is **Dolphin Heads** (named for its distinctive headland), where you can stay at the four-star **Dolphin Heads Resort** (1800 075 088, 4954 9666; www.dolphinheadsresort.com.au; Beach Rd, Dolphin Heads; d $180-220;). The resort overlooks an attractive (but rocky) headland. The swimming pool dominates the central courtyard and you can choose from poolside, garden or oceanfront units. The Seabreeze restaurant and bar sprawls out onto a deck overlooking the pool.

North of Dolphin Heads is **Eimeo**, where the **Eimeo Pacific Hotel** (4954 6105; Mango Ave, Eimeo; mains $15-28; 10am-midnight) beckons you with magnificent Coral Sea views. It's at least worthy of stopping for a drink although the meals warrant a longer stay. Indeed, lunch at the Eimeo is one thing you should do if you're in the area. It's deservedly popular with locals as well.

Bucasia and **Shoal Point** are across Sunset Bay from Eimeo and Dolphin Heads. The beachfront parks of these holiday towns offer shady barbecue and picnic areas, and Bucasia beach has a safe swimming enclosure. **Bucasia Beachfront Caravan Resort** (4954 6375; www.bucasiabeach.com.au; 2 The

Esplanade; sites $27-37, villas $160; ⊛) has camp sites but they aren't on the beach. The small villa has total glass frontage and a large deck with comfy outdoor lounges, and it's only a short stroll across the lawn to the beach.

Pioneer Valley

Travelling west, Mackay's urban sprawl gives way to the lush greenness of the beautiful Pioneer Valley. The unmistakable smell of sugar cane wafts through your nostrils, and loaded cane trains busily work their way along the roadside. The first sugar cane was planted here in 1867, and today almost the entire valley floor is planted with the stuff. The route to Eungella National Park (p235), the Mackay–Eungella Rd, branches off the Peak Downs Hwy about 10km west of Mackay and follows the river through vast fields of cane to link up with the occasional small town or steam-belching sugar mill and the odd local attraction.

Marian is dominated by an enormous sugar mill that crushes much of the valley's cane. **Melba House**, where Dame Nellie Melba and her husband (manager of the mill) lived, is on the right as you approach Marian from Mackay. It operates as a **tourist information centre** (☎4954 4299; ⊙9am-3pm), a gallery and home to Melba memorabilia. At Marian there's a turn-off to **Kinchant Dam** (8km), which is well stocked with sooty grunter, barramundi and even the odd sleepy cod or two.

The next town is **Mirani**, where there's a **local history museum** (☎4961 9230; Victoria St; adult/child $4/1.50; ⊙9.30am-2.30pm Tue-Fri) behind the library. If you fancy lunch or a drink, drive on for another 17km to the **Pinnacle Hotel** (Eungella Rd, Pinnacle; mains $10-20). The pub has an alfresco cafe where you can dine overlooking the cane fields or enjoy a cruisy Sunday afternoon listening to live music.

About 27km west of Mirani is the turn-off for Finch Hatton Gorge, part of Eungella National Park. About 1.5km past the turn-off is the pretty township of **Finch Hatton**. The historic **railway station** (⊙10am-3pm) hasn't seen a train for a while now, but it has an interesting collection of photos and brochures on local history. The **Criterion Hotel** (9 Eungella Rd; mains $10-27) has seen better days but it's worth having a beer and a chat with the locals.

From Finch Hatton it's another 18km to Eungella, a quaint mountain village overlooking the valley, and the gateway to the Broken River section of Eungella National Park. The last section of this road climbs suddenly and steeply, with several incredibly sharp corners – towing a large caravan up here is not recommended.

Eungella

Pretty little Eungella (*young*-gluh; meaning 'land of clouds') sits perched on the edge of the Pioneer Valley. The cool mountain air is invigorating and there are some good walks in the area. There's a general store with snacks, groceries and fuel, and a couple of accommodation and eating options.

Eungella Mountain Edge Escape (☎4958 4590; www.mountainedgeescape.com.au; 1-/2-bedroom cabins $115/135; ⊛) has three wooden cabins perched on the edge of the escarpment with superb views of the valley below. The fully self-contained cabins are a great choice and close to everything.

Eungella Chalet (☎4958 4509; www.eungellachalet.com.au; 1-/2-bedroom cabins $115/135; ⊛) exudes a rustic charm in a once-grand kind of way. The chalet is perched on the edge of a mountain and the views are spectacular. The cabins are large and spacious but furnishings are quite dated. Cyclone damage in 2010 destroyed the hostel-style rooms in the chalet but renovations will see the opening of new motel-style units ($100). There's a small bar, the dining room has fantastic views, and there's live music most Sunday afternoons. Hang-gliding is possible from the backyard here.

Eungella Holiday Park (☎0437 479 205; www.eungella.com; sites $20-22, cabins $85-120) is a small and very basic campground located just north of the township, right on the edge of the escarpment. You'll need to self-register on arrival. Prices are for two people.

It's worth stopping in for lunch at the interesting **Hideaway Café** (☎4958 4533; Broken River Rd; light meals $4-10; ⊙9am-4pm), which may or may not be open, and where the eccentric owner may or may not be welcoming. If it's open – and welcoming – sit on the picturesque little balcony and enjoy decent home-cooked dishes such as Weiner schnitzel and potato salad, or lentil vegetable casserole. Afterwards take a stroll around the whimsical garden or check out some of the local art and crafts in the attached gallery.

Stoney Creek

Just south of the town of **Eton**, on the Peak Downs Hwy about 28km southwest of Mackay, is a deservedly popular farmstay and horse-riding centre.

Stoney Creek Farm Stay (☎4954 1177; www.stoneycreekfarmstay.com; Peak Downs Hwy; camp sites $20, dm $25, cottages $145) is a place where you can park your campervan, pitch a tent, bunk in a dorm, or sleep in a rustic room above the horse stables. But best of all is the handmade wood-and-stone cottage, which has a 'bog in a log'. The three-hour horse ride costs $85 per person. After the ride, cool down in a secluded swimming hole or wash in the outside bush shower. There's a $290 three-day package that's designed for backpackers and includes budget accommodation, meals and activities. It's possible to get to Stoney Creek by bus, leaving Mackay at 1.45pm. Otherwise the farm-stay owners will pick you up if you ring ahead (minimum of two people). Willing Workers on Organic Farms (WWOOFs) are welcome.

Eungella National Park

Stunning Eungella National Park is 84km west of Mackay, and covers nearly 500 sq km of the Clarke Range, climbing to 1280m at Mt Dalrymple. The mountainous park is largely inaccessible, except for the walking tracks around Broken River and Finch Hatton Gorge. The large tracts of tropical and subtropical vegetation have been isolated from other rainforest areas for thousands of years and now boast several unique species. The Eungella honeyeater is a Holy Grail for birders, while spotting the Eungella gastric brooding frog, which incubates its eggs in its stomach and then gives birth by spitting out the tadpoles, would be a rare treat.

However, it's the platypuses that steal the show. Most days of the year you can be pretty sure of seeing a platypus or two in the Broken River. The best times to see the creatures are the hours immediately after dawn and before dark; you must remain patiently silent and still. Platypus activity is at its peak from May to August, when the females are fattening themselves up in preparation for gestating their young.

Other river life you're sure to see are the large northern snapping turtles and, flitting above the feeding platypuses, brilliant azure kingfishers.

There are no buses to Eungella or Finch Hatton, but Reeforest Adventure Tours and Jungle Johno (see p229) both run day trips from Mackay and will drop off and pick up those who want to linger; however, tours don't run every day and your stay at Eungella may be longer than intended.

BROKEN RIVER

There's an unmanned **QPWS information office** (☎4958 4552; ⏲8am-4pm), picnic area and **kiosk** (⏲9.30am-5.30pm Wed-Mon) near the bridge over the Broken River, 5km south of Eungella. A **platypus-viewing platform** has been built near the bridge, and bird life is prolific. There are some excellent walking trails between the Broken River picnic ground and Eungella; maps are available from the information office, which is (unfortunately) rarely staffed.

For accommodation, you have the choice of camping or cabins. **Broken River Mountain Resort** (☎4958 4000; www.brokenrivermr.com.au; d $105-160; ❄@📶🏊) has comfortable cedar cabins ranging from small motel-style units to a large self-contained lodge sleeping up to six. There's a cosy guest lounge with an open fire and the friendly **Possums Table Restaurant & Bar** (mains $21-37; ⏲breakfast & dinner) with a good selection of steak, seafood and chicken dishes, and a moderately priced wine list. You can also preorder a picnic lunch. The resort organises several (mostly free) activities for its guests, including spotlighting, birdwatching and guided walks, and will organise shuttle transfers for longer walks.

Fern Flat Camping Ground (sites per person/family $6/21) is a lovely place to camp, with shady sites adjacent to the river where the platypuses play. Inquisitive brush turkeys and rufous bettongs (small marsupials) watch your every move, and there's the most amazing bird chorus in the morning. Indeed, you really are sharing your bedroom with the wildlife here. This is a walk-in camping ground and is not vehicle accessible. Camp sites are about 500m past the information centre and kiosk and you need to self-register.

Crediton Hall Camping Ground (sites per person/family $6/21), 3km after Broken River, is accessible to vehicles. Turn left into Crediton Loop Rd and turn right after the

Wishing Pool circuit track entrance. The camping ground has toilets.

FINCH HATTON GORGE

Located about 27km west of Mirani, just before the town of Finch Hatton, is the turn-off for the Finch Hatton Gorge. The last 2km of the 10km drive from the main road is unsealed with several creek crossings that can become impassable after heavy rain. A 1.6km walking trail leads from the car park to **Araluen Falls**, with its spectacular waterfalls and swimming holes. A further 1km takes you to the **Wheel of Fire Falls**, another tumbling cascade and excellent swimming hole.

Easily the best way to experience the forest from a bird's perspective is to do the ultrafun **Forest Flying** (☎4958 3359; www.forestflying.com; rides $60). Get harnessed to a 350m-long cable suspended up to 25m above the ground and glide through the rainforest canopy to get a whole new angle on forest life. It's deservedly popular and you'll need to book ahead. There's a full safety briefing; the ride is not suitable for those weighing less than 18kg or more than 120kg. There's also a seasonal fruit-bat colony (August to May) to see.

The following accommodation places are signposted on the road to the gorge.

Platypus Bushcamp (☎4958 3204; www.bushcamp.net; Finch Hatton Gorge; camp sites $10, dm/d $35/100) is a totally amazing, true bush retreat hand-built by Wazza, the eccentric owner. If you're looking for a castaway paradise, this is it. The basic huts are a real back-to-nature experience. They are all open-air, allowing the fresh rainforest atmosphere to seep in. Mosquito nets are available, but rarely needed. A creek with platypuses and great swimming holes runs next to the camp, and the big alfresco communal kitchen/eating area is the heart of the place. There are wonderful hot bush showers and a cosy stone hot tub. Bring your own food and linen. WWOOFs are welcome.

The only luxury accommodation in Eungella National Park is the **Rainforest B&B** (☎4958 3099; www.rainforestbedandbreakfast.com.au; 52 Van Houweninges Rd; cabins $300). There's a touch of Balinese to this rainforest retreat with its garden sculptures, wooden cabin and romantic decor. The candelabra lighting the double spa on the deck sets the scene for a night of romancing. There's a private creekside picnic table, and a five-course home-cooked meal ($60) is available on request. Complimentary afternoon tea greets you on arrival.

The self-contained cabins at **Finch Hatton Gorge Cabins** (☎4958 3281; www.finchhattongorgecabins.com.au; d $95, extra person $20; ❄) sleep up to five, which is perfect if you're travelling with young kids or with a group. The cabins are quite basic but have wonderful views of the forest, and linen is provided. Dine on the large deck while listening to birdsong at the **River Rock Café** (breakfast & lunch Tue-Sun).

Brampton Island

Brampton Island Resort proudly announces there are no day-trippers (except for Sundays) to interrupt the peace and solitude on the island. It's a classy resort that's popular with couples, honeymooners and those wanting a relaxed island experience. It's definitely not a party island, and kids (especially those under 12) are not catered for. There's no mobile-phone coverage on the resort side of the island – it's that kind of place.

This mountainous island is a national park and wildlife sanctuary with lush forests surrounded by coral reefs. There are stunning beaches and a couple of good walking trails, as well as all the frills associated with a big resort.

In the 19th century the island was used by the Queensland government as a nursery for palm trees, of which there are still plenty. The Bussutin family, which moved to the island in 1916 to raise goats and horses, established the first resort here in 1932. Brampton is connected by a sandbar that you can sometimes walk across at low tide to nearby Carlisle Island, which has a couple of national-park camp sites.

Activities

The resort has two swimming pools: one saltwater, one freshwater. There are tennis courts and a small six-hole golf course, as well as complimentary snorkelling gear, catamarans, windsurfers and surf skis. Motorised water sports cost extra.

There are 12 beaches on the island, seven of them easily accessible via the national-park walking trails. The main beach at Sandy Point is very pleasant. There's good snorkelling over the coral in the channel between Brampton and Carlisle Islands.

There are two excellent **walking trails** on the island. The 7km walk circumnavigates the central section of the island, and side tracks lead down to Dinghy and Oak Bays. The 2km steady climb to the top of 219m Brampton Peak takes about two hours, and is rewarded with fine views along the way.

Of course, if being energetic is not your style, the **Sea Spa**, set among tropical gardens, offers all sorts of remedies for a weary body ranging from massage therapy to spa treatments as well as a special men-only package. All treatments cost extra.

Day-trippers ($120 per person) can use all the resort facilities. Transfers depart on Sundays only. Contact the resort for more details.

Sleeping & Eating

Brampton Island Resort RESORT **$$$**
(☎1300 134 044, 4951 4499; www.bramptonholidays.com.au; s $290-640, d $310-660;) There are four grades of room depending on the view and facilities and, naturally, the rates increase the closer you get to the ocean. You'll be comfortable here. The premium ocean views are stunning, but even the standard rooms are classy. The Bluewater Restaurant serves a buffet breakfast and lunch and a scrumptious à la carte dinner as well as beach barbecues. Prices are often much cheaper if you book a five-night package or wait for stand-by rates.

Getting There & Away

Organise your transfers with the resort when booking accommodation.

Air

Australasian Jet (☎4953 3261; www.ausjet.com.au) departs twice daily from Mackay airport (15 minutes) at 11am and 5pm. It leaves Brampton Island for Mackay airport at 9am and 2pm. One-way/return flights cost $85/170.

Boat

The resort has its own launch that leaves Mackay Marina daily at 2pm. The trip takes 1¼ hours. The return voyage to Mackay departs at 3pm. There's a courtesy bus connecting passengers to/from the airport. A one-way/return ticket for an adult is $68/136.

To access the national park, **Reefstar Cruises** (☎4955 0393; www.reefstarcruises.com.au; adult/child $55/10) operates a daily ferry service that leaves Mackay at 8.30am and returns at 4pm.

Cumberland Islands

There are about 70 islands in the Cumberland group (including Brampton Island), which is sometimes referred to as the southern Whitsundays. The islands are all designated national parks except for Keswick, St Bees and part of tiny Farrier Island. Although the islands are accessible, getting there can be difficult.

Carlisle Island is connected to Brampton by a narrow sandbar, and at some low tides it's possible to walk or wade from one island to the other. Carlisle is uninhabited and covered in dense eucalypt forests, and there are no walking trails. However, there are national-park camping grounds at Southern Bay, which is directly across from the Brampton Island Resort, and at another site further north at Maryport Bay.

Scawfell Island, 12km east of Brampton, is the largest island in the group. Refuge Bay, on its northern side, has a safe anchorage, a beach, a camping ground with water (but always bring your own supply), barbecues and toilets. In the Sir James Smith Island Group, just northwest of Brampton, **Goldsmith Island** has a safe anchorage on its northwestern side, good beaches and a camping ground with toilets, tables and fireplaces.

Keswick Island is a quiet, inhabited island that is part national park and part freehold. There are grand plans for future development of this idyllic island, but for now you are unlikely to bump into many people other than the few who already live here, or those staying at the guesthouse.

Keswick Island Guest House (☎4965 8002; www.keswickislandguesthouse.com.au; 26 Coral Passage Dr; full board s $365-385, d $550-590, minimum 2-night stay) offers four comfortable double rooms with ocean views and three scrumptious home-cooked meals a day. All rooms have access to the huge deck with its fantastic ocean views. It's a place to relax (no kids, thanks) and perhaps hit the water for a leisurely swim or snorkel. In addition, there's kayaking, fishing or exploring the island's bush tracks and sandy beaches.

Camp site bookings and permits for Carlisle, Scawfell and Goldsmith Islands, and the more remote islands are best made online or by phoning ☎13 74 68. Bookings can also be made at **Mackay QPWS** (www.derm.qld.gov.au; sites per person/family $6/21), at the Mackay Visitor Information Centre, or at the Mackay Town Hall Visitor Information Centre.

Carlisle Island can be reached from Brampton Island via the sand spit at low tide, or by chartering a boat at Brampton resort. Scawfell and Goldsmith Islands are reached by charter boat, which can be organised through the Mackay Visitor Information Centre. Transfers out to these islands depend on the weather, how many people are travelling, and so forth. Keswick Island transfers can be arranged for you by the guesthouse.

Cape Hillsborough National Park

Despite being so easy to get to, this small coastal park feels like it's at the end of the Earth. Ruggedly beautiful, it takes in the rocky, 300m-high Cape Hillsborough, and Andrews Point and Wedge Island, which are joined by a causeway at low tide. The park, 58km north of Mackay, features rough cliffs, a broad beach, rocky headlands, sand dunes, mangroves, hoop pines and rainforest. Kangaroos, wallabies, sugar gliders and turtles are common in the park; the roos are likely to be seen on the beach in the evening and early morning. There are also the remains of Aboriginal middens and stone fish-traps, which can be accessed by good walking tracks. On the approach to the foreshore area there's also an interesting boardwalk leading out through a tidal mangrove forest. If you have a hire car that prevents you from driving off-road, be sure to take the sealed road at Yakapari rather than the bumpy dirt track from Mt Ossa to Seaforth.

Smalleys Beach Campground (☎13 74 68; www.derm.qld.gov.au; sites per person/family $6/21) is a small, grassed camping ground hugging the foreshore and jumping with kangaroos. There's no longer self-registration here and you'll need to book a permit.

Cape Hillsborough Nature Resort (☎4959 0152; www.capehillsboroughresort.com.au; sites $25-30, r $95, cabins $65-120; @) is in a quiet spot on a long stretch of beach. Motel-style rooms are large but basic, and the beach huts on the foreshore are looking tired and run-down. The caravan sites are a better option. If you're lucky you can sometimes see kangaroos on the beach. Alcohol can be purchased here.

Newry Island Group

The Newry Island Group is a cluster of small islands just off the coast from Seaforth, about 50km northwest of Mackay. They are rocky, wild-looking continental islands with grassy, open forests and small patches of rainforest. From November to January green turtles nest on the beaches.

The largest of the Newry Island Group is **Rabbit Island**. Its campground has toilets and a rainwater tank (which can be empty in dry times). It also has the only sandy beaches in the group, although, because of its proximity to the mainland, box jellyfish may be present in summer. **Newry Island** and **Outer Newry Island** each have a camping ground with shelter, water (depending on rainfall) and toilets. If you don't have your own boat, access to the islands is difficult. However, camping permits can be obtained online at www.derm.qld.gov.au or at the **Mackay QPWS** (☎4944 7800; 20 Tennyson St).

THE WHITSUNDAYS

The Whitsunday group of islands off the northeast Queensland coast is, as the cliché goes, a tropical paradise. The 74 islands that make up this stunning archipelago are really the tips of mountaintops jutting out from the Coral Sea, and from their sandy fringes the ocean spreads towards the horizon in beautiful shades of crystal, aqua, blue and indigo. Sheltered by the Great Barrier Reef, the Whitsundays have no crashing waves or deadly undertows, and the waters are perfect for sailing.

Weaving between the islands and the mainland, the Whitsunday Passage was named by Lieutenant James Cook, who sailed through here on 3 June 1770. Cook called the islands the Cumberland Isles, but this grouping was later subdivided and the islands scattered around the Whitsunday Passage became the Whitsunday Islands. All are within 50km of Shute Harbour. The Great Barrier Reef proper is at least 60km out from Airlie Beach; Bait Reef is the nearest part of it.

Only seven of the islands have tourist resorts (from backpacker to five-star), most are uninhabited, and several offer the chance of back-to-nature beach camping and bushwalking. All but four islands – Dent, Hamilton, Daydream and Hayman – are predominantly or completely national park, and the surrounding waters fall within the Great Barrier Reef Marine Park. Of the numerous stunning beaches and secluded bays, Whitehaven Beach stands out for its pure white silica sand. It is undoubtedly the finest beach in the Whitsundays, and possibly one of the finest in the world.

Airlie Beach is the mainland gateway to the Whitsundays, with a bewildering array of accommodation options, travel agents and tour operators. Shute Harbour, about 10km east of Airlie, is the port for some day-trip cruises and island ferries, while most of the yachts and other cruise companies berth at Abel Point Marina about 1km west of Airlie Beach.

Activities

Most activities that take place around the islands, either in, under or on top of the water, attract a Great Barrier Reef Marine Park levy of $5.50 per person per day. Check to see if it is included in quoted prices.

Sailing

What could be better than sailing from one island paradise to another? There are plenty of sailing tours itching to get your landlubber's feet on deck, but if you've got saltwater in your veins, a bareboat charter might be more your style. No, there are no bare butts involved although, since a bareboat charter means you rent a boat without skipper, crew or provisions, you could conceivably bare whatever bits you want. You don't need formal qualifications to hire a boat but you (or one of your party) have to prove you can competently operate a vessel.

Expect to pay between $500 and $800 a day in the high season (September to January) for a yacht that will comfortably sleep four to six people. A booking deposit of $500 to $750 and a security bond of between $200 and $2000 is payable before departure and refunded after the boat is returned undamaged. Bedding is usually supplied, and provisions can be provided at extra cost. Most companies have a minimum hire period of five days.

It's worth asking if the company belongs to the Whitsunday Bareboat Operators Association, a self-regulatory body that guarantees certain standards. Also check that the latest edition of David Colfelt's *100 Magic Miles* is stowed on board.

There are a number of bareboat charter companies around Airlie Beach:

Charter Yachts Australia (☎1800 639 520; www.cya.com.au; Abel Point Marina)

Cumberland Charter Yachts (☎1800 075 101; www.ccy.com.au; Abel Point Marina)

Queensland Yacht Charters (☎1800 075 013; www.yachtcharters.com.au; Abel Point Marina)

Whitsunday Escape (☎1800 075 145, 4946 5222; www.whitsundayescape.com; Abel Point Marina)

Whitsunday Rent A Yacht (☎1800 075 000; www.rentayacht.com.au; Trinity Jetty, Shute Harbour)

If you want to know why those old salts at the bar keep smiling into their drinks, learn to sail:

Whitsunday Marine Academy (☎1800 810 116; www.explorewhitsundays.com; 4 The Esplanade) Run by Explore Whitsundays.

Whitsunday Sailing Club (☎4946 6138; www.whitsundaysailingclub.com.au; Airlie Point)

Diving

The ultimate diving experience to be had here is on the actual Great Barrier Reef, at places such as Black, Knuckle, Fairy, Bait and Elizabeth Reefs. However, the fringing reefs around the islands (especially on their northern tips) are often more colourful and abundant than most of the walls on the outer reef, and there's usually a greater variety of softer coral. These waters are all part of the Great Barrier Reef Marine Park so wherever you dive, you won't be disappointed.

The Whitsundays are a great place to learn how to dive. Many of the day trips and overnight sailing cruises offer dive instruction or 'introductory dives'. Be sure about what you are paying for. Costs for open-water courses with several ocean dives start at around $500, and any cheaper courses you may dig up will probably have you spending most of your 'dives' in a pool. It is worth paying more so that you do get to enjoy what you have learned and, more importantly, build up invaluable open-water experience. Generally speaking, courses involve two or three days' tuition on the mainland, with the rest of the time diving in the Great Barrier Reef Marine Park. Check that the Great Barrier Reef Marine Park levy and any other additional costs are included in the price.

A number of sailing cruises include diving as an optional extra. Prices start from $75 for introductory or certified dives. Most of the island resorts also have their own dive schools and free snorkelling gear.

Whitsunday Dive Adventures DIVING (☎4948 1239; www.adventuredivers.com.au; 303 Shute Harbour Rd) This company offers a range

SAILING THE WHITSUNDAYS

Dream of an island holiday and alongside the swaying palms, sand-fringed bays and calm blue seas there's usually a white sailboat skimming lightly across the water. In the Whitsundays it isn't hard to put yourself in the picture but with the plethora of charters, tours and specials on offer, deciding how to go about it can be confusing. Before booking, compare what you get for the price you pay. Cheaper companies often have crowded boats, bland food and cramped quarters. If you're flexible with dates, last minute stand-by rates can considerably reduce the price, and you'll also have a better idea of weather conditions.

Aside from day trips, most overnight sailing packages are for three days and two nights, or two days and two nights. Again, check what you pay for. Some companies set sail in the afternoon of the first day and return by mid-morning of the last while others set out early and return late. Be sure of what you're committing to – don't set sail on a party boat if you're after a chilled-out cruise.

Most vessels offer snorkelling on the fringing reefs (the reefs around the islands). The softer coral here is often more colourful and abundant than what you see on the outer reef. Check if snorkel equipment, stinger suits and reef taxes are included in the package. Diving usually costs extra.

Once you've decided what suits, book at one of the many agencies in town or a management company such as **Whitsunday Sailing Adventures** (☎4940 2000; www.whitsundaysailing.com; 293 Shute Harbour Rd) or **Explore Whitsundays** (☎4946 4999; www.explorewhitsundays.com; 4 The Esplanade).

Recommended sailing trips:

» **Camira** (day trip $165) This good-value day trip includes Whitehaven Beach, snorkelling, morning and afternoon tea, a barbecue lunch, and all refreshments (including wine and beer).

» **Maxi Action Ragamuffin** (day trip $156) Cruise to Whitehaven Beach (Thursday and Sunday) or snorkel at Blue Pearl Bay (Monday, Wednesday, Friday and Saturday) where diving ($90) is also available.

» **Derwent Hunter** (3-day & 2-night trip from $590) A very popular sailing safari on a timber gaff-rigged schooner. Good for couples and those wanting to experience nature and the elements.

» **Whitsunday Magic** (3-day & 3-night trip from $779) This beautiful three-masted schooner is the largest vessel sailing the Whitsundays and cruises to the outer reef. One of the more upmarket tours.

» **Wings 2** (2-day & 2-night trip from $475) Comfortable, well-maintained fast cat for those wanting to sail, dive and make new friends.

» **Solway Lass** (3-day & 3-night trip from $549) At 28m, this is the only authentic tall ship in Airlie Beach. A popular choice for backpackers.

» **Pride of Airlie** (3-day & 2-night trip $349) A raucous booze cruise popular with young backpackers. Nights are spent at Adventure Island Resort on South Molle Island.

Crewing

Adventurous types might see the 'Crew Wanted' ads posted in backpackers or at the marina and yacht club and dream of hitching a ride on the high seas. In return for a free bunk, meals and a sailing adventure you get to hoist the mainsail, take the helm, and clean the head. You could have the experience of a lifetime – whether good or bad depends on the vessel, skipper, other crew members (if any), and your own attitude. Think about being stuck with someone you don't know on a 10m boat, several kilometres from shore, before you actually find yourself there. For safety reasons, let someone know where you're going, with whom, and for how long.

of PADI dive courses including Scuba Diver ($490), Open Water Diver ($565), and Rescue Diver ($695) courses, PADI Dive Master and Instructor courses, referral, tune-up and refresher courses, as well as half-day dive trips ($175).

Fantasea DIVING
(☎4967 5455; www.fantasea.com.au) Offers introductory and certified dives on its day trip to Reef World, a floating pontoon located on the edge of Hardy Reef.

Cruise Whitsundays DIVING
(☎4946 4662; www.cruisewhitsundays.com) Runs day trips to the Barrier Reef Marine Base, a similar pontoon located in Knuckle Reef Lagoon.

Sea Kayaking

Go where you want, when you want, and leave when you want. No cruise-boat skipper telling you to pack up because it's time to go home. Paddling serenely in search of an island with dolphins and turtles as company would have to be one of the best ways to experience the Whitsundays.

Ngaro Sea Trail combines sea-kayaking trails with island bushwalks. Pick up the guide *Whitsunday National Park Islands and Ngaro Sea Trail* from the QPWS office to help you plan your itinerary. Don't forget to book camp sites on the islands before you paddle out from Shute Harbour.

Salty Dog Sea Kayaking KAYAKING
(☎4946 1388; www.saltydog.com.au) This company offers guided tours and kayak rental. Half-/full-day tours from Shute Harbour cost $70/125. There are also overnight trips ($365) and a brilliant six-day expedition ($1500) that covers 15km to 20km per day and is suitable for beginners. Kayak rental costs $50/60 for a half-/one-day single kayak and $80/90 for a double.

Tours

It can be confusing figuring out the best and most convenient way to see the islands. There are so many operators, but it needn't be too difficult.

Island & Reef Cruises

Not everyone has the time or the money to sail and therefore must rely on the faster catamarans to whisk them to several different islands on a day trip. If snorkelling, lying on the beach or exploring the rainforests of a few of the Whitsunday Islands appeals, then it's just a matter of hunting down the tour that will suit you.

Most day trips include activities such as snorkelling or boom netting, with scuba-diving as an optional extra. Children generally pay half fare.

The majority of cruise operators run out of Abel Point Marina but those that run from Shute Harbour do coach pick-ups from Airlie Beach and Cannonvale. You can take a public bus to Shute Harbour.

Following are some (but by no means all) of the day trips on offer, and bookings can be made at any of the tour agents in Airlie Beach.

Voyager 3 Island Cruise CRUISES
(☎4946 5255; www.wiac.com.au; Shute Harbour Rd; adult/child $140/80) This is a good-value day cruise that includes snorkelling at Hook Island, beachcombing and swimming at Whitehaven Beach, and checking out Daydream Island.

Cruise Whitsundays CRUISES
(☎4946 4662; www.cruisewhitsundays.com; Shingley Dr, Abel Point Marina; full-day adventure cruise adult/child $199/95) One of the Whitsundays' largest tour companies, Cruise Whitsundays operates as an island ferry, offers day trips to Daydream and Long Islands, and also has a huge wave-piercing catamaran that speeds out to a pontoon moored at Knuckle Reef Lagoon on the Great Barrier Reef. There you'll find spectacular snorkelling as well as an underwater observatory, a water slide and a children's swimming enclosure, plus optional extras such as diving. A hefty buffet lunch is included in the price and there's an expensive, but thrilling, option of flying in or out by helicopter. Alternatively, to hop on and off the islands at leisure you can buy a daily Island Hopper pass ($79/49 per adult/child). Cruise Whitsundays also operates a popular sailing day trip aboard the Camira ($165/85 per adult/child), a fast catamaran that takes in Whitehaven Beach. This good value full-day trip includes morning and afternoon tea, lunch and all drinks.

Ocean Rafting CRUISES
(☎4946 6848; www.oceanrafting.com; 25 Ocean View Ave; adult/child/family $120/78/360) Visit the 'wild' side of the islands in a very fast, big yellow speedboat. Swim at Whitehaven Beach, view Aboriginal cave paintings at Nara Inlet, snorkel the reef at Mantaray Bay or Border Island. Lunch is extra. Book before turning up to the jetty.

Fantasea CRUISES
(☎4967 5455; www.fantasea.com.au; Shute Harbour) Another large tour operator in Airlie Beach, and the only ferry service to Hamilton Island marina, Fantasea offers high-speed catamaran cruises to its Reef World pontoon on the Great Barrier Reef, where you can snorkel, take a trip in a semisubmersible and check out the underwater viewing chamber (adult/child/family $225/102/589). An overnight 'Reefsleep' costs from $460.

Big Fury CRUISES
(☎4948 2201; Abel Point Marina; adult/child/family $130/70/350) Small operator with a maximum of 35 passengers that speeds out to Whitehaven Beach on an open-air sports boat for lunch and then snorkelling at a secluded reef nearby.

Scenic Flights

Air Whitsunday SCENIC FLIGHTS
(☎4946 9111; www.airwhitsunday.com.au; Terminal 1, Whitsunday Airport) Flying is the only way to do day trips to exclusive Hayman Island ($195). Other tours include a three-hour Reef Adventure (adult/child $315/280), a Whitehaven experience ($240/210), and the signature four-hour Panorama Tour ($425/390) where you fly to Hardy Lagoon to snorkel or ride a semisubmersible then fly to Whitehaven Beach for a picnic lunch.

HeliReef SCENIC FLIGHTS
(☎4946 9102; www.avta.com.au) Offers flights to the reef (from $129), day trips to Hayman Island ($399) and a picnic lunch on Whitehaven Beach ($399).

Aviation Adventures SCENIC FLIGHTS
(☎4946 9988; www.av8.com.au; 2927 Shute Harbour Rd) Helicopter flights ranging from scenic island trips ($99) to picnic rendezvous ($199) and reef adventures ($649).

Sleeping

Camping

QPWS (www.derm.qld.gov.au) manages the **Whitsunday Islands National Park** camping grounds on several islands for both independent and commercial campers (tour companies). There's also a privately run camping ground at Hook Island (p252).

You must be self-sufficient to camp in the national-park sites. You're advised to take 5L of water per person per day, plus three days' extra supply in case you get stranded. You should also have a fuel stove – wood fires are banned on all islands.

The national-parks leaflet *Whitsunday National Park Islands and Ngaro Sea Trail* describes the various sites and provides detailed information on what to take and do. Camping permits are available online, from the Whitsunday QPWS office and from the Whitsunday Information Centre in Proserpine (p243). Permits cost $6/21 per person/family.

Get to your island with **Whitsunday Island Camping Connections – Scamper** (☎4946 6285; www.whitsundaycamping.com.au), which leaves from Shute Harbour and can drop you at South Molle, Denman or Planton Islands ($65 return); Whitsunday Island ($105 return); Whitehaven Beach ($155 return); and Hook Island ($160 return). Camping transfers also include complimentary snorkelling gear and water containers. You can also hire camp kits ($40 per night). A food drop-off service can be provided at extra cost.

Northern islands such as Armit, Gloucester, Olden and Saddleback are harder to reach since the water taxi and cruises from Shute Harbour don't usually go there. Gloucester and Saddleback are best reached from Dingo Beach or Bowen.

Independent campers can stay on the islands at all times of the year, provided they have a permit.

Resorts

There are resorts on seven of the Whitsunday Islands. Each resort is quite different from the next, ranging from Hayman's five-star luxury to the family-friendly Daydream, and from the high-rise development of Hamilton to the basic cabins on Hook.

The rates quoted in this section are the standard high-season rates, but most travel agents can put together a range of discounted package deals that combine airfares, transfers, accommodation and meals that are much more inexpensive.

It's also worth noting that, unless they're full, almost all resorts offer discounted stand-by rates. The limiting factor is that you usually have to book less than five days in advance. All the agents in Airlie Beach can provide information on the resorts.

Information

Whitsunday Information Centre (☎1300 717 407, 4945 3711; www.whitsundaytourism.com) On the Bruce Hwy on the southern entry to Proserpine.

The Whitsunday district office of the **QPWS** (p250) is 3km past Airlie Beach on the road to Shute Harbour.

Getting There & Around

Air

The two main airports for the Whitsundays are Hamilton Island (p255) and Proserpine (p243; Whitsunday Coast).

There is also the Whitsunday Airport (p250), which has regular flights from the mainland to the islands – light planes, seaplanes and helicopters.

Boat

The services to the islands all operate out of Shute Harbour or Abel Point Marina near Airlie Beach. **Cruise Whitsundays** (☎4946 4662; www.cruisewhitsundays.com) provides ferry transfers to Daydream, Long and South Molle Islands, and the Hamilton Island airport. **Fantasea** (☎4946 5111; www.fantasea.com.au) provides ferry transfers to Hamilton Island; see the individual islands for details.

The Whitsunday Sailing Club is at the end of Airlie Beach Esplanade; check the noticeboards here and at the Abel Point Marina for possible rides or crewing opportunities on passing yachts.

Bus

Greyhound (☎1300 473 946; www.greyhound.com.au) and **Premier Motor Service** (☎13 34 10; www.premierms.com.au) buses detour off the Bruce Hwy to Airlie Beach. **Whitsunday Transit** (☎4946 1800; www.whitsundaytransit.com.au; 7 Orchid Ave, Cannonvale) connects Proserpine, Cannonvale, Abel Point, Airlie Beach and Shute Harbour. Timetables are readily available at travel agencies and bus stops, and from your accommodation. **Whitsundays 2 Everywhere** (☎4946 4940; www.whitsundays2everywhere.com.au) operates airport transfers from both Proserpine ($15 per person) and Mackay ($60 per person) airports to Airlie Beach.

Midge Point

There's not much to do at Midge Point but it is a quiet and tranquil beachside town. Located on a good stretch of sandy beach, **Travellers Rest Caravan & Camping Park** (☎4947 6120; travellersrest2@bigpond.com; 29 Jackson St; sites $25-30, cabins $75-105; ❄🏊) is a picturesque park, shaded by plenty of trees with well-manicured grounds.

Located a little north of town is a popular golf resort. Sadly, **Laguna Whitsundays** (☎4947 7777; www.lagunawhitsundays.info; Kunapipi Springs Rd; ❄🏊) suffered severe cyclone damage in March 2010 and at the time of research was still undergoing repairs. Although accommodation is still available (at considerably reduced rates), no activities were on offer and the golf course was indefinitely out of action. Check with the resort before booking.

Proserpine

Proserpine airport decided on changing its name to Whitsunday Coast, no doubt in an effort to spruce up its image, but there's still no reason to linger in this industrial sugar-mill town, which is the turn-off point for Airlie Beach and the Whitsundays. It's worth stopping at the helpful **Whitsunday Information Centre** (☎1300 717 407, 4945 3711; www.whitsundaytourism.com; Bruce Hwy; ⏲9am-5pm Mon-Fri, 10am-4pm Sat & Sun), just south of town, for advice on the Whitsundays and the surrounding region. You can also pick up information on bushwalking trails and national-park camping permits here.

Fans of eclectic jewellery, clothing and homewares will want to detour into town to **Colour Me Crazy** (☎4945 2698; 2b Dobbins Lane; ⏲8.30am-5.30pm Mon-Fri, 8.30am-3.30pm Sat, 9.30am-2.30pm Sun), a zany boutique that showcases an amazing range of goodies from all over the world.

The airport is 14km south of town and is serviced from Brisbane and Sydney (as well as some other capitals) by **Jetstar** (☎13 15 38; www.jetstar.com.au) and **Virgin Blue** (☎13 67 89; www.virginblue.com.au).

In addition to meeting all planes and trains, **Whitsunday Transit** (☎4946 1800; www.whitsundaytransit.com.au) has a number of scheduled bus services daily from Proserpine to Airlie Beach. One way/return from the airport costs $15/28, and from the train station it's $9/16.

Whitsunday Taxis (☎13 10 08) operates a share taxi ($15 per person) service from the airport to Airlie Beach.

Airlie Beach

POP 6770

Framed by a backdrop of soft hills, and with white yachts gracing the aqua-blue ocean just metres offshore, Airlie Beach should be a picturesque little town. As the mainland gateway to the magnificent Whitsunday Islands, one would expect no less. Unfortunately, the pretty esplanade is hidden behind

DON'T MISS

TOP THREE BEACHES

If the Whitsundays has some of the finest beaches in Australia, and Australian beaches are some of the best in the world, then beach connoisseurs have hit the jackpot. Although there are plenty of secluded, postcard-perfect, sandy bays in this tropical paradise, the following places are reasonably accessible with most tour companies.

Whitehaven Beach – with azure blue waters lapping the pure white silica sand, Whitehaven, on Whitsunday Island, is absolutely stunning.

Chalkies Beach – another pure white silica sand beach, on Haslewood Island, and opposite Whitehaven Beach. As it's not on the usual tourist circuit, charter a boat and make like a castaway.

Langford Island – at high tide, Langford is a thin strip of sand on the rim of a coral-filled turquoise lagoon.

the tacky main drag, a busy and unattractive road but the heart and soul of the action. And action there is aplenty! After a day sailing to the islands, the bustling backpacker-set fill the street, partying hard, fast and frequently. Although at times it seems there's nary an Aussie accent to be heard, look around – local yachties, couples and families have just as much fun, they're just not as loud.

Abel Point Marina, where the Cruise Whitsundays ferries depart and where many of the cruising yachts are moored, is about 1km west along a pleasant boardwalk, and Shute Harbour, where the Fantasea ferries depart, is about 12km east. The new marina precinct, at the Shute Harbour end of town, was under construction at the time of writing, but by the look of the works going on, it's bound to be big.

 Activities

For details on sailing, diving and kayaking around the islands, see p239.

Swimming & Water Sports

The gorgeous lagoon on Airlie's foreshore provides year-round safe swimming and is an attractive, popular public space for those wanting to work on their tan. The beaches at Airlie Beach and Cannonvale are OK for swimming, but the presence of stingers (box jellyfish) means swimming in the sea isn't advisable between October and May. There are (seasonal) operators in front of the Airlie Beach Hotel that hire out jet skis, catamarans, windsurfers and paddle skis.

Bushwalks

The Conway Range behind Airlie Beach is part national park (see p251) and part state forest, and provides some great walking in coastal rainforest. With information supplied at the tracks, you can learn about the forest ecology and the traditional life of local Indigenous people. Try the 2.4km climb up Mt Rooper for great views, the short Coral Beach Track at Shute Harbour, or the three-day Whitsunday Great Walk. For advice and track notes on these and other walks visit the QPWS office.

Skydiving and Scenic Flights

Other active pursuits include tandem skydiving with **Tandem Skydive Airlie Beach** (☎4946 9115; www.skydiveairliebeach.com.au), with prices starting at $249. For a more sedate aerial turn you can always take a scenic flight (p242). These activities can easily be booked through your accommodation or one of the agents in Airlie Beach.

 Tours

Finding an operator to take you on a tour of the Whitsundays and the Great Barrier Reef is a confusing business. While you're spoilt for choice with island cruises, finding the right one to suit your needs can be overwhelming. The best plan of attack is to talk to other travellers.

Reeforest Adventure Tours RAINFOREST
(☎1800 500 353; 4959 8360; www.reeforest.com) This operator has a day-long Platypus & Rainforest Eco Safari ($145 per person) to Finch Hatton Gorge and visits the platypuses of Broken River. It includes lunch at a secluded bush retreat near the gorge and an interpretive walk.

Fawlty's 4WD Tropical Tours RAINFOREST
(☎4946 6665; adult/child $65/50) This tour departs daily at 10.30am, and returns at 4pm. It's a great way to see the beautiful Cedar Creek Falls (when they're running, that is) and some rainforest close up. Lunch and pick-ups are included in the price.

Whitsunday Crocodile Safari WILDLIFE
(☎4948 3310; www.crocodilesafari.com.au; adult/child $110/55) This is the best way to

Airlie Beach

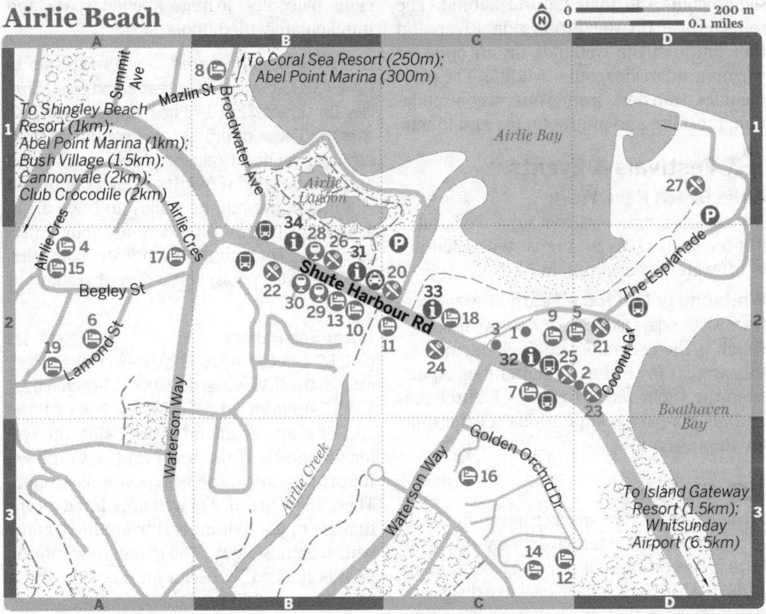

0 — 200 m
0 — 0.1 miles

To Coral Sea Resort (250m); Abel Point Marina (300m)
To Shingley Beach Resort (1km); Abel Point Marina (1km); Bush Village (1.5km); Cannonvale (2km); Club Crocodile (2km)
To Island Gateway Resort (1.5km); Whitsunday Airport (6.5km)
Airlie Bay
Airlie Lagoon
Boathaven Bay
Shute Harbour Rd
The Esplanade
Coconut Gr
Summit Ave
Mazlin St
Broadwater Ave
Airlie Cres
Begley St
Lamond St
Waterson Way
Airlie Creek
Golden Orchid Dr

Airlie Beach

Activities, Courses & Tours

1 Explore Whitsundays C2
2 Whitsunday Dive Adventures D2
3 Whitsunday Sailing Adventures C2

Sleeping

4 Airlie Apartments A2
5 Airlie Beach Hotel D2
6 Airlie Beach Motor Lodge A2
7 Airlie Beach YHA C2
8 Airlie Waterfront B&B B1
9 Airlie Waterfront Backpackers C2
10 Beaches Backpackers B2
11 Magnums Backpackers C2
12 Martinique C3
13 Nomads Backpackers B2
14 Pinnacles Resort & Spa C3
15 Sunlit Waters A2
16 Water's Edge Resort C3
17 Waterview A2
18 Whitehaven Beachfront Holiday Units C2
19 Whitsunday Organic B&B A2

Eating

20 Airlie Supermarket C2
21 Capers D2
Deja Vu .... (see 16)
22 Extreme Bean B2
23 Fish D'vine D2
24 KC's Steak & Seafood C2
25 Mangrove Jack's Café Bar C2
26 Marino's Deli B2
Village Cafe .... (see 11)
27 Whitsunday Sailing Club D1

Drinking

Beaches .... (see 10)
Magnums .... (see 11)
28 Mama Africa B2
29 Paddy's Shenanigans B2
30 Uber B2

Information

31 Airlie Beach Visitors Centre B2
32 Destination Whitsundays C2
33 Where? What? How? Whitsundays C2
34 Whitsundays Central Reservation Centre B2

see crocodiles in their natural habitat. The tours cruise up the Proserpine River and then through the wetlands on an open-air wagon train to view other wildlife. The price includes transfers from your accommodation, morning and afternoon tea and lunch.

Festivals & Events

Airlie Beach Race Week YACHT RACES
(www.airliebeachraceweek.com.au) A week of full-on yacht races in August with plenty of off-water entertainment.

Whitsunday Fun Race Festival YACHT RACES
(www.whitsundaysailingclub.com.au) Airlie Beach is the centre of activities during this annual festival each September. Apart from the yacht races, the Miss Figurehead and Mr Six-pack competitions set the tone for the festivities.

Sleeping

Airlie Beach is a backpacker haven but, with so many hostels, standards vary and bedbugs are a common problem. Most of the resorts in Airlie Beach have package deals, and stand-by rates that are much cheaper than their regular ones. The new marina development in Boathaven Bay has spoilt the view for those who stay in some of the prestigious resorts and apartments on the hill. Until the development is complete, look elsewhere for ocean views.

With nightclubs thumping beats into the main street, avoid accommodation in the centre of town – unless you intend to party into the wee hours.

TOP CHOICE **Waterview** APARTMENTS $$
(4948 1748; www.waterviewairliebeach.com.au; 42 Airlie Cres; studio/1-bedroom units from $135/149;) An excellent choice for location and comfort, this boutique accommodation overlooks the main street and has gorgeous views of the bay. The rooms are modern, airy and spacious and have kitchenettes for self-caterers.

Water's Edge Resort APARTMENTS $$$
(4948 4300; www.watersedgewhitsundays.com.au; 4 Golden Orchid Dr; 1-bedroom apt $210-260, 2-bedroom apt $275-345;) Stepping into the reception area, you immediately feel that you're on holiday. Its open-air plan and gently revolving ceiling fans stir the languid, tropical heat. The rooms feature soft colours, cane headboards and shutters that seal off the bedroom from the living space. There are wonderful views from the spacious balconies, a huge kitchen space and immaculately tiled floors.

Shingley Beach Resort APARTMENTS $$
(4948 8300; www.shingleybeachresort.com; 1 Shingley Dr; studios $150, 1-/2-bedroom apt $170/230;) These midrange, self-contained holiday apartments are close to Abel Point Marina and feature good views. It's a quiet option but still only a five-minute walk into town along a pleasant boardwalk. There are four different room configurations, private balconies, two saltwater pools, and a decent restaurant on-site.

Coral Sea Resort RESORT $$$
(1800 075 061, 4946 1300; www.coralsearesort.com; 25 Ocean View Ave; d $220-370, 1-bedroom apt $330, 2-bedroom apt $350-400;) At the end of a low headland overlooking the water just north of the town centre, Coral Sea Resort has one of the best positions around. There's a huge range of well-appointed rooms that are motel style and self-contained, many with stunning views. The massive swimming pool is flanked by ocean on one side and a bar-restaurant on the other.

Sunlit Waters APARTMENTS $$
(4946 6352; www.sunlitwaters.com; 20 Airlie Cres; studios from $92, 1-bedroom apt $115;) One of the best-value options in Airlie Beach, these large studios have everything you could want including a self-contained kitchenette and stunning views from the loooong balconies.

Summit Apartments APARTMENTS $$
(1800 463 417, 4946 3400; www.summitairliebeach.com.au; 15 Flame Tree Court; 1-/2-bedroom apt from $175/199;) On a hill behind town, these excellent-value apartments are stylish, spacious and in a quiet location. Featuring large glass windows and doors, these modern contemporary apartments have spectacular ocean views. It's a 15-minute walk into town. To get here, follow Waterson Way into Seaview Dr, then turn left into Flame Tree Ct.

Bush Village Budget Cabins HOSTEL $
(1800 809 256, 4946 6177; www.bushvillage.com.au; 2 St Martins Rd; dm from $30, d $93;) These boutique backpacker cabins only 1.5km west of Airlie have undergone a revamp and are the best budget accommodation in town. There are 17 self-contained cabins set in leafy gardens – some furnished as four- and six-bed dorms, others as doubles and two-bedroom cabins. Travellers who are

over the party scene and young couples who are into each other will want to head here. It's worth the extra bucks to stay in the swish king studios ($100 to $130). There's off-street parking, it's close to the supermarket, and there's a courtesy bus into town.

Marina Shores APARTMENTS **$$$**
(☎1800 813 066, 4964 1500; www.marinashores.com.au; Shingley Dr; 1-bedroom apt $230-260, 2-bedroom apt $270-375, 3-bedroom apt $395-650; ❄@🏊) These luxurious fully self-contained apartments have the best views overlooking Abel Point Marina and the Whitsunday Islands. The modern contemporary design makes full use of space, light and glass. And it's only a five-minute stroll into town along the boardwalk.

Pinnacles Resort & Spa APARTMENTS **$$$**
(☎4948 4800; www.pinnaclesresort.com; 16 Golden Orchid Dr; 1-/2-/3-bedroom apt from $215/285/350; ❄🏊) At the top of a steep hill, Pinnacles rewards you with five-star luxury. King-sized beds, spa baths and impeccable views make this one of the best in town.

Airlie Waterfront B&B B&B **$$$**
(☎4946 7631; www.airliewaterfrontbnb.com.au; cnr Broadwater Ave & Mazlin St; d $259-285; ❄@) Absolutely gorgeous views and immaculately presented from top to toe, this sumptuously furnished B&B oozes class and is a leisurely five-minute walk into town along the boardwalk. Some rooms have a spa, and if you tire of the ocean views (how could you?) there are enough TVs and DVD and CD players to distract your attention.

Martinique APARTMENTS **$$$**
(☎4948 0401; www.martiniquewhitsunday.com.au; 18 Golden Orchid Dr; 1-/2-/3-bedroom apt $195/260/395; ❄📶🏊) French Caribbean is the theme in these luxury digs on the hillside above Airlie. The views are stunning, especially from the spectacular tiled wet-edge pool on the third level of this five-level complex.

Nomads Backpackers HOSTEL **$**
(☎4999 6600; www.nomadsairliebeach.com; 354 Shute Harbour Rd; dm/d $28/90; ❄@📶🏊) The newest hostel to open in the heart of Airlie, Nomads is the pick of the lot. Set on 3 hectares in the centre of town, the rooms are clean and bright. The camping sites out the back are in a good shady spot (away from the noisy main street), all dorm rooms have en suites (and beds have reading lights!), and private rooms have a TV, fridge and kitchenette. There's a large kitchen and a small bar in the complex.

Whitsunday Organic B&B B&B **$$**
(☎4946 7151; www.whitsundaybb.com.au; 8 Lamond St; s/d $155/210) Rooms are comfortable, but it's the organic-garden walk and the orgasmic three-course organic breakfasts that everyone comes here for (nonguests $22.50). You can book a healing essential-oil massage, meditate in the garden teepee, or just indulge in all things organic. Lavender oil and fresh herbs surround the place to keep insects at bay and there's a 500L rainwater tank with fresh filtered water on offer as well as organic tea and coffee available all day.

Airlie Apartments APARTMENTS **$$**
(☎4946 6222; www.airlieapartments.com.au; 22-24 Airlie Cres; 1-/2-bedroom apt $120/180; ❄📶🏊) Airlie Apartments is a good-value option that's ideal for families. Although all of the apartments have loads of space, furnishing standards vary. The Superior Ocean View apartments ($260 to $320) have just that – superior ocean views – and are modern, stylish and comfortable. There's a three-night minimum stay here.

Airlie Beach Hotel HOTEL **$$**
(☎1800 466 233, 4964 1999; www.airliebeachhotel.com.au; cnr The Esplanade & Coconut Grove; s/d $129/139, apt $179-289; ❄📶🏊) The motel units are looking decidedly shabby but the sea-facing apartments are clean and spacious. With three restaurants on-site and a perfect downtown location, you could do far worse than stay here.

Club Crocodile RESORT **$$**
(☎1800 075 151, 4946 7155; www.oceanhotels.com.au; Shute Harbour Rd, Cannonvale; dm from $30, s/d $120/140; ❄🏊) Favoured by tour groups and families, Club Croc, 2km west of Airlie, has opened up budget options for backpackers. The motel-style units are looking worn and tired but they overlook an attractive central courtyard featuring a tropical pool, fountains, a tennis court, restaurants and a bar.

Whitehaven Beachfront Holiday Units APARTMENTS **$$**
(☎4946 5710; 285 Shute Harbour Rd; r $120; ❄) Smack-bang in the centre of Airlie Beach, these six older-style ground-floor studio apartments are looking a little weary but open directly onto the park in front of the beach.

Airlie Beach Motor Lodge MOTEL $$
(☎1800 810 925, 4946 6418; www.airliebeachmotorlodge.com.au; 6 Lamond St; d $130-140, 2-bedroom apt $240;) Ignore the drab exterior; although some rooms are looking tired, the renovated units are perfectly comfortable. It's in a quiet residential area just a short walk from the Shute Harbour Rd action and the lagoon.

Airlie Waterfront Backpackers HOSTEL $
(☎1800 089 000, 4948 1300; www.airliewaterfront.com; 6 The Esplanade; dm $25-33, d & tw $60-130;) Up a couple of flights of stairs, and tucked under a big A-frame roofline, the rooms can feel a bit closed in. Thank goodness for the great balconies, clean kitchen and lounge. Security is good, and all dorms have en suites and TVs. And if you get the munchies, there's a food court downstairs.

Beaches Backpackers HOSTEL $
(☎1800 636 630; 4946 6244; www.beaches.com.au; 356 Shute Harbour Rd; dm/d $25/85;) You must at least enjoy a drink at the big open-air bar, even if you're not staying here. Rivalling Magnums as party-central, Beaches has the edge with its clean rooms (metal bunks), free continental breakfast, and TV and bar fridge in every room. Custom-made tour packages are available at the travel desk.

Backpackers by the Bay HOSTEL $
(☎1800 646 994, 4946 7267; www.backpackersbythebay.com; 12 Hermitage Dr; dm $28, d & tw $70;) Located on the road to Shute Harbour and a short walk into town, this friendly, homey hostel will suit travellers who are over the party scene. The bright walls on the corridors are painted with a nautical theme and there's a relaxed barbecue area and a small bar that opens at 5.30pm. Dorms contain just four beds. Unfortunately, construction of the new marina has temporarily interfered with the usually great ocean views.

Magnums Backpackers HOSTEL $
(☎1800 624 634, 4946 1199; www.magnums.com.au; 366 Shute Harbour Rd; sites $22-24, dm/d $19/56, cabins $25;) A loud party bar, loads of alcohol, and a bevy of pretty young things…must be Magnums. Forget the tent sites close to the bar – you won't sleep unless you're comatose. Once you get past the busy reception, you'll find simple dorms in a tropical garden setting. There's a small breakfast room but no kitchen to speak of.

Airlie Beach YHA HOSTEL $
(☎1800 247 251, 4946 6312; airliebeach@yha.com.au; 394 Shute Harbour Rd; dm $27, d $70-78;) Central, but just far enough removed from the hubbub, this good, clean hostel is small and reasonably quiet. All doubles have a balcony, although the view here is nothing special.

Flametree Tourist Village CARAVAN PARK $
(☎4946 9388; www.flametreevillage.com.au; Shute Harbour Rd; sites $21-29, cabins from $77;) Not as glitzy as the other big parks, but the spacious sites are scattered through lovely, bird-filled gardens and there's a good camp kitchen and barbecue area. The park is 6.5km east of Airlie.

Island Gateway Caravan Resort CARAVAN PARK $
(☎4946 6228; www.islandgateway.com.au; Shute Harbour Rd, Jubilee Pocket; sites $30-37, cabins $80-135, chalets $145-225;) This is a big park 1.5km east of Airlie Beach. The sites are shady and the facilities are excellent and include a camp kitchen, a shop, half-court tennis and minigolf.

Eating

TOP CHOICE **Fish D'vine** SEAFOOD $$
(☎4948 0088; www.fishdvine.com.au; 303 Shute Harbour Rd; mains $10-25; ⊙lunch & dinner) Of course, rum and fish – what a perfect combination! But somehow this quirky concept has taken off like a storm. Maybe those early rum-drinking buccaneers were onto something. Dishes served from Neptune's realm will keep you happy. And the selection of more than 100 different rums is bound to unleash your inner pirate.

Alain's Restaurant FRENCH $$$
(☎4946 5464; www.alainsrestaurant.com.au; 44 Coral Esplanade, Cannonvale; mains $25-35; ⊙dinner Thu-Sat) For fine dining you can't go past this intimate French restaurant opposite Cannonvale Beach. White linen, silverware and soft candlelight add up to romance. Indulge in the six-course *table d'hôte* menu and you'll have time to ask about that Citröen parked in the corner.

Sorrento ITALIAN $$
(☎4946 7454; www.sorrentowhitsunday.com; Shingley Dr, Abel Point Marina; mains $14-30; ⊙lunch & dinner daily, breakfast Sat & Sun) This casual restaurant on the mezzanine level serves up large portions of good Italian food. Come for lunch to appreciate the superb ocean

views. The downstairs bar is full of cruising yachties.

Waterline MODERN AUSTRALIAN $$
(☎4948 1023; 1 Shingley Dr; mains $20-30; ⊙lunch & dinner Wed-Sun, breakfast Sun) With stunning views over the marina, this restaurant at Shingley Beach Resort has one of the best locations for waterfront dining. The decor is tropical-beach chic. Recommended by the locals for its good service, great food and consistent quality.

Capers MODERN AUSTRALIAN $$$
(☎4946 1777; The Esplanade; mains $27-43; ⊙7am-late) On the ground floor of the Airlie Hotel complex, this is a casual but classy affair and a local favourite. There's lots to choose from the extensive menu. It's also a great spot for a sundowner.

Deja Vu FUSION $$$
(☎4948 4309; www.dejavurestaurant.com.au; Golden Orchid Dr; lunch mains $15-21, dinner mains $27-40; ⊙lunch Wed-Sun, dinner Wed-Sat) Consistently rated as one of Airlie's best, this Polynesian-themed restaurant concocts contemporary dishes with Asian and Mediterranean influences. Be sure to while away a few hours at the famous long Sunday lunch (eight courses $39.50).

Village Café CAFE $
(www.villagecafe.com.au; 366 Shute Harbour Rd; mains $10-21; ⊙breakfast, lunch & dinner) Always busy with hungover backpackers, and those after good coffee, this popular cafe serves up breakfasts that are just the tonic to get the day started. For lunch or dinner be sure to order a 'hot rock' ($26 to $34) and watch your protein of choice cook to perfection on a volcanic rock that's been heated for 12 hours. Divine.

Mangrove Jack's Café Bar CAFE $$
(☎4964 1888; 297 Shute Harbour Rd; mains $20-24; ⊙lunch & dinner) It may be a chain restaurant, and it may be located at the Airlie Beach Hotel, but people love sitting outside at this breezy streetside bar and eatery to watch the passing parade on Shute Harbour Rd. Good pizza.

KC's Steak & Seafood STEAKHOUSE $$
(☎4946 6320; 282 Shute Harbour Rd; mains $16-40; ⊙3pm-3am) KC's happy hour(s) are followed by dinner, between 6pm and 9pm, and then there's usually live music. It's lively and licensed, and the menu has croc and roo grills, as well as steak and seafood.

Whitsunday Sailing Club PUB FARE $$
(☎4946 7894; www.whitsundaysailingclub.com.au; Airlie Point; mains $14-32; ⊙lunch & dinner) The sailing-club terrace (don't sit inside) is a great place for a meal and a drink and wonderful ocean views. Choose from the usual steak and schnitzel culprits.

Marino's Deli DELI $
(☎4946 4207; 269 Shute Harbour Rd; dishes $6-15; ⊙11am-8pm Mon-Sat) Takeaway pasta, soup and gourmet rolls with delicious fillings dominate the menu at this unpretentious little deli-cafe. It's best to stock up on antipasto offerings and have a picnic beside the lagoon.

Extreme Bean CAFE $
(346 Shute Harbour Rd; meals $7-15; ⊙breakfast & lunch). To get rid of that hangover, you need an Extreme Bean espresso. Also renowned for its frappés.

Banjo's PUB FARE $
(☎4946 7220; cnr Shute Harbour Rd & Island Dr, Cannonvale; mains $16-30; ⊙lunch & dinner) If you want to meet the locals, this unpretentious, often rowdy, bar and grill is the place to come. The fare is stock-standard chicken, steak and seafood, but there's plenty to choose from. On Wednesday and Sunday you get two meals for the price of one. It's on the corner at the Cannonvale Shopping Centre.

Airlie Supermarket SELF-CATERING $
(277 Shute Harbour Rd) If you are preparing your own food, there's a small, expensive, and horribly crowded supermarket, which is open daily and located in the centre of town. Both Woolworths and Coles are in Cannonvale.

Drinking

According to the locals, Airlie Beach is a drinking town with a sailing problem. The bars at Magnums and Beaches, the two big backpackers in the centre of town, are always crowded, and everyone starts their night at one, or both, of them.

Uber BAR
(www.uberairliebeach.com; 350 Shute Harbour Rd; ⊙2pm-11pm Tue-Thu, to 2am Fri & Sat) This ubercool bar and restaurant is the classiest in town. Come for cocktails, lounge in comfortable nooks on the alfresco deck, or just savour the uberambience.

Paddy's Shenanigans BAR

(352 Shute Harbour Rd; ⊙5pm-3am) Paddy's has live music late at night, and proudly encourages the Irish penchant for hard drinking.

Mama Africa NIGHTCLUB

(263 Shute Harbour Rd; ⊙10pm-5am) Just a stumble across the road from the main party bars, this African-style safari nightclub throbs a beat that both hunter and prey find hard to resist.

Information

Shute Harbour Rd is littered with privately run tour-booking and ticket agencies, all able to answer queries on island transport, and book tours and accommodation. Check out their noticeboards for stand-by rates on sailing tours and resort accommodation.

Internet access is widely available; all of the hostels have terminals, and there are several dedicated internet cafes.

Airlie Beach Visitors Centre (☎4946 6665; 277 Shute Harbour Rd) Information and booking agent.

Destination Whitsundays (☎4946 7172; 297 Shute Harbour Rd) Books tours.

Doctors (☎4948 0900; 283 Shute Harbour Rd; ⊙8am-6pm Mon-Fri, 9am-5pm Sat) Medical service.

Post Office (Cannonvale Shopping Centre; ⊙9am-5pm Mon-Fri, to 12.30pm Sat)

QPWS (☎4967 7355; www.derm.qld.gov.au; cnr Shute Harbour & Mandalay Rds; ⊙9am-4.30pm Mon-Fri) Very helpful advice on planning your camping trip. Information and permits for camping in the Conway and the Whitsunday Islands National Parks. It's 3km towards Shute Harbour.

Where? What? How? Whitsundays (☎4946 5255; 283 Shute Harbour Rd)

Whitsundays Central Reservation Centre (☎1800 677 119, 4946 5299; www.airliebeach.com; 259 Shute Harbour Rd; ⊙7am-7pm) Extremely helpful family-run tour agency. Books tours, accommodation, sailing trips. Also has internet.

Getting There & Away

Air

The closest major airports are Hamilton Island (p255) and Proserpine (p243). **Whitsunday Airport** (☎4946 9180), a small airfield 6km east of Airlie Beach, is midway between Airlie Beach and Shute Harbour. Half a dozen different operators are based here, and you can take a helicopter, a light plane or a seaplane out to the islands or the reef.

Air Whitsunday Seaplanes (☎4946 9111; www.airwhitsunday.com.au) flies to Hayman and Long Island. **Helireef** (☎4946 9102; www.avta.com.au) and Air Whitsunday Seaplanes run joy flights over the reef.

Boat

Transfers between Abel Point Marina and Daydream, Long and South Molle Islands are provided by **Cruise Whitsundays** (☎4946 4662; www.cruisewhitsundays.com). It also runs airport transfers from Abel Point Marina to Hamilton Island. Transfers between Shute Harbour and Hamilton Island are provided by **Fantasea** (☎4946 5111; www.fantasea.com.au); see the Getting There & Away sections of the individual islands for details. There are noticeboards at the Whitsunday Sailing Club and Abel Point Marina showing when rides or crewing are available.

Bus

Greyhound (☎1300 473 946; www.greyhound.com.au) and **Premier Motor Service** (☎13 34 10; www.premierms.com.au) buses detour off the Bruce Hwy to Airlie Beach. There are buses between Airlie Beach and all the major centres along the coast, including Brisbane ($230, 19 hours), Mackay ($38, 2 hours), Townsville ($58, 4½ hours) and Cairns ($140, 11 hours).

Long-distance buses stop on the Esplanade, between the sailing club and the Airlie Beach Hotel. Any of the booking agencies along Shute Harbour Rd can make reservations and sell bus tickets.

Whitsunday Transit (☎4946 1800) connects Proserpine (Whitsunday Coast Airport), Cannonvale, Abel Point, Airlie Beach and Shute Harbour. Buses operate from 6am to 10.30pm. Schedules are readily available from any tour agency or accommodation, and are also posted at the bus stops.

Whitsundays 2 Everywhere (☎4946 4940; www.whitsundays2everywhere.com.au) operates airport transfers from both Proserpine ($15 one-way) and Mackay ($60 one-way) airports.

Getting Around

Airlie Beach is small enough to cover by foot, and all the cruise boats have courtesy buses that will pick you up from wherever you're staying and take you to either Shute Harbour or Abel Point Marina. To book a taxi, call **Whitsunday Taxis** (☎13 10 08); there's a taxi rank on Shute Harbour Rd, opposite Magnums.

There are several car-rental agencies in town:

Avis (☎4946 6318; www.avis.com.au; 366 Shute Harbour Rd)

Europcar (☎4946 4133; www.europcar.com.au; 398 Shute Harbour Rd)

Fun Rentals (☎4948 0489; www.funrentals.com.au; 344 Shute Harbour Rd)

Hertz (☎4946 4687; www.hertz.com.au; Shute Harbour Rd)

Conway National Park

The mountains of this national park and the Whitsunday Islands were once part of the same coastal mountain range, but rising sea levels after the last ice age flooded the lower valleys and cut off the coastal peaks from the mainland.

The road from Airlie Beach to Shute Harbour passes through the northern section of the national park. Several **walking trails** start from near the picnic and day-use areas, including a 1km-long circuit track to a mangrove creek. About 1km past the day-use area and on the northern side of the road, there's a 2.4km walk up to the **Mt Rooper lookout**, which provides good views of the Whitsunday Passage and Islands. Further along the main road, and up the hill towards Coral Point (before Shute Harbour), there's a pleasant 1km track leading down to Coral Beach and the **Beak lookout**. This track was created with the assistance of the Giru Dala, the traditional custodians of the Whitsunday area; a brochure available at the start of the trail explains how the local Aborigines used plants growing in the area.

To reach the beautiful **Cedar Creek Falls**, turn off the Proserpine–Airlie Beach road on to Conway Rd, 18km southwest of Airlie Beach. It's then about 15km to the falls; the roads are well signposted.

At the end of Conway Rd, 20km from the turn-off, is **Conway Beach**. A small coastal community on the shores of Repulse Bay and at the southern end of the Conway National Park, it consists of a few old houses and pleasant picnic areas along the foreshore, but the beach isn't one of the best and is notorious for sharks and stingers. **Conway Beach Tourist Park** (☎4947 3147; www.conwaybeach.com.au; 10 Daniels St, Conway Beach; camp sites $26, cabins $95-120;) is a friendly van park with an impressively colourful ladies amenities block.

Long Island

Underrated Long Island has the best of everything. With three resorts, each with a different personality, this rugged island is suitable for everybody. It's about 9km long but not much more than 1.5km wide, and a channel only 500m wide separates it from the mainland. There are 13km of walking tracks and some fine lookouts, and day-trippers can use the facilities at Long Island Resort.

Activities

The **beaches** on Long Island are some of the best in the Whitsundays. Walks are through dry rainforest vine thicket and are gentle to moderately steep. There's a **national park camp site** (sites per person/family $6/21) at Sandy Bay.

Sleeping & Eating

Paradise Bay RESORT $$$
(☎4946 9777; www.paradisebay.com.au; 3-night packages per person from $1800) This secluded lodge on Paradise Bay consists of 10 spacious, waterfront bungalows made from Australian hardwood, with high cathedral ceilings. The bungalows are positioned to make the most of the sea breezes and the huge front window opens for magnificent views. The resort uses solar power, natural gas and collected rainwater and the whole lodge complex aims to consume less energy than the average suburban home – while still maintaining its standards of 'eco-luxury'. The maximum number of guests is just 20 and there are no phones, no TV and no kids. All meals, beer, wine and soft drinks are included in the tariff. There is a three-night minimum stay, no day visitors, and no motorised water sports, so you are guaranteed peace and tranquillity. The tariff is inclusive of helicopter transfers from Hamilton Island, sailing tours and activities.

Long Island Resort RESORT $$
(☎1800 075 125, 4946 9400; www.oceanhotels.com.au/longisland; d incl all meals $260-380;) A resort for everyone and, yep, the kids are more than welcome here. Sitting on Happy Bay at the north of the island, Long Island Resort is a comfortable, mid-range place that offers guests beachfront- or garden-view motel-style rooms and a budget lodge option. There are some fabulous short walks around the island that start from here, from the 600m stroll to Humpy Point to the 4.4km walk to Sandy Bay. There are plenty of activities to keep all age groups busy. The resort is currently undergoing some much needed renovations, especially the backpacker accommodation in the Barefoot Lodge. Even after the reno, the lodge dorms will share bathroom facilities, and although there's a new camp kitchen in the works, you're better off spending the extra to stay in the beachfront rooms. As well as a wide selection of free activities on offer including snorkelling, bird feeding and beach volleyball, you can hire jet skis ($70

for 20 minutes), go water-boarding ($70 for 20 minutes) or waterskiing ($60 for 20 minutes). Always check the internet or the agents in Airlie Beach for stand-by rates, as they can be significantly cheaper.

Getting There & Away

Cruise Whitsundays (☎4946 4662; www.cruisewhitsundays.com) connects Long Island Resort to Abel Point Marina by frequent daily services. The direct trip takes about 20 minutes, and costs $30/20 per adult/child.

Hook Island

The second largest of the Whitsundays, 53-sq-km Hook Island is predominantly national park and rises to 450m at Hook Peak. There are a number of good beaches dotted around the island, and Hook boasts some of the best diving and snorkelling locations in the Whitsundays. The resort itself is a no-frills, budget place. Many travellers come here enticed by the low prices and have left disappointed because it's not what they expected. If you want five-star luxury, don't come to Hook Island...try Hayman instead!

The southern end of the island is indented by two very long fjord-like bays. Beautiful **Nara Inlet** is a popular deep-water anchorage for yachts, and Aboriginal rock paintings have been found there. Hook has an old underwater observatory that is no longer functioning.

There are some wonderful camping opportunities in basic national-park **camping grounds** (per person/family $6/21), which are located at Maureen Cove, Steen's Beach, Bloodhorn Beach, Curlew Beach and Crayfish Beach.

Hook Island Wilderness Resort (☎4946 9380; www.hookislandresort.com; camp sites per person $20, d $100-120; ❄☒) has seen better days. Amenities and rooms are basic and maintenance is an issue. The simple, adjoining units each sleep up to six or eight people; the bathrooms are *tiny*. Private rooms have no en suite, but the camp sites have a superb beachfront location. However, the barbecues are out of action and the camp kitchen isn't much better. On the plus side, there's great snorkelling just off shore from the resort. So if snorkelling is your main priority and you don't mind roughing it, you might want to head here.

Food is not a priority at the resort. The licensed **restaurant** (mains $14-18) serves seafood, steak and pasta, and there is usually a vegetarian option on offer at night; snacks are available during the rest of the day and there is also the Barefoot Bar, which opens at noon.

Transfers to the resort are arranged when you book your accommodation. Return transfers are by regular tour boat. The **Voyager** (☎4946 5255) does a daily three-island cruise (Hook Island, Whitehaven Beach and Daydream Island) and can drop you off at Hook ($40) but you'll have to complete the three-island cruise on the return ($120). With enough notice the resort can organise a more economical option. **Whitsunday Island Camping Connections – Scamper** (☎4946 6285; www.whitsundaycamping.com.au) can organise drop-offs to the camping grounds for around $160 return.

Daydream Island

Gorgeous little Daydream Island would be dreamy if it wasn't always so busy. At just more than 1km long and 200m wide, and the closest resort to the mainland, Daydream is a very popular day-trip destination. It's suitable for everybody, but especially busy families, swinging singles, and couples looking for a romantic island wedding. There is a wide range of nonmotorised water-sports gear (including catamarans and kayaks) available for hire (free for resort guests). Daydream also offers a variety of motorised **water sports** for guests, including parasailing, jet-skiing, and waterskiing, all at the northern end of the island. You can also go diving (introductory dive $110).

A steep, rocky path, taking about 20 minutes to walk, links the northern end with the much quieter southern end of the island. There's another short walk to the tiny but lovely **Lover's Cove**, and a concreted path leads around the eastern side of the island. And once you've done these walks, you've just about covered Daydream from head to foot.

Surrounded by beautifully landscaped tropical gardens, and with the largest open-air aquarium in the Southern Hemisphere (filled with stingrays, sharks, and tropical fish), **Daydream Island Resort & Spa** (☎1800 075 040, 4948 8488; www.daydreamisland.com; 3-night packages $900-2500; ❄☒) has 296 rooms. With tennis courts, a gym, catamarans, windsurfers, three swimming pools, and an open-air cinema, all of which are included in the tariff, this resort barely offers time for daydreaming. There are five grades of accommodation and most package deals include a buffet breakfast. There is a club with constant activities to keep children occupied and they will love the **stingray splash** ($38) and fish-feeding sessions held at the small coral reef pool near the main atrium. This is a large resort on a small island, so it's not the place to head if you're seeking isolation. It's much cheaper in low season, and keep an eye out for standby rates from the mainland.

Breakfast is served up buffet-style at the Waterfalls Restaurant, which stays open all day, serving snacks, lunch and dinner. **Boathouse Bakery** provides coffee, sandwiches and other lunchtime snacks. The Neptune-themed **Fishbowl Tavern** offers the usual pizza, steak, risotto and salad. More formal is **Mermaids**, which is situated right on the beachfront.

In addition, the resort has three bars: Lagoon, which has nightly entertainment, Splashes Pool and Gilligans. After all that frenzied activity, make time for a pamper session at the **Rejuvenation Spa**, which offers naturopathic treatments as well as indulgent massages.

Cruise Whitsundays (☎4946 4662; www.cruisewhitsundays.com; one-way adult/child $30/20) connects Daydream Island to Abel Point Marina with frequent daily services. **Voyager** (☎4946 5255; adult/child $140/80) visits Daydream on its daily three-island cruise to Hook Island, Whitehaven Beach and Daydream Island.

South Molle Island

South Molle Island offers an impressive array of short or long walks through gorgeous rainforest, making it an ideal destination for those wanting to put their legs to good use. The resort, which is decidedly nonglitzy, also has a nine-hole golf course, a gym, and tennis and squash courts. There is also a wide range of nonmotorised water-sports gear available for day-trippers to hire. Of course, if relaxation is more your style, South Molle doesn't disappoint, with some superb beaches and a huge pool surrounded by inviting sun lounges.

Largest of the Molle group of islands at 4 sq km, South Molle is virtually joined to Mid Molle and North Molle Islands – indeed, you can walk across a causeway to Mid Molle. Apart from the resort area and golf course at Bauer Bay in the north, the island is all designated national park. There is some forest cover around the resort, and the trees are gradually reclaiming the once overgrazed pastures. The island is criss-crossed by 11km of walking tracks and has some superb lookout points. The highest point is **Mt Jeffreys** (198m), but the climb up **Spion Kop** will reward you with fantastic sunset views. The track to Spion Kop passes an ancient Ngaro stone quarry – look out for an area of shattered rock spilling down the hillside.

The island is known for its prolific birdlife. The most noticeable birds are the dozens of tame, colourful lorikeets and black currawongs. The endangered stone curlews are also common and rather intimidating. The beaches are reasonably good at high tide, but severe tidal shifts mean some time will be spent at the pool.

There are national-park **camping grounds** (sites per person/family $6/21) located at Sandy Bay in the south and at Paddle Bay near the resort.

Adventure Island Resort (☎1800 464 444; www.koalaadventures.com.au; dm from $49-100, d $180-240, 3-night minimum stay; ❄@≋), formerly known as South Molle Island Resort, is far from luxurious and is in dire need of a spruce-up but the rooms (pretty much your basic motel-style) are clean, comfortable and functional. The bungalows on the beachfront are the best option – each with its own spa, and balcony to catch the sea breeze. There are also four-, five- and six-share dorm rooms with en suites.

The Discovery Bar, and restaurants, surround a large swimming pool and this is the heart of the resort's active nightlife. Attracting a more adventurous, young-at-heart crowd, Adventure Island is *the* party island but cocktails, party games and dancing aren't the only activities on offer. Archery, tennis, paddle skis, bushwalking, fish-feeding and beach volleyball are free while sailing, diving, snorkelling and paddle safaris incur a minor cost. There's also a nine-hole golf course at the resort. Plans are afoot to host a regular full-moon party with DJs and entertainment – check with the resort.

Make the most of the Adventure Island experience by cruising on the *Pride of Airlie,* which stops at South Molle for two nights on its three-day trip (adult $349). The journey also includes Whitehaven Beach. You can also extend the sailing trip by opting to stay for two extra nights at the resort for only $49 per night. Book through **Koala Adventures** (☎1800 466 444; www.koalaadventures.com.au).

Cruise Whitsundays (☎4946 4662; www.cruisewhitsundays.com) offers connections to South Molle (via Daydream Island) from Abel Point Marina (adult/child $30/20).

Hamilton Island

Hamilton Island can come as quite a shock for the first-time visitor. Swarms of people and heavy development make Hamilton seem like a busy town rather than a resort island. Although this is not everyone's idea of a perfect getaway, it's hard not to be impressed by the sheer range of accommodation options, restaurants, bars and activities. The great thing about Hamilton is there's something for everyone here.

Sights & Activities

The sheer size of this resort means there are plenty of entertainment possibilities, which makes Hamilton an interesting day trip from Shute Harbour as you can use some of the resort facilities.

Before leaving Hamilton marina, wander down to **Foots Artwork** (☎4946 8308; www.foot.com.au), a gallery featuring the unique work of Airlie Beach local, Foot Young. The beautiful marble and bronze sculptures of mermaids, dolphins, marine creatures and fantasy creations are fascinating.

A few dive shops by the harbour organise dives and certificate courses. **H2O Sportz** (☎4946 9888; www.h2osportz.com.au) offers PADI dive courses, introductory dives, and snorkel safaris. **Cruise Indigo** (☎4946 8613; www.cruiseindigo.com.au) has a 1½-hour sunset cruise (adult/child $60/40), which includes complimentary drinks and nibbles, but you can find a variety of cruises to other islands and the outer reef. Half-day fishing trips cost around $125 per person, with fishing gear supplied.

From **Catseye Beach**, in front of the resort, you can hire windsurfers, catamarans, jet skis and other equipment, and go parasailing, wakeboarding or water-skiing. Among the other options are helicopter joy rides and game fishing. The resort has tennis courts, squash courts, a gym, a golf driving range and a minigolf course. There's also an 18-hole championship **golf course** on nearby Dent Island. Ferries leave from the marina on the hour every hour, and take five minutes to reach Dent. The clubhouse here is a popular lunch outing.

There are a few **walking trails** on Hamilton Island, the best being from behind the Reef View Hotel up to Passage Peak (230m) on the northeastern corner of the island. Hamilton also has a day spa, and day care and a Clownfish Club for kids.

Sleeping

Hamilton Island Resort RESORT **$$$**
(☎13 73 33, 4946 9999; www.hamiltonisland.com.au;) The resort has a number of accommodation options ranging from hotel rooms to self-contained apartments to penthouses and luxury bungalows. Rates listed on the website are for one night although almost everyone stays for at least three nights, when the cheaper package deals come into effect. All bookings need to be made through the central reservations number.

Qualia RESORT **$$$**
(☎13 73 33; d $1450-3500) The newest and most luxurious resort in the Whitsundays (and possibly Australia), Qualia has a relaxed modern design that makes full use of its stunning natural setting to draw the outside in. With large windows, glass doors and warm timber fittings, the private villas (called pavilions) appear like heavenly tree houses in the leafy hillside. Leeward Pavilions have a private sun deck, Windward Pavilions have an infinity plunge pool, while the ultimate Beach House has the lot. With a private beach, two restaurants and two swimming pools, you won't need to venture out of the resort's 30-acre grounds.

Beach Club RESORT **$$$**
(☎13 73 33; d $700) Once the star of Hamilton Island, the Beach Club is looking a little dated but the rooms are spacious and all have beachfront positions. The infinity pool overlooking Catseye Beach is sublime and, since this is an adults-only resort, serene and peaceful.

Whitsunday Holiday Apartments APARTMENTS **$$$**
(☎13 73 33; d $385) These serviced one- to four-bedroom apartments are on the resort side of the island and are very popular with families.

Palm Bungalows CABINS **$$$**
(☎13 73 33; d $315) These attractive individual units behind the resort complex are closely packed but buffered by lush gar-

dens. Each has a double and a single bed, and a small patio with a hammock.

Self-Catering Accommodation APARTMENTS **$$$**
(☎13 73 33; d $380-2000) There are several types of fully self-contained units, from standard to luxury. There's a four-night minimum stay.

Reef View Hotel HOTEL **$$$**
(☎13 73 33; d from $385) This large and ugly 20-storey, four-star hotel has 386 spacious rooms, mostly balconied; some have Coral Sea views, others garden views. Popular with families.

Eating & Drinking

The main resort complex has a number of restaurants, but it's probably more fun strolling up and down the marina several times and finding an independently run restaurant along the waterfront. There's also a supermarket and general store for those in apartments preparing their own meals.

Bommie Restaurant MODERN AUSTRALIAN **$$$**
(☎4948 9433; Hamilton Island Yacht Club; mains $20-45; ⌚dinner) This fine-dining restaurant at the stunning new yacht club has superb water views. The menu isn't extensive but has an interesting twist on its mouth-watering selections. There's also the casual alfresco **cafe** (tapas $7-15; ⌚lunch), where a glass of chilled white wine and a small selection of tapas is the civilised way to ease into the afternoon.

Romano's ITALIAN **$$$**
(☎4946 8212; Marina Village; mains $28-40; ⌚dinner Wed-Sun) This is a relaxed Italian restaurant with a large enclosed deck built right out over the water. This is a great option if you're not sure where to go as it caters equally well for groups, couples and families.

Manta Ray Café CAFE **$$**
(☎4946 8213; Marina Village; mains $17-30; ⌚lunch & dinner) The food is popular here because it's simple and very tasty. The wood-fired gourmet pizzas are a favourite although the salt-and-pepper squid and the Spanish paella provide worthy competition.

Mariners Seafood Restaurant SEAFOOD **$$$**
(☎4946 8628; Marina Village; mains $38-47; ⌚dinner) In a big, enclosed verandah overlooking the harbour, Mariners is both licensed and BYO. While the emphasis is on seafood, grills are also available; it's a stylish restaurant with a menu to match.

Steakhouse STEAKHOUSE **$$$**
(☎4946 8019; Marina Village; mains $14-40; ⌚dinner) Carnivores will be in their element. If it's dead animal, then it's cooked here. You just need to choose between the steak, lamb rump, ribs, lamb shanks or the huge chicken parma.

Sails MODERN AUSTRALIAN **$$**
(☎4946 8562; Hamilton Island Resort; mains $22-30; ⌚breakfast, lunch & dinner) Enjoy a casual poolside breakfast or a lazy lunch at this cool cafe overlooking Catseye Beach. Go for dinner, or just settle in for a drink and nibble from the snack menu while listening to live music.

Marina Tavern PUB FARE **$**
(☎4946 8839; Marina Village; mains $14-20; ⌚lunch & dinner) Formerly the yacht club, this busy harbourside pub affords wonderful views of the marina. It's a great place for a decent pub feed or a drink.

Ice Cream Parlour ICE CREAM **$**
(Marina Village; ⌚8am-10pm) Responsible for dirty little faces (and grown-up ones!) for years, this busy kiosk serves all kinds of frosty delights.

Entertainment

Some of the bars in the resort and harbourside offer nightly entertainment and there's always **Boheme's NightClub** (Marina Village; ⌚9pm-late Thu-Sat).

Getting There & Away

Air

Hamilton Island airport is the main arrival centre for the Whitsundays. **Qantas** (☎13 20 30; www.qantas.com.au) and **Jetstar** (☎13 15 38; www.jetstar.com.au) have flights to/from Brisbane, Sydney and Melbourne. **Virgin Blue** (☎13 67 89; www.virginblue.com.au) has flights to/from Brisbane and Sydney.

Boat

Fantasea (☎4946 5111; www.fantasea.com.au) connects Hamilton Island marina (adult/child $125/62) and the airport ($49/27) to Shute Harbour by frequent daily services. **Cruise Whitsundays** (☎4946 4662; www.cruisewhitsundays.com) connects Hamilton Island airport and Abel Point Marina in Airlie Beach (adult/child $59/37).

Getting Around

There's a free shuttle-bus service operating around the island from 7am to 11pm.

Everyone hires a golf buggy ($45/55/60 per one/two/three hours, $65 all day) to whiz around the island. They are available from the office near the reception of Hamilton Island Resort or from the Charter Base near the ferry terminal.

Hayman Island

The most northern island of the Whitsunday group, Hayman is just 4 sq km in area and rises to 250m above sea level. It has forested hills, sandy beaches and a luxurious five-star resort, but at low tide the beach fronting the resort becomes a wide, shallow reef.

Hayman is closer to the outer reef than the other islands, and there is good diving around its northern end and at nearby Hook Island. There are several small, uninhabited islands close to Hayman: Langford Island, 2km southwest, has some good coral around it, as do Black and Bird Islands nearby.

Activities

Hayman Island Resort guests have free use of catamarans, windsurfers, paddle skis, and tennis and squash courts. There's also a driving range for golf, a putting green and a well-equipped gym.

The resort has a dive shop and a range of diving and snorkelling trips to the Great Barrier Reef, including the increasingly popular night dives. Learn to dive at Blue Pearl Bay (introductory dives from $270).

Bushwalks include an 8km island circuit, a 4.5km walk to Dolphin Point at the northern tip of the island, and a 1.5km climb up to the Whitsunday Passage lookout. To enjoy the water views, take a scenic seaplane flight or sunset sail.

Spa Hayman offers all the pampering you could possibly handle so drop the kids off at **Hernando's Hideaway**, a kids club and crèche that keeps children and toddlers entertained, and let the treatments begin.

Tours

Air Whitsunday Seaplanes SCENIC FLIGHT
(☎4946 9111; www.airwhitsunday.com.au) This company offers several options for seaplane tours for resort guests. Destinations include a three-hour stop at Whitehaven Beach ($300) and a three-hour reef adventure to Hardy Reef ($390).

Mt Hook Sunset Tour SCENIC FLIGHT
(per person $210) For a romantic sunset, you can be dropped off by helicopter on top of Mt Hook on nearby Hook Island. With a picnic rug, cushions, champagne and a cheese platter, and a magnificent tropical sunset, you can't go wrong. Book at the reception of Hayman Island Resort.

Sleeping

Hayman Island Resort RESORT $$$
(☎1800 075 175, 4940 1234; www.hayman.com.au; r $595-3900 incl breakfast;) An avenue of stately 9m-high date palms leads to the main entrance of this five-star resort. With its 210 rooms, a hectare of swimming pools, landscaped gardens, an awesome collection of antiques and arts, and exclusive boutiques, Hayman is certainly impressive. The resort's original '80s-style architectural design and furnishings has recently undergone a makeover with emphasis on light and space. With rooms that open directly onto the fabulous pool (including stepladders from your balcony into the water), and the introduction of eight contemporary and stylish beachfront villas, Hayman is definitely one of the most luxurious resorts on the Great Barrier Reef.

Eating & Drinking

Breakfast is served buffet-style in **Azure**, a relaxed indoor/outdoor restaurant with a great outlook over the beach.

There are quite a few restaurants, including **La Trattoria** (mains $28; dinner), a casual Mediterranean restaurant with live music; the **Oriental** (mains $34; dinner), in a beautiful Japanese garden; and **La Fontaine** (mains $42; dinner), the most formal of the restaurants, with a Louis XIV–style dining room and classic French and modern European cuisine.

Not to be missed is the **Chef's Table**, a weekly behind-the-scenes look into the main kitchen with the head chef. It's a six-course banquet (with matching wines) and costs $245. Also not to be missed is a tour of the Chocolate Room where you get to sample a variety of delicious homemade chocolates.

Sunset cocktails are a must at the Beach Pavilion.

The Hayman wine cellar stocks more than 20,000 bottles of Australian and European wine, and La Fontaine has an additional 400 vintages.

Getting There & Away

Guests flying into Hamilton Island are met by Hayman staff and escorted to one of the resort's fleet of luxury cruisers (return adult/child $290/145) for a pampered transfer to the resort. **Air Whitsunday Seaplanes** (☎4946

BEST WHITSUNDAY ISLAND RESORTS...

Only seven of the Whitsunday Islands have resorts, each with its own unique flavour and style. Depending on whether you want to romance, party or pamper, check the list below.

...For Ecotourism

Paradise Bay (p251) is an exclusive ecoresort with an environmental conscience. Recognising the impact large resorts have on the natural environment, Paradise Bay has just 10 simple bungalows and implements 'earth-kind' sustainable operations without compromising on luxury. The resort even plants 1200 trees a year to offset carbon-dioxide emissions from guests' travel.

...For Luxury

Qualia (p254) on Hamilton Island is divine. Guests stay in luxurious pavilions amongst the trees and feast on stunning Coral Sea views from their own private plunge pool. Qualia raises the bar for a new generation of resorts.

Hayman Island Resort (p256) epitomises old-fashioned views of pampering and luxury with a focus on sensory and gustatory indulgence and impeccable service, and has a whopping big pool.

...For Families

Daydream Island Resort (p252) is always buzzing with activity. There's fun stuff for all age groups on and off the water, and with a kiddies club, an open-air cinema, and plenty of restaurants, cafes and a pool bar, you (and better still, the kids) won't be bored.

Long Island Resort (p251) is decidedly less glitzy but still has plenty of activities to keep the kids busy while you laze on the beach or lounge beside the pool with a pink cocktail in hand.

Club Med (p258) on Lindeman Island is the Energiser bunny of the island resorts. If you've got hyperkids, head here – the famous kids' club and its limitless choice of activities will use up any surplus energy.

...For Romance

Paradise Bay (p251), on Long Island, is not only an ecoresort, it's a favourite honeymoon hot spot. It's exclusive and intimate but don't expect glitzy-glam; this is simple nature-based elegance.

...For Fun

Adventure Island Resort (p253), on South Molle Island, carries the Airlie Beach party crowd into the wee hours. With DJs, hot bands and full-moon parties, good times are only as far away as the next drink. The resort has plenty of water-sport activities and fantastic bushwalks to cure those nasty hangovers so, come nightfall, you can start all over again.

9111; www.airwhitsunday.com.au) provides a seaplane charter service from Hamilton Island ($1590 per plane).

Flying is also the only way to do day trips to Hayman ($195 per person).

Lindeman Island

Sitting snugly at the southern end of the Whitsundays, pretty little Lindeman Island is far enough away from the hubbub of Hamilton Island and Airlie Beach to be 'remote', but compensates with an energy all its own.

Club Med took over the resort in 1992 and while it's a little dated in appearance, a vibrant, youthful atmosphere seems to radiate from everywhere you go. The 8-sq-km island is mostly national park, and while the resort will appeal to travellers of all ages, those who don't have kids, or don't want to share the island with lots of kids, should look elsewhere.

Activities

The resort boasts an archery range, an excellent golf course, tennis and all number of daily classes from power walking to aerobics, dance and stretching.

The usual range of **water-sports** equipment is available, and a **diving school** offers various dive courses and snorkelling trips. Children are also kept busy with all sorts of organised activities.

For a less strenuous experience, the **Whitsunday Club Spa** offers body pampering at an extra (hefty!) cost.

There is some excellent **walking** on the 20km of trails. A must is the 3.6km journey to the top of Mt Oldfield (210m) where you will be rewarded with stunning vistas of the Whitsundays.

Sleeping

Club Med RESORT **$$$**

(1300 855 052, 4946 9333; www.clubmed.com.au; 1-night full-board packages per 2 people from $720;) It's all hustle and bustle at Club Med and it's no secret this resort will appeal to energetic types. However, it's not too difficult to slow the pace down if that's what you prefer. The staff ensure there are plenty of activities to keep you entertained, and the famous kids club may well ensure you don't see the little ones all day (good news for most parents!). The accommodation serves a purpose, but don't expect luxury. Unless you want to hoof it up a mountain of steps, splash out a bit and ask for a resort-side room.

Eating

All meals and drinks (yep, including alcohol – oh, those cocktails!) are included in the tariff. The Main Restaurant serves buffet-style breakfasts, lunches and dinners. The food is plentiful and varied, but the heaped plates of pastas, rice dishes, lasagnes etc can get a bit tiresome. Try to visit the pleasant Nicholson's restaurant, a smaller à la carte place (open only two nights per week), at least once.

Entertainment

Every night there's a live show in the main theatre performed by the young and energetic staff. It's great fun, but put it into perspective. These are not highly paid actors and dancers. They're just young people making a couple of bucks while travelling and it's all very amateur in a fun kind of way. Yep, it's corny, but that only adds to the appeal. You're likely to find yourself singing and dancing along. There's usually a live band from 6.30pm and the 'disco' gets going from 10.30pm.

Getting There & Away

Club Med has its own launch that connects with flights from Hamilton Island and is included in your package.

Whitsunday Island

TOP CHOICE **Whitehaven Beach** is touted as one of the most beautiful beaches in the world. A pristine 7km-long stretch of dazzling white silica sand on Whitsunday Island, it's bounded by lush tropical vegetation and a brilliant blue sea. From Hill Inlet at the northern end of the beach, the swirling pattern of pure white sand through the turquoise and aquamarine water paints a magical picture. There's excellent snorkelling from its southern end.

Whitsunday Island itself is the largest of the Whitsunday group, covering 109 sq km and rising to 438m at Whitsunday Peak. It has some fine bushwalking tracks. There's no resort, but there are national-park **camping grounds** (per person/family $6/21) at Dugong, Nari's and Joe's Beaches in the west, and at Chance Bay in the south; at the southern end of Whitehaven Beach; and Peter Bay in the north.

Dingo Beach, Hydeaway Bay & Cape Gloucester

Back on the mainland, north of Airlie Beach, there's a lonely road leading to some lovely coastal retreats, where peace and tranquillity (and fish) are virtually guaranteed. **Dingo Beach** is a quiet little place with an evocative name, and is set on a long sandy bay backed by low, forested mountains.

There are two islands a little way off either end of the bay. **Gloucester Island** is to the northwest and **Saddleback Island** sits to the northeast. Both have small national-park **camping grounds** (sites per person/family $6/21).

At secluded **Hydeaway Bay**, there's the friendly **Hydeaway Bay Caravan Park** (4945 7170; www.hydeawaybaycaravanpark.com.

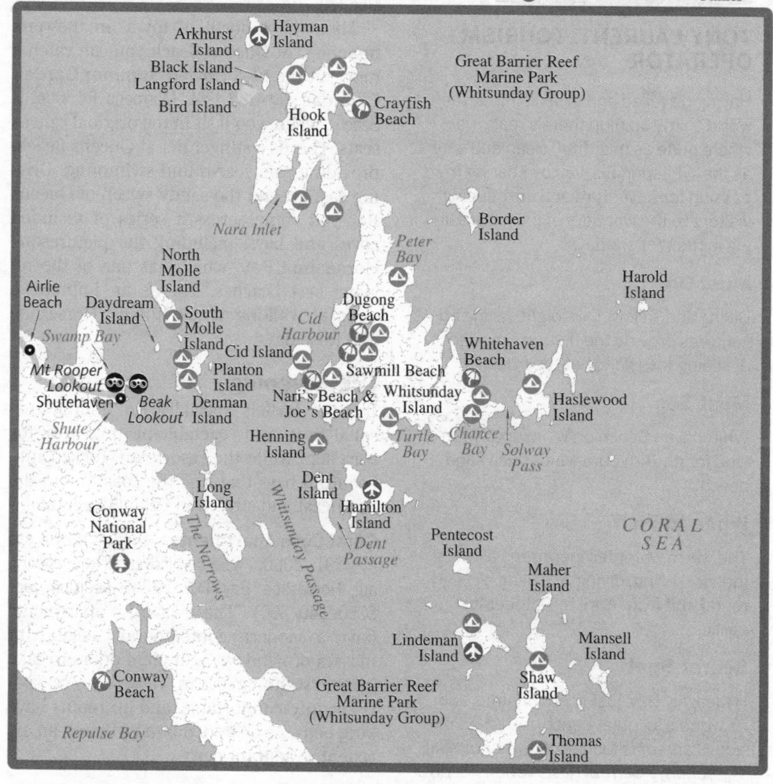

au; 414 Hydeaway Bay Dr; sites $24/28), where shade is at a premium. Further down the track are a couple of real surprises. **Cape Gloucester Eco-Resort** (☎4945 7242; www.capeg.com.au; d $100-300; ❄📶🏊) has comfortable bungalows and motel-style rooms facing the sandy beach. The outdoor bar and the **Oar** (mains $21-34; ⏲lunch & dinner) restaurant have great beachfront views. You can borrow a glass-bottomed kayak or just swim in the 25m saltwater pool. Pick-ups can be arranged from Whitsunday Coast (Proserpine) Airport. If you have your own boat, the resort has its own mooring and you can use the resort's facilities for $25/125 per day/week.

Also along the rough dirt track out to Cape Gloucester is an older, more understated resort set on 20 acres of bushland. **Montes Reef Resort** (☎4945 7177; www.montesreefresort.com.au; d from $140) has beachfront bungalows that are looking a bit worn and run-down but the brilliant location more than compensates. It's quiet and secluded, and lunch at the lovely open-air beachfront bar and bistro is well worth a day trip from Airlie.

If beachcombing or fishing aren't enough to keep you happy, hop on a jet ski with **Ecojet Safari** (☎4946 6610; www.coralseaecojetsafari.com.au; half-day safari per ski $375, incl lunch & transfers from Airlie Beach), which is based at Montes Reef Resort and runs eco-educational safaris around the Edgecumbe Bay area.

Bowen

POP 7850

Bowen is a classic reminder of the typical small Queensland coastal towns of the 1970s – wide streets, low-rise buildings, wooden Queenslander houses, and laid-back friendly locals. The foreshore with its newly

LOCAL KNOWLEDGE

TONY LAURENT: TOURISM OPERATOR

Having travelled and sailed all over the world, in my opinion there's really nowhere quite as beautiful, clean and safe as the Whitsundays. I enjoy sharing my passion for adventure and introducing visitors to the wonders of pleasure sailing in the Whitsundays.

Must Do

Diving and sailing. Overnight sailing adventures provide the unique experience of seeing the islands at their best.

Must See

Whitehaven Beach on Whitsunday Island for its 7km pure white silica sand beach.

When to Visit

The warm water temperatures allow for snorkelling, diving or sailing all year round, but from April to October it's idyllic.

Secret Spot

Hydeaway Bay, just north of Airlie, and its wonderful quiet beach.

Tony Laurent is founder & owner of Whitsundays Central Reservations Centre

landscaped esplanade and picnic tables and barbecues is a focal point. Although the town itself holds little of interest to travellers (except those who are keen on fruit-picking between April and November), there are some stunning beaches and bays northeast of the town centre.

Sights & Activities

For a spectacular view of the Coral Sea and the Whitsunday Islands, head up to **Flagstaff Hill**, overlooking Kings Beach and to the east of the town centre. Several walls and buildings around the centre of town are decorated with terrific **murals** depicting the town's history, painted by Queensland artists. There are currently 24 mural sites, most within the block formed by Gregory, Powell, Herbert and George Sts. The town's early history is displayed at the **Bowen Historical Museum** (☎4786 2035; 22 Gordon St; adult/child $5/2; ⏰9.30am-3.30pm Mon-Fri).

About 2km north of town are Bowen's **beaches**. At Queens Beach you can catch a movie at the 1948 **Bowen Summer Garden Cinemas** (☎4785 1241; Murroona Rd, Queens Beach), where you'll sit in the original canvas seats. There's a stinger net at Queens Beach, providing safe year-round swimming. Driving east around the sandy sweep of Queens Bay you come across a series of secluded coves and bays, including the picturesque **Horseshoe Bay**, which has one of the regions best beaches. There's an impressive **coastal walking track** linking Horseshoe and Rose Bays.

Sleeping

Bowen's hostels specialise in finding seasonal fruit- and vegetable-picking work for travellers while the resorts are tucked into beautiful bays that line the coastline to the northeast and stretch to Cape Edgecumbe.

Coral Cove Apartments APARTMENTS **$$$**
(☎4791 2000; www.coralcoveapartments.com.au; Horseshoe Bay Rd; 1-/2-/3-bedroom apt $250/340/360) These swish apartments have a modern contemporary edge with masses of windows and glass doors to take in the stunning ocean view. They're spacious, ultracomfortable, and all rooms have king beds. As an added bonus, there's an excellent restaurant here.

Rose Bay Resort RESORT **$$**
(☎4786 9000; www.rosebayresort.com.au; 2 Pandanus St, Rose Bay; r $145-290, minimum 2-night stay; ❄@≋) In a beautiful location right on the beach, these spacious studios and comfy units will ensure plenty of quiet time. Good location and good value.

Horseshoe Bay Resort CARAVAN PARK **$**
(☎4786 2564; horseshoe@bigpond.net.au; Horseshoe Bay; sites $32-36, cabins $62, self-contained units $80-115; ≋) You can hear the small waves lapping at Horseshoe Bay from this decent park, which is nestled among the granite boulders. The cabins look a little shabby but it's walking distance to the beautiful Horseshoe Bay beach and close to the Horseshoe Bay Cafe.

Aussiemates Backpackers HOSTEL **$**
(☎4786 3100; aussiemates@live.com; dm/d per week $160/190) In a lovely old Queenslander in the centre of town, this family-run and ultrafriendly hostel is like a home away from home. It's clean and freshly painted, has

two kitchens, and a large upstairs verandah overlooking the main street. Weekly rates include transfers to working farms.

Whitsunday Sands Resort RESORT $$
(☎4786 3333; www.whitsundaysandsresort.com; Horseshoe Bay; d $98-166;) Out on the headland of Cape Edgecumbe, this resort is in a pleasant setting, with access to several coves and beaches. The complex has decent enough motel-style rooms, small self-contained units, a bar, a kiosk and a so-so restaurant.

Bowen Backpackers HOSTEL $
(☎4786 3433; www.bowenbackpackers.net; cnr Herbet & Dalrymple Sts; dm per week $185; @) Has beds in four- and eight-bed dorms. The rooms don't have en suites but there's a decent amenities block. Weekly rates include transfers to working farms.

Bowen Coral Coast Beachfront Holiday Park CARAVAN PARK $
(☎4785 1262; www.big4bowen.com.au; Soldiers Rd; sites from $33, 1-/2-bedroom villas from $120/130;) This small and cosy beachfront park has good amenities but overlooks a rocky beach.

Eating

Cove ASIAN FUSION $$
(☎4791 2050; Coral Cove Apartments, Horseshoe Bay Rd; mains $15-25; lunch & dinner Tue-Sun) The spectacular views of the Coral Sea from the timber deck demands a long lunch, or at least a sunset drink before dinner. There's an interesting fusion of Chinese and Malay dishes.

360 on the Hill CAFE $
(☎4786 6360; Flagstaff Hill; mains $6-16; breakfast & lunch daily, dinner Fri) Browse through the small interpretive centre and then take a seat outside at this brilliant cafe perched proudly on top of Flagstaff Hill. There are amazing views that accompany the excellent seafood mains but you can also have a light salad or sandwich.

Horseshoe Bay Café CAFE $$
(☎4786 2565; Horseshoe Bay; mains $14-25; 10am-10pm) As the only cafe in the vicinity of Horseshoe Bay's stunning beach, it's a pity the view from your table overlooks the car park. The menu isn't extensive and is quite pricey for what's on offer.

Grandview Hotel PUB FARE $$
(☎4786 4022; cnr Herbert & Dalrymple Sts; mains $15-30; lunch & dinner) This huge corner pub is consistently recommended by the locals for its quality meals and sizeable portions.

Jochheims Pies CAFE $
(☎4786 1227; 49 Gregory St; 5.30am-3.30pm Mon-Fri, 6am-1pm Sat) Be sure to grab one of the region's famously great pies ($4.50) at this unpretentious pie shop.

Information

Post Office (cnr Powell & Herbert Sts)

Tourism Bowen (☎4786 4222; www.tourismbowen.com.au; 8.30am-5pm Mon-Fri, 10.30am-5pm Sat & Sun) About 7km south of Bowen on the Bruce Hwy. Look for the enormous mango. There's also an **information booth** (☎4786 2602; Santa Barbara Pde; 10am-5pm, 10.30am-5pm Sat & Sun) on the esplanade in town.

Getting There & Away

Bus

Long-distance buses stop outside **Bowen Travel** (☎4786 2835; 40 William St), where you can book and purchase bus tickets. **Greyhound Australia** (☎1300 473 946; www.greyhound.com.au) and **Premier Motor Service** (☎13 34 10; www.premierms.com.au) have frequent services to/from Rockhampton ($110, eight hours), Airlie Beach ($28, 1½ hours) and Townsville ($50, four hours). Premier's prices are cheaper, but services are less frequent.

Getting Around

Bowen Transit (☎4786 4414; www.bowenbus.com; 10 Powell St) runs local buses to Queens Beach, Rose Bay and Horseshoe Bay, Monday to Friday and Saturday morning, from near the post office.

Townsville to Innisfail

Includes »

Townsville 264
Magnetic Island 275
Ravenswood 281
Charters Towers. 281
North of Townsville . . .284
Paluma Range National Park 284
Hinchinbrook Island. 289
Tully 290
Mission Beach 291
Dunk Island. 298
Mission Beach to Innisfail. 299
Innisfail & Around . . 300

Best Places to Eat

» A Touch of Salt (p271)
» Man Friday (p278)
» Monsoon Cruising (p303)
» Benny's Hot Wok (p272)
» New Deli (p297)

Best Places to Stay

» Elandra (p294)
» Noorla Heritage Resort (p286)
» Sanctuary (p296)
» Reef Lodge (p269)

Why Go?

In between the tourist magnets of Cairns and Airlie Beach, Townsville is a real, living, breathing city with a pulse. North Queensland's largest urban centre, Townsville is often bypassed by visitors, yet it has a surprising number of attractions: a palm-lined beachfront promenade, gracious 19th-century architecture, and a host of cultural and sporting venues and events. In addition, Magnetic Island's national park, walking trails and wildlife are just offshore.

To the north of Townsville, through canefields and tropical coastline known as the Cassowary Coast, Cyclone Yasi carved a path of destruction in February 2011, mainly around Mission Beach, Tully and Cardwell. However, most services and attractions should be open by the time you read this.

Charters Towers and Ravenswood, inland to the southwest, offer an accessible slice of the dusty outback, or take a short boat trip to forested Hinchinbrook and Dunk Islands.

For a low-key getaway, this stretch of north Queensland is the real deal.

When to Go

Townsville

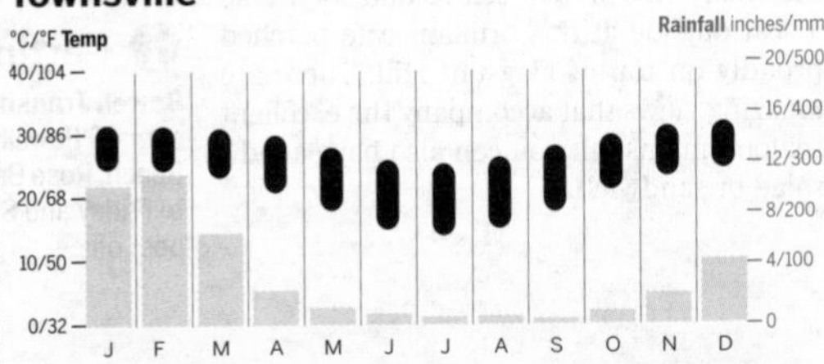

May Ingham celebrates with pasta, vino and music during its Australian Italian Festival.

July Charters Towers cranks its Venus Gold Battery into action during the Gold Fever Festival.

August Townsville shows off its cultural side during the Australian Festival of Chamber Music.

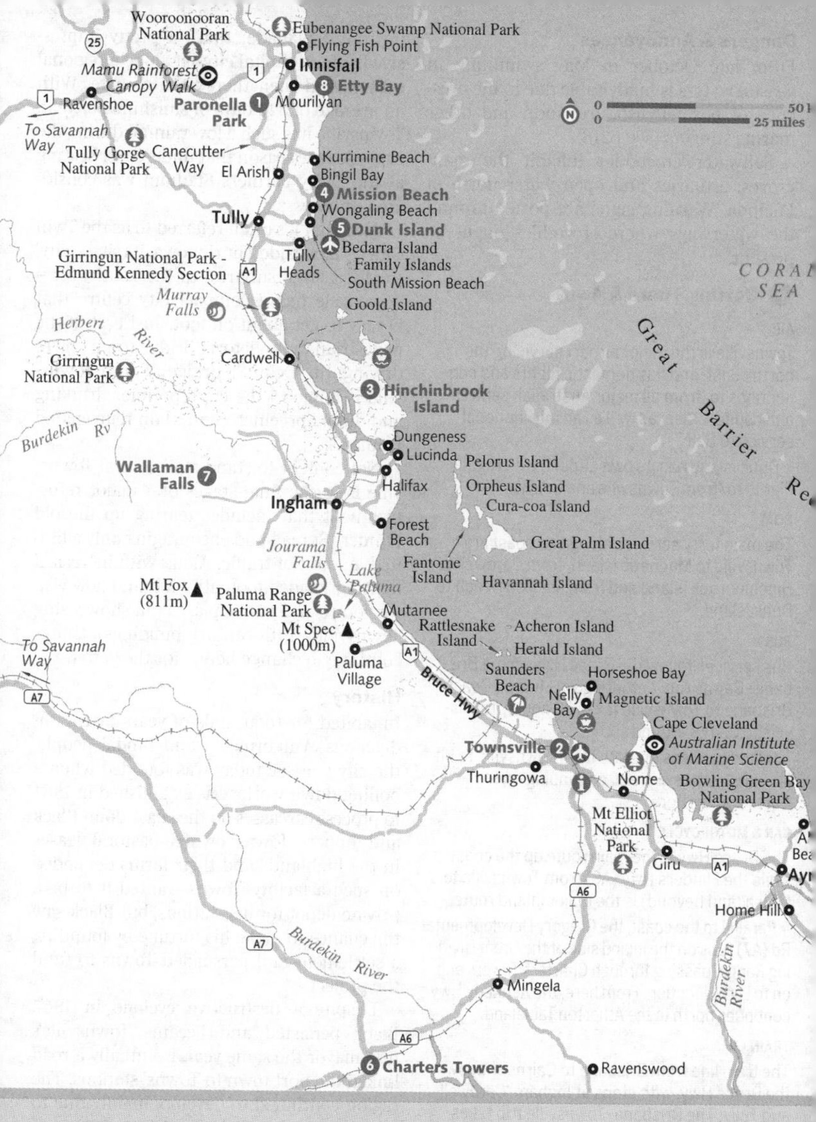

Townsville to Innisfail Highlights

1. Hearing the fascinating story behind the ruined castles of **Paronella Park** (p300) on an atmospheric tour
2. Cheering on the Cowboys, north Queensland's revered National Rugby League Team, or the Crocodiles National Basketball League team, in **Townsville** (p274)
3. Tackling the 32km-long Thorsborne Trail on pristine **Hinchinbrook Island** (p289)
4. Skydiving onto a reassuringly soft, sandy landing at **Mission Beach** (p292)
5. Searching out a secluded beach on **Dunk Island** (p298)
6. Getting goosebumps during a Ghosts After Dark outdoor film screening in the outback gold-rush town of **Charters Towers** (p281)
7. Photographing Australia's highest single-drop waterfall, **Wallaman Falls** (p286)
8. Watching wild cassowaries wander along the beach at picturesque **Etty Bay** (p300)

Dangers & Annoyances

From late October to May swimming in coastal waters is inadvisable due to the presence of box jellyfish, Irukandji and other marine stingers (see p216).

Saltwater crocodiles inhabit the mangroves, estuaries and open water north of Lucinda. Warning signs are posted around the waterways where crocodiles might be present.

Getting There & Away

AIR

Townsville is the major airport servicing the north coast, and has domestic flights and connections to/from all major Australian centres and capital cities, as well as an international service to Bali.

Dunk Island has its own airport, with regular flights to/from Townsville and Cairns.

BOAT

The main ferry services along this coast are from Townsville to Magnetic Island, from Cardwell to Hinchinbrook Island and from Mission Beach to Dunk Island.

BUS

Bus services follow the Bruce Hwy on the Brisbane–Cairns run, detouring via Mission Beach. Brisbane to Townsville takes 22 hours, Townsville to Cairns around six.

Inland services operate from Townsville to Mt Isa via Charters Towers, continuing on to the Northern Territory.

CAR & MOTORCYCLE

The Bruce Hwy is the main route up the coast, while the Flinders Hwy (A6) from Townsville to Mt Isa (and beyond) is the major inland route.

Parallel to the coast, the Gregory Developmental Rd (A7) runs on the inland side of the Great Dividing Range, passing through Charters Towers and on to Lynd Junction. From here, the Kennedy Hwy continues north to the Atherton Tableland.

TRAIN

The train line from Brisbane to Cairns shadows the Bruce Hwy, with stops at Ingham, Cardwell and Tully. The Brisbane–Townsville trip takes around 24 hours. The trip from Townsville to Cairns is just under eight hours.

The *Inlander* (p275) runs between Townsville and Mt Isa twice a week taking 21 hours; the trip from Townsville to Charters Towers takes three hours.

Townsville

POP 181,740

Excellent museums, a huge aquarium, world-class diving, two major sporting teams, vibrant nightlife and a stunning waterfront esplanade…that's a pretty impressive list for a capital city, let alone a regional centre. And then there's the climate. With an average of 320 days of sunshine per year, Townsville has such a low rainfall during the rugby league season that undercover seating at the Dairy Farmers Stadium was considered unnecessary.

Although it's often referred to as the Twin Cities – alongside Thuringowa, its sister 'city' (really a large suburb), to the southwest – Townsville has a compact city centre that is easy to get about on foot. Just east of the pedestrian-only Victoria Bridge (or, if you're driving, the Dean St Bridge), South Townsville is home to the city's premier drinking and dining precinct, centred on rejuvenated Palmer St.

Not content to stand still, central Townsville is in the final stages of a major refurbishment that includes tearing up the old Flinders St mall and encouraging only a limited amount of traffic. Along with increased lighting, shaded footpaths, a brand new visitor centre and public piazza (all showcasing Townsville's 19th-century buildings), things continue to change here – for the better.

History

Inhabited for thousands of years by the Indigenous Wulgurukaba and Bindal people, the city you see today was founded when a boiling-down works was established in 1864 to process carcasses on the coast. John Black and Robert Towns owned pastoral leases in the highlands and their farms depended on such a facility. Towns wanted it to be a private depot for his stations, but Black saw the chance to make his fortune by founding a settlement and persuaded Towns to fund the project.

Despite a destructive cyclone in 1867, Black persisted and became Townsville's first mayor the same year. Eventually a road linked the port town to Towns' stations. The region continued to develop, mainly due to Chinese and 'kanaka' labour (see p281).

Townsville's location makes it a strategic centre for military defence. During WWII its population of 30,000 boomed to more than 100,000 when it became a major base for Australian and US forces, and today some 70% of the Australian Army is based here.

Sights & Activities

Strand SWIMMING, PARK

Stretching 2.2km, Townsville's waterfront is interspersed with parks, pools, cafes and

CYCLONE YASI

When Tropical Cyclone Yasi began to form in the Coral Sea early in 2011, residents of North Queensland prepared for the worst. Coming almost five years after the destructive Cyclone Larry, many feared Category 5 Yasi would be even more damaging, prompting thousands of residents between Cairns and Townsville to evacuate.

The cyclone hit the coast around Mission Beach early on 3 February, with winds estimated at up to 300kmh ripping through the hardest hit towns of Tully and Cardwell, and islands including Dunk, Bedarra and Hinchinbrook.

Hundreds of homes along the coast between Innisfail and Ingham were severely damaged, banana plantations and canefields flattened and areas of national park rainforest pummelled, but fortunately there were no deaths or serious injuries. Cairns was spared the full brunt of the cyclone as it veered southwest before hitting the coast, while Townsville suffered only superficial damage.

Despite the estimated $800 million bill, recovery should be swift and travellers won't notice too many changes. At the time of writing, most national parks between Cairns and Townsville – including Hinchinbrook Island, Dunk Island, Goold Island, Orpheus Island, Girringun and Eubenangee Swamp – were either closed or partially closed while rangers assessed damaged and made access and walking trails safe. All are expected to be open by mid-2011. Contact **DERM** (☎13 74 68; www.derm.qld.gov.au) for information.

playgrounds – with hundreds of palm trees providing shade. Walkers and joggers take to the path from first light, beachgoers take over by midmorning and evening strollers are at it by late afternoon. Its golden-sand beach is patrolled and protected by two stinger enclosures from November to May.

At the northern tip is the **rock pool** (admission free; ⏲24hr), an enormous artificial swimming pool surrounded by lawns and sandy beaches; a huge filtration system keeps it clean and stinger-free. If you want to be 100% sure there are no jellyfish nearby, head to the chlorinated safety of the heritage-listed, Olympic-sized swimming pool, **Tobruk Memorial Baths** (www.townsville.qld.gov.au; Strand; adult/child $2.50/1.50; ⏲5.30am-7pm Mon-Thu, to 6pm Fri, 7am-4pm Sat, 8am-5pm Sun).

Kids will revel in the brilliant little **water playground** (admission free; ⏲10am-8pm Dec-Mar, to 6pm Sep-Nov, Apr & May, to 5pm Jun-Aug). Water is pumped through all sorts of tubes and culminates with a big bucket filling and then dumping its load onto the squealing little ones below.

Castle Hill — LOOKOUT

The striking 286m-high red hill (an isolated pink granite monolith) that dominates Townsville's skyline offers stunning views of the city and of Cleveland Bay. Walking up here is a popular way to keep fit: access the rough 'goat track' (2km one way) from Hillside Cres. If walking sounds too energetic, you can drive up via Gregory St along the narrow, winding 2.6km Castle Hill Rd. At the car park up top, a signboard details short trails that lead to various lookout points, or pick up a map from Townsville's Visitor Information Centre.

Reef HQ — AQUARIUM

(☎4750 0800; www.reefhq.com.au; Flinders St E; adult/child $24.75/12.10; ⏲9.30am-5pm) Townsville's excellent aquarium is a living reef on dry land. A staggering 2.5 million litres of water flow through the coral-reef tank, which is home to 130 coral and 120 fish species. The backdrop of the predator exhibit is a replica of the bow of the SS *Yongala*, which sank in 1911 off the coast of Townsville during a wild cyclone with 125 passengers, and wasn't located until 1958; these days it's a popular diving spot. The **fish-feeding** display will excite younger guests, particularly the sea snakes and shy eels (impeccable table manners, those guys!). To maintain the natural conditions essential for the survival of this complex ecosystem, a wave machine simulates the ebb and flow of the ocean, circular currents keep the water in motion and marine algae are used in the purification system. Kids will also love feeding and touching turtles at the aquarium's newest attraction, the **turtle hospital**, which rehabilitates sick and injured turtles. It's well worth joining one (or a few) of the **talks and tours** throughout the day, which focus on different aspects of the reef and the aquarium.

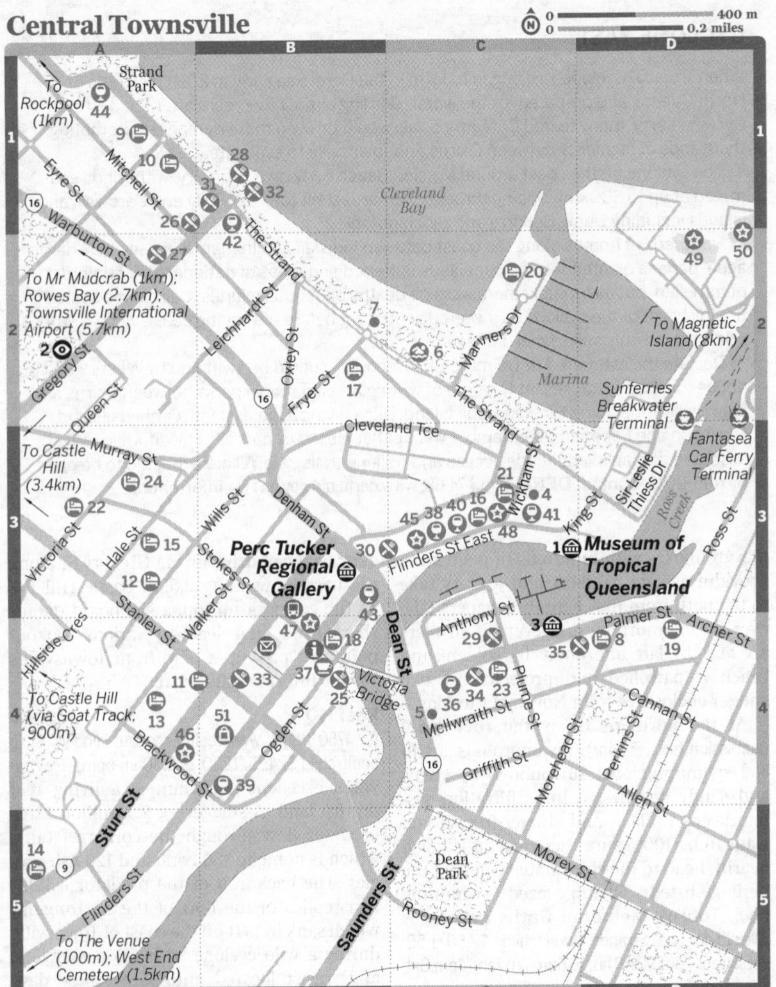

IMAX Cinema CINEMA
(adult/child $14/9; ⌚10.30am-4.30pm) IMAX is next door to the aquarium. With its 18m-high screen and surround sound you can experience just what it's like to live underwater. Without getting wet! Combined aquarium and IMAX entry is $39/21 per adult/child.

FREE **Cultural Centre** ART GALLERY, MUSEUM
(☎4772 7679; www.cctownsville.com.au; 2/68 Flinders St E; ⌚9.30am-4.30pm) Showcasing the history, traditions and customs of the Wulgurukaba and Bindal people, this impressive Aboriginal and Torres Strait Islander museum/gallery offers guided tours of the art works and artefacts – contact the centre for tour times.

Museum of Tropical Queensland MUSEUM
(www.mtq.qld.gov.au; 70-102 Flinders St E; adult/child $13.50/8; ⌚9.30am-5pm) Not your ordinary, everyday museum, the Museum of Tropical Queensland reconstructs scenes using detailed models with interactive displays. The wreck of the *Pandora* is showcased, with some fascinating artefacts from the ship. At 11am and 2.30pm, you can load and fire a cannon 1700s-style. Other galleries include the kid-friendly **MindZone science centre** and displays on north

Central Townsville

Top Sights

Museum of Tropical Queensland C3
Perc Tucker Regional Gallery B3

Sights

1 Cultural Centre C3
2 Queens Gardens A2
Reef HQ .... (see 1)
3 Townsville Maritime Museum C4

Activities, Courses & Tours

4 Adrenalin Dive C3
5 Remote Area Dive C4
6 Tobruk Memorial Baths C2
7 Water Playground B2

Sleeping

8 Adventurers Resort D4
9 Aquarius on the Beach A1
10 Beach House Motel A1
11 Central City Motel A4
12 City Oasis Inn A3
13 Civic Guest House A4
14 Classique Bed & Breakfast A5
15 Coral Lodge A3
16 Globetrotters Hostel C3
17 Historic Yongala Lodge Motel B2
18 Holiday Inn B4
19 Hotel M D4
20 Mariners North C2
Orchid Guest House .... (see 15)
21 Reef Lodge C3
22 Ridgemont A3
23 Rydges Southbank C4
24 Summit A3

Eating

25 A Touch of Salt B4
Benny's Hot Wok .... (see 23)
26 Bountiful Thai A1
27 Café Bambini A2
28 Cbar B1
29 Deli on Palmer C4
30 Get India C3
Globe .... (see 16)
31 Harold's Seafood B1
32 Jamaica Joe's B1
33 Ladah B4
34 Salt Cellar C4
35 Scirocco D4
Souvlaki Bar .... (see 31)

Drinking

36 Australian Hotel C4
37 Coffee Dominion B4
38 Exchange Hotel C3
39 Great Northern Hotel B4
40 Mad Cow Tavern C3
41 Molly Malones C3
42 Seaview Hotel B1
43 The Brewery B3
44 Watermark Hotel A1

Entertainment

45 Bank C3
46 BCC Cinemas A4
Consortium .... (see 38)
47 Cowboys Leagues Club B4
48 Flynns C3
IMAX Cinema .... (see 1)
49 Jupiters Casino D2
Shed .... (see 41)
50 Townsville Entertainment Centre D2

Shopping

51 John Melick & Co B4

Queensland's history, from the dinosaurs to the rainforest and the reef.

FREE Perc Tucker Regional Gallery ART GALLERY

(www.townsville.qld.gov.au; cnr Denham & Flinders Sts; ⏲10am-5pm Mon-Fri, to 2pm Sat & Sun) This contemporary art gallery, in an 1885-built former bank, has a packed schedule of exhibitions each year. Shows feature work by international and local artists, though the focus is on north Queensland artists.

Townsville Maritime Museum MUSEUM

(www.townsvillemaritimemuseum.org.au; 42-68 Palmer St; adult/child $6/3; ⏲10am-4pm Mon-Fri, noon-3pm Sat & Sun) The highlight of a visit to Townsville's Maritime Museum is the gallery dedicated to the wreck of the *Yongala*. Maritime buffs can also check out historical exhibits on northern Queensland's naval industries.

North Queensland Military Museum MUSEUM

(www.army.gov.au; Mitchell St, Kissing Point; admission by donation; ⏲9am-12.30pm Mon, Wed & Fri, 10am-2pm Sun) Photo ID is required to enter this military museum in the grounds of the Jezzine Army Barracks. Apart from the paraphernalia atmospherically displayed in the old gun stores, there are stunning 360-degree views from Kissing Point at the northern end of the Strand.

National Trust Heritage Centre HISTORIC BUILDING
(www.heritagecentre.org.au; 5-7 Castling St, West End; adult/child $6/2; ⏲10am-2pm Wed, 1-4pm Sat & Sun Feb-Nov) For an insight into life in Townsville in the 19th and early 20th centuries, head 2km west of the city centre along Ingham Rd. Three historic houses make up Townsville's heritage centre: a miners cottage (c 1884), a beautiful verandah-wrapped villa (1888), and a farmhouse (c 1921).

A block east is **West End Cemetery**, with graves dating from the 1880s.

Botanic Gardens GARDENS
(admission free; ⏲sunrise-sunset) Townsville's botanic gardens are spread across three locations: each has its own character, but all have tropical plants and are abundantly green.

The **Queens Gardens** (cnr Gregory & Paxton Sts) are 1km northwest of the town centre at the base of Castle Hill. These are the town's original gardens, which were first planted in 1870 with trial plants (including mango and coffee) to potentially boost the economy. They've since been thoroughly redesigned – after 100,000 US soldiers squatted there during WWII – and are now formal ornamental gardens, with a children's playground and a herb garden.

Anderson Park (Gulliver St, Mundingburra), established in 1932, is 6km southwest of the centre. The large gardens cover a 20-hectare site and were originally planted in taxonomic lots. They feature plants and palms from northern Queensland and Cape York Peninsula, lotus ponds and a tropical-fruit orchard.

The **Palmetum** (University Rd), 15km southwest of the centre, is a 17-hectare garden devoted to just one plant family, the palm. More than 300 species are represented here, including around 60 native to Australia.

Barra Fishing FISHING
(☎4789 3093; www.barrafishing.net; Allambie Lane, Kelso; per hr from $20; ⏲10am-6pm Fri-Mon) You're pretty much guaranteed to catch something at this fish farm 19km southwest of the city centre. Rod hire is an additional $3; if you want to keep your catch, it costs $14 per kilogram extra. If you just want to watch, there's a $2 charge. Real anglers will shudder at the thought of this place, but it's not a bad option for kids and families.

Skydive Townsville SKYDIVING
(☎4721 4721; www.skydivetownsville.com.au; tandem jumps $395-445) Hurl yourself from a perfectly good plane and land right on the Strand. Tandem jumps require no prior knowledge, just a lot of guts (but not too much: there's a weight limit of 95kg). The price gets more expensive the higher up the plane takes you.

Tours

Several companies operate Great Barrier Reef trips and dive courses. For tours to the excellent Billabong Sanctuary wildlife park, 17km south of Townsville, see p280.

Woodstock Trail Rides HORSE RIDING
(☎4778 8888; www.woodstocktrailrides.com.au; Jones Rd, Woodstock; half-/full-day rides $80/150) Situated 43km south of the city, Woodstock offers trail rides that take you deep into the huge property; full-day trips stop for a barbecue lunch along Ross Creek. All riding abilities are catered for. **Cattle musters** ($150) include herding cattle on horseback, a camp-oven lunch and learning to crack a whip, shear a sheep and even brand calves. Prices include transfers from Townsville for full-day rides and cattle; bookings for all rides are essential.

Kookaburra Tours SCENIC
(☎0448 794 798; www.kookaburratours.com.au) Highly recommended day trips in Townsville and further afield, with enthusiastic, informed commentary. Options include 'Heritage and Highlights' city tours (adult/child $40/18), Wallaman Falls (adult/child $125/55), rainforest tours in Mount Spec National Park (adult/child $125/55) and Aboriginal cultural tours (adult/child $140/65).

Townsville Ghost Tours GHOST TALES
(☎0404 453 354; www.townsvilleghosttours.com.au) Five spooky options, from city haunts aboard the 'ghost bus' (from $65) to an overnight trip to Ravenswood ($295 including meals and accommodation).

Nautilus Aviation SCENIC FLIGHTS
(☎4725 6056; www.nautilusaviation.com.au) Helicopter flights over Townsville (from $180 for five minutes for two people).

Coral Princess CRUISE
(☎1800 079 545, 4040 9999; www.coralprincess.com.au) Three-night cruises (from $1496 per person, twin share) between Cairns and Townsville.

GREAT BARRIER REEF TRIPS FROM TOWNSVILLE

The Great Barrier Reef lies further offshore from Townsville than it does from Cairns and Port Douglas, hence fuel costs push up the prices. On the upside, it's less crowded (and suffers fewer effects from crowds). Trips from Townsville are dive-oriented and include a number of reefs, as well as the SS *Yongala* wreck and Wheeler Reef. If you just want to snorkel, take a day trip that only goes to the reef; the *Yongala* is for diving only. It takes around 2½ hours to reach the *Yongala* from Townsville, but only 30 minutes from Alva Beach near Ayr, so if your main interest is wreck diving, you may want to consider a trip with Alva Beach–based Yongala Dive (p280).

Several Townsville-based operators offer Professional Association of Diving Instructors (PADI) learn-to-dive courses, with two days' training in the pool, plus at least two days and one night living aboard the boat. Prices start at around $615; you'll need to obtain a dive medical, which the course providers can arrange (around $50).

Adrenalin Dive (☎4724 0600; www.adrenalinedive.com.au; 9 Wickham St) Day trips to the *Yongala* (from $220) and Wheeler Reef (from $280), both including two dives. Also offers snorkelling (from $180) on Wheeler Reef as well as live-aboard trips, and open-water and advanced diving certification courses.

Remote Area Dive (RAD; ☎4721 4424; www.remoteareadive.com; 16 Dean St) Runs day trips (from $220) to Orpheus and Pelorus Islands. Also live-aboard trips and dive courses.

Salt Dive (☎4721 1760; www.saltdive.com.au; 2/276 Charters Towers Rd, Hermit Park) *Yongala* and reef diving day trips (from $199) aboard a fast boat; dive courses available.

Festivals & Events

The city has a packed calendar of festivals and annual events, as well as regular sporting fixtures (see p274).

Townsville Offshore BOAT RACING
(www.superboat.com.au) Early July sees boat motors running when Townsville hosts the Townsville Offshore (also known as the Offshore Superboat Championship).

Townsville 400 MOTOR SPORTS
(www.v8supercars.com.au) V8 Supercars roar through a purpose-built street circuit each year in mid-July during the V8 Supercar Championship.

Magnetic Island to Townsville Open Water Swim SWIMMING
(www.magneticislandswim.com.au) In mid-July, join around 100 competitors braving the sharks between Magnetic Island and Townsville's Strand beach, or just cheer them on.

Australian Festival of Chamber Music MUSIC
(www.afcm.com.au) Townsville gets cultural during this internationally renowned festival each September. Spin-off events include the Taste of Townsville food and wine festival.

Sleeping

You wouldn't think a city Townsville's size could fill to capacity, but it does during festivals and events – book ahead. Midrange motels and self-catering units stretch along the Strand, while international chains and backpacker places cluster in the city centre and around Palmer St.

Historic Yongala Lodge Motel MOTEL $$
(☎4772 4633; www.historicyongala.com.au; 11 Fryer St; motel $99-110, 1-bedroom apt $115-120, 2-bedroom apt $150-160;) Built in 1884 as a private residence by Mr Matthew Rooney, who perished aboard the *Yongala* shipwreck in 1911, these historic premises reside in a quiet side street a short stroll from the Strand and the city. Sympathetically styled motel rooms and 10 self-contained one- and two-bedroom apartments are built around the original heritage building, which now houses an excellent **restaurant** (mains $20-38; dinner Mon-Sat) serving classy Greek cuisine.

Reef Lodge HOSTEL $
(☎4721 1112; www.reeflodge.com.au; 4 Wickham St; dm $22-26, d $62-76;) The cruisy atmosphere at Townsville's best hostel extends from Buddhist sculptures and hammocks strewn through the garden to an outdoor 'cinema' with swinging lounges

and more than 1200 DVDs. There's a games room with bench presses, free weights and a retro video-game machine (with *Space Invaders*, *Frogger*, *Pacman*...very cool). The sizeable kitchen, dorms (including a female-only dorm) and private rooms are all spotless.

Coral Lodge B&B $
(☎4771 5512; www.corallodge.com.au; 32 Hale St; s $65-80, d $70-85; ❄) If you're looking to stay in a charmingly old-fashioned Aussie home, don't miss this century-old property. The upstairs self-contained units are like having your own apartment, while the downstairs guest rooms share bathrooms. Breakfast is available for an extra $5 per person. The welcoming owners will pick you up from the bus, train or ferry.

Holiday Inn HOTEL $$
(☎4772 2477; www.townsville.holiday-inn.com; 334 Flinders St; d $114-199; ❄📶🏊) Dubbed the 'sugar shaker' (for reasons that are immediately obvious), this 20-storey, 1976-built circular building (the city's tallest) is a Townsville icon. Its 199 rooms are much more contemporary than the exterior suggests, and there's a great rooftop pool and unrivalled views over the city.

Rowes Bay Caravan Park CARAVAN PARK $
(☎4771 3576; www.rowesbaycp.com.au; Heatley Pde, Rowes Bay; sites $25-33, cabins $65-95, villas $98; ❄@📶🏊) Directly opposite Rowes Bay's beachfront (2.7km from town), this leafy campground has first-rate facilities including a children's playground and half-size tennis court. Facing the pool, brand-new villas are smaller than cabins but spiffier.

Hotel M HOTEL $$
(☎1800 760 144; www.oakshotelsresorts.com; 81 Palmer St; d $144-189; ❄📶🏊) Soaring up behind the revamped 1887 Metropole Hotel, this 2009-built, 11-storey hotel has space-agey rooms with metallic and lime colour schemes, kitchens and laundries, a gym, plus handy 24-hour reception. Higher-priced rooms have glittering skyline views from the balconies.

Orchid Guest House GUESTHOUSE $
(☎4771 6683; www.orchidguesthouse.com.au; 34 Hale St; dm $26, s $50-70, d $60-80; ❄) A guesthouse in every sense of the word. Fran will pick you up for free from the bus, train or ferry. All of the cosy, old-fashioned rooms – even the dorms – come with TV, fridge and air-con, and guaranteed peace and quiet, thanks to a no-noise policy after 10pm. There's free laundry, a well-equipped kitchen and parking.

Adventurers Resort HOSTEL $
(☎4721 1522; www.adventurersresort.com; 79 Palmer St; dm/s/d $25/45/55; ❄@📶🏊) Roomy, multilevel dorms await at this sociable motel-style complex, which puts on regular falafel nights and theme parties, and has its own egg-laying chicken. The highlight is the rooftop pool and barbecue area with views of the city skyline, Magnetic Island and Castle Hill. Camper-vans are welcome in the car park for $5 per night, including full use of the hostel's facilities.

Beach House Motel MOTEL $$
(☎4721 1333; www.beachhousemotel.com.au; 66 Strand; d $99-118; ❄📶🏊) This sky-blue '60s-style motel is a good option if you just want a clean, comfortable, well-equipped room and friendly service without unnecessary trimmings. You can gawk at passers-by from the pool out front.

Mariners North APARTMENTS $$$
(☎4722 0777; www.marinersnorth.com.au; 7 Mariners Dr; 2-/3-bedroom apt from $250/390; ❄📶🏊) In Townsville's only absolute oceanfront location, these self-contained apartments have generous living areas, brilliant balconies overlooking Cleveland Bay, and big bathrooms. Work out in the gym, or just splash in the huge, palm-fringed saltwater pool. Minimum stay is two nights.

Aquarius on the Beach HOTEL $$
(☎1800 622 474, 4772 4255; www.aquariusonthebeach.com.au; 75 Strand; d $125-145; ❄@📶🏊) The full-width balcony views from all 130 apartments impress almost as much as the size of this place, the tallest building on the Strand. Don't be put off by the dated facade – this is one of the better places around, especially its refurbished 'executive rooms' (tiles instead of carpets, flat-screens instead of hefty TVs).

Classique Bed & Breakfast B&B $$
(☎4721 0898; www.classiquebnb.com.au; 495 Sturt St; d $150-170; ❄@📶) Tropical breakfast is included in the rate at this gorgeous old Queenslander. Built in 1890, original features include lofty pressed-tin ceilings and hoop-pine floors. Each of its three en suite rooms has wrought-iron or timber sleigh beds. You can unwind over a game of pool or in the outdoor spa.

Ridgemont MOTEL $$
(☎4771 2164; www.ridgemont.com.au; 15-19 Victoria St; d $118-148;) The impressive one- and two-bedroom self-contained units here are especially popular and with great balcony views of Magnetic Island it's not hard to see why. Views also extend from the **restaurant** (mains $23-34; breakfast daily, dinner Mon-Sat) and bar.

Bayside APARTMENTS $$
(☎4721 1688; www.baysideapartments.com.au; 102 Strand; 1-/2-bedroom apt $125/140;) Tiled floors keep the rooms cool in this value-for-money place on the Strand. The two-bedroom apartments have balconies overlooking the beach, and there's a lovely landscaped pool for a dip. Kitchens are spacious and modern and you can do your washing for free in the laundry. Minimum stay is two nights.

Rydges Southbank HOTEL $$
(☎4726 5265; www.rydges.com/townsville; 17-29 Palmer St; d from $129;) Rooms at this hotel are geared towards business travellers, but even if work's the last thing on your mind, you'll love the palatial executive suites with lounge rooms, spa baths and views over the river, marina and buzzing restaurants below.

City Oasis Inn HOTEL, APARTMENTS $$
(☎4771 6048; www.cityoasis.com.au; 143 Wills St; d from $140;) The decor's modern, rather than contemporary, but there are so many sparkling white surfaces that you'll have to allow time for your eyes to adjust upon entering. The fabulous loft apartments have an upstairs bedroom separate from the downstairs kitchen, or you can opt for even more space between you and the kids by going for the two-bedroom apartments. Facilities include a restaurant, children's playground and laundry.

Globetrotters Hostel HOSTEL $
(☎1800 008 533, 4771 5000; www.globetrottersaustralia.com; 121 Flinders St E; dm $22-24, s/d $60/75;) Surrounded by pubs and clubs, the basic dorms and private rooms (all with bathroom) at this hectic hostel teeter above steep staircases, so it's not suitable for light sleepers or anyone with mobility problems. An extra $5 per night gets you dinner at the adjacent restaurant-bar, **Globe** (☎4721 2222; www.globetownsville.com; mains $14-18; dinner), which has a beer garden hosting regular jelly wrestling (yes…).

Summit MOTEL $$
(☎4721 2122; www.summitmotel.com.au; 6-8 Victoria St; d $105-115;) There's not a lot of difference between the standard and executive rooms, so save yourself 10 bucks and go for the cheaper version. The rooms are standard motel style, but clean and comfortable.

Central City Motel MOTEL $$
(☎4724 0233; www.centralcitymotel.com; 164 Stanley St; d $102-130;) Exactly what it says on the tin: this is Townsville's most central motel, with streamlined, modernised rooms that are perfectly acceptable if you reckon motels are for sleeping only.

Civic Guest House GUESTHOUSE $
(☎1800 646 619, 4771 5381; www.civicguesthouse.com; 262 Walker St; dm $22-24, d $54-59, with bathroom d $75;) Behind the palms and bushes bursting out of the cyclone-wire fence, this converted home has clean, tidy rooms (higher-priced rooms have air-con) and a relaxed ambience.

Townsville Seaside Apartments APARTMENTS $$
(☎4721 3155; www.townsvilleseaside.com.au; 105 Strand; studios $100, 1-/2-bedroom units $120/170;) In a strip of renovated 1960s apartments, these dated units (sporting a kitsch but cute logo of a sun wearing sunglasses) are comfortable nonetheless and equipped with kitchens. Two-night minimum stay.

Eating

Palmer St is Townsville's premier dining strip, offering a diverse range of cuisines: wander along and take your pick. Running perpendicular to the Strand, Gregory St has a clutch of cafes and takeaway joints. Many of Townsville's bars and pubs also serve food.

TOP CHOICE **A Touch of Salt** MODERN AUSTRALIAN $$
(☎4724 4441; www.atouchofsalt.com.au; cnr Stokes & Ogden Sts; mains $30-36; lunch Thu & Fri, dinner Tue-Sat) At this family-run riverside establishment, delectable seafood is accompanied by an extensive wine list and genuinely good service. Even the pies (such as lamb, green pea and mint or peppered beef) with hand-cut chips are gourmet, and desserts (try the butterscotch cheesecake) are divine. When we visited, the same team was putting the finishing touches on a Palmer St tapas and wine bar, the **Salt Cellar**

(☎4724 5866; www.thesaltcellar.com.au; 13 Palmer St; ⊙dinner Mon-Sat).

Benny's Hot Wok ASIAN $$
(☎4724 3243; www.bennyshotwok.com.au; 17-21 Palmer St; mains $14-29; ⊙lunch Fri & Sun, dinner daily) Outdoor seating, savvy staff and a good wine list set the scene for some of the finest pan-Asian cuisine in north Queensland – from freshly made sushi and sashimi to Peking duck rolls, steaming laksas, sizzling Mongolian lamb, or create-your-own stir fries.

Cafe Bambini CAFE $$
(www.cafebambini.com.au; 47 Gregory St; mains $12-20; ⊙5.30am-5pm Mon-Fri, 6.30am-4pm Sat & Sun; ✎) Spawning five branches around town at last count, this local success story cooks up the best breakfasts in Townsville: lamb's fry and bacon, smashed avocado on multigrain, breakfast bruschettas, and pork, apple and sage sausages. Lunches have international flavours, from smoked salmon with pappadams to French steak sandwiches.

Jamaica Joe's CARIBBEAN $$
(☎4724 1234; www.jamaicajoes.com; Strand, opposite Gregory St; mains $17-43; ⊙lunch & dinner) The best time to head to this funky Jamaican-American diner-bar on the waterfront is on Sunday afternoons, when entertainment includes live music and DJs spinning old-school reggae vinyl. But it's a worthy dining option any time for Caribbean dishes like Jamaican goat curry and spicy jerk chicken breast.

Mr Mudcrab SEAFOOD $
(www.mrmudcrab.com.au; 1 Rose St; dishes $3-10; ⊙8am-8pm) If mud crab's on offer here, you know it's fresh – Mr Mudcrab refuses to get it in frozen. This excellent seafood shop sells fresh catches to cook yourself, as well as fish and chips (with homemade tartare sauce) and yummy daily-baked seafood pies.

Get India INDIAN $$
(☎4772 5828; 215 Flinders St E; mains $15-19; ⊙lunch & dinner; ✎) Amid the clubs of Flinders St East, with a bar of its own, this spot cooks authentic Indian cuisine according to your own spice-o-meter. There are standards like butter chicken and lamb korma, and seafood options including prawn vindaloo and fish masala.

Deli on Palmer CAFE $$
(☎4724 5298; 30-34 Palmer St; mains $11-21; ⊙breakfast & lunch; ✎) Churning out hearty omelettes, scrambled eggs, croissants, fresh fruit salad and strong coffee at breakfast, this small, busy continental-style deli switches to grilled Turkish breads, antipasto, pasta and gourmet rolls at lunch.

Ladah CAFE $$
(cnr Sturt & Stanley Sts; mains $14-23; ⊙7am-4pm Mon-Fri, 8am-1pm Sat & Sun; ✎) The energy that radiates from the busy kitchen and funky contemporary art on the walls is an early indication of the quality food at this licensed cafe. Try the haloumi and egg tortilla wrap or homemade baked beans for breakfast. For lunch, you can't go past the chickpea burger or chicken nicoise salad.

Cbar CAFE $$
(www.cbar.com.au; Strand, opposite Gregory St; mains $16-26; ⊙7am-10pm; ✎) Your best bet if you're hungry outside regular dining hours, Cbar serves full meals throughout the day, from coconut prawns with mango salsa to Moroccan-style beef tagines.

Harold's Seafood SEAFOOD $
(cnr Strand & Gregory St; meals $4-10; ⊙lunch & dinner) More than your average takeaway joint, Harold's has bug burgers of the Moreton Bay variety. Watch the goings-on at the Strand across the road while you wait for your order.

Scirocco FUSION $$
(www.sciroccocafe.com; 61 Palmer St; mains $27-36; ⊙dinner Mon-Sat) Asia meets the Med on the menu of this laid-back spot, sparking some serious deliberation, but you can't go wrong with the vodka-flamed king prawn linguine.

Souvlaki Bar GREEK $
(Shop 3 & 4, 58 Strand; mains $7-18; ⊙10.30am-9pm Mon-Fri, to 10pm Sat & Sun) It's simple, but it's cheap, quick and damn good. Grab a big Greek breakfast of bacon, eggs, sausage, souvlaki, grilled tomatoes, haloumi and pita bread.

Bountiful Thai THAI $$
(Shop 1/52 Gregory St; mains $13-21; ⊙lunch Mon-Fri, dinner daily) Pokey little takeaway Thai cafe whipping up noodle and rice dishes, curries and soups in huge portions and quick time.

Drinking & Entertainment

Perhaps it's the sunny climate, but Townsville sure loves a sip. Most nightlife concentrates around Flinders St East, while Palmer St and the Strand offer lower key spots. Establishments come and go; locals can point you to the latest hot spots, or check listings in Friday's edition of the *Townsville Bulletin* newspaper. Opening hours vary according to the season and the crowds; nightclubs generally stay open until 5am.

Coffee Dominion CAFE $
(www.coffeedominion.com.au; cnr Stokes & Ogden Sts; ⌚6am-5pm Mon-Wed, to 5.30pm Thu & Fri, 7am-1pm Sat & Sun) OK, there's no food, and just a handful of seats. But if you drop by between 8am and 11.30am on weekdays, you can watch – and smell – this eco-conscious establishment roasting beans from Mareeba to Brazil and Zambia. If you don't find a blend you like, invent your own and they'll grind it fresh.

TOP CHOICE **The Brewery** MICROBREWERY
(www.townsvillebrewery.com.au; 252 Flinders St; ⌚Mon-Sat) Brews made onsite at Townsville's stunningly restored 1880s former post office (admire the paisley wallpaper, original fireplaces and exposed brickwork) include local favourite Townsville Bitter (midstrength lager), Bandito Loco (citrusy Mexican pilsner), the five-malt Ned's Red (Irish-style red ale), plus a seasonal brew (ask what's on tap). Soak them up with a meal at its refined **restaurant** (mains $17-36; ⌚lunch & dinner Mon-Sat).

Watermark Hotel BAR
(www.watermarktownsville.com.au; 72-74 Strand) *The* place to be seen in Townsville. Well, if it's good enough for Missy Higgins and silverchair, then it's good enough for the rest of us. Some serious Sunday sessions take place in the tavern bar. There's also a more upmarket bar and an excellent Mod Oz **restaurant** (mains $28-36; ⌚breakfast Sun, lunch & dinner daily).

Australian Hotel PUB
(11 Palmer St) A rejuvenated and revamped landmark along Palmer St since 1888, this pub played host to Errol Flynn in the 1930s. Its stylish front bar has a good range of draught beers while the big beer garden out the back is a convivial spot to knock back a few on a Sunday afternoon.

Molly Malones PUB, NIGHTCLUB
(www.mollymalonesirishpub.com.au; 87 Flinders St E) This boisterous Irish pub stages live music on Friday and Saturday nights, or you can shake it on the dance floor of its adjacent nightclub, the **Shed** (⌚8pm-5am Tue, Fri & Sat). Wrist-snapping plates of food include rissoles and mash, and Irish stew, or consume your weekly iron requirements in a steak and Guinness.

Seaview Hotel PUB
(www.seaviewhotel.com.au; cnr Strand & Gregory St) Renowned for its Sunday sessions in the huge concrete beer 'garden', the Seaview serves ice-cold schooners and has live music and entertainment. Its immense **restaurant** (mains $21-44; ⌚lunch & dinner) serves steaks on a par with the size of the premises.

Exchange Hotel PUB, NIGHTCLUB
(www.exchangehoteltownsville.com.au; 151 Flinders St E; ⌚Tue-Sun) Not only are there several bars inside this revamped 1882 hotel, but also a swish **cocktail bar** (⌚from 4pm Tue-Sun), **bistro** (mains $17-34; ⌚lunch Tue-Fri, dinner Tue-Sun), and an upstairs **nightclub** (⌚10pm-late Fri & Sat).

Consortium NIGHTCLUB
(www.consortiumtownsville.com.au; 159 Flinders St E; ⌚9am-5am Tue & Thu-Sun) Resident DJs, DJ comps and events like 'fetish and fantasy' balls make this big-city-style venue Townsville's hippest nightclub.

Mad Cow Tavern BAR
(129 Flinders St E) Although it seems there are more bouncers than patrons at the black-and-white-splotched Mad Cow, it does have its supporters, especially from the military.

Flynns LIVE MUSIC
(www.flynnsirishbar.com; 101 Flinders St E; ⌚5pm-late Tue-Sun) A jolly Irish pub that doesn't try too hard to be Irish. Wildly popular for its $8 jugs and live music every night except Wednesdays, when karaoke takes over.

Bank NIGHTCLUB
(169 Flinders St E; ⌚9pm-5am Tue-Sun) House and dance beats; slinky surrounds in an 1887 former bank.

Venue LIVE MUSIC
(www.thevenuetownsville.com.au; 719 Flinders St W) Multilevel place with regular gigs by Aussie acts (Grinspoon et al) and four bars.

BCC Cinemas CINEMA
(cnr Sturt & Blackwood Sts) Screens mainstream films.

Jupiters Casino CASINO
(www.jupiterstownsville.com.au; Sir Leslie Thiess Dr) The place to head for a waterside flutter.

Great Northern Hotel PUB
(500 Flinders St; ⌚10am-midnight Mon-Thu, 10am-1am Fri & Sat, 10am-10pm Sun) This

COWBOYS & CROCS

You won't leave Townsville without hearing (in minute detail) about the **North Queensland Cowboys** (☎4773 0700; www.cowboys.com.au) National Rugby League (NRL) team. While the club represents the whole of north Queensland, its home ground is Townsville's **Dairy Farmers Stadium** (www.dairyfarmersstadium.org.au; Golf Links Dr, Kirwan), 15km southeast of the city centre. The stadium was originally a harness-racing track, but was converted into a rugby-league venue for the Cowboys' inaugural season in 1995. It holds 26,500 people and the atmosphere is brilliant (tickets to a game against arch rivals the Brisbane Broncos sell out fast). The season runs from March to September; shuttle buses to the stadium leave from opposite the **Cowboys Leagues Club** (335 Flinders St) and Park and Ride facilities.

Townsville's other major sporting team, the **Crocodiles** (☎4778 4222; www.crocodiles.com.au) compete in the National Basketball League (NBL) and play home games at **Townsville Entertainment Centre** (www.tecc.net.au; 2 Entertainment Dr, Breakwater Island), aka 'the Swamp'. The season runs from mid-October to April. If you don't believe how popular basketball can be in Australia, you will when you see locals driving around with croc tails handing out of their car boots.

Tickets for both teams are available online.

down-to-earth, 1900-built Aussie pub has loads of character, icy beer and cheap, filling meals.

Shopping

Cotters Market MARKET
(www.townsvillerotarymarkets.com.au; Flinders St; 8.30am-1pm Sun) Around 200 quality craft and food stalls, as well as live entertainment.

John Melick & Co OUTDOOR GEAR
(481 Flinders St) Good range of camping and bushwalking gear, Driza-Bone oilskins and Akubra hats.

Strand Night Market MARKET
(www.townsvillerotarymarkets.com.au; Strand; 5-9.30pm 1st Fri of month May-Jun & Sep-Dec, 2nd Fri of month Jul & Aug) Browse stalls on the Strand for curios, crafts and knick-knacks.

Information

Department of Environment & Resource Management (DERM; ☎13 74 68; www.derm.qld.gov.au; 1-7 Marlow St)

Internet Den (☎4721 4500; 265 Flinders St; per 90min $5; 8am-10pm) More than just a full-service internet cafe (with superfast computers), this home-away-from-home has a dedicated room for reading, storytelling, and Indigenous art workshops, and traveller-friendly services like luggage storage.

Post office (Post Office Plaza, Shop 1, Sturt St)

Townsville Hospital (☎4796 1111; www.health.qld.gov.au/townsville; 100 Angus Smith Dr, Douglas)

Visitor Information Centre (☎4721 3660; www.townsvilleonline.com.au; cnr Flinders & Stokes Sts; 9am-5pm) Extensive visitor information on Townsville, Magnetic Island and nearby national parks. There's another branch on the Bruce Hwy 10km south of the city.

Getting There & Away

Air

From **Townsville Airport** (www.townsvilleairport.com.au), **Virgin Blue** (☎13 67 89; www.virginblue.com.au), **Qantas** (☎13 13 13; www.qantas.com.au), **Jetstar** (☎13 15 38; www.jetstar.com) and **Regional Express** (REX; ☎13 17 13; www.rex.com.au) fly to Cairns, Brisbane, the Gold Coast, Sydney, Melbourne, Cloncurry, Gladstone, Mackay, Mount Isa and Rockhampton, with connections to other major cities. **Strategic Airlines** (☎13 53 20; www.flystrategic.com.au) runs a twice-weekly direct service to/from Bali.

Boat

See p279 for ferries to/from Magnetic Island.

Bus

Greyhound Australia (☎1300 473 946; www.greyhound.com.au) has three daily services to Brisbane ($270, 23 hours), Rockhampton ($149, 12 hours), Airlie Beach ($71, 4½ hours), Mission Beach ($63, 3¾ hours) and Cairns ($83, six hours). There's also a service four times a week to Charters Towers ($36, 1¾ hours) continuing to the Northern Territory. Buses pick up and drop off at Townsville's Sunferries passenger ferry terminal.

Premier Motor Service (☎13 34 10; www.premierms.com.au) has one service a day to/from Brisbane and Cairns, stopping in Townsville at Townsville's Fantasea car ferry terminal (p279).

Car

Major car-rental agencies are represented in Townsville and at the airport.

Train

Townsville's **train station** (Charters Towers Rd) is 1km south of the centre.

The Brisbane–Cairns *Sunlander* travels through Townsville three times a week. Journey time between Brisbane and Townsville is 24 hours (one way from $190).

The *Inlander* heads from Townsville to Mt Isa on Thursday and Sunday (one way from $127, 21 hours) via Charters Towers ($28, three hours).

Contact **Queensland Rail** (☎1800 872 467; www.traveltrain.com.au) for details.

Getting Around

To/From the Airport

Townsville airport is 5km northwest of the city centre at Garbutt. A taxi to the centre costs about $20. The **Airport Shuttle** (☎4775 5544; one way/return $10/18) services all arrivals and departures, with pick-ups and drop-offs throughout the central business district (bookings essential).

Bus

Sunbus (☎4725 8482; www.sunbus.com.au) runs local bus services around Townsville, including the Redbus service – a dedicated loop stopping at key tourist attractions in the city. Fares start from $1.60. Route maps and timetables are available at the visitor information centre.

Taxi

Taxis congregate outside the Sunbus **bus interchange** (cnr Flinders & Stokes Sts), or call **Townsville Taxis** (☎13 10 08).

MAGNETIC ISLAND

POP 2107

'Maggie', as it's affectionately called, is a 'real' island. Permanent residents live and work here and some even make the daily commute to Townsville. Half of this mountainous, triangular-shaped island's 52 sq km is national park, with scenic walks and abundant wildlife, including one of the largest concentrations of wild koalas in Australia. Stunning beaches offer adrenaline-pumping water sports or just the chance to bask in the sunshine. Each of the four tiny beach villages has its own distinct personality, and the granite boulders, hoop pines and eucalypts are a change from your typical tropical island paradise. Although battered by Cyclone Yasi, the island emerged largely unscathed.

Long known as Yunbenun by the Indigenous Wulgurukaba people, Captain Cook named it Magnetic Island in 1770, when his ship's compass went haywire and he sailed by without stopping. Cook missed out, big time. Even if you just do a day trip, don't make the same mistake.

Sights & Activities

There's one main road across the island, which goes from Picnic Bay, past Nelly and Geoffrey Bays, to Horseshoe Bay. Local buses ply the route regularly.

PICNIC BAY

Since the ferry terminal was relocated to Nelly Bay, Picnic Bay now resembles a ghost town. Shopfronts have been abandoned as businesses suffered from the decreased tourist traffic. But that curious, elegant bird, the curlew, has made the bay its own, and the twinkling night views of Townsville from the esplanade are magical, especially during a stroll along the jetty. Without the ferry traffic, the jetty is now one of the best spots on the island for fishing.

Activities in the area also include swimming in the beach's stinger enclosure (November to May) or hitting balls around the nine-hole golf course at the **Magnetic Island Country Club** (☎4778 5188; www.magneticislandgolf.com.au; Hurst St, Picnic Bay; ⏲from 8am). West is **Cockle Bay**, with the HMS *City of Adelaide* wreck languishing on the ocean floor, followed by **West Point**, some 4km further northwest, with its sunsets and secluded beach. Heading east round the coast from Picnic Bay is **Rocky Bay**, where a short, steep walk leads down to a beautiful, sheltered beach.

NELLY BAY

Crowds swarm off the ferry and onto the bustling marina at the newly developed Nelly Bay terminal. This is where your holiday on Magnetic will begin, but its busy vibe is the total opposite to what you'll probably experience during your stay here.

That said, Nelly Bay has a wide range of eating and sleeping options and a decent beach. There's a children's playground towards the northern end of the beach and good snorkelling on the fringing coral reef.

ARCADIA

Arcadia village has the island's main concentration of shops, eateries and accommodation. Its main beach, **Geoffrey Bay**, has a reef at its southern end (DERM discourages reef walking at low tide). By far its prettiest beach is **Alma Bay** cove, with huge boulders tumbling into the sea. There's plenty of shade, along with picnic tables and a children's playground here.

If you head to the end of the road at **Bremner Point**, between Geoffrey Bay and Alma Bay, at 5pm, you can have wild rock wallabies – which have become accustomed to being fed at the same time each day – literally eating out of your hand.

RADICAL BAY & THE FORTS

Townsville was a supply base for the Pacific during WWII, so forts were strategically designed to protect the town from naval attack. If you're going to do just one walk, then the **forts walk** (2.8km, 1½ hours return) is a must. It starts near the Radical Bay turn-off, passing lots of ex-military sites and gun emplacements. At the top of the walk is the observation tower and command post, which both have spectacular views up and down the coast, and you'll almost certainly spot the odd koala or two lazing about in the treetops. Return the same way or continue along the connecting paths, which run past Radical and Balding Bays, eventually depositing you at Horseshoe Bay (you can catch the bus back to the start of the walk).

You can also head north to Radical Bay via a rough vehicle track, with walking tracks leading off it to secluded **Arthur** and **Florence Bays** (both great for snorkelling) and the old searchlight station on the headland between the two.

From Radical Bay you can walk across the headland to beautiful **Balding Bay** (an unofficial nude-bathing beach) and Horseshoe Bay.

HORSESHOE BAY

Horseshoe Bay, on the north coast, is the island's water-sports hub. Its crescent-shaped, golden-sand beach is easily the best of the island's accessible beaches, and there is a string of cafes and a good pub.

Experience the thrill of blasting about on Horseshoe Bay by hiring a **jet ski** (☎4758 1100; Horseshoe Bay beach; per 15/30/60min $50/90/165; ⏰closed Tue & Thu). Prices are for two-seater jet skis, so you can split the cost between two. You'll find the makeshift 'office' on the beach near the stinger net. It's open daily during school holidays.

Magnetic Island Hire Boats (☎4778 5327) rents boats ($220 per day plus fuel) that can carry up to eight people – great for fishing, snorkelling, or just finding your own private cove.

Bungalow Bay Koala Village has a **wildlife park** (adult/child $19/10; ⏰2hr tours 10am, noon & 2.30pm), where you can cuddle koalas ($14 including photos), or tuck into a **bush tucker gourmet breakfast** (adult/child $25/12.50) of lemon myrtle pancakes, reef fish with bush tomatoes, guava champagne and more – all in the company of friendly native birds and critters.

Pick up local arts and crafts at Horseshoe Bay's monthly **market** (⏰9.30am-2pm last Sun of month), which sets up along the beachfront.

☞ Tours

Unique ways to tour the island range from horseback to tall ship. If you'd rather explore under your own steam, **DERM** (☎13 74 68; www.derm.qld.gov.au) produces a leaflet for Magnetic Island's excellent bushwalking tracks. Walks are mainly along the east coast, and vary in length from half an hour to half a day. Alternatively, rent your own boat or jet ski, or zoom around by Moke or scooter.

Reef Safari DIVING
(☎4778 5777; www.reefsafari.com; 1 Nelly Bay Rd, Nelly Bay) Maggie has a couple of outfits operating courses and dive trips. At Base Backpackers in Nelly Bay, Reef Safari runs four-day open-water courses from $299, in addition to advanced courses, introductory dives and certified dives.

Pleasure Divers DIVING
(☎1800 797 797, 4778 5788; www.pleasuredivers.com.au; 10 Marine Pde, Arcadia) Adjacent to Magnums in Arcadia; it offers three-day PADI open-water courses from $339, as well as advanced courses and Yongala wreck dives.

Tropicana Tours ISLAND TRIPS
(☎4758 1800; www.tropicanatours.com.au; full-day tours adult/child $198/99) If you're time poor, this full-day tour with well-informed guides takes in the island's best spots in its stretch 4WD. Enjoy close encounters with wildlife, lunch at a local cafe and a sunset cocktail (all included in the price). Shorter tours are available.

Horseshoe Ranch HORSE RIDING
(☎4778 5109; www.horseshoebayranch.com.au; 38 Gifford St, Horseshoe Bay) Popular two-hour

rides ($100) take you through bushland to the beach, where your horse can swim. Also on offer are 3½-hour rides ($130), plus 20-minute pony rides ($20) for kids.

Providence V SAILING, SNORKELLING
(☎4778 5580; www.providencesailing.com.au) Six-hour sailing trips aboard a 62-ft gaff rigged schooner (including snorkelling gear) for $129, or 2½-hour champagne sunset cruises.

Magnetic Island Sea Kayaks KAYAKING
(☎4778 5424; www.seakayak.com.au; 93 Horseshoe Bay Rd; tours from $69) Eco-oriented morning tours to Balding Bay (from $85, including breakfast) and sunset tours (from $60 including drinks). Also offers kayak rental (single/double kayak per day $75/150).

Reef EcoTours SNORKELLING
(☎0419 712 579; www.reefecotours.com) One-hour guided snorkelling tour (adult/child $80/70) with a marine biologist. Good for families.

Adrenalin Jet Ski Tours JET-SKIING
(☎4758 5533) Circumnavigate Maggie on the back of a jet ski (from $175) to spot sea turtles, dolphins, dugongs and (from July to September) humpback whales.

Sleeping

Maggie is especially popular with families and couples, but backpackers also have plenty of options. Much of the accommodation on the island is holiday rental cottages – contact **First National Real Estate** (☎4778 5077; 21 Marine Pde, Arcadia) or **Smith & Elliott** (☎4778 5570; 4/5 Bright Ave, Arcadia).

PICNIC BAY

Tropical Palms Inn MOTEL $$
(☎4778 5076; www.tropicalpalmsinn.com.au; 34 Picnic St; s/d $100/110;) With a terrific little swimming pool right outside your front door, the self-contained motel units here are bright and comfortable. Reception hires out 4WDs (from $75 per day).

Magnetic Island Holiday Units APARTMENTS $$$
(☎4778 5246; www.magnetic-island.com.au/mi-units.htm; 16 Yule St; 1-/2-bedroom units from $264/303;) These self-contained units, each with their own private courtyard, are in a secluded part of the island amid leafy gardens and manicured lawns.

NELLY BAY

TOP CHOICE **Base Backpackers** HOSTEL $
(☎1800 242 273, 4778 5777; www.stayatbase.com; 1 Nelly Bay Rd; camping $10 per person, dm $24-30, d without/with bathroom from $65/120;) Famous for its wild full-moon parties, this huge backpackers resort vibrates with energy at any time of the year. With a concentration of A-frame cabins (some oceanfront), facilities including a massive deck overlooking the deep blue of the ocean, and an adjoining **cafe** (mains $7-16, lunch & dinner;), you'd have to try hard not to have a good time here. Great-value package deals include two nights' dorm accommodation, return ferry from Townsville, return bus transfer from Nelly Bay terminal, dinner, breakfast and snorkelling gear for $95.

Shambhala Retreat APARTMENTS $$
(☎0448 160 580; www.shambhala-retreat-magnetic-island.com.au; 11-13 Barton St; d $110;) Feel the serenity…these three tropical-hued units have Buddhist wall hangings and books scattered about and their own tree-screened patios attracting local wildlife. Two have outdoor courtyard showers, and all have fully equipped kitchens, large bathrooms and laundry facilities. The saltwater pool's scarcely bigger than a puddle, but the property is entirely green powered. Minimum stay is two nights.

Peppers Blue on Blue Resort HOTEL $$$
(☎4758 2400; www.peppers.com.au/blue-on-blue; 123 Sooning St; d/1-bedroom apt/2-bedroom apt from $229/321/379;) A glinting vision of glass and steel alongside the Nelly Bay ferry terminal, this is the island's newest and by far its ritziest resort. There are citified neutral-toned rooms and apartments, and even a day spa. The casually chic **Boardwalk Restaurant & Bar** (mains $25-32; breakfast, lunch & dinner;) opens onto an enormous deck, where you can watch the ferries dock.

Island Leisure Resort APARTMENTS $$
(☎4778 5000; www.islandleisure.com.au; 4 Kelly St; d from $155;) A block back from the bay, and with palm trees sprouting up all over the place, Island Leisure Resort is well situated, but cramped, with dated units squashed close together. Still, the spacious interiors have high ceilings, and there's a gym and a pool large enough for a swim team to train in.

ARCADIA

Arcadia Beach Guest House GUESTHOUSE $$
(4778 5668; www.arcadiabeachguesthouse.com.au; 27 Marine Pde; dm $30, safari tent $50, d $80-100, d with bathroom $120-150;) Super-friendly owners have created a stunningly different place to stay, with bright, beachy rooms named after Magnetic Island's bays and coves. You can turtle-spot from the balcony, and rent a canoe, a Moke or a 4WD. Free ferry pick-ups.

Magnums on Magnetic HOSTEL $
(1800 663 666, 4778 5177; www.magnums.com.au; 7 Marine Pde; dm $20-24, d $75-85;) Fresh from a facelift, Magnums tries its best to trade off the success of its namesake at Airlie Beach. All dorms and doubles have bathrooms; make sure you ask for one with an ocean view. Doubles come with a small fridge and TV. The hub of Arcadia Bay is the onsite bistro and bar, the **Island Tavern** (mains $19.50-28; lunch & dinner), which keeps punters happy with $10 jugs, cane-toad races every Wednesday night and a large swimming pool accessible to the public.

Brooke Haven Holiday Units APARTMENTS $$
(4778 5262; www.brookehavenholidayunits.com; 5 Horden Ave; d $150;) Set among tropical gardens with their own courtyards, these stylishly renovated units have beachy decor (striped bedspreads, light-toned leather lounges). OK, they're not right on the beach, but it's only a five-minute stroll to find some sand. There's a two-night minimum stay.

HORSESHOE BAY

Bungalow Bay Koala Village HOSTEL $
(1800 285 577, 4778 5577; www.bungalowbay.com.au; 40 Horseshoe Bay Rd; unpowered/powered sites per person $13/15, dm $30, d without/with bathroom $74/90;) Not only a resort-style, YHA-associated hostel but a nature wonderland (with its own wildlife park). Less than five minutes' walk from the beach, A-frame bungalows are strewn throughout leafy grounds backing onto national park. Cool off at the breezy outdoor bar area, go coconut bowling on Thursdays, or dine at the onsite **restaurant** (mains $16-24; lunch & dinner), specialising in fragrant curries.

Shaws on the Shore APARTMENTS $$$
(4778 1900; www.shawsontheshore.com.au; 7 Pacific Dr; 1-/2-/3/-bedroom apt $195/270/325;) Natural light floods these sparkling apartments, which feature balconies overlooking Horseshoe Bay's arc of sand. Flowing living areas and tiled surfaces give rooms a tropical air; larger apartments have en suites off the master bedroom. Staff are genuine and helpful.

Eating & Drinking

Oh, Maggie. You might have natural beauty in spades, but (with a few exceptions) your culinary skills aren't much. Sure, everything has to be brought over from the mainland but, still, it's surprisingly hard to find a decent meal on the island.

Several hotels and hostels have restaurants and bars that are at least as popular with locals as they are with guests and visitors. Opening hours can fluctuate according to the season and the crowds.

PICNIC BAY

Picnic Bay Hotel PUB
(Picnic Bay Mall) Settle in for a drink with Townsville's city lights sparkling across the bay. Locals love sinking a few pots at this big, friendly pub and enjoying a punt on the horses in the onsite TAB. Its **R&R Cafe Bar** (mains $11-26; lunch & dinner) has an all-day grazing menu and huge salads including Cajun prawn.

NELLY BAY

TOP CHOICE **Man Friday** INTERNATIONAL $$
(4778 5658; 37 Warboy St; mains $14-39; dinner Wed-Mon;) Man Friday's imaginative international cuisine is easily the best Mexican food on Maggie (and no, it's not the only Mexican food on Maggie). Relax in the rustic, fairy-lit garden and bring your own wine (it's unlicensed) but book ahead or risk missing out.

Fat Possum Cafe CAFE $
(55 Spooning St; mains $7-17; breakfast & lunch;) This slightly alternative spot is aptly named for the well-fed possums scampering around the island. The best pickings are on the specials board – pancakes with fresh fruit salad, bacon and avocado wraps and grilled ciabatta breads. Sunday's $15 all-you-can-eat breakfast buffet is something of a village social event.

Terrace MEDITERRANEAN $$
(4778 5200; www.allseasons.com.au; 61 Mandalay Ave; mains $22-44; lunch Sat & Sun, dinner Mon-Sat;) Overlooking the pool of the dated All Seasons Hotel (so dated, in fact, that it won't be too long before it's retro-cool again), the Terrace is one of the better places

on the island to dine on the likes of pan-roasted duck or oven-baked spring lamb on kumara mash.

Le Paradis FRENCH $$
(www.leparadis.com.au; 8/98-100 Sooning St; mains $23-26; ⏲lunch & dinner) It *looks* like an authentic French restaurant (complete with Eiffel Tower–emblazoned menus written in French). But it's severely let down by its overpriced and, in our experience, ultimately inedible takeaway fare (ordered from a neon-pink-lit booth in the car park, despite coming out of the same kitchen) – not promising if you were planning a romantic meal here. *C'est dommage.*

ARCADIA

Butler's Pantry CAFE, DELI $$
(2-3/5 Bright Ave; mains $15-21; ⏲breakfast & lunch Wed-Mon;) The island's best brekkies are served at this bang-up-to-date gourmet grocery store and cafe, including pancakes, eggs every which way, and stacks of veggie options. Great lunches too – from Thai fish cakes to Greek lamb salad – and attentive service.

caffè dell' isola ITALIAN $$
(Shop 1, Arcadia Village; mains $15-26; ⏲breakfast & lunch Tue, Thu & Sun, breakfast, lunch & dinner Wed, Fri & Sat, daily during school holidays) The Italian radio station reverberating through the outdoor courtyard attests to the authenticity of the crisp-crust pizzas here (as does the menu that reads 'please do not even ask for pineapple'). No credit cards.

Banister's Seafood SEAFOOD $$
(☎4778 5700; 22 McCabe Cres; mains $10-22; ⏲lunch & dinner) You can do the whole sit-down thing and order off the menu chalked on the blackboard of this BYO-only seafood joint, or grab some takeaway and head to a nearby beach.

Arcadia Night Market MARKET $$
(Hayles Ave, Arcadia; ⏲5-8pm Fri) If you're here on a Friday night, pick up sizzling Indonesian food or seafood to cook up yourself at this small but lively night market next door to the RSL club.

HORSESHOE BAY

Marlin Bar PUB $$
(3 Pacific Dr; mains $16-24; ⏲lunch & dinner) You can't leave Maggie without enjoying a cold one by the window as the sun sets across the bay at this busy seaside pub. The meals are on the large side and (surprise!) revolve around seafood. Great value.

Barefoot MODERN AUSTRALIAN $$
(☎4758 1170; www.barefootartfoodwine.com.au; 5 Pacific Dr; mains $16-30; ⏲lunch & dinner Thu-Mon) Set back from the street, this ode to contemporary design also houses an art gallery. Dishes like artichoke risotto with truffle oil, and Egyptian-spiced kangaroo burgers are accompanied by a good wine list.

☆ Entertainment

Stage Door CABARET
(☎4778 5448; www.stagedoortheatre.com.au; 5 Hayles Ave, Arcadia; dinner & show $75; ⏲Fri & Sat) Whether taking off country stars like 'Dolly Pardon Me' or Broadway legends, this cabaret's energetic performing duo, Bernadette and Phill, sing, dance and impersonate their way through an entertaining 90-minute show while you dine on a set three-course dinner. Not suitable for kids under 13.

ℹ Information

There's no official visitor information centre on Magnetic Island, but Townsville's visitor information centre has comprehensive info and maps, and can help find accommodation. Maps are also available at both ferry terminals in Townsville and at the terminal at Nelly Bay.

ATMs are scattered throughout the island, although there are no banks. The **post office** (Sooning St, Nelly Bay) also has an ATM.

ℹ Getting There & Away

All ferries arrive and depart Maggie from the terminal at Nelly Bay.

Sunferries (☎4726 0800; www.sunferries.com.au) operates a frequent passenger ferry between Townsville and Magnetic Island (adult/child return $29/14.50), which takes around 20 minutes. Ferries depart Townsville from the Sunferries Breakwater Terminal at 2/14 Sir Leslie Thiess Dr.

Fantasea (☎4796 9300; www.magneticislandferry.com.au; Ross St, South Townsville) operates a car ferry crossing eight times daily (seven on weekends) from the south side of Ross Creek, taking 35 minutes. It costs $164 (return) for a car and up to three passengers, and $26/15.50 (return) for an adult/child foot passenger only. Bookings are essential. Bicycles are transported free.

Both Townsville terminals have car parking.

ℹ Getting Around

Bicycle

Magnetic Island is ideal for cycling although some of the hills can be hard work. Most places to stay rent bikes for around $15 a day and a number of places offer them free to guests.

Bus

The **Magnetic Island Bus Service** (4778 5130) ploughs between Picnic Bay and Horseshoe Bay at least 18 times a day, meeting all ferries and stopping at major accommodation places. A hop-on, hop-off day pass costs $6.

Moke & Scooter

Moke and scooter rental places abound around the island. Expect to pay around $75 to $85 per day (plus extras such as petrol and a per-kilometre fee after the first 40km) for a Moke. You'll need to be over 21, have a current international or Australian driver's licence, and leave a credit-card deposit. Scooter hire starts at around $30 per day. Try **MI Wheels** (4778 5491; 138 Sooning St, Nelly Bay) for a classic Moke or 'topless' (open-topped) car, or **Roadrunner Scooter Hire** (4778 5222; 3/64 Kelly St, Nelly Bay) for scooters and trail bikes.

SOUTH OF TOWNSVILLE

Wildlife-spotting opportunities abound south of the city.

Billabong Sanctuary (www.billabongsanctuary.com.au; Bruce Hwy; adult/child $30/19; 8am-5pm) is an eco-certified wildlife park just 17km south of Townsville, which offers up-close-and-personal (but not too up-close-and-personal) encounters with Australian wildlife – from dingoes to cassowaries – in their natural habitat. You could easily spend all day at the 11-hectare park, which has feedings, shows and talks every half-hour or so. There's a cafe and a swimming pool. Transfers are available from Townsville with **Abacus Tours** (4775 5544; adult/child $50/30 incl park entry).

The unique wetlands of **Bowling Green Bay National Park** foster an assortment of wildlife in mudflats, mangroves and salt marshes. Various species of bird wade through the waters, and the seagrass beds in the bay are home to turtles and dugongs. The turn-off from the Bruce Hwy to the park is at **Alligator Creek**, 28km south of Townsville. Alligator Creek tumbles down between two rugged ranges that rise steeply from the coastal plains. The taller range peaks with Mt Elliot (1234m), whose higher slopes harbour some of Queensland's most southerly tropical rainforest. A sealed road heads 6km inland from the highway to the park entrance, from where a good gravel road leads to picnic areas. Further on, its campground is due to have reopened following redevelopment by the time you're reading this; contact **DERM** (13 74 68; www.derm.qld.gov.au; per person $5.15). Alligator Creek has some superb swimming holes, and there are two walking trails: one to Hidden Valley and Alligator Falls (17km, five hours return), the other following Cockatoo Creek (3km, one hour return).

Australian Institute of Marine Science (AIMS; 4753 4444; www.aims.gov.au; tours 10am Fri Mar-Nov), a marine-research facility at Cape Ferguson, runs free two-hour tours covering the institute's research (such as coral bleaching and management of the Great Barrier Reef) and how it relates to the community; bookings are essential. The turn-off from the Bruce Hwy is 35km southeast of Townsville.

On the delta of the Burdekin, one of the state's biggest rivers, **Ayr** (population 8093), 90km southeast of Townsville, is the major commercial centre for the rich farmlands of the Burdekin Valley. The town and its surrounds are devoted to the production and harvesting of sugar cane, melons and mangoes.

Yongala Dive (4783 1519; www.yongaladive.com.au; 56 Narrah St, Alva Beach) does dive trips ($220 including gear) out to the *Yongala* wreck from Alva Beach, 17km northeast of Ayr. It only takes 30 minutes to get out to the wreck from here, instead of a 2½-hour boat trip from Townsville. Book ahead for backpacker-style accommodation at its onshore **dive lodge** (dm $27, d $65; @), with free pick-ups from Ayr.

The **Burdekin visitor centre** (4783 5988; www.burdekintourism.com.au; Bruce Hwy; 9am-4pm), in Plantation Park on the southern side of Ayr, is able to help with finding accommodation.

WEST OF TOWNSVILLE

The north coast's sparse, open hinterland is in stark contrast to the verdant rainforests along the coast. This is the Dry Tropics, after all, where you can almost always see a horizon cutting across a giant sky.

The Flinders Hwy (A6) heads inland from Townsville and runs virtually due west for its entire length – almost 800km from Townsville to Cloncurry. The first section of the highway takes you 138km southwest from Townsville to the gold-mining town

SLAVERY OF SORTS: QUEENSLAND'S EARLY SUGAR LABOURERS

Queensland's sugar industry boomed between 1863 and 1891. It was during this time that the government brought 46,387 South Pacific Islanders to Australia to work primarily in the cane fields as cheap labour. The men, known as kanakas, worked 10-hour days for four pence per day, under three-year contracts. Stories abound of men going without pay and working in terrible conditions. Mortality figures of the time reinforce this: for non–Pacific Islanders the mortality rate was 13.03 per 1000, for Pacific Islanders it was 62.89.

Australia introduced its White Australia Policy in 1901 when there were around 9000 kanakas still working in Queensland's cane fields. By 1914 more than 7000 Islanders had been repatriated.

of Charters Towers, with a turn-off around two-thirds of the way to the tiny gold-mining village of Ravenswood. Both are easily accessible on a day trip from Townsville.

Ravenswood

POP 150

A ghost town for much of the 20th century, Ravenswood is thriving once more. At Mingela, 88km from Townsville, a road leads 40km south to this tiny mining town among scattered red-earth hills, which is classified by the National Trust for its preserved historic buildings from its gold-rush days.

Gold was discovered here by chance in 1868 by a pastoralist who, while on a cattle muster, dipped his pannikin into the river and found more than he bargained for in his drinking water. And so the rush was on. Ravenswood experienced a number of booms and subsequent busts, reaching its climax between 1900 and 1912, when it produced 12,500kg of gold and supported a population of around 5000 – with 48 pubs in an eight-mile radius.

From the old post office and **Mining & Historical Museum** (☎4770 2047; adult/child $2/1; ⌚11am-1pm Mon-Fri, 11am-2pm Sat & Sun) housed in the restored courthouse, police station and lock-up, a walking trail leads to a viewing platform over an old open-cut mine.

More recently gold-mining operations (now underground) have again moved into Ravenswood: hop on a stool at one of the two remaining ornate pubs and chat to Ravenswood's new generation of miners.

The grandiose, two-storey **Imperial Hotel** (☎4770 2131; 23 Macrossan St; s/d incl breakfast $48/68; wi-fi) has character for mortar. Its solid red-brick facade and iron-lace-trimmed verandah are features of the architectural style known as 'goldfields brash'. The timber-lined bedrooms upstairs, some with old brass beds and opening out onto the verandah, are clean and well presented (all share bathrooms). Decent pub **meals** (mains $15-22; ⌚lunch Thu-Sun, dinner daily) are served from the magnificent red-cedar bar.

An imposing, solid, red-brick pub, the **Railway Hotel** (☎4770 2144; Barton St; s/d $39/55) was originally built in 1871, but what you see today was built in the same year as the Imperial, 1902. A great ancient staircase leads up to basic bedrooms (all sharing bathrooms) with tin ceilings; most rooms open onto the big front verandah. **Meals** (mains $10-24; ⌚lunch & dinner) are available, though the focus is firmly on the beer.

Charters Towers

POP 7980

The name might conjure up thoughts of high-rises, but the 'towers' for which this historic outback town is named are its surrounding tors (hills). William Skelton Ewbank Melbourne (WSEM) Charters was the gold commissioner during the gold rush, when the town was the second largest, and wealthiest, in Queensland.

Gold was discovered with a bang: Hugh Mosman and Aboriginal horseboy Jupiter Mosman (his adopted son), among others, had been prospecting south of here when their horses bolted during a crashing thunderstorm. Searching for the horses the next day, Jupiter first found gold here. It didn't take long for the population to explode to around 30,000; almost 100 mines, some 90 pubs (albeit most little more than tents serving alcohol) and a stock exchange to open; and for the town to become known simply as 'the World'.

Today, a highlight of a visit to the Towers is strolling past its glorious facades recalling the grandeur of those heady days. Ghosts apparently abound in the town's buildings; everyone has a ghost story to tell. And at night the words 'the World' shine brightly over the town from the sides of Towers Hill's massive water tanks.

While Charters Towers is easily reached without venturing too far inland, it's worth staying at least one night to explore its architecture, museums and easygoing outback pace.

Sights & Activities

Stock Exchange Arcade HISTORIC BUILDING
(www.nationaltrustqld.org; Mosman St; gold coin donation) History oozes from the walls of this beautiful little 1888-built arcade, which housed the stock exchange from 1890. It was connected to the 'outside' world via telegraph with three calls per day, six days a week. After watching a film about the town's history at the visitor centre next door, ask the staff to activate the automated **calling of the cards**. This quaint re-enactment takes five minutes; allow 20 minutes all-up including the tiny **mining museum** of old mining equipment, photos and minerals.

One Square Mile Trail HISTORIC BUILDINGS
Pick up a free brochure from the visitor centre and set off on the One Square Mile trail around the town centre's beautifully preserved 19th-century buildings. Highlights include the original Australia Bank of Commerce building, built in 1891, which now houses the **World Theatre** (82 Mosman St), comprising a theatre, cinema and restaurant; and the 1878 **Northern Miner offices** (73 Gill St). The twice-weekly *Northern Miner* newspaper (Tuesday and Friday) was first published in 1872 and still serves a readership area the size of Tasmania.

Zara Clark Museum MUSEUM
(www.nationaltrustqld.org; 36 Mosman St; adult/child \$5/2; 10am-2pm) Offering a wonderful place to escape back in time, this private collection has been amassed by local Zara Clark. The clutter of memorabilia here – from old photos and farming equipment to period costumes and military items – is fascinating.

Venus Gold Battery MUSEUM
(Millchester Rd; tours adult/child \$12/6; 10am-3pm) Gold-bearing ore was crushed and processed until as recently as 1973 at the largest and best-preserved battery in Australia. An imaginative tour tells the story of this huge relic, departing hourly from April to October and twice daily from November to March. Follow the signs 3.5km west of town from Gill St.

FREE **Towers Hill Lookout** LOOKOUT, CINEMA
Reached via Mosman St on the town's southern edge, Towers Hill, the site where gold was first discovered, has inspiring views over the plain and interpretive panels. Come nightfall, it's the atmospheric setting for a free **open-air cinema** showing the 20-minute film *Ghosts After Dark* each evening – check seasonal screening times with the visitor centre.

Miner's Cottage MUSEUM, GOLD-PANNING
(www.theminerscottage.com.au; 26 Deane St; adult/child \$5/3, gold-panning from \$11; 11am-2pm Mon-Fri, 10am-2pm Sat & Sun) If you've got gold fever by now, you can pan for gold at this classic wooden 19th-century miner's cottage, and check out its collection of mining tools. A winner with kids.

Lissner Park PARK, SWIMMING
(bordered by Anne, Deane, Church & Plummer Sts) In the northeastern corner of the town centre, the **Boer War memorial** at this oasis-like park honours local soldier and poet Harry 'Breaker' Morant, who was executed by the British after shooting a prisoner and went on to become an Aussie folk hero. It remains a controversial chapter in Australian military history – in late 2010, the British government again refused to allow Morant a royal pardon.

Charters Towers' community **swimming pool** is in the park's northeastern corner.

Festivals & Events

Dalrymple Sales Yards Cattle Sales CATTLE SALES
(www.charterstowers.qld.gov.au) Catch the excitement of cattle sales at Charters Towers' huge cattle yards every Wednesday.

Goldfield Ashes CRICKET
(www.goldfieldashes.com.au) For three days over the Australia Day long weekend in late January, the largest gathering of amateur cricket teams in the world – 214 at last count! – descends on Charters Towers.

Charters Towers Country Music Festival MUSIC
(www.charterstowerscountrymusic.com) Three days of big-name Aussie country music stars and lotsa line dancing in late April/early May.

Gold Fever Festival GOLD

(www.charterstowers.qld.gov.au) Mid-July's Gold Fever Festival is the only time of year the Venus Gold Battery cranks into action.

Sleeping

Good-value motels are strung along Dalrymple Rd as you approach the town from Townsville.

TOP CHOICE **Royal Private Hotel** HOTEL $$

(☎4787 8688; 100 Mosman St; s/d without bathroom $45/55, d $90-115;) This grand old former pub reminds you that the townsfolk back in the gold-rush era were very well-to-do. Nowadays it's one of the best-value places around. Couples should ask for room 7, with a huge bed, a spa big enough to do laps in (well, almost), and gorgeous period furniture, which opens onto the broad 1st-floor verandah.

Park Motel MOTEL $$

(☎4787 1022; www.parkmotel.com.au; 1 Mosman St; s/d $95/105;) With spacious rooms, Charters Towers' closest motel to the town centre is an excellent choice, so long as you don't mind sharing with resident ghost Bridget Clancy. In 1901, 24-year-old Bridget took over running the property. Three years later, she took her own life by overdosing on cyanide after the object of her affection, her brother-in-law Watson Nixon, was killed in a mining accident. Staff can fill you in on her antics (opening doors, switching off TVs, etc), if you don't experience them yourself. The fine-dining **restaurant** (mains $15-30; breakfast & dinner) specialises in steaks.

Charters Towers Motel MOTEL $$

(☎1800 217 002, 4787 1366; www.charterstowersmotel.com.au; 95 Hackett Tce; s $85-125, d $95-125;) It might look like an ordinary motel from the outside, but two things make this family-run spot stand out. First are the city-chic 2008-built 'deluxe' units, with gleaming tiles and fittings. Second are the Nikken magnetic mattress underlays in some rooms, providing a blissful night's sleep (so much so that you'll probably want to buy one for your own bed back home).

Aussie Outback Oasis CARAVAN PARK $

(☎4787 8722; 76 Dr George Ellis Dr; unpowered/powered site $18/30, cabins $98-120;) Charters Towers' best caravan park is situated 3km northeast of the town centre, but its facilities more than make up for that: an enormous saltwater swimming pool amid rocks and waterfalls, loads of shady sites, and a huge 'jumping pillow' for kids.

Bluff Downs FARMSTAY $

(☎4770 4084; www.bluffdowns.com.au; powered sites/dm/d from $20/28/90;) For a taste of tough outback life without roughing it, this historic homestead, on a working cattle station 110km northwest of Charters Towers, has a range of accommodation packages including meals and activities such as river swimming, boating and fishing. No credit cards.

Eating

Despite the number of day trippers from Townsville, many of Charters Towers' cafes and restaurants have surprisingly limited opening hours on weekends.

Henry's MODERN AUSTRALIAN $$

(☎4787 4333; 82-90 Mosman St; mains $25-32; 9am-late Tue-Sat, 10am-2pm Sun) Formerly Lawson's, but still named after the Aussie poet Henry Lawson, this upmarket spot has an extensive menu spanning lamb loin chops to baked coral trout with lime butter, and vegetarian couscous. There's a sense of occasion to the setting beneath the World Theatre building's towering ceilings.

Stock Exchange Café CAFE $

(76 Mosman St; dishes $5-10; breakfast & lunch Mon-Sat) You could play a game of chess on the chequer-board floor, but the food is a worthy distraction. Just about everything is dished up at this good old-fashioned cafe, such as salmon patties served with chips and salad.

Gold City Chinese CHINESE $

(☎4787 2414; 118 Gill St; mains $9-16; lunch Wed-Fri, dinner Tue-Sun) You can eat well for very little at this BYO Chinese place on the main street. All-you-can-eat buffets (lunch Wednesday to Friday, $11; dinner Wednesday, Friday and Sunday, $16), pack in locals and visitors alike; soup, dessert and tea or coffee are included.

Towers Bakery BAKERY $

(114 Gill St; pies $3.90-4.30; 5am-3pm Mon-Fri, 5am-1pm Sat) A venture to Charters Towers is incomplete without scoffing down one of this bakery's award-winning pies. It's just got to be done.

Peppers Cafe CAFE $

(58 Gill St; dishes $6-15; 8am-4pm Mon-Fri, 8am-noon Sat, 9am-1pm Sun) Fresh, wholesome dishes including gourmet sandwiches are whipped up at this friendly local cafe.

Leaning Towers Pizza PIZZA $$
(☎4787 7333; 56 Mosman St; pizzas $11-18; ⊙3-9pm Mon-Thu, 11am-9pm Fri-Sun) No wonder it takes so bloody long for your pizza to cook – the toppings are piled sky-high. Try the fiery 'devil's delight' with jalapeños and pepperoni on a chilli-flake base.

Drinking & Entertainment

Tors Drive-In Cinema CINEMA
(www.torsdrive-in.com; cnr New Queen Rd & Flinders Hwy; adult/child $7.50/5.50; ⊙gates open 6pm Fri & Sat) Built in the '60s out of secondhand materials, this fabulous old drive-in is 5km north of the centre.

Irish Molly's PUB
(www.irishmollys.com.au; 120 Gill St) At the historic Courthouse Hotel, Molly's Irish-themed bar has live music every Friday night and great craic.

White Horse Tavern PUB
(cnr Gill & Deane Sts) Charters Towers' party pub guarantees a good crowd during its regular theme nights (from Mr Abs night to Nurse Party night!), two pool tables and cheap drinks.

Information

Services along Gill St include ATMs, the post office, and the **Charters Towers visitor centre** (☎4752 0314; www.charterstowers.qld.gov.au; 74 Mosman St; ⊙9am-5pm), which can book all tours in town.

Getting There & Away

Greyhound Australia (☎1300 473 946; www.greyhound.com.au) has a service from Townsville to Charters Towers ($36, 1¾ hours) four times a week, on Tuesday, Thursday, Friday and Sunday, continuing to the Northern Territory. The long-distance bus stop is outside the Catholic church on Gill St.

The **train station** (cnr Gill St & Enterprise Rd) is 1.5km east of the centre. The twice-weekly *Inlander* runs from Townsville to Charters Towers on Sunday and Thursday, and from Charters Towers to Townsville on Tuesday and Saturday ($28, three hours).

In town, the travel agent **Travel Experience.com** (☎4787 2622; 13 Gill St) can book travel tickets.

NORTH OF TOWNSVILLE

As you leave Townsville, you also leave the Dry Tropics. The scorched-brown landscape slowly gives way to sugar-cane plantations lining the highway and tropical rainforest shrouding the hillsides.

Much of the tourist infrastructure between Townsville and Innisfail centres on the beaches and islands, while waterfalls, national parks and small villages hide up in the hinterland. This area was hardest hit by Cycle Yasi in February 2011 (and by Cyclone Larry in 2006), with damage to the coastline, islands, national parks and farmland.

Paluma Range National Park

Part of the Wet Tropics World Heritage Area, Paluma Range National Park and the teeny village of Paluma provide a secluded respite from the drone of the Bruce Hwy.

MT SPEC SECTION

It's not uncommon for the lofty rainforest in this part of the park to be veiled in mist or capped by cloud. Straddling the summit and escarpment of the Paluma Range, the Mt Spec Section stands over the Big Crystal Creek flood plain below. As you head up, the landscape changes from eucalypt stands to the closed canopy of the rainforest, containing a range of habitats to support diverse bird species.

There are two bitumen roads into this section of the park, both leading off a bypassed section of the Bruce Hwy: either 61km north of Townsville or 40km south of Ingham.

Take the northern access route and follow the partly sealed road 4km to **Big Crystal Creek** where goannas scamper away from your approaching footsteps as you walk the few hundred metres from the picnic area to the popular Paradise Waterhole. Its **DERM campground** (☎13 74 68; www.derm.qld.gov.au; per person $5.15) is well equipped with toilets, gas barbecues and drinking water, but it's popular so book ahead.

The southern access route, the sealed Mt Spec Rd, was built by relief labour during the 1930s Depression. It's a dramatic, narrow road (with lose-your-lunch twists) that weaves its way up the mountains to the village of Paluma. After 7km you come to **Little Crystal Creek**, where a pretty stone bridge (built in 1932) arches across the creek. This is a great swimming spot, with waterfalls and a couple of deep rock pools, and there's a small picnic area opposite the car park. From here it's another steep 11km up to Paluma village.

TOP CHOICE **Frosty Mango** (☎4770 8184; www.frostymango.com.au; Bruce Hwy; dishes $6-15; ⏲8am-6pm; ✎) is a roadside restaurant on the Bruce Hwy, 70km north of Townsville at Mutarnee. It's easy to drive past, but it's definitely worth breaking your journey for everything and anything to do with mangoes: fresh-squeezed mango juice, mango muffins with mango jam and cream, mango trifle, and scrumptious mango ice cream, as well as inexpensive fresh-picked fruit. Hot dishes include jackfruit curry.

PALUMA VILLAGE & AROUND

POP 25

Chimneys billow smoke in winter at the cosy little mountain-top village of Paluma – a reminder that it can get chilly here in July and August. The town was founded in 1875 when tin was discovered in the area, but these days there's little activity to disturb the cool, clear mountain air.

A number of walks lead through the rainforest surrounding the village. If not cushioned in cloud, **McClelland's Lookout** (300m return, 15 minutes), 100m before Paluma village, provides humbling views out to Halifax Bay and the Palm Islands. (This was also the site of a US Army radar station during WWII.) About 200m from here a trail leads to **Witts Lookouts** (3km return, two hours) and the steep **Cloudy Creek Falls** (4km return, 2½ hours). Otherwise take the **H Track** (1.1km return, one hour) circuit walk, which leads from the rear of Lennox Cres along a former logging road containing evidence of the tin-mining industry.

Stop by for a chat with local potter Len Cook at his gallery/workshop, **Paluma Pottery** (www.lencookpottery.com; 29 Lennox Cres; ⏲9am-5pm).

Paluma Rainforest Inn (☎4770 8688; www.rainforestinnpaluma.com; 1 Mt Spec Rd; d $125; ❄) has large rooms with comfy, stylish beds in rainforest brown and green tones. The gardens contain more than 50 rhododendrons; some are normally in bloom throughout the year. Kangaroo burgers and roast pumpkin wraps are among the choices at its licensed **restaurant** (mains $19-29; ⏲lunch Wed-Mon, breakfast & dinner by reservation; ✎), which is the pick of the village's limited dining options for guests and nonguests.

About 10km beyond Paluma is **Lake Paluma**, a drinking-water storage dam, with a dedicated foreshore area for swimming and picnicking.

Hidden Valley Cabins (☎4770 8088; www.hiddenvalleycabins.com.au; homestead s/d $69/79, cabins $139/149; ≋), a solar-powered, carbon-neutral eco-retreat, has small, cosy homestead rooms with shared bathrooms and a clutch of en suite log cabins grouped close together. A range of **tours** (2hr from $20), including platypus-spotting safaris and night walks, run daily; two-night tours are available from Townsville (from $449 including accommodation and meals). Its bar and **restaurant** (mains $24-31; ⏲breakfast, lunch & dinner; ✎), serving country-style home cooking, are open to guests only. Bringing your own alcohol is not allowed. Hidden Valley is 24km west of Paluma Village; the last 4km stretch is along a bumpy unsealed road.

There's no fuel in Paluma, so fill up before heading out this way.

JOURAMA FALLS SECTION

Jourama Falls and a series of cascades and rapids tumble along Waterview Creek, which is enclosed by palms and umbrella trees. It's a small area that's well developed, with a few lookouts, picnic areas and a **DERM campground** (☎13 74 68; www.derm.qld.gov.au; per person $5.15) with water (treat before drinking), toilets and cold showers.

This part of the park is reached via a 6km dirt road, 91km north of Townsville and 24km south of Ingham; access may be restricted during the wet season.

Ingham & Around

POP 6127

Laid-back Ingham is the proud guardian of the 120-hectare **Tyto wetlands** (Tyto Wetlands Information Centre; ☎4776 4792; www.hinchinbrooknq.com.au; cnr Cooper St & Bruce Hwy; ⏲8.45am-5pm Mon-Fri, 9am-4pm Sat & Sun), which has 4km of walking trails and attracts around 230 species of birds, including far-flung guests from Siberia and Japan, as well as hundreds of wallabies at dawn and dusk. From the information centre, a wheelchair-accessible boardwalk leads across the lagoon to the stylish cafe-restaurant **Pepper for Passion @ Tyto** (☎4776 6212; 24-30 Macrossan Ave; mains $17-25; ⏲10am-4pm Mon-Thu, 10am-9pm Fri & Sat, 8am-4pm Sun; ✎). Sit out on the deck watching the birdlife and tuck into chef Craig Lyons' creations like creamy

PUB WITHOUT BEER

One of Ingham's most famous sons was Dan Sheahan (1882–1977): canecutter, horseman and poet. Dan's poems carried on the Australian literary tradition, started by AB 'Banjo' Paterson and Henry Lawson, of investigating Australian bush identity through verse. Sheahan's focus, however, was on examining the Australian identity during WWII. Though Sheahan enjoyed mild success from his poetry, one of his poems was to become wildly popular as a song. Sheahan penned 'Pub Without Beer' (over a glass of wine) at Ingham's Day Dawn Hotel, after arriving to find that US troops had just been through his local and drained it dry of beer. (The Day Dawn was demolished in 1960; Lees Hotel now stands in its place.) The weekly *North Queensland Register* published the poem in 1944.

It wasn't until 1956 that Gordon Parsons used Sheahan's poem as inspiration to compose the song 'Pub with No Beer' (over whisky) at a pub in Taylors Arm, New South Wales. The song was then immortalised by the late Australian country-music icon Slim Dusty, who went on to record 'Duncan' ('love to have a beer with...') in 1980, and whose album *Beer Drinking Songs* (1986) went gold within three weeks of its release. Yes, Aussies love their beer....

banana curry king prawns. A state-of-the-art gallery and library should be open next door by the time you're reading this.

Ingham is the jumping-off point for a trip out to magnificent **Wallaman Falls**, the longest single-drop waterfall in Australia at 305m. Located in **Girringun National Park**, 51km southwest of the town (sealed road except for 10km; not suitable for caravans), the falls look their best in the Wet, though are spectacular at any time of year. Nearby, the **DERM campground** (☎13 74 68; www.derm.qld.gov.au; per person $5.15) has showers and barbecues; the swimming hole is visited by the occasional platypus. Two- and three-day walking trails start from the falls, with campsites along the way – pick up a *Wallaman Falls Section Girringun National Park* leaflet from the Tyto Wetlands Information Centre.

Mungalla Station (☎4777 8718; www.mungallaaboriginaltours.com.au; Forrest Beach, Allingham; 2hr tours adult/child $40/10), 15km east of Ingham, runs insightful Aboriginal-led tours including boomerang throwing and stories from the local Nywaigi culture. Definitely book in for a traditional **Kup Murri** (incl tour $80/20) lunch of meat and veggies wrapped in banana leaves and cooked underground in an earth 'oven'. If you have a self-contained caravan or campervan, you can **camp** (per van $10) overnight.

In mid-May the **Australian Italian Festival** (www.australianitalianfestival.com.au) celebrates the fact that 60% of Ingham residents are of Italian descent, with pasta flying, wine flowing and music playing over three days.

TOP CHOICE **Noorla Heritage Resort** (☎4776 1100; www.hotelnoorla.com.au; 5-9 Warren St; sites $15-22, dm $28, d $89, d with bathroom $139;), once the domain of Italian canecutters, is now a wonderful 1920s art deco guesthouse with magnificently restored high-ceilinged rooms, plus cheaper container-style rooms in the garden. A photomontage of local stories lines the walls, bringing the town's history to life, as do the stories told around its aqua-tiled guest-only bar.

A main-street icon with a statue of a mounted horseman on the roof, good old Aussie pub **Lees Hotel** (☎4776 1577; www.leeshotel.com.au; 58 Lannercost St; s/d $55/65; mains $10-28; ⏲lunch & dinner Mon-Sat;) occupies the site of the Day Dawn Hotel, of 'Pub Without Beer' fame. Don't be put off by the dingy corridors: the en suite rooms, while not flash, are perfectly acceptable. Decent meals and, fear not, beer, are served in the bar and bistro out back.

For a gourmet picnic, head to **Lou's Food Emporium** (73 Lannercost St), where marinated olives, hams, pepperoni, biscuits and other imported Italian goodies cram the shelves.

Greyhound Australia (☎1300 473 946; www.greyhound.com.au) has services to Townsville ($39) and Cairns ($63). **Premier** (☎13 34 10; www.premierms.com.au) buses on their Cairns–Brisbane runs stop in the centre of town on Townsville Rd, near the corner of Lannercost St ($26 to Townsville; $34 to Cairns).

Ingham is on the **Queensland Rail** (☎1300 131 722; www.traveltrain.com.au) Brisbane–Cairns train line.

Lucinda

POP 450

The big reason camera-wielding tourists head to little Lucinda, 27km northeast of Ingham, is to snap a photo of its 5.76km-long jetty. The roofed structure, with a continuous conveyor belt running its length, is the world's longest bulk sugar-loading jetty, allowing enormous carrier ships to dock. Public access is off-limits, but it's an impressive sight nonetheless.

Offshore, Hinchinbrook Island is seemingly within touching distance. You can take a four-hour cruise along the Deluge Inlet or a 2½-hour tour along the channel with **Hinchinbrook Wilderness Safaris** (☎4777 8307; www.hinchinbrookwildernesssafaris.com.au; inlet/channel cruise $80/60), which also offers transfers to Hinchinbrook for hikers to/from the southern end of the Thorsborne Trail.

Fishing is a popular pastime at Lucinda. Pick up bait, tackle and more at the **Lucinda Jetty Store & Take-Away** (☎4777 8280; 2 Rigby St; mains $16-20; ⏲6am-7pm), which serves great barramundi, crumbed steak and king salmon as well as takeaway fare like burgers and filled rolls. Friendly staff have an encyclopaedic knowledge of the jetty's operations and the sweetest fishing spots.

The well-equipped caravan park **Wanderer's Holiday Village** (☎4777 8213; www.wanderers-lucinda.com.au; Bruce Pde; unpowered/powered sites $26/30, cabins $87-102; ❄📶🏊) is a relaxed place, but then, so is Lucinda.

Opening to a wide verandah, Lucinda's local pub, the **Lucinda Point Hotel-Motel** (☎4777 8103; www.lucindahotel.com.au; cnr Halifax & Dungeness Rds; d without/with bathroom $85/110; ❄🏊) has comfortable en suite motel rooms and dongas sleeping up to three with shared bathrooms. Its **restaurant** (mains $20-35; ⏲lunch & dinner) is especially popular for its Saturday night buffet ($28.50) and Sunday afternoon barbecue ($18.50), when even nonovernight guests can use the swimming pool.

Around 1.5km up the road from Lucinda in Dungeness, **Hinchinbrook Marine Cove** (☎4777 8377; www.hinchinbrookmarinecove.com.au; d $125, cabin $150-195; ❄🏊), overlooking a busy little fishing port, has airy, contemporary rooms and cabins, as well as a **cafe** (dishes $5-15; ⏲7am-6pm Mon-Fri, 6am-6pm Sat & Sun) and **restaurant** (mains $22-30; ⏲dinner Wed-Sat). It also rents out **houseboats** (from $415) to cruise the waters at your own pace (no boat licence required). Rates include two days and one night, with good deals for longer rentals.

Orpheus Island

The traditional land of the Manbarra Aboriginal people, secluded Orpheus Island lies about 25km off the coast near Ingham. Only 11km long and about 1km wide, Orpheus is the second largest of the Palm Islands Group. There are 10 other islands in the group; apart from Orpheus and nearby council-run Pelorus, all of the islands are Aboriginal communities with restricted access.

Orpheus is mostly national park, protecting macaranga trees, with their huge heart-shaped leaves, and eucalypts standing on a foundation of volcanic rocks. However, it's the magnificent fringing reef that is the main attraction here.

Large coral bommies can be found in Little Pioneer Bay, Cattle Bay and around the Yank's Jetty area. Snorkelling is best around the island's northeast tip. The beaches at Mangrove Bay, Yank's Bay and Pioneer Bay are simply beautiful, but shallow at low tide.

During the early 19th century, goats were released on the island as part of a madcap scheme to provide food for possible shipwreck survivors. The goats thrived to the extent that at one stage they numbered more than 4000. A national parks 'control program' significantly reduced numbers.

Established in the 1940s, the luxurious **Orpheus Island Resort** (☎4777 7377; www.orpheus.com.au; d $1600-2000; ❄@🏊) trades on its isolation from the outside world: no interlopers, no kids under 15, and no phones or TVs in the 21 rooms, but private patios and spas. Meals (including seven-course dinners), snacks, snorkelling and tennis are included in the price. The resort also runs diving trips, sunset cruises, guided walks and courses, including chef-run canapé-making classes, for guests.

The resort has a seaplane that handles transfers from Townsville (per person $450 return, 30 minutes).

Charter boat access from Lucinda is the only way to reach the island's three **bush camping sites** at Yank's Jetty, South Beach and Pioneer Bay. Yank's Jetty and Pioneer Bay have toilets, and all have picnic tables, but you'll need to be self-sufficient: bring drinking water and a fuel stove. Obtain permits from **DERM** (☎13 74 68; www.derm.qld.gov.au; per person $6).

Cardwell & Around

POP 1250

Most of the Bruce Highway runs several kilometres inland from the coast, so it comes as something of a shock to see the sea lapping right next to the road as you come into the small town of Cardwell. Poor Cardwell took a beating from Cyclone Yasi, with many of the town's older homes smashed and the new marina switched to spin cycle.

The area offers superb fishing and access to Hinchinbrook Island offshore, as well as walking and swimming opportunities in nearby Girringun National Park.

Sights & Activities

Girringun National Park NATIONAL PARK

From the town centre, the **Cardwell Forest Drive** is a scenic 26km round trip through the national park, with lookouts, walking tracks and picnic areas signposted along the way. There are super swimming opportunities at **Attie Creek Falls**, as well as the aptly named Spa Pool, where you can sit in a hollow in the rocks as water gushes over you.

Murray Falls tumbles into fine rock pools suitable for swimming; take care as the rocks are slippery. There's a wheelchair-accessible viewing platform and a rainforest walk (1.8km return, one hour), as well as a barbecue and camping area. The falls are 22km west of the highway, signposted about 27km north of Cardwell.

Just west of the Bruce Hwy, about 7km south of Cardwell, the **Five Mile Swimming Hole** is another good swimming spot with picnic facilities. The final 700m is along a dirt track suitable for 2WDs; camping is not permitted.

The challenging **Dalrymple Gap Walking Track** (10.2km one way, six hours) was originally an Aboriginal foot track which was made into a stock route and road by George Dalrymple in the 1860s. It passes an old stone bridge registered by the National Trust. Watch out for stinging trees! (They're not dangerous but they 'inject' tiny silicon needles into your skin and are very painful. If you get stung the best way to remove them is to use masking tape to pull them out.) The turn-off to the track is signposted off the highway 15km south of Cardwell.

On the eastern side of the Bruce Hwy, 4km north of Cardwell, Clift Rd leads to the **Edmund Kennedy section** of the national park. Two walking trails run through this section of the park: the mangrove boardwalk (3.5km, two hours return), and the Wreck Creek walk (2.5km one way, 90 minutes) trail, both to the beach just south of the creek mouth. At low tide only, you can return to the picnic area via the beach. Bring *plenty* of insect repellent.

In town, the following are worth a visit:

FREE **Historic Cardwell Post Office & Telegraph Station** MUSEUM

(53 Victoria St; ⏰10am-1pm Mon-Fri, 9am-noon Sat) Check out the original postal room and old telephone exchange at this 1870-built wooden building, which has survived cyclones and termites.

Girringun Aboriginal Corporation Arts ART GALLERY

(www.girringun.com.au; 235 Victoria St; ⏰8.30am-5pm Mon-Thu, 8.30am-2pm Fri) Traditional woven baskets are among the works for sale at this corporation of Aboriginal artists.

Cardwell Gallery ART GALLERY

(www.hinchinbrookregionalarts.org.au; 2 Balliol St; ⏰10am-3pm Tue, Wed, Fri & Sun, 9am-3pm Thu & Sat) Glass, pottery, timber, jewellery, oils, acrylics, pastels and watercolours are among the media represented at this local artists' co-op in Cardwell's historic School of the Arts building.

Sleeping & Eating

Mudbrick Manor B&B $$

(☎4066 2299; www.mudbrickmanor.com.au; Lot 13 Stony Creek Rd; s/d $90/120; ❄🏊) Hand-built from mud bricks, natural timber and stone, this family home has huge, beautifully appointed rooms grouped around a fountained courtyard. Spend long, lazy evenings on the verandah or in the large lounge area. Rates include hot breakfast; book at least a few hours ahead for delicious three-course **dinners** (per person $30).

Beachcomber CARAVAN PARK $

(☎4066 8550; www.cardwellbeachcomber.com.au; 43a Marine Pde; sites $25-30, motel d $75-100, cabins & studios $90-110; ❄@📶🏊) There's a happy holiday vibe at this large park, which offers a range of accommodation options from camping through to snazzy new studios with timber decks and bright, tropical decor. Its licensed **restaurant** (mains $25-37; ⏰breakfast daily, lunch & dinner Mon-Sat) is the best in town, serving the likes of rosemary-crusted lamb, slow-roasted pork, and sweet and sour flathead, as well as pizzas.

Port Hinchinbrook Resort RESORT **$$**
(☎4066 2000; www.porthinchinbrook.com.au; Bruce Hwy; d $130-225; ❄🏊) The resort and marina here were badly damaged by Cyclone Yasi – an aerial photo of the marina boats tossed around like toys was one of the enduring images from the disaster. It's likely that the luxury cabins – and probably the Marina Restaurant – will be refurbished and open mid-to-late 2011.

Kookaburra Holiday Park CARAVAN PARK **$**
(☎4066 8648; www.kookaburraholidaypark.com.au; 175 Bruce Hwy; sites $22-29, dm/s/d $25/45/50, cabins $65, units with bathroom $85-105; ❄@🏊) Over 1.2 green, tree-shaded hectares, accommodation options at this well-run park include airy dorms in a large Queenslander house at the back. You can borrow a fishing rod, prawn nets and crab pots to catch dinner, and tents to head off for some bush camping.

Cardwell Central Backpackers HOSTEL **$**
(☎4066 8404; www.cardwellbackpackers.com.au; 6 Brasenose St; dm $20; @📶🏊) Friendly hostel with partitioned dorms in high-ceilinged former squash courts. Caters mostly to banana and prawn workers (management helps find work), but accepts overnighters. Free internet and pool table.

Vívia Café CAFE **$**
(135 Victoria St; mains $9-20; ⏰7am-4pm; 🍷) Smart, contemporary surrounds for dining on gourmet fare and fresh seafood dishes.

ℹ Information

The **DERM Rainforest & Reef Centre** (☎4066 8601; www.derm.qld.gov.au; ⏰8.30am-5pm Mon-Fri, 9am-3pm Sat & Sun Apr-Oct, to 1pm Sat & Sun Nov-Mar; @), next to Cardwell's town jetty, has an interactive rainforest display and detailed info on Hinchinbrook Island and other nearby national parks.

ℹ Getting There & Away

Greyhound Australia (☎1300 473 946; www.greyhound.com.au) has buses to Cairns ($47) and Townsville ($49). **Premier** (☎13 34 10; www.premierms.com.au) buses on the Brisbane–Cairns route stop at Cardwell ($30 to Cairns; $26 to Townsville).

Cardwell is on the Brisbane–Cairns train line; contact **Queensland Rail** (☎1300 131 722; www.traveltrain.qr.com.au) for details.

Boats depart for Hinchinbrook Island from Port Hinchinbrook Marina, 2km south of town.

Hinchinbrook Island

Its resort might have closed its doors, but Australia's largest island national park remains a holy grail for walkers. Granite mountains rise dramatically from the sea; rugged Mt Bowen (1121m) is the island's highest peak. The mainland side is dense with lush tropical vegetation, while long sandy beaches and tangles of mangrove curve around the eastern shore. All 399 sq km of the island is national park, ensuring plenty of wildlife such as the aptly named pretty-faced wallaby and the iridescent-blue Ulysses butterfly.

Hinchinbrook's rainforest sustained a considerable amount of damage during Cyclone Yasi. The island was closed at the time of writing but should be reopened by the time you read this.

Hinchinbrook's highlight is the **Thorsborne Trail** (also known as the East Coast Trail), a 32km coastal track from Ramsay Bay past Zoe Bay, with its beautiful waterfall, to George Point at the southern tip. **DERM campsites** (☎13 74 68; www.derm.qld.gov.au; per person $5.15) are interspersed along the route. It's recommended that you take three nights to complete the trail, allowing for swimming stops and quiet time. Return walks of individual sections are also possible. This is the real wilderness experience; you'll need to use plenty of insect repellent, protect your food from ravenous rats, draw water from creeks as you go (water is reliably available at Nina, Little Ramsay and Zoe Bays), and be alert to the possible presence of crocs around the mangroves.

The trail is ungraded and at times rough, including challenging creek crossings; you should carry a map, drinking water and a fuel stove. Beach fishing is permitted from Zoe Bay south only.

A maximum of 40 walkers are allowed to traverse the trail at any one time. DERM recommends booking a year ahead for a place during the high season and six months ahead for other dates. Cardwell's Rainforest & Reef Centre stocks the imperative *Thorsborne Trail* brochure and screens the 15-minute *Without a Trace* video, which walkers are required to view. Cancellations for places on the trail are not unheard of, so it's worth asking if you've arrived without a booking.

Hinchinbrook Island Ferries (☎4066 8585; www.hinchinbrookferries.com.au) runs a service from Cardwell's Port Hinchinbrook Marina to Hinchinbrook's Ramsay Bay boardwalk (one way $85, 90 minutes). It also operates a five-hour **day tour** (adult/child $99/50; ⏲daily Easter-Sep, Wed, Fri & Sun Oct-Easter) including a cruise between Goold and Garden Islands spotting dolphins, dugongs and turtles, and docking at Ramsay Bay boardwalk for a walk on the 9km-long beach and a picnic lunch.

Thorsborne Trail walkers can pick up a one-way transfer back to the mainland with **Hinchinbrook Wilderness Safaris** (☎4777 8307; www.hinchinbrookwildernesssafaris.com.au; one way $50) from George Point at the southern end of the trail.

Goold & Garden Islands

These uninhabited islands provide the perfect castaway setting. Both are national parks and off the tourist radar, so you could have them to yourself. Goold Island, just 17km northeast of Cardwell, supports open forest, mangroves and a sandy beach on both the west and south sides. There's a **DERM campground** (☎13 74 68; www.derm.qld.gov.au; per person $5.15) on the island's west, with toilets, picnic tables and a gas barbecue. Bring drinking water.

Just south of Goold Island is tiny Garden Island, with a recreation reserve controlled by the local council. Permits to camp are required and are available from the **Cardwell Newsagency** (☎4066 8622; 83 Victoria St; per person $6). The island has a good sandy beach but no fresh water; children aged under six aren't permitted.

Hinchinbrook Island Ferries (☎4066 8270; www.hinchinbrookferries.com.au) can ferry campers on request; it's $150 for a return to Goold or Garden Island transfer.

Tully

POP 2460

Surrounded by banana plantations – most of which were flattened by Cyclone Yasi – the sugar-mill town of Tully, 44km north of Cardwell, takes pride in its reputation as the wettest place in Australia. Its big 7.9m **golden gumboot** at the entrance to town boasts that Tully received 7.9m of rain in 1950. Climb the spiral staircase to the viewing platform to get a sense of just how much that is! All that rain ensures plenty of raftable rapids on the nearby Tully River. The town's family-friendly **Golden Gumboot Festival** (www.tullygumbootfestival.com), with parade floats and games, takes place in May.

The **Tully Visitor & Heritage Centre** (☎4068 2288; Bruce Hwy; ⏲8.30am-4.45pm Mon-Fri, 9am-3pm Sat & Sun) has a brochure outlining a self-guided **heritage walk** around town, with 17 interpretative panels including one dedicated to Tully's UFO sightings.

Book at the visitor centre for 90-minute **Tully Sugar Mill Tours** (adult/child $12/8; ⏲daily late Jun-early Nov) during the crushing season, when the mill processes around two million tonnes of cane and generates its own power by burning fibre residue. Wear closed shoes and a shirt with sleeves. Tour times depend on the weather and crushing conditions.

The visitor centre stocks walking maps for trails along former logging tracks in the Tully-accessed section of the **Misty Mountains** (www.mistymountains.com.au); 640m-high **Mt Tyson**; and **Tully Gorge National Park**, 40km west of town (the road dead-ends, so you can't drive to Ravenshoe from here). Tully Gorge has picnic facilities, but crocs inhabit the area. If you want a swim, head to the croc-free (and alligator-free) **Alligator's Nest**, 7km north of town via Murray St.

Practically all accommodation in Tully is geared for banana workers, with cheap weekly rates and help finding farm work. The visitor centre has a list, or try the excellent **Banana Barracks** (☎4068 0455; www.bananabarracks.com; 50 Butler St; dm without/with bathroom $24/26, bungalows $60; @) bang in the town centre, with lots of corrugated iron, pool tables, and decent dorms and bungalows out back. It's also the hub of Tully's nightlife, with an onsite **nightclub** (⏲Thu-Sat) where DJs hit the decks on Friday and Saturday nights.

For non-workers, the only real option is the corporate-oriented **Tully Motel** (☎4068 2233; www.tullymotel.com; Bruce Hwy; d $89-110;), with large, well-appointed rooms done out in heritage colours, and Tully's only restaurant, **Plantations** (mains $27-38; ⏲dinner Mon-Fri).

The **Mt Tyson Hotel** (23 Butler St; mains $9-17; ⏲lunch & dinner Mon-Sat) and **Hotel Tully** (5 Butler St; mains $18-26; ⏲lunch & dinner Mon-Sat), aka the 'top pub', both serve hearty meals, while **Joe's Pizza Parlour** (☎4068 1996; 46

Butler St; pizzas $12-21; ⏱dinner, days can vary) has steaming, thick-crust old-school pizzas. Sweetshop **Lola** (23 Butler St) whips up icy-cold smoothies, slushies, flurries and thick-shakes.

Greyhound Australia (☎1300 473 946; www.greyhound.com.au) buses stop at Cairns ($22) and Townsville ($54) and **Premier** (☎13 34 10; www.premierms.com.au) buses on the Brisbane–Cairns route stop in town; it's $26 to Cairns, $30 to Townsville. Tully is on the Brisbane–Cairns train line; contact **Queensland Rail** (☎1300 131 722; www.traveltrain.qr.com.au) for details.

See also p298.

DON'T MISS

TULLY RIVER RAFTING

The Tully River provides thrilling white water year-round thanks to all that rain and the river's hydroelectric floodgates. Rafting trips are timed to coincide with the daily release of the floodgates, resulting in Grade 4 rapids, with stunning rainforest scenery as a backdrop.

Day trips with **Raging Thunder Adventures** (☎4030 7990; www.ragingthunder.com.au/rafting.asp; standard trip $185, 'xtreme' trip $215) or **R'n'R White Water Rafting** (☎4041 9444; www.raft.com.au; $185) include a barbecue lunch and transport from Tully or nearby Mission Beach. It only costs an extra $10 for transfers from Cairns and as far north as Palm Cove, but you'll save yourself several tedious hours return by bus if you pick up a trip here.

Mission Beach

POP 2590

Less than 30km east of the Bruce Hwy's rolling sugar-cane and banana plantations, the hamlets that make up greater Mission Beach are hidden amongst World Heritage rainforest. The rainforest extends right to the Coral Sea, giving this 14km-long palm-fringed stretch of secluded inlets and wide, empty beaches the castaway feel of a tropical island.

Sadly, Mission Beach was one of the worst-affected areas following Cyclone Yasi, with much of the rainforest and vegetation stripped bare – though the experience of Cyclone Larry in 2006 shows it can recover quickly. The communities here certainly recovered quickly – within two weeks water and power were restored and most businesses and tourist operators were running normally.

Although collectively referred to as Mission Beach or just 'Mission', the area comprises a sequence of individual villages strung along the coast. **Bingil Bay** (sometimes called North Mission) lies 4.8km north of Mission Beach proper. **Wongaling Beach** is 5km south; from here it's a further 5.5 km south to **South Mission Beach**. Mission Beach and her sister villages are like four siblings who are close in character and style, but who live separate lives and are not jealous of each other in the slightest. Each has its own distinct personality, but you can tell they're all from the same pod. Most amenities are in Mission Beach proper and Wongaling Beach; South Mission Beach and Bingil Bay are mainly residential

One of the closest access points to the Great Barrier Reef, and the gateway to Dunk Island, Mission Beach has many walking tracks, and Australia's highest density of cassowaries (see the boxed text, p294) roaming the rainforest.

History

Peaceful Mission Beach has a tumultuous history. The area's Indigenous Djiru people lived in *mijas* or *gunyahs* (semipermanent shelters), but were removed to the 1914-established Queensland Government mission from which the town takes its name. By 1916, around 490 Aboriginal people lived at the settlement; 200 died of malaria in 1917. The following year the mission was razed by one of the state's worst cyclones. Every building was ruined by the 150km/h winds, giant waves and flooding, and it's estimated that at least 40 people lost their lives. Survivors were rounded up and removed to Palm Island. A small, hard-to-find memorial marks the Old Mission Site on Mission Drive in South Mission.

Explorer Edmund Kennedy commenced his doomed 1848 expedition to Cape York from South Mission Beach. Assisted by an Indigenous man named Jackey Jackey, Edmund Kennedy led 13 men, 28 horses and a flock of sheep north from Tam O'Shanter Point. Only Jackey Jackey made it to the ship waiting at Cape York, and he guided officials to locate the other members of the expedition. Kennedy had been speared, most of

Mission Beach

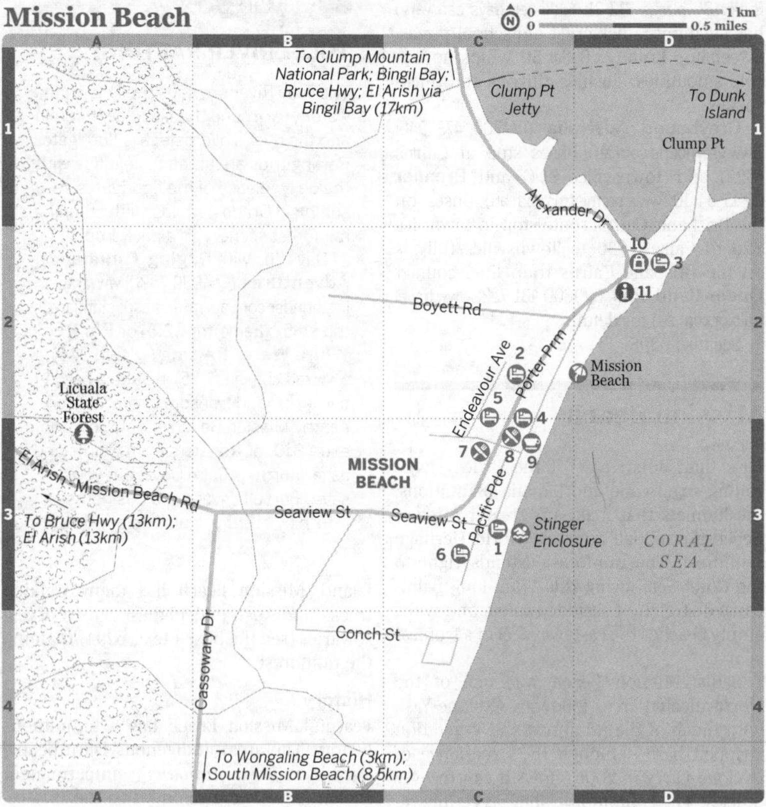

the men had starved to death and the others were never found. There's a memorial to the expedition at Tam O'Shanter Point.

Sights & Activities

Adrenaline junkies flock to Mission Beach for extreme and water-based sports, including white-water rafting on the nearby Tully River. And, if you've got your own board, Bingil Bay is one of the rare spots inside the reef where it's possible to surf, with small but consistent swells of around 1m.

Mission Beach is one of the most popular spots in Queensland for skydiving. Both **Jump the Beach** (☎1800 444 568; www.jumpthebeach.com.au) and **Skydive Mission Beach** (☎1800 800 840; www.skydivemissionbeach.com) offer tandem dives from 9000ft ($249), 11,000ft ($310) and 14,000ft ($334). There's soft sand to cushion your landing but a 100kg weight limit.

Rainforest walks are your best chance to spot a cassowary, especially early morning. The visitor centre has walking guide information about trails in the area. From David St in central Mission Beach, the **Ulysses Link** – named for the bright-blue Ulysses butterflies that flit through the area – is a gentle 2km stroll (around one hour return) along the foreshore to Clump Point. Sweeping views unfold from the **Bicton Hill Track** (4km, two hours return) through Clump Mountain National Park. The superb coastal **Kennedy Track** (7km, four hours return) leads past secluded Lovers Beach and a lookout at Lugger Bay. **Licuala State Forest** has a number of rainforest walks, including a 10-minute children's walk marked with cassowary footprints, and the **Rainforest Circuit & Fan Palm Boardwalk** (1.2km, 30 minutes return) with interpretive signage and a cassowary display.

Mission Beach

Activities, Courses & Tours

Mission Beach Adventure Centre.......................................(see 1)

Sleeping

1 Castaways Resort & Spa C3
2 Hideaway Holiday Village....................C2
3 Mission Beach Ecovillage D2
4 Mission Beach Retreat........................C2
5 Rainforest Motel C2
6 Sejala on the Beach............................C3

Eating

7 Cafe Gecko C3
Early Bird Cafe ....(see 7)
8 Friends C3
New Deli ....(see 9)
Oceania Bar & Grill ....(see 5)

Drinking

9 Coffee Tree C3

Shopping

10 Mission Beach Markets.......................D2

Information

11 Mission Beach Visitor Centre.............D2
Post Office ....(see 5)
Wet Tropics Environment Centre.......................................(see 11)

Stinger enclosures at Mission Beach and South Mission Beach provide safe year-round swimming.

Calypso Dive & Snorkel SNORKELLING, DIVING
(Map p296; ☎4068 8432; www.calypsodive.com; Wongaling Beach Rd, Wongaling Beach) Calypso runs reef dives (from $264 including gear), wreck dives of the *Lady Bowen* ($245), and three-day PADI open-water courses ($625). Alternatively, you can snorkel the reef ($169), or take a jet-ski tour around Dunk Island (from $224).

Spirit of the Rainforest CULTURAL TOURS
(☎4088 9161; www.echoadventure.com.au; 4hr tour adult/child $80/60; ⏲Tue, Thu & Sat) Local Aboriginal guides offer a unique insight into the ancient rainforest, creeks, waterholes and waterfalls around Mission Beach, including plant and animal life, and Dreaming stories. Prices include pick-ups from Mission Beach.

Coral Sea Kayaking KAYAKING
(☎4068 9154; www.coralseakayaking.com; half-/full-day tours $77/128) Paddle over to Dunk Island for the day or bob around the coastline for half a day. Trips depart from South Mission Beach; courtesy pick-ups are available. Experienced kayakers can also rent sea kayaks.

Dunk Jet Sports JET-SKIING
(☎4068 8432; www.dunkjetsports.com; full-day tour for 2 people $330) An action-packed day trip, Dunk Jet Sports' great-value two-person package includes a 90-minute jet-ski tour around Dunk Island departing from Mission Beach, an hour's paddle-ski hire, and two Dunk Island Resort day passes (see p298).

Mission Beach Adventure Centre WATER SPORTS
(Map p292; ☎0429 469 330; www.missionbeachadventurecentre.com.au; Seaview St, Mission Beach) This little hut by the beach runs the gamut of water and beach sports, including kayak hire (single/double $15/30 per hour), three-hour kayak tours ($60), stand-up board hire ($15 per hour), and, when the wind's up, blokarting ($30/50 per half-hour/hour). Its **cafe** (dishes $5-8.50) is famed for its hot dogs.

Fishin' Mission FISHING
(☎4088 6121; www.fishinmission.com.au; half-/full-day tours $130/190) Half-day island fishing trips and full-day reef fishing trips are ideal for anglers keen for local knowledge and guidance. Trips depart from Clump Point jetty, and include tackle, bait and lunch, as well as snorkelling gear; barramundi, mangrove jack and Spanish mackerel are common catches. Sole charters are available; alternatively, the visitor centre has a list of operators renting boats.

Mission Beach Tropical Fruit Safari FOOD TASTING
(☎4068 7099; www.missionbeachtourism.com; Mission Beach Visitor Centre, Porter Promenade; admission $4; ⏲1-2pm Mon & Tue) Tastings and presentations of tropical fruit from the surrounding region.

NQ Heli-Worx SCENIC FLIGHTS
(☎0407 771 009; www.nqheliworx.com.au) Hover over the reef, rainforest and tropical islands in a helicopter. Flights start from $173 for 15 minutes.

Festivals & Events

Mission Beach Film Festival FILM
(www.missionbeachfilmfestival.com.au) Outdoor screenings, guest speakers, Q&A panels and short-film comps over three days in mid-September.

THE CASSOWARY: ENDANGERED NATIVE

Looking like something out of *Jurassic Park*, a flightless prehistoric bird struts through the rainforest. It's as tall as a grown man, has three razor-sharp, dagger-style clawed toes, a bright-blue head, red wattles (the lobes hanging from its neck), a helmet-like horn and luxuriant shaggy black feathers similar to an emu's. Meet the cassowary, the shy native of these northern forests. The Australian cassowary, also known as the Southern cassowary, is only found in north Queensland; other species inhabit Papua New Guinea.

The cassowary is an important link in the rainforest ecosystem. It's the only animal capable of dispersing the seeds of more than 70 species of trees whose fruit is too large for other rainforest animals to digest and pass. Cassowaries swallow fruit whole and excrete the fruit's seed intact, which acts as fertilizer encouraging the seed's growth. It takes four years for a cassowary to reach maturity, which can then live for around 50 years. Traditional gender roles are reversed: the male incubates the egg and rears the chicks on his own. You're most likely to see cassowaries in the wild around Mission Beach, Etty Bay, and the Cape Tribulation section of the Daintree National Park. They can be aggressive, particularly if they have chicks. Do not approach them; if one threatens you, don't run – give the bird right-of-way and try to keep something solid between you and it, preferably a tree.

There are thought to be between 1500 and 2500 cassowaries in the wild in north Queensland, and up to 200 in the immediate cyclone-affected area. An endangered species, the cassowary's biggest threat is loss of habitat, and most recently the cause has been natural – Tropical Cyclone Yasi stripped much of the rainforest around Mission Beach bare, threatening the struggling population with starvation from the lack of forest fruits. The birds are also exposed to the elements and more vulnerable to dog attacks and being killed by cars as they venture out in search of food – following Cyclone Larry, more birds died crossing the road than from starvation. A conservation effort was launched soon after Cyclone Yasi hit in February 2011, with remote feeding stations established at some 80 locations around Mission Beach, Tully, Cardwell and Etty Bay, as well as aerial food drops. Local conservation groups and park rangers – supported by cassowary campaigner Bob Irwin (father of the late Steve Irwin) – continue to monitor the cassowary population, with remote-sensing cameras set up at a number of feed stations. Experience from Cyclone Larry suggests it will take the rainforest at least 12 months to sufficiently recover as a food resource.

Next to the Mission Beach visitor centre, there are cassowary conservation displays at the **Wet Tropics Environment Centre** (Map p292; ☎4068 7197; www.wettropics.gov.au; Porter Promenade, Mission Beach; ⏲10am-4pm, hr can vary), which is staffed by volunteers from the Community for **Cassowary & Coastal Conservation** (C4; www.cassowaryconservation.asn.au). Proceeds from gift-shop purchases go towards buying cassowary habitat. The website www.savethecassowary.org.au is also a good source of info.

Rainforest Rescue (www.rainforestrescue.org.au) is a conservation NGO working with government authorities in the campaign to save the cassowary.

Mission Evolve Music Fest MUSIC
(www.missionevolvemusicfest.com) Two days of live music in mid-October featuring local blues, roots, soul, funk and other genres from around Far North Queensland.

Sleeping

There's no shortage of accommodation in the Mission Beach area across all budgets. Mission and Wongaling Beaches are the most popular areas; South Mission and Bingil Bay are quieter. Hostels have courtesy-bus pick-ups. Holiday house and apartment rentals proliferate throughout the area – the visitor centre has a list of booking agents.

SOUTH MISSION BEACH

TOP CHOICE **Elandra** RESORT $$$
(☎4068 8154; www.elandraresorts.com; 1 Explorer Dr; d $270, ste $370-520; ❄@🛜≋) Mission's most upmarket resort isn't snooty in the slightest, with a breezy, beachy vibe. All 52 contemporary rooms and suites at this secluded piece of paradise front the ocean and most have balconies to take full advantage of the views. Interiors have limed

floors and sparing African and Asian decor (headdresses, carvings and raised soapstone basins), and the huge Dunk Island–facing pool area houses the Elandra's fabulous restaurant and cocktail bar. It's hidden away at the southern end of South Mission Beach.

Beachcomber Coconut Caravan Village CARAVAN PARK $
(Map p296; ☎1800 008 129, 4068 8129; www.beachcombercoconut.com; Kennedy Esplanade; sites $42-33, cabins & villas $100-175; ❄@📶≋) Cabins are packed tightly together and are showing their age. And it's pretty pricey (even en suite cabins incur a linen hire fee). But there are good playground facilities for kids, an onsite shop-cafe, and it's right on the beach.

WONGALING BEACH

Hibiscus Lodge B&B B&B $$
(Map p296; ☎4068 9096; www.hibiscuslodge.com.au; 5 Kurrajong Close; r $95-120; ❄≋) Wake to the sound of birds chirping and, more than likely, spot a cassowary or two during breakfast on the rainforest-facing deck of this lovely B&B. Each of its three rooms has its own en suite; you can play croquet on the pitch out front.

Scotty's Mission Beach House HOSTEL $
(Map p296; ☎1800 665 567, 4068 8676; www.scottysbeachhouse.com.au; 167 Reid Rd; dm $24-29, d $61, d with bathroom $71; ❄@📶≋) Clean, comfy rooms (including girls-only dorms with Barbie-pink sheets) are grouped around this sociable hostel's grassy pool area – a great spot for catching some rays. Out front, **Scotty's Bar & Grill** (mains $10-30; ⏰dinner), open to nonguests, has something happening virtually every night, from fire-twirling shows to pool comps and live music.

Licuala Lodge B&B $$
(Map p296; ☎4068 8194; www.licualalodge.com.au; 11 Mission Circle; s/d $99/130; 📶≋) Up in the rainforest just west of Tully Mission Beach Rd, a resident teddy bear guards each of the five rooms at this state-of-the-art B&B. Bonuses include a huge lounge, guest kitchen, barbecue and laundry, a fridge stashed with complimentary beer, soft drinks and fruit juices, and a gorgeous rock-sculpted 'jungle pool'.

Absolute Backpackers HOSTEL $
(Map p296; ☎4068 8317; www.absolutebackpackers.com.au; Wongaling Beach Rd; dm $22-26, d $56; ❄@📶≋) Past the pool area festooned with hammocks, refurbished rooms here are bright and airy, music is piped into the bathrooms, and the whole place is well managed and relaxed. There's a bank of lockers and a huge 24-hour kitchen; you can bring your own drinks onto the premises.

Shores APARTMENTS $$
(Map p296; ☎4068 9716; www.missionbeachshores.com; 137-139 Reid Rd; d from $159; ❄📶≋) Shores' open-plan Balinese-style bungalows are set in lush tropical gardens. Stretch out on your personal patio or lounge beside the big pool.

Wongalinga APARTMENTS $$$
(Map p296; ☎4068 8221; www.wongalinga.com.au; 64 Reid Rd; 1-/2-/3-bedroom apt $240/310/340; ❄≋) These beachfront apartments are so massive you may need to take a compass in case you get lost. Open the shutters and let the cool breezes waft through.

MISSION BEACH

Mission Beach Ecovillage CABINS $$
(Map p292; ☎4068 7534; www.ecovillage.com.au; Clump Point Rd; d $145-190; ❄📶≋) It's not eco-certified, but with its own banana and lime trees scattered around its tropical gardens and a direct path through the rainforest to the beach, this 'ecovillage' makes the most of its natural environment. The self-contained bungalows here are huge; the more expensive ones have spas, and the brilliant free-form pool is perfect for all ages. It's a short stroll along the beachfront to Mission's eateries, or you can cocoon at the onsite licensed **restaurant** (mains $19; ⏰dinner Tue-Sat).

Sejala on the Beach CABINS $$$
(Map p292; ☎4088 6699; www.missionbeachholidays.com.au/sejala; 26 Pacific Pde; d $239; ❄≋) Your first steps down into the bathrooms reveal shutter doors that open onto rainforest, allowing you to shower with nature. These three beach huts have loads of character, kitchenettes and your own private barbecue on the front deck; the pick are the two huts facing the beach. Kids aged over six welcome.

Castaways Resort & Spa RESORT $$
(Map p292; ☎1800 079 002, 4068 7444; www.castaways.com.au; Pacific Pde; d $145-185, 1-/2-bedroom unit $205/295; ❄@📶≋) The cheapest rooms at this beachfront resort don't have balconies, so it's worth splashing out a bit for one of the 'Coral Sea' rooms, which have an extended deck and day bed. Even the units are small, but perks include two elongated pools, luxurious treatments at its **spa**

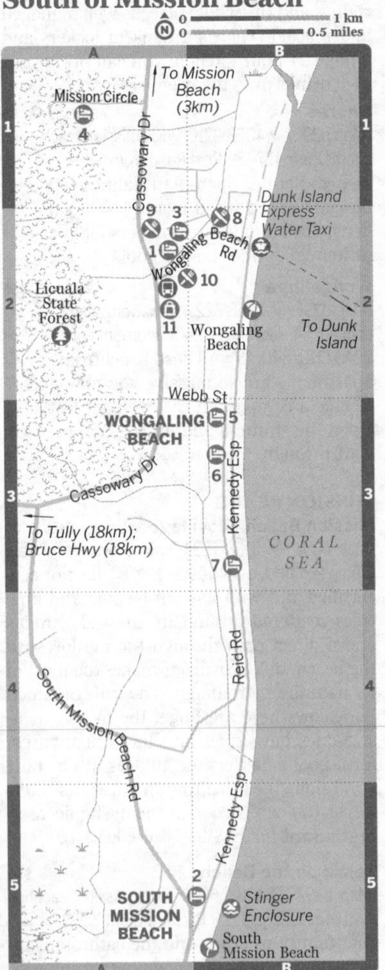

South of Mission Beach

Activities, Courses & Tours
Calypso Dive & Snorkel.................(see 1)

Sleeping
1 Absolute Backpackers........................A2
2 Beachcomber Coconut Caravan Village..............................B5
3 Hibiscus Lodge B&B..........................A2
4 Licuala Lodge..................................A1
5 Scotty's Mission Beach House..........B3
6 Shores..B3
7 Wongalinga....................................B3

Eating
8 Caffe Rustica..................................B2
Scotty's Bar & Grill.....................(see 5)
9 Spicy Thai Hut................................A2
10 Woolworths Supermarket................A2

Shopping
11 Mission Beach Rotary Market............A2

(www.driftspa.com.au), and regular entertainment including live bands during 'sangria Sunday' afternoons at its **bar-restaurant** (mains $12-32; ⊙breakfast, lunch & dinner).

Hideaway Holiday Village CARAVAN PARK **$$**
(Map p292; ☎1800 687 104, 4068 7104; www.missionbeachhideaway.com.au; 58-60 Porter Promenade; unpowered/powered sites $29/35, cabins without/with bathroom $85/105; ❄@🛜≋) Plenty of shade keeps things cool at this central holiday park, which backs onto the rainforest and overlooks the beach. Grassy sites and cabins are well-spaced and amenities are in tip-top condition.

Rainforest Motel MOTEL **$$**
(Map p292; ☎4068 7556; www.missionbeachrainforestmotel.com; 9 Endeavour Ave; s/d $89/109; ❄@🛜≋) If only all motels could be like this. Immaculate, tiled rooms come with coffee infusions and quality shampoos, and free bikes are available.

Mission Beach Retreat HOSTEL **$**
(Map p292; ☎4088 6229; www.missionbeachretreat.com.au; 49 Porter Promenade; dm $21-24, d $56; ❄@🛜≋) This intimate 35-bedroom beachfront hostel in the heart of Mission with an open-sided kitchen offers an escape from the party scene.

BINGIL BAY

Sanctuary CABINS **$**
(☎1800 777 012, 4088 6064; www.sanctuaryatmission.com; 72 Holt Rd; dm $35, s/d huts $65/70, s/d cabins $145/160; ⊙mid-Apr–mid-Dec; @🛜≋) Reached by a steep 600m-long rainforest walking track from the car park (4WD pick-up available), Sanctuary has a range of sleeping options. You can be surrounded only by flyscreen on a platform in simple huts, or opt for en suite cabins featuring glass-walled showers with floor-to-ceiling rainforest views. About 95% of the land is set aside for conservation; in addition to walks you can take yoga classes ($15), indulge in a massage ($80 per hour), cook in the self-catering kitchen or dine on wholesome fare at the **restaurant** (mains $19-33; ⊙breakfast,

lunch & dinner;). Eco-initiatives include its own sewerage system, use of rainwater (for drinking etc), and biodegradable detergents. Not suitable for kids under 11.

Treehouse HOSTEL $
(☎4068 7137; www.treehousehostel.com.au; Frizelle Rd; unpowered sites $12, dm/d $25/55;) Musical instruments and no TV set the chilled-out scene at this timber-pole-framed YHA-associated hostel high in the rainforest. Heavy wooden tables on the balcony are strewn with board games and books, or join like-minded travellers zenning out in shaded hammocks.

Eating & Drinking

The majority of bars and/or restaurants are clustered in Mission Beach proper along Porter Promenade and its adjoining spider's web of tiny walkways and arcades. There's a small supermarket here, and a huge new Woolworths supermarket at Wongaling Beach, which also has a handful of eateries, bars and bottleshops.

SOUTH MISSION BEACH

Elandra MODERN AUSTRALIAN $$$
(☎4068 8154; www.elandraresorts.com; 1 Explorer Dr; mains $28-42; breakfast, lunch & dinner;) Even if you can't afford a room at the Elandra resort, don't miss chef Kurt Goodban's stunning cuisine, such as wattle-seed-spiced kangaroo or coconut-dusted squid with pawpaw and mango. Goodban uses local and/or organic produce and makes his own jams and pastries. If that's still beyond your budget, at least stop by for a sunset Mission Rumble cocktail of Frangelico, banana liqueur, banana ice cream and honey.

WONGALING BEACH

Caffe Rustica ITALIAN $$
(Map p296; ☎4068 9111; www.caffe-rustica.com.au; 24 Wongaling Beach Rd; mains $18-22; lunch Sun, dinner Wed-Sun;) Book ahead if you want to dine in this contemporary corrugated-iron beach shack. There are nearly a dozen authentic Italian pastas and almost two dozen types of traditional crispy-crusted pizzas accompanied by Italian wines. Delicious desserts include homemade gelato.

Spicy Thai Hut THAI $$
(Map p296; ☎4068 8401; Shop 5, 2042 Tully Mission Beach Rd; mains $16-25; dinner Wed-Sun;) Mission Beach's best Thai is served up to eat in or take away from this hip new place. Soups, stir fries and salads are all made fresh; choose whether you want your curry mild, moderate or 'damn hot!'

MISSION BEACH

TOP CHOICE **New Deli** CAFE, DELI $
(Map p292; Shop 1, 47 Porter Promenade; mains $8-16; 9.30am-6pm Sun-Fri;) Tuck into blueberry pancakes or smoked salmon and brie bagels for breakfast, or zucchini and feta tart for lunch. You can even stock up on goodies for a gourmet picnic at this aromatic deli-cafe where most produce is organic and everything is homemade, including scrumptious biscuits.

Cafe Gecko CAFE $
(Map p292; cnr Porter Promenade & Campbell St; mains $7-14; 7am-4pm Mon-Fri, to 2pm Sat & Sun;) The pies here are awesome – chunks of real steak and nothing artificial. Sandwiches are made fresh right in front of you. Gecko serves cream teas ($12) and high teas ($19) – not very tropical but a sight for sore eyes for homesick Brits.

Oceania Bar & Grill MODERN AUSTRALIAN $
(Map p292; 52 Porter Promenade; mains $10-18; 1pm-midnight) Grab a draught beer at 'the Oshee', or browse through the lengthy wine list before ordering a meal, which will inevitably consist of steak or seafood. The chilled seafood plate goes well with a Sauv Blanc, or perhaps a T-bone and a Stella might hit the spot.

Early Bird Cafe CAFE $
(Map p292; Shop 2, 46 Porter Promenade; mains $6-15; 6am-3pm;) Early Bird's all-day tropical Aussie Brekkie of bacon and eggs, grilled tomato and local banana, toast, and tea or coffee goes down a treat after a morning swim.

Friends MODERN AUSTRALIAN $$
(Map p292; ☎4068 7107; Porter Promenade; mains $22-34; dinner Fri-Tue, annual closures vary seasonally) Fine dining (minus the dress code) in elegant surrounds, with a short, inventive, Mediterranean-accented menu. Vegetarians will struggle.

Coffee Tree CAFE $
(Map p292; Shop 3, 47 Porter Promenade, Mission Beach; dishes $3.50-6; 9.30am-5pm Tue-Sun) Strong espresso, handmade chocolates and a tantalising array of cakes.

BINGIL BAY

TOP CHOICE **Bingil Bay Cafe** CAFE $$
(29 Bingil Bay Rd; mains $14-22; breakfast, lunch & dinner;) A lavender-painted

landmark, this retro corner store has been transformed into a groovy licensed cafe with original aqua tiles, and burgundy leather seats salvaged from vintage train carriages. The menu spans felafel wraps to fish and chips, German sausages with sauerkraut to seafood linguine. Groceries and ice creams to take to the beach are also available.

Shopping

Local arts, crafts, jewellery, tropical fruit, homemade gourmet goods and more overflow from stalls at the **Mission Beach Markets** (Map p292), held opposite Hideaway Holiday Village caravan park on the first and third Sunday of the month. An even bigger range of goods, including handmade log furniture, is for sale at the **Mission Beach Rotary Market** (Map p296; Marcs Park, Cassowary Dr, Wongaling Beach) on the last Sunday of the month from April to November.

Information

The efficient **Mission Beach Visitor Centre** (Map p292; ☎4068 7099; www.missionbeachtourism.com; Porters Promenade; ⏰9am-4.45pm Mon-Sat, 10am-4pm Sun; @) has reams of info in multiple languages.

Internet cafes with tour-booking desks include **Intermission@the Beach** (David St, Mission Beach; per 20min/hr $2/5; ⏰8.30am-6pm Mon-Sat) and **Mission Beach Information Station** (www.missionbeachinfo.com, 4 Wongaling Shopping Ctr, Cassowary Dr, Wongaling Beach; per 20min/hr $2/5; ⏰9am-7pm).

Getting There & Around

Greyhound Australia (☎1300 473 946; www.greyhound.com.au) has trips to Cairns ($21) and Townsville ($40) and **Premier** (☎13 34 10; www.premierms.com.au) buses also service Cairns ($19) and Townsville ($46); pick-up is from the stop in Wongaling Beach next to the 'big cassowary'. **Sun Palm** (☎4087 2900; www.sunpalmtransport.com) has daily services to Cairns and Cairns airport ($49) as well as Innisfail and Tully.

The hail-and-ride **Mission Impossible Beach Shuttle** (www.calypsocoaches.com.au; day pass $8; ⏰Mon-Sat) runs roughly every hour between Bingil Bay and South Mission Beach, and also serves Tully (one way $10); the visitor centre has timetables.

Sugar Land Car Rentals (☎4068 8272; www.sugarland.com.au; 30 Wongaling Beach Rd, Wongaling Beach; ⏰8am-5pm) rents small cars from $59 per day.

See the Dunk Island section for boat transfers to Dunk Island.

Mission Beach Adventure Centre rents bikes ($10/20 per half-day/day).

Call ☎13 10 08 for a taxi.

Dunk Island

The water surrounding Dunk Island seems too blue to be true. It's the first thing you notice when you step off the ferry and onto the long jetty. As you make your way to terra firma and peer over the edge of the old wooden structure, myriad fish swarm below as if they take it upon themselves to be the island's unofficial welcoming party (and also offer fantastic fishing). Whether you're a resort guest or a day tripper, Dunk is pretty much your ideal tropical island.

Dunk Island was severely battered by Cyclone Yasi in February 2011 and the resort was closed. At the time of writing, no bookings were being taken until at least late August. It's likely that there will be no regular day trips out to the island until the resort reopens – call ahead to check.

Known to the Djiru Aboriginal people as Coonanglebah (the Island of Peace and Plenty), Captain Cook dubbed it 'father isle', nearby Bedarra the 'mother isle' and the remaining 14 islands of the Family Islands group 'the children'. Only 4.5km east of Mission Beach, Dunk Island is the largest and most northerly of the group.

Its abundant species of birds (more than 100), butterflies, coral gardens and marine life were the inspiration for the transcendentalist EJ Banfield, who wrote four novels while living here between 1897 and 1923. Of them, *The Confessions of a Beachcomber* is probably the most well known. **Banfield's grave** is a short walk from the jetty towards Muggy Muggy. Visual artists also use the island as inspiration, staying at the artists' colony established in 1974 by Bruce Arthur (known for his tapestries).

You can almost circumnavigate the island along the park's well-marked **walking trails** (9km, three hours). Otherwise, a walk to the top of Mt Kootaloo (271m; 5.6km, 1½ hours return) allows you to look back to the mainland and see Hinchinbrook Channel fanning out before you. There's good **snorkelling** over bommies at Muggy Muggy and great **swimming** at Coconut Beach.

Otherwise, day trippers can utilise a limited number of Dunk Island Resort's facilities by purchasing a **day pass** (adult/

child $40/20), available from the Watersports Centre near the jetty, including a two-course lunch at one of the resort's excellent cafes and an hour's **paddle-ski hire**, as well as pool access and use of the nine-hole **golf course** with boardwalks through dense rainforest.

The standard beachfront rooms at **Dunk Island Resort** (☎4068 8199, reservations 1300 384 403, 4047 4740; www.dunk-island.com; s/d incl breakfast, lunch & dinner from $386/475; ❄@📶🏊) are just as nice as the more expensive beachfront suites. Step out your sliding door to the water's edge then while away your day in a sun lounger, before heading to the bar and pool at dusk. Kids under 12 sharing their parents' room stay and eat free; you can lose your little angels – temporarily – at the kids' club.

Permits for the **DERM campground** (☎13 74 68; www.derm.qld.gov.au; per person $5.15) need to be organised through the resort. Just back from the jetty, sites occupy a gravel patch; there are toilets and showers.

Air transfers (adult/child return $390/290, 45 minutes, two daily) to/from Cairns can be booked through the resort.

Calypso (☎4068 8432; www.calypsoadventures.com.au; adult/child same-day return $40/20, one way $25/12.50), departing from Mission Beach's Clump Point jetty, and **Mission Beach Dunk Island Water Taxi** (☎4068 8310; Banfield Pde, Wongaling Beach; adult/child return $35/18), departing from Wongaling Beach, make the 20-minute trip to Dunk Island. Calypso also operates an amphibious marine craft, **Sealegs** (adult/child return $30/15), which can pick up from a dozen departure points along Mission's beachfront and drop you over on Dunk.

Bedarra Island

Like something lifted from the pages of a glossy lifestyle magazine, Bedarra Island, 7km offshore, is the sort of place you go whenever the 'who cares, it's only money' mood strikes. Yes, it's expensive, but they don't cut any corners here.

As with Dunk Island, Bedarra was closed until at least late August 2011 following Cyclone Yasi.

The 16 timber-and-glass beachfront villas at **Bedarra Island Resort** (☎1300 384 417, 4047 4747; www.bedarraisland.com; s/d from $1168/1444; ❄@📶🏊) are the very essence of luxury and seclusion – there are often more beaches than guests! Each stunning split-level villa overlooks Wedgerock Bay and has its own private plunge pool and outdoor area with a day bed. You'll have a bucket of ice and a plate of canapés delivered here daily. The bar opens 24/7 and all meals are included; kids under 12 aren't accepted.

Return air/coach and boat transfers via Dunk Island cost $490/150, bookable through Bedarra Island Resort.

Mission Beach to Innisfail

The road north from Mission Beach rejoins the Bruce Hwy at **El Arish** (population 230), home to not much, bar a golf course and the memorabilia- and character-filled **El Arish Tavern** (38 Chauvel St), built in 1927.

From El Arish you can take the more direct route north by continuing straight along the Bruce Hwy, with turn-offs leading to beach communities, or detour west via the Old Bruce Hwy, also known as the Canecutter Way.

BRUCE HWY

Directly opposite the southern turn-off to the Old Bruce Hwy, the road leading east to Kurrimine Beach passes **Murdering Point Winery** (☎4065 2327; www.murderingpointwinery.com.au; 161 Murdering Point Rd, Silkwood East; ⏲9am-5pm). Started by the Berryman family in 2003 to reduce wastage from their commercial orchards, it produces some stunning tropical wines made from mango, passionfruit and Davidson plum, among others, spiced with ginseng and ginger, with free tastings (yum!).

The fishing at the small township of Kurrimine Beach (population 840), 9km east of the Bruce Hwy, is as good as it gets along north Queensland's coast. Or get in the water with your horse on a trek with **Kurrimine Beach Horse Rides** (☎4065 6054; http://kurriminebeachhorserides.info; 1hr $88). A surprising array of accommodation options include the beachfront **King Reef Resort** (☎4065 6144; www.kingreef.com.au; powered sites $30, motel r/cabins from $100/150; ❄🏊), with cabins right on the beach, plus a pub, casino (ie pokies) and **restaurant** (mains $15-29; ⏲lunch & dinner).

About 7km south of Innisfail, the Bruce Hwy passes through **Mourilyan** (population 420), home to the **Australian Sugar Industry Museum** (www.sugarmuseum.com.au; Bruce

Hwy; adult/child $10/5; ⌚9am-5pm Mon-Sat, 9am-3pm Sun May-Oct, 9am-5pm Mon-Fri, 9am-3pm Sat, 9am-noon Sun Nov-Apr). In a refurbished old cinema, the museum houses a fascinating collection of artefacts – historic tractors, locomotives, harvesters and steam-driven crushing engines – as well as photographs and oral histories.

Turn off at Mourilyan to drive 9km to **Etty Bay**, an exquisite little beach surrounded by rocky headlands and rainforest, with cassowaries roaming along the shore and a large stinger enclosure. You can let the world pass you by at the simple **Etty Bay Caravan Park** (☎4063 2314; Esplanade; unpowered/powered sites $23/25, cabins $66; 📶). There's no mobile-phone reception here, and none of the cabins have en suites, but there are cooking facilities, or you can fill up on fish, chips and towering burgers at the park's **cafe** (dishes $6.50-15; ⌚breakfast, lunch & dinner; 📶).

CANECUTTER WAY

The Old Bruce Hwy, ie **Canecutter Way** (www.canecutterway.com.au) or Japoonvale Rd, is the more scenic route north. From the small beef cattle village of **Silkwood** (population 350), it runs along banana and sugar-cane plantations, with cane trains intermittently cutting across the road during harvest (the season is officially June to December).

In a lush pocket of rainforest at the tiny township of **Mena Creek** are the enchanting ruins of two once-grand castles at the 5-hectare **Paronella Park** (☎4065 0000; www.paronellapark.com.au; Japoonvale Rd; adult/child $34/17; ⌚9am-7.30pm). The complex was built in the 1930s to bring a whimsical entertainment centre to the area's hard-working folk. Today the mossy Spanish ruins have an almost medieval feel, and walking trails lead through rambling gardens past a waterfall and swimming hole. Take the 45-minute daytime tour and/or one-hour night tour to hear the full, fascinating story. Guides also fill you in on its 1933-built hydroelectric system, which began generating power again in 2009.

Admission includes both tours, as well as one night at its powered campground. Alternatively book in to one of the newly constructed timber **cabins** (d $75; ❄), which share a brand-new bathroom block. Wi-fi is planned. Tickets to Paronella Park are valid for one year.

Further north at **South Johnstone** (population 480), during the cane-cutting season you'll see how the charming little art gallery–cafe–secondhand bookshop **Off the Rails** (Hynes St; mains $8-18; ⌚10am-5pm Wed-Sun; 🥬) got its name: cane trains from the South Johnstone sugar mill literally run down the middle of the street right past its pavement tables. As well as homemade cakes and great coffee, local produce is used in dishes like fresh, baked and marinated veggie platters.

Follow the signposted back roads from South Johnstone to rejoin the Bruce Hwy at Innisfail.

Innisfail & Around

POP 8260

Just 80km south of the mayhem of Cairns, Innisfail may come as a surprise to anyone expecting a ho-hum town that exists purely to serve the agricultural industry. At the confluence of the North and South Johnstone Rivers, this buzzing regional hub has a real community feel and some gorgeous art deco architecture (Australia's largest concentration, no less).

Flying Fish Point is 8km northeast of the town centre on the beach, while national parks and nature activities, including the Mamu Rainforest Canopy Walk, are within a short drive.

Leaving the Bruce Hwy 4km northwest of Innisfail, the Palmerston Hwy follows the original route taken in 1882 by the bushman, gold prospector and explorer Christie Palmerston, assisted by Aboriginal guides.

The Palmerston Hwy continues west to Millaa Millaa, passing the entrance to the Waterfalls Circuit (p348) just before the town.

Sights & Activities

Johnstone River Crocodile Farm

CROCODILE FARM

(www.crocpark.com.au; Flying Fish Point Rd; adult/child $28/14; ⌚8.30am-4.30pm, feeding times 11am & 3pm) Head east over Geraldton Bridge on the road to Flying Fish Point to reach this croc-breeding facility. Frequent half-hour tours from 9.30am let you watch guides sit on 1-tonne, 5m-long Gregory – the farm's fattest reptile – and meet its oldest croc, 90-year-old Johnny. (Don't get so attached that you don't taste the croc skewers at the kiosk.) Other wildlife includes cassowaries, pythons, roos and wallabies.

Wooroonooran National Park NATIONAL PARK
The **Palmerston (Doongan) section** of Wooroonooran National Park is home to some of the oldest continually surviving rainforest in Australia.

At the southeast corner of the park, **Crawford's Lookout** has views of the white water of the North Johnstone River, but it's worth the walk down to view it at closer range. Among the park's walks is the lovely **Nandroya Falls Circuit** (7.2km, three to four hours), which crosses a swimming hole. A number of platypus-viewing areas are marked in the park; dawn or dusk are the best times of day to spot them.

 **Mamu Rainforest Canopy Walkway** WALKING
(www.derm.qld.gov.au/mamu; Palmerston Hwy; adult/child $20/10; ⏲9.30am-5.30pm, last entry 4.30pm) About 27km along the Palmerston Hwy, this elevated rainforest walkway gives you eye-level views of the canopy's fruits, flowers and birds, and a bird's-eye perspective from its 100-step, 37m-high tower. Built along the path Cyclone Larry took in 2006, the walkway is constructed from sustainable materials, including decking made from more than 900,000 recycled 2L plastic milk bottles. Allow at least an hour to complete the 2.5km, wheelchair-accessible circuit.

Eubenangee Swamp National Park NATIONAL PARK
About 20km north of Innisfail on the Bruce Hwy is the turn-off to the bird-rich wetlands of this national park. During the Wet the water level of the Russell River rises such that it causes the Alice River to flow backwards, which floods the swamp. A 1km walking trail follows the river (home to a healthy croc population) through the mangroves and leads to an elevated grassy knoll overlooking the lily-studded wetlands. From here there are also views over to Mt Bartle Frere in Wooroonooran National Park.

Art Deco Walk HISTORIC BUILDINGS
(www.artdeco-innisfail.com.au) Following a devastating 1918 cyclone, Innisfail rebuilt in the art deco style of the day, and 2006's cyclone resulted in many of these striking buildings being refurbished. Pick up a free **town walk brochure** from the visitor centre, detailing more than two dozen key points of interest.

Local History Museum MUSEUM
(11 Edith St; adult/child $5/2; ⏲10am-noon & 1-3pm Mon-Fri) In the old School of Arts building, with displays covering Innisfail's history, including Cyclone Larry.

Lit Zing Khuong TEMPLE
(Temple of the Universal God; Owen St; admission by donation; ⏲temple 9am-5pm, shop 9am-2pm Sat & Sun) Behind its red facade, this temple with its wafting incense is a reminder of the area's Chinese heritage. Its inspiring caretaker dispenses healing Chinese herbs, and runs t'ai chi and calligraphy classes.

Memorial Baths SWIMMING
(McGowan Dr; admission $3; ⏲6am-6pm Mon-Fri, 8am-5pm Sat, 10am-5pm Sun) Cool down with a dip.

THE CROCODILE ROCK (& DEATH ROLL)

In 1991 Charlie was awarded the title of 'Queenslander of the Year' for his outstanding contribution to tourism. Charlie was a crocodile who, for 65 years, entertained thousands of tourists to Hartley's Creek by snapping for dangling chickens and performing the occasional death roll.

Crocodiles have been a protected species in Queensland since 1974. Since it became illegal to harm or kill a wild crocodile, the once-dwindling population has recovered greatly. Some argue that numbers are too high; whenever there's a crocodile encounter in a built-up area, there are cries for controlled culling. Problem (or rogue) crocs – those deemed a threat to landowners – are ideally captured and relocated to commercial crocodile farms.

Croc farms like Innisfail's Johnstone River Crocodile Farm and Hartley's Crocodile Adventures (p335), near Cairns, see khaki-clad tough guys enter the croc's pen and take on the risks, while you're safely entertained from the bleachers. A number of crocodile farms also operate to breed crocs for restaurant dishes or handbags, wallets or shoes. Crocs can also end up as taxidermied trophies, known as 'stuffies', and as souvenirs such as stuffed crocodile feet back-scratchers.

These giant beady-eyed predators will attack humans – see p456 to avoid unwanted encounters.

LOCAL KNOWLEDGE

ROBERT STEPHENS: RANGER, MAMU RAINFOREST CANOPY WALKWAY

Mamu's Origins?

Several sites had been under consideration for a rainforest walkway, then Cyclone Larry came along; he'd done the hard work for us, all the clearing – we just came in and cleaned it up. The construction helped inject money back into the Innisfail area. We planted 7000 trees, and another couple of thousand since it opened.

Relationship with the Ma:Mu People?

Ma:Mu represents five separate clans, including Waribara, whose land we're on; we've found quite a few artefacts here. We've got a traditional owner on staff and part of every entry fee goes back to the traditional owners. Long-term, it's anticipated the Ma:Mu people will take over from DERM and generate income and jobs from the project.

Typical Tasks?

Weed and feral-animal control, track and infrastructure maintenance, recording photo databases and assisting visitors. Previously I was a zoo keeper, so it's similar in terms of public awareness and education. I want to make a difference, fixing the problems of the past to preserve native species.

Job Highlight?

I walk this track every day and see stuff on a daily basis that I haven't seen before. There's so much diversity.

Festivals & Events

The four-day **Feast of the Senses** (www.feastofthesenses.com.au), which takes place in late March, showcases produce from the local area, with foodie events including street stalls and celebrity chefs.

Sleeping

Innisfail's hostels primarily cater to banana pickers who work the surrounding plantations; several offer weekly rates only (around $175 for a week's dorm accommodation). Contact the visitor centre for a full list of hostels, which often provide courtesy transport to work.

Just off the highway, 38km from Innisfail, Henrietta Creek has a **DERM campground** (☎13 74 68; www.derm.qld.gov.au; per person $5.15) with composting toilets and coin-operated gas barbecues. Water is available from the creek (boil before drinking).

Barrier Reef Motel MOTEL $$
(☎4061 4988; www.barrierreefmotel.com.au; Bruce Hwy; s/d $100/110, units $130-150; ❄@📶🏊) The best place to stay in Innisfail, this comfortable motel next to the visitor centre has 41 airy, tiled rooms with large bathrooms. If you're self-catering, book into one of the units with kitchenettes, otherwise head to the **restaurant** (mains $28-31; ⏰breakfast & dinner; 🖉), or just stop by the bar for a drink.

Flying Fish Point Tourist Park CARAVAN PARK $
(☎4061 3131; www.ffpvanpark.com.au; 39 Elizabeth St, Flying Fish Point; unpowered/powered sites $26/31, dm $30, cabins $50-65, cabins & villas with bathroom $85-105; ❄@📶🏊) You can fish right off the beach across the road from this minivillage, or organise boat rental through the friendly managers. Facilities are first-rate and the Flying Fish Point Cafe is right next door.

Codge Lodge HOSTEL $
(☎4061 8055; www.codgelodge.com; 63 Rankin St; dm $33; ❄@📶🏊) Housed in an atmospheric turn-of-the-20th-century Queenslander, with a wide verandah and rambling corridors, this cheerful hostel has plenty of farm workers bunking down for an extended stay, but also welcomes overnight travellers. Staff organise regular tours to nearby swimming spots, rainforest walks and fishing and crabbing trips.

River Drive Van Park CARAVAN PARK $
(☎4061 2515; riverdrv@bigpond.net.au; Bruce Hwy; unpowered/powered sites $20/25, cabin $80; ❄@🏊) Fronted by neon-blue palm

trees and with a camp kitchen right by the river, this caravan park is Innisfail's most central. Book ahead for its four cabins.

Moondarra Motel MOTEL $$
(☎4061 7077; www.moondarramotel.com.au; 21 Ernest St; s $85, d $90-100; ❄) Considering the dated turquoise exterior, the much more up-to-date rooms here are a pleasant surprise.

Eating

Monsoon Cruising CAFE $
(☎0427 776 663; 1 Innisfail Wharf; mains $10-14; ⏰10am-5pm Wed-Sun, yr-round weather permitting; ✍) When this cruiser isn't out travelling the waterways, you can dine aboard up on deck or down below by the waterline. Everything is locally sourced and/or organic, from foccacia baked fresh on the boat each day to local hand-smoked chicken and black tiger prawns straight off the trawlers. Or just drop by for Mareeba coffee with organic milk and a slice of deliciously sticky macadamia toffee cake.

Flying Fish Point Cafe CAFE $$
(9 Elizabeth St, Flying Fish Point; mains $13-19; ⏰7.30am-8.30pm; ✍) Sitting on the deck of this breezy beachside cafe is an easy way to while away some time. Seafood is a specialty – you're doing well if you can make it through the seafood basket of battered and crumbed fish, barbecued calamari, wonton prawns, tempura scallops and more.

Oliveri's Continental Deli DELI $
(www.oliverisdeli.com.au; 41 Edith St; sandwiches $7.50-8.50; ⏰8.30am-5.30pm Mon-Fri, 8.30am-1pm Sat; ✍) Step back in time at this authentic Italian delicatessen. An Innisfail institution for decades, it has more than 60 varieties of European cheese, ham and salami, and row upon row of smallgoods and jarred goodies like antipasto and olives. Stock up or pick up gourmet sandwiches for a riverside picnic.

Roscoe's Piazza ITALIAN $$
(☎4061 6888; www.roscoes.com.au; 3b Ernest St; mains $22-36, buffets $24-39; ⏰lunch & dinner) Roscoe's is a hugely popular local haunt for its authentic pizzas, pastas and seafood, and especially for its enormous buffets, complete with homemade desserts such as tiramisu. Fantastic value.

Innisfail Fish Depot SEAFOOD $
(51 Fitzgerald Esplanade; ⏰7.30am-6pm Mon-Fri, 8am-4pm Sat, 10am-4pm Sun) Fresh-as-it-gets fish to throw on the barbie and organic cooked prawns by the bagful ($18/kg).

Famishes CAFE $
(64 Edith St; mains $5-15; ⏰from 5am Mon-Fri, 6am Sat, 7am Sun to at least 2pm; ✍) Dependable as they come, this central local cafe serves light meals such as lasagne, and wraps and rolls that will tide you over until dinnertime.

Information

The **visitor centre** (☎4061 2655; www.innisfailtourism.com.au; cnr Eslick St & Bruce Hwy; ⏰9am-5pm Mon-Fri, 9.30am-12.30pm Sat, 10am-1pm Sun; @) has free discount vouchers for many of the area's attractions.

Getting There & Away

Bus services operate once daily with **Premier** (☎13 34 10; www.premierms.com.au) to Townsville ($52) and Cairns ($19). Services run five times daily with **Greyhound Australia** (☎1300 473 946; www.greyhound.com.au) from Innisfail to Townsville ($70, 4½ hours) and Cairns ($32, 1½ hours). **Sun Palm** (☎4087 2900; www.sunpalmtransport.com) runs to Cairns ($35), including Cairns airport, and south as far as Tully ($25). Buses depart from the bus stop opposite King George Sq on Edith St.

Innisfail is on the Cairns–Brisbane train line; contact **Queensland Rail** (☎1300 131 722; www.traveltrain.com.au) for information.

Byrne Travel (☎4061 2177; 23-25 Edith St) handles travel tickets.

Cairns, Islands & Highlands

Includes »

Cairns 306
Machans Beach 331
Holloways Beach ...332
Yorkeys Knob 332
Palm Cove..........333
Ellis Beach 335
Green Island........335
Fitzroy Island 336
Atherton Tableland ..337
Kuranda............338
Mareeba 342
Ravenshoe 347
Yungaburra.........349
Lake Tinaroo.........351

Best Places to Eat

» Yorkeys Knob Boating Club (p332)
» Ochre (p316)
» L'Unico Trattoria (p333)
» Beach Almond (p334)

Best Places to Stay

» Crater Lakes Rainforest Cottages (p352)
» Tropic Days (p313)
» Sebel Reef House (p334)

Why Go?

Cairns has a heady reputation as Australia's reef-diving capital – with the Great Barrier Reef's dazzling marine life and coral-fringed islands a short boat ride offshore – and as tropical Far North Queensland's party-central. But although you could easily spend your entire trip here, some spectacular natural attractions lie just beyond the city limits.

Lush rainforest, waterfalls, volcanic-crater lakes, and a winding coastline of coves, bays and beach communities are all within a couple of hours of Cairns, as are the rich pastoral Atherton Tableland's gourmet food producers, farms and orchards.

The entire region is impressively – and at times overwhelmingly – geared for tourism. Tour operators are an art form in themselves: as well as scuba diving or snorkelling the reef, you can sail, kayak, skydive, fish, golf, birdwatch, hot-air balloon, horse-ride... The only limitations are your budget and your imagination (not necessarily in that order!).

When to Go

Cairns

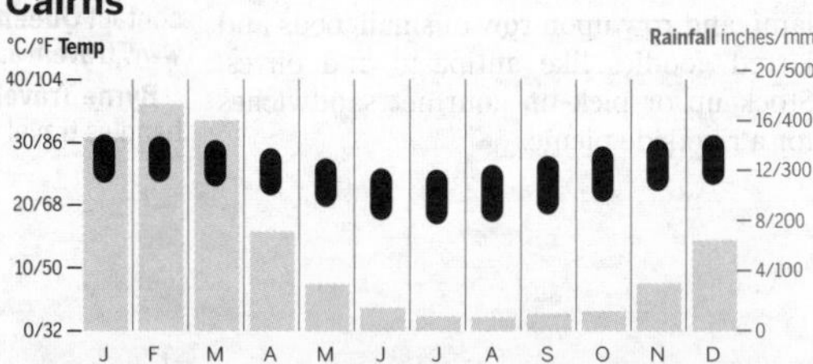

July Bucking broncos and country music entertain the crowds at Mareeba's annual rodeo.

September Party-hard Cairns parties even harder during the Cairns Festival.

October Roots and blues bands headline the Yungaburra Folk Festival.

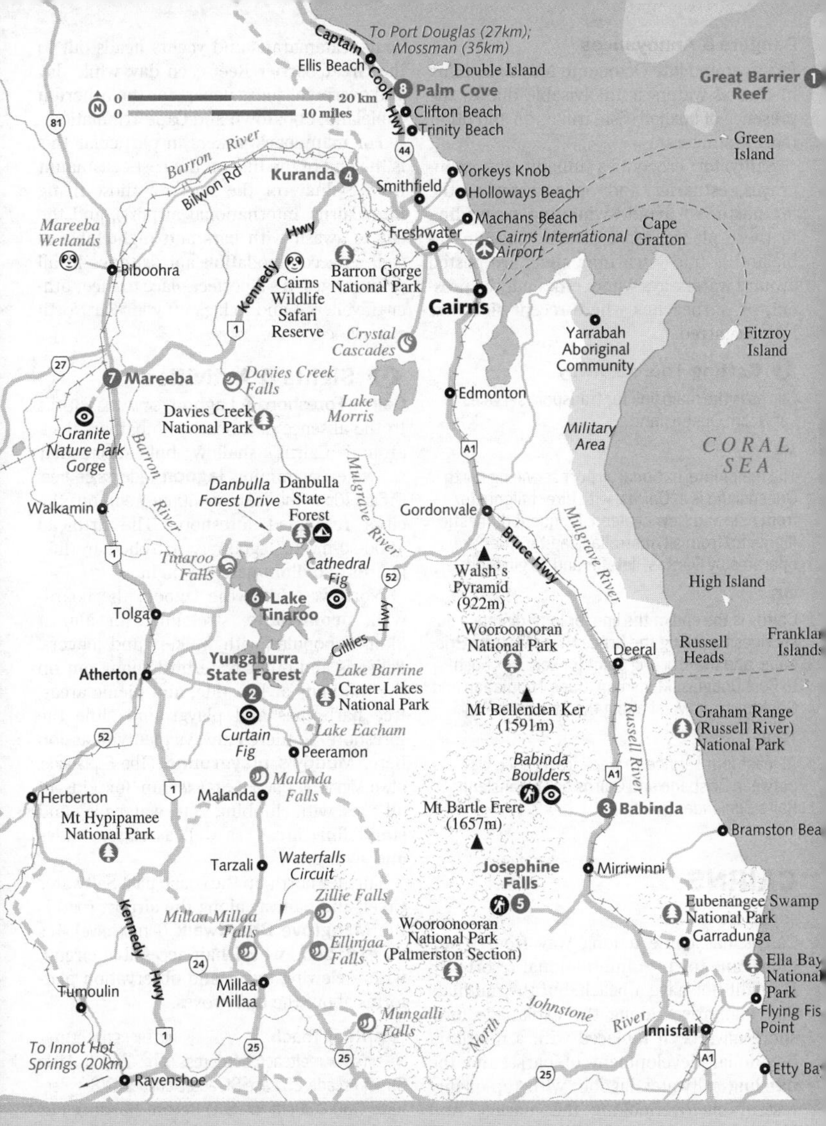

Cairns, Islands & Highlands Highlights

1. Diving, snorkelling and swimming among the fish, turtles and anemones that live in the multicoloured corals of the **Great Barrier Reef** (p311) from Cairns
2. Platypus-spotting along the creek in the picturesque village of **Yungaburra** (p349)
3. Making your own didgeridoo with local Aboriginal artists in **Babinda** (p330)
4. Riding the Skyrail cable car through the rainforest to the alternative market town of **Kuranda** (p342) and returning to Cairns by Scenic Railway
5. Splashing in the natural pools and waterfalls at **Josephine Falls** (p331)
6. Fishing, barbecuing or simply watching the sun set on a **Lake Tinaroo** cruise (p351)
7. Drifting up, up and away over the Atherton Tableland in a hot-air balloon from **Mareeba** (p312)
8. Donning the shades and people-watching on the esplanade at **Palm Cove** (p333

Dangers & Annoyances

From around late October to May swimming in coastal waters is inadvisable due to the presence of box jellyfish, irukandji and other marine stingers.

Saltwater crocodiles inhabit the mangroves, estuaries and open water of the far north, so avoid swimming or wading in these places. Most of the Atherton Tableland is fine – warning signs are posted around waterways where crocs may be present, or on beaches where recent sightings have occurred.

Getting There & Away

Cairns is the main link for transport services to Far North Queensland.

AIR

The major international airport servicing north Queensland is in Cairns, with direct flights to/from Asia and New Zealand. Frequent domestic flights to/from all Australian capital cities are operated by Qantas, Jetstar and Virgin Blue.

BUS

Cairns is the end of the line for long-distance bus services travelling the Bruce Hwy (A1) from Brisbane, and the starting point for services north to Port Douglas, Mossman, Cape Tribulation and Cooktown and west along the Savannah Way.

TRAIN

At least four services a week travel each way between Brisbane and Cairns on Queensland Rail's *Sunlander* (p476).

CAIRNS

POP 147,120

Cairns has come a long way from struggling cane town to international resort city. It might not have a beach, but the mudflats and mangroves along the Esplanade foreshore have been replaced with a multimillion-dollar development of parks and the dazzling saltwater lagoon, with top-quality restaurants overlooking the marina. And if you do want some sand, it's a short local bus ride or easy drive to Cairns' Northern Beaches.

Old salts claim Cairns has lost some of its character and sold its soul, but it has an infectious holiday vibe and a tropical aura, and it ticks to the tune of tourism. The central business district (CBD) is more boardshorts than briefcases – a mini urban jungle of tour shops, booking agents, car-hire agents and internet cafes. There's no limit to the activities you can organise here: a flotilla of cruise boats, catamarans and yachts heads out to the Great Barrier Reef each day, while day and overnight tours depart for the Atherton Tableland, Cooktown and Cape Tribulation.

For many backpackers in particular this is the end of the line on the east-coast jaunt from Sydney (or the start for those flying into Cairns' international airport), and the city is awash with bars and nightclubs, as well as accommodation and eateries in all price ranges. It's a perfect place to meet other travellers – and to kick off your Far North experience.

Sights & Activities

Cairns Foreshore & Lagoon SWIMMING, WALKING

In the absence of a beach, sunbathers flock around Cairns' shallow but spectacular saltwater swimming **lagoon** (admission free; 6am-10pm Thu-Tue, noon-10pm Wed) on the city's reclaimed foreshore. The artificial 4800-sq-metre lagoon is patrolled by lifeguards and illuminated at night.

Northwest from the lagoon, the boardwalk **promenade**, stretching for almost 3km, is popular with walkers and joggers. Pelicans and other waterbirds hang out on the mudflats at low tide, and picnic areas, free barbecues and playgrounds line the foreshore, so there's always plenty of action here. **Muddy's playground** (The Esplanade, btwn Minnie & Upward Sts) is fun for kids of all ages, with climbing nets, water-play and storytelling areas, as well as classic slides and swings.

Further north up the coast, past Saltwater Creek and halfway along the airport road is the **Mangrove Boardwalk** (Airport Ave). It's an easy 2km, wheelchair-accessible circuit, with a viewing tower and observation platforms above the mangroves.

Reef Teach INTERPRETIVE CENTRE

(www.reefteach.wordpress.com; 2nd fl, Main Street Arcade, 85 Lake St; adult/child $15/8; lectures 6.30-8.30pm Tue-Sat) Before heading out to the reef, take your knowledge to greater depths at this excellent and informative centre, where marine experts explain how to identify specific types of coral and fish and how to treat the reef with respect.

Flecker Botanic Gardens & Around GARDEN

(www.cairns.qld.gov.au; Collins Ave, Edge Hill; admission free; 7.30am-5.30pm Mon-Fri, 8.30am-5.30pm Sat & Sun) These beautiful tropical gardens are an explosion of greenery and rainforest plants. Sections include an area for bush-tucker plants and the Gondwanan

Evolutionary Trail, which traces the 415-million-year heritage of tropical plants. Free guided walks, lasting approximately two hours, depart on Tuesday and Thursday at 10am and 1pm from the **information centre** (⌚8.30am-5pm Mon-Fri), or you can pick up a map and self-guided-walks brochure and go it alone. Twitchers will want to sign up for free 90-minute birdwatching tours departing from the information centre at 8.30am on Tuesday.

Across the road, a rainforest boardwalk leads from the botanic gardens through lowland swamp forest to the **Centenary Lakes**. The area covers 38 hectares and includes a freshwater lake and a saltwater lake leading off from Saltwater Creek (which has been known to harbour crocs). There are barbecues, picnic areas and children's play areas at both lakes, which can also be accessed by car and local bus from Greenslopes St in the south.

Just behind the botanic gardens is the **Mt Whitfield Conservation Park**. Its two walking tracks lead through rainforest with patches of eucalyptus and grasslands, climbing to viewpoints over the city; follow the Red Arrow circuit (1.3km, one hour) or the more demanding Blue Arrow circuit (5.4km, three hours).

Tanks Arts Centre ART GALLERY, THEATRE

(☎4032 2349; www.tanksartscentre.com; 46 Collins Ave, Edge Hill; ⌚gallery 10am-4pm Mon-Fri) Adjacent to the botanic gardens, Cairns' community arts centre isn't your run-of-the-mill art space. Three gigantic ex-WWII fuel-storage tanks have been transformed into studios, galleries showcasing local artists' work and an inspired performing-arts venue. A lively market takes place here on the last Sunday of the month from April to September.

Cairns Regional Gallery ART GALLERY

(www.cairnsregionalgallery.com.au; cnr Abbott & Shields Sts; adult/child under 16yr $5/free; ⌚10am-5pm Mon-Sat, 1-5pm Sun) Exhibitions at Cairns' acclaimed regional gallery, housed in a 1936 colonnaded heritage building, reflect the consciousness of the tropical north region, with an emphasis on local and Indigenous works. Its shop stocks some truly beautiful craft items, including jewellery, ceramics and glassware.

Tjapukai Cultural Park CULTURAL CENTRE

(☎4042 9900; www.tjapukai.com.au; Kamerunga Rd, Smithfield; adult/child $35/17.50; ⌚9am-5pm) Combining fascinating aspects of Aboriginal culture with showbiz, this Indigenous-owned cultural extravaganza presents a variety of inspirational and educational performances. It incorporates the Creation Theatre, which tells the story of creation using giant holograms and actors, a Dance Theatre and a gallery, as well as boomerang- and spear-throwing demonstrations around an Aboriginal camp. You can also learn to paint message stones, play the didgeridoo or turtle-spot during a canoe ride on the lake. Allow at least three hours. It offers shuttle service from Cairns and the Northern Beaches for $25/14 per adult/child; shuttles for the night show cost $22/11.

A fireside corroboree is the centrepiece of the **Tjapukai By Night** (adult/child $99/49.50, transfers extra $22/11; ⌚7-10pm) dinner-and-show deal.

The park is about 15km north of the city centre, just off the Captain Cook Hwy (Hwy 44) near the Skyrail terminal (combined park entry, Skyrail and Scenic Railway tickets cost from $154/79 per adult/child, including transfers).

Centre of Contemporary Arts ART GALLERY, THEATRE

(www.coca.org.au; 96 Abbott St; ⌚10am-5pm Tue-Sat) CoCA houses the **KickArts** (www.kickarts.org.au) galleries of contemporary visual art, as well as the **Jute Theatre** (www.jute.com.au) and the **End Credits Film Club** (www.endcredits.org.au). Artists from all over Far North Queensland and the Torres Strait Islands exhibit in the ever-changing galleries. The attached shop sells locally made art and design products.

Cairns Museum MUSEUM

(www.cairnsmuseum.org.au; cnr Lake & Shields Sts; adult/child $5/2; ⌚10am-4pm Mon-Sat) Housed in the 1907-built former School of the Arts, the city's historical museum recounts Cairns' early years and the development of the region. Exhibits include the construction of the Cairns–Kuranda railway, the contents of a Chinese temple and displays on the Palmer River and Hodgkinson River goldfields. There's an excellent bookshop here.

Cairns Wildlife Dome ZOO

(www.cairnsdome.com.au; 35-41 Wharf St; adult/child $22/11; ⌚9am-6pm) If it's a rainy day, or if you're not heading to one of the wildlife parks out of town, Cairns Wildlife Dome might merit a visit. Oddly perched in the

Central Cairns

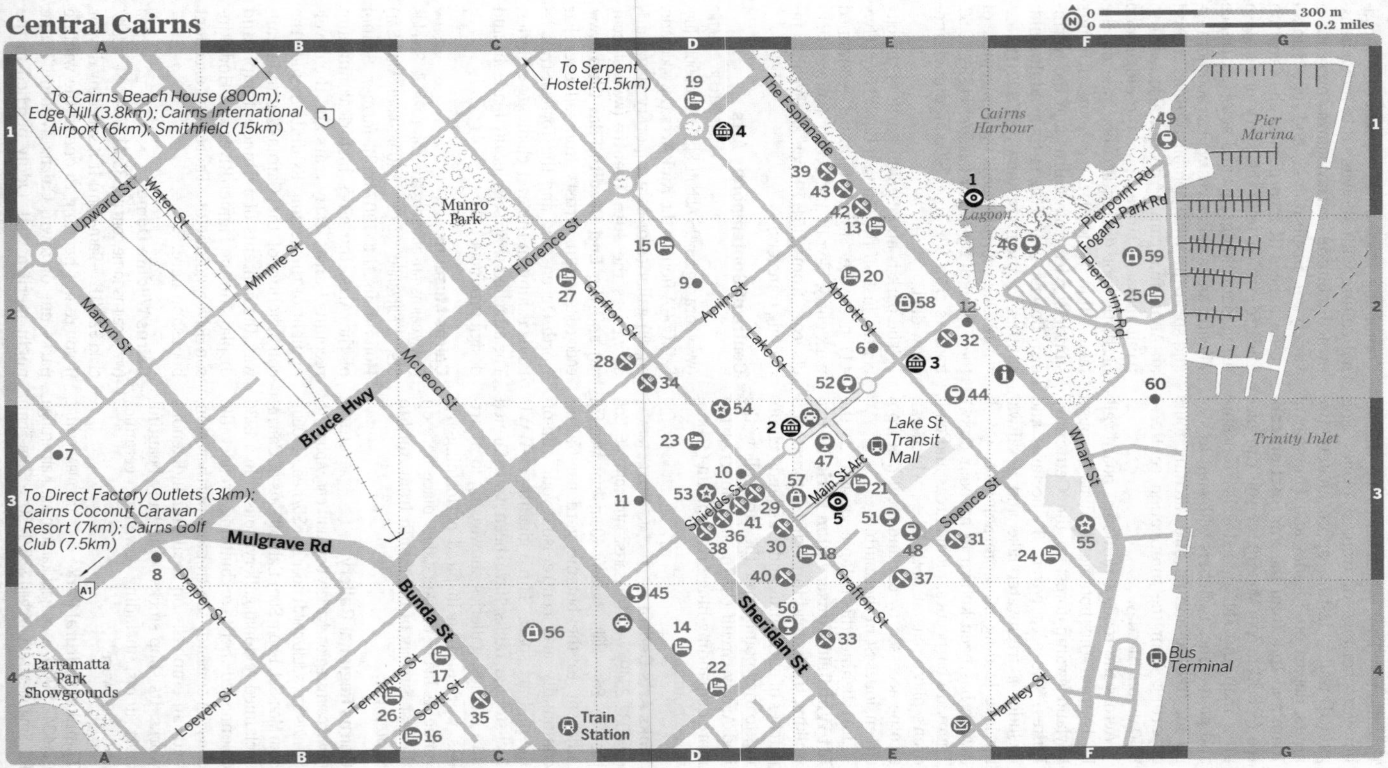

0 — 300 m
0 — 0.2 miles

To Cairns Beach House (800m); Edge Hill (3.8km); Cairns International Airport (6km); Smithfield (15km)
To Serpent Hostel (1.5km)
To Direct Factory Outlets (3km); Cairns Coconut Caravan Resort (7km); Cairns Golf Club (7.5km)

Cairns Harbour
Pier Marina
Lagoon
Trinity Inlet
Munro Park
Parramatta Park Showgrounds
Lake St Transit Mall
Bus Terminal
Train Station

The Esplanade
Pierpoint Rd
Fogarty Park Rd
Wharf St
Abbott St
Lake St
Aplin St
Grafton St
Shields St
Main St Arc
Spence St
Sheridan St
Hartley St
Florence St
McLeod St
Bruce Hwy
Mulgrave Rd
Bunda St
Terminus St
Scott St
Draper St
Loeven St
Martyn St
Upward St
Water St
Minnie St

1 2 3 4 5 6 7 8 9 10 11 12 13 14 15 16 17 18 19 20 21 22 23 24 25 26 27 28 29 30 31 32 33 34 35 36 37 38 39 40 41 42 43 44 45 46 47 48 49 50 51 52 53 54 55 56 57 58 59 60

Central Cairns

Sights
1 Cairns Foreshore & Lagoon ... E1
2 Cairns Museum ... D3
3 Cairns Regional Gallery ... E2
Cairns Wildlife Dome ... (see 55)
4 Centre of Contemporary Arts ... D1
5 Reef Teach ... E3

Activities, Courses & Tours
6 Cairns Dive Centre ... E2
Cairns Heliscenic ... (see 59)
7 Deep Sea Divers Den ... A3
8 Down Under Dive ... A3
Great Adventures ... (see 60)
9 Mike Ball Dive Expeditions ... D2
10 Pro-Dive ... D3
11 Skydive Cairns ... D3
Taka Dive ... (see 7)
12 Tusa Dive ... E2

Sleeping
13 Bellview ... E2
14 Cairns Central YHA ... D4
15 Cairns Girls Hostel ... D2
16 Cairns Sharehouse ... C4
17 Gecko's Backpackers ... C4
18 Gilligan's ... E3
19 Hotel Cairns ... D1
20 Il Palazzo ... E2
21 Inn Cairns ... E3
22 Mid City ... D4
23 Northern Greenhouse ... D3
24 Sebel Cairns ... F3
25 Shangri-La ... F2
26 Travellers Oasis ... B4
27 Villa Vaucluse ... C2

Eating
28 Adelphia Greek Taverna ... D2
29 Asian Foods Australia ... D3
30 Beethoven Cafe ... D3
31 Cherry Blossom ... E3
32 Dolce & Caffe ... E2
33 First House ... E4
34 Fusion Organics ... D2
35 Green Ant Cantina ... C4
36 La Fettuccina ... D3
37 Marinades ... E3
Meldrum's Pies in Paradise ... (see 30)
Night Markets ... (see 58)
38 Ochre ... D3
Perrotta's at the Gallery ... (see 3)
39 Raw Prawn ... E1
40 Rusty's Markets ... D3
41 Sushi Zipang ... D3
42 Vanilla Gelateria ... E1
43 Villa Romana Trattoria ... E1

Drinking
44 Court House Hotel ... E2
45 Grand Hotel ... D4
Hotel Cairns ... (see 19)
46 Pier Bar & Grill ... F2
47 PJ O'Briens ... E3
48 Rhino Bar ... E3
49 Salt House ... F1
50 Shenannigans ... D4
51 Vibe Bar & Lounge ... E3
52 Woolshed Chargrill & Saloon ... E2

Entertainment
53 12 Bar Blues ... D3
BCC Cinemas ... (see 56)
54 Cairns City Cinemas ... D3
Gilligan's ... (see 18)
Jute Theatre ... (see 4)
55 Pullman Reef Hotel Casino ... F3
Velvet Underground ... (see 55)
Vertigo Bar & Lounge ... (see 55)

Shopping
Absells Chart & Map Centre ... (see 5)
Bookshelf ... (see 30)
56 Cairns Central Shopping Centre ... C4
57 Exchange Bookshop ... E3
58 Night Markets ... E2
59 Pier Marketplace ... F2

Transport
60 Reef Fleet Terminal ... F2

glass atrium on top of the Reef Casino, this mini-zoo has a simulated rainforest environment with free-flying birds, wallabies, koalas, snakes, lizards and freshwater crocs. Admission to the Dome includes feeding tours as well as reptile and 'furry friends' shows.

Lake Morris & Crystal Cascades

LAKE, WATERFALLS

A spectacular drive along the Lake Morris Rd (off Reservoir Rd, Kanimbla) takes you on a narrow 16km winding road high above Cairns to **Lake Morris** (8am-5pm). Also known as the Copperlode Dam, this is the city's drinking water supply, so swimming

DIVE COURSES

Cairns is the scuba-diving capital of the Great Barrier Reef and a popular place to attain Professional Association of Diving Instructors (PADI) open-water certification. There's a plethora of courses on offer, from budget four-day courses that combine pool training and reef dives to five-day courses that include two days of pool theory and three days living aboard a boat. Live-aboard courses are generally more rewarding as you'll dive less-frequented parts of the reef.

Dive-school standards are first-rate, and there is little to differentiate between them. All operators require you to have a dive medical certificate, which they can arrange (around $50). Many operators also offer advanced courses for certified divers. Following is a selection of reputable dive schools:

Cairns Dive Centre DIVING
(☎1800 642 591, 4051 0294; www.cairnsdive.com.au; 121 Abbott St) One of the cheapest operators; affiliated with Scuba Schools International (SSI) rather than PADI. Live-aboard tours (two/three days $355/470) and day tours ($120).

Deep Sea Divers Den DIVING
(☎1800 612 223, 4046 7333; www.diversden.com.au; 319 Draper St) Long-established school running multiday live-aboard courses and trips from $570.

Down Under Dive DIVING
(☎1800 079 099, 4052 8300; www.downunderdive.com.au; 287 Draper St) Multilingual instructors. Four- and five-day live-aboard trips from $520.

Pro-Dive DIVING
(☎1800 353 213, 4031 5255; www.prodivecairns.com; cnr Grafton & Shields Sts) One of Cairns' most experienced operators. Runs a comprehensive five-day learn-to-dive course incorporating a three-day live-aboard trip for $825.

Tusa Dive DIVING
(☎4047 9100; www.tusadive.com; cnr Shields St & The Esplanade) Inexpensive four-day learn-to-dive courses ($650) including two day-trips of diving.

is not allowed. There are a few short walks around the dam and a **kiosk** (⏲8am-3pm Tue-Sun), with a deck overlooking the lake.

If you do want to swim, another popular drive leads to **Crystal Cascades**, about 20km from Cairns, reached by a turn-off south along Redlynch Intake Rd (just past the Skyrail). Accessed by a 1.2km (30-minute) pathway, this series of waterfalls and pools is croc-free and especially popular in summer when the stingers arrive at the beaches.

Crystal Cascades and Lake Morris are linked by a *steep* rainforest **walking trail** (allow for three hours return). It starts near the picnic area at Crystal Cascades and climbs steadily uphill, coming out on Lake Morris Rd, about 300m from Copperlode Dam (turn right).

Other Activities

A plethora of tour operators run adventure-based activities from Cairns, most offering transfers to/from your accommodation – see p311.

In and around the city, activities of varying adrenalin levels include the following:

AJ Hackett Bungy & Minjin BUNGEE JUMPING
(☎1800 622 888; www.ajhackett.com; McGregor Rd, Smithfield; bungee jump $139, minjin swing $89, bungee & minjin swing combo $194; ⏲10am-5pm) Bungee from the purpose-built tower or swing from the trees on the minjin (a harness swing). Rates include transfers.

Cable Ski WATERSKIING
(☎4038 1304; www.cableskicairns.com.au; Captain Cook Hwy, Smithfield; adult/child 1hr $36/31, per day $69/64; ⏲10am-6pm) Learn to waterski, wakeboard or kneeboard without the boat at this watersports park near the Skyrail.

Cairns Golf Club GOLF
(☎4054 1494; www.cairnsgolfclub.com.au; Bruce Hwy, Woree) Established in 1929; scenic 18-hole course south of the city centre. Hires out equipment; rates depend on the day and tee time.

Fishing Cairns FISHING
(☎4041 1169; www.fishingcairns.com.au) Arranges river, reef and game fishing trips.

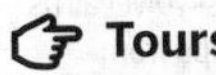

Tours

A staggering 600-plus tours bus, boat, fly and drive out of Cairns each day. See p335 for tours to Green, Fitzroy and the Frankland Islands, and p386 for day tours to Lizard Island. See p328 for cargo freighter trips from Cairns to the Cape.

Great Barrier Reef

Reef operators generally include transport, lunch and snorkelling gear in their tour prices. Many have diving options including introductory dives requiring no prior experience. When choosing a tour, consider the vessel (catamaran or sailing ship), its capacity (from six to 300 people), what extras are offered and the destination. The outer reefs are more pristine; inner reef areas can be patchy, showing signs of damage from humans, coral bleaching and crown-of-thorns starfish. Of course, companies that are only licensed to visit the inner reef have cheaper tours; in most cases you pay for what you get. Some operators offer the option of a trip in a glass-bottomed boat or semisubmersible.

The majority of boats depart from the Pier Marina and Reef Fleet Terminal at about 8am, returning around 6pm. As well as the popular day trips, a number of operators also offer multiday live-aboard trips, which include specialised dive opportunities such as night diving. Dive-course companies (p310) also offer tours.

Not up for scuba diving but want to get down with the fishes? Several dive boats offer helmet diving (from $140). Hoses attached to the helmet deliver air, so you can breathe normally. Because you're 'walking' on a submerged platform, it's ideal for non-swimmers, kids over 12 and anyone who doesn't like to get their hair wet.

Following is a list of reef trip operators worth considering.

Coral Princess REEF TRIPS
(☎1800 079 545, 4040 9999; www.coralprincess.com.au) Three-night cruises (from $1496 per person, twin share) between Cairns and Townsville, and four-night return trips between Cairns and Lizard Island (from $1896).

Great Adventures REEF TRIPS
(☎4044 9944; www.greatadventures.com.au; adult/child from $190/95) Fast catamaran does day trips to its floating pontoon, with an optional stopover on Green Island (from $210/105), as well as semisubmersibles and a glass-bottomed boat.

Passions of Paradise REEF TRIPS
(☎1800 111 346; www.passions.com.au; adult/child $139/89) Sexy sailing catamaran taking you to Michaelmas Cay and Paradise Reef for snorkelling or diving.

Silverswift REEF TRIPS
(☎4044 9944; www.silverseries.com.au; adult/child from $167.50/125.50) Popular catamaran snorkelling/diving three outer reefs.

Sunlover REEF TRIPS
(☎4050 1333; www.sunlover.com.au; adult/child from $180/65) Fast catamaran day cruises to a pontoon on the outer Moore Reef. Options include semisubmersible trips and helmet diving. Good for families.

Vagabond REEF TRIPS
(☎4031 9959; www.vagabond-dive.com; 2-day tours from $290) Luxury yacht carrying a maximum of 11 guests.

Cod Hole & Coral Sea

Cod Hole, near Lizard Island, is one of Australia's premier diving locations, so these extended live-aboard trips are mainly for keen certified divers.

Mike Ball Dive Expeditions LIVE-ABOARD TRIPS
(☎4053 0500; www.mikeball.com; 143 Lake St; trips from $1480) Long-running three-day live-aboard expeditions to the Cod Hole; four- and seven-day trips available.

Spirit of Freedom LIVE-ABOARD TRIPS
(☎4047 9150; www.spiritoffreedom.com.au; 3-/4-/7-day tours from $1350/1675/2775) Three-deck vessel with live-aboard trips to the Cod Hole and Ribbon Reefs.

Taka Dive DIVING
(☎4051 8722; www.takadive.com.au; 319 Draper St; 4-/5-/7-day tours from $1290/1610/2650) Dives the Cod Hole and the remote Osprey Reef (Coral Sea). Also offers speciality courses such as underwater photography, and the chance to swim with dwarf minke whales from June to August.

Scenic Flights

Cairns Heliscenic SCENIC FLIGHTS
(☎4031 5999; www.cairns-heliscenic.com.au; Pier Marketplace; 15/30min flight per person from $220/295) Helicopter flights departing from Green Island (from 10 minutes $148) to an hour-long reef and rainforest trip ($529).

Cairns Seaplanes SCENIC FLIGHTS
(☎4031 4307; www.cairnsseaplanes.com; Cairns Airport; 30min flights from $219) Scenic reef flights, including Green Island.

White-Water Rafting

The excitement level of white-water rafting down the Barron, Russell and North Johnstone Rivers is hitched to the season: obviously the wetter the weather, the whiter your water. The Tully River has rapids year-round – see p291.

Trips are graded according to the degree of difficulty, from armchair rafting (Grade 1) to white knuckle (Grade 5).

Major rafting companies departing from Cairns:

Foaming Fury RAFTING
(☎1800 801 540, 4031 3460; www.foamingfury.com.au) Full-day trips on the Russell River ($139); half-day on the Barron ($124), with options for kids aged over 10.

Raging Thunder RAFTING
(☎4030 7990; www.ragingthunder.com.au) Full-day Tully trips (standard trip $195, 'xtreme' trip $225) and half-day Barron trips ($133).

R'n'R White Water Rafting RAFTING
(☎4035 3555; www.raft.com.au) Full-day Tully ($195) and half-day Barron ($130) trips.

Tubing

Floating in an inner tube is a tranquil way to see beautiful Behana Gorge.

Aussie Drifterz TUBING
(☎0401 318 475; www.aussiedrifterz.net; half-day tour adult/child $59/39) Includes two hours on the water.

Ballooning

The dawn skies above Cairns and the highlands see a multitude of colourful balloons seemingly suspended in the air. Most hot-air balloon flights take off from the Mareeba region in the Atherton Tableland and include champagne breakfast afterwards.

Hot Air Cairns BALLOONING
(☎4039 9900; www.hotair.com.au; 30min flights from $215)

Raging Thunder BALLOONING
(☎4030 7990; www.ragingthunder.com.au; 30min flights from $225)

Skydiving

The higher you go, the higher the price: 9000ft gives you up to 28 seconds' freefalling, while up to 14,000ft gives you over 60 seconds plummeting back to earth.

Skydive Cairns SKYDIVING
(☎1800 444 568, 4031 5466; www.skydivecairns.com.au; 59 Sheridan St; tandem jumps from 9000ft $249) Licensed skydivers can jump solo for $50.

Atherton Tableland

Food Trail Tours FOOD & WINE TOURS
(☎4041 1522; www.foodtrailtours.com.au; adult/child from $154/77; ⏰Mon-Sat) Taste your way around the Tableland visiting farms producing macadamias, tropical-fruit wine, cheese, chocolate and coffee.

On the Wallaby ADVENTURE TOURS
(☎4033 6575; www.onthewallaby.com; day/overnight tours $99/169) Excellent activity-based tours including cycling, hiking and canoeing.

Uncle Brian's Tours DAY TRIPS
(☎4033 6575; www.unclebrian.com.au; tours $109; ⏰Mon-Wed, Fri & Sat) Lively small-group day trips covering forests, waterfalls and lakes.

Cape Tribulation & the Daintree

After the Great Barrier Reef, Cape Trib is the next most popular day trip, which usually includes a cruise on the Daintree River. Access is via a well-signposted sealed road, so don't discount hiring your own vehicle instead, especially if you want to take your time.

Billy Tea Bush Safaris DAY TRIPS
(☎4032 0077; www.billytea.com.au; day trips adult/child $170/120) Exciting eco daytours to Cape Trib and along the 4WD Bloomfield Track to Emmagen Creek.

BTS Tours DAY TRIPS
(☎4099 5665; www.btstours.com.au; day trips adult/child $159/115) Small-group tours including swimming and canoeing.

Cape Trib Connections DAY TRIPS
(☎4041 7447; www.capetribconnections.com; day trips $124) Includes Mossman Gorge, Cape Tribulation Beach and Port Douglas. Also overnight tours.

Trek North Safaris DAY TRIPS
(☎4033 2600; www.treknorth.com.au; adult/child $160/110) Full-day tours include Mossman Gorge and a river cruise.

Tropical Horizons Tours DAY TRIPS
(☎4035 6445; www.tropicalhorizonstours.com.au; day tours from $161) Day trips to Cape Trib and the Daintree; overnight tours available.

Tropics Explorer DAY TRIPS
(☎1800 801 540; www.tropicsexplorer.com.au; day tours from $119) Fun Cape Trib day trips; overnight tours available.

Cooktown & Cape York

See p390 for tours through Cape York Peninsula.

Adventure North Australia ADVENTURE TOURS
(☎4053 7001; www.adventurenorthaustralia.com; 1-day tour $235) 4WD trips to Cooktown via the coastal route, returning via inland route. Also two- and three-day tours, fly-drive and Aboriginal cultural tours.

Wilderness Challenge 4WD TOURS
(☎4055 4488; www.wilderness-challenge.com.au; 3-day tours from $845; ⏲May-Nov) Does 4WD tours to Cooktown via Cape Tribulation and the Bloomfield Track, returning via Cape York rock-art sites.

Undara Lava Tubes

Undara Experience LAVA-TUBES TOURS
(☎4097 1411; www.undara.com.au; 2-day tour adult/child $389/270) Coach tours to the Undara Lava Tubes. Day trips available by light aircraft and helicopter (from $540 per person, minimum four people).

City Tours

Cairns Discovery Tours CITY TOURS
(☎4053 5259; www.cairnsdiscoverytours.com; adult/child $65/32; ⏲Mon-Sat) Half-day afternoon tours run by horticulturists; includes the botanic gardens and Palm Cove. Northern Beaches transfers are available for an extra $5.

Festivals & Events

Cairns Festival ARTS
(www.festivalcairns.com.au) This regional festival takes over the city for three weeks each September with a packed program of performing arts, music, visual arts and family events such as sand sculpting.

Sleeping

Cairns has a vast range of accommodation for all budgets. Prices peak from 1 June to 31 October; prices quoted here are high-season rates. Even during this time, you may find reduced walk-in or stand-by rates, though you'll invariably get the best deals online. The rest of the year, prices can drop dramatically, especially at midrange and top-end places. Lower weekly rates are par for the course.

Commercial accommodation agencies are scattered throughout town; the government-run Cairns & Tropical North Visitor Information Centre (p327) has up-to-date listings and can help find and book places to stay.

Cairns is a backpacker hot spot, with around 40 hostels at last count – from intimate converted houses to hangar-sized resorts. Competition means many offer extras such as cheap or free evening meals and/or drinks. If you're planning on sticking around for four weeks or more, **Cairns Sharehouse** (☎4041 1875; www.cairns-sharehouse.com; 17 Scott St; s/d from per week $135/240) has a range of budget share accommodation around the city. The properties have single, double and twin rooms, share bathrooms, kitchens, lounge areas and usually a swimming pool and a garden; female-only apartments are available.

Cairns' wealth of self-contained accommodation works well for groups or families. Dozens of virtually identical motels are lined up along Sheridan St with rates from as little as $75 for a standard room. If you want to escape the urban tumult, consider basing yourself at one of Cairns' Northern Beaches (p331). The beaches are served by public transport and most tour operators can pick up and drop off at beach accommodation.

TOP CHOICE **Tropic Days** HOSTEL $
(☎1800 421 521, 4041 1521; www.tropicdays.com.au; 28 Bunting St; camping $11, tent $16, dm $26, d $64-74; ❄@📶🏊) Tucked behind the showgrounds (with a courtesy bus into town), Cairns' best hostel is a haven of tropical gardens strung with hammocks, and has a pool table, board games and a chilled vibe that makes it easy to stay longer than planned. Three- to four-bed dorms are bunk-free, doubles share spotless bathrooms, the kitchen's stocked with spices, and even non-guests can book for Monday night's croc, emu and roo barbecue ($12 including a didge show).

Floriana Guesthouse GUESTHOUSE $$
(☎4051 7886; www.florianaguesthouse.com; 183 The Esplanade; s $69, d $79-120; ❄@📶🏊) Cairns-of-old still exists at this old-fashioned place run by charismatic jazz musician Maggie. Picture original polished floorboards and art deco fittings. A swirling staircase leads to 10 individually decorated rooms; some have bay windows with window seats, others have balconies, and all come with en suites.

Shangri-La HOTEL **$$$**
(☎4031 1411; www.shangri-la.com; Pierpoint Rd; r from $270; ❄@📶🏊) In an unbeatable waterfront setting, towering over the marina, Shangri-La is Cairns' top hotel, a super-swish five-star that ticks all the boxes for location, views, facilities (including a gym and pool bar) and attentive service. The Horizon Club rooms are top-notch.

Floriana Villas APARTMENTS **$$**
(☎4041 2637; www.florianavillas.com.au; 187-189 The Esplanade; 1-/2-bed apt $140/180; ❄📶🏊) Next to the Floriana Guesthouse, this distinctive complex – built by a Maltese family in the 1940s – has been converted into enormous, contemporary self-contained apartments. Minimum stay is three nights; extras include free bike hire, a shaded pool with spa jets and a landscaped barbecue area.

Hotel Cairns HOTEL **$$$**
(☎4051 6188; www.thehotelcairns.com; cnr Abbott & Florence Sts; d $195-265; ❄📶🏊) There's a real tropical charm to this sprawling bone-white hotel, built in a traditional Queenslander plantation style. Rooms have an understated elegance and the huge 'tower' rooms and suites offer luxury touches such as wicker chaise longues and private balconies.

Reef Palms APARTMENTS **$$**
(☎1800 815 421, 4051 2599; www.reefpalms.com.au; 41-7 Digger St; apt $125-145; ❄@📶🏊) The crisp white interiors of Reef Palms' apartments will have you wearing your sunglasses inside. All rooms in this traditional Queenslander-style place have kitchen facilities; larger ones include a lounge area and a spa. Good for couples and families.

Northern Greenhouse HOSTEL **$$**
(☎1800 000 541, 4047 7200; www.friendlygroup.com.au; 117 Grafton St; dm/tw/apt $28/95/120; ❄@📶🏊) It fits into the budget category with dorm accommodation and a relaxed attitude, but this friendly place is a cut above, with neat studio-style apartments that have kitchens and balconies. The central deck, pool and games room are great for socialising. Freebies include breakfast and a Sunday barbie.

Cairns Holiday Park CARAVAN PARK **$**
(☎1800 259 977, 4051 1467; www.cairnscamping.com.au; 12-30 Little St; unpowered/powered/ensuite sites $32/39/50, cabins $60-85; ❄@📶🏊) The closest caravan park to central Cairns is 3.5km north of the city centre. A recent overhaul has resulted in smartly appointed bathroom and camp kitchen facilities, along with tidy backpacker cabins and free internet.

Travellers Oasis HOSTEL **$**
(☎4052 1377; www.travellersoasis.com.au; 8 Scott St; dm $26, s $45, d $64-74; ❄@📶🏊) Handmade timber furniture, sculptures, bright colours and a brand-new barbecue area make this soulful 50-bed backpacker hostel a laid-back place to hang out with like-minded travellers. Dorms are bunk-free, and private rooms share squeaky-clean bathrooms.

Il Palazzo BOUTIQUE HOTEL **$$$**
(☎1800 813 222, 4041 2155; www.ilpalazzo.com.au; 62 Abbott St; d from $195; ❄📶🏊) A replica of Michelangelo's *David* greets you in the foyer of this central boutique high-rise. It's quietly stylish, in a soft-focus, terracotta-urns Mediterranean kind of way, and the welcome and service are intimate compared with the big hotels. Opulent apartments have balconies, laundries and full kitchens, and there's a rooftop sundeck and on-site beauty salon.

Inn Cairns APARTMENTS **$$**
(☎4041 2350; www.inncairns.com.au; 71 Lake St; apt $125-188; ❄@📶🏊) Behind the unassuming facade, this is true inner-city apartment living. Take the lift up to the 1st-floor pool or to the rooftop garden for a sundowner. The elegant self-contained apartments come with wrought-iron and glass furnishings.

Cairns Girls Hostel HOSTEL **$**
(☎4051 2767; www.cairnsgirlshostel.com.au; 147 Lake St; dm/tw $20/48; @📶) Sorry, boys! With three well-equipped kitchens, spacious lounge areas and a manager who looks after you as if you were a guest in her own home, this 1900s-built, white glove–test clean, female-only hostel is one of the most accommodating budget stays in Cairns.

Serpent Hostel HOSTEL **$**
(☎1800 666 237, 4040 7777; www.serpenthostel.com; 341 Lake St; dm $24-28, d $55-75; ❄@📶🏊) About 2km north of the centre, this spiffing Nomads resort (*not* to be confused with Cairns' Nomads Esplanade) is a good-time backpacker bubble with a huge pool, beach volleyball, a sports bar, free evening meals and a free shuttle bus into town.

Bay Village RESORT **$$**
(☎4051 4622; www.bayvillage.com.au; cnr Lake & Gatton Sts; d $150-170; ❄@🏊) Smart units encircle a central pool at this sprawling resort. It's popular with package tours but no worse for that. Pricier rooms are self-contained, with kitchens and lounges; Balinese chefs

cook up aromatic cuisine at the on-site **Bay Leaf Restaurant** (mains $15-24; ⏲lunch Mon-Fri, dinner daily).

Mid City APARTMENTS **$$**
(☎4051 5050; www.midcity.com.au; 6 McLeod St; 1-/2-bedroom apt $175/200; ❄@📶🏊) The immaculate, terracotta-tiled apartments in this arctic-white building are truly self-contained, with superb kitchens, washing machines and dryers. Each has its own balcony, so try for a room with a view.

Acacia Court HOTEL **$$**
(☎1300 850 472; www.acaciacourt.com; 223-227 The Esplanade; d $120-145; ❄📶🏊) A stroll along the foreshore from town, this waterfront high-rise is great value for money. Rooms have beachy touches such as bright aqua bedspreads and a choice of ocean or mountain views; most have private balconies. Famed buffet restaurant Charlie's is downstairs.

Bellview GUESTHOUSE **$**
(☎4031 4377; www.bellviewcairns.com.au; 85-87 The Esplanade; dm/s/d $22/35/55, motel units $59-75; ❄🏊) Right on the Esplanade, this longstanding, family-run spot offers a central alternative to the rowdy backpacker scene. Budget rooms are pokey (it's worth paying extra for a motel unit) but overall it's a good-value, secure choice.

Cairns Beach House HOSTEL **$**
(☎1800 229 228; 239 Sheridan St; dm $13-20, d $50; ❄@📶🏊) Amped-up music greets you at the bar/bistro out front, but the converted motel-room dorms and doubles (with share bathrooms) at the rear are surprisingly quiet. Lots of freebies (brekkie cereal, evening meals and airport pick-ups) and plenty of travellers up for a party.

Waterfront Terraces APARTMENTS **$$$**
(☎4031 8333; www.cairnsluxury.com; 233 The Esplanade; 1-/2-bedroom apt $212/289; ❄📶🏊) Set in lush tropical grounds, these low-rise luxury apartments have handsomely furnished separate tiled lounges and kitchen areas and all the trimmings, including big balconies looking out over the ocean.

Balinese MOTEL **$$**
(☎1800 023 331, 4051 9922; www.balinese.com.au; 215 Lake St; d from $138; ❄@📶🏊) Bali comes to Cairns at this low-rise complex: waking up among the authentic wood furnishings and ceramic pieces, you may be taken with the sudden urge to have your hair beaded.

Sebel Cairns HOTEL **$$$**
(☎4031 1300; www.sebelcairns.com.au; 17 Abbott St; r $256-316; ❄@🏊) Sebel's exterior looks a little dated but the hotel is still the granddaddy of Cairns' five-stars, with a fine location, a colonial charm and surprisingly contemporary rooms with city, mountain or harbour views. Decadent touches include marble en suites and an on-site spa.

Gilligan's HOSTEL **$**
(☎4041 6566; www.gilligansbackpackers.com.au; 57-89 Grafton St; dm $26-32, d $130; ❄@📶🏊) The 'G spot' is pricey, impersonal and very loud, but all rooms at this flashpacker resort have en suites and most have balconies; higher-priced rooms come with fridges and TVs. There are several bars, as well as nightly entertainment such as jelly wrestling; a beauty salon; and a gym to work off all that beer. See also p326.

Cairns Coconut Caravan Resort CARAVAN PARK **$**
(☎1300 262 668, 4054 6644; www.coconut.com.au; cnr Bruce Hwy & Anderson Rd; powered/en-suite sites $43/60, cabins $70-125, villas $150-320; ❄@🏊) The last word in five-star caravan-park luxury, 8km south of the city centre. Spas, minigolf, an outdoor cinema and a slew of accommodation options.

Tropical Queenslander RESORT **$$**
(☎4051 0122; www.queenslanderhotels.com.au; 287 Lake St; apt from $125; ❄@📶🏊) Double dip here in the two pools, and relax in the smart apartments with kitchenettes, bathrooms and balconies.

Gecko's Backpackers HOSTEL **$**
(☎4031 1344; www.geckosbackpackers.com.au; 187 Bunda St; dm/s/d $23/35/56; ❄@📶🏊) Big old Queenslander behind the train station with a hippie-style vibe – great for travellers wanting to chill out away from the party scene. No en suites.

Villa Vaucluse APARTMENTS **$$**
(☎4051 8566; www.villavaucluse.com.au; 141-3 Grafton St; 1-bedroom apt $175; ❄🏊) Mediterranean decor meets with tropical influences. There is a central atrium, a secluded saltwater swimming pool and sumptuous self-contained apartments.

Cairns Central YHA HOSTEL **$**
(☎4051 0772; www.yha.com.au; 20-26 McLeod St; dm $26.50-36; ❄@🏊) Bright, spotless and professionally staffed.

Eating

Cairns' status as an international city is reflected in its multicultural restaurants, which often incorporate a tropical Aussie twist. Along the waterfront outside the Pier Marketplace, half a dozen restaurants with international cuisine share a boardwalk overlooking the marina – just wander along and take your pick.

If you want something cheap and quick, the Night Markets, between the Esplanade and Abbott St, have a busy Asian-style food court.

Some of Cairns' pubs dish up amazingly cheap meals to the thrifty backpacker hordes and they're not half bad. For some you need a meal token, available at hostels or from the free *Backpacker Xpress* magazine, or just ask about the special. Some of the best are at PJ O'Brien's, the Woolshed and Shenannigan.

TOP CHOICE Ochre MODERN AUSTRALIAN **$$$**
(☎4051 0100; www.ochrerestaurant.com.au; 43 Shields St; mains $30-36; ⊙lunch Mon-Fri, dinner nightly; ✎) In the ochre- and plum-toned dining room of this innovative restaurant, the changing menu utilises native Aussie fauna (such as croc with native pepper, or roo with quandong chilli glaze) and flora (from sides like wattle-seed damper loaf with peanut oil and native dukka, to desserts such as lemon-myrtle panacotta). If you can't decide, try a tasting plate ($23 to $36), or go all-out with a six-course tasting menu ($90, with wines $130). It also sells its house-speciality jams, spices and sauces to take home.

Green Ant Cantina MEXICAN **$$**
(☎4041 5061; www.greenantcantina.com; 183 Bunda St; mains $17-40; ⊙dinner) This funky little slice of Mexico behind the railway station is worth seeking out for its homemade quesadillas, enchiladas and Corona-battered tiger prawns. Great cocktail list, cool tunes (including an open-mic night on Sunday) and two-for-one backpacker meals on Monday.

Botanic Gardens Restaurant Cafe CAFE **$**
(www.cafebotanic.com.au; Collins Ave, Edge Hill; mains $14-19; ⊙7am-4.30pm) Under the rainforest canopy just inside the botanic gardens' main entrance, this lovely licensed cafe proudly boasts no fried food. Instead, choose from delicious dishes such as champagne-ham eggs benedict for brekkie, or roast chicken and macadamia nut salad or oven-baked baguette for lunch.

Charlie's SEAFOOD **$$**
(www.acaciacourt.com; 223-227 The Esplanade; buffet $28.50; ⊙dinner) It's not the fanciest place in town but Charlie's, at the Acacia Court hotel, is legendary for its nightly all-you-can-eat seafood buffet. Fill your plate (over and over) with prawns, oysters, clams or hot food and eat out on the poolside terrace. Great cocktails too.

Fusion Organics CAFE **$**
(www.fusionorganics.com; cnr Grafton & Aplin Sts; dishes $4-20; ⊙7am-4pm Mon-Fri, 7am-1pm Sat; ✎) In the wicker chair–strewn corner courtyard of an historic 1921 red-brick former ambulance station, Indian chefs spice up Fusion's organic, allergy-free fare such as quiches, frittatas, corn fritters and filled breads. Healthy brekkie options include buckwheat waffles and pick-me-up 'detox' juices.

Perrotta's at the Gallery MEDITERRANEAN **$$**
(☎4031 5899; 38 Abbott St; mains $27-33; ⊙breakfast, lunch & dinner; ✎) This chic spot adjoining the Cairns Regional Gallery tempts you onto to its covered deck's wrought-iron furniture for a breakfast of eggs, French toast with vanilla-roasted pear and superb coffee. An inventive Med-inspired menu takes over at lunch and dinner.

Marinades INDIAN **$$**
(☎4041 1422; 43 Spence St; mains $14-30; ⊙lunch & dinner Tue-Sun) A long, *long* menu of aromatic dishes such as lobster marinated in cashew paste, or Goan prawn curry, along with restrained decor in its dining room, make Marinades the pick of Cairns' Indian restaurants.

Edge CAFE **$**
(www.theedgefoodstore; 1/138 Collins Ave, Edge Hill; mains $10-18; ⊙7am-5.30pm Mon-Sat, 8am-3pm Sun; ✎) Up the road from the botanic gardens in the boutique shopping strip of Edge Hill, this gourmet fruit-and-veg grocer doubles as a sophisticated cafe serving great coffee, focaccias and locally produced sauces, jams and chocolate.

Naked Nut MEDITERRANEAN **$$$**
(☎4032 2136; 120 Collins Ave, Edge Hill; mains $29-37; ⊙lunch Fri & Sun, dinner Wed-Sun) Prawn, scallop and mussel vol-au-vent with dill *velouté* sauce, and traditional Italian lasagne with béchamel, hint at the mostly Mediterranean influences at this creative Edge Hill restaurant. It's licensed but you can BYO wine.

(Continued on page 325)

The Great Barrier Reef

Gateways to the Reef »
Top Reef Encounters »
Nature's Theme Park »
The Perfect Reef Trip »

A diver explores the wonderland of Kelso Reef (p27)

Gateways to the Reef

There are numerous ways to approach Australia's massive undersea kingdom. You can head to a popular gateway town and join an organised tour, sign up for a multiday sailing trip exploring less-travelled outer fringes of the reef, or fly out to a remote island, where you'll have the reef largely to yourself.

Port Douglas

1 An hour's drive north of Cairns, Port Douglas (p355) is a laid-back beach town with dive boats heading out to over a dozen sites, including more pristine outer reefs such as the Agincourt Reefs.

Townsville

2 Australia's largest tropical city (p264) is far from the outer reef (2½ hours by boat) but has some exceptional draws: access to Australia's best wreck dive, an excellent aquarium and marine-themed museums, plus multiday live-aboard dive boats departing from here.

Cairns

3 The most popular gateway to the reef, Cairns (p306) has dozens of boat operators offering both day trips and multiday reef explorations on live-aboard vessels. For the uninitiated, Cairns is a good place to learn to dive.

The Whitsundays

4 Home to turquoise waters, coral gardens and palm-fringed beaches, the Whitsundays (p238) have many options for reef-exploring: base yourself on an island, go sailing or stay on Airlie Beach and island-hop on day trips.

Southern Reef Islands

5 For an idyllic getaway off the beaten path, book a trip to one of several remote reef-fringed islands (p213) on the southern edge of the Great Barrier Reef. You'll find fantastic snorkelling or diving right off the island.

Clockwise from top left
1. A windswept vista at Port Douglas (p355) 2. Townsville's marina 3. Kewarra Beach (p333), northern Cairns

1

3

Top Reef Encounters

Donning a mask and fins and getting an up-close look at this marine wonderland is one of the best ways to experience the Great Barrier Reef. You can get a different take aboard a glass-bottomed boat tour, on a scenic flight or on a land-based reef walk.

Semisubmersibles

1 A growing number of reef operators (especially around Cairns) offer semi-submersible or glass-bottomed boat tours, which give cinematic views of coral, rays, fish, turtles and sharks – without ever getting wet.

Scenic Flights

2 Get a bird's-eye view of the vast coral reef and its cays and islands from a scenic flight. You can sign up for a helicopter tour (such as those offered from Cairns) or a seaplane tour (particularly memorable over the Whitsundays).

Diving & Snorkelling

3 The classic way to see the Great Barrier Reef is to board a catamaran and visit several different coral-rich spots on a long day trip. Nothing quite compares to that first underwater glimpse, whether diving or snorkelling.

Sailing

4 You can escape the crowds and see some spectacular reef scenery aboard a sailboat. Experienced mariners can hire a bareboat, others can join a multiday tour – both are easily arranged from Airlie Beach (p239), near the Whitsundays.

Reef Walking

5 Many reefs of the southern Great Barrier Reef are exposed at low tide, allowing visitors to walk on the reef top (on sandy tracks between living coral). This can be a fantastic way to learn about marine life, especially if accompanied by a naturalist guide.

MICHAEL AW / LONELY PLANET IMAGES ©

1

3

DAVID WALL / LONELY PLANET IMAGES ©

Clockwise from top left

1. View vivid anemone fish on a semisubmersible trip (p311)
2. Take a seaplane flight on Hayman Island (p256)
3. Experience the reef with a snorkel and flippers (p29)

CORAL AIR
WHITSUNDAY
HAYMAN

Nature's Theme Park

Home to some of the greatest biodiversity of any ecosystem on earth, the Great Barrier Reef is a marine wonderland. It's home to 30-plus species of marine mammals along with countless species of fish, coral, molluscs and sponges. Above the water, 200 bird species and 118 butterfly species have been recorded on reef islands and cays.

Commonly encountered fish species include dusky butterfly fish, which are a rich navy blue, with sulphur-yellow noses and back fins; large and lumbering graphic turkfish, with luminescent pastel coats; teeny neon damsels, with darting flecks of electric blue; and six-banded angelfish, with blue tails, yellow bodies and tiger stripes.

The reef is also a haven to many marine mammals, such as whales, dolphins and dugongs. Dugongs are listed as vulnerable, and a significant number of them live in Australia's northern waters; the reef is home to around 15% of the global population. Humpback whales migrate from Antarctica to the reef's warm waters to breed between May and October. Minke whales can be seen off the coast from Cairns to Lizard Island in June and July. Porpoises and killer and pilot whales also make their home on the reef.

One of the reef's most-loved inhabitants is the sea turtle. Six of the world's seven species (all endangered) live on the reef and lay eggs on the islands' sandy beaches in spring or summer.

LEONARD ZELL / LONELY PLANET IMAGES ©

1

3

BOB HALSTEAD / LONELY PLANET IMAGES ©

Clockwise from top left

1. Barracuda are among many fish species that inhabit the reef **2.** Nesting turtle, Lady Elliot Island (p214) **3.** Giant soft coral, Coral Sea

The Perfect Reef Trip

A Two-Week Itinerary

Along with experiencing the majesty of the Great Barrier Reef on snorkelling and diving trips, this itinerary includes a sailing excursion around coral-trimmed cays, rainforest walks and idyllic stays on tropical islands fronting white-sand beaches.

BOB CHARLTON / LONELY PLANET IMAGES ©

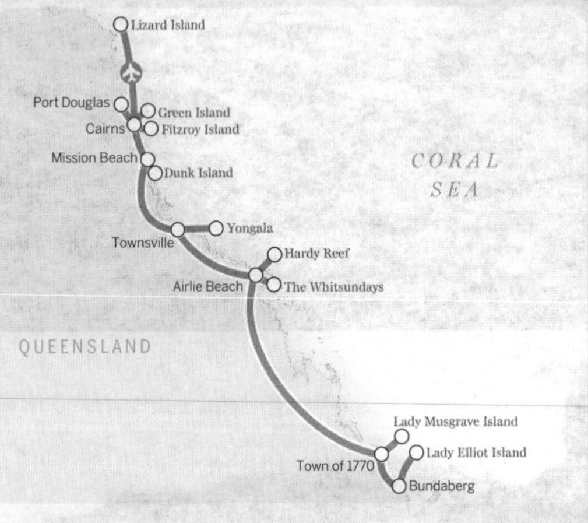

ANDREW BAIN / LONELY PLANET IMAGES ©

» After arriving in Bundaberg, take a seaplane to **Lady Elliot Island** (p214), an island resort with superb snorkelling and diving.

» Head north to the **Town of 1770** (p215) and day-trip out to **Lady Musgrave Island** (p214), for semisubmersible coral-viewing, plus snorkelling or diving in a pristine blue lagoon.

» Continue to **Airlie Beach** (p243) and book a two-night sailing cruise exploring the Whitsundays' white-sand beaches and coral gardens.

» Back at Airlie, board a catamaran to **Hardy Reef** (p241), a spectacular 13km-long reef with a suspended lagoon and 'waterfalls' that drain it.

» Go north to **Townsville** (p264), visiting the excellent Reef HQ aquarium; if you're an experienced diver, book a trip on a live-aboard boat to dive the **Yongala** (p269).

» Unwind on **Mission Beach** (p291), with rainforest walks, and overnight on nearby **Dunk Island** (p298), which has good bushwalking, swimming and snorkelling.

» Head to **Cairns** (p306), and take day trips to stunning **Green and Fitzroy Islands** (p335), both with rainforest and fringing coral.

» Pretty **Port Douglas** (p355) is next. From here visit the Agincourt Reefs, home to excellent diving and snorkelling sites.

» If time and money allow, add on a trip to **Lizard Island** (p385), gateway to some of Australia's best diving sites.

Above
1. Idyllic Lady Musgrave Island (p214) **2.** Rainforest trek to Mt Kootaloo, Dunk Island (p298)

(Continued from page 316)

Cherry Blossom JAPANESE $$$
(☎4052 1050; www.cherryblossom.com.au; cnr Spence & Lake Sts; mains $29-53; ⏰lunch Tue-Fri, dinner Mon-Sat) This 1st-floor restaurant is reminiscent of an *Iron Chef* cook-off, with two chefs working at opposite ends of the restaurant floor. Book ahead for sushi, teppanyaki and plenty of theatre.

First House VIETNAMESE $$
(☎4051 5153; 55 Spence St; mains $11-20; ⏰11am-9pm) Serving continuously throughout the day (a rarity for Cairns restaurants), this small, simple Vietnamese restaurant is a good bet if you like pork, which appears in virtually every dish. Unlicensed but BYO.

Adelphia Greek Taverna GREEK $$
(☎4041 1500; www.adelfiagrektaverna.com; cnr Aplin & Grafton Sts; mains $21-30; ⏰lunch Fri, dinner Tue-Sun) Plate-smashing, Mediterranean music, belly dancing and heaping portions of authentic Greek cuisine make this taverna, run by a trio of brothers, a fun family night out. Call for entertainment times and kids' specials.

Villa Romana Trattoria ITALIAN $$
(www.villaromana.com.au; cnr Aplin St & The Esplanade; mains $19-34; ⏰lunch & dinner) With solid Italian credentials (its other branch is on Lygon St, Melbourne) and enormous portions, Villa Romana's meat and seafood dishes would do Mama proud. Vegetarian options are limited, especially at lunch.

Beethoven Cafe CAFE $
(105 Grafton St; dishes $7-16; ⏰7am-5pm Mon-Thu, 6.30am-5pm Fri, 6.30am-3pm Sat; ✎) Continental open-face rolls and sandwiches the size of doormats are the signature of this busy bakery-cafe. Choose from the 30-odd combinations suggested – such as *Buendnerfleisch* (air-dried beef, Swiss cheese and gherkin) – or invent your own. Leave room for homemade strudel or cheesecake.

Meldrum's Pies in Paradise PIES $
(97 Grafton St; pies $4.50-5.50; ⏰7am-5pm Mon-Fri, 7am-2.30pm Sat; ✎) A Cairns institution, Meldrum's bakes some 40 inventive varieties of the humble Aussie pie – from chicken and avocado to pumpkin gnocchi or tuna mornay.

Raw Prawn SEAFOOD $$$
(☎4031 5400; www.rawprawnrestaurant.com.au; The Esplanade Centre, The Esplanade; mains $29-40; ⏰lunch & dinner) Fine-dining affair especially renowned for its seafood platters ($54 to $90 per person). The priciest include succulent mud crab.

Dolce & Caffe CAFE $$
(Shop 1, Mantra Esplanade, Shields St; dishes $5.50-18.50; ⏰6am-4.30pm Mon-Sat, 7am-4.30pm Sun; ✎) A local fave for its sublime coffee and super-fresh salads.

La Fettuccina ITALIAN $$
(www.lafettuccina.com; 41 Shields St; mains $24-30; ⏰dinner) Homemade sauces are a speciality at this small, atmospheric Italian restaurant. Try for a seat on the tiny, internal wrought-iron mezzanine balcony. Licensed and BYO.

Vanilla Gelateria ICE CREAM $
(cnr The Esplanade & Aplin Sts; cone or cup $3.80-5.80; ⏰9.30am-11pm) Cairns has several hole-in-the-wall gelatarias like this one, with icy concoctions such as Toblerone, and lemon, lime and bitters – even Red Bull!

Sushi Zipang JAPANESE $
(39 Shields St; sushi $3-8, mains $13-20; ⏰lunch & dinner) The novelty of a sushi-laden conveyor belt wending its way around the bar just never wears off, does it? Zipang also serves traditional noodle and rice dishes.

Self-Catering

Rusty's Markets (Grafton St, btwn Shields & Spence Sts; ⏰5am-6pm Fri, 6am-3pm Sat, 6am-2pm Sun) Cairns' main food market; in among the souvenirs, jewellery, crafts and clothing you'll find seafood, fresh fruit and veg, herbs and honey, as well as juice bars and food stalls.

Asian Foods Australia (101-5 Grafton St) Sells food products from all over Asia.

Drinking & Entertainment

Cairns holds the mantle as the party capital of the north Queensland coast and the number of places to go out for a drink is intoxicating. The busiest inner-city bars and clubs are geared towards the lucrative backpacker market. Thursdays tend to be the biggest night of the week, but you'll find plenty of action on any given night, even in the Wet.

Most venues are multipurpose, offering food, alcohol and some form of entertainment, and you can always find a beer garden or terrace to enjoy balmy evenings. Live music hits stages all over town; the Tanks Arts Centre (p307) hosts well-known pop, rock, indie and folk artists. Jazz buffs should check the weekly roster for performances at www.tropicjazz.org.au. Nightclubs come and go; ask locally about what's hot (and not). Clubs generally close at 3am or later; cover charges usually apply.

The website www.entertainmentcairns.com and the free *Backpacker Xpress* magazine list the hot spots.

TOP CHOICE **Salt House** BAR
(www.salthouse.com.au; 6/2 Pierpoint Rd; 9am-2am) Next to Cairns' new yacht club, Salt House has a sleek nautical design. It has become the city's most sought-after bar since it opened a couple of years ago. Actually two bars: the luxury yacht–styled Sailing Bar, with live music, and the Balinese-influenced Deck Bar, with killer cocktails and DJs hitting the decks.

Vibe Bar & Lounge BAR
(www.vibebarcairns.com; 39 Lake St; 10.30am-1am Mon-Thu, 10.30am-5am Fri, noon-5am Sat, 5am-3am Sun) Walk through the unassuming street entrance to the cathedral-like back room with funky artworks adorning the walls and couches in the corners at this gay-friendly 'Melbourne-style' lounge bar. The dance floor cranks from 9pm nightly.

Pullman Reef Hotel Casino CASINO, BARS
(www.reefcasino.com.au; 35-41 Wharf St; 9am-3am Sun-Thu, 9am-5am Fri & Sat) Cairns' casino has table games (blackjack, roulette, baccarat et al), as well as hundreds of bling-bling poker machines. Also four restaurants; four bars, including **Vertigo Bar & Lounge**, with free live music; and a pumpin' nightclub, **Velvet Underground** (www.myspace.com/clubvelvetunderground), which also hosts ticketed shows.

Gilligan's BARS, NIGHTCLUB
(www.gilligansbackpackers.com.au; 57-89 Grafton St; 9am-late) You're guaranteed a crowd at Cairns' biggest and busiest backpacker resort, with 400-odd backpackers staying here. But it's also popular with locals for its immense beer deck, live bands, and DJs spinning house tunes, and cocktails in its upstairs lounge bar.

Court House Hotel PUB
(38 Abbott St; 9am-late) In Cairns' gleaming white former courthouse building, dating from 1921, the Court House pub is replete with a polished timber island bar and Scales of Justice statue – and cane-toad races on Wednesday nights.

12 Bar Blues JAZZ
(62 Shields St; 7pm-late Tue-Sun) The best place in Cairns for loungy live music, this intimate bar grooves to the beat of jazz, blues and swing. Songwriter open-mic nights take place on Thursdays, with general open-mic nights on Sundays.

Shenannigans BAR
(www.shenanniganshotel.com.au; 48 Spence St; daily until late) The huge beer garden with barrels for tables, big screens and a music stage is the stand-out at this marginally Irish-themed pub attached to a backpacker hostel. Entertainment spans trivia nights and karaoke to live bands.

Pier Bar & Grill BAR
(www.pierbar.com.au, Pierpoint Rd; 11.30am-late) A local stalwart for its waterfront location and well-priced meals. The Pier's Sunday session is a must.

Grand Hotel PUB
(33 McLeod St; 11am-1am) This laid-back local is worth a visit just so you can rest your beer on the bar – an 11m-long carved crocodile!

Starry Night Cinema CINEMA
(www.endcredits.org.au; Flecker Botanic Gardens, Collins Ave, Edge Hill; admission $10; May-Nov) Every third Wednesday of the month, classic films screen in the tropical outdoors of the botanic gardens. Gates open at 6.30pm, shorts start at 7.30pm.

PJ O'Briens BAR
(www.pjobriens.com.au; cnr Lake & Shields St; daily until late) Sticky carpets and the smell of stale Guinness but Irish-themed PJ's packs 'em in with party nights, pole dancing and dirt-cheap meals.

Woolshed Chargrill & Saloon BAR
(24 Shields St; daily until late) Another backpacker magnet. A young crowd of travellers and dive instructors gets hammered and dances on the tables.

Hotel Cairns BAR
(www.thehotelcairns.com; cnr Abbott & Florence Sts; daily until late) This grand dame hotel is a low-key alternative to Cairns' hurdy-gurdy party scene, with nightly piano and double bass performances.

Rhino Bar BAR
(http://rhinobarcairns.com; cnr Spence & Lake Sts; from 8pm) A high-energy crowd downs cocktails and shots and spills out onto the enormous 1st-floor balcony. Can get messy.

Jute Theatre THEATRE
(☎4031 9555; www.jute.com.au; CoCA, 96 Abbott St; tickets $17-30) Stages a variety of con-

temporary Australian works and indie plays in the Centre of Contemporary Arts.

Rondo Theatre THEATRE
(☎4031 9555; www.cairnslittletheatre.com; Greenslopes St) The Cairns Little Theatre Co puts on a season of community plays and musicals at this theatre opposite Centenary Lakes.

Cairns City Cinemas CINEMA
(108 Grafton St) Mainstream flicks.

BCC Cinemas CINEMA
(Cairns Central Shopping Centre) First-release films.

Shopping

Cairns offers the gamut of shopping opportunities, from high-end boutiques like Louis Vuitton to garishly kitsch souvenir barns. You'll have no trouble finding a box of macadamia nuts, some emu or crocodile jerky, fake designer sunglasses and tropical-fish fridge magnets.

Markets MARKETS
Head to the **Night Markets** (The Esplanade; ⏲4.30pm-midnight) and **Mud Markets** (Pier Marketplace; ⏲Sat morning) if your supply of 'Cairns Australia' T-shirts is running low, or you need your name on a grain of rice.

The Tanks Arts Centre (p307) hosts a monthly **market day** (last Sun of month Apr-Sep) with high-quality local arts and crafts as well as entertainment.

Shopping Centres MALLS
Central Cairns has two multilevel shopping centres, where you can browse in a climate-controlled bubble: the enormous **Cairns Central Shopping Centre** (www.cairnscentral.com.au; McLeod St; ⏲9am-5.30pm Mon-Wed, Fri & Sat, 9am-9pm Thu, 10am-4.30pm Sun), with a couple of supermarkets and a huge range of speciality stores selling everything from books to bikinis; and the smaller **Pier Marketplace** (Pierpoint Rd), which was developed as a waterfront shopping mall but at the time of writing had only a limited range of specialist boutiques.

Over 100 fashion and homewares brands are massively discounted at the **Direct Factory Outlets** (DFO; www.dfo.com.au; 274 Mulgrave Rd; ⏲9am-5pm) shopping mall south of the city centre.

Bookshops BOOKS, MAPS
Secondhand bookshops in Cairns include **Bookshelf** (www.thebookshelfcairns.com.au; 95 Grafton St), whose proceeds go to a women's centre, and **Exchange Bookshop** (www.exchangebookshop.com; 78 Grafton St). **Absells Chart & Map Centre** (☎4041 2699; Main Street Arcade, 85 Lake St) carries an impressive range of quality regional maps, topographic maps and nautical charts.

Information

Emergency

Cairns Police Station (☎4030 7000)

Internet Access

Most tour-booking agencies and accommodation places have internet access; dedicated internet cafes are clustered along Abbott St, between Shields and Aplin Sts. They have fast connections, cheap international phone calls, printing facilities, CD burning and wi-fi, and charge around $3 to $5 per hour. Cairns Central Shopping Centre and Pier Marketplace both have basic self-serve, coin-operated terminals and wi-fi. Most of the public wi-fi hot spots in Cairns require payment.

Call Station (123 Abbott St; per hr $3; ⏲9am-9pm)

Global Gossip (www.globalgossip.com; 125 Abbott St; per hr $4; ⏲9am-11pm Mon-Fri, 10am-10pm Sat & Sun)

Medical Services

Cairns Base Hospital (☎4050 6333; The Esplanade) Has a 24-hour emergency service.

Cairns City 24 Hour Medical Centre (☎4052 1119; cnr Florence & Grafton Sts) General practice and dive medicals.

Cairns Travel Clinic (☎4041 1699; 15 Lake St; 8.30am-5.30pm Mon-Fri, 9am-noon Sat) Vaccinations, medical kits and advice.

Money

Major banks have branches with ATMs throughout central Cairns. Most banks exchange foreign currency; private currency-exchange bureaux line the Esplanade and are open longer hours.

American Express (63 Lake St) In Westpac Bank.

Travelex (75 Abbott St)

Post

Main post office (www.auspost.com; 13 Grafton St) Handles poste restante. There are branches in Orchid Plaza and in Cairns Central Shopping Centre.

Tourist Information

The glut of tourist information available can either inspire you to do something wild, or baffle you with its sheer volume. Most places to stay have tour-booking desks, and dozens of commercial tour-booking agents operating in Cairns call themselves 'information centres' and brandish an 'i' symbol (white on a blue background, with an upright 'i'). The only officially accredited visitor information centre (represented by a yellow, italicised '*i*' on a blue background) is the government-run **Cairns & Tropical North Visitor Information Centre** (☎4051 3588; www.tropicalaustralia.com.au; 51 The Esplanade; ⌚8.30am-6.30pm). In addition to impartial advice, the centre books accommodation and tours, houses an interpretive centre, and distributes the *Welcome to Cairns* directory and map. It's also the main point of contact for the wider region stretching north to Cape York and south to Mission Beach.

Other useful contacts:

Cairns Discount Tours (☎4055 7158; www.cairnsdiscounttours.com.au) Knowledgeable booking agent for day trips and tours, specialising in last-minute deals.

Department of Environment & Resource Management (DERM; ☎13 74 68; www.derm.qld.gov.au; 5b Sheridan St) Information on national parks and state forests, walking trails and camping permits.

Far North Queensland Volunteers (☎4041 7400; www.fnqvolunteers.org; 68 Abbott St) Arranges volunteer positions with nonprofit community groups.

Royal Automobile Club of Queensland (RACQ; ☎4033 6433; www.racq.com.au; 537 Mulgrave Rd, Earlville) Maps and information on road conditions state-wide including Cape York. It also has a recorded **road-report service** (☎1300 130 595).

Getting There & Away

Air

International routes from **Cairns Airport** (www.cairnsairport.com) include **Jetstar** (www.jetstar.com.au) to Auckland, Singapore, Tokyo and Osaka; **Cathay Pacific** (www.cathaypacific.com) to Hong Kong; and **Air New Zealand** (www.airnewzealand.com) to Auckland.

Domestically, **Jetstar** (☎13 15 38; www.jetstar.com.au), **Qantas** (☎13 13 13; cnr Lake & Shield Sts, City Pl; www.qantas.com.au) and **Virgin Blue** (☎13 67 89; www.virginblue.com.au) fly to major destinations including Brisbane (two hours), Sydney (four hours), Melbourne (five hours), Adelaide (four hours) and Darwin (two hours). Perth and Hobart usually require a change in Sydney or Melbourne.

Skytrans (☎1800 818 405, 4046 2462; www.skytrans.com.au) services Cape York with regular flights to Cooktown, Coen, Bamaga and Lockhart River, as well as Burketown, Normanton in the Gulf and Mt Isa and Cloncurry.

Hinterland Aviation (☎4035 9323; www.hinterlandaviation.com.au) has one to four flights daily except Sunday to/from Cooktown (one-way $150, 40 minutes), and two to Lizard Island (bookable through Lizard Island Resort, p386).

Bus

Cairns is the hub for Far North Queensland buses.

Greyhound Australia (☎1300 473 946; www.greyhound.com.au; Reef Fleet Terminal) has four daily services down the coast to Brisbane ($310, 29 hours), via Townsville ($81, six hours), Airlie Beach ($139, 11 hours) and Rockhampton ($215, 18 hours). Bus passes can reduce costs. Departs from outside Reef Fleet Terminal at the southern end of the Esplanade.

Premier (☎13 34 10; www.premierms.com.au) also runs one daily service to Brisbane ($205, 29 hours) via Innisfail ($19, 1½ hours), Mission Beach ($19, two hours), Tully ($26, 2½ hours), Cardwell ($30, three hours), Townsville ($55, 5½ hours) and Airlie Beach ($90, 10 hours).

CAIRNS TO CAPE YORK (& BACK) BY CARGO FREIGHTER

A unique and relaxing way to see the Cape is aboard the **MV Trinity Bay** (www.seaswift.com.au), the supply ship for the Cape York Peninsula and the Torres Strait. Sure, there's no pool and no shuffleboard. But watching the crew unloading everything from crates of bananas to council garbage bins to ambulances is fascinating, air-conditioned cabins (some en suite) are comfortable, and the on-board bar opens each afternoon.

The MV *Trinity Bay could* be a one-way ride: three days unwinding on deck as the Cape floats by and cargo is transferred by crane to a barge offshore from Lockhart River, docking at historic Horn Island and the Torres Strait's maritime hub, Thursday Island, then disembarking on the mainland at Seisia near the Tip (with the chance to visit by 4WD if the ship's schedule allows) and flying down from Bamaga. (Or joining a 4WD safari, or transporting your own vehicle and driving in the Dry.) But you'd be missing out on two more tranquil days on board back to Cairns, feasting on crew-sustaining buffets; watching leaping dolphins, coral-coloured sunsets and star-filled skies; and being rocked to sleep by the sea.

See p392 for details.

Cheaper bus passes available. Departs from Stop D, Lake St.

Trans North (☎4061 7944; www.transnorthbus.com) has two to five daily bus services connecting Cairns with the Tableland, serving Kuranda ($4, 30 minutes, five daily), Mareeba ($16.80, one hour), Atherton ($22, 1¾ hours) and Ravenshoe ($33, 2½ hours), as well as three services weekly to Herberton ($28, two hours), continuing on to Karumba ($140, 12 hours). Departs from 46 Spence St.

John's Kuranda Bus (☎0418 772 953) A service between Cairns and Kuranda ($4, 30 minutes) two to five times daily, departing from Lake St Transit Mall.

Sun Palm (☎4087 2900; www.sunpalmtransport.com) runs two northern services from Cairns to Cape Tribulation ($78, three hours) via Port Douglas ($35, 1½ hours) and Mossman ($40, 1¾ hours) with additional services direct to Port Douglas; and south to Mission beach ($49, two hours).

Country Road Coachlines (☎4045 2794; www.countryroadcoachlines.com.au) runs a service between Cairns and Cooktown on the coastal route via Port Douglas and Cape Tribulation three times a week ($75) leaving Cairns Monday, Wednesday and Friday and returning from Cooktown Tuesday, Thursday and Saturday, depending on the condition of the Bloomfield Track. Another service takes the inland route via Mareeba on Monday, Wednesday and Friday ($75; same day return).

Car & Motorcycle

Most car rental companies restrict the driving of conventional 2WD vehicles to sealed roads; to travel to Cooktown via the unsealed Bloomfield Track (the coastal route), you'll need a 4WD. If you're in for the long haul, check out the noticeboard on Abbott St for used campervans and ex-backpackers' cars.

All the major car rental companies have branches in Cairns and at the airport, with discount car and campervan rental companies proliferating throughout town. Daily rates start at around $45 for a late-model small car and around $80 for a 4WD.

Choppers Motorcycle Tours & Hire (☎0408 066 024; www.choppersmotocycles.com.au; 150 Sheridan St) Hire a Harley from $160 to $250 a day, or smaller bikes from $95 a day. Also offers motorcycle tours, from one hour to a full-day ride to Cape Trib.

Train

Cairns' **train station** (Bunda St) is on the southwest side of the Cairns Central Shopping Centre. The *Sunlander* departs Cairns on Tuesday, Thursday and Saturday for Brisbane (one-way from $219, 31½ hours). There's also the Scenic Railway (p342) to Kuranda. For more details, contact **Queensland Rail** (☎1800 872 467; www.traveltrain.com.au).

ℹ Getting Around

To/From the Airport

The airport is about 7km north of central Cairns; many accommodation places offer courtesy pick-ups. **Sun Palm** (☎4087 2900; www.sunpalmtransport.com; adult/child $10/5) meets all incoming flights and runs a shuttle bus to the CBD. **Black & White Taxis** (☎13 10 08) charges around $26.

Bicycle

Bike hire is available from some accommodation places or try the following:

Bike Man (☎4041 5566; www.bikeman.com.au; 99 Sheridan St; per day/week $20/60) Hire, sales and repairs.

Cairns Bicycle Hire (☎4031 3444; www.cairnsbicyclehire.com.au; 47 Shields St; per day/week from $15/45, scooters from $85 per day) Groovy bikes and scooters.

Bus

Sunbus (☎4057 7411; www.sunbus.com.au) runs regular services in and around Cairns from the Lake St Transit Mall, where schedules are posted. Useful routes include: Flecker Botanic Gardens/Edge Hill and Machans Beach (bus 7), Holloways Beach and Yorkeys Knob (buses 1C, 1D and 1H), Trinity Beach, Clifton Beach and Palm Cove (buses 1N, 1X, 2, 2A). Most buses heading north go via Smithfield. All are served by the (almost) 24-hour night service (N) on Friday and Saturday. Heading south, bus 1 runs as far as Gordonvale.

Taxi

Black & White Taxis (☎131 008) has a rank near the corner of Lake and Shields Sts, and on McLeod St, outside Cairns Central Shopping Centre.

SOUTH OF CAIRNS

South of Cairns, a lush pocket of rainforest offers a rewarding trip for walkers and wildlife watchers. The surrounding towns and settlements also provide fascinating windows onto the area's heritage.

The first town, **Gordonvale** (population 4420), 24km south of Cairns, is a delightfully old-fashioned community, with a disproportionate number of timber pubs set around its central park, an enormous sugar mill – and the dubious honour of being the first place where cane toads were released in 1935. It's backed by the looming 922m peak **Walsh's**

Pyramid, one of the world's highest free-standing natural pyramids. A hard-going but worthwhile walking track (6km return, six hours) runs from the base to the summit. Start out early and take plenty of water.

The Gillies Hwy (Hwy 52) heads south-west from Gordonvale through the ranges to the southern Atherton Tableland. To the east, a turn-off leads to the Yarrabah Aboriginal Community. At the time of writing, the Cairns & Tropical North Visitor Information Centre (p327) was advising visitors that the community was not generally accessible to the public – check for updates.

Babinda

POP 1170

On the Bruce Hwy, 60km south of Cairns, Babinda is a small working-class town that leads into mythical rainforest and boulders. It's the traditional home of the Yidinyji people, and the town's name comes from the Aboriginal *bunna binda,* loosely meaning 'waterfall'. Increasingly, it's known as the 'umbrella town', and paintings of umbrellas throughout the village centre attest to its claim as the wettest town in Australia – giving Tully and its gumboot a run for its money.

Babinda's main attraction is 7km inland. At the **Boulders**, a fast-running creek rushes between 4m-high granite rocks. It's croc-free, though beware of surging water after heavy rain and take care on the slippery rocks at any time. The point where swimming is out of bounds – downstream from the main pool – is clearly signposted; numerous drownings have occurred here over the years. According to Aboriginal legend, the boulders were formed when a tremendous upheaval shook the local tribe. A young couple, whose love was forbidden, was discovered and forcibly separated at this spot. Rather than go back to her tribe without her lover, the young woman threw herself into the creek. The moment she did, calling for her lover, rushing water flooded the area and the land shuddered, throwing up the giant boulders. It's said that her spirit still guards the rocks, and that her cries can sometimes be heard, luring young men into the dangerous waters.

Walking trails lead to **Devil's Pool Lookout** (470m) and the **Boulders Gorge Lookout** (600m).

Just before the picnic area at the car park is the free **Boulders Camping Ground** (two-night maximum), which has toilets, cold showers and free barbecues. There are just five sites, with a maximum of five people per site.

South of the Boulders, 3.3km from the town centre, you can kayak the clear waters of Babinda Creek almost all the way back to town with **Babinda Kayak Hire** (☎4067 2678; www.babindakayakhire.com.au; 330 Stager Rd; per half-/full day $35/50). Prices include pick-ups.

In town, the excellent Aboriginal-run art gallery, **Babinda Heritage Blessing** (☎4067 2333; 29-33 Munro St; ⏲8am-5pm Mon-Fri, 8am-4.30pm Sat, 3-5pm Sun) is around the corner from the visitor centre. The gallery is operated by artists Judy Ross-Kelly and Mat Kadir, who offer the opportunity to **make your own didgeridoo** ($200). Start with an authentic, ready-to-use plain didge, come up with a design (you can paint or burn it), and finish with some expert playing lessons before taking it home. The day includes lunch, a trip to the Boulders and Dreaming stories thrown in, as well as transfers from Cairns. Bargain.

Queensland's only remaining state-owned pub is the **Babinda State Hotel** (73 Munro St). The pub was built in 1917 by the government, which controlled the sale of alcohol (otherwise prohibited within the Babinda Sugar Works Area). Not surprisingly, it was regularly flooded with canecutters at the end of a shift, and remains popular today for its cold beer and good-value **Chinese restaurant** (mains $11-15; ⏲dinner Tue-Sun).

If you're in town on the weekend, try to catch a film while reclining in a hessian-slung seat at the timeless, 1950s-built **Munro Theatre** (www.babindacentre.com.au; Munro St; tickets $7; ⏲screenings 7.30pm Fri-Sun).

The **Babinda visitor centre** (☎4067 1008; www.cairnsgreatbarrierreef.org.au; cnr Munro St & Bruce Hwy; ⏲9am-4pm) has stacks of information on the area.

Bramston Beach

POP 300

About 6km south of Babinda, turn east at tiny Mirriwinni down a 17km road winding through rolling cane fields and patches of rainforest (keep an eye out for cassowaries) to one of the north coast's undiscovered gems, peaceful Bramston Beach.

Overlooked by most tourists – who don't know what they're missing – this long stretch of coarse golden sand is practically deserted and undeveloped compared to beaches north of Cairns, and is an idyllic spot to get away for a while. A stinger net is erected during summer; watch out for crocs at the estuaries either end of the beach.

Bramston Beach Camping Ground (☎4067 4121; The Esplanade; unpowered sites $16.50) is basic but right on the foreshore, with hot showers, gas barbecues and a laundry.

Also just a few metres stroll from the beach, the stylish little motel **Bramston Beach Seaside Haven** (☎4067 4139; www.bramstonbeachmotorinn.com; 1-3 Dawson St; d $90-110; ❄≋) was undergoing a change of ownership at the time of research – check for updates on its spacious units, restaurant and bar.

The heart of Bramston Beach's small residential community is the **Bramston Beach Cafe & Store** (☎4067 4129; 67 Evans Rd; mains $7-14; ⏲9am-6pm Mon-Thu, 9am-8pm Fri, 8am-7pm Sat, 8am-6pm Sun). As well as fab food (fresh Spanish mackerel, spicy African Mama fish burgers, veggie burgers), and chilled roots and blues tunes playing on the wooden deck, it stocks groceries, has fuel and a post office outlet, and rents bikes ($15 per day) to explore the surrounding national park.

Wooroonooran National Park

Part of the Wet Tropics World Heritage Area, Wooroonooran National Park is a veritable *Who's Who* of natural spectacles: it has the state's highest peak, dramatic falls and everything in between.

The rugged tropical rainforest in the Josephine Falls section of the park covers the foothills and creeps to the peak of Queensland's highest mountain, **Mt Bartle Frere** (1622m). It provides a shielded and exclusive environment for a number of plant and animal species. The car park for **Josephine Falls** – a spectacular series of waterfalls and pools – is signposted 6km off the Bruce Hwy, about 10km south of Babinda.

The falls are a steep but paved 600m walk through the rainforest and along a mossy creek. At the bottom pool you can swim in a circle of clear pools fringed by the massive roots of towering trees, and scamper up the rock face to a natural water slide – kids love it. Beware: the smooth rocks connecting the pools are slippery and can be treacherous, and the flow can be powerful after rain, when flash flooding can occur, so be extremely careful.

The falls are at the foot of the Bellenden Ker Range. The **Mt Bartle Frere Summit Track** (15km, two days return) leads from the Josephine Falls car park to the summit. Don't underestimate this walk: the ascent is for fit, experienced and well-equipped walkers only. Rain and cloud can close in suddenly. There's also an alternative 10km (eight-hour) return walk to Broken Nose. Pick up a trail guide from the nearest visitor centre or contact **DERM** (☎13 74 68; www.derm.qld.gov.au; 5b Sheridan St, Cairns). Camping (sites per person $5.15) is permitted along the trail; book ahead as self-registration is not possible.

For the Palmerston (Doongan) section of Wooroonooran National Park, see p300.

CAIRNS' NORTHERN BEACHES

A string of independent communities cling to the 26km stretch of coast north of Cairns, each separated by the twists and turns of the coastline and reached by signposted turn-offs from the Captain Cook Hwy. Closer to Cairns – and in places where the water is too shallow to swim – residential neighbourhoods enjoy the quiet life on the city's hem. Where the beach becomes more inviting, you'll find sunbeds, seasonal stinger nets, resorts and restaurants bunched along the waterfront esplanades. There's a distinctive beach-holiday vibe and each has its own character: Yorkeys is popular with sailors and Trinity with families, while Palm Cove is a swanky honeymoon haven. Only Ellis Beach and Palm Cove have camping grounds.

Machans Beach

Heading north from Cairns, the first turn-off you come to is to Machans Beach, a small community strung along the waterfront. Apart from private holiday rentals, there's no accommodation here, but there is a welcoming, low-key restaurant and bar. **Ebony & Ivory** (☎4055 0398; 169 O'Shea Esplanade; mains $15-30; ⏲4-10pm Tue-Fri, 9am-10pm Sat & Sun) serves pub-style steaks and seafood on its deck overlooking the beach.

Holloways Beach

The Coral Sea meets a rough ribbon of sand at quiet Holloways Beach. It's a mostly residential area, with beachside homes making way for a handful of tourist developments.

Pacific Sands (☎4055 0277; www.pacificsandscairns.com; 1-19 Poinciana St; d $140; ❄📶🏊) is a complex of bright self-contained two-bedroom apartments stretching one block back from the beach.

There's a flash tropical ambience to the one-bedroom apartments at **Cairns Beach Resort** (☎1800 150 208, 4037 0400; www.cairnsbeachresort.com.au; 129 Oleander St; d $163-225; ❄@🏊), which are as close to Cairns as you can get for pure beachfront accommodation. Sea-view apartments are more expensive than garden-view apartments, but worth it.

Breezy cafe **Strait on the Beach** (100 Oleandar St; mains $9-19; ⏰7.30am-5.30pm Mon-Thu, 7.30am-7.30pm Fri, 7.30am-6pm Sat & Sun) has a chunky timber deck overlooking the beach – perfect for reading the paper over coffee or breakfast. It carries the beach theme through to its driftwood-inspired seating, and has a small shop where you can stock up on the basics, as well as fuel.

For something classier, reserve a table by the sand at **Coolum's on the Beach** (☎4055 9200; www.coolums.com.au; cnr Hibiscus & Oleandar Sts; mains $27-39; ⏰dinner Tue-Sat). Beef and reef fare includes seafood linguine and rib-eye steak.

Bogeys on Palm (22 Palm St; mains $10-18; ⏰from 3pm) dishes up pizzas, curries and live music on Thursdays.

Yorkeys Knob

The most appealing of Cairns' Northern Beaches, Yorkeys is a sprawling, low-key settlement on a white-sand beach. In the crescent-shaped Half Moon Bay is the marina, supporting 200 bobbing boats.

'Yorkey' was the nickname of a fisherman who originally hailed from Yorkshire and worked here in the 1880s. Known for his gumption and dogged nature, he attempted to grow pumpkins on the top of the knob and established a bêche-de-mer (p336) curing station on Green Island.

The 'knob' is the rocky headland that cradles the bay to the north, allowing the wind to whip the water south. This wind is fuel for the many kitesurfers and windsurfers. **Kite Rite** (☎0409 283 322; www.kiterite.com.au; Shop 1, 471 Varley St; per hr $79) offers instruction, including gear hire, and a two-day certificate course ($499). Its booking office and shop is in the **Yorkeys Knob shopping centre** (Varley St), which has a supermarket, a bottle-shop, cafes and takeaway food.

Nonmembers are welcome at the **Half Moon Bay Golf Club** (4055 7933; www.halfmoonbaygolf.com.au; 66 Wattle St; 18 holes $35), a lovely lush course with sea views.

A block-or-so back from the beach, adjoining a patch of rainforest, **Villa Marine** (☎4055 7158; www.villamarine.com.au; 8 Rutherford St; d $119-159; ❄📶🏊) is the best-value spot in Yorkeys. Friendly owner Peter is a mine of info on the area and makes you feel at home in the retro-style, single-storey self-contained apartments arranged around a sparkling pool.

The mid-size complex **York Beachfront Apartments** (☎4055 8733; www.yorkapartments.com.au; 61-63 Sims Esplanade; apt $135-170; ❄@📶🏊) has apartments with fully equipped kitchens and laundries, and separate bedrooms with en suite. Throw open the sliding doors to your balcony and breathe in the sea views.

Hidden down a side road at Yorkeys' southern end, a private path leads to the beach from **Golden Sands** (☎4055 8033; www.goldensandsresort.com.au; 12-14 Deauville Close; 1-bedroom apt $145-165, 2-bedroom apt $210; ❄📶@🏊). First-rate facilities include a solar-heated pool, a tennis court and small gym, and a French restaurant incongruously named **Water Dragon** (mains $22-29; ⏰dinner Wed-Sun).

TOP CHOICE **Yorkeys Knob Boating Club** (☎4055 7711; www.ykbc.com.au; 25-29 Buckley St; mains $17-29; ⏰lunch & dinner daily, breakfast Sat & Sun; 🖉) is a diamond find – it serves up some of the freshest seafood in north Queensland (which is really saying something!). Go for the cod if it's on the menu, or the cooked-to-perfection calamari, order a schooner (or two – there's a local courtesy bus) and take a seat on the deck and dream about sailing away on one of the luxury yachts moored out front.

Trinity Beach & Around

High-rise developments detract from Trinity Beach's long stretch of sheltered white sand, but holidaymakers love it – turning their backs to the buildings and focusing on what is one of Cairns' prettiest Northern Beaches.

Around the next bay to the north is residential **Kewarra Beach**, home to a prestigious golf course at **Paradise Palms Resort & Country Club** (☎4059 9999; www.paradisepalms.com.au; 457/9 Paradise Palms Dr; 18 holes incl cart hire $120).

From its lofty position atop Trinity's headland, the soaring high-rise complex **Amaroo** (☎4055 6066; www.amarooresort.com; 92-94 Moore St; d $149-159;) has tasteful self-contained apartments and commanding views of the beach below. Steps lead down to the sand; there's a two-night minimum stay.

Self-contained apartments are just footsteps from the beach at **Castaways** (☎4057 6699; www.castawaystrinitybeach.com.au; cnr Trinity Beach Rd & Moore St; 1-/2-bedroom apt $132/165;), which has three pools, spas, tropical gardens and good stand-by rates.

Comfort Inn & Suites Trinity Beach Club (☎4055 6776; www.trinitybeachclub.com.au; 19-23 Trinity Beach Rd; 1-/2-bedroom apt $150/180;) has spacious single-level one-bedroom apartments and mezzanine two-bedroom apartments a 200m stroll to the beach. Don't be fooled by the 'vacancy' sign, which stays up out front even when it's full (because, they told us, they can't be bothered taking it down). Still, families will find it worth booking ahead for facilities including kitchen hobs and full laundries. Minimum stay is three nights.

TOP CHOICE **L'Unico Trattoria** (☎4057 8855; www.lunico.net.au; 75 Vasey Esplanade; mains $22-44; lunch & dinner, breakfast Sat & Sun;) opens to a wraparound wooden deck. The stylish Italian cuisine at this beachside find includes veal medallions in marsala sauce, homemade four-cheese gnocchi and wood-fired pizzas, along with superb specials such as scallops in creamy chilli sauce – accompanied by a stellar wine list and professional service.

Bangkok Rose (www.bangkokrose.com.au; 81 Vasey Esplanade; lunch & dinner;) cooks up aromatic Thai fare.

Clifton Beach

Local and leisurely, Clifton Beach has a good balance of residential and holiday accommodation and services. You can walk north along the beach about 2km to Palm Cove.

Clifton Palms (☎4055 3839; www.cliftonpalms.com.au; 35-41 Upolu Esplanade; cabins/units from $69/108, 2-bedroom apt from $145;) has freestanding single-storey apartments backed by a curtain of green hills. There's a big poolside barbecue area, a range of accommodation options to suit any budget or family group, and value for money is jaw-droppingly good.

Opposite Clifton Palms, **Clifton Capers Bar & Grill** (14 Clifton Rd; mains $23-25; lunch & dinner Wed-Sun) is highly rated among locals with a range of pastas and pizzas – from prawns with pineapple and bacon to roast lamb with Mediterranean veggies and rosemary. Casual service in a pleasant, relaxed setting; live music most Sundays.

Palm Cove

The St-Tropez of Cairns' Northern Beaches, Palm Cove is all about glamour and indulgence. More intimate than Port Douglas and much more upmarket than its southern neighbours, Palm Cove is essentially one big promenade along Williams Esplanade, with a gorgeous stretch of white-sand beach and top-notch restaurants luring sunlovers out of their luxury resorts.

Sights & Activities

Beach strolls, shopping and leisurely swims will be your chief activities here but there's no excuse for not getting out on the water.

Palm Cove Watersports KAYAKING, HIKING
(☎0402 861 011; www.palmcovewatersports.com) Offers 1½-hour early-morning sea-kayaking trips ($56) and half-day paddles to Double Island (adult/child $96/68), offshore from Palm Cove. It also runs a half-day hike to Lake Placid and the Barron Gorge (adult/child $92/72).

Beach Fun Co WATER SPORTS
(☎0411 848 580; www.tourismpalmcove.com) Hires catamarans ($50 per hour), jet skis ($60/80 per single/double for 15 minutes), paddle boats ($30) and boogie boards ($10), and organises jet-ski tours around Double Island and Haycock Island (single/double from $120/180). Fishing boats start at $100 per two hours.

Cairns Tropical Zoo ZOO
(☎4055 3669; www.cairnstropicalzoo.com.au; Captain Cook Hwy; adult/child $32/16; 8.30am-5pm) Just west of Palm Cove, this zoo offers an up-close wildlife experience with crocodiles and snakes, koala photo sessions and kangaroo feeding…and, if you're planning a Palm Cove honeymoon, a Wildlife Wedding Chapel.

Its **Cairns Night Zoo** (adult/child $97/48.50; ⏲7-10pm Mon-Thu & Sat) experience includes a barbecue dinner, a guided tour of the zoo's nocturnal creatures, a spot of stargazing and campfire entertainment.

Transfers are available from Palm Cove, Port Douglas and Cairns and the Northern Beaches.

Sleeping

Most of Palm Cove's accommodation has a minimum three-night stay.

TOP CHOICE **Sebel Reef House** HOTEL $$$
(☎1800 079 052, 4055 3633; www.reefhouse.com.au; 99 Williams Esplanade; d from $299; ❄@📶🏊) The Sebel is more intimate and understated than most of Palm Cove's resorts – more like an old British Empire tropical mansion. Hardly surprising since it was once the private residence of an army brigadier. The whitewashed walls, wicker furniture and big beds romantically draped in muslin all add to the air of refinement. The Brigadier's Bar works on a quaint honesty system; complimentary punch is served by candlelight at twilight.

Peppers Beach Club & Spa HOTEL $$$
(☎1300 987 600, 4059 9200; www.peppers.com.au; 123 Williams Esplanade; d from $290; ❄@📶🏊) Step through the opulent lobby at Peppers and into a wonder-world of swimming pools – there's the sand-edged lagoon pool and the leafy rainforest pool and swim-up bar, along with tennis courts and spa treatments. Even the standard rooms have private balcony spas and the penthouse suites (from $540) have their own rooftop pool. Service exceeds even the highest expectations.

Double Island HOTEL $$$
(☎1300 301 992; www.doubleisland.com.au; d from $595; ❄@📶🏊) Privately owned Double Island is an ultraluxe retreat. Until recently, only one group at a time could rent the whole island (and, for around $33,000, up to 10 people still can), but individual rooms are now available for a minimum of three nights. Rates include the 10-minute transfer by boat across from Palm Cove.

Angsana Resort & Spa HOTEL $$$
(☎4055 3000; www.angsana.com; 1 Veivers Rd; d from $315; ❄@📶🏊) Pure beachfront luxury. Some rooms are split-level and a few have private pools. Spa treatments include two-hour massages.

Palm Cove Camping Ground CAMPING GROUND $
(☎4055 3824; 149 Williams Esplanade; unpowered/powered sites $16.50/23) Council-run beachfront camping ground near the jetty, with a barbecue area and laundry. No cabins but the only way to do Palm Cove on the cheap!

Silvester Palms APARTMENTS $$
(☎4055 3831; www.silvesterpalms.com; 32 Veivers Rd; 1-/2-/3-bedroom apt $110/130/190; ❄📶🏊) These bright self-contained apartments are an affordable alternative to Palm Cove's city-sized resorts. Good for families.

Melaleuca Resort APARTMENTS $$$
(☎1800 629 698, 4055 3222; www.melaleucaresort.com.au; 85-93 Williams Esplanade; d $195-218; ❄🏊) Named for the melaleuca trees that line Palm Cove's esplanade, this charming boutique resort has 24 one-bedroom apartments, all with kitchens, balconies and laundry facilities.

Eating & Drinking

Palm Cove has some fine restaurants and cafes strung along the Esplanade. All of the resort hotels have swish dining options open to nonguests.

TOP CHOICE **Beach Almond** MODERN ASIAN $$$
(☎4059 1908; www.beachalmond.com; 145 Williams Esplanade; mains $14-40; ⏲lunch & dinner) A rustic beach house near the jetty is the setting for Palm Cove's most inspired dining. Black-pepper prawns, ginger pork belly, Singaporean mud crab and Balinese barra are among the fragrant, freshly prepared innovations.

Nu Nu MODERN AUSTRALIAN $$$
(☎4059 1880; www.nunu.com.au; 123 Williams Esplanade; mains $31-47; ⏲breakfast, lunch & dinner) With one of the highest profiles on the coast, you'll need to book way ahead at the retro Nu Nu, which specialises in 'wild foods' such as beet-poached Angus tenderloin or roast chicken with leatherwood honey–grilled figs.

Colonies Cafe Bar & Grill FUSION $$
(☎4055 3058; www.palmcoveonline.com/colonies; 117 Williams Esplanade; mains $24-41; ⏲breakfast, lunch & dinner) Alfresco Colonies is a popular Mediterranean- and Mod Oz–style spot with world-music beats and a few Asian dishes spicing up the menu. It's licensed and BYO, with an easygoing ambience.

Apres Beach Bar & Grill BISTRO **$$**
(www.apresbeachbar.com.au; 119 Williams Esplanade; mains $23-39; ⏲breakfast, lunch & dinner) The most happening place in Palm Cove, with a zany interior of old motorcycles, racing cars and a biplane hanging from the ceiling, regular live music, and crowds spilling out onto the open deck. The menu runs the gauntlet from beer-battered prawns to jungle curry, but it's all pretty pricey for the venue.

Annie's Upstairs BISTRO **$$**
(Level 1, Palm Cove Shopping Village, Williams Esplanade; mains $21-29; ⏲dinner Wed-Mon; ✍) A clothing boutique by day, this casual spot creates Asian-inspired curries, kangaroo fillet and seafood. Licensed; BYO wine.

Surf Club Palm Cove LICENSED CLUB **$**
(www.thesurfclubpalmcove.com; 135 Williams Esplanade; meals $14-28; ⏲dinner) A great local for a drink in the sunny garden bar and bargain-priced seafood, plus decent kids meals.

El Greko GREEK **$$**
(www.elgrekostaverna.com.au; Level 1, Palm Cove Shopping Village, Williams Esplanade; mains $22-34; ⏲dinner; ✍) Souvlaki, spanakopita and moussaka are among the staples at this lively taverna. Good meze platters; belly dancing on Friday and Saturday nights.

ℹ Information

Commercially run tour-booking companies are strung along Williams Esplanade; Cairns & Tropical North Visitor Information Centre (p327) can help with bookings.

The two-storey, ice cream–coloured **Paradise Village Shopping Centre** (113 Williams Esplanade) has a post office (with internet access for $4 per hour), a small supermarket and a newsagent.

Ellis Beach

Ellis Beach is the last of the Northern Beaches and the closest to the highway, which runs right past it. The long sheltered bay is a stunner, with a palm-fringed, patrolled swimming beach and stinger net in summer. The view is spectacular as you drive in from the south. This is where the coastal drive to Port Douglas really gets interesting.

TOP CHOICE **Ellis Beach Oceanfront Bungalows** (☎1800 637 036, 4055 3538; www.ellisbeach.com; Captain Cook Hwy; unpowered sites $26, powered sites $32-38, cabins $85, bungalows $149-185; ❄@) offers camping and cabins, including contemporary bungalows, all of which enjoy widescreen ocean TV at this palm-shaded beachfront park. Paradise, except when the horse flies are out in force.

Across the road, **Ellis Beach Bar 'n' Grill** (Captain Cook Hwy; mains $8-24; ⏲breakfast, lunch & dinner) is the place for a feed. There's live music some Sunday afternoons and best of all, pinball.

One of the best opportunities in the north to see monster saltwater crocs from a safe distance, **Hartley's Crocodile Adventures** (☎4055 3576; www.crocodileadventures.com; adult/child $32/16; ⏲8.30am-5pm) also has plenty of other wildlife including cassowaries, koalas and snakes. Events throughout the day include croc-farm tours, crocodile-feeding, 'crocodile attack' shows, and boat cruises on its large lagoon. For more on croc farms, turn to p301.

ISLANDS OFF CAIRNS

A short skim across the water from Cairns, Green and Fitzroy Islands make for great day trips; spend the afternoon snorkelling in crystal waters, walking in rainforest or just lazing on the beach. Each has a resort, so you can play five-star castaway for a few days, and there's a camping ground on Fitzroy Island. To really leave the day-trippers behind, cruise to and camp on the picturesque Frankland Islands.

Green Island

Green Island's long, dog-legged jetty heaves under the weight of boatloads of day-trippers. It's hardly surprising since this beautiful coral cay is only 45 minutes from Cairns and has a rainforest interior with interpretive walks, a fringing white-sand beach and snorkelling just offshore. As well as gentle walks through the leafy interior, you can walk around the island in about 30 minutes.

Before Green Island was named after the astronomer on Cook's *Endeavour*, the Gungandji people used it as a retreat to perform initiation ceremonies for the young men of their group. Commercial activity began around 1857 when the waters around Green Island were heavily fished for bêche-de-mer (see p336). The animals were cured here before export, and many of the island's trees were logged in the process. The resultant traffic around the island and reports of people going missing inspired

BÊCHE-DE-MER

Those black sluglike creatures languishing on the ocean floor are variously known as bêche-de-mer, sea cucumbers, and *hai shen* to the Chinese, who consider them a delicacy.

Hai shen (which roughly translates as 'sea ginseng') is dried and used in soup and is said to be a longevity tonic and disease preventive. And, of course, there are the aphrodisiac claims – bêche-de-mer is believed to aid impotence caused by kidney problems.

There are hundreds of species of bêche-de-mer. What they all have in common are extraordinary physiological characteristics, which enable them to breathe through their anus and purge their innards. If sufficiently irritated, the bêche-de-mer's defence is to eject most of its internal organs, which it quickly regenerates.

the government to plant coconut palms on the island – thinking that shipwreck survivors could live on coconut meat and milk until they were found.

Today the island and its surrounding waters are protected by their national- and marine-park status. **Marineland Melanesia** (www.marinelandgreenisland.com; adult/child $17/8) has an aquarium with fish, turtles, stingrays and crocodiles, as well as a collection of Melanesian artefacts.

The luxurious **Green Island Resort** (☎1800 673 366, 4031 3300; www.greenislandresort.com.au; ste $570-670; ❄@☒) has stylish split-level suites, each with its own private balcony. Island transfers are included. The resort has an exclusive feel but it's partially open to day-trippers (using a separate pool), so even if you're not staying you can enjoy the restaurants, bars, ice-cream parlour and water-sports facilities.

Great Adventures (☎4044 9944; www.greatadventures.com.au; 1 Spence St, Cairns; adult/child $75/37.50) has Green Island transfers by fast catamaran, departing Cairns' Reef Fleet Terminal at 8.30am, 10.30am and 1pm and returning at noon, 2.30pm and 4.30pm. Snorkelling gear is included; pricier packages include glass-bottomed boat coral view tours, diving and scenic flights.

Big Cat (☎4051 0444; www.greenisland.com.au; adult/child from $75/37.50) also runs half- and full-day tours departing Cairns' Reef Fleet Terminal at 9am and 1pm. Prices include snorkelling gear or a glass-bottomed boat tour (extra $12 for both); add-ons such as semisubmersible trips are also available.

Alternatively you can sail to the island on the family-owned yacht **Ocean Free** (☎4052 1111; www.oceanfree.com.au; adult/child from $135/90), spending most of the day offshore at Pinnacle Reef, with a short stop on the island as well as a snorkel tour and fish feeding, and optional diving.

Fitzroy Island

A steep mountaintop rising from the sea, Fitzroy Island has coral-strewn beaches, woodlands and walking tracks, camping and a flash refurbished resort.

The Indigenous Gungandji people, who know this island as Gabarra, have hunted and fished from the island for centuries. Cook named the island Fitzroy, after the prime minister of the day, when the *Endeavour* left for its Pacific journey. In 1877 the island was used to quarantine Chinese immigrants bound for the goldfields. Thousands were compulsorily detained for 16 days and observed for signs of smallpox. Squalid conditions contributed to the deaths of hundreds of Chinese, and a number of unmarked graves remain.

Today the island is a national park, with the resort occupying a small portion. The most popular snorkelling spot is around the rocks at **Nudey Beach** (1.2km from the resort), which, despite its name, is not clothing-optional, so bring your togs.

On the island there are two walking tracks where you should spot some of the island's resident birds and butterflies. The 20-minute **Secret Garden Walk** is a leisurely stroll through rainforest that returns along the same path. The hour-long **Lighthouse & Summit Trail** leaves from the northern end of Welcome Bay and heads steeply up to the lighthouse, which was the last staffed lighthouse in Australia. From here there are views to Little Fitzroy Island below.

You can pitch a tent at the **Fitzroy Island Camping Ground** (☎4044 3044; sites $28), run by Cairns Regional Council. It has showers, toilets and barbecues; advance bookings are essential.

The **Fitzroy Island Resort** (☎4044 6700; www.fitzroyisland.com; studios $195, cabins $299, 1-/-2-bedroom ste $350/515) has luxurious accommodation, from sleek studios and beachfront cabins through to a decadent-and-then-some penthouse ($1899). Its restaurant, bar and kiosk are open to day-trippers.

Raging Thunder (☎4030 7900; www.ragingthunder.com.au; Reef Fleet Terminal, Cairns; island transfers adult/child $58/31.50) runs island transfers twice a day, leaving Cairns at 8.30am and 10.30am and returning at 3pm and 5pm. There are also a range of day trips including lunch and a glass-bottomed boat tour.

Frankland Islands

If the idea of hanging out on one of five uninhabited coral-fringed islands with excellent snorkelling and stunning white sandy beaches appeals – and if not, why not? – cruise out to the Frankland Group National Park. These continental islands consist of High Island to the north and four smaller islands to the south: Normanby, Mabel, Round and Russell.

Camping is available on High or Russell Islands, which both feature rainforest areas. Numbers are limited on Russell where camping is only permitted on weekdays outside peak season. Camping on Russell is free but permits must be obtained in advance from the **DERM** (☎13 74 68; www.derm.qld.gov.au) office in Cairns. Book online for High Island ($5.15 per person). You must be fully self-sufficient as there is no water on the islands; advance bookings during the Dry are essential. There's a four-night maximum stay at this time (seven nights in the Wet) – in case you were getting any ideas about dropping out of the rat race for a while.

Frankland Islands Cruise & Dive (☎4031 6300; www.franklandislands.com.au; adult/child from $136/84) runs excellent day trips, which include a cruise down the Mulgrave River, snorkelling gear and lunch. Guided snorkelling tours with a marine biologist and diving packages are also offered. Transfers for campers to/from Russell Island are available. Boats depart from Deeral; transfers from Cairns and the Northern Beaches cost $16 per person.

You'll need to organise your own boat or charter to reach High Island.

ATHERTON TABLELAND

The beauty of the Cairns region doesn't end at the reef. Climbing back from the coast between Innisfail and Cairns are the highlands known as the Atherton Tableland. It's the fertile food bowl of the region, where altitude does its best to defeat humidity and quaint rural towns are sprinkled between patchwork fields, pockets of rainforest, and spectacular lakes, waterfalls and Queensland's highest mountains: **Bartle Frere** (1622m) and **Bellenden Ker** (1591m).

Non-Indigenous Australians and other migrants first came to the Tableland in the 1870s in search of gold. Mining spurred the development of roads and railways, though farming soon became the chief commercial activity. European occupation of the country severely impacted on the original inhabitants (from the Djirbal language group), who were displaced from their lands, trade routes and ceremonial areas. Today, efforts are being made to protect areas of cultural significance through education and site management.

Your own wheels are ideal for exploring the Tableland's fruit wineries and coffee farms, lake fishing, swimming and hiking, and seeking out eco-wilderness lodges and luxurious B&Bs.

Four main roads lead in from the coast: Palmerston Hwy (Hwy 25) from Innisfail, Gillies Hwy from Gordonvale, Kennedy Hwy (Hwy 1) from Cairns, and Rex Range Rd between Mossman and Port Douglas. The following section follows the Kennedy Hwy from Cairns and heads south before looping up along the Gillies Hwy back to Cairns.

Getting There & Around

There are bus services to the main towns from Cairns (generally three services on weekdays, two on Saturday and one on Sunday), but not to the smaller towns or all the interesting areas *around* the towns.

Trans North (☎0400 749 476; www.transnorthbus.com) has regular bus services connecting Cairns with the Tableland, departing from 46 Spence St and running to Kuranda ($4, 30 minutes), Mareeba ($16.80, one hour), Atherton ($22, 1¾ hours) and Herberton ($28, two hours, three per week). **John's Kuranda Bus** (☎0418 772 953; www.kuranda.org; one-way $4) runs a service between Cairns and Kuranda two to five times daily. Buses depart from Cairns' Lake St Transit Mall. **Kerry's** (☎0427 841 483) serves Ravenshoe ($33, 2½ hours).

Kuranda

POP 1430

Reached by a switchback road, a scenic railway or Australia's longest gondola cableway from Cairns, artsy, alternative Kuranda is the Tableland's most popular day trip. Between about 10am and 3.30pm, this tiny rainforest village is crawling with tourists poking through its ever-expanding markets and visiting its wildlife sanctuaries. Even at its most crowded, you can still appreciate the beautiful setting and superb walking trails. But it's outside peak hours that you'll see it transform into the mellow spot that made it so popular with hippies in the late '60s, many of whom still live here today.

Sights & Activities

Art Galleries ART GALLERIES

Djurri Dadagal Art Enterprises (DDAE; ☎0428 645 945; 9 Coondoo St; ⏲9.30am-3.30pm) Many of the authentic paintings, artefacts, screen prints and textiles at this Indigenous art cooperative are produced on-site by local artists. Community leader and proprietor Wanegan (Glenis Grogan; p340) commissions artworks and buys authentic pre-completed works, and is passionate about giving visitors an insight into her people.

For works by local artists using a wide range of media, check out the artist-run **Kuranda Arts Co-op** (www.artskuranda.asn.au; Shop 5, 20 Coondoo St; ⏲10am-4pm).

For information on Kuranda's well-known markets, see p342.

Walking WALKS

Walking trails wind in and around the village. Many are the traditional pathways of the Indigenous Djabagny; some paths later became pack routes linking the goldfields with the coast. Across the train line by the station a path leads down to the Barron River. Follow the path downstream to the railway bridge (1km, 20 minutes). This bridge marks the start of the **Jungle Walk section** (0.8km, 15 minutes), a paved track that runs between Barron Gorge Rd meeting the **Jumrum Creek Walk** (800m, 15 minutes). You can walk the 3.5km loop or take one section as a short return walk. The Jumrum Creek Walk starts/finishes on Coondoo St and links to a 2km walk along a narrow road (no footpath) to the beautiful **Barron Falls**, or you can drive to the falls lookout and follow the trail.

For a **guided walk** after dark, when the rainforest's inhabitants are at their most active, join **Dr Dave's Night Walks** (75min walk

Kuranda

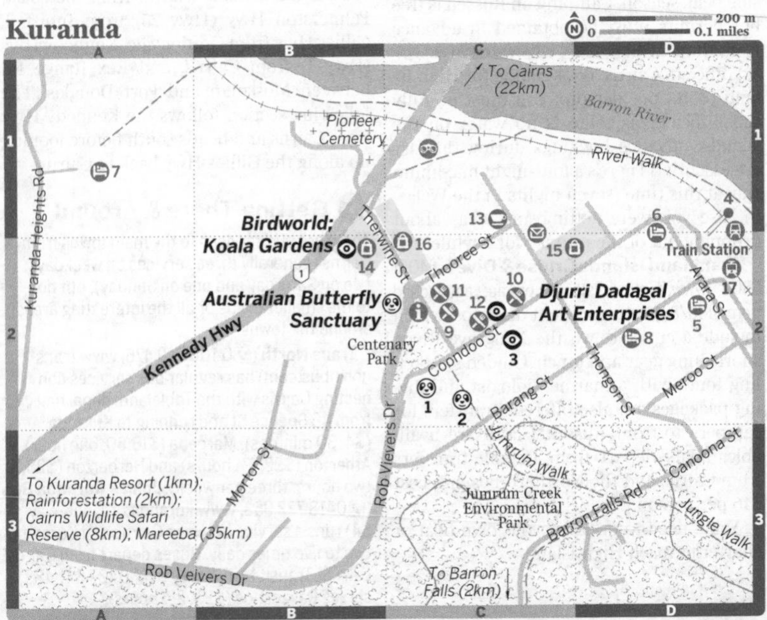

$25), departing from the Kuranda Rainforest Park caravan park.

Kuranda Riverboat BOAT CRUISE

(☎4093 7476; www.kurandariverboat.com.au; adult/child $15/7; ⏲hourly 10.30am-2.30pm) One of the most relaxing ways to see the Barron River is aboard a 45-minute cruise. The departure dock is behind the train station, over the footbridge; buy tickets on board.

Wildlife Sanctuaries & Zoos SANCTUARIES, ZOOS

There's loads of wildlife in Kuranda – in zoos and sanctuaries as well as the rainforest.

BatReach BAT-RESCUE CENTRE

(☎4093 8858; www.batreach.com; Jumrum Walk; admission by donation; ⏲10.30am-2.30pm Tue-Fri & Sun) BatReach invites visitors to see the volunteer work being done at this rescue and rehabilitation centre for troubled fruit bats (flying foxes).

At the back of the Heritage Markets is a trio of hits for kids (and nature-lovers of any age). If you can wake 'em from their gum-leaf coma, you can cuddle a koala (there are wombats and wallabies too) at the **Koala Gardens** (www.koalagardens.com; adult/child $16/18; ⏲9am-4pm). The **Australian Butterfly Sanctuary** (www.australianbutterflies.com; 8 Rob Veivers Dr; adult/child $18/9; ⏲9.45am-4pm) is a fluttering butterfly aviary where you can see butterflies being bred in the lab and take a free 30-minute tour on request. **Birdworld** (www.birdworldkuranda.com; adult/child $16/8; ⏲9am-4pm) is an expansive aviary displaying free-flying native and exotic birds. Combination tickets for all three cost $42/21 per adult/child.

If you've ever worried about the creepies and crawlies outside your tent, the **Australian Venom Zoo** (www.tarantulas.com.au; 8 Coondoo St; adult/child $16/10; ⏲10am-4pm) will either ease your mind or scare the pants off you. A close-up look at Australian tarantulas, scorpions and venomous snakes – the zoo breeds creatures for venom extraction and, believe it or not, pets.

Rainforestation (www.rainforest.com.au; Kennedy Hwy; adult/child $40/20; ⏲8.30am-4pm) is an enormous tourist nature park located 3km west of Kuranda ($8 return bus transfers are available from Kuranda's visitor centre). The park is divided into three sections: native wildlife, river cruises and an Aboriginal show with boomerang- and spear-throwing. There's a lot to see; you can choose to do a particular section at a reduced cost.

Cairns Wildlife Safari Reserve (www.cairnswildlifesafarireserve.com.au; Kennedy Hwy; adult/child $28/14; ⏲9am-4.30pm), which isn't located in Cairns but 9km southwest of Kuranda, is as close as you'll get to an African safari in Queensland. Lions, cheetahs, hippos, rhinos and the odd tiger and bear roam the free-range zoo. Don't stick your

Kuranda

Top Sights

Australian Butterfly Sanctuary ... C2
Birdworld ... B2
Djurri Dadagal Art Enterprises ... C2
Koala Gardens ... B2

Sights

1 Australian Venom Zoo ... C2
2 BatReach ... C2
3 Kuranda Arts Co-op ... C2

Activities, Courses & Tours

4 Kuranda Riverboat ... D1

Sleeping

5 Kuranda Backpackers Hostel ... D2
6 Kuranda Hotel Motel ... D1
7 Kuranda Rainforest Park ... A1
8 Kuranda Villas ... D2

Eating

9 Annabel's Pantry ... C2
Fanny O'Reilly's Bar & Grill ... (see 6)
10 Frogs ... C2
11 German Tucker ... C2
Kuranda Rainforest Restaurant ... (see 7)
Nevermind Cafe ... (see 14)
12 Village Vibe ... C2

Drinking

13 Kuranda Coffee Republic ... C1

Shopping

14 Heritage Markets ... B2
15 New Kuranda Markets ... C2
16 Kuranda Original Rainforest Markets ... C2

Transport

17 Skyrail Rainforest Cableway Terminal ... D2

LOCAL KNOWLEDGE

WANEGAN (GLENIS GROGAN)

Proprietor, Djurri Dadagal Art Enterprises (DDAE)

Background? I'm a nurse and midwife and worked in academia; I set up the gallery in 2007 to stop the exploitation of our cultural products.

How many artists are involved?About 100...one lady still knows how to weave baskets traditionally used for fishing, she's keeping the culture alive by teaching younger ones to find the pandanus leaves, then cleaning, cutting, soaking, preparing and weaving them. My elderly uncle is teaching someone to make boomerangs. I love to paint; I also work with dancers and musicians.

Gallery philosophy? To be more than just a gallery: profits go back to the community, including a healing centre using Aboriginal ways, helping people overcome transgenerational grief, loss and trauma and helping them understand how they got so far removed from tribal culture.

Is exploitation of Aboriginal art still a big problem? Yes! Places sell 'Aboriginal' souvenirs made by non-Indigenous artists, including from overseas; they don't pay artists what their work is worth...there's no legislation in this country to prevent it. I couldn't just complain and not do anything, so the gallery is my 'doing'. It's all self-funded. Discerning visitors want to know what they're buying.

fingers outside the cage when a pride of lions prowl around during **Breakfast with the Beasts** (adult/child $49.50/29.50; ⏲7.30-10.30am)! Feedings and talks take place during the day.

Billabong Adventures HORSE RIDING
(☎4093 8929; www.billabongadventures.com.au; Mt Haren Rd; adult/child half-day tours from $102/79; ⏲daily) Take in the mountain views astride a horse or ATV quad bike at this adventure centre. No experience is necessary for either, but you'll need to wear long pants and closed shoes. Billabong is 5km northwest of Kuranda.

Sleeping

Central accommodation is thin on the ground, but the information centre has a list of places in the surrounding region.

Kuranda Hotel Motel MOTEL $$
(☎4093 7206; www.fireflykuranda.com.au; cnr Coondoo & Arara Sts; d $100-120; ❄🏊) This hotel motel is locally known as the 'bottom pub' (and is rebadging its accommodation section as 'Firefly'). The back of the Kuranda Hotel Motel has spacious '70s-style motel rooms with exposed brick and tinted crinkle-cut glass, enhanced with eye-catching artworks, quality linens, groovy light fittings and flat-screen TVs. All come with microwaves and fridges.

Kuranda Rainforest Park CARAVAN PARK $
(☎4093 7316; www.kurandarainforestpark.com.au; 88 Kuranda Heights Rd; unpowered/powered sites $26/28, s/d backpacker rooms $30/55, cabins $90-110; 📶🏊) This excellent, well-tended park lives up to its name, with grassy camping sites enveloped in rainforest. The basic but cosy private 'backpacker rooms' open on to a tin-roofed timber deck, cabins come with poolside or garden views, and the Kuranda Rainforest Restaurant is on-site. It's a 10-minute walk from town via a forest trail.

Miju Rainforest Retreat B&B $$
(☎4093 9304; www.mijurainforestretreat.com; 47 Bangalow Pl; d $125; 📶🏊) Situated 4km east of Kuranda off Saddle Mountain Rd, this self-contained two-bedroom brick property sits under the same roof as the home of its hosts, Mike and Julie (hence 'Miju'), with a private deck, kitchen with breadmaker, and use of their 12m pool. Mike and Julie are serious collectors of green tree frogs: at last count, they had over 840 (stuffed, crocheted, ceramic, you name it) scattered about. Rates include continental breakfast and a half-bottle of mango wine.

Kuranda Villas UNITS $$
(☎4093 7556; www.kurandavillas.com.au; 12 Barang St; d $130) Pair of bright, modern self-contained villas, one two-bedroom and one three-bedroom, right in the village. Coffee, tea and port included.

Kuranda Resort RESORT $$
(☎4093 7556; www.kurandaresort.com.au; 3 Green Hills Rd; dm $19, d $99-199;) Vast, mossy resort 2km west of town, getting back on its feet after a long decline. Bare-bones dorms and loft villas (most with ladder-accessed beds), two enormous pools, a tennis court, gym and **restaurant** (mains $15-40; by reservation).

Kuranda Backpackers Hostel HOSTEL $
(☎4093 7355; www.kurandabackpackershostel.com; cnr Arara & Barang Sts; dm/s/d $19/46/49;) This creaky, falling-apart Queenslander was operating under receivership at the time of writing, despite most utilities being cut off. Check for updates.

Eating & Drinking

TOP CHOICE **Kuranda Coffee Republic** CAFE $
(www.kurandacoffeerepublic.com.au; 10 Thongon St; coffee $1-5.50; 8am-4pm Mon-Fri, 9am-4pm Sat & Sun) Food is basically limited to biscotti, but who cares when the coffee's this good? You can see – and smell – the locally-grown beans being roasted on-site. Go for the silky Dark Matter blend – unless you're here for the three days leading up to the full moon, which is the only roasting time for the Full Moon Roast, infused with vanilla pod.

Frogs CAFE $$
(www.frogsrestaurant.com.au; 11 Coondoo St; mains $14-32; 10am-3pm Sun-Wed, 10am-7pm Thu-Sat;) Barra, prawns and a brilliant brekkie omelette (which they'll cook up at any time of day, if you ask nicely) are the staples of this breezy, family-run cafe. In the back garden, **Aboriginal dance shows** (admission by donation; 1pm) take place daily, weather permitting.

Kuranda Rainforest Restaurant SRI LANKAN $$
(88 Kuranda Heights Rd; mains $14-36; dinner Wed-Sun;) The fiery reef-fish red curry will blow your head off at this hidden spot at the back of the Kuranda Rainforest Park caravan park. If you're not a spice fan, ask for dishes, including roasted coconut pork curry and lamb marsala, to be served mild, or opt for the 'non curry eater' menu of pasta and steak.

Village Vibe CAFE $$
(5b Coondoo St; mains $8-15; breakfast & lunch;) With a cool name and cool decor (sunflower-yellow and cornflower-blue walls and funky artworks), this newcomer is winning over locals and visitors alike with its creamy hot chocolate and gourmet salads.

German Tucker GERMAN, AUSTRALIAN $
(☎4057 9688; Therwine St; dishes $6-10; 10am-2.30pm) Emu, crocodile or kangaroo sausages with sauerkraut? German Tucker serves extreme Australiana/traditional German fare and German beer.

Fanny O'Reilly's Bar & Grill PUB $$
(cnr Coondoo & Arara Sts; mains $17-27; lunch daily, dinner Mon-Sat) The full-length deck is a great place to watch the passing parade, and the Irish-style bar has good pub grub including a speciality Guinness pot pie.

Annabel's Pantry PIES $
(15 Therwine St; pies $4.10-4.50; breakfast & lunch;) With around 25 pie varieties, including kangaroo, and spinach-and-feta rolls, Annabel's is great for lunch on the run.

Nevermind Cafe ORGANIC $
(Heritage Markets; mains $13; breakfast & lunch;) Epitomising Kuranda's hippie vibe with organic smoothies, herbal teas and light meals such as nachos, but the reluctant service might see you saying 'never mind'...

WILDLIFE CONSERVATION VOLUNTEERING

If you're keen to get involved in wildlife conservation, the Tableland has some good opportunities for volunteers. Contact the organisations in advance to find out their requirements.

BatReach (☎4093 8858; www.batreach.com; Jumrum Walk, Kuranda; admission by donation; 10.30am-2.30pm Tue-Fri & Sun) Rescue and rehabilitation centre for orphaned fruit bats (flying foxes).

Tolga Bat Hospital (☎4091 2683; www.tolgabathospital.org; 134 Carrington Rd, Tolga; visitor centre adult/child $12/6; 3-6pm Wed-Sun Jun-Sep) Set up to save fruit bats threatened by ticks and loss of habitat. Volunteers are especially needed during tick paralysis season (October to January).

Eagle's Nest Wildlife Hospital (☎4097 6098; www.wildlife-sanctuary.info; Ravenshoe) Cares for wildlife, particularly birds.

Shopping

Kuranda Original Rainforest Markets MARKETS

(www.kurandaoriginalrainforestmarket.com.au; Therwine St; ⏲9am-3pm) With revamped boardwalks terraced in the rainforest and wafting incense, these markets first opened in 1978 and are still the best place to see artists such as glassblowers at work, pick up hemp products, and sample local produce such as honey and fruit wines.

Heritage Markets MARKETS

(www.kurandamarkets.com.au; Rob Veivers Dr; ⏲9am-3pm) Across the road from Kurunda, these markets overflow with souvenirs and crafts such as ceramics, emu oil, jewellery, clothing (lots of tie-dye) and pistachio-nut figurines.

New Kuranda Markets MARKETS

(www.kuranda.org; 21-23 Coondoo St; ⏲9am-4pm) The first place you come to if you're walking up from the train station, these markets are essentially just an ordinary group of shops.

Information

Kuranda visitor centre (☎4093 9311; www.kuranda.org; ⏲10am-4pm) Located in Centenary Park.

Getting There & Away

The Skyrail and Scenic Railway between Kuranda and Cairns are themselves big attractions and most people go up one way and down the other. Otherwise, it's only a 20-minute drive or cheap bus ride (p337) to/from Cairns.

Kuranda Scenic Railway (☎4036 9333; www.ksr.com.au; Cairns train station, Bunda St; adult/child one-way $45/23, return $68/34) winds 34km from Cairns to Kuranda through picturesque mountains and 15 tunnels. The line took five years to build and opened in 1891. The trip takes 1¾ hours and trains depart Cairns at 8.30am and 9.30am daily, returning from pretty Kuranda station (known for its floral displays) on Arara St at 2pm and 3.30pm.

Skyrail Rainforest Cableway (☎4038 1555; www.skyrail.com.au; adult/child one-way $42/21, return $61/30.50; ⏲9am-5.15pm) at 7.5km is one of the world's longest gondola cableways. The Skyrail runs from the corner of Kemerunga Rd and the Cook Hwy in the northern Cairns suburb of Smithfield (15 minutes' drive north of Cairns) to Kuranda (Arara St), taking 90 minutes. It includes two stops along the way with boardwalks and interpretive panels. The last departure from Cairns and Kuranda is at 3.30pm. Combination Skyrail and Scenic Railway deals are also available. As space is limited, only daypacks are allowed on board; advance bookings are recommended.

Mareeba

POP 6810

At the centre of industrious cattle, coffee and sugar enterprises, Mareeba is essentially an administrative and supply town for the northern Tableland and parts of Cape York Peninsula. The main street boasts some quaint old facades, and the region's natural beauty is typified by the expansive wetlands to the north.

Sights & Activities

A growing number of Mareeba's food producers have opened their doors for tours; see also p345. With over 300 days of sunshine annually, Mareeba is a hot-air ballooning mecca – see p312 for operators, which you can link up with in the Mareeba area.

Mareeba Heritage Museum & Tourist Information Centre MUSEUM

(☎4092 5674; www.mareebaheritagecentre.com.au; Centenary Park, 345 Byrnes St; admission free; ⏲8am-4pm) First stop in Mareeba should be this small but excellent museum with displays on the area's past and present commercial industries, as well as its natural surrounds. The attached visitor centre gives out discount vouchers for many of the area's attractions.

Mareeba Wetlands WILDLIFE RESERVE

(☎1800 788 755,4093 2514; www.jabirusafarilodge.com.au; adult/child $12/6; ⏲9am-4.30pm Apr-Jan) This 20-sq-km reserve of woodlands, grasslands, swamps and the expansive Clancy's Lagoon, is a birdwatchers' nirvana. A huge range of bird species flock here and you might see other animals such as kangaroos and freshwater crocs. Over 12km of walking trails crisscross the wetlands and various safari tours (from $38) depart during the week, or you can take a 30-minute eco-cruise (adult/child $15/7.50) or paddle in a canoe ($15 per hour). The on-site **Jabiru Safari Lodge** (cabins incl breakfast s $125-159, d $190-250) has solar-powered en suite tented cabins and a spa.

Take the Pickford Rd turn-off from Biboohra, 7km north of Mareeba.

Military Museums MUSEUMS

Aviation and military buffs should check out the **Beck Museum** (☎4092 3979; nbeck@ledanet.com.au; Kennedy Hwy; adult/child $12.50/6; ⏲10am-4pm Sat & Sun or by appointment). It's the biggest collection in Queensland and includes American fighter planes used over the Coral Sea during WWII.

WORTH A TRIP

CHILLAGOE

Even on a day trip, the charismatic former gold-rush town of Chillagoe, about 140km west of Mareeba, can fulfil any romantic notion you may have of the outback. With a raw, unhurried quality, it's at the centre of an area imbued with impressive limestone caves, Indigenous rock-art sites, and the ruins of an early-20th-century smelting plant.

From Mareeba, take the Dimbulah Hwy, which is also known as the Wheelbarrow Way, in honour of the early miners who pushed their barrows along the route. Each May, the three-day **Great Wheelbarrow Race** sees runners (solo and in teams) push a wheelbarrow the length of the route.

Leaving the Tableland, the landscape gradually changes from fertile farmland to dry woodland savannah. The road is sealed most of the way, save for 18km of the final 30km into Chillagoe (traversable by 2WDs in dry conditions). After passing through Dimbulah (population 500), a regional centre that developed in the 1930s around tobacco, you cross Eureka Creek. It's here that the terrain becomes characteristic of the outback, with rugged rusty plains supporting spindly vegetation, termite hills and hump-backed Brahman cattle. About 25km past Petford (population 20) is Almaden (population 30), a stop on the *Savannahlander* train, from where passengers are bussed to Chillagoe. Soon you'll start to see the limestone bluffs for which Chillagoe is known, and the giant marble pits that are dotted around the region. In 1910 Chillagoe's population peaked at 10,000. These days it's home to 350 people, and, in ice-to-Eskimo fashion, currently exports marble to Italy.

Chillagoe's excellent visitor centre, the **Hub** (☎4094 7111; www.chillagoehub.com.au; Queen St; ⏱8am-5pm Mon-Fri, to 3.30pm Sat & Sun), has interesting historical displays. Knowledgeable staff can direct you to Aboriginal **rock-art sites**, the local **swimming hole**, the old **smelter site**, a hodge-podge little **history museum** with a piano played during silent movies, and an eccentric local with a cool old **Ford collection**. It also books ranger-guided tours of Chillagoe's **limestone caves** (tours adult/child $21/16.50). Three of the 500-plus caves can be visited: **Donna** (⏱1hr tour at 9am), **Trezkin** (⏱45min tour at 11am) and **Royal Arch** (⏱90min tour at 1.30pm).

The annual **Chillagoe Rodeo** takes place in May.

Rustic-on-the-outside, modern-on-the-inside miners shacks make up **Chillagoe Cabins** (☎4094 7206; www.chillagoe.com; Queen St; d $140; ❄🏊), where the owner has a small wildlife-rescue menagerie and offers **town tours** ($20). There's a camp kitchen and barbecue, or you can order home-cooked **meals** (3-course meals $35).

Chillagoe's former post office is now the **Chillagoe Guesthouse** (☎4222 1135; www.chillagoeguesthouse.com.au; 16-18 Queen St; s/d from $100/120; ❄). Rates include a hamper with bacon and eggs to cook your own brekkie.

Chillagoe Observatory & Eco Lodge (☎4094 7155; www.coel.com.au; Hospital Ave; unpowered/powered sites $20/24, s/tw $30/45, d $80-100; ❄🏊) has a licensed **restaurant** (mains $18-25) and an **observatory** (90min tour adult/child $15/8; ⏱Apr-Oct) where you can scan the southern night sky.

The **Chillagoe Bus Service** (☎4094 7155; adult/child $36/27) departs from Chillagoe on Monday, Wednesday and Friday, returning from Mareeba on the same days. Billy Tea Bush Safaris (p312) runs day tours from Cairns.

At **Warbird Adventures** (☎4092 7391; www.warbirdadventures.com.au; Mareeba Airport, Kennedy Hwy; museum adult/child $7.50/4; ⏱10am-4pm Wed-Sun) you can see restored vintage planes as well as take a half-hour joy flight ($355 to $850) in a Nanchang, Winjeel, Harvard or Kittyhawk; an extra $50 includes swooping aerobatics. An **air show** takes place in August.

Granite Gorge Nature Park WALKING, SWIMMING
(☎4093 2259; www.granitegorge.com.au; adult/child $10/2) This privately owned nature park occupies a volcanic region of huge granite boulders populated by rock wallabies, **walking tracks** and waterfalls tumbling into a croc-free **swimming hole**. There are picnic areas and a **camping ground** (per person unpowered/powered sites $12/16; incl park entry). Granite Gorge is 12km southwest of Mareeba.

Follow Chewko Rd south of Mareeba for 7km, from where the turn-off is signposted to your right.

Wine & Whiskey Producers WINERY, DISTILLERY
For a tropical tipple, **Golden Drop Mango** (☎4093 2750; www.goldendrop.com.au; 227 Bilwon Rd; ⏰8am-6.30pm), 2km off the highway north of Mareeba, offers tastings of its sweet mango wine.

Queensland's only whisky distillery is the stunningly designed **Mt Uncle Distillery** (☎4086 8008; www.mtuncle.com; 1819 Chewko Rd, Walkamin; ⏰10am-5pm), which also produces seasonal liqueurs and spirits using local bananas, coffee, mulberries and lemons (tastings available, of course). Its gin is made from 14 Australian native botanicals including peppermint gum and bunya pine.

Don't miss a meal at the classy **Bridges Cafe** (mains $10-18), hand-built by the owners from the timber of a former local bridge. It's signposted along Chewko Rd, 15.5km south of Mareeba.

Festivals & Events

Mareeba Rodeo RODEO
(www.mareebarodeo.com.au) Mareeba's annual rodeo in July is one of Australia's biggest and best. Catch bull and bronco riding, and 'cowboy protection' courtesy of rodeo clowns, along with events such as agricultural shows, wood-chopping, a 'beaut ute' muster and country music bands.

Cattle Saleyards CATTLE SALES
(www.saleyards.info) Every Tuesday from 9am, these cattle saleyards just north of town on the road to Mt Molloy provide a genuine taste of country Australia.

Sleeping & Eating

Decent dining and accommodation is in short supply.

Jackaroo Motel MOTEL $$
(☎4092 2677; www.jackaroomotel.com; 340 Byrnes St; d $115; ❄📶🏊) Facilities at Mareeba's most upmarket motel include a saltwater swimming pool and barbecue area.

Mareeba Lodge MOTEL $$
(☎4092 2266; www.mareebalodge.com.au; 21 Byrnes St; s $90, d $100-110; ❄) This central, lime green–coloured motel is run by a friendly, well-travelled family. Farm work can be arranged for those staying in the separate backpacker wing (dorm per week $175).

Mareeba Rodeo Grounds CAMPGROUND $
(☎4092 1654; www.mareebarodeo.com.au; Kerribee Park, 614 Dimbulah Rd; unpowered/powered sites $12/14) Amazingly cheap camping (rates are for two people), and free during the rodeo. Facilities include hot showers and a laundry. The catch? No shade.

Ant Hill Hotel & Steakhouse STEAKHOUSE $$
(☎4092 2147; 79 Byrnes St; mains $16-25; ⏰lunch & dinner) The restaurant at this friendly pub in the town centre has good-value specials with all the pub favourites – steak, barra and burgers, and a bargain bar menu (mains $10).

Nastasi's CAFE $
(210 Byrnes St; mains $9-19; ⏰breakfast, lunch & dinner; @) Fried everything, plus burgers, pizzas and pasta. Nastasi's doubles as the local internet cafe (30 minutes for $3).

Atherton & Around

POP 6250

Unofficial 'capital' of the Tableland, the commercial and agricultural hub of Atherton takes its name from one of the first white settlers to find tin, and later farm in the region, John Atherton.

The small, historic village of Tolga, 5km north of Atherton, also has a couple of worthwhile stops.

Sights & Activities

Hallorans Hill LOOKOUT
From this panoramic lookout, the surrounding farmland looks like an earth-coloured patchwork quilt. The hill features an outdoor sculpture park and is adjacent to an interpretive rainforest trail. Head up Robert St from the information centre and follow the signs.

Crystal Caves GEMSTONE GALLERY
(www.crystalcaves.com.au; 69 Main St; adult/child $22.50/15; ⏰8.30am-5pm Mon-Fri, to 4pm Sat, 10am-4pm Sun, closed Feb) To see the life's work of a collector of geodes, thunder eggs and assorted minerals, head to this impressive mineralogical wonderland, which descends into an artificial fairy-cave setting. Don a hard hat and check out the pièce de résistance – the world's largest amethyst geode, a 3.25m, 2.7-tonne giant excavated from Uruguay. Last entry is one hour before closing; you can view the display cases in the shop for free.

HOME-GROWN CUPPA

All the ingredients for a cuppa – coffee, tea, milk and sugar – are produced on and around the Atherton Tableland.

Coffee is one of the area's biggest crops; producers open to the public include the following:

» **North Queensland Gold Coffee Plantation** (☎4093 2269; www.nqgoldcoffee.com.au; Dimbulah Hwy; tours $5; ⏲8am-5pm) Local icon Bruno Maloberti leads entertaining personal tours of his family's plantation. Be sure to try his dark chocolate–covered coffee beans. Located 10.2km southwest of Mareeba.

» **Jaques Coffee Plantation** (☎4093 3284; www.jaquescoffee.com; 232 Leotta Rd; tours adult/child $15/8; ⏲9am-5pm) Ride around Jaques' plantation in its 'bean machine' and sip its coffee liqueur. Signposted off the Kennedy Hwy, 8km east of Mareeba.

» **Skybury Coffee Plantation** (☎4093 2190; www.skybury.com.au; Dimbulah Hwy; adult/child $23.75/11.90; ⏲tours 10.30am, 11.45am & 2.15pm) Snazzy plantation and visitor centre; tours include a film and laboratory tasting. There's also a licensed on-site restaurant. Situated 9km west of Mareeba.

» **Coffee Works** (☎4092 4101; www.arabicas.com.au; 136 Mason St; adult/child $19/10; ⏲9am-4pm) In-town roaster.

See p348 to tour Australia's largest tea plantation; p348 for dairy factory tours; and p290 and p364 for sugar mill tours.

Atherton Chinatown TEMPLE, MUSEUM
(www.nationaltrustqld.org; 86 Herberton Rd; adult/child $10/5; ⏲11am-4pm Wed-Sun) More than 500 Chinese migrants came to the region in search of gold in the late 1800s, but its only remaining building from those heady days is the **Hou Wang Temple**, which features a handcrafted altar panel. Museum admission includes a guided tour.

Less than 100m north is **Platypus Park** where, with luck, you might spot a monotreme along Piebald Creek.

Galleries GALLERIES
The Aboriginal-owned and -run **Magarra Gallery** (www.magarragallery.com.au; Shop 7, Herberton Rd; ⏲10.30am-4.30pm Tue-Sat) sells striking artworks; ask about upcoming cultural landscape Tableland tours.

Tolga Woodworks Gallery & Cafe (☎4095 4488; www.tolgawoodworks.com.au; Kennedy Hwy, Tolga; ⏲9am-5pm Mar-Jan) has amazingly crafted wood pieces for sale or just to stare at. Local artisans' skills extend to ceramics, leatherwork and glassware.

Food Producers FARMS
All the sweet smells are indoors at **Gallo Dairyland** (www.gallodairyland.com.au; Malanda Rd; ⏲9.30am-4.30pm), a working dairy farm 7km southeast of Atherton that doubles as a cheese and chocolate factory (great combination!). It produces 30-plus types of chocolate and over a dozen gourmet cheeses, with a few free samples of both. At various times of day you can see the production process, or just taste the end result at the on-site cafe.

At **Shaylee Strawberries** (☎4091 2962; cnr Gillies Hwy & Marks Lane; ⏲9am-5pm Jun-Nov), a family-run commercial farm supplies 6km east of Atherton, you can pick your own succulent strawberries (from $10 per 10kg) from mid-September to the end of November. The rest of the season, watch as strawberries are sorted and packed, and taste them in jams, gelati and sorbets.

A ginormous, smiling 'peanut man' sculpture greets you at the **Peanut Place** (☎4095 5333; www.thepeanutplace.com.au; Kennedy Hwy, Tolga; ⏲8.30am-5pm), which sells roasted, flavoured and boiled peanuts, as well as homemade peanut butter.

Sleeping & Eating

Atherton Blue Gum B&B B&B $$
(☎4091 5149; www.athertonbluegum.com; 36 Twelfth Ave; d $130-180; ❄🏊) Breakfast (continental included, cooked $10 extra) comes with superb views from the verandah of this double-storey B&B perched on Hallorans Hill. There's a range of rooms with pine panelling and big windows, and a heated pool and spa.

Barron Valley Hotel PUB $
(☎4091 1222; www.bvhotel.com.au; 53 Main St; s/d $40/60, with bathroom s/d $60/75; ❄📶) A heritage-listed beauty, the grand art deco 'BV', built in the early 1940s, has tidy budget pub rooms upstairs; en suite rooms have air-con. Its restaurant (mains $12 to $30) serves hearty meals, including giant steaks.

Tolga Country Lodge HOSTEL, MOTEL $
(☎4095 5166; 36-38 Kennedy Hwy, Tolga; dm/s/d $30/50/80; @) This peacefully set timber lodge has country-style doubles, excellent dorms with private lockable wardrobes and a polished timber and corrugated-iron dining room.

Atherton Woodlands CARAVAN PARK $
(☎4091 1407; www.woodlandscp.com.au; 141 Herberton Rd; unpowered/powered sites $25/33, cabins $85-130; ❄🏊) The best of Atherton's three van parks, Woodlands is 1.5km south of the centre.

Indonesian Bistro MD Hot Wok INDONESIAN $
(63 Main St; mains $13-20; ⏲lunch Tue-Fri, dinner Tue-Sat) Paintings, carvings and a rickshaw decorate this aromatic restaurant, where fresh, authentic nasi goreng, laksas and curries are cooked up in a flash.

Tolga Bakery BAKERY $
(56 Main St, Tolga; pies $3.50-4; ⏲6am-4.30pm Mon-Fri, 6am-1pm Sat) Famed throughout the area; everything is freshly baked on the premises including pies such as sweet chilli, and chunky lamb.

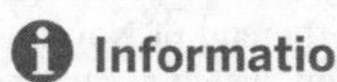

Atherton Tableland Information Centre
(☎4091 4222; www.athertoninformationcentre.com.au; cnr Main St & Silo Rd; ⏲9am-5pm) Useful information on the region includes brochures outlining the network of heritage trails.

Herberton

POP 1000

Peaceful Herberton is tucked in the crease of one of the area's rolling hills. It was founded on the Wild River after the discovery of a tin lode in 1880. Dozens of mines opened in the area, and by the early 1900s Herberton supported two newspapers and 17 pubs. The establishment of the town decimated the Indigenous Bar Barrum community – members of the now extinct Mbabaram language group. The shire has reinstated Native Title to Herberton and acknowledged the cultural significance of certain areas to the Bar Barrum.

Herberton's star attraction is the **Herberton Historic Village** (www.herbertonhistoricvillage.com.au; 6 Broadway; adult/child $24/12; ⏲9am-5pm), a collection of 50 original buildings dating back as far as 1870, which have been moved here from various locales, restored and filled with some fascinating historic exhibits. Highlights include a pub, a blacksmith's workshop, Ada's frock salon, a school house and a grocery store. Allow at least a couple of hours.

On the site of an old tin mine, the **Herberton Mining Museum & Information Centre** (☎4096 3473; www.herbertonvisitorcentre.com.au; Great Northern Mining Centre, 1 Jacks Rd; museum adult/child $5/3; ⏲9am-4pm) has an informative display on the region's mining history and geology, including a gallery of minerals. It's the starting point for a number of **historic walking trails** (from 1km to 12km) and stocks trail maps.

You can let someone else do most of the work and get a donkey to carry your gear on a guided trek with **Wilderness Expeditions** (☎4096 2266; www.wildex.com.au; day treks from $125); overnight treks are also available.

James Bond wannabes won't want to miss the **Spy & Camera Museum** (☎4096 2092; www.spycameramuseum.com.au; 49 Grace St; adult/child $14/12; ⏲9.30am-5pm Mar-Jan), with rare 19th-century cameras, tiny spy cameras and Russian KGB models – the original owner was reputed to be a secret agent.

Accommodation is limited; try Herberton's original post office, which is now the **Herberton Heritage Cottage B&B** (☎0427 962 670; 2 Perkins St; s/d $100/130; ❄). Heritage-style rooms (polished-wood surfaces, pot-belly heating and high beds) incorporate mod cons such as spas and DVD players.

Mt Hypipamee National Park

Between Atherton and Ravenshoe, the Kennedy Hwy passes the eerie, and hard to pronounce, **Mt Hypipamee crater**, which could be a scene from a sci-fi film and certainly adds some vertigo to the itinerary. It's anomalous due to the granite rock, which is not associated with volcanic activity. From the picnic area, it's a scenic 700m return walk, past **Dinner Falls**, to the narrow, 138m-deep crater; the moody-looking lake far below makes for one giant wishing well.

Ravenshoe

POP 910

If you're on your way to or from the Savannah Way, this may be your first or last taste of the Tableland. Ravenshoe (pronounced *ravens*-hoe, not *raven*-shoe) is Queensland's highest town at a modest 930m – it gets chilly up here in winter! Founded on the timber industry, it's known these days for more sustainable resources, with wind farms harnessing those prevailing breezes.

The **Ravenshoe visitor centre** (☎4097 7700; www.ravenshoevisitorcentre.com.au; 24 Moore St; ⏲9am-5pm Apr-Sep, 9am-4pm Oct-Mar) houses the **Ngayaji Interpretive Centre**, which explains the Jirrbal people's traditional lifestyle.

Nearby waterfalls (no swimming) include **Little Millstream Falls**, 3km south of Ravenshoe, and **Tully Falls**, around 20km further south on the Tully Falls Rd (which doesn't go through to Tully). The 13m-high **Millstream Falls** (signposted off the Savannah Way towards Innot Hot Springs, from where it's 1km to the car park) are said to be the widest in Australia in flood.

Train enthusiasts and kids will love a ride on the restored steam train *Capella* with the **Ravenswood Railway Co** (☎4097 6005; www.ravenshoesteamrail.com.au; Grigg St; adult/child $20/10; ⏲departs 1.30pm Sun), which chugs 7km north to Tumoulin – Queensland's highest railway station – and back. Check for annual closures.

You can sleep knowing you're a notch above everyone else at **Hotel Tully Falls** (☎4097 6136; 34 Grigg St; s/d $32/42), a grand hotel with a reasonable claim to being Queensland's highest hotel. Rooms are basic pub style with shared bathrooms.

Possum Valley B&B (☎4097 8177; www.bnbnq.com.au/possumvalley; Evelyn Central, via Ravenshoe; s/d $60/75), off the Kennedy Hwy, down a 4.5km unsealed road, has two cottages clinging to the fringe of World Heritage–listed rainforest. It uses solar and hydroelectricity and tank water.

Millaa Millaa

POP 250

Tiny Millaa Millaa is the gateway to the Tableland from the south (Innisfail) and the closest village to the Waterfalls Circuit (p348). Surrounded by rolling farmland dotted with black-and-white Friesian cows, this is also the centre of a thriving local dairy industry. There's no visitor centre, but information is available at www.millaamillaa.com.au.

The village's heart is its only pub, the **Millaa Millaa Hotel** (☎4097 2212; 15 Main St; mains $14-26; ⏲restaurant lunch & dinner Mon-Sat), which serves mountain-sized meals and has six spick-and-span brick one-bedroom motel units (singles/doubles $70/80) out back. Publican Terry organises regular events like gumboot throwing.

TOP CHOICE **Falls Teahouse** (☎4097 2237; www.fallsteahouse.com.au; Palmerston Hwy; s/d $65/110, meals $7-16; ⏲10am-5pm) tempts you to go inside by its aroma of fresh baking – even the bread for sandwiches is homemade. In the country-style kitchen of this heritage teahouse, Ray cooks dishes such as pan-fried barra, and pies made from local beef. Sit next to the pot-belly stove, or on the back verandah overlooking rolling

WORTH A TRIP

INNOT HOT SPRINGS

Who can resist a dip in thermal springs? This inland trip along the Savannah Way chases the warm waters that spring up from the volcanic ground. Take the Kennedy Hwy about 32km west of Ravenshoe to the tiny township of **Innot Hot Springs**, where a spring measuring 73°C heats up the cool waters of the town's Nettle Creek. The spring water is said to be therapeutic, and after a steaming soak you'll probably agree. You can 'take the waters' at **Innot Hot Springs Health Waters** (☎4097 0136; innotspa@hotmail.com; unpowered/powered sites $23/27, cabins $65-120; ❄≋). Visitors have free use of the park's six indoor and outdoor **thermal pools** (nonguest adult/child $7/5; ⏲8am-6pm) of varying temperatures up to 44°C. Otherwise, just dig a hole in the sand and soak in Nettle Creek itself (BYO shovel).

Have a beer or stay the night in the **Innot Hotel** (☎4097 0203; Kennedy Hwy; s/d $45/55), a friendly country pub with five motel units and home-cooked meals (mains $14 to $22).

DON'T MISS

WATERFALLS CIRCUIT

Passing some of the Tableland's most picturesque waterfalls, this 15km circuit makes for a leisurely drive or cycle. Enter the circuit by taking Theresa Creek Rd, 1km east of Millaa Millaa on the Palmerston Hwy. Surrounded by tree ferns and flowers, the **Millaa Millaa Falls**, 1.5km along, are easily the best for swimming and have a grassy picnic area. The star of Qantas' ads, the spectacular 12m falls are reputed to be the most photographed in Australia. **Zillie Falls**, 8km further on, are reached by a short walking trail that leads to a lookout peering down on the falls from above. The next, **Ellinjaa Falls**, have a 200m walking trail down to a rocky swimming hole at the base of the falls. A further 5.5km down the Palmerston Hwy there's a turn-off to **Mungalli Falls**.

farmland. Its three guest rooms are individually decorated with period furniture. It's at the intersection of the Millaa Millaa Falls turn-off.

Mungalli Creek Dairy (www.mungallicreekdairy.com.au; 254 Brooks Rd; mains $15-17; ⏲10am-4pm Mar-Jan) is about 6km southeast of the village. You can tuck into free tasting platters of yoghurt and cheese at this biodynamic dairy, or order them cooked in dishes like three-cheese pie followed by a sinfully rich Sicilian cheesecake (with chocolate, on a cinnamon base).

Millaa Millaa Tourist Park (☎4097 2290; www.millaapark.com; cnr Malanda Rd & Lodge Ave; unpowered/powered sites $20/25, s/d without bathroom $35/40, d with bathroom $60-80; @) has a range of cabins on large grounds.

Malanda & Around

POP 1930

Milk runs through the proverbial veins of Malanda – ever since 500 bedraggled cattle made an arduous 16-month overland journey from New South Wales in 1908. There's still a working dairy here, producing 120 million litres of milk each year, and a dairy-research centre. The town is surrounded by lush rainforest that's one of the best places in Queensland to spot tree kangaroos.

Sights & Activities

Malanda Falls SWIMMING, WALKING

(Malanda–Atherton Rd) These falls don't 'fall' particularly spectacularly, but the resulting pool, surrounded by lawns and forest, is a shady, croc-free swimming spot. **Guided rainforest walks** ($15, by appointment) led by members of the Ngadjonji community can be organised through Malanda's **visitor centre** (☎4096 6957; www.malandafalls.com; ⏲9.30am-4.30pm). A new centre is currently being built next to the falls after a fire destroyed the previous building; in the meantime, it's housed at the Malanda Dairy Centre.

Malanda Dairy Centre INTERPRETIVE CENTRE

(8 James St; ⏲9.30am-3pm, closed 3 weeks during Oct) Malanda Dairy Centre can tell you more than you ever wanted to know about cows, with 40-minute **factory tours** (adult/child $10.50/6.50; ⏲10am & 11am Mon-Fri), including a cheese platter or milkshake; the 'Udder Experience' with historical exhibits and costumed dummies; and a shop stuffed with all sorts of black-and-white cow-related souvenirs.

Malanda Hotel NOTABLE BUILDING

(cnr James & Edith Sts) The southern hemisphere's largest wooden structure, Malanda's enormous 1911-built hotel is lined with black-and-white photos.

Bromfield Swamp NATURE RESERVE

(Upper Barron Rd) This important waterbird sanctuary, particularly for brolgas and cranes, lies 6km west of Malanda. It's on private property, but a viewing area opposite Stonehouse Rd (best late afternoon) overlooks an eroded volcanic crater.

Nerada Tea TEA PLANTATION

(☎4096 8328; www.neradatea.com.au; Glen Allyn Rd; ⏲9am-4pm) Australia's largest tea plantation is 6km southeast of Malanda. It has a visitor centre, a tea-tasting house and **factory tours** (adult/child $12.50/6) on request.

Tarzali Lakes Fishing Park FISHING

(www.tarzalilakes.com; Millaa Millaa Rd, Tarzali; fishing adult/child from $18/12, unpowered sites per person $10; ⏲10am-5pm Thu-Tue) This aquaculture farm has several artificial lakes stocked with jade perch and barramundi, so you're sure to catch something – or just buy it at the on-site smokehouse. There's plenty of birdlife here, plus **platypus-spotting tours** (adult/child $10/5; ⏲tours at 2pm & 3.30pm). It's about halfway between Malanda and Millaa Millaa; look for the giant fish.

Sleeping

Quality B&B accommodation is tucked away in the forests and farms around Malanda.

Canopy B&B $$$
(4096 5364; www.canopytreehouses.com.au; Hogan Rd, Tarzali via Malanda; d $227-339;) A pristine patch of old-growth rainforest is the stunning setting for this superbly designed group of all-timber pole houses, where even the soaps are handmade. There's a minimum two-night stay.

Rivers Edge Rainforest Retreat B&B $$$
(4095 2369; www.riversedgeretreat.com.au; d from $298;) Surrounded by forest on the Johnstone River are two secluded luxury timber lodges with lavish touches such as a sliding glass wall in the spa bathroom and a wood fire. Minimum two-night stay.

Lumholtz Lodge B&B $$$
(4095 0292; www.lumholtzlodge.com.au; Upper Barron Rd; d incl breakfast $180, full-board d $300;) Enveloped in foliage, this is a prime spot to watch the surrounding wildlife. Guests have free rein of the lodge, which includes shelves stocked with books about nature, and a spa.

Travellers Rest B&B $
(4096 6077; www.travrest.com.au; Millaa Millaa Rd, Tarzali; s/d inc breakfast $50/90) This English-style country farmhouse 5km south of Malanda is a cosy budget place (no en suites) with a billiard room, formal dining room and fresh, floral rooms. Book ahead for Saturday's murder-mystery nights.

Malanda Falls Caravan Park CARAVAN PARK $
(4096 5314; www.malandafalls.com.au; 38 Park Ave; unpowered/powered sites $16/22, cabins $75-85) Right next to Malanda Falls, this site has tidy en suite cabins and camp sites where you can hear the water flowing.

Eating

Malanda Dairy Centre CAFE $$
(8 James St; mains $12-18; 9.30am-3pm, closed 3 weeks during Oct;) The centre's licensed cafe is the best place to eat in town, serving leg ham, cranberry sauce and Swiss cheese focaccias through to homemade lasagne.

Malanda Hotel PUB FARE $$
(cnr James & Edith Sts; mains $12.50-25.50; breakfast, lunch & dinner) Serves reasonably priced counter meals.

Entertainment

Majestic Theatre CINEMA
(4096 5726; www.majestictheatre.com.au; Eacham Place; Fri, Sat & Sun) Built in 1929, with traditional oak-framed and lay-back canvas bleachers, this theatre screens mainstream movies on weekend evenings.

Yungaburra

POP 1200

Home to a shy colony of platypus (the jury is still out on the plural – some experts say platypode!), tiny Yungaburra is one of the unassuming gems of the Tableland. Queensland's largest National Trust village – with 18 heritage-listed buildings – its quaint chocolate box–pretty architecture, central location and superb boutique accommodation have made it a popular weekend retreat for those in the know.

Sights & Activities

The shops in the village centre make for a pleasant place to stroll. Lakes Tinaroo, Eacham and Barrine are within a short drive.

Platypus Viewing WILDLIFE-SPOTTING, WALKS
Yungaburra has two **platypus-viewing platforms** on Peterson Creek – one by the bridge on the Gillies Hwy and another at a spot known as Allumbah Pocket (the town's original name) further west. The two are joined by a **walking trail** along the creek which continues east to Railway Bridge. End to end, the 2km walk takes less than an hour.

Curtain Fig NATURE RESERVE
The magnificent curtain fig tree, about 3km out of town, is a must-see. Like a prop from *The Lord of the Rings*, this 500-year-old strangler fig has aerial roots that hang down to create a feathery curtain. A wheelchair-accessible viewing platform snakes around the tree, while brush turkeys forage in the leaf litter below.

Wild Mountain Cellars WINE TASTING
(www.wildmountain.com.au; 23 Eacham Rd) In the village centre, this small local producer offers tastings of its tropical-fruit wines, such as dragonfruit or persimmon and lychee, ports, and a mind-blowing coffee liqueur.

Tours

On the Wallaby CANOEING, BIKING
(4095 2031; www.onthewallaby.com; 34 Eacham Rd; tours $30) The eco-oriented folk at this

hostel run excellent half-day bike and canoe tours. It's also the only operator in Queensland offering **night canoeing**, when you've a good chance of spotting snakes, tree kangaroos and more. Nonguests are welcome.

Tableland Adventure Guides KAYAKING, BIKING
(TAG; ☎0448 517 979; www.tablelandadventureguides.com.au) Guided biking along tracks and rail trails, kayaking on Lake Tinaroo and hiking in World Heritage rainforest are among the activities run by this enthusiastic and knowledgeable local outfit. Half-day trips start from $95; multiday trips and combo packages are available.

Festivals & Events

Yungaburra Markets MARKET
(www.yungaburramarkets.com; Gillies Hwy; ⏲7.30am-noon 4th Sat of month) Day trippers descend on the village to hunt through crafts and food products at Yungaburra's vibrant markets.

Yungaburra Folk Festival FOLK FESTIVAL
(www.yungaburrafolkfestival.org; ⏲late Oct) A fabulous weekend-long community event featuring music, workshops, poetry readings and kids activities.

Sleeping

Most places raise their rates on weekends. The visitor centre can help find cottage rentals in the surrounding area.

TOP CHOICE **On the Wallaby** HOSTEL $
(☎4095 2031; www.onthewallaby.com; 34 Eacham Rd; camping $10, dm/d $24/55; @) Some hostels just feel like home and this one does, with handmade timber furniture and mosaics, spotless rooms – and no TV! Nature-based tours depart daily; tour packages (p349) and transfers (one-way $30) are available from Cairns.

Williams Lodge B&B $$$
(☎4095 3449; www.williamslodge.com; Cedar St; d incl breakfast $180-285; ❄@📶🏊) Built in 1911 and still owned and run by the Williams family, all of the rooms at this heritage Queenslander home open onto the verandah, including enormous suites fitted with original period furniture and four-poster beds (some with spa baths). Grand touches include a pianola lounge, wine bar and billiard table. Kids under 12 years aren't allowed.

Eden House Retreat & Mountain Spa BOUTIQUE HOTEL $$$
(☎4089 7000; www.edenhouse.com.au; 20 Gillies Hwy; d incl breakfast $180-295; ❄@📶🏊) Amid the gardens behind this historic 1912 homestead in the village centre are romantic cottages with large spa baths and high beds, and family-oriented villas. Nonguests can book into the full-service day spa and highly regarded **restaurant** (mains $26-34; ⏲dinner Tue-Sat).

Foxwell Park B&B $$$
(☎4096 6183; www.foxwellpark.com.au; Foxwell Rd; d $200, ste $250; @📶) In rolling countryside 7km southwest of Yungaburra, Foxwell's beautifully restored pair of century-old timber buildings have original tiles and pressed-tin ceilings. Suites open onto deep, private verandahs. Also on the 24-hectare estate are a private, barra-stocked lake and a garden producing fruit, vegetables, fresh herbs and eggs, which are served up at its French-inspired **restaurant** (mains $25-35; ⏲dinner Wed-Sun, nightly for guests).

Mt Quincan Crater Retreat CABINS $$$
(☎4095 2255; www.mtquincan.com.au; Peeramon Rd; d $245-350; 📶) In secluded rainforest, these luxurious pole cabins and tree houses have been built for sheer countryside indulgence, with double spas, indoor and outdoor showers, wood fires and stupendous views – and supreme peace and quiet (children aren't permitted). It's 3km south of town; follow the road to Peeramon to the sign-posted turn-off.

Lake Eacham Hotel PUB $
(☎4095 3515; www.yungaburrapub.com.au; 6-8 Kehoe Pl; d $55-85) This hotel is better known as the 'Yungaburra Pub'. The downstairs **dining room** (mains $17-30; ⏲lunch & dinner) and the swirling wooden staircase of this grand old hotel are inspirational, the circular pool table is unconventional and the en suite rooms are basic but functional.

Kookaburra Lodge MOTEL $
(☎4095 3222; www.kookaburra-lodge.com; cnr Oak St & Eacham Rd; s/d $80/90; ❄) Stylish little rooms opening out to an inviting barbecue patio amid tropical gardens. Breakfast (extra charge) includes homemade muesli, porridge with cream and brown sugar, or buttermilk pancakes.

Gumtree on Gillies B&B $$$
(☎4095 3105; www.gumtreeongillies.com.au; Gillies Hwy; d incl breakfast $175; 🏊) Individually themed cabins skirt the globe, with

Australian-, African-, Moroccan- and Egyptian-inspired fittings. All have open fireplaces, spa baths and king beds.

Eating

TOP CHOICE **Flynn's** MEDITERRANEAN **$$$**
(☎4095 2235; www.flynnsyungaburra.com; 17 Eacham Rd; mains $27-29, 3-course menu $45; ⊙lunch Sun, dinner Fri-Tue) Between ducking outside to pick his own veggies and running Flynn's almost single-handedly, Kiwi culinary maestro Liam has managed to put Yungaburra on the foodie map. The menu changes daily but expect dishes like duck-liver cognac pâté and fish of the day, along with a superb wine list. Book ahead.

Nick's Restaurant SWISS-ITALIAN **$$**
(☎4095 3330; www.nicksrestaurant.com.au; 33 Gillies Hwy; mains $16-23; ⊙lunch Fri-Sun, dinner Tue-Sun) This Swiss chalet-style number makes for a fun night out with costumed staff, beer steins, a piano-accordion serenade and possibly some impromptu yodelling. Food spans schnitzels to smoked pork loin with sauerkraut, but there are a couple of vegetarian options.

Whistlestop Cafe CAFE **$**
(cnr Cedar St & Gillies Hwy; mains $8-14; ⊙7.30am-5pm Wed-Mon; ✎) Sure, this laid-back garden-set cafe serves healthy rice slices and veggie lasagne, but the real reason everyone's here is its soufflé-style Tuscany cakes, which explode with deliciously gooey chocolate when you unwrap them. Great 'Funky Monkey' smoothies (with a shot of coffee), too.

Information

Visitor centre (☎4095 2416; www.yungaburra.com; Cedar St; ⊙10am-6pm; @) Staffed by friendly local volunteers.

Lake Tinaroo

Also known as Tinaroo Dam, Lake Tinaroo was originally created for the Barron River hydroelectric power scheme. When it was filled in 1959, the village of Kulara was submerged below water, with residents relocated to Yungaburra and the surrounding area.

Barramundi fishing is legendary in the croc-free artificial lake and is permitted year-round. Fishing permits (per week/year $7/35, children free, covering all of Queensland's dams) are readily available from local businesses and accommodation places, can be ordered online at **Queensland's Department of Primary Industries** (www.dpi.qld.gov.au/fishweb). Head out for a fish or simply a sunset cruise with a glass of wine aboard the super-comfy 'floating lounge room' skippered by **Lake Tinaroo Cruises** (☎0457 033 016 www.laketinaroocruises.com.au; 2hr/half-day/full-day boat charter $240/380/550). Rates are for the whole boat (up to 12 people). There's an on-board fridge and barbecue (barbecue packs cost $10 per person), plus binoculars for wildlife spotting. The **Barra Bash** fishing competition is held annually at the end of October around the full moon; it's a great event attracting loads of people, but avoid it if you're after a quiet escape.

The **Danbulla Forest Drive** winds its way through rainforest and softwood plantations along the north side of the lake. It's 28km of unsealed but well-maintained road passing a number of picnic areas and attractions, including pretty **Lake Euramoo** and the **Cathedral Fig** – a gigantic strangler fig tree shouldering epiphytes nestling in its branches, accessed by a boardwalk (also signposted along a sealed road off the Gillies Hwy). There are five **DERM campgrounds** ☎13 74 68; www.derm.qld.gov.au; sites per person $5.15) in the Danbulla State Forest – Platypus, School Point, Downfall Creek, Kauri Creek and Fong-On Bay. All have water, barbecues and toilets; advance bookings are essential.

Across from the lake foreshore in the small settlement of Tinaroo Falls, **Discovery Lake Tinaroo Holiday Park** (☎4095 8232; www.discoveryholidayparks.com.au; 3 Tinaroo Falls Dam Rd; unpowered/powered sites $24/29, cabins $70-140; ❄@🛜≋) is a modern, well-equipped and shady camping ground with fuel, a small shop and an on-site **cafe** (mains $10-17). It also rents tinnies (per half-day $90) and canoes (per hour $10).

Lake Tinaroo Terraces (☎4095 8555; www.laketinarooterraces.com.au; cnr Church & Russell Sts; d $109-160; ❄≋) has great-value one- and two-bedroom self-contained lodges (some with air-con) in a prime lakefront location.

Crater Lakes National Park

Part of the Wet Tropics World Heritage area, the two mirrorlike crater lakes of Lake Eacham and Lake Barrine are both croc-free and nestled among rainforest. Walking tracks fringe the lakes, which are easily reached by sealed roads off the Gillies Hwy. Camping is not permitted.

LAKE BARRINE

The larger of the two lakes, Lake Barrine is cloaked in thick old-growth rainforest; a 5km walking track around the lake takes about 1½ hours. The **Lake Barrine Rainforest Tea House** (☎4095 3847; www.lakebarrine.com.au; Gillies Hwy; mains $7-17; ⏲breakfast & lunch) sits out over the lakefront. Upstairs you'll feel like you're aboard a boat as you take Devonshire tea or order a meal. To actually board one, there's a booking desk downstairs for 45-minute **lake cruises** (adult/child $16/8). There are four daily. It also rents out a lakeside, self-contained **cottage** (d incl breakfast & cruise $140).

A 100m stroll from the teahouse are two enormous, neck-tilting, 1000-year-old kauri pines.

LAKE EACHAM

The crystal-clear waters of Lake Eacham are idyllic for swimming and spotting turtles; there are sheltered lakeside picnic areas, a swimming pontoon and a boat ramp. The 3km lake-circuit track is an easy walk and takes less than an hour. Stop in at the **Rainforest Display Centre** (McLeish Rd; ⏲9am-1pm Mon, Wed & Fri) at the rangers' station for information on the area, the history of the timber industry and the rebuilding of the rainforest.

TOP CHOICE **Crater Lakes Rainforest Cottages** (☎4095 2322; www.craterlakes.com.au; Eacham Close, off Lakes Dr; d $230; ❄@) has four individually themed timber cottages – 'Bali', 'beach shack', 'Tuscany' and 'pioneer'. Ideally spaced in its own private patch of rainforest, each is a romantic hideaway filled with candles, fresh flowers and logs for the wood-stoves, with spa baths, fully fitted kitchens and breakfast hampers with bacon, eggs, chocolates and fruit to feed the birds. Unlike many places around here, there's no minimum stay, but trust us, you won't want to leave.

Rose Gums (☎4096 8360; www.rosegums.com.au; Land Rd, Butcher's Creek; d from $286) has ecofriendly pole and timber treetop pads that are totally private, and fitted out with spas, wood-burning heaters and king-sized beds. All come with breakfast hampers, kitchens and barbecues, but you can also dine on Mediterranean cuisine at the on-site **restaurant** (mains $30-35; ⏲dinner; 🖉). Minimum two nights.

Lake Eacham Caravan Park (☎4095 3730; www.lakeeachamtouristpark.com; Lakes Dr; unpowered/powered sites $19/22, cabins $90-110; @), 1km down the Malanda road from Lake Eacham, is a pretty camping ground with cosy cabins.

Port Douglas & the Daintree

Includes »

Port Douglas........355
Mossman.......... 364
Julatten 365
Mossman to the Daintree........... 365
The Daintree........366
Daintree Village 367
Daintree River to Cape Tribulation.....370
Cape Tribulation.....373
North to Cooktown .. 377
Inland Route........377
Coastal Route.......379
Cooktown.......... 380
Lizard Island Group............. 385

Best Places to Eat

» Mojo's (p365)
» Julaymba Restaurant (p369)
» Beach Shack (p362)

Best Places to Stay

» Mungumby Lodge (p380)
» Cape Trib Exotic Fruit Farm Cabins (p375)
» Daintree Eco Lodge & Spa (p368)

Why Go?

Dominated by a World Heritage–listed rainforest and reef, this extraordinary corner of Queensland teems with diverse natural environments. The dramatic coastal drive winding from Cairns to the ritzy resort town of Port Douglas – with reef cruise and dive boats departing daily from its marina – is the start of the Far North experience. But it's once you're past Mossman and the Daintree River that the adventure really begins.

The magnificent Daintree National Park stretches up the coast, its rainforest tumbling right onto the white-sand beaches in places. Indigenous culture remains strong here, with tracts of land shared between the traditional custodians and non-Indigenous settlers. The road is peppered with small village communities, from where you can take rainforest walks, croc-spotting river tours, sea-kayaking trips or just beachcomb. Further north, the Bloomfield Track from Cape Tribulation to Cooktown is one of the country's greatest 4WD journeys.

When to Go

Port Douglas

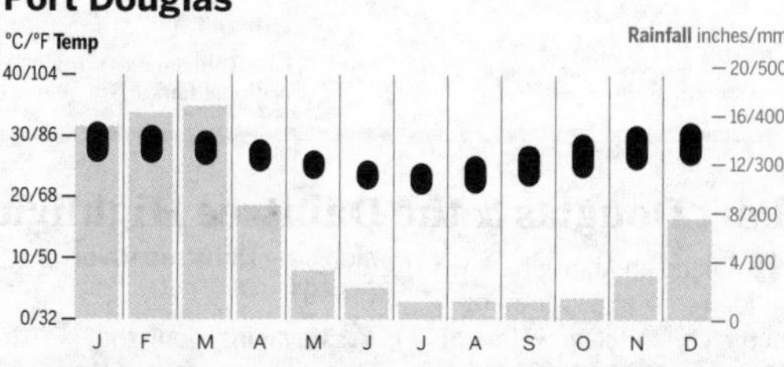

June A re-enactment of Captain Cook's landing is the centrepiece of the Cooktown Discovery Festival.

September Reggae, funk, roots and blues artists play in the rainforest for the Wallaby Creek Festival.

October Port Douglas' Go Troppo festival displays the creativity of artists living in the tropics.

Port Douglas & the Daintree Highlights

1 Taking an Aboriginal guided walk and swimming in the crystal-clear waters of **Mossman Gorge** (p364)

2 Heading out for a free afternoon sail with members of the local yacht club in **Port Douglas** (p357)

3 Scanning the riverbanks for saltwater crocs on a cruise along the **Daintree River** (p369)

4 Kayaking along the shoreline in search of turtles off **Myall Beach** (p373)

5 Toasting the completion of the 4WD Bloomfield Track from Cape Trib at the iconic **Lion's Den Hotel** (p380)

6 Joining the locals fishing from the wharf at **Cooktown** (p380)

7 Catching an outdoor concert or theatre performance at the lakeside Karnak Playhouse in the lush **Whyanbeel Valley** (p366)

8 Cantering along the water's edge at **Wonga Beach** (p366)

Dangers & Annoyances

From around late October to May, swimming in coastal waters is not advised due to the presence of box jellyfish, irukandji and other marine stingers (see p456).

Saltwater crocodiles inhabit the mangroves, estuaries and open water of the Far North, so avoid swimming or wading in these places. Warning signs are posted around waterways where crocs may be present, or on beaches where recent sightings have occurred.

 Getting There & Away

AIR

The closest commercial airport to Port Douglas is in Cairns, 67km south, with direct bus services. Cooktown's airport has regular flights to/from Cairns (see p385).

BUS

Buses serve major destinations throughout the region, including Port Douglas, Mossman, Cape Tribulation and Cooktown.

TRAIN

The area covered in this chapter is not served by passenger trains; the nearest terminus is in Cairns.

PORT DOUGLAS

POP 3000

Port Douglas is the flashy playground of tropical north Queensland. Like a spoilt child, it thumbs its nose at Cairns by being more sophisticated and intimate, and (perhaps most of all) by having a beautiful, white-sand beach right on its doorstep.

From the Captain Cook Hwy, a 6km low spit of land passes swanky village-sized resorts and golf courses to the township. There's no question: this is a purpose-built holiday hub, so there's a happy, relaxed vibe and clearly plenty of money floating around. Yet although those swish seafood restaurants, boutique clothing stores and four-star apartments contradict the Far North frontier image, Port Douglas (or 'Port', as it's locally known) retains an endearing character with all the comforts of a big city condensed into a surprisingly small town.

Port's town centre juts out into the Coral Sea with Dickson Inlet and the gleaming marina on the west side and Four Mile Beach on the east. The Great Barrier Reef is less than an hour away and getting to it is as easy (or hard) as choosing which boat to hop on. Just don't forget there's more to explore further north!

History

Port Douglas has a history of infamy, influence and affluence. What you see today was largely developed by businessman Christopher Skase, an archetype of the greed-is-good 1980s. Among other ventures, his company backed what was to be the genesis of Port Douglas: its first luxury resort, the Mirage. Within a few years, the eponymous port attracted a great deal of investment, which resulted in multimillion-dollar resorts, a golf course, heliport, marina, shopping complex and an avenue of palms lining the road from the highway to the township. In 1991, Skase's company filed for bankruptcy and he fled to Spain, kicking off a decade-long battle with the Australian government, which attempted to bring Skase back to Australia to repay a reputed $172 million in debt. Skase died in 2001 without ever returning to Australia.

Before Skase, Port Douglas was a sleepy village founded in 1877 as the port town for the Hodgkinson River goldfields. After initially flourishing, its prosperity came to a grinding halt in the mid-1880s when Cairns was chosen ahead of it as the terminal for the new rail line from Kuranda and Mareeba. Port was largely destroyed by a cyclone in 1911.

The traditional custodians, the Kuku Yalarij people, have inhabited the region for thousands of years, from Port Douglas north to Cooktown and west to Chillagoe.

Sights

Most visitors come to Port Douglas to swim, sun-lounge, sip cocktails (or sink ice-cold schooners) and cruise out to the reef. Although the town itself is short on sights, there are a few you shouldn't miss.

Four Mile Beach BEACH

Backed by palms, the broad band of white sand of Four Mile Beach reaches as far as your squinting eyes can see. At the northern end is a **Surf Life Saving Club**, in front of which is a swimming enclosure patrolled and protected with a stinger net during summer.

For a fine view over Four Mile Beach, follow Wharf St and then the steep Island Point Rd to **Flagstaff Hill Lookout**.

Wildlife Habitat Port Douglas WILDLIFE PARK

(☎4099 3235; www.wildlifehabitat.com.au; Port Douglas Rd; adult/child $30/15; ⏰8am-5pm)

Port Douglas

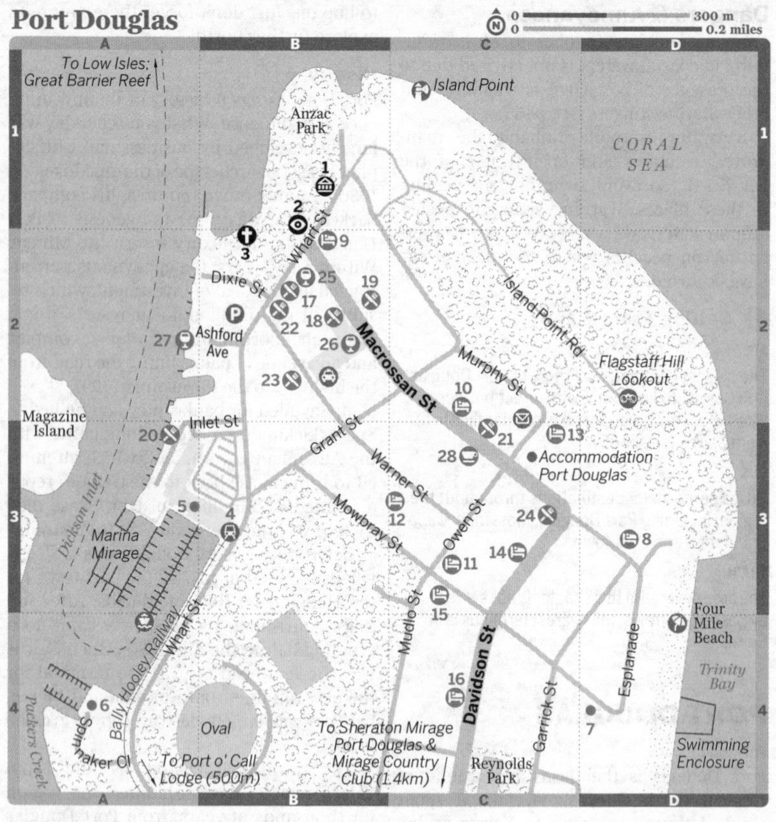

Port Douglas

Sights

1	Court House Museum	B1
2	Port Douglas Markets	B1
3	St Mary's By the Sea	B2

Activities, Courses & Tours

4	Ballyhooley Steam Railway	B3
5	Port Douglas Boat Hire	A3
6	Port Douglas Yacht Club	A4
7	Surf Life Saving Club	D4

Sleeping

8	By the Sea Port Douglas	D3
9	Club Tropical Resort	B2
10	Global Backpackers	C2
11	Hibiscus Gardens	C3
12	ParrotFish Lodge	C3
13	Port Douglas Cottage & Lodge	C3
14	Port Douglas Motel	C3
15	Port Douglas Retreat	C3
16	Tropic Sands Holiday Apartments	C4

Eating

17	2 Fish Restaurant	B2
18	Coles Supermarket	B2
19	Nautilus Restaurant	B2
20	On the Inlet Restaurant	A3
21	Re:hab	C3
22	Salsa Bar & Grill	B2
23	Seafood House	B2
24	Zinc	C3

Drinking

25	Court House Hotel	B2
26	Iron Bar	B2
	Port Douglas Yacht Club	(see 6)
27	Tin Shed	A2
28	Whileaway	C3

There's no shortage of wildlife tourist parks in north Queensland, but this one is up there with the best. The sanctuary endeavours to keep and showcase native animals in enclosures that closely mimic their natural environment – wetlands, grasslands and rainforest – but also allows you to get up close. It's home to koalas, kangaroos, crocs and tree kangaroos, as well as parrots, wading birds, kookaburras, flying foxes and the prehistoric-looking cassowary – take your time as your ticket is valid for three days. Come early to have **Breakfast with the Birds** (adult/child incl park entry $44/22; 8-10.30am) or book in for **Lunch with the Lorikeets** (adult/child incl park entry $44/22; noon-2pm). The sanctuary also operates a wildlife care centre for sick or injured animals.

Port Douglas Markets MARKET
(Anzac Park, Macrossan St; 8am-1.30pm Sun) The grassy foreshore of Anzac Park spills over every Sunday morning with stalls selling arts, crafts and jewellery, as well as locally produced tropical fruits, ice creams and coconut milk, and hot food stalls. You'll find treasure without the trash: only wares made by stallholders or their families are allowed to be sold here. Arrive early for maximum browsing potential.

Court House Museum MUSEUM
(www.douglas-shire-historical-society.org; 18 Wharf St; admission $2; 10am-3pm Tue, Thu, Sat & Sun) Located near Anzac Park, this small but absorbing museum is housed in Port Douglas' 1879-built former courthouse. After police use ceased in 1963, the timber building lay dormant until 1993, when it was restored by the council and the Port Douglas Restoration Society, whose volunteers run the museum. Interesting exhibits on the town's early history include displays on the Chinese community, which in the late 19th century comprised two-thirds of the district's population, the 1887 trial of Ellen Thomson, the only woman legally hanged in Queensland, and the 1942 Battle of the Coral Sea.

St Mary's by the Sea CHURCH
(6 Dixie St) Worth a peek inside (when it's not overflowing with wedding parties), this quaint, nondenominational, white-timber church was built in 1911 and relocated to its seaside position in 1989.

Activities

What Port Douglas lacks in sights, it makes up for with a smorgasbord of activities and tours.

FREE **Port Douglas Yacht Club** SAILING
(www.portdouglasyachtclub.com.au; Spinnaker Close) Already been to the reef? Port's yacht club offers free sailing with club members every Wednesday afternoon. You might have to do some sweet-talking if places are limited but it's a great way to get out on the water and meet some locals.

Ballyhooley Steam Railway MINIATURE TRAIN
(www.ballyhooley.com.au; adult/child day pass $8/4; Sun) Kids will get a kick out of this cute miniature steam train. Every Sunday (and some public holidays), it runs from the little station at Marina Mirage to St Crispins station at 11am, 1pm and 2.30pm, stopping at Dougies Backpackers Resort (p360), Mirage Country Club (p357) and **Rydges Sabaya Resort** (87 Port Douglas Rd). A round trip takes about one hour; discounts are available for shorter trips. Buy tickets on board.

Golf GOLF
Port Douglas has two of north Queensland's finest public-access golf courses. They're not cheap, but if you're a keen golfer it's an opportunity too good to miss. If the green fees are too steep, try the nearby Mossman Golf Club (p364). **Tropical Golf Tours** (4098 4929; www.portdouglasgolftours.com.au) offers a range of packages including transport, golf cart and green fees starting at $290 for three rounds.

Designed by Peter Thomson (which should get golf fans excited), the **Mirage Country Club** (4099 5537; www.miragecountryclub.com.au; Port Douglas Rd; 18 holes $98) course sprawls around the Sheraton Mirage Port Douglas.

Located at the Sea Temple Resort & Spa, the **Sea Temple Golf Club** (4087 2222; www.seatemplegolfclub.com.au; Old Port Rd; 18 holes $130; 6.30am-4pm) is a championship links course that is rated in the top 50 in Australia.

WindSwell KITE SURFING
(0427 498 042; www.windswell.com.au; Four Mile Beach) At the southern end of Four Mile Beach, this enthusiastic outfit offers two-hour intro lessons from $100, and two-hour rental from $150. It also runs tours, including tours to the Low Isles.

Port Douglas Boat Hire BOAT HIRE
(☎4099 6277; pdboathire@bigpond.com; Berth C1, Marina Mirage) Rents a range of boats, including dinghies (per hour $31) and canopied, family-friendly pontoon boats (per hour $41) to take on the inlet. Fishing gear (rod and reel $13, hand lines $7, including bait and tackle) is also available here.

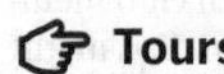

Tours

Port Douglas is a hub for tours. The number-one destination is the reef, with the rugged rainforests of Cape Tribulation the next most popular tour.

Many tours based out of Cairns (p311), including some white-water rafting and hot-air ballooning trips, also pick up from Port Douglas. Conversely, many of the following tours departing from Port Douglas also offer pick-ups from Cairns and Cairns' Northern Beaches.

GREAT BARRIER REEF

The outer reef lies closer to Port Douglas than it does to Cairns, and the unrelenting surge of visitors has had a similar impact on its condition here. You'll still see colourful corals and marine life, but it's patchy in parts. Access to the majority of spots that operators visit is around an hour from Port Douglas. From May to September, sightings of dwarf minke and humpback whales are common.

Most day tours depart from Marina Mirage. Tours generally make two to three stops on the outer and ribbon reefs, including St Crispins, Agincourt, Chinaman and Tongue Reefs. Tour prices include reef tax, snorkelling, transfers from your accommodation, lunch and refreshments. An introductory dive – a controlled scuba dive with no certification or experience necessary – costs around $240, with additional dives around $40; certified divers will pay around $250 for two dives with all gear included.

Reef Tours

Aristocat REEF TRIPS
(☎4099 4727; www.aristocat.com.au; adult/child $195/135) Fast cat to three sites; maximum 45 passengers.

Calypso REEF TRIPS
(☎4099 6999; www.calypsocharters.com.au; adult/child $195/140) Large catamaran visiting three outer reefs.

Haba REEF TRIPS
(☎4098 5000; www.habadive.com.au; Marina Mirage; adult/child $180/104) Long-standing, well-regarded local dive company; also offers 25-minute glass-bottomed boat tours (adult/child $16/8).

Poseidon REEF TRIPS
(☎4099 4772; www.poseidon-cruises.com.au; adult/child $195/135) Friendly family-owned and -operated luxury catamaran with trips to Agincourt Reef.

Quicksilver REEF TRIPS
(☎4087 2100; www.quicksilver-cruises.com; adult/child $204/105) Major operator with fast cruises to Agincourt Reef. If you don't want to get your hair wet, try an 'ocean walk' helmet dive ($142) on a submerged platform, with hoses attached to your helmet so you can breathe normally (great for nonswimmers and kids over 12). Also offers scenic helicopter flights from the pontoon on the reef ($148, minimum two passengers).

Sail Tallarook REEF TRIPS
(☎4099 4990; www.sailtallarook.com.au; adult/child $110/85) Historic 90ft yacht sailing to Tongue Reef. Sunset cruises ($50, Tuesday and Thursday) include cheese platters; BYO drinks. Introductory dives available.

Silversonic REEF TRIPS
(☎4087 2100; www.silverseries.com.au; adult/child $180/129) Smooth trips out to Agincourt Reef.

Synergy REEF TRIPS
(☎4084 2800; www.synergyreef.com.au; adult/child $270/200) With a maximum of just 12 passengers, the *Synergy* sails to the outer reefs; snorkelling only (no diving).

Wavelength REEF TRIPS
(☎4099 5031; www.wavelength.com.au; adult/child $200/150) Outer reef snorkelling at three sites with a marine biologist. Maximum 30 passengers; no diving.

Low Isles

Several operators visit the Low Isles: an idyllic little island with a lighthouse and fringing coral just 15km offshore, offering your best chance for spotting turtles.

Aquarius LOW-ISLES TRIPS
(☎4099 6999; www.portdouglascruises.com; trips $230) Guided island walks and snorkelling only, with glass-bottomed boat trips. Maximum 23 passengers; not suitable for kids under 14.

Reef Sprinter LOW-ISLES TRIPS
(☎4099 3175; www.reefsprinter.com.au; adult/child $100/80) Superfast 15-minute trip to the Low Isles for speed snorkelling (and no seasickness!); departs from beside On The Inlet Restaurant.

Sailaway LOW-ISLES TRIPS
(☎4099 4772; www.sailawayportdouglas.com; adult/child $190.50/120.50) Popular sailing and snorkelling trip to the Low Isles that's great for families; maximum 27 passengers. Also offers 90-minute twilight sails ($50, Monday to Friday).

Dive Schools

A couple of Port Douglas–based schools offer PADI dive courses, including open-water and advanced certificates:

Reef Dive School DIVING
(☎4099 6980; www.reefdiveschool.com; 4- to 5-day open-water courses from $550) Friendly instruction; also offers advanced courses.

Tech Dive Academy DIVING
(☎4099 6880; www.tech-dive-academy.com; 4-day open-water courses from $1390) High-quality, one-on-one instruction (additional person $590); also advanced and technical dive courses.

THE DAINTREE & AROUND

Numerous operators offer day trips to the Daintree and Cape Tribulation, some via Mossman Gorge.

BTS Tours DAY TRIPS
(☎4099 5665; www.btstours.com.au; adult/child $154/110) Tours to the Daintree Rainforest and Cape Trib, including canoeing.

Deluxe Safaris DAY TRIPS
(☎4099 6406; www.deluxesafaris.com.au; adult/child $165/135) Upmarket tour taking in Cape Trib and Mossman Gorge; also offers Bloomfield Track 4WD tours to Bloomfield Falls.

Fine Feather Tours CRUISES, BIRDWATCHING
(☎4094 1199; www.finefeathertours.com.au; half-/full-day tours $175/245) Half-day Daintree River cruises; serious ornithologists and amateur twitchers alike will love the birdwatching hinterland tours, led by an expert guide.

Flames of the Forest ABORIGINAL CULTURE
(☎4099 3144; www.flamesoftheforest.com.au; dinner, show & drinks adult/child from $204/160; ⏱Tue, Thu & Fri) Just 10 minutes from town you can dine at communal tables in flame- and candle-lit rainforest surroundings in a silk marquee while watching Aboriginal cultural shows with storytelling, didgeridoo playing and singing. Saturday nights don't have performances, but do have private tables (adults only) and a six-course tasting menu. Prices include transfers to and from Port Douglas.

Reef and Rainforest Connections DAY TRIPS
(☎4099 5333; www.reefandrainforest.com.au; adult/child $163/105) A big range of day-long ecotours that combine a number of attractions. In addition to its flagship Cape Trib and Mossman Gorge trip, there are various trips to Kuranda and wildlife tours to the region's parks and sanctuaries.

FISHING

Reef-, river- and land-based fishing charters operate regularly out of Port Douglas. Fishing gear and bait is included.

Norseman Port Douglas FISHING
(☎4099 6668; www.mvnorseman.com.au; Closehaven Marina; day tours adult/child $195/175) Private charters also available (per day $3510; maximum 18 people).

Fishing Port Douglas FISHING
(☎4099 4058; www.fishingportdouglas.com.au) Fishing on the river (share/sole charter per day $200/800) and reef (share/sole charter per day $225/3200).

Tropical Fishing & Eco Tours FISHING, WILDLIFE
(☎4099 4272; www.fishingecotours.com) Half-day fishing trips from $90; wildlife-spotting inlet tours from $30.

RIVER CRUISES & DRIFT SNORKELLING

Lady Douglas CRUISES
(☎4099 1603; www.ladydouglas.com.au; 1½hr cruises adult/child $30/15) Lovely paddleboat running croc-spotting cruises along the Dickson Inlet.

Back Country Bliss Adventures CRUISES
(☎4099 3677; www.backcountryblissadventures.com.au; trips $80) Drift with the current along the river, spotting turtles and freshwater fish, with an interpretative guide. Easy and enjoyable, including for kids.

SCENIC FLIGHTS

GBR Helicopters SCENIC FLIGHTS
(☎4099 6030; www.gbrhelicopters.com.au; Port Douglas Rd; flights $359-529) Scenic reef and/or rainforest helicopter flights.

Port Douglas Microlights SCENIC FLIGHTS
(☎4099 3046; pdm@nothi.com.au; 30/60min flights from $150/240) Low-level flying, 300m off the ground, in an open-cockpit microlight (a bit like a motorised hang-glider). After some basic instructions from the pilot, you're ready to take the controls yourself.

Skysafari SCENIC FLIGHTS
(☎4099 3666; www.skysafari.com.au) Chopper flights from 10 minutes to an hour over Port Douglas ($110 per person), plus various flights over the reef, rainforest and Mossman Gorge, as well as the outback and Great Dividing Range ($479).

Festivals & Events

Port Douglas Carnivale CARNIVAL
(www.carnivale.com.au) It's not Rio, but Port Douglas' 10-day Carnivale in late May includes a colourful street parade, live music and food and wine galore.

Go Troppo Arts Festival ARTS
(www.go-troppo-arts-festival.com) Pottery workshops, painting classes and storytelling; held in late October.

Sleeping

Befitting a holiday town, Port Douglas is swimming in accommodation, most of it in self-contained apartments or upmarket resorts (mostly located a few kilometres from the centre on the way into town). There are a few budget options, but nothing like the scale of Cairns, and price brackets here generally move up a notch. Signboards often promote standby rates, but you'll invariably get much better discounts online. Prices can drop significantly during quieter times.

Accommodation Port Douglas (☎1800 079 030, 4099 5355; www.accomportdouglas.com.au; 1/48 Macrossan St; ⏲9am-5pm Mon-Sat) is a useful agent for holiday rentals.

TOP CHOICE **Pink Flamingo** BOUTIQUE RESORT $$
(☎4099 6622; www.pinkflamingo.com.au; 115 Davidson St; r $125-195; ❄@🛜🏊) Flamboyant fuchsia-, purple- and orange-painted rooms opening onto private courtyards (with hammocks and outdoor baths and showers) and a groovy mirror-balled alfresco bar make the Pink Flamingo Port Douglas' hippest digs. At night, movies are screened under the palms; you can watch while floating in the pool! Tone your abs in the gym or rent a bike for a spin around town. Gay-owned, gay-friendly and all-welcoming (except for kids).

Port Douglas Cottage & Lodge COTTAGE, LODGE $$$
(☎1800 603 401, 4098 5432; www.portdouglascottage.com; 4 Owen St; cottages/lodges $375/475; ❄@🛜🏊) Beach hut meets Queenslander at these two free-standing, centre-of-town properties, each with their own private plunge pools. The two-storey, timber-floored cottage has views from the marble bath and a hidden kitchen; both have stainless-steel appliances and fittings, and loads of privacy.

Hibiscus Gardens RESORT $$$
(☎1800 995 995, 4099 5315; www.hibiscusportdouglas.com.au; 22 Owen St; d from $205; ❄@🏊) Balinese influences of teak furnishing and fixtures, bifold doors and plantation shutters – as well as the occasional Buddha – give this stylish resort an exotic ambience. The in-house day spa, specialising in Indigenous healing techniques and products, has a local reputation as the best (of many) places to be pampered in town.

Dougies Backpackers Resort HOSTEL $
(☎1800 996 200, 4099 6200; www.dougies.com.au; 111 Davidson St; tent sites per person $12, dm $26, safari tents $23, d $75; ❄@🛜🏊) At this laid-way-back hostel, it's easy to hang about the sprawling grounds in a hammock by day and move to the bar at night. If you do decide to leave the premises for a bit, rent a bike and/or fishing gear from reception, which also stocks groceries. Free pick-up from Cairns on Monday, Wednesday and Saturday.

Sea Temple Resort & Spa RESORT $$$
(☎1800 833 762, 4084 3500; www.mirvachotels.com.au; Mitre St; d from $309; ❄@🛜🏊) Port Douglas' most luxurious five-star resort and its prestigious golf course are set in lush tropical gardens near the southern end of Four Mile Beach. Rooms range from spa studios to the opulent 'swim out' penthouse with direct access to the enormous lagoon pool. Decadent day-spa treatments include hot stones.

Port Douglas Motel MOTEL $
(☎4099 5248; www.portdouglasmotel.com; 9 Davidson St; d $96; ❄🏊) For value and location this friendly little motel is hard to beat and as a result is often full. There are no views, but rooms are bright and well furnished; some have basic kitchen facilities (ie fridge, microwave and toaster). Wi-fi is on its way.

ParrotFish Lodge HOSTEL $
(☎1800 995 011, 4099 5011; www.parrotfishlodge.com; 37-39 Warner St; dm $25-33, d with/without bathroom $95/85; ❄@≋) Mural-sized contemporary art covers the bright-yellow walls at this energetic central backpackers. The extreme beach decor extends to the swirling iridescent-blue floors in the common areas and four- to eight-bed dorms (some with en suite). The on-site bar is a great meeting place; freebies include pick-ups from Cairns. Wi-fi is also on its way here.

Lychee Tree APARTMENTS $$
(☎4099 5811; www.lychee-tree.com.au; 95 Davidson St; 1-/2-bedroom apt $155/180; ❄≋) Families will fit right in at these single-storey, self-contained apartments. They're simply decorated and well equipped with kitchens, washing machines and dryers, DVDs and balconies overlooking tropical gardens. Minimum two-night stay.

Port o' Call Eco Lodge HOSTEL $
(☎4099 5422; www.portocall.com.au; cnr Port St & Craven Cl; dm $35, d $99-119; ❄@≋) This solar- and wind-powered, YHA-associated hostel was once a motel, so all of its squeaky-clean rooms have en suites. The good-value **bistro** (mains $16-25; dinner) and bar are both well patronised, but the vibe here is lower key than Port's other backpackers, so it's a good bet if you've outgrown the party scene or just need some time to recover.

Sheraton Mirage Port Douglas RESORT $$$
(☎4099 5888; www.starwoodhotels.com; Davidson St; d from $329; ❄@≋) Not to be confused with the separately located Marina Mirage, Port Douglas' original luxury resort is surrounded by five acres of swimmable lagoons – it looks amazing from the air. There's no doubt it's past its prime but it still has its own beachfront, golf course (p357), child-care facilities, a shuttle service into town, tennis courts and a gym.

Global Backpackers HOSTEL $
(☎1800 682 647, 4099 5641; www.globalportdouglas.com.au; 38 Macrossan St; dm $27-32, d $80; ❄@) Location, location... Port's most central hostel doesn't have a pool, but it's bang in the middle of Macrossan St above the Rattle n Hum restaurant and bar. Rooms are decked out in sleek dark-brown tones, doubles have en suites, and the kitchen and common room open onto a big balcony.

By the Sea Port Douglas APARTMENTS $$
(☎4099 5387; www.bytheseaportdouglas.com.au; 72 Macrossan St; d from $175; ❄@≋) Close to the beach and town centre, the 12 self-contained rooms are spread over three levels – the upper rooms have 'filtered' views through the palm trees to the beach. Its refitted rooms have neutral tones livened up with bright splashes of colour.

Club Tropical Resort APARTMENTS $$
(☎4099 5885; www.clubtropicalresort.com; cnr Macrossan & Wharf Sts; d $150; ❄≋) The good news? Apartment kitchens are set out on deep, shuttered balconies, and the town-centre location is awesome. The bad news? Street-facing (ie pub-facing) apartments can be seriously loud. The *really* bad news? Club Trop has no overnight managers, and attracts lots of groups, so screaming, singing, and spewing in the pool isn't dealt with until morning (yep, that pretty much ruined our stay...). Minimum two-night stay.

Pandanus Caravan Park CARAVAN PARK $
(☎4099 5944; Davidson St; unpowered/powered sites $30/35, cabins with/without bathroom $95/72; ❄@≋) Five minutes' stroll from the beach, this large, shady park has a good range of cabins as well as free gas barbecues.

Port Douglas Retreat APARTMENTS $$
(☎4099 5053; www.portdouglasretreat.com.au; 31-33 Mowbray St; d $149-179; ❄≋) Recline on a sun lounge on the wide wooden decking that surrounds the palm-lined swimming pool at this traditional Queenslander-style complex of 36 apartments.

Tropic Sands APARTMENTS $$
(☎4099 4533; www.tropicsands.com.au; 21 Davidson St; d from $175; ❄@≋) Handsome open-plan rooms in a beautiful, white, colonial-style building. From your private balcony, you can catch a whiff of the sea or whatever's cooking in your fully equipped kitchen. Kids aren't catered for.

Eating

For a town its size, Port Douglas has some of the most sophisticated dining north of Noosa. Chairs and tables spill out of cafes, and candlelit gardens are a romantic setting for lingering dinners. Chefs are in hot demand and frequently move around, so menus tend to be fairly similar. Advance reservations are recommended, and essential for really popular places.

Duck down tiny Grant St for juice bars, pie shops and pizzerias.

TOP CHOICE **Beach Shack** MODERN AUSTRALIAN $$
(☎4099 1100; www.the-beach-shack.com.au; 29 Barrier St, Four Mile Beach; mains $21-29; ⏰dinner; 🖉) There'd be an outcry if this local favourite took its macadamia-crumbed eggplant (with grilled and roast veggies, goat's cheese and wild rocket) off the menu. But it's the setting that makes it really worth heading to the southern end of Four Mile Beach: a lantern-lit garden with sand underfoot. Good reef fish, sirloins and blackboard specials.

Zinc MODERN AUSTRALIAN $$
(☎4099 6260; www.zincportdouglas.com; cnr Macrossan & Davidson Sts; mains $25-34; ⏰7am-midnight) Over 70 wines (40 by the glass) and 110 spirits and liqueurs set Zinc apart from its neighbours – as do dishes such as pan-seared Moreton Bay bugs with apple- and vanilla-scented sweet potato purée and candied cashews, and twice-cooked duck with Queensland blue (pumpkin) and port. Don't leave without checking out the floor-to-ceiling, fish-filled aquarium in the bathrooms!

On the Inlet SEAFOOD $$
(☎4099 5255; www.portdouglasseafood.com; 3 Inlet St; mains $22-39; ⏰lunch & dinner) Jutting out over Dickson Inlet, tables spread out along a huge deck where you can wave to the passing boats and await the 5pm arrival of George the groper, who comes to feed most days. Take up the bucket of prawns and a drink deal for $18 between 3.30pm and 5.30pm, or you can choose your own crayfish and mud crabs from the live tank. Great service, cool atmosphere.

Nautilus MODERN AUSTRALIAN $$$
(☎4099 5330; www.nautilus-restaurant.com.au; 17 Murphy St; mains $32-52; ⏰dinner) A hidden pathway leads through tropical gardens to intimate white-clothed tables amid tall palms at this decades-old fine-dining institution. Seafood is its speciality, such as wok-tossed mud crab with kaffir lime and lemongrass laksa. The pièce de résistance is the chef's six-course tasting menu ($110; $160 with paired wines). Children under eight aren't accepted.

Re:hab CAFE, GALLERY $
(Map p356; www.rehabportdouglas.com.au; 7/42 Macrossan St; ⏰8am-6pm; @📶) Coffee is literally an art form at this chilled cafe and local art gallery, with astoundingly intricate designs etched in the froth of its hot brews. Also has home-baked cakes, muffins and slices, and a little Zen courtyard out back.

2 Fish SEAFOOD $$$
(☎4099 6350; www.2fishrestaurant.com.au; 7/20 Wharf St; mains $25-39; ⏰lunch & dinner) Seafood dominates most menus in Port Douglas, but 2 Fish takes it to new levels. More than 15 types of fish, from coral trout to red emperor and wild barramundi, are prepared in a variety of innovative ways, or go for a hot or cold seafood platter for two ($130).

Salsa Bar & Grill MODERN AUSTRALIAN $$
(☎4099 4922; www.salsaportdouglas.com.au; 26 Wharf St; mains $17-30; ⏰lunch & dinner; 🖉) In a white Queenslander, Salsa is a stayer on Port's often-fickle scene. Try the Cajun jambalaya (rice with prawns, yabbies, crocodile and smoked chicken) or the gingerbread-dusted kangaroo with polenta and chocolate ganache, but save space for the soft cheeses made on-site.

OTZ DELI $$
(☎4099 3373; Four Mile Beach Plaza, Barrier St, Four Mile Beach; mains $14-29; ⏰7.30am-6pm Mon-Fri, 8am-6pm Sat & Sun, plus dinner Wed & Thu) Organic-oriented gourmet deli at the southern end of Four Mile Beach serving twice-weekly dinners.

Four Mile Seafood & Takeaway SEAFOOD, BURGERS $
(Four Mile Beach Plaza, Barrier St, Four Mile Beach; dishes $5.50-14; ⏰9am-8pm Mon-Sat, 11am-8pm Sun) Lots of places claim to have the best burgers in North Queensland. While this takeaway doesn't, burger combos such as fresh coral trout with avocado will convince you it actually does.

Whileaway CAFE, BOOKSHOP $
(www.whileaway.com.au; 2/43 Macrossan St; 9am-5.30pm; 📶) Excellent independent bookshop with well-read staff and potent coffee.

Self-Catering

Stock up on supplies at the large **Coles Supermarket** (11 Macrossan St) in the Port Village shopping centre. Or for locally caught seafood, including prawns, mud crabs and a big range of fish, head to **Seafood House** (11 Warner St).

Drinking & Entertainment

Drinking and dining go hand in hand in Port Douglas and the local clubs and hotels all serve up inexpensive pub-style meals. Even before the cutlery is packed away, many restaurants are inviting places for a drink.

TOP CHOICE **Tin Shed** LICENSED CLUB
(www.thetinshed-portdouglas.com.au; 7 Ashford Ave) Port Douglas' Combined Services Club is a locals' secret. This is a rare find: bargain dining on the waterfront – even the drinks are cheap. Sign in, line up and grab a table on the river- or shore-fronting deck.

Iron Bar PUB
(5 Macrossan St) A bit of whacky outback shearing shed decor never goes astray in Queensland. It's well done – all rustic iron and ageing timber; even the outdoor furniture is old wood and hessian. After polishing off your Don Bradman eye fillet (the steaks are named after famous Aussies), head upstairs for a flutter on the cane toad races. Usually the latest closer in town.

Court House Hotel PUB
(www.at-the-courty.com; cnr Macrossan & Wharf Sts; mains $15-25; ⊙lunch & dinner) Commanding a prime corner location, the 'Courty' is a lively local, with cover bands on weekends.

Port Douglas Yacht Club LICENSED CLUB
(www.portdouglasyachtclub.com.au; Spinnaker Close) Another local favourite, there's a spirited nautical atmosphere at Port's yacht club. Inexpensive meals are served nightly.

Information

There's no official (ie noncommercial) tourist information centre in Port Douglas but booking agencies have mountains of brochures and maps and, of course, can book any tour. In Cairns, the government-run Cairns & Tropical North Visitor Information Centre (p327) covers Port Douglas and the Daintree region, and can provide info and make bookings.

All the major banks have branches with ATMs along Macrossan St, where you'll also find internet cafes charging around $5 per hour. The main post office is on Owen St.

Getting There & Away

Coral Reef Coaches (☎4098 2800; www.coralreefcoaches.com.au) connects Port Douglas with Cairns ($36, 1¼ hours) via Cairns airport and Palm Cove.

Sun Palm (☎4087 2900; www.sunpalmtransport.com) has frequent daily services between Port Douglas and Cairns ($35, 1½ hours) via Cairns' northern beaches and the airport, and up the coast to Mossman ($10, 20 minutes), Daintree village and the ferry ($20, one hour), and Cape Tribulation ($48, three hours).

Airport Connections (☎4099 5950; www.tnqshuttle.com; ⊙3.20am-5.20pm) runs an hourly shuttle-bus service ($36) between Port Douglas, Cairns' Northern Beaches and Cairns airport, continuing on to Cairns CBD.

Country Road Coachlines (☎4069 5446; www.countryroadcoachlines.com.au) has a bus service between Port Douglas and Cooktown on the coastal route via Cape Tribulation three times a week ($63); weather permitting.

For more information on getting to Cairns, see p328.

Getting Around

Bicycle

Cycling around Port Douglas is a stress-free way to get about. Some accommodation places hire out bikes; otherwise try **Port Douglas Bike Hire** (☎4099 5799; www.portdouglasbikehire.com; cnr Wharf & Warner Sts; hire per day $19).

Bus

Sun Palm (☎4087 2900; www.sunpalmtransport.com; ⊙7am-midnight) runs in a continuous loop every half-hour from Wildlife Habitat Port Douglas to the Marina Mirage, stopping regularly en route. Flag down the driver at marked bus stops.

Car & Motorcycle

Port Douglas has plenty of small, local car-hire companies as well as major international chains. With the exception of Daintree Wild Zoo (p366), Port Douglas is the last place before Cooktown where you can hire a 4WD. Vehicle hire is pricier in Port than in Cairns; expect to pay around $65 per day for a small car and $130 per day for a 4WD, plus insurance.

Latitude 16 (☎4099 4999; www.latitude16.com.au; 54 Macrossan St) rents open-sided 4WDs (per day from $49).

Taxi

Port Douglas Taxis (☎13 10 08) offers 24-hour service and has a rank on Warner St.

NORTH OF PORT DOUGLAS

Once you drag yourself away from the cushy comforts of Port Douglas, the road north narrows and passes through the mill town of Mossman on the way to Daintree National Park and Cape Tribulation. Along this path are turn-offs to the rustic beachside communities of Wonga Beach and Newell Beach to the east, and the lush Whyanbeel Valley to the west.

On Mossman's southern edge, the road to the mountain-top hamlet of Julatten continues to Mt Molloy, from where you can head south to the Atherton Tableland, or north via the inland route to Cooktown.

Mossman

POP 1740

After the holiday hype of Port Douglas, Mossman – only 20km north – brings you back to earth. It's a pleasant, unpretentious cane town with a working sugar mill and cane trains to prove it. Mossman should be an obligatory stop to visit Mossman Gorge (and Mojo's restaurant!), and it's also a good place to fill up the tank and stock up on supplies if you're heading north.

Sights & Activities

Mossman Gorge NATIONAL PARK

(Map p354) In the southeast corner of Daintree National Park, 5km west of Mossman town, Mossman Gorge forms part of the traditional lands of the Kuku Yalanji people. Carved by the Mossman River, the gorge is a boulder-strewn valley where sparkling water washes over ancient rocks. **Walking tracks** loop along the river to a refreshing **swimming hole** where you can take a dip with the slow-moving jungle perch (identified by two black spots on their tails) – take care here, particularly after downpours, as the currents can be swift. Beyond the swimming hole, the Rex Creek swing bridge takes you across the river to a 2km elevated trail through the lowland rainforest. The wheelchair-accessible trail passes interpretive signs and trees dripping with jungle vines. The complete circuit back to the entrance takes about an hour. There's a picnic area here but no camping.

Kuku Yalanji Dreamtime Walks WALKING

(adult/child $38.50/22; ⌚9am, 11am, 1pm & 3pm Mon-Fri) To truly appreciate the cultural significance of Mossman Gorge, join the excellent 1½-hour guided walks run by Kuku Yalanji Dreamtime Walks. Indigenous guides lead you through the rainforest pointing out and explaining the significance of rock-art sites, plants and natural features, followed by damper and tea. Book Dreamtime Walks through the cultural and visitor centre, **Mossman Gorge Gateway** (☎4098 2595; www.yalanji.com.au; ⌚8.30am-5pm Mon-Fri), run by the Kuku Yalanji community. Its **gallery** displays Indigenous art and artefacts by local artists.

At the time of writing, Mossman Gorge Gateway was preparing to shift its location to the new car park along the road to the Gorge, from where electric buses will run to the Gorge entrance.

Janbal Gallery ART GALLERY

(☎4099 5599; www.janbalgallery.com.au; 5 Johnston Rd; ⌚Tue-Sat or by appointment) Not only can you browse and buy the art at this welcoming Indigenous gallery, you can also create your own under the guidance of its artist in residence, Binna. **Art classes** include painting an A4 canvas (adult/child $65/30, two hours), a boomerang ($48/30, one hour), painting (and playing) a didgeridoo ($165/80, three hours), and one-on-one lessons, while learning about local reef and rainforest heritage.

Mossman Sugar Mill Tours TOUR

(☎4030 4190; www.mossag.com.au; Mill St; adult/child $25/15; ⌚11am & 1.30pm Mon-Fri Jul-Oct) With all the cane fields around, you'll probably be curious to know how all that giant tropical grass gets turned into sugar. During crushing season, tours reveal all. Wear closed shoes; kids under five aren't allowed.

Mossman Golf Club GOLF

(☎4098 1570; Newell Beach Rd; 18 holes $30) If the prices at the flashy manicured resort golf courses of Port Douglas make your head spin, do as many of the locals do and play a round in pretty, tropical surrounds on this 18-hole course 3km northeast of town.

Sleeping & Eating

Silky Oaks Lodge CABINS $$$

(☎4098 1666; www.silkyoakslodge.com.au; Finlayvale Rd; treehouse/cabins from $598/798;

THE BAMA WAY

From Cairns to Cooktown, you can see the country through Aboriginal eyes along the **Bama Way** (www.bamaway.com.au). Bama (pronounced bumma) means 'person' in the Kuku Yalanji and Guugu Yimithirr languages. Take a tour with Aboriginal guides, such as the Walker Family Tours (p379) on the Bloomfield Track, or Willie Gordon's enlightening Guurrbi Tours (p383) from Cooktown. Pick up a Bama Way map from visitor centres.

(❄@📶≈) Spend languorous afternoons in the hammock strung on your private verandah in regenerated rainforest, take a guided nature walk, canoe along the river, or book in for a pampering spa treatment. This international resort woos honeymooners and soothes stressed-out execs with polished-timber cabins complete with aromatherapy oil burners. If you want to check out the lodge without sleeping there, the resort's stunning **Treehouse Restaurant & Bar** (mains $34-38; ⏲breakfast, lunch & dinner) is open to interlopers.

Demi View Motel MOTEL **$$**
(☎4098 1277; www.demiview.com.au; 41 Front St; s $69-79, d $89-99; ❄@📶≈) Airy, tiled rooms are on offer at this central spot on Mossman's main street, but the biggest draw is its proximity to the separately run restaurant out front, Mojo's (p365), which has inspired many guests to book in here for another night.

Mossman Gorge B&B B&B **$$**
(☎4098 2497; www.bnbnq.com.au/mossgorge; Lot 15 Gorge View Cres; s $125-135, d $145-165; ❄≈) Take a left turn on the road to the gorge to this intimate little timber B&B. Breakfast, including homemade bread, is served on the verandah, with uninterrupted views of the national park. Kids under 10 aren't catered for.

TOP CHOICE **Mojo's** INTERNATIONAL **$$**
(☎4098 1202; www.mojosbarandgrill.com.au; 41 Front St; mains $24-29; ⏲lunch Mon-Fri, dinner Mon-Sat; 🖉) Save yourself a round-the-world plane ticket: French-Australian team Remi Pougeard-Dulimbert and Michael Hart (who caters for the summer and winter Olympics) are the creative forces behind exquisite dishes such as feather-light gnocchi with blue cheese and caramelised pear, spicy samosas with tamarind chutney, soft-shell prawn tacos, and a *divine* scallop pie, followed by their 'Flaming Mojo' chocolate fondue with Bundy rum. Incredible value and well worth the trip from Port Douglas (or Paris, or anywhere, actually).

Raintrees Cafe CAFE **$$**
(☎4098 2139; 2 Front St; mains $10-14; ⏲breakfast & lunch) This country-style cafe opening onto a shady outdoor area is renowned for its burgers' secret sauce (no, they wouldn't tell us what's in it). It also doubles as an informal **visitor centre**, whose friendly staff can help with bookings.

Information

Department of Environment and Resource Management (DERM; ☎4098 2188; www.derm.qld.gov.au; Centenary Bldg, 1 Front St; ⏲8am-4pm Mon-Fri) Provides information on the Daintree National Park up to and beyond Cape Tribulation.

Getting There & Away

Sun Palm (☎4087 2900; www.sunpalmtransport.com) has three daily buses between Mossman and Cairns ($70, 1¾ hours) via Cairns airport, and Port Douglas ($10, 20 minutes), on its run to Cape Trib.

Julatten

POP 979

From the turn-off just south of Mossman the Rex Hwy climbs and winds through pretty, productive tropical-fruit farms and cattle country for around 20km to this smattering of buildings on the hillsides, which links up with the inland route to Cooktown.

Keen twitchers should head to **Kingfisher Park Birdwatchers Lodge** (☎4094 1263; www.birdwatchers.com.au; Lot 1 Mt Kooyong Rd; unpowered/powered sites $26/28, bunkhouse s/d $44/60, en suite unit s/d from $135/149; ❄), a birdwatchers' lodge where you can listen for the haunting cry of the wompoo pigeon or try to spot a buff-breasted paradise kingfisher. Not suitable for kids under 10.

Julatten Mountain Spa Retreat (☎4094 1282; www.julattenretreat.com; English Rd, via Euluma Creek Rd; d incl breakfast $200; ≈) includes yoga classes, or you can replenish your body and soul with an ayurvedic facial, massage or spiritual healing. Stay the night in one of the three secluded A-frame cottages, each with its own outdoor rainforest shower.

Mossman to the Daintree

Travelling north from Mossman, it's 26km through cane fields and farmland before the crossroads to either Daintree village or the Daintree River ferry, with some worthwhile stops en route.

NEWELL BEACH

Five kilometres from Mossman you'll come to the first 2.5km-long palm-fringed stretch of sand, Newell Beach. It's a small community where lazing around or fishing for dinner off the beach take priority.

Drop out of your life for a while at **Newell Beach Caravan Park** (☎4098 1331; www.newellbeachcaravanpark.com.au; 44 Marine Pde; unpowered/powered sites $23/30, cabins $75-90;), a block from the beach, with shady sites and comfy cabins.

WHYANBEEL VALLEY

About 8km northwest of Mossman, follow the turn-off to Miallo in the Whyanbeel Valley. Highlights of this hidden, fertile haven include the horticultural gardens and orchards of **High Falls Farm** (☎4098 8231; www.highfallsfarm.com.au; Old Forestry Rd, Miallo; mains $11.50-19.50; lunch Fri-Tue, breakfast & lunch Sun Jun-Oct;), by the river, serving simple but delicious meals such as open-faced focaccias with fried plantain bananas. Ask about self-guided orchard tours and tropical fruit tastings.

Nearby, **Karnak Playhouse** (Map p354; ☎4098 8111; www.karnakplayhouse.com.au; Upper Whyanbeel Rd, via Miallo; Jun-Oct) is a performance amphitheatre in a magical setting: the seats look down onto a timber stage set beside a small lake, with a backdrop of rainforest-covered hills. The brainchild of Diane Cilento – former actress and first wife of Sean Connery – it stages a limited number of musical and theatrical performances each year by acclaimed performers. Even if there's not a performance on, stop by its **cafe and gallery** (10am-4pm Jun- Oct) for coffee and home-baked cakes.

Stunning works of art are on display, and on sale, at the open-sided **Höglund Art Glass** (www.hoglundartglass.com; 580 Whyanbeel Rd; 10am-4pm Fri-Tue Jun-Oct) studio and gallery. Artists Ola and Marie Simberg-Höglund produce one-off pieces including multicoloured vases and fruit bowls or, if they won't fit in your suitcase, jewellery.

High-octane activities at the **Australian Muster Experience** (☎4098 1149; www.australianmusterexperience.com; Kingston Rd; by reservation) include horse riding (half-day $125), quad biking ($125) and tumbling downhill inside a clear, water-filled 'jungle ball' (per ride $50), as well as a whip-cracking stockman's muster show (adult/child $63/36 including an all-you-can-eat barbecue lunch). Transfers are available from Cairns and Port Douglas.

WONGA BEACH

The turn-off to Wonga Beach, 22km north of Mossman, leads to this peaceful 7km ribbon of beach backed by palms and calophyllum trees. **Wonga Beach Equestrian Centre** (Map p354; ☎4098 7583; www.beachhorserides.com.au; group rides $115) offers three-hour morning and afternoon rides along the beach. Personal guided rides start at $180; beginners can book in for a lesson (per hour $60).

You can almost feel the waves lapping at your campervan at **Wonga Beach Caravan Park** (☎4098 7514; 1 Esplanade; unpowered/powered sites $18.50/20), a simple, low-key camping ground with absolute beach frontage.

Pinnacle Village Holiday Park (☎4098 7566; www.pinnaclevillage.com; Vixies Rd; unpowered/powered sites $27/36, cabins with/without bathroom $95/75; @) is a huge, family-friendly beachfront site with grassy surrounds, a games room, a kiosk and a camp kitchen.

Back on the main road about 5km north of Wonga Beach, en route to the intersection to Daintree village or the Daintree River ferry, wildlife at **Daintree Wild Zoo** (☎4098 7272; www.daintreewild.com.au; 2054 Daintree Rd; adult/child $26/13; 8.30am-4.30pm) includes fresh and saltwater crocs, roos, dingoes and a cacophony of birds. It also has cosy farmstay accommodation, a BYO restaurant and tours from Cairns and Port Douglas, with various package deals available; good deals on 4WD rental for the Bloomfield Track can also be arranged.

THE DAINTREE

The Daintree represents many things: a river, a rainforest national park, a reef, a village, and the home of its traditional custodians, the Kuku Yalanji people. It encompasses the coastal lowland area between the Daintree and Bloomfield Rivers, where the rainforest meets the coast. It's an ancient but fragile ecosystem, once threatened by logging and development but now largely protected as a World Heritage area. For travellers it's an opportunity to immerse yourself in a sublime natural environment – the fan palms, ferns and mangroves are just some of around 3000 plant species and the forest is alive with a chorus of birds, frogs and insects.

The Daintree National Park stretches inland from Mossman Gorge to the Bloomfield River, while tiny Daintree village sits on the river about 12km upstream from the ferry crossing.

The Daintree was named after British-born geologist, gold prospector and photographer Richard Daintree (1832–78), the first government geologist for north Queensland,

DAINTREE NATIONAL PARK: THEN & NOW

The greater Daintree Rainforest is protected as part of the Daintree National Park. The area has a controversial history: despite conservationist blockades, in 1983 the Bloomfield Track was bulldozed through lowland rainforest from Cape Tribulation to the Bloomfield River, and the ensuing international publicity led indirectly to the federal government to nominate Queensland's wet tropical rainforests for World Heritage listing. The move drew objections from the Queensland timber industry and the state government, but in 1988, the area was inscribed on the World Heritage List, resulting in a total ban on commercial logging in the area.

World Heritage listing doesn't affect land ownership rights or control, and since the 1990s, efforts have been made by the Queensland State Government and conservation agencies to buy back and rehabilitate freehold properties, adding them to the Daintree National Park and installing visitor interpretation facilities such as the Marrdja and Dubuji boardwalks. Sealing the road to Cape Tribulation in 2002 opened the area to rapid settlement, triggering the buy-back of hundreds more properties. Coupled with development controls, these efforts are now bearing the fruits of forest regeneration. Check out the **Rainforest Rescue** (www.rainforestrescue.org.au) website for more information.

Biodiversity

Far North Queensland's Wet Tropics World Heritage Area has amazing pockets of biodiversity. It stretches from Townsville to Cooktown and covers 894,420 hectares of coastal zones and hinterland, diverse swamp and mangrove-forest habitats, eucalypt woodlands and tropical rainforest. It covers only 0.01% of Australia's surface area, but has:

» 36% of all mammal species

» 50% of bird species

» around 60% of butterfly species

» 65% of fern species

Making a difference

Increased tourism is undoubtedly having an impact on the Daintree. When visiting, leave only footsteps behind: take your rubbish with you, stick to designated trails and watch out for wildlife on the roads.

Other ways to help preserve this impossibly beautiful part of the world:

» Check whether tour companies have eco-certification (www.ecotourism.org.au).

» Use natural, chemical-free toiletries.

» Ask about volunteer opportunities to clean up beaches or monitor wildlife, or contact Austrop (Bat House; p373) to assist with forest rehabilitation and planting.

» Consider donating to a nonprofit environment group, such as Rainforest Rescue, the Wilderness Society or the Australian Conservation Foundation.

» Choose accommodation that encourages recycling and low energy and water consumption.

whose pioneering work included geological surveys and a collection of plant specimens.

Daintree Village

POP 130

You may be racing to the beaches of Cape Trib, but it's worth taking the 20km detour to tiny, low-key Daintree village to spot crocs along the broad Daintree River. Settlement here began in the 1870s when loggers sought the area's red cedars for their strength, versatility and beauty, and the logs were floated down the Daintree River for onward transportation. While neither the village nor the surrounding countryside are part of the Wet Tropics World Heritage Area, there are still pockets of untouched rainforest.

DAINTREE PRACTICALITIES

Despite the number of tourists that make their way to the Daintree, this is still remote country. There's no mains power north of the Daintree River – electricity is supplied by generators or, increasingly, solar power. As a result, air-con is rare and, if available, comes at a premium.

Shops and services are limited; self-caterers should consider stocking up at Mossman, which also has the closest banks – though most places to stay and eat and the general stores have Eftpos and credit-card facilities, and there's an ATM at the IGA supermarket in Cape Trib. The only fuel between the Daintree River and the Bloomfield Track Takeaway & Middleshop (p379) is at Rainforest Village (p372), just south of Cooper Creek. Mobile phone reception (with any network) is largely nonexistent due to the rainforest canopy. A number of places have internet, but wi-fi is not widespread.

Although Cape Trib is a popular day trip from Port Douglas and Cairns, accommodation here can still be booked solid in peak periods – plan ahead.

Sights & Activities

Croc-spotting cruises on the Daintree River are the village's main attraction (see boxed text, p369). The Daintree Eco Lodge & Spa (p368) organises Aboriginal-led walks and art classes for guests and nonguests.

Daintree Argo Rainforest Tours OFF-ROAD TOURS
(☎0409 627 434; Upper Daintree Rd; 1hr tour $40) Head into the rainforest and cattle country aboard an Argo 8x8 (a tank-like amphibious, open-topped, all-terrain vehicle) to take in panoramic mountaintop views on this family cattle property 1km from the village.

Sleeping

There are some beautiful B&Bs and boutique accommodation in the village and the surrounding forest and farmland.

Daintree Eco Lodge & Spa BOUTIQUE RESORT **$$$**
(☎4098 6100; www.daintree-ecolodge.com.au; 20 Daintree Rd; d $550-598; ❄@📶≋) The 15 boutique 'banyans' (pole cabins; 10 with private spas) sit high in the rainforest canopy a few kilometres south of Daintree Village. Despite its cachet, staff are genuinely warm, and even the **day spa** is eco-minded, with its own range of organic products and methods borrowed from the Indigenous community, including a spiritual waterfall treatment at the property's ancient falls. Guests and nonguests can take 90-minute **guided rainforest walks** ($40) and two-hour **Aboriginal art classes** ($68) with members of the Kuku Yalanji community, and dine at its superb restaurant (p369).

Kenadon Homestead Cabins CABINS **$$**
(☎4098 6142; www.daintreecabins.com; Dagmar St; d incl breakfast $130; ❄≋) On the fringe of a 400-acre, fifth-generation cattle station, Kenadon's timber cabins can sleep up to five, making them ideal for families. Clustered together near the pool, they face the vast pastures.

Red Mill House B&B **$$$**
(☎4098 6233; www.redmillhouse.com.au; 11 Stewart St; s/d $160/200; ❄@≋) Birdwatchers will love the Red Mill. The owners of this pair of timber Queenslanders are enthusiastic birders and the large verandah overlooking the rainforest garden is a prime spot to observe the resident wildlife. There are four well-appointed en suite rooms, a large communal lounge and library, and a two-bedroom family unit. Guided birding walks are available on request.

Daintree Valley Haven CABINS **$$**
(☎4098 6206; www.daintreevalleyhaven.com.au; Stewart Creek Rd; s/d incl breakfast $135/170; ❄) Secluded farm-style accommodation, 8km south of the village. Kids aren't allowed.

Daintree Riverview CARAVAN PARK **$**
(☎4098 6119; www.daintreeriverview.com; Stewart St; unpowered/powered sites $20/30, cabins $99) Riverside camping and good-value en suite cabins.

Daintree Escape CABINS **$$**
(☎4098 6021; www.daintreeescape.com.au; 17 Stewart St; d $175; ❄@≋) Cute cabins amid grassy gardens; strolling distance from the village.

DON'T MISS

DAINTREE RIVER CROC-SPOTTING CRUISES

Sightings of resident saltwater crocodiles are frequent, though not guaranteed, on the Daintree River, but there's plenty to see in any case – birds and butterflies in particular. At the end of Daintree Village's main street, the public-access wharf is the departure point for a number of small tour operators. More tour operators have their own departure points along Daintree Rd between the Daintree River ferry crossing and the village.

Departure times vary seasonally; tours can be booked directly or at visitor centres and booking agencies in the village.

Bruce Belcher's Daintree River Cruises CRUISES
(☎4098 7717; www.daintreerivercruises.com; adult/child $25/10) One-hour cruises on a covered boat.

Chris Dahlberg's Daintree River Tours BIRDWATCHING
(☎4098 7997; www.daintreerivertours.com.au; Daintree Village; 2hr cruise adult/child $55/35) Sunrise tours specialising in birdwatching.

Crocodile Express CROCODILE-SPOTTING
(☎4098 6120; www.daintreeconnection.com.au; Daintree Village; 1hr cruise adult/child $25/13; ⊙daily from 8.30am) The original Daintree River cruise operator.

Daintree River Experience BIRDWATCHING
(☎4098 7480; www.daintreecruises.com.au; 2hr cruise adult/child $50/35) Serene sunrise and sunset cruises specialising in birdwatching.

Daintree River Wild Watch BIRDWATCHING, CRUISES
(☎4098 7068; www.daintreeriverwildwatch.com.au; 2hr cruise adult/child $50/35) Informative sunrise birdwatching cruises and sunset nature photography cruises.

Dan Irby's Mangrove Adventures CRUISES
(☎4090 7017; www.mangroveadventures.com.au; 2hr cruise $55) Personalised cruises on a small aluminium punt.

Electric Boat Cruises CRUISES
(☎1800 686 103; www.electricboatcruises.com; 1hr cruise adult/child $24/12) Quiet, canopied electric boat.

Solar Whisper CROCODILE-SPOTTING, CRUISES
(☎4098 7131; www.solarwhisper.com; 1¼hr cruise adult/child $22/11) Electric boat fitted with a croc-cam.

Thundacroc CROCODILE-SPOTTING, CRUISES
(☎4098 6146; 1½hr cruise adult/child $35/20) Also runs one-hour cruises (adult/child $24/12). Book at the general store (p370).

Eating

TOP CHOICE **Julaymba Restaurant** MODERN AUSTRALIAN $$$
(☎4098 6100; www.daintree-ecolodge.com.au; 20 Daintree Rd; mains $29-32; ⊙breakfast, lunch & dinner) At Daintree Eco Lodge & Spa, a timber terrace looks over a lagoon and dense rainforest, and Aboriginal art decorates the walls. Dishes are prepared using local produce, including native berries, nuts, leaves and flowers. Don't miss a Flaming Green Ant cocktail, made with frozen green ants. It's high-end dining, but accommodating chefs are willing to whip up dishes such as delicious toasted sandwiches on request.

Daintree Tea House Restaurant MODERN AUSTRALIAN $$
(☎4098 6173; 3-5 Stewart St; mains $17-40; ⊙10am-4pm Mon-Wed, Fri & Sat, 10am-3pm Thu & Sun) The 'Taste of the Daintree' platter, with treats such as crocodile wontons and sugarcane prawns, is a signature dish at this timeless wooden teahouse. Fish and chips and beef pies sit alongside nasi goreng and delicately prepared barramundi.

Big Barramundi SEAFOOD $$
(☎4098 6186; 12 Stewart St; mains $5-18; ⊙lunch) Proving that even tiny rainforest towns aren't immune to the Australian propensity for building really big things, a gigantic

silver fish welcomes you to the Big Barra. The semi-open-air restaurant is an informal place for a barra burger, tropical fruit smoothie or Devonshire tea.

Daintree Village General Store

CAFE, GROCERIES **$$**

(1 Stewart St; mains $20-30; ⏲breakfast, lunch & dinner) The village's general store has an attached cafe serving beef-and-reef style meals. BYO from the attached bottle shop.

Information

Visitor Centre (☎4098 6120; www.daintreeconnection.com.au; 5 Stewart St; ⏲8.30am-4.30pm) On the main street; efficient and independent.

Daintree Tourism Information (www.daintree.info) A good online resource.

Service Station There's no fuel available in Daintree Village.

Daintree River to Cape Tribulation

Crossing the Daintree River by ferry gives the feeling that you're about to enter a frontier wilderness. From here the road narrows and winds north for 35km, hugging the coast for most of the way to Cape Tribulation. Along the way are tiny hamlets, isolated beaches and attractions that make getting to Cape Trib half the fun.

The Kuku Yalanji name for the area is Kulki; Captain Cook called it Cape Tribulation after his ship ran aground on an outlying reef.

Part of the Wet Tropics World Heritage Area, the region from the Daintree River north to Cape Tribulation is extraordinarily beautiful and famed for its ancient rainforest, sandy beaches and rugged mountains, including **Thornton Peak** (1375m) and **Mt Sorrow** (770m). Of the tropical lowland rainforest that existed before settlement, 96% has been cleared for cane, cattle and residences. Only north of the Daintree River does the forest remain relatively intact. It's one of the few places in the world where the tropical rainforest meets the sea.

In recognition of this unique environment, much of the area is protected as the Daintree National Park, which was declared in 1981. The Cape Tribulation section reaches from the Daintree River to the Bloomfield River, with the mountains of the McDowell Range providing the western boundary. The Cow Bay area is largely privately owned and excluded from the national park, but development is restricted.

Cow Bay and Cape Tribulation are loosely termed 'villages', but the length of Cape Tribulation Rd is scattered with places to stay and eat.

The lovable **Daintree River ferry** (car/motorcycle/bicycle & pedestrian one way $12/5/1; ⏲6am-midnight) carries you and your vehicle across the river, departing every 15 minutes or so (no booking required).

CAPE KIMBERLEY BEACH & AROUND

About 3km beyond the Daintree River crossing, a 5km unsealed road leads to Cape Kimberley Beach, a beautiful quiet beach with **Snapper Island** just off shore. The island is national park, with a fringing reef. Access is by private boat; **Crocodylus Village** (p371) runs sea-kayaking tours here. You'll need to obtain a permit for the **DERM Campground** (☎13 74 68; www.derm.qld.gov.au; per person $5.15) on the southwest side of Snapper Island, where there's a toilet and picnic tables. Take a fuel stove, as fires are not permitted.

At the junction of the road to Cape Kimberly, turning west and following the road for 12km (4km unsealed) leads you to **Daintree Forest Trails** (www.daintreeforesttrails.com; Old Forest Creek Rd, off Forest Creek Rd; adult/child $10/free; ⏲dawn-dusk), with six walking trails (from 15 minutes to one hour) in 5 sq km of rainforest wilderness.

COW BAY

On the steep, winding road between Cape Kimberly and Cow Bay is the **Walu Wugirriga (Alexandra Range) lookout**, with an information board and sweeping views over the range and the Daintree River inlet, which are especially breathtaking at sunset.

The award-winning rainforest interpretive centre **Daintree Discovery Centre** (Map p374; ☎4098 9171; www.daintree-rec.com.au; Tulip Oak Rd; adult/child $28/14; ⏲8.30am-5pm) has an **aerial walkway**, which takes you high into the forest canopy including climbing up a 23m-high **tower** (used to study carbon levels). There are a few short **interpretive walks** – including superb life-size sculptures of now-extinct giant wombats and echidnas, hidden among the foliage – and a small theatre running films on cassowaries, crocodiles, conservation and climate change (part of your admission fee goes towards carbon offsetting). You can spend about an hour meandering along the boardwalks and looking out for wildlife, but if you hire an audio guide allow at least a couple of hours. The audio guide offers an excellent interpretation of the rainforest from an Indigenous Australian perspective. Tickets are valid for seven days, with good rates for families.

Just past the centre, the **Jindalba Boardwalk** (Map p374) snakes a 700m circuit through the rainforest.

Cow Bay Horse Rides (Map p374; ☎4098 9202; Cape Tribulation Rd; 1/2hr rides $65/110) takes very personalised rides – from one to four people – on its forested property.

Serious anglers might want to take a helifishing jaunt with Cow Bay–based **Bungie Scott Helicopters** (☎0409 325 442; www.bungiehelicopters.com.au). Prices start from $1700 per person per day for a two-day trip including meals, accommodation and tackle.

Daintree Rainforest Retreat (Map p374; ☎4098 9101; www.daintreeretreat.com.au; 1473 Cape Tribulation Rd; d $121-149, f $190-210;) is set back from the main road amid rainforest. The boutique motel rooms are done out in striking tropical colour schemes and glossy woodwork. Some have kitchenettes, or you can dine at its on-site restaurant, **Tree Frogs** (Map p374; mains $15-36; dinner Mon-Sat), which is open to nonguests.

TOP CHOICE **Jambu** (Map p374; www.daintreecoffeecompany.com.au; 335 Cape Tribulation Rd; mains $9.50-15; breakfast & lunch;) This funky little find dishes up 12-inch wraps, fantastic burgers including tofu with homemade peanut sauce, rib steak, and reef fish (all somewhat unnecessarily served with additional side salads, but no matter), as well as boutique Australian beers like Little Creatures, and its own Daintree Coffee Company brews served in 10 different styles (espresso, ristretto, affogato et al).

If you're craving a counter meal and pot of beer, the **Cow Bay Hotel** (Map p374; ☎4098 9011; Cape Tribulation Rd; s/d $77/99, mains $12-25; lunch & dinner), adjacent to the turn-off to the beach, is the only real pub in the whole Daintree region (takeaway alcohol available), with an adjacent block of basic motel-style rooms.

Floravilla Ice Cream Factory (Map p374; ☎4098 9016; Bailey Creek Rd; ice creams $5; 8am-5.30pm), next door to the pub, has at least 26 flavours of organic ice cream using local ingredients such as macadamia and Davidson's plum, dragonfruit and ginger, as well as Guinness. The attached **gallery** displays photographs and plants.

Along the sealed Buchanan Creek Rd (often called Cow Bay Rd, or simply 'the road to the beach'), ultrabasic green canvas safari-style huts merge with the surrounding foliage at the YHA-associated **Crocodylus Village** (Map p374; ☎4098 9166; www.crocodyluscapetrib.com; Buchanan Creek Rd; dm/d $25/85;). If you prefer solid walls, go for the four- to six-bed dorms or private rooms. Its **restaurant** (mains $15; dinner) and bar are both open to the public, as are activities including half-day kayaking trips ($65) and adventurous two-day **sea-kayaking tours to Snapper Island** (tours $220; Mon, Wed & Fri).

Laidback **Epiphyte B&B** (Map p374; ☎4098 9039; www.rainforestbb.com; 22 Silkwood Rd; s/d/cabins $70/95/140) is set on a lush 3.5-hectare property with individually styled rooms of varying sizes but all with en suites and their own verandahs. Even better is the spacious, super-private cabin with a patio, kitchenette and sunken bathroom. From the front deck of the house you can kick back with views of imposing Thornton Peak. Rates include breakfast.

The best-value accommodation in the area, hands-down, is at **Daintree Rainforest Bungalows** (Map p374; ☎4098 9229; www.daintreerainforestbungalows.com; Lot 40 Spurwood Rd; d $90). Its freestanding wooden cabins are simple but stylish, with violet- and lilac-toned fabrics, en suites and sheltered decks overlooking the rainforest. Minimum stay is two nights.

Of course, Cow Bay's real highlight lies at the end of the road, where the beautiful white-sand **Cow Bay Beach** rivals any coastal paradise.

COW BAY TO COOPER CREEK

Strung out the main road from Cow Bay to Cooper Creek are a handful of accommodation and dining options.

Daintree Ice Cream Company (Map p374; ☎4098 9114; Lot 100 Cape Tribulation Rd; ice cream $5; 11am-5pm) No agonising decisions at this ice cream producer – you get a cup of four exotic flavours that change daily. It could be wattleseed, black sapote, macadamia, mango, coconut or jackfruit – they're all delicious. Work it off on a 20-minute self-guided **orchard walk** – pick up a free trail map from the kiosk.

Curtained by lush rainforest, **Daintree Wilderness Lodge** (Map p374; ☎4098 9105; www.daintreewildernesslodge.com.au; 83 Cape Tribulation

DON'T MISS

FRUITS OF THE FOREST

Black sapote, mangosteen, durian and jackfruit are just some of the delicious tropical fruits grown in the pristine conditions of the Daintree rainforest. Hit the brakes to taste the fruits of the labour of these eco-minded entrepreneurs:

» **Daintree Ice Cream Company** (p371) Four flavours of ice cream made everyday from fruit picked straight from the surrounding orchards.

» **Cape Trib Exotic Fruit Farm** (p373) Organic farm offering tastings of some of its 100-plus seasonal tropical fruits.

» **Floravilla Ice Cream Factory** (p371) Over two-dozen flavours of homemade organic ice cream.

Rd; d $280-300;) has seven timber cabins connected by a series of boardwalks. Each has a ceiling window to watch the rainforest canopy. There's a classy **restaurant** (mains $27-33; dinner), and you can end a night-time nature walk with a soak in the 'jungle jacuzzi'.

The family-friendly **Lync-Haven Rainforest Retreat** (Map p374; 4098 9155; www.lynchaven.com.au; Lot 44 Cape Tribulation Rd; unpowered/powered sites $24/28, d $120-160) is set on a 16-hectare property on the main road about 5km north of Cow Bay, with its own walking trails, hand-reared kangaroos and resident croc, Boris (who you can watch being fed each morning). Its **restaurant** (mains $16-28; breakfast, lunch & dinner) serves robust steaks, good pasta and fish.

The **Daintree Tea Company** (Map p374; www.daintreetea.com) sells its all-natural tea at a stall on the plantation, which operates on a cash-based honesty system.

COOPER CREEK

A smattering of sights nestles in the bend of Cooper Creek at the base of dramatic **Thornton Peak**.

Just south of the creek itself, **Rainforest Village** (4098 9015; 7am-7pm) sells groceries, ice and fuel, and has a small **camping ground** (unpowered/powered sites $24/32) with hot showers and a camp kitchen.

Also known as Jungle Bugs & Butterflies, the **Daintree Entomological Museum** (Map p374; 4098 9045; www.daintreemuseum.com.au; Turpentine Rd; adult/child $10/5; 10am-4pm) displays a large private collection of local and exotic bugs, butterflies and spiders pinned inside large glass cases. There are a few live exhibits of giant cockroaches and a butterfly enclosure.

Book ahead for a walk with **Cooper Creek Wilderness** (Map p374; 4098 9126; www.ccwild.com; Cape Tribulation Rd; guided walks $45). Bring your togs for the day walks (departing at 9am, 2pm and 3pm), which take you through Daintree rainforest and include a dip in Cooper Creek. Night walks (departing at 8pm) focus on spotting nocturnal wildlife. There's also a full-day tour including lunch and a river cruise ($130).

Cape Tribulation Wilderness Cruises (Map p374; 4033 2052; www.capetribcruises.com; Cape Tribulation Rd; adult/child $25/18) has one-hour mangrove cruises down Cooper Creek in search of crocs.

There are few better settings to practice, or learn, meditation and yoga than the ancient rainforest of the Daintree. **Prema Shanti** (Map p374; 4098 9006; www.premashanti.com; Turpentine Rd; tw per person $80) yoga retreats include meditation every morning and two hours of daily instruction. Share bathroom accommodation includes breakfast and dinner. Drop-in classes cost $18 per hour; by reservation only.

THORNTON BEACH

A sliver of vegetation separates Cape Tribulation Rd from magnificent crescent-shaped Thornton Beach. There's a small, rocky offshore island, and opportunities for snorkelling. Best of all is the licensed **Cafe on Sea** (Map p374; Cape Tribulation Rd; mains $12-20; 9am-4pm), only a towel-length back from the beach.

Directly across the road, **Thornton Beach Bungalows** (Map p374; 07-4098 9179; www.thorntonbeach.com; Cape Tribulation Rd; cabins/houses $85/250) has two petite cabins, plus a beach house sleeping four (there's a two-night minimum).

NOAH BEACH & AROUND

Marrdja Botanical Walk (Map p374) is a beautiful 540m interpretive boardwalk that follows the creek through a section of rainforest packed with fan palms and past mangroves to a lookout over Noah Creek. It takes about 30 minutes; wear insect repellent to beat the midges.

The **Noah Beach Campground** (Map p374; 13 74 68; www.derm.qld.gov.au; Cape Tribulation Rd; sites per person $5.15) at Noah Beach has 15 sites set 100m from the beach beneath red-trunked trees. There are toilets but no showers. Boil water before drinking – and watch out for crocs.

Noah Valley Mountain Treks (☎4098 9292; noahvalleymountaintreks@activ8.net.au; half-day/night treks $55/35) runs challenging, enviro-oriented treks through the Noah Valley.

Cape Tribulation

Walking along beautiful Cape Tribulation Beach in the gathering sunset, it's hard not to wonder what Captain Cook was thinking when he gave this little piece of paradise such a depressing name. Of course, he was too busy weaving his way through (and eventually running aground on) the reef to be awed by the dramatic coastline.

The rainforest tumbles right down to two magnificent beaches, Myall and Cape Trib, separated by a knobby cape. The village of Cape Tribulation marks the end of the road, literally, and the beginning of the 4WD-only coastal route along the Bloomfield Track. Discovered by hippies in the '70s, backpackers in the '80s and everyone else in the '90s, Cape Trib retains a frontier quality, with low-key development, road signs alerting drivers to cassowary crossings and crocodile warnings that make beach strolls that little bit less relaxing.

Sights & Activities

Beaches & Waterholes SWIMMING, WALKING

Emerge from the rainforest and you're on Cape Trib's main attraction – the beach. Long walks on the stunning swathes of **Cape Tribulation Beach** or **Myall Beach** (Map p354) are a favourite pastime and you can swim in the shallows of the Coral Sea outside stinger season, though heed any warning signs and local advice about croc sightings. From the main car park it's a short walk to Cape Trib Beach; also from the car park, a trail leads for 500m over a ridge through rainforest to Myall Beach. You can walk about 1.5km south along the beach (crossing a small creek) and return to the village along the **Myall Creek boardwalk**. Look out for lace monitors (goannas), birdlife and the tiny mud crabs that inhabit the creek beds.

Just south of PK's Jungle Village is another car park, from where the **Dubuji Boardwalk** (Map p374) is an easy 1.8km wheelchair-accessible loop through mangroves and rainforest.

Alternatively, you can take a dip in the crystal-clear, croc-free **swimming hole** (admission by gold coin donation) adjacent to Mason's Store (p377).

Ocean Safari REEF TRIPS

(☎4098 0006; www.oceansafari.com.au; adult/child $108/69; ⊙9am & 1pm) The Great Barrier Reef is just half an hour offshore, but Ocean Safari is one of the few, if not the only, outfits running trips to the reef. You'll be one of a maximum of 25 people onboard; prices include snorkelling gear. It's professionally run and very popular, so book ahead.

Jungle Surfing FLYING FOX

(☎4098 0043; www.junglesurfing.com.au; $90) Get right up into the rainforest on an exhilarating zipline flying fox through the rainforest canopy, stopping at five tree platforms. Tours depart eight times daily from Cape Tribulation Pharmacy (next to the IGA Supermarket). It's not possible to self-drive to the property, and spectators aren't allowed.

The same outfit also runs guided **night walks** ($40) at 7.30pm in which zany biologist guides help shed light on the dark jungle; offers free pick-ups throughout Cape Trib.

Cape Trib Exotic Fruit Farm FARM TOUR

(Map p374; ☎4098 0057; www.capetrib.com.au; tastings $20; ⊙tastings at 2pm) Bookings are essential for tours of these magnificent tropical orchards and a tasting of 10 of the 100-plus seasonal organic fruits grown here using permaculture methods. It also has a couple of stunning private cabins (p375).

Bat House CONSERVATION CENTRE

(Map p374; ☎4098 0063; Cape Tribulation Rd; www.austrop.org.au; admission $2; ⊙10.30am-3.30pm Tue-Sun) This information and education centre is run by volunteers from local conservation organisation **Austrop**. As the name suggests, it's also a nursery for injured or orphaned fruit bats (flying foxes), and there's always one hanging around for you to meet. Austrop also welcomes forest rehabilitation and planting **volunteers** for a minimum of one week (on-station bunkhouse accommodation and meals included).

Mt Sorrow WALKING

Serious, fit walkers should lace up early for the **Mt Sorrow Ridge Walk** (7km, five to six hours return); it's strenuous but worth it. The start of the marked trail is about 150m

Cape Tribulation Area

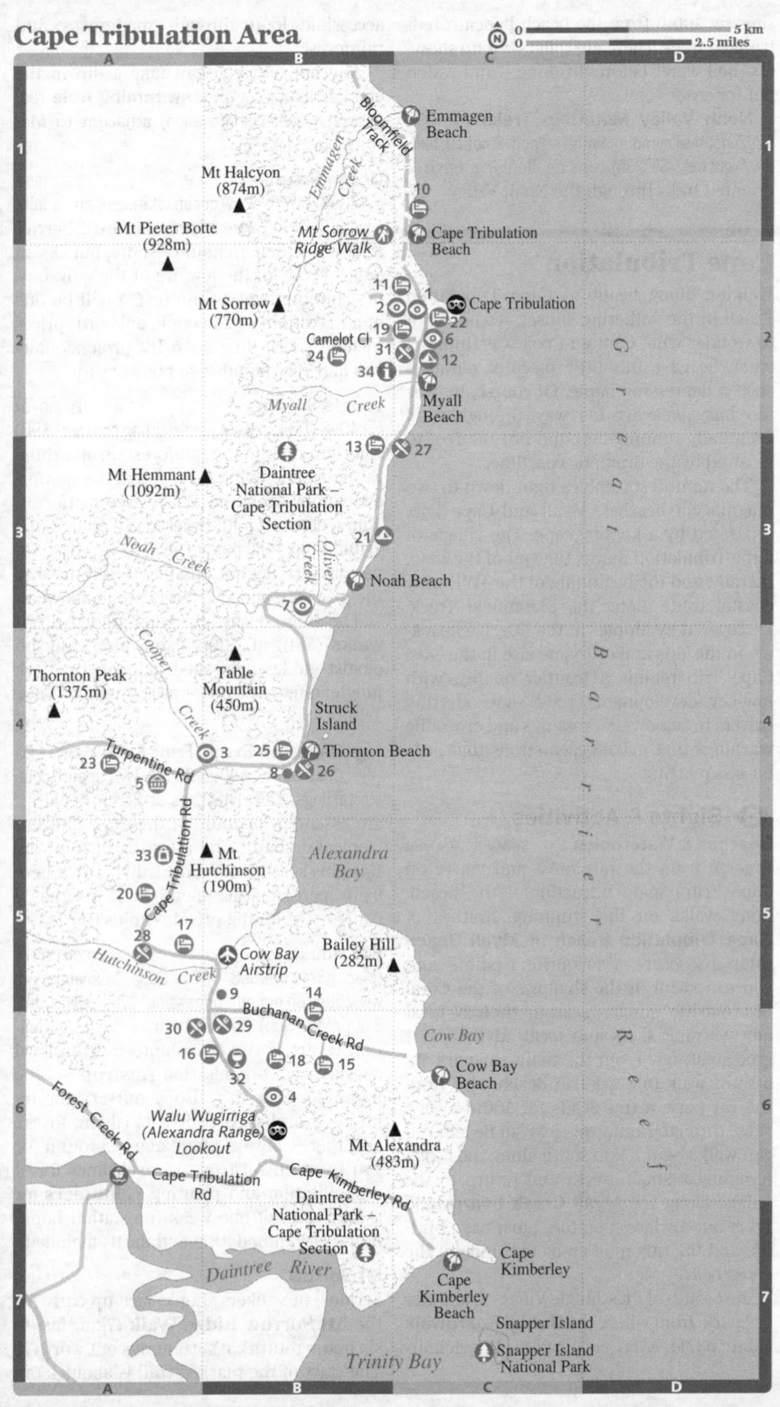

0 5 km
0 2.5 miles
Emmagen Beach
Bloomfield Track
Emmagen Creek
Mt Halcyon (874m)
Mt Pieter Botte (928m)
Mt Sorrow Ridge Walk
Cape Tribulation Beach
Mt Sorrow (770m)
Cape Tribulation
Camelot Cl
Myall Creek
Myall Beach
Great Barrier Reef
Mt Hemmant (1092m)
Daintree National Park – Cape Tribulation Section
Noah Creek
Oliver Creek
Noah Beach
Cooper Creek
Table Mountain (450m)
Thornton Peak (1375m)
Struck Island
Thornton Beach
Turpentine Rd
Cape Tribulation Rd
Mt Hutchinson (190m)
Alexandra Bay
Bailey Hill (282m)
Cow Bay Airstrip
Hutchinson Creek
Buchanan Creek Rd
Cow Bay
Cow Bay Beach
Forest Creek Rd
Walu Wugirriga (Alexandra Range) Lookout
Mt Alexandra (483m)
Cape Tribulation Rd
Cape Kimberley Rd
Daintree National Park – Cape Tribulation Section
Daintree River
Cape Kimberley
Cape Kimberley Beach
Snapper Island
Snapper Island National Park
Trinity Bay

Cape Tribulation Area

Sights

1 Bat House ... C2
2 Cape Trib Exotic Fruit Farm ... C2
3 Cooper Creek Wilderness ... B4
4 Daintree Discovery Centre ... B6
5 Daintree Entomological Museum ... A4
6 Dubuji Boardwalk ... C2
Jindalba Boardwalk ... (see 4)
7 Marrdja Botanical Walk ... B3

Activities, Courses & Tours

Mason's Tours ... (see 34)
8 Cape Tribulation Wilderness Cruises ... B4
9 Cow Bay Horse Rides ... B5

Sleeping

Cape Trib Exotic Fruit Farm Cabins ... (see 2)
10 Cape Trib Beach House ... C1
11 Cape Trib Farmstay ... C2
12 Cape Tribulation Camping ... C2
13 Cape Tribulation Resort ... B3
14 Crocodylus Village ... B5
15 Daintree Rainforest Bungalows ... B6
16 Daintree Rainforest Retreat ... B6
17 Daintree Wilderness Lodge ... A5
18 Epiphyte B&B ... B6
19 Ferntree Rainforest Resort ... C2
20 Lync-Haven Rainforest Retreat ... A5
21 Noah Beach Campground ... B3
22 PK's Jungle Village ... C2
23 Prema Shanti ... A4
24 Rainforest Hideaway ... B2
25 Thornton Beach Bungalows ... B4

Eating

26 Cafe on Sea ... B4
27 Cape Restaurant & Bar ... C3
28 Daintree Ice Cream Company ... A5
29 Floravilla Ice Cream Factory ... B6
IGA Supermarket ... (see 22)
30 Jambu ... A6
Jungle Bar ... (see 22)
Mason's Store & Cafe ... (see 34)
Tree Frogs ... (see 16)
31 Whet Restaurant ... C2

Drinking

32 Cow Bay Hotel ... B6

Shopping

33 Daintree Tea Company ... A5

Information

34 Mason's Store ... B2

north of the Kulki picnic area car park, on your left. The steep climb takes you through a forest of palms, cycads and acacias to a lookout (680m), with awesome views across the windswept vegetation of the cape and south along the coast.

Tours

Cape Trib Horse Rides HORSE RIDING
(☎1800 111 124; 4098 0030; rides per person $95; ⏰8am & 1.30pm) Leisurely rides along the beach.

Cape Tribulation Kayaks KAYAKING
(☎4098 0077; www.capetribcamping.com.au; 2hr tours $60) Runs guided kayaking trips and rents kayaks (single/double kayak per hour $20/30).

D'Arcy of the Daintree 4WD
(☎4098 9180; darcyofdaintree@yahoo.com.au) Entertaining 4WD trips up the Bloomfield Track as far as Cooktown (adult/child $185/90) and down Cape Tribulation Rd (adult/child from $55/35); free pick-ups from Cape Trib and Cow Bay.

Mason's Tours WALKING, 4WD
(Map p374; ☎4098 0070; www.masonstours.com.au, Mason's Store, Cape Tribulation Rd) There are interpretive walks lasting two hours (adult/child $49/40) or a half-day ($70/55), and a croc-spotting night walk ($49); also offers 4WD tours up the Bloomfield Track (from $135/114).

Paddle Trek KAYAKING
(☎4098 0040; www.capetribpaddletrek.com.au; morning 3½hr tours $79, afternoon 2½hr tours $69) Guided kayaking trips.

Sleeping & Eating

Restaurants at Cape Trib's resorts are all open to nonguests.

TOP CHOICE **Cape Trib Exotic Fruit Farm Cabins** CABINS $$
(Map p374; ☎4098 0057; www.capetrib.com.au; d incl breakfast $180) Right on the burbling World Heritage creek boundary, amid the orchards of Cape Trib Exotic Fruit Farm (p373), this pair of timber pole cabins are far enough apart for you to feel like you're

alone in the forest. With exposed timber floors, ceilings and huge decks, cabins are simple but elegant, and equipped with electric Eskies. Enjoy bountiful breakfast hampers filled with tropical fruit from the farm. Minimum two-night stay.

Rainforest Hideaway B&B **$$**
(☎4098 0108; www.rainforesthideaway.com; 19 Camelot Close; d incl breakfast $95-135) This colourful B&B has been single-handedly built by its owner, artist and sculptor 'Dutch Rob' – even the furniture and beds are handmade. Choose from a room in the house, a detached cabin with a stunning outdoor shower, or a rustic, raised octagonal cabin along a track deep in the rainforest, also with an outdoor shower open to the rainforest, which is extremely private – if you don't count the cassowary that occasionally pops past. A sculpture trail winds through the property.

Cape Trib Beach House HOSTEL **$**
(Map p374; ☎4098 0030; www.capetribbeach.com.au; dm $26-32, d $75, cabins $130-230;) Hidden down a pedestrian-only path from its car park, this beachfront place is a low-key alternative for backpackers. Neat rainforest huts range from air-con dorms to pricey timber cabins with bathrooms. There's a tidy communal kitchen as well as a breezy **restaurant** (mains $11.50-26.50; breakfast, lunch & dinner), with a bar, a pool table and board games. Wi-fi is on its way.

Cape Tribulation Resort HOTEL **$$$**
(Map p374; ☎4098 0033; www.capetribulationresort.com.au; Cape Tribulation Rd; d $298; May-Nov;) In the jungle about 2km south of the village, the luxurious individual cottages here have polished floorboards, rattan furniture, and baths with essential-oil burners. Across the road, reached by a candlelit boardwalk, the cathedral-like **Cape Restaurant & Bar** (mains $28-31; breakfast, lunch & dinner May-Nov) is worth visiting for a drink on the deck after a stroll on Coconut Beach.

Cape Tribulation Camping CAMPGROUND **$**
(Map p374; ☎4098 0077; www.capetribcamping.com.au; unpowered/powered sites $30/40, safari huts s/d $45/70;) Right on the beachfront, this sociable spot has a good range of facilities, including beach showers and a camp kitchen with barbecues. A communal fire is lit every evening. Its friendly managers and kayaking guides (p375) are experts on the area.

Cape Trib Farmstay FARM STAY **$$**
(Map p374; ☎4098 0042; www.capetribfarmstay.com; Cape Tribulation Rd; d $88, cabins $135-155;) Lined up in a lovely 30-hectare fruit orchard yielding mangosteen, rambutan, breadfruit and bananas – which you might find on your breakfast plate – cute stilted cabins (some with air-con, one with wheelchair access) look out at **Mt Sorrow** from their verandahs. There are also three cosy rooms in the farmhouse (with a shared bathroom) as well as a communal kitchen.

PK's Jungle Village HOSTEL **$**
(Map p374; ☎4098 0040; www.pksjunglevillage.com; unpowered sites per person $15, dm $25, cabins d $125, cabins without bathroom $48;) A longstanding backpacker hub, PK's en suite cabins are definitely overpriced, but you can reach Myall Beach by boardwalk, and its open-plan restaurant and bar, the **Jungle Bar** (dishes $5-18; restaurant lunch & dinner, bar noon-midnight), remains the entertainment epicentre of Cape Trib.

Ferntree Rainforest Resort HOSTEL, CABINS **$$**
(Map p374; ☎4098 0033; www.ferntreerainforestlodge.com.au; Camelot Close; dm $28, d $98, lodge $198;) Spread through the rainforest (making it easy to get lost – take a torch after dark), this resort combines slick dorms and private rooms in the hostel wing with stylish loft-style timber lodges with big bathrooms and huge beds. Facilities include two pools and the on-site **Cassowary Cafe** (mains $16-30; breakfast, lunch & dinner).

Whet Restaurant MODERN AUSTRALIAN **$$**
(Map p374; ☎4098 0007; 1 Cape Tribulation Rd; mains $27-33; lunch & dinner) Loungy Whet is Cape Trib's coolest address, but its food (barbecued ox tongue, chilli crab pasta), while passable, tends to be over-hyped throughout the Daintree – perhaps because it's the only place you can get a meal much after 8pm. Whet also shows films – call for screening times.

Mason's Store & Cafe GROCERIES, CAFE **$**
(Map p374; Cape Tribulation Rd; mains $12; 10am-4pm Sun-Thu, 10am-7pm Fri & Sat) Laid-back cafe dishing up good fish and chips and huge steak sandwiches. The store sells limited groceries and takeaway alcohol.

IGA Supermarket GROCERIES **$**
(Map p374; PK's Jungle Village; 8am-6pm) The Daintree's largest supermarket.

Information

Mason's Store (☎4098 0070; Cape Tribulation Rd; ⏰8am-6pm; @) Stop in at Mason's, about 1.5km south of the Cape, for info on the region including Bloomfield Track conditions.

Getting There & Away

For details of buses between Cape Tribulation, Cairns and Cooktown, see p363.

NORTH TO COOKTOWN

There are two routes to Cooktown from the south: the coastal route from Cape Tribulation via the 4WD-only Bloomfield Track, and the inland route, which is sealed all the way via the Peninsula and Cooktown Developmental Rds. If you can, use both, travelling north up the inland route and returning via the coastal route or vice versa.

Inland Route

The inland route to Cooktown skirts along the western side of the Great Dividing Range and stoically retains its arid, outback character whatever the season. It's 332km (about 4½ hours' drive) from Cairns to Cooktown, past the ghosts of the gold- and copper-mining boom. Access the Peninsula Developmental Rd from Mareeba, or via the turn-off just before Mossman. The road travels through rugged ironbarks and cattle-trodden land, and climbs two ranges before joining the Cooktown Developmental Rd at Lakeland.

MT MOLLOY TO PALMER RIVER

The historical township of Mt Molloy (population 275) marks the start of the Peninsula Developmental Rd, about 40km north of Mareeba. Since its heady gold- and copper-mining days, the town centre has shrivelled to comprise a pub, bakery, post office and cafe. Irish prospector James Venture Mulligan is buried in the cemetery just south of town. Credited with first finding gold in the Palmer and Hodgkinson Rivers (which dominoed into the establishment of Cairns and Port Douglas), he mined copper around Mt Molloy in the 1890s, and bought the town pub where he sustained injuries breaking up a brawl that eventually killed him.

Despite the unappealing name, **Abattoir Swamp Environment Park** is a beautiful wetland area blanketed in lotus flowers, which is popular with birdwatchers.

About 1km north of town, there's a rest area where you can **camp** (free; 2-night maximum). There are toilets and cold showers.

Taking centre stage in town, the **National Hotel** (☎4094 1133; www.mountmolloynationalhotel.com.au; Main St; s/d $35/70, mains $7.50-22.50; ⏰lunch & dinner) is a welcoming local with tidy upstairs rooms (no en suites), most opening onto the wide verandah. At the jack-of-all-trades **Mt Molloy Cafe & Takeaway** (Main St; mains $6-15; ⏰10am-midnight), also known as 'Lobo Loco', you can get everything from dim sims and burritos to boxes of cornflakes, or a shot of bourbon at its bar.

Mt Carbine, 28km northwest of Mt Molloy, is a one-pub town, literally – that's about all there is. The **Mt Carbine Hotel** (☎4094 3108; mains $14-20; ⏰lunch & dinner) was established for wolframite (a mineral used for tungsten) miners in the area, and was well known for an old Brahmin bull that used to come into the bar and drink beer. Sadly the bull is no more, but there are pictures on the wall to prove it! Look up above the door to see what's claimed to be the world's longest playable didgeridoo (4.7m – that's a *lot* of lungpower); the pub also sells locally made didges. Its handful of motel-style rooms (doubles $70) have en suites.

The mine closed in 1988 and the abandoned Brooklyn mining village has been transformed into the **Mt Carbine Caravan Park** (☎4094 3160; www.mtcarbine.com; 6806 Mulligan; unpowered/powered sites $14/18, units $60-80; ❄). Set on a large bush property south of the pub, the park has good, clean facilities and enormous self-contained units. The area is visited by no less than 245 species of birds and other wildlife, and retains evidence of the village's former life with a disused Olympic-sized pool, a playground and a recreation hall. The friendly manager leads a 700m return walk to the lookout every evening at 5pm.

After crossing the McLeod River, 15km west of Mt Carbine, the road winds up through the Desailly Range, with panoramic views over the savannah. The road continues north reaching the Palmer River 60km from Mt Carbine, and all that's left of a once thriving mining town. You'll find food and fuel at the **Palmer River Roadhouse** (☎4060 2020; mains $13.50-20; ⏰breakfast, lunch & dinner; @). You can also pitch a tent, park your van (unpowered/powered sites $10/20) or stay in

WORTH A TRIP

PALMER RIVER

The Palmer River's alluvial gold deposits spurred a mighty gold rush, which created thriving, if transitory, townships. The remains of two major townships from the Palmer River rush (1873 to 1883) lie inland from the Palmer River Roadhouse. There's an unmarked turn-off from the Peninsula Developmental Rd, which runs west for 35km to the ghost town of **Maytown**, and **Palmerville** 30km further on. This is rugged 4WD-only territory where the only passing traffic you might see is the odd cow from the neighbouring cattle station. The turn-off is about 17km south of the Palmer River Roadhouse, just before the Whites Creek crossing.

The Palmer goldfields are legendary not only for the 46°C days and lack of comforts that prospectors endured but also for the thousands who walked overland to get here. Maytown was the second settlement to be established after Palmerville, and it became the major centre in 1875.

All that remains of Maytown's 12 hotels, three bakeries, butcher and lemonade factory are a few stumps, some plaques and slate roads that the earth is gradually reclaiming. The population of 252 Europeans and 422 Chinese had largely abandoned Maytown by 1945, when the gold dried up. There's a **DERM Campground** (☎13 74 68; www.derm.qld.gov.au; sites per person $5.15) near Maytown, before you cross the river. Check with DERM for an update on the current condition of the track. You'll need to backtrack the same way you came in.

This remote area will be anything but deserted during the **total solar eclipse** on 13 November, 2012. The onset of the Wet means visibility is likely to be impeded along the coast, so the Palmer River area, which has an average monthly rainfall of only 62mm for November, is set to be the epicentre for thousands of sky-watchers and revellers from around the world.

the roadhouse's safari tents (singles/doubles $30/40) overlooking the river.

LAKELAND TO COOKTOWN

From Palmer River it's another 15km to Lakeland, a hamlet at the junction of the Peninsula Developmental Rd and the Cooktown Developmental Rd. Lakeland is in the fertile volcanic basin of the Laura Valley, producing cereal grains, sugar and coffee (almost the full complement for the breakfast table). Head west and you're on your way to Laura and Cape York; continue straight northeast and you've got another 80km to Cooktown.

Lakeland Downs Hotel-Motel (☎4060 2142; www.lakelandhotel.com.au; Peninsula Developmental Rd; s/d $65/99; ❄) has slate-floored, motel-style rooms and doubles as the local **pub** (mains $12-22; ⊙dinner).

Lakeland Caravan Park (☎4060 2033; lakelandcaravanpark@bigpond.com; Sesame St; unpowered/powered sites $20/25, s/d $50/65; @) has new rooms with bathrooms and offers van storage (per week $36) if you're unhitching it to head up the Cape.

Across the road from the caravan park, **Lakeland Coffee House** (Sesame St; mains $6.50-17; ⊙6.30am-6pm Mon-Fri, 7am-5pm Sat & Sun) serves fabulous Laura Valley coffee, smoothies, sandwiches and burgers. It also has fuel, basic supplies and an ATM.

About 50km past Lakeland is the **Annan River Gorge**, which has a natural swimming hole and a picnic area. Downstream the river has carved an impressive gorge through solid rock; the water pools briefly before cascading into impressive falls.

A little further down the road is the turn-off to Helenvale and the coastal route to Cape Tribulation.

Continuing to Cooktown, the road passes the staggering **Black Mountain National Park**, with thousands of stacked, square, black granite boulders that look unnervingly precarious, as though they might tumble down with the slightest movement. The mountain is home to unique species of frogs, skinks and geckoes. It was formed 260 million years ago by a magma intrusion below the surface, which then solidified and was gradually exposed by erosion. Black Mountain marks the northern end of the Wet Tropics World Heritage Area. From here, it's another 30km to Cooktown.

Coastal Route

The Bloomfield Track from Cape Tribulation to Cooktown is the great adventure drive of Queensland's Far North coast. It's a 4WD-only route that traverses creek crossings, diabolically steep climbs and patchy surfaces that can be boggy or bald. This infamous stretch of road can be impassable for many weeks on end during the Wet, and even in the Dry you should check road conditions locally, as creek crossings are affected by tide times. The Bloomfield Track runs for around 80km before linking up with the sealed Cooktown Developmental Rd 30km south of Cooktown. Although this is a remote region, there are quite a few accommodation places and attractions along the way.

The track was originally forged as far back as 1968 but for many years it was little more than a remote walking track. The road was built in 1983 – two years after the Cape Tribulation National Park was created – despite vociferous opposition from locals. The official justification for the track was to open up the region to tourism and to halt the illegal trade in drugs, wildlife and plants. Many locals, supported by scientific reports, expressed concern over the environmental impact of the track on the surrounding rainforest and reef – see boxed text p367. The debate over the Bloomfield Track continues, with some locals seeking its staged closure over the next decade or so.

CAPE TRIBULATION TO THE BLOOMFIELD RIVER

It's 5km from Cape Trib to Emmagen Creek, the official start of the Bloomfield Track. Just before you reach the creek, you'll see a huge strangler fig, from where a walking path leads down to the pretty, crescent-shaped **Emmagen Beach**.

Beyond the Emmagen Creek crossing, the road climbs and dips steeply and turns sharp corners over fine, slippery bull dust. This is the most challenging section of the drive, especially after rain. The road then follows the broad Bloomfield River before crossing it 30km north of Cape Trib – check for tide times.

Turn left immediately after the bridge to see the **Bloomfield Falls**. The falls are for looking only: crocs inhabit the river and the site is significant to the Indigenous Wujal Wujal community who live just north of the river. Residents of Wujal Wujal run the **Walker Family Tours** (☎4060 8069; www.bamaway.com.au; adult/child $15/8), highly recommended half-hour **walking tours** of the falls and surrounding forest, departing daily – advance bookings are essential.

From Wujal Wujal to the Cooktown Developmental Rd the track is unsealed, but this stretch is possible to traverse (slowly) in a 2WD in dry conditions.

About 5km north of Wujal Wujal, the **Bloomfield Track Takeaway & Middleshop** (☎4060 8174; dishes $7-27.50; ⏲8am-10pm Tue-Sat, 8am-8pm Sun & Mon) serves pizzas and burgers (call ahead and they'll have your order waiting), and has fuel, fishing tackle and groceries.

A further 5km north is the small hamlet of **Ayton** (named after Great Ayton, the birthplace of Captain Cook) where the Bloomfield River empties out into the Coral Sea; there's a small shop here, but no fuel. Just north of Ayton, **Haley's Cabins & Camping** (☎4060 8207; www.haleyscabins.com.au; 20 Bloomfield Rd, Ayton; unpowered/powered sites per person $10/15, d $85; ❄) has a great setting, with tall, shady gum trees. A path from the property leads to a 9km walk to **Weary Bay** (during which you'll appreciate its name). Cabins don't have en suites, but there are in-room fridges.

Accessible only by sea, the luxury resort **Bloomfield Lodge** (☎4035 9166; www.bloomfieldlodge.com.au; Weary Bay; 4-night d $1745-2477; ❄🏊) is gloriously remote (no internet, no mobile-phone reception). Its cabins are spaced well apart, with verandahs overlooking the rainforest and/or the sea. All meals and fishing gear are included; optional extras range from spa treatments to excursions. It's a honeymooners' haven but children over 10 are welcome. Minimum stay is four nights; prices include transfers from Cairns (a charter flight, a boat trip and a 4WD journey).

BLOOMFIELD RIVER TO COOKTOWN

North of Bloomfield, the road passes through the **Cedar Bay (Mangkal-Mangkalba) National Park**. Access to the park is either by boat, which is difficult in most conditions, or by a walking trail (17km, seven hours). There's a camp site at Cedar Bay; permits must be obtained over-the-counter from **DERM** (☎13 74 68; www.derm.qld.gov.au; sites per person $5.15) branches in Cairns, Mossman or Atherton. This and other walks begin from **Home Rule Wilderness Cabins** (☎4060 3925; www.home-rule.com.au; Rossville; unpowered sites per adult/child $10/5, r adult/child $25/15), at the end of a bumpy 3km driveway. Spotless facilities include a communal kitchen; cooked breakfasts ($12) and evening meals ($15) are available, as well as canoe hire (per half-day $10) for a paddle on crystal-clear, croc-free **Wallaby Creek**. The turn-off is signposted from Rossville, 33km north of the Bloomfield River crossing. Home Rule is ground zero for the weekend-long **Wallaby Creek Festival** (www.wallabycreekfestival.org.au; ⏲Sep), with roots and blues music on two stages, alternative workshops and events including 'breakfast with the poets' and street theatre, plus food and market stalls, and kids entertainment.

It's only another 9km to the welcoming sight of the **Lion's Den Hotel** (Map p354; ☎4060 3911; www.lionsdenhotel.com.au; Helenvale; unpowered/powered sites $20/26, s/d $40/50, d safari tents $70;). This legendary watering hole with genuine corrugated, graffiti-covered decor dates back to 1875 and still attracts a steady stream of travellers and local characters. There's fuel and ice-cold beer, and its **restaurant** (mains $18-23; ⏲breakfast, lunch & dinner) serves up excellent pub grub all day, including oven-baked barra and schnitzels, plus famous Lion's Den pizzas.

Mungumby Lodge (☎4060 3158; www.mungumby.com; Helenvale; s/d incl breakfast $260/279;) In 2009 David Attenborough came to film at this verdant oasis 5km east of the Bloomfield Track – you'll see why as you explore its surrounding rainforest walks and nearby waterfall. Individual timber bungalows (TV-free) are scattered on the lawns among mango trees, and the semi-open communal lounge area overlooks the shaded pool. Lunch (mains $11.50 to $30), dinner (two-/three-course meal $39/48) and **nature tours**, including a 90-minute nocturnal walk (adult/child from $35/25), are available.

About 4km north, the Bloomfield Track meets the sealed Cooktown Developmental Rd, from where it's a dust-free 28km to Cooktown.

Cooktown

POP 2093

At the southeastern edge of Cape York Peninsula, Cooktown is a small place with a big history: for thousands of years Waymbuurr was the place the Guugu Yimithirr and Kuku Yalanji people held as a meeting ground, and it was here that Lieutenant (later Captain) Cook first set foot on the Australian continent.

After years of isolation and hard living that's imbued the locals with a down-to-earth character and great sense of humour, the inland route from Mareeba was finally sealed all the way in 2005. Tourism is now a growing industry. It's still remote territory, though, and getting here is an adventure, especially if you take the 4WD Bloomfield Track from Cape Tribulation. And Cooktown exists despite tourism, firmly believing that happiness is a fishing rod and an Esky full of beer.

As well as historical sites relating to early European contact, there's increasing recognition for the area's Indigenous heritage and unspoilt natural environment of wetlands, mangroves, rainforest and long, lonely beaches.

History

On 17 June 1770, James Cook beached his bark, the *Endeavour*, on the banks of its estuary at Waymbuurr. The *Endeavour* had earlier struck a reef off shore from Cape Tribulation, and Cook and his crew spent 48 days here while they repaired the damage – making it the site of Australia's first, albeit transient, non-Indigenous settlement. During this time, Joseph Banks, the chief naturalist, and botanist Daniel Solander kept busy studying the plants and animals along the banks of the Endeavour River, while artist Sydney Parkinson illustrated their finds. Banks collected 186 plant species, and 'observed, described, sketched, shot, ate and named the kangaroo' (from the Guugu Yimithirr word, *gangurru*).

In 1874 Cooktown became a large and unruly port town at the centre of the Palmer River gold rush. At its peak there were no fewer than 94 pubs and the population was more than 30,000. A large percentage of this population was Chinese, and their industrious presence led to some wild race-related riots. And here, as elsewhere in the country, the Indigenous population was overrun and outcast, with much blood shed.

Cooktown's gold-rush glory was short-lived, and as the gold ran out, the population dwindled. Two cyclones – in 1907 and 1949 – likewise had an impact, but the biggest decline in the population followed the evacuation in WWII, when the overwhelming majority of residents left. Many Indigenous people died after being forcibly removed from their traditional lands, and many Indigenous and white families never returned. Things started to turn around by 1970, when Queen Elizabeth II opened the James Cook Historical Museum…and a rock, commemorating the point where Cook ran aground.

Although Cooktown is no longer an isolated outpost, its frontier spirit remains unchanged.

Sights & Activities

Cooktown hibernates during summer (the Wet; locals call it 'the dead season'), and many attractions and tours close or have reduced hours.

Nature's Powerhouse & Botanic Gardens

GALLERIES, GARDENS

(www.naturespowerhouse.com.au; Walker St; galleries adult/child $3.50/free; 9am-5pm) This environment interpretive centre is home to two excellent galleries. The **Charlie Tanner Gallery** is dedicated to Cooktown's 'snake man'. Charlie's backyard pets included venomous snakes that he milked to make antivenins, and he had a particular passion for the deadly coastal taipan. The gallery displays pickled and preserved exhibits of only-on-the-Cape wildlife (such as the nightmare-inducing bare-backed fruit bat), inspirational stories from taipan-bite survivors, and displays on termites and barramundi. The **Vera Scarth-Johnson Gallery** is a collection of intricate and beautiful botanical illustrations of the region's native plants.

The centre doubles as Cooktown's official visitor centre (p385), with brochures outlining some of the area's excellent **walking trails**. Also here is a bookshop, and the Verandah Cafe (p384).

Nature's Powerhouse is at the entry to Cooktown's 62-hectare **Botanic Gardens** (unrestricted access). Filled with native and exotic tropical plants, including rare orchids, the gardens are among Australia's oldest and most magnificent. Highlights include the Palmetum palm collection and wetlands.

James Cook Museum

MUSEUM

(www.nationaltrustqld.org; cnr Helen & Furneaux Sts; adult/child $10/3; 9.30am-4pm) Built as a convent in 1889, Cooktown's finest historical building houses well-preserved and presented relics from Cook's time in the town, including journal entries and the cannon and anchor from the *Endeavour*, retrieved from the sea floor in 1971. Photographs, artefacts and interpretive panels explain other topics that were influential to the shaping of Cooktown including its Indigenous culture, the gold rush and the Chinese presence.

Bicentennial Park & Around

PARK, MONUMENTS

Bicentennial Park is home to the much-photographed bronze **Captain Cook statue**. Nearby, the **Milbi Wall (Story Wall)** tells the story of European contact from the local Gungarde (Guugu Yimithirr) community's perspective. The 12m-long mosaic begins with creation stories and moves through European contact, WWII and recent attempts at reconciliation. Sitting just out in the water from Bicentennial Park is the **rock** marking the spot where Cook ran aground and tied up to a tree (part of the original tree is on display at the James Cook Museum); the **Queen's Steps** were constructed so Her Majesty could reach it.

Cooktown's **wharf** is one of Queensland's sweetest spots for fishing; get gear and local advice at the **Lure Shop** (142 Charlotte St).

Grassy Hill

LOOKOUT, WALKS

A winding road in the shape of the rainbow serpent (a sacred character in Indigenous Dreaming stories) snakes all the way up to the top of Grassy Hill Lookout, with 360-degree views of the town, river and ocean. If you're feeling fit, you can also reach it by a steep 15-minute walk, which is especially worthwhile at sunrise. Cook climbed this hill looking for a passage out through the reefs. Crowning the hill, the compact, corrugated, 19th-century iron lighthouse was built in England and shipped to Cooktown in 1885.

Another walking trail (800m one-way; 25 minutes) leads from the summit down to the beach at **Cherry Tree Bay**.

Old Bank & Cooktown Archive Research Centre

HISTORICAL BUILDINGS

(Old Bank, 122 Charlotte St; adult/child $5/free; 9am-3pm Mon-Sat Easter-Oct) Cooktown's magnificent 1891 Old Bank still contains the Cooktown Historical Society's local history collection, from information about Indigenous inhabitants to the Palmer River gold rush, as well as a family-history database. However, financial pressure on the volunteer-run organisation means that the collection is likely to relocate across the street to the **Cooktown Archive & Research Centre** (121 Charlotte St; hr vary), housed in the 1878-built former post and telegraph office. Check with the visitor centre for updates.

Keatings Lagoon Conservation (Mulbabidgee) Park NATURE RESERVE
Birds frequent the melaleuca swamps at this peaceful woodland located 5km south of Cooktown off the Cooktown Developmental Rd. There's a bird hide, a picnic area and a walking trail (1.5km return; 30 minutes). No camping.

Trevathen Falls WATERFALL, SWIMMING
Accessible only by 4WD, Trevathen Falls is a hidden treasure, with a safe, secluded swimming hole under the forest canopy. Head south from Cooktown and turn left at Mt Amos Rd. After about 9km you'll see a track to your right; take it for about 1km until you reach a fork. Take the right-hand path for about 2km until you reach a gate. Don't go through the gate; turn left, which will lead you to the falls. Take a picnic. It's private land, so there's no camping.

Hopevale Arts Cultural Centre GALLERY
(www.hopevalearts.com; 1 Flierl St, Hopevale; admission free; ⌚9am-4.30pm Mon-Thu, 9am-2pm Fri, 10am-2pm Sat) In the Aboriginal community of Hopevale, 45km north of Cooktown (accessible by 2WD in dry conditions), this cultural centre's **Nganthanun Bamawi Bayan Gallery** has beautiful works by local artists and organises traditional dance performances.

Festivals & Events

The **Cooktown Discovery Festival** (www.cooktowndiscoveryfestival.com.au; ⌚early Jun) is held over the Queen's Birthday Weekend to commemorate Captain Cook's landing in 1770 with a costumed re-enactment and fancy dress grand parade, as well as Indigenous workshops such as didgeridoo making, spear throwing and basket weaving, and a traditional corroboree.

Sleeping

Cooktown has accommodation across all budgets, but book well ahead during the Dry.

Sovereign Resort Hotel HOTEL $$
(☎4043 0500; www.sovereign-resort.com.au; cnr Charlotte & Green Sts; d $170-185, 2-bed apt $210; ❄@📶🏊) Cooktown's swishest digs are right on the main street, with a warren of breezy tropical-style rooms with wooden-slat blinds and tile floors. Kick back in the landscaped garden pool area and the **Balcony Restaurant and Cafe-Bar** (p384).

Pam's Place & Cooktown Motel HOSTEL, MOTEL $
(☎4069 5166; www.cooktownhostel.com; cnr Charlotte & Boundary Sts; dm/s/d $27/50/55, motel d $90; ❄@📶🏊) Cooktown's YHA-associated hostel is everything a backpackers should be: welcoming and cosy, with sociable common areas to meet other travellers, spotless facilities and a leafy garden. Adjacent to the hostel, its spiffy motel units are so new there's still a faint scent of fresh woodwork and paint. The friendly managers can help find harvest work.

Endeavour Falls Tourist Park CARAVAN PARK $
(☎4069 5431; www.endeavourfallstouristpark.com.au; Endeavour Valley Rd; unpowered/powered sites $24/28, cabins $115; ❄🏊) Situated 32km northwest on the road to Hopevale (15km unsealed), this well-run, peaceful park backs onto the Garden of Eden–like Endeavour Falls (inhabited by a resident croc – don't swim!). It's a handy spot if you're self-driving to take a Guurrbi tour, which starts nearby, or if you're heading to Lakeland National Park. Its well-stocked shop serves takeaways (dishes $6.50 to $13.50) and has fuel, as well as barra swimming in a fish tank, which the owners will let you feed.

Alkoomie Cattle Station & Mountain Retreat FARMSTAY $$
(☎4069 5463; www.alkoomie.com.au; Alkoomie Station; tents with bathroom $80, self-contained units $100, d incl meals $199-225; ❄🏊) You'll need a 4WD (or a light plane or helicopter) to reach this 18,000-hectare working cattle station 45km west of Cooktown. As well as watching cattle being rounded up and branded, activities include horse riding, feeding the farm animals, swimming below waterfalls, and gazing at the star-filled night sky, as well as day tours.

Milkwood Lodge CABINS $$
(☎4069 5007; www.milkwoodlodge.com; Annan Rd; d $135; ❄🏊) Among giant milkwood trees in a patch of rainforest 2.5km south of town, these six split-level, timber-pole cabins are beautifully designed with bushland views opening out from private balconies. Cabins come with king beds and kitchenettes but aren't suitable for kids.

Seaview Motel MOTEL $$
(☎4069 5377; seaviewmotel@bigpond.com.au; 178 Charlotte St; d $99-155, townhouses $220; ❄🏊) The location is the biggest draw of this low-rise motel, which sits across the main street from the wharf. Sunlight fills the modern

TOURS FROM COOKTOWN

Some interesting tours operate out of Cooktown from May to October, with scaled-back schedules from November to April. But this is not Cairns or Port Douglas, and although the reef is not far away, there are no regularly scheduled dive or snorkelling trips. Water-based tours depart from the wharf.

Guurrbi Tours INDIGENOUS CULTURE

(☎4069 6259; www.guurrbitours.com; 2/4hr tours $95/120, self-drive $65/85; ⊙Mon-Sat) Nugal-warra family elder Willie Gordon runs revelatory tours that use the physical landscape to describe the spiritual landscape, providing a powerful insight into Aboriginal culture and lore. The morning Rainbow Serpent tour involves some walking, bush tucker and rock-art sites including a birthing cave. The afternoon Great Emu tour is shorter and visits three rock-art sites. Cooktown pick-ups are from your accommodation; self-drivers meet near the Hopevale Aboriginal Community.

Catch-a-Crab CRAB-CATCHING

(☎4069 6289; cook.cac@bigpond.com; adult/child $100/50) Local seafood supplier Nicko runs river tours on the Endeavour and Annan Rivers in search of mud crabs. Great for kids and very popular – book well ahead.

Maaramaka Walkabout Tours ABORIGINAL CULTURE

(☎4060 9389; irenehammett@hotmail.com) Aboriginal cultural stories, rainforest walks, bush tucker and home cooking in a gorgeous setting near Hopevale.

Cooktown Barra Fishing Charters FISHING

(☎4069 5346; www.cooktownbarracharters.com; half-/full-day $100/200) Barra, mangrove jack, giant trevally and estuary cod are all potential catches, thanks to local knowledge. Also runs croc-spotting, birdwatching, mud-crabbing and ecotours.

Cooktown Reef Charters FISHING, SNORKELLING

(☎4069 5396; www.reefcharters.com.au; trips from $230 per person) Game-fishing day trips with the option of snorkelling.

Cooktown Tours COOKTOWN TOURS

(☎1300 789 550; www.cooktowntours.com) Two-hour town tours (adult/child $55/33) and half-day trips to Black Mountain and the Lion's Den Hotel (adult/child $110/77).

Cooktown Bush Adventures DAY TOURS, SAFARIS

(☎4069 5005; helipete@gmail.com; day tours from $250) Runs a variety of local day tours and overnight safaris (per vehicle per day from $1350).

Cooktown Cruises RIVER CRUISES

(☎4069 5712; www.cooktowncruises.com; 2hr cruise adult/child $55/35; ⊙Tue-Sun Jun-Sep, 3 days per week Apr-Jun & Oct-Dec) Scenic cruises up the Endeavour River.

Gone Fishing FISHING

(☎4069 5980; www.fishingcooktown.com; half-/full-day $100/200) River-fishing tours. Prices are per person, with a minimum of four people.

rooms, and the grassy area around the pool is a great spot to unwind. Higher-priced rooms have private balconies.

Peninsula Caravan Park CARAVAN PARK $

(☎4069 5107; pen.park@bigpond.com; 64 Howard St; unpowered/powered sites $24/30, cabins $80-100; ❄≋) On the eastern edge of town, this shady park has a beautiful bush setting with stands of big, old paperbark and gum trees and resident wildlife including birds and wallabies. Cabins are priced according to size; all have en suites. *Fawlty Towers*–style management is haphazard.

Seagren's HOTEL $

(☎4069 5357; seagrens-inn@bigpond.com; 124 Charlotte St; d $95; ❄≋) A century-old main street landmark, Seagren's has undergone a change of management, but it still has unadorned pub-style rooms with lots of wood, high puffy beds and heaps of character. The small front rooms open onto the breezy verandah; some

WORTH A TRIP

HOPE ISLANDS

Adventurous souls can play Robinson Crusoe out on the Hope Islands, with just you and nature (and the odd passing boat). **East Hope** and **West Hope Islands** are sand cays about 10km offshore from the mainland, 37km southeast of Cooktown. Both are national parks, which protects the hardy mangroves and shrub vegetation. West Hope is an important nesting site for pied-imperial pigeons – access is not permitted during nesting, from 1 September to 31 March. Snorkelling is excellent around both islands, but best on the leeward margin of the East Hope Island reef; beware of strong currents. East Hope Island has three camp sites, toilets, tables and fireplaces. Permits are required and there's a seven-day limit; contact **Cooktown DERM** (p385). Take drinking water, food and a fuel stove.

Getting here isn't cheap; contact **Cooktown Travel Centre** (p385) to check availability for boat charters.

share a bathroom. A wine and tapas bar is planned for downstairs.

Alamanda Inn HOSTEL, MOTEL $
(☎4069 5203; sayahscott@tpg.com.au; cnr Hope & Howard Sts; guesthouse s/d $50/60, motel s/d $60/70, units s/d $75/85; ❄🏊) Budget accommodation at this easygoing spot ranges from rooms in the guesthouse (share bathroom and kitchen) to basic motel rooms with bathrooms and units with kitchenettes.

Cooktown Holiday Park CARAVAN PARK $
(☎4069 5417; www.cooktownholidaypark.com.au; 31-34 Charlotte St; powered sites $35, budget cabins $90, motel units $110-120, cabins with bathroom $120-140; ❄@📶🏊) Cooktown's best-equipped caravan park is also its priciest ('budget' cabins don't have en suites). Flash facilities include a great camp kitchen and two big saltwater pools.

Eating & Drinking

Eating out in Cooktown these days is more than just a counter meal at the local pub. Drinking is a favourite pastime here, and the local pubs and licensed clubs are a good place to mix with the locals.

Restaurant 1770 MODERN AUSTRALIAN $$
(☎4069 5440; 7 Webber Esplanade; mains $20-32; ⏱breakfast, lunch & dinner; 🖉) Opening onto a romantic waterside deck right next to the wharf, fresh fish – such as beer-battered barra and Spanish mackerel – takes top billing, but save space for mouth-watering desserts such as mocha mousse, white chocolate mud cake, and the house-speciality bongo bongos (profiteroles with vanilla ice cream and homemade chocolate sauce).

Verandah Cafe CAFE $
(www.naturespowerhouse.com.au; Walker St; mains $9-16; ⏱10am-2.30pm; 🖉) Attached to Nature's Powerhouse at the entrance to the botanic gardens, the broad, shady deck of this cafe is a serene setting for lunch mains such as Thai chicken salad or gado gado with coconut damper, or to test its claim to the best scones in Queensland.

Cooktown Bowls Club LICENSED CLUB $$
(☎4069 5819; Charlotte St; mains $14-25; ⏱lunch Wed-Fri, dinner daily) Sign yourself in at the door and join the bowlo for the night. As well as big servings of bistro meals, such as fish or steak, there's no limit on trips to the salad bar. You can join in social bowls on Wednesday and Saturday afternoon and barefoot bowls on Wednesday evening.

Balcony Restaurant MODERN AUSTRALIAN $$
(☎4069 5400; Sovereign Resort, cnr Charlotte & Green Sts; mains $23-30; ⏱breakfast & dinner) Upstairs, the Sovereign Resort's formal Balcony Restaurant serves French-inspired Mod Oz cuisine like duck confit with sweet potato purée or pistachio-crusted rack of lamb (along with seafood, of course). The **Cafe-Bar** (mains $11-21.50; ⏱11am-8pm; @🖉) has reasonably priced seafood, pizzas and BLTs, as well as pool tables and free internet.

Cooktown Hotel PUB $$
(www.cooktownhotel.com; 96 Charlotte St; mains $10.50-25; ⏱lunch & dinner) The double-storey timber 'Top Pub' is a local landmark at the top (southern) end of Charlotte St. Plenty of character, plenty of locals and a side beer garden to sit with a beer, kangaroo pie or Sunday roast.

Gill'd & Gutt'd FISH & CHIPS $
(☎4069 5863; Fisherman's Wharf, Webber Esplanade; mains $7-12; ⏱lunch & dinner) Fish and chips the way it should be – fresh and right on the waterside wharf. Check ahead for daily closing times to avoid the last-minute rush.

Cornett's IGA SUPERMARKET $
(cnr Helen & Hogg Sts; 8am-6pm Mon-Sat, 9am-5pm Sun) Groceries.

Information

The **Cooktown & Cape York Peninsula** (www.cooktownandcapeyork.com) website has information on the town and surrounding areas.

Cooktown DERM (13 74 68; www.derm.qld.gov.au; Webber Esplanade; 9am-3pm Mon-Fri) Information and camping permits for national parks, including Lizard Island.

Cooktown Library (4069 5009; Helen St; 9am-5pm Mon-Fri) Internet access; per hour $4.

Nature's Powerhouse (4069 6004; www.naturespowerhouse.com.au; Walker St; 9am-5pm) Incorporates the visitor centre.

Cooktown Travel Centre (4069 5446; 113 Charlotte St) Information and bookings for tours, transport and accommodation.

Getting There & Around

Cooktown's airfield is 10km west of town along McIvor Rd. **Hinterland Aviation** (4035 9323; www.hinterlandaviation.com.au; one-way $150) has one to four flights daily, except Sunday, to/from Cairns (one-way $150, 40 minutes).

Country Road Coachlines (4045 2794; www.countryroadcoachlines.com.au) runs a daily bus service between Cairns and Cooktown ($75) on either the coastal route (Bloomfield Track) or inland route (via Mareeba), depending on the day of departure and the condition of the track.

To get to sights outside town, the Sovereign Resort Hotel (p382) rents 4WDs starting at $120 per day.

For a taxi call 4069 5387.

Lizard Island Group

The spectacular islands of the Lizard Island Group are clustered just 27km off the coast about 100km from Cooktown. **Lizard Island** is a continental island with a dry, rocky and mountainous terrain offering bushwalking, glistening white swimming beaches, and a relatively untouched fringing reef for snorkelling and diving. Apart from the ground where the luxury resort stands, the entire island is national park, so it's open to anyone who makes the effort to get here.

There are four other smaller islands in the Lizard group. Right in front of the resort, **Osprey Island**, with its nesting birds, is within wading distance. Around the edge of Blue Lagoon, south of the main island, are **Palfrey Island**, with an automatic lighthouse, and **South Island** – both have beaches accessible by dinghy. **Seabird Islet**, further south, is a popular nesting site for terns – visitors should keep their distance.

History

The traditional custodians, the Dingaal people, know Lizard Island as Jiigurru. In the Dingaal creation story, the island group is associated with the stingray – with Jiigurru forming the head and the other islands snaking south forming the tail. Historically, the Dingaal used the islands as a place for important meetings and initiation ceremonies; they were also used as a base for collecting shellfish, fish, turtles and dugongs.

Cook and his crew were the first non-Indigenous people to visit Lizard Island. Having successfully patched up the *Endeavour* in Cooktown, they sailed north and stopped on Lizard Island, where Cook and the botanist Joseph Banks climbed to the top of what's now known as Cook's Look to search for a way through the Great Barrier Reef maze and out to the open sea. Banks named the island after its large lizards, known as Gould's monitors, which are from the same family as Indonesia's komodo dragons.

LIZARD ISLAND RESEARCH STATION

Operated by the Australian Museum, Lizard Island's permanent research facility, the **Lizard Island Research Station** (4060 3977; www.lizardisland.net.au) has examined topics as diverse as marine organisms for cancer research, the deaths of giant clams, coral reproductive processes, sea-bird ecology, and life patterns of reef fish during their larval stage.

If you're interested in giving them a hand, it runs one- to two-week **volunteer programs**, which involve helping with maintenance around the station, rather than helping researchers. Accommodation is included but not food or transport to the island. Application details are posted on the website.

Sights & Activities

Lizard Island has plenty of wildlife. There are 11 species of lizard, including Gould's monitors, which can grow up to 1m long. More than 40 species of birds have also been recorded on the island and a dozen or so actually nest here, including the beautiful little sunbirds with their long, hanging nests. Bar-shouldered doves, crested terns, Caspian terns and a variety of other terns, oystercatchers and large sea eagles are other resident species.

Beaches SWIMMING, SNORKELLING

Lizard Island's 24 beaches are nothing short of sensational, and range from long stretches of white sand to idyllic little rocky bays. The water is crystal clear and magnificent coral surrounds the island – **snorkelling** here is superb.

Immediately south of the resort are three postcard beaches – Sunset, Pebbly and Hibiscus Beaches. Watson's Bay to the north of the resort is a wonderful stretch of sand with great snorkelling at both ends and a giant-clam garden in between. There are also plenty of other choices right around the island – most of them deserted.

Diving DIVING

There are good dives right off the island, and the outer Barrier Reef is less than 20km away, including two of Australia's best-known dive sites – Cod Hole and Pixie Bommie. Lizard Island Resort offers a full range of diving facilities to its guests. Some live-aboard tours from Cairns (p311) dive the Cod Hole.

Cook's Look LOOKOUT, WALK

The climb to the top of Cook's Look is a great walk (three hours return). Near the top there are traces of stones marking an Aboriginal ceremonial area. The trail, which starts from the northern end of Watson's Bay near the camp site, is clearly signposted and, although it can be steep and a bit of a clamber at times, it's easy to follow. The views from the top are sensational, and on a clear day you can see the opening in the reef where Cook made his exit.

Sleeping & Eating

Accommodation is only available on Lizard Island, and the choices couldn't be more extreme – camping or supreme five-star luxury.

Lizard Island Resort HOTEL $$$

(☎1300 863 248; www.lizardisland.com.au; Anchor Bay; d from $1700; ❄@📶🏊) As one of a maximum of 80 guests in 40 villas, expect some serious pampering. On one of Queensland's most exclusive and luxurious resorts, you're likely to see someone rich and famous sharing the **Osprey Restaurant**, indulging in spa treatments, or using the wi-fi in the lounge (the only place it works). Rates include all meals and a range of activities; minimum stay is two nights. Children aren't allowed.

DERM Campground CAMPGROUND $

(☎13 74 68; www.derm.qld.gov.au; sites per person $5.15) At the northern end of Watson's Bay, the national park's bush camp site has toilets, gas barbecues, tables and benches. Untreated water (boil first) is available from a pump about 250m from the site. Bring all supplies as there are no shops on the island.

Getting There & Away

Unless you have your own boat or can organise a private charter in Cooktown, flying is the easiest way to reach Lizard Island.

Book through the resort for all air transfers to/from Cairns (return $530). Flight time is one hour.

Daintree Air Services (☎1800 246 206, 4034 9300; www.daintreeair.com.au) has full-day tours from Cairns at 8am ($690). The trip includes lunch, snorkelling gear, transfers and a local guide.

Cape York Peninsula & the Savannah Way

Includes »

Cape York Peninsula 390
Musgrave to Archer River 393
Archer River to Lockhart River 394
Archer River to Weipa 394
Archer River to Bramwell Junction .. 395
Torres Strait Islands 397
The Savannah Way 400
Normanton to Burketown 404
Burketown to the Border 406

Best Places to Eat

» Raptis Fish Markets (p405)

» Sunset Tavern (p405)

» Mt Surprise Tourist Van Park, Motel & BP Roadhouse (p402)

Best Places to Stay

» Punsand Bay Camping Resort (p397)

» End of the Road Motel (p405)

» Burketown Pub (p406)

Why Go?

Rugged and remote Cape York Peninsula has one of the wildest tropical environments on earth. The Great Dividing Range forms the spine of the Cape, with tropical rainforests and palm-fringed beaches on its eastern flanks and sweeping savannah woodlands, dry eucalypt forests and coastal mangroves on its west. The overland trip to the tip of Australia is simply one of the greatest 4WD routes on the continent, an exhilarating trek into Australia's last great frontier.

Running west from the Cape across to the Northern Territory border, the Gulf Savannah is a vast, flat and mostly empty landscape of tropical grasslands, shimmering horizons, saltpans and impenetrable mangroves. Connecting the scattering of historic mines, gem-fossicking centres, geological wonders and colourful fishing towns are the vital but tenuous Gulf roads – the main one being the Savannah Way, which shoots across the continent from Cairns to Broome. A journey out here will give you a sense of what Australia's primordial outback is all about.

When to Go

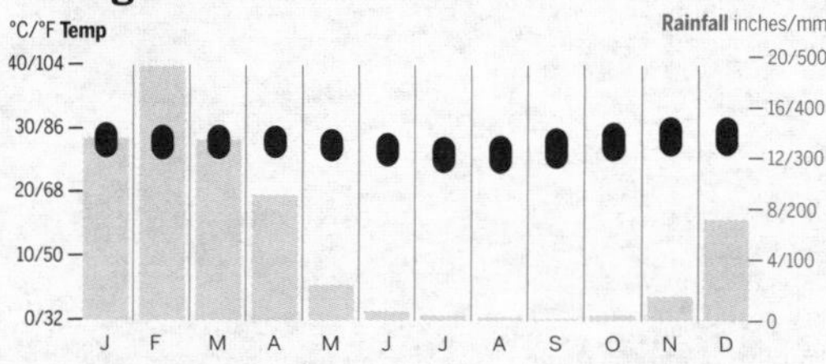

June–July The best time in the Cape is early in the dry season, with warm days and cool evenings.

August–November Cloud-surf the 'morning glory' phenomenon in the skies above Burketown.

October Undara's bushland is the magical setting for 'Opera in the Outback'.

Cape York Peninsula & the Savannah Way Highlights

1 Exploring the remote and wild **Lakefield National Park** (p393)

2 Swimming in the idyllic freshwater pools at **Twin Falls and Eliot Falls** (p396)

3 Popping champagne at the end of the epic journey to reach the **'Tip of Australia'** (p397)

4 Hauling in a big barramundi and watching a blazing sunset over an icy beer at the colourful Gulf port of **Karumba** (p405)

5 Canoeing the emerald-green waters beneath towering red cliffs in the outback

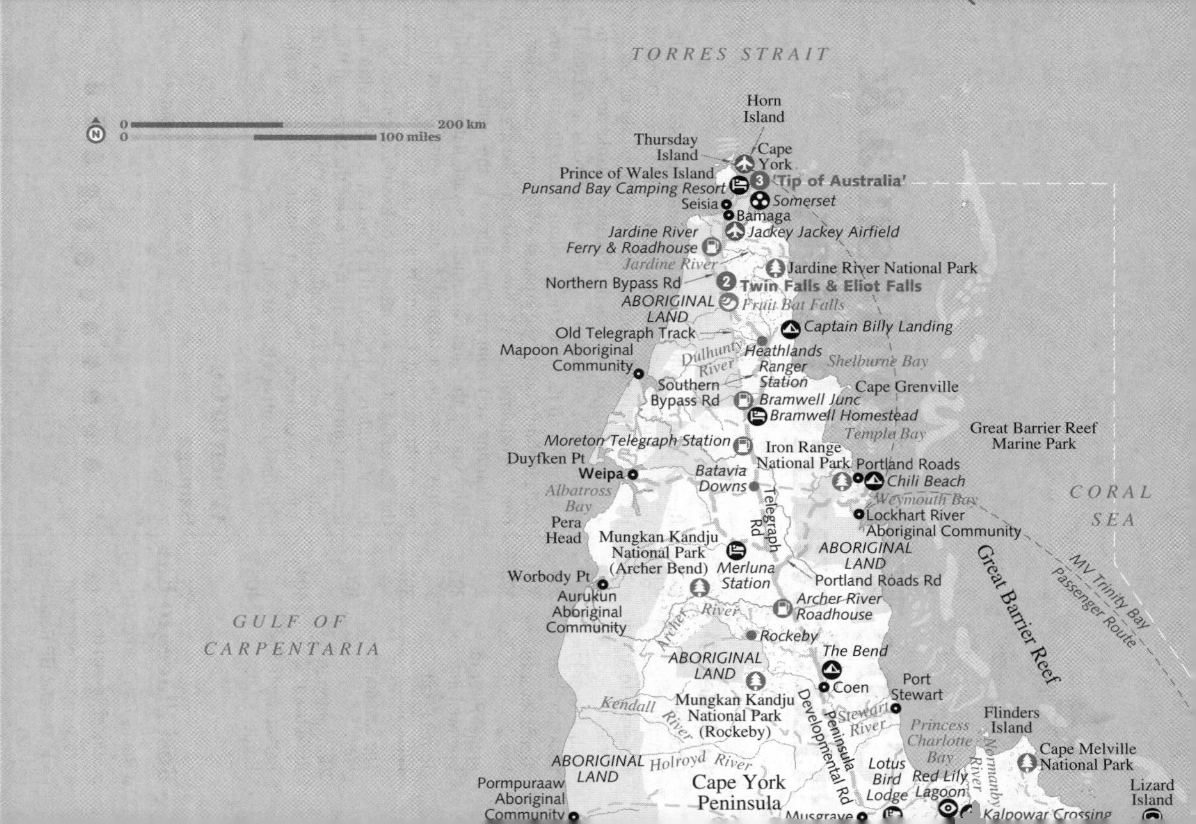

TORRES STRAIT
0 200 km
0 100 miles
Horn Island
Thursday Island
Cape York
Prince of Wales Island
Punsand Bay Camping Resort
3 'Tip of Australia'
Somerset
Seisia
Bamaga
Jardine River Ferry & Roadhouse
Jackey Jackey Airfield
Jardine River
Jardine River National Park
Northern Bypass Rd
2 Twin Falls & Eliot Falls
ABORIGINAL LAND
Fruit Bat Falls
Old Telegraph Track
Captain Billy Landing
Mapoon Aboriginal Community
Dulhunty River
Heathlands Ranger Station
Shelburne Bay
Southern Bypass Rd
Cape Grenville
Bramwell Junc
Bramwell Homestead
Moreton Telegraph Station
Templa Bay
Great Barrier Reef Marine Park
Duyfken Pt
Iron Range National Park
Portland Roads
Weipa
Batavia Downs
Chili Beach
Albatross Bay
Telegraph Rd
Weymouth Bay
CORAL SEA
Lockhart River Aboriginal Community
Pera Head
Mungkan Kandju National Park (Archer Bend)
ABORIGINAL LAND
Merluna Station
Portland Roads Rd
Great Barrier Reef
MV Trinity Bay Passenger Route
Worbody Pt
Aurukun Aboriginal Community
Archer River
Archer River Roadhouse
GULF OF CARPENTARIA
Rockeby
The Bend
ABORIGINAL LAND
Coen
Port Stewart
Kendall River
Mungkan Kandju National Park (Rockeby)
Peninsula Developmental Rd
Stewart River
Princess Charlotte Bay
Flinders Island
Normanby River
Cape Melville National Park
ABORIGINAL LAND
Holroyd River
Lotus Bird Lodge
Red Lily Lagoon
Lizard Island
Pormpuraaw Aboriginal Community
Cape York Peninsula
Musgrave
Kalpowar Crossing

oasis of **Boodjamulla (Lawn Hill) National Park** (p403)

6 Fossicking for precious stones in the gem fields around **Mt Surprise** (p402)

7 Escaping the tropical heat inside the cool, cavernous lava tubes at **Undara Volcanic National Park** (p401)

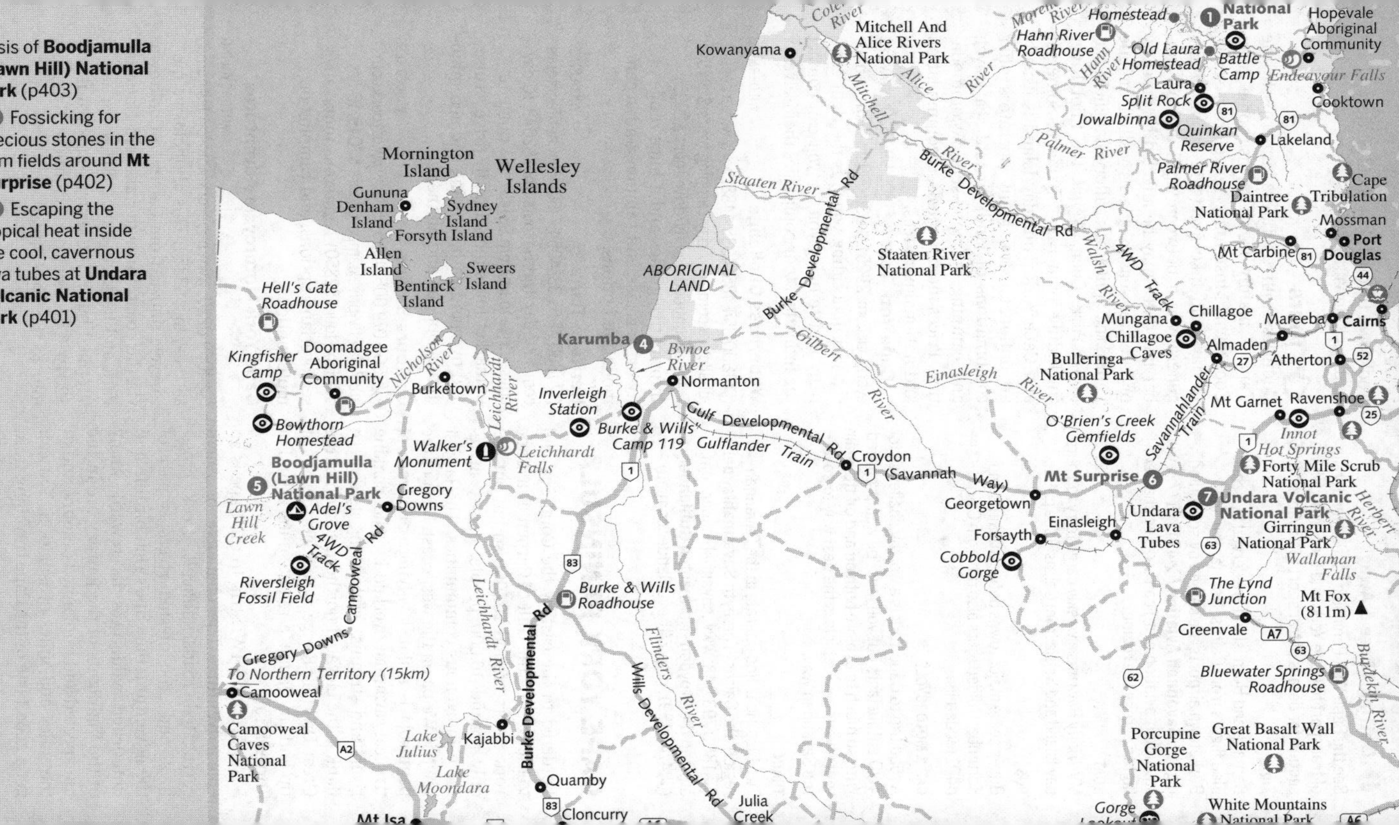

Getting There & Away

See the Cape York Peninsula section for details of transport to Cape York, and the Savannah Way section for details of transport to Savannah Way.

AIR

Bamaga and Horn Island are served by scheduled flights from Cairns. Normanton and Burketown airports are served by scheduled flights. **Savannah Aviation** (☎4745 5177; www.savannah-aviation.com) can arrange charter flights across the region.

BOAT

MV *Trinity Bay* runs a weekly cargo ferry to Thursday Island and Seisia from Cairns – see p392.

BUS

Buses serve major towns between Cairns and Karumba. Guided tours also run from Cairns – see p401 for details.

CAR & MOTORCYCLE

A road trip to Cape York is a worthy challenge for 4WD enthusiasts but you must be well-prepared. With so much to explore both on and off the main route, your own vehicle is the best way to cover the Savannah Way.

TRAIN

Two historic trains operate in the Savannah region: the Cairns–Forsayth **Savannahlander** (☎1800 793 848; www.savannahlander.com.au) and the Croydon–Normanton **Gulflander** (☎4745 1391; http://thegulflander.com.au).

CAPE YORK PENINSULA

Bordered to the east by the Coral Sea and to the west by the Gulf of Carpentaria, Cape York covers around 207,000 sq km but has only around 16,000 people, mostly in remote Indigenous communities. The largest town is Weipa on the west coast. Most of the peninsula is a flat, low-lying patchwork of tropical savannah overlaid by wild, snaking rivers and streams, while along its eastern flank is the elevated northern section of the Great Dividing Range, whose northernmost tip ends in Dauan, a remote outer island of Torres Strait.

An overland 4WD trip to the Cape is an epic adventure. The challenge of rough corrugated roads, difficult creek crossings, and croc-infested rivers is part of the adventure, the Cape's rich birdlife and untouched wilderness its reward. Many of the highlights of the journey are in the unexpected and unplanned detours, and in the miles and miles of isolation. You can get a good taste of the Cape travelling from Cooktown through Lakefield National Park and back down to Cairns.

Tours

Countless tour operators run trips to the Cape – mainly from Cairns, some from Cooktown. Most tours range from six to 14 days and take five to 12 people. Tours generally run between April and November but dates may be affected by an early or late wet season. Places visited include Laura, the Split Rock gallery, Lakefield National Park, Coen, Weipa, the Eliot River (including Twin Falls), Bamaga, Somerset and Cape York. Thursday Island is usually an optional extra. Many operators offer combinations of land, air and sea travel, and camping or motel-style accommodation. Prices include meals, accommodation and national park fees.

Cape York Tour (☎1800 994 620; www.capeyorktour.com; 21-25 Lake St; ⏲9am-5pm) can assist you in deciding which is the right company and tour for you, or you can contact the individual tour companies themselves.

Wilderness Challenge WILDERNESS
(☎1800 354 486, 4035 4488; www.wilderness-challenge.com.au; 7-day camping tours $1945, 7-day accommodated fly/drive tours $2995) Informative guides and a huge range of fly-drive-cruise and camping and accommodation options.

Heritage Tours WILDERNESS
(☎1800 77 55 33, 4054 7750; www.heritagetours.com.au; 7-day fly-drive tours from $2049, 10-day cruise-drive tours from $3745) Big range of upmarket tours including fly-drive, cruise and overland with camping and accommodation options and all meals.

Oz Tours Safaris WILDERNESS
(☎1800 079 006, 4055 9535; www.oztours.com.au; 7-day fly-drive camping tours $2049, 16-day overland tours $2850) Numerous tours, air/sea/overland options, and camping or motel options.

Cape York Motorcycle Adventures MOTORCYCLING
(☎4059 0220; www.capeyorkmotorcycles.com.au; 5-day tour $3250) This all-inclusive motorcycle tour is from Cairns to Cooktown via the coast, through Lakefield National Park and back via Laura. Bikes are supplied but if you bring your own it's $2340. There's also an eight-day fly-ride tour to the Tip ($4950).

Aurukun Wetland Charters INDIGENOUS (☎4058 1441; www.aurukunwetlandcharters.com; 3-day tour $700) In the remote western Cape south of Weipa, this cultural and wildlife tour is led by Aboriginal guides from the Aurukun community. Accommodation is aboard the MV *Pikkuw* (maximum eight passengers). These remote wetlands are exceptional for birdwatching.

 Information

The foremost consideration of a Cape trip is good preparation. Carry spares, tools and equipment, and check **RACQ road reports** (☎1300 130 595; www.racq.com.au). Water can be scarce along the main track, especially late in the dry season, and roadhouses stock only basic food supplies.

Dangers & Annoyances

This is serious crocodile country. Be aware that many stretches of water can hold a big hungry saltie. Heed the warning signs and, if in doubt, don't swim.

Emergency

As well as emergency assistance, the following police stations can provide up-to-date information on road conditions to travellers:

Bamaga (☎4069 3156)

Coen (☎4060 1150)

Cooktown (☎4069 5688)

Hopevale Aboriginal Community (☎4060 9266)

Laura (☎4060 3244)

Lockhart River Aboriginal Community (☎4060 7120)

Weipa (☎4069 9119)

Maps & Books

The Hema maps *Cape York & Lakefield National Park* and the RACQ maps *Cairns/Townsville* and *Cape York Peninsula* are the best. Ron and Viv Moon's *Cape York – an Adventurer's Guide* is the most comprehensive guide for 4WD and camping enthusiasts.

Medical Services

Hospitals and medical clinics on Cape York Peninsula:

Bamaga (☎4069 3166) Hospital.

Coen (☎4060 1166) Clinic.

Cooktown (☎4069 5433) Hospital.

Laura (☎4060 3320) Clinic.

Weipa (☎4082 3900) Hospital.

ALCOHOL RESTRICTIONS

On the way up to the Cape you'll see signs warning of alcohol restrictions, which apply to all visitors. The restrictions are part of a Queensland government alcohol-management plan covering remote communities. It's worth knowing the rules because the fines for breaking them are huge – up to $37,500. In some communities alcohol is banned completely and cannot be carried in. In the Northern Peninsula Area (north of the Jardine River) you can carry a maximum of 11.25L of beer (or 9L of premixed spirits) and 2L of wine per vehicle (not per person). Alcohol is still available at taverns in some communities (such as Bamaga) and roadhouses, but the rules are designed to stop people bringing in large quantities. For up-to-date information see www.mcmc.qld.gov.au.

Money

Banking facilities are limited on Cape York, and full banking facilities are only available at Cooktown, Weipa and Thursday Island. There are ATMs at Laura and Coen, and Eftpos is readily available at most roadhouses, hotels and general stores. Credit cards, including MasterCard and Visa, are widely accepted.

Permits

Once you are north of the Dulhunty River you will need a permit to camp on Aboriginal land, which in effect is nearly all the land north of the river. The Injinoo people are the traditional custodians of much of this land, and the Injinoo Aboriginal Community, which runs the ferry across the Jardine River, includes a camping permit in the ferry fee.

Travelling across Aboriginal land elsewhere on the Cape may require an additional permit, which you can obtain by contacting the relevant community council. The website of the **Aboriginal and Torres Strait Islander Services** (www.atsip.qld.gov.au) lists contact details for all the Cape York Aboriginal communities. Permits can take up to six weeks.

 Getting There & Around

Air

QantasLink (☎13 13 13; www.qantas.com.au) flies daily from Cairns to Weipa and Horn Island. **Skytrans** (☎1300 759 872; www.skytrans.com.au) and **Regional Pacific Airlines**

WORTH A TRIP

JOWALBINNA

To visit some of the more remote Quinkan rock-art sites – and stay in a lovely bush-camp setting – head 36km southwest of Laura on a 4WD track to Jowalbinna.

Jowalbinna Rock Art Safari Camp (☎4060 3236; www.jowalbinna.com.au; camping $10, cabins per person $45) offers secluded camping and accommodation with good facilities including toilets and showers, a cafe and campfire cooking.

From the camp there are **guided walks** (2hr/half-day walk $45/75) to ancient rock-art sites with experienced interpretive guides. There are also self-guided bush walks and a safe swimming hole near the camp. The camp is usually open from April to October; call ahead to book tours and accommodation.

(☎4040 1400; www.regionalpacific.com.au) both have daily flights from Cairns to Bamaga.

Boat

MV Trinity Bay (☎4035 1234; www.seaswift.com.au; per person twin share incl meals 2-day one-way $710, 5-day return $1255) runs a weekly cargo ferry to Thursday Island and Seisia, which takes up to 38 passengers. It departs from Cairns every Friday and returns from Seisia on Monday. Prices are for high season. See also the boxed text, p328.

Car & Motorcycle

From Cairns to the top of Cape York is 952km via the shortest and most challenging route. The first 175km of the Peninsula Developmental Rd from Mareeba to Lakeland is sealed. The journey from Lakeland to Weipa is nearly 600km of wide and reasonably well-maintained but often corrugated, unsealed road.

As you head north of the Weipa turn-off, the real adventure begins along the Telegraph Rd (also known as the Overland Telegraph Track) to Cape York. The creek crossings become more numerous and more challenging: this is pure 4WD territory.

Further north you have the choice of continuing on Telegraph Rd or taking the better-maintained bypass roads.

Lakeland to Musgrave

LAKELAND TO LAURA

At Lakeland, the Peninsula Developmental Rd (known as the PDR) heads northwest up the Cape as a wide, well-maintained dirt road. Lakeland has a general store, a small caravan park and a hotel-motel.

Leaving Lakeland you enter Quinkan country, so named for the Aboriginal spirits depicted at the rock-art sites scattered throughout this area. More than 1200 galleries have been discovered in the escarpment country south of Laura. Unesco lists Quinkan country in the top 10 rock-art regions in the world. About 50km north of Lakeland is the turn-off to **Split Rock Gallery**. The sandstone escarpments here are covered with paintings dating back 14,000 years.

LAURA

POP 230

This sleepy settlement comes alive during June in odd-numbered years with the three-day **Laura Aboriginal Dance Festival** (www.quinkancc.com.au/laura-dance-festival; tickets $69), the largest traditional indigenous gathering in Australia.

The historic, corrugated-iron **Quinkan Hotel** (☎/fax 4060 3393; Terminus St; unpowered/powered sites $20/26, r $69) burnt down in 2002 and although the rebuilt pub is clean and functional it lacks the rustic character of the original. The park opposite the pub has a 'lock-up' dating from the 1880s.

Quinkan & Regional Cultural Centre (☎4060 3457; www.quinkancc.com.au; adult/child $5.50/2; ⏲8.30am-5pm Mon-Fri, 9am-3.30pm Sat & Sun) is a cultural and heritage centre covering the history of the region in photos, murals and interpretive boards. Profiles of local Aboriginal elders and stories of pioneering settlement plaster the walls. This is the place to organise guided tours of the Split Rock art sites with an Aboriginal guide.

The **Laura Store & Post Office**, next to the pub, sells a range of groceries, including fruit and veggies, ice, gas and fuel. Laura also has a **roadhouse** (☎4060 3419; ⏲6am-10pm) with food, fuel and an ATM.

LAURA TO MUSGRAVE

North from Laura some of the creek crossings, such as the Little Laura and Kennedy Rivers, offer great places to bush camp. Sections of road are sealed between Laura and Musgrave, making the going a bit easier.

WORTH A TRIP

LAKEFIELD NATIONAL PARK

The 275km 4WD route from Cooktown to Musgrave via Lakefield National Park is a great alternative to the main road north. This route, however, is very isolated, without any facilities or fuel stops along the way, and you must carry enough water to get between the permanent water points.

Taking the McIvor Rd from Cooktown, you'll reach **Endeavour Falls** after just 33km, most of which is along a sealed road. Here there's a tourist park with a swimming pool, and a grocery and fuel store. At the 36km mark is the turn-off for Battle Camp and Lakefield.

Continue straight on (north) to get to the **Hopevale Aboriginal Community**, established as a Lutheran Mission in 1949. Back on the Cooktown road, turn northwest to continue to **Battle Camp**. About 5km further on there is a stony river crossing and the magical **Isabella Falls** – well worth a stop and a cooling swim.

Lakefield National Park, Queensland's second largest national park, is renowned for its vast river systems, spectacular wetlands and prolific birdlife. Covering more than 537,000 hectares, the park encompasses a rich and diverse landscape across the flood plains of the Normanby, Kennedy, Bizant, Morehead and Hann Rivers. This extensive river system drains into Princess Charlotte Bay on the park's northern perimeter.

Old Laura Homestead, near the junction with the Battle Camp Rd from Cooktown, was built soon after the 1874 Palmer River gold rush. The **QPWS ranger station** (☎4060 3260) is located at New Laura Homestead, about 25km north of the junction.

The best camping facilities (with toilets and showers) are at **Kalpowar Crossing** (per person/family $5.15/20.60) beside the Laura River. Obtain permits from the self-registration stand near the **Lakefield QPWS ranger station**, 3km south of the campground.

The picturesque **Red Lily** and **White Lily Lagoons**, about 8km north of the Lakefield ranger base, attract masses of birdlife including jabirus, brolgas and magpie geese. The red lotus lilies at Red Lily Lagoon are best appreciated in the morning when the lotus blossoms are in full bloom.

Soon after **Hann Crossing** the flat, treeless landscape of **Nifold Plain** stretches from horizon to horizon, its spectacular monotony broken only by sweeping grasslands and giant termite mounds.

About 26km before Musgrave, **Lotus Bird Lodge** (☎4060 3400; www.lotusbird.com.au; Marina Plains Rd; s/d $375/550; ⏰May-Dec), a favourite with birdwatchers, has comfortable timber cabins overlooking a lagoon.

On the banks of the Hann River, 76km north of Laura, the **Hann River Roadhouse** (☎4060 3242; Peninsula Developmental Rd; camp sites $6) sells fuel, groceries and takeaways, and has a licensed restaurant (mains $5 to $19), as well as a camping area with shower and toilet facilities.

MUSGRAVE

The **Musgrave Roadhouse** (☎4060 3229; camp sites $10, r $88), built in 1887, was originally a telegraph station. It's now a licensed restaurant and roadhouse selling fuel, basic groceries and takeaway food. The rooms are simple and the camping area is popular as a first overnight stop on the road up to the Tip.

From near here, tracks run east to the Lakefield National Park or west to Edward River and the Pormpuraaw Aboriginal Community on the far western side of the Cape.

Musgrave to Archer River

About 95km north of Musgrave you come to a road junction. The Peninsula Development Rd leads left to Coen, while a rough road swings right, crossing the **Stewart River** and heading 63km to **Port Stewart** on the eastern coast of the Cape, with reasonable bush camping and good fishing.

COEN

POP 250

Coen is the biggest town in the central Cape area but there's not much to it: a pub, two general stores with fuel and supplies, a hospital, a police station, a small museum and a couple of accommodation options.

A repeater station relocated from the Overland Telegraph line, **Coen Heritage House** has been restored as a museum.

Coen Camping Ground (☎4060 1134; unpowered/powered sites $20/25), next to Rosin general store, has toilets and hot showers.

Homestead Guest House (☎4060 1157; s/d $77/99; ❄) has clean, comfortable rooms with ceiling fans (some with air-con) and shared bathrooms.

The rowdy **'S'Exchange Hotel** (☎4060 1133; r from $75, units from $100; ❄) has dongas, rooms with shared bathrooms or self-contained motel rooms with en suites. After a boozy prank, the 'S' on top of the pub has become a permanent fixture.

A picturesque riverside spot for campers is at **The Bend**, about 5km north of Coen.

The road is sealed for the first 23km north of Coen, but once you pass the Coen airfield it deteriorates. A little further is the rugged access track to **Mungkan Kandju National Park**, an isolated wilderness park that straddles much of the Archer River and its tributaries. The **ranger station** (☎4060 3256) at Rokeby Homestead is about 70km west from the Peninsula Developmental Rd, or you can visit the district ranger in Coen for more information.

ARCHER RIVER

Archer River Roadhouse (☎4060 3266; archerriverroadhouse@bigpond.com; camp sites adult/child $10/5, r $65; ⏲7.30am-10pm) is a great place to stop and enjoy a cold beer and the famous Archer Burger. Look for the memorial dedicated to Toots, a tough-talking female truck driver, and a Cape York legend.

Just down the hill from the roadhouse, the Archer River's wide, tree-lined sandy bed is an ideal spot to camp. The banks are lined with tall paperbark trees (melaleucas) attracting hordes of birds and fruit bats that love the sweet-smelling nectar.

Archer River to Lockhart River

About 36km north of the Archer River Roadhouse, Portland Roads Rd turns off northeast towards Iron Range National Park and the Lockhart River Aboriginal Community. It's another 110km to the **ranger station** (☎4060 7170) at King Park Homestead.

Iron Range National Park is of world significance and conserves the largest area of lowland tropical rainforest in Australia. Birdlife in the area is rich and includes the southern cassowary – this is one of the only habitats where the bird isn't endangered. Also look out for the spotted and the grey cuscus – a monkeylike marsupial with a prehensile tail. Some 10% of Australia's butterfly species also resides in this park; of these, 25 species are found no further south and the park is their stronghold.

There are four bush-camp sites in the park. Near the East Claudie River are the Rainforest and Cooks Hut camping grounds, while further east is the Gordon Creek site. Most campers head for the self-registration Chili Beach site on the coast at the end of the road. Self-registration permits for the first three sites can be obtained at the ranger station.

From the ranger station it's only another 11km to Lockhart River, which is worth a visit for the **Lockhart River Art Centre** (☎4060 7341; www.artgang.com.au), a gallery and cultural centre exhibiting the works of local Indigenous artists known as the 'art gang'. Some of these artists, such as Rosella Namoko and Silas and Samantha Hobson, have received national acclaim and their works sell for big bucks. Note that alcohol restrictions apply in the community.

About 45km north of Lockhart River at Portland Roads, **Portland House** (☎4060 7193; www.portlandhouse.com.au; per person $85) must be one of Australia's most remote holiday houses. The beachfront cottage is the ultimate getaway.

Archer River to Weipa

About 50km north of Archer River, the road splits: the route straight up to the Tip becomes the Telegraph Rd, while the well-maintained Peninsula Development Rd heads northeast for 145km to Weipa on the Western Cape. At Sudley Homestead, 74km in, a rough track turns east to rejoin the Telegraph Rd at Batavia Downs. While it's often chopped up with a couple of creek crossings, it's a shortcut if you're heading up to the Tip after Weipa.

Merluna Station (☎4060 3209; www.merlunastation.com; unpowered sites $10, cabins $110, s/d without bathroom$77/88; ❄✖), about 80km northwest of Archer River Roadhouse, has accommodation in converted workers' quarters. Guests gather in the 'wreck shed' to play pool, throw darts, or sizzle a few snags on the barbie.

WEIPA

POP 2830

Weipa is a bauxite-mining town of red dirt, coconut palms and intermittent danger signs. The mine here works the world's largest deposits of bauxite (the ore from which aluminium is processed), but for most visitors Weipa is a fishing town, renowned for barramundi. All of Weipa's accommodation places can book various tours and fishing charters. A good way to start is to take the **town and mine tour** (adult/child $30/15) from the Weipa Camping & Caravan Park.

In the suburb of Nanum there's a credit union and ATM, post office and supermarket. At Rocky Point you'll find the police and a hospital.

Weipa Camping & Caravan Park (☎4069 7871; www.campweipa.com; Newbold Dr; unpowered/powered sites $26/30, cabins $60-85, units $120, lodges from $155; ❄@≋) is a relaxed camping ground by the waterfront and something of a town hub, operating as an informal tourist office, and booking mine and fishing tours.

Near the waterfront, the **Albatross Bay Resort** (☎1800 240 663, 4090 6666; www.albatrossbayresort.com.au; Duyfken Cres; bungalows $130, r $155; ❄≋) is a large resort with well-appointed motel rooms and cheaper dongas.

The **Heritage Resort** (☎4069 8000; www.heritageresort.com.au; Nanum; s/d $150/160; ❄≋) has relatively comfortable rooms and a Thai restaurant that doubles as a pizzeria.

Weipa Air (☎4069 7807; www.weipaair.com.au) has scenic and charter flights over the coast and Cape York.

Archer River to Bramwell Junction

Back on the northward journey, the Telegraph Rd starts at the Weipa turn-off, 50km north of the Archer River. The road begins to deteriorate here and can be rough and sandy in places. The Wenlock River was once a major challenge on the way north to the Cape, but it is now bridged. The sturdy concrete bridge is raised about 6m above the river, though it still floods in the wet season (when the waters might reach 14m).

On the northern bank of the Wenlock, the **Moreton Telegraph Station** (☎4060 3360; unpowered sites per person $10, safari tents per person $84), formerly a station on the Overland Telegraph Line, has hot showers and meals available.

TURTLE RESCUE

At Mapoon, 86km north of Weipa, **Cape York Turtle Rescue** (☎4069 7266; www.capeyorkturtlerescue.com) is a conservation project where researchers and members of the local Indigenous community work to save turtles and other marine animals such as dolphins and dugong from stray fishing nets and other hazards. Volunteers are welcome to join the project, identifying turtle-nesting sites, collecting research information and helping the rangers and researchers. Volunteering is organised in three- and five-day camps, staying at Camp Chivaree. The camp includes tented accommodation, meals and transfers from Weipa, and costs $1275 for three days and $2125 for five days. Apart from the conservation aspect, it's an opportunity to visit a remote community and work with the indigenous residents – and there's free time for fishing and bush walks.

Bramwell Junction Roadhouse (☎4060 3230; unpowered sites per person $10) marks the junction of the new Southern Bypass Rd and the historic Old Telegraph Track. This is the last fuel stop before the Jardine River Ferry (which is only open from 8am to 5pm).

Fifteen kilometres before the roadhouse is the turn-off to Australia's most northern cattle station, **Bramwell Homestead** (☎4060 3300; bramwellstn@bigpond.com.au; s/d $50/80), which offers accommodation, camping and meals.

Bramwell Junction to Jardine River

After Bramwell Junction there are two possible routes to the Jardine River ferry. The longer route on the graded and reasonably well-maintained Southern and Northern Bypass Rds is quicker and avoids most of the creeks and rivers between the Wenlock and Jardine Rivers.

The more direct but far more challenging route down the **Old Telegraph Track** (commonly called the OTT or 'the Track') is where the real Cape York adventure begins. The OTT follows the remnants of the Overland Telegraph Line, which was constructed during the 1880s to allow communications from Cairns to the Cape via a series of repeater stations and an underwater cable link to Thursday Island. The OTT is a serious 4WD experience with deep corrugations, powdery sand and difficult creek crossings (especially the **Dulhunty River** crossing).

A road leaves the OTT 2km north of the Dulhunty and heads for **Heathlands Ranger Station** (☎4060 3241), looping past the difficult Gunshot Creek crossing. However, if you continue 11km past the ranger station you will reach the Southern Bypass Rd. The track to **Captain Billy Landing**, on the eastern coast, continues straight ahead, but if you stay on the bypass road for the next 45km you rejoin Old Telegraph Rd 14km north of Cockatoo Creek.

To make the most of the OTT, just follow the loop around Gunshot Creek and back onto the OTT. The road becomes sandy for a stretch and after a few more creek crossings joins up with the Southern Bypass Rd after Cockatoo Creek.

Just 9km further north on Telegraph Rd, the second major bypass, Northern Bypass Rd, heads west to the Jardine River ferry crossing. At this point there's a turn-off and it's another 3km to **Fruit Bat Falls**, a lovely swimming area with a popular day-use picnic area (no camping). If you continue on Telegraph Rd, the turn-off to **Twin Falls and Eliot Falls** is a further 6.5km north. The Twin Falls track leads less than 2km to an excellent camping ground. This is the most popular camping spot on the trip north, and although it gets crowded, it's still very enjoyable and well worth spending a day or two lazing away at the falls and cooling off in the long swimming hole.

There are several challenging creeks to cross over the next 23km to the Jardine River, and several bush camping spots.

Note that the old vehicular crossing of the Jardine River on the OTT is closed. The only access to the Jardine River Ferry is on the Northern Bypass Rd.

JARDINE RIVER

The Jardine River is Queensland's largest perennial river, spilling more fresh water into the sea than any other river in Australia. The **Jardine River Ferry & Roadhouse** (☎4069 1369; unpowered sites $5; ⏲8am-5pm), run by the Injinoo Community Council, sells fuel and operates a ferry during the dry season ($88 return, plus $11 for trailers). The fee includes a permit for bush camping between the Dulhunty and Jardine Rivers, and in designated areas north of the Jardine.

LOCAL KNOWLEDGE

TOM WARNES: TOUR OPERATOR

Standing at the tip of the Australian mainland is an emotional experience – with goose bumps. I've been guiding tours to Cape York for the past 21 years and still enjoy sharing Cape York's wonderful wilderness with visitors.

Best Way to Experience the Cape

On a 4WD tour with a reputable tour operator who has knowledge of Cape York's changing landscapes, wonderful wildlife and history, both Indigenous and European.

Natural Wonders

Lots of Australia's wildlife is nocturnal, but you can expect to see wallabies and goannas and it's not unusual to see dingoes and wild pigs. However, the most wildlife you will see are birds and Cape York is home to many fabulous endemic species.

Must-see

Split Rock, Quinkan Aboriginal rock art, Lakefield National Park, Iron Range National Park, Telegraph Track, Eliot Falls, Cape York.

When to travel

Soon after the wet season, in May and June, is the most adventurous. Later, in September and October, it's warmer, with less people and it's great for swimming and birdwatching. July and August is the most popular time because it's cold in southern states.

My best time? September and October.

Stretching east to the coast from the main track is the impenetrable country of **Jardine River National Park**. It includes the headwaters of the Jardine and Escape Rivers, where explorer Edmund Kennedy was killed by Aborigines in 1848.

Northern Peninsula Area

Everything north of the Jardine River is known as the Northern Peninsula Area (NPA to the locals).

BAMAGA

POP 780

In 1947, Chief Bamaga Ginau decided to move his community to the mainland from Saibai Island, just 8km from Papua New Guinea, to escape flooding and a lack of fresh water. Today Bamaga is the largest Torres Strait Islander community on Cape York Peninsula. The town has good facilities, with a hospital, police station, supermarket, bakery, newsagency and service station, but most travellers carry on to Seisia, 5km further north.

Resort Bamaga (☎4069 3050; http://resortbamaga.com.au; cnr Lui & Adidi Sts; r $200; ❄☒), overlooking Mosby Creek, is a very basic four-star resort, and has a restaurant.

SEISIA

POP 180

Australia's most northerly mainland settlement, the tiny Torres Strait Islander town of Seisia, gazes out over a blue-green sea to the outlying islands. It's an idyllic spot to relax after the long journey through the Cape and many people, including those on tours, spend a night here before making the final pilgrimage to the Tip. It's also the jumping-off point for ferries to Thursday Island and the cargo-passenger ferry to Cairns.

Cape York Helicopters (☎4035 9400; www.capeyorkhelicopters.com) offers a number of scenic flights including a quick trip to the Tip (from $190 per person) to a 75-minute bird's-eye view of the island-scattered Torres Strait.

Cape York Adventures (☎4069 3302; www.capeyorkadventures.com.au) has half-day and full-day fishing trips and cruises.

Peddells (☎4069 1551; www.peddellsferry.com.au; adult/child $56/28; ⏲8am & 4pm Mon-Sat Jun-Sep, Mon, Wed & Fri Oct-May) runs regular ferries from Seisia jetty to Thursday Island.

Loyalty Beach Camp Ground & Fishing Lodge (☎4069 3372; www.loyaltybeach.com; unpowered/powered sites $22/24; lodge s/d $105/135, villa $210), 2km north of Seisia, has great beachfront camp sites and a fishing lodge. Here you can book tours, helicopter flights and the ferry to Thursday Island. Also here, **DJs Beer Garden** (⏲5.30-9pm), at the lodge, is an excellent beach-bar for sunset drinks.

Seisia Holiday Park (☎1800 653 243, 4069 3243; www.seisiaholidaypark.com; unpowered/powered sites per person $12/15, lodge s/d $80/120, cottage $160-230; ❄@) looks out over the waters near the wharf, and is the town's accommodation hub. As well as shady sites – some with prime beachfront – there are rooms in a lodge, and neat self-contained A-frame cottages. The park also has a restaurant (open dinner Monday to Thursday), and acts as the booking agent for scenic flights and the ferry to Thursday Island.

THE TIP

From Bamaga, the road north passes the ruins of **Lockerbie Homestead**. The **Croc Tent** (☎4069 3210; www.croctent.com.au; ⏲7.30am-6pm), located across the road, sells souvenirs and provides an unofficial tourist information service. The road then passes through the northernmost rainforest in Australia, **Lockerbie Scrub**, before reaching a Y-junction.

The track right leads to the pretty foreshore of **Somerset** (for information on its history, see the boxed text, p398). The left track leads 15km down the road to the now defunct Pajinka Wilderness Lodge. A 1km walk through the forest and along the beach (over the headland if the tide's in) takes you to **Cape York**, the northernmost 'Tip of Australia'.

On the western side of the Tip, the idyllic **Punsand Bay Camping Resort** (☎4069 1722; www.punsand.com.au; unpowered/powered sites per person $10, on-site tents per person $140-200, air-con cabins $220; ☒) is a remote haven in the wilderness. A dip in the pool, or a cold beer in the breezy restaurant, tops off the Tip experience. **Dato's Venture** (☎4090 2005) operates a ferry (May to October) to Thursday and Horn Islands from here.

Torres Strait Islands

Scattered across the reef-strewn waters of Torres Strait, running like stepping stones from the top of Cape York to the southern

THE JARDINES OF SOMERSET

In 1864, Captain John Jardine was selected to supervise Somerset, a Government Residency and remote outpost at the tip of Cape York. Big plans were afoot for Somerset: the refuge for shipwrecked sailors was earmarked to become a port for the increasing shipping trade, and the foundation for a 'Singapore' of the north. Jardine set his sons, Frank and Alec, the task of droving a mob of cattle from Rockhampton to stock the outpost. It took 10 months to drive the cattle 2000km through searing heat, a long Wet, and numerous Aboriginal attacks.

Frank Jardine's epic expedition set the tone for one of Cape York's most influential pioneers. A tough hard-headed man, Frank Jardine developed a notorious reputation as a mass-murderer of Aborigines and Islanders. He was also cited for bravery (rescuing many shipwrecked sailors), married a Samoan princess, and in 1868 took over his father's role as Government Resident at Somerset. He left after five years to pursue pearling interests but returned in 1877 when the government administration moved to Thursday Island (due to Somerset's poor anchorage and Thursday Island's booming pearling industry). The port never eventuated and all that's now left at Somerset are the lonely graves of Frank Jardine and his wife, Sana.

coast of Papua New Guinea, are the far-flung Torres Strait Islands.

The 70-odd islands include the rocky northern extensions of the Great Dividing Range including Thursday Island; a central group of islands east of the Great Barrier Reef, which are little more than coral cays; and the picturesque Murray Islands in the far east of the strait. It was a successful claim by Torres Strait Islander Eddie Mabo to traditional ownership of Murray Island that led to the federal government's 1993 Native Title legislation (see the boxed text, p434).

While Thursday Island (or 'TI' as it's casually known) is the 'capital' of Torres Strait, there are 17 inhabited islands, the northernmost being Saibai and Boigu Islands, just kilometres from the Papuan coast.

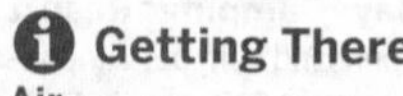

Getting There & Around

Air

Qantaslink (☎13 13 13; www.qantas.com.au) flies daily from Cairns to Horn Island.

Boat

Peddells Ferry Service (☎4069 1551; www.peddellsferry.com.au; Engineers Jetty, Thursday Island) runs regular services between Seisia and Thursday Island. From June to September it has two daily services from Monday to Saturday (adult/child one way $56/28), and from October to May it operates only on Monday, Wednesday and Friday. The ferry departs from Thursday Island for Seisa at 6.30am and 2.30pm, and Seisia for Thursday Island at 8am and 4pm.

McDonald Charter Boats (☎1300 664 875, 4034 2907; www.tiferry.com.au) runs ferries between Thursday Island and Horn Island roughly hourly between 6.30am and 6.30pm (adult/child one way $20/10, 15 minutes), as well as a water-taxi service between other Torres Strait islands. McDonald's also operates a bus service to and from the Horn Island Airport.

Rebel Marine (☎4069 1586; info@rebeltours.com.au) operates a water taxi between Thursday Island and Horn Island Airport connecting with all Qantaslink flights ($18 one way).

THURSDAY ISLAND

POP 2550

Tiny Thursday Island, or 'TI' as it's locally known, was once a major pearling centre. Although it's only 3 sq km and lacks its own fresh water supply, Thursday Island's deep harbour, sheltered port and proximity to major shipping channels made it the logical hub to become the administrative capital of the Torres Strait. The legacy of TI's pearling industry has resulted in a friendly, easy-going cultural mix of Asians, Europeans and Islanders.

Sights

Gab Titui Cultural Centre ART GALLERY
(☎4090 2130; www.gabtitui.com.au; cnr Victoria Pde & Blackall St; admission $6; ⏲9am-5pm Mon-Sat & 2-5pm Sun Apr-Oct, 10am-3pm Mon-Sat Nov-Mar) This modern gallery displays the cultural history of the Torres Strait, hosts cultural events and exhibitions by local artists, and has a popular outdoor cafe.

All Souls Quetta Memorial Church CHURCH
This church was built in 1893 in memory of the shipwreck of the *Quetta*, which struck an uncharted reef in the Adolphus Channel

in 1890, with 133 lives lost. Today its walls are adorned with curious memorabilia, including a porthole recovered from the *Quetta* in 1906.

Japanese Pearl Memorial MONUMENT
The Japanese section of the town's cemetery is crowded with hundreds of kanji-inscribed graves of pearl divers who died from decompression sickness. The memorial is dedicated to them.

Green Hill Fort HISTORIC SITE
Fears of a Russian invasion prompted the erection of this fort in 1893. The small **Torres Strait Museum** is also here.

 Tours

Peddells DAY TRIPS
(☎4069 1551; www.peddellsferry.com.au) Peddells offers bus tours of Thursday Island (adult/child $31/15.50) and also runs Cape York 4WD day trips and Horn Island WWII tours.

Tony's Island Adventures FISHING
(☎4069 1965; www.tonysislandadventures.com.au) Local TI guide, Tony, runs fishing trips and tours of various Torres Strait Islands including Friday, Hammond and Goodes Islands.

Sleeping & Eating

Jardine Resort MOTEL $$
(☎4069 1555; www.jardinemotel.com.au; cnr Normanby St & Victoria Pde; s/d $180/200; ❄@🛜🏊) Although looking a little jaded, this is still the best deal on the island. There's a popular restaurant here.

Thursday Island Motel MOTEL $$
(☎4069 2500; www.thursdayislandmotel.com.au; cnr Jardine & Douglas Sts; s/d incl breakfast $190/200; ❄@) These new and comfortable motel units at the back of the Federal Hotel are a good choice.

Grand Hotel HOTEL $$
(☎4069 1557; www.grandhotelti.com.au; 6 Victoria Pde; s/d from $165/180; ❄@) On a hill behind the wharf, the Grand Hotel has comfortable, modern rooms with ocean and mountain views. The hotel's **Malu Paru restaurant** (⊙dinner Mon-Sat) has a balcony with sweeping views.

Federal Hotel HOTEL $$
(☎4069 1569; www.federalhotelti.com.au; cnr Victoria Pde & Jardine St; s/d incl breakfast $160/180; ❄@) The Federal's motel-style rooms are looking quite tired but are spacious and comfortable enough.

Ilan Café CAFE $
(cnr Victoria Pde & Blackall St; mains $6-20; ⊙breakfast & lunch Mon-Sat, dinner Wed-Sat) After browsing through the local gallery be sure to grab a bite to eat at this modern outdoor cafe.

Information

The island is little more than 3 sq km in area, with the town of Thursday Island on its southern shore.

Hospital (☎4069 1109)

Peddells' Ferry Island Tourist Bureau (☎4069 1551; Engineers Wharf) For tourist information.

Police station (☎4069 1520)

HORN ISLAND

POP 590

During WWII, Horn Island became a battle zone, suffering eight Japanese air raids. Among the 5000 troops once stationed on the island was the 830-strong Torres Strait Light Infantry Battalion. Today Horn Island, and its small town of Wasaga, is very quiet and undeveloped. The story of Horn Island is told in the **Torres Strait Heritage Museum & Art Gallery** (☎4069 2222; www.torresstrait.com.au; adult/child $6.50/3.50) in the grounds of the Gateway Resort.

Gateway Torres Strait Resort (☎4069 2222; www.torresstrait.com.au; 24 Outie St; r $169-249; ❄@🏊), near the wharf, has basic self-contained units with kitchenettes and TVs but is looking decidedly worn and tired. The restaurant, lacking any sort of atmosphere, serves lunch and buffet dinners during the dry season.

OTHER TORRES STRAIT ISLANDS

On Friday Island, the **Kazu Pearl Farm** (☎4069 1268; adult/child incl seafood lunch $70/45; ⊙11.30am-2.30pm) demonstrates pearl cultivation, seeding and harvesting, and has pearls for sale at 'farm' prices.

The inhabited outer islands are difficult to visit, and you must plan well in advance. The islands have very small populations and virtually no tourist infrastructure. To visit any island other than Thursday or Horn, you usually need permission from the island's council; contact the **Torres Strait Regional Council** (☎4069 1247; www.tsirc.qld.gov.au; Torres Strait Haus, Victoria Pde, Thursday Isand).

Most inhabited islands have an airstrip and quite a few airlines operate light aircraft in the strait. Although it's only a few kilometres away, you cannot travel to Papua New Guinea from the northern islands of the Torres Strait. Under the Torres Strait Treaty between Australia and Papua New Guinea, only traditional inhabitants are permitted to cross the border here.

THE SAVANNAH WAY

The epic Savannah Way stretches all the way across the top of Australia from Cairns to Broome. In Queensland, it traverses one of the least-travelled and most spectacular parts of the state, the Gulf Savannah. The world has a different tint out here: the green cloud-tipped mountains and sugarcane fields of the east coast give way to a flat, often red-dust-coated landscape of sweeping grass plains, scrubby forest and mangroves engraved by an intricate network of seasonal rivers and croc-filled tidal creeks that drain into the Gulf of Carpentaria. The fishing here is legendary, particularly for barramundi (barra season runs from mid-January to the end of September).

Vast distances between attractions are interspersed with a scattering of cattle stations and historic towns that have been through the cycles of boom and bust over and over again, and retain a hardy independent spirit and some extraordinary outback characters. Stop by the rusting roadhouses and you'll meet folk with stories to tell, and not many people to tell them to (mobile phone service is nonexistent in some places). Best of all, you don't even need a 4WD vehicle to explore most of it, just a sense of adventure.

Information

Gulf Savannah Development (☎4031 1631; www.gulf-savannah.com.au) has details of tourist operators in the Savannah region.

The website www.savannahway.com.au has information covering the length of the road.

Getting There & Around

Air

Skytrans (☎1300 759 872; www.skytrans.com.au) flies several times a week between Cairns and Normanton (from $179) and Burketown (from $179); and between Mt Isa and Burketown (from $200).

Bus

TransNorth (☎4061 7944; www.transnorthbus.com) has a service from Cairns to Karumba ($140, 12 hours, three times weekly), departing from Cairns Monday, Wednesday and Friday, stopping at the Undara turn-off ($61, 5½ hours), Georgetown ($79, seven hours), Croydon ($101, 9½ hours) and Normanton ($135, 11 hours). The return service runs Tuesday, Thursday and Saturday.

No buses run between Normanton and Mt Isa or Burketown.

Car & Motorcycle

The sealed Gulf Developmental Rd forms the major section of this stretch of the Savannah Way, passing through Georgetown and Croydon en route to Normanton, from where you can continue on bitumen up to Karumba, or continue on the gravel Gulf Track to Burketown and beyond to the Northern Territory border.

Heading south from Burketown the unsealed road to Camooweal runs via Gregory Downs and the Boodjamulla (Lawn Hill) National Park, while the Nardoo-Burketown Rd cuts across to meet the Burke Developmental Rd at the Burke & Wills Roadhouse.

There aren't many options apart from these major routes, particularly if you don't have a 4WD. Even if you do, remember that this is very remote country. If you're thinking of attempting the Savannah Way's alternate routes (such as the continuation of the Burke Developmental Rd, which takes you east from between Normanton and Karumba to Mareeba via Chillagoe), you'll need to be well prepared and carry good maps, plenty of water and preferably a UHF radio. If you want to hire a 4WD, you should organise one in Cairns.

Even sealed roads are often single-file, so you need to slow down and move over to the shoulder as oncoming traffic approaches. If a road train's coming your way, pull over completely and wait for it to pass – and for the blinding dust clouds to settle. (The same applies if a vehicle's overtaking yours – pull off the road and wait for it to pass.)

Unfenced cattle and kangaroos can appear on the road as if from nowhere, and hitting one will probably kill the animal and ruin your car for good (not to mention endanger your own life); *always* avoid driving at dawn, dusk and night.

Train

A must for rail buffs, the historic **Savannahlander** (☎1800 793 848; www.savannahlander.com.au; one-way/return fare-only $210/355), fondly known as the 'Silver Bullet', chugs its way along a traditional mining-route from Cairns to Forsayth and back over four days, departing from Cairns on Wednesday at 6.30am and returning on Saturday at 6.40pm. A range of tours (including side trips to Chillagoe, Undara and Cobbold Gorge) and accommodation can be booked through the website.

The quaint, snub-nosed **Gulflander** (☎4745 1391; http://thegulflander.com.au; one-way/return fare-only $63/107) runs once weekly in each direction between Normanton and Croydon on the 1891 gold-to-port railway line alongside the Gulf Developmental Rd. It leaves Normanton on Wednesday at 8.30am, returning from Croydon on Thursday at 8.30am; shorter trips are available.

Tours

Several operators run guided tours from Cairns. Their itineraries are all pretty similar, taking in a combination of Chillagoe, Undara, Cobbold Gorge, Normanton, Karumba and Boodjamulla (Lawn Hill) National Park.

Heritage Tours HERITAGE
(☎1800 77 55 33, 4054 7750; www.heritagetours.com.au; 9-day tours from $3095)

Oz Tours Safaris WILDLIFE
(☎1800 079 006, 4055 9535; www.oztours.com.au; 7-/9-day tours from $2495/3095)

Wilderness Challenge WILDLIFE, CAMPING
(☎1800 354 486, 4035 4488; www.wilderness-challenge.com.au; 9-day accommodated tours from $2995, 11-day camping safari from $2995)

Mt Garnet to Undara

Around 15km west of Innot Hot Springs, the landscape starts to thin out at the small mining town of **Mt Garnet** (population 400), revealing outback features of woodland savannah and multicoloured termite mounds. There's a pub, roadhouse and a couple of cafes along the main street. Just north of town is the Wurruma Swamp, a wetlands area that attracts a huge range of birdlife.

About 60km past Mt Garnet, the Kennedy Hwy passes through **Forty Mile Scrub National Park**. It's named not for its length, but because it's '40 miles' from Mt Garnet – a common system of distance markers used by early travellers, miners and drovers. There are toilets, picnic facilities (watch your crumbs – the leaf litter is home to the giant cockroach!) and a wheelchair-accessible circuit boardwalk (300m, 10 minutes).

UNDARA VOLCANIC NATIONAL PARK

About 190,000 years ago, the Undara shield volcano erupted not with a bang but with a flow, like an overboiled pot of tomato soup, sending molten lava coursing through the surrounding landscape. The results are the world's longest continuous (though fragmented) lava tubes. They formed when the lava flows drained towards the sea, following the routes of ancient river beds, and while the surface of the lava cooled and hardened, hot lava continued to race through the centre of the flows, eventually leaving enormous basalt tubes.

All-up there are over 160km of tubes, but only a fraction can be visited, on **guided tours** only. Most are operated by **Undara Experience** (☎1800 990 992, 4097 1900; www.undara.com.au; full-day/half-day/2hr/sunset tours $128/82/46/43). Full- and half-day tours only run in the Dry. If you take the sunset tour during the 'green' (ie wet) season (December to March), you're likely to see nature's food chain in full swing: every evening around dusk, thousands of microbats fly out of their cave en masse in search of an insect feed, while tree snakes known as 'night tigers' hang in wait to snatch the tiny bats in midflight.

Alternatively, **Bedrock Village Caravan Park & Tours** (☎1800 447 982, 4062 3153; 23 Garland St; half-day tour adult/child $74/37, full-day tour $120/60) in Mt Surprise runs tours. Both are members of **Savannah Guides** (www.savannah-guides.com.au), an association of expert interpreters of Australia's tropical savannahs.

The closest accommodation to the tubes and national park is at **Undara Experience** (☎1800 990 992, 4097 1900; www.undara.com.au; unpowered/powered sites $20/30, swag tent d from $40, carriage s from $75, carriage d without/with bathroom from $150/170;). Its resort-like complex combines bush camping and van sites with accommodation in 'swag tents' and pricey but atmospheric restored railway carriages with original fittings converted into comfy rooms (some with bathrooms). Facilities include barbecues, hot showers, laundries and campfire entertainment. You can boil billy tea and cook toast over the campfire during the daily bush breakfast (adult/child $22.50/11.25), but even though all meals need to be booked in advance, the bistro (lunch buffet adult/child $22.50/11.25, dinner mains $15.50 to $32.50) can shut early without warning, and there's nowhere else to eat out here – don't get caught out!

Undara's biggest weekend of the year is **Opera in the Outback** in October, a cultural extravaganza of opera, theatre and Broadway music in a bush setting.

WORTH A TRIP

COBBOLD GORGE

About 32km west of Mt Surprise, the 150km **Explorers' Loop** detour takes you through the old mining townships of **Einasleigh** (population 40), home to the character-filled, corrugated-iron **Einasleigh Pub** (☎4062 5222; Daintree St; s/d $38.50/49.50) containing its publican's hand-carved, miniature period furniture; **Forsayth** (population 90), the last stop on the *Savannahlander*, which also has accommodation; and on to the main attraction, **Cobbold Gorge**.

With swimming holes, rugged cliffs and an abundance of wildlife, this spring-fed oasis is one of those startling outback discoveries. Access to the gorge is by guided tour only. Savannah Guides–member **Cobbold Gorge Village** (☎1800 669 922, 4062 5470; www.cobboldgorge.com.au; unpowered/powered sites $18/29, sites with bathroom $45, s/d cabins $75/109; ⏲Apr-Oct; ❄@☒) runs three-hour tours (adult/child $69/35; from April to October), including a boat cruise. Facilities at the village include a restaurant (all-day snacks $7 to $12, dinner mains $22), a bar and groceries, so it's not hard to hang around for a few days.

The Explorers' Loop is mostly unsealed and rough in sections but is usually passable for 2WD vehicles during the Dry. It rejoins the Savannah Way at Georgetown, from where Cobbold Gorge tours can pick up.

The turn-off to Undara is 66km south of Mt Garnet, from where it's 15km along a sealed road. In addition to TransNorth buses, overnight tours run from Cairns (p311).

Mt Surprise

POP 160

Back on the Gulf Developmental Rd, 39km past the Undara turn-off, the 'jewel of a town' Mt Surprise lives up to both its moniker and its name. The town welcomes – and farewells – you with twin sculptures of a black cockatoo and a scrap-metal miner. Between them are a couple of pubs and a community that loves collecting: gem collections, snake collections and even miniature horses. It's a good base for fossicking in the nearby gemfields. The knowledgeable owners of **Mt Surprise Gems** (☎4062 3055; www.thegemden.com.au; Garland St), Pete and Pam, run fossicking tours from April to September (half-day tours including transport/self-drive $65/45), rent out tools (per day $22) and can issue licences (per month $6.50, Queensland-wide). There's also a gem shop, a post office and a cafe (mains $10.50 to $25; open 7am to 7pm April to October).

At **Planet Earth Adventures** (☎4062 3127; p.e.a.@bigpond.com.au; unpowered/powered sites $10/17 per person, dishes $5-12; ⏲cafe 7am-8pm), Russell Dennis has a snake museum (gold coin donation) where you can see deadly taipans and king brown snakes, and free snake shows (open 10am Sunday; otherwise $10 by arrangement), including – God forbid – snake bite education. He also has a Midas touch for curing even the most entrenched snake phobias – you'll be wrapping a black-headed python around your neck in no time (seriously!).

Mt Surprise Tourist Van Park, Motel & BP Roadhouse (☎1800 447 982, 4062 3153; 23 Garland St; unpowered/powered sites $20/24, cabins $55-89; ❄☒) is set amid lush, shady gardens, a miniature horse stud and bird aviary. Another surprise: its BYO cafe (mains $5 to $19; open 7am to 7pm) serves authentic, homemade Chinese Mongolian beef, tofu and mushroom soup, chilli hotpot chicken – and delicious dim sims for just 50 cents.

Bedrock Village Caravan Park & Tours (☎4062 3193; www.bedrockvillage.com.au; Garnet St; unpowered/powered sites $20/27, cabins $65-85; ❄@☒) is another excellent park set in native bushland just north of the main road, with cabins, meals on request, and tours to Undara.

Georgetown

POP 300

During the days of the Etheridge River gold rush, Georgetown was a bustling commercial centre, but these days there's not much here, bar a resident monitor lizard, a free swimming pool, and the flash **Terrestrial Centre** (☎4062 1485; ⏲8am-5pm Apr-Sep, 8.30am-4.30pm Mon-Fri Oct-May; @), which is home to the **visitor centre**, the town **library** and the outstanding **Ted Elliot Mineral Collection** (adult/child $11/9), a shimmering display of more than 4500 minerals, gems and crystals from all over Australia.

Georgetown has a post office, a pub, fuel and a handful of places to stay and/or eat. The pick is the modern **Latara Resort Motel** (☎4062 1190; www.georgetownaccommodation.com; North St; s/d $92/105; ❄≋) and its restaurant (mains $25 to $32; open dinner Saturday to Thursday). **Midway Caravan Park & Service Station** (☎4062 1219; unpowered/powered sites $18/20, s/d cabins from $40/52; ❄≋) has shady sites and a good range of cabins (all share a bathroom).

Croydon

POP 320

Connected to Normanton by the *Gulflander,* this old gold-mining town was once the biggest in the Gulf. Gold was discovered here in 1885, and within a couple of years there were 8000 diggers working 5000 gold mines, and more than 30 pubs. By the end of WWI the gold had run out and Croydon became little more than a ghost town.

Croydon's **visitor information centre** (☎4745 6125; Samwell St; ⏲9am-4.30pm; @) has details of the remaining historic buildings.

The town's water supply, **Lake Belmore,** 4km north of the centre, was built in 1995 and is stocked with barramundi. On the way to the lake are the Chinese Temple and cemetery ruins, remnants of Croydon's once-thriving Chinatown.

The 1887-built **Club Hotel** (☎4745 6184; cnr Brown & Sircom Sts; d $70, units $120; ❄≋) is the only pub left from the mining heyday, serving up huge meals (mains $16 to $25; open lunch and dinner), ice-cold beer, and views of the sun setting over the orange-glowing plains from the front verandah. Campers can pitch up at the **Croydon Caravan**

WORTH A TRIP

BOODJAMULLA (LAWN HILL) NATIONAL PARK

One of the most rewarding side trips off the Savannah Way is the beautiful, unexpected oasis of Lawn Hill Gorge. Stuck between a rock (the Constance Range) and a hard place (the Gulf Savannah), a series of deep flame-red sandstone gorges, fed by spring water and lined with palms, provides a haven for wildlife. Aboriginal people have inhabited the area for some 30,000 years, and paintings and old camp sites abound. Book well ahead for accommodation including camping.

In the southern part of the park is the World Heritage–listed **Riversleigh Fossil Field**, with a small **Department of Environment & Resource Management (DERM) bush camp** (☎13 74 68; www.derm.qld.gov.au; per person $5.15; ⏲Mar-Oct). The fossils include everything from giant snakes and carnivorous kangaroos to pocket-sized koalas.

Some 20km of walking tracks fan out around the gorge, while the emerald-green waters are idyllic for a swim or a paddle in a canoe with the red cliffs towering above.

The main hub for accommodation and activities is at **Adel's Grove** (☎4748 5502; www.adelsgrove.com.au; unpowered sites/permanent tent/d $32/80/130; ⏲camping year-round, other accommodation & facilities Easter-late Oct), 10km east of the park entrance. Set amid trees close to the creek, there are camp sites, permanently set-up tents (including beds and linen) and basic rooms, a bar and restaurant (breakfast $12.50, lunch mains $10 to $15, two-course dinner $30). Fuel, food packs and basic groceries are available, as well as fascinating Savannah Guide–led Riversleigh fossil field tours (half-day tours $65), and canoe hire (per hour from $20).

Also near the gorge is a **DERM camping ground** (☎13 74 68; www.derm.qld.gov.au; sites per person $5.15) with showers and toilets.

The park entrance is 100km west of **Gregory Downs** (population 40) on the beautiful Gregory River, via a gravel road suitable for conventional vehicles in the Dry. Fuel is available at the **Gregory Downs Hotel** (☎4748 5566; sites per person $12, motel unit d $100; ❄), a laid-back spot to quench your thirst and tuck into decent pub meals (mains $10 to $22; open lunch daily and dinner Monday to Saturday).

The 334km unsealed road from Burketown to Gregory Downs is the most direct route to Boodjamulla (Lawn Hill) National Park. For 2WDs, the easiest route to Gregory Downs is the sealed road from the Burke & Wills Roadhouse.

MORNING GLORY

Between approximately August and November, Burketown becomes the home of intrepid cloud-surfers, when 'morning glory' clouds frequently (but unpredictably) roll in. A rare meteorological phenomenon, these tubular clouds come in wave-like sets of up to eight. Each can be up to 1000km long by 2km high, and travel at speeds of up to 60km per hour. As the sun rises, gliders head up in the hope of catching one; ask around in town and chances are someone will take you along for the ride. For a close-up look at the clouds aboard a light plane, Gulf-wide charter company **Savannah Aviation** (☎4745 5177; www.savannah-aviation.com; per hr for up to 4 people $550) has plenty of expertise – owner Paul Poole heads up Australia's branch of the Cloud Appreciation Society.

Park (☎4745 6238; admin@croydon.qld.gov.au; cnr Brown & Alldridge Sts; unpowered/powered sites $18/25, en-suite cabins $80; ❄🏊).

Normanton

POP 1330

Capital of the gigantic Carpentaria Shire, Normanton is a disproportionately small, peaceful community essentially consisting of one long main street. Normanton's boom years were the 1890s, when it acted as the port for the Croydon gold rush. Since those heady days, it's existed as a major supply point for the surrounding cattle stations.

The Norman River produces whopping barramundi; every Easter the **Barra Bash** lures big crowds, as do the **Normanton Rodeo & Show** (mid-June) and the **Normanton Races** (September).

Housed in the historic Burns Philp & Co Ltd store, the **visitor information & heritage centre** (☎4745 1065; www.carpentaria.qld.gov.au; cnr Caroline & Landsborough Sts; ⏲9am-4.30pm Mon-Fri, 9am-noon Sat, noon-3pm Sun Apr-Sep, 9.30am-3.30pm Mon-Fri, 9am-noon Sat Oct-Mar; @) has local history displays. Normanton's **train station** is a charming Victorian-era building. When it's not running, the *Gulflander* rests under its arched roof.

The main street's most impressive sight is the life-size model of **Krys the Crocodile** in the LEW Henry Park. The real beast was shot by crocodile hunter Krystina Pawloski in 1958 – at a staggering 8.64m it's the largest recorded croc in the world. Stand next to it and imagine meeting *that* when you're out fishing!

The other impossible-to-miss main-street icon is the **Purple Pub** (☎4745 1324; cnr Landsborough & Brown Sts; s/d $95/120; ❄), painted a lurid shade of aubergine several decades ago because it was the only cheap paint available in the area at the time. Comfortable motel rooms congregate out back, and there are meals available for $12 to $25.

In a mercifully shady setting, the huge 25m swimming pool at the welcoming **Normanton Tourist Park** (☎1800 193 4699, 4745 1121; 14 Brown St; unpowered/powered sites $20/25, cabins without/with bathroom $55/90; ❄🏊) adjoins an artesian spa.

The iron-roofed **Albion Hotel** (☎4745 1218; cnr Landsborough & Haig Sts; d $95; ❄) has cool, clean motel rooms, a pool table, as well as the best barra and chips in town (mains $8 to $15).

Normanton to Burketown

From Normanton the Savannah Way (Gulf Track) sweeps across the flat plains of the Gulf to Burke and beyond to the Northern Territory. This 233km, partly sealed route is accessible for 2WDs in the Dry, and there are plans to seal it all the way to Burketown.

The turn-off to get back on the Savannah Way to Burketown is 5km south of Normanton. After 33km you come to a signposted turn-off leading 2km to **Burke and Wills' Camp 119**, the northernmost camp of the Burke and Wills expedition (which came within just 5km of reaching the Gulf). It's marked by a ring of trees surrounding a tree blazed by Burke and Wills.

Back on the Gulf Track, it's 113km to the **Leichhardt River**. The best place to pull over is at the small, sandy, tree-covered island about halfway across the river's rocky bed, just past the narrow bridge. From here it's a short walk downstream to the spectacular **Leichhardt Falls** (don't swim in the big stretch of water above the road crossing – there are crocs), where trees offer shade and the birdlife is rich and varied.

It's only a couple of kilometres on to a road junction: continue straight to Burketown, or head south to the sealed Wills Developmental Rd (69km) from where you can

WORTH A TRIP

KARUMBA

Ay Karumba! Although technically not on the Savannah Way, you can't come all this way and not drive the extra 70km north from Normanton. When the fish are biting and the sun sinks into the Gulf in a fiery ball of burnt ochre, this is a little piece of outback paradise. Even if you don't like fishing, it's the only town accessible by sealed road on the entire Gulf coast.

Karumba (population 520) is a tale of two towns. **Karumba Town** is on the banks of the Norman River, while **Karumba Point** – the best place to stay – is about 6km away by road on the beach. By the time you're reading this, a new 3.2km **boardwalk** with solar-powered lighting will link the two.

Established as a telegraph station in the 1870s, Karumba was brought alive by prawning in the Gulf in the 1960s. Barra, grunter, queenfish and bream are common catches, as are prawns; most shops sell fishing gear, permits and bait. You can fish right off the beach at Karumba Point, or go out on a charter with **Kerry D Fishing Charters** (☎4745 9275; www.kerrydfishing.com.au; half-/full-day charter per person $100/200) or **Ferryman Cruises** (☎4745 9155; www.ferryman.net.au; half-/full-day charter $90/180).

Ferryman also offers two-hour River & Gulf Sunset cruises (adult/child $35/15), morning birdwatching cruises ($45/20) and night croc-spotting cruises ($45/20). **Croc & Crab Tours** (☎0428 496 026; www.crocandcrabtours.com.au; half-day tour adult/child $119/30) include live crab-pot lifting and fresh-cooked mud crabs. Alternatively, go heli-fishing with **Tremain-Hill Helicopter Services** (☎4745 9777; tours per person $400).

To learn everything you ever wanted to know about barra (eg, that most start life as males and change sex to females after about seven years!), take a 45-minute guided tour at the **Barramundi Discovery Centre** (☎4745 9359; 148 Yappar St; adult/child $12.50/5; ⏲10am-3pm Mon-Sat, call for wet season hr), a breeding centre and hatchery, where you can hand-feed the fish and buy wacky, locally made wallets, bags and more fashioned from barramundi, crocodile, sea snake, stingray and cane toad leather.

Karumba's **visitor information centre** (☎4745 9582; www.carpentaria.qld.gov.au; Walker St, Karumba Town; ⏲hr vary; @) can help find accommodation – book ahead in the Dry.

End of the Road Motel MOTEL $$

(☎4745 9599; www.endoftheroadmotel.com.au; 26 Palmer St, Karumba Point; d $130-160; ❄🏊) These breezy, stylish beachside units are Karumba's premium accommodation.

Karumba Point Sunset Caravan Park CARAVAN PARK $

(☎4747 9277; www.sunsetcp.com.au; 53 Palmer St, Karumba Point; sites $28-32, cabins $95, villas $110; ❄🏊) Superbly equipped palm-shaded park; spotless amenities.

Ash's Holiday Units & Café MOTEL, CABINS $

(☎4745 9132; www.ashsholidayunits.com.au; 21 Palmer St, Karumba Point; s/d $85/90; ❄@📶🏊) Spacious motel-style rooms and compact but cute cabins. The cafe (mains $6.50 to $17; open 7am to 7.30pm) out front serves up legendary barra and chips.

Karumba Lodge Hotel HOTEL $

(☎4745 9143; cnr Yappar & Gilbert Sts, Karumba Town; d $95; ❄) Comfortable motel rooms and two very different bars. The open-sided **Animal Bar** was reputedly Australia's roughest pub when the prawning industry was in full swing.

Raptis Fish Markets SEAFOOD $

(☎4745 9122; www.raptis.com.au; Massey Dr, Karumba Town; ⏲8am-3pm Mon-Fri, 9am-1pm Sat) Unless you catch it yourself, ready-to-cook seafood doesn't come fresher than from this waterside shed, which also sells bargain-priced 1kg bags of mouth-watering cooked prawns ($15) that alone justify the drive to Karumba.

Sunset Tavern TAVERN $$

(☎4745 9183; The Esplanade, Karumba Point; mains $15-28; ⏲10am-midnight) The place to take in those glorious sunsets, ice-cold schooner in hand, especially from the waterfront beer garden. Excellent meals range from burgers to kangaroo tenderloins, plus seafood, of course.

head southeast to the **Burke & Wills Roadhouse** (☎4742 5909; unpowered/powered sites $18/22, d $65; ❄), or west to Gregory Downs. A little further along the Burketown road is the turn-off to Floraville Station. A 'Historic Site' sign indicates the 1.3km diversion to **Walker's Monument**. Frederick Walker, who'd been sent out to find Burke and Wills, died here in 1866. Although he didn't find them, he did discover Camp 119, and his maps opened up much of the Gulf country.

BURKETOWN

POP 220

Isolated Burketown is a fishing mecca just 30km from the waters of the Gulf of Carpentaria. Founded in 1865, it almost came to a premature end a year later when a fever wiped out most of the residents. In 1887 a huge tidal surge almost carried the town away and, while nothing so dramatic has occurred since, the township is often cut off from the rest of the country by floodwaters.

Besides excellent fishing, Burketown is the best place in the world to witness the extraordinary 'morning glory' phenomenon – see the boxed text on p404. The biggest events on the town's social calendar are the **World Barramundi Fishing Championship** (Easter), and **Burketown Rodeo** (late September/early October).

TOP CHOICE **Burketown Pub** (☎4745 5104; www.burketownpub.com; Beames St; s/d $65/85, units $100-140; ❄) is the heart and soul of Burketown, an outback pub originally built as the local customs house in the late 1860s. It's the oldest building in town – all its contemporaries have been blown or washed away. Swap stories with locals and travellers in the palm-fringed beer garden, or over a meal (mains $8 to $25, open lunch and dinner). If you bring in your catch, the kitchen will cook it to order for $10. Comfortable motel units are set far enough away to be quiet.

Across the park from the pub, the bushy **Burketown Caravan Park** (☎4745 5118; www.burketowncaravanpark.com.au; Sloman St; powered sites $30, d & cabins with bathroom $99-110, d & cabins without bathroom $66-88; ❄) has a takeaway van (mains $8 to $22) dishing up *Ben Hur*–sized brekkies and two-handed barra burgers for lunch and dinner.

Burketown to the Border

This 228km section of the Savannah Way is along unsealed roads, although a 4WD vehicle isn't required during the Dry. Travel (in any vehicle) isn't recommended during the Wet, when heavy rains can close the roads. A useful fuel stop for the 486km run between Burketown and Borroloola (NT) is the **Doomadgee Aboriginal Community** (☎4745 8188). While you're welcome to buy fuel and shop at the store here, village access is subject to council permission, and alcohol is restricted.

It's another 80km of Melaleuca scrub to the re-opened **Hell's Gate Roadhouse** (☎4745 8258; unpowered sites $20), 50km from the NT border. It has fuel, camping (no power) and basic snacks such as pies, but bring cash as there are no credit card facilities. Roughly midway between the two, a signposted turn-off leads down a 42km track to remote **Kingfisher Camp** (☎4745 8212; www.kingfisherresort.com.au; day pass adult/child $5/free, sites per person/family $10/25) on Bowthorn Station. It's set beside a gorgeous 5km-long waterhole on the Nicholson River, which you can explore by boat (per hour $25) and canoe (per hour $10). Camping facilities include hot showers.

From Kingfisher, it's another 33km south to Bowthorn Homestead, from where you can head east 72km to join up with the Savannah Way (Gulf Track) east of the Nicholson River, or detour south 100km or so to Boodjamulla (Lawn Hill) National Park.

Journeys into the Outback

Includes »

Charters Towers to Cloncurry 409
Cloncurry 409
Mt Isa 410
Mt Isa to Charleville 413
Winton 413
Barcaldine 417
Charleville 418
Mt Isa to Birdsville 419
Birdsville 419
Birdsville Track 420
Simpson Desert National Park 420
Birdsville to Charleville 420

Best Places to Eat

- Wagon Wheel Hotel (p410)
- FJ Holden's (p409)
- Livingstone's (p412)
- Rodeo Bar & Grill (p412)
- Young Tiger (p418)

Best Places to Stay

- Blacksmith's Cottage (p418)
- Hotel Corones (p418)
- Nardoo Station (p414)
- Wagon Wheel Hotel (p410)

Why Go?

Australia's mystical outback is less a place than a state of mind, and its mythical, spiritual power retains an inexplicable hold on this most urbanised of peoples. Geographically, it lies anywhere west of the Great Dividing Range. Yet to experience it can be elusive.

Driving west from Townsville, you come upon the outback's open spaces within a few hundred kilometres, but if you go expecting cattlemen on horseback or *Crocodile Dundee* types entertaining the crowds in every outback pub, you may be disappointed. Instead, you'll find tiny towns linked by long, roo-strewn roads that slice through vast pastoral plains dotted with surprises: fascinating fossils, eccentric local festivals, blissfully deserted national parks and even striking public art.

The outback can't be experienced on a day trip, but the all-embracing skies, fiery sunsets, star-studded nights and the laconic characters you meet along the way are more than enough reward for all those kilometres.

When to Go

Mt Isa

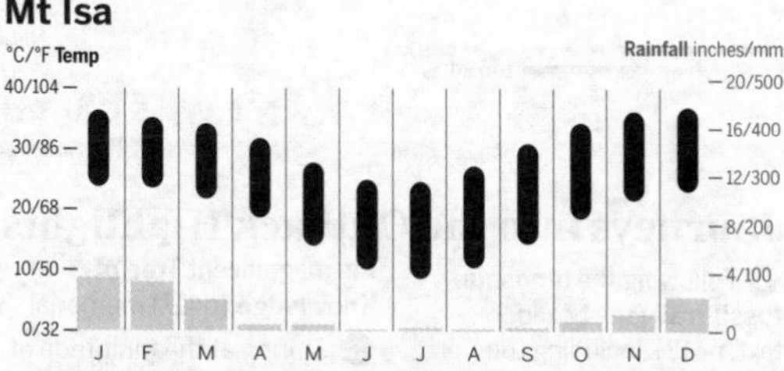

April–October Mild weather and extended opening hours through the winter.

June–September Racing festivals and rodeos take place throughout outback Queensland.

November–March Temperatures soar, rivers swell and roads can flood – take care.

Journeys into the Outback Highlights

1. Following the **dinosaur-fossil trail** (see boxed text, p413), including the prehistoric stampede at Lark Quarry Dinosaur Trackways and the fossil museums at Richmond and Winton
2. Making a short pub crawl of the iconic timber pubs of Barcaldine, stopping to admire the magnificent **Tree of Knowledge** (p417) memorial
3. Staring at the multitude of stars above **Nardoo Station** (see boxed text, p414) while soaking in a warm artesian spa with a cold beer in hand
4. Listening to a yarn and propping up the bar at Charleville's grand **Hotel Corones** (p418)
5. Joining in the festivities and revelry at the absurdly popular **Birdsville Races** (p419)
6. Descending into the **Hard Times Mine** (p410) and drilling a rock face at Mt Isa

Getting There & Around

AIR

Qantas (☎13 13 13; www.qantas.com.au) flies daily to Mt Isa, while Qantaslink flies from Brisbane to Barcaldine, Blackall, Charleville and Longreach.

Skytrans (☎1300 759 872; www.skytrans.com.au) covers most of the outback with flights between Brisbane and Birdsville via Charleville, Quilpie and Windorah; Birdsville and Mt Isa with stops at Bedourie and Boulia; Brisbane and Thargomindah via Cunnamulla and St George; and from Cairns and Mt Isa direct. Skytrans also services the northwestern corner of the state, connecting Mt Isa and Cairns with Doomadgee, Burketown and Normanton.

Regional Express (☎13 17 13; www.rex.com.au) also services the outback with flights connecting Townsville with Hughenden, Richmond, Julia Creek, Mt Isa, Winton and Longreach.

BUS

Greyhound Australia (☎1300 473 946; www.greyhound.com.au) has a regular coach service from Townsville to Mt Isa via Hughenden, and from Brisbane to Mt Isa via Roma and Longreach. From Mt Isa, buses continue to Tennant Creek in the Northern Territory (NT); from there you can head north to Darwin or south to Alice Springs.

Paradise Coaches (☎1300 300 156; www.paradisecoaches.com.au) makes the run from Rockhampton to Longreach (twice weekly) via Emerald.

CAR & MOTORCYCLE

If you like driving, you're in for a treat here, because you'll be doing a lot of it! Although sparsely settled, the outback is well serviced by major roads: the Flinders and Barkly Hwys, which together form the Overlander's Way, connect northern Queensland with the NT; the Capricorn Hwy runs along the tropic of Capricorn from Rockhampton to Longreach; and the Landsborough and Mitchell Hwys, which together make up the epic Matilda Hwy, run from the New South Wales (NSW) border south of Cunnamulla up to Cloncurry and Karumba on the Gulf of Carpentaria.

TRAIN

Queensland Rail (☎1800 872 467, 3235 1122; www.queenslandrail.com.au) has three trains servicing the outback, and all run twice weekly. The *Spirit of the Outback* runs from Brisbane to Longreach via Rockhampton and Emerald, with connecting bus services to Winton; the *Westlander* runs from Brisbane to Charleville via Roma, with connecting bus services to Cunnamulla and Quilpie; and the *Inlander* runs from Townsville to Mt Isa via Cloncurry.

Charters Towers to Cloncurry

The 246km route from Charters Towers to Hughenden is a former Cobb & Co coach run, and is dotted along the way with tiny townships that were established as stopovers for the coaches.

It's about 200km to the aptly named town of **Prairie**, where the quiet little **Prairie Hotel** (☎4741 5121; Flinders Hwy; unpowered/powered sites $12/20, s/d with shared bathroom $50/85, motel units with bathroom $90-99; ❄) serves pub meals amid outlandish outback decor. Further along is **Hughenden**, with its interesting display of dinosaur fossils, and excellent burger joint **FJ Holden's** (☎4741 5121; Brodie St; meals $5-24; ⏰8am-8pm Mon-Sat, 9am-8pm Sun).

Porcupine Gorge National Park (☎13 74 68; www.qld.gov.au/camping; sites per person/family $5/20) is an oasis in the dry country north of Hughenden. You can camp at **Pyramid Lookout** and it's an easy 30-minute walk into the gorge and its creek.

Richmond has even more dinosaur bones in its admirable little museum at **Kronosaurus Korner** (☎4741 3429; www.kronosauruskorner.com.au; 91 Goldring St; adult/child $12/6; ⏰8.30am-4.45pm). The centre houses what is easily the best collection of marine fossils in the region, most found by local landholders. Pride of place goes to an almost-complete 4.25m pliosaur skeleton, one of Australia's best vertebrate fossils, and a partial skeleton of *Kronosaurus queenslandicus,* the largest known marine reptile ever to have lived in the area. A video explains some of the prehistory and the background of the finds.

Further along the road, you hit tiny **Julia Creek** – if you're there in April be sure to stop by the **Dirt 'n' Dust Festival**.

Cloncurry

POP 3,380

Some 135km west of Julia Creek, the 'Curry' was the centre of a copper boom in the 19th century, and was once the largest copper producer in the British Empire. Today it's a busy pastoral centre with a reinvigorated mining industry.

The **Mary Kathleen Park & Museum** (☎4742 1361; McIlwraith St; adult/child $8/3.60; ⏰8am-4.30pm Mon-Fri, 9am-3pm Sat & Sun, closed weekends Oct-Apr) is the tourist information centre. Relics of the Burke and Wills expedition and displays of local rocks and minerals are housed in buildings transported from the ghost town at the former nearby uranium mine of Mary Kathleen.

John Flynn Place (☎4742 4125; cnr Daintree & King Sts; adult/child $8.50/4; ⏰8am-4.30pm Mon-Fri, 9am-3pm Sat & Sun Apr-Oct) commemorates the pioneering work of Dr John Flynn in setting up the invaluable Royal Flying Doctor Service here in Cloncurry.

Wagon Wheel Hotel (☎4742 1866; 54 Ramsay St; s $70, d $74-85; ❄️) is the oldest licensed premises in this part of Queensland and is a friendly place with historic charm. The lodgings were transported here from abandoned Mary Kathleen, and the excellent restaurant (mains $12 to $30) serves up some of the outback's best meals.

Built from rammed red earth and trimmed with corrugated iron, **Gidgee Inn** (☎4742 1599; www.gidgeeinn.com.au; Matilda Hwy; r $136-156) is a modern, spotless motel with a good restaurant.

A little way out of town on the road to Julia Creek, **Gilbert Park Tourist Village** (☎4742 2300; www.gilbertpark.com.au; Flinders Hwy; unpowered/powered sites $20/26, cabins from $90) is the better of Cloncurry's two van parks.

Bug and Ox Café (☎4742 2325; 37 Ramsay St; mains $5-12; ⏰8am-4.30pm Mon-Fri, weekends 9am-3pm May-Oct) makes a good pit-stop on the main road, offering huge breakfasts, milkshakes and toasted sandwiches.

Mt Isa

POP 28,256

The first things that catch your eye as you drive through the spectacular red hills of the Selwyn Ranges into Mt Isa are the smoke stacks, pointing skyward and puffing away. This is a mining town and the immensely rich lead, zinc, silver and copper ore bodies lying beneath the red ridges west of the city have turned it into Queensland's biggest outback town.

Prospector John Campbell Miles was recovering his wayward horse 'Hard Times' when he stumbled upon a heavy ore outcrop in 1923, or so the story goes. It was during and after WWII that Mt Isa really took off, with mine-related jobs attracting people of more than 50 different nationalities to this isolated but now richly multicultural town. Today the mine is among the world's top producers of silver, copper and zinc.

If you are in town during the second week in August, saddle up for Australia's largest **rodeo** (www.isarodeo.com.au).

Sights & Activities

Outback at Isa INFORMATION/MUSEUM

(☎1300 659 660, 4749 1555; www.outbackatisa.com.au; 19 Marion St; ⏰8.30am-5pm) This site hosts the tourist information centre along with a number of attractions. Get kitted out in mining attire and descend into the **Hard Times Mine** (adult/child $45/26), which is a purpose-built – and perfectly safe – underground mine complete with fuming, roaring and rattling machinery. Your entertaining guide will most likely be a local miner. Also located in the complex is the fascinating **Riversleigh Fossil Centre** (adult/child $12/7.50), as well as the **Isa Experience Gallery** and **Outback Park** (admission for gallery & park adult/child $12/7.50), showcasing the natural, Indigenous and mining heritage of Mt Isa. There's a good-value, two-day Deluxe Pass (adult/child $55/36) that combines all the attractions.

Kalkadoon Tribal Council Keeping Place ART GALLERY

(☎4749 1001; Marion St; admission $2; ⏰9am-5pm Mon-Fri) Adjacent to Outback at Isa, it has a small gallery displaying local Indigenous art, history and artefacts.

City Lookout LANDMARK

Early evening is the best time to go to the lookout, off Hilary St, when a glorious sunset is followed by the lights going up on the mine.

Xstrata Black Star Open Cut Mine MINE

(⏰11am Mon-Sat; adult/child $28.50/17.50) Find out what makes the Isa tick via a surface tour of the enormous mine. Tour departures and tickets at Outback at Isa.

Underground Hospital Museum MUSEUM

(☎4743 3853; Joan St; adult/child $10/4; ⏰10am-2pm Apr-Sep) With the threat of Japanese bombing raids in WWII, and a ready supply of miners and equipment, Mt Isa Hospital decided to go underground. The bombs never came but the 1940s hospital was preserved.

School of the Air SCHOOL

(☎4744 9100; Kalkadoon High School, Abel Smith Pde; admission $2.50; ⏰tour 10am Mon-Fri during school term) Covering an area of around 800,000 sq km, this service teaches kids in remote communities via the airwaves and,

Mt Isa

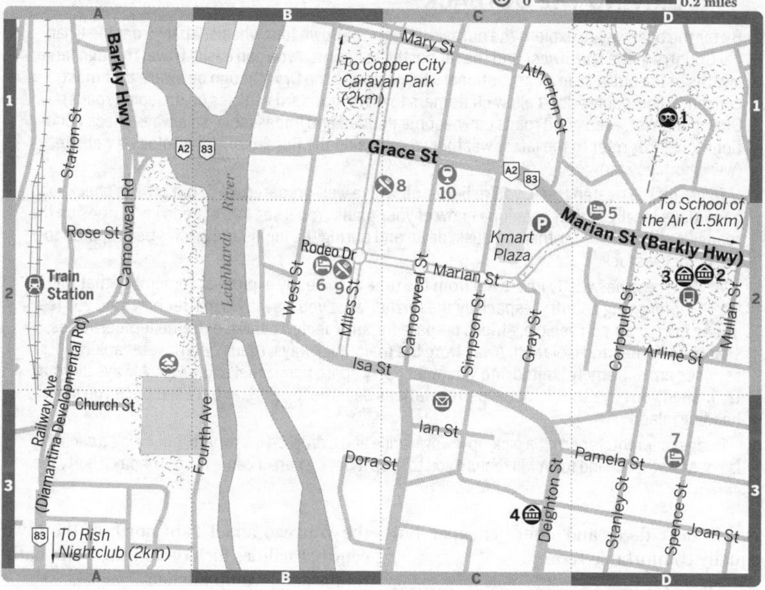

more recently, via virtual classrooms over the internet. The guided tour includes listening in on a lesson.

Lake Moondarra, 16km north of town, is a popular spot for swimming, boating, waterskiing, fishing and birdwatching. It's difficult to find, but ask the locals about the **Poison Waterhole**, a dramatic 15m-high, water-filled quarry east of town.

Tours

Various tours and activities can be booked through the information desk at Outback at Isa (p413), including **Yididi Aboriginal Guided Tours** (adult/child $990/475), which offers all-inclusive three-day camping safaris to Boodjamulla (Lawn Hill) National Park, including the Riversleigh fossil sites.

Westwing Aviation (☎4743 2144; www.westwing.com.au; Mt Isa Airport) takes passengers on its mail-run services. Wednesday's run ($330; from 9am to 5pm) to the Gulf has a dozen stops. Friday's run ($220, 9am to 1pm) flies southwest over the Barkly Tablelands.

Sleeping

Red Earth Hotel HOTEL **$$$**
(☎1800 603 488; www.redearth-hotel.com.au; Rodeo Dr; d $220-250; ❄@) Mt Isa's smartest address features antique-style furniture along with good business facilities such as broadband internet. The top rooms have private balconies and spas, and there's an excellent restaurant and coffee shop here. If the Red Earth is full, its sister hotel, The

Mt Isa

Sights
- 1 City Lookout ... D1
- Hard Times Mine ... (see 3)
- Isa Experience Gallery ... (see 3)
- 2 Kalkadoon Tribal Council Keeping Place ... D2
- 3 Outback at Isa ... D2
- Outback Park ... (see 3)
- Riversleigh Fossil Centre ... (see 3)
- 4 Underground Hospital Museum ... C3

Sleeping
- 5 Central Point ... D2
- Red Earth ... (see 6)
- 6 Red Earth Hotel ... B2
- 7 Travellers Haven ... D3

Eating
- 8 Livingstone's ... C1
- 9 Rodeo Bar & Grill ... B2

Drinking
- 10 Buffs Club ... C1

DRIVING THE OUTBACK

By far the best way to explore the outback is with your own four wheels. Apart from the Channel Country in the southwest and the far northwest corner, you can easily travel through large swaths of the outback in a conventional vehicle during the Dry (though be aware that most car-rental companies don't allow customers to drive standard vehicles on unsealed roads). During the Wet, even good roads can become flooded and impassable, so always check conditions locally or refer to the latest weather warnings on the Bureau of Meteorology's website (www.bom.gov.au).

To get off the beaten track, you're better off with a well-prepared 4WD, but always check road conditions locally and let someone know of your plans. You'll see lots of dead kangaroos on the roadside – watch out for them at dusk, dawn and during the night, and always be prepared to brake for livestock.

While access has vastly improved from the time of the early explorers, remember that this is harsh, unforgiving country, especially the further west you travel. No matter how safe you feel sitting in your air-con vehicle, always prepare for unexpected delays, extreme temperatures, scarcity of water and isolation. Away from the major highways, roads deteriorate rapidly; services are extremely limited and you must carry spare parts, fuel and water. Always fill your tank when you have the chance – petrol stations become few and far between once you start heading inland.

Budget car rentals permit a pick-up in Townsville and a drop-off elsewhere, but hiring a car in Mr Isa or any other inland town will require you to drop it back where it came from – or pay a hefty fee.

Isa, is next door, and offers cheaper but equally comfortable rooms.

Travellers Haven HOSTEL $

(☎4743 0313; www.travellershaven.com.au; 75 Spence St; dm/s/d $25/50/66;) Mt Isa's only real hostel has a mixture of backpackers stopping over on the long haul and itinerant workers. Its lino-tiled floor is a little worn but lends a retro-charm to this place, whose owner Polly is happy to share her wealth of local knowledge and her passion for the area. There's a decent kitchen, lounge area and pool, and the owners will pick you up from the bus station if you call ahead.

Spinifex MOTEL $$

(☎4749 2944; www.spinifexmotel.com.au; 79 Marion St; r $160-180;) Just a few blocks from Outback at Isa, the Spinifex has very spacious rooms, each with its own outdoor area, and offers a common barbecue area, wireless internet and free laundry.

Central Point MOTEL $$

(☎4743 0666; 6 Marion St; s/d $110/130;) Across from Outback at Isa, this friendly motel has a tropical atmosphere and well-equipped kitchenettes in all the sunny rooms. There's also a free laundry and a common barbecue area. Ask about weekend rates.

Copper City Riverside Caravan Park CARAVAN PARK, CABINS $

(☎4743 4676; 185 West St; unpowered/powered sites $20/26, sites with bathroom $32, cabins $70;) This excellent, shady park backs onto the Warrego about 2km north of the town centre. Facilities include van sites with bathrooms and a camp kitchen.

Eating & Drinking

Livingstone's MODERN AUSTRALIAN $$

(☎1800 603 488; 26 Miles St; mains $15-38; ⏲lunch & dinner daily, breakfast Sat & Sun) Locals tip this as the town's best eatery. Lunch specials ($14 to $24) include gourmet sandwiches and salads; the more formal dinner crowd sups on pricier dishes while gazing over the strangely romantic, twinkling mine. For a bargain, try Wednesday's trattoria night with specials from $15.

Rodeo Bar & Grill STEAKHOUSE $$

(☎4749 8888; 11 Miles St; mains $25-32; ⏲10am-late) If you've made it as far as Mt Isa, you may already have swallowed enough steaks to turn you vegetarian, but in the land of beef, this place can't be beat. Huge steaks sizzle away on the open grill, and all come served with a large salad and potato on the side. There are also pizzas, tapas-style snacks and an airy deck that's always filled on a warm evening.

Dom's ITALIAN $$

(☎4743 4444; 57 Marion St; mains $18-34; ⏲from 8.30am Tue-Sat) Dom's is an authentic little Italian place serving three meals a day: from the morning coffee and toast through to classics such as pizza and calzones, antipasto, linguini and risotto. Book ahead for dinner.

Buffs Club NIGHTCLUB
(☎4743 2365; www.buffs.com.au; cnr Grace & Camooweal Sts; ⏰10am-midnight Sun-Mon, to 2am Fri & Sat) The Carpentaria Buffalo Club is the Isa's most central, with the busy Billabong Bar, a sundeck, a pokie lounge and live entertainment on weekends.

Rish NIGHTCLUB
(☎4743 2577; 19th Ave) At the bountiful Irish Club, the Rish is Isa's biggest nightclub, with a disco and karaoke bar, and free entry before 11pm. If that's too much, go upstairs and kick back in the piano bar.

Information

Miles St News (☎4743 9105; 25b Miles St; per hr $5.50; ⏰7am-8pm) Internet cafe at the rear; there's space to plug in your own laptop.

Outback at Isa (☎1300 659 660, 4749 1555; www.outbackatisa.com.au; 19 Marion St; ⏰8.30am-5pm) Visitor centre, internet cafe and the Greyhound long-distance bus terminal.

QPWS (☎4744 7888; cnr Mary & Camooweal Sts) Provides information on the national parks in the area.

Getting There & Around

Qantas (☎13 13 13; www.qantas.com.au) flies daily between Brisbane and Mt Isa. **Skytrans** (☎1300 759 872; www.skytrans.com.au) flies from Mt Isa to Burketown, Mt Isa to Cairns and Mt Isa to Birdsville with stops at Bedourie and Boulia. **Regional Express** (REX; ☎13 17 13; www.rex.com.au) flies direct from Mt Isa to Townsville.

Greyhound Australia (☎1300 473 946; www.greyhound.com.au) has a regular service to Townsville via Hughenden, and to Brisbane via Longreach and Roma.

Queensland Rail (☎1300 131 722; www.traveltrain.com.au) operates the *Inlander* train twice a week between Townsville and Mt Isa. It departs Townsville on Sunday and Thursday and leaves Mt Isa on Monday and Friday. The full journey takes about 20 hours.

Avis (☎4743 3733), **Hertz** (☎4743 4142) and **Thrifty** (☎4743 2911) have car rental desks at the airport. For a taxi to town ($20 to $30) call **Mt Isa Taxis** (☎4743 2333).

THE DINOSAUR TRAIL

Western Queensland cockies (cattle farmers) have been stumbling upon priceless old bones ever since 1963, when a farmer near Hughenden unearthed some fossils that would piece together to become *Muttaburrasaurus*. A few hundred kilometres away a station owner discovered fossilised footprints at Lark Quarry – the world's only recorded evidence of a dinosaur stampede.

More than 100 million years ago, much of central Queensland was a vast inland sea harbouring marine dinosaurs, while the surrounding tropical forest was home to many land-dwelling species. These days local farmers play amateur palaeontologists, taking great pride in their finds and the museums they've helped build.

Both Hughenden and Richmond (p409) have a museum devoted to local fossil finds, while near Winton (p415) you'll find the Lark Quarry Dinosaur Trackways and the very fine Australian Age of Dinosaurs museum, where you can even take part in a dig. Visit http://aaodl.com for details.

Mt Isa to Charleville

About 14km east of Cloncurry, the narrow Landsborough Hwy turns off the Flinders Hwy (A6) and heads southeast to Winton via the one-pub towns of McKinlay and Kynuna. The first section of this 341km route, from Cloncurry to McKinlay, passes through a rugged and rocky landscape of low, craggy hills; these gradually give way to the flat, grassy plains that typify most of the outback.

McKinlay is a tiny settlement that would probably have been doomed to eternal insignificance had it not been used as a location in the film *Crocodile Dundee*. The **Walkabout Creek Hotel** (☎746 8424; Landsborough Hwy; unpowered/powered sites $22/25, s $88; ❄) has some fading photos and movie memorabilia on the walls, but is otherwise a pretty ordinary outback pub. There's a dusty camping ground out the back and some basic air-con lodgings.

Winton

POP 1321

Winton makes the most of its connections to 'Banjo' Paterson and Australia's unofficial anthem 'Waltzing Matilda' (see p430), reputedly written after a visit to the region. It's also the richest stop (after Hughenden and Richmond) on the outback dinosaur trail, with Lark Quarry's dinosaur stampede prints and the Australian Age of Dinosaurs

OUTBACK FARMSTAYS

One of the best ways to experience western Queensland is to stay on one of the area's vast cattle stations, where you can get a close-up look at the way of life – and the economic lifeblood – of the outback. Most offer station tours and other activities. **Nardoo Station** (☎4655 4833; www.nardoo.com.au; Mitchell Hwy; unpowered/powered sites $17/20, dm/cabins $82/27; ❄), a 45,000-hectare sheep and cattle station with spotless lodgings in old shearer's quarters, is one of the best. As you're soaking in a hot artesian spa under a billion stars you'll feel a world away from civilisation. Offering similar experiences are **Thurlby Station** (☎4654 2430; Adavale Rd; unpowered/powered sites $24/26, cabins $104), just 9km west of Charleville, and **Carisbrooke Station** (see p415) outside Winton.

museum both nearby. Winton's other claim to fame is as the official birthplace of Qantas airlines in 1920. Winton's sunsets are truly a sight to behold, and the town's old cemetery is the perfect place for an evening stroll as you watch the sky turn crimson. The town holds a **Bush Poetry Festival** in July, followed by the annual **camel races**.

Sights & Activities

Waltzing Matilda Centre MUSEUM

(☎4657 1466; www.matildacentre.com.au; 50 Elderslie St; adult/child/family $20/1/49; ⏲9am-5pm) Winton's biggest attraction doubles as the visitor centre. For a museum devoted to a song, there's a surprising amount here, including an indoor billabong recreation (complete with a squatter, troopers and a jolly swagman), talking billy cans, a nifty hologram display oozing nationalism and the **Jolly Swagman** statue – a tribute to the unknown swagmen who lie in unmarked graves in the area. The centre also houses the **Qantilda Pioneer Place**, which has displays on the founding of Qantas. You can purchase the creatively named 'shin plaster' ($24 to $52; ask at the desk for a quick history of the phrase) for entry into a number of the area's attractions.

Corfield & Fitzmaurice Building MUSEUM

(☎4657 1486; 63 Elderslie St; adult/child $5/1; ⏲9am-5pm Mon-Fri, to 1pm Sat, 11am-3pm Sun) Here you'll find a gem and mineral collection, a slightly inaccurate recreation of the dinosaur stampede that occurred at Lark Quarry, and a dinosaur-fossil display. It also sells a range of delightful handicrafts (think crocheted baby bonnets) made by locals.

Royal Theatre THEATRE

(☎4657 1296; 73 Elderslie St; adult/child $6.50/4; ⏲screenings 8pm Wed Apr-Sep) At the rear of Wookatook Gift & Gem, this is a wonderful open-air theatre with canvas-slung chairs, corrugated tin walls and a star-studded ceiling. It also houses the **world's biggest deck chair**.

Arno's Wall LANDMARK

(Vindex St) Winton's quirkiest attraction is a 70m-long work-in-progress by local sculpture artist Arno Grotjahn, featuring a huge range of recycled industrial and household items – from TVs to motorbikes – ensnared in the mortar. Find it behind the North Gregory Hotel. A few blocks away is the runner-up for quirkiest attraction: a **musical fence** made from a variety of found objects whose drum-kit provides an irresistible photo opportunity.

Sleeping & Eating

North Gregory Hotel HOTEL $

(☎4657 1375; 67 Elderslie St; r $80-90, with shared bathroom $60; ❄) This friendly hotel holds its place in history as the venue where 'Waltzing Matilda' reportedly was first performed on 6 April 1895, although the original building burnt down in 1900. There are basic pub rooms and comfortable rooms with bathrooms upstairs, and free caravan parking at the rear.

Tattersalls Hotel PUB FARE $$

(☎4657 1309; 78 Elderslie St; mains $7.50-30; ⏲lunch & dinner daily) This charming old timber pub has a lively atmosphere, outdoor tables and a better-than-average cook whose roast chicken comes flavoured with bush herbs such as lemon myrtle.

Twilight Cafe CAFE $$

(☎4657 1301; 68 Elderslie St; mains $12-18.50; ⏲8am-2pm & 3-8pm) Take a bottle of wine along to the best little cafe in Winton and hop into country fare such as lamb shanks.

Getting There & Away

Regional Express (REX; 13 17 13; www.rex.com.au) flies to Townsville, Mt Isa and Longreach. **Greyhound Australia** (1300 473 946; www.greyhound.com.au) operates a daily bus from Winton to Brisbane and Mt Isa. Buses depart from the Waltzing Matilda Centre.

Around Winton

About 95 million years ago – give or take a few million – a herd of small dinosaurs got spooked by a predator and scattered. The resulting stampede left thousands of footprints in the stream bed, which nature remarkably conspired to fossilise and preserve. The **Lark Quarry Dinosaur Trackways** (4657 1188; www.dinosaurtrackways.com.au; guided tour adult/child $11/6; 55min tours 10am, noon & 2pm), 110km southwest of Winton, is outback Queensland's mini Jurassic Park, where you can see the remnants of the prehistoric stampede. Protected by a sheltered walkway, the site can only be visited by guided tour, conducted three times a day. There are no facilities to stay (or eat) but it's a signposted drive on the unsealed but well-maintained Winton–Jundah road, which is suitable for 2WD vehicles in the Dry. Contact the Waltzing Matilda Centre in Winton to book tours.

The **Australian Age of Dinosaurs** (4657 0778; http://aaodl.com; guided tour adult/child $22/11; 8.30am-5pm, tours 9am, 11am, 1pm & 3pm) is housed on a local cattle station atop a rugged plateau offering spectacular views. Essentially an enormous shed, the centre was opened in 2006 and has grown to include a museum display, including a life-sized model of the dinosaur thought to be responsible for the stampede at Lark Quarry. In 2012 a new facility is set to open on site. Fossil enthusiasts can book in advance for a day's ($60) or week's worth of bone preparation. To get here, follow the Landsborough Hwy 15km east of Winton (about a 20-minute drive).

Carisbrooke Station (4657 3885; www.carisbrooketours.com.au; unpowered/powered sites from $17/22, tw per person with/without bathroom $45/40;) is a sheep and cattle property 85km southwest of Winton where you can experience outback station life. There's camping and accommodation in self-contained units, and the owners run tours of the area.

Longreach

POP 3673

Longreach is a busy little town with some big attractions. It was the pioneering home of Qantas early last century, but these days it's equally renowned for the Australian Stockman's Hall of Fame & Outback Heritage Centre. The Tropic of Capricorn passes through Longreach, and so do more than a million sheep and cattle.

Sights & Activities

Longreach, along with Winton, Barcaldine and Ilfracombe, hosts **Easter in the Outback** annually. Longreach also hosts the **Outback Muster Drovers Reunion** on the Labour Day weekend in May.

Australian Stockman's Hall of Fame & Outback Heritage Centre MUSEUM
(4658 2166; www.outbackheritage.com.au; Landsborough Hwy; adult/child/family $25/14/55; 9am-5pm) This museum is a tribute to the region's early stockmen and explorers (check out the nifty maps) and has a range of galleries covering Aboriginal culture – though scant attention is paid to Queensland's notoriously bitter frontier wars. It's 2km east of town towards Barcaldine. Admission is valid for two days.

Qantas Founders Outback Museum MUSEUM
(4658 3737; www.qfom.com.au; Landsborough Hwy; adult/child/family $19/10/45; 9am-5pm) It's not hard to spot as you drive along the highway east of town – it's the one with the enormous jumbo jet parked out the front. The museum houses a life-size replica of an Avro 504K, the first aircraft owned by the fledgling airline. Interactive multimedia and working displays tell the history of Qantas. Next door, the original 1921 Qantas hangar houses a mint-condition DH-61. Towering over everything is a bright and shiny **747-200B Jumbo** (museum & jumbo tour $34/18/75; tours 9.30am, 11am, 1pm & 3pm) on whose wings you can **walk** (adult/child $85/55, bookings essential).

Kinnon & Co Station Store SOUVENIRS, THEATRE
(4658 2006; www.kinnonandco.com.au; 126 Eagle St) is where you go for high-quality outback souvenirs such as handmade stockwhips and saddles, riding boots and Aussie bush hats and clothing. At the back is the excellent Changing Station Cafe, and the **Australian Bush Picture Show** (adult/child $7.50/3.50). You can also see the **Star-**

Longreach

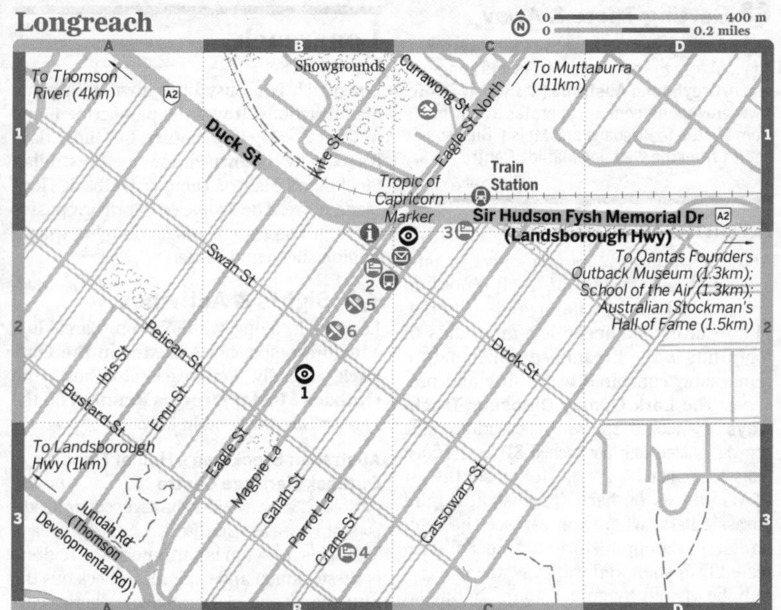

Longreach

Sights

1 Kinnon & Co Station Store B2

Sleeping

2 Commercial Hotel B2
3 Longreach Motor Inn C1
4 Old Time Cottage B3

Eating

5 Eagle's Nest Bar & Grill B2
6 Merino Bakery B2

light Spectacular Live Show (adult/child $15/10; shows at noon), which recounts the story of local cattle duffer Captain Starlight. Book here for the **Cobb & Co Coach Experience** (adult/child $49/29; 10am & 1.30pm Mon-Fri, Apr-Sep), a 45-minute ride on an authentic replica Cobb & Co coach, which includes morning and afternoon tea and the bush movie. You can also ride the coach on an overnight swag camp-out with dinner and breakfast included ($198/99).

School of the Air SCHOOL
(4658 4222; Landsborough Hwy; adult/child $4.50/2.50; tours 9am & 3.30pm) Takes you into a virtual outback classroom; the tour includes listening in on a live lesson.

Tours

Longreach Outback Travel Centre CRUISE
(4658 1776; www.lotc.com.au; 115a Eagle St) Tours include **Billabong Cruises** (adult/child $50/36), a sunset cruise on the Thomson River, followed by dinner under the stars and campfire entertainment. The **Longreach Lookabout** (adult/child $187/154) tour combines the town's main attractions with the dinner cruise. There's also an **outback station tour** (adult/child $109/79).

Outback Aussie Tours OUTBACK
(4658 3000; www.oat.net.au; Landsborough Hwy) Based at the railway platform, it offers a variety of multiday tours from a five-day Longreach and Winton tour (from $1879) to outback garden tours and rail journeys.

Sleeping & Eating

Old Time Cottage RENTAL HOUSE $$
(4658 1550, 4658 3555; 158 Crane St; r $105;) This quaint little corrugated-iron cottage is a good choice for a group or a family. Set in an attractive garden, the self-contained home sleeps up to five.

Longreach Motor Inn MOTEL $$
(4658 2322, 4658 2411; 84 Galah St; r $124-134;) This centrally located motel has somewhat tired but thoroughly comfortable

rooms, and a lovely pool area complete with palm trees and a rockery.

Discovery Holiday Park & Cabins CARAVAN PARK, CABINS **$**
(☎4658 1781; 12 Thrush Rd; unpowered/powered sites $29/32, with bathroom $41, cabins $96-171; ❄☒) This neat, modern park has comfy cabins, and if recent rains have brightened the lawns, mobs of kangaroo will visit for a feed.

Commercial Hotel PUB, MOTEL **$**
(☎4658 1677; 102 Eagle St; s/d with shared bathroom $28/45, s/d with bathroom $70/90, cabins $80-120; ❄☒) This hotel has basic but comfy rooms, and its friendly, bougainvillea-filled beer garden hosts bargain steak nights.

Merino Bakery BAKERY **$**
(☎4658 1715; 120 Eagle St; light meals $3-8; ⏲5am-5pm Mon-Fri, to 12.30pm Sat) Busy Merino is the best place for fresh sandwiches, pies and typical Australian treats such as lamingtons and finger buns.

Eagle's Nest Bar & Grill MODERN AUSTRALIAN **$$**
(☎4658 0144; 110 Eagle St; meals $20-33; ⏲lunch & dinner Wed-Sun, breakfast Sat & Sun) Recommended by locals, this cafe has outdoor seating and the usual variety of pasta and seafood, plus the obligatory steak.

ℹ Information

Longreach Library (☎4658 0735; 124 Eagle St) Has some computers with free internet access.

Outback Queensland Internet (☎4658 3937; 127 Galah St; per 30min $3; ⏲8.30am-5pm Mon-Fri, 9am-noon Sat) Allows you to surf its wireless internet ($3 per hour) from inside or from outside in your van or car.

Visitor centre (☎4658 3555; 99 Eagle St; ⏲8.30am-5pm Mon-Fri, 9am-noon Sat & Sun, closed Sat & Sun Oct-Mar)

ℹ Getting There & Away

Qantaslink (☎13 13 13; www.qantas.com.au) flies from Brisbane to Longreach daily. **Regional Express** (REX; ☎13 17 13; www.rex.com.au) flies between Longreach and Townsville.

Greyhound Australia (☎1300 473 946; www.greyhound.com.au) has a daily bus service to Brisbane (17 hours) via Charleville (6¾ hours), and Mt Isa via Winton and Cloncurry. Buses stop behind the Commercial Hotel.

Paradise Coaches (☎1300 300 156; www.paradisecoaches.com.au) makes the twice-weekly run to Rockhampton, returning via Emerald. Buses stop at Outback Aussie Tours next to the train station.

Queensland Rail (☎1300 131 722; www.traveltrain.com.au) operates the twice-weekly *Spirit of the Outback* train service between Longreach and Brisbane via Rockhampton.

Barcaldine

POP 1496

Barcaldine (bar-*call*-din) is a colourful little pub town with a long, colourful past. Popping up at the junction of the Landsborough and Capricorn Hwys 108km east of Longreach, its wide, tree-lined streets are dotted with brightly painted colonial pubs, and delightful wooden churches and houses – all on stilts.

The original inhabitants of Barcaldine were the Inningai who 'disappeared' soon after explorer Thomas Mitchell arrived in 1824.

The town gained a place in Australian history in 1891 when it became the headquarters of a major shearers' strike. The confrontation led to the formation of a workers party that went on to become the Australian Labor Party. The organisers' meeting place was the **Tree of Knowledge**, a ghost gum planted near the train station that long stood as a monument to workers and their rights. It was poisoned in 2006 but the remains of the heritage-listed tree are now sheltered by a magnificent $5 million timber-and-steel **memorial** that honours its place in Australian history.

The **visitor centre** (☎4651 1724; Oak St) is next to the train station. The **Australian Workers Heritage Centre** (☎4651 2422; www.australianworkersheritagecentre.com.au; Ash St; adult/child/family $12/7.50/28; ⏲9am-5pm Mon-Sat, 10am-5pm Sun) provides a rundown on Australian social, political and industrial movements. Set in landscaped gardens, Barcaldine's main attraction features the **Australian Bicentennial Theatre**, with displays tracing the history of the shearers' strike, as well as a school, hospital and powerhouse.

Barcaldine Historical Museum (☎4651 1310; cnr Beech & Gidyea Sts; admission $3; ⏲7am-5pm) is crammed with fascinating regional memorabilia.

It's worth stopping for a while in town, and picking up a guide to Barcaldine's **historic walk** ($2) at the visitor centre. It takes you through the town's pretty streets, which are lined with typical timber Queenslanders, while signposts tell interesting tales of the district's past.

Artesian Country Tours (☎4651 2211; www.artesiancountrytours.com.au; adult/child $145.65;

⏲Wed & Sat, weather permitting) runs a highly regarded historical tour to local Aboriginal rock-art sites, lava caves and cattle stations.

You can stay in the tiny wood-and-tin **Blacksmith's Cottage** (☎4651 1724; 7 Elm St; d/tr/q $70/80/90), which dates from the late 19th century and was once home to a blacksmith, his wife and nine kids; it's now filled with antiques and quirky knick-knacks.

Barcaldine Country Motor Inn (☎4651 1488; 1 Box St; s/d $89/99; ❄) is just around the corner from the main street's iconic pubs, most of which have their own basic rooms with shared facilities, as well as hearty pub meals. The **Shakespeare Hotel** (☎4651 1111; 95 Oak St; s/d/cabins $35/55/75) has the pick of the pub rooms.

Charleville

POP 3500

More than 750km west of Brisbane, Charleville is the grand old dame of Central Queensland and the largest town in Mulga Country. Due largely to its prime locale on the Warrego River, the town was an important centre for early explorers (Cobb & Co had their largest coach-making factory here), but the town has maintained its prosperity as a major Australian wool centre.

The **Visitor Information Centre** (☎4654 3057; Sturt St), on the southeast side of town, offers two handy heritage trail maps to follow by either car or foot.

The finest sights in Charleville are light years away. The **Cosmos Centre** (☎4654 3057; www.cosmoscentre.com; per ticket/family $7/21, night observatory session adult/child/family $24/16/60; ⏲10am-6pm Mon, Wed & Fri), offers a spectacular view of the night sky via a telescope and an expert guide. The 90-minute sessions start soon after sunset. The centre lies 2km south of town, off Airport Dr.

Charleville's QPWS runs a captive-breeding program for the endangered bilby, which you can meet in person at the **Bilby Experience** (1 Park St; admission $5; ⏲6pm Mon, Wed, Fri & Sun, Apr-Oct). Book at the Cosmos Centre. You'll learn about the plight of this cute animal before seeing the critters scampering about in their enclosure. The bilby is a long-eared, desert-dwelling marsupial that once thrived in many parts of Australia – there are now fewer than 600 in the wild in Queensland.

The most majestic hotel in Central Queensland, **Hotel Corones** (☎4654 1022; 33 Wills St; r $50-90; ❄) is a stunningly restored country pub. Bypass the motel rooms in favour of its resurrected upstairs interior where rooms feature fireplaces, leadlight windows and elegant Australian antiques. You can eat in the grandiose, yet affordable, dining room (mains $15 to $20) or the bare-bones public bar (mains $10 to $12).

Thurlby Station (see the boxed text, p414), 9km west of Charleville, runs a caravan park and farmstay.

If you can't bear to look at another steak, try **Young Tiger** (☎4654 2996; 95 Galatea St; mains $16-20; ⏲lunch & dinner Tue-Sat). It's the best (maybe the only?) Thai eatery in the outback.

THE CHANNEL COUNTRY

If you wanted the outback, here it is: miles and bloody square miles of it! The Channel Country is an unforgiving, eerily empty region where red sand hills, the odd wildflower and strange luminous phenomena run across prime beef-grazing land. The channels are formed by water rushing south from the summer monsoons to fill the Georgina, Hamilton and Diamantina Rivers and Cooper Creek. Despite deluges in 2007, 2009 and 2010, rain itself rarely falls in southwest Queensland, which borders NT, South Australia (SA) and NSW. Avoid the summer months (October to April) unless you're into searing heat and dust.

The main destination for most is Birdsville, but there are a few interesting towns along the way – and miles of empty road in between.

ℹ Getting There & Around

There are no train or bus services in the Channel Country, and the closest car rental is in Mt Isa. Fools perish out here; roads are poorly marked and getting lost is easy. In fact, it's required that you write your name, destination and expected date of arrival on a blackboard at the station where you start, so search and rescue services can come looking if you don't show up within a few days. Some roads from the east and north to the fringes of the Channel Country are sealed, but between October and May even these can be cut off when dirt roads become quagmires. Visiting this area requires a sturdy vehicle (a 4WD if you want to get off the beaten track) with decent clearance. Always carry plenty of drinking water and petrol.

The main road through this area is the Diamantina Developmental Rd. It runs south from Mt Isa through Boulia to Bedourie, then east through Windorah and Quilpie to Charleville. It's a long and lonely 1340km, about two-thirds of which is sealed. Take extra caution if driving at dusk, when the warm road attracts wild camels and kangaroos.

Mt Isa to Birdsville

The 300km northern section of the Diamantina Developmental Rd from Mt Isa to Boulia is a narrow but sturdy bitumen road. Halfway along is the small settlement of **Dajarra**, with a pub, a shop and a roadhouse with expensive fuel – it's better to fill up in Mt Isa or Boulia.

BOULIA

POP 300

Boulia is the 'capital' of the Channel Country, and the region is home to a supernatural phenomenon known as the Min Min Light. Said to resemble a car's headlights – but quite often appearing as a green floating light – this 'earthbound UFO' has been terrifying locals for years, hovering a metre or so above the ground before vanishing and reappearing elsewhere.

The best time to be in town is the third weekend in July, when Boulia holds Australia's premier camel-racing event, the **Desert Sands Camel Races**.

Min Min Encounter (☎4746 3386; Herbert St; adult/child/family $15/12/35; ⏰8.30am-5pm Mon-Fri, 8am-5pm Sat & Sun) is an hourly show that tells the story of the Min Min Light in a thoroughly entertaining, laconic Aussie way but with a (relatively) hi-tech show. The 45-minute walk-through show features animatronic characters amid imaginative sets and eerie lighting – it attempts to convert the nonbelievers and is all good fun. The centre doubles as the town's tourist information centre and there's a cafe attached.

The quirky **Stone House Museum** (cnr Pituri & Hamilton Sts; adult/child $5/3; ⏰8am-noon & 1-4pm Mon-Fri, 8am-noon Sat & Sun) has sheds full of outback stuff, space junk, local history, Aboriginal artefacts and the preserved 1888 home of the pioneering Jones family (the Stone House). The fossil collection has bits and pieces collected from around the region.

Peer over the fence of the house next to the Shell garage on Herbert St to see a map of Australia made entirely of local moon rocks and showing the inland sea of 100 million years ago.

Boulia Caravan Park (☎4746 3320; Herbert St; swag sites $10, unpowered/powered sites $20/25, cabins with bathrooms $75-95) is a simple park with shady sites on the banks of the sandy Burke River.

Australian Hotel (☎4746 3144; Herbert St; s/d/motel units $44/55/99; ❄) is the only pub in town (it gets lively on weekends) and has decent pub rooms, motel units and a good bistro.

Desert Sands Motel (☎4746 3000; Herbert St; s/d $110/120; ❄) is the best of Boulia's accommodation with spacious rooms.

From Boulia, the sealed Kennedy Developmental Rd (Min Min Way) heads 368km east to Winton through an eerily flat and empty landscape punctuated by mirage-like mesas (flat-topped hills). The only stop along the way is the old Cobb & Co staging post of **Middleton**, 175km from Boulia, where there's a pub and fuel.

BEDOURIE

POP 120

Almost 200km south of Boulia, Bedourie was first settled in 1880 as a Cobb & Co depot and is now the administrative centre for the huge Diamantina Shire. You can get tourist information from the **council offices** (☎4746 1202; Herbert St; ⏰9.30am-4.30pm). A big attraction is the free public swimming pool and **artesian spa**.

There's a caravan park and comfortable motel units at the **Simpson Desert Oasis** (☎4746 1291; 1 Herbert St; unpowered sites free, powered sites $26, cabins $103-139, motel rooms $114-156 ❄), a roadhouse with fuel, a supermarket and a restaurant.

Birdsville

POP 120

Off-the-beaten track travellers can't claim the title until they visit Birdsville, an iconic Australian settlement on the fringe of the Simpson Desert, and Queensland's most remote 'town'. During the first weekend in September, the annual **Birdsville Cup** (www.birdsvilleraces.com) horse races draw up to 7000 fans from all over the country to drink, dance and gamble for three dusty days. Parking is free for all light aircraft. Following rare but spectacular floods in recent years, bird enthusiasts and other curious folk flocked to Birdsville to see, among thousands of other species, coastal pelicans enjoying the Diamantina River and Eyre Creek running at capacity.

The **Birdsville Working Museum** (☎4656 3259; Macdonald St; adult/child $7/5; ⏰8am-5pm Apr-Oct, tours 9am, 11am & 3pm) is an impressive private collection of droving gear, saddles, shearing equipment, wool presses, road signs, toys and trinkets. John Menzies will happily show you around his big tin shed.

Another highlight is the **Birdsville Studio** (☎4656 3221; www.birdsvillestudio.com.au; Graham St; ⏰9am-10pm Jun-Sep; @), where you can inspect and buy outback art by exceptional local artist Wolfgang John.

Standing strong in sandstone since 1884 is the much-loved **Birdsville Hotel** (☎4656 3244; www.theoutback.com.au; Adelaide St; s/d $130/150; ❄). It's a humbling experience to sip a stubbie on the verandah with loose-lipped locals and big-hearted adventurers and watch the sun set deep into the desert. When you've had a gutful, the motel-style units are tasteful and spacious, while the restaurant (mains $15 to $20) is surprisingly slick. Try to arrive on a Friday when happy hour runs late and loud.

Birdsville Track

The 517km Birdsville Track stretches south of Birdsville to Maree in SA, taking a desolate course between the Simpson Desert to the west and Sturt Stony Desert to the east. The first stretch from Birdsville has two alternative routes, but only the longer, more easterly Outside Track is open these days. Before tackling the track, it's a good idea to keep friends or relatives informed of your movements so they can notify the authorities should you fail to report in on time. Contact the **Wirrarri Centre** (☎4656 3300) for road conditions.

Simpson Desert National Park

The waterless Simpson Desert occupies a massive 200,000 sq km of central Australia and stretches across the Queensland, NT and SA borders. The Queensland section, in the state's far southwestern corner, is protected as the 10,000-sq-km Simpson Desert National Park, and is a remote, arid landscape of high red sand dunes, spinifex and cane grass.

While conventional vehicles can just about tackle the Birdsville Track in dry conditions, the Simpson crossing requires a 4WD and far more preparation. Crossings should only be undertaken by parties of at least two 4WD vehicles equipped with suitable communications to call for help if necessary. You can hire a satellite phone from **Birdsville police** (☎4656 3220) and return it to **Maree police** (☎08-8675 8346) in SA.

Permits are required to camp anywhere in the park and are can be obtained online (www.qld.gov.au/camping) or at the QPWS in Birdsville or Longreach, and at Birdsville's service stations. You also need a separate permit to travel into the SA parks, and these are available through the **South Australian National Parks & Wildlife Service** (☎1800 816 078).

Birdsville to Charleville

The Birdsville Developmental Rd heads east from Birdsville, meeting the Diamantina Developmental Rd after 277km of rough gravel and sand. The old pub that constituted the 'township' of **Betoota** between Birdsville and Windorah closed its doors in 1997, meaning motorists must carry enough fuel and water to cover the 395km distance.

Just west of Cooper Creek, **Windorah** has a pub, a general store and a basic caravan park. The **Western Star Hotel** (☎4656 3166; www.westernstarhotel.com.au; 15 Albert St; pub s/d $50/60, motel s/d $90/100; ❄), originally built in 1878, has pub rooms and motel units. **Yabbie races** are staged here on the Wednesday before the Birdsville Races.

Quilpie is an opal-mining town and the railhead from which cattle are sent to the coast. The name comes from an Aboriginal word for stone curlew, and all but two of the town's streets are named after native birds. The **Quilpie Museum & Visitors Centre** (☎4656 2166; 51 Brolga St; ⏰8am-5pm Mon-Fri year-round, 10am-4.30pm Sat & Sun Apr-Nov) has tourist information, historical displays and regular opal-cutting demonstrations. Fossicking tours can be organised here.

South of Quilpie and west of Cunnamulla are the remote **Yowah Opal Fields** and the town of **Eulo**, which cohosts the **World Lizard Racing Championships** with Cunnamulla in late August. **Thargomindah**, 130km west of Eulo, has a couple of motels and a guesthouse. **Noccundra**, another 145km further west, was once a busy little community. It now has just one hotel supplying basic accommodation, meals and fuel. If you have a 4WD you can continue west to Innamincka, in SA, on the rough and stony Strzelecki Track, via the site of the famous **Dig Tree**, where William Brahe buried provisions during the ill-fated Burke and Wills expedition in 1860–61.

Understand Queensland

QUEENSLAND TODAY **422**

Economic boom and bust, green initiatives and reconciling the past: big changes are underway in modern-day Queensland.

HISTORY **425**

From the early convict settlements to the postwar boom days, there's never a dull moment in Queensland's rugged history.

ENVIRONMENT **437**

Tim Flannery's portrait of ancient tropical rainforests, ever-changing underwater landscapes and the unusual wildlife that call these places home.

THE ARTS IN QUEENSLAND **446**

Music, film, painting and Indigenous rock art are all part of Queensland's captivating artscape.

CULINARY QUEENSLAND **450**

Top tips on Queensland's bountiful seafood, its rising wine industry and venerable restaurants sprinkled across the state.

people per sq km

Queensland Today

A Topsy-Turvy Economy

When the global financial crisis erupted in 2008, Queensland was in a fine position to weather the storm. Over the previous two decades, it had enjoyed an economic boom fuelled by tourism and the mining industries, with a flourishing capital city (Brisbane) and an annual growth rate that often soared well above the national average.

The good times, however, didn't last. As economies across the globe came to a standstill (or sometimes shrank), Queensland saw its economy enter a slump with a lacklustre 0.8% growth rate from 2008 to 2009, a depressed housing market, a downturn in manufacturing and construction, and a drop in tourism. The soaring Australian dollar brought more spending power to Aussies heading overseas, but hurt domestic tourism and exports, particularly in farming and manufacturing. To help combat the stagnant economy, Queensland Premier Anna Bligh announced investments in public works, with $18.2 billion earmarked towards infrastructure projects.

» Litre of petrol: $1.25

» Car/4WD hire: from $30/175 per day

» Great Barrier Reef day/3-night cruise: $200/1400

» 2hr surf lesson: $60

» Seafood feast for 2 people: $200

How About That Weather?

The end of 2010 brought record rainfall to Queensland. Farmers initially welcomed the announcement that the 10-year drought was over, then saw their crops waterlogged and destroyed. As the rains continued, things grew progressively worse, and by early 2011 flood waters had inundated Brisbane and dozens of towns, affecting 1 million sq km – the size of France and Germany combined. The floods killed 35 people and ruined over 30,000 homes and businesses; damage costs were estimated at $5 billion. Then just weeks later the massive Category 5 Cyclone Yasi ripped through North Queensland, causing another $800 million worth of damages and taking one life. For some climatologists this was just one more piece of evidence that the effects of human-induced climate

Myths

» That Queenslanders are rough-edged larrikins living in the bush. In fact, most live along the coast, with 60% within 150km of Brisbane.

» That most Queenslanders are a sporty, outdoors bunch. Not quite: 55% of the state is obese.

Queensland Stars

Charles Kingsford Smith (1897–1935) Made the first flight from the USA to Australia.

George Miller (b 1945) Film-maker; directed the *Mad Max* films.

Geoffrey Rush (b 1951) Toowoomba-born actor and Academy Award winner.

Steve Irwin (1962–2006) The 'Crocodile Hunter'; a charismatic wildlife lover and conservationist.

Keith Urban (b 1967) Country singer with 10 number-one hits on US country charts.

Cathy Freeman (b 1973) Aboriginal athlete and Olympic champion.

belief systems

(% of population)

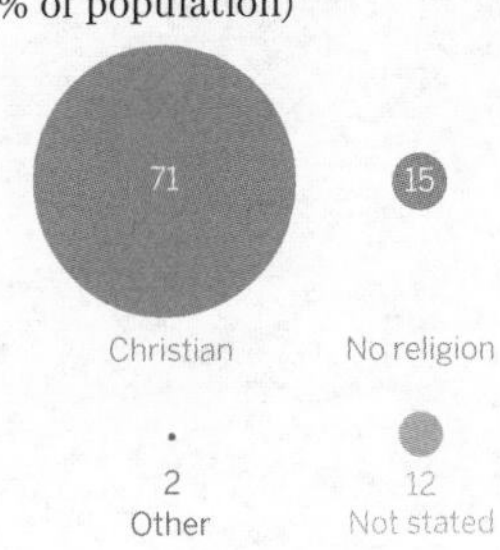

if Queensland were 100 people

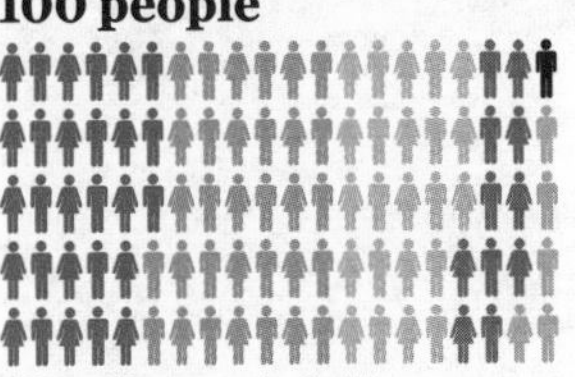

32% would live as a couple with children
28% would live as a couple with no children
23% would live alone
11% would be a one-parent family
5% would live as a group household
1% would be other family household

change were wreaking havoc on the state's weather patterns. Speaking of climate change, when it comes to Queensland's biggest tourist attraction, the Great Barrier Reef, the future looks grim. As sea temperatures continue to rise, marine researchers predict disastrous consequences for the Great Barrier Reef, with some estimates placing the near total devastation of the reef within the next 50 years, if rising carbon levels continue on their present course. The destruction of one of Earth's most diverse ecosystems is unthinkable on many fronts, not least of which are the catastrophic economic consequences: the Great Barrier Reef generates an estimated $4 billion in annual tourism revenue.

An Uncertain Future

Following the devastating floods, the federal government devised a plan to help pay for the clean-up costs. Ironically, environmental projects – rather than taxpayer subsidies to fossil-fuel companies – were to be slashed by a staggering $1.5 billion. This included gutting climate-change and solar projects, a move that angered many environmentalists. Conservation groups called for mining and gas companies to pitch in as well. Currently, Australian taxpayers provide $6 billion in annual subsidies to the fossil-fuel industry – a practice that keeps prices artificially low and raises greenhouse-gas emissions, and not an ideal scenario where such catastrophic (and costly) events may be at stake.

Queensland has made a few tentative steps towards greening its economy. In 2010 Bligh backed a multibillion-dollar project to construct an 1800MW hydropower plant in Papua New Guinea (PNG), which could provide clean energy for PNG, as well as much of Queensland, meeting up to 20% of the state's energy needs. This would also help Bligh's Labor government meet the ambitious goals it had set in 2009: to cut by

» Area: 1.9 million sq km

» Nickname: Sunshine State

» Population: 4.5 million

» Gross State Product: $255 billion

» State income per capita: $53,865

» Unemployment: 5.5%

» Inflation: 3%

Top Musicians

Powderfinger Well loved rock band with five platinum albums; retired in 2010.

Kate Miller-Heidke Classically trained singer of edgy pop.

Christine Anu Torres Strait Islander who blends Creole-style rap and Islander chants with English.

Key Aussie Slang

Aussie salute the action of brushing flies away from your face

rough as guts very rough, uncivilised

blow-in an unexpected or uninvited guest

perve to look at lustfully

gutless wonder a coward

tinnie a can of beer

put on the wobbly boot to get drunk

legless; pissed as a fart/parrot/newt extremely drunk

like a stunned mullet in a state of complete confusion

a dog's breakfast a dreadful mess

one-third Queensland's carbon footprint by 2020. The government also aimed to increase the amount of land in national parks by 50% over the next decade. More immediate was Bligh's creation of a $57 million 'Green Army' program that would create 3000 jobs in planting trees, building boardwalks in national parks and improving riverbanks and foreshores.

Queensland for All

» Rainiest town: Tully (4490mm yearly, on average)

» Highest-recorded temperature: 53.1°C at Cloncurry

» Highest point: Mt Bartle Frere (1622m)

Queensland has come a long way since the administration of Joh Bjelke-Petersen (premier from 1968 to 1987), or the anti-immigrant statements of One Nation party founder Pauline Hanson (who in 1996 famously said that Australia was at risk of being 'swamped by Asians').

Most Queenslanders have rejected the xenophobic White Australia policy of the past, but are still coming to grips with the dark legacy of abuse inflicted upon the Indigenous population. In 2008 Prime Minister Kevin Rudd opened the door to reconciliation when he issued an apology for wrongs of the past, and announced a call for bipartisan action to improve the lives of Indigenous Australians. Rudd's apology was particularly directed to the stolen generations (Indigenous children taken from their parents and placed with white families during the 19th and 20th centuries).

Rudd's speech resonated in many parts of Queensland, which is home to more than one-quarter of the nation's Indigenous people, and the call for action has in some cases been answered. In 2009 the Queensland government launched a Reconciliation Action Plan, which set goals for improving relationships and creating more opportunities in higher education and the workforce. These were important steps, though Bligh acknowledged that government alone cannot close the gap, and that reconciliation is in the interest of all, so that Queensland can be a great place 'for everyone to live and call home'.

Top Reads

On Our Selection (1899) Steele Rudd's humorous and insightful sketches of life in the Australian bush.

It's Raining in Mango (1987) Historical saga by Thea Astley tracing the fortunes and failures of a pioneer family in Cooktown.

Must-See Films

Praise (1998) A strange and surprising love story involving two mismatched twenty-somethings in down-and-out Brisbane.

Muriel's Wedding (1998) Follows the socially awkward dreamer Muriel (Toni Collette) on comedic misadventures.

Quirky Sights

Arno's Wall A 70m-long wall in Winton studded with toilet bowls, lawnmower parts, motorbikes and other mechanical relics.

Hard Times Mine Don your headlamp and go deep into the earth at mineral-loving Mt Isa.

History

Michael Cathcart & Regis St Louis

Michael Cathcart presents history programs on ABC TV, is a broadcaster on ABC Radio National and teaches history at the Australian Centre, University of Melbourne.

Human settlement in Queensland dates back 60,000 years, though historians know little of its inhabitants prior to Captain Cook's arrival in 1770. In Australia's early frontier days, Queensland was largely ignored until the 1820s, when Redcliffe and subsequently Brisbane became convict settlements. By 1840, Brisbane was on the rise, with explorers and settlers discovering the fertile hinterland (around Toowoomba).

Queensland formally separated from New South Wales (NSW) in 1859, as settlers moved north and west. Wealth brought by sugar cane and livestock helped spur growth. Meanwhile, tensions simmered between European settlers and displaced Aboriginal groups, sometimes erupting into small-scale warfare.

In the 1870s gold was discovered in the hinterland, bringing thousands (including Chinese workers) to the state and fuelling Brisbane's growth. Within two decades the gold was gone, and the depression of the 1890s was underway. As wages fell, workers formed trade unions and organised strikes, some of which ended in violence. Class warfare took centre stage. Out of this emerged the Australian Labor Party, thereafter a strong force in the political scene. The 1890s also shaped a kind of Queenslander pride – an admiration for the tough, independent frontier folk who stood up to those in power.

In 1900, Australia instituted its White Australia policy, designed to keep nonwhite immigrants out of the country. Thousands of Pacific Islanders were deported over subsequent years. The following decade brought Australia into WWI, with enormous losses (more than 60,000 deaths) felt across Australia, including in many Queensland towns.

Robert Hughes' bestseller *The Fatal Shore* (1987) is a highly readable if sometimes harrowing portrait of Australian history, told through the experience of convicts, free settlers and the Indigenous peoples they displaced.

TIMELINE

60,000 BC

Although the exact start of human habitation in Australia is still uncertain, according to most experts this is when Aborigines settled on the continent.

6000 BC

Rising water levels due to global warming force many Indigenous groups off their fertile flatlands homes along the coast. Vast sections of land disappear into the sea.

3000 BC

The last known large migration to the continent from Asia occurs (at least until about 1970). Humans introduce the dingo, which along with hunting drives some native species to extinction.

Mining brought new wealth to Queensland in the 1920s, though the Great Depression soon overshadowed it: one in three households experienced unemployment. As the economy rebounded, Australia was whisked once again into world war. Brisbane became headquarters for US forces, and Queenslanders lived in fear of a Japanese invasion (indeed, north Queensland was bombed by Japanese planes).

Raymond Evans' award-winning *A History of Queensland* (2007) is a good single-volume work covering the major events and power shifts in Queensland, from precontact Aboriginal times up to the present.

Following the war, Queensland experienced boom days, with a growing demand for Queensland products (metals, coal and wool), and families benefited from affordable housing and an expanded social-welfare system. In the 1960s long-time injustices against Aborigines received more attention, and they began winning major victories in their struggle for land rights. The 1970s also saw the dismantling of the White Australia policy, bringing a flood of non-English-speaking immigrants into the country. Queensland saw fewer immigrants than elsewhere and maintained a more insular approach – in part owing to the long-running tenure of premier Joh Bjelke-Petersen, whose administration faced allegations of corruption in the 1980s.

Intruders

In April 1770, Aborigines standing on a beach in southeastern Australia saw an astonishing spectacle out at sea. It was an English ship, the *Endeavour*, under the command of then-Lieutenant James Cook. His gentleman passengers were English scientists visiting the Pacific to make astronomical observations and to investigate 'new worlds'. As they sailed north along the edge of this new-found land, Cook began drawing the first British chart of Australia's east coast. This map heralded the beginning of conflicts between European settlers and Indigenous peoples.

A few days after that first sighting, Cook led a party of men ashore at a place known to the Aborigines as Kurnell. Though the Kurnell Aborigines were far from welcoming, the *Endeavour*'s botanists were delighted to discover that the woods were teeming with unfamiliar plants. To celebrate this profusion, Cook renamed the place Botany Bay.

Before Europeans arrived, Queensland contained more than 200 of Australia's 600 to 700 Aboriginal nations. Among them, they spoke at least 90 Indigenous languages and dialects.

As his voyage northwards continued, Cook strewed English names the entire length of the coastline. In Queensland, these included Hervey Bay (after an English admiral), Dunk Island (after an English duke), Cape Upstart, the Glass House Mountains and Wide Bay.

One night, in the seas off the great rainforests of the Kuku Yalanji Aborigines in what is now known as Far North Queensland, the *Endeavour* was inching gingerly through the Great Barrier Reef when the crew heard the sickening sound of ripping timbers. They had run aground near a cape which today is a tourist paradise. Cook was in a

1607

Spanish explorer Luis Torres manages to sail between Australia and New Guinea and not discover the rather large continent to the south. The strait bears his name today.

1770

English Captain James Cook maps Australia's east coast in the scientific ship *Endeavour*. He runs aground on the Great Barrier Reef near a place he names Cape Tribulation.

1823

Government explorer John Oxley surveys Redcliffe for a convict settlement. It is established the following year and becomes known as a place of blood, sweat and tears.

1840

Squatters from New South Wales establish sheep runs on the Darling Downs, which had first been explored 13 years earlier; it's some of the most fertile agricultural land in the country.

glowering mood: he named it Cape Tribulation, 'because here began all our troubles'. Seven days later Cook managed to beach the wounded ship in an Aboriginal harbour named Charco (Cook renamed it Endeavour), where his carpenters patched the hull.

Back at sea, the *Endeavour* finally reached the northern tip of the Cape York Peninsula. On a small, hilly island (Possession Island), Cook raised the Union Jack and claimed the eastern half of the continent for King George III. His intention was not to dispossess the Aborigines, but to warn off other European powers – notably the Dutch, who had already charted much of the coastline.

A classic biography is *The Life of Captain James Cook* (1974), by JC Beaglehole. Another fascinating read is Tony Horwitz's *Blue Latitudes: Boldly Going Where Captain Cook Has Gone Before* (2002), both travelogue and biography.

Settlement

In 1788 the English were back. On 26 January, 11 ships sailed into a harbour just north of Botany Bay. The First Fleet was under the command of a humane and diligent officer named Arthur Phillip. Under his leadership, the settlers cut down trees, built shelters and laid out roadways. They were building a prison settlement in the lands of the Eora people. Phillip called the place Sydney.

In the early years of the settlement, both the convicts and the free people of Sydney struggled to survive. Their early attempts to grow crops failed and the settlement relied on supplies brought by ship. Fortunate or canny prisoners were soon issued with 'tickets of leave', which gave them the right to live and work as free men and women on the condition that they did not attempt to return home before their sentences expired.

The convict system could also be savage. Women (who were outnumbered five to one) lived under constant threat of sexual exploitation. Female convicts who offended their jailers languished in the depressing 'female factories' (women's prisons). Male offenders were cruelly flogged and could be hanged even for such crimes as stealing. In 1803, English officers established a settlement to punish reoffenders at Port Arthur, on the wild southeast coast of Tasmania.

Tom Petrie's *Reminiscences of Early Queensland* (1904) is a bushman's story of life with Aborigines. A Queensland classic.

The impact of these settlements on the Aborigines was devastating. Multitudes were killed by unfamiliar diseases such as smallpox and, in the years that followed European settlement, many others succumbed to alcoholism and despair as they felt their traditional lands and way of life being wrenched away.

Convicts to Queensland

By the 1820s Sydney was a busy port, teeming with soldiers, merchants, children, schoolmistresses, criminals, preachers and drunks. The farms prospered, and in the streets, children were chatting in a new accent that we would probably recognise today as 'Australian'.

1844–45

The first guidebook to Australia is written in the form of a journal by Ludwig Leichhardt. It chronicles his party's exploration from Brisbane almost to Darwin. In 1848 he vanishes without a trace.

1846

Sole survivor of a shipwreck off Queensland, Jemmy Morrill is rescued by Aboriginal people. He lives with them for 17 years, and later plays a key role in improving European-Aboriginal relations.

1859

Queen Victoria gives approval to establish the new colony of Queensland, which formally separates from New South Wales and is named in her honour (rather than 'Cooksland', another proffered option).

1860s

Queensland becomes a pioneer in the nation's education system when the government subsidises municipalities to set up grammar schools – the first free education in Australia.

The authorities now looked north to the lands of the Yuggera people, where they established another lonely penal colony at Redcliffe. Here, men laboured under the command of the merciless Captain Patrick Logan, building their own prison cells and sweating on the farms they had cleared from the bush. These prisoners suffered such tortures that some welcomed death, even by hanging, as a blessed release.

Logan himself met a brutal end when he was bashed and speared while riding in the bush. Shortly after his murder, a group of soldiers reported that they had seen him on the far bank of a river, screaming to be rescued. But as they rowed across to investigate, his tormented ghost melted into the heat...

Logan's miserable prison spawned the town of Brisbane, which soon became the administrative and supply centre for the farmers, graziers, loggers and miners who occupied the region. But the great hinterland of Queensland remained remote and mysterious – in the firm control of its Aboriginal owners.

Vestiges from a Convict Past

» St Helena Island, Moreton Bay

» Old Windmill & Observatory, Brisbane

» The Barracks (former Petrie Terrace Gaol), Brisbane

» Heritage Centre, Maryborough

Explorers & Settlers

The hinterland frontier was crossed in 1844, when an eccentric Prussian explorer named Ludwig Leichhardt led a gruelling 15-month trek from Brisbane to Port Essington (near today's Darwin). His journal – the first European travel guide to Australia's Top End – would have secured his place in Australian history, but today he is remembered more for the manner of his death. In 1848 his entire party vanished in the desert during an attempt to cross the continent. Journalists and poets wrote as if Leichhardt had been received into a silent mystery that lay at the heart of Australia. It might seem strange that Australians should sanctify a failed explorer, but Leichhardt – like two other dead explorers, Burke and Wills – satisfied a Victorian belief that a nation did not come of age until it was baptised in blood.

The Commissariat Stores Building in Brisbane was built in 1829 by convicts; the original section of the building is the second-oldest structure in Queensland.

As Queensland formally separated from NSW in 1859, graziers, miners and small farmers were pushing further west and north. Some European settlers established cooperative relations with local tribes, sharing the land and employing Aborigines as stockmen or domestics. Conversely, others saw settlement as a tough Darwinian struggle between the British race and a primitive Stone Age people – a battle the Europeans were destined to win. Indeed, settlers who ran sheep on the vast grasslands of the Darling Downs sometimes spoke as if they had taken possession of a great park where no other humans had ever lived. Today, Aborigines across the country tell stories of how European settlers shot whole groups of their people or killed them with poisoned food. Some Aboriginal tribes fought back, but the weapons of the white people were formidable – including the notorious Native Police, a government-backed squad made

1870s

Thousands of Chinese people arrive to work in the goldfields. In 1877 the government imposes restrictions on Chinese immigration and access to the goldfields.

1872

The gold rush sweeps into Charters Towers, funding the construction of magnificent homes and public buildings. Queensland is connected to Europe by telegraph.

» World Theatre (p282), Charters Towers

up of Aborigines recruited from distant tribes who violently suppressed any uprisings.

Meanwhile, on the tropical coast, growers were developing a prosperous sugar-cane industry that relied on the sweat of thousands of labourers from the Solomon Islands, Vanuatu and other Pacific islands. Known as 'kanakas', these workers endured harsh and sometimes cruel conditions that were considered intolerable for white workers (see boxed text, p281).

Delving into History

- Newstead House, Brisbane
- Queensland Maritime Museum, Brisbane
- Cobb & Co Museum, Toowoomba
- Australian Age of Dinosaurs Museum, Winton
- Jondaryan Woolshed Complex, Darling Downs

Gold & Revolution

In 1871 an Aboriginal stockman named Jupiter spotted gold glinting in a waterhole near Charters Towers. His find triggered a gold rush that attracted thousands of prospectors, publicans, traders, prostitutes and quacks to the diggings. For a few exhilarating years, any determined miner, regardless of class, had a real chance of striking it rich. By the 1880s, Brisbane itself had grown prosperous on wool and gold but, by then, life on the goldfields was changing radically. The easy gold was gone. The free-for-all had given way to an industry in which the company boss called the shots.

As displaced prospectors searched for work, the overheated economy of eastern Australia collapsed, throwing thousands of labouring families into the miseries of unemployment and hunger. The depression of the 1890s exposed stark inequalities as barefoot children scavenged in the streets. But this was Australia, 'the working man's paradise' – the land where the principle of 'a fair day's pay for a fair day's work' was sacred.

A LAST STAND

The Kalkadoon (also known as Kalkatungu) people of the Mt Isa region in western Queensland were known for their fierce resistance to colonial expansion. As pastoralism and mining concerns pushed into their country in the 1860s, some of the Kalkadoon initially worked for the settlers as labourers and guides. However, competition for land and resources eventually led to conflict, and the Kalkadoon waged guerrilla-style warfare against settlers and their stock. They soon gained a reputation as ferocious warriors who seemingly melted away into the bush. In 1883 they killed five Native Police and a prominent pastoralist – an incident that turned the tide of the conflict against them.

In September 1884, some 600 Kalkadoon retreated to a defensive site known as Battle Mountain, where they fought one last battle against the Native Police and armed settlers. Despite heroic resistance, which included a charge against cavalry positions, the Kalkadoon warriors were mercilessly slain, their spears and clubs no match for guns. In all, an estimated 900 Kalkadoon were killed between 1878 and 1884.

1884

In a tragic last stand, the defiant Kalkadoon Indigenous nation is defeated in a massacre at Battle Mountain, near Mt Isa.

1891

A violent shearers' strike around Barcaldine, where 1000 men camp around the town, establishes a labour legend. The confrontation leads to the birth of the Australian Labor Party.

1901

The new federal government removes kanakas from Queensland, in line with the White Australia policy. Mortality figures for these Pacific Islanders were almost five times those of whites.

1902

The first trans-Pacific cable between Australia and Canada is completed, terminating on the Gold Coast. The cable also allows Australia to join the England cable link.

River of Gold, by Hector Holthouse, is a high-spirited novel set in the wild days of Queensland's Palmer River gold rush.

As employers tried to drive down wages, a tough Queensland working class began to assert itself. Seamen, factory workers, miners, loggers and shearers organised themselves into trade unions to take on Queensland's equally tough bosses and shareholders.

The result was a series of violent strikes. The most famous of these erupted in 1891 after angry shearers proclaimed their socialist credo under a great gum tree, known as the 'Tree of Knowledge', at Barcaldine in central Queensland. As the strike spread, troopers, right-wing vigilantes and union militants clashed in bitter class warfare. The great radical poet Henry Lawson expected revolution: 'We'll make the tyrants feel the sting/O' those that they would throttle;/They needn't say the fault is ours/If blood should stain the wattle!'

ONCE A JOLLY SWAGMAN

Written in 1895 by AB 'Banjo' Paterson (1864–1941), 'Waltzing Matilda' is widely regarded as Australia's unofficial national anthem. While not many can sing the entire official anthem, 'Advance Australia Fair', without a lyric sheet, just about every Aussie knows the words to the strange ditty about a jolly swagman who jumped into a billabong and drowned himself rather than be arrested for stealing a jumbuck (sheep). But what the hell does it mean?

For the song's origins to be understood, it has to be seen in the political context of its time. The 1890s was a period of political change in Queensland. Along with nationalistic calls for Federation, economic crisis, mass unemployment and severe droughts dominated the decade. An ongoing battle between pastoralists and shearers led to a series of strikes that divided the state and led to the formation of the Australian Labor Party to represent workers' interests.

In 1895 Paterson visited his fiancée in Winton, and together they travelled to Dagworth Station south of Kynuna, where they met Christina Macpherson. During their stay they went on a picnic to the Combo Waterhole, a series of billabongs on the Diamantina River, where Paterson heard stories about the violent 1894 shearers' strike on Dagworth Station. During the strike rebel shearers burnt seven woolsheds to the ground, leading the police to declare martial law and place a reward of £1000 on the head of their leader, Samuel Hoffmeister. Rather than be captured, Hoffmeister killed himself near the Combo Waterhole.

Paterson later wrote the words to 'Waltzing Matilda' to accompany a tune played by Christina Macpherson on a zither. While there is no direct proof he was writing allegorically about Hoffmeister and the shearers' strikes, a number of prominent historians have supported the theory and claimed the song was a political statement. Others maintain it is just an innocent but catchy tune about a hungry vagrant, but the song's undeniable anti-authoritarianism and the fact that it was adopted as an anthem by the rebel shearers weigh heavily in favour of the historians' argument.

1908

Queensland's first national park is established on the western slope of Tamborine Mountain. Today, the national park stretches onto the Tamborine plateau and into surrounding foothills.

1915

In line with Australia's close ties to Britain, Australian and New Zealand troops (the Anzacs) join the Allied invasion of Turkey at Gallipoli.

1918

The Great War ends. Out of a country of 4.9 million, 320,000 were sent to war in Europe and almost 20% were killed. Cracks appear in Australian-British relations.

1923

Vegemite, a savoury, yeasty breakfast spread, is invented. Given it is a byproduct of brewing that had gone to waste, it is a modern marketing triumph.

The striking shearers were defeated and their leaders jailed by a government determined to suppress the unrest. Despite this loss, trade unions remained a powerful force in Australia and the Barcaldine strike contributed to the formation of a potent new force in Australian politics: the Australian Labor Party.

Nationalism

Whatever their politics, many Queenslanders still embody the gritty, independent outlook that was so potent in colonial thinking. At the end of the 19th century, Australian nationalist writers and artists idealised the people of 'the bush' and their code of 'mateship'. The most popular forum for this 'bush nationalism' was the *Bulletin* magazine, whose pages were filled with humour and sentiment about daily life, written by a swag of writers, most notably Henry Lawson and AB 'Banjo' Paterson.

While these writers were creating national legends, the politicians of Australia were forging a national constitution.

Federation & WWI

On 1 January 1901, Australia became a federation. When the bewhiskered members of the new national parliament met in Melbourne, their first aim was to protect the identity and values of a European Australia from an influx of Asians and Pacific Islanders. Their solution was the infamous White Australia policy. Its opposition to nonwhite immigrants would remain a core Australian value for the next 70 years.

For European settlers, this was to be a model society, nestled in the skirts of the British Empire. Just one year later, in 1902, white women won the right to vote in federal elections. In a series of radical innovations, the government introduced a broad social-welfare scheme and protected Australian wage levels with import tariffs. This mixture of capitalist dynamism and socialist compassion became known as the 'Australian Settlement'.

When war broke out in Europe in 1914, thousands of Australian men rallied to the Empire's call. They had their first taste of death on 25 April 1915, when the Anzacs (the Australian and New Zealand Army Corps) joined an Allied assault on the Gallipoli Peninsula in Turkey. Eight months later, the British commanders acknowledged that the tactic had failed. By then, 8141 young Australians were dead. Soon, Australians were fighting in the killing fields of Europe. When the war ended, 60,000 Australian men had died. Ever since, on 25 April, Australians have gathered at the country's many war memorials for the sad and solemn services of Anzac Day.

Peter Weir's epic film *Gallipoli* (1981) shows the utter brutality and senselessness of WWI through the eyes of two young mates (played by Frank Lee and a young Mel Gibson).

1928

Reverend John Flynn starts the Royal Flying Doctor Service in Cloncurry – an invaluable service that now has networks around the country.

1929

The Great Depression: thousands go hungry and one in three households experiences unemployment. Irene Longman becomes the first woman elected to Queensland's parliament.

1937

Thousands of cane toads are released into the wild in an effort to control pests damaging Queensland's sugar cane fields. The action proves disastrous to Australian biodiversity.

1941

The Japanese bomb Townsville – a strategic centre for defence, with a major base for US and Australian military forces.

Turbulent '20s

Australia careered wildly into the 1920s, continuing to invest in immigration and growth. In Queensland, breathtakingly rich copper, lead, silver and zinc deposits were discovered at Mt Isa, setting in motion a prosperous new chapter in the history of Queensland mining.

This was also the decade in which intrepid aviators became international celebrities. For Queensland, a state that felt its isolation profoundly, the aeroplane was a revolutionary invention. The famous airline Qantas (an acronym for Queensland and Northern Territory Aerial Services) was founded at Longreach, in the centre of the state, in 1920. Eight years later, veteran Queensland aviator Bert Hinkler flew solo from England to Darwin in just 16 days.

It was not just aeroplanes that linked Australia to the rest of the world. Economics, too, was a global force. In 1929 the Wall St crash and high foreign debt caused the Australian economy to collapse into the abyss of the Great Depression. Once again, unemployment brought shame and misery to one in three households, but for those who were wealthy or employed, the Depression made less of a dent in day-to-day life.

Avian Cirrus, Bert Hinkler's tiny plane that made the first England-to-Australia solo flight, is on display at the Queensland Museum in Brisbane.

In the midst of this hardship, sport diverted a nation in love with games and gambling. Down south, the champion racehorse Phar Lap won an effortless and graceful victory in the 1930 Melbourne Cup ('the race that stops a nation'). In 1932 the great horse travelled to the racetracks of the USA where he mysteriously died. Back in Australia, the gossips insisted that the horse had been poisoned by envious Americans: thus grew the legend of Phar Lap – a hero cut down in his prime.

WWII & Growth

As the economy began to recover, the whirl of daily life was hardly dampened when Australian servicemen and -women sailed off to Europe to fight in a new war in 1939. Though Japan was menacing, Australians took it for granted that the British navy would keep them safe. In December 1941, Japan bombed the US fleet at Pearl Harbor. Weeks later, the 'impregnable' British naval base in Singapore crumbled, and soon thousands of Australians and other Allied troops were enduring the savagery of Japan's prisoner-of-war camps.

As the Japanese swept through Southeast Asia and into Papua New Guinea, the British announced that they could not spare any resources to defend Australia. But the legendary US general Douglas MacArthur saw that Australia was the perfect base for US operations in the Pacific and established his headquarters in Brisbane. As the fighting intensified, thousands of US troops were garrisoned in bases the length of Queensland: Australians and Americans got to know each other as never

1942

The Battle of the Coral Sea is fought off northern Queensland between Japan and US–Australian forces. Although there is no clear winner, the USA loses the carrier USS *Lexington*.

1950s–1960s

The postwar boom is on as Queensland experiences strong growth in manufacturing and other industries. Affordable housing is the norm with rampant construction in the suburbs.

LAWRIE WILLIAMS / LONELY PLANET IMAGES ©

» Industrial boom: one of Queensland's many sugar mills

before. In a series of savage battles on sea and land, Australian and US forces gradually turned back the Japanese advance. The days of the Australian–British alliance were numbered.

As the war ended, a new slogan rang through the land: 'Populate or Perish!' The Australian government embarked on an ambitious scheme to attract thousands of immigrants. With government assistance, people flocked from Britain and from non-English-speaking countries. They included Greeks, Italians, Slavs, Serbs, Croatians, Dutch and Poles, followed by Turks, Lebanese and others.

This was the era when Australian families basked in the prosperity of a 'long boom' created by skilful government management of the economy. Manufacturing companies such as General Motors and Ford operated with generous tariff support. The social-welfare system became more extensive and now included generous unemployment benefits. The government owned many key services, including Qantas, which it bought in 1947. This, essentially, was the high point of the 'Australian Settlement' – a partnership of government and private enterprise designed to share prosperity as widely as possible.

David Malouf's novel *Johnno* (1975) is a beautifully written coming-of-age story set in postwar Brisbane.

At the same time, there was growing world demand for the type of primary products produced in Queensland: metals, coal, wool, meat and wheat. By the 1960s mining dominated the state's economy and coal was the major export. That same decade, the world's largest bauxite mine roared into life at Weipa on the Cape York Peninsula.

This era of postwar growth and prosperity was dominated by Robert Menzies, the founder of the modern Liberal Party of Australia, and Australia's longest-serving prime minister. Menzies had an avuncular charm, but he was also a vigilant opponent of communism. As the Cold War intensified, Australia and New Zealand entered a formal military alliance with the USA – the 1951 Anzus security pact. It followed that when the USA became involved in a civil war in Vietnam more than a decade later, Menzies committed Australian forces to the conflict. In 1966 Menzies retired, leaving his successors a bitter legacy: an antiwar movement that divided Australia.

A Question of Tolerance

In the 1960s, increasing numbers of Australians saw that Aborigines had endured a great wrong that needed to be put right. From 1976 until 1992 Aborigines won major victories in their struggle for land rights. As Australia's imports from China and Japan increased, the White Australia policy became an embarrassment. It was officially abolished in the early 1970s, and soon thereafter Australia was a little astonished to find itself leading the campaign against the racist apartheid policies of white South Africa.

1962

Indigenous Australians gain the right to vote in federal elections – but they have to wait until 1967 to receive full citizenship.

1965

Merle Thornton and Rosalie Bogner chain themselves to a Brisbane bar to protest public bars being open to men only. Their action marks the beginnings of the feminist movement in Australia.

1968

Setting the political scene in Queensland for the next 19 years, Joh Bjelke-Petersen becomes premier. His political agenda was widely described as development at any price.

1970s

Inflation, soaring interest rates and rising unemployment bring the golden postwar days to an end. As house prices skyrocket, home ownership slips out of reach for many.

By the 1970s more than one million migrants had arrived from non-English-speaking countries, filling Australia with new languages, cultures, food and ideas. At the same time, China and Japan far outstripped Europe as Australia's major trading partners. As Asian immigration increased, Vietnamese communities became prominent in Sydney and Melbourne. In both those cities a new spirit of tolerance known as multiculturalism became a particular source of pride.

The Australian Stockman's Hall of Fame & Outback Heritage Centre at Longreach shamelessly celebrates Queensland's bush legends – explorers, pastoralists, Aborigines and cattlemen. See www.outbackheritage.com.au.

The impact of postwar immigration was never as great in Queensland, and the values of multiculturalism made few inroads into the state's robustly old-time sense of what it means to be Australian. This Aussie insularity was well understood by the rough-hewn and irascible Joh Bjelke-Petersen, premier of Queensland for 19 years from 1968. New Zealand–born Johannes Bjelke-Petersen was the longest-serving (1968–1987) and longest-lived (1911–2005) premier of Queensland. He was described as a paradox of piety, free enterprise and political cunning or, more succinctly, as 'a Bible-bashing bastard' by Prime Minister Gough Whitlam in 1975.

Kept in office by malapportionment (which gave more voting power to his rural base – he never won more than 39% of the popular vote), he established a policy of development on the state. Under his tenure,

TERRA NULLIUS TURNED ON ITS HEAD

In May 1982 Eddie Mabo led a group of Torres Strait Islanders in a court action to have traditional title to their land on Mer (Murray Island) recognised. Their argument challenged the legal principle of *terra nullius* (literally 'land belonging to no one') and demonstrated their unbroken relationship with the land over a period of thousands of years. In June 1992 the High Court of Australia found in favour of Eddie Mabo and the islanders, rejecting the principle of *terra nullius* – this became known as the Mabo decision. The result has had far-reaching implications in Queensland and the rest of Australia, including the introduction of the Native Title Act in 1993.

Eddie Mabo accumulated more than 20 years' experience as an Indigenous leader and human-rights activist. He had 10 children, was often unemployed, established a Black Community School – the first institution of its kind in Australia – and was involved in Indigenous health and housing. In the late 1960s he worked as a gardener at James Cook University, returning there in 1981 for a conference on land rights, where he delivered a historic speech that culminated in the landmark court case.

Eddie Mabo died of cancer six months before the decision was announced. After a customary period of mourning he was given a king's burial ceremony on Mer, reflecting his status among his people – such a ritual had not been performed on the island for some 80 years.

1974

The audacious Beerburrum mail robbery is pulled off – the most lucrative mail robbery in Australian history at the time.

1975

The Great Barrier Reef Marine Park is proclaimed, protecting 2000km of reef – the most extensive reef system in the world.

1981

The Great Barrier Reef becomes a Unesco World Heritage Site, a move furiously opposed by Queensland Premier Joh Bjelke-Petersen, who intended to do exploratory mining for oil on the reef.

1982

Brisbane hosts the Commonwealth Games. Australia tops the medal tally, winning 107 medals overall. Matilda, a 13m-high winking kangaroo, was the mascot for the Games.

forests were felled to make way for dams, coal mines, power stations and other burgeoning infrastructure projects.

Bjelke-Petersen's administration strongly encouraged the development of the Gold Coast. There were few environmental restrictions as hotels and high-rise apartment blocks transformed quiet seaside towns into burgeoning holiday resorts. Among many projects under his term was the building of a highway through the Daintree rainforest and the demolition of historic or heritage buildings to make way for new developments (Brisbane's Bellevue Hotel, dating from the 1880s, was demolished – in the middle of the night – despite public attempts to save it). His plans to drill for oil in the Great Barrier Reef came to nothing when the reef was declared a World Heritage Site in 1981. Meanwhile, Queensland spent less on social infrastructure than any other state in Australia.

In the 1970s there were widespread reports of police brutality against student demonstrations at the University of Queensland, a well-known haven for anti–Bjelke-Petersen sentiment. In 1977 street marches were banned.

Things took a turn in the late 1980s, when a series of investigations revealed that Bjelke-Petersen presided over a compromised system. His police commissioner was jailed for graft (bribery), and in 1991 Bjelke-Petersen faced his own criminal trial (for perjury, and allegations of corruption were also incorporated into the trial). Although the jury was deadlocked and didn't return a verdict, the tides had turned against him, and most Queenslanders were eager to put the Bjelke-Petersen days behind them.

POLITICS

For more on one of Queensland's formidable politicians, read Hugh Lunn's *Joh: The Life and Political Adventures of Johannes Bjelke-Petersen* (1978).

Queensland Today

Today Australia faces new challenges. Since the 1970s, Australia has been dismantling the protectionist scaffolding that allowed its economy to develop. Wages and working conditions, which used to be fixed by an independent authority, are now much more uncertain. Two centuries of development have also placed great strains on the environment – on water supplies, forests, soil, air quality and the oceans. Australia is linked more closely than ever to the USA (exemplified by its involvement in the 21st century's Afghanistan and Iraq wars). Some say this alliance protects Australia's independence; others insist that it reduces Australia to a fawning 'client state'.

In Queensland, old fears and prejudices continue to struggle with tolerance and an acceptance of Asia, and Indigenous issues seem as intractable as ever. Aboriginal leaders acknowledge that poverty, violence and welfare dependency continue to blight the lives of too many Aboriginal communities. In the Cape York Peninsula, Aboriginal leaders,

1988

Over a six-month period between April and October, Brisbane hosts a World Fair called Expo '88. The theme is 'Leisure in the Age of Technology'.

1990s

Queensland experiences rapid population growth – mostly from domestic migration – even while a full-blown recession is underway, with high unemployment and huge bank and corporate collapses.

1992

After 10 years in the courts, the landmark Mabo decision is delivered by the High Court. Effectively, this gives recognition to Indigenous land rights across the country.

1997

Warning of being 'swamped by Asians', Pauline Hanson founds the anti-immigrant One Nation party, and later publishes a book on supposed Aboriginal cannibalism. Popularity wanes following a 2003 fraud conviction.

cattle ranchers, the government and mining companies displayed a new willingness to work with each other on land issues when they signed the Cape York Heads of Agreement in 2001. In late 2007, worrying newspaper reports (such as those appearing in *The Australian* and *New York Times*) of child sexual abuse in the Cape York Aboriginal communities highlighted the enormous social problems within Indigenous communities in Queensland and across the country.

In 2008 an official apology to the stolen generations (Aboriginal children taken from their parents and placed with white families during the 19th and 20th centuries) delivered by the Australian government was an important step on the road to addressing long-standing grievances afflicted on Australia's first peoples.

2006

The legendary 'Crocodile Hunter' Steve Irwin is killed by a stingray while shooting the wildlife documentary *Ocean's Deadliest*. His conservation work continues via the Steve Irwin Foundation.

2007

Peter Beattie, the longest-serving Labor premier in Queensland history, retires. His deputy, Anna Bligh, becomes the state's first female premier.

2008

On behalf of parliament, Prime Minister Kevin Rudd delivers a moving apology to Aborigines for laws and policies that 'inflicted profound grief, suffering and loss'.

2011

Powerful floods inundate vast areas of the state (including Brisbane), killing 35 people and causing billions of dollars in damages. Cyclone Yasi follows weeks later, devastating parts of north Queensland.

Environment

Tim Flannery

Tim Flannery is a scientist, explorer and writer. He has written several award-winning books including *The Future Eaters, Throwim Way Leg* and *The Weather Makers*.

Australia's plants and animals are just about the closest things to alien life you are likely to encounter on earth. That's because Australia has been isolated from the other continents for a very long time – at least 45 million years. The other habitable continents have been able to exchange various species at different times because they've been linked by land bridges. Just 15,000 years ago it was possible to walk from the southern tip of Africa right through Asia and the Americas to Tierra del Fuego. Not Australia, however. Its birds, mammals, reptiles and plants have taken their own separate and very different evolutionary journey, and the result today is the world's most distinct – and one of its most diverse – natural realms.

The first naturalists to investigate Australia were astonished by what they found. Here the swans were black – to Europeans this was a metaphor for the impossible – while mammals such as the platypus and echidna were discovered to lay eggs. It really was an upside-down world, where many of the larger animals hopped, where each year the trees shed their bark rather than their leaves, and where the 'pears' were made of wood.

If you are visiting Australia for a short time, you might need to go out of your way to experience some of the richness of the environment. That's because Australia is a subtle place, and some of the natural environment – especially around the cities – has been damaged or replaced by trees and creatures from Europe. Places like Brisbane, however, have preserved extraordinary fragments of their original environment that are relatively easy to access. Before you enjoy them, though, it's worthwhile understanding the basics about how nature operates in Australia. This is important because there's nowhere like Australia, and once you have an insight into its origins and natural rhythms, you will appreciate the place so much more.

Australia is currently moving north at a rate of 73 millimetres per year. According to NASA, in 250 million years Australia will collide with Asia as Africa smashes into Europe – all of which will create the new supercontinent of Pangaea Ultima.

If Queensland were an independent nation, it would be the 18th largest country on earth – larger than Iran, but slightly smaller than Libya.

An Extraordinary Continent

There are two really big factors that go a long way towards explaining nature in Australia: its soils and its climate. Both are unique. Australian soils are the more subtle and difficult to notice of the two, but they have been fundamental in shaping life here. On other continents, in recent geological times processes such as volcanism, mountain building and glacial activity have been busy creating new soil. Just think of the glacier-derived soils of North America, north Asia and Europe. They feed the world today, and were made by glaciers grinding up rock of differing chemical composition over the last two million years. The rich soils of

India and parts of South America were made by rivers eroding mountains, while Java in Indonesia owes its extraordinary richness to volcanoes.

All of these soil-forming processes have been almost absent from Australia in more recent times. Only volcanoes have made a contribution, and they cover less than 2% of the continent's land area. In fact, for the last 90 million years, beginning deep in the age of dinosaurs, Australia has been geologically comatose. It was too flat, warm and dry to attract glaciers, its crust too ancient and thick to be punctured by volcanoes or folded into mountains.

Under such conditions no new soil is created and the old soil is leached of all its goodness by the rain, and is blown and washed away. Even if just 30cm of rain falls each year, that adds up to a column of water 30 million kilometres high passing through the soil over 100 million years, and that can do a great deal of leaching! Almost all of Australia's mountain ranges are more than 90 million years old, so you will see a lot of sand here, and a lot of country where the rocky 'bones' of the land are sticking up through the soil. It is an old, infertile landscape, and life in Australia has been adapting to these conditions for aeons.

Australia's misfortune in respect to soils is echoed in its climate. In most parts of the world outside the wet tropics, life responds to the rhythm of the seasons – summer to winter, or wet to dry. Most of Australia experiences seasons – sometimes very severe ones – yet life does not respond solely to them. This can clearly be seen by the fact that although there's plenty of snow and cold country in Australia, there are almost no trees that shed their leaves in winter, nor do any Australian animals hibernate. Instead, there is a far more potent climatic force that Australian life must obey: El Niño.

The cycle of flood and drought that El Niño brings to Australia is profound. Our rivers can be miles wide one year, yet you can literally step over its flow the next. This is the power of El Niño, and its effect, when combined with Australia's poor soils, manifests itself compellingly. As you might expect from this, relatively few of Australia's birds are seasonal breeders, and few migrate. Instead, they breed when the rain comes, and a large percentage are nomads, following the rain across the breadth of the continent.

LAND MASS

Of Australia's enormous 7.4 million sq km of land mass, only about 6.5% is arable – this is roughly the size of Spain.

UNESCO WORLD HERITAGE SITES

Queensland is home to five of Australia's 18 Unesco World Heritage Sites. Some advocates are also lobbying to add Cape York Peninsula to this list.

» **Fraser Island** – the world's largest sand island and home to a diversity of fragile and complex ecosystems, including coloured sand cliffs, freshwater lakes and rainforests growing right in sand.

» **Gondwana Rainforests** – straddling Queensland and New South Wales, sheltering temperate and unique rainforests, including the world's most extensive subtropical rainforest. Includes Lamington and Main Range National Parks.

» **Riversleigh Australian Fossil Mammal Site** – in northwest Queensland, this is among the richest and most extensive fossil sites on earth. Some of the fossils here date back 25 million years.

» **Great Barrier Reef** – comprising 2900 individual reefs and home to a staggering array of aquatic life, the Great Barrier Reef is one of the world's most diverse ecosystems.

» **Wet Tropics** – spanning 9000 sq km of Queensland's northern coast and harbouring the highest concentration of primitive flowering plant families in the world (creating a near perfect record of plant life evolution on earth). Includes Daintree, Barron Gorge and Wooroonooran National Parks.

So challenging are conditions in Australia that its birds have developed some extraordinary habits. The kookaburras, magpies and blue wrens you are likely to see – to name just a few – have developed a breeding system called 'helpers at the nest'. The helpers are the young adult birds of previous breedings, which stay with their parents to help bring up the new chicks. Just why they should do this was a mystery until it was realised that conditions in Australia can be so harsh that more than two adult birds are needed to feed the nestlings. This pattern of breeding is very rare in places like Asia, Europe and North America, but it is common for many Australian birds.

Australian icon Steve Irwin died while shooting *Ocean's Deadliest*, a 2007 documentary he produced with Philippe Cousteau, Jr. It features all sorts of deadly critters from Queensland's waters but not the ray that stung Irwin.

Strange & Wondrous Wildlife

Australia is, of course, famous as the home of the kangaroo (roo) and other marsupials. Unless you visit a wildlife park, such creatures are not easy to see as most are nocturnal. Their lifestyles, however, are exquisitely attuned to Australia's harsh conditions. Have you ever wondered why kangaroos, alone among the world's larger mammals, hop? It turns out that hopping is the most efficient way of getting about at medium speeds. This is because the energy of the bounce is stored in the tendons of the legs – much like in a pogo stick – while the intestines bounce up and down like a piston, emptying and filling the lungs without needing to activate the chest muscles. When you travel long distances to find meagre feed, such efficiency is a must.

Marsupials are so energy-efficient that they can survive on one-fifth less food than equivalent-sized placental mammals (everything from bats to rats, whales and ourselves). But some marsupials have taken energy efficiency much further. If you visit a wildlife park or zoo you might notice that faraway look in a koala's eyes. It seems as if nobody is home – and this in fact is near the truth. Several years ago biologists announced that koalas are the only living creatures that have brains that don't fit their skulls. Instead they have a shrivelled walnut of a brain that rattles around in a fluid-filled cranium. Other researchers have contested this finding, however, pointing out that the brains of the koalas examined for the study may have shrunk because these organs are so soft. Whether soft-brained or empty-headed, there is no doubt that the koala is not the Einstein of the animal world, and we now believe that it has sacrificed its brain to energy efficiency. Brains cost a lot to run – our brains typically weigh 2% of our body weight, but use 20% of the energy we consume. Koalas eat gum leaves, which are so toxic that koalas use 20% of their energy just detoxifying this food. This leaves little energy for the brain, and living in the tree tops where there are so few predators means that they can get by with few wits at all.

The first platypus sent to England for study was dismissed as a hoax. Evidently a critter with a duck's bill and a beaver's tail that also laid eggs yet suckled its young was considered an impossibility.

The peculiar constraints of the Australian environment have not made everything dumb. The koala's nearest relative, the wombat (of which there are three species), has a large brain for a marsupial. These creatures live in complex burrows and can weigh up to 35kg, making them the largest herbivorous burrowers on earth. Because their burrows are effectively air-conditioned, they have the neat trick of turning down their metabolic activity when they are in residence. One physiologist, who studied their thyroid hormones, found that biological activity ceased to such an extent in sleeping wombats that, from a hormonal point of view, they appeared to be dead! Wombats can remain underground for a week at a time, and can get by on just a third of the food needed by a sheep of equivalent size. One day, perhaps, efficiency-minded farmers will keep wombats instead of sheep. At the moment, however, that isn't possible; the largest of the wombat species, the northern hairy-nose, is one of the

The stately brolga – a member of the crane family – performs graceful courtship displays that have been absorbed into Aboriginal legends and ceremonies.

world's rarest creatures, with only around 100 surviving in a remote nature reserve in central Queensland.

Megafauna – large animal species – once flourished in Australia, but became extinct around 40,000 to 60,000 BC. Species included the diprotodon (a 2000kg, 3m-high wombat).

Among the more common marsupials you might catch a glimpse of in national parks around Australia's major cities are the species of antechinus. These nocturnal, rat-sized creatures lead an extraordinary life. The males live for just 11 months, the first 10 of which consist of a concentrated burst of eating and growing. Like teenage males, the day comes when their minds turn to sex, and in the antechinus this becomes an obsession. As they embark on their quest for females they forget to eat and sleep. Instead they gather in logs and woo passing females by serenading them with squeaks. By the end of August – just two weeks after they reach 'puberty' – every male is dead, exhausted by sex and by carrying around swollen testes. This extraordinary life history may also have evolved in response to Australia's trying environmental conditions. It seems likely that if the males survived mating, they would compete with the females as they tried to find enough food to feed their growing young. Basically,

WILDLIFE WATCHING

One of the most biologically diverse places on earth, Queensland is home to many animal species found in Australia – in all some 239 species of native mammals, 562 native birds, 125 native frogs and 473 native reptiles. Remember that many are nocturnal and/or extremely shy, so a torch comes in handy if you're staying in a national park.

Birds

Queensland has more bird species than any other Australian state or territory. Two huge flightless birds here are unusual, because only the males incubate the eggs and care for the young: the emu, found in woodlands and grasslands west of the Great Dividing Range; and the elusive cassowary, found in the rainforests of Far North Queensland.

Dingoes

Australia's only native dog, dingoes are believed to descend from a Southeast Asian wolf family. They don't bark, but do howl at night. Fraser Island has one of the country's most genetically pure breeds (p192).

Kangaroos

Kangaroos are perhaps the most famous inhabitants of the bush, and the eastern grey kangaroo is commonly encountered in Queensland woodlands. The family of about 50 species also includes many smaller species such as wallabies and the adorable pademelon, which is smaller than a wallaby.

Koalas

Common along Australia's entire eastern seaboard, this endearing creature is adapted to life in trees, feeding exclusively on eucalyptus leaves. The female carries her baby in her pouch until it is old enough to cling to her back.

Good places to spot them in the wild are Magnetic Island (p275) and Daisy Hill Koala Sanctuary (p64) in Brisbane.

Platypuses & Echidnas

The platypus and echidna are monotremes, a group containing only three species (the third lives in New Guinea). Both animals lay eggs, but suckle their young on milk secreted directly through the skin from mammary glands. The shy and elusive platypus lives in freshwater streams and is rarely seen by the casual observer. A good place to look for it is in Eungella National Park (p235).

The echidna, or spiny anteater, eats only ants and protects itself by digging into the ground or by rolling itself into a bristling ball. It is found throughout Queensland, from Brisbane's suburbs up to Cape York.

antechinus dads are disposable. They do better for antechinus posterity if they go down in a testosterone-fuelled blaze of glory.

One thing you will see lots of in Australia are reptiles (see p457). Snakes are abundant, and they include some of the most venomous species known. Where the opportunities to feed are few and far between, it's best not to give your prey a second chance, hence the potent venom. Snakes will usually leave you alone if you don't fool with them. Observe, back quietly away and don't panic, and most of the time you'll be OK.

Some visitors mistake lizards for snakes, and indeed some Australian lizards look bizarre. One of the more abundant is the sleepy lizard. These creatures, which are found throughout the southern arid region, look like animated pine cones. They are the Australian equivalent of tortoises, and are harmless. Other lizards are much larger. Unless you visit the Indonesian island of Komodo you will not see a larger lizard than the desert-dwelling perentie. These beautiful creatures, with their leopard-like blotches, can grow to more than 2m long, and are efficient predators of introduced rabbits, feral cats and the like.

Australia's plants can be irresistibly fascinating. The sheer variety of flowers is amazing, with 4000 species crowded into the southwestern corner of the continent. This diversity of prolific flowering plants has long puzzled botanists. Again, Australia's poor soils seem to be the cause. The sand plain is about the poorest soil in Australia – it's almost pure quartz. This prevents any single fast-growing species from dominating. Instead, thousands of specialist plant species have learned to find a narrow niche, and so coexist. Some live at the foot of the metre-high sand dunes, some on top, some on an east-facing slope, some on the west and so on. Their flowers need to be striking in order to attract pollinators, for nutrients are so lacking in this sandy world that even insects such as bees are rare.

Ecotourism Australia (www.ecotourism.org.au) has an accreditation system for environmentally friendly and sustainable tourism in Australia. You can browse ecofriendly accommodation, attractions and tours by state.

Current Environmental Issues

Headlining the environmental issues facing Australia's landscape at present are climate change, water scarcity, nuclear energy and uranium mining. All are interconnected. For Australia, the warmer temperatures resulting from climate change spell disaster to an already fragile landscape. At the time of research, Australia was suffering its worst drought on record. Dams throughout the country are at record lows and mandatory water restrictions have been imposed. A 2°C climb in average temperatures on the globe's driest continent will result in an even drier southern half of the country and greater water scarcity. Scientists also agree that hotter and drier conditions will exacerbate bushfire conditions and increase cyclone intensity, two natural phenomena that have cost lives and a great deal of money.

Australia is a heavy greenhouse-gas emitter because it relies on coal and other fossil fuels for its energy supplies. The most prominent and also contentious alternative energy source is nuclear power, which creates less greenhouse gases and relies on uranium, in which Australia is rich. But the radioactive waste created by nuclear power stations can take thousands of years to become harmless. Moreover, uranium is a finite energy source (as opposed to yet-cleaner and renewable energy sources such as solar and wind power), and even if Australia were to establish sufficient nuclear power stations now to make a real reduction in coal dependency, it would be years before the environmental and economic benefits were realised.

Uranium mining produces polarised opinions. Because countries around the world are also looking to nuclear energy, Australia finds itself in a position to increase exports of one of its top-dollar resources.

Top Books About Climate Change

- *Field Notes From a Catastrophe*, Elizabeth Kolbert
- *The Vanishing Face of Gaia*, James Lovelock
- *The Weather Makers*, Tim Flannery
- *Eaarth, Making Life on a Tough New Planet*, Bill McKibben

THE GREAT BARRIER REEF

Larger than the Great Wall of China and the only living thing visible from space, the Great Barrier Reef is one of the seven wonders of the natural world. The kaleidoscope of colour stretches along the Queensland seaboard from south of the Tropic of Capricorn to the Torres Strait. It's the planet's biggest reef system, where 2900 reefs form an outer ribbon parallel to the coast. The 900 islands dotting the reefs also play an important role in the ecosystem. Some are home to lush rainforests and mangroves, and key habitats for nesting seabirds and sea turtles. Other islands are sandy deserts that get washed away during fierce storms.

Unlike mainland Australia, the reef is relatively young (geologically speaking). It first formed around 500,000 years ago, but has gone through dramatic changes in response to changing sea levels. The present structure of the reef is only about 6000 to 8000 years old, growing atop fossil remains of reefs formed during eras of higher sea levels.

At a Glance

» **Area** 344,000 sq km (slightly smaller than Germany)
» **Length** 2300km from north of Bundaberg to the Torres Strait
» **Width** Between 60km and 250km
» **Distance from shore** 300km in the south, 30km in the north

From Little Polyps, Mighty Reefs Grow

An industrious family of tiny animals, the coral polyp is responsible for creating the Great Barrier Reef and other reefs. All corals are primitive hollow sacs with tentacles on the top, but it is the hard corals that are the architects and builders. These corals excrete a small amount of limestone as an outer skeleton that protects and supports their bodies. As polyps die and new ones grow on top, their billions of skeletons cement together into an ever-growing natural bulwark. The coral's skeletons are white, while the reef's kaleidoscopic colours come from the living polyps.

Although coral can catch small fish and plankton using stinging cells on their tentacles, most coral obtain their nutrient requirements from algae called zooxanthellae, which live in the gastric cells of the coral. Like plants, the zooxanthellae use photosynthesis (energy from the sun) to supply coral with essential nutrients. Owing to this symbiotic relationship – and need for sunlight – coral can grow no deeper than 30m below the water's surface. It also needs clear and salty water to survive and consequently does not grow around river mouths.

The speed in which corals and other reef organisms grow, are smothered, buried, broken or otherwise altered is astounding. Different times of day, tide or year, as well as El Niño, La Niña, crown-of-thorns invasions, cyclonic or storm damage, bleaching events or coastal run-off all contribute to this constantly changing world.

Coral Spawning

One of the most spectacular sights of the Great Barrier Reef occurs for a few nights after a full moon in late spring or early summer each year, when vast numbers of corals spawn at the same time. The tiny bundles of sperm and eggs are visible to the naked eye, and together they look like a gigantic underwater snowstorm. Many other reef organisms reproduce around this time, giving their spawn a greater chance of surviving predators.

Astounding Biodiversity

Marine environments demonstrate the greatest biodiversity of any ecosystems on earth. The Great Barrier Reef is home to marine mammals such as whales, dolphins and dugongs (sea cows). With new varieties still being found, its flora and fauna includes the following:

» 1500 species of fish
» 400 types of coral
» 5000 to 8000 breeds of clams and other molluscs
» 600 species of echinoderm, including starfish, sea urchins and sea cucumbers
» 400 to 500 varieties of marine algae

» 1500 different sponges
» six types of turtle
» 17 species of sea snake
» 30 species of cetacean (whales and dolphins)
» 13,000 dugong (of the world population of 90,000)

Sorting the Reef from the Cays

Reefs fall into three categories: barrier (or ribbon) reefs, platform reefs and fringing reefs. The barrier reef proper lies on the outer, seaward edge of the reef system, lining the edge of the continental shelf in an often-unbroken formation.

Platform reefs grow on the land side of these barrier reefs and often support coral cay islands. These occur when the reef grows above sea level; dead coral is ground down by water action to form sand, and sometimes vegetation takes root. Many famous islands – eg Green Island, Heron Island and Lady Musgrave Island – are coral cays.

Closer to shore you'll find fringing reefs surrounding the hillier, continental islands. Great Keppel, most of the Whitsundays, Hinchinbrook and Dunk, for example, were once the peaks of mainland coastal ranges, but rising sea levels submerged most of these mountains, leaving only the tips exposed.

Taking the Temperature of the Barrier Reef

Coral polyps need a water temperature of 17.5°C to 28°C to grow and can't tolerate too much sediment. There are three main threats to the reef: land-based pollutants, overfishing and global warming. Global warming causes parts of the world's oceans to overheat, and the rise in temperature bleaches the reef. As the brightly coloured living polyps die, only the white skeletons remain. Pollution has also poisoned some coral, plus some questions persist about the long-term effects of crown-of-thorns starfish.

Some environmentalists and scientists predict that under current conditions, coral cover within the reef may be reduced to less than 5% by 2050. Because all the living organisms in the reef are symbiotic, the diverse ecosystem we see today may be gone forever.

Fortunately it's not all doom and gloom. In 2004 the Australian government introduced new laws that increased 'no-take' zones, where it is forbidden to remove animal or plant life (eg no fishing), to 33.33% of the reef (it was previously only 4.5%). The Queensland government also unveiled the Great Barrier Reef Marine Park, a state park encompassing the actual coastline from just north of Bundaberg to the tip of Cape York – a total of 3600km. And collectively the federal and Queensland governments have launched a Reef Water Quality Protection Plan in an effort to deal with land-based pollutants. On a micro level, the Great Barrier Reef Marine Park Authority (www.gbrmpa.gov.au) looks after the welfare of most of the reef. It monitors bleaching and other problems and works to enforce the reef's 'no-take' zones.

This increased awareness means it's even more important to take all litter with you, even biodegradable material like apple cores. Admire, but don't touch or harass, marine animals and be aware that if you touch or walk on coral you'll damage it.

Experiencing the Reef

Snorkelling and diving will get you up close and personal with the reef. However, you can also view fish and coral from a glass-bottomed or semisubmersible boat. You can visit the Reef HQ aquarium in Townsville (p265) to see a living coral reef without leaving dry land. Apart from all the psychedelically patterned tropical fish, there's the chance to swim with manta rays, squid, turtles and more. There's nothing to be too alarmed about, but make sure you avoid scorpion fish, stonefish and jellyfish. No reef shark has ever attacked a diver, and sea snakes have fangs in the back of their throats so present no threat to humans.

For more information on planning a visit to the reef, see p26. If you'd like more in-depth knowledge of dive sites, you might also check out Lonely Planet's *Diving & Snorkelling the Great Barrier Reef*.

QUEENSLAND'S NATIONAL PARKS

Queensland has over 500 areas of environmental or natural importance, totalling some 8 million hectares, which makes up nearly 5% of the gigantic state. Of these areas, 219 are national parks, some of which comprise only a single hill or lake, while others are vast expanses of wilderness. The remainder are a mix of state parks, resources reserves and nature refuges. The good news for conservationists is that Queensland's government hopes to dramatically expand this protected area, with a goal of protecting nearly 13 million hectares by 2020.

You can get information about these areas from the Queensland Parks & Wildlife Service (www.derm.qld.gov.au), a wing of the Department of the Environment and Resource Management. There are QPWS regional offices scattered across the state, or you can use the website to access and download a wealth of information and make camping bookings for many of the parks.

Our Favourite National Parks

PARK	FEATURES	ACTIVITIES	BEST TIME	PAGE
Carnarvon	ancient Aboriginal paintings, rich birdlife, gaping Ward's Canyon, spectacular views	overnight bushwalks, birdwatching	cooler months, Apr-Oct	p222
Eungella	unique wildlife, including platypuses, tumbling Araluen Falls	wildlife watching, bushwalking, swimming, scenic drives	Apr-Nov, Aug for platypuses	p235
Great Barrier Reef	coral cays, fringing reefs, islands	snorkelling, diving, reef-walking, wildlife-watching (marine mammals, birds, turtles)	Apr-Sep	p26
Great Sandy	vast tracts of beach, freshwater lakes, rainforests, mangrove forests	bushwalking, swimming, 4WD touring, fishing	drier months, Apr-Dec	p163
Hinchinbrook Island	unspoiled wilderness, towering mountains, dense rainforest, idyllic beaches, the Thorsborne Trail	bushwalking, birdwatching, swimming, bush camping	cooler months, Apr-Sep	p289
Lakefield	mighty rivers, wetlands, freshwater crocodiles, immense grasslands	barramundi fishing, wildlife watching, bush camping	dry months, Apr-Oct	p393
Lamington	rugged mountains, cascading waterfalls, gorges, subtropical rainforest, wildlife such as pademelons (a type of small wallaby), spotted quolls, Richmond birdwing butterflies, satin bowerbirds and other bird species	bushwalking, wildlife watching, bush camping, abseiling	year-round; Nov-Mar are the hottest months	p140
Lizard Island	stark and sandy terrain, sublime and remote beaches, diverse wildlife	swimming, snorkelling, scuba diving, bushwalking, wildlife watching	cooler, dry months, May-Oct	p385

But uranium mining in Australia has been met with fierce opposition for decades, not only because the product is a core ingredient of nuclear weapons, but also because much of Australia's uranium supplies sit beneath sacred Indigenous land. Supporters of increased uranium mining and export suggest that the best way to police the use of uranium is to manage its entire life cycle; that is, to sell the raw product to international buyers, and then charge a fee to accept the waste and dispose of it. Both major political parties consider an expansion of Australia's uranium export industry to be inevitable for economic reasons.

Pizzey and Knight's *Field Guide to Birds of Australia* is an indispensable guide for birdwatchers and anyone else even peripherally interested in Australia's feathered tribes. Knight's illustrations are both beautiful and helpful in identification.

National & State Parks

Australia has more than 500 national parks – nonurban protected wilderness areas of environmental or natural importance. Each state defines and runs its own national parks, but the principle is the same throughout Australia. National parks include rainforests, vast tracts of empty outback, strips of coastal dune land and rugged mountain ranges.

Public access is encouraged as long as safety and conservation regulations are observed. In all parks you're asked to do nothing to damage or alter the natural environment. Camping grounds (often with toilets and showers), walking tracks and information centres are often provided for visitors. In most national parks there are restrictions on bringing in pets.

State parks and state forests are other forms of nature reserves; owned by state governments, they have fewer regulations than national parks. Although state forests can be logged, they are often recreational areas with camping grounds, walking trails and signposted forest drives. Some permit horses and dogs.

Watching Wildlife

For those intrigued by the diversity of tropical rainforests, Queensland's World Heritage Sites are well worth visiting. Birds of paradise, cassowaries and a variety of other birds can be seen by day, while at night you can search for tree-kangaroos (yes, some kinds of kangaroo do live in the tree tops). In your nocturnal wanderings you are highly likely to see curious possums, some of which look like skunks, and other marsupials that today are restricted to a small area of northeast Queensland. Fossils from as far afield as western Queensland and southern Victoria indicate that such creatures were once widespread.

Australia's deserts are a real hit-and-miss affair as far as wildlife is concerned. If you're visiting in a drought year, all you might see are dusty plains, the odd mob of kangaroos and emus, and a few struggling trees. Return after big rains, however, and you'll encounter something close to a Garden of Eden. Fields of white and gold daisies stretch endlessly into the distance, perfuming the air. The salt lakes fill with fresh water, and millions of water birds – pelicans, stilts, shags and gulls – can be seen feeding on the superabundant fish and insect life of the waters. It all seems like a mirage, and like a mirage it will vanish as the land dries out, only to spring to life again in a few years' or a decade's time.

The Arts in Queensland

Queensland painters, writers and musicians have made substantial contributions to Australia's artistic heritage. Following the fall of the National Party in the 1990s, the new Labor government did much to stimulate and encourage artistic and cultural development. Brisbane in particular has experienced a cultural renaissance with the building of world-class museums and exhibition spaces. It's home to one of Australia's biggest arts fests; it's also a place where you can tap into theatre, opera, alternative cinema, poetry, music and other artistic activities happening every night of the week.

The Brisbane Writers Festival (www.brisbanewritersfestival.com.au) is a great chance to mingle with distinguished writers and editors from around the globe. Over five days in early September, the fest features writing seminars, masterclasses, round-table discussions and plenty of writing tips from the pros.

Outside the capital, you'll find arts scenes in Cairns and Townsville, both of which have a mix of galleries and cultural centres that showcase the best of north Queensland and beyond. Cairns also has a lively arts and culture fest to rival Brisbane's, though on a smaller scale.

The Aboriginal art scene in Queensland is quite vibrant, though you have to know where to look. The state has some captivating rock-art sites, where you can connect to ancient arts traditions dating back tens of thousands of years. You can also encounter fine works by living Aboriginal artists at galleries scattered around the state, though Brisbane is still the best place to begin the cultural journey.

Music

Indigenous music is one of the Australian music industry's great success stories of recent years, and Queensland has produced some outstanding Indigenous musicians. Christine Anu is a Torres Strait Islander who was born in Cairns. Her debut album *Stylin' Up* (1995) blends Creole-style rap, Islander chants and traditional languages with English, and was followed by the interesting *Come My Way* (2000) and *45 Degrees* (2003) – highly recommended listening. Ever evolving, she even released a colourful children's album *Chrissy's Island Family* (2007).

Brisbane's pub-rock scene has produced a couple of Australia's all-time greatest bands. The Saints, considered by many to be one of the seminal punk bands, started out performing in Brisbane in the mid-1970s before moving on to bigger things in Sydney and, later, London.

Queensland's musicians have given their counterparts elsewhere a run for their money in recent years. Powderfinger played a dominant role in the music industry from the 1990s until their breakup in 2010. Their albums make excellent driving soundtracks – get your hands on *Odyssey Number Five* (2000), *Vulture Street* (2003), their best-of album *Fingerprints* (2004), or their last one, *Golden Rule* (2009). They played their final concert in Brisbane in late 2010 before a crowd of 10,000. Lead singer Bernard Fanning also released a solo album, *Tea and Sympathy*, in 2005.

The Australian Record Industry Association (ARIA) award-winning debut album *Polyserena* (2002) by Queensland band George is deliciously haunting and well worth a listen. Katie Noonan (George's lead singer) released a solo album, *Skin*, in 2007. Another star hailing from the Sunshine State is Pete Murray. His acoustic licks and chocolate-smooth voice have earned him national and international acclaim. Listen to his debut *Feeler* (2003) or his latest offerings *See the Sun* (2005) and *Summer at Eureka* (2008).

Another Queensland success story is The Veronicas, twins of Sicilian descent whose pop style is a hit with teenagers. More interesting is Kate Miller-Heidke, a classically trained singer, who channels a bit of Björk, Kate Bush and Cyndi Lauper in her works. Chase down a copy of *Little Eve* (2007); or *Curiouser* (2008), which received moderate success (especially 'The Last Day on Earth', which became a top-10 single).

Representing Far North Queensland, the McMenamins are a talented brother and sister folk duo who are receiving increasing airplay and have performed around the country. Their self-titled debut released in 2003 as well as their second album, *In this Light* (2006), are both worth seeking out.

For a dose of 100% Australian music talent, tune in to the national radio station Triple J (www.abc.net.au/triplej) for 'Home and Hosed', 9pm to 10pm Monday to Thursday.

QUEENSLAND ON FILM

Although Australia's film industry has been firmly lodged in Victoria and New South Wales, Queensland has spent more than a decade making significant inroads, which in turn has fostered new growth in the artistic wing of the industry.

The commercial industry is based around the Warner Roadshow Studios at Movie World on the Gold Coast, which has made films targeted at the family market, including *Scooby Doo* (2002) and *Peter Pan* (2003). Other commercial films produced here include the horror thriller *Ghost Ship* (2002); and *The Great Raid* (2002), which tells the story of a WWII rescue mission of American prisoners in a Japanese prisoner-of-war camp in the Philippines. In the horror genre, *Undead* (2002), shot in southeast Queensland, is about a town that becomes infected with a zombie virus.

Other international titles filmed in the state include the following:

» *Australia* (2008), Baz Luhrmann's epic, was partly filmed in Bowen. The second-highest grossing Australian film of all time (after *Crocodile Dundee*) relates the adventure of an English aristocrat (played by Nicole Kidman) in northern Australia against the backdrop of WWII.

» *Ocean's Deadliest* (2007), the last documentary Steve Irwin made before his untimely death, features Philippe Cousteau, grandson of renowned oceanographer Jacques Cousteau.

» *Gettin' Square* (2003), directed by Jonathan Teplitzky, is an exquisitely funny and dark story about two low-grade criminals trying to extricate themselves from their past.

» *Swimming Upstream* (2002) is the autobiographical story of Anthony Fingleton, a Queensland swimmer. It captures the hardship of his life with his alcoholic father (played by Geoffrey Rush) in gritty 1960s Brisbane.

» *The Thin Red Line* (1998) is Terrence Malick's critically acclaimed tale of WWII soldiers in the Pacific.

» *Praise* (1998), adapted from the novel by Andrew McGahan, is a toothy, honest tale of mismatched love in down-and-out Brisbane.

» *Muriel's Wedding* (1994) is a hit comedy that strips the lino off the suburban dream as Muriel attempts to escape a monotonous life.

» *Crocodile Dundee* (1986), Paul Hogan's record-breaking vehicle to stardom, as well as its two sequels, were partially shot in Queensland.

Painting & Photography

Queensland's art scene was slow to emerge, with paintings by early settlers first appearing in the second half of the 19th century. In the 20th century a few seminal figures helped put Queensland on the map.

Ian Fairweather (1891–1974) is described by some critics and fellow artists as Australia's greatest painter. He used muted colours and shied away from typical Australian themes, such as gum trees and pastoral and rugged landscapes, and incorporated Asian elements (gouaches of villages and market scenes, influenced by his years living in China from 1930 to 1933). An enigmatic figure, he spent the last years of his life as a recluse on Bribie Island.

The long-lived Lloyd Rees (1895–1988) has an impressive body of work and is one of Queensland's best-known artists of the 20th century. A master of light and texture, he was obsessed with capturing a spiritual element in the landscapes he painted. He was born in Brisbane and painted right up until his death.

One of Queensland's most successful living artists is William Robinson (b 1936). He has worked in a variety of styles and completed some of his most successful work after moving from Brisbane to a large property in the Gold Coast hinterland. His paintings capture the magical quality of the rainforest and the awe-inspiring power of the mountains near Springbrook. His work is on display in Brisbane's Old Government House (p53).

Brisbane-based Richard Bell (b 1953) is an Aboriginal artist who creates provocative works that touch on politics, religion and Aboriginal relations (words over one controversial but prize-winning piece read 'Aboriginal art – it's a white thing'). He also explores black-white relations in large Lichtenstein-like cartoon tableaus.

Tracey Moffatt (b 1960), who also hails from Brisbane, blends cinema, photography and visual arts in carefully constructed 'film stills' with underlying themes of poverty and violence. Her work hangs in galleries all over the world and she has been described as one of Australia's '50 most collectable artists'.

For galleries in Brisbane, see p64.

Tina Cooper, one of Australia's leading glass-blowing artists, creates exquisite and richly textured works. Her gallery, Tina Cooper Glass (www.tinacooper.com) in Eumundi, on the Sunshine Coast, showcases her sculptures and colourful pieces, as well as works by other artists.

In 1964 Oodgeroo Noonuccal from North Stradbroke Island became the first Aboriginal woman to be published (under the name of Kath Walker), with her collection of verse *We Are Going*. The publication sold out in three days and during the 1970s and '80s her subsequent work received international acclaim.

Aboriginal Rock Art

Rock art is a diary of human activity by Australia's Indigenous peoples stretching over tens of thousands of years. Queensland has plenty of sites, especially hidden around the Far North. Try to see some while you're here – the experience of viewing rock art in the surroundings in which it was painted is far more profound than seeing it in a gallery.

Carnarvon Gorge (p222), in Carnarvon National Park, houses rock engravings, freehand drawing and over 2000 mouth-sprayed stencils,

READING QUEENSLAND

Lebanese-Australian author David Malouf (b 1934) is one of Queensland's most internationally recognised writers, having been nominated for the Booker Prize. Among other titles, he is well known for his evocative tales of an Australian boyhood in Brisbane – *Johnno* (1975), as well as his memoir *12 Edmondstone Street* (1985) – and for *The Great World* (1990), his Australian epic that spans two world wars. Set on the Gold Coast, his 1982 novel *Fly Away Peter* tells the poignant story of a returned soldier struggling to come to terms with ordinary life and the unjust nature of social hierarchy. His latest work is a collection of short stories titled *Every Move You Make* (2006), which dissects Australian life across the continent, including Far North Queensland.

which are of deep spiritual significance to the present-day Bidjarra people of the area.

Kuku Yalanji sites, in Mossman Gorge, feature Dreaming legends depicted in cave paintings (see p364). The Kuku Yalanji community offers excellent guided walks to see and understand the art. High-quality works are also sold in an on-site gallery.

Split Rock and Guguyalangi Galleries, on the Cape York Peninsula, have some of the best-known examples of Quinkan art, a painting style in northern Australia that's named after human-like spirit figures with oddly shaped heads. There are hundreds of ancient rock-art sites displaying this style around Laura in Cape York. The most accessible is the Split Rock site; tours are led by Aboriginal guides from Laura (p392). Check out the Quinkan & Regional Cultural Centre site (www.quinkancc.com.au) for more information about Cape York Peninsula rock art and how to access it.

Wangaar-Wuri sites, near Cooktown, depict different aspects of local society and Aboriginal culture, including family stories, mythical figures, spiritual beliefs and practical guidance. Difficult to find on your own, they are best visited with local guides on Guurrbi Tours (p383), who can help explain the fascinating works.

Culinary Queensland

The long legacy of steak-and-three-veg is a distant memory in Queensland, which today harbours some of the most dynamic places in the country for a bite. Thanks to a diverse expatriate community, ever-inventive chefs and an open-minded public, restaurant-goers face dizzying choices when it comes to dining. Culinary riches come from every corner of the globe: Vietnamese, Indian, Thai, Italian, Spanish, Greek and Japanese influences are just a small part of the Queensland foodie experience.

The total at the bottom of a restaurant bill is all you really need to pay. It should include 10% GST, and no 'optional' service charge added. Waiters are paid a reasonable salary, so they don't rely on tips to survive. Increasingly though, people leave a few coins in a cafe and up to 15% at high-end places.

Brisbane has firmly established itself as a gastronomic Goliath, rivalling the feats of Sydney and Melbourne, and can claim to be a destination worthy of touring gourmands. Noosa is renowned for its award-winning restaurants, with its fine cuisine the subject of cookbooks and food guides. The Gold and Sunshine Coasts have their share of fine and imaginative eateries, fuelled by the growing number of tourists visiting the southeast. Further north, Townsville and Cairns have a global palate, with eclectic offerings to suit all budgets. Outside of these top spots you should expect simpler fare. But whereas 'pub grub' once meant a lamb roast, bangers and mash or chicken parmigiana, it now encompasses everything from salt-and-pepper squid to a butter-chicken curry.

Australia has readily embraced the moniker Modern Australian, or Mod Oz, to describe the nation's cuisine. If it's a melange of East and West, it's Modern Australian. If it's not authentically French or Italian, it's Modern Australian – a sometimes challenging attempt to classify the unclassifiable. Dishes usually aren't too fussy and the flavours are often bold and interesting.

Local Delicacies

Australia's best food comes from the sea. Nothing compares to this continent's seafood, harnessed from some of the purest waters you'll find. Right along the Queensland coast, even a simple dish of fish and chips (and that includes the takeaway variety) is superfresh and cooked with care.

Connoisseurs prize Queensland's sea scallops and blue-swimmer crabs. One of the state's iconic delicacies is the Moreton Bay bug – like a shovel-nosed lobster and priced accordingly (around $40 per kilogram when we last checked). The prawns and calamari here are also delicious. Add to that countless wild fish species and Queensland has one of the greatest bounties on Earth.

Queenslanders love their seafood, but they've not lost their yen for a hefty chunk of steak. Rockhampton is the beef capital of Australia and visiting carnivores would be foolish not to cut into a sizzling steak. Elsewhere beef and lamb remain staples, but they are now done with tandoori, Greek or Provinçal flavourings…or served as just chops or steak.

Queensland's size and diverse climate – from the humid, tropical north to the mild, balmy south – mean there's an enormous variety of produce on offer. If you're embarking on a road trip throughout the state, you're bound to encounter rolling banana, sugar or mango plantations or quilted orchards. In summer, mangoes are so plentiful that Queenslanders actually get sick of them. But this is not the case with macadamias. This native nut with its smooth, buttery flavour grows throughout southeastern Queensland and fetches hefty prices. Queenslanders use it in everything – you'll find it tossed in salads, crushed and frozen in ice cream and petrified to a sticky consistency in gooey cakes and sweets.

There's a small but brilliant farmhouse-cheese movement, hampered by the fact that all the milk must be pasteurised (unlike in Italy and France, home to some of the world's best cheeses). Despite that, the results can be great. Keep an eye out for goat's cheese from Gympie and anything from the boutique Kenilworth Country Foods company (p167).

Serious foodies should pick up a copy of *The Food & Wine Guide Queensland*, which also covers northern NSW and the Northern Territory, produced by the *Courier Mail*.

Tasting Tours

In the Atherton Tableland in north Queensland, you can get a firsthand look at the nation's best coffee-growing plantations. Even better, you'll get to sample the good stuff – not just incredibly rich, freshly made coffee, but also coffee liqueur and dark chocolate–coated coffee beans (see the boxed text on p345).

Further north, the Daintree offers gustatory temptations of a different sort. You can sample delectable ice cream made from freshly picked produce grown in the surrounding orchards, or feast on tropical fruit grown at the Cape Trib Exotic Fruit Farm (see p373).

In the south of Queensland, the wine-growing region of the Granite Belt also has a marvellous climate for growing fruit. Even if you're not a wine lover, it's worth visiting to sample farmhouse cheeses, apples, berries and other fruit, plus Belgian-style chocolate; the bimonthly Market in the Mountains (p108) showcases the best of the region. For tips on where to go, see the boxed text on p107.

Tim Tam bombs (also known as exploding Tim Tams or Tim Tam slams) are a delicious Aussie ritual. Take a Tim Tam biscuit, nibble off two diagonally opposite corners, dunk one nibbled corner into a hot drink (tea, coffee or hot chocolate) and suck through the fast-melting biscuit like a straw. Ugly but good.

TOP QUEENSLAND RESTAURANTS

» **Anise** (p82), Brisbane, has phenomenal *amuse-bouches* (entrees) for sharing and expertly matched wines by the glass.

» **Oskars** (p132), Burleigh Heads, has sweeping views and sassy seafood.

» **Berardo's on the Beach** (p149), Noosa, is a highly acclaimed restaurant with heavenly ambience and inventive cuisine.

» **Waterview Bistro** (p174), Rainbow Beach, has excellent cuisine and magnificent sea views.

» **Shio Kaze** (p206), Yeppoon, serves mouth-watering sushi and sashimi alongside ocean views in a quaint little beach town.

» **Fish D'vine** (p248), Airlie Beach, serves superb seafood and dazzling cocktails.

» **Yorkeys Knob Boating Club** (p332), on Cairns' northern beaches, is a local secret for delectable, fresh-as-it-gets seafood.

» **Mojo's** (p365), Mossman, serves exceptional and creative fusion fare at incredibly reasonable prices.

» **Julaymba Restaurant** (p369), in the Daintree Rainforest, features indigenous produce including berries, nuts, leaves, flowers and green ants!

» **Rodeo Bar & Grill** (p412), Mt Isa, fires up the best steaks in the outback.

Wine Country

Queensland's climate is generally too warm to produce good wines, but there are a few pockets where you can find respectable locally grown vines. The Atherton Tableland, the Sunshine and Gold Coast hinterlands and the countryside around Kingaroy are all home to vineyards, but the state's best-known wine region is the Granite Belt in the Darling Downs.

'Shouting' is a revered custom where people rotate paying for a round of drinks. Just don't leave before it's your turn to buy!

Still under the radar in most parts of Australia (and virtually unknown abroad), the Granite Belt has slowly been carving a name for itself in recent years, buoyed by an excellent response at international awards shows. The first vines were planted here by Sicilian immigrants in the 1800s, and some of the best-known wineries are still family-run affairs, with vines dating back many generations. Today more than 50 boutique wineries dominate the region, producing an impressive variety of wines – grapes from Italy, South Africa, Portugal, Spain and France all flourish in the diverse microclimate of the Granite Belt, which remains cooler than coastal Queensland owing to its higher elevations (topping 954m).

Most wineries are open to visitors, and have free tastings, though some keep limited hours (opening only on weekends). See p107 for a list of top wineries in the region.

For something completely different, don't miss a chance to try 'tropical wine'. Just north of Mission Beach, you can stop in for a free tasting at Murdering Point Winery (p299), which produces highly drinkable wines made from plum, passionfruit and mango, among other fruits.

In Queensland, when ordering a beer you can order a five or small (140mL), a pot, 10 or middy (all 285mL), a schooner (425mL), a pint (568mL) or a jug (1125mL).

Beer, Breweries & Bundaberg

There's a bewildering array of beer available in bottle shops, pubs, bars and restaurants. The Queensland staple is XXXX (pronounced 'Four X'), which has been around since 1924. It's much maligned elsewhere in the country, but the locals swear by it. The widely bandied joke is that Queenslanders call it XXXX because they don't know how to spell 'beer'. You can learn about the history of the brew and sample the good stuff on a tour at the Castlemaine Perkins XXXX Brewery in Brisbane (p70).

In addition to XXXX, you'll find other domestic lagers (Tooheys, Carlton and Victoria Bitter in particular) on tap in every pub and bar,

EXOTIC TASTES

After being ignored for about 200 years, Australia's native produce – aka bush tucker – is finally appearing on menus. Kangaroo meat is even carried by major supermarkets. It's a deep purple-red meat, very lean and best served rare. Crocodile is also appearing on some menus (and on pizzas!), and has a chickenlike consistency and a fishy taste. Much of the native flora contains chemicals not fit for human consumption, but notable exceptions include fiery bush pepper; sweet, aromatic lemon myrtle; wattle seed; acidic bush tomato; and the macadamia nut.

If you're in the outback and after something a bit more challenging, give witchetty grubs a go. Although they look like giant maggots, they have a nutty flavour and squishy texture. Green ants are another bush tucker – to eat them pick 'em up and bite off their lightly acidic bottoms. Now you know you're in Australia...

Brisbane, Cairns and Noosa all have restaurants featuring bush food. In Brisbane, **Tukka** (☎3846 6333; 145 Boundary St, West End; mains $28-32) offers a gourmet menu based entirely around native produce: sink your fangs into some smoked Cairns crocodile fillet, confit Tasmanian possum, homemade damper, native berries and even lilly-pilly salad with macadamia and bunya nuts.

but the appearance of imported lagers, ales and pilsners in city pubs and bars is increasing. Microbreweries are scattered throughout the state and offer the opportunity to try some unique brews.

» New in 2008, **Blue Sky Brewery** (www.blueskybrewery.com.au) is an award-winning Cairns brewery with a good range of beers – from a crisp lager (the FNQ) to a traditional Czech-style pilsner, as well as cider and stout.

» **Burleigh Brewing Co** (www.burleighbrewing.com.au) is based on the Gold Coast and produces the Duke label, including a smooth lager that's easy drinking on hot days.

» **Mt Tamborine Brewery** (www.mtbeer.com) produces some of Queensland's best microbrews with no additives or chemicals. Top picks include a Belgian-style ale, a hops-loving IPA (India Pale Ale) and a rich imperial stout.

» **Sunshine Coast Brewery** (www.sunshinecoastbrewery.com) is a respectable boutique brewery with a refreshing Belgian-style wheat beer, a bright summer ale and unique brews made with ginger and chilli.

Most beers have an alcohol content between 3.5% and 5%. That's less than many European beers, but more than the main producers in North America. Light beers contain less than 3% alcohol and are finding favour with people observing the superstringent drink-driving laws.

Bundaberg rum, or 'Bundy', is another feather in Queensland's cap. The famous rum, with its emblematic polar bear – a rather distant relative of the kangaroo – makes fine use of the endless sea of sugar cane growing in tropical Queensland. You can learn all about the spirit on a tour of the distillery in the town for which it's named (p186).

Survival Guide

DEADLY & DANGEROUS...... 456
Bushfires.............. 456
Critters that Bite & Sting 456
Environmental Hazards.. 457

DIRECTORY A–Z....459
Accommodation........ 459
Business Hours 460
Discount Cards......... 460
Electricity 460
Gay & Lesbian Travellers 460
Health.................461
Insurance.............. 462
Internet Access......... 462
Legal Matters 462
Maps.................. 462
Money................. 462
Photography & Video ... 463
Post................... 463
Public Holidays......... 463
Safe Travel 463
Telephone 463
Time.................. 465
Tourist Information 465
Travellers with Disabilities............. 465
Volunteering 465
Women Travellers....... 465
Work................. 466

TRANSPORT 467
GETTING THERE & AWAY................ 467
Air.................... 467
Land.................. 468
GETTING AROUND...... 468
Air.................... 468
Bicycle 469
Bus................... 469
Car & Motorcycle........471
Local Transport..........475
Train...................475

Deadly & Dangerous

Home to bushfires, treacherous surf, blazing heat, jellyfish, snakes, spiders, sharks, crocodiles, ticks and mosquitoes, Queensland certainly has its share of hazards. Thankfully, the real threat to travellers is often greatly exaggerated – and those who take basic precautions are unlikely to encounter serious problems. For info on road hazards and outback travel, see p474.

Bushfires

Bushfires happen every year in Queensland. In hot, dry, windy weather, be extremely careful with any naked flame and don't throw live cigarette butts out in the open. On a day of total fire ban it is forbidden to use even a camping stove in the open.

If you're out in the bush and you see smoke, even at a great distance, take it seriously. Go to the nearest open space, downhill if possible. A forested ridge is the most dangerous place to be. Bushfires move very quickly and change direction with the wind. Last but not least, always take seriously the advice of authorities and follow their warnings, regulations and instructions.

Critters that Bite & Sting

Stingers & Marine Animals

Marine spikes and poisonous spines, such as those found on sea urchins, catfish, stingrays, scorpion fish and stonefish, can cause severe local pain. If you're stung, immediately immerse the affected area in hot water (as hot as can be tolerated) and seek medical care.

Contact with blue-ringed octopuses and Barrier Reef cone shells can be fatal, so don't pick them up. If someone is stung, apply a pressure bandage, monitor breathing carefully and conduct mouth-to-mouth resuscitation if breathing stops. Seek immediate medical care.

Marine stings from jellyfish such as the potentially deadly box jellyfish and the rare and tiny irukandji (1cm to 2cm across), also occur in Australia's tropical waters. It's particularly unwise to swim north of Agnes Water between November and May unless there's a stinger net. 'Stinger suits' (full-body lycra swimsuits) prevent stinging, as do wetsuits. Swimming and snorkelling are usually safe activities around the reef islands throughout the year. However, irukandji have been recorded on the outer Reef and islands.

If you are stung, wash the affected skin with vinegar to prevent any further discharge by the remaining stinging cells, then transfer to a hospital immediately. Do not attempt to remove the tentacles. See p36 for more information.

Mosquitoes

Mozzies can be a problem just about anywhere in Queensland. Fortunately, malaria is not present in Australia, although dengue fever is a danger in northern Queensland, particularly during the wet season (November to April). This viral disease is spread by a species of mosquito that feeds primarily during the day. Most people recover in a few days, but more severe forms of the disease can occur.

To minimise bites:

- » Wear loose, long-sleeved clothing
- » Apply repellent with at least 30% DEET on exposed skin
- » Wear permethrin-impregnated clothing
- » Use mosquito coils and nets
- » Sleep under ceiling fans set to high speed

Sharks & Crocodiles

The risk of an attack from sharks on divers in Queensland is extremely low, as sharks tend to favour southerners – er, southern states.

The risk of a crocodile attack in tropical Far North Queensland is real, but with some common sense it is entirely avoidable. 'Salties' are estuarine crocodiles that can grow to 7m. They inhabit coastal waters and are mostly seen in the tidal reaches of rivers, though on occasion they're spotted on beaches and in freshwater lagoons. Always heed any advice, such as crocodile warning signs, that you might come across. Don't assume it's safe to swim if there are no signs: if you're not sure, don't swim.

If you're away from popular beaches anywhere north of Mackay, avoid swimming in rivers, waterholes and in the sea near river outlets. Don't clean fish or prepare food near the water's edge, and camp at least 50m away from waterways. Crocodiles are particularly mobile and dangerous during the breeding season (October to March).

Snakes

Australian snakes have a fearsome reputation owing to the potency of their venom, but they only pose a small actual risk to travellers. Snakes are usually timid in nature and in most instances will move away if disturbed. Their fangs are small, making it easy to prevent bites to the lower limbs (where 80% of bites occur) by wearing decent footwear and protective clothing (such as gaiters) around the ankles when bushwalking.

If bitten, apply an elastic bandage (as you would do for a sprained ankle; you can improvise with a T-shirt). Wrap it firmly – but not tightly enough to cut off circulation – around the entire limb, and immobilise with a splint or sling. Don't use a tourniquet, and *don't* try to suck out the poison.

Spiders

Australia has poisonous spiders, although the only one to have caused a single death in the last 50 years, the Sydney funnel-web, isn't found in Queensland. Common species include the following:

» Redback – its bites cause increasing pain followed by profuse sweating. Apply ice and transfer to a hospital.

» Whitetail (brown recluse) – blamed for causing slow-healing ulcers. If bitten, clean the wound and seek medical assistance.

» Huntsman – large, tarantula-like spider with a painful but harmless bite.

Ticks

The common bush tick (found all along the eastern coast) can be dangerous if left lodged in the skin, because the toxin the tick excretes can cause partial paralysis and, in theory, even death. Check your body (and that of children and dogs) every night if walking in tick-infested areas. Remove ticks by dousing them with methylated spirits or kerosene and levering them out intact.

Tick typhus cases have been reported in Queensland. A week or so after the bite occurs, a dark area forms around the bite, followed by a rash and possibly fever, a headache and inflamed lymph nodes. The disease is treatable with antibiotics (doxycycline).

Environmental Hazards

Coral Cuts

Coral can be extremely sharp: you can cut yourself by merely brushing against the stuff. Make sure to clean cuts thoroughly and douse with antiseptic to avoid infection.

Drowning

Around 80 people a year drown at Australia's beaches, where pounding surf and rips (strong currents) can create serious hazards. If you happen to get caught in a rip and taken out to sea, swim parallel to the shore – *don't* try to swim back against the rip, you'll only exhaust yourself.

Heat Sickness

Very hot weather is experienced year-round in some parts of Queensland and can lead to heat exhaustion or more severe heatstroke (resulting from extreme fluid depletion). When arriving from a temperate or cold climate, remember that it takes around two weeks to acclimatise.

Unprepared and under-prepared travellers die from dehydration each year in

A BIT OF PERSPECTIVE

Australia's plethora of critters that bite and sting is impressive, but don't let this put you off. There's approximately one shark-attack fatality per year in Australia, and a similar number of croc-attack deaths. Blue-ringed-octopus deaths are rarer – only two in the last century – and there's only ever been *one* confirmed death from a cone shell. Jellyfish do better, disposing of about two people each year. You're still over 40 times more likely to *drown* than be killed by one of these nasties.

On land, snakes kill one or two people per year (about the same as bee stings, or less than a thousandth of the number of people killed on the roads). There hasn't been a recorded death from a tick bite for more than 50 years, nor from spider bites in the last 20.

BASIC REEF SAFETY RULES

» Don't touch any marine life.

» Wear shoes with strong soles when walking near reefs.

» Don't eat fish you don't know about or can't identify.

» Don't swim in murky water; try to swim in bright sunlight.

outback Australia. This can be prevented by following these simple rules:

» Carry sufficient water for any trip, including extra to see you through in case of breakdown.

» Always let someone know where you are going and when you expect to arrive.

» Carry communications equipment of some form.

» If in trouble, stay with the vehicle rather than walk for help.

» When out bushwalking, always stay hydrated and carry water with you at all times, even on short hikes.

Sunburn & Skin Cancer

Australia has one of the highest rates of skin cancer in the world. Monitor exposure to direct sunlight closely. Ultraviolet (UV) radiation is greatest between 10am and 4pm, so avoid skin exposure during these times. Wear a wide-brimmed hat and a long-sleeved shirt with a collar. Always use SPF 30+ sunscreen, and apply it 30 minutes before exposure and repeated regularly to minimise sun damage.

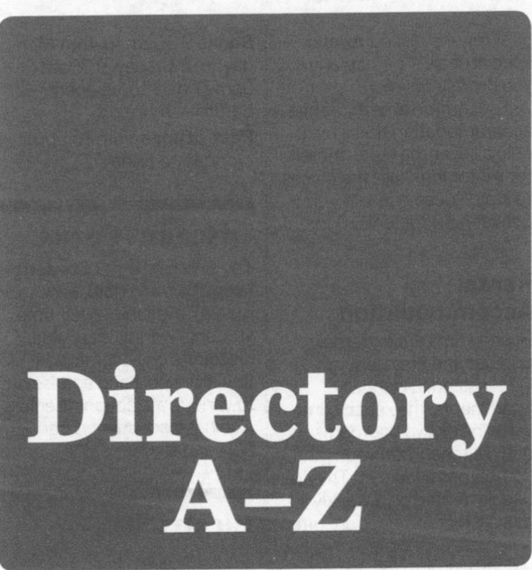

Accommodation

Queensland has an excellent range of sleeping options, including charming guesthouses and B&Bs, high-end seaside resorts, festive hostels, camping grounds and cabins, as well as no-fuss hotels and motels. The listings in the Sleeping sections of this guidebook are in order of preference, from most to least desirable.

Prices

$ Less than $100 per double

$$ Between $100 and $200 per double

$$$ More than $200 per double

In most areas you'll find seasonal price variations. Prices rise by about 25% during school and public holidays, during breaks around Easter and Christmas, and during the high-season months between June and September.

Weekends are often busier and pricier in major holiday areas, and two-night minimum bookings may apply. For more information on climatic seasons and holiday periods, see p14.

Booking Online

Some sites for discounted or last-minute accommodation:

Lastminute.com (www.au.lastminute.com)

Quickbeds.com (www.quickbeds.com.au)

Wotif.com (www.wotif.com.au)

B&Bs

B&B options include restored miners' cottages, converted barns, rambling old houses, upmarket country manors, beachside bungalows and simple bedrooms in family homes. Tariffs are typically in the $100 to $180 (per double) bracket, but can be much higher.

Local tourist offices can usually give you a list of B&B options. For online information, try the following:

Bed & Breakfast and Farmstay Association of Far North Queensland (www.bnbnq.com.au)

Bed & Breakfast Site (www.babs.com.au)

OZBedandBreakfast.com (www.ozbedandbreakfast.com)

Camping

Camping in the bush is for many people one of the highlights of a visit to Australia, with magnificent camping grounds in state and national parks. Permits are mandatory and can be purchased online or over the phone from **Queensland Parks & Wildlife Service** (☎13 74 68; www.derm.qld.gov.au). The cost is $5.15 per person per night, or $21 per family. Some camping grounds fill up at holiday times, so you may need to book well ahead.

You can also pitch your tent in one of the hundreds of caravan parks that are scattered across Queensland; most have pools, toilets, laundry facilities, barbecues and camp kitchens.

Unpowered sites $20 to $30 per night

Powered sites $22 to $35 per night

On-site vans $60 per night

Self-contained cabins $75 to $150 per night, depending on the facilities provided

You should also note that it's illegal to stop overnight in a campervan anywhere that's not a designated camp site. Plenty of backpackers pull up by a beach or even in a Cairns car park, for example, for a free night, and rangers or council people often hand out fines.

Farmstays

A handful of hinterland farms offer a bed for the night and the chance to see rural Australia at work. Some farms offer

BOOK YOUR STAY ONLINE

For more accommodation reviews by Lonely Planet authors, check out http://hotels.lonelyplanet.com. You'll find independent reviews, as well as recommendations on the best places to stay. Best of all, you can book online.

accommodation where you can just sit back and watch how it's done, while others like you to get more actively involved in the day-to-day activities. Check out options at www.babs.com.au under Family Holidays/Farmstays. For travellers who don't mind getting their hands dirty, there's **Willing Workers on Organic Farms** (WWOOF; www.wwoof.com.au). Regional and town tourist offices should also be able to tell you what's available in their area.

Hostels

Queensland has a staggering number of backpacker hostels, with standards ranging from the magnificent to the abysmal, depending on how they are run. You'll find everything from small, low-key, family-run places in converted Queenslanders (timber houses) to massive, custom-built places with hundreds of beds, extensive facilities and a party attitude.

Dorm beds typically cost $20 to $30, with private doubles costing between $70 and $100. Single rooms are also sometimes available.

A warning for Australian and Kiwi travellers: some hostels will only admit overseas backpackers, mainly because they've had problems with local males harassing the backpackers.

Useful organisations, with annual memberships ($37 to $43) that yield lodging and other discounts:

Nomads (www.nomadsworld.com)

VIP Backpackers (www.vipbackpackers.com)

YHA (www.yha.com.au)

Hotels & Motels

There are many excellent four- and five-star hotels and quite a few lesser places. The best tend to have a pool, restaurant or cafe, room service and various other facilities. We quote 'rack rates' (official advertised rates) throughout this book, but often hotels and motels offer regular discounts and special deals – particularly if you browse online.

For comfortable midrange accommodation that's available all over the state, motels (or motor inns) are the places to stay. Prices typically run between $90 and $120 for a room.

Rental Accommodation

Holiday flats are extremely popular and prevalent in Queensland. Essentially apartments, they each come with one or two bedrooms, and a kitchen, bathroom and sometimes a laundry. They're usually rented on a weekly basis – higher prices are often reserved for shorter stays. For a one-bedroom flat, expect to pay anywhere from $90 to $180 per night. An alternative in major cities is to rent a serviced apartment.

If you're interested in a shared flat or house for a long-term stay, delve into the classified advertisements section of the daily newspapers; Wednesday and Saturday are usually the best days. Noticeboards in universities, hostels, bookshops and cafes are also good to check out.

Business Hours

Reviews in this book don't list operating hours unless they deviate from the following normal opening times:

Restaurants Breakfast 8am to 10.30am, lunch noon to 3pm, dinner 6pm to 9pm

Cafes 8am to 5pm

Shops 9am to 5pm Monday to Friday, 9am to noon or 5pm Saturday, late-night shopping to 9pm Thursday or Friday; Sunday trading in most cities and tourist areas

Shopping centres 9am to 9pm

Supermarkets 9am to 8pm

Pubs and bars Noon to 2am

Nightclubs 11pm to 4am Thursday to Saturday

Banks 9.30am to 4pm Monday to Thursday, 9.30am-5pm Friday, some open Saturday morning

Post offices 9am to 5pm Monday to Friday

Discount Cards

The **International Student Identity Card** (ISIC; www.isic.org), available to full-time students worldwide, yields discounts on accommodation, transport and admission to various attractions. Seniors also net discounts on transport and sights.

Electricity

Gay & Lesbian Travellers

Historically, Queensland has a poor reputation when it comes to acceptance of gays and lesbians. Homosexuality was only decriminalised in Queensland in 1991, after the fall of the National Party government.

Brisbane has a small but lively gay and lesbian scene centred on the inner-city suburbs of Spring Hill and

Fortitude Valley, with a few nightclubs, pubs and guesthouses (see p87). There are also gay- and lesbian-only accommodation options in some of the more popular tourist centres, including Brisbane and Cairns. Elsewhere in Queensland, however, there can be a strong streak of homophobia, and violence against homosexuals is a risk, particularly in rural communities.

The website of **Gay & Lesbian Tourism Australia** (GALTA; www.galta.com.au) is a good place to look for general information and gay-friendly listings. **Pink Guide** (www.pinkguide.com) is also useful.

Health

Although there are plenty of hazards in Queensland (see p456), few travellers should experience anything worse than an upset stomach or a bad hangover. If you do fall ill, the standard of hospitals and health care is high.

Availability & Cost of Health Care

Australia has an excellent health-care system, with a mixture of privately run medical clinics and hospitals, and a system of government-funded public hospitals. Medicare covers Australian residents for some health-care costs. Visitors from countries with which Australia has a reciprocal health-care agreement (New Zealand, the UK, the Netherlands, Sweden, Finland, Italy, Malta, Belgium, Norway and Ireland) are eligible for benefits to the extent specified under the Medicare program. If you are from one of these countries, check program details before departure. For further information visit www.health.gov.au.

In remote locations there may be significant delays in emergency services reaching you in the event of serious accident or illness – do not underestimate the vast distances between most major outback towns. An increased level of self-reliance and preparation is essential; consider taking a wilderness first-aid course, such as those offered by **Equip Wilderness First Aid Institute** (www.equip.com.au). Always take a comprehensive first-aid kit that's appropriate for the activities planned and ensure that you have adequate means of communication. Queensland has extensive mobile phone coverage, but radio communications are important for remote areas. The Royal Flying Doctor Service provides a backup for remote communities.

Chemists (Pharmacies) & Prescription Medication

Over-the-counter medications are available at chemists throughout Queensland. These include painkillers, antihistamines and skincare products. You may find that medications readily available over the counter in some countries are only available in Australia by prescription. These include the oral contraceptive pill, some medications for asthma and all antibiotics. If you take medication on a regular basis, bring an adequate supply and ensure you have details of the generic name, as brand names may differ between countries.

Further Reading

Lonely Planet's *Healthy Travel Australia, New Zealand & the Pacific* is a handy, pocket-sized guide packed with useful information including pretrip planning, emergency first-aid, immunisation and disease information, and what to do if you get sick on the road. *Travel with Children*, from Lonely Planet, also includes advice on travel health for younger children.

Health Insurance

Health insurance is essential for all travellers. While health care in Queensland is of a high standard and not overly expensive by international standards, considerable costs can build up if you require medical care, and repatriation is extremely expensive. Find out in advance if your insurance plan will make payments directly to providers or reimburse you later for overseas health expenditures. If your health insurance doesn't cover you for medical expenses abroad, consider purchasing some extra insurance.

Recommended Vaccinations

Proof of yellow fever vaccination is required only from travellers entering Australia within six days of having visited a yellow-fever-infected country. For a full list of these countries, visit the website of the **World Health Organization** (WHO; www.who.int) or that of the **Centers for Disease Control and Prevention** (CDC; wwwnc.cdc.gov/travel).

The WHO recommends that all travellers be vaccinated for diphtheria, tetanus, measles, mumps, rubella, chickenpox and polio, as well as hepatitis B, regardless of their destination.

Tap Water

Tap water is generally quite safe to drink – but not always delicious – anywhere in Queensland. In recent years, there have been rare failures of water-treatment plants in Far North Queensland, and locals were advised to boil tap water due to contamination fears. It's best to inquire locally about tap-water safety.

Water taken directly from streams, rivers and lakes should be treated before drinking.

Insurance

Don't underestimate the importance of a good travel-insurance policy that covers theft, loss and medical problems – nothing will ruin your holiday plans quicker than an accident or having that brand-new digital camera stolen. There are a wide variety of policies available, so compare the small print.

Some policies specifically exclude designated 'dangerous activities' such as scuba diving, parasailing, bungee jumping, motorcycling, skiing and even bushwalking. If you plan on doing any of these activities, make sure the policy you choose fully covers you.

You may prefer a policy that pays doctors or hospitals directly rather than you having to pay on the spot and claim later. If you have to claim later, make sure you keep all documentation. Some policies ask you to call back (reverse charge or collect) to a centre in your home country, where an immediate assessment of your condition is made. Check that the policy covers ambulances and emergency medical evacuations by air.

Worldwide travel insurance is available at www.lonelyplanet.com/travel_services. You can buy, extend and claim online anytime – even if you're already on the road.

For information on car insurance, see p473.

Internet Access

Internet is relatively accessible in Queensland. Typical costs for casual use are around $6 per hour. Many hostels, B&Bs and hotels offering guest terminals with internet access are identified in this book with an internet symbol (@).

Most public libraries have internet access, but generally there are a limited number of terminals and you need to book in advance (although they are the best option for towns in the outback). You'll find internet cafes in cities, sizeable towns and pretty much anywhere that travellers congregate.

Wireless access is widespread throughout the state, and common in cities and large towns. We've indicated places that offer access (either free or paid) with the 📶 symbol. Unfortunately, free access is rare and most hot spots require you to buy credit (with a credit card) before use – though some hotels, motels and caravan parks may provide free access (others may charge as much as $20 for 24 hours). Most libraries offer free wi-fi access.

Telstra, Optus, Vodafone and other big carriers sell mobile broadband devices with USB connectivity that work with most laptops and allow you to get online just about anywhere in the country. Prices are around $80 for 30 days of access, including up to 2GB of data.

Legal Matters

Drinking & Driving

Australia is very strict when it comes to drinking and driving – or driving while under the influence of drugs. There is a significant police presence on the roads, with the power to stop you and ask to see your licence (you're required to carry it), check your vehicle for roadworthiness and ask you to take a breath test for alcohol.

The legal limit is 0.05 blood alcohol concentration. Swab drug testing is also common. If you're over, or test positive to illegal drugs, you'll be in serious trouble, facing a fine of anywhere from a few hundred dollars to $3300 and a suspension of licence.

Drugs & Overstaying a Visa

First offenders caught with small amounts of illegal drugs are likely to receive a fine rather than go to jail, but the recording of a conviction may affect visa status. Speaking of which, if you remain in Australia beyond the life of your visa, you will officially be an 'overstayer' and could face detention and expulsion, and then be prevented from returning to Australia for up to three years.

Maps

The **Royal Automobile Club of Queensland** (RACQ; www.racq.com.au) publishes a good series of regional road maps that show almost every drivable road in the state – these are free to RACQ members and to members of affiliated motoring organisations. You can also plan your route using its online trip planner. There are also plenty of good road maps for sale at service stations.

Queensland's Department of Environment and Resource Management produces the Sunmap series, which, together with commercial maps by companies including Hema, Gregory's and UBD, are available from most newsagents and many bookshops in Queensland. **World Wide Maps & Guides** (www.worldwidemaps.com.au; Shop 30, Anzac Sq, 267 Edward St, Brisbane) has one of the best selections of maps in the state.

For bushwalking and other activities that require large-scale maps, the topographic sheets put out by **Geoscience Australia** (☎1800 800 173; www.ga.gov.au) are the ones to get.

Money

In this book all prices given in dollars refer to Australian dollars. Exchange rates are listed on p15. ATMs are prominent throughout Queensland and are the best way to get local currency. MasterCard and Visa are widely accepted. You can use debit cards at most retail outlets, which carry Eftpos (Electronic Funds Transfer at Point of Sale) facilities.

You can change foreign currency or travellers cheques at most banks throughout Queensland and at foreign exchange counters such as Travelex or Amex, found in major cities. American Express, Thomas Cook and other well-known international brands of travellers cheques are all widely accepted. Tipping is not common in Australia.

Photography & Video

Digital cameras and gear are widely available at electronics shops and department stores across the state. For tips on shooting images, see Lonely Planet's *Travel Photography: A Guide to Taking Better Pictures*.

Cheap, disposable underwater cameras are widely available at most beach towns and resorts. These are OK for snapshots when snorkelling or shallow diving and can produce reasonable results in good conditions, but without a flash the colours will be washed out. These cameras won't work below about 5m because of the water pressure. If you're serious about underwater photography, good underwater cameras with flash units can be hired from many of the dive shops along the coast.

As in any country, politeness goes a long way when taking photographs; ask before taking pictures of people. Indigenous Australians generally do not like to have their photograph taken, even from a distance.

Post

Australia Post (www.auspost.com.au) is efficient and reasonably cheap. Posting standard letters or postcards within the country costs 60 cents. The international rate for airmail letters up to 50g is $2.20; postcards cost $1.45.

Public Holidays

New Year's Day 1 January
Australia Day 26 January
Easter (Good Friday to Easter Monday inclusive) March or April
Anzac Day 25 April
Labour Day First Monday in May
Queen's Birthday Second Monday in June
Royal Queensland Show Mid-August, Brisbane only
Christmas Day 25 December
Boxing Day 26 December

School Holidays

Key times when prices are highest and many accommodation options are booked out well in advance:

» Christmas holiday season (mid-December to late January)
» Easter (March or April)
» Shorter (two-week) school-holiday periods generally fall in mid-April, late June to mid-July, and late September to mid-October

Safe Travel

Queensland is a relatively safe place to visit, but it's better to play it safe and take reasonable precautions.

The Gold Coast is notorious for car crime, and more than a few travellers have lost all their belongings from locked vehicles in public car parks. The golden rule is to never leave valuables in your car. A steering wheel lock is also a worthwhile investment.

Most accommodation places have somewhere they can store your valuables.

Telephone

To make a reverse-charge (collect) call within Australia, dial ☎1800 REVERSE/1800 738 3773 from any public or private phone. Toll-free numbers (prefix ☎1800) can be called free of charge. Calls to numbers beginning with ☎13 or ☎1300 are charged at the rate of a local call.

Mobile Phones

Local numbers with the prefix ☎04xx belong to mobile phones. Brisbane and coastal towns get good reception, but it can be haphazard or nonexistent in the interior.

Australia's digital network is compatible with GSM 900 and 1800 (used in Europe), but generally not with networks in the USA or Japan. It's easy and cheap enough to get connected short-term, as the main service providers (Telstra, Optus and Vodafone) all have prepaid mobile systems. In more remote areas, Telstra is often the only provider with service – though in some areas, such as the Daintree, the remote north and the outback – there is simply no service.

To get connected, just buy a starter kit, which may include a phone. If you have your own phone, buy a SIM card (under $10) and a prepaid charge card. Purchase recharge cards at convenience stores and newsagents.

Phone Codes

To call overseas from Australia, dial ☎0011 or ☎0018, the country code and the area code (without the initial zero). So for a London number you'd dial ☎0011-44-171, then the number. If dialling Queensland from overseas, the country code is ☎61, and you need to drop the zero in the ☎07 area code.

INTERNATIONAL VISITORS

Entering the Region

Before leaving for Australia, make sure you have your visa in order. Arriving in Australia is a straightforward affair, just be mindful not to bring in any food or contraband. If you plan to drive in Australia, you can use your own driving licence, as long as it's in English – if not, you'll need an International Driving Permit along with it.

Customs Regulations

For comprehensive information on customs regulations, contact the **Australian Customs Service** (www.customs.gov.au). When entering Australia you can bring in most articles free of duty provided that customs is satisfied they're for personal use and you'll be taking them with you when you leave. Australia's duty-free quota:

» 2.25L alcohol
» 250 cigarettes
» dutiable goods up to the value of $900 per person

Prohibited goods include drugs (all medicines must be declared) and food – Australia is very strict on this, so declare all food items, even leftover edibles taken from the plane.

Practicalities

» Videos use the PAL system.

» Plugs have angled pins. The voltage is 220V to 240V; 50Hz.

» The *Courier-Mail* is Queensland's daily newspaper; the *Australian* is the national daily newspaper.

» The metric system is used for weights and measures.

» Between 2010 and 2013 Australia is switching from analogue to digital television. Free-to-air TV offers the government-sponsored, ad-free ABC, multicultural SBS and three commercial stations – Seven, Nine and Ten. These five networks offer several secondary digital channels as well.

Visas

All visitors to Australia need a visa. Only New Zealand nationals are exempt; they receive a 'special category' visa on arrival.

Visa application forms are available from Australian diplomatic missions overseas, travel agents and the **Department of Immigration and Citizenship** (DIAC; www.immi.gov.au). For working-holiday visas, see p466.

SHORT-TERM TOURIST VISAS

For stays of less than three months (working not allowed), the most straightforward visa is the short-term tourist visa. Where to apply and how much it costs depends on your citizenship. Visitors from the USA, Canada, Japan, South Korea, Hong Kong, Singapore, Malaysia and Brunei should apply for an **Electronic Travel Authority** (ETA; www.eta.immi.gov.au). The cost is $20 and it can be done online. Approval is rapid – usually within 12 hours. Travel agents and airlines can also submit ETA applications. Visitors from the UK and European nations should apply for an **eVisitor** (www.immi.gov.au). This visa is free and can be rapidly obtained online.

OTHER VISAS

If you're from a country not covered by ETA or eVisitor, or you want to stay longer than three months, you'll need to apply for a **tourist visa, subclass 676**. Standard visas (which cost $105) allow one entry (or in some cases multiple entries) and stays of up to three, six or 12 months.

VISA EXTENSIONS

Visitors are allowed a maximum stay of 12 months, including extensions. Visa extensions are made through DIAC and it's best to apply at least two or three weeks before your visa expires. The application fee is currently $255 – it's nonrefundable, even if your application is rejected.

Useful codes in Australia:

STATE/ TERRITORY	AREA CODE
Queensland	☎07
Australian Capital Territory, New South Wales	☎02
Northern Territory, South Australia & Western Australia	☎08
Tasmania, Victoria	☎03

Phonecards

Purchase phonecards at newsagents and post offices. You can use them with public or private phones by dialling a toll-free access number and then the PIN on the card. Some public phones also accept credit cards.

Time

Australia is divided into three time zones:

» **Eastern Standard Time** (EST; Greenwich Mean Time plus 10 hours) Used in the Australian Capital Territory (ACT), New South Wales (NSW), Queensland, Tasmania and Victoria

» **Central Standard Time** (half-hour behind EST) Used in the Northern Territory and South Australia

» **Western Standard Time** (two hours behind EST) Used in Western Australia

Queensland remains on EST all year, while most other states switch to daylight-saving time in summer. From around October through March, Queensland is one hour behind NSW, Victoria and Tasmania.

Tourist Information

Information posts are widespread in Queensland, and you could easily drown yourself in brochures, booklets, maps and leaflets. Keep in mind that some tourist information places are also booking agents and will steer you towards the tour that will pay them the best commission.

There are official tourist offices in just about every city and town in Queensland, staffed largely by friendly and knowledgable volunteers.

Australian Tourist Commission (www.australia.com) National organisation with information in over 15 languages.

Queensland Parks & Wildlife Service (www.derm.qld.gov.au) Provides information on conservation areas throughout the state, including national parks.

Tourism Queensland (www.queenslandholidays.com.au) This government-run body offers a website stacked with information, from accommodation options to diving the Great Barrier Reef.

Travellers with Disabilities

Disability awareness in Australia is pretty high and getting higher. Legislation requires that new accommodation meet accessibility standards, and discrimination by tourism operators is illegal. Many of Queensland's key attractions provide access for those with limited mobility, and a number of sites have also begun to address the needs of visitors with visual or aural impairments; contact attractions in advance to confirm the facilities available for people with disabilities.

Tour operators with accessible vehicles operate from most major cities. Travellers with disabilities with some form of identification are often eligible for concession prices.

There are a number of organisations that can supply information for travellers with disabilities visiting Queensland:

Accessible Tourism Website (www.australiaforall.com) Good site for tourists with disabilities to obtain accessibility information.

Disability Information Service (☎1800 177 120, TTY 1800 010 222; www.communities.qld.gov.au/disability) Provides information on disability services and support throughout Queensland.

National Disability Services (☎3357 4188; www.nds.org.au) The national industry association for disability services; a good place to start for information.

Spinal Injuries Association (☎3391 2044; www.spinal.com.au) In Brisbane; another useful resource.

Wheelie Easy (☎4091 4876; www.wheelieeasy.com.au) This company runs specialised tours in Far North Queensland for travellers with impaired mobility. It also has useful information about Cairns. See p93 for more information.

Volunteering

The following places have volunteering opportunities:

Atherton Tableland (p341) Rescue and rehabilitation of fruit bats, eagles and other bird species.

Lizard Island Research Station (p385) One- to two-week volunteer opportunities to help researchers studying marine ecology and seabirds.

Daintree Rainforest (p373) Forest rehabilitation and planting for volunteers (one-week minimum).

Women Travellers

Queensland is generally a safe place for women travellers, although it's probably best to avoid walking alone late at night. Sexual harassment is rare, although the Aussie male culture does have its sexist elements.

Some women have reported problems at party hostels on the Gold Coast. If you're out on the town, always keep enough money aside for a taxi back to your accommodation. The same applies for outback and rural towns, where there are often a lot of unlit, semideserted streets between you and your temporary home. When the pubs and bars close and there are inebriated people roaming around, it's not a great time to be out and about.

Lone women should also be wary of staying in basic pub accommodation unless it looks safe and well managed.

Lone female hitchers are tempting fate – while hitching with a male companion is safer, hitching is never entirely safe in any country in the world, and we don't recommend it.

Work

Finding Work

Some of the backpacker hostels in Brisbane have job boards with notices of available employment, while many of the bigger hostels have job clubs that aim to find work for guests. Telemarketing, door-to-door sales and table waiting are the most common jobs.

If you're in Brisbane and happy with bar work or waiting on tables, the best advice may be to go knocking on doors in Fortitude Valley or New Farm. Many places want staff for longer than three months, though, so it may take a bit of footwork to find a willing employer. The *Courier-Mail* has daily Situations Vacant listings – Wednesday and Saturday are the best days to look.

Harvest work is popular elsewhere in Queensland. The main spots are Bundaberg, Childers, Stanthorpe, Bowen, Tully and Innisfail, where everything from avocados to zucchini is harvested almost year round and hostels specialise in finding travellers work. The **National Harvest Labour Information Service** (www.jobsearch.gov.au/harvesttrail) is a good source of information on where to pick up seasonal work.

Other useful websites:

Australian Job Search (www.jobsearch.gov.au)

Career One (www.careerone.com.au)

Seek (www.seek.com.au)

Working Holiday Visas

Visitors aged 18 to 30 years old from Canada, Denmark, France, Germany, Hong Kong, Ireland, Japan, Korea, the Netherlands, Sweden, the UK and the USA are eligible for a working-holiday visa, which allows you to visit for up to 12 months and gain casual employment. Two visa options are available for those wishing to obtain a working-holiday visa in Australia: subclass 417 and subclass 462. Check out www.immi.gov.au for more information, including application fees and eligibility requirements, or to apply online.

Working-holiday visa holders may be eligible to apply for a second 12-month working-holiday visa if they have done at least three months of 'specified work' (including harvest work, fishing, pearling, mining and construction) in regional Australia. Working-holiday visa holders are only supposed to work for any one employer for a maximum of three months.

Transport

GETTING THERE & AWAY

All flights from Europe make a stop in Asia, usually in Bangkok, Hong Kong, Singapore or Kuala Lumpur. Flights into Australia are heavily booked during the European and US summer holidays and at Christmas time. Flights, tours and rail tickets can be booked online at lonelyplanet.com/bookings.

Air

International

Many international flights head to Sydney or Melbourne before flying to Queensland, but Brisbane receives a growing number of direct international flights. Cairns has some Asia and New Zealand flights, as does Coolangatta airport on the Gold Coast.

Because of Australia's size and diverse climate, any time of the year can prove busy for inbound tourists – if you plan to fly during a particularly popular period (Christmas, for example) or on a particularly popular route (such as via Hong Kong, Bangkok or Singapore), make your arrangements well in advance.

Brisbane Airport (http://bne.com.au)

Cairns Airport (www.cairnsairport.com)

Gold Coast Aiport (www.goldcoastairport.com.au)

Australia's national carrier is **Qantas** (www.qantas.com), which has an exemplary safety record.

TICKETS

Round-the-world tickets can be a good option for getting to Australia.

For online bookings, try the following:

Airbrokers (www.airbrokers.com) US company specialising in round-the-world tickets.

Cheap Flights (www.cheapflights.com) Flight searches from the USA and other regions.

Cheapest Flights (www.cheapestflights.co.uk) Cheap worldwide flights from the UK.

Kayak (www.kayak.com) Best site in US for finding flight deals.

Opodo (www.opodo.com) Pan-European company with UK, German and French sites.

Orbitz (www.orbitz.com) Excellent site for web-only fares for US airlines.

Travel Online (www.travelonline.co.nz) Good place to check worldwide flights from New Zealand.

Travel.com.au (www.travel.com.au) Probably one of the best Australian sites; look up fares and flights into and out of the country.

Roundtheworld.com (www.roundtheworldflights.com) This excellent site allows you to build your own trips from the UK with up to six stops.

CLIMATE CHANGE & TRAVEL

Every form of transport that relies on carbon-based fuel generates CO_2, the main cause of human-induced climate change. Modern travel is dependent on aeroplanes, which might use less fuel per kilometre per person than most cars but travel much greater distances. The altitude at which aircraft emit gases (including CO_2) and particles also contributes to their climate change impact. Many websites offer 'carbon calculators' that allow people to estimate the carbon emissions generated by their journey and, for those who wish to do so, to offset the impact of the greenhouse gases emitted with contributions to portfolios of climate-friendly initiatives throughout the world. Lonely Planet offsets the carbon footprint of all staff and author travel.

QANTAS AIRPASS

International travellers planning to visit more than a few destinations in Australia should have a look at the Qantas **Aussie Airpass**, allowing travel to up to three cities for a heavily discounted price. The Qantas **Walkabout Pass** allows visitors to customise their itinerary, visiting major destinations at set prices across the country (including the following in Queensland: Brisbane, Cairns, Gold Coast, Hamilton Island, Mackay, Maroochydore, Rockhampton and Townsville). The catch is that the itinerary must include a Qantas international flight, and all itineraries must be booked together.

The fee structure places all flights into three zones: flights within one zone are $58 (US$59) for each leg of the journey; flights between zones are $117 (US$119). One zone comprises Queensland, New South Wales, South Australia, Tasmania and the Australian Capital Territory (ACT). Zones two and three include Western Australia and the Northern Territory.

Zuji (www.zuji.com.au) Good Asia Pacific–based site.

Land

Border Crossings

Travelling overland to Queensland from elsewhere in Australia will really give you an impression of just how big this country is. The journey from Brisbane to the nearest state capital, Sydney, is a torturous 1030km, and the journey from Brisbane to Cairns, the next biggest city in Queensland, covers 1700km! To give you a sense of scale, Melbourne is 1735km away from Brisbane, Adelaide is 2130km distant, Perth is a mere 4390km away, and the shortest route to Darwin covers 3495km.

The Pacific Hwy is the main access point into Queensland from the south, crossing the border at Tweed Heads and Coolangatta. It runs along the coast between Sydney and Brisbane and passes through a number of popular tourist spots and some great scenery. A lesser-used route from the south is the New England Hwy, which crosses the border at Tenterfield. It's a quieter, longer inland route from Sydney, and the road is the undisputed territory of road trains (a string of trailers pulled by a semitrailer) and kangaroos at night.

The Newell Hwy is the most direct route to Brisbane from Melbourne or Adelaide. It's a good road through the heart of rural New South Wales (NSW), crossing the border at Goondiwindi, before becoming the Leichhardt and Gore Hwys.

The other major route into southern Queensland is the Mitchell Hwy. It crosses the border at Barringun and links Bourke in outback NSW with Charleville in outback Queensland. In the state's far west, the Birdsville Track crosses the South Australian–Queensland border at Birdsville. This road is in various stages of being paved but a 4WD is still recommended.

For those wanting to travel further into the outback, have a look at Lonely Planet's *Central Australia (Adelaide to Darwin)*.

The main road from the west is the Barkly Hwy, which crosses the NT–Queensland border around 15km west of Camooweal and cuts across to Mt Isa. From Mt Isa, you can continue eastward along the Flinders Hwy to Townsville on the coast, or head southeast along the Landsborough (Matilda) Hwy towards Brisbane.

See p471 for information on road rules, driving conditions and buying and renting vehicles.

GETTING AROUND

Air

Queensland is well serviced by airlines. The following regional carriers access these locations from within Queensland:

Hinterland Aviation (☎4035 9323; www.hinterlandaviation.com.au) Flies daily (except Sundays) between Cairns and Cooktown.

Jetstar (☎13 15 38; www.jetstar.com.au) Flies between Brisbane and many coastal destinations, as well as Hamilton Island.

Qantas (☎13 13 13; www.qantas.com.au) Flies to over two-dozen locations in Queensland, including Brisbane, Cairns, Townsville, Mt Isa, Hamilton Island and Horn Island.

Skytrans (☎1300 759 872; www.skytrans.com.au) Serves northern Queensland, flying from Cairns to Bamaga (Tip of Australia) and Mt Isa among other (more obscure) locations.

Tiger Airways (☎03-9335 3033; www.tigerairways.com) Flies from Melbourne to Brisbane, the Gold Coast and a few other Queensland destinations.

Virgin Blue (☎13 67 89; www.virginblue.com.au) Flies between Brisbane and many coastal destinations, as well as Hamilton Island.

Bicycle

Queensland can be a good place for cycling, although you need to choose your areas. There are bike tracks in most cities, but in the country they're variable. Roads such as the Bruce Hwy, from Brisbane to Cairns, can be long, hot and not particularly safe, as there are limited verges and heavy traffic. The humid weather can be draining too. The best areas for touring are probably the Gold Coast hinterland, the Sunshine Coast secondary roads and the area north of Cairns.

Bicycle helmets are compulsory, as are front and rear lights for night riding; you can receive an on-the-spot fine if you don't follow these regulations.

Cycling has always been popular in Australia, and not only as a sport: some shearers would ride for huge distances between jobs rather than use less reliable horses. It's rare to find a reasonable-sized town that doesn't have a shop stocking at least basic bike parts.

If you're coming specifically to cycle, it makes sense to bring your own bike. Check with your airline for costs and the degree of dismantling/packing required. Within Australia you can load your bike onto a bus or train to skip the boring bits of road. Note that bus companies require you to dismantle your bike, and some don't guarantee that it will travel on the same bus as you. Trains are easier, but you should supervise the loading and, if possible, tie your bike upright, otherwise you may find that the guard has stacked crates of spare tyres on your fragile alloy wheels.

Many towns in the east were established as staging posts, a day's horse ride apart, which is pretty convenient if you want a pub meal and a bed at the end of a day's riding. Camping is another option, and it's usually warm enough that you won't need a bulky sleeping bag. You can get by with standard road maps, but as you'll probably want to avoid both the highways and the low-grade, unsealed roads, the government map series is best.

Remember that you need to maintain your body as well as your bike. Exercise is an appetite suppressant, so stock up on carbohydrates at regular intervals, even if you don't feel that hungry. Drink plenty of water: dehydration is no joke and can be life-threatening. Summer in Queensland isn't a great time for cycling. It can get very hot and incredibly humid, and torrential downpours that are commonplace during the Wet.

Of course, you don't have to follow the larger roads and visit towns. It's possible to fill your mountain bike's panniers with muesli, head out into the mulga and not see anyone for weeks (or ever again – outback travel is very risky if not properly planned). Water is the main problem, and you can't rely on it being available where there aren't settlements, whatever your map may say.

Always check with locals if you're heading into remote areas, and notify the police if you're about to do something particularly adventurous. That said, you can't rely too much on local knowledge of road conditions – most people have no idea about what a heavily loaded touring bike is like to ride. What they think of as a great road may be pedal-deep in sand or bull dust, and cyclists have happily ridden along roads that were officially flooded out.

Bicycle Queensland (☎3844 1144; www.bq.org.au) is worth contacting for more information. Additionally, the Queensland Department of Transport has an informative website, including road rules, maps and other resources. Click onto www.transport.qld.gov.au/cycling.

Some of the better bike shops can also be good sources of information on routes, suggested rides, tours and cycling events. For more information on seeing Australia from two wheels, check out Lonely Planet's *Cycling Australia*.

Hire

It is possible to hire touring bikes and equipment from a few of the commercial touring organisations. You can also hire mountain bikes from bike shops in many cities, although these are usually for short-term hire (around $20 to $30 a day).

Purchase

If you want to buy a good steel-framed mountain bike that will be able to endure touring, you'll need to spend from $600 up to $1500. You'll also need to add equipment, including panniers, and a bike helmet, which can increase your expenditure to upwards of $1700.

Secondhand bikes are worth checking out in the cities, as are the post-Christmas sales and midyear stocktakes, when newish cycles can be heavily discounted.

Good websites for reselling your bike include the following:

Bike Exchange (www.bikeexchange.com.au)

Gumtree (www.gumtree.com.au)

Trading Post (www.tradingpost.com.au)

Bus

Queensland's bus network is reliable, but not always the cheapest way to get around; it requires planning if you intend to diverge very far from the coast. Most long-distance buses are equipped with air-con, toilets and videos, and all are smoke-free zones. The smallest towns eschew formal bus terminals for a single drop-off/pick-up point, usually outside a post office, a newsagent or a shop.

Bus Companies & Routes

Greyhound Australia (☎1300 473 946; www.greyhound.com.au) Queensland's most extensive network, servicing the coast from Coolangatta to Cairns, as well as inland to Toowoomba; it also has a route from Townsville to Mt Isa. Has interstate services to the NT and NSW.

Premier Motor Service (☎13 34 10; www.premierms.com.au) Popular Brisbane-to-Cairns route that has fewer services per day but typically costs less than Greyhound.

Coachtrans (☎3358 9700; www.coachtrans.com.au) Runs between Brisbane and Surfers Paradise or Coolangatta/Tweed Heads on the Gold Coast. Also services the Sunshine Coast and Byron Bay, NSW.

Coral Reef Coaches (☎4098 2800; www.coralreefcoaches.com.au) Runs from Cairns to popular destinations on the way north to Cape Tribulation.

Country Road Coachlines (☎4045 2794; www.countryroadcoachlines.com.au) Runs three times weekly from Cairns to Cooktown on the inland (via Mareeba) and coastal (via Cape Tribulation) routes.

Crisps Coaches (☎3236 5266; www.crisps.com.au) Has extensive services throughout the Darling Downs area, with services from Brisbane to Toowoomba, Stanthorpe and south to Tenterfield in NSW.

Paradise Coaches of Rockhampton (☎4933 1127; www.paradisecoaches.com.au) Runs from Rockhampton to Emerald and Longreach, and between Emerald and Mackay.

Sun Palm (☎4087 2900; www.sunpalmtransport.com) Operates services between Cairns, Port Douglas, Mossman and Cape Tribulation, as well as southern routes as far south as Tully, including Mission Beach.

Veolia (☎1300 826 608; www.vtb.com.au) Has an express service from Brisbane to Noosa twice daily.

See the Getting There & Away and Getting Around sections in the destination chapters for information on fares.

Backpacker Buses

Several party tour buses operate along the coast, stopping at sights and pubs along the way and checking into big party hostels each night.

These trips are economically priced and will get you from A to B, and can be more fun than conventional buses: the buses are usually smaller and you'll meet other travellers – but you may not see much of Australia except through the bottom of a glass. **Oz Experience** (☎1800 555 287; www.ozexperience.com) is the main player.

Bus Passes

Greyhound offers the following passes that can save you a significant amount of money if bus travel is going to be your main mode of transport over a decent chunk of time (for example, four or more weeks):

Kilometre Pass Gives you go-anywhere flexibility, including the choice to backtrack; choose 500km to 20,000km.

Mini Traveller Pass Allows up to 90 days to travel from Sydney to Cairns ($350), stopping as often as you like. Cairns to Darwin, NT, is $381.

Explorer Pass Set routes that contain a slice of Queensland including Aussie Coast & Red Centre (which takes in towns such as Airlie Beach and Cairns, as well as Alice Springs and Kakadu for $1301 ex-Cairns; valid 183 days) and the Central Coaster between Sydney and Brisbane ($211; valid for 90 days).

Premier Motor Service also offers bus passes along the eastern coast, between Sydney and Cairns, which are slightly less expensive than Greyhound's.

ONE-WAY BUS FARES

ROUTE	FARE ($)	DURATION (HR)
Airlie Beach–Townsville	70	4½
Brisbane–Cairns	310	29
Brisbane–Hervey Bay	75	5½
Cairns–Mt Isa	233	19
Hervey Bay–Rockhampton	95	5½
Mackay–Airlie Beach	38	2
Rockhampton–Mackay	73	5
Townsville–Cairns	81	5½

For most travel, you can expect a 10% discount for members of the Youth Hostel Association (YHA), VIP Backpackers, Nomads and other approved organisations, as well as card-carrying seniors/pensioners.

Reservations

Over summer, school holidays and public holidays, you should book well ahead on the more popular routes, including intercity and coastal services. At other times you should have few problems getting a seat on your preferred service. But if your long-term travel plans rely on catching a particular bus, book at least a day or two ahead just to be safe.

You should make a reservation at least a day in advance if you're using a Greyhound pass.

Car & Motorcycle

Queensland is a big, sprawling state and among the locals driving is the accepted means of getting from A to B. More and more travellers are also finding it the best way to see the country. With three or four people the costs are reasonable and the benefits many, provided, of course, that you don't have a major mechanical problem.

In fact, if you want to get off the beaten track – and in parts of Queensland the track is *very* beaten – then having your own transport is the only way to go, as many of the destinations covered in this book aren't accessible by public transport.

Motorcycles are another popular way of getting around. Between April and November the climate is just about ideal for biking around Queensland and you can bush camp just about anywhere.

Bringing your own motorcycle into Australia will entail an expensive shipping exercise, valid registration in the country of origin and a *Carnet De Passages en Douane*. This is an internationally recognised customs document that allows the holder to import their vehicle without paying customs duty or taxes. To get one, apply to a motoring organisation/association in your home country. You'll also need a rider's licence and a helmet.

The long, open roads are really made for large-capacity machines above 750cc, which Australians prefer once they outgrow their 250cc learner restrictions.

The **Department of Transport and Main Roads** (☎13 23 80; www.tmr.qld.gov.au) is the Queensland government body in charge of roads. It provides a wealth of free information on Australian road rules and conditions, and downloadable brochures including the extremely useful *Guide to Queensland Roads*, which includes distance charts, road maps and other helpful information.

For more advice on driving in the outback check out www.exploroz.com.

ROAD DISTANCES (KM)

	Airlie Beach	Brisbane	Bundaberg	Cairns	Cape York	Hervey Bay	Mackay	Mission Beach	Mt Isa	Noosa Heads	Rockhampton	Surfers Paradise
Brisbane	1114											
Bundaberg	770	362										
Cairns	633	1699	1356									
Cape York	1580	2648	2304	949								
Hervey Bay	877	291	124	1463	2411							
Mackay	149	968	623	735	1683	730						
Mission Beach	520	1588	1244	139	1087	1351	623					
Mt Isa	1131	1827	1612	1111	1492	1719	1234	1137				
Noosa Heads	1011	138	259	1598	2545	188	865	1485	1821			
Rockhampton	482	633	288	1068	2016	395	336	956	1333	529		
Surfers Paradise	1197	79	445	1784	2731	374	1051	1671	1881	221	715	
Townsville	288	1356	1011	349	1297	1118	391	237	905	1253	724	1439

These are the shortest distances by road; other routes may be considerably longer. For distances by coach, check the companies' leaflets.

Driving Licence

You can use your own foreign driving licence in Australia, as long as it is in English (if it's not, a translation must be carried). If you're buying a car and want comprehensive insurance, you'll need an international licence or Australian driving licence.

Hire

Competition between car-hire firms can be pretty fierce, so rates are flexible and special deals pop up all the time. However you travel on the long stretches, it can be very useful to have a car for local travel.

You must be at least 21 years old to hire from most firms because car-hire companies cannot obtain insurance for people younger than this. If you are 20 years or under, however, and you want to rent a car, certain companies will oblige, but you will need to obtain an original insurance certificate of currency from an insurance company, which will indemnify the car-hire company in the event of an accident. Regardless of your age, you will also require a credit card in order to leave a bond for the car. You may be able to get around this with some rental agencies by leaving a wad of cash, but you're looking at a security deposit of several hundred dollars and upwards. See p473 for important information regarding insurance.

A small car costs between $30 and $50 per day to hire, depending on the length of your rental. A sedan that will seat a family of four comfortably generally costs between $50 and $75 per day. Rates become cheaper if you take a car for a week or more.

Major companies with offices throughout Queensland:

Avis (www.avis.com.au)
Budget (www.budget.com.au)
Europcar (www.europcar.com.au)
Hertz (www.hertz.com.au)
Thrifty (www.thrifty.com.au)

Smaller companies that often have great deals:

Abel Rent A Car (www.abel.com.au) Based in Brisbane.
Bargain Wheels (www.bargainwheels.com.au) Searches local hire companies for the best deals.
East Coast (www.eastcoastcarrentals.com.au) Some of Queensland's best prices; offices in Brisbane, Cairns and the Gold Coast.

4WD VEHICLES

Having a 4WD enables you to get right off the beaten track and out to some of the natural wonders in the wilderness and the outback that most travellers don't see.

Renting a 4WD is within the scope of a reasonable budget if a few people share the cost. Something small like a Suzuki costs around $120 per day; for a Toyota Land Cruiser you're looking at around $170, which should include insurance and some free kilometres (typically 100km per day, although unlimited kilometres are common in the far north and outback though). Check the insurance conditions, especially the excesses, as they can be onerous – in Queensland $4000 is typical, although this can often be reduced to around $1000 on payment of an additional daily charge (around $30). Even for 4WDs most insurance does not cover damage caused when travelling 'off-road'.

Britz (www.britz.com.au) is among the most reputable 4WD-hire outfits. Hertz and Avis have 4WD rentals, with one-way rentals possible between the eastern states and the NT. Budget also rents 4WDs from Darwin and Alice Springs.

CAMPERVANS

Campervan hire is extremely popular in Australia. There are several major hire nationwide outfits, and you'll find branches in Cairns, Brisbane and other major cities. One-way hire between certain destinations incur a surcharge of around $200. Reliable companies:

Britz Australia (☎1800 331 454; www.britz.com.au)

RACQ

If you decide to purchase a car, it's well worth joining the **Royal Automobile Club of Queensland** (RACQ; ☎13 19 05; www.racq.com.au). The RACQ offers emergency breakdown cover for $74 per year, which will get you prompt roadside assistance and a tow to a reputable garage if the problem can't be fixed on the spot. Membership gives reciprocal cover with the equivalent automobile associations in other states, and with similar organisations overseas, for example the AAA in the USA or the RAC or AA in the UK.

The RACQ also produces a particularly useful set of regional maps of Queensland, which are free to members. Its offices sell a wide range of travel and driving products, including good maps and travel guidebooks; book tours and accommodation; and provide advice on weather and road conditions. It can arrange additional insurance on top of your compulsory third-party personal liability cover, and give general guidelines about buying a car.

Camperman Australia (☎1800 216 223; www.campermanaustralia.com.au)

Jucy (☎1800 150 850; www.jucy.com.au) In Brisbane and Cairns.

Travellers Auto Barn (☎1800 674 374; www.travellers-autobarn.com.au) Hire or sales.

Wicked Campervans (☎1800 246 869; www.wickedcampers.com.au)

Insurance

In Queensland, third-party personal-injury insurance is always included in the cost of vehicle registration. This ensures that every registered vehicle carries at least the minimum insurance. You'd be wise to extend that minimum to include third-party property insurance as well – minor collisions with other vehicles can be amazingly expensive.

When it comes to hire cars, know exactly what your liability is in the event of an accident. Rather than risk paying out thousands of dollars if you do have an accident, you can take out your own comprehensive insurance on the car, or (the usual option) pay an additional daily amount to the rental company for an 'insurance excess reduction' policy. This brings the amount of excess you must pay in the event of an accident down from between $2000 and $5000 to a few hundred dollars.

Be aware that if you're travelling on dirt roads you will not be covered by insurance even if you have a 4WD – in other words, if you have an accident you'll be liable for all the costs involved. Also, most companies' insurance won't cover the cost of damage to glass (including the windscreen) or tyres. Always read the small print.

Purchase

Australian cars are not cheap (a result of the small population) but secondhand prices can be quite acceptable, particularly if split between several travellers. If you're buying a secondhand vehicle, reliability is all important. Breakdowns in the outback can be inconvenient, expensive and downright dangerous – help could be very long in coming. It's also wise to buy a locally manufactured vehicle, such as a Holden Commodore or Ford Falcon, or one of the mainstream VW, Toyota, Mitsubishi or Nissan campervans. Life gets much simpler if you can get spare parts anywhere from Cairns to Cunnamulla.

When buying or selling a car in Queensland, the vehicle needs to be re-registered locally with Queensland Transport at the time of sale, for which the buyer and seller must complete a vehicle registration transfer application form, available from Queensland Transport or the RACQ. The seller will usually add the cost of any outstanding registration to the overall price of the vehicle. Before the vehicle can be offered for sale, the seller must also obtain a safety certificate from a Queensland Transport–approved vehicle-inspection station.

Stamp duty has to be paid when you buy a car and, as this is based on the purchase price (2% for hybrids, 3% for four-cylinder vehicles, 3.5% for six-cylinder vehicles and 4% for V8s), it's not unknown for buyer and seller to agree privately to understate the price. It's much easier to sell a car in the state in which it's registered, otherwise the

CAMPING ON WHEELS

Once the preserve of grey nomads and round-Australia backpackers, camper-vanning has exploded in recent years and nowhere more so than in Queensland. The advantages are obvious: a self-contained home on wheels, meaning transport, accommodation, usually cooking gear, and no mucking around with tents. It combines the freedom of camping with a level of comfort that's only limited by your budget – the biggest models are luxurious vehicles with toilets, showers, TVs and air-con.

Every town has at least one caravan park where you can find a site and plug into power. National parks usually have self-registration or prebook campsites. There are also lots of off-track free camping options – with a good map and a bit of planning you can always find a secluded spot.

Campervans start with budget two-berth vans. Seating folds down to a double bed and there's generally room for a basic gas stove and hand-pump sink. But there's usually no fridge, so storing food is a pain, and they're too cramped for extended trips. Next up are pop-top or hi-top campervans that can sleep three or four, have a gas stove, a watertank and a fridge, and plug into 240V power – economical and brilliant for a couple or a small family. From there you can go to a four- or five-berth campervan. Lots of companies hire out campervans, starting from less than $50 a day for small ones, and going up to $200 a day for the big ones, with discounts for long-term rentals. Make sure it comes with tables and chairs, cooking equipment, bedding and preferably an awning for shade.

buyer will eventually have to re-register it in the new state.

Shopping around for a used car involves the same rules as anywhere in the Western world. You'll probably get a car cheaper by buying through classifieds rather than through a dealer. Among other things, dealers are not required to give you a warranty when you buy a car in Queensland, regardless of cost.

BUY-BACK DEALS

One way of getting around the hassles of buying and selling a vehicle privately is to enter into a buy-back arrangement with a car or motorcycle dealer. But many dealers will find ways of knocking down the price when you return the vehicle – even if a price has been agreed upon in writing – often by pointing out spurious repairs that allegedly will be required to gain the dreaded safety certificate. The cars on offer have usually been driven around Australia a number of times, often with haphazard or minimal servicing, and are generally pretty tired. The main advantage of these schemes is that you don't have to worry about being able to sell the vehicle quickly at the end of your trip.

Road Conditions

Australia doesn't have the traffic volume to justify multilane highways, so most of the country relies on single-lane roads, which can be pretty frustrating if you're stuck behind a slow-moving caravan. Passing areas are usually only found on uphill sections or steep descents, so you may have to wait a long time for an opportunity to overtake.

There are a few sections of divided road, most notably on the Surfers Paradise–Brisbane road. Main roads are well surfaced and have regular rest stops and petrol stations.

You don't have to get very far off the beaten track to find yourself on dirt roads, though most are well maintained. A few useful spare parts are worth carrying. Also look out for the hybrid dirt road: a single, bidirectional strip of tarmac with dirt verges. It's okay to drive down the central strip but be ready to pull into the verges to pass oncoming traffic.

Between cities, signposting on the main highways is generally OK, but once you hit the back roads you'll need a good map – see p462 for suggestions.

Road Hazards

Many Australians avoid travelling altogether once the sun drops because of the risks posed by animals on the roads.

Kangaroos are common hazards on country roads, as are cows and sheep in the unfenced outback – hitting an animal of this size can make a real mess of your car and result in human casualties, depending on the speed at which you're travelling. Kangaroos are most active around dawn and dusk. They often travel in groups, so if you see one hopping across the road in front of you, slow right down, as its friends may be just behind it.

If you're travelling at night and an animal appears in front of you, hit the brakes, dip your lights (so you don't dazzle and confuse it) and only swerve if it's safe to do so – numerous people have been killed in accidents caused by swerving to miss animals.

Flooding can occur with little warning, especially in outback areas and the tropical north. Roads can be cut off for days during floods, and floodwaters sometimes wash away whole sections of road.

A not-so-obvious hazard is driver fatigue. Driving long distances (particularly in hot weather) can be so tiring that you might fall asleep at the wheel – it's not uncommon. So on a long haul, stop and rest every two hours or so – do some exercise, change drivers or have a coffee.

Motorcyclists need to beware of dehydration in the dry, hot air. Force yourself to drink plenty of water, even if you don't feel thirsty, and *never* ride at night: a road train can hit a kangaroo without stopping, but a motorcycle has no chance. Make sure you carry water – at least 2L on major roads in central Australia, more off the beaten track. And finally, if something does go hopelessly wrong in the back of beyond, park your bike where it's clearly visible and observe the cardinal rule – *don't leave your vehicle*.

Road Rules

Australians drive on the left-hand side of the road just like in the UK, Japan and some countries in South and East Asia and the Pacific.

There are a few variations to the rules of the road as applied elsewhere. The main one is the 'give way to the right' rule. This means that if you approach an unmarked intersection, traffic on your right has right of way. Most places do have marked intersections; Mt Isa doesn't!

The speed limit in towns and built-up areas is 50km/h or 60km/h, sometimes rising to 80km/h on the outskirts and dropping to 40km/h in residential areas and around schools. On the highway it's usually 100km/h or 110km/h, depending on the area.

The police have radar speed traps and speed cameras, and are fond of using them. When you're far from the cities and traffic is light, you'll see many vehicles moving a lot faster than 100km/h. Oncoming drivers who flash their lights at you may be giving you a friendly indication of a speed trap ahead (it's illegal to do so, by the way).

Wearing seat belts is compulsory, and small children must be restrained in an approved safety seat. Drink-driving is a real problem, especially in country areas. Serious attempts to reduce the resulting road toll are ongoing and random breath-tests are not uncommon in built-up areas. If you're caught with a blood-alcohol level of more than 0.05%, be prepared for a hefty fine and the loss of your licence.

Outback Travel

If you really want to see outback Queensland, there are lots of roads where the official recommendation is that you report to the police before you leave one end, and again when you arrive at the other. That way if you fail to turn up at your destination, the police can send out search parties.

Many of these roads can be attempted confidently in a conventional car, but you do need to be carefully prepared and to carry important spare parts. Backtracking 500km to pick up a replacement for some minor malfunctioning component or, much worse, to arrange a tow, is unlikely to be easy or cheap.

When travelling to really remote areas it's advisable to travel with a high-frequency outpost radio transmitter that is equipped to pick up the Royal Flying Doctor Service bases in the area. Some 4WD-hire outfits such as Britz also hire out satellite phones. They're costly (at $18 per day), but handy in an emergency.

You will, of course, need to carry a fair amount of water in case of disaster (around 20L a person is sensible), stored in more than one container. Food is less important – the space might be better allocated to an extra spare tyre or spare fuel.

The RACQ can advise on preparation and supply maps and track notes.

Most tracks have an ideal time of year – in Queensland's southwest, it's not wise to attempt the tough tracks during the heat of summer (November to March), when the dust can be severe, the chances of mechanical trouble much greater and water scarce. In the north, travelling in the wet season (December to March) may be impossible because of flooding and mud.

You should always seek advice on road conditions when you're travelling into unfamiliar territory. The local police will be able to advise you as to whether roads are open and whether your vehicle is suitable for a particular track.

The RACQ has a 24-hour telephone service with a prerecorded report on road conditions throughout the state – dial ☎1300 130 595. For more specific local information, you can call into the nearest RACQ office.

If you do run into trouble in the back of beyond, stay with your vehicle. It's easier to spot a car than a human being from the air and plenty of travellers have wandered off into the wilderness and died of exposure long after their abandoned car was found!

Local Transport

Bus & Train

Brisbane has a comprehensive public transport system with buses, trains and river ferries. The **Translink** (☎13 12 30; www.transinfo.qld.gov.au; ⏲6am-10pm) provides schedule information for Brisbane, the Sunshine and Gold Coasts, and parts of the Darling Downs.

Larger cities such as Surfers Paradise, Toowoomba, Mt Isa, Bundaberg, Rockhampton, Mackay, Townsville and Cairns all have local bus services. There are also local bus services throughout the Gold and Sunshine Coasts.

At the major tourist centres, most of the backpacker hostels and some resorts and hotels have courtesy coaches that will pick you up from train or bus stations or the airport. Most tour operators include in their prices courtesy coach transport to/from your accommodation. Elsewhere, all of the larger towns and cities have at least one taxi service.

Taxi

Brisbane and Cairns have plenty of taxis, but outside of these two cities their numbers are far fewer. Taxi fares vary throughout the state, but shouldn't differ much from those in Brisbane, where a 5km cross-town jaunt runs to about $20. Try the following:

Black & White Cabs (Brisbane) (☎13 32 22)
Black & White Cabs (Cairns) (☎13 10 08)
Gold Coast Cabs (☎13 10 08)
Suncoast Cabs (☎13 10 08)
Townsville Taxi (☎13 10 08)
Yellow Cab (Brisbane) (☎13 19 24, 13 22 27)

Train

Queensland has a good rail network that services the coast between Brisbane and Cairns, with several routes heading inland to Mt Isa, Longreach and Charleville. There are seven services in total, including the Kuranda Scenic Railway, which is primarily a tourist route in northern Queensland. All services are operated by **Queensland Rail** (☎1300 131 722; www.queenslandrail.com.au).

NSW's **CountryLink** (☎13 22 32; www.countrylink.nsw.gov.au) has a daily XPT (express passenger train) service between Brisbane and Sydney (economy seat/1st-class seat $111/156, 13½ to 15 hours).

Classes & Costs

Travelling by rail within Queensland is generally slower and more expensive than bus travel, although some of the economy fares are comparable to bus fares. The trains are almost all air-conditioned and you can get sleeping berths on most trains for around $50 extra a night in economy, and approximately $170 in 1st class. The *Sunlander*, which runs from Brisbane to Cairns, also has the exclusive 'Queenslander Class', which includes comfortable berths, meals in the swanky restaurant car and historical commentary along the way.

You can break your journey on the *Tilt Train* service between Brisbane and Cairns by using a stopover fare, where you pay slightly extra for up to four stops within a period of 28 days.

Half-price concession fares are available to kids under 16 years of age and students with an International Student Identity Card (ISIC). There are also discounts for seniors and pensioners.

Reservations

There are Queensland Rail travel centres throughout the state – these are basically booking offices that can advise you on all rail travel, sell you tickets and put together rail-holiday packages that include transport and accommodation:

Brisbane Central Station (cnr Edward & Ann Sts); Roma St Transit Centre (171 Roma St)

Cairns (Cairns Railway Station, Bunda St)

Rockhampton (Rockhampton Railway Station, Murray St)

Townsville (Townsville Railway Station, Flinders St)

You can also purchase train tickets through travel agencies. Telephone reservations can be made through one of the Queensland Rail travel centres or through **Queensland Rail's** (☎1300 131 722; www.queenslandrail.com.au) centralised booking service from anywhere in Australia.

Train Services

GULFLANDER

The *Gulflander* is a strange, snub-nosed little train that travels once a week between the remote Gulf towns of Normanton and Croydon – it's a unique and memorable journey. See p400 for details.

INLANDER

The *Inlander* goes from Townsville to Mt Isa (economy/sleeper/1st-class sleeper $127/187/288, 21 hours, noon Sunday and Thursday). Returning from Townsville, departure is at 1.30pm Monday and Friday.

KURANDA SCENIC RAILWAY

One of the most popular tourist trips out of Cairns is the Kuranda Scenic Railway – a spectacular 1½-hour trip on a historic steam train through the rainforests west of Cairns. See p342 for details.

SAVANNAHLANDER

A classic 1960s train, the *Savannahlander* (www.savannahlander.com.au) travels between Cairns (departs Wednesday) and Forsayth (departs Friday). It coasts up the scenic Kuranda Railway and into the outback. The journey costs $210/355 for a single/return trip.

SPIRIT OF THE OUTBACK

The *Spirit of the Outback* travels the 1326km from Brisbane to Longreach ($190/250/385 economy/sleeper/1st-class sleeper, 24 hours, departs 6.25pm Tuesday and 1.10pm Saturday). A connecting bus service operates between Longreach and Winton. Returning from Longreach, departure is at 7.15am on Monday and Thursday.

You can also take a shorter trip from Brisbane to Rockhampton ($108/168/261 economy/sleeper/1st-class sleeper, 10 hours).

SUNLANDER

The *Sunlander* travels from Brisbane to Cairns three times a week ($219/279/430/784 economy seat/sleeper/1st-class sleeper/Queenslander-class, 31 hours, Tuesday, Thursday and Sunday). Return from Cairns is on Tuesday, Thursday and Saturday.

TILT TRAIN

The *Tilt Train*, a high-speed economy and business train, makes the trip from Brisbane to Cairns ($328, 24 hours, departs 6.25pm Monday and Friday). Returning from Cairns, departure is at 9.15am Sunday and Wednesday.

There are also shorter trips from Brisbane to Bundaberg ($68/102 economy/business, five hours) and Brisbane to Rockhampton ($108/162 economy/business, eight hours).

A second train, which will add additional services, was scheduled to begin operating as this book went to press.

WESTLANDER

The *Westlander* heads inland from Brisbane to Charleville ($127/166/252 economy/sleeper/1st-class sleeper, 17 hours, Tuesday and Thursday). There are connecting bus services from Charleville to Cunnamulla and Quilpie. Return from Charleville is on Wednesday and Friday.

behind the scenes

SEND US YOUR FEEDBACK

We love to hear from travellers – your comments keep us on our toes and help make our books better. Our well-travelled team reads every word on what you loved or loathed about this book. Although we cannot reply individually to postal submissions, we always guarantee that your feedback goes straight to the appropriate authors, in time for the next edition. Each person who sends us information is thanked in the next edition – and the most useful submissions are rewarded with a free book.

Visit **lonelyplanet.com/contact** to submit your updates and suggestions or to ask for help. Our award-winning website also features inspirational travel stories, news and discussions.

Note: we may edit, reproduce and incorporate your comments in Lonely Planet products such as guidebooks, websites and digital products, so let us know if you don't want your comments reproduced or your name acknowledged. For a copy of our privacy policy visit lonelyplanet.com/privacy.

OUR READERS

Many thanks to the travellers who used the last edition and wrote to us with helpful hints, useful advice and interesting anecdotes:

Fiona Anderson, Robert Autrique, Christine Birch, Leanne Brandt, David Brown, Vicky Brown, Dick Butler, Laurel Colton, Helen Cornelius, Tracey Crittenden, Rachel Fitzpatrick, Barbara Fox, Shanshan Fu, Amelie Furler, Mike Hill, Mark Holmes, Hans Hooyberghs, Andrew Hunt, Eve Jones, Indy Jones, Tracy Lewis, Harriet Mansergh, Anika Menkens, Lisa Molloy, Sean O'Shea, Jaime Parnell, Adinda Slingerland-Telkamp, Lee Su Jin, Nhu Tran, Gerhard Vaculik, Steven Vale, Marie Weder

AUTHOR THANKS

Regis St Louis

Thanks to the many Brisbanites who shared tips and insights into their lovely city. I'd also like to thank master chef Philip Johnson and winemaker extraordinaire Mark Ravenscroft for insightful interviews. Other thanks go to the many winemakers who plied me with viticultural insight (plus free wine) in the Granite Belt, and the many helpful Queenslanders elsewhere in the state. At Lonely Planet, thanks to Maryanne Netto for inviting me onboard and my co-authors for all their hard work. Special thanks to Cassandra and daughters Magdalena and Genevieve for a memorable stay in Brisbane. Hugs and handshakes to Leonie and Col for providing a home away from home, and to Tim, Leone, Nadina, August and Luca for all their hospitality.

Sarah Gilbert

Thanks to my Lonely Planet colleagues, particularly Regis and Maryanne. I'll always be grateful to my loving and beloved parents, Danny and Kathleen, and to my brother and sister, James and Mary. Thanks most of all to Nico, for his company on the road, and in life.

Catherine Le Nevez

Cheers to the countless locals, tourism professionals and fellow travellers who provided insider tips and invaluable insights throughout Far North Queensland. Thanks especially to Robert Stephens at Mamu and Wanegan (Glenis Grogan) in Kuranda, Russell (and Clancy!) in Mt Surprise, the Burketown crew, Jason in Normanton, everyone at Bramston Beach, and, of course, to Julian. Thanks too to Maryanne for signing me up, and to Regis and all at Lonely Planet. As ever, *merci surtout* to my family.

Olivia Pozzan

At Lonely Planet, thanks to Maryanne for the opportunity to again research and write about this land I love so much. Thanks also to Regis and the team – Catherine and Sarah. A huge thanks to everyone I met, especially in the Whitsundays, where tourism officials and operators went out of their way to show me the beauty of the islands. A special thank you to Tony – serendipity at work? And a very heartfelt thanks to Andrew for making my trip fun and memorable.

ACKNOWLEDGMENTS

Climate map data adapted from Peel MC, Finlayson BL & McMahon TA (2007) 'Updated World Map of the Köppen-Geiger Climate Classification', *Hydrology and Earth System Sciences*, 11, 163344.

Cover photograph: parrotfish, Great Barrier Reef

Image on p5: *The skin speaks a language not its own*, Bharti Kher, 2006

Purchased 2007, Queensland Art Gallery Foundation

Collection: Queensland Art Gallery

Photograph: Natasha Harth

Many of the images in this guide are available for licensing from Lonely Planet Images: www.lonelyplanetimages.com.

THIS BOOK

This is the 6th edition of Lonely Planet's *Queensland* guide. The 1st edition was researched and written by Mark Armstrong; the 2nd edition by Hugh Finlay and Andrew Humphries; research on the 3rd was led by Joe Bindloss; the 4th by Justine Vaisutis; and the 5th by Alan Murphy. Regis St Louis was the coordinating author on this edition. He was joined by co-authors Sarah Gilbert, Catherine Le Nevez and Olivia Pozzan; see Our Writers (p500) to find out which destinations each of them researched. Dr Michael Cathcart wrote the History chapter. Dr Tim Flannery wrote the Environment chapter, with sidebars and boxed texts added by Regis St Louis. This guidebook was commissioned in Lonely Planet's Melbourne office and produced by the following:

Commissioning Editor Maryanne Netto

Coordinating Editors Carolyn Boicos, Trent Holden, Alison Ridgway

Coordinating Cartographer Hunor Csutoros

Coordinating Layout Designer Mazzy Prinsep

Managing Editor Liz Heynes

Senior Editor Susan Paterson

Managing Cartographer David Connolly

Managing Layout Designer Jane Hart

Assisting Editors Susie Ashworth, Pete Cruttenden, Andrea Dobbin, Victoria Harrison, Gabrielle Innes, Bella Li, Andi Lien, Karyn Noble, Sophie Splatt, Gabrielle Stefanos

Assisting Cartographer Brendan Streager

Cover Research Naomi Parker

Internal Image Research Rebecca Skinner

Thanks to Jessica Boland, Helen Christinis, Melanie Dankel, Kate Evans, Ryan Evans, Anna Metcalfe, Darren O'Connell, Celia Wood

4WD travel 195, 412, 472
- Birdsville Track 420
- Bloomfield Track 12, 379-80, **12**
- Old Telegraph Track 395-6

4WD tours
- Cooktown 313
- Daintree 359, 375
- Fraser Island 146-7, 157, 194-5
- Moreton Island 105
- North Stradbroke Island 102
- Rainbow Beach 173

A

Abattoir Swamp Environment Park 377
Abbey Museum 152
Aboriginal people, *see* Indigenous people
abseiling 65-6
accommodation 459-60, *see also individual locations,* farmstays
activities 19-21, 34-41, *see also individual activities*
Agnes Water 27, 215-18
air travel 467-8
Airlie Beach 27, 243-50, **245**
Akarra Lagoons 178
alcohol restrictions 391
Alexandra Park & Zoo 188
Alligator Creek 280
Alligator's Nest 290
Alma Park Zoo 64
animals, *see individual animals*
Annan River Gorge 378
antechinus 440-1
Anu, Christine 446
aquariums
- Daydream Island Resort & Spa 252
- Reef HQ 265
- Reef World 177

Araluen Falls 236
Arcadia 275-6
Archer River 394
area codes 463, 465
Arno's Wall 414
art deco architecture
- Innisfail 300, 301
- Mackay 227

art galleries, *see* galleries, museums
arts 446-9, *see also* Indigenous rock art
Atherton 344-6
Atherton Tableland 337-52
ATMs 463
Australia Day 19
Australia Day Cockroach Races 67, 70
Australia Zoo 153
Australian Butterfly Sanctuary 339
Australian Institute of Marine Science 280
Australian Labor Party 114, 417, 425, 431
Australian Outback Spectacular 130
Australian Stockman's Hall of Fame & Outback Heritage Centre 415
Australian Venom Zoo 339
Avian Cirrus 432
Ayr 280
Ayton 379

B

Babinda 330
Ballandean 106-11
ballooning, *see* hot-air ballooning
Baloon Cave 223
Bama Way 364
Bamaga 397
Banfield, EJ 298
Banjo Paterson 430
Barcaldine 417-18
Bargara 190
Baroon Pocket Dam 167
barracuda 29, 214, **322-3**
barramundi 40, 351, 395, 400, 404, 405, 406
basketball 274
Bat House 373
BatReach 339, 341
beaches 16
- Bargara 190
- Blacks Beach 233
- Brampton Island 236
- Bramston Beach 330-1
- Broadbeach 129
- Burleigh Heads 130
- Caloundra 152-3
- Cape Kimberley Beach 370
- Cape Tribulation 373
- Catseye Beach 254
- Chalkies Beach 244
- Clifton Beach 333
- Coolangatta 133
- Dingo Beach 258
- Eighteen Mile Beach 101
- Elliot Heads 190
- Ellis Beach 335
- Emmagen Beach 379
- Fisherman's Beach 208
- Fitzroy Island 336
- Four Mile Beach 355
- Frankland Islands 337
- Halfway Island 210
- Harbour Beach 228-9
- Holloways Beach 332
- Humpy Island 210
- Illawong Beach 228
- Lizard Island 386
- Long Beach 208
- Long Island 251
- Machans Beach 331
- Mackay 228-9
- Main Beach 117
- Maroochydore 155
- Middle Island 210
- Monkey Beach 208
- Mooloolaba 155
- Moore Park 190
- Myall Beach 373
- Newell Beach 365-6
- North Stradbroke Island 101
- Palm Cove 333
- Sarina Beach 232
- Sunshine Beach 161
- Surfers Paradise 122
- Thornton Beach 372
- Town Beach 228
- Trinity Beach 332-3
- Whitehaven Beach 244, 258
- Wonga Beach 366
- Yorkeys Knob 332

bêche-de-mer 336
Beck Museum 342
Bedarra Island 299
Bedourie 419
beer 452-4
Bell, Richard 448
Best of All Lookout 139
Betoota 420
bicycle travel, *see* cycling
Big Crystal Creek 284
bilbies 418
Billabong Sanctuary 280
Bingil Bay 291
Binna Burra 140
birds, *see individual birds,* birdwatching
Birdsville 419-20

000 Map pages
000 Photo pages

Birdsville Cup horse races 12, 21, 419, **12**
Birdsville Track 420
birdwatching 439, 440, 445
Dunk Island 298
Etty Bay 300
Eungella National Park 235
Iron Range National Park 394
Julatten 365
Kuranda 339
Lady Elliot Island 214
Lady Musgrave Island 214
Lakefield National Park 393
Lizard Island 386
Mareeba 342
Masthead Island 215
Mission Beach 294
North West Island 215
South Molle Island 253
Tryon Island 215
Tyto wetlands 285
Birdworld 339
Bjelke-Petersen, Joh 434-5
Black Mountain National Park 378
Blackdown Tableland National Park 219
Blacks Beach 233
Bloomfield Track 12, 379-80, **12**
Blue Lake 101
Blue Sky Brewery 453
Bluff Point 207
boat travel, *see* cruises, sailing
Boodjamulla (Lawn Hill) National Park 403
books 424, *see also* literature
bushwalking 36
food 451
health 461
history 425, 426, 427, 430
politics 435
Boolimba Bluff 223
border crossings 468
Boreen Point 162-3
Boulia 419
Bowen 259-61
Bowling Green Bay National Park 280
box jellyfish 36, 216, 264, 306, 355, 456
Brampton Island 236-7
Bramston Beach 330-1
breweries 452-3, *see also* distilleries, wineries
Blue Sky Brewery 453
Bundaberg Barrel 186-7
Burleigh Brewing Co 453
Carlton & United Brewhouse 70
Castlemaine-Perkins XXXX Brewery 70
Mt Tamborine Brewery 137, 453
Sunshine Coast Brewery 453
Bribie Island 151
Brisbane 5, 45, 52-96, **54-5**, **56**, **60**, **62**, **73**, **76**, **80**
accommodation 52, 72-8
activities 65-7
attractions 53-64
children, travel with 67
climate 52
courses 67
cruises 64, 71
drinking 84-7
emergency services 91-2
entertainment 87-90
festivals & events 72
food 52, 78-84
gay travellers 87, 460-1
highlights 54-5
history 53
internet access 92
itineraries 61, 68-9, **68**
lesbian travellers 87, 460-1
medical services 93
shopping 90-1, 92
tourist offices 93
tours 70-1
travel seasons 52
travel to/from 93-5
travel within 95-6
Brisbane Botanic Gardens 62
Brisbane Festival 20, 71, 72
Brisbane Go Club 70
Brisbane International Film Festival 72
Brisbane Open Air 89
Brisbane Pride Festival 72
Broadbeach 129-30
Broken River 235-6
brolgas 439
Bromfield Swamp 348
Brown Lake 102
Bucasia 233-4
budgeting 14
Bundaberg 186-90, **187**
Bundaberg Barrel 186-7
Bundaberg Rum Distillery 186, 453
bungee jumping 39-40, 310
Burke & Wills' Camp 119, 404
Burketown 404, 406
Burleigh Brewing Co 453
Burleigh Heads 130-3, **131**
Burrum Coast National Park 186
bus travel 469-71, 475
bush tucker 452
bushfires 456
bushwalking 34-6
Airlie Beach 244
books 36
Bowen 260
Brampton Island 236-7
Cape Tribulation 373, 375
Carnarvon Gorge 35, 223
Conway National Park 251
Cooloola Wilderness Trail 172
Dalrymple Gap Walking Track 288
Dunk Island 298
Fitzroy Island 336
Fraser Island Great Walk 35, 196
Great Keppel Island 208
Hamilton Island 254
Hayman Island 256
Hinchinbrook Island 289
Kuranda 338
Lamington National Park 140
Lindeman Island 258
Magnetic Island 276
Mamu Rainforest Canopy Walkway 301
Marrdja Botanical Walk 372
Mission Beach 292
Mt Bartle Frere Summit Track 331
North Stradbroke Island 101
Paluma Range National Park 284-5
Sunshine Coast hinterland 35, 167, 168
Thorsborne Trail 289
Whitsunday Island 35, 258
Wooroonooran National Park 301
business hours 460
butterflies 292, 339
Byfield 207-8

C

Caboolture Warplane Museum 152
Cairns 11, 27, 48, 304-29, **308**, **318**
accommodation 304, 313-15
activities 306-11
attractions 306-11
climate 304
drinking 325-7
emergency services 327
entertainment 325-7
festivals & events 313
food 304, 316, 325
highlights 305
internet access 327
medical services 327
shopping 327
tourist offices 327-8
tours 311-13
travel seasons 304
travel to/from 328-9
travel within 329
Cairns Festival 20, 313
Cairns Tropical Zoo 333
Cairns Wildlife Dome 307, 309

Cairns Wildlife Safari Reserve 339-40
Calliope River Historical Village 211
Caloundra 152-5, **154**
camel races 414, 419
camel rides 162
campervans 472-3
camping 32-3, 459
Canecutter Way 300
Cania Gorge National Park 193
canoeing 38, 173, *see also* kayaking, rafting
Canyon Lookout 139
Cape Hillsborough National Park 238
Cape Kimberley Beach 370
Cape Trib Exotic Fruit Farm 373
Cape Tribulation 373-7, **374**
  tours from Cairns 312-13
Cape York 397
Cape York Peninsula 8, 49, 390-400, **338**, **8**
  accommodation 387
  climate 387
  food 387
  highlights 388
  tours from Cairns 313
  travel seasons 387
Cape York Turtle Rescue 395
Capricorn Caves 203
Capricorn Coast 47, 198-224, **199**
  accommodation 198
  climate 198
  food 198
  highlights 199
  hinterland 218-24
  travel seasons 198
Captain Cook, *see* Cook, James
car travel 15, 471-5, *see also* 4WD travel
Cardwell 288-9
Carisbrooke Station 415
Carlisle Island 237
Carlo Sandblow 172
Carlton & United Brewhouse 70
Carnarvon Creek 223
Carnarvon Gorge 9, 17, 222, 223, **9**, **17**
Carnarvon National Park 9, 222-4, **9**, **17**
casinos 58, 129, 273, 326
cassowaries 292, 294, 300, 394, 445
Castlemaine-Perkins XXXX Brewery 70
Cathedral Cave 222, 223
Cathedral Fig 351

000 Map pages
000 Photo pages

cathedrals, *see* churches & cathedrals
Catseye Beach 254
Causeway Lake 207
caves
  Baloon Cave 223
  Capricorn Caves 203
  Cathedral Cave 222, 223
  Chillagoe 343
  Kenniff Cave 222
Cedar Bay (Mangkal-Mangkalba) National Park 379-80
Cedar Galleries 212
cell phones 15, 463
Centenary Lakes 307
Chalkies Beach 244
Channel Country 418-20
Charleville 418
Charters Towers 281-4, **328**
Childers 184-6
children, travel with 18, 42-4, 67
Chillagoe 343
churches & cathedrals
  All Souls Quetta Memorial Church 398-9
  St John's Cathedral 61
  St Mary's by the Sea 357
Clifton Beach 333
climate 14, 19, 20, 21, 27, 422-3, *see also individual regions*
climate change 441
Cloncurry 409-10
Cobb & Co Museum 111
Cobbold Gorge 402
Cod Hole 311
Coen 393-4
coffee plantations 345
Coloured Sand Cliffs (Rainbow Beach) 172
Commissariat Stores Building 58
conservation 341
Conway National Park 251
Cooberrie Park 205
Cook, James 215, 380-1, 385, 426-7
Cooktown 28, 380-5
  coastal route to 379-80
  inland route to 377-8
  tours from Cairns 313
Cooktown Discovery Festival 19-20, 382
Coolangatta 133-6, **134**
Coolangatta Gold 21, 135
Cooloola Coast 162-3
Cooloola Wilderness Trail 172
Coolum 160-1
Cooper Creek 372
coral cuts 457
Cosmos Centre 418
costs 14, 15

courses
  cooking 67
  diving 30, 36-7
Cow Bay 370-1
Crater Lakes National Park 351-2
credit cards 463
cricket 90, 282
Crocodile Dundee 413
crocodiles 207, 264, 300, 301, 306, 335, 355, 369, 456-7
Crows Nest 114
Crows Nest Falls National Park 114
Croydon 403-4
cruises
  Brisbane 64, 71
  Bundaberg 188
  Caloundra 153
  Coolangatta 134
  Daintree River 369
  Everglades 147
  Gladstone 211-12
  Great Barrier Reef 29-30, 311
  Great Keppel Island 209
  Hervey Bay 180
  Lake Tinaroo 351
  Main Beach 120
  Manly 100
  Maryborough 176
  Mooloolaba 156
  Noosa 146
  Port Douglas 359
  Rainbow Beach 173
  Redcliffe 99
  St Helena 100
  South Stradbroke Island 117-18
  Southport 120
  Whitsundays 241-2
Crystal Cascades 310
Crystal Caves 344
culture 424, 446-9
Cumberland Islands 237-8
currency 14
Currumbin 130-3
Currumbin Wildlife Sanctuary 130
Curtain Fig 349
Curtis Island 214
customs regulations 464
cycling 65, 469
Cyclone Yasi 265, 422-3

D

D'Aguilar Range National Park 62-3, 66
Daintree 5, 48, 366-77, **5**
  tours from Cairns 312-13
  tours from Port Douglas 359
Daintree Discovery Centre 370-1
Daintree Ice Cream Company 371

Daintree National Park 367
Daintree River 369, 370-3
Daintree Village 367-70
Daintree Wild Zoo 366
Daisy Hill Koala Centre 64
Dajarra 419
Dalrymple Gap Walking Track 288
dangers, *see* safety
David Fleay Wildlife Park 130-1
Daydream Island 252-3
Deepwater National Park 218
Depression, the 432
Dig Tree 420
digital photography 463
Dilli Village 192
Dingo Beach 258
dingoes 175, 192, 440, **7**
dinosaur fossils 409, 413, 415
disabilities, travellers with 93, 465
distilleries 453, *see also* breweries, wineries
  Bundaberg Rum Distillery 186, 453
  Mt Uncle Distillery 344
  Tamborine Mountain Distillery 137
diving 16, 36-7
  Bundaberg 37, 188
  Cairns 310, **11**
  Cod Hole 311
  courses 30, 36-7
  Great Barrier Reef 29-31, 33, 311, 359
  Great Keppel Island 208-9
  Hamilton Island 254
  Hayman Island 256
  Heron Island 214-5
  insurance 31
  Lady Elliot Island 214
  Lady Musgrave Island 214
  Lindeman Island 258
  Lizard Island 386
  Magnetic Island 276
  Main Beach 119
  Mission Beach 293
  Mooloolaba 37, 155-6
  Moreton Island 37, 105
  North Stradbroke Island 37, 101
  Rainbow Beach 37, 173
  safety 31
  Southport 119
  Whitsundays 239, 241
  Yongala wreck 280
Djurri Dadagal Art Enterprises 338, 340
Dolphin Heads 233
dolphin watching
  Fraser Island 190, 193
  Hervey Bay 180
  Noosa 144
  North Stradbroke Island 101
  Rainbow Beach 173
  Tangalooma 105
  Tin Can Bay 185
Doomadgee Aboriginal Community 406
Double Head 207
Dreamtime Cultural Centre 201
Dreamworld 123
drinks 17, 391, 452-4, *see also* breweries, distilleries, wineries
driving, *see* car travel
dunes
  Carlo Sandblow 172
  Fraser Island 190
  Simpson Desert National Park 420
Dunk Island 298-9, **324**
Dunwich 101

E

Eagle's Nest Wildlife Hospital 341
echidnas 440
economy 422, 423-4, 432
Egan, Luke 132
Eighteen Mile Beach 101
Eimeo 233
Einasleigh 402
'Ekka' Royal National Agricultural (RNA) Show 20, 72
El Arish 299
El Niño 438
electricity 460
Eli Creek 192
Eliot Falls 396
Elliot Heads 190
Ellis Beach 335
Emerald 219-20
emergencies 15
Emmagen Beach 379
Emu Park 207
environmental issues 423-4, 441, 444-5
Eton 235
Etty Bay 300
Eubenangee Swamp National Park 301
Eulo 420
Eumundi 163-5
Eungella 234-5
Eungella National Park 235-6
Eurimbula National Park 218
Eurong 192
events 17, 19-21, *see also* festivals
  Airlie Beach Race Week 246
  Australia Day Cockroach Races 67, 70
  Beef Australia Expo 201
  Birdsville Cup horse races 12, 21, 419, **12**
  Brass Monkey Season 108
  Brisbane Open Air 89
  Carnival of Flowers 112
  Coolangatta Gold 21, 135
  Dalrymple Sales Yards Cattle Sales 282
  Desert Sands Camel Races 419
  'Ekka' Royal National Agricultural (RNA) Show 20, 72
  Gold Coast International Marathon 125
  Goldfield Ashes 282
  Great Brisbane Duck Race 70
  Great Wheelbarrow Race 343
  Magnetic Island to Townsville Open Water Swim 269
  Moonlight Cinema 88
  Noosa Triathlon 147
  Queensland Winter Racing Carnival 72
  Quicksilver Pro-Surfing Competition 124
  Schoolies 125
  Surf Life-Saving Championships 124
  Townsville 400 269
  Townsville Offshore 269
Everglades 147
exchange rates 15
ex-HMAS *Brisbane* 155-6

F

Fairweather, Ian 448
farms
  Cape Trib Exotic Fruit Farm 373
  Gallo Dairyland 345
  Scrub Hill Community Farm 178
  Whyanbeel Valley 366
farmstays 459-60
  Myella Farmstay 204
  outback Queensland 414
  Stoney Creek 227, 235
festivals 17, 19-21, *see also* events
  Apple & Grape Festival 108
  Australian Festival of Chamber Music 269
  Australian Italian Festival 286
  Big Day Out 124
  Brisbane Festival 20, 71, 72
  Brisbane International Film Festival 72
  Brisbane Pride Festival 72
  Bush Poetry Festival 414
  Cairns Festival 20, 313
  Charters Towers Country Music Festival 282
  Cooktown Discovery Festival 19-20, 382
  Feast of the Senses 302

festivals *continued*
Festival of Cultures 185
Gemfest Festival of Gems 221
Go Troppo Arts Festival 360
Gold Fever Festival 283
Golden Gumboot Festival 290
Hervey Bay Whale Festival 20, 181
Jazz on Quay 201
Laura Aboriginal Dance Festival 392
Mission Beach Film Festival 293
Mission Evolve Music Fest 294
Muster 171
National Festival of Beers 67
Noosa Food & Wine Festival 19, 147
Noosa Jazz Festival 147
Noosa Long Weekend 147
Paniyiri Festival 72
Port Douglas Carnivale 360
Queensland Music Festival 72
Tropfest 72
Valley Fiesta 72
Wallaby Creek Festival 380
Whitsunday Fun Race Festival 246
Wintermoon Folk Festival 229
Woodford Folk Festival 21, 165
Yungaburra Folk Festival 350
films 424, 431, 447
Finch Hatton 234
Finch Hatton Gorge 236
fishing 40-1
Burketown 406
Cairns 311
Cooktown 383
Emerald 219
Hervey Bay 180
Karumba 405
Kurrimine Beach 299
Lake Tinaroo 351
Lucinda 287
Malanda 348
Mission Beach 293
North Stradbroke Island 101
Port Douglas 359
Rainbow Beach 172
Townsville 268
Fitzroy Island 336-7
Flames of the Forest 359
floods 58, 113, 422-3
Floravilla Ice Cream Factory 371
flying foxes 339, 341, 373
food 17, 450-4
Forsayth 402
Forty Mile Scrub National Park 401

000 Map pages
000 Photo pages

fossicking 40, 220-1, 402
Frankland Islands 337
Fraser Coast 47, 171-90, **170**
accommodation 169
climate 169
food 169
highlights 170
travel seasons 169
Fraser Island 7, 47, 190-7, 438, **191**, **7**
Fraser Island Great Walk 35, 196
frogs 10, **10**
Fruit Bat Falls 396
fruit bats 339, 341, 373
fruit wines 299, 312, 344, 349, 452

G

Gab Titui Cultural Centre 398
Gabba 90
galleries
Artspace Mackay 227
Bundaberg Regional Art Gallery 187-8
Cairns Regional Gallery 307
Cardwell Gallery 288
Cedar Galleries 212
Centre of Contemporary Arts 307
Childers Palace Memorial & Art Gallery 184
Crystal Caves 344
Djurri Dadagal Art Enterprises 338, 340
Fireworks 64
Foots Artwork 254
Gallery of Modern Art 59
Girringun Aboriginal Corporation Arts 288
Gold Coast Art Gallery 122
Institute of Modern Art 64
Jan Murphy 64
Janbal Gallery 364
Judith Wright Centre for Contemporary Arts 64
Kalkadoon Tribal Council Keeping Place 410
Lockhart River Art Centre 394
Magarra Gallery 345
Milani 64
Mill Gallery 205
Nature's Powerhouse 381
Nob Creek Pottery 208
Perc Tucker Regional Gallery 267
Philip Bacon Gallery 64
Queensland Art Gallery 59, **5**
Rockhampton City Art Gallery 200
Split Rock Gallery 392
Stanthorpe Regional Art Gallery 108
Suzanne O'Connell Gallery 17, 64
Tanks Arts Centre 307
Tolga Woodworks Gallery & Cafe 345
Torres Strait Heritage Museum & Art Gallery 399
Townsville Cultural Centre 266
Gallery of Modern Art 59
Garden Island 290
gardens, *see* parks & gardens
gay travellers 87, 460-1
gemfields 40, 220-2, 402
geography 437-8
geology 437-8
Georgetown 402-3
Ginger Factory 164
Girraween National Park 66, 110
Girringun Aboriginal Corporation Arts 288
Girringun National Park 286, 288
Gladstone 27, 211-13
Glass House Mountains 66, 151-2
Gloucester Island 258-9
glow worms 137
Go Card 95
Gold Coast 8, 46, 115-41, **116**, **8**
accommodation 115
climate 115
food 115
highlights 116
hinterland 136-41
itineraries 120
travel seasons 115
travel to/from 117
travel within 117
Gold Coast International Marathon 125
gold rush 429-31
golden gumboot 290
Goldsmith Island 237
golf
Brisbane 66-7
Cairns 310
Hamilton Island 254
Magnetic Island 275
Mossman 364
Paradise Palms 333
Port Douglas 357
Yeppoon 205
Yorkeys Knob 332
Goold Island 290
Gordonvale 329-30
gorges
Annan River Gorge 378
Carnarvon Gorge 9, 17, 222, 223, **9**, **17**
Cobbold Gorge 402
Finch Hatton Gorge 236
Mossman Gorge 364
Granite Belt 106-11
Granite Belt Maze 108

Granite Gorge Nature Park 343-4
Great Barrier Reef 4, 26-33, 317-24, 438, 442-3, **4**, **317**, **320-1**, **322-3**, **324**
camping 32-3
climate 27
cruises 29-30, 311
diving 29-31, 33, 311, 359
environmental issues 423
internet resources 28
planning 27-9
resorts 31-2
responsible travel 32
safety 458
snorkelling 29-31, 311
tours from Cairns 311
tours from Cape Tribulation 373
tours from Port Douglas 358-9
tours from Townsville 269
Great Brisbane Duck Race 70
Great Keppel Island 208-10, **209**
Great Sandy National Park 162, 163, 172
Green Island 28, 335-6
Green Mountains 140
Gulflander 476
Gympie 171-2

H

Halfway Island 210
Hamilton Island 28, 254-6
hang-gliding 40
Hard Times Mine 410
Hayman Island 256-7
health 461
heat exhaustion 457-8
Herberton 346
Heron Island 28, 214-15
Hervey Bay 7, 177-84, **178**
Hervey Bay Whale Festival 20, 181
Highfields 114
hiking, *see* bushwalking
Hinchinbrook Island 11, 289-90, **11**
Hinkler Hall of Aviation 186
history 425-36
Australian Labor Party 114, 417, 425, 431
books 425, 426, 427, 430
Cook, James 215, 380-1, 385, 426-7
Depression, the 432
exploration 215, 291-2, 380-1, 385, 426-9
federation 431
gold rush 429-31
Indigenous land rights 434
postwar immigration 434
shearers' strike 430-1, 417
stolen generations 424, 436
White Australia policy 425, 426, 431, 433
white settlement 53, 264, 398, 427-9
WWI 425, 431
WWII 152, 201, 264, 276, 342-3, 380-1, 399, 410, 432-3
holidays 463
Holloways Beach 332
homesteads, *see* stations & homesteads
Hook Island 28, 252
Hope Islands 384
Hopevale Aboriginal Community 393
Hopevale Arts Cultural Centre 382
Horn Island 399
horse racing 12, 21, 419, **12**
horse riding
Cape Tribulation 375
Gold Coast hinterland 136
Hervey Bay 181
Kuranda 340
Lake Cooroibah 162
Mackay 227
Magnetic Island 276-7
Noosa 146
Surfers Paradise 123-4
Townsville 268
Wonga Beach 366
Yeppoon 205
Horseshoe Bay 260, 276
hot-air ballooning
Brisbane 66
Cairns 312
Surfers Paradise 122-3
Hou Wang Temple 345
Hughenden 409
Hummock 186
humpback whales 7, 175, 178, 180, 182, **7**
Humpy Island 210
Hydeaway Bay 258

I

Indian Head 193
Indigenous galleries & cultural centres
Babinda Heritage Blessing 330
Cultural Centre (Townsville) 266
Djurri Dadagal Art Enterprises 338, 340
Dreamtime Cultural Centre 201
Gab Titui Cultural Centre 398
Girringun Aboriginal Corporation Arts 288
Hopevale Arts Cultural Centre 382
Janbal Gallery 364
Kalkadoon Tribal Council Keeping Place 410
Lockhart River Art Centre 394
Magarra Gallery 345
Murra Wolka Creations 164
Tjapukai Cultural Park 307
Indigenous people 302, 429
festivals 392
food 452
land rights 434
stolen generations 424, 436
Indigenous rock art 218-19, 222, 223, 343, 364, 392, 448-9, **17**
Indigenous tours 19, 173, 293, 359, 364, 383, 391, 411
Ingham 285-6
Inlander 476
in-line skating 66
Innisfail 48, 300-3
Innot Hot Springs 347
insurance
diving 31
health 461
travel 462
vehicle 473
internet access 462
internet resources 15, 28, 467-8
Iron Range National Park 394
irukandji 216, 306, 355, 456
Irwin, Steve 153, 422, 436, 439
Isabella Falls 393
islands 16, *see also individual islands*
itineraries 22-5, **22**, **23**, **24**, **25**
Brisbane 61, 68-9, **68**
Gold Coast 120
Sunshine Coast 146

J

James Cook Museum 381
Janbal Gallery 364
Japanese Pearl Memorial 399
Jardine, Captain John 398
Jardine, Frank 398
Jardine River 396-7
Jardine River National Park 397
jellyfish 36, 216, 264, 306, 355, 456
jet-skiing
Main Beach 119
Mission Beach 293
Johnson, Philip 78
Johnstone River Crocodile Farm 300
Jondaryan Woolshed Complex 114
Josephine Falls 331
Jourama Falls 285
Jowalbinna Rock Art Safari Camp 392
Julatten 365
Julia Creek 409
Jumpinpin 101

K

Kalkadoon people 429
Kalkadoon Tribal Council Keeping Place 410
kangaroos 439, 440
Karumba 405
kayaking 16, 38-9, *see also* canoeing, rafting
  Agnes Water 215
  Babinda 330
  Boreen Point 163
  Caloundra 153
  Cape Tribulation 375
  Everglades 147
  Magnetic Island 39, 277
  Mission Beach 39, 293
  Mooloolaba 156-7
  Moreton Island 105
  Noosa 39, 146
  North Stradbroke Island 39
  Rainbow Beach 173
  South Stradbroke Island 118
  Surfers Paradise 122
  Whitsundays 39, 241
Kazu Pearl Farm 399
Keatings Lagoon Conservation (Mulbabidgee) Park 382
Kenilworth 167
Kennedy, Edmund 291-2, 397
Kenniff Cave 222
Keswick Island 237
Kinchant Dam 234
kite surfing 37-8
  Noosa 144-5
  Port Douglas 357
  Redcliffe 99
Koala Gardens 339
koalas 275, 339, 439, 440
Koorana Crocodile Farm 207
Kronosaurus Korner 409
Kuku Yalanji Dreamtime Walks 364
Kuranda 11, 338-42, **338**
Kuranda Scenic Railway 11, 476, **11**
Kurrimine Beach 299

L

Lady Elliot Island 9, 28, 181, 188, 214
Lady Musgrave Island 214
Lake Awoonga 211
Lake Barrine 352
Lake Cooroibah 162
Lake Cootharaba 162-3
Lake Eacham 352
Lake Maraboon 219
Lake Moondarra 411
Lake Morris 309-10
Lake Paluma 285
Lake Tinaroo 351
Lake Wabby 192
Lakefield National Park 393
Lakeland 378
Lamington National Park 140-1
Langford Island 244
language 14
Lark Quarry Dinosaur Trackways 415
Laura 392
Laura Aboriginal Dance Festival 20
Leichhardt Falls 404
Leichhardt, Ludwig 428
lesbian travellers 87, 460-1
Licuala State Forest 292
Lindeman Island 257-8
Lit Zing Khuong 301
literature 448, *see also* books
Little Crystal Creek 284
Lizard Island Group 385-6
Lizard Island Research Station 385
lizards 386, 441
Lockhart River Art Centre 394
Lone Pine Koala Sanctuary 63-4
Long Island 251-2
Longreach 415-17, **416**
Lucinda 287

M

Mabo, Eddie 434
macadamia nuts 451
Machans Beach 331
Mackay 227-32, **228**
Magnetic Island 275-80
Main Beach 117-21, **118**
Majestic Theatre 164
Malanda 348-9
Maleny 165-6
Malouf, David 433, 448
Ma:Mu people 302
Mamu Rainforest Canopy Walkway 301
Manly 100-1
Mapleton 168
Mapoon 395
maps 462
Mareeba 342-4
Mareeba Rodeo 20, 344
Mareeba Wetlands 342
Marian 234
Marine Research & Education Centre 105
Maritime Museum 59-60
markets
  Brisbane 92
  Calliope River Historical Village 211
  Eumundi 163
  Kuranda 342
  Port Douglas 357
  Yungaburra 350
Maroochydore 155-60, **156**
Mary Cairncross Scenic Reserve 165
Maryborough 175-7
Masthead Island 215
Maytown 378
McKinlay 413
measures 464
medical services 461
Melba House 234
Mena Creek 300
Middle Island 210
Midge Point 243
Millaa Millaa 347-8
Min Min Light 419
mines
  Blackwater International Coal Centre 219
  Hard Times Mine 410
  Miners Heritage Walk-in Mine 220-1
  Mt Morgan 205
  Ravenswood 281
  Weipa 395
  Xstrata Black Star Open Cut Mine 410
Mirani 234
Miriam Vale Historical Society Museum 215
Mission Beach 27, 291-8, **292**, **296**
Misty Mountains 290
mobile phones 15, 463
Moffatt, Tracey 448
Mon Repos 188
money 14, 15, 460, 462-3
Montville 166-8
Mooloolaba 155-60, **159**
Moonlight Cinema 88
Moore Park 190
Moreton Island 104-6
morning glory 404
mosquitoes 456
Moss Garden 222
Mossman 364-5
Mossman Gorge 364
motion sickness 30
motorcycle travel 15, 471-5
Mourilyan 299
Mt Archer 201
Mt Barney National Park 141
Mt Bartle Frere 331
Mt Beerwah 152
Mt Bowen 289
Mt Carbine 377
Mt Castle Tower National Park 211
Mt Coolum 160

000 Map pages
000 Photo pages

Mt Coonowrin 152
Mt Coot-tha Reserve 61-2
Mt Cougal 140
Mt Garnet 401
Mt Hypipamee National Park 346
Mt Isa 410-13, **411**
Mt Moffatt 222
Mt Molloy 377
Mt Morgan 205
Mt Sorrow 370, 373, 375
Mt Surprise 402
Mt Tamborine Brewery 137, 453
Mt Tyson 290
Mt Uncle Distillery 344
Mt Whitfield Conservation Park 307
Mudjimba Island 160
Mungalla Station 286
Mungkan Kandju National Park 394
Murra Wolka Creations 164
museums
  Abbey Museum 152
  Archer Park Rail Museum 201
  Australian Age of Dinosaurs 415
  Australian Stockman's Hall of Fame & Outback Heritage Centre 415
  Australian Sugar Industry Museum 299-300
  Beck Museum 342
  Bowen Historical Museum 260
  Brennan & Geraghty 176
  Caboolture Warplane Museum 152
  Cairns Museum 307
  Central Queensland Military & Artefacts Association 201
  Cobb & Co Museum 111
  Corfield & Fitzmaurice Building 414
  Dreamtime Cultural Centre 201
  Gympie Gold Mining & Historical Museum 171
  Heritage Village 201
  Hinkler Hall of Aviation 186
  Historic Cardwell Post Office & Telegraph Station 288
  James Cook Museum 381
  Kronosaurus Korner 409
  Mareeba Heritage Museum 342
  Maritime Museum 59-60
  Maryborough Military & Colonial Museum 175
  Mining & Historical Museum 281
  Miriam Vale Historical Society Museum 215
  Mt Morgan Historical Museum 205
  Museum of Brisbane 53
  Museum of Tropical Queensland 266-7
  North Queensland Military Museum 267-8
  North Stradbroke Historical Museum 101
  Old Pharmacy 184
  Outback at Isa 410
  Qantas Founders Outback Museum 415
  Queensland Air Museum 153
  Queensland Museum 58-9
  QUT Art Museum 58
  Redcliffe Historical Museum 99
  Sciencentre 59
  Stanthorpe Heritage Museum 108
  Torres Strait Heritage Museum & Art Gallery 399
  Townsville Cultural Centre 266
  Townsville Maritime Museum 267
  Underground Hospital Museum 410
  Venus Gold Battery 282
  Waltzing Matilda Centre 414
  Woodworks Forestry & Timber Museum 171
  Zara Clark Museum 282
Musgrave 393
music 423, 446-7
Myall Beach 373
Myora Springs 102

N

Nardoo Station 414
National Basketball League (NBL) 274
National Festival of Beers 67
national parks 444-5
  Black Mountain National Park 378
  Blackdown Tableland National Park 219
  Boodjamulla (Lawn Hill) National Park 403
  Bowling Green Bay National Park 280
  Brampton Island 236-7
  Bribie Island National Park 151
  Burrum Coast National Park 186
  Byfield National Park 207-8
  Cania Gorge National Park 193
  Cape Hillsborough National Park 238
  Carnarvon National Park 9, 222-4, **9**, **17**
  Cedar Bay (Mangkal-Mangkalba) National Park 379-80
  Conway National Park 251
  Crater Lakes National Park 351-2
  Crows Nest Falls National Park 114
  D'Aguilar Range National Park 62-3, 66
  Daintree National Park 367
  Deepwater National Park 218
  Eubenangee Swamp National Park 301
  Eungella National Park 235-6
  Eurimbula National Park 218
  Forty Mile Scrub National Park 401
  Girraween National Park 66, 110
  Girringun National Park 286, 288
  Glass House Mountains National Park 152
  Great Sandy National Park 162, 163, 172
  Hinchinbrook Island 11, 289-90, **11**
  Iron Range National Park 394
  Jardine River National Park 397
  Kondalilla National Park 167
  Lakefield National Park 393
  Lamington National Park 140-1
  Mapleton Falls National Park 168
  Mt Archer 201
  Mt Barney National Park 141
  Mt Castle Tower National Park 211
  Mt Hypipamee National Park 346
  Mt Moffatt 222
  Mungkan Kandju National Park 394
  Noosa National Park 144
  Paluma Range National Park 284-5
  Porcupine Gorge National Park 409
  Simpson Desert National Park 420
  Springbrook National Park 138-40
  Tamborine Mountain National Park 137
  Tully Gorge National Park 290
  Undara Volcanic National Park 401-2
  Wooroonooran National Park 301, 331
National Rugby League (NRL) 274
Natural Bridge 140
Nelly Bay 275
Newell Beach 365-6
Newry Island Group 238
newspapers 464
Newstead House 61
Ngungun 152
Noah Beach 372-3
Noccundra 420
Noosa 46, 144-51, **145**, **148**
Noosa Food & Wine Festival 19, 147
Normanton 404
North Keppel Island 211
North Queensland Cowboys 274
North Queensland Military Museum 267-8
North Stradbroke Island 66, 101-4, **102**
North West Island 215
nuclear energy 441

O

oceanariums 155
octopuses 456
Old Rainworth Fort 222
Old Telegraph Track 395-6

Old Windmill & Observatory 57-8
Oodgeroo Noonuccal 448
opening hours 460
Orpheus Island 28, 287-8
Outback at Isa 410
outback Queensland 49, 407-20, **408**
  accommodation 407
  climate 407
  food 407
  highlights 408
  travel seasons 407
  travel to/from 409
  travel within 409, 412, 475
Outer Newry Island 238

P

painting 448
Palm Cove 333-5
Palmer River 377-8
Palmerville 378
Paluma Range National Park 284-5
Paluma Village 285
paragliding 40
  Gold Coast hinterland 136
  Rainbow Beach 172-3
parasailing 40
parks & gardens
  Abattoir Swamp Environment Park 377
  Alexandra Park & Zoo 188
  Bicentennial Park 381
  Brisbane Botanic Gardens 62
  Bundaberg Botanic Gardens 187
  Cooktown Botanic Gardens 381
  Emerald Botanic Gardens 219
  Flecker Botanic Gardens 306-7
  Granite Gorge Nature Park 343-4
  Heritage Village 201
  Ju Raku En Japanese Garden 111
  Keatings Lagoon Conservation (Mulbabidgee) Park 382
  Kershaw Gardens 201
  Laurel Bank Park 111
  Mackay Regional Botanic Gardens 227
  Mt Coot-tha Reserve 61-2
  Paronella Park 300
  Queens Park 175-6
  Rainforestation 339
  Rockhampton Botanic Gardens 200
  Roma St Parkland 53, 57-8
  South Bank Parklands 59
  Toondoon Botanic Gardens 211
  Toowoomba Botanic Gardens 111
  Townsville Botanic Gardens 268
Parliament House 58
Paterson, AB 'Banjo' 430
pearl farming 399
Perc Tucker Regional Gallery 267
Peregian 161-2
phonecards 465
photography 448, 463
Picnic Bay 275
Pinnacle Point 207
Pioneer Valley 234
planning, *see also individual regions*
  budgeting 14
  calendar of events 19-21
  children 42-4
  Great Barrier Reef 27-9
  itineraries 22-5, 61, 68-9, 120, 146, **22**, **23**, **24**, **25**, **68**
  Queensland's regions 45-9
  travel seasons 14
plants 441
platypuses 235, 301, 348-9, 439, 440
Poison Waterhole 411
politics 431, 434-6
Polstone Sugar Cane Farm 233
Pomona 164
population 422, 423
Porcupine Gorge National Park 409
Port Douglas 27-8, 48, 318, 355-63, **356**, **318-19**
  climate 353
  cruises 359
  highlights 354
  travel seasons 353
Portside Wharf 79
possums 445
postal services 463
Powderfinger 446
Prairie 409
Proserpine 243
public holidays 463
Pumpkin Island 211
Purling Brook Falls 139

Q

Qantas Founders Outback Museum 415
Qantilda Pioneer Place 414
QDeck 122
Queensland Art Gallery 59, **5**
Queensland Museum 58-9
Queensland Music Festival 72
Queensland Winter Racing Carnival 72
Quicksilver Pro-Surfing Competition 124
Quilpie 420
QUT Art Museum 58

R

Rabbit Island 238
Radical Bay 276
rafting 38, *see also* canoeing, kayaking
  Cairns 312
  Tully River 10, 291, **10**
Rainbow Beach 172-5
Rainforestation 339
Ravenshoe 347
Ravenswood 281
Redcliffe 99
Reef HQ 265
Reef Teach 306
Rees, Lloyd 448
religion 423
reptiles 441
responsible travel 32
Richmond 409
Riversleigh Australian Fossil Mammal Site 438
Riversleigh Fossil Field 403
Robinson, William 448
rock art 218-19, 222, 223, 343, 364, 392, 448-9, **17**
rock climbing
  Brisbane 59, 65-6
  Glass House Mountains 152
Rockhampton 200-5
rodeos
  Burketown Rodeo 406
  Chillagoe 343
  Mareeba Rodeo 20, 344
  Mt Isa Rodeo 20, 410
  Normanton Rodeo & Show 404
Roma St Parkland 53, 57-8
Royal Queensland Yacht Squadron 100
rugby league 90

S

Saddleback Island 258
safaris 339-40
safety 456-8, 463
  animals & insects 456-7
  bushfires 456
  coral cuts 457
  diving & snorkelling 31
  reefs 458
  road hazards 474-5
  swimming 306, 355, 456, 457
  theft 463
sailing 38-9
  Main Beach 118
  Manly 100
  Port Douglas 357
  Southport 118
  Whitsundays 239, 240

000 Map pages
000 Photo pages

Sarina 232
Sarina Beach 232
Savannah Way 49, 400-6, **388**
  accommodation 387
  climate 387
  food 387
  highlights 388
  travel seasons 387
Savannahlander 476
Scawfell Island 237
Schoolies 125
scenic flights
  Airlie Beach 244
  Cairns 311-12
  Fraser Island 193
  Hayman Island 256
  Hervey Bay 180-1
  Mackay 229
  Mission Beach 293
  Port Douglas 359-60
  Seisia 397
  Townsville 268
  Whitsundays 242
School of the Air (Longreach) 416
School of the Air (Mt Isa) 410-11
Sciencentre 59
Scrub Hill Community Farm 178
sea cucumbers 336
sea wasps 216
Sea World 123
seafood 450
Seisia 397
senior travellers 460
sharks 456-7
Sheahan, Dan 286
shearers' strike 417, 430-1,
Shoal Point 233-4
Silkwood 300
Simpson Desert National Park 420
Sir Thomas Brisbane Planetarium 62
skydiving 39-40
  Airlie Beach 244
  Brisbane 66
  Cairns 312
  Caloundra 153
  Coolum 160
  Hervey Bay 181
  Mission Beach 292
  Rainbow Beach 173
  Townsville 268
Skywalk 137
slang words 423
snakes 457
snorkelling 36-7
  Great Barrier Reef 29-31, 311
  Great Keppel Island 208
  Hamilton Island 254
  Hayman Island 256
  Heron Island 214
  Hook Island 252
  Lady Elliot Island 214
  Lady Musgrave Island 214, 216
  Lindeman Island 258
  Magnetic Island 277
  Mission Beach 293
  Moreton Island 105
  North Stradbroke Island 101
  safety 31
  Whitsunday Island 258
  Wilson Island 214
  Yeppoon 205
Somerset 397, 398
South Bank Parklands 59
South Johnstone 300
South Mission Beach 291
South Molle Island 253-4
South Stradbroke Island 121-2
Southport 117-21, **118**
spas 139
spiders 457
Spirit of the Outback 476
Split Rock Gallery 392
sports, *see individual sports*
Springbrook National Park 138-40
Springsure 222
St Helena 100-1
Stanthorpe 106-11
stations & homesteads, *see also* farmstays
  Bramwell Homestead 395
  Carisbrooke Station 415
  Greenmount Homestead 233
  Kroombit Lochenbar Station 204
  Merluna Station 394
  Mungalla Station 286
  Nardoo Station 414
  outback Queensland 414
steam-train trips
  Brisbane 71
  Gympie 171
  Port Douglas 357
  Ravenshoe 347
stingers 216, 306, 456
stolen generations 424, 436
Stoney Creek 235
Stradbroke Island, *see* North Stradbroke Island, South Stradbroke Island
Streets Beach 59
sugar mills 229, 232, 234, 290, 364, 429, **432**
sugar-cane farms 233, 234, 300
sunburn 458
Suncorp Piazza 59
Sunlander 476
Sunshine Beach 161-2, **161**
Sunshine Coast 6, 46, 142-68, **143**, **6**
  accommodation 142
  climate 142
  food 142
  highlights 143
  hinterland 165-8
  itineraries 146
  travel seasons 142
  travel to/from 144
  travel within 144
Sunshine Coast Brewery 453
Surf Life-Saving Championships 124
Surfers Paradise 6, 122-9, **124**
surfing 16, 37-8
  Agnes Water 38, 215
  Burleigh Heads 38, 131-2
  Caloundra 153
  Coolangatta 38, 133
  Coolum 160
  Main Beach 119
  Mooloolaba 155
  Noosa 38, 144-6
  North Stradbroke Island 38, 101
  Surfers Paradise 122
  Town of 1770 38
surfing carnivals 8, 124, **8**
Suzanne O'Connell Gallery 17, 64
swimming
  Airlie Beach 244
  Brisbane 66
  Cairns 306
  Cape Tribulation 373
  Fraser Island 193
  Mackay 227
  safety 306, 355, 456, 457
  Streets Beach 59

T

Tamborine Mountain 137-8
Tangalooma 105
Tanks Arts Centre 307
taxis 475
tea plantations 348
Teewah coloured sand cliffs 162
Telegraph Rd 395
telephone services 15, 463, 465
temples 301, 345
Thargomindah 420
theme parks 123
Thornton Beach 372
Thornton Peak 370
Thorsborne Trail 289
Thursday Island 398-9
Tibrogargan 152
ticks 457
Tilt Train 476
time 465

Tin Can Bay 185
Tip of Australia 397
tipping 450
Tjapukai Cultural Park 307
Tolga Bat Hospital 341
Toondoon Botanic Gardens 211
Toowoomba 111-14, **112**
Torres Strait Islands 397-400
tourist information 465
tours, *see also individual locations*, 4WD tours, cruises, scenic flights
food & drink 70, 107, 186-7, 312
glow worms 137
Indigenous tours 19, 173, 293, 359, 364, 383, 391, 411
rainforests 244, 246
sugar mills 229
Town of 1770 9, 27, 215-18, **9**
Townsville 27, 48, 264-75, 318, **266**, **318-19**
accommodation 262, 269-71
activities 264-8
attractions 264-8
climate 262
drinking 272-4
entertainment 272-4
festivals & events 269
food 262, 271-2
highlights 263
history 264
internet access 274
medical services 274
shopping 274
tours 268
travel seasons 262
travel to/from 274-5
travel within 275
train travel 475-6, *see also* steam-train trips
Kuranda Scenic Railway 11, 476, **11**
travellers cheques 463
Tree of Knowledge 417
trekking, *see* bushwalking
Trevathen Falls 382
Trinity Beach 332-3
Tropfest 72
Tryon Island 215
tubing 312
Tully 290-1
Tully Gorge National Park 290
Tully River 10, 291, **10**

000 Map pages
000 Photo pages

turtles 9, 16, 175, 188, 214, 215, 218, 265, 395, **9**, **323**
TV 464
Tyto wetlands 285

U

Ulysses butterflies 292
Undara lava tubes 313, 401
Undara Volcanic National Park 401-2
Underground Hospital Museum 410
Underwater World 155
uranium 441, 444-5

V

vacations 463
vaccinations 461
Valley Rattler 171
Venus Gold Battery 282
Vic Hislop's Greath White Shark & Whale Expo 178
video systems 464
vineyards, *see* wineries
visas 15, 462, 464, 466
volcanoes 138, 186, 401, 438
volunteering 328, 341, 373, 385, 395, 465

W

Walkabout Creek 63
Walkabout Creek Hotel 413
Walker, Kath 448
walking, *see* bushwalking
Wallaby Creek 380
Wallaman Falls 286
Walsh's Pyramid 329-30
'Waltzing Matilda' 413, 414, 430
Waltzing Matilda Centre 414
Wanggoolba Creek 192
Ward's Canyon 222
Warner Bros Movie World 123
water 461
waterfalls
Araluen Falls 236
Attie Creek Falls 288
Bloomfield Falls 379
Crystal Cascades 310
Eliot Falls 396
Ellinjaa Falls 348
Fruit Bat Falls 396
Isabella Falls 393
Josephine Falls 331
Jourama Falls 285
Kondalilla Falls 167
Leichhardt Falls 404
Malanda Falls 348
Millaa Millaa Falls 348
Mungalli Falls 348
Murray Falls 288
Purling Brook Falls 139
Ravenshoe 347
Tamborine Mountain National Park 137
Trevathen Falls 382
Twin Falls (Springbrook National Park) 139
Twin Falls (Cape York Peninsula) 396
Wallaman Falls 286
Wheel of Fire Falls 236
Zillie Falls 348
waterskiing 252, 310, 411
weather 14, 19, 20, 21, 27, 422-3, *see also individual regions*
websites, *see* internet resources
weights 464
Weipa 395
Westlander 476
Wet'n'Wild 123
Wetside 178
whale watching
Coolangatta 133-4
Fraser Island 192-3
Hervey Bay 7, 178, 180, **7**
Main Beach 119
Mooloolaba 156
North Stradbroke Island 101
Redcliffe 99
Southport 119
Surfers Paradise 123
Wheel of Brisbane 60
Wheel of Fire Falls 236
White Australia policy 425, 426, 431, 433
Whitehaven Beach 244, 258
white-water rafting, *see* rafting
WhiteWater World 123
Whitsunday Coast 47, 225-61, **226**
accommodation 225
climate 225
food 225
highlights 226
travel seasons 225
Whitsunday Island 258
Whitsundays 6, 238-61, 318, **259**, **6**, *see also individual islands*
cruises 241-2
diving 239, 241
kayaking 39, 241
sailing 239, 240
scenic flights 242
Whyanbeel Valley 366
wildlife sanctuaries
Akarra Lagoons 178
Australian Butterfly Sanctuary 339

Bat House 373
BatReach 339, 341
Billabong Sanctuary 280
Birdworld 339
Bromfield Swamp 348
Cape York Turtle Rescue 395
Cooberrie Park 205
Currumbin Wildlife Sanctuary 130
Daisy Hill Koala Centre 64
David Fleay Wildlife Park 130-1
Eagle's Nest Wildlife Hospital 341
Koala Gardens 339
Lone Pine Koala Sanctuary 63-4
Tolga Bat Hospital 341
Walkabout Creek 63
Wildlife Habitat Port Douglas 355, 357
Wilson Island 214-15
Windorah 420
wineries 452, *see also* breweries, distilleries
Golden Drop Mango 344
Granite Belt 106, 107, 108
Mareeba 344
Murdering Point Winery 299
Wild Mountain Cellars 349
Winton 413-15
wombats 439-40
women travellers 465-6
Wonga Beach 366
Woodford Folk Festival 21, 165
Woodgate 186
Woodworks Forestry & Timber Museum 171
Wooroonooran National Park 301, 331
work 466, *see also* volunteering
World Heritage Sites 438
WWI 425, 431
WWII 152, 201, 264, 276, 342-3, 380-1, 399, 410, 432-3

X

Xstrata Black Star Open Cut Mine 410

Y

yabbie races 420
yachting, *see* cruises, sailing
Yeppoon 205-7
Yongala wreck 280
Yorkeys Knob 332
Yowah Opal Fields 420
Yungaburra 349-51

Z

Zillie Falls 348
zoos, *see also* wildlife sanctuaries
Alexandra Park & Zoo 188
Alma Park Zoo 64
Australia Zoo 153
Australian Venom Zoo 339
Cairns Tropical Zoo 333
Cairns Wildlife Dome 307, 309
Daintree Wild Zoo 366

how to use this book

These symbols will help you find the listings you want:

- Sights
- Activities
- Courses
- Tours
- Festivals & Events
- Sleeping
- Eating
- Drinking
- Entertainment
- Shopping
- Information/ Transport

These symbols give you the vital information for each listing:

- Telephone Numbers
- Opening Hours
- Parking
- Nonsmoking
- Air-Conditioning
- Internet Access
- Wi-Fi Access
- Swimming Pool
- Vegetarian Selection
- English-Language Menu
- Family-Friendly
- Pet-Friendly
- Bus
- Ferry
- Metro
- Subway
- London Tube
- Tram
- Train

Reviews are organised by author preference.

Look out for these icons:

- TOP CHOICE — Our author's recommendation
- FREE — No payment required
- A green or sustainable option

Our authors have nominated these places as demonstrating a strong commitment to sustainability – for example by supporting local communities and producers, operating in an environmentally friendly way, or supporting conservation projects.

Map Legend

Sights
- Beach
- Buddhist
- Castle
- Christian
- Hindu
- Islamic
- Jewish
- Monument
- Museum/Gallery
- Ruin
- Winery/Vineyard
- Zoo
- Other Sight

Activities, Courses & Tours
- Diving/Snorkelling
- Canoeing/Kayaking
- Skiing
- Surfing
- Swimming/Pool
- Walking
- Windsurfing
- Other Activity/ Course/Tour

Sleeping
- Sleeping
- Camping

Eating
- Eating

Drinking
- Drinking
- Cafe

Entertainment
- Entertainment

Shopping
- Shopping

Information
- Post Office
- Tourist Information

Transport
- Airport
- Border Crossing
- Bus
- Cable Car/ Funicular
- Cycling
- Ferry
- Metro
- Monorail
- Parking
- S-Bahn
- Taxi
- Train/Railway
- Tram
- Tube Station
- U-Bahn
- Other Transport

Routes
- Tollway
- Freeway
- Primary
- Secondary
- Tertiary
- Lane
- Unsealed Road
- Plaza/Mall
- Steps
- Tunnel
- Pedestrian Overpass
- Walking Tour
- Walking Tour Detour
- Path

Boundaries
- International
- State/Province
- Disputed
- Regional/Suburb
- Marine Park
- Cliff
- Wall

Population
- Capital (National)
- Capital (State/Province)
- City/Large Town
- Town/Village

Geographic
- Hut/Shelter
- Lighthouse
- Lookout
- Mountain/Volcano
- Oasis
- Park
- Pass
- Picnic Area
- Waterfall

Hydrography
- River/Creek
- Intermittent River
- Swamp/Mangrove
- Reef
- Canal
- Water
- Dry/Salt/ Intermittent Lake
- Glacier

Areas
- Beach/Desert
- Cemetery (Christian)
- Cemetery (Other)
- Park/Forest
- Sportsground
- Sight (Building)
- Top Sight (Building)

Contributing Authors

Dr Michael Cathcart wrote the History chapter. Michael teaches history at the Australian Centre, University of Melbourne. He is well known as a broadcaster on ABC Radio National and has presented history programs on ABC TV. His most recent book is *The Water Dreamers* (2009), which details how water has shaped the history of Australia.

Dr Tim Flannery wrote the Environment chapter. Tim is a scientist, explorer and writer. He has written several award-winning books, including *The Future Eaters*, *Throwim Way Leg* and *The Weather Makers*. He lives in Sydney, where he is a professor in the faculty of science at Macquarie University.

OUR STORY

A beat-up old car, a few dollars in the pocket and a sense of adventure. In 1972 that's all Tony and Maureen Wheeler needed for the trip of a lifetime – across Europe and Asia overland to Australia. It took several months, and at the end – broke but inspired – they sat at their kitchen table writing and stapling together their first travel guide, *Across Asia on the Cheap*. Within a week they'd sold 1500 copies. Lonely Planet was born.

Today, Lonely Planet has offices in Melbourne, London and Oakland, with more than 600 staff and writers. We share Tony's belief that 'a great guidebook should do three things: inform, educate and amuse'.

OUR WRITERS

Regis St Louis

Coordinating Author; Brisbane; Around Brisbane Regis' love of Australia has taken him to every corner of the country, exploring remote pockets of the Kimberley, around Tasmania and through the rainforests and tropical islands of Queensland. On his most recent trip, he walked the waterlogged streets of Brisbane during the rainiest spring on record, introduced his daughters to cuddly koalas at Lone Pine Koala Sanctuary and enjoyed a bit of mayhem during the lively Brisbane Festival. Regis has contributed to more than 30 Lonely Planet titles, including the latest edition of *East Coast Australia*. When not travelling the world, he splits his time between New York City and Sydney.

Sarah Gilbert

Capricorn Coast; Journeys into the Outback Sarah is a Sydneysider who has also made her home in Amsterdam, New York and Buenos Aires. As a writer, she cut her teeth on the Big Apple's tabloids before moving home to work in TV current affairs. Once more based in Sydney, she makes her living both writing and working in TV. She's contributed to several Lonely Planet guides and is writing her first book of literary nonfiction.

Catherine Le Nevez

Townsville to Innisfail; Cairns, Islands & Highlands; Port Douglas & the Daintree; Cape York Peninsula & the Savannah Way Catherine's first writing for Lonely Planet was on Far North Queensland while completing her Doctorate of Creative Arts in Writing, during a 65,000km lap-and-a-half of the continent, including driving through two cyclones. Since then, Catherine has authored or co-authored more than two dozen guidebooks worldwide, including Lonely Planet's *Australia* and *East Coast Australia* guides – and relived one of those cyclone-pounded drives for a Lonely Planet feature story. She jumped at the chance to return to tropical paradise for this assignment.

Olivia Pozzan

Gold Coast; Noosa & the Sunshine Coast; Fraser Island & the Fraser Coast; Whitsunday Coast; Cape York Peninsula & the Savannah Way Raised in Queensland, Olivia had a sun-soaked beachside upbringing that shaped a lifelong addiction to balmy days and gorgeous beaches. Before her veterinary career led her to the deserts of the Middle East, her bikini collection graced every sandy shore between Cairns and the Gold Coast. After years of travelling the globe, Olivia had a craving for sand between her toes that finally drew her back to the Sunshine Coast. While revisiting her favourite coastal hot spots for this edition, she fell in love with the beautiful Whitsunday Islands.

ER GE MORE WRITERS

Published by Lonely Planet Publications Pty Ltd
36 005 607 983
edition – July 2011
978 1 74179 463 2

8 7 6 5 4 3 2 1
Printed in Singapore